Gender in Agriculture

SOURCEBOOK

AGRICULTURE AND RURAL DEVELOPMENT

Seventy-five percent of the world's poor live in rural areas, and most are involved in farming. In the 21st century, agriculture remains fundamental to economic growth, poverty alleviation, and environmental sustainability. The World Bank's Agriculture and Rural Development publication series presents recent analyses of issues that affect agriculture's role as a source of economic development, rural livelihoods, and environmental services. The series is intended for practical application, and we hope that it will serve to inform public discussion, policy formulation, and development planning.

Other titles in this series:

Sustainable Land Management Sourcebook

Forests Sourcebook: Practical Guidance for Sustaining Forests in Development Cooperation

Changing the Face of the Waters: The Promise and Challenge of Sustainable Aquaculture

Enhancing Agricultural Innovation: How to Go Beyond the Strengthening of Research Systems

Reforming Agricultural Trade for Developing Countries, Volume 1: Key Issues for a Pro-Development Outcome of the Doha Round

Reforming Agricultural Trade for Developing Countries, Volume 2: Quantifying the Impact of Multilateral Trade Reform

Sustainable Land Management: Challenges, Opportunities, and Trade-Offs

Shaping the Future of Water for Agriculture: A Sourcebook for Investment in Agricultural Water Management

Agriculture Investment Sourcebook

Sustaining Forests: A Development Strategy

Gender in Agriculture Sourcebook

Enabling poor rural people
to overcome poverty

ISBN: 978-0-8213-7587-7
eISBN: 978-0-8213-7588-4
DOI: 10.1596/978-0-8213-7587-7

Library of Congress Cataloging-in-Publication Data

Gender in agriculture sourcebook / The World Bank, Food and Agriculture
Organization, and International Fund for Agricultural Development.
    p. cm.
  ISBN 978-0-8213-7587-7 — ISBN 978-0-8213-7588-4 (electronic)
    1. Women in agriculture. 2. Women agricultural laborers. 3. Agricultural laborers. 4. Women in agriculture—Developing countries. 5. Women agricultural laborers—Developing countries. 6. Agricultural laborers—Developing countries. I. World Bank. II. Food and Agriculture Organization of the United Nations. III. International Fund for Agricultural Development.

  HD6077.G46 2008
  338.1082'091724—dc22
                                                        2008026383

Cover photos: Michael Foley (Afghanistan and Bangladesh) and Curt Carnemark/World Bank (Burkina Faso and Mexico).
Cover design: Patricia Hord Graphik Design.

CONTENTS

FIGURES

TABLES

FOREWORD

Three out of every four poor people in developing countries live in rural areas, and most of them depend directly or indirectly on agriculture for their livelihoods. In many parts of the world, women are the main farmers or producers, but their roles remain largely unrecognized. The *2008 World Development Report: Agriculture for Development* highlights the vital role of agriculture in sustainable development and its importance in achieving the Millennium Development Goal of halving by 2015 the share of people suffering from extreme poverty and hunger. Climate change and rising food prices are reminders of the need to focus on food security and agriculture for development; and the material presented in the *Gender in Agriculture Sourcebook* suggests that accounting for the different roles of women and men and gender equality in access to resources and opportunities is a necessary condition for doing so.

Gender inequalities limit agricultural productivity and efficiency and in so doing, undermine development agendas. Failure to recognize the different roles of men and women is costly because it results in misguided projects and programs, forgone agricultural output and incomes, and food and nutrition insecurity. It is time to take into account the role of women in agricultural production and to increase concerted efforts to enable women to move beyond production for subsistence and into higher-value, market-oriented production.

This *Sourcebook* is a particularly timely resource. It combines descriptive accounts of national and international experience in investing in agriculture with practical operational guidance on to how to design agriculture-for-development strategies that capitalize effectively on the unique properties of agricultural growth and rural development involving women and men as a high-impact source of poverty reduction. It looks at gender equality and women's empowerment, and the associated principles have the potential to make a difference in the lives of hundreds of millions of rural poor.

This *Sourcebook* is a joint project of the World Bank, the Food and Agriculture Organization (FAO) of the United Nations, and the International Fund for Agricultural Development (IFAD). We are grateful to the teams in these organizations for their tremendous efforts to bring over 100 experts together and to produce this significant contribution to our development work.

Juergen Voegele
Director
Agriculture and Rural Development
The World Bank

Marcela Villarreal
Director
Gender, Equity and Rural Employment Division
Food and Agriculture Organization (FAO) of the
United Nations

Rodney Cooke
Director
Technical Advisory Division
International Fund for Agricultural Development
(IFAD)

ACKNOWLEDGMENTS

The *Gender in Agriculture Sourcebook* was managed by a core team led by Eija Pehu (World Bank), Yianna Lambrou Food and Agriculture Organization (FAO), and Maria Hartl International Fund for Agricultural Development (IFAD). The overall coordination was provided by Catherine Ragasa (Consultant), supported by Chitra Deshpande (Consultant). Excellent overall guidance was offered by Anne Nicolaysen (FAO), Annina Lubbock (IFAD), Meena Munshi (World Bank), and Lynn Brown (World Bank).

The preparation of this *Sourcebook* involved many people from within several units of the World Bank, FAO, and IFAD, and a variety of partner organizations. Many individuals played a leading role as the main author or coordinator in the preparation of the modules. They are as follows: Module 1— Lynn Brown (World Bank) and Yianna Lambrou (FAO); Module 2—Regina Birner (International Food Policy Research Institute [IFPRI]); Module 3—Linda Mayoux (Consultant) and Maria Hartl (IFAD); Module 4—Malcolm Childress (World Bank) and Susan Lastarria-Cornhiel (University of Wisconsin–Madison); Module 5—Cathy Rozel Farnworth (Consultant) and Catherine Ragasa (Consultant); Module 6—Anne Kuriakose (World Bank); Module 7—Eija Pehu (World Bank) and Maria E. Fernandez (Center for Integrating Research and Action [CIRA] at the University of North Carolina–Chapel Hill); Module 8—Elena Bardasi (World Bank) and Kristy Cook (Consultant); Module 9— Dominique Lallement (Consultant); Module 10—Carolyn Sachs (Pennsylvania State University); Module 11—Ian Bannon (World Bank) and Sanam Naraghi-Anderlini (Consultant); Module 12—Sabine Gündel (Consultant); Module 13—Christine Okali (Consultant); Module 14— Catherine L. M. Hill (Consultant); Module 15—Christine Holding-Anyonge (Consultant); Module 16—Riikka Rajalahti (World Bank) and Pamela White (Consultant).

Many other individuals made written contributions to the Module Overviews and Thematic Notes. These include the following: Jacqueline Ashby (International Potato Centre [CIP]); Marilyn Carr (Consultant); Mari H. Clarke (Consultant); Suman Gautam (Consultant); Renee Giovarelli (Consultant); Jeanette Gurung (Women Organizing for Change in Agriculture and Natural Resources [WOCAN]); Katrien Holvoet (FAO); Leah Horowitz (IFPRI); Eriko Hoshino (Consultant); Natalie Hufnagl (Consultant); Helga Josupeit (FAO); Leena Kirjavainen (Consultant); Marina Laudazi (Consultant); M. C. Nandeesha (Central Agricultural University, Tripura); Yvette Diei Ouadi (FAO); Juan A. Sagardoy (Consultant); Christine Sijbesma (Consultant); Anushree Sinha (National Council for Applied Economic Research Council [NCAER]); Nidhi Tandon (Consultant); Barbara van Koppen (Consultant).

Many individuals contributed Innovative Activity Profiles of ongoing or completed projects or project components as follows: Reshad Alam (Danish International Development Assistance [DANIDA]); Mary Arimond (IFPRI); Shweta Banerjee (World Bank); Marie-Louise Beerling (RDP Livestock Services); Lisa Bhansali (World Bank); Paricia Colbert (FAO); Christine E. Cornelius (World Bank); Francesca Dalla Valle (FAO); Harvey Demaine (DANIDA); Grahame Dixie (World Bank); Hadiza Djibo (FAO); Christian Fauliau (Consultant); Dian Fiana (Coral Reef Rehabilitation and Management Program [COREMAP]); Charles Greenwald (COREMAP); John Hourihan (FAO); Sagipa Jusaeva (United Nations Development Fund for Women

[UNIFEM]); Vijaysekar Kalavakonda (World Bank); Vijay Kumar (Society for Elimination of Rural Poverty, Hyderabad); Jan W. Low (CIP); Sitaramachandra Machiraju (World Bank); Ira Matuschke (Consultant); Grant Milne (World Bank); Marietha Owenya (Consultant); Francisco Pichon (World Bank); Aleyda Ramirez (FAO–Honduras); Vanaja Ramprasad (Genetic Resource Ecology Energy Nutrition Foundation); K. P. Rao (Society for Elimination of Rural Poverty, Hyderabad); Parmesh Shah (World Bank); Monawar Sultana (Asian Development Bank [ADB]); Mona Sur (World Bank); Mio Takada (World Bank); Arine Valstar (FAO); Robina Wahaj (Consultant).

Many other individuals inside and outside the World Bank, FAO, and IFAD provided useful inputs to this *Sourcebook*. They include the following: Festus Akinnifesi (World Agroforestry Center [ICRAF]); Keith Clifford Bell (World Bank); David Boerma (FAO); Fatiha Bou-Salah (FAO); Carol Djeddah (FAO); Nora Dudwick (World Bank); Carla Ferreira (IFAD); Ambra Gallina (Consultant); Brian Griffin (FAO); Lenyara Khayasedinova (IFAD); Aichi Kitalyi (ICRAF); Dominique Lantieri (FAO); Annabelle Lhommeau (IFAD); Jens-Peter Barkenow Lilleso (ICRAF); Sibyl Nelson (FAO); Rasha Omar (IFAD); Anna Pietikainen (IFAD); Laura Puletti (IFAD); John Keith Rennie (World Bank); Andrea Rossi (FAO); Dieter Schoene (FAO); Reuben Sessa (FAO); Iain G. Shuker (World Bank); Alessandro Spairani (Consultant); Cristiana Sparacina (IFAD); Silvia Sperandini (IFAD); Vivek Srivastava (World Bank); Miguel Trossero (FAO); Dina Umali-Deininger (World Bank); Rosemary Vargas-Lundius (IFAD); Doris Voorbraak (World Bank); Briana Wilson (IFC).

Each Module was peer reviewed, usually by two technical staff from each partner organization and one external reviewer. The team appreciates the substantive comments and suggestions from the following reviewers: Kaori Abe (FAO); Moses Abukari (IFAD); Nilufar Ahmad (World Bank); Harold Alderman (World Bank); Sriani Ameratunga (International Labour Organization [ILO]); Jamie Anderson (IFAD); Jock Anderson (World Bank); Tom Anyonge (IFAD); Henry Bagazonzya (World Bank); Douglas Barnes (World Bank); Daniela Battaglia (FAO); Diji Chandrasekharan Behr (World Bank); Rupert Best (International Center for Tropical Agriculture [CIAT]); Nienke Bientema (IFPRI); Magdalena Blum (FAO); Hubert Boirard (IFAD); Luz Caballero (World Bank); Karel Callens (FAO); Alice Carloni (Consultant); Elizabeth Cecelski (Consultant); Delgermaa Chuluunbaater (IFAD); Bill Clay (FAO); Rudolph Cleveringa (IFAD); Patricia Colbert (FAO); Edward Cook (World Bank); Eve Crowley (FAO); John Curry (FAO); Rekha Dayal (Consultant); Henri Dommel (IFAD); Samuel Eremie (IFAD); Katuscia Fara (IFAD); Erick Fernandes (World Bank); Ilaria Firmian (IFAD); Nicole Franz (IFAD); René Fréchet (IFAD); Theodor Friedrich (FAO); Neela Gangadharan (FAO); Rosalia Garcia (FAO); Zoraida Garcia (FAO); Michelle Gauthier (FAO); Sophie Grouwels (FAO); Natasha Hayward (World Bank); Jennifer Heney (FAO); Peter Hurst (ILO); Mary Kawar (ILO); Kieran Kelleher (World Bank); Siobhan Kelly (FAO); Karin Kemper (World Bank); Sean Kennedy (IFAD); Josef Kienzle (FAO); Renate Kloeppinger-Todd (World Bank); Ib Kollavick-Jensen (FAO); Sasha Koo (FAO); Regina Laub (FAO); Harold Liversage (IFAD); Niels Louwaars (Nageningen University and Research Centre [WUR]); Mohamed Manssouri (IFAD); Susan Maybud (ILO); Anni McLeod (FAO); Kerry McNamara (World Bank); Robin Mearns (World Bank); Kayoko Shibata Medlin (World Bank); Ruth Meinzen-Dick (IFPRI); Samia Melhem (World Bank); Rebecca Metzner (FAO); Victor Mosoti (FAO); Sheila Mwanundu (IFAD); Ajai Nair (World Bank); Audrey Nepveu (IFAD); Anne Nicolaysen (FAO); Martin Oelz (ILO); Clare O'Farrell (FAO); Yvette Diei Ouadi (FAO); Sabine Pallas (International Land Coalition); David Palmer (FAO); Pawan Patil (World Bank); George Politakis (ILO); Suzanne Raswant (FAO); Melba Reantaso (FAO); Francesco Rispoli (IFAD); Anne Ritchie (Consultant); Simmone Rose (FAO); Antonio Rota (IFAD); Dan Rugabira (FAO); Bill Saint (Consultant); Daniel Sellen (World Bank); Andrew Shepherd (FAO); Susan Siar (FAO); Paolo Silveri (IFAD); Ilaria Sisto (FAO); Jimmy Smith (World Bank); Libor Stloukal (FAO); Laurent Stravato (IFAD); Rohana Subasinghe (FAO); Ratna M. Sudarshan (Institute of Social Studies Trust); Burt Swanson (University of Illinois); Florence Tartanac (FAO); Paola Termine (FAO); Brian Thompson (FAO); Catherine Tovey (World Bank); Richard Trenchard (FAO); Robert Tripp (Overseas Development Institute [ODI]); Kees van der Meer (World Bank); Steve Wiggins (ODI); Tanja Winther (Oslo University).

In addition to the peer review, several people provided an overall review on the concept note and final *Sourcebook* draft: Nata Duvvury (Consultant); Indira Ekanayake (World Bank); Anita Kelles-Vitanen (Consultant); Shyam Khadka (IFAD); Rekha Mehra (World Bank); Gajanand Pathmanathan (World Bank); Thomas Price (FAO); Nitya Rao (University of East Anglia); Mary Hill Rojas (Consultant); Deborah Rubin (Cultural Practice).

The team would like to acknowledge Juergen Voegele (World Bank), Mark E. Cackler (World Bank), Marcela Villarreal (FAO), and Rodney Cooke (IFAD), who contributed invaluable guidance and support throughout the preparation of the *Sourcebook.*

Technical edits from Kelly Cassaday (Consultant), Mike Donaldson (Consultant), and Gunnar Larson (Consultant) improved the readability and sharpened the key messages substantially. Hild Rygnestad (Consultant) and Annu Ratta (Consultant) are acknowledged for their help in shortening and editing the documents. The team is very grateful for their patience and attention to detail.

The team thanks Patricia Katayama (World Bank), Lisa Lau (World Bank), and Dina S. Towbin (World Bank) for their assistance in the production.

The team acknowledges the support and guidance of the Poverty Reduction and Economic Management–Gender and Development (PREMGE), under the leadership of Mayra Buvinić (World Bank). They also acknowledge the support and financial assistance from the FAO Investment Centre, especially William Sorrenson (FAO). Thanks also to the IFAD Technical Advisory Division for both technical and financial support.

Finally, the team recognizes the assistance provided by Felicitas Doroteo-Gomez (World Bank), Claudia Escutia (FAO), and Simone Zein (IFAD).

ABBREVIATIONS

ACE	civic extension association
ACT	African Conservation Tillage network
ADB	Asian Development Bank
ADR	alternative dispute resolution
AET	agricultural extension and training
AIDS	acquired immune deficiency syndrome
AIS	agricultural innovation systems
AL	alternative livelihood
ALMP	active labor market program
ANADER	Agence Nationale d'Appui au Développement Rural
APC	Asian-Pacific countries
APDPIP	Andhra Pradesh District Poverty Initiatives Project
APRPRP	Andhra Pradesh Rural Poverty Reduction Project
ASCA	accumulating savings and credit association
ASNAPP	Agribusiness in Sustainable Natural African Plant Products
ATM	automatic teller machine
ATMA	Agricultural Technology Management Agency
AusAID	Australian Agency for International Development
AWLAE	African Women Leaders in Agriculture and Environment
AWM	agriculture water management
B2B	business to business
BINP	Bwindi Impenetrable National Park
BLGWIP-III	Bhairahawa Lumbini Groundwater Irrigation Project
BRAC	Bangladesh Rural Advancement Committee
CA	conservation agriculture
CATIE	Centro Agronomico Tropical de Investigacion y Enseñanza
CBD	community-based development; Convention on Biological Diversity
CBDP	community-based disaster preparedness
CBNRM	community-based natural resource management
CBO	community-based organization
CeC	community e-center
CDD	community-driven development

CDF	community development fund
CEDAW	Convention on the Elimination of All Forms of Discrimination against Women
CEM	Country Economic Memorandum
CGA	country gender assessment
CGIAR	Consultative Group on International Agricultural Research
CIAT	International Center for Tropical Agriculture
CIFOR	Center for International Forestry Research
COHRE	Centre on Housing Rights and Evictions
COREMAP	Coral Reef Rehabilitation and Management Program
COVERCO	Commission for the Verification of Corporate Codes of Conduct
CREPA	Centre for Low-Cost Drinking Water Supply and Sanitation (Burkina Faso)
CSR	corporate social responsibility
CWANA	Central and West Asia and North Africa
DAC	Development Assistance Committee
DANIDA	Danish International Development Assistance
DEWA	Division for Early Warning and Assessment
DFID	Department for International Development (U.K.)
DLS	Department of Livestock Services
DOF	Department of Forests
DPIP	District Poverty Initiatives Project
DTW	deep tubewell
EALA	East African Legislature Assembly
ECLAC	Economic Commission of Latin America and the Caribbean
EDI	Economic Development Institute
EFTA	European Fair-Trade Association
ENAM	Enhancing Child Nutrition through Animal Source Food Management
ESW	economic and sector work
FAC	farmer advisory committee
FAESIS	Food and Agriculture Education Information System
FAO	Food and Agriculture Organization
FARC	Revolutionary Armed Forces of Colombia
FARM	Farmer-Centered Agricultural Resource Management
FEDEV	Femmes et Développement
FFS	Farmer Field School
FIAS	Foreign Investment Advisory Service
FLG	functional literacy group
FLO	Fair-Trade Labelling Organisations International
FLS	Farmer Life School
FRIEND	Foundation for Rural Integrated Enterprises N Development
FSVGD	Food Security for Vulnerable Group Development Women and Their Dependents
FTD	farmer training demonstration
GAL	Gender in Agricultural Livelihoods
GAP	Gender Action Partnership
GBI	gender budget initiative
GDP	gross domestic product
GEF	Gender Environment Faculty
GENRD	Gender and Rural Development Thematic Group

GGA	gender and growth assessment
GM	genetically modified
GNAEP	Greater Noakhali Aquaculture Extension Project
GNI	gross national income
GOLDA	Greater Options for Local Development through Aquaculture
GoSL	government of Sri Lanka
GOWE	Growth Oriented Women Enterprise
GRBI	Gender Responsive Budgeting Initiative
GRTI	Gender and Rural Transport Initiative
GTZ	Gesellschaft für Technische Zusammenarbeit (also German Technical Cooperation)
HIV	human immunodeficiency virus
HLFFDP	Hills Leasehold Forestry and Forage Development Project
HPAI	highly pathogenic avian influenza
IADB	Inter-American Development Bank
IAP	indoor air pollution
IASC	Inter-Agency Standing Committee
ICECD	International Centre for Entrepreneurship and Career Development
ICESCR	International Covenant on Economic, Social and Cultural Rights
ICM	integrated crop management
ICRAF	World Agroforestry Center (International Council for Research in Agroforestry)
ICRC	International Committee of the Red Cross
ICT	information and communication technology
IDA	International Development Association
IDP	internally displaced person
IDRC	International Development Research Centre
IFAD	International Fund for Agricultural Development
IFAT	International Federation for Alternative Trade
IFC	International Finance Corporation
IFPRI	International Food Policy Research Institute
IGA	income-generating activity
IIM	Indian Institute of Management
IISD	International Institute for Sustainable Development
IK	indigenous knowledge
IKP	Indira Kranthi Patham
ILO	International Labour Organization
IMF	International Monetary Fund
IMT	intermediate means of transport; irrigation management transfer
INCAGRO	Peruvian Agro-Innovation and Competitiveness Project
INSTRAW	International Research and Training Institute for the Advancement of Women
IPCC	Intergovernmental Panel on Climate Change
IPM	integrated pest management
IPPM	integrated production and pest management
IRAD	Integrated Research and Action for Development
IRAP	integrated rural accessibility planning
IRRI	International Rice Research Institute
JFFLS	Junior Farmer Field and Life School
JSA	joint staff assessment
KARI	Kenya Agricultural Research Institute

KRC	Kabarole Research and Resource Centre
KWDP	Karnataka Watershed Development Project
LAC	Latin America and the Caribbean
LACOSREP	Upper East Region Land Conservation and Smallholder Rehabilitation Project (Ghana)
LADEP	Lowlands Agricultural Development Programme
Lao PDR	Lao People's Democratic Republic
LARC	Legal Assistance to Rural Citizens
LCC	Land Claims Court
LDW	local development window
LEAF	Livelihood Empowerment and Agroforestry
LinKS	Local Indigenous Knowledge Systems
LPG	liquid propane gas
LSA	livelihood support activity
LTTE	Liberation Tamil Tigers of Eelam
M&E	monitoring and evaluation
MACEMP	Marine and Coastal Environment Management Project
MADER	Ministry of Agriculture and Rural Development (Mozambique)
MAMS	Maquette for MDG Simulations
MARENASS	Management of Natural Resources in the Southern Highlands Project (Peru)
MBFO	membership-based financial organization
MDG	Millennium Development Goal
ME	marketing extension
MEA	Millennium Ecosystem Assessment
MENA	Middle East and North Africa
MFA	microfinance association
MFI	microfinance institution
MIGEPROFE	Ministry of Gender and the Promotion of Women (Rwanda)
MINECOFIN	Ministry of Economics and Finance
MIS	management information system
MOA	Ministry of Agriculture
MS	*mandal samakhyas*
NAADS	National Agricultural Advisory Service
NABARD	National Bank for Agriculture and Rural Development
NCEUS	National Commission for Enterprises in the Unorganized Sector
NCU	national coordination unit
NERICA	New Rice for Africa
NEWS	Network of European World Shops
NGO	nongovernmental organization
NOPEST	New Options for Pest Management
NPIU	national project implementation unit
NPM	New Public Management
NRM	natural resource management
NSSO	National Sample Survey Organisation
NTFP	nontimber forest product
NWFP	nonwood forest product
ODI	Overseas Development Institute
OECD	Organisation for Economic Co-operation and Development
OECD/DAC	Development Assistance Committee of the OECD

PA	protected area
PACTA	Proyecto Acceso a la Tierra (Land Access Pilot Project)
PAF	performance assessment framework
PALS	Participatory Action Learning System
PARIMA	Pastoral Risk Management on East African Rangelands
PARPA	Action Plan for the Reduction of Absolute Poverty (Mozambique)
PBAEP	Patuakhali Barguna Aquaculture Extension Project
PCUWA	Policy Coordinating Unit for Women in Agriculture
PER	public expenditure review
PL	post-larvae
PMU	project management unit
PNASA	Projet National d'Appui aux Services Agricoles
PO	producers organization
PPB	Participatory Plant Breeding
PRA	participatory rapid appraisal
PRGA	Participatory Research and Gender Analysis
PRMT	Poverty Resource Monitoring and Tracking
PRS	poverty reduction strategy
PRSC	Poverty Reduction Support Credit
PRSP	Poverty Reduction Strategy Paper
PTD	Participatory Technology Development
RCU	regional coordination unit
RDC	rural development society
RDI	Rural Development Institute
ROPPA	Reseau des Organisations Paysannes et des Producteurs Agricoles de l'Afrique de l'ouest
ROSCA	rotating savings and credit association
RPO	rural producer organization
SACEP	South Asia Cooperative Environment Programme
SADC	South African Development Community
SAFE	Safe Access to Firewood and Alternative Energy
SARD	Sustainable Agriculture and Rural Development
SARI	Selian Agricultural Research Institute
SASKI	Sustainable Agriculture Systems, Knowledge, and Institutions
SDC	Swiss Agency for Development and Cooperation
SEAGA	Socio-Economic and Gender Analysis Programme
SEI	Stockholm Environment Institute
SEWA	Self-Employed Women's Association
SFLP	Sustainable Fisheries Livelihoods Programme
SHG	self-help group
SIDA	Swedish International Development Agency
SIEMBRA	Servicios Integrales a Mujeres Emprendedoras
SIMS	sectoral information and monitoring system
SLA	Sri Lanka army; Sustainable Livelihoods Approach
SMC	site management committee
SMS	short message system
SOPPEXCCA	Sociedad de Pequeños Productores Exportadoras y Compradores de Café
SSA	sub-Saharan Africa
SSDP	Seed Systems Development Project

STFC	SEWA Trade Facilitation Centre
SWAP	sectorwide approach
SWOT	strengths, weaknesses, opportunities, threats
T&V	training and visit
TA	technical assistance
TRIPS	Trade-Related Aspects of Intellectual Property Rights
UER	Upper East Region
UN	United Nations
UNCCD	United Nations Convention to Combat Desertification
UNDAW	United Nations Division for the Advancement of Women
UNDHR	Universal Declaration on Human Rights
UNDP	United Nations Development Programme
UNEP	United Nations Environment Programme
UNESCAP	United Nations Economic and Social Commission for Asia and the Pacific
UNFCCC	United Nations Framework Convention on Climate Change
UNFF	United Nations Forum on Forests
UNHCR	United Nations High Commission for Refugees
UNIDO	United Nations Industrial Development Organization
UNIFEM	United Nations Development Fund for Women
UNIMAS	University of Malaysia Sarawak
UNPF	United Nations Population Fund
USAID	U.S. Agency for International Development
UWA	Uganda Wildlife Authority
VAC	vuong/ao/chuong (garden/pond/animal husbandry)
VD	village development (association)
VDC	village development committee
VFFP	Village and Farm Forestry Project
VO	village organization
VREL	Volta River Estates, Ltd.
VSHLI	Village Self-Help Learning Initiative
WFP	World Food Programme
WHO	World Health Organization
WID	Women in Development
WIEGO	Women in Informal Employment: Globalizing and Organizing
WIN	Empowerment of Women in Irrigation and Water Resources Management for Improved Food Security, Nutrition and Health
WIND	Work Improvement in Neighbourhood Development
WOUGNET	Women of Uganda Network
WRDS	women's rural development society
WUA	water user association
WUG	water user group
WWF	World Wildlife Fund

Currency is in U.S. dollars unless otherwise noted.

Sourcebook Overview

Agriculture is central to the livelihoods of the rural poor and in the attainment of the Millennium Development Goals (MDGs). Agriculture can be the engine of growth and is necessary for reducing poverty and food insecurity, particularly in sub-Saharan Africa (IFAD 2001; World Bank 2007a). Understanding the dynamic processes of change is crucial to better position the sector for faster growth and sustained development, which is vital for food and livelihoods security for millions of men and women worldwide.

The rapid changes occurring in the agriculture sector present opportunities and challenges for the sector's central role in poverty reduction and food security. Markets and the demand for agricultural commodities are changing rapidly, especially for higher-value products. These changes may create opportunities for greater market participation for both women and men; however, for women in particular, to date, equal access to these markets is still limited. Advances in agricultural knowledge and technology that accompany the changes in the sector are creating an array of new choices for producers, altering what is produced, where it is produced, and how it is produced. Factors outside of the sector, such as widespread environmental change, are also altering agricultural potential throughout the world. In particular, climate change is now affecting water supply and weather conditions and consequently is impacting agricultural production.

The composition of rural households is changing considerably as a consequence of HIV and AIDS, with deaths of young adults and farm households left in the hands of children and grandparents with subsequent impacts on agriculture. Migration, arising mainly from poverty or prompted by natural disasters or violent conflict, now forms a dynamic force, changing the landscape of the rural population. Remittances sent back home by migrants form substantial sources of funds supporting household consumption and productive investments in rural areas. Migration shows stark gendered differences. In some regions, men more than women are likely to abandon agricultural work at home and migrate first to seek income in other sectors. Women are being left to carry the full burdens of agricultural production, but often with no legal protection or rights to property ownership.

Although the changes in agriculture create new sources of opportunities for livelihoods and food security, they also pose significant uncertainties. Equity concerns are being raised. Poor and small producers, often women, may be excluded from the lucrative high-value markets because they may not be able to compete in terms of costs and prices with larger producers. Globalization and trade liberalization have opened more market opportunities internationally and have induced greater innovations and efficiencies in many cases. But, at the same time, globalization has led to painful transition periods for some economies and has favored the producers who have more resources and the information, education, and capacity to cope with increasingly stringent market demands. Thus, these changes may increase the vulnerability of individuals with few resources, especially poor women, who have traditionally had limited access to crucial services and opportunities because of persistent cultural, social, and political biases.

Within the development community, a renewed interest has been expressed in support of agriculture. The *World Development Report of 2008: Agriculture for Development* has helped spearhead renewed thinking about the sector, calling for more and better investments in agriculture. Increased investment in the sector is also flowing from the private foundations (such as the Bill and Melinda Gates Foundation). In light of such renewed interest and resources, this is an opportune time to rethink agriculture strategies for better development outcomes. Concerted efforts are required to use fully the strengths and diversity among the rural people and their institutions, to manage innovatively the risks and challenges associated with rapid changes in the sector, and to ensure that growth reaches poor women and men. For instance, women play a major role in agriculture, but these roles are often unrecognized. The design of many development policies and projects continues to assume wrongly that farmers and rural workers are mainly men (World Bank 2007b). Failure to recognize the roles, differences, and inequalities poses a serious threat to the effectiveness of the agricultural development agenda.

WHY GENDER EQUALITY IS IMPORTANT IN AGRICULTURE

Gender equality is crucial for agricultural development and the attainment of the MDGs. The definition of *gender* used in the *Sourcebook* is the economic, social, political, and cultural attributes and opportunities associated with being man or woman. The *Sourcebook* uses the definition in the *Global Monitoring Report 2007* on gender equality, which means equal access to the "opportunities that allow people to pursue a life of their own choosing and to avoid extreme deprivations in outcomes," highlighting gender equality in rights, resources, and voice (World Bank 2007c: 106).

Gender issues must be addressed in development. First, gender dimension is crucial for economic reasons and from the efficiency point of view. This is especially true in the agriculture sector, where gender inequalities in access to and control over resources are persistent, undermining a sustainable and inclusive development of the sector. Second, equity or distributional issues are related to gender differences in outcomes. Gender differences, arising from the socially constructed relationship between men and women, affect the distribution of resources between them and cause many disparities in development outcomes. Third, gender

roles and relations affect food security and household welfare, critical indicators of human development. Last, but not least, gender equality is a basic human right, one that has value in and of itself.

In many parts of the world—for example, sub-Saharan Africa (SSA) and South Asia—despite women being the main farmers or producers, their roles are largely unrecognized. In Uganda, broadly illustrative of SSA, 75 percent of agricultural producers are women.[1] In other areas, where migration and HIV and AIDS are affecting rural demographics, agriculture is becoming feminized as women increasingly become major actors in the sector. Women also play active roles as traders, processors, laborers, and entrepreneurs, despite facing many obstacles (compared to their men counterparts) in market access. However, the design of many development policies and projects continues to assume incorrectly that farmers and rural workers are mainly men (World Bank 2007b).

Significant gender inequalities can be found in peoples' access to other key productive assets and services: land, labor, financial services, water, rural infrastructure, technology, and other inputs. Available evidence indicates that the distribution of land ownership is heavily skewed toward men. For example, roughly 70 to 90 percent of formal owners of farmland are men in many Latin American countries (Deere and Leon 2003), and similar patterns are seen in SSA (Doss 2005; Quisumbing, Estudillo, and Otsuka 2004). Evidence also suggests that strengthening women's land rights can significantly increase income and families' welfare (for example, a new law adopted in several countries in SSA certifying women's title to land had a positive impact on women's and household welfare). In many countries, providing land titles is not enough because complementary services (such as in the Lao Peoples' Democratic Republic and the Philippines) also need to be in place (see Module 4).

The poor, especially women, face obstacles in making their voices heard even in democratic systems and in increasing accountability and governance reforms in many areas (World Bank 2007a). For instance, recent studies stress that women's representation and gender integration into national plans and agricultural sector strategies remain a challenge (World Bank 2005b).[2]

Women face considerable gender-related constraints and vulnerabilities compared to men because of existing structures in households and societies. Property grabbing from women and children is common, particularly in communities affected by HIV and AIDS. Also, exposure to risk arising from violent conflicts or natural disaster is different for men and women; it is often influenced by existing gender-based inequalities in the allocation of food within the household, mobility restrictions, and other sociocultural factors. For example, in the aftermath of Hurricane Mitch in Honduras and Nicaragua in 1998, women's household tasks and care responsibilities increased to such an extent that they found it difficult to return to work. Women's participation and voice in organizations are limited, they are less likely to receive critical information for emergency preparedness, and they have limited savings or assets to ensure them against external shocks (see Module 11).

The World Bank (2001) documented that ignoring gender inequalities comes at great cost to people's well-being and countries' abilities to grow sustainably and thereby reduce poverty. Not taking gender issues into account may result in projects that are technically successful but that negatively affect both women and children and augment social and economic stratification. In SSA the "missed potential" in agriculture is considerable, as evidenced in country studies by the World Bank (2005a):

- *Burkina Faso:* Shifting labor and fertilizer between men's and women's plots could increase output by 10 to 20 percent.
- *Kenya:* Giving women farmers the same inputs and education as men could increase yields by more than 20 percent.
- *Tanzania:* Reducing time burdens of women could increase cash incomes for smallholder coffee and banana growers by 10 percent.
- *Zambia:* If women enjoyed the same overall degree of capital investment in agricultural inputs, including land, as their men counterparts, output in Zambia could increase by up to 15 percent.

As is evident from just the few preceding examples, efforts to reach the MDGs—especially the goals of halving poverty and hunger (MDG 1) and promoting gender equality (MDG 3) and maternal and child health (MDG 4) by 2015—must fully address and integrate gender into operations in the agriculture sector. Growth and development in the sector simply cannot be done while ignoring women, who are the major actors.

Recognizing the role of gender equality, key development organizations have engaged in a process of mainstreaming gender into agricultural development. The World Bank, Food and Agriculture Organization (FAO), and International Fund for Agriculture Development (IFAD) have made some progress in their gender-mainstreaming strategies and have recently embarked on more action-oriented processes of gender integration (Curry and Tempelman

2006; FAO 2007; IFAD 2003; World Bank 2006, 2008). Analytical capacity is being strengthened, and data collection and analysis have been improved to include gender-specific variables and indicators in these three agencies. The Gender and Development Program of the International Food Policy Research Institute has contributed significantly toward this strengthening of analytical capacity (see also IFPRI 2007a, 2007b; Quisumbing and McClafferty 2006a, 2006b). Capacity building of staff has also been implemented (see Module 2) with the development community, and improvement has occurred in the way gender issues and women's empowerment are addressed throughout the project cycle, starting with project design (GENRD 2006, 2007; IFAD 2003; World Bank 2006). However, studies have highlighted the need to ensure greater continuity between design and implementation to integrate women more fully into mainstream development activities, and the current challenge is to shift the emphasis toward actual implementation and supervision (GENRD 2006, 2007; IFAD 2003).

One of the often-cited reasons for inadequately addressing gender is that practitioners lack the tools, know-how, and good practices to integrate gender perspectives in their work, especially now that the sector itself is undergoing profound changes. Some cite the abundance of tools, the many available handbooks and toolkits, but often one wonders where to start. Others mention lack of training of development practitioners in using the tools, lack of accountability in processes to show results on gender equality, and lack of resources: budget and competent human resources to deliver well-thought-out design, implementation, and monitoring. Although these concerns can be addressed effectively only through concerted efforts, the *Gender in Agriculture Sourcebook* is developed to respond to some of these needs. The *Sourcebook* compiles the good practices and innovative activities that successfully integrated gender into their project and program design for sharing and learning. It synthesizes in one place knowledge, experience, and tools, which are currently scattered in many different places, and it provides an up-to-date understanding of gender issues and the complexities linking gender equality, sustainable livelihoods, and food security in one volume, especially in the context of the rapidly changing agriculture sector.

GENDER IN AGRICULTURE SOURCEBOOK

The *Sourcebook* is the outcome of joint planning, continued interest in gender and agriculture, and concerted efforts by the World Bank, FAO, and IFAD. The purpose of the *Sourcebook* is to act as a guide for practitioners and technical staff in addressing gender issues and integrating gender-responsive actions in the design and implementation of agricultural projects and programs. It speaks not with gender specialists on how to improve their skills but rather reaches out to technical experts to guide them in thinking through how to integrate gender dimensions into their operations. The *Sourcebook* aims to deliver practical advice, guidelines, principles, and descriptions and illustrations of approaches that have worked so far to achieve the goal of effective gender mainstreaming in the agricultural operations of development agencies. It captures and expands the main messages of the *World Development Report 2008: Agriculture for Development* and is considered an important tool to facilitate the operationalization and implementation of the report's key principles on gender equality and women's empowerment.

The *Sourcebook* focuses on agricultural livelihoods, with *agriculture* defined broadly as "agriculture, forestry, fisheries, livestock, land and water, agro-industries, and environment," following the FAO definition.[3] The *Sourcebook* is grounded in the notion of agriculture's central role in providing rural livelihoods, food security, and broad-based poverty reduction. Although the *Sourcebook* focuses on the agriculture sector, it is also aware of the fluctuations of agricultural livelihoods so that poverty reduction and rural development require a holistic approach. Both nonagriculture-specific sectors, such as rural finance, rural infrastructure, and rural labor with a reference to agriculture-driven activities, and social protection policies are addressed in the *Sourcebook*.

The *Sourcebook* is targeted to key actors within international and regional development agencies and national governments, specifically, operational staff who design and implement lending projects and technical officers who design thematic programs and technical assistance packages. The *Sourcebook* can also be an important resource to the research community and nongovernmental organizations.

The *Sourcebook* is one of a few interorganization partnerships to take advantage of complementarities in moving toward greater coherence and harmonization of development support, particularly in the area of gender mainstreaming in agriculture. The *Sourcebook* capitalizes on the comparative strengths of the three organizations to lead the development of the Modules. In addition, it uses the expertise in each organization for technical contributions, good practice selection, innovative project examples, and a series of reviews and quality control. The contents are assembled from across all the geographic regions, with inputs from the experiences of the African Development Bank, the Asian Development Bank, the Inter-American Development Bank, and many other development organizations.

SUSTAINABLE LIVELIHOODS THROUGH A GENDER LENS

The *Sourcebook* adopts the Sustainable Livelihoods Approach (SLA), popularized by the U.K. Department for International Development (DFID) to provide a conceptual framework for the complexities and synergies of gender equality, livelihoods, food security, and poverty reduction.[4] The SLA's holistic concept of livelihood strategies—based on human, physical, financial, natural, and social assets—is a helpful approach in understanding the livelihoods of the poor. Livelihoods have been defined as comprising "the capabilities, assets (including both material and social resources) and activities required for a means of living. A livelihood is sustainable when it can cope with and recover from stresses and shocks and maintain or enhance its capabilities and assets both now and in the future, while not undermining the natural resource base."[5]

The following factors are the central defining ones in the SLA used by the *Sourcebook*:

- *Assets:* Sustainable livelihoods depend on the access to and control over assets, namely, human, social, physical, natural, and financial capital. Gender differences in access to and control over assets dictate power asymmetries and negotiating power between men and women within the household and community.
- *Markets:* Access to agricultural markets is an important source of income, assets, and factors of production and consumption to sustain the needs of the household and welfare of the family. Agricultural markets include product, input, labor (in agriculture and agribusiness), financial, land, and water markets. In many areas, participation in lucrative markets is often dependent on access to and control of capital, mobility, and sociocultural factors, where potential gender asymmetries persist.
- *Risk and vulnerability:* Risks include natural hazard risk, human conflict, human and animal disease epidemics, food insecurity, agroecological and geographic factors such as water variability and drought proneness, and market and price risks (including trade shocks). Vulnerability to these risks is a result of poverty and socioeconomic position, influenced by social dimensions such as income levels, asset ownership, ethnicity, age, class, and gender.
- *Knowledge, information, and organization:* Access to and engagement in organizations affect access to assets and markets as well as risk and vulnerability and, thus, impact sustainable livelihoods. Gender asymmetries in organization and information often reinforce or intensify gender

asymmetries in these three areas. Information includes market information, information on risks and hazards, legal rights, and skills to use to develop the rights to access markets, improve income, and manage risks. Organization includes formal and informal forms of collective action, including the political and governance structures.

The gender perspective has been structured, using the SLA, to capture the gender inequalities in these four factors. Gender inequalities in rights, resources, and voice addressed in the *Sourcebook* specifically look at the following:

- Gender asymmetries in access to and control over assets
- Gender asymmetries in participation and power in land, labor, financial, and product markets

- Gender-differentiated distribution of risks and gains along value chains
- Gender asymmetries in market information, extension services, skills, and training
- Gender asymmetries in participation and leadership in rural organizations
- Gender asymmetries in rights, empowerment, and political voice
- Gender asymmetries in household composition and labor availability (dependency ratios, migration, and disability)
- Physical and agroecological risks and their gender-differentiated impacts and vulnerability.

A simplified framework of analyzing agricultural livelihoods through a gender lens is presented in figure O.1, in

Figure O.1   Sustainable Livelihoods through a Gender Lens

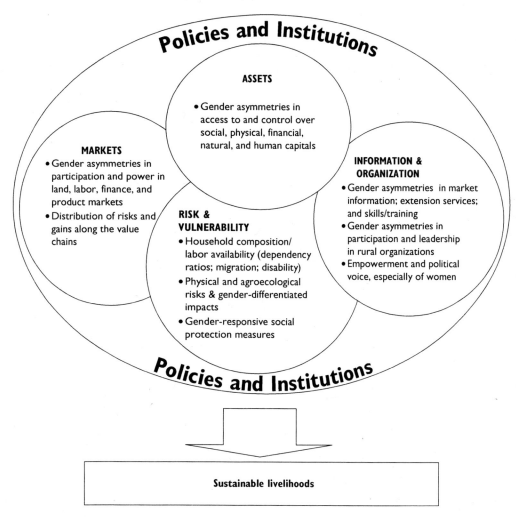

Source: Sourcebook task force.

which sustainable livelihoods are conceptualized as influenced by access to and control over assets, access to markets, access to information and organization, and effective management of risk and vulnerability, and by the interaction of these factors with policies and institutions at the global, national, and local levels.

Policies are defined as actions or strategies that directly influence rights and equity as well as prices of goods and services (World Bank 2005a). Institutions are defined as a set of formal rules (for example, law and regulations) and informal norms, as well as their enforcement characteristics (North 2005); they also include processes guiding interactions between groups of people. The *Sourcebook* looks at livelihoods at the household level, and the policies and institutions (at the global, national, and local levels) are discussed in terms of their impact on the processes affecting livelihood outcomes. The *Sourcebook* also focuses on design of agricultural projects and programs at the country level, although important regional and global issues specific to those projects and programs are also covered. Different forms of support—transformative, mainstreaming gender perspectives, and targeted project approaches[6]—are discussed, explicitly in some cases and implicitly in others. At the project level, recommendations and guidelines are made on what approaches and strategies can be implemented at different stages of the project cycle, and at different levels of development support (for example, national, local, and project levels).

KEY CONSIDERATIONS IN THE CREATION OF THE SOURCEBOOK

Several principles govern the writing of the *Sourcebook:*

Focus on people

The *Sourcebook* puts people at the center of the discussion. This focus on people is equally important at both the higher levels (when thinking about the achievement of objectives, such as poverty reduction, economic reform, or sustainable development) and at the micro- or community level. Assets, resources, markets, infrastructure, and political structures are discussed in relation to their impact on people and their livelihoods.

Holistic approach

The *Sourcebook* recognizes the importance of an integrated and multisectoral approach in promoting sustainable livelihoods. It attempts to bring together different aspects of people's livelihoods in relation to development planning, implementation, and evaluation by exploring the possibilities of unifying different sectors and stakeholders toward a common framework. Emphasizing holistic approaches, the *Sourcebook* discusses trade-offs accompanying the different sector changes and varying responses of stakeholders. Although the *Sourcebook* reflects on the various options available to the readers, it attempts to provide balanced analysis, guidance, and key principles to inform their decisions.

Macro-micro links

Development activity tends to focus on either the macro- or the microlevel. The *Sourcebook* attempts to bridge this gap by emphasizing the importance of macrolevel policy and institutions to the livelihood options of communities and individuals. It also stresses the need for higher-level policy development and planning to be informed through lessons learned and insights gained at the local level. This simultaneously gives local people a stake in policy and increases overall effectiveness. The treatment of the different topics and themes aims at comprehensive inclusion by drawing in relevant partners active in rural areas (the government, civil society, and private sector; local, national, and international levels).

Building on strengths

The *Sourcebook* focuses on strengths and opportunities, rather than on needs and weaknesses. This implies recognition of potentials, such as strong social networks, access to physical resources and infrastructure, the ability to influence core institutions, or any other factor that has poverty-reducing potential. The *Sourcebook* provides strategies on assisting women to become even stronger and more effective partners and major players in agricultural development.

Timing matters

In response to the dynamics of agricultural development, the *Sourcebook* includes anchoring the present in past developments, describing the main drivers of change, and providing a vision for the future. This discussion can help in understanding the sequencing of development support. The *Sourcebook* seeks to understand and learn from changes so that it can support positive patterns of change and help mitigate negative patterns. It explicitly recognizes the effects on livelihoods of external shocks and trends, which are more predictable than shocks but not necessarily less damaging. The *Sourcebook* aims to uncover the nature of complex, two-way cause-and-effect relationships and iterative chains of events and to provide feedback mechanisms.

Context matters

The *Sourcebook* also brings forth the diversity and heterogeneity of the poor. The context—who they are, where they are, and what they do—matters in how effectively gender integration and development goals are achieved. Particular attention is paid to regional differences in the *Sourcebook*. The policy environment and governance structure are important determinants of what development support will work. Projects with gender components will be effective only if current structures are in place. Transformative approaches and changes in institutions in many instances are necessary to break the structural gender-related constraints in societies. The *Sourcebook* aims to look at modes of providing support to the rural poor that best fit the specific structural conditions and development priorities of their area or country instead of the one-size-fits-all strategies that were adopted in the past in some cases.

Heterogeneity of the rural poor

One of the largest groups of the rural poor consists of *market-oriented smallholders*, who have small pieces of land for economic activities but are largely constrained by liquidity, risk, and transactions costs (Berdegue and Escobar 2001). With improved market opportunities and greater support services, many of these farmers can build their asset base, adopt production processes that are more suitable to the environment, and make the transition to commercially oriented farming (World Bank 2005a). These groups are the ones with the greatest potential for growth; close attention thus must be paid to associating both women and men in smallholders' programs to correct the current bias in favor of men. As illustrated by many examples in the *Sourcebook*, several gender-specific constraints limit women's active participation; and assessing and easing these constraints are vital not only for equity but also for an efficiency perspective (see Module 5). Another of the large groups, the *subsistence-oriented farmers*, frequently operates in less-favored and marginal production environments with poor access to markets; this group is made up of a large proportion of women. The major development challenge is promoting stable production and food security among these people. Another important group consists of *laborers*

on farms and agribusinesses. Occupational segregation by gender is particularly strong in many countries in South Asia, Southeast Asia, and Latin America, where a high prevalence of women in casual, low-paid employment with limited security leads to other abuses (see Module 8). The *Sourcebook* pays attention to providing options for development support differentiated by these groups of rural poor.

STRUCTURE OF THE SOURCEBOOK

Using the agricultural sector strategies and gender policies of the three partner organizations, the *Sourcebook* addresses the subsectors and topics that would foster the realization of the development objectives. The *Sourcebook* addresses agricultural livelihoods in specific investment or programmatic areas of the World Bank, FAO, and IFAD (table O.1). The Modules are selected based on themes of cross-cutting importance for agriculture and rural development with strong gender dimensions (policy and governance; agricultural innovation and education; food security; product and input markets; rural finance; rural infrastructure; water; land; labor; natural resource management; and crises) and specific subsectors in agriculture (crops, livestock, forestry, and fisheries). A separate Module on monitoring and evaluation is included, responding to the need to track implementation and development outcomes.

The Modules use the conceptual framework of agricultural livelihoods by discussing assets, markets, information and organization, and risk and vulnerability in the subsectors and themes. Political economy is intertwined throughout the *Sourcebook*, especially in Module 2, and the sociocultural dimension is captured in all Modules.

Table O.1	The Sourcebook Modules
1	Gender and Food Security
2	Gender and Agricultural Livelihoods: Strengthening Governance
3	Gender and Rural Finance
4	Gender Issues in Land Policy and Administration
5	Gender and Agricultural Markets
6	Gender Mainstreaming in Agricultural Water Management
7	Gender in Agricultural Innovation and Education
8	Gender Issues in Agricultural Labor
9	Gender in Rural Infrastructure for Agricultural Livelihoods
10	Gender and Natural Resource Management
11	Gender and Crises: Implications for Agriculture
12	Gender in Crop Agriculture
13	Gender in Fisheries and Aquaculture
14	Gender and Livestock
15	Gender and Forestry
16	Gender Issues in Monitoring and Evaluation

Source: World Bank, FAO, and IFAD 2009.

Each Module contains three different types of subunits and can function as a stand-alone document:

- A *Module Overview* is intended as a broad introduction to the topic and provides a summary of the major development issues in the sector, key gender considerations, the rationale of looking at gender dimensions in the sector, and a presentation of the framework that guides the analysis and links different themes, issues, and examples in the Modules.
- *Thematic Notes* provide a brief but technically sound guide in gender integration in selected themes within the Module topic. These Notes summarize what has been done and the success and lessons learned from projects and programs. They provide guidelines in terms of key considerations, checklists, organizing principles, key questions, and key performance indicators that would guide the design and implementation of projects.
- *Innovative Activity Profiles[7]* describe the design and innovative features of recent and exciting projects and activities that have been implemented or are ongoing and can be considered for scaling up or replication. Activities profiled here have often not been sufficiently tested and evaluated in a range of settings to be considered "good practice," but they should be closely monitored for potential scaling up. These Profiles provide the important details about the design and implementation that have contributed to the budding success of certain activities or projects, which technical experts can adopt into their operations. These Profiles are aimed at igniting the imagination of task managers and technical experts about possibilities that they can explore and adopt in their project designs.

The *Sourcebook* draws on a wide range of experience from donor agencies, governments, institutions, and other groups active in agricultural development. However, in this first edition of the *Sourcebook,* the initial contributions draw mainly from the World Bank, FAO, and IFAD experiences.

The themes and topics covered in the *Sourcebook* are not always comprehensive and are constrained by both the availability of materials and specialists and experts willing to contribute examples and share experiences. The Modules generally address the priority issues within a thematic area or areas in which operational guidance is needed, but important gaps exist that should be filled in future editions. Migration, rural-urban interlinkages, biofuels, genetically modified foods, agricultural finance, and food safety are a few areas only briefly mentioned in the *Sourcebook* that need to be more thoroughly addressed in future updates.

THE PROCESS OF THE SOURCEBOOK

The *Sourcebook* is not a primary research product, advocacy piece, or toolkit; it capitalizes on the real development experiences of task managers and operational staff in designing and implementing gender-responsive agricultural projects. The Modules have undergone an iterative process of development and review:

- *A review of existing toolkits and checklists on gender:* A preliminary evaluation of existing toolkits on gender revealed that a few toolkits are available. However, the organizers felt that a distinct need exists for a more operationally relevant, updated, concise reference source to assist task managers and technical officers in their efforts toward greater gender inclusion in agricultural policies, projects, and programs. A more detailed review of these existing toolkits was done as part of the *Sourcebook* preparation to distill relevant information.
- *Subsector reviews:* The *Sourcebook* examines key gender issues present across the concerned subsectors at the conceptual level. It identifies the range of project design emphases and approaches implemented in the sector to date. Sources of data and information include the use of secondary sources and the experiences of task managers and technical officers. Project lessons learned and challenges encountered are also identified.
- *Consultative sessions with technical experts:* Although the main sources of information are project documents and studies as well as the experience of the Module coordinators, authors, and contributors, consultative sessions and discussions were used to draw on the experiences of a wide range of experts in the World Bank, FAO, IFAD, and other relevant organizations. This process was very useful in identifying and verifying project examples with strong gender components, in documenting good practices, and in describing the context into which these practices and innovations would fit best in future operations.

LESSONS LEARNED AND WAYS FORWARD

The *Sourcebook* is a good practice example of the potential of interorganization cooperation. The gender and sector expert teams in the World Bank, FAO, and IFAD worked very well together. The interest and willingness of over 100 technical experts to provide input and reviews are admirable. The *Sourcebook* also witnessed great complementarities in approaches, expertise, and networks in the three organizations. The preparation of the *Sourcebook* encountered difficulty in getting good practice examples that are based on sound impact assessment. Not many projects have incorporated gender-disaggregated impact assessments. Good practices and innovative projects used in the *Sourcebook* relied largely on the expert judgment of the authors and thematic experts and on a rigorous review process involving experts in the three organizations to check and verify the examples. Intensifying efforts to undertake sound gender-disaggregated impact assessment is an area of great importance for further partnership.

The *Sourcebook* is a living document that provides a good start but that remains open to dialogue and new, imaginative ways of doing gender-responsive agricultural development. The authors expect the *Sourcebook* to be expanded and updated as new experience is gained and new approaches and initiatives arise. Most Module Overviews and Thematic Notes should be valid for a number of years. Individual Modules can be used as stand-alone documents, and it may be expected that in time some of the Modules will be developed into their own *Sourcebook*.

To ensure the material in the *Sourcebook* is updated, a wide dissemination strategy is planned with easy access for readers to provide updates and experiences from their development projects. The authors encourage readers to update, verify, offer feedback, and, most important, adapt key principles and relevant guidelines to individual agricultural projects and programs.

NOTES

1. "Gender and 'Shared Growth' in Sub-Saharan Africa," briefing notes on critical gender issues in sub-Saharan Africa, http://siteresources.worldbank.org/EXTABOUTUS/Resources/GenderGrowth.pdf.

2. See also Elaine Zuckerman, "Poverty Reduction Strategy Papers and Gender," background paper for the Conference on Sustainable Poverty Reduction and PRSPs—Challenges for Developing Countries and Development Cooperation, www.genderaction.org/images/PRSPs&Gender-GTZ.pdf.

3. See www.fao.org/unfao/bodies/council/cl115/w9751e.htm. Manufacturing of agricultural inputs and machinery, regional and river development, and rural development, which are also part of FAO's definition, are not discussed in this *Sourcebook*.

4. For more details on the Sustainable Livelihoods Approach (SLA), see www.ifad.org/sla/about/index.htm

(IFAD n.d.) and www.livelihoods.org/info/guidance_sheets_pdfs/section1.pdf.

5. Robert Chambers and Gordon Conway, "Sustainable Rural Livelihoods: Practical Concepts for the 21st Century," IDS Discussion Paper 296 (1992), cited in www.livelihoods.org/info/guidance_sheets_pdfs/section1.pdf.

6. Transformative programs are designed to transform gender relations by tackling the underlying structural causes and effects of inequality, such as initiatives to change inheritance laws and related practices (at the community level). Mainstreaming gender perspectives in macro- or regular programming and strengthening the capacity of institutions to mainstream gender are crucial in supporting changes in policy and legal frameworks. Targeted project approaches through agricultural initiatives can be specifically focused on either women only or men only to redress inequalities and lack of access or skills (see Module 11).

7. The selection of the Innovative Activity Profiles was largely based on the expert judgment of relevant technical staff in the three organizations on projects and programs, with a strong gender dimension or component, that worked or has a strong potential of success. These suggested projects and programs were then traced, and more information and details were gathered. However, not many of these have good documentation, and only a few have gender-disaggregated impact assessments, which meant that there were not many actual project examples for these Profiles.

REFERENCES

Berdegue, Julio, and Germán Escobar. 2001. "Agricultural Knowledge and Information Systems and Poverty Reduction." AKIS/ART Discussion Paper, World Bank, Rural Development Department, Washington, DC.

Curry, John, and Diana Tempelman. 2006. "Improving the Use of Gender and Population Factors in Agricultural Statistics: A Review of FAO's Support to Member Countries in Gender Statistics." Food and Agriculture Organization (FAO), Rome.

Deere, Carmen Diana, and Magdalena Leon. 2003. "The Gender Asset Gap: Land in Latin America." *World Development* 31: 925–47.

Doss, Cheryl. 2005. "The Effects of Intrahousehold Property Ownership on Expenditure Patterns in Ghana." *Journal of African Economies* 15: 149–80.

Food and Agriculture Organization (FAO). 2007. "Progress Report on the Implementation of the FAO Gender and Development Plan of Action." FAO, Rome.

Gender and Rural Development Thematic Group (GENRD). 2006. "FY06 Gender Portfolio Review." World Bank, Washington, DC.

———. 2007. "FY07 Gender Portfolio Review." World Bank, Washington, DC.

International Food Policy Research Institute (IFPRI). 2007a. "Proceedings of the Consultation on Strengthening Women's Control of Assets for Better Development Outcomes." IFPRI, Washington, DC.

———. 2007b. *Engendering Better Policies: Two Decades of Gender Research from IFPRI.* CD-ROM. Washington, DC: IFPRI.

International Fund for Agricultural Development (IFAD). 2001. *Rural Poverty Report 2001: The Challenge of Ending Rural Poverty.* New York: Oxford University Press.

———. 2003. "Mainstreaming a Gender Perspective in IFAD's Operations: Plan of Action 2003–2006." IFAD, Rome.

———. n.d. "Sustainable Livelihoods Approach (SLA)." IFAD, Rome. Accessed on April 10, 2007 at www.ifad.org/sla/about/index.htm.

North, Douglass. 2005. *Understanding the Process of Economic Change.* Princeton: Princeton University Press.

Quisumbing, Agnes, and Bonnie McClafferty. 2006a. "Gender and Development: Bridging the Gap between Research and Action," IFPRI Issue Brief No. 44. IFPRI, Washington, DC.

———. 2006b. "Using Gender Research in Development," Food Security in Practice No. 2, IFPRI, Washington, DC.

Quisumbing, Agnes, Jonna P. Estudillo, and Keijiro Otsuka. 2004. *Land and Schooling: Transferring Wealth across Generations.* Baltimore: Johns Hopkins University Press.

World Bank. 2001. *Engendering Development—Through Gender Equality in Rights, Resources, and Voice.* Washington, DC: World Bank.

———. 2005a. *Agricultural Growth for the Poor: An Agenda for Development.* Directions in Development Series. Washington, DC: World Bank.

———. 2005b. "Evaluating a Decade of World Bank Gender Policy: 1990–99." Operations Evaluation Department, World Bank, Washington, DC.

———. 2005c. *World Development Report 2006.* Washington, DC: World Bank.

———. 2006. "Implementing the Bank's Gender Mainstreaming Strategy: Annual Monitoring Report for FY04 and FY05." World Bank, Washington, DC.

———. 2007a. *World Development Report 2008: Agriculture for Development.* Washington, DC: World Bank.

———. 2007b. "Agriculture for Development: The Gender Dimensions." Agriculture for Development Policy Brief, World Bank, Washington, DC.

———. 2007c. *Global Monitoring Report 2007: Millennium Development Goals—Confronting the Challenges of Gender Equality and Fragile States.* Washington, DC: World Bank.

———. 2008. "Gender Equality as Smart Economics: World Bank Group Gender Action Plan, First Year Progress Report (January 2007–January 2008)." World Bank, Washington, DC.

World Bank, FAO, and IFAD. 2009. *Gender in Agriculture Sourcebook.* World Bank: Washington, DC.

Gender and Food Security

INTRODUCTION

Food Security, at the individual, household, national, regional, and global levels [is achieved] when all people, at all times, have physical, social, and economic access to sufficient, safe, and nutritious food to meet their dietary needs and food preferences for a healthy and active life.

FAO (2001)

Today the world has enough food to feed everyone, yet an estimated 854 million people worldwide are still undernourished (FAO 2006) (fig. 1.1).[1] Poverty—not food availability—is the major driver of food insecurity. Improvements in agricultural productivity are necessary to increase rural household incomes and access to available food but are insufficient to ensure food security. Evidence indicates that poverty reduction and food security do not necessarily move in tandem. The main problem is lack of economic (social and physical) access to food at national and household levels and inadequate nutrition (or hidden hunger). Food security not only requires an adequate supply of food but also entails *availability, access,* and *utilization* by all—men and women of all ages, ethnicities, religions, and socioeconomic levels.

Gender-based inequalities all along the food production chain "from farm to plate" impede the attainment of food and nutritional security. Maximizing the impact of agricultural development on food security entails enhancing women's roles as agricultural producers as well as the primary caretakers of their families. Food security is a primary goal of sustainable agricultural development and a cornerstone for economic and social development, and so this Module serves as a road map that indicates how addressing gender in agriculture development in the other Modules can be optimized to maximize the impact on food security. Unlike the other Modules, it does not contain thematic notes but instead guides the reader to Modules that provide more in-depth discussions. It also demonstrates the vital and often unacknowledged role that women play in agriculture, as well as how their critical role in ensuring sustainable agricultural development translates into household-level improvements in food and nutritional security.

FROM AGRICULTURE TO FOOD SECURITY

Agriculture and food security are inextricably linked (see fig. 1.2). The agricultural sector in each country is dependent on the available natural resources, as well as on national and international policy and the institutional environment that governs those resources. These factors influence women and men in their choice of crops and levels of potential productivity. Agriculture, whether domestic or international, is the only source of food both for direct consumption and as raw material for refined foods. Agricultural production determines food availability. The stability of access to food through production or purchase is governed by domestic policies, including social protection policies and agricultural investment choices that reduce risks (such as droughts) in the agriculture production cycle. Yet the production of food

Figure 1.1   Undernourished People Worldwide

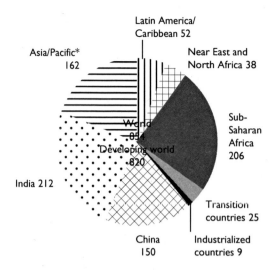

*Excluding China and India

Sources: FAO 2006; www.ifad.org/hfs/thematic/rural/rural_2.htm.

National food security requires both the production and the ability to import food from global markets to meet a nation's consumption needs.

Household food security is year-round access to an adequate supply of nutritious and safe food to meet the nutritional needs of all household members (men and women, boys and girls).

Nutritional security requires that household members have access not only to food, but also to health care, a hygienic environment, and knowledge of personal hygiene. Food security is necessary but not sufficient for ensuring nutrition security. (International Fund for Agricultural Development [IFAD])

---

is not the only goal of agricultural systems that also produce feed for livestock and fuel (see Module 10 for a more in-depth discussion). Therefore, demand for and policies related to feed and fuel also influence food availability and access.

Staple grains are the main source of dietary energy in the human diet and are more likely to be available through national and international markets, even in developing countries, given their storage and transport characteristics. Fruits, vegetables, livestock, and aquaculture products are the key to micronutrient, that is, vitamins and minerals, sufficiency. However, most of these products are more perishable than grains, so that in the poorest countries where lack of infrastructure, such as cold storage and refrigerated transport, predicates short food chains, local agriculture determines the diversity of diets. Food security can become a reality only when the agricultural sector is vibrant.

Other elements are necessary to achieve food and nutritional security as shown in figure 1.2. These are largely assigned to women, who play a key role in ensuring food security and are the focus of this Module.

WOMEN'S ROLE IN FOOD AND NUTRITIONAL SECURITY

Agricultural interventions are most likely to affect nutrition outcomes when they involve diverse and complementary processes and strategies that redirect the focus beyond agriculture for food production and toward broader consideration of livelihoods, women's empowerment, and optimal intrahousehold

uses of resources. Successful projects are those that invest broadly in improving human capital, sustain and increase the livelihood assets of the poor, and focus on gender equality.

World Bank (2007b)

Women are crucial in the translation of the products of a vibrant agriculture sector into food and nutritional security for their households. They are often the farmers who cultivate food crops and produce commercial crops alongside the men in their households as a source of income. When women have an income, substantial evidence indicates that the income is more likely to be spent on food and children's needs. Women are generally responsible for food selection and preparation and for the care and feeding of children. *Women are the key to food security* for their households (Quisumbing and others 1995).

In rural areas the availability and use of time by women is also a key factor in the availability of water for good hygiene, firewood collection, and frequent feeding of small children. In sub-Saharan Africa transportation of supplies for domestic use—fetching fuelwood and water—is largely done by women and girls on foot. In Ghana, Tanzania, and Zambia women expend most of their energy on load-carrying activities involving transport of fuelwood, water, and grain for grinding. Fields dedicated to food crops are often farther from home than those related to cash crops. Because women must also perform domestic tasks, they must spend a considerable amount of time traveling between their home and the fields. This burden, together with other domestic and

Figure 1.2 Elements in Achieving Food and Nutrition Security

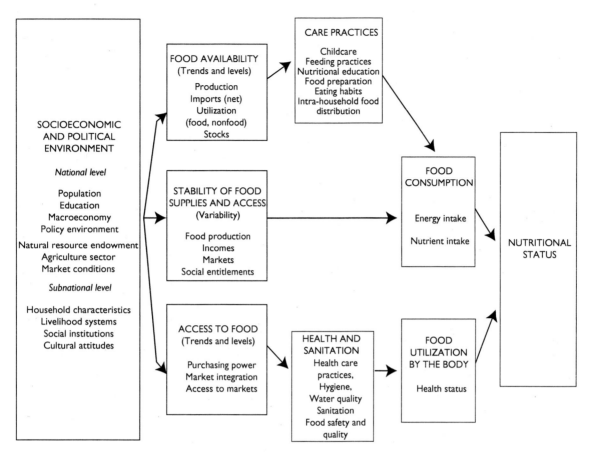

Source: IFAD, FAO, and WFP 2000.

reproductive activities, severely constrains the amount of time available to women (see Modules 9 and 7, particularly Technical Note 4 in the latter). As women's time constraints increase because of engagement in wage labor and other factors, they will need to build "strategic alliances with men" to meet all the needs of the household. In the WIN project (Empowerment of Women in Irrigation and Water Resources Management for Improved Food Security, Nutrition and Health) in Nepal, one woman trained as a para-veterinarian convinced her husband to care for their children and perform other domestic tasks while she made her rounds.[2]

Changes in the availability of natural resources, due to the depletion of natural resources and/or impacts of climate change, can compromise food security by further constraining the time available to women. As discussed in Module 10, water degradation and pollution can force women to travel farther to collect water, reduce the amount they collect, and compromise hygiene practices in the household. Recognizing women's needs for environmental resources, not only

for crop production but also for fuel and water, and building these into good environmental management can release more time for women to use on income generation, child care, and leisure.

Agriculture has an additional impact on food security through its impact on health. For example, poorly managed irrigation infrastructures may become a breeding ground for mosquitoes, and excessive use of groundwater for irrigation may compromise water sources needed by women to ensure good hygiene practices and clean food preparation, without which children suffer more frequently from diarrhea and compromised growth.

Poverty is a major driver of food insecurity, but the two are not always linked. Poorer households headed by women have demonstrated that they often succeed in providing more nutritional food for their children than those headed by men (Kennedy and Peters 1992). This demonstrates the importance of gender-based knowledge and roles with regard to food security. Men who lack knowledge about food preparation may not be able to translate food availability into nutritional security for their households.

The following sections examine in detail the three key components of food security and show how women's contribution to agriculture and its translation into nutritional security can be promoted.

FOOD SECURITY

Food security is essentially built on three pillars: food availability, food access, and food utilization. An individual must have access to sufficient food of the right dietary mix (quality) *at all times* to be food secure. Those who never have sufficient quality food are chronically food insecure. Those whose access to an adequate diet is conditioned by seasonality are food insecure and are generally called *seasonally* food insecure. Individuals who normally have enough to eat but become food insecure in the face of disasters triggered by economic, climatic, and civil shocks (war and conflict) are *transitorily* food insecure. The "at all times" element of the food security definition makes risk and associated vulnerability an important element of the food security concept.

The definition of food security is often applied at varying levels of aggregation, despite its articulation at the individual level. The importance of a pillar depends on the level of aggregation being addressed. At a global level, the important pillar is food availability. Does global agricultural activity produce sufficient food to feed all the world's inhabitants? The answer today is yes, but it may not be true in the future given the impact of a growing world population, emerging plant and animal pests and diseases, declining soil productivity and environmental quality, increasing use of land for fuel rather than food, and lack of attention to agricultural research and development, among other factors.

When food security is analyzed at the national level, an understanding not only of national production is important, but also of the country's access to food from the global market, its foreign exchange earnings, and its citizens' consumer choices. Food security analyzed at the household level is conditioned by a household's own food production and household members' ability to purchase food of the right quality and diversity in the market place. However, it is only at the individual level that the analysis can be truly accurate because only through understanding who consumes what can we appreciate the impact of sociocultural and gender inequalities on people's ability to meet their nutritional needs.

The third pillar, food utilization, essentially translates the food available to a household into nutritional security for its members. One aspect of utilization is analyzed in terms of distribution according to need. Nutritional standards exist for the actual nutritional needs of men, women, boys, and girls of different ages and life phases (that is, pregnant women), but these "needs" are often socially constructed based on culture. For example, in South Asia evidence shows that women eat after everyone else has eaten at a meal and are less likely than men in the same household to consume preferred foods such as meats and fish.

Hidden hunger commonly results from poor food utilization: that is, a person's diet lacks the appropriate balance of macro- (calories) and micronutrients (vitamins and minerals). Individuals may look well nourished and consume sufficient calories but be deficient in key micronutrients such as vitamin A, iron, and iodine. People may live in unhealthy environments with inadequate hygiene and sanitation, which results in frequent illnesses and compromised nutritional outcomes despite sufficient food being available. Infants and very young children may have mothers who are so time constrained, particularly at peak times in the agricultural calendar, that they are unable to feed a child as often as necessary to provide good nutrition. Malnutrition is economically costly: it can cost individuals 10 percent of their lifetime earnings and nations 2 to 3 percent of gross domestic product (GDP) in the worst-affected countries (Alderman 2005).

Achieving food security is even more challenging in the context of HIV and AIDS. HIV affects people's physical ability to produce and use food, reallocating household labor, increasing the work burden on women, and preventing widows and children from inheriting land and productive resources (Izumi 2006). A study of rural households in Mozambique has shown that an adult death due to illness, which is likely to be AIDS related, reduces the amount of staple foods produced by these households by 20–30 percent, contributing to household food insecurity (Donovan and Massingue 2007).

Policy responses differ according to the underlying determinants of the food insecurity. These responses range from legal reforms to economic incentives to infrastructure investment to the provision of insurance instruments. The following sections will address the specific gender issues in each pillar of food security, drawing out the links to the other Modules of the *Sourcebook*.

Food availability

Women are key players in the farming sector as shown in figure 1.3. Their role in agriculture self-employment is

Figure 1.3   Rural Employment by Sector of Activity

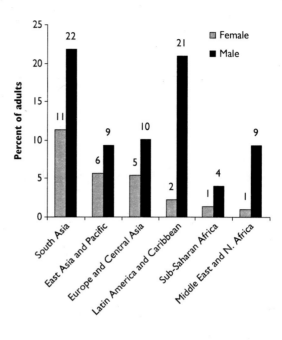

Agriculture Self-Employment by Sex

Agriculture Wage Labor by Sex

Source: World Bank 2007c.

notable in sub-Saharan Africa and the Middle East and North Africa. Women's role in food production within agriculture is even greater. In many societies women supply most of the labor needed to produce food crops and often control the use or sale of food produce grown on plots they manage.

However, the asymmetries in ownership of, access to, and control of livelihood assets (such as land, water, energy, credit, knowledge, and labor) negatively affect women's food production. Women are less likely to own land and usually enjoy only use rights, mediated through a man relative. Studies cited in Deere and Doss (2006) indicate that women held land in only 10 percent of Ghanaian households while men held land in 16–23 percent in Ghana; women are 5 percent of registered landholders in Kenya, 22.4 percent in the Mexican *ejidos* (communal farming lands), and 15.5 percent in Nicaragua. On average, men's land holdings were almost three times the women's land holdings. This compromised land access leads women to make suboptimal decisions with regard to crop choices and to obtain lower yields than would otherwise be possible if household resources were allocated efficiently.

Insecurity of tenure for women results in lower investment and potential environmental degradation; it compromises future production potential and increases food insecurity. In Ghana the primary investment in land, given the lack of availability of fertilizer, is fallowing. However, longer fallows are likely to lead to loss of land when tenure is insecure, but shorter fallows reduce yields as soil fertility is compromised. Goldstein and Udry (2005) demonstrate that those with less political capital in a village have less tenure security and as a result leave their land fallow for shorter periods. Within households, profits per hectare of a maize-cassava intercrop from similar plots vary according to individuals and length of fallow. Women have less tenure security and sacrifice profits per hectare with shorter fallows. The lower production reduces not only women's potential income, but also the availability of food for household consumption.

Legal reforms need to take into account multiple-use rights to land, particularly women's rights, as well as the different means by which women gain access to land, including divorce and inheritance systems (see Module 4, particularly Thematic Notes 2 and 4). The Lowlands Agricultural Development Projects in The Gambia (see Module 6, particularly Innovative Activity Profile 2) provide a good example of how understanding the way that women obtain land rights affects the design of a successful project. The project resulted in previously landless women obtaining secure rights to land through a land reclamation program.

Agricultural production depends on natural resources: land, soil, water, and plant genetic resources. Women often have unique perspectives on as well as understanding of local biodiversity and can be key partners for plant breeders as they work to develop adapted and improved varieties. In Rwanda women farmers have shown they can be more effective at selecting improved varieties for local cultivation than the men plant breeders (Sperling and Berkowitz 1994). The LinKS project,[3] discussed in Module 10 (in particular Innovative Activity Profile 1), demonstrates how to work with a broad spectrum of stakeholders to promote food security by understanding local women and men farmers' unique understanding of agrobiodiversity.

Agricultural technology transfer capacity development is one of the prime policy levers to increase agricultural productivity. But often women are not targeted because it is assumed that their husbands or fathers will share the knowledge with them, and often they are supplied with technologies that do not meet their needs. For example, early dissemination of hybrid maize in Zambia failed to recognize that women use the crop for home consumption, which requires milling. The hybrid that was introduced required hammer mills, but only traditional mills were available locally. Poorer storage characteristics of the hybrid also compromised women's ability to conserve their agricultural produce, so women returned to growing traditional maize varieties (see Module 12). Involving young women and men in training opportunities from the start has proved to be a successful strategy in ensuring food security and sustainable livelihoods for households, as can be seen in the example provided by the approach used in the Junior Farmer Field Life School (see Module 7, in particular Innovative Activity Profile 3).

However, adoption of new technology depends on many things, including the availability of required assets to implement the technology, how local women and men view the perceived benefits, the way information is shared, and local gender roles and other sociocultural constraints. Even when women have access to land for food production and access to improved technologies, they face more constraints than men in accessing complementary resources for success. They have less access to credit (see Module 3) and less access to inputs such as fertilizer, and they are less likely to benefit from agricultural extension services (see Module 7), and therefore they have less access to improved technologies (see fig. 1.4). Women tend to process their crops more on the farm than men do theirs, but little is invested in technology research into on-farm crop processing.

These constraints are not only costly to food security but also to economic growth. If women farmers in Kenya had the same access to farm inputs, education, and experience as their men counterparts, their yields for maize, beans, and cowpeas could increase as much as 22 percent (Quisumbing 1996). This would have resulted in a one-time doubling of Kenya's GDP growth rate in 2004 from 4.3 percent to 8.3 percent (World Bank 2007a). More important, household productivity in agriculture and food supplies could often be increased at no extra cost by reallocating existing resources inside the household toward women.

Figure 1.4   Roles and Access to Assets by Women and Men in the Agriculture Sector

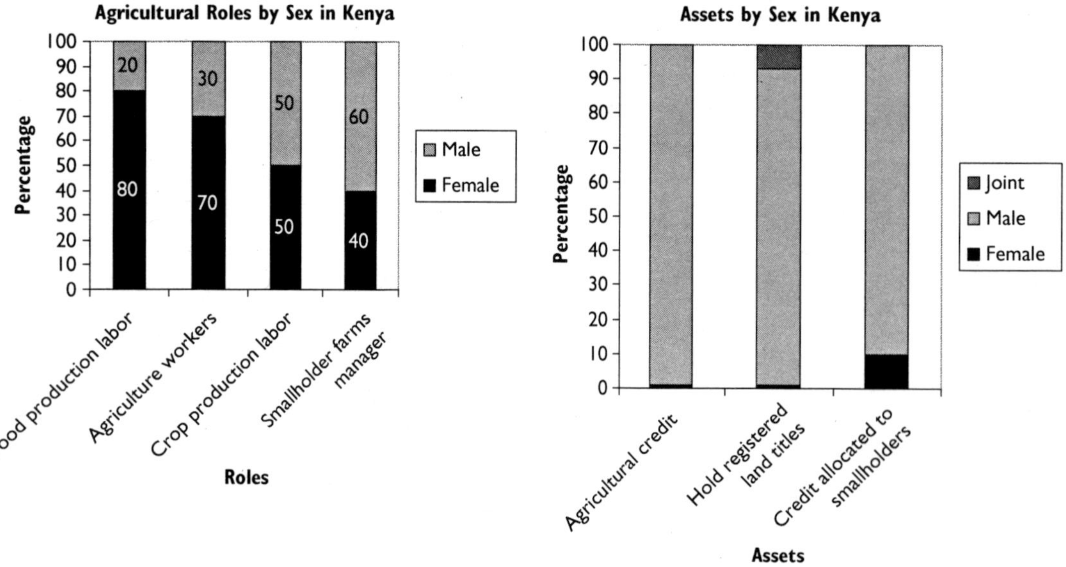

Source: World Bank 2007a.

Soil fertility is an important component of agricultural productivity. As shown in Module 12, particularly Thematic Note 2, legumes can be used to improve soil fertility to enhance crop productivity as well as human nutrition. Recognition and adaptation of this approach in Malawi demonstrated that women had a preference for a legume intercrop production system for their plots. This approach helped improve soil fertility and increased the productivity of their main crop as well as improved household food security by providing an additional source of nutritious food.

Food access

Access to food can be constrained physically—washed-out roads in a rainy season may cut off access to the nearby market town—or, more usually, economically. Ironically, food insecurity has a largely rural face. Despite the fact that the majority of food is grown in rural areas, most of the rural poor are net food buyers, not sellers, in many countries. Hence, economic access to markets, or lack thereof, is a fundamental determinant of food insecurity. The role of agriculture in income generation for the poor, particularly women, is more important for food security than its role in food production (Sanchez and others 2005).

The Andhra Pradesh Rice Credit Line Project (Module 3, Innovative Activity Profile 1) and Niger's Food Bank Project (Module 11, Innovative Activity Profile 2) are examples of initiatives in which improved income generation and food-linked credit systems for women enhanced household food security and the overall well-being of the family.

During conflict and crises, food aid and agricultural assistance are both necessary components of effective interventions. The intertwining forces of food aid and agricultural support affect women's and men's food security, nutrition, health, and livelihoods. During times of crisis, women and girls are often forced to reduce their intake in favor of other household members, particularly men and boys, which results in increased incidence of malnutrition among women. However, men are at greater risk during famines, and in many recorded famines, mortality rates are higher among men than women. Insecure conditions can also limit women's mobility and access to humanitarian aid or markets (see Module 11).

When crises disrupt agricultural production and distribution, displace populations, and render land unusable, food aid is of critical importance, especially in the short term. The key to sustainability, however, is to ensure that the aid provided does not create dependency or harm the communities and stakeholders it hopes to assist. To plan emergency interventions properly requires substantial knowledge of the ways in which the agricultural sector works, as well as knowing what the sociocultural reality is locally and how that dictates who does what, who has what, and who controls what. Because women (and children to some extent) are typically responsible for food production, preparation, storage, and marketing, it is crucial to include them in emergency-related food security planning and decision making as potential change agents and decision makers, rather than as the "victims" they are often portrayed to be. A key aspect of program design is to understand the differing roles, responsibilities, capacities, and constraints of women and men in the region in question. This includes understanding the traditional division of labor in the agricultural sphere, as well as any changes that may have resulted from a crisis. Lessons learned reveal that food security interventions and livelihoods-saving strategies within an emergency setting are more efficient, cost effective, and timely when gender-based differences and gender-differentiated impacts on the affected population have been properly understood and addressed (FAO 2005; see Module 11).

The Household Food Security and Nutrition Project in Ethiopia illustrates that it is vital that beneficiaries have a strong sense of ownership of the project and that the ability of men and women to assess their own situation and their ability to improve their livelihoods are important steps in the empowerment process.[4] Moreover, identifying gender-differentiated opportunities and constraints for improving nutrition and food security during the design phase of a project often leads to better food security interventions.

Addressing poverty issues in and of themselves, while vital, does not necessarily mean that we are addressing food insecurity. India has been remarkably successful in using agricultural development to foster economic growth and poverty reduction. It has moved from food deficits to food surpluses on the national level. India has a higher gross national income (GNI) per capita at $730 than most of sub-Saharan Africa. However, its child stunting rates are high at 46 percent. Niger's GNI per capita is just $240, but its stunting rate is 40 percent. The Gambia demonstrates what can be achieved despite poverty, with a stunting rate of just 19 percent against a GNI per capita income of $290.[5] Afghanistan, Bangladesh, India, and Nepal occupy four of the top five positions in the global ranking of underweight children. Bangladesh and India rank among the highest incidences of low-birth-weight babies, an indicator of maternal malnutrition. Many would argue that the inferior status of women in South Asia is a key factor in the failure to translate agriculture-led poverty reduction into nutritional improvements.

Welfare improvements at the household level are not just a function of increasing incomes for households; they are related to who accrues the income within the household. In Côte d'Ivoire, significantly more is spent on food and education and less on alcohol and cigarettes when a higher share of household cash income accrues to women. To achieve the same improvements in children's nutrition and health with a $10 increase in women's income would require a $110 increase in men's income (Hoddinott and Haddad 1995).

Although men often control labor input and the sale of "cash crops," women often manage production of subsistence crops, albeit some of the same crops that are sold in local markets. Therefore, improving women's productivity in agriculture not only increases food availability for the household but also raises women's incomes and enhances food security due to women's spending patterns. As discussed in Module 8, public works programs are often used as elements of social protection programs to benefit poor, landless households. Cash wages provide flexibility, but women often prefer that these programs pay food wages. In a World Food Programme project to improve watershed management in Rajasthan, India, women were glad that the program paid food wages as opposed to cash wages because if the program paid cash, then their husbands would participate, and they would not see any additional resources dedicated to household food security.[6]

However, women often face constraints to market engagement. Cash crops are often collected at the farm gate, whereas food crops need to be transported by the grower to local markets. In Africa this is commonly done by women headloading. Studies have found that women transport 26 metric ton kilometers per year compared to less than 7 for men. This leads some people to argue that women account for two-thirds of rural transport in sub-Saharan Africa (Blackden and Bhanu 1999). Hammer mills, which are needed to grind many maize hybrids, are often less common and are centralized at a greater distance from individual households. Given that women bear the transport burden, they may be less likely to adopt hybrid varieties and continue to favor their traditional but lower-yielding varieties.

Investment in transport and infrastructure is necessary to support women's market engagement (see Module 9). This is an important step toward integrating women into value chains (see Module 5). Changes in policy and regulatory frameworks are also needed to create an equal playing field for women and men in market participation. Greater access to information, organizations, and resources is important for poor women, who disproportionately lack access compared to their men counterparts. Finally, capacity building is needed for poor women in particular, as cultural and other gender-specific constraints have hindered them from greater engagement in markets (see Module 5).

Food utilization

Having access to food of sufficient quality does not automatically translate into good nutritional status for individuals. Women's role in food utilization for food security is perhaps the most critical and outweighs the importance of their role in food production and how they spend the income they earn.

Sixty percent of the calories and proteins consumed by humans today come from just three plant species: maize, rice, and wheat. Seventy-five percent of our food supply comes from just 12 plants and five animal species (Lambrou and Laub 2004), but yet dietary diversity is extremely important. Diets dominated by cereals lack an adequate array of micronutrients such as iron, vitamin A, B vitamins (niacin, thiamine), vitamin C, zinc, iodine, and folate. Deficiencies in micronutrients are costly in economic terms and in terms of people's well-being. Deficiencies in vitamin A, iron, and zinc all rank within the top 10 leading causes of death through disease in developing countries (WHO 2002). In Sierra Leone iron deficiency among women agricultural workers will cost the economy $100 million in the next five years (Darnton-Hill and others 2005).

Women are typically responsible for food preparation and thus are crucial to the dietary diversity of their households. Women are generally responsible for selecting food purchased to complement staple foods and to balance the household's diet. Even in the Sahel where men control the granaries, women are responsible for supplying the "relishes" that go with the grains, and it is these that provide the bulk of the micronutrients.

The prime sources for micronutrients are fruits, vegetables, and animal source foods, including fish. Animal source foods are particularly good; they are high density in terms of micronutrients, and those micronutrients are also more bioavailable to the human body (see Modules 13 and 14). Agriculture is thus a key to dietary diversity, particularly in areas that have less access to markets given the perishable nature of fruits, vegetables, and animal source foods.

An extensive review of the nutritional impacts of agricultural interventions, disaggregated into staple crops, fruits and vegetables, and animal source foods, found that the role of women was critical. Studies of the commercialization of staple food production determined that those people who increased the share of women's income were more likely to increase expenditures on food, although not necessarily improve nutritional outcomes. Interventions focused on fruits and vegetables were more likely to produce biochemical indicators of improved nutritional status when they included educational behavior change designed to empower women. Many of the reviewed livestock and aquaculture interventions resulted in gains in production, income, and food availability, and significantly greater nutritional improvements when the interventions were combined with capacity development training that promoted women's empowerment, education, and behavior change (see Modules 13 and 14). A good example of this type of intervention is that of the introduction of orange-fleshed sweet potatoes in Mozambique. These contain higher levels of provitamin A carotenoids and when introduced with nutrition education can lead to reductions in vitamin A deficiency.[7] Fisheries also offer powerful opportunities for women, as demonstrated in Module 13, particularly Thematic Note 2, which shows how CARE Bangladesh introduced a sustainable, high-income fisheries component that improved family nutrition. As discussed in Module 12, Thematic Note 2, vegetables can be cultivated on the homestead because they require very little land and do not displace other crops. Women do not need to leave the homestead, and so they do not need to violate local cultural restrictions, which would have lowered their participation rates in projects.

MONITORING AND EVALUATION

Disaggregated monitoring of food security is critical. Many of the following Modules contain specific information and indicators regarding production and access to food under different production systems. Table 1.1 provides examples of indicators that might be used in monitoring the access of women and their families to food of adequate quality and quantity.

Depending on the country or region, it may be relevant also to consider ethnicity and caste alongside gender (both as comparative indicators and when collecting data), because women of lower castes or ethnic minorities are usually in the most disadvantaged situation.

CONCLUDING REMARKS

Women play a triple role in agricultural households: productive, reproductive, and social. The productive role, performed by both men and women, focuses on economic activities; the reproductive role, almost exclusively done by women, includes child bearing and rearing; household maintenance, including cooking, fetching water, and fuelwood; and the social role or community building, often dominated by women, which includes arranging funerals, weddings, and social events.

If sustainable agricultural development is to be translated into food and nutrition security, then the active engagement of women is absolutely necessary. Their involvement will require that development agents go beyond traditional approaches to sustainable agricultural development. Food and nutritional security will mean that women are included in crop breeding and selection strategies so that crops are not selected on their behalf that they cannot market or process, such as hybrid maize when they do not have a hammer mill, and it will necessitate incorporating women in marketing chains (see Module 5).

Food security is not just a goal of sustainable agricultural development; it is a right enshrined in the Universal Declaration of Human Rights, and amplified by Article 11 of the International Covenant on Economic, Social and Cultural Rights. Women also have the right to be equal partners in the agriculture sector, and to that end the Convention for the Elimination of Discrimination against Women protects women's equal access to land, credit, and income. In South Africa (Integrated Food Security Strategy) and Uganda (Food and Nutrition Policy), governments call for a rights-based approach to food security that includes gender equity. Public policies, written from a human rights perspective, recognize the interrelatedness of all basic rights and assist in the identification of those whose rights are not fully realized. In this way they facilitate corrective action and appropriate strategies to enable equal protection for all. Equal representation and active engagement of both women and men in the policy-making processes are required so that their varying needs and priorities are appropriately targeted. More often than not, however, access to the legal system may be more problematic for women than men, but technical and financial support is also needed if institutions that advance and implement women's rights are to fulfill their mandate (see Module 2).

This Module has outlined the basic concepts regarding food security and how it may be achieved by addressing gender inequalities in agricultural development. For a more in-depth understanding of how food security can be achieved through a specific agricultural sector, refer to the relevant Modules or the further reading listed below.

Table 1.1   Monitoring and Evaluation Indicators for Gender and Food Security

Indicator	Sources of verification/tools
Relative contributions of fruits, vegetables, animal products, fish, and grains to diet, disaggregated by gender and age	• Household survey • Nutritional survey
Change in food consumption by women, men, boys, and girls per quarter	• Household survey • Nutritional survey
Change in amount of milk, eggs, fish, and animal protein consumed by household family members (disaggregated by women, men, boys, and girls)	• Child health records • Household surveys • Rapid nutrition surveys
Change in nutritional status of children under age five, before and after program activities (disaggregated by boys and girls)	• Child health records • Household surveys • Rapid nutrition surveys
Change in birth weight of babies, before and after program activities	• Child health records • Household surveys
Time spent or distance walked by household members to collect potable water or firewood, disaggregated by gender and age	• Household surveys • Participatory Rapid Appraisal (PRA)
Percentage of time spent daily in household on paid and nonpaid activities, disaggregated by gender and age	• Gender analysis • Time-use studies
Uptake of new or intermediate technologies, such as low fuel stoves, solar cookers, rope pumps, small grain mills, and new types of food, disaggregated by age and education level	• Observation • Sample surveys • Stakeholder interviews
Number of persons accessing credit for food production annually, disaggregated by gender	• Bank records • Savings and loan group records
Changes in soil, crop, and pasture condition in farmland, before and after program activities (such as nutrient levels and percentage ground cover)	• Department of Agriculture surveys • Farm records • Participatory monitoring by villagers/herders
In postdisaster situations, number of women with cooking utensils	• Sample surveys
Changes to livelihood sources (on-farm and nonfarm) among resettled or postdisaster men, women (especially women-headed households), and other disadvantaged groups	• Case studies • Community monitoring committees • PRA • Sample surveys
Changes in access to food markets, before and after infrastructure development	• Household surveys, before and after • Project management information system
Changes over x-year period of project activities in household nutrition, health, education, vulnerability to violence, and happiness, disaggregated by gender	• Household surveys, before and after • Project management information system • School records

Source: Authors, with inputs from Pamela White, author of Module 16.

NOTES

This Module was written by Lynn Brown (World Bank), Chitra Deshpande (Consultant), Catherine L. M. Hill (Consultant), Yianna Lambrou (FAO), and Marina Laudazi and Catherine Ragasa (Consultants), with inputs from Anne Nicolaysen (FAO), and reviewed by Deborah Rubin (Cultural Practice); Karel Callens, Bill Clay, Patricia Colbert, Brian Thompson and Marcela Villarreal (FAO); Maria Hartl, Sean Kennedy, and Annina Lubbock (IFAD); and Harold Alderman and Mio Takada (World Bank).

1. Based on FAO's 2001–03 estimates; see FAO (2006).

2. The project is funded by the United Nations Foundation and implemented by FAO. See e-GAL *Sourcebook* for more details on the WIN project at www.worldbank.org.

3. See www.fao.org/sd/LINKS/GEBIO.HTM.

4. Available in the e-GAL *Sourcebook*, Module 11, Innovative Activity Profile 3, at www.worldbank.org.

5. Nutrition statistics from *State of the World's Children 2007* (UNICEF 2006), GNI per capita statistics from *World Development Indicators 2007* (World Bank 2007d).

6. Personal communication with Lynn Brown, April 1, 2008.

7. Available in the e-GAL *Sourcebook*, Module 12, Innovative Activity Profile 1, at www.worldbank.org.

REFERENCES

Alderman, Harold. 2005. "Linkages between Poverty Reduction Strategies and Child Nutrition: An Asian Perspective." *Economic and Political Weekly* 40 (46): 4837–42.

Blackden, Mark, and Chitra Bhanu. 1999. "Gender, Growth and Poverty Reduction," 1998 SPA Status Report on Poverty in sub-Saharan Africa, World Bank Technical Paper 428, World Bank, Washington, DC.

Darnton-Hill, Ian, Patrick Webb, Philip W. J. Harvey, Joseph M. Hunt, Nita Dalmiya, Mickey Chopra, Madeleine J. Ball, Martin W. Bloem, and Bruno de Benoist. 2005. "Micronutrient Deficiencies and Gender: Social and Economic Costs." *American Journal of Clinical Nutrition* 81 (5): 1198S–1205S.

Deere, Carmen D., and Cheryl Doss. 2006. "Gender and the Distribution of Wealth in Developing Countries." *UNU-WIDER* (World Institute for Development Economics Research of the United Nations University), Research Paper No. 2006/115, UNU-WIDER, Helsinki.

Donovan, Cynthia, and Jaqualino Massingue. 2007. "Illness, Death and Macronutrients: Adequacy of Rural Mozambican Household Production of Macronutrients in the Face of HIV/AIDS." *Food and Nutrition Bulletin* 28 Supp.: S331–38.

Food and Agriculture Organization (FAO). 2001. *FAO's State of Food Insecurity 2001*. Rome: FAO.

———. 2005. *Breaking Ground: Gender and Food Security*. Rome: FAO.

———. 2006. *The State of Food Insecurity in the World 2006: Eradicating World Hunger—Taking Stock Ten Years after the World Food Summit*. Rome: FAO. Also available at www.fao.org/sof/sofi.

Goldstein, Markus, and Christopher Udry. 2005. "The Profits of Power: Land Rights and Agricultural Investment in Ghana." Economic Growth Center Discussion Paper No. 929, Yale University, New Haven, CT.

Hoddinott, John, and Lawrence Haddad. 1995. "Does Female Income Share Influence Household Expenditures? Evidence from Côte D'Ivoire." *Oxford Bulletin of Economic and Statistics* 57 (1): 77–96.

International Fund for Agricultural Development (IFAD), Food and Agriculture Organization (FAO), and World Food Programme (WFP). 2000. *System-Wide Guidance on Household Food Security and Nutrition*. Administrative Committee on Coordination (ACC) Occasional Policy Papers. Rome: IFAD, FAO, and WFP.

Izumi, Kaori. 2006. *Reclaiming Our Lives: HIV and AIDS, Women's Land and Property Rights and Livelihoods in East and Southern Africa—Narratives and Responses*. Cape Town: HSRC Press.

Kennedy, Eileen, and Pauline Peters. 1992. "Household Food Security and Child Nutrition: The Interaction of Income and Gender of Household Head." *World Development* 20 (8): 1077–85.

Lambrou, Yianna, and Regina Laub. 2004. *Gender Perspectives on the Conventions on Biodiversity, Climate Change and Desertification*. Rome: FAO.

Quisumbing, Agnes. 1996. "Male-Female Differences in Agriculture Productivity: Methodological Issues and Empirical Evidence." *World Development* 24 (10): 1579–95.

Quisumbing, Agnes R., Lynn R. Brown, Hilary S. Feldstein, Lawrence Haddad, and Christin Peña. 1995. *Women: The Key to Food Security*. Food Policy Statement 21. Washington, DC: International Food Policy Research Institute.

Sanchez, Pedro, M. S. Swaminathan, Philip Dobie, and Nalan Yuksel. 2005. *Halving Hunger: It Can Be Done*. New York: Millennium Project.

Sperling, Louise, and Peggy Berkowitz. 1994. *Partners in Selection: Bean Breeders and Women Bean Experts in Rwanda*. Washington, DC: Consultative Group on International Agricultural Research.

United Nations Children's Fund (UNICEF). 2006. *State of the World's Children 2007*. New York: UNICEF.

World Bank. 2007a. *Gender and Economic Growth in Kenya*. Washington, DC: World Bank.

———. 2007b. "From Agriculture to Nutrition: Pathways, Synergies, and Options." Report 40196-GLB, World Bank, Washington, DC.

———. 2007c. *World Development Report 2008: Agriculture for Development*. Washington, DC: World Bank.

———. 2007d. *World Development Indicators 2007*. Washington, DC: World Bank.

World Health Organization (WHO). 2002. *The World Health Report 2002: Reducing Risks, Promoting Health Life*. Geneva: WHO.

FURTHER READING

Azad, Nandini. n.d. "Engendered Mobilization, the Key to Livelihood Security: IFAD's Experience in South Asia." Rome: IFAD. Available at www.ifad.org/hfs/thematic/southasia/south_toc.htm.

Bamberger, Michael, and Annabel Davis. 2001. *Women and Rural Transport in Development*. Washington, DC: World Bank.

Food and Agriculture Organization (FAO). 2003a. *Participatory Appraisal of Nutrition and Household Food Security Situations and Planning from a Livelihoods Perspective—Methodological Guide*. Rome: FAO.

———. 2003b. *Trade Reforms and Food Security: Conceptualizing the Linkages.* Rome: FAO.

———. 2006. *The Double Burden of Malnutrition, Case Studies from Six Developing Countries.* Rome: FAO.

Haddad, Lawrence, and John Hoddinott. 1994. "Women's Income and Boy-Girl Anthropometric Status in the Côte d'Ivoire." *World Development* 22 (4): 543–53.

International Fund for Agricultural Development (IFAD). n.d. IFAD India projects Web site, "Impact of Market-Oriented Production on Household Food Security." Available at www.ifad.org/hfs/learning/in_3.htm.

Johnson-Welch, Charlotte, Kerry MacQuarrie, and Sandra Bunch. 2005. "A Leadership Strategy for Reducing Hunger and Malnutrition in Africa: The Agriculture-Nutrition Advantage." Project report for the U.S. Agency for International Development (USAID), and U.S. Department of Agriculture (USDA). International Center for Research on Women (ICRW), Washington, DC.

Mechlem, Kerstin. 2004. "Food Security and the Right to Food in the Discourse of the United Nations." *European Law Journal* 10 (5): 631–48.

Patel, Mahesh. 2001. *Human Rights as an Emerging Development Paradigm and Some Implications for Programme Planning, Monitoring and Evaluation.* Nairobi: UNICEF.

Rae, Isabella. 2006. *Gender Dimensions of the Right to Food.* Rome: Food and Agriculture Organization.

Rahman, Osmani. n.d. "Food Security, Poverty and Women: Lessons from Rural Asia." Rome: IFAD. Available at www.ifad.org/hfs/thematic/rural/rural_toc.htm.

Roberts, S. L. 2001. "Women: The Key to Food Security." Paper presented at the International Congress on Dietetics, Chicago, IL, May.

Theis, Joachim. 2003. "Rights-Based Monitoring and Evaluation." Discussion Paper, Save the Children, Bangkok.

Van Esterik, Penny. 1999. "Right to Food; Right to Feed; Right to Be Fed: The Intersection of Women's Rights and the Right to Food." *Agriculture and Human Values* 16 (2): 225–32.

Further information on developing and using food security indicators at different levels

Beerlandt, Hannelore, and Stijn Huysman. 1999. *Manual for Bottom-Up Approach in Food Security Interventions: Analysis of Target Groups.* Rome: IFAD. Available at www.ifad.org/hfs/tools/hfs/bsfpub/manual_toc.htm.

Committee on World Food Security. 2000. Twenty-sixth session, Rome, Italy, September 18–21. Available at www.fao.org/docrep/meeting/X8228E.htm.

Maxwell, Simon, and Timothy Frankenberger. 1992. "Household Food Security: Concepts, Indicators and Measurements." Rome: IFAD. Available at www.ifad.org/hfs/tools/hfs/hfspub/index.htm.

Further case studies

Available via the Innovative Activity Profiles prepared for the *Gender in Agricultural Livelihoods* (GAL) *eSourcebook* available at www.worldbank.org: Module 12 (Gender in Crop Agriculture), Innovative Activity Profile 1 (Promoting Orange-Fleshed Sweet Potatoes).

Gender and Agricultural Livelihoods: Strengthening Governance

Overview

Governance has taken center stage in the international development debate. As Kofi Annan, then-Secretary-General of the United Nations (UN), told world leaders in 1998: "Good governance is perhaps the single most important factor in eradicating poverty and promoting development." Good governance has been defined in different ways by development organizations. The definition offered by the United Nations Development Programme highlights participation, accountability, transparency, consensus, sustainability, and the rule of law as elements of good governance and emphasizes the inclusion of the poorest and most vulnerable people in making decisions about allocating development resources.[1] A widely used set of aggregate data from a broad range of sources compiled by the World Bank Institute measures the following six dimensions of good governance: (1) voice and accountability, (2) political stability and absence of violence, (3) the rule of law, (4) regulatory quality, (5) government effectiveness, and (6) control of corruption (Kaufmann, Kraay, and Mastruzzi 2007).

Reforms that aim at promoting good governance have become an important policy area increasingly supported by international financial institutions and donor agencies. In 2007, 14 percent of the World Bank's total lending was spent on public sector governance (World Bank 2007a). Programs, projects, and investments that support governance reforms are relevant for agricultural livelihoods in two respects: First, agriculture can benefit from overall reforms that aim at improving governance, such as decentralization,

promotion of community-driven development, public sector management reforms, legal reforms, and anticorruption measures (column a in table 2.1). Second, agricultural livelihoods can be promoted by governance reforms specific to the agricultural sector, such as strategies to improve agricultural policy making and reforms of agricultural service provision (column b). As shown in table 2.1, one can further distinguish approaches to improve governance that require institutional and legal changes (row a), and approaches that can be pursued within an existing institutional and legal framework (row b).

Although all four types of reforms create significant opportunities for improving agricultural livelihoods by making agricultural policies and programs more effective, one cannot take it for granted that any of these governance reforms will also promote gender equity in the agricultural sector. If implemented in a "gender-blind" way, such reforms can even increase gender inequalities. Therefore, specific efforts are needed to make governance reforms gender sensitive and to address the specific challenges of gender inequality in the agricultural sector, which have been outlined in the *Sourcebook* Overview. One can consider governance reforms that are relevant for agriculture to be "gender sensitive" if they are (1) *sensitive to gender differentials,* for instance, by making sure that women in the agricultural sector do not lose out in the reform process; (2) *gender specific,* that is, by addressing specific needs that differ between men and women engaged in agriculture; (3) *empowering to women,* for instance, by making provisions for affirmative action

Table 2.1   Investment Options to Improve Governance

Activities supported by investment projects and programs	General governance reforms (a)	Agriculture-specific governance reforms (b)
(a) Governance reforms requiring institutional and legal change	• Political, fiscal, and administrative decentralization • Public administration and civil service reforms • Access to justice reforms • Changes in procurement rules and procedures • Right to information laws	• Decentralization of agricultural services and functions (transfer of functions, staff, and resources to lower levels of government) • Institutional reforms of Ministries of Agriculture (including creation of autonomous agencies and transfer of management to local groups)
(b) Approaches to improving governance within existing legal and institutional structures	• Participatory policy planning and budgeting • Citizen report cards • Governance and integrity surveys • Improved audits, including introduction of social audits • Leadership training • Civic education	• Promoting participation in agricultural policy processes • Improving management systems in Ministries of Agriculture • Community-driven agricultural development projects • Support for rural self-help groups' producer organizations

Source: Authors.

and creating more opportunities for rural women's participation in political processes; or (4) *transformative,* for instance, by attempting to change prevalent attitudes and social norms that lead to discrimination against rural women. The objective of this Module is to identify and discuss opportunities for making governance reforms gender sensitive, focusing on those reforms that are particularly relevant for agricultural livelihoods.

CONCEPTUAL FRAMEWORK

The following sections discuss several strategies and approaches to reform governance.

Strategies to reform governance

To understand how the gender dimension can best be addressed in governance reforms that are relevant to agriculture, it is useful to define good governance for the agricultural sector and to identify the major mechanisms or strategies by which such reforms attempt to lead to better governance. Applying the definitions and concepts of good governance quoted above, one can derive the following dimensions of good governance in the agricultural sector (fig. 2.1): quality of agricultural policies and regulations (regulatory quality); efficiency and equity in the provision of agricultural services and infrastructure (government effectiveness); reduction of corruption, that is, the abuse of public office for private gain, in the agricultural sector (control of corruption); and access to justice and enforcement of

rights that are related to food and agriculture, including rights to land and the right to food (rule of law). All these dimensions of good governance are essential for the improvement of agricultural livelihoods, because they make agricultural policies and programs more effective and lead to a more efficient use of the funds invested in agriculture.

In figure 2.1 one can distinguish two types of approaches that can lead to improved governance outcomes. They can be referred to as "demand-side" and "supply-side" strategies, even though one must acknowledge that public service provision does not follow the principles of a functioning market. The term "demand-side" strategies has become widely used to cover strategies that aim at strengthening people's and communities' ability to demand better public services and hold public officials accountable, including politicians and the public administration. These strategies capture the "voice and accountability" dimension of good governance. The term "supply-side" strategies is used to cover all approaches that strengthen the capacity of the public administration and other public service providers to supply services more effectively and efficiently and to be more responsive to citizens' priorities and needs. These strategies refer to the "government effectiveness" dimension of good governance.

Making demand-side strategies gender sensitive

An important example of a demand-side strategy is decentralization, which holds promise for better service provision by "bringing government closer to the people." One can distinguish between political, administrative, and fiscal

Figure 2.1 Demand- and Supply-Side Strategies to Improve Governance

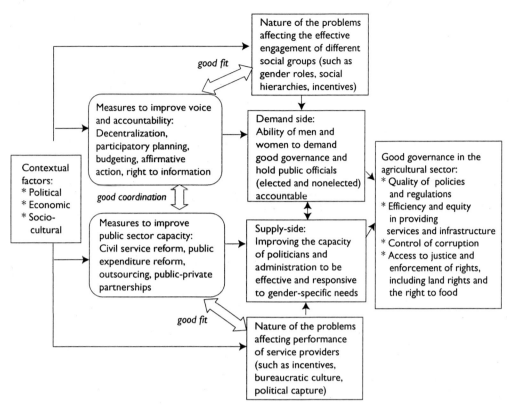

Source: Authors.

decentralization, depending on whether political authority, administrative functions and staff, or financial resources are transferred to lower levels of government. If accompanied by fiscal and administrative decentralization, political decentralization has considerable potential for making public service provision more accountable to rural citizens and more responsive to their needs. Other examples of demand-side approaches include participatory planning and budgeting and strengthening citizen's rights to information. Demand-side approaches that are specific to the agricultural sector include decentralizing agricultural ministries and departments, making service providers accountable to locally elected governments, using participatory methods in agricultural policy formulation and in agricultural advisory services, and using social audits for agricultural infrastructure projects. Demand-side approaches are often promoted by civil society organizations, and they are particularly effective if they are driven by civil society organizations' grassroots movements rather than external interventions (Ackerman 2004).

To make demand-side reforms gender sensitive, taking into account that gender roles and existing forms of discrimination against women may prevent them from exercising demand and holding public officials accountable are both

important. The design of governance reforms can help to address such problems; but no simple solutions are to be found. A prominent example is the reservation of seats for women in local government bodies, an affirmative action measure that was introduced together with decentralization in India, Pakistan, Uganda, and other countries. A considerable challenge to making this strategy work is the fact that many men politicians deeply resent the reservation of seats for women. As a consequence, it is a common strategy that they have their wives run on their behalf, who are then considered to be proxies for their husbands. Another challenge is low levels of literacy among women, which limit their effectiveness as politicians, as studies in India and Uganda have shown (Jayal 2006; Johnson, Kabuchu, and Vusiya 2003). Women who stand for elections may also suffer from physical intimidation and violence (Jayal 2006). One also has to take into account that women do not necessarily advocate for gender equity once they assume political functions. Studies from India suggest that women representatives often align their policy emphasis along caste rather than gender lines (Vyasulu and Vyasulu 2000). Research from southern Africa indicates that women politicians dismissed the idea to give up party solidarity in support of gender concerns

(Geisler 1995). Despite these limitations, evidence suggests that reservations may lead to women's empowerment and better representation, eventually. Chattopadhyay and Duflo (2004) found that local council presidents in three Indian states invest more in types of infrastructure directly relevant to the needs of their own gender (see further discussion, lessons learned from past experience, and entry points for improved interventions in Thematic Note 3).

In participatory planning approaches—a type of intervention that can be introduced within existing legal and institutional structures—special provisions may be required to ensure women's participation in the planning process, such as holding planning meetings with women's groups prior to general planning meetings. Gender-disaggregated information is a key input in demand-side strategies, because citizens need to know how the state has allocated public resources and to whose benefit. Right-to-information legislation, such as India's Right-to-Information Act, helps to improve access to information. Citizen report cards, which are based on surveys among citizens regarding their satisfaction with the quality of public service provision, have become an important approach to increase transparency (Samuel 2002). Women may have comparative advantages in some types of demand-side strategies. For example, women's groups are effectively monitoring food prices in ration shops in India to reduce corruption (Goetz and Jenkins 2002). Demand-side approaches may lead to repression of citizens who try to disclose irregularities in the public administration. Women may be particularly vulnerable to such repression. Therefore, ensuring women's access to justice is often important to make demand-side approaches work.

Making supply-side strategies gender sensitive

Examples of supply-side reforms include civil service reforms, public expenditure management reforms, the reform of procurement and audit procedures, training programs for public officials, and improved coordination between different government agencies and departments. Because the agricultural administration is part of the general public administration, such general reforms typically have implications for agriculture. Also, however, supply-side reforms exist that are specific for agriculture. For example, the introduction of new technologies, such as information and communication technologies (ICTs) for agricultural advisory services or land administration, can help to improve agricultural sector governance. Another supply-side approach consists in involving nongovernmental organizations and private sector enterprises in agricultural service provision, for example, through outsourcing of agricultural advisory services, public-private partnerships in agricultural research, devolution of authority for natural resources to user groups, and privatization (for example, of formal seed supply systems).

Gender-sensitive supply-side reforms build the capacity and willingness of state actors and other public service providers to perform their tasks in such a way that women are served equally, and that gender equality is one of the goals of public management. Awareness creation and training for men and women staff members remain an important approach to reach this goal. Another avenue to make supply-side reform more gender sensitive consists in strengthening the role of women staff members within agricultural agencies. Not only is this a measure to reduce discrimination in the workplace for the women employed there, but it also may increase the capacity of the respective agencies to serve women clients better, as the theory of representative bureaucracy suggests. For example, women extension agents may have a better understanding of the needs of women farmers. Another important approach is the development of "machineries" for the promotion of gender equity, such as special units in agricultural ministries that have the task of mainstreaming gender concerns. To make supply-side reforms gender sensitive, one also has to take into account that reforms may affect men and women differently. For example, special provisions may be necessary to make sure that women, whose literacy level is often lower than that of men, can participate in agricultural e-governance initiatives, such as Internet-based agricultural extension.

Going from "best practice" to "good fit"

The experience with governance reforms shows that "blue print" or "one-size-fits-all" approaches have limited chances for success. In fact, the reform approaches have to be tailored to the context-specific conditions (Levy and Kpundeh 2004), indicated by the "good fit" arrows in figure 2.1. As highlighted above, the design of demand-side approaches needs to take into account the challenges that different groups, including women, face in exercising voice and demanding accountability. Likewise, supply-side reforms need to address the specific problems that prevent public agencies and other service providers from performing their tasks effectively. Moreover, demand- and supply-side approaches need to be coordinated. Little value can be found in increasing people's ability to demand better services if the service providers lack the incentives or the capacity to respond, indicated by the "good coordination" arrow in figure 2.1.

One also needs to take into account that reforming governance is essentially a political process. Experience shows that it is often necessary to focus on those types of governance reforms first for which political commitment can be created (Grindle 1997; Levy and Kpundeh 2004). Governance reforms that require a change in legal and institutional frame conditions (table 2.1) typically depend on higher levels of political commitment than strategies that can be used within the existing legal and institutional framework.

POLICY PROCESSES

As indicated above, developing sound policies and regulations is an important aspect of good governance. In recent years, the international development community and civil society have placed increasing emphasis on making processes of policy formulation more participatory and consultative. Because of democratization, the role of parliaments in policy making has been strengthened in many countries too. Likewise, democratic decentralization has improved the possibilities of locally elected council members to engage in policy formulation. In terms of the framework above, these trends are "demand-side" approaches, which strengthen the ability of citizens to formulate demands by involving them in policy making, directly, through interest groups, and through elected representatives. These developments have created important opportunities for making policies more gender sensitive. The contemporary challenge is to seize these opportunities, as women face particular obstacles of making their political voice heard. With regard to agricultural livelihoods, the following five types of policy processes are of particular interest.

1. *Formulation of general development strategies and plans.* National development strategies and plans form an important basis for economic policies. In many countries, they take the form of Poverty Reduction Strategy Papers (PRSPs), which are developed with a strong emphasis on stakeholder participation. Other countries, such as India, have five-year development plans formulated by national planning commissions. The way in which agriculture and gender are addressed in these strategies and plans has far-reaching implications for the formulation of agricultural policies and programs.
2. *Formulation of agricultural sector policies and plans.* Most countries have specific agricultural sector policies, which are often developed with support from international organizations. These policies are an important entry point for mainstreaming gender concerns.

3. *Formulation of plans at the local level.* Decentralization and community-driven development approaches have introduced or strengthened planning processes at the local level, such as community-action plans and district-level plans. Integrating agriculture as well as gender concerns into such local plans is important to ensure that local development efforts improve agricultural livelihoods in a gender-sensitive way. Moreover, local plans are important because they are increasingly used to feed into regional and national agricultural and general development strategies.
4. *Development of budget processes.* The national and local budget processes are of crucial importance, as they determine to which extent policies are actually translated into practice. Gender budgeting, which is now promoted actively in many countries, provides important entry points for gender mainstreaming (box 2.1). One also needs to pay attention to the range of policy documents related to the budget process, such as Medium-Term Budget Frameworks, Annual Budget Framework Papers, and Sector Investment Plans. Mainstreaming gender concerns in these documents is essential for achieving adequate budget allocations.
5. *Development of political processes leading to institutional reforms.* Another type of process that deserve attention are political processes that lead to the reform of agricultural sector institutions, such as agricultural extension reforms or land administration reforms. The content of such policy reforms is covered in different Modules of this *Sourcebook*. The *political process* of bringing about such reforms is an important entry point for gender concerns. This is also true for the political processes by which general governance reforms (such as decentralization reforms) are pursued, because those have important implications for gender and agriculture too.

As further detailed in Thematic Note 1, different entry points make these policy processes gender sensitive by strengthening the capacity of women and their organizations to (1) participate effectively in policy-making processes; (2) conduct relevant analyses, such as gender-specific agricultural expenditure reviews and gender analysis of agricultural budgets; (3) use research-based knowledge in the policy process (for instance, by providing training in policy communication); and (4) analyze the political economy of specific policy processes through a gender lens and engage in policy change management, for example, by building coalitions and influencing public opinion.

Box 2.1 Gender Budgeting

Public expenditure analysis can be a powerful tool for gender equity when gender-disaggregated analyses of public budgeting and expenditure expose gender bias in macroeconomic policy. Public expenditure management portfolios conventionally focus on fiscal discipline and good operational management. However, how public money is allocated and spent is the most concrete representation of policy priorities in a country, and gender-sensitive analyses can be used to hold policy makers accountable for spending real money to achieve their political promises. One prominent strategy in this realm is gender-responsive budgeting. Gender-responsive budget initiatives are usually multistep policy analysis projects that compare the adequacy of policy and budgetary allocations for addressing the specific nature of

gender inequity in a country. They can be sectoral, focusing on a particular gender-equity issue, or may involve a more comprehensive disaggregation of government accounts. Such initiatives also increase the transparency of government and discourage the use of public office for private gain, especially in ways that siphon off resources that should be of special benefit to women. Civil society groups play an important role in gender budgeting. The United Nations Development Fund for Women (UNIFEM) has been supporting gender-responsive budgeting and operates a Web site with resources in several languages (www.gender-budgets.org). Although gender budgeting has gained increasing importance, a need still exists to use opportunities created by this tool more effectively in agricultural budgets.

Source: Authors.

PUBLIC ADMINISTRATION AND PUBLIC SECTOR REFORM

Although good policies are important, they are not enough. To improve agricultural livelihoods in a gender-sensitive way, public institutions must have the will and the capacity to implement policies and programs that are targeted at gender equity in the agricultural sector. In other words, "supply-side" factors must accompany demand-side processes to strengthen governance. Understanding the public administration is especially important to achieve gender-sensitive governance because research has shown that the bureaucracy plays a significant role in creating gender relations in the broader society. The agricultural administration can maintain existing gender relations in the agricultural sector by providing unequal access to social and economic resources, and it can help to transform them through recognizing men's and women's different needs and positions in this sector. Moreover, public administration staff in frontline service agencies such as agricultural extension are often the first, and perhaps the only, contact that women and men in rural areas have with the state. The implementation of public policy through the agricultural administration thus determines how policy directives developed at a central level are actually experienced on the ground. Agricultural bureaucracies are also gendered in their own internal cultures—in the relationships of and opportunities for the men and women who work within them. Improving public sector management in agriculture is thus essential for the alleviation of poverty for rural women.

National and local machineries for promoting gender equity

Since the First World Conference on Women in the mid-1970s, the international women's movement and the donor community have pressed countries to establish state institutions specifically tasked with the promotion of the status of women. These "national machineries" take many forms, including self-standing ministries, gender focal points, gender units or "gender desks" within existing ministries such as Finance or Agriculture, or a central advisory body within the Executive Office. Early machineries tended to be isolated structures that actually implemented welfare-oriented projects, but it is now generally recognized that the machinery should act as a catalyst for gender mainstreaming in all areas of policy and administration, rather than as an implementer. As of 2004, 165 countries had established some type of national machinery for promoting gender equity.

Because agriculture is the primary source of women's livelihoods in most developing countries, the way in which the agricultural bureaucracy institutionalizes gender policy and planning functions is particularly important for poverty alleviation. Both the International Fund for Agricultural Development (IFAD) and the Food and Agriculture Organization (FAO) support the establishment of gender units that specifically serve the rural sector as part of a country's broader machinery for the promotion of gender equity. Women's desks or gender focal points in Ministries of Agriculture and/or in decentralized district agricultural offices can provide guidance to sector practitioners on how to mainstream gender in agricultural planning, budgeting, and implementation. For example, the Unit for the Strengthening of and Support to Gender Policies at the El Salvador Ministry for Agriculture and Livestock helped the extension program tailor training to women farmers, thus enhancing productivity. The Gender Strategy in the reconfigured Ministry of Agriculture in Côte d'Ivoire led fully a quarter of the ministry's programs to have an explicit gender focus (see Innovative Activity Profile 2). Broad-based practitioner evidence suggests that separate, small women-specific agricultural and rural development programs are usually not successful in reaching large numbers of rural women. Instead, it is more effective to design mainstream agricultural programs so that they reach both men and women. Having dedicated gender staff sit inside sectoral ministries increases the gender relevance of their work (see further discussion specific to the agricultural sector, lessons learned from past experience, and entry points for improved interventions in the Thematic Note 2).

Public sector reform

In addition to creating dedicated institutional bodies to advocate for women's issues, gender sensitivity can be integrated into the daily operations of the public sector. Periods of reform often provide strategic opportunities to do this.

REFORM MODELS. Public administration reforms have been on the development agenda ever since developing countries achieved their independence, but with the increasing commitment to good governance, public sector management has gained particular prominence. The models that have guided public sector reforms have changed over time (UN & AF 2005). The New Public Management (NPM) approach, which replaced the traditional public administration model, focused on the introduction of private sector management approaches in public agencies, emphasizing entitlements, efficiency and results, outcomes, and professionalism. Treating citizens as "customers" is an important guiding principle in NPM. Creating semiautonomous agencies to remove the public administration from direct political influence has also been a major approach in NPM. These principles remain relevant for public sector reform, and they create scope for gender mainstreaming by recognizing the entitlements of women "customers," disaggregating results and outcomes by gender, and introducing gender mainstreaming as an element of professionalism in public service. In current reform approaches, a stronger focus lies on combining public sector reforms with demand-side approaches by emphasizing stakeholder participation and transparency. The "responsive governance" model of public sector reform describes this trend. To make this reform approach gender responsive, it is crucial to involve stakeholders that represent women in participatory processes.

Although public sector reforms have potentially far-reaching impacts on agricultural administration, it is important to determine which activities are best addressed through sectoral instruments, and which through a more cross-cutting approach. Administrative reforms within Ministries of Agriculture and other relevant government agencies can be important tools for creating incentives for service responsiveness to women-specific needs, as well as those of men. Projects focusing on building administrative capacity can experiment with innovative incentive systems that reward the extra effort needed to work for women's advancement. Performance reviews and indicators, bureaucratic communication flows, trainings, management techniques, and informal professional cultures all can be strengthened to value the work necessary to tailor services specifically to the needs of women clients and to help women clients overcome barriers to accessing these. In Chile, for example, the public sector Management Improvement Program links performance evaluations to achievement of specific gender targets and has led a high proportion of government agencies and services to incorporate gender.

Civil service reform is another area with potentially significant gender impacts. Practitioner evidence suggests that public sector downsizing often impacts women disproportionately, especially in places where women are overrepresented in the secretarial and administrative ranks of the bureaucracy that are thinned. Gender-sensitive reform projects begin with an ex ante analysis of the gender impacts of public sector downsizing, such as that conducted by the World Bank in Vietnam, to understand how the reforms impact the roles of women and men who work inside the administration. Important positive benchmarks for civil service reforms include whether they diminish job discrimination, increase equity and opportunities, and give consideration to issues relevant to women in the workplace such as sexual harassment and family leave policies. In addition to improving the job quality of women bureaucrats, these gender-equity practices in the public administration can improve the quality of service provided by the public sector. The theory of representative bureaucracy suggests that organizations perform their missions more effectively if their workforces reflect the characteristics of their constituent populations. Keeping women in the public administration means they may be better able to tailor agricultural services and policies to the needs of rural women. A study of two rural credit and development programs in Bangladesh showed that women field workers and managers identified with some of the problems of their poor women clients and acted as advocates for them within the managers' organizations (Goetz 2001).

PUBLIC SECTOR REFORMS BY INVOLVING THE PRIVATE SECTOR AND CIVIL SOCIETY. Another set of supply-side reforms aims at improving public sector governance by involving private sector agencies, user organizations, and nongovernmental organizations (NGOs) in the provision of public services. The combination of approaches discussed here that is most suitable depends on country-specific conditions, as highlighted earlier ("best fit"):

- *Outsourcing.* Contracting, or outsourcing, is suitable for functions that require public finance but not necessarily public provision. For example, in Uganda's new National Agricultural Advisory Services system, the provision of agricultural advisory services is contracted out to private sector enterprises, individual consultants, and NGOs that compete for the contracts. The approach is combined with a demand-side strategy, because committees of farmers' representatives at the subcounty level make decisions on awarding the contracts. A quota for women farmers in these committees aims to ensure gender responsiveness.
- *Public-private partnerships and privatization:* Going beyond outsourcing, public-private partnerships create joint responsibilities for financing and provision of services and infrastructure, including irrigation infrastructure. For services that are not confronted with market failure, privatization can be a useful reform approach. Veterinary services, for example, have been increasingly privatized in many developing countries. However, if market failures exist because of, for example, natural monopolies, as with water and electricity supplies, privatization needs to be combined with regulation to ensure that the rural poor, including rural women, retain access to such services. Regulation can be combined with demand-side approaches, for example, by making regulatory decisions subject to public consultations, as they are for electricity regulation in India. Special provisions can help to ensure that women's interests are equally represented in such approaches.

A range of reform strategies represent mixed demand- and supply-side approaches because they involve citizens directly in public functions such as service provision and regulation.

- *Representation of the private sector and civil society in management boards of public sector agencies:* One important public sector reform approach is the creation of semi-autonomous agencies, which are governed by boards that include representatives of the private sector and civil society, for example, Guatemala's forest administration and Uganda's national agricultural research system (Birner and Wittmer 2006).
- *Public-private people partnerships:* These partnerships involve civil society organizations, such as farmer organizations, along with public sector agencies and private business enterprises. An example is the "Sustainable Uptake of Cassava as an Industrial Commodity" project in Ghana. Cassava is widely grown by women and traditionally viewed as a subsistence food crop. The project established systems that link farmers, especially women, to new markets for cassava products, such as flour, baking products, and plywood adhesives (World Bank 2007b).
- *Devolvement of management authority to user groups:* This strategy is widely applied in natural resource management. Community forestry in India and Nepal is a prominent example. The strategy is also important in irrigation. The Office du Niger irrigation scheme in Mali is a particularly successful African example of this approach (Aw and Diemer 2005).
- *Development of service cooperatives:* Formed and owned by producers, including smallholder farmers, service cooperatives can be important for providing services helping the poor. In India, for example, dairy cooperatives provide livestock services to more than 12 million households.

Such mixed approaches create opportunities for involving women: for example, by involving organizations that represent rural women. Yet it cannot be taken for granted that such opportunities will be used. Special provisions, such as reserving seats in governing bodies for women representatives, and enabling measures, such as training coaching and mentoring, may be necessary to make such approaches gender sensitive. Moreover, strengthening the capacity of organizations that represent rural women is often an important prerequisite to make such approaches work (see further discussion on civil society and women organizations in Thematic Note 4).

Reforms to reduce corruption

The emphasis on good governance has stimulated a wide range of reforms aimed at combating corruption. Corruption affects the agricultural sector in many ways. National integrity surveys show that land administration is often one of the most corrupt government agencies.[2] Large agricultural infrastructure projects, such as those for irrigation, are particularly prone to corruption, as is water allocation in public irrigation systems (Rinaudo 2002). Companies may bribe regulators, as in biotechnology regulation in Indonesia (BBC News 2005), and pesticide regulation in India. Pesticides may cause particular health hazards for women, who often do the planting and weeding work. Reducing public sector involvement into input supply and marketing of agricultural products may reduce the scope for corruption, which is often associated with such interventions (see, for example, Jeffrey 2002). However, outsourcing and privatization also create new scope for corruption, and the agricultural sector is equally affected by such problems. For example, concerns have been expressed that outsourcing agricultural advisory services in Uganda has created scope for corruption in the contracting process.

Both demand- and supply-side approaches can overcome corruption in agriculture (World Bank 2007b). Public expenditure management reforms and procurement reforms are typical supply-side approaches, which are often part of general public sector reform. A successful demand-side example is the monitoring of food prices in ration shops by women's groups in India, as mentioned above. A study of strategies to reduce corruption in village road projects applied a randomized experimental design to compare social audits, a demand-side approach, and government audits, a supply-side approach (Olken 2007). The study suggests that grassroots monitoring may reduce theft more when community members have substantial private stakes in the outcome. New technologies, especially ICTs (e-government), can reduce the scope for corruption, as with computerizing land records in Karnataka. As box 2.2 shows, a vivid debate exists on the extent to which involving women in politics and public sector management will reduce the scope for corruption.

DECENTRALIZATION, LOCAL GOVERNANCE, AND COMMUNITY-DRIVEN DEVELOPMENT

Decentralization—the transfer of political, administrative, and fiscal authority to lower levels of government—is one

---

Box 2.2   Gender and Corruption

Two papers by the World Bank launched women into the global debate on anticorruption and good governance. In two cross-country studies, Swamy and others (2001) and Dollar, Fisman, and Gatti (2001) found that a greater proportion of women in parliament was associated with lower levels of corruption. Swamy and others (2001) also used data from the World Values Survey as well as a survey of business owners in Georgia to show gender differentials in attitudes about and involvement in bribery. Do these studies show that women are intrinsically more honest, and thus are a "tool" to combat corruption?

Several political scientists who study gender dynamics in developing countries argue no. They suggest *opportunities* for corruption are what is gendered, not people's reactions to it. In particular, in socially conservative societies, it is difficult for women to become either clients or patrons in the men-dominated patronage networks through which corrupt exchanges occur. Where corrupt acts are condoned by social networks, or even required by social convention, women have been shown to be no less willing than men to engage in such behavior, especially if required to create a sustainable livelihood.

These scholars argue that the central question in the gender and corruption debate is not whether women or men are less corrupt as a group, but how to combat gender-specific accountability failures. These include gendered capture, such as when money destined for women's development is more easily stolen by state actors because women tend to be less aware of their rights and less willing than men to demand that public authorities account for missing funds, and gender bias in purportedly impartial law and policy, which exacerbates existing forms of discrimination. Women may also be more susceptible to "sexual currencies" of corruption, such as having sexual services demanded in lieu of money bribes. Because corruption takes the largest toll on the poor, and women make up a disproportionate share of the poor in many places, the effects of corruption are thus disproportionately borne by women. The key question to ask is whether anticorruption measures equally address the types of corruption faced by women and men.

Sources: Alhassan-Alolo 2007; Goetz 2007; Goetz and Jenkins 2005.

---

of the major governance reforms that many developing countries have been undertaking. Eighty percent of all developing countries have experimented with some form of decentralization (Work 2002). Community-driven development (CDD) is a related approach. Broadly defined, CDD gives community groups control over planning decisions and investment resources. By mobilizing community groups, CDD aims at making the rural poor active partners rather than targets of poverty alleviation measures. In early phases of decentralization, local governments often do not reach down to the community level. However, decentralization and CDD can go hand in hand by making local governments, rather than higher-level state agencies, responsible for the implementation of CDD approaches.

Decentralization

As indicated earlier, decentralization holds great promise for making public service provision more responsive to the needs of rural citizens, including rural women, by "bringing government closer to the people." With regard to agriculture, acknowledging that this sector is best served by a mix of centralized and decentralized functions is important. For example, public functions of strategic relevance—such as ensuring food safety and controlling epidemic diseases—need to remain national responsibilities, even though their implementation may require considerable administrative capacity at intermediate and local levels. For applied agricultural research, agroecological zones may be the appropriate level of decentralization. Agricultural extension, however, is often best organized at lower tiers of local government to be responsive to diverse local conditions and extension needs (World Bank 2007b). Decentralization is inherently a political process that shifts power and authority, and so agricultural ministries at the central level, like other ministries, often resist the transfer of their fiscal resources and their staff to local governments. This resistance limits the possibilities of the elected local leaders, including women leaders, to become active players in promoting agriculture. Hence, building political support is important to avoid fiscal and administrative decentralization falling behind political decentralization.

Decentralization also involves the challenge of "local elite capture," which implies that local elites use public resources to their advantage. However, whether elite capture is indeed more important at the local than at higher levels depends on country-specific conditions (Bardhan and Mookherjee 2000). The gender dimension of the elite capture problem is complex, since women are part of local and national elites, and they do not necessarily prioritize gender concerns when they assume political office. The system of reserving seats in local councils in India aims at addressing both elite capture and gender-inequality problems, as seats are reserved for women and for disadvantaged castes. Efforts to reserve seats for women in state assemblies and the national parliament have been unsuccessful so far. The challenges involved in the reservation of seats for local council members have been discussed earlier.

Community-driven development

Once a visionary idea, CDD has become a reality on a large scale. More than 9 percent of World Bank lending uses this approach to development (World Bank 2007b). Other international development organizations also use this mechanism to a large extent. Experience shows that CDD can speed up the implementation of projects, increase cost effectiveness, make fiscal transfers more efficient, improve the quality of infrastructure, and increase income from agriculture. Considerable experience has been accumulated in scaling up, but drawing definitive conclusions requires more rigorous impact evaluation (World Bank 2005).

As further detailed in Thematic Note 3, experience has shown that communities that manage resources under CDD programs typically concentrate first on meeting basic needs for health, education, and infrastructure. Once they turn to income-generating activities, however, agricultural projects—including those that link smallholders to high-value markets—become an important choice. Community-driven projects in northeast Brazil that promote agricultural income generation show that success depends not only on community capacity but also on market demand, technical assistance, and capacity building (van Zyl and others 2000). Income-generating projects in the agricultural sector often provide private goods, such as livestock, seeds, and access to irrigated plots, rather than public goods, such as schools. Such projects need special provisions to avoid elite capture and to make sure that women benefit equally. Without such provisions, agricultural CDD projects that provide private goods may disadvantage women by one-sidedly increasing the asset base of men.

Although CDD approaches attempt to avoid market and state failure, they may be confronted with the problem of community failure. Therefore, developing accountability is an important condition for enabling communities to implement agricultural projects. Unlike local governments, communities do not usually have formal structures of authority and accountability, and they can be riddled with abuses of power, social exclusion, social conservatism, and conflict. Where customary traditions deny rights and privileges to women, relying on customary community institutions for project implementation can deepen gender inequality (Beall 2005). Therefore, CDD projects need to invest considerable resources in changing community practices by encouraging more transparent information flows, broad and gender-sensitive community participation in local decision making, and participatory monitoring of local institutions. Special provisions, such as quorum rules for women's participation in community meetings, may help to achieve gender equity. One needs to acknowledge that accountability evolves over time, and that solutions need to be specific to country context. Yet, when associated with predictable resource flows, CDD approaches can change community dynamics beyond the project time frame (World Bank 2007b).

GLOBAL GOVERNANCE OF AGRICULTURE

In today's global world, much of the architecture of agricultural governance is created at a supranational scale. As the *World Development Report 2008: Agriculture for Development* (World Bank 2007b) makes clear, action at the global level is essential for successful realization of national agendas to use agriculture for development. Even though agriculture is primarily a private sector activity, it relies heavily on the provision of public goods, as well as on the regulation of the international commons for sustainable development. Agricultural development is also influenced by the globalization of the economy, and reducing barriers and transaction costs in trade requires international coordination. Agriculture is increasingly susceptible to transboundary issues, such as pandemic animal and plant diseases and invasive species that require regional solutions. Progress in agriculture is also essential to meet other great global challenges of our day, including environmental change, disease, poverty, and security. For all of these reasons, international cooperation through the types of organizations listed in table 2.2 is necessary to support strategies for strong agricultural livelihoods at the national and local levels.

Because activities, agreements, and institutions that operate at an international scale influence outcomes at the

Table 2.2 Types of Global Organizations Relevant for Agriculture

Sector and specialization	Intergovernmental organizations	Nongovernmental organizations and networks, private sector enterprises, and organizations with mixed membership
Specialized organizations in the agricultural sector	Food and Agriculture Organization Global Donor Platform on Rural Development International Fund for Agricultural Development World Food Program World Organization for Animal Health	Global networks of farmers' organizations (for example, International Federation of Agricultural Producers and Via Campesina) Multinational agribusiness enterprises (for example, Dow Chemicals and Monsanto) Supermarket chains Consultative Group on International Agricultural Development
Cross-sectoral organizations that include agriculture	Codex Alimentarius	*Harvest Plus*
Development organizations and funding agencies with agricultural programs	United Nations Development Programme World Bank Group	Private foundations and funding agencies (for example, Gates and Rockefeller foundations) Nongovernmental development organizations (for example, CARE and Oxfam)
Specialized environmental organizations	Global Environmental Facility Intergovernmental Panel on Climate Change United Nations Environment Programme	Environmental NGOs (for example, Greenpeace and World Wide Fund for Nature) International Union for the Conservation of Nature
Specialized organizations in other sectors	United Nations Development Fund for Women World Health Organization World Trade Organization	Multinational pharmaceutical and biotechnology companies International Organization for Standardization
General global governance bodies	G-8 Summit United Nations Secretariat, Assembly and Security Council	

Source: World Bank 2007b.

national and local scales within developing countries, it follows that institutions of global governance must be gender sensitive for their country-level impacts to be gender sensitive as well. For example, trade liberalization has differential effects on women and men when women are disproportionately employed in industries affected by the removal of tariffs, such as agriculture or textile manufacturing. Analysis of these country-level effects must be available during international trade negotiations. Likewise, recent agreements relating to agricultural inputs, such as the International Treaty on Plant Genetic Resources for Food and Agriculture (commonly known as the International Seed Treaty), have important gender aspects, because men and women are often stewards of different crops and species, and the farmers' rights of women need to be equally protected. Hence, it is important to include gender-sensitive language and concepts in such agreements.

Making sure that women are at the negotiating table when international agreements relevant to agriculture and global governance are written and that gender interests are represented in international policy and regulatory vehicles is essential for truly mainstreaming gender in agricultural governance. Similar to the programs and investments discussed above in mainstreaming gender in national agricultural policy processes, donors and governments can build the capacity of both men and women to bring relevant gender concepts to the world of international agriculture diplomacy. In particular, trade capacity-building programs should involve significant training in gender analysis, because trade negotiations are particularly data intensive. Activities such as exchange programs or study tours for elected officials or diplomats can also expand their awareness of positive gender practices in other countries. Support programs and investments should focus on both government representatives and civil society actors.

MEASURING CHANGE: GENDER-SENSITIVE MONITORING AND EVALUATION INDICATORS

It is important to be able to measure the impact that governance initiatives have on men and women beneficiaries, their families, and communities. Table 2.3 gives some ideas for indicators and sources of verification, although clear modifications are required for each program. Further detail is also available in Module 16.

Depending on the country or region, it may be relevant also to consider ethnicity and caste alongside gender (both as comparative indicators and when collecting data), because women of lower castes or ethnic minorities are usually in the most disadvantaged situation.

Table 2.3 Monitoring and Evaluation Indicators for Gender and Governance

Indicator	Sources of verification and tools
Number of women and men actively participating in local-level planning and policy-setting processes	• Citizen's scorecards • Community meeting minutes • Participatory monitoring records
Number of women and men employed at each level in the public service	• Staff records
Percentage of women and men in new recruitment in public service at each level	• Staff records
Percentage of elected women officials (at national, state, and local levels)	• Government electoral records
Number of women and men (bureaucrats or elected officials) participating in training per quarter	• Training records
Change in knowledge and attitudes of women and men in public service regarding issues such as sexual harassment, child care access, and family leave policies, measured annually	• Focus groups • Surveys • Stakeholder interviews
Number of government officials participating in gender training annually	• Government records • Training records
Percentage of women and men extension workers and project staff	• Government agricultural extension and business support services records • Project records
Perceptions of incidence of corruption, disaggregated by gender	• Stakeholder interviews • Surveys
Percentage of women and men actively involved in committees writing PRSPs, national policies, and so on	• Government minutes • Poverty Reduction Strategy Paper (PRSP) records
Use or otherwise of gender-disaggregated monitoring in PRSPs, national budgets, project logical frameworks, government socioeconomic development plans, and so on	• Documents: PRSPs, budgets, and others • Gender analysis of budgets • Public expenditure reviews
Satisfaction of entrepreneurs with their access to government services (such as land titles and business registration), training, information, and infrastructure, disaggregated by gender	• Average time taken by government offices to issue certificates • Focus groups • Stakeholder interviews
Changes in community knowledge regarding government policies, laws, or services, disaggregated by gender	• Focus groups • Sample survey • Stakeholder interviews
Percentage of time spent daily in household on paid and nonpaid activities, disaggregated by gender and age	• Gender analysis • Time use studies
Numbers of women and men community trained in group management and leadership skills	• Training records
Active participation of women and men in community-based rural organizations, including holding leadership roles	• Bank account signatories • Organization minutes • Stakeholder interviews
Changes over x-year period of project activities in household nutrition, health, education, vulnerability to violence, and happiness, disaggregated by gender	• Household surveys, before and after • Project management information system • School records

Source: Authors, with inputs from Pamela White, author of Module 16.

Gender in Policy-Making Processes

Democratization and the rise of participatory policy making have increased the possibilities for smallholders and the rural poor to raise their political voice. Diverse institutional arrangements involving citizens directly in service provision and regulation have started to be adopted, including (1) representation of the private sector and civil society on management boards of public sector agencies, (2) public-private partnerships, (3) devolving management authority to user groups, and (4) service cooperatives (see Module Overview). Reforms in the public sector and in many agricultural institutions have escalated in recent years; they also create special opportunities for greater representation and inclusion, especially involving women, who historically have been underrepresented in processes and neglected in policy outcomes. However, it cannot be taken for granted that such opportunities will be used. Increasing voice and accountability in rural areas remains a challenge even in democratic systems, and rural women face particular obstacles in making their voices heard (World Bank 2007). This suggests a vital need for a critical look across countries at the processes of policy formulation, participation of women and men, and the different obstacles that they face to seize the opportunities presented by recent governance reforms.

GENDER IN DIFFERENT TYPES OF POLICY PROCESSES

Following the discussion in the Module Overview on the different types of policy processes, we discuss here the level of inclusion of gender issues in various policy documents and the equality of participation between women and men in the different policy processes.

Process of developing national development strategies and plans. National development strategies and plans form an important basis for economic policies. In many countries they take the form of PRSPs,[1] which are developed with a strong emphasis on stakeholder participation. However, recent studies have stressed that representation by women and the incorporation of gender issues in the PRSP processes remain a challenge (World Bank 2005; Zuckerman 2002). A World Bank survey covering the PRSP process in 32 countries shows that agricultural stakeholders, especially women, are often well represented in the preparatory phases when issues are diagnosed and studied, but their involvement in actually setting priorities is much weaker (World Bank 2004). In the rural sector, the attention to gender issues and follow-through in the recommendations or priorities in the document are even more challenging. In 2004 the World Bank conducted a review of rural development aspects of 12 PRSPs (in 2000–04). Only six PRSPs brought up gender issues in the poverty diagnosis, and only three included a detailed discussion. Only one PRSP (Rwanda) used gender as one of the criteria for prioritizing actions in the policy matrix. Gender-related targets are generally absent in the PRSPs, and only two PRSPs (Kyrgyz Republic and Mali) had a set of gender indicators. Only three had follow-up in the instruments for policy changes, in the form of Poverty Reduction Support Credits, and only two had follow-up in the lending program of the Bank and other donors (World Bank 2004).

Process of developing agricultural sector policies and plans. Most countries have specific rural or agricultural sector policies, which are often developed with support from the World Bank or international organizations. In a recent analysis of seven rural development strategies supported by the World Bank (2005–06),[2] only three reports included substantial discussion of gender-related issues including specific recommendations (Cambodia, Mozambique, and Vietnam). Two of the reports presented country-specific findings on the differences between men and women in the rural sector, with less focus on recommendations (Argentina and Lao People's Democratic Republic). These strategy documents most commonly discuss gender issues related to education, nonfarm employment, and woman-headed households. Often focus is given to women's access to health care, property rights, credit, women's limited access to relevant extension services, and limited participation in local planning processes.

In the seven documents, no discussion is given to the consultation processes undertaken before the strategy writing. However, the Cambodia document recommended increased women's participation at the village level, and the Vietnam document noted how local planning processes need to become more transparent and inclusive to ensure that all groups—including ethnic minorities and women—have a voice in the decisions that affect their lives.

Budget processes. Gender-responsive budgeting aims at mainstreaming gender into public finance. Gender-responsive budgets are not separate budgets for women,[3] but instead, general budgets that are planned, approved, executed, monitored, and audited in a gender-sensitive way. In the aftermath of the Fourth World Conference on Women (1995), gender-responsive budgeting work has been carried out in more than 60 countries. Schneider (2007) summarized some successes:

- Awareness has increased that budgetary decisions may have an impact on gender relations and gender equity.
- The capacity to analyze budgets from a gender perspective has increased.
- In some countries, budget allocations have been reprioritized in favor of women and girls.
- In some countries, budget guidelines and formats have been changed.
- Debates on gender issues have taken place in parliament, and gender issues have been mentioned in the budget speeches of ministers of finance.
- Budget processes have become more transparent.
- The participation of the civil society in the budgetary process has increased.

However, Schneider noted that gender budget work in many countries was partial in scope. In some cases, the impact was limited because the initiatives referred to a stylized approach that was not suitable for the respective national budget system. Yet gender budgeting work in many countries remained a one-off activity (for example, sensitization workshops, training, and analyses) and was not institutionalized. Moreover, gender-responsive budgeting activities were not linked with recent reforms in many countries' public finance systems (for example, a more results-oriented budgeting and establishment of mid-term

economic frameworks to link planning and budgeting more closely).

One challenge is that government ministries responsible for women's affairs and advocacy groups tend to have limited expertise in macroeconomic issues and are therefore at a disadvantage when it comes to negotiating gender-equitable policies (World Bank 2005). They also often lack authority and/or budget allocations for follow-up action.

Political processes leading to institutional reforms. As is the case for public system reforms, gender-responsive actions rarely accompany recent or ongoing general governance reforms (for example, decentralization reforms) and more specific agricultural reforms (for example, national agricultural extension, land administration). Although the political process of bringing about such reforms is an important entry point for gender concerns, gender-responsive actions are seldom incorporated in such processes.

WOMEN AS POLICY MAKERS

In agriculture, women account for more than 50 percent of the labor force, and they are responsible for three-quarters of food production in sub-Saharan Africa, but the design of many development policies continues to assume wrongly that farmers and rural workers are men (World Bank 2007). The rigidities of some gender-blind policies, institutions, programs, and projects are perpetuated by the underrepresentation of women as policy makers or their limited participation in policy and institutional change processes.

At the national level, the number of women in parliaments remains low: 17 percent in parliament, 14 percent as ministers, and 7 percent as heads of government in 2006 (IPU 2006). Signs of progress have been seen in terms of women's participation in parliaments over the years; however, the proportion of women remains low. In addition, despite the increasing role of civic society organizations in shaping the research and policy agenda, it remains a challenge for these organizations to be representative and inclusive of women.

At the local level, women have enjoyed more success at gaining access to decision-making positions in local government than at the national level (UNIFEM 2007).[4] These positions tend to be more accessible to them and have less competition than for parliamentary seats. In all likelihood women's decision-making roles in city and community government may be more easily accepted because they are seen as an extension of women's involvement in their community. Yet, in many countries, women's participation in local politics is often undermined by gender inequality within families, by an inequitable division of labor within households, and by deeply entrenched cultural attitudes about gender roles and the suitability of women for decision-making positions (UNIFEM 2007).

MISSED OPPORTUNITY FROM LIMITED ANALYTICAL WORK

Good analytical work can lead to more and better treatment of agricultural issues in policy debates, which in turn can result in more and better projects and programs. In the agriculture sector, significant analytical strengthening has occurred in several organizations. For instance, FAO, IFAD, and the World Bank have made some progress in their gender-mainstreaming strategies and have recently embarked on more action-oriented processes of gender integration (Curry and Tempelman 2006; FAO 2007; GENRD 2006, 2007; IFAD 2003; World Bank 2008). Analytical capacity is being strengthened, and data collection and analyses have been improved to include gender-specific variables and indicators in these three agencies. The International Food Policy Research Institute (IFPRI)'s Gender and Development Program has also contributed in analytical capacity strengthening for gender in agriculture (see also IFPRI 2007a, 2007b; Quisumbing and McClafferty 2006a, 2006b). Capacity building of staff in these organizations has also been implemented (see also Thematic Note 2). However, several gaps still remain. For instance, in a recent review of 130 economic and sector work (ESW) programs by GENRD (2008), at least 50 percent of the reviewed ESW do not include any gender-related issues; of the remainder, several reports include a minimal to moderate level of diagnosis of and recommendations for gender issues, and only one to four ESW programs include detailed coverage. Of the 39 technical assistance (TA) documents, between 63 and 76 percent of the reviewed TA reports do not include any gender-related issues; and of the remainder, only one provides detailed coverage of gender issues (GENRD 2008). In the IFAD, while the checklist on "prerequisites of gender-sensitive design" is being used widely, application remains uneven across regions. Opportunities for consultation and capacity building with local NGOs or women's groups were often missed.

GOOD PRACTICES AND LESSONS LEARNED

Some good approaches and examples emerge that can be scaled up to effect greater gender equity across a broader spectrum of countries. The different lessons learned from past experience and good entry points for investments are summarized below. The roles of national governments are crucial in reducing the barriers for greater gender inclusion in the policy processes and outcomes, but an important role also is available for the international development community. Effective partnerships and capturing the comparative advantages of both national governments and the international community, along with other stakeholders, are critical for scaling up activities and venturing other innovative approaches.

Unified policy framework

Having a unified, national framework guiding general gender policies and mainstreaming gender into agricultural policies and institutions is important. Some countries have already moved in this direction. For instance, Chile's Equal Opportunities Plans are the framework documents guiding the country's gender-mainstreaming processes, leading to a recent success story of effective gender mainstreaming in the public sector, including agriculture.

Representation of women in political institutions

Getting more women in the policy making and research institutions is an important step toward getting gender issues into the focus of national strategies and policies. Political reservations for women are often proposed as a way to rapidly enhance women's ability to participate in policy making. Quotas for women in assemblies or on parties' candidate lists are in force in the legislation of over 30 countries (World Bank 2001). Reservation policies clearly have a strong impact on women's representation; however, this does not necessarily imply that reservation for women has an impact on policy decisions. Despite the importance of this issue for the design of institutions, little is known about the causal effect of women's representation on actual policy decisions (Chattopadhyay and Duflo 2004).[5]

In Uganda, women are particularly visible in national politics due to affirmative action, which has also contributed to women's participation in regional political decision making. Women hold four of the Ugandan representative positions in the East African Legislature Assembly (EALA) and are two of the five Ugandan members of the African Parliament. The enabling laws derived from the 1995 constitution have seen the need for affirmative action, mainly as a result of women's groups' activism: (1) the Land Act of 1998 provides for the protection of the land rights of the poor, the majority of whom are women, and the (2) the Local

Government Act of 1997 explicitly states that women shall form one-third of all local councils at all levels. As a result the proportion of women in local councils rose from 6 percent in the early 1990s to 44 percent in 2003.[6]

At the same time, one needs to recognize that the setup of political institutions (for example, whether or not parliaments or political parties have quotas) is hardly an entry point for donor-funded projects per se, because these are sovereign decisions that the citizens of a country and their representatives need to make. However, donor interventions can aim at strengthening the capacity of women in political institutions (for example, women members of Parliamentary Committees on Agriculture). Capacity building and training are important for enhancing women's role in decision making, at all policy-making levels, and for providing women with skills to ensure that they are fully conversant with their roles and accountabilities. Capacity strengthening of women policy makers and administrators has proven to be a pillar of the Gender Strategy of Côte d'Ivoire's National Agricultural Services project. A series of data collection processes and staff training to analyze these data have dramatically built competencies for gender and other staff in analyzing agricultural themes sensitive to specific gender issues at both the national and regional levels. The presence of the head of the national office for gender issues in all strategic discussions was also key to more effective gender mainstreaming in the agriculture sector (see Innovative Activity Profile 2).

Support can also be provided for activities that support women candidates to run for elections at different levels. In countries where education levels of women are low, governments can have a pipeline of well-qualified women candidates for senior positions in public and private organizations, which would require increased emphasis on women's education, including scholarships and cash transfers for the education of girls for vocational and university training in agricultural science and policy (see also Module 7).

Participation of women in political processes

The participation of women in political processes is an important entry point. The rise of participatory policy making and stakeholder consultation provides important opportunities. Projects can aim at strengthening the capacity of women to participate. Because participatory processes are often managed by donor agencies, they can place emphasis on an adequate participation of women in such processes, and a systematic evaluation of such processes with regard to the participation of women would be an instrument that donors could use more effectively.

Increasing women's political participation may not be easy. Despite Chile's many successes in its gender mainstreaming, political participation of women is the area in which less progress has been made. The work, led by the national "women's machinery" called the Servicio Nacional de la Mujer (National Women's Service), has found few allies within the public sector, and progress on women's participation in formal politics has been sparse. Thus, it is not surprising that studies have recommended continued promotion of women's active participation in forums of citizen's control, strengthening women's organizations, and piloting quota mechanisms for formal politics.

In most cases around the developing world, institutional support is needed to ensure that gender issues are effectively represented in the policy processes. For instance, one reason why only a few PRSPs have a gender dimension is that they were prepared based on the assumption that participatory processes would automatically feed into PRSPs. In fact, participatory processes have often not fed into PRSPs (Zuckerman 2002). In Ghana previously disaggregated data were aggregated, obscuring gender differences and inequalities, thereby undermining the potential to challenge gender-blind policies (Derbyshire 2002). Other countries have had weaker participatory exercises, and some countries restrict PRSP participation to a very short list of government-recognized NGOs (Zuckerman 2002). Even if women's groups are integrated into participatory exercises, women generally remain marginalized from government, civil society, and grassroots decision making, and women's organizations feel removed from macroeconomic debates central to PRSPs (Derbyshire 2002). However, various emerging good-practice examples can be highlighted (box 2.3).

Participatory processes do not guarantee gender integration in PRSPs because of a possible disconnect between participants of the consultation processes and writing teams. In most cases PRSP writers have scarcely integrated participatory inputs into PRSPs; this reflects their lack of commitment to reflecting citizens' inputs and mainstreaming gender into the PRSP. PRSP writers have consisted mainly of government finance and economic ministry staff, often men who may lack sensitivity to gender issues (Zuckerman 2002). In a few countries, external consultants have played key PRSP writing roles, but gender integration was not always guaranteed. The Rwanda PRSP is a good example where gender integration was achieved from the consultation and institutional support in writing the PRSP (box 2.4).

Assessments of the PRSPs and other national development strategies conducted by donor agencies also provide a good venue to incorporate gender perspective. For instance,

Box 2.3   Institutional Support for Gender Integration in PRSPs

Bangladesh: The Ministry of Women's Affairs with the support of several donors facilitated the establishment of a "Gender Platform," with representatives from both government and civil society, which consulted and negotiated with the interministerial PRSP task force to incorporate gender analysis and concerns in the PRSP.

Pakistan: The World Bank conducts a gender dialogue with the government either directly or through the Interagency Gender and Development Group (INGAD) and supports INGAD's participation in the subgroups working on the interim PRSP. This gender dialogue is a regular ongoing Bank activity with special focus on political participation, poverty reduction, and strengthening of institutional mechanisms.

Sri Lanka: The World Bank supported the government's Strategy on Gender as part of the PRSP process. The strategy includes (1) increased emphasis on the protection of women's rights in conformity with the UN Convention on the Elimination of All Forms of Discrimination against Women (CEDAW), (2) introduction of an employment policy to promote equal training and employment opportunities for women, (3) continued support for entrepreneurship programs for women, (4) greater support for victims of gender-based violence, (5) specific rehabilitation programs targeting women affected by conflict, and (6) introduction of gender sensitization programs for the public and private sectors.

Vietnam: The National Committee for the Advancement of Women (NCAFW), together with some donors, established a Task Force for mainstreaming gender into the Comprehensive Poverty Reduction and Growth Strategy in Vietnam. A group of donors funded and facilitated research on gender-based violence and on equality of economic opportunity under Vietnam law, particularly with respect to land titling.

Sources: World Bank 2004a, 2004b.

Box 2.4   Rwanda: Steps toward Effective Gender Integration in a PRSP

- The Ministry of Gender and the Promotion of Women (MIGEPROFE) hired an external gender expert to facilitate the process. The expert analyzed in detail the potential areas where gender could be integrated in the IPRSP and suggested specific steps on how these steps could be done in the Rwandan context.
- The consultant worked with the PRSP writing group at the Ministry of Economics and Finance (MINECOFIN) to ensure its members were committed to mainstreaming gender into the PRSP.
- PRSP stakeholders including MIGEPROFE and PRSP writing team members tried to persuade the participatory exercise facilitators, also headed by an external consultant, of the importance of ensuring women's as well as men's views.
- MIGEPROFE and MINECOFIN cosponsored a workshop to promote engendering the PRSP for some 50 representatives from a broad range of sectors. Two dynamic civil society activists cofacilitated the workshop. The MIGEPROFE and MINECOFIN ministers opened and closed the workshop, giving it a high profile. Presentations focused on the importance of integrating gender into the PRSP to achieve poverty reduction and tools to engender the PRSP. Participants practiced using these PRSP engendering tools through a teamwork exercise to engender IPRSP sectors, and teams formulated recommendations on how to engender the interim PRSP text using tools provided.
- An interagency PRSP Engendering Committee was established to promote PRSP gender mainstreaming. Committee members consisted of the PRSP writing team director, the MIGEPROFE Gender and Development Department director, and a representative of Pro-Femmes, the women's civil society groups' umbrella organization.

Source: Zuckerman 2002.

in the World Bank over half of the 17 joint staff assessments (JSAs) of PRSPs reviewed in 2003 provided concrete advice for improving attention to gender inequalities in the sectors considered in the PRSP. Almost all JSAs acknowledged the treatment of gender inequalities in the PRSP's poverty diagnosis or the consultative process or made a general statement about insufficient attention to gender in the PRSP. Aside from describing the deficit of attention to gender issues in PRSP processes and documents, these JSAs often provide useful recommendations on further steps in diagnosis and sex-disaggregated data collection and monitoring.

Gender-responsive budgeting

Gender analysis of public budgets is an emerging tool for determining the different impact of expenditures on women and men to help ensure the equitable use of existing resources. Although more resources are usually needed, in some cases the problem is not allocating more resources, but efficient spending on different activities or better coordination between sectors. Intersectoral coordination and impact monitoring should be strengthened. For instance, the objective of increasing girls' completion rates in primary schools will be achieved only if investments are made in transport or water provision. Gender analyses contribute to making public spending more effective. The development community can support the capacity to perform regular gender analysis in public budgets, and it can strengthen the capacity of the national "women machinery" to identify main gender issues and coordinate the gender mainstreaming in planning and budgeting needs to be built up (see also Thematic Note 2 and Innovative Activity Profile 2).

Governments and donors should ensure that all tools used to assess public financial management systems—such as public expenditure reviews (PERs), Public Expenditure Tracking Surveys, Public Expenditure and Financial Accountability, and Country Financial Accountability Assessments—incorporate a gender perspective. Good examples include PERs initiated by the World Bank for Bangladesh, Cambodia, and Morocco. The Bangladesh PER recommends using area-based poverty indicators to allocate public funds to social sectors, such as to the Female Secondary Stipends program. This not only helps correct gender disparities, but also strengthens the overall impact of public spending. Cambodia's PER includes gender-disaggregated benefit-incidence analysis; identifies the barriers to public service access faced by women and girls, especially in education and agriculture; and proposes ways of addressing these issues. Based on the gender analysis of the budget conducted as

part of the Morocco PER, Morocco's Ministry of Finance and Privatization endorsed the integration of the gender dimension in Morocco's budgetary reform process. Although no impact assessment has been made to date, hopes are high that this will advance the institutionalization of gender considerations in public policy.

Strengthening analytical capacity

Research-based knowledge can play an important role in the policy processes. Country gender assessments and gender mainstreaming in economic and sector work, technical assistance, macroeconomic models, and other regular activities need to be intensified.

The World Bank's country gender assessments (CGAs) seek to diagnose the gender-related barriers to poverty reduction and economic growth in client countries and use this diagnosis to identify priority interventions. In 2005 CGAs had been completed for 41 of 91 client countries, and many of them have been instrumental in intensifying gender inclusion into lending and nonlending activities of the World Bank. CGA preparation processes for most countries have involved extensive consultations with stakeholders including the World Bank, other donors, and civil society groups. This good practice has enhanced the analysis and fostered greater country ownership of the CGA.

Gender issues are also increasingly being incorporated into the World Bank's other instruments for country-level analytical work, such as a Country Economic Memorandum (CEM). For example, the Kenya CEM analyzed the linkage between gender inequality and economic growth and advocated reform of succession laws as applied to women as a key element in promoting stronger pro-poor reform. In a recent case using the Downsizing Options Simulation Exercise tool, analysis in Vietnam found that displaced women employees benefit more from lump-sum compensation than from standard severance packages.[7] Based on this finding, the Vietnamese government modified its assistance package during its state-owned enterprise-downsizing program to include substantial lump-sum components. The World Bank has an ongoing project to mainstream gender perspective in *Doing Business,* a book widely used by researchers, the private sector, and policy makers on the status of the business climate and regulations in 175 countries.[8] Also, the gender-disaggregated MAMS (Maquette for MDG Simulations) presents a few attempts to mainstream gender into macroeconomic modeling and planning (Morrison 2007).

Lessons from IFAD-supported projects show that, for women's economic advancement to be significant and sustained, income-generating activities need to be linked to market opportunities. However, also essential is accompanying support for production and marketing with complementary measures that include awareness and confidence building, information and communication, the sensitization of men and local leaders, general capacity building (in areas such as literacy, leadership, and management skills), organizational support, reduction of women's workloads to enable women to participate more fully, and, occasionally, social welfare measures. Increased emphasis in IFAD's country programs on these critical action areas could be at risk in view of the fact that borrowing governments are becoming less inclined to incorporate capacity building and social investments in loan agreements.

Completion of CGAs and other ESWs is an important element of strategy implementation, but of equal importance is the dissemination and use of research-based findings by donor agencies and strengthening partnerships in producing and disseminating the findings. Moreover, there could be more intensified and concerted efforts in bridging the remaining disconnect between the analytical work and actual policy dialogues initiated and projects implemented by donor agencies.

Interventions can also aim at strengthening the capacity of stakeholders in the countries to conduct relevant analyses (for example, gender-specific expenditure reviews, gender budget analysis, and macroeconomic policy). Strengthening their capacity to use such knowledge in the policy process (for example, training in policy communication) is also important.

Gender in policy instruments

Donors have assisted countries in terms of providing financial and technical support in undertaking policy reforms. For instance, the World Bank and International Monetary Fund (IMF) have lending instruments called Poverty Reduction Support Credits (PRSCs), a new name for Structural Adjustment Loans—and the IMF's Poverty Reduction and Growth Facilities. In Vietnam the latest PRSC promotes gender equity in the labor force and the protection of women's rights, which has helped facilitate a national employment policy to promote equal training and employment opportunities for women as well as support for entrepreneurship programs for women. Several examples related to agriculture and rural development policies also include Mali, Rwanda, and Vietnam (box 2.5). These donor policy-lending instruments are crucial entry points for addressing gender-related constraints and obstacles for agriculture and

rural development. Donors must ensure the inclusion of gender perspective in these instruments. Debate continues on the relative effectiveness of conditionality. On the one hand, the Millennium Challenge Corporation's conditionality to Lesotho has paved the way for changing the country's minority status of women.[9] On the other hand, some experts believe that policy dialogues between a wide range of participants, both governmental and nongovernmental, are likely to prove more productive than donor conditionality (Elson and McGee 1995) and that they emphasize that policy reform processes with the highest chances of success are those which are locally designed and implemented.

Although most countries have national gender policies that guide the implementation of the gender-equity agenda (and a few more countries are in the process of finalizing their national gender policies), the greater challenge is the alignment of the gender policies and approaches to the macroeconomic and trade policies and budget processes in the countries. The existing "cultural" divide separating gender staff from technical staff and economists needs to be narrowed by increasing mutual understanding of the concepts, priorities, strategies, and instruments deployed by both groups. Critical to the development of a better collective understanding of gender and macroeconomic issues is interdonor dialogue; and these policy dialogues should be centered on key processes, for example, PER, poverty assessment, sectoral policy reforms, and market development strategies. As a focus for policy dialogues, a concept of a "gendered economy" (Elson and McGee 1995) is important, in which gender relations are seen as an important social and economic variable at macro-, meso-, and microlevels, rather than viewing the economy as something external and not having an impact on women. A broader understanding is needed, one that recognizes that the issues are both social and economic and that matters of efficiency as well as equity are important. It would be crucial to intensify research and impact assessments that bring into the picture the impact of gender relations on the achievement of policy reforms and rural development, to complement the existing focus on the impact of policy reforms on women.

At the project design stage, donors can focus mainly on the design of the policy reforms. This involves not only checking social policy, but also examining particular elements of the economic policy reform program supported by the reform package to see how far they contribute to influencing gender relations. Improvement in the quality and availability of gender-disaggregated data, training that integrates gender analysis and economic analysis at the national and sectoral levels, and access of women's groups

Box 2.5   The World Bank's Poverty Reduction Support Credit

The Mali Economic Management Credit supports the government's efforts to improve women's access to land and financial services. It has facilitated the preparation of an action plan that was included in the overall financial sector action plan approved in 1998, which resulted in budget support for women's income-generation activities. The operation has also facilitated and increased women's access to land in the Office du Niger region and raised public awareness of women's legal rights and the benefits of women's participation in the development process. In addition, the operation has resulted in the creation of a Ministry of Women's Affairs.

The Rwanda Economic Recovery Credit supports legislation to eliminate discrimination against women. The credit is designed to promote legal and institutional changes in the agricultural sector and labor market that will foster economic growth and reduce rural poverty. In this context, amendments will be made to the labor code to consolidate minimum wages in the rural labor market to one national minimum wage and remove provisions that discriminate against women.

The Vietnam Poverty Reduction Support Credit has been particularly strong in analyzing the likely gender impacts of state-owned enterprise reform and integrating this analysis into the design of safety net provisions for displaced workers. The gender analysis for the credit focused on women and men as separate stakeholders on whom the reform might have different impacts. It found that men are more likely to be laid off, but that women who are laid off are likely to experience a sharper drop in earnings. It also found that men benefit more from compensation packages defined as a multiple of earnings, whereas women benefit more from lump-sum packages. Informed by this analysis, the Vietnam Poverty Reduction Support Credit proposes a unified compensation package (not a separate one for women) that has an important lump-sum component.

Source: "Integrating Gender into the World Bank's Work: A Strategy for Action," http://siteresources.worldbank.org/INTGENDER/Resources/strategypaper.pdf.

to policy-making processes are crucial toward this gendered economy perspective. Some donor agencies, such as the Swedish International Development Agency (SIDA), have started on this. To support the implementation of its gender-equity policy, the gender-equity manual and training that integrates gender and economic analyses have been adopted as one of SIDA's gender strategies (SIDA 2005). Peer review is a tool also used by the Development Assistance Committee of the Organisation for Economic Co-operation and Development (OECD/DAC), in which a panel of peers assesses a multilateral agency's evaluation systems and processes. The OECD/DAC has also developed a gender-equity marker that allows donors to record whether activities have the explicit goal of achieving gender equity. The gender-equity index, which represents another effort to measure progress or regression in gender equity internationally as a result of new aid modalities,[10] uses a set of indicators for which data are available in most countries. Gender audits have also been used increasingly as a self-assessment tool for measuring gender equity among institutions, including development agencies and NGOs (see Module 16).

GUIDELINES AND RECOMMENDATIONS FOR PRACTITIONERS

Representation of women in political institutions. The representation of women in governments and parliaments is an important avenue to making agricultural policies more gender responsive. Donor interventions can aim at strengthening the capacity of women in political institutions, such as women members of parliamentary Committees on Agriculture. Support can also be provided for activities that support women candidates with a rural background to run for elections at different levels. Reservation policies can be adopted and promoted; however, reservation should be coupled with capacity building in decision making and negotiations for women. Training for women needs to provide them with the required skills, particularly in countries where education levels for women are low, and to ensure that they are fully conversant with their roles and accountabilities. Emphasis on women's education, including incentives and scholarships for women in science and policy, is important to ensure a pipeline of well-qualified women candidates for senior positions in public and private organizations.

Participation of women in political processes. Explicit and concerted efforts are needed to ensure the participation of women and inclusion of gender constraints in the strategies. A truly gender-integrated strategy is critical so as to include genuine participation of women in the consultation process and gender-sensitive writing teams. Moreover, in most cases, institutional support for women's groups is needed to strengthen their voice in the national and agricultural policy and strategy development process. Projects can aim at strengthening the capacity of women and their organizations to participate effectively in such processes.

Development cooperation strategies, such as country cooperation strategies, corresponding country plans, and strategies for working in partnership with multilateral organizations, are important entry points for a better integrated gender perspective. In these strategies donors should be guided by priorities and initiatives expressed in the partner country's PRSPs, or similar national and sectoral plans, and by the international conventions and agendas to which the partner country has subscribed. If national priorities and plans do not include gender-equity issues, donors could raise this in the bilateral dialogue and promote further steps to be taken. Donors could also promote and support the capacity of civil society to influence the national plans and priorities in order to close an existing gender gap.

Gender-responsive budgeting. Initiatives toward gender-responsive budgeting should be continued and intensified.

Capacity building for stakeholders to conduct relevant analyses (for example, gender-specific agricultural expenditure reviews, gender analysis of agricultural budgets, and macroeconomic policy analysis) is crucial. National women's machinery needs to be strengthened, along with their capacity for negotiation, to have an effective voice in the budget processes.

Strengthening analytical support. Many gaps need to be explored to understand the obstacles and constraints faced by women and men. Analytical work on gender issues should be heightened, and more should be done to strengthen the capacity of organizations to do gender analysis and gender impact assessments and improve mechanisms to collect gender-disaggregated data to inform policy effectively. Strengthening their capacity to use research-based knowledge in the policy process, for example, by providing training in policy communication, is also important.

Analyzing the political economy of policy making and strengthening the capacity for policy change management. Making policies more gender responsive is inherently a question of political economy. Powerful interests are likely to prevent changes, such as the introduction of land titles for women. Interventions can aim at strengthening the capacity of women policy makers and advocacy NGOs to analyze the political economy of specific policy processes and to engage in policy change management, for example, by building coalitions and influencing public opinion.

Institutionalizing Gender in the Agriculture Sector

Getting the right policies is critical, but equally important are effective institutions and approaches to implement the policies. *Gender mainstreaming* is often a term that encompasses these institutions and approaches.[1] The international women's movement and the donor community have urged countries to establish national institutions (called national machineries) specifically tasked for gender mainstreaming.[2] The Mexico Declaration and Plan of Action in the 1970s, the first international instrument to introduce the concept of national machinery, called for the establishment of national machineries for the advancement of women to advocate for attention to women's advancement, provide policy direction, undertake research, and build alliances. As of 2004, at least 165 countries have established national machineries.[3] A number of world conferences have assessed the status and provided recommendations on strengthening national machineries, and discussions on the role of national machineries have been held at the regional and subregional levels.

Over the last decade, the role of national machineries has evolved in many countries. Transformations in global and national systems of production and governance (including market liberalization and governance reforms, the HIV and AIDS pandemic, urbanization, new forms of conflict, increased migration, and new communication and other technologies) have intensified in the last decade, with important implications for gender relations and for the role, relevance, and impact of national mechanisms for promoting gender equity (see also *Sourcebook* Overview). These changes pose big challenges, but they also present an important opportunity to national mechanisms for gender equity to influence reforms to ensure that they promote women's human rights, market access, and political participation. For example, the shared commitment to meeting the Millennium Development Goals (MDGs) presents an opportunity to mainstream gender-equity perspectives into key development goals, and the Monterrey Consensus offers a chance to incorporate gender equity centrally in economic governance reforms.[4] Governance reforms introducing new accountability jurisdictions at the regional and local levels provide national mechanisms for gender equity with an opportunity to influence policy making at multiple levels.

The emerging new mechanisms (apart from the national machineries) serve as new opportunities to promote the status of women, but they also highlight the need for more coordinated efforts for more effective gender mainstreaming. Some countries have a combination of women's ministry, parliamentary caucus, gender focal points in line ministries, an ombudsperson, and a gender-equity commission, which is a multistakeholder body with high-level participation, monitoring, and reporting to top political leadership. In India associations of elected women in local government are mobilizing themselves across party lines, voicing their demands, and finding a place in the political structure, at a more influential level as they carry political power, votes, and local constituencies (Jain 2005).

This Thematic Note reviews the experiences of national machineries and is divided into two subtopics: one at a national level and the other at the level of the Ministry of Agriculture. Although the focus of the *Sourcebook* is on agriculture, the broader macroeconomic planning and simultaneously the coordination of competition among the different structures of the government also affect the agricultural sector. The second part reviews the experiences of selected countries (Côte d'Ivoire, Arab Republic of Egypt, Morocco, and Sudan)[5] in terms of their design and implementation of national and agriculture sector-specific institutions to support gender approaches. The aim of this exercise is to draw lessons learned from these experiences to inform key principles and entry points for improved investments toward gender-responsive interventions. That governments learn from international success stories in setting up gender units in Ministries of Agriculture and other sectoral ministries to encourage change in what can be a particularly conservative sector is essential.

NATIONAL MACHINERIES FOR THE ADVANCEMENT OF WOMEN

The structure and effectiveness of national machineries vary across countries.[6] National machineries take three general structures: (1) units located at the highest level of government, that is, the president's office (for example, in South Africa and Zambia); (2) fully fledged ministries responsible for gender or women's affairs, with additional responsibilities to coordinate other policy issues (Angola, Democratic Republic of Congo, Lesotho, Malawi, Mozambique, Namibia, Nepal, Tanzania, Uganda, Zimbabwe); and (3) departments or units within a bigger structure (Botswana, Swaziland).

Most of these structures have evolved from small structures to their current size, and their mandate has been changing, an indication of greater focus being given to gender mainstreaming. In general, the mandate, role, and responsibilities of the gender structures are clearly defined to include facilitation, coordination, and monitoring. National machineries in many countries are facilitating exchange and sharing of experiences as well as information and best practices among stakeholders; developing gender competency of stakeholders to influence engendering of policies, programs, and projects; and lobbying for increased measures to address the gender-equity agenda. However, in many countries, the mandates of national machineries are quite broad compared to the resources allocated to fulfill the roles, responsibilities, and functions they are assigned.

Several studies show that national machineries have played catalytic roles in facilitating gender mainstreaming as elaborated in the Beijing Platform for Action, particularly by sensitizing different sectoral ministries and agencies to address gender concerns in their policies and programs. Many countries have enacted gender-equity laws and legal reforms and adopted national gender-equity policies, action plans, and national strategies. Gender-sensitive budgeting has also been introduced in many countries (see Thematic Note 1).

The UNDAW (United Nations Division for the Advancement of Women) conference concluded that some national machineries have had major successes while others have been constrained by lack of clear mandates, political support, and resources and have experienced problems in balancing demands for project implementation, including those from their constituents at a grassroots level, with the need to actively influence policy and program development at the national level from a gender perspective. Many national machineries are constrained by the lack of expertise and conflicting demands on their scarce time and resources, particularly in cases in which women/gender-equity units are part of larger ministries with the responsibility for many issues, and gender-equity issues still remain marginalized in the competition for attention and resources. The gender machineries in many countries also lack coordination, that is, they are not efficiently connected to each other and the other departments. This is in part because of limited human and other resources allocated to these structures and in part to limited clarity on the role and mandate of the national machinery in terms of coordination and monitoring as opposed to implementation of programs, which most national machineries are involved in. The above scenario points to the need for innovative arrangements and structures for sustained financing, which can be achieved in part by better coordination of gender structures within countries to reduce duplication of activities and create synergies to better outcomes.

With about three decades of worldwide experience, lessons have been learned and good practices can be highlighted (box 2.6).

Experiences by various countries also show that the structure and institutional arrangements matter in the effectiveness of the national machineries in gender mainstreaming. For instance, national machineries of South Africa demonstrate a good practice example in terms of interrelationships between the different components of the national machinery (Warioba 2005). The relevant departments and even some of the private sector firms are taking the processes of mainstreaming gender seriously. They have structured relationships between the Office of the Status of Women and the other structures, and they have a clear calendar of events on when they convene planning and monitoring meetings, how they operate, and when consultative meetings are held at the different levels. The role of the Office of the Status of Women in coordination and monitoring is clearly visible. The annual gender audits by this office regularly monitor progress made by its stakeholders in addressing the assigned responsibilities and tasks. Most government departments have developed gender policies to enable gender mainstreaming to happen within their respective departments. The gender focal points are appointed at a very senior level: the director, deputy director, or assistant director levels. Some departments have established structures that are provided with more than one staff member to coordinate gender mainstreaming and women's empowerment programs. Because of better coordination, the national machineries of South Africa are able to influence policy decision-making processes at all levels, at cabinet, national parliament, and provincial levels. Gender mainstreaming and women empowerment programs in the various sectors of the economy are a living example. South

- A clear vision and intellectual leadership that harnesses the knowledge of many relevant partners in the society
- The development of a strategic plan of action to support policy development and implementation
- The utilization of research and data collection, in formulation and review of policies, programs, and plans
- The establishment of alliances with strategic actors within government (head of governments, line ministries, and local governments), parliaments, professional organizations, academic institutions, civil society, community-based organizations, and the media to create synergies to enhance outcomes
- For effective coordination and collaboration, development and implementation of different types of national gender-equity machineries, including joint meeting, plans, and annual reports
- The implementation of a package of actions—such as legislation, gender-mainstreaming action at policy and program levels, and pilot projects

- Capacity development through training of government officials and other relevant actors to support gender-sensitive policy formulation and implementation
- Allocation of adequate personnel and budgetary resources to government bodies and other partners to implement the various activities
- Innovative special incentives (such as awards to gender-sensitive judges or earmarked seed funds to sectoral ministries) to encourage further actions
- Establishment of targets, development of appropriate monitoring tools, and regular tracking of progress
- Regular meeting with partners inside and outside government to assess progress, identify gaps, and devise collaborative strategies to address obstacles
- Mobilization of political will through public awareness programs and broad dissemination of information.

Source: UNDAW conference (see note 1 in Thematic Note 2).

Africa was also able to present comprehensive and detailed national progress reports on the implementation of the various gender-equity instruments to which their country is partly compared to other countries, in which in most cases the national reports omit much information that could have been added.

Another example is Tanzania: although a structured relationship is lacking between the national machinery and NGOs that are promoting the gender-equity and women's empowerment processes, the Ministries of Finance and Planning Commission and NGOs have been able to establish a working relationship in promoting gender-sensitive planning and budgeting processes that were initiated through a Gender-Responsive Budgeting Initiative. These processes resulted in the establishment of a gender macro-policy working group that is coordinated by the national machinery and convenes regular meetings to facilitate mainstreaming gender in macroeconomic policy frameworks, such as PRSPs and Medium Term Expenditure Review Frameworks. In Uganda women are particularly visible in national politics because of affirmative action. Affirmative action has also contributed to women's participation

in regional political decision making. Women hold four of the nine positions of Ugandan representatives in the EALA and are two of the five Uganda members of the African parliament. The enabling laws derived from the 1995 constitution have seen the need for affirmative action, mainly as a result of activism by women groups: (1) the Land Act of 1998 provides for the protection of the land rights of the poor, the majority of whom are women, and (2) the Local Government Act of 1997 explicitly states that women shall form one-third of all local councils at all levels. As a result, the proportion of women in local councils rose from 6 percent in the early 1990s to 44 percent in 2003.[7]

GENDER UNITS AND FOCAL POINTS IN THE AGRICULTURE SECTOR

The Ministries of Agriculture are the main agencies responsible for mainstreaming gender into agricultural policies, projects, and programs. The first step in the gender mainstreaming in the selected countries was an information campaign and sensitization of the "gender" and women empowerment concepts usually initiated with technical and funding support from international organizations (including FAO, IFAD, and the World Bank). Plans of action for the integration of the gender dimension in rural and agricultural development policies and programs were also designed, starting with situation assessment (for men and women) in the agricultural sector and identifying gender roles in agriculture, constraints, potentialities (natural resources, human resources), priorities, needs, and solutions. A second step was training for trainers and national officers about gender approaches and gender analysis, and technical support often came from international agencies. Pilot testing was performed for effective adaptation of gender approaches and methodological tools to the sociocultural context of the countries.

A third step was the introduction of gender focal points and creation of gender units within the Ministries of Agriculture (MOAs) to address gender issues in the sector. The name given to these gender units differs from one country to another (for example, Office for the Promotion of Rural Women's Socioeconomic Promotion, Women and Agricultural Development Directorate, Women Promotion Units, Policy Coordinating Unit for Women in Agriculture, and National Gender Service). These gender units and focal points are either independent units under MOAs or a part of the extension services or policy and economic planning units. Donors often partner with gender units to implement key programs and projects. For instance, the IFAD supported the Lao People's Democratic Republic's Women's Union to mainstream gender issues in all project activities. In many countries in Asia (China, Lao PDR, Mongolia), the IFAD is collaborating with women's organizations under the Communist Party; these are often the de facto operational force for the national machinery and plans to be replicated in Cambodia and Vietnam. In Azerbaijan an IFAD-financed project targeting rural women in the mountainous areas is being implemented in cooperation with the MOA and the Ministry for Women's Affairs. This collaboration is taking place at the central level as well as local government and community levels and is enhancing the national machinery's capacity to address gender inequalities through practical measures.

GOOD PRACTICES AND LESSONS LEARNED

The effectiveness of these gender units varies across countries. For example, the unit for the Strengthening of and Support to Gender Policies in the El Salvador Ministry for Agriculture and Livestock helped the extension program tailor training to women farmers, thus enhancing produc-

tivity. The Gender Services unit in the reconfigured MOA in Côte d'Ivoire led to fully one-quarter of the ministry's programs having an explicit gender focus (see also Innovative Activity Profile 2). In most North African countries (including Egypt, Morocco, and Sudan), the gender-mainstreaming concept was introduced around 1995 through projects and programs funded in cooperation between governments and international or bilateral agencies. Mainstreaming gender became a prerequisite for the design of development projects and programs, but the implementation has started slowly, and little progress was made during the first five years. The initial challenges were due to several factors: (1) the concept was new, and the national researchers have not produced the relevant data to make the concept more comprehensive; (2) the "new" concept has been perceived as a theoretical one without operational use; and (3) the decision makers have not been targeted as beneficiaries of information and sensitization sessions: those officials in charge of women's affairs or women's NGOs participated in the sessions. However, the situation has evolved, and progress has been made in the adoption of gender approaches in development policy and program design. Gender-sensitive governance is becoming the rule in these countries.

But for some countries, similar to the national machineries discussed above, the focal strategy has had limited effectiveness because the often junior women staff who are appointed are given few extra resources or time for new responsibilities, as well as little training, support, and clarity about their role. Gender desks themselves have often suffered from lack of political will and insecure institutional tenure. Crucial lessons and experiences in gender units and focal points in the agriculture sector include the following:

Strategic location of gender units and focal points. The location of the gender unit is important to ensure that gender equity is taken into account when designing, implementing, and evaluating agricultural development policies and programs. For instance, this approach has been more successful in Sudan compared to Morocco and other countries, where the gender unit was located within the extension directorate (box 2.7). Gender units established and focal points identified within permanent structures for planning had greater access to gender databases in agriculture because their activities are included in the work plan and budget. Others had difficulties performing their tasks because the units had neither power nor a hierarchical coordinating role, the units depended on external funds (government or donor), and they had no relation with universities and research centers. In some cases the autonomous gender unit stopped the activities on completion of the project, when the unit was not included in the official chart of the MOA.

Networks established that connect different levels of governance. Networks connecting the central and local governments, private sector, and the community were proven to ease the integration of gender dimension at the earliest step of the program and project design and during the projects' implementation and evaluation. The gender units can also serve as vehicles to connect local agents with national entities that could facilitate change in spheres in which rural development projects cannot intervene directly, for example, domestic violence against women and girls. Another area is improvement of health, which, in the case of rural women, is usually neglected because of lack of accessibility and cultural barriers. In this case the national machinery can also facilitate contacts with governmental institutions to make services available.

In Egypt the approach for gender mainstreaming in the agricultural sector through the pilot governorates is said to be innovative since it involves a multisectoral approach and a wide range of stakeholders to participate in key activities and share information related to constraints, needs, priorities, and proposed solutions. The activities involve women and men farmers and agricultural workers, extension agents, rural development specialists, authorities of extension structures, the private sector, and women's NGOs. To date, the gender-mainstreaming concept in Egypt's agriculture sector is said to be integrated in the agricultural research programs (box 2.8). In El Salvador,

Unidad de Fortalecimiento y Apoyo en Aspectos de Género works closely with the gender units in the different projects at the local level not only to provide support but also to learn about the different challenges, constraints, and opportunities that arise in the project implementation process.

Political commitment. Securing high-level political commitment is important, and the national commitment to and generalization of gender policy making, implementation, and monitoring and evaluation through gender units are all crucial. This should be followed by a clear objective and quantifiable indicator to measure progress over time effectively. The need is present for defining and applying impact indicators to measure how gender-equity measures impact the lives of women and men in communities. The national machinery could be crucial in the dissemination of such tools and could be very effective when convincing Ministries of Finance (which in the case of the IFAD are very important) to allocate resources to finance gender-related budgets and activities. Vargas-Lundius (2007) illustrates the importance of introducing affirmative actions to reduce the gender gap at the community level, as well as the importance of measuring the impact such measures could have in terms of reducing poverty, generating income and employment, and increasing women's self-esteem, empowerment, and economic autonomy.

Moreover, gender approaches need to be institutionalized in the governmental planning process and curriculum for planners and statisticians. In Morocco curricula Modules

Box 2.8 Egypt: Integrated Approach to Gender Mainstreaming

The women-equity machinery in the Ministry of Agriculture and Land Reclamation is called the Policy Coordinating Unit for Women in Agriculture (PCUWA). This autonomous structure is located at a central level. The unit team is composed of researchers and officers from the Agricultural Research and Extension Institutes. Gender-related projects also contribute to the funding of the unit expenses. PCUWA works with the technical services at central and decentralized levels, mainly with extension agents. It cooperates with the rural women's associations, particularly in newly reclaimed lands. The unit works in an integrated approach—involving governorate authorities, stakeholders, and the local population: rural men and women.

The main activities performed by the unit team are related to (1) preparation of agriculture and gender studies, (2) integration of women in the agricultural policies and programs, and (3) promotion of income-generating activities in agriculture on old and newly reclaimed lands. Awareness and training sessions on gender approaches and related topics were organized with the support of governmental and bilateral or international agencies through development projects. Among the integrated activities, the experience gained during the last five years in the framework of integration of women into the agricultural policy and practice project is of particular interest.

Source: Personal communication with Fatiha Bou-Salah (FAO), January 18, 2008.

on gender approach were integrated into the agricultural education institutes including the university. This leads to approach sustainability and improvement.

Holistic approach. Broad-based practitioner evidence suggests that separate, small women-specific agricultural and rural development programs are usually not successful in reaching large numbers of rural women. Instead, design of mainstream agricultural programs so that they reach both men and women is more effective (Innovative Activity Profile 2). Mainstreaming gender in the policies, programs, and projects requires much more than just a unit or organization, but should be tackled at the different technical divisions as well as in administrative, human resources, and financial services divisions.

Human and technical expertise. Providing high-quality technical support on gender analysis by the main coordinating body of the national gender machinery is important. Sound analysis of what the MOA and gender units are currently doing and then the analysis and dissemination of gendered impacts are very important processes. Crucial to these processes are the training and support of national and decentralized staff to (1) build gender monitoring and evaluation of their current activities, (2) quantify existing gender gaps, (3) agree on the necessity of change, and (4) build the new strategy and instruments. Effective facilitation of a sustainable national commitment is often based on solid, credible knowledge of gender issues.

Moreover, appointing gender focal points in MOAs with the most extensive knowledge of technical and research issues and the authority to encourage change is crucial. Women should be encouraged to participate at all levels of the hierarchy, particularly at managerial and technical levels; however, identifying posts or tasks that can be performed only by women does not help the cause. Having dedicated gender staff sit within sectoral ministries increases the gender relevance of their work. These staff need to have exceptional competencies in mobilizing other partners, have great field knowledge of the agricultural women producers, and display a high university-level education to exhibit recognized technical credibility in front of men directors. They would also need to have a specific budget to facilitate missions, networks, and training.

A need exists to provide support to ensure that MOAs' human resources policies become genderized and introduce the necessary measures and incentives to increase the participation of qualified women at managerial and technical levels. For example, the terms of reference for all staff, particularly those for new recruits, ought to highlight their engagement to promote gender equity actively in all their activities and programs. Ministries should also be encouraged to introduce quotas to improve gender balance among technical and managerial staff.

Last, looking at and devising incentives are important strategies. Linking gender targets to economic incentives for public sector employees is needed. Presenting gender as a principle of excellence in public sector management, rather than as an additional burden, can be adopted as an effective strategy.

GUIDELINES AND RECOMMENDATIONS FOR PRACTITIONERS

Several entry points for more effective support through donor programs and projects, in partnership with governments and civil society organizations, are the following:

- Capacity building and support to national women machinery, gender units, and focal points in critical areas such as poverty reduction strategies, MDGs, national economic planning, statistical systems, budgeting processes, and agriculture sector approaches
- Providing women machinery, gender units, and focal points with adequate human and financial resources to enable them to respond more effectively to the challenges of changed global and national environments and to enhance their important monitoring and reporting roles

- Strengthening the capacity of women machinery, gender units, and focal points to undertake gender analysis and to develop the methodologies and tools needed to play a catalytic role in gender mainstreaming across all sectors of government in collaboration with line ministries
- Mandatory training on gender mainstreaming for all governmental bodies, including at the local level, to ensure understanding of their roles and responsibilities
- Developing effective accountability mechanisms, particularly through the introduction of gender perspectives and gender-equity indicators in budgetary processes at all levels of government
- Facilitating the establishment of alliances between women machineries and strategic actors within parliaments, professional organizations, academic institutions, civil society, community-based organizations, and the media to create synergies
- Assisting in the effective coordination and collaboration among the different types of women machineries and gender units, which may include joint meetings, plans, and annual reports.

Decentralization and Community-Driven Development

As reported in the *World Development Report 2008*, governance issues are crucial to achieving an agriculture-for-development agenda to fulfill the MDGs and reduce world poverty. Although democratic processes and the rise of participatory policy making have increased the opportunities for small landholders and the rural poor to make gains from agriculture over the last 25 years, the complexity and diversity of agriculture require special efforts to ensure gender equity and accountability and inclusion to disadvantaged groups, including women, in relation to their access to technology, natural resources, finance, markets, and nonfarm opportunities.

In the last two decades, many large international development agencies have turned increasingly to decentralization and the use of demand-driven (community-based and community-driven) development approaches to address poverty by involving rural women and other beneficiaries in choices regarding project activities and resource allocation, making use of a special development fund to ensure delivery of goods and services to rural communities. Social funds and community development funds (CDFs) are mechanisms used by the World Bank and IFAD to channel grant resources to CDD projects; they are currently viewed by many in the donor community as *the* delivery model best suited for large-scale implementation of community-based, demand-driven development and decentralization based on their attractiveness to beneficiaries as grants instead of loans and their flexibility and potential for poverty targeting. Other agencies, including CARE, the U.K. Department for International Development's Sustainable Livelihoods Program, and the United Nations Development Programme–supported Decentralization Program, utilize CDD approaches that do not fully meet the strict definition of the term because they rely less on a fund mechanism (Gillespie 2006). CDD is believed not only to lead to better allocation of resources to help communities by building social capital and fostering empowerment, but

also to reduce corruption and misuse, and to increase transparency and accountability by working directly with communities (Mansuri and Rao 2004).

The term "CDD" is widely adopted and assumes a different meaning and connotations depending on which development agency has tried to apply it in practice, but in all cases, CDD is an approach to reduce rural poverty through more equitable, sustainable, and efficient use of resources by (1) establishing an enabling institutional environment for the emergence of robust community organizations, (2) developing community-level infrastructure, (3) supporting the local economy at the community level, and (4) diversifying sources of external support for community-based organizations (see also box 2.9). The approach supports participatory decision making, self-reliance, empowerment, local capacity building, and community control of resources by channeling resources to activities proposed by community groups. Various forms of social fund financing and technical assistance are available from outside the community; these are usually implemented through decentralized local governments. Projects can have low or high CDD content depending on the extent of devolution and institutional development at the community level.

An important distinction between the two is that CDD has a tendency to reach down to the village level, whereas decentralization interventions tend to be clustered at a somewhat higher administrative level, municipality, or district. Complementarities may exist between the two that can improve the welfare of rural women.

One of the recognized benefits of these approaches is their potential to reach goals of capacity building, empowerment, and sustainability of community-based organizations and self-help groups, including those of the most marginalized groups, such as poor women, for the development of public goods and services. To varying degrees, donor agencies use targeting as an approach to build the capacities of those who have less power, to influence

Decentralization is the transfer of administrative, political, and fiscal authority to lower levels of government to make policy making and implementation more responsive to the needs of rural people. It is a political process that shifts power and authority and has been tried in some form in over 80 percent of all developing countries. Fiscal decentralization has as its goal the improvement of revenue generation while building accountability of local governments to local taxpayers. Devolution refers to the delegation of responsibilities and power from a central to a subordinate level.

Community-based development (CBD) is an umbrella term that refers to projects that actively include beneficiaries in their design and management;

community-driven development provides a mechanism to design and implement projects that facilitates access to social and physical capital assets for the poor by creating conditions for the following:

- Transforming development agents from top-down planners into client-oriented service providers
- Empowering communities to take initiatives for their own socioeconomic development
- Enabling community-level organizations to play a role in the design and implementation of policies and programs affecting their livelihoods, including the management of funds
- Enhancing the impact of public expenditure on the local economy at the community level.

Source: Author.

---

decisions, and to participate in development (see examples from projects in Indonesia and the Philippines in box 2.10).

Donor agency policy documents often state that grants allocated to CDD programs will go to the very poor and women, who are perceived as key agents of change (and victims of social and economic inequalities) in agricultural production and food security programs. As a result, CDD projects hold out hope as an approach to fortify women's agency and decision making for benefit sharing in the agricultural sector. CDD projects build the capacity of community and women's groups (including producer associations, microenterprise groups, credit and savings groups, natural resource management and common property groups, and groups formed for agricultural extension and adaptive research purposes), promote an enabling environment through policy and institutional reform (decentralization, sector policies, and so on), strengthen local governance relationships (including forging linkages between community-based organizations and local governments), enable community-level organizations to play a broader role in the design and implementation of policies and programs affecting their livelihoods, and enhance the impact of public expenditure on the local economy at the community level.

Yet CDD involves trade-offs between building the capacities of marginalized groups, such as poor women, and responding to community demands for social and physical infrastructure, which leaves the process subject to decision-making systems already in place. Thus, without due attention to gender issues and without changes in existing power structures, women's interests can be harmed both socially—by undermining their decision-making roles and sidelining their priorities—and materially (GENRD 2008).

KEY GENDER ISSUES

Agriculture requires a mix of centralized and decentralized services. Some tasks are best organized at the central level, such as food security, whereas the intermediate level is most suited for research, and the local level is best for extension. In cases where agricultural goods and services are provided through private services, capture by elites and exclusion of women are much higher than in development programs that provide public goods, such as drinking water supplies and schools.

Decentralization has generally been considered a positive step toward making governments more accountable to the poor by bringing decision making down to a local level. Research has shown that where resources are available, decentralization has resulted in the greater participation of poor and marginalized groups such as women in decision making and in monitoring the activities of local governments (Baden 2000). However, projects that work through existing decentralized public administration to devolve investment authority to decentralized entities at the district

Box 2.10 Indonesia and the Philippines: Gender Targeting

The *Indonesia Kecamatan Development Program (KDP)* began in 1998 and is partially funded by the World Bank. Its aims are to alleviate poverty, strengthen local government and community institutions, and improve local governance through the delivery of block grants to *kecamatans* (subdistricts) for productive infrastructure and social and economic investments identified through a participatory planning process. From 1998 to July 2006, KDP covered 34,233 of the poorest villages in 30 provinces (260 districts and 1,983 subdistricts), approximately 48 percent of all of Indonesia's 71,011 villages.

The KDP gender strategy has been developed since its first phase to identify key activities that can promote gender equity, including (1) creation of an affirmative action recruitment program for field staff, (2) hiring and training of equal numbers of men and women village facilitators, (3) opening up subproject menus to a broader range of options that reflect women's choices, (4) improving opportunities for women's participation in developing proposals and decision making, (5) ensuring that a share of block grants goes only through preexisting women's groups, (6) furthering women's active roles in project implementation, including speaking competitions for shy women, and (7) creating internships for women engineers.

The *Kapitbisig Laban Sa Kahirapan-Comprehensive and Integrated Delivery of Social Services Project (KALAE-*

CIDSS) is the flagship poverty reduction project of the government of the Philippines. The objectives are to (1) empower communities to manage their assets, lives, and livelihoods; (2) strengthen their social networks and link them up with policy and administrative structures of the state; and (3) promote representation and accountability at different levels of the decision-making pyramid. The Midterm Review notes that awareness of KALAE-CIDSS is quite high (75–92 percent) and so is the level of participation in the preparatory and planning stages (61–90 percent).

KALAE-CIDSS gave priority to subprojects if they target women's participation in all phases of decision making. In a few regions participation in the preparatory phase was slightly higher among women than men members. Most of those who did not participate claimed that they did not have spare time, were afraid to attend evening meetings, were not properly informed, were discouraged, or were not interested. Other lessons include the following: (1) lack of confidence prevents women from contributing during meetings; (2) women's capacity to exert their voice and interact productively is gradually increasing; (3) contrary to what was expected, both men and women are partners in terms of work inside their home and in the field; and (4) encouraging women's participation in indigenous peoples' communities has proven to be a long process.

Sources: Balisacan, Edillon, and Ducanes 2000; Balisacan and Edillon 2003; Joint Donor and Government Mission 2007; World Bank 2002, 2003, 2007b.

---

level are less likely than community-driven processes at the subdistrict level to favor poor women. Factors that account for this are women's greater accessibility to community-level decision making, less stringent eligibility criteria, and greater relevance to issues and services that directly impact women's private lives. Although in many areas local politics are more suited to women than are national politics (because of restrictions on mobility and lack of experience), patriarchal structures and norms that are often strong at the local level and may well be combined with nonaccountable customary or informal bodies and community relationships mean that in many cases it is even harder for women to exert meaningful influence (Baden 2000).[1] At the local level, inequalities due to class and caste make it equally difficult

for poor women to participate, as at any other level. Similarly, the shape, structure, and politics of the decentralization program in countries affect both men and women policy makers' ability to wield the power of the state in women's interests (Horowitz 2007). A common constraint is that in many countries decentralized structures of government are created but given very few resources, capacity-building investment, or power actually to enact an agenda defined by local citizens.

Institution building that could provide sustainable solutions is problematic; innovations and organizational changes that facilitate gender equity and women's empowerment are not easily accepted by civil servants and local politicians. Without strong external intervention, implementation of

CDD has been known to revert to conventional ways of implementing top-down projects, sidelining participation and empowerment. In part for this reason, some donors adopt a targeting approach: a range of measures that ensure that the most marginalized social groups are able to claim their rights to receive an equitable share of the benefits of development interventions, expand their influence over public policy and institutions, and enhance their bargaining power in the marketplace through special enabling, empowering, and self-targeting measures.

An inherent contradiction exists between traditional poverty targeting, which is usually top-down and uses quotas or earmarked funds for special groups, and CDD approaches that grant resources to community groups best able to influence decision-making and granting processes. Women's participation in decentralized processes and community organizations is hampered by gender inequities that are particularly acute at the local level. Due to their lack of free time, literacy, and language barriers, low levels of confidence, and gender norms within households and cultures, women often are excluded from CDD processes that require them to develop proposals and compete for funds (IADB 1998).

Finally, CDD projects are reluctant to impose gender-equity concerns on existing institutions and rarely set targets for percentages of women among project beneficiaries, or for women's representation in decision-making bodies or in user groups for project-supported facilities. No gender earmarking exists for development funds, gender sentization, or affirmative action on gender balance in staffing. Staff are not assigned responsibility for gender or poverty targeting. Going against this trend, World Bank projects in Indonesia, the Philippines, and Vietnam incorporate affirmative action and targeted capacity building to enable gender equity (box 2.10).

EXPERIENCES, IMPACTS, AND BENEFITS FROM GENDER-RESPONSIVE ACTIONS

Some lessons have been learned from earlier development projects, but it is unclear whether women have been able to benefit as fully as men in the CDD processes, or whether they have been harmed by the process. A review of IFAD CDD projects in 2003 revealed that it is difficult to evaluate impacts on women in projects that do not explicitly target women because of insufficient information. Basic infrastructure development projects, which have reported more success than those of capacity building, have a strong potential to benefit the whole community; these are commonly used to develop roads, markets, irrigation and water systems, community-based natural resource management, and income-generating activities. The impact of community projects themselves on women has been shown to be positive or negative, depending on the type of activities financed (boxes 2.10–2.13).

Yet there is abundant evidence that untargeted CDD can bypass women and the poor. Evidence suggests that infrastructure investments need to be accompanied by investments in user group empowerment to increase the likelihood that the poorest women and men will benefit from the facilities. Women's marginalized status within the community renders their voices less significant than those of men; they have less access to decision making and to the resources for development, and limited time and mobility to attend meetings that determine women's needs and priorities. In some cases CBD/CDD approaches have resulted in more women's participation, but this inclusion has not always translated into active participation and equal access to benefits for women. Without additional measures to empower women to articulate their own needs for technical assistance or form and strengthen groups, these approaches differ little from more traditional top-down approaches to community development. However, as noted by Horowitz (2007), limited evidence exists of this kind of transformation in practice.

To date, the evidence of the impacts of CDD approaches is limited; most CDD projects have not yet been subjected to rigorous evaluation (World Bank 2005), and few studies have attempted rigorous and credible evaluation of their social impacts (Mansuri and Rao 2004). Existing literature also does not provide a sufficient understanding of how decisions are made by communities in CDD projects (Labonne and Chase 2007), much less an understanding of the roles and impacts on women.

Recent studies have led to a pause in the optimism for women to benefit significantly from CDD approaches and decentralization. The World Bank and IFAD have found that the link between CBD/CDD projects and social capital and community empowerment is weak, and that there is "mixed and limited evidence on the impacts of CBD/CDD projects in relation to empowerment and poverty reduction." A review of IFAD's experiences (IFAD 2004a, 2006) reported that current information on gender aspects and impacts in the CDFs is superficial; assessments of CDD and CDFs have not measured gender impacts or participation of women in the capacity-building activities. Reports show that less than half of CDFs go to the targeted poor because elites favor groups who are more educated, better connected to information channels, more politically influential—and better off. Positive impacts on poor women's livelihoods cannot be taken for granted. Investments in supporting empowerment initiatives through CBD/CDD projects alone are often insufficient and can even be counterproductive if the better-off sections of the community gain more than the less well-off. The views and priorities of poor women are likely to remain excluded from collective decision-making processes.

GOOD PRACTICES AND LESSONS LEARNED

To date, the documentation and evaluation of decentralization and CDD on building accountability to rural women and transforming gender relations are extremely limited. Knowledge generated by both the IFAD and World Bank gives some preliminary findings on gender impacts of these policy and implementation instruments.

Capacity building

Building internal leadership and accountability. Poor women's participation in publicly visible activities, such as those of CDD projects, is severely constrained as well by their own lack of confidence. Experience has shown that building women's leadership, capacity, and self-esteem can result in more active participation and benefit sharing. Although women's membership in groups may have been achieved, members may not be the type of people envisaged, or all women may not participate and benefit equally. In the case of IFAD's project in Chattisgarh, India, participation in self-help groups was found to build women's confidence to enable them to challenge those abusing power. Yet a big constraint is the lead time required to build women's self-esteem, which ideally should exist before a CDD project is initiated.

Training and skill development. Women with low levels of literacy find it impossible to participate in decision-making processes that are heavily dependent on written work and agendas, minutes, and reports and are thus significantly disadvantaged under CDD. Their capacity to participate meaningfully in the drafting of microproject requests and participatory procurement mechanisms is thus seriously constrained.

Women members of self-help groups and elected officials in local government also require more specific training in procedures, group management, and leadership. Women's self-help groups as well as NGO-created and -funded women's *sanghas* in several Indian states have served as important training grounds for women to develop and define their leadership skills (Horowitz 2007).

IFAD projects in Peru and Nepal have provided women leaders and knowledge holders from within the beneficiary groups with contracts to work as providers of extension services and skills in technical aspects of agricultural production and agroforestry as well as in group formation, bookkeeping and accounting, and leadership, thus contributing to the women's abilities to build local institutional capacities to address their own needs.

Participation

Inclusion of the poorest. A major lesson learned from CDD projects is the need to avoid assumptions about social homogeneity of communities and to understand the livelihood strategies of women as compared to men, and as compared to women of other socioeconomic status. Assumptions by project managers about who constitutes the poorest are often found to be very different from the perceptions of local community members. Even in successful targeting projects, a "middle class effect" occurs, wherein the better-off section of the poor benefits as a result of being more able to negotiate and communicate their desires. Poor women also face a high opportunity cost by participating, especially if it displaces income-earning opportunities (Horowitz 2007).

Recognizing the complexity of targeting within CDD projects, the IFAD has found that a combination of enabling and affirmative action measures directed at the poor, reinforced by disincentives for the wealthier, to "mainstream a pro-poor perspective" minimizes the risk of elite capture. In Peru participatory social mapping and wealth ranking were valuable exercises that proved essential to the design of a targeting strategy and project activities that included the poorest (Peña-Montenegro 2004), although it remains unclear to what extent their participation was included in the later stages of the project cycle. The Indonesia Kecamatan Development Program and Vietnam Community-Based Rural Infrastructure Project selectively target the poorest communities (boxes 2.10 and 2.11).

Strategies for supporting women's participation in different types of groups and ensuring accountability to them. Within CDD projects, project-approved groups are the gatekeepers of the resources and decisions and are therefore more powerful than in traditional projects. Existing groups are found to have more community credibility, cohesion, and established decision-making procedures than newly formed groups; by selecting target groups, donors can influence the targeting of benefits to women. There is no strong recommendation that can be made about trying to achieve high levels of homogeneity in these groups, as some groups

The objective of the Community Based Rural Infrastructure Project (CBRIP) is to reduce rural poverty in the poorest rural communes in 13 provinces in central Vietnam by (1) increasing the capacity for decentralized and participatory planning and management of development activities; (2) providing essential small-scale, community-based infrastructures; and (3) generating direct income for the poor through providing construction employment. The project initially targets 540 poor communes with a population of about 1.4 million. The communes selected for the project are defined as "poor," based on nationally established criteria. The poor are mostly women and ethnic people. Women's participation has been a key objective and successful component of CBRIP, but its full potential remains to be realized as women make up 50–60 percent of village meeting participants, 20–30 percent of participants in training courses, 40 percent of members of CPCC, 42–51 percent of participants in subprojects, and 20–30 percent of operation and maintenance groups.

Lessons learned. The benefits to women were particularly recognized in activities including (1) recognizing women's customary rights in determining compensation for land and assets, (2) opportunities for practicing training skills in workshops on gender mainstreaming, (3) revised and improved communication content of leaflets and posters focusing on gender equality, and (4) separate meetings for men and women to select subprojects. Women interviewees were very satisfied with their participation from selection, implementation, and monitoring the subprojects. Although women have benefited from new employment opportunities, they usually receive low pay for "simple" work. The Vietnam Women's Union has not been fully made aware of CBRIP and its gender initiatives.

Sources: World Bank 2001a, 2006a, 2006b, 2007c.

prefer (as in the case of a project with people who own no land in Nicaragua) to have some better-connected members in their groups to perform advocacy or functions requiring more education.

In the case of very poor and overworked women, total inclusiveness is extremely difficult to achieve. Contributions of cash, labor, and local materials that must be provided by communities as proof of commitment and a condition to obtain community-driven funds are often unaffordable by women who have few material resources and little time for labor contributions. In some cases, "artificial groups" form to access CDF funds, undermining legitimate groups that exist for credit purposes and collective investments.

In India all adult women in villages were organized into self-help groups by the IFAD to compensate for their exclusion from project groups. Criteria for group membership may exclude the poorest; projects need to understand the reasons for exclusion and encourage nonparticipants to group themselves on the basis of common interests and affinities.

Quotas and earmarked funds have been used to ensure women's representation in decision-making bodies or recipient groups. These measures alone have not been fully effective in ensuring benefits, however; when transparency was stressed, as in a project in Peru, the directing of funds to women of easily identified groups had the desired impact. But despite the fact that quotas for women's inclusion in recipient groups in projects in India and Nicaragua were met, they were often filled by women who lacked the assets to use profitably the technical assistance services provided (such as women without livestock for livestock-related activities). Furthermore, the East Asia Region CDD Flagship Report concludes that women's frequent attendance in meetings does not always mean that they will be able to influence the decision making (box 2.12).

Gender relations within the community groups and community-based organizations that represent their communities are key to equitable participation and impact. In some cases, decentralized decision making works more smoothly than in others; success depends on the capacity of the community organizations for democratic decision making. Associations such as the Cape Verde community associations may have a majority of women members, but they tend to be less informed and active and are led by better-educated men leaders. The number of women in leadership positions in rural producer organizations, for example, is extremely limited; women in these groups—and many others—are not always able to hold their representatives—both men and women—accountable to their needs. As a result,

Box 2.12   Enabling East Asian Communities to Drive Local Development

The East Asia Region CDD Flagship Report refers in particular to experiences from Cambodia, Indonesia, the Philippines, and Vietnam. Its main findings related to gender issues include the following:

Increased women's involvement. If women, minorities, and the poor remain uninvolved, elites are far more likely to retain control within the community. Evidence on the success of CDD operations in promoting participation among these groups comes from Cambodia, Indonesia, and the Philippines. Analysis shows increased women's involvement compared to other villages where there are no CDD operations. Women in Indonesia also expressed satisfaction that their voice was being heard.

Involvement leading to decision-making power. Although quantitative evidence points toward frequent attendance at meetings by women in Cambodia and Indonesia, women may not influence the actual decision-making process, which is often because women lack capacity or because of their language barriers. Despite these results, evidence from Indonesia shows active participation by women in particular in

women-only meetings. Data show that women in CDD operations attend decision-making activities more frequently compared to limited evidence in non-CDD projects.

Indicators of women's participation. Project outcome indicators should be SMART (Specific, Measurable, Attributable, Realistic, and Targeted). By targeted is meant that the indicator identifies the particular group the project should impact. An example of a strongly targeted indicator is "40 percent participation rate of women and poorest community members in planning and decision-making meetings." An example of a weakly targeted indicator is "improved social capital and organizational development." Outcome indicators could include "percentage change in the number of women in local decision-making bodies in the targeted communities." The facilitators should be able to obtain the necessary information during their first and their last visits to the village. For day-to-day management purposes, data should be collected, such as percentage of poor and women (or any other marginalized group) involved in planning, execution, and maintenance.

Source: World Bank 2007e.

women's roles are still overlooked by those who fail to internalize the fact that agriculture is dominated by women through their labor, knowledge, and other inputs at the field level.

Institutional linkages

CDD design efforts usually do a good job of articulating the demand side, that is, the processes whereby demands will be elicited in a participatory manner from local populations. However, they often fall seriously short in analyzing the supply side. To have positive impacts on women, the menu of goods and services available within CDD projects must include those that are of relevance and interest to women. Poor landless women could not gain much benefit from a project's land improvement activities in India, for example; nor could Nicaraguan women without animals benefit from livestock activities (IFAD 2004b). In Vietnam one project aimed to avoid transferring agricultural technology innovations to women farmers if it increases their already heavy workload (box 2.13). In-depth preliminary

poverty and livelihood analyses are necessary before determining the menu of the types of goods and services to be funded and supported to match the interests and livelihoods of women.

Even when menus of eligible microprojects are appropriate, a rigorous analysis of the capacity to deliver such goods and services and follow-up on implementation is frequently lacking. This then leads to unacceptably large numbers of low-quality microprojects. Effective participation may occur, and even a degree of empowerment. This empowerment must, however, be a means to an end of improved living conditions and higher incomes. To this end, a project in Vietnam now aims to improve communication with organizations such as the Vietnam Women's Union to facilitate monitoring, dissemination, and training opportunities (box 2.12).

The IFAD has found that the process of mobilizing community demands is often rushed, uninformed, and influenced by either government or NGO actors who often are not representing women's interests. To counteract this tendency, the IFAD uses self-targeting by communities to determine activities and investments appropriate to a specific group. Adequate identification of target groups and their characteristics in terms of assets and livelihood strategies, conducted through gender-sensitive poverty analysis, is a precondition for the design and implementation of an effective targeting strategy. In the case of a CDD project in Peru, this analysis turned up much more variation in women's livelihood strategies than was initially recognized. Similarly, it was discovered in a project in the Philippines that—contrary to expectations—men and women share the workload in terms of work inside the home as well as in the field (box 2.10).

Networking and communication. Most CDD projects use both mass media and field personnel such as extension agents, NGOs, and promoters to provide information. A careful communication strategy is needed to ensure that women are provided with full information on what is available from the fund, to whom, and how to obtain access in a language and at a level that suits their abilities

(boxes 2.12 and 2.13). Poor women's lack of capacity, information, and knowledge hampers their ability to participate equally with men in CDD processes. Women often lack information about the process of applying for funds, as well as the time to attend meetings and the confidence to speak up if they do. Class, caste, and other nongender aspects of identity also affect women's ability to participate and the issues that motivate them. In Cape Verde, India, and Peru, planners observed that information can ensure that women (1) know what goods and services they can choose, (2) are able to make informed choices, (3) know where to go to obtain the necessary forms, (4) are able to prepare and present acceptable proposals or seek help to produce these, (5) understand their responsibilities, and (6) know what to do with the goods and services once provided, to gain full benefit (IFAD 2004b). Yet a lesson learned is to separate the role of promoter from service provider, as marginalized groups are often vulnerable to a slick "sales pitch." An unclear division of responsibilities between these two has created conflicts of interest at times between profit and non-profit-oriented suppliers who engage with poor women.

In Cape Verde the community facilitators who assist the promoters are selected by the groups themselves. This was a result of a lesson learned from Peru, where promoters hired from outside the community with strong patriarchal attitudes affected women's participation negatively.

Sustainability depends on the existence of enabling environments in which policy and institutional reforms are oriented toward increasing control of decisions and resources by community groups or elected governments. Political and institutional environments often prove unsupportive to the process of CDD, in part because they lack cadres of competent facilitators. Sustained community action often rests on the abilities of external mediators to unlock and activate local social capital (Mansuri and Rao 2004).

Measures required by project management to ensure the participation and benefits to women are new to many governments, NGOs, and private sector partners and as such are often slow to be adopted. Resistance is also found where this approach is perceived as a threat to established ways of doing things and the interests of dominating groups. IFAD found that men often saw no reason to include women in decision making and to target benefits to them. Broad enabling and empowerment targeting measures are found to be easier to apply and more effective than narrow measures based on eligibility criteria; the concept of inclusion is generally more acceptable than targeting, which suggests top-down and exclusionary measures.

Financing modalities

To date, the effectiveness of demand-driven mechanisms and funds has been strongly enhanced or undermined by the specific procedures for the application for funds and review and selection of proposals. The complexity and technical difficulty of preparing proposals, time allocated for submission, distance to be traveled for submission, criteria and processes for selection of groups—all affect women's abilities to participate and benefit from CDD projects. Women with less education and free time and whose mobility is constrained require special assistance by not-for-profit groups such as NGOs or promoters to prepare proposals. Investments to build the capabilities of poor women to become leaders and to choose good representatives and hold them accountable must be supported by governments and donors as needed. The process requires full transparency and publicity in procedures, including selection, signing of agreements, and contracts.

Contributions of cash, labor, and local materials that must be provided by communities as proof of commitment and a condition to obtain community-driven funds are often unaffordable by women who have little time for labor contributions and few material resources to provide. In some cases artificial groups form to access CDF funds, undermining legitimate groups that exist for credit purposes and collective investments. Many borrower governments have not been convinced that allowing community control over investment decisions and resources is the best means of engaging communities; they have concerns about local capacities but also feel threatened by devolution of authority (World Bank 2005).

To date, CDD projects have been rarely designed with sufficient investments to provide the types of follow-up support and complementary investments that poor women require to overcome their multiple constraints and to achieve the expected level of benefits (Perrett 2004)—a point that clearly requires mitigation to realize the potential of CDD and decentralization for gender-equity goals.

Empowering measures are arguably the most important ones to increase poor women's bargaining power and their participation in public decisions, as evidenced by the case of women members of self-help groups in a project in Chattisgarh, India (IFAD 2004b). It is clear that a demand-led process and the availability of funding are not sufficient to ensure outreach to poor rural women. Specific empowerment measures are needed to enable the poorest and most marginalized groups to transform their needs into effective demands. Women in communities participating in the management of natural resources in the Southern Highlands Project in Peru demonstrated higher levels of self-esteem and more active participation in community decision making through various instruments, including gender mainstreaming and affirmative action, gender sensitization and training for both men and women, and the creation of a special fund for support of economic activities undertaken by women (IFAD 2004b). The Self-Help Learning Initiative of the Gemidiriya project in Sri Lanka illustrates how women's participation in decision making and in managing village-level financial institutions can be achieved (see Innovative Activity Profile 3).

On the supply side, the capacity of service providers to respond to the needs of poor women needs to be strengthened with services and extension methods appropriate for women, requiring a complete reversal from the established way of providing assistance as per the decisions and methods of technical staff. Projects in India and Peru demonstrate that inculcating gender sensitivity and commitment within the implementing organizations and service providers while simultaneously building women's leadership and capacity was critical to achieve women's substantial participation and accountability to them. There it was learned that existing institutional and policy environments are often critical constraints and that pro-active measures to instill a strong commitment by project management can catalyze positive results (IFAD 2004b).

GUIDELINES AND RECOMMENDATIONS FOR PRACTITIONERS

Cases of well-designed CBD/CDD projects have taken place, but most have not taken sufficient account of the limitations in the enabling environment to achieve gender-equitable impacts from these approaches. Specific improvements in the design of these projects, based on qualitative analyses of gender aspects of livelihood strategies, community organizations, and project partner institutions (as well as those of the donor agencies themselves), could go far in promoting the success of CBD/CDD approaches to address the needs of poor rural women. Guidelines and principles used in gender mainstreaming are useful references for this purpose.

Inclusion of the poorest women. To ensure that the poorest women are able to participate in and benefit from CDD project activities, project management procedures and policies must mandate the use of tools of gender-sensitive poverty and livelihood analysis to first identify them, understand their livelihood-related constraints and opportunities, and incorporate their views before determining the menu of the types of goods and services to be funded and supported to match the interests and needs of women. All CDD projects—even those that work through existing decentralized public administration—must incorporate an explicit strategy to ensure that the resources reach and benefit women and men of poor rural households. This implies an adoption of enabling, empowering, menu-based, procedural, and other targeting measures and continuous monitoring of effectiveness.

Enabling policy environments. The presence or absence of an enabling environment for CDD as an innovation makes a significant impact on its success. The design of projects should anticipate resistance to CDD and include measures targeted at the implementing agencies themselves, such as capacity building for gender mainstreaming, to build support for the CDD process at all levels. Bringing about changes in attitudes and ways of interacting with poor women builds sustainable organizational and individual accountability of public and private service providers to rural women.

As a result of the importance that local governance issues assume in the elaboration of a CDD project policy, new tools must be adopted to complement existing methodologies of project formulation, appraisal, implementation monitoring, and performance evaluation. Gender-sensitive institutional analysis is a tool that would greatly improve the understanding of the system within and around communities and would help to identify enabling and disabling agencies and actors, to properly map implementation arenas, and to streamline project organization and management arrangements.

At the community level, institutional analysis will help to (1) understand the community institutions, the rules of the game accepted by everyone, and how these can be used to devise self-targeting instruments in favor of women; (2) acquire insights on how socioeconomic and political factors affect change and community preferences and demands; and (3) monitor the reactions to project conditions of "inclusiveness" and monitor the impact of formal inclusiveness on the effective role of women in the management of the public affairs of the community.

At the level "around" the communities, institutional analysis will help to (1) understand the institutional systems and how they really work; (2) identify enabling and disabling agencies and actors that can or should work to improve the livelihood of members of the rural communities, their roles, motivations, organizational culture, and behavior; (3) establish a dialogue with both women and men; (4) negotiate enabling instruments, including solutions to the key issues of inappropriate processes and disabling

procedures, transparency, and accountability mechanisms; and (5) facilitate the role of enabling actors in the application of agreed-to enabling instruments.

Institutional analysis brings stakeholders together to examine how best they can make use of the resources and authority they will get from CDD and can inform questions of linkages and feedback loops between enablers, service providers, and client groups (Binswanger and Aiyar 2003).

The experience of CDD project implementation in West and Central Africa suggests that partnerships that join together CBOs, local government administrators, civil society organizations working for local development, and the private sector provide more effective mechanisms to unleash the development potential of the rural communities than do mechanisms that operate exclusively through the government administration (Patanali 2007).

Accountability, monitoring, and evaluation. One shortcoming of many CDD projects is that if one of the primary goals is to build grassroots capacity, appropriate monitoring tools are rarely employed to assess the evolution of this capacity, but good practical tools exist for doing this. Monitoring and evaluation (M&E) are especially critical to ensure that decentralization and CDD approaches have the intended impacts for women and gender equity. Innovation always requires more careful M&E; in this case a careful watch is needed to monitor who does or does not obtain access to funds and decision-making processes, and why. Such monitoring starts with the first process (often information dissemination about the project) and should continue to the distribution and use of benefits within a group.

CHALLENGES

Further information is needed to answer questions such as the following. What are the consequences of decentralization and CDD for poor rural women, for gender relations in households and institutions, and for agricultural productivity and food insecurity? Are poor rural women able to demand accountability, and do they play a significant role in decision making for project activity selection? Do women and their households benefit substantially from CDD projects? Under what circumstances are poor rural women harmed by CDD? Does a CDD approach hold greater promise to improve the condition of women than thematic project interventions related to issues of particular relevance to women such as microfinance, small-scale marketing assistance, and food crop development?

Is the goal of CDD pro-poor women institutional development or poverty reduction through women's increased access to infrastructure? What is the likelihood that devolution of decision making on public resources to communities will lead to greater equity? What is the likelihood that government will devolve decision making on public resources and use their authority to support women's decision making in this?

In addition, a need exists for a broad search for innovations that have aided women to benefit from decentralization and CDD projects to address the current gap in the knowledge of whether or not, as well as how, these processes have significantly impacted gender relations and women's poverty levels.

Gender, Self-Help Groups, and Farmer Organizations in the Agricultural Sector

SOCIAL CAPITAL, EMPOWERMENT, AND DECISION-MAKING AGENCY

Good governance involves effective collective organization, and without question this has proven to have value for improving the livelihood opportunities and empowerment of poor women who depend on agricultural or rural livelihoods in developing countries. Participation in group organization has clear benefits for poor women in terms of increased assets, income, and gains in control over decision-making processes that affect their lives. Poor rural women form and belong to many types of groups related to agriculture, including self-help groups, producer associations, and businesses as well as voluntary associations. Here the focus is on groups that involve agriculture-driven, joint activities initiated around an economic purpose, where this includes the production of goods or services or collective management of natural resources important for agriculture. This focus identifies several types of groups summarized in box 2.14: agricultural cooperatives, self-help groups (including microcredit and rotating savings and credit groups), user groups for natural resource management, agricultural extension and field schools, and farmer research groups. The last are a specific, agriculture-related case of groups that form in the rural sector to provide several kinds of public services, such as sanitation or schooling. Groups may be formal, in the sense of having agreed-on rules and procedures that give the group a status that enables the group to own or manage its assets legally, as in the case of formal cooperatives, or they may be informal, as is the case with self-help groups, but the legal status of groups is not a primary determinant of important gender issues. Rural women may be involved in other kinds of interest groups and political organizations with noneconomic objectives, such as advocacy, or that pursue different concerns, such as health, education, religion, or political representation, that are important to rural women but not agriculture driven. In most cases, as discussed in more detail below, organized groups in the agricultural sector are rarely formed exclusively by or for women. Important gender issues are therefore related to the inclusion of women and their membership status, and policies that enable women to participate in decision making or take leadership roles in groups.

This Thematic Note addresses key gender issues that cut across different types of group organization in the agricultural sector, following the topical outline that guides all the Thematic Notes in this *Sourcebook,* to synthesize current knowledge about the advantages and disadvantages of group organization for women. Discussion is organized under the following topics: aspects of experience in group formation related to the impacts and benefits of groups for women, key implementation problems and constraints due to gender relations, good practices and lessons learned, and principles and guidelines for designing and implementing group organization in the agricultural sector that is inclusive of women.

GROUP FUNCTIONS, ADVANTAGES, AND DISADVANTAGES

Groups in the agricultural sector have several functions affected by gender relations that, in turn, influence how much women benefit from participation in group organization. A central function of groups is to overcome market failures, cases in which collective action helps members to overcome high transaction costs, or risks that increase the vulnerability of the poor. For example, cooperatives and self-help groups facilitating savings and credit for agroenterprise development are important for overcoming market failure, which makes it difficult for women producers to diversify and engage in commercial farming. Another function of groups is to produce public goods and externalities associated with nonexcludability, as is the case with common property management of natural resources, including water, forests, and fisheries, that may be of critical importance to women's agricultural livelihoods. Groups may also function to advance

Producer associations and cooperatives are businesses owned and often managed by farmers to transform, package, distribute, and market their produce. Agricultural cooperatives encompass several functions or may specialize in marketing, input supply, or savings and credit.

Self-help groups (SHGs) are voluntary associations of not more than 10 to 20 members who are usually poor people with the aim of solving their common problems through mutual help. Typically an SHG promotes internal savings and lending among its members; this capital eventually may be deposited with a bank.

Rotating savings and credit associations (ROSCAs) are groups of about 6–12 individuals who make regular contributions to a common fund, which is then given as a lump sum to one member in each saving cycle. In this way a member lends money to other members through contributions, and members alternate between being lenders and borrowers.

Women's subgroups in village development associations (VDs) are vehicles for mobilizing local resources, especially labor, for projects such as the construction of bridges and community halls, renovation of school buildings and health centers, digging and maintenance of earthen roads, irrigation, soil conservation works, and the provision of piped water.

Women's groups in watershed management associations may be traditional groups for collective management of common property resources or may be externally catalyzed by projects for the management of natural resources. They are mainly oriented toward carrying out soil and water conservation measures, reforestation and forest conservation, training, and conflict resolution and may have specific functions like water users committees, forest protection committees, fodder development committees, or seed distribution committees that represent sectoral interests in watershed development.

Agricultural extension field schools or farmer research groups are formed to promote learning about production technologies or to contribute to the development of innovations. Women's groups formed for these purposes can help to ensure that innovation is more relevant to women producers, although they may also be marginalized into "traditional" semisubsistence production.

Source: Authors.

claims of their members to rights and resources or enforce existing rights important for agriculture: these include land-rights groups, labor unions, cooperatives, and associations that perform this function.

Gender relations affect the extent to which women enjoy important advantages obtained by membership in groups, such as economic gains from collective marketing, agroprocessing, or input supply. Group membership helps to build different kinds of internal and external social capital, solidarity, and bargaining power, as well as experience with democratic decision making and leadership. In all kinds of groups, gender relations affect the extent to which women are included as group members, participate in decision making, and exercise leadership, but it is important to keep in mind that women's socioeconomic resources and ethnic, religious, or caste identity may compound any effect of gender on its own. One of the most important effects of group membership for poor women is the development of self-esteem, solidarity, and shared identity. The potential to forge empowering social and political identities for poor women makes groups a powerful channel for women to demand and effect social change, especially when large numbers of groups federate and act together. Women's empowerment through participation in groups is especially important for attacking root causes of rural women's poverty: lack of entitlement to key economic resources, drudgery and weak bargaining power within the household, domestic violence, and sexual oppression.

Against the advantages of participation in groups for women must be considered the low probability of successful participation in groups by very poor women, especially in highly stratified and unequal societies. Very poor women seldom join or form strong, sustainable groups without external catalysts to initiate and support group formation with long-term training and facilitation. Nonetheless, it is also clear that once rural women have had the experience of belonging to a successful group, even the poorest groups can produce women leaders who are fully capable of inspiring and teaching other women to form groups. Recent studies show that building self-esteem and self-worth among poor women and their organizational skills is perceived by them as the most important result of participation in groups and may be as or more important than the economic benefits of group action.

EXPERIENCE, IMPACTS, AND BENEFITS FROM GENDER-RESPONSIVE ACTIONS

Rural women's groups and producer associations have exploded recently in developing countries. In Mali, for example, it is not uncommon for a woman farmer to belong to four, five, or even six associations. Participation in groups for mutual assistance such as communal labor or rotating credit and savings associations is a feature of traditional village life in many rural areas, but recently a dramatic expansion of women's self-help groups (SHGs) has been driven by the microfinance revolution. In 2006 microcredit SHGs numbered 2.23 million with approximately 33 million members. These groups have proved remarkably effective as a mechanism for extending microfinance services to the very poor. Women's SHGs formed for microcredit, especially in India, have expanded vigorously into other development domains, including education, water management, housing, sanitation, and disaster prevention, effecting significant changes in women's status. In general, self-help groups with microcredit as their primary purpose have not proved effective for financing agricultural production because of the difficulty they have in providing the relatively large infusions of capital required for farming at key points in the production calendar, but they have proved important for group agroenterprise development by women producers (box 2.15).

The experience of PRADAN, a large rural livelihoods development NGO reaching over 80,000 poor women in seven of the poorest states in India, illustrates the empowerment impact of women's SHGs. PRADAN (Professional Assistance for Development Action) targets women in the poorest and most socially marginalized groups with the goal of enhancing the capacity of women to exercise voice and influence within the wider community, and so it builds secondary-level federations, networks, or clusters of these groups to improve their bargaining power. Federations are developed to function as self-sustaining organizations with a variety of livelihood-focused interventions, which include microcredit for agroenterprise development, although this is not the primary objective of group formation. An impact assessment of PRADAN's SHGs shows that group members have higher levels of awareness and knowledge than nonmembers about issues that affect women's ability to control certain aspects of their lives, such as family planning and government policies. Group members had greater mobility outside the home and a higher proportion kept a portion of household income for their own use.[1]

Box 2.15 India: Example of the Broad Impact of SHGs on Poor Women's Livelihoods and Empowerment

In India the IFAD's North Eastern Region Community Resource Management Project for Upland Areas has mobilized women's organization into SHGs to achieve a wide array of benefits. Women members make weekly savings used for income-earning, health, and education needs of the village. The group acquired a rice and maize dehusking mill to save labor and effort on the part of villagers who had to travel long distances for this. Additionally, the group has revived the local market in Nonglang, which previously opened once a week. Now it opens daily, making the procurement of food and other items much easier for all in the village. SHG members value meeting every week to discuss common problems. Eradication of illiteracy has become one of the group's goals. With the encouragement of the project, the group has organized a school for young children, who previously either did not attend classes or did so only in the morning. Now each family sends at least one child to this school. Women volunteers teach here. Members know that the school needs more supplies and better resources for the students and are looking at using the group's savings to arrange for these. The most important impact of SHGs has been this mobilization of poor women to assume responsibility for their own development.

Source: Authors.

The empowerment impact of group organization may be more important for women, especially poor women, than the direct economic benefits of group membership. Although the intensive support required for financially sustainable microcredit SHGs may not be profitable for lenders in the long run, numerous studies find that participation in SHGs, notably in India, has assisted the development of women's self-confidence in working collectively to influence change in their communities. An example is the Women's Empowerment Program in Nepal, which focused on literacy and savings for 6,500 women's groups in which many participants started businesses and increased their decision-making authority in the home. In addition, SHGs have provided a platform for the development of women's leadership both at the community level and in local politics, where group members are taking an active role in electoral politics. In India SHGs have created a role for women in local politics, and a growing number of SHG members now fill elected local government positions.

Women's SHGs have formed effectively for a variety of purposes that enable them to have an impact on public service provision, although they often also include group savings as an activity. SHGs often evolve from existing women's organizations that, like the Women's Councils in Maharashtra, India, can provide an important source of leadership for group formation. SHGs involved in service provision have successfully expanded women's access to health, literacy, and agricultural extension services. Such groups provide an important forum for women to access and share information from which they are otherwise excluded, a function that deserves explicit attention in group formation. For example, the Agha Khan Rural Support Program has formed women's organizations that have had the dual purpose of income generation and providing a civic forum for social development. A different approach is that used by the International Development Bank MAG-PAES project in El Salvador, which sets up municipality-level gender committees (*comités de genero*) to explicitly address issues of gender equity. The committees funnel training and microfinance to women's groups, which have launched several of the program's more successful agroenterprise initiatives.

Watershed development strategies to address land degradation and improve agricultural productivity rely heavily on decentralization of decision making to farmer groups. The focus of watershed management on land, to which mainly men have title, means that women's groups have been marginalized, even though it is well known that women often play a key role in managing common pool resources such as communal forest and grazing. Non-land-based income generation has been higher on the agenda than land management or land rights for most women's SHGs in watershed development programs. Women's microcredit SHGs have been mobilized to meet quotas for women's participation in many watershed development schemes but seldom have direct links to natural resource management unless an explicit effort is made to link women into participatory watershed governance, such as watershed committees. When women are brought into watershed planning, very different outcomes have been observed. For example, the AKRSP (Aga Khan Rural Support Programme) in Gujarat used gender sensitization exercises that led men to conclude that women were contributing about 50 percent of the labor for watershed improvement and should receive part of the wages that were being paid to men as the land owners. The women

deposited their wages into the common fund of their women's association and used it for collective activities addressing women's priorities (Seeley, Batra, and Sarin 2000).

Several decades of experience with the formation of producer associations and agricultural cooperatives for women, supported by governments, NGOs, and national women's organizations, have had mixed results. Notable examples of success are the work of the Self-Employed Women's Association (SEWA) and Working Women's Forum in India or Femmes et Développement (FEDEV: Women's Development Project) in Mali. SEWA, a registered trade union with a membership of 800,000 women, two-thirds of whom are small farmers or landless agricultural laborers, has a strategy of empowering women by improving women's assets and employment opportunities and has created the All-India Women Farmers Association. Some benefits are clear in terms of enhancing the skills, opportunities, and prestige of women who are active leaders in these organizations. In many cases participation in producer associations or cooperatives has enabled women to break down cultural restrictions on their mobility and to expand their social and economic networks. So long as organizations forming SHGs provide long-term, high-quality, nonfinancial support (typically one or two years) for capacity building, groups have low dropout and turnover rates, reflecting their utility to poor women. But the vast majority of women farmers' associations have not been able to sustain income generation for members without outside support.

POLICY AND IMPLEMENTATION ISSUES

Similar implementation problems in forming and sustaining women's groups are found whether at the small scale of self-help groups or at larger scales of producer associations and cooperatives because of the persistent handicaps women experience from unequal gender relations. Frequently in producer cooperatives or farmer associations, women members have been oriented to compete with traditional "women's" products in weak markets that often cannot absorb expanded production of these products, or they have not been provided with the skills and technology required to compete successfully. Collective organization for production has not automatically improved women's status or control over key assets, such as land or capital, or over the income generated. Insecure access to land and land tenure remains a pressing issue for women producers, as does the need for public policy to support small-scale farming. Poor women still face the problem of adequately establishing user rights allotted to them by law. Thus, even when organized in groups and associations, women producers face political as well as economic disadvantages that force them to compete on relatively unfavorable terms.

An important obstacle to implementation, although the evidence is contradictory, tends to be the problem that cooperative organization has not led to redistribution of work between women and men in the household, increasing already heavy demands on women's time and energy. This especially affects poorer women, who find it difficult to absorb the costs of participation in collective decision making, and are less likely to join groups. In the case of PRADAN, for example, membership in self-help groups did not alter the gendered pattern of decision making about household resource allocation, which remained very similar in member and nonmember households.

Another obstacle to implementing successful group organization is the difficulty of providing incentives to group participation that promote the inclusion of resource-poor women. The advantages of cooperative organization frequently accrue primarily to better-off women who are more likely to have the formal education needed for leadership roles. However, research shows that more educated rural men and women alike tend to participate less in community-level groups, in part because they are more likely to be engaged in nonfarm, income-generating activities (these are becoming a major source of income to smallholders in developing countries). The cost of participation in groups, associations, or cooperatives can be a disincentive to those with more profitable ways of investing their time outside of groups. Even so, more educated women are more likely to fill positions of authority in SHGs and producer associations alike. This can lead to conflicts of interest between them and poorer members over the distribution of benefits.

Even when group participation is broadly inclusive of women with different levels of resources, cooperative organization is frequently overly ambitious relative to women's skill base, and corruption resulting from weak leadership or high turnover in management is common. Problems of distrust and conflict between members and management are frequently cited as reasons for the failure of women's cooperatives. The so-called middle-class effect of participation can lead to the disempowerment of the majority of poor women in a producers association when, for example, patronage resources are arrogated to a select group of women from the wealthier families in a community. Mistrust, class conflict, and limited participation may delegitimize a cooperative or association for most of the women who are nominally members.

Group formation can be seriously hampered by underlying structural disadvantages and inequities that underpin the poverty of women. The assumption that participation in groups assists women in escaping from poverty and inequity has been severely criticized for its neglect of the "dark side" of social capital, referring to the possibility that association can lead to the exclusion of women and to reproduction of existing structures of inequality. Multiple factors militate against group participation for the poorest women: for example, ill-health and their physical inability to participate, their inability to afford reciprocal relationships and maintain more than "threadbare" social networks, their lack of assets needed to make regular contributions to group fees and activities, and discriminatory norms that restrict their mobility and relegate them to lower status within groups. Although groups have clear benefits for some women, entrenched class, caste, and ethnic differences exist among women that groups cannot in and of themselves overcome.

Building coalitions and federations of SHGs and producer organizations is crucial for sustaining their socioeconomic viability. A key gender issue is the extent to which women can access and undertake leadership roles at different levels of federated producer organizations or SHGs. Participatory decision making and the management of organizations require special skills that poor women seldom have and for which they need special training. Scaling up from small groups to federations requires long-term capacity building and mentoring to develop women producers' organizational as well as technical skills at all levels. The training of professional social mobilizers and financial support for them are frequently insufficient for them to provide the type of capacity building required to build sustainable federations of women's organizations. Inadequate investment in either members' or facilitators' capacity has led to the postproject collapse of numerous federations.

GOOD PRACTICES AND LESSONS LEARNED

This section draws together some of the more effective practices derived from learning to overcome several of the main problems of implementation highlighted above (box 2.16). One of the most important lessons concerns the importance of formulating and putting into practice specific policies to alleviate gender inequalities that are widely understood to be basic constraints to the success of women's self-help groups and producer organizations in agriculture. Few programs explicitly include such policy measures, but these are needed to address the lack of child care and onerous domestic

- Use group formation strategies that are easily replicable (such as the SHG approach) and lead to scaling up and federation of groups.
- Provide long-term, high-quality capacity development and mentoring over at least one to two years from inception of groups and federations.
- Include an explicit effort to include women with different resource endowments in governance and decision making.
- Include specific policies to alleviate gendered work and power relations unfavorable to women.
- Develop group management and leadership skills as well as technical skills, for women as well as for men.
- In the early stages of group organization, consider creating relatively homogeneous subgroups of women facing similar constraints to create a safe

place where the most disadvantaged can develop new skills and empowerment.
- Assess the need for intensive social awareness and gender sensitization training for women and men to build mutual confidence, esteem, and capacity to negotiate.
- Include specific policies, such as selective targeting, to enable women to control some key inputs and resources critical to project success.
- Ensure groups have mechanisms that include women as well as men in performance evaluation of groups and their leaders, and some enforceable sanctions such as the ability to withhold membership fees.
- Promote inclusive information sharing that enhances women's understanding of their rights and opportunities.

Source: Author.

conditions that place heavy demands on women's time spent in unpaid domestic work and limit the time they have for group activities. Evidence suggests that participation in groups, especially if these generate tangible, short-term income under women's control, can improve women's bargaining capacity within the household to negotiate changes in their domestic workload and responsibilities. An important lesson is that to benefit poor women, strategies for their collective organization in agriculture need to include explicit measures to alleviate unfavorable work and power relations in the home as well as in the wider social context. It is essential for interventions based on women's participation in agriculture-driven group organization to build their confidence and self-esteem so they can both increase participation in groups *and* negotiate for important changes elsewhere in their lives.

An important lesson is that the heterogeneity of women's social class and ethnic differences needs to be factored into the formation of and support for women's groups, associations, and cooperatives. A relatively homogeneous class or ethnic composition of small groups may be needed to create a safe space for the most disadvantaged women to develop their skills. Avoiding the "middle-class effect" of participation is extremely difficult at larger scales. Gender targeting and quotas are not enough, because forming women's groups, associations, or cooperatives will not guarantee that poor women reap benefits from membership. A good practice is

to provide intensive social awareness training for women's group members. In SHGs engaged in microcredit, this type of intervention has had an important influence on the capacity of women to negotiate change in intrahousehold decision making and to transform their groups into actors of local institutional change.

Development interventions aimed at benefiting women need to include policies designed to enhance women's control over all types of development inputs and to target women for this purpose. The expansion of women's self-help groups in India into multiple areas of intervention, including health, education, domestic violence mitigation, and local politics, is strong evidence of an expressed demand among women for this type of multifaceted approach. The strategy of targeting women-only beneficiaries, validated by numerous rural women's empowerment programs, has had positive results in terms of helping poor women to overcome their lack of self-confidence and in making socioeconomic and political change, including expanding women's income generation opportunities. In this respect there is some evidence that women's organizations have outperformed men's organizations (for examples, see Liamzon 2006).

Project design needs to include a careful targeting strategy to enhance women's control over public investments. An example is the Sunamganj community-based resource management project in Bangladesh, in which 50 percent of community organizations were planned from the start to have trained women managers, and 50 percent of the land made available to the poor was allocated to women-headed households.[2] Representation for active women leaders in decision-making bodies such as watershed committees, village associations, and cooperatives that give them voice in planning processes consistently leads to different outcomes from those obtained when women are excluded.

Building capacity to represent and negotiate women's interests is a priority issue for women producers, while recognizing that there is no uniform "women's interest." Men-dominated producer organizations in developing countries that seek to create a policy voice for farmers give a degree of representation to women but seldom have an operational gender-based program. For example, Reseau des Organisations Paysannes et des Producteurs Agricoles de l'Afrique de l'ouest (ROPPA: Network of Farmers' and Agricultural Producers' Organizations of West Africa) country delegations must include at least one woman representative, and the top executive committee of 10 members must include two women, but ROPPA did not at the time of writing have specific gender initiatives. In contrast, the International Federation of Agricultural Producers has a separate committee on Women in Agriculture, established in 1992 to promote the status of women farmers, empower their participation in farmer organizations at all levels, and advocate women farmer's interests. The formation of women-managed organizations for women producers is an alternative strategy that has gained ground in some countries, notably in West Africa, where there are several regional federations of organizations representing women producers.[3]

Meeting quotas for women's representation or forming women-managed producer organizations and federations does not guarantee that the interests of the least-advantaged women will be addressed unless mechanisms for accountability exist, as the Ndulo case illustrated. It is vital, therefore, for these organizations to have the mechanisms that enable their members to evaluate leadership and monitor how different types of women benefit from the organization. Accountability requires building capacity for women to take responsibility for monitoring and evaluating activities, whether at the scale of individual SHGs, producer associations, or larger-scale federations. Participation in monitoring and evaluating performance is not sufficient, unless accompanied by performance incentives and enforceable sanctions, such as the ability of members to withhold fees.

An important lesson is that building capacity for social action within each SHG and then clustering or federating groups at larger scales can increase the capacity of women's groups to advocate for policy change, as well as to take responsibility for local development. For example, in Mysore, India, SHGs with 20,000 members have been organized so that each group includes a small task force that undertakes to represent village interests and claims with local government. In an area of tribal conflict in Tripura, India, SHGs in which women make up 80 percent of membership are active in social justice issues, campaigning against alcoholism and wrongful arrest.

Farmer organizations that operate beyond the level of SHGs that act as an interface between local communities and national and global policy-making bodies sometimes have the capacities and mandates to engage in advocacy activities at national, regional, and global levels. For example, building the capacity of farmer organizations is IFAD's goal. Through its Farmer Forum, IFAD aims to increase farmer participation in policy dialogue with their governments and within intergovernmental bodies and forums, via a bottom-up process of consultation and dialogue with small farmers and rural producers organizations that IFAD and governments convene every two years. Yet in most bodies such as this, whether international or national, as in farmer organizations in general, there is a notable absence of women's voices and leadership. To address this, IFAD organizes separate working sessions and side events with women leaders, from organizations such as the national women's organization SEWA. At the February 2008 meeting of the Farmer Forum, its members recommended that IFAD support farmer organizations to engage their women members in the management and decision-making processes of their organizations, with a minimum quota of 30 percent women farmers in all IFAD programs, events, and initiatives.

Other spaces for advocacy by women farmers exist through the UN's mechanism of major groups of civil society for sustainable development, wherein women have their own major group that facilitates their participation in the UN Commission for Sustainable Development and the various conventions related to agriculture and environment.

GUIDELINES AND RECOMMENDATIONS FOR PRACTITIONERS

Experience shows that a combination of empowering and capacity development measures works best for realizing the development potential of women's groups, associations, or cooperatives. This involves combining several measures so that they are flexible: for example, quotas to ensure women are in key leadership positions and participate as members, targeting specific resources and opportunities at the poorest women, sharing information to make sure women know about rights and opportunities, and building beneficiary capacity. Long-term support is needed for processes that foster women's involvement in and leadership of democratic decision making. Finally, women members need to have the means and the authority to undertake monitoring of an organization's performance, using well-defined, locally appropriate indicators of change in women's welfare in domestic as well as other domains.

A key principle for forming and supporting sustainable women's SHGs and producer associations is to invest from the beginning in skill formation, especially among the least advantaged. Building the skill base for women's empowerment and leadership development, especially for the poorest women, requires work in small groups in which self-confidence and self-esteem can develop more easily. However, up-scaling and clustering into associations and federations is crucial for gaining the bargaining power and influence needed for women producers to effect change. Planning the long-run up-scaling strategy and its expected results from an early stage in group formation is one key to success. Self-replication has occurred on a large scale among women's self-help savings and microcredit groups in South Asia, for example, which highlights the importance for poor women in particular of using group formation strategies that are easily replicable (see box 2.16).

Advocacy

Farmer organizations that operate beyond the level of SHGs acting as an interface between local communities and national and global policy-making bodies have the capacities and mandates to engage in advocacy activities at national, regional, and global levels. Building the capacity of farmer organizations is a focus of the IFAD: for example, to increase their participation in policy dialogue with their governments and within intergovernmental bodies and forums, particularly through its Farmers' Forum, which is a bottom-up process of consultation and dialogue between small farmers and rural producers' organizations, the IFAD, and government that convenes every two years. Yet within these meetings, and within farmer organizations in general, a notable absence of women's voices and leadership is present. To address this, the IFAD organizes separate working sessions and side events with women leaders, including those of SEWA. At the February 2008 meeting of the forum, its members recommended that the IFAD support farmer organizations to engage their women members in the management and decision-making processes of their organizations, with a minimum quota of 30 percent women farmers in all IFAD programs, events, and initiatives.

Other spaces for advocacy by women farmers exist through the UN's mechanism of Major Groups of civil society for sustainable development, wherein women have their own Major Group that facilitates their participation in the UN Commission for Sustainable Development and the various conventions related to agriculture and environment.

Bangladesh, Nepal, and Pakistan: Gender and Governance Issues in Local Government

Decentralization is an important governance reform that holds promise for making public service provision more responsive to the rural population by bringing government closer to the people. Yet it is a challenge to involve women in local governments and to ensure that the services they require to improve their agricultural livelihoods are met. In Bangladesh, Nepal, and Pakistan, legislative reforms of local government bodies have led to quotas for women. Approximately 12,000 women representatives participate in local governments in Bangladesh and more than 36,000 in Pakistan. In Nepal more than 39,000 women were elected in 1997. Although these quotas created space for the participation of rural women in local governments, elected women have faced a range of challenges, especially because many come from poor households and did not enjoy the benefit of schooling. Low levels of literacy, time constraints, lack of confidence, and limited access to relevant social networks restrict the effectiveness of women as local politicians. In view of traditional patriarchical power structures, men members of local councils often restrict women's participation, for example, by not informing elected women about council meetings and by not including them in important committees. Moreover, officials of line departments often do not give sufficient recognition to the women members of local councils. Among various projects created to address these problems, the "Gender and Governance Issues in Local Government" project (Regional Technical Assistance Project—RETA 6008)— jointly funded by the Asian Development Bank, Japan Special Fund, and Canadian International Development Agency) has developed an innovative approach to address the multiple problems faced by women representatives in local governments.

PROJECT OBJECTIVES AND DESCRIPTION

The objective of this project was to promote gender and good governance by assisting women representatives of local governments to carry out their roles more confidently and to serve their constituents, who are mainly poor women, more effectively. The project included the following components:

- Creating an interface among women representatives, poor communities, and government officials that established the credibility and effectiveness of elected women and involved officers from line agencies in transparent and accountable interaction with community members
- Providing social mobilization of key stakeholders, particularly the poor, elected women representatives and women leaders, and officers of line agencies
- Developing the capacity of elected women and men representatives of local government bodies, and of women and men community leaders.

Past experience with poverty reduction and local development projects suggests that when only one stakeholder in a complex social environment is provided with training,

---

What's innovative? The project combines capacity development, formalizing interactions and creating local forums for stakeholders. The forums provided women representatives with visibility and status and helped them to establish links with government line agencies, NGOs, and private sector representatives. The forums also provided support networks and opportunities to discuss experiences, problems, and issues and to plan actions to increase the accountability of both government officers and women members to their poor and other constituents.

---

assets, or resources, the results are often not effective. For example, line officers are often trained to deliver services more effectively, but reaching their target populations is hampered because locally elected officials responsible for providing accurate recipient lists are not involved. Moreover, the groups targeted for assistance often are unaware of resources designated for them, miss out on benefits to which they are entitled, and cannot act as pressure groups to hold government officials and locally elected members accountable.

The project addressed these problems by combining capacity development with the creation of an interface for stakeholders and with social mobilization. Creating an interface implied formalizing interactions among key stakeholders involved in delivering services in rural communities. The project brought together stakeholders in local forums on a monthly basis that provided women representatives with visibility and status and helped them to establish links with government line agencies, NGOs, and private sector representatives in all three countries. The forums also provided support networks and opportunities to discuss experiences, problems, and issues and to plan actions to increase the accountability of both government officers and women members to their poor and other constituents.

The forums made local people aware of various programs like development schemes or the *zakat* (charity funds) and community development projects in Pakistan and the poverty and social protection programs provided by *union parishads* (local government bodies). Local people also learned about the agriculture and rural development programs offered by the line agencies and about the microcredit programs provided by NGOs. In Nepal the forums demanded and received funds for development projects from village development committees (VDCs) and other agencies.

Capacity-building training was provided by local NGOs in each country to enhance the knowledge and skills of local women representatives and women community leaders so that they could be more effective in their roles in local government and forums. The goal was to provide women with basic knowledge about local government (their roles, budgets, meetings, record keeping, agendas, development projects, monitoring committees; council project funds); about how to run meetings, mediate disputes, and negotiate for development programs and local resource mobilization; and about gender issues.

It was recognized, however, that without the support of their men counterparts, women representatives would still not be able to realize their potential. Therefore, each country created capacity-building programs for women and

men, and in all cases training in gender sensitivity was also provided to men representatives, and in some cases to other men stakeholders, as well.

BENEFITS AND IMPACTS

The combined effects of project activities did much to improve the confidence and ability of the elected women in Bangladesh and Pakistan and former representatives of the VDCs and community leaders in Nepal to represent the interests of all their constituents. Creating visible networks between women representatives and the officials of line agencies, including agricultural departments, proved to be a key element in improving the effectiveness of women representatives. Moreover, gender sensitivity training of men representatives of local bodies in the project area increased their awareness of the role and potential of elected women, which in turn led to better collaboration.

The women representatives made significant contributions to the well-being of the poor in their constituencies. Through the cooperation with government officers and NGOs in Bangladesh, women's forums made it possible for women representatives to provide poor women and young people with access to extension programs in the fields of agriculture, livestock, and fishery. The forums also increased the access of poor women and children to social protection programs and to other income-generating activities. Women local government members were also involved in mediating disputes and in mediating cases of woman and child repression, divorces, and theft.

In Nepal the forums were able to mobilize funds from VDC budgets for projects in the fields of agriculture, forest, and environmental management. Active links were made with government line agencies, NGOs, and community-based organizations engaged in savings and credit cooperatives, health, education, and hygiene. Women's forums promoted citizenship certificates and the registration of births, deaths, and marriages. The women's forums also mediated gender and social disputes related to domestic violence against women, polygamy, and witchcraft and were active in campaigns against alcoholism, drugs, and child trafficking.

In Pakistan forums in two districts of North West Frontier Province have established links with government departments, NGOs, and savings and credit programs and have implemented a range of development schemes. Women were also provided with income-generating opportunities, and some obtained jobs through government, private, or NGO sources. As in the other two countries, women were also involved in mediating disputes, including cases of land disputes, fights between neighbors, child custody, provision of education for young girls, and waiving school fees for poor students.

LESSONS LEARNED AND ISSUES FOR WIDER APPLICABILITY

Quotas create space for the political participation of women in local governments, but additional measures are needed to increase the effectiveness of women representatives. The experience in South Asia shows that low levels of women literacy, patriarchical power structures, and blocking access of women from poor households to social networks limit their effectiveness as local politicians. Project interventions are more likely to be successful if they address these multiple obstacles in an integrated way.

Training women representatives is important, but not sufficient to increase their effectiveness. Elected women clearly benefit from improved knowledge about local government procedures, such as meetings, record keeping, negotiating for development programs, local resource mobilization, budget management, monitoring, and dispute resolution. However, the training of women representatives needs to be combined with strategies to address other challenges they face beyond knowledge and skill gaps.

Increasing the awareness of men stakeholders in local government about gender issues is crucial. The project showed that efforts to promote gender equity in local governments should not be limited to interventions that target women representatives. It is equally important to increase the awareness of men stakeholders about the role that women can play in local government and about the obstacles that they face. Hence, gender sensitivity training needs to be targeted to both men and women representatives, community leaders, and other stakeholders, such as line department officials.

Creating visible interfaces between women representatives and service providers from line agencies and NGOs is a promising approach to improve service delivery in rural areas. The project showed that regularly held forums can create an important interface between elected women and service providers and address a number of key constraints that women representatives face, especially if they come from poor backgrounds: lack of recognition, lack of access to social networks, and lack of contacts with stakeholders outside their villages, such as NGOs and the public administration.

Social mobilization is needed to increase the awareness of women about projects and programs that support agricultural livelihoods. Because the forums promoted by the project involved not only elected representatives, but also the constituents, they provided an important avenue for social mobilization. They increased the awareness of the rural poor, including rural women, about the availability of development programs that support agricultural livelihoods, thus facilitating their access to such programs. Moreover, the forums provided an avenue to create transparency and improve accountability.

NGOs can play an important role in strengthening the confidence and ability of locally elected women to operate in predominantly men-oriented environments. In all three countries the project showed that NGOs can be important partners in improving the effectiveness of women representatives in local governments and their commitment to gender equity.

Côte d'Ivoire: Gender in Agricultural Services Reforms

PROJECT OBJECTIVES AND DESCRIPTION

At the beginning of 1991, the government of Côte d'Ivoire requested World Bank support to reform the institutions of the agricultural sector. The first five-year phase of the national project was focused on rationalizing and strengthening all the agricultural extension services and adaptive research. Plans were to have an Adaptable Lending Program for 11 years. One of the three main project components of the Projet National d'Appui aux Services Agricoles (PNASA: National Agricultural Services Project) was designed to help, create, and support the initial operation of the new National Agricultural Services Agency. The strategy aimed at closing the three big public administrations for agricultural services and to merge the selected best staff into one national institution. This new institution would be semiprivate and have a decentralized structure: the Agence Nationale d'Appui au Développement Rural (ANADER: National Agency for Rural Development). Being a semiprivate institution meant having no civil servant staff and one board, including an equal number of representatives from (1) the public administration, (2) the private sector, and (3) the producers organizations. The

producers organizations (POs) were becoming a key institutional element to achieving the project's goals. ANADER was built as an autonomous institution: the board led ANADER and appointed the general and central directors. The general directorate had full power to manage the budget, human resources, and strategy only under the control of the board. The PO's representatives on the board were freely elected by the POs for each main agricultural production chain area (for example, food crops, livestock, coffee, cocoa, cotton, and pigs). In each specific agricultural production organization, ANADER support was improving the participation of women to guarantee that PO representatives were efficiently defending women producers' interests. ANADER was implementing (1) agricultural advice (extension), (2) adaptive research, (3) PO development support, and (4) training and information.

GENDER APPROACH

A pilot Women in Development (WID) stand-alone project was closed because of a number of difficulties in implementing activities isolating the support of women from the global development strategy. The knowledge of the women's role in the agricultural national production was just emerging with the quick transition from a self-agriculture consumption of food crops to a need to feed an increasing urban population. To avoid similar problems during WID, the national staff supported by Bank staff decided to implement a national gender-mainstreaming approach. Three main steps were undertaken.

1. *Speaking about gender issues:* At the beginning of PNASA I, the gender-mainstreaming strategy was announced to all staff: support to women producers' development was becoming a mandatory goal for ANADER staff. The different workshops for managers and field staff demonstrated that they were permanently arguing that women

---

What's innovative? The creation of the Gender National Services was instrumental to the gender- mainstreaming activity of Côte d'Ivoire. The Service led to fully one-quarter of the ministry's programs having an explicit gender focus. Selecting a highly qualified and strongly committed head of this Service was crucial to the effectiveness of this mainstreaming effort. Staff training, sound impact assessment and research, and effective monitoring and evaluation were the cornerstones of this effort.

producers were already fully integrated into their strategies. However, when monitoring and evaluation started to be more precise, asking for proof of field results, it became evident that the majority of the staff were working only with men producers. The gender approach adopted earlier was used only to make politically correct speeches for headquarters or international visits without specific instruments and obviously without field results.

2. *The creation of the national service for gender policy implementation:* The ANADER general directorate supported by Bank staff decided to create a National Gender Service. A woman staff member was selected with a university diploma, wide experience, and strong qualifications. She was very committed. However, she was quickly disappointed. The majority of the staff, including those at managerial levels, thought that gender issues and the related work were the responsibility of the National Gender Service and not their own. They continued to maintain that the gender issue was not a problem: they claimed that they knew what they had to do in the field. The chief of the National Gender Service sponsored a number of quantitative studies and organized two large regional workshops to demonstrate to all staff the gap between what they were reporting about gender issues and the reality in the field. The necessity for change became evident to everyone.

3. *The generalization of gender policy making, implementation, monitoring, and evaluation led by the Gender National Service and the general directorate:* Under the leadership of the general directorate, the National Gender Service began a general national training program, which aimed to provide all staff with tools for analyzing gender issues and tools to design and implement gender-sensitive projects. Support from the general directorate was high, and an annual budget was provided. Gender issues became a part of the daily agenda of all ANADER staff.

INNOVATIVE FEATURES

Several innovations of this project are worth mentioning: national strategy change, policy implementation, and capacity strengthening.

Policy making

Mainstreaming gender in the national and subnational strategy and policy. The past policies and strategies were aimed at supporting small associations and groups of women

farmers. With the creation of ANADER, the inclusion of women producers' empowerment into the national agricultural services strategy was made possible as the explicit objective in the plan. This objective states that 25 percent of technical packages and advisory services respond to the needs of women. Evaluation of existing practice indicated that the actual percentage of women being reached by these services was far lower than 25 percent of the total number of producers. Supervision missions demonstrated that field advisors were mainly using top-down advice and were not responding to the women producers' needs and requests. These findings legitimized the urgent need to look more closely at gender equality.

Policy implementation/public administration

The results of the baseline study were very clear: women staff in the agricultural services delivery were only 1 percent. ANADER launched an experiment in recruiting five young women staff just after the end of their economic study to become PO advisers in the field. Women staff demonstrated that they could perform the job without problems. However, the availability of suitable trained women staff was limited, and thus the ANADER strategy has been limited in increasing the number of women staff. Gender policy was limited by the low number of girls entering into agricultural education and training at the secondary and university levels.

Capacity strengthening

Studies and pilot experiments provided reliable data for advocacy and policy change. These data were facilitating the task of the chief of the National Gender Service and other staff in building instruments for policy implementation in the field. New instruments and new training built solid competencies for staff in analyzing agricultural issues sensitive to specific gender issues. The positive changes are very evident at the regional and national levels. Credible data and sound studies facilitated strategic discussions, which transformed staff's approaches and knowledge about the gender issues in the agricultural sector.

BENEFITS AND IMPACTS

The objective to have 25 percent of packages advice respond to the needs of women was almost achieved in 2001, with 21 percent according to an independent field study at the time (World Bank 2003). Sixty-one focal points were implemented in the different regions. In 2003, 720 groups of producers have been supported, including at least 26 percent of women producers. The majority of the groups were focused on food crop production and trading. They were receiving support from the new ANADER PO advisers. At least 100 women group leaders have emerged and are playing an increasing role in the POs and consequently positively influencing the place of the women producers in the ANADER board orientations. The proportion of women receiving agricultural advice has increased from 8 percent at the start of the project to 30 percent in 2003. At the request of women, new technologies were introduced and adopted to reduce women's time burden: for example, pedal pumps, oil presses, and solar dryers. The Service Gender and Development was fully implemented with a budget, credibility, and support from all members of the general directorate. Women staff in ANADER increased from 1 to 14 percent. Beneficiaries' evaluation demonstrated high women's satisfaction with the project. The project concluded with a better integration of women's needs into the agricultural services policy and investment.

LESSONS LEARNED AND ISSUES FOR WIDER APPLICABILITY

Functional national lead unit for gender mainstreaming. Gender approach needs a high national commitment. Although having a gender component at the start of the project or program is important, more crucial are the implementation, evaluation, and impact assessment. Training and support of the national staff are necessary (1) to build gender monitoring and evaluation of their current activities, (2) to quantify the gender-related gaps in access to resources and opportunities, (3) to build a consensus for the necessity to change, and (4) to build a new national strategy for gender equality and effective instruments and tools to implement it.

Strategic choice of the chief of the gender implementation strategy. A highly competent woman or gender-sensitive man at the director level is needed. He or she needs to have great field knowledge of the agricultural women producers and needs to have achieved a high university level and/or a recognized technical credibility in front of the men direc-

tors. He or she needs to have exceptional competencies in mobilizing other partners. The gender unit needs to have a specific budget to facilitate contact missions, training, and other activities.

Support sharing of studies and evaluation results. The most important constraint in implementing gender strategies is changing staff perception at all levels. Staff often believe that they know the problems of women and that they are responding to these needs. Sound and credible research and impact assessments are needed to help staff realize the intensity of gender issues in the country. Workshops and conferences at local, regional, and national levels using the results of those studies can facilitate the change of perception by staff and policy makers and should be included as a regular activity in the project cost.

Incentives and rewards for staff. Implementation of a win-win strategy in human resources management is important. The staff need to change, but they are the ones who decide whether to change or not. If they expect some benefits from change, the gender strategy will be implemented easily. Gender issues need to be part of the daily agenda of all staff and need to be evaluated as an essential part of their job, not as a supplemental activity. Human resources management needs to be gender sensitive.

Intensified agricultural education and training for girls. The low rate of girls' enrollment in the agricultural schools at the secondary level or in the universities is conditioning the opportunity of agricultural services to appoint women staff into the public or private agricultural sector institutions. According to the importance of the sector, affirmative actions need to be implemented in numerous countries to avoid this constraint.

Strengthened the producer organizations. Agricultural field advisers are all working with groups of farmers. The efficiency of the adviser generally depends on the organization, cohesion, and sustainability of the group. For agricultural development, technical advice is important but not sufficient. Technical advice needs to be implemented with an enabling environment and equal playing field for farmers: access to land, input, credit, and power to negotiate. Particularly for women farmers, membership in a strong and well-established group is crucial to gain access to necessary productive resources.

Sri Lanka: Gemidiriya Community Development and Livelihood Improvement Project

PROJECT OBJECTIVES AND DESCRIPTION

The Gemidiriya project aims to enable the rural poor to improve their livelihood and quality of life. In Sinhalese *gemidiriya* means "village strength." As part of a longer-term 12-year program, this 4-year project is implemented in about 1,000 village communities (510 Grama Niladhari Divisions) in five districts (Badulla, Galle, Hambantota, Matara, and Moneragala) of Uva and Southern provinces in Sri Lanka. This covers approximately 150,000 households and is expected to directly benefit approximately 700,000 people (about 20 percent of the population of the two provinces).

Uva Province continues to be one of the most economically backward regions in the country because of problems of accessibility, connectivity, poor infrastructure, and poor quality of economic services. Production of primary commodities, mainly seasonal crops and livestock, is the main source of economic sustenance. Access to health and education and other basic services is less than satisfactory. Although the Southern Province shows a remarkable disparity between its districts (Galle, Hambantota, and Matara), it has a significantly high average poverty incidence along with high adult illiteracy and lack of access to electricity, safe water, and safe sanitation. The social assessment indicates that women in different villages contribute

between 35 and 60 percent of household income, whereas, on average, they contribute 36 percent of agricultural labor and 79 percent of domestic labor. In general, women are not willing to take loans because of the risk. Women's participation in community-based organizations is high, but their voice is typically not fully heard and their participation in decision making is relatively low. Data also indicate that although women heads of household have lower education than man household heads, their income and consumption capacity are at least as good.

The project demonstrates an innovative approach in employment generation and rural poverty through five components: (1) strengthening village organizations (VOs) and funding priority subprojects; (2) building the capacity of local and national agencies and support organizations to respond to community demands; (3) creating an innovative seed fund to pilot innovative ideas that need experimentation, learning, and incubation; (4) facilitating overall coordination, implementation, and management of the project; and (5) creating a pilot Village Self-Help Learning Initiative (VSHLI).

GENDER APPROACH

In recognizing that women's empowerment and their participation in development opportunities will benefit not only women but also the entire community of the current and future generations, the project aims to mainstream gender in all project-related activities. Gender equity is a cross-cutting aspect of the project, and measures to establish and sustain gender equity have been set in the entire project design and implementation arrangements. In addition, the project sets gender empowerment and participation as a trigger for the next phase. The trigger states that women should participate in decision making by holding 30 percent of management positions either as members of the VO Board of Directors or as members of VO subcommittees in the first two years of Phase 1.

> **What's innovative?** Gender equity is a cross-cutting aspect of the Gemidiriya project. Measures to establish and sustain gender equity have been integrated in the design and implementation arrangements, such as in the leadership of community finance organizations. In addition, the project sets gender empowerment and participation targets as a trigger for the next phase.

The overall gender goals of the project are threefold: (1) social balancing (power balancing) through awareness and sensitization, (2) economic empowerment of women through their livelihood improvements, and (3) promotion of village-level initiatives toward social issues.

The project's Gender Strategy and Action Plan consists of three components, addressing three objectives:

- Gender mainstreaming and awareness building
- Ensuring women's equitable participation and benefit sharing
- Provisioning of special assistance to the most vulnerable women.

Because a risk exists that women may not be permitted to participate in key decisions and in operation and maintenance management, project rules of inclusion dictate their participation. For example, a specific results indicator has been created for the village development component that at least 50 percent of the decision-making positions should be women and youth at the village level (that is, chairperson or treasurer of various subcommittees). In addition, at least 50 percent of the project benefits should go to women. This would be monitored closely and accompanied by gender-specific training and capacity building.

BENEFITS AND IMPACTS

The midterm report indicates that as part of the VSHLI pilot program villages, 60 percent of the decision-making positions on the board of directors were women at the end of 2006—exceeding the goal of 30 percent set during the project appraisal. Further, women have broad representation and participate in many decision-making positions in the various VO bodies, as shown in tables 2.4 and 2.5.

In the community-managed microcredit program, most of the necessary ingredients have been included to achieve the success of a credit project of this nature for the poor, including establishing village savings and credit committees through social mobilization, group formation, group decision making, training for skills development to receive credit, establishment of a credit insurance fund, and registration of village societies as companies. Finally, the committees have obtained majority women's participation, and women have been empowered to manage these financial institutions—an area previously dominated by rich men.

LESSONS LEARNED AND ISSUES FOR WIDER APPLICABILITY

Through in-built project rules and targets, participation of women and youth in decision-making positions was

Table 2.4 Representation of Women, Youth, and the Poorest in Decision-Making Positions of Village Organizations
percent

Village organization officials	Women	Youth	Poorest
Board of Directors	56	40	11
Finance Committee	60	42	8
Procurement Committee	51	39	10
Social Audit Committee	53	31	8
Subproject Committees	48	40	9
Village Savings and Credit Committees	75	36	5

Source: Project Midterm Review, September 2007.

Table 2.5 Participation in Village Organization Activities by Selected Groups

Category	Attendance at meetings	Participation in planning activities	Participation in decision-making activities	Participation in monitoring	Participation in implementation
Women	1.60	1.90	2.00	2.11	2.13
Youth	2.75	2.67	2.68	2.79	2.82
Poorest	1.85	2.38	2.50	2.58	2.38

Source: Project Midterm Review, September 2007.
Note: Reported value is the mean score. The standard errors of the mean are consistently below 0.125. The five-point scale used: Very high—1, high—2, satisfactory—3, low—4, and very low—5. Sample size = 90 VOs. The lower the score, the better the participation.

encouraged from the start and reached expected levels. Core participation of women and youth has injected an important level of commitment and energy to community activities. This is also a very important factor for sustainability. An additional outcome is that the status of women in the project communities has increased.

The earlier pilot villages under the VSHLI have demonstrated that a high degree of women and youth participation in project activities also had high positive benefits to outcomes and to accountability (for example, through active and effective Social Audit Committees).

Additional benefits of the community-managed credit program that were not considered initially include the fact that group members—mostly women—have their capacity and employability increased through accounting and bookkeeping knowledge, and committee members are trained in how to prepare simple business plans. On the other hand, to overcome a bookkeeping turnover problem, a lesson was learned by the project to also target and train as bookkeepers unemployed, senior women members who are unlikely to leave the village.

NOTES

Overview

This Overview was written by Regina Birner and Leah Horowitz (IFPRI) and reviewed by Chitra Deshpande, Nata Duvvury, and Catherine Ragasa (Consultants); Neela Gangadharan (FAO); Maria Hartl (IFAD); and Rekha Mehra and Eija Pehu (World Bank).

1. United Nations Development Programme (1997), *Governance for Sustainable Human Development–A UNDP Policy Document,* http://mirror.undp.org/magnet/policy.

2. See Transparency International India (New Delhi), "India Corruption Study 2005," www.tiindia.in.

Thematic Note 1

This Thematic Note was prepared by Catherine Ragasa (Consultant), with inputs from Regina Birner and Leah Horowitz (IFPRI), and reviewed by Nata Duvvury (Consultant); Maria Hartl (IFAD); and Jock Anderson and Rekha Mehra (World Bank).

1. In 2005, 49 countries have prepared national PRSPs, and these PRSPs are currently guiding assistance strategies of donor agencies, including the Asian Development Bank, DFID, International Monetary Fund, government of Japan, and the World Bank, among others (World Bank and IMF 2005).

2. This is based on the review done by Hild Rygnestad. Seven reviewed strategy documents are for Angola, Argentina,

Armenia, Cambodia, Lao PDR, Mozambique, and Vietnam. Initial selection was based on whether "Rural/Agriculture Strategy" is in the report title. This review excludes reports that deal only with specific sectors such as livestock, water, cotton—rather than agriculture or the rural sector as a whole.

3. In contrast to the other budget work that focuses on the distributional impact of budgets, such as pro-poor budgeting, gender-responsive budgeting does not treat households as a single unit but highlights that the access to and control over resources and bargaining power of household members differ. It is carried out by different actors in different countries. Some of the so-called Gender Responsive Budgeting Initiatives (GRBIs) were initiated by the Ministry of Women or Ministry of Finance, some by parliamentarians, and some by NGOs.

4. According to a comparative analysis by UNIFEM (2007) of women in local government in 13 countries in East Asia and the Pacific.

5. The available evidence, based on a cross-sectional comparison, is difficult to interpret because women who are better represented in a particular country or locality may reflect the political preferences of the group that elects them. The correlation between policy outcomes and women's participation thus may not imply a causal effect from women's participation (Chattopadhyay and Duflo 2004).

6. G. Bantebya-Kyomuhendo, "The Role of National Mechanisms in Promoting Gender Equality and the Empowerment of Women: Uganda Experience," background paper for the Expert Group Meeting "The Role of National Mechanisms in Promoting Gender Equality and the Empowerment of Women," Rome, November 29–December 2, 2004, www.un.org/womenwatch/daw/egm/nationalm2004.

7. See also http://siteresources.worldbank.org/INTGENDER/Resources/BeyondVietnam.pdf.

8. See the report at www.doingbusiness.org/documents/Women_in_Africa.pdf.

9. Not only is there gender inequality under customary law, but, until recently, married women were legal minors under civil law. The reality was that women could not enter into contracts, get a loan, serve on a board, or engage in other economic activities without permission of their husbands.

10. Social Watch, "Gender Equity Index 2007," www.socialwatch.org/en/avancesyRetrocesos/IEG/tablas/SWGEI.htm.

Thematic Note 2

This Thematic Note was written by Catherine Ragasa (Consultant), with inputs from Fatiha Bou-Salah (FAO) and Rosemary Vargas-Lundius (IFAD), and reviewed by Nata Duvvury (Consultant); Maria Hartl (IFAD); Regina Birner (IFPRI); and Rekha Mehra and Eija Pehu (World Bank).

1. Gender mainstreaming is defined "as the process of assessing the implications for women and men of any planned action, including legislation, policies, or programmes, in all areas and at all levels. It is a strategy of making women's as well as men's concerns and experiences an integral dimension of the design, implementation, monitoring and evaluation of policies and programmes in all political, economic and societal spheres so that women and men benefit equally and inequality is not perpetuated. The ultimate goal is to achieve gender equality." See United Nations Division for the Advancement of Women (UNDAW), *The Role of National Mechanisms in Promoting Gender Equality and the Empowerment of Women,* Final Report of the Expert Group Meeting, Rome, Italy, November 29–December 2, 2004, www.un.org/womenwatch/daw/egm/nationalm2004.

2. The term "national machinery for the advancement of women" referred to the mechanisms established by government to promote and support the achievement of gender equality, including through implementation of the commitments made in global processes, such as the four world conferences on women. See the UNDAW report cited ibid.

3. See note 1 above.

4. Ibid.

5. The selection of countries was based on the available information that the authors gathered from existing literature and interviews of experts from FAO, IFAD, and the World Bank.

6. This section draws mainly on the papers presented during the UNDAW Expert Group Meeting; see note 1 above and background papers for more details.

7. See note 6 in Thematic Note 1.

Thematic Note 3

This Thematic Note was prepared by Jeannette Gurung (WOCAN), with inputs from Robin Mearns (World Bank) and Hild Rygnestad (Consultant), and reviewed by Catherine Ragasa (Consultant); Alice Carloni, Maria Hartl, and Annina Lubbock (IFAD); Regina Birner (IFPRI); and Eija Pehu (World Bank).

1. A. M. Goetz and R. Jenkins, "Re-thinking Accountability. Briefing on the Gender-Poverty-Governance Nexus: Key Issues and Current Debates," paper prepared for Development Cooperation Ireland by C. Server, www.bridge.ids.ac.uk/reports_gend_gov.htm.

Thematic Note 4

This Thematic Note was prepared by Jacqueline Ashby (International Potato Centre [CIP]), with inputs from Jeannette Gurung (WOCAN), and reviewed by Alice Carloni and Catherine Ragasa (Consultants); Maria Hartl and Annina Lubbock (IFAD); Regina Birner (IFPRI); and Eija Pehu (World Bank).

1. SHG membership also generated clear benefits for members' household livelihoods. An impact study conducted in 2005 found that group members experienced fewer months of food shortage than nonmembers, had better sources of drinking water, owned more consumption assets such as radios and bicycles, had 57 percent of children between 5 and 16 attending school compared to 18 percent among nonmembers, had a better harvest each year and higher fertilizer use, and had lower reliance on moneylenders (Kabeer and Noponen 2005).

2. See IFAD, "Rural Poverty in Bangladesh," www.ifad.org/operations/projects/regions/PI/factsheets/bd.pdf.

3. Examples from West Africa are Reseau des Femmes Sahéliennes, a regional network of Sahelian women that seeks to develop the capacity of women's groups, the Fédération Nationale des Groupements Féminines, which includes about 1 million women and aims to improve credit and market access for women, and the Directoire de Femmes en Elevage, with 15,000 members, which works on improving livestock production and marketing.

Innovative Activity Profile 1

This Innovative Activity Profile was written by Monawar Sultana (ADB) and reviewed by Regina Birner (IFPRI) and Eija Pehu (World Bank).

Innovative Activity Profile 2

This Innovative Activity Profile was written by Christian Fauliau (Consultant) and reviewed by Catherine Ragasa (Consultant) and Regina Birner (IFPRI). This Profile was drawn heavily from the author's field experiences and knowledge of the project, with consultations on World Bank (1998) and World Bank (2003).

Innovative Activity Profile 3

This Innovative Activity Profile was written by Hild Rygnestad (World Bank) and reviewed by Catherine Ragasa (Consultant); Maria Hartl (IFAD) and Natasha Hayward (World Bank). This Profile was drawn from project-specific World Bank documents: "Project Appraisal Document" March 2004, the "Midterm Review Report," September 2007, and the "Progress Report," Fourth Quarter 2007.

REFERENCES

Overview

Ackerman, John. 2004. "Co-Governance for Accountability: Beyond 'Exit' and 'Voice.'" *World Development* 32: 447–63.

Alhassan-Alolo, Namawu. 2007. "Gender and Corruption: Testing the New Consensus." *Public Administration and Development* 27: 227–37.

Aw, Djibril, and Geert Diemer. 2005. *Making a Large Irrigation Scheme Work. A Case Study of Mali.* Washington, DC: World Bank.

Bardhan, Pranab, and Dilip Mookherjee. 2000. "Relative Capture of Government at Local and National Levels." *American Economic Review* 90: 135–39.

BBC News. 2005. "Monsanto Fined $1.5m for Bribery." BBC News, January 7.

Beall, Jo. 2005. "Decentralizing Government and Centralizing Gender in Southern Africa: Lessons from the South African Experience." Report No. 8, United National Research Institute for Social Development, Geneva.

Birner, Regina, and Heidi Wittmer. 2006. "Better Public Sector Governance through Partnership with the Private Sector and Civil Society: The Case of Guatemala's Forest Administration." *International Review of Administrative Sciences* 72: 459–72.

Chattopadhyay, Raghabendra, and Esther Duflo. 2004. "Women as Policymakers: Evidence from Randomized Policy Experiment in India." *Econometrica* 72 (5): 1409–43.

Dollar, David, Raymond Fisman, and Roberta Gatti. 2001. "Are Women Really the Fairer Sex? Corruption and Women in Government." *Journal of Economic Behavior and Organization* 46: 423–29.

Geisler, Gisela. 1995. "Troubled Sisterhood: Women and Politics in Southern Africa: Case Studies from Zambia, Zimbabwe, and Botswana." *African Affairs* 94: 545–78.

Goetz, Anne Marie. 2001. *Women Development Workers: Implementing Rural Credit Programmes in Bangladesh.* Dhaka: University Press.

———. 2007. "Political Cleaners: Women as the New Anti-Corruption Force?" *Development and Change* 38: 87–105.

Goetz, Anne Marie, and Rob Jenkins. 2002. "Accountability to Women in Development Spending—Experiments in Service-Delivery Audits at the Local Level." Draft, Institute of Development Studies, Brighton and Birkbeck College, London, U.K.

———. 2005. *Reinventing Accountability: Making Democracy Work for Human Development.* Baskingstoke, U.K.: Palgrave Macmillan.

Grindle, Merilee S. 1997. *Getting Good Government: Capacity Building in the Public Sectors of Developing Countries.* Cambridge, MA: Harvard University Press.

Jayal, Niraja Gopal. 2006. "Engendering Local Democracy: the Impact of Quotas for Women in India's Panchayats." *Democratization* 13: 15–35.

Jeffrey, Craig. 2002. "Caste, Class, and Clientelism: A Political Economy of Everyday Corruption in Rural North India." *Economic Geography* 78: 21–42.

Johnson, Deb, Hope Kabuchu, and Santa Vusiya. 2003. "Women in Ugandan Local Government: The Impact of Affirmative Action." *Gender and Development* 11: 8–18.

Kaufmann, Daniel, Aart Kraay, and Massimo Mastruzzi. 2007. "Governance Matters VI: Governance Indicators for 1996–2006." World Bank Policy Research Working Paper No. 4280, World Bank, Washington, DC.

Levy, Brian, and Sahr Kpundeh. 2004. *Building State Capacity in Africa.* Washington, DC: World Bank and Oxford University Press.

Olken, Benjamin. 2007. "Monitoring Corruption: Evidence from a Field Experiment in Indonesia." *Journal of Political Economy* 115: 200–49.

Rinaudo, Jean-Daniel. 2002. "Corruption and Allocation of Water: The Case of Public Irrigation in Pakistan." *Water Policy* 4: 405–22.

Samuel, Paul. 2002. *Holding the State to Account: Citizen Monitoring in Action.* Bangalore: Books for Change.

Swamy, Anand, Stephen Knack, Young Lee, and Omar Azfar. 2001. "Gender and Corruption." *Journal of Development Economics* 64: 25–55.

United Nations and Academic Foundation (UN & AF). 2005. "Unlocking the Human Potential for Public Sector Performance." World Public Sector Report 2005, Department of Economic and Social Affairs, New Delhi, and United Nations Academic Foundation.

van Zyl, Johan, Tulio Barbosa, Andrew N. Parker, and Loretta Sonn. 2000. "Decentralized Rural Development, Enhanced Community Participation, and Local Government Performance: Evidence from North-East Brazil." World Bank, Washington, DC.

Vyasulu, Poornima, and Vinod Vyasulu. 2000. Women in the Panchayati Raj: Grassroots Democracy in India. In *Women's Political Participation and Good Governance: 21st Century Challenges,* ed. L. Hammadeh-Bannerjee, 41–49. New York: United Nations Development Programme.

Work, R. 2002. "Overview of Decentralisation Worldwide: A Stepping Stone to Improved Governance and Human Development." Paper presented at the 2nd International Conference on Decentralisation, "Federalism: The Future of Decentralizing States?" Manila, Philippines.

World Bank. 2005. "The Effectiveness of World Bank Support for Community-Based and -Driven Development—An OED Evaluation." Operations Evaluation Department, World Bank, Washington, DC.

———. 2007a. *Annual Report 2007.* Washington, DC: World Bank.

———. 2007b. *World Development Report 2008: Agriculture for Development.* Washington, DC: World Bank.

Thematic Note 1

Chattopadhyay, R., and E. Duflo. 2004. "Women as Policy-makers: Evidence from Randomized Policy Experiment in India." *Econometrica* 72 (5): 1409–43.

Curry, J., and D. Tempelman. 2006. "Improving the Use of Gender and Population Factors in Agricultural Statistics: A Review of FAO's Support to Member Countries in Gender Statistics." FAO, Rome.

Derbyshire, Helen. 2002. "Evaluation of Gender Mainstreaming in Oxfam's Advocacy Work on Poverty Reduction Strategy Papers." Oxfam, Oxford (Stage 1: Briefing Paper for Country Case Studies).

Elson, Diane, and Rosemary McGee. 1995. "Gender Equality, Bilateral Program Assistance and Structural Adjustment: Policy and Procedures." *World Development* 23 (11): 1987–95.

Food and Agriculture Organization (FAO). 2007. "Progress Report on the Implementation of the FAO Gender and Development Plan of Action." FAO, Rome.

Gender and Rural Development Thematic Group (GENRD). 2006. "FY06 Gender Portfolio Review." World Bank, Washington, DC.

———. 2007. "FY07 Gender Portfolio Review." World Bank, Washington, DC.

———. 2008. "Economic and Sector Work and Technical Assistance in ARD Portfolio." World Bank, Washington, DC.

International Food and Agriculture Organization (IFAD). 2003. "Mainstreaming a Gender Perspective in IFAD's Operations: Plan of Action 2003–2006." IFAD, Rome.

International Food Policy Research Institute (IFPRI). 2007a. "Proceedings of the Consultation on Strengthening Women's Control of Assets for Better Development Outcomes." IFPRI, Washington, DC.

———. 2007b. "Engendering Better Policies: Two Decades of Gender Research from IFPRI—CD ROM." IFPRI, Washington, DC.

Inter-Parliamentary Union (IPU). 2006. "Women in Politics: 60 Years in Retrospect." Data Sheet No. 4. Note, IPU, Geneva, February.

Morrison, Andrew. 2007. "Does Gender Equality Matter for Shared Growth?" Paper presented for Poverty Reduction and Economic Management-Gender and Development (PREMGE), World Bank, Washington, DC, April 25.

Quisumbing, Agnes, and Bonnie McClafferty. 2006a. "Gender and Development: Bridging the Gap between Research and Action," IFPRI Issue Brief No. 44, International Food Policy Research Institute, Washington, DC.

———. 2006b. "Using Gender Research in Development." Food Security in Practice No. 2, International Food Policy Research Institute, Washington, DC.

Schneider, Katrin. 2007. "Public Finance Management, Including Gender-Responsive Budgeting." Draft, UN Division for the Advancement of Women, New York.

Swedish International Development Agency (SIDA). 2005. "Policy Promoting Gender Equality in Development Cooperation." SIDA, Stockholm.

UNIFEM. 2007. *The State of the World's Children 2007.* New York: United Nations.

World Bank. 2001. *Engendering Development: Through Gender Equality in Rights, Resources, and Voice.* Oxford: Oxford University Press and World Bank.

———. 2004a. "Implementing the Bank's Gender Mainstreaming Strategy: Second Annual Monitoring Report, FY03." World Bank, Washington, DC.

———. 2004b. "A Review of Rural Development Aspects of PRSPs and PRSCs, 2000–2004." Agriculture and Rural Development Internal Report, World Bank, Washington, DC.

———. 2005. "Evaluating a Decade of World Bank Gender Policy: 1990–99." Operations Evaluation Department, World Bank, Washington, DC.

———. 2007. *World Development Report 2008: Agriculture for Development.* Washington, DC: World Bank.

———. 2008. "Gender Equality as Smart Economics: World Bank Group Gender Action Plan, First Year Progress Report (January 2007–January 2008)." World Bank, Washington, DC.

World Bank and International Monetary Fund. 2005. "2005 Review of PRS Approach: Balancing Accountabilities and Scaling Up Results." World Bank, Washington, DC.

Zuckerman, Elaine. 2002. "Poverty Reduction Strategy Papers and Gender." Background paper for the Conference "Sustainable Poverty Reduction and PRSPs—Challenges for Developing Countries and Development Cooperation," Berlin, May 13–16.

Thematic Note 2

Jain, Devaki. 2005. "Rethinking the Need for and Structure of the National Machineries for Women's Advancement." Background paper for the Expert Group Meeting "The Role of National Mechanisms in Promoting Gender Equality and the Empowerment of Women," Rome, November 29–December 2, 2004.

Vargas-Lundius, Rosemary, in collaboration with Annelou Ypeij. 2007. *Polishing the Stone. A Journey through the Promotion of Gender Equality in Development Projects.* Rome: International Fund for Agricultural Development.

Warioba, Christine. 2005. "The Role of National Mechanisms in Promoting Gender Equality and the Empowerment of Women: SADC Experience." Background paper for the Expert Group Meeting "The Role of National Mechanisms in Promoting Gender Equality and the Empowerment of Women," Rome, November 29–December 2, 2004.

Thematic Note 3

Baden, Sally. 2000. "Gender, Governance and the Feminization of Poverty." In *Women and Political Participation: 21st Century Challenges*. New York: United Nations Development Programme.

Balisacan, Arsenio, and Rose Edillon. 2003. "Second Poverty Mapping and Targeting Study for Phases III and IV of KALAHI-CIDSS." Asia-Pacific Policy Center, Quezon City, Philippines.

Balisacan, Arsenio, Rose Edillon, and Geoffrey Ducanes. 2000. "Poverty Mapping and Targeting for KALAHI-CIDSS."

Binswanger, Hans P., and Swaminathan S. Aiyar. 2003. "Scaling Up Community-Driven Development: Theoretical Underpinnings and Program Design Implications." World Bank Policy Research Working Paper 3039, World Bank, Washington, DC.

Gender and Rural Development Thematic Group (GENRD). 2008. "Does Unfettered CDD Hurt Women More than It Helps Them?" Proceedings of the debate session during the Sustainable Development Network Week, February 22, World Bank, Washington, DC.

Gillespie, Stuart. 2006. *Scaling Up Community Driven Development: A Synthesis of Experience*. FCND Discussion Paper No. 181, Food Consumption and Nutrition Division, International Food Policy Research Institute, Washington, DC.

Horowitz, Leah. 2007. "Getting Good Government for Women: A Literature Review." Draft report, IFPRI, Washington, DC.

Inter-American Development Bank (IADB). 1998. *The Use of Social Investment Funds as an Instrument for Combating Poverty: Strategy Paper*. Washington: IADB.

International Fund for Agricultural Development (IFAD). 2004a. *Community Development Funds in IFAD Projects: Some Emerging Lessons for Project Design*. Rome: IFAD.

————. 2004b. *Innovative Approaches to Targeting in Demand-Driven Projects*. Rome: IFAD.

————. 2006. "Initiative on Community Driven Development Regional Workshop Report." Accra, FIDAFRIQUE program, IFAD. Also available at http://fidafrique.net/rubrique282.html.

Joint Donor and Government Mission. 2007. "Gender in Community Driven Development Projects: Implications for PNPM Mandiri." Working paper, Report No. 40765, World Bank, Washington, DC.

Labonne, Julien, and Rob Chase. 2007. "Who's at the Wheel When Communities Drive Development? The Case of the KALAHI-CIDSS in the Philippines." Working paper No. 43037, World Bank, Washington, DC.

Mansuri, Ghazala, and Vijayendra Rao. 2004. "Community-Based and Driven Development: A Critical Review." *World Bank Research Observer* 19: 1–39.

Patanali, R. 2007. "IFAD's Approach to Community Driven Development in West and Central Africa: Lessons of Experience." IFAD Paper No. 107, International Fund for Agricultural Development (IFAD), Washington, DC, September.

Peña-Montenegro, Raquel. 2004. *Case Study: Scaling Up Innovative Project Strategy Approaches for Poverty Reduction in the Southern Highlands of Peru*. Rome: International Fund for Agricultural Development.

Perrett, Heli. 2004. "Review Development Funds in IFAD Projects: Some Emerging Lessons." Unpublished report, Rome, October.

World Bank. 2001a. "Vietnam: Community Based Rural Infrastructure Project." Project Appraisal Document, World Bank, Washington, DC.

————. 2001b. "Vietnam: Northern Mountains Poverty Reduction Project." Project Appraisal Document, World Bank, Washington, DC.

————. 2002. "Kapitbisig Laban Sa Kahirapan—Comprehensive and Integrated Delivery of Social Services Project (KALAE-CIDSS)." World Bank, Washington, DC.

————. 2003. "Kecamatan Development Program." Implementation Completion Report, World Bank, Washington, DC.

————. 2005. *The Effectiveness of World Bank Support for Community-Based and Driven Development: An OED Evaluation*. Washington, DC: World Bank.

————. 2006a. "Vietnam: "Community Based Rural Infrastructure Project—Project Process Monitoring Consulting Services." Progress Report, World Bank, Washington, DC.

————. 2006b. "Report on Project Implementation Issues in First Half of 2006 and Outline of Tasks in Second Half of 2006 of the Community-Based Rural Infrastructure Project." Progress Report, World Bank, Washington, DC.

————. 2007a. "Strengthening Governance, from Local to Global." In *The World Development Report 2008*, chapter 11. Washington, DC: World Bank.

————. 2007b. "Tracking Progress towards Community Empowerment and Welfare: KALAHI-CIDSS Midterm Evaluation Report." World Bank, Washington, DC.

————. 2007c. "Vietnam: Community Based Rural Infrastructure Project." Progress Report, World Bank, Washington, DC.

————. 2007d. "Vietnam: Northern Mountains Poverty Reduction Project." Project Completion and Results Report, World Bank, Washington, DC.

————. 2007e. "Enabling East Asian Communities to Drive Local Development: East Asia Region CDD Flagship Report." World Bank, Washington, DC.

———. 2008. "Vietnam: Northern Mountains Poverty Reduction Project." Final Report, World Bank, Washington, DC.

Thematic Note 4

Kabeer, Nailer, and Helzi Noponen. 2005. *Social and Economic Impacts of PRADAN's Self Help Group Microfinance and Livelihoods Promotion Program.* Brighton, U.K.: Institute of Development Studies, University of Sussex.

Liamzon, Cristina. 2006. "Strengthening Capacities of Organization of the Poor: Experience in Asia—IFAD's Experience in Building and Strengthening Rural Organizations in Asia." ANGOC/IFAD, Quezon City, Philippines.

Seeley, Janet, Meenakshi Batra, and Madhu Sarin. 2000. *Women's Participation in Watershed Development in India.* Gatekeeper Series No. 92. London: International Institute for Environment and Development.

Innovative Activity Profile 2

World Bank. 1998. "Republic of Côte d'Ivoire—Second National Agricultural Services Support Project." Project Appraisal Document, World Bank, Washington, DC.

———. 2003. "Republic of Côte d'Ivoire—Second National Agricultural Services Support Project." Implementation and Completion Report, World Bank, Washington, DC.

Innovative Activity Profile 3

World Bank. 2004. "Gemidiriya Community Development and Livelihood Improvement Project." Project Appraisal Document, World Bank, Washington, DC.

———. 2007a. "Gemidiriya Community Development and Livelihood Improvement Project." Midterm Review Report, World Bank, Washington, DC.

———. 2007b. "Gemidiriya Community Development and Livelihood Improvement Project." Progress Report, Fourth Quarter, World Bank, Washington, DC.

FURTHER READING

Thematic Note 1

Norris, Pippa, and Ronald Inglehart. 2000. "Cultural Barriers to Women's Leadership: A Worldwide Comparison." International Political Science Association paper.

Quisumbing, Agnes, Jonna P. Estudillo, and Keijiro Otsuka. 2004. *Land and Schooling: Transferring Wealth across Generations.* Baltimore: Johns Hopkins University Press.

World Bank. 2006. "Implementing the Bank's Gender Mainstreaming Strategy: Annual Monitoring Report for FY04 and FY05." World Bank, Washington, DC.

Thematic Note 2

International Fund for Agricultural Development. 2005. "Issues and Action Note on IFAD's Experience Working with National Mechanisms in Support of Gender Equality." Background paper for the Expert Group Meeting "The Role of National Mechanisms in Promoting Gender Equality and the Empowerment of Women," Rome, November 29–December 2, 2004.

Thematic Note 3

Food and Agriculture Organization (FAO). 2005. *Rapid Guide for Missions: Analysing Local Institutions and Livelihoods.* Rome: Institutions for Rural Development, FAO.

International Fund for Agricultural Development. n.d. "Empowering the Poor by Shifting from a Supply to a Demand Driven Approach." Available at www.ifad.org/events/reducingpoverty/peru.htm.

Thematic Note 4

Catholic Relief Services. 2007. *The Organization and Development of Farmer Groups for Agroenterprise: Conclusions from a CRS and RII-CIAT Study Tour in Asia, Africa and Latin America.* Baltimore: Catholic Relief Services.

Cornwall, Andrea. 2001. "Whose Voices? Whose Choices? Reflections on Gender and Participatory Development." *World Development* 31 (8): 1325–42.

Weinberger, Katinka, and Johannes Jutting. 2001. "Women's Participation in Local Organizations: Conditions and Constraints." *World Development* 29 (8): 1391–1404.

Wilson, Kimberly. 2002. "The New Microfinance: An Essay on the Self-Help Group Movement in India." *Journal of Microfinance* 4 (2): 218–45.

Gender and Rural Finance

Overview

RURAL FINANCE AND RURAL LIVELIHOODS: INTRODUCTION

The critical role of financial services in rural livelihood development is broadly recognized. In recent years there has been an increasing emphasis on establishing an "inclusive financial sector"—in other words, on supporting the whole diversity of financial institutions that can provide funds for pro-poor development.[1] "Rural finance" as defined here refers to the range of financial services available in rural areas—not only agricultural finance, but also finance for nonagricultural development in rural areas (fig. 3.1). It is important that gender issues be considered across the entire range of rural financial service providers.

Rural finance includes the range of retail and wholesale institutions that have the capacity or potential to offer financial services to the poor and extremely poor (commonly referred to as "microfinance"). Beginning in the 1990s many donors, including the World Bank, International Fund for Agricultural Development (IFAD), and Food and Agriculture Organization (FAO), increasingly focused on the sustainable and large-scale delivery of financial services for the poor, especially small loans for both farm and off-farm activities, savings and microinsurance services, and, more recently, remittance transfer services. Access to well-designed financial services can help poor households build assets, engage more effectively with markets, and reduce their vulnerability to crises, especially when access to services is planned as part of household livelihood strategies and sustained over time.

The provision of financial services can effectively complement—and provide a means of accessing—different types of training and other nonfinancial services. Rural finance providers can also provide a forum for grassroots collective action and advocacy where people meet regularly over a sustained period to access financial services (as in group-based microfinance but also in other meetings of people who obtain finance on a more individual basis). Interest is also increasing in going beyond the establishment and expansion of financial institutions per se, to look at the ways in which financial service providers can strategically promote pro-poor growth—for example, through interventions at different levels of marketing and supply chains—and contribute to environmental management.

Pro-poor development has many requirements extending beyond interventions targeted at alleviating poverty. Interventions are needed at other levels to promote economic growth in ways that benefit the poor, such as by increasing employment, providing consumption goods, and improving markets. The provision of financial services for the poor, therefore, should be seen as a complement to, and not a substitute for, the provision of financing for larger-scale agricultural activities and rural development (World Bank 2007a). More attention must be paid to providing innovative types of rural finance for rural development. These innovations can address the shortcomings of earlier agricultural finance programs, with respect not only to economic growth but also to their contribution to sustainable development and poverty reduction.

Figure 3.1   Interplay of Financial Services in Rural Areas

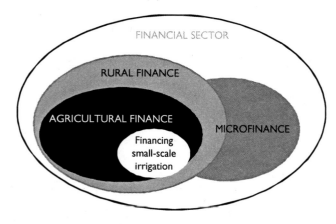

Source: Kloeppinger-Todd 2007.

Examples include the provision of larger and longer-term loans to commercial farmers, value chain finance, finance for natural resource management, and improvements in the legal environment to facilitate the provision of financial services (Fries and Akin 2004; Hollinger 2004; World Bank 2007a). The development of financial services for the poor also needs to be placed in the context of debates about corporate social responsibility and consumer protection.

Rural financial services are currently provided by a range of institutions, including the following:

- *Informal private sector providers:* Large-scale farmers, traders, processors, and employers provide credit as part of sharecropping or leasing agreements, putting-out systems, market transactions, or employment arrangements. Retail stores offer consumer goods under credit or lease-to-own arrangements. Moneylenders, pawnbrokers, and informal deposit collectors are also included in this group.
- *Informal mutual financial mechanisms:* Examples include rotating or accumulating savings and credit associations (ROSCAs or ASCAs), burial societies for death insurance, cash or in-kind advances, or savings arrangements with relatives and patrons.
- *Formal sector providers:* Examples include private commercial banks, state-owned banks, post offices, insurance companies, and companies specializing in products such as leasing, housing finance, and remittance transfers.
- *Specialist microfinance institutions:* These institutions provide financial services to poor and low-income populations. They use either their own funds or funds borrowed from private banks and other sources of funding by individuals and/or groups.

- *Membership-based financial organizations:* These organizations include rural financial cooperatives, credit unions, and other village-based entities. Some of these may also lend external funds to members.
- *Integrated rural development programs and multisector nongovernmental organizations (NGOs) that offer financial and nonfinancial services as part of integrated development strategies:* These programs or organizations may mobilize rural populations, often through groups of various types, to gain access to financial services, either directly from the NGO or indirectly through links between rural communities and other financial institutions.

The organizational distinctions and organizational gender policy related to these providers are discussed in more detail in Thematic Note 1.

Rural finance covers a range of products, such as the following:

- Loans of varying amounts, with varying time frames and conditions, to pursue a range of livelihood activities (including both agricultural and off-farm activities) or to permit asset-building and consumption
- Savings services of different types to meet different needs, from managing day-to-day household cash flows to building assets over the long term
- Insurance to reduce risk and vulnerability
- Leasing arrangements for assets
- Remittance transfer services enabling migrants to send more of their earnings home for investment in livelihoods and asset building, for consumption, and for reducing the vulnerability of family members left behind
- Bill payment services
- Pensions to reduce long-term vulnerability.

The gender dimensions of different products are discussed in more detail in Thematic Note 2.

Rural finance may or may not differ substantially from urban finance. Many institutions offer services (often the same services) in rural and urban areas, and rural and urban areas are obviously on a geographical continuum—there is rarely a sharp division between one and the other. In many contexts, however, rural finance faces specific challenges:

- A lack of market development and infrastructure, and hence greater limitation in the kinds of livelihoods that can be pursued by the rural population, leads to broad-based "geographical" poverty.

- The means of gaining a livelihood may be seasonal, especially in agriculture but also in cases in which processors or manufacturers depend on local agriculture to source raw materials or on local incomes to create demand for their products.
- Interrelated covariant economic risks are present, such as climatic and environmental risks, price and market fluctuations, or pests and diseases.
- Information and transaction costs for service providers can be higher in rural areas, where populations are more dispersed (sometimes very remote), have lower levels of literacy and education, and have less access to the complementary support that people may need to translate access to financial services into improved livelihoods.
- Rural communities may face different types of social opportunities and risks. Rural communities may be more closely knit, have concentrated local power structures, experience sharper ethnic divisions, or may be characterized by more than one of these.
- Property rights are ill defined and frequently characterized by complex land, crop, and resource use rights and sharing arrangements based on kinship, marriage, or community.

These factors may make financial services more costly to provide in rural than in urban areas, particularly in more remote areas or those suffering from particularly severe environmental risks. These factors may also make financial services less effective unless services are also supported by other interventions. Like urban areas, rural areas have a range of target groups that could benefit from financial services and that must be reached as part of a pro-poor development process. In some rural areas or for some target groups, the efficient provision of financial services may require delivery mechanisms that differ from those in urban areas, as well as different types of integration with other development interventions.

BENEFITS FROM GENDER-RESPONSIVE ACTION: POTENTIAL VIRTUOUS SPIRALS

Concerns over women's access to financial services and the degree to which women benefit from these services are not new; nor are they part of a donor- or Western-led agenda. Beginning in the early 1970s, women's movements in many countries became increasingly interested in the extent to which women actually use poverty-focused credit programs and credit cooperatives, as well as in the lack of secure savings facilities to help women increase their control over assets. Both concerns were fundamental to setting up the Self-Employed Women's Association in India (Rose 1992) (see Innovative

Activity Profile 1). The first International Women's Conference in 1975 in Mexico, where the Women's World Banking network was established, gave the problem of women's access to savings and credit services particular emphasis. Following the second International Women's Conference in Nairobi in 1985, government and NGO-sponsored programs to generate income for women proliferated. Many of these programs channeled savings and credit services through women's groups.

Beginning in the 1990s microfinance programs were increasingly directed at women—partly because of evidence that women's repayment rates were higher than men's but also because donors supported microfinance for women as an effective gender strategy to increase women's role in production. In contrast to most economic development interventions, in many prominent microfinance programs women eventually formed the majority of clients, including programs modeled after the Grameen Bank program and many of the Finca Village Banking affiliates.[2] In some cases the emphasis on women clients often continued as microfinance programs evolved into more formal microfinance institutions.

Although the provision of financial services to rural women has focused largely on microfinance and poverty reduction, some parties have raised concerns with increasing women's access to financial services at all levels to help them increase their incomes as medium- or large-scale entrepreneurs, exporters, and farmers (World Bank 2006, 2007b).

Gender-responsive action to remove discrimination in women's access to rural financial services is likely to have many significant benefits, both for the development process and for women themselves.

First, *efficiency and economic growth:* Women have been targeted for microfinance programs largely because they have proved to be more reliable clients than men. Women have often proved to be better savers than men, better at repaying loans, and more willing to form effective groups to collect savings and decrease the cost of delivering many small loans. Targeting women may therefore improve the financial sustainability of rural finance institutions. This benefit is in addition to the efficiency benefits to the rural economy of enabling over half the rural population to save and gain access to loans, insurance, and other services so that they can contribute to rural economic growth (World Bank 2006). Efficiency and economic growth will also be supported by paying attention to the rapidly increasing numbers of women migrants who require remittance transfer services and to the increasing numbers of women left behind in rural areas who now bear major responsibility for developing the rural economy. Attention must also be given to the needs of large-scale women entrepreneurs (such as those in

West Africa who control most of the trade in food), women exporters in global markets, and women engaging in cross-border trade (Burjorjee, Deshpande, and Weidemann 2002).

Second, *poverty reduction:* To reduce poverty, specific attention must be given to women in poor households. Women are generally poorer than men. They are more vulnerable within households because they lack control over productive assets. Research also indicates that women tend to invest any additional earnings in the health and nutritional status of the household and in schooling for the children (Burjorjee, Deshpande, and Weidemann 2002). Channeling economic resources such as credit or savings facilities to households through women can enable them to play a more active role in household decision making—both in addressing risks facing the household and in advocating for increased investment in family welfare. Increasing household expenditure in areas like nutrition and education, particularly for girls, may not only benefit children but can also improve women's well-being by enabling them to reduce gender inequalities in the household.

Third, *gender equality and empowerment:* Promoting gender equality of access to financial services has been part of the agenda of the international women's movement since 1975, as part of women's economic rights. Evidence indicates that access to microfinance can initiate the virtuous spirals of economic empowerment, increased well-being, and social and political empowerment of women themselves (Cheston and Kuhn 2002). Women—in some contexts, many women—show enormous resourcefulness and initiative when provided with a loan or the opportunity to save without interference from family members (Kabeer 2001). Most microfinance organizations can cite instances of women who were very poor before entering the program, started an economic activity with a loan, and thereby improved well-being, relationships in the household, and involvement in local community activities. Impact studies that differentiate by poverty level often find these benefits particularly for the "better-off poor" who have some education and contacts to build on for operating a successful enterprise.

Women can become economically empowered in several ways by greater access to financial services. Women can increase their understanding of and control over household finances. Through savings, credit, and insurance facilities, women can promote their own economic activities, create and protect assets, enter markets, and diversify their economic activities. By strengthening women's economic roles and enhancing respect for women's decision making, access to financial services may also increase women's own share of the benefits from greater household well-being.

The combination of women's increased economic activity and increased decision making in the household can spur wider social and political empowerment. The positive effects on women's confidence and skills—as well as expanded knowledge, support networks, and market access for some women—can enhance the status of all women within a community. In societies in which women's mobility has been very circumscribed and women previously had little opportunity to meet other women outside their immediate families, very significant changes have occurred when women have started to be involved in paid economic activities. Individual women who gain respect in their households and communities may become role models for others, which leads to a wider process of change in community perceptions and men's willingness to accept change. Particularly in societies in which women do not already have extensive networks, these empowerment effects can be enhanced through well-designed, group-based models for financial services. Even individual bank savings and lending products that are gender inclusive may bring about change by developing women's confidence in negotiating with men staff and initiating wider impacts in their relations with men in other arenas.

Women's economic empowerment as individuals is potentially significant at both the community and higher levels because it heightens women's visibility as agents of economic growth and magnifies their voice as economic actors in policy decisions. Microfinance groups may form the basis for collective action to address gender inequalities within a community, including issues such as gender violence, access to resources, and local decision making. Microfinance groups have been used strategically by some NGOs as an entry point for wider social and political mobilization of women around gender issues (see Thematic Note 1). Local changes may be reinforced by higher-level organization and lead to wider movements for social and political change and the promotion of women's human rights at the macrolevel.

These wider impacts are not necessarily confined to the effects of having access to financial services. They could also be promoted by strengthening women's participation in agricultural organizations and cooperatives, strengthening individual services to women members of entrepreneurship associations to advocate for women's interests, and strengthening gender-equitable policies at the macrolevel.

GENDER CHALLENGES: POTENTIAL VICIOUS CIRCLES

Despite the considerable potential of rural financial services for women, there is still a long way to go before women have equal access to these services or fully benefit from them. Achieving both of these goals does not depend only on expanding financial services per se, but also on the specific types of financial services that are delivered in different contexts to women from different backgrounds and by different types of institutions or programs (Mayoux 1999, 2008).[3] What follows in this section should, however, be taken as an indication of the types of issues to be borne in mind in designing gender-equitable services and why the points and suggestions in the rest of this Module are important, rather than an indication that rural finance should not be considered as a potentially effective and important part of a gender strategy.

The gender dimensions of the constraints to rural finance mentioned earlier affect women's access to finance and the degree to which they benefit:

- Gender restrictions on women's mobility in many cultures and the gender-discriminatory pattern of most rural development mean that women are likely to have less access than men to markets and infrastructure and greater limitations on the types of economic activity that they can undertake.
- Most cultures generally view women as bearing the main responsibility for household subsistence. Women thus may have more interest in seasonally specific strategies to diversify their livelihoods, decrease household vulnerability, and maintain consumption levels in lean times, and less incentive and ability to take risks on economic activities that may yield a higher income.
- Women's concentration in a narrow range of activities with insufficient resources for investment may make them more susceptible to climatic and environmental risks, price and market fluctuations, and epidemics of pests and disease. Women tend to be at the bottom of the hierarchy in local and global value chains and are thus the least protected from fluctuations in employment and income caused by economic and environmental factors.
- Women, on average, have lower levels of literacy and education than men in the same area.
- Women are generally subject to higher levels of "social control" within households and communities and are less likely to have their interests represented by local power hierarchies.
- Women often have few formal property rights. The rights they do have may be undermined through land reform and rural development programs that grant property titles to the household head (generally automatically assumed to be the man) and that do not protect or reinforce women's informal rights (see also Module 4).

These contextual disadvantages are compounded by institutionalized discrimination, which hinders women's access to formal financial services (Anderson-Saito, Dhar, and Pehu 2004). Women's use of financial services has increased significantly over the past two decades, but considering the types of services they receive and the broader spectrum of rural finance as a whole, it is clear that access to financial services is still unequal. The extent to which microfinance programs are directed at women varies among countries, and the perception that such programs focus largely on women is not true everywhere (for example, Pakistan).[4] In most financial institutions, women generally receive smaller loans than men, even for the same activities. Women are mainly involved in microfinance programs with small savings and credit services and some types of microinsurance. Their participation relative to men decreases as financial organizations grow and introduce services for better-off clients, often as a way to improve financial viability.[5] It is unclear how much of this trend can be attributed to institutional discrimination of the types outlined previously, to women's lower demand for larger loans, and to a tendency for better-off households to take loans in men's names.[6] It is important to note that women are vastly underrepresented as borrowers and members in many rural finance programs and cooperatives that focus on larger agricultural production loans.

Financial indicators of access—such as the numbers of women clients, numbers and size of loans obtained, and repayment data—should not be used as stand-alone indicators of women's actual use of financial services or as proxy indicators of women's well-being or empowerment. For women, as for men, credit is also debt. It must be repaid and thus carries risk when it is taken on by people with fragile livelihoods and high levels of economic insecurity. Savings, insurance, or pension premiums and remittance transfers are foregone investment or consumption. The extent of the benefit from financial services, therefore, depends on the type of service provided and the extent to which it enables livelihoods to improve. In addition, specific gender dimensions affect the degree to which women benefit. The registration of loans in women's names does not necessarily ensure their participation in decisions about how the loan will be used, particularly if it is for an economic activity operated by a man or by a family rather than an economic activity managed by the woman. Similarly, high repayment levels by women do not of themselves indicate that women have used the loans. Men may take the loans from women, or women may choose to invest the loans in men's activities. Loans may be repaid from men's earnings or any of the economic activities engaged in by the household, through women forgoing their own or the family's consumption, or from borrowing from other sources. Although women may still benefit from accessing finance for the household, this outcome can by no means be assumed. In relation to savings, insurance, and remittance transfers, there are questions about how far women are benefiting or about whether they are now expected to use their own scarce resources for household welfare—resources previously provided by men.

The contribution of financial services to increasing incomes varies widely. The degree to which credit contributes to increased incomes for women, as well as men, depends to a large extent on how well the delivery of credit is adapted to the economic activities being financed. Agricultural loans that arrive late or are not large enough to pay for inputs may simply burden a woman with debt that she cannot repay through proceeds from the activity she wished to finance. In many contexts, only a minority of women use credit and savings to develop lucrative new activities of their own. Evidence suggests that in some instances women invest in current activities that yield little profit or in their husband's activities. Although a decrease in household vulnerability may be as important as an actual increase in income for many very poor women, many women seek to increase their own incomes significantly. Some women have extremely good business ideas requiring larger loans, but they face discrimination in accessing such loans, with the result that their businesses collapse because they are forced to purchase inferior equipment or materials (Mayoux 1999). Negative impacts on incomes are not confined to loans. Compulsory savings and insurance premiums constitute a further drain on resources for investment, unless they are designed with the interests of the woman in mind and not just to limit risk and increase financial sustainability for the financial institution.

Clearly, women's choice of livelihood activity and their ability to increase their income are seriously constrained by gender inequalities in access to other resources for investment, responsibility for household subsistence expenditure, lack of time because of unpaid domestic work, low levels of mobility, and vulnerability—all of which limit women's access to markets in many cultures. These gender constraints occur in addition to market constraints on expansion of the informal sector and resource and skill constraints on the ability of poor men as well as women to move up from survival activities to expanding businesses. The rapid expansion of loans for poor women may saturate the market for "women's" activities and cause profits to plummet.

Women's contribution to increased income for their households does not ensure that women necessarily benefit

or that there is any challenge to gender inequalities within the household. Women's perceptions of value and self-worth are not necessarily translated into actual changes in well-being, benefits, or gender relations in the household. Although in some contexts women may seek to increase their influence within joint decision-making processes rather than seek independent control over income, neither of these outcomes can be assumed to occur. Evidence indicates alarmingly that men, in response to women's increased (but still low) incomes, may withdraw more of their contribution to the household budget for their own expenditure on luxuries. Men are often very enthusiastic about women's savings and credit programs because their wives no longer "nag" them for money (Mayoux 1999). Small increases in access to income may come at the cost of heavier workloads, increased stress, and diminished good health. Women's expenditure patterns may replicate rather than counter gender inequalities and continue to disadvantage girls. Without providing substitute care for small children, the elderly, and the disabled and providing services to reduce domestic work, many organizations report that women's outside work adversely affects children and the elderly. Daughters in particular may be withdrawn from school to assist their mothers. Although in many cases women's increased contribution to household well-being has considerably improved domestic relations, in other cases it intensifies tensions. This problem affects not only poor women but also women from all economic backgrounds, which indicates that the empowerment process must have effective strategies to change men's attitudes and behaviors.

Women's individual economic empowerment and/or participation in group-based microfinance programs is not necessarily linked to social and political empowerment. Women's increased productive role often reduces their time for social and political activities. Earning an income and finding time to attend group meetings for savings and credit transactions may also take women away from other social and political activities—and experience suggests that when meetings focus only on savings and credit transactions, women commonly want to decrease the length and frequency of group meetings over time. Women's existing financial networks may come under serious strain if women's own loan repayments or savings contributions, or those of other group members, become a problem. The contribution of financial services to women's social and political empowerment depends to a great extent on other factors, such as staff attitudes in interacting with women and men, the types and effectiveness of core and other capacity building, and the types of nonfinancial support services or collaboration with other organizations.

Finally, very little research has been done on the gender impacts of financial services for men. Any financial intervention available to any household member has the potential to reinforce or challenge existing inequalities in ways that may contribute to or undermine both the poverty and the potential of other household members. As noted earlier, research suggests that financial services targeted to men contribute less to household well-being and food security. When financial services automatically treat men as the head of the household, they may reinforce what are often only informal rights that men have over household assets, labor, and income. In other words, they may seriously undermine women's informal rights. As in other areas of development, such outcomes may have consequences not only for the women and households involved but also for the effectiveness of the intervention and sustainability of the institutions involved.

GENDER MAINSTREAMING IN AN INCLUSIVE FINANCIAL SECTOR FOR PRO-POOR DEVELOPMENT: GOOD PRACTICE AND CURRENT AREAS OF DEBATE AND INNOVATION

Given the contextual and institutional constraints, gender mainstreaming in rural finance requires more than increasing women's access to small savings, loan, and microinsurance programs or to a few products designed specifically for women. Instead, gender mainstreaming requires the promotion of gender equality of opportunity across the entire range of financial services, including remittance transfer services, leasing arrangements, and larger loans for productive investment, as well as enhanced opportunities to participate in natural resource management and value chain development initiatives.

To mainstream gender in an inclusive financial sector, providers must go beyond access alone and consider how access can enable women and men to challenge and change gender inequality as well as household and community poverty. This task requires not only attention to product design but also attention to the organizational mechanisms employed to deliver services and the ways in which financial services are integrated with or complemented by other types of support from the same or other local organizations. Finally, gender mainstreaming in an inclusive financial sector requires innovative thinking about how women's access and gender equity can be incorporated into the large-scale rural finance programs for agricultural development and macrolevel policy reform that are being given renewed emphasis.

Women must lead efforts to mainstream gender, given that it is women who are currently most disadvantaged in relation to all economic and human development indicators. First, to promote gender equity, we must also examine the gender dimensions of financial and other services for men to see to what extent these support rather than undermine strategies for women. Second, it must be recognized that not all women (any more than all men) have the same needs. Considerable diversity exists across regions of the world in gender differences and inequalities in economic roles, in cultural opportunities and constraints, and in the ways that these factors interact with economic market and institutional factors. Even in one geographical area, not all women or men are in the same position. The financial and other service needs of women and men involved in different economic activities and with different levels of experience and resources, different ethnic backgrounds, ages, marital status, education levels, and so forth will be different. Individual women and men are also likely to have a diversity of financial needs, which will change over time with the life cycle and personal circumstances. The aim must therefore be to develop a diversified, inclusive rural finance sector in which different types of institutions provide different and diverse services adapted to the needs of different women and support men's ability to promote equitable change. This endeavor should not be seen as an additional burden but as an integral part of any serious strategy for growth and poverty reduction.

First, gender mainstreaming must promote *gender equality of opportunity and access to all types of rural finance* at all levels, from microfinance directed at the very poor to gender-equitable financial services for women farmers and entrepreneurs who have moved higher up in the value chain. "Access" means more than just physical proximity; it means removing direct and indirect gender discrimination in the design, promotion, and delivery of all services. It is important to establish graduation procedures so that women do not remain entrenched and confined to small savings and credit schemes. These women need clear avenues for upward mobility through the financial sector as their needs and skills evolve. Economic growth and poverty reduction both require the gender-equitable development of economic sectors employing large numbers of women, along with strategies to help women enter new sectors. It is crucial that current debates about agricultural and value chain finance, remittance transfers, and commercialization incorporate gender equity in their strategies for economic growth and poverty reduction.

Second, gender mainstreaming must ensure that women not only access but also *benefit from the use of these services in terms of their well-being and empowerment.* Ensuring that financial services actually benefit women clients, members, and other intended beneficiaries is not only a concern for donor agencies and governments seeking to comply with organizational gender mandates and international agreements. It must be a concern of any financial service provider that obtains funds from these donor agencies and of any commercial providers with claims to corporate social responsibility and ethical standards. Corporate social responsibility and ethical standards are becoming increasingly important in relation to environmental protection and child labor, but they need to be extended to address international agreements on gender equity and women's human rights.

Third, gender mainstreaming will require *action, advocacy, and linkages with movements that address the underlying bases of gender discrimination,* which affect both women's access to opportunities and the degree to which they are able to benefit. Particular areas of concern include property rights, sexual violence, and political participation to increase women's voice in economic and rural policy.

The most cost-efficient and developmentally effective strategies for mainstreaming gender equality of opportunity and for promoting women's empowerment will differ, depending on the type of financial institution, local context, and capacities. However, some things can be done by rural financial institutions of *all types*—from banks, insurance companies, and remittance transfer agencies to specialized microfinance institutions, member-based financial organizations, and integrated rural development programs and NGOs with savings and credit components. Moreover, although some of these strategies will require a different way of "doing business" and some shift in priorities for resource and funding allocation (possibly including the use of "smart subsidies"), gender mainstreaming is likely to increase rather than undermine sustainability.

Most of what is discussed in this Module is not concerned with "women's empowerment projects" as optional add-ons, although these projects can also have their role if they are well designed. We are concerned with mainstreaming gender and empowerment throughout the financial sector—not only to benefit women but in the process also to improve the longer-term financial and organizational sustainability of financial services themselves and the sustainability and dynamism of the rural economy in general.

Thematic Note 1, on models and strategies for institutional gender mainstreaming, discusses how institutional structure and governance affect women's access to rural financial services and the empowerment outcomes for women. It contains an additional discussion on internal gender policy.

Thematic Note 2, on financial products, describes types of products, discusses the issues involved in product design, and describes innovations to increase women's access. It also discusses the likelihood that women will be able to use services to benefit their economic activities or households and increase their own status and control over resources and decision making.

The Innovative Activity Profiles illustrate many of these points through case studies:

- Indira Kranthi Patham in India has supported the creation of self-managed grassroots institutions of poor women, helped to expand and diversify their livelihood base, sustained food security among poor households, and enabled participants to discover and influence market mechanisms for sustaining growth and equity.
- The Kabarole Research and Resource Centre in Uganda has developed self-managed microfinance associations under a gender policy to promote women's leadership. It has also developed a sustainable, gender-mainstreamed participatory action learning system for training.

GUIDELINES AND RECOMMENDATIONS FOR PRACTITIONERS

Specific recommendations in regard to different aspects of rural finance are provided in the Thematic Notes. Broad guidelines are listed below.

At the national level:

- Ensure that gender experts and women's organizations are involved in designing financial regulations to ensure that regulations do not inadvertently exclude women (for example, through definitions of ownership) and that all regulations comply with and promote gender equality of opportunity in fulfillment of international women's human rights agreements. The aim must be to promote a diversified sector, spanning the range from commercial enterprises to NGOs, that caters to the needs of all women as well as men and does not impose unnecessary regulations and blueprints that favor particularly powerful financial lobbies or networks.
- Promote and support the collection of gender-disaggregated data on access to financial services across the sector, as well as cross-institutional research into the reasons, and potential solutions, for any gender differences identified.

- Promote networks of practitioners and gender experts who can work together to identify, develop, and monitor good practices and innovation for increasing women's equal access to rural financial services and increasing the extent to which they benefit from these services—bearing in mind that credit is also debt, and that there is danger in selling financial products inappropriately to vulnerable people.
- Appraise the national training programs for bankers, agriculturalists, rural development staff, and other government development staff and assess and improve the integration of gender and participatory gender planning skills.
- Promote linkages between the financial sector, rural development planning, and other agencies promoting gender equity, particularly in relation to property rights and women's participation in economic decision making.

At the intermediate level:

- Facilitate and support collaboration between different rural finance providers in an area so that they can work together to (1) promote innovation in financial services for different target groups and ensure that women from different economic and social backgrounds are included, (2) reduce the costs of providing complementary support for livelihoods and gender-equity strategies, and (3) advocate and promote gender equity at the local and national levels.

At the local level, for practitioners:

- Conduct a gender audit of their organization's structures and practices to assess the degree to which gender equality of opportunity is present across the range of services

and the degree to which affirmative gender strategies may be needed.

- To ensure that women have equal access to financial services and benefit from them, avoid simplistic replication of models from elsewhere. Design services and structures based on a sound understanding of the local context, the target group and their financial needs, and any needs for complementary support for livelihood development and gender equity.
- Identify contextual gender constraints and consider how they can be addressed through interorganizational collaboration, collective action, and lobbying the financial sector or government.

GENDER INDICATORS AND CHECKLIST

Detailed checklists for conducting gender assessments of different types of institutional structures and product designs are given below. Box 3.1 lists general questions that need to be asked in assessing the gender impact of rural finance development interventions. In each case it is important to conduct a thorough contextual analysis rather than make assumptions about existing forms of gender inequality, to assess the magnitude of change, and to determine the degree to which changes are caused by better access to financial services or by specific aspects of the services, organizational structure, or nonfinancial services rather than other contextual factors. Table 3.1 provides sample monitoring and evaluation indicators.

Depending on the country or region, it may be relevant to also consider ethnicity and caste alongside gender (both as comparative indicators and when collecting data), as women of lower castes or ethnic minorities are usually in the worst situation.

Box 3.1   Gender Impact Checklist for Rural Finance

How far and in what ways has women's access to rural financial services increased? Is there gender equality of opportunity?

What informal and formal financial services (such as credit, savings, insurance, and remittance transfers) exist in the area? Which financial services did women normally use before the intervention? Which ones did men normally use? What were the gender differences

and reasons for any differences? Has access to these sources changed since the intervention? If so, what and why?

Does the institution or intervention track gender-disaggregated data? What gender differences appear in the data with respect to access to different financial services?

If differences exist in numbers of women and men using different financial services, what are the reasons

(Box continues on the following page)

Box 3.1   Gender Impact Checklist for Rural Finance (continued)

for this behavior? Differences in aspirations and motivation? Explicit or implicit institutional gender discrimination?

How far and in what ways have rural financial services increased women's economic empowerment?

What economic activities did women already pursue? What economic activities did men pursue?

How were assets, income, and resources distributed within households? Did women and men have different degrees of access? Different degrees of control?

Have financial services enabled women to increase incomes or production from their economic activities? To enter new and more profitable or productive activities? To increase assets? To decrease economic vulnerability?

How far do women control this income or these assets? For what do women use the income? Investment in livelihoods? Or consumption?

Has women's market access increased? In existing markets only? In new markets? Has vulnerability to market fluctuations decreased?

Even if women do not use the income for their own economic activities, has their role in household decision making and their control over household income or assets increased?

How far and in what ways have rural financial services contributed to increased well-being for women and their families?

What was the extent of gender inequality in well-being before? Food security? Health? Literacy and education? Freedom from violence? Did gender inequality with respect to these characteristics change significantly or only a little following the intervention?

What have been the impacts of financial services on women's own nutritional and food security, health, education, vulnerability to violence, and happiness?

What have been the impacts on the nutrition, health, education, vulnerability to violence, and happiness of other women household members—girls and the elderly?

What have been the impacts on the well being of boys and men?

How far and in what ways have rural finance programs contributed to women's social and political empowerment?

Did women have personal autonomy and self-confidence before the intervention? Did they have freedom of mobility or social and political activity? If not, in what ways were they limited compared to men?

How far and in what ways did access to financial services or rural finance programs increase women's self-confidence and personal autonomy?

How far and in what ways have financial services or rural finance programs extended and strengthened women's networks and mobility?

How far and in what ways have financial services or rural finance programs enabled women to challenge and change unequal gender relations? In property rights? Sexual violence? Political participation? Other?

Source: Author.

Table 3.1   Monitoring and Evaluation Indicators for Gender and Rural Finance

Indicator	Sources of verification and tools
Percentage of women and men among officials and staff trained in leadership and management, systems, and procedures	• Financial institution records
Percentage of women, men, and other disadvantaged groups sitting on management boards and committees	• Administrative records • Project management information system
Number of men, women, and ethnic minorities who received training in household budgeting and SME financial management	• Financial institution records • Training records
Number of men, women, and ethnic minorities who received training in loan application procedures	• Financial institution records • Training records
Number of men, women, indigenous people, and ethnic minorities who accessed financial services per quarter	• Financial institution records • Project management information system • Savings and loans group records

(Table continues on the following page)

Indicator	Sources of verification and tools
Payment defaults, disaggregated by gender, per quarter	• Financial institution records • Savings and loans group records
Among surveyed beneficiaries in target group, at least x percent of both women and men rate their access to rural finance as having improved during the period covered by the program or project	• Interviews with beneficiaries in target groups; ideally the interviews should be conducted before and after any project/program activities
Changes in on-farm or enterprise earnings of women-headed households and other disadvantaged groups as a result of access to financial services and training support	• Case studies • Gender analysis • Sample surveys
Percentage of new investments in nontraditional businesses (that is, not basic food crops or selling merchandise)	• Interviews • Project records
Changes over x-year period of project activities in household nutrition, health, education, vulnerability to violence, and happiness, disaggregated by gender	• Household surveys, before and after • Project management information system • School records
At least x percent increase of annual household income compared with baseline, measured at end of project period	• Household surveys • Project management information system

Source: Inputs from Pamela White, author of Module 16.

Organizational Gender Mainstreaming: Models and Strategies

ORGANIZATIONAL MODELS AND DIMENSIONS OF VARIATION

Rural finance is probably as old as the rural cash economy itself. Money lending and the provision of credit in kind under varying terms from relatives, traders, employers, and patrons for centuries if not millennia have been important means for farmers and households to make investments and address seasonal or extraordinary income and consumption demands. Despite their notoriety, money lending and patronage systems may be relatively well adapted to balancing needs, risks, and costs (Rutherford 1999). They offer immediacy of loan disbursement, small loans, flexible repayment schedules, and minimal and flexible collateral requirements because the borrower and lender are known to one another. The transaction costs are low because of the proximity of the borrower and lender. In many cultures indigenous systems of mutual assistance, such as rotating savings and credit associations and accumulated savings and credit associations, enjoy a very long history.[1] In some regions, particularly West Africa, very sophisticated informal systems are common for both economic and social purposes. In designing rural finance services, the full range of existing informal services must be fully understood, taken into account, and complemented rather than undermined by providers if informal services already address some of the intended clients' financial needs.

Beginning in the 1950s many newly independent governments set up credit programs in agriculture and industry as a major aspect of poverty alleviation and development strategies. In South Asia subsidized or low-interest credit was extended through some state banking systems to small-scale farmers and producers. In Africa resources were mobilized for development through the stimulation of traditional credit and savings groups and their formalization into cooperatives and credit unions. In the 1970s and 1980s, multilateral and bilateral aid agencies increasingly supported

such organizations under their rural development programs. Some programs targeting women were introduced by private banks such as Barclays Kenya. Public and private rural finance mechanisms have often been inadequate and unsustainable, however, with very low repayment rates, especially in the public sector. More recently some commercial banks—aided by improved technology and infrastructure—have become interested in rural areas, in part in response to government lending requirements that give priority to poverty alleviation and in part because they perceive these sectors as potentially profitable and wish to establish an early commercial advantage. For example, ICICI Bank in India is exploring how to place automated teller machines (ATMs) in rural areas for individual lending at normal bank interest rates, significantly lower than microfinance institutions (MFIs); how to link with MFIs and membership-based financial organizations (MBFOs); and how to upgrade entire value chains by providing financial services for enterprises at specific points in the chain. Remittance transfer services have become crucial for capturing the increasing volume of overseas transfers and linking them to local development in rural areas that are the original home of many migrants.

The "microfinance revolution" of the 1980s and 1990s saw the rise and expansion of new organizations such as Grameen Bank and microfinance networks such as Acción and Finca. These organizations aimed to provide financial services on a large enough scale to reduce poverty significantly on a financially sustainable and even profitable basis. Most are still confined to urban areas, but some, like Grameen Bank, are based in rural areas. Some MFIs originated as integrated development NGOs that saw themselves as pioneers of participatory development for the poor.

The MBFOs also have a long history. Credit unions and financial cooperatives were set up in many countries under colonial rule and as part of burgeoning cooperative movements. In some African countries, **missionaries set up savings clubs** for rural households to cope with the agricultural cycle. Small-scale informal systems and self-managed federations, based on rotating systems and self-help groups, were more frequently set up, particularly for women, beginning in the mid-1980s. In some countries, such as India, various government programs widely promoted these organizations; elsewhere, they have been promoted by rural development programs. In some cases the groups have been self-replicating (for example, the Women's Empowerment Program in Nepal). Many are developing more sophisticated methods in scaling up, diversifying their products, and accessing services from banks and large MFIs.

An MBFO can operate cost effectively in rural communities in which banks and professionally managed MFIs do not exist, cannot be attracted, or are uninterested in serving the poor. Like cooperatives, MBFOs should follow a savings-first approach, but this approach takes time, and quick results in terms of loans disbursed should not be expected. As with cooperatives, external capitalization may damage these organizations, especially if external loan funds are injected before groups have organized and operated successfully using their own savings. Relationships can be developed with banks if they are located within a reasonable distance of the MBFO and if members are interested. This relationship may start quite modestly with the opening of a bank account, but even that simple step can be empowering for people, especially women, who have never had access to a bank account (see also Ritchie 2007).

Box 3.2 outlines broad distinctions between rural finance institutions, which are generally required to conform to legislative norms, although significant differences in the legal

---

Box 3.2   Rural Finance Institutions

Formal sector providers include commercial banks and state banks with rural development or poverty portfolios. Banks can either deliver services directly to rural areas and poor people (individually or in groups) or provide services through retail microfinance institutions, such as agricultural development and rural banks, development banks, postal banks, post offices that capture savings and offer transfer services, commercial banks (such as ICICI Bank in India), and remittance transfer providers (such as Western Union).

Specialist microfinance institutions provide financial products to poor and low-income populations. This category encompasses many organizational types, such as Grameen Bank affiliates, trust banks (such as the Opportunity network), and "village banks" (such as the Finca model). Some MFIs originated as catalyst, intermediary, or parallel programs operated by NGOs and then officially registered as MFIs or banks. Depending on national regulations, registration lets them collect deposits and offer insurance and other financial services as well as loans. They have professional staff and aim at reaching very large numbers of poor borrowers on a financially sustainable basis. Some MFIs may serve the nonpoor to subsidize services for the poor. Some act as retail intermediaries for banks to their clients as individuals or as groups, providing referrals, helping with loan applications, and offering training, technical assistance, and guarantees to lenders (which reduce the

implicit costs of formal borrowing and reduce the bank's costs and risks of lending to the poor).

Membership-based financial organizations include financial cooperatives, credit unions, and self-help groups, as well as their apex organizations and federations. These registered membership organizations are governed by different types of state legislation. They are formed and owned by members who (in theory at least) make the main decisions, and they may be managed on a day-to-day basis by elected officers or salaried staff. These MBFOs may supplement the funds available from members' savings through linkages with banks or arrangements with donor agencies.

Integrated provision of financial services through rural development programs and NGOs can include very large rural development programs, such as those funded by the International Fund for Agricultural Development, Food and Agriculture Organization, and the World Bank, as well as small, local organizations that provide basic financial services as part of a broader development agenda. These programs may work with any of the institutions described earlier and directly mobilize small savings and credit groups, often as networks or federations or by linking groups to the formal banking system or microfinance institutions. Such programs seek to be cost effective and have a development impact but not necessarily to be financially sustainable.

Source: Author.

framework for each type of institution will affect how each is established and develops. For example, national legislation (which differs among countries) affects the kinds of products that an institution can develop and offer. The same institution may combine one or more organizational forms in different areas, for different target groups, or for different programs or projects funded by different donors. For example, a registered bank or MFI may serve one area with individual lending, but in another area self-help groups may be linked to government rural development programs. The ways in which particular organizations operate also depend on whether and how they attempt to comply with legal requirements and donor guidelines or adapt them to their aims. Some MBFOs, MFIs, and NGOs are in transition from one legal category to another as a result of changes in donor requirements, growth and internal change, and change in the regulatory environment.

It is important to recognize that the distinguishing features of each model and organizational form have become blurred as particular models (such as the Grameen model or cooperatives) have been adapted to different contexts. The parent models themselves have evolved to adopt promising innovations and address emerging challenges. Some commercial banks increasingly look to microfinance to fulfill government requirements or for its potential profits. NGOs have increasingly adopted elements of the financial sustainability approach. As mutual and self-managed organizations grow, they more often employ staff to manage operations, and members' participation in decision making may become more limited.

Organizations nominally following the same model can differ significantly in their governance and in the products and services they offer. Some rural finance is directed at particular groups (large- or medium-scale farmers, women, the poorest, or particular social groups). The details of group structure and decision-making procedures vary, as do levels and conditions of external funding (national and international). All of these differences can further or hinder the potential for change.

KEY GENDER ISSUES AND BENEFITS OF GENDER MAINSTREAMING: EMPOWERMENT VERSUS SUSTAINABILITY

The variations among organizational models can significantly influence gender outcomes and have implications for the most effective ways in which gender can be mainstreamed. Some service providers in all categories described in box 3.2 mainly or exclusively target women or have a written or an informal gender policy, or both.

A conflict is often perceived between empowerment strategies and institutional sustainability. In particular it is often asserted that gender strategies are inappropriate in banks, and hence irrelevant to the rapid expansion of commercial or large-scale rural finance, including profit-oriented or financially sustainable MFIs.

Gender mainstreaming should not be seen as a diversion from the serious, "hard-nosed" business of banking but as an integral part of all good business practice. The perceived opposition between sustainability and empowerment overlooks the ways in which systemic change, rather than increasing programs, can help increase gender opportunity of access and women's empowerment. It also overlooks the ways in which such changes contribute to financial sustainability in addition to development and organizational sustainability. Women at all levels of society are an underserved market and—apart from extremely poor women—an underdeveloped and potentially profitable market.[2] Women (like men) who are confident, make good livelihood and household decisions, have control over resources, and can use larger loans effectively to increase their incomes are potentially very good long-term clients. They can contribute substantial amounts of savings and use a range of insurance and other financial products and can pay for services that benefit them. The task for all rural finance providers is therefore to ensure that their systems are women friendly and contribute as far as possible to women's economic empowerment and well-being, providing avenues of upward mobility and support for the benefit of both women and the provider. Even commercial banks can contribute to women's social and political empowerment through changes in institutional culture and collaboration with other development organizations.

ORGANIZATIONAL GENDER MAINSTREAMING: GOOD PRACTICES AND LESSONS LEARNED

The most cost-effective means of maximizing contributions to gender equality and empowerment is to develop an institutional culture that is women-friendly and empowering, that manifests these traits in all interactions with clients, and that addresses the institutional constraints (box 3.3).

Most of these measures have a minimal cost but expand the numbers of women clients, which in turn expands outreach and increases the pool of reliable, successful, and (in most cases) profitable clients. These measures, therefore, would enhance rather than detract from financial sustainability. The best way of integrating gender policy with existing practices and contexts can be assessed through a gender

Box 3.3   Institutional Measures Contributing to Women's Empowerment

- The institutional culture is expressed in the way the organization chooses to promote itself. What sorts of images and messages does it send through the images in its offices, its advertising, and the consistency of its gender aims in the community with its internal gender policy? The institution's routinely issued promotional leaflets, calendars, and advertising are a very powerful means of presenting alternative models and challenging stereotypes. No extra cost should be needed in ensuring that promotional materials achieve these goals. It is just a question of vision—and of ensuring that the designers of promotional materials understand that vision.

- The application process for products or other services involves asking questions about the applicant's background and capacities. Without increasing the time needed to answer these questions, they could be reworded or adapted to promote a vision of empowerment, help applicants think through their financial planning, and help them challenge

inequalities in power and control in the household for both women and men.[3]

- A sectoral focus can include activities in which women are concentrated and can look at ways of developing such activities through marketing and supply chains.

- Extension services and business advice sections can ensure that they recruit staff members who can work with women as well as men and thus increase women's participation even in activities normally dominated by men.

- Even in basic savings and credit training and group mobilization, it is possible to integrate empowerment concerns. Many issues within the household and community need to be discussed for women to anticipate problems such as repayment and continuing membership. Discussions need to equip women to devise solutions that also address the underlying gender inequalities that cause the problems in the first place. Men, including some progressive men leaders, can also be invited to these meetings.

Source: Author.

audit, a simple gender SWOT (strengths, weaknesses, opportunities, threats) analysis, or a well-designed participatory process.[4] This effort would entail an initial cost that is likely to be recouped within a short period through better outreach to good women clients.

Underpinning this women-friendly and empowering institutional culture are four main dimensions of a strategy for mainstreaming gender equality and women's empowerment: (1) staff gender policy (discussed below), (2) mainstreaming gender concerns in product development (Thematic Note 2), (3) structures for participation (box 3.4), and (4) effective integration of complementary nonfinancial services and collaboration with complementary service providers (box 3.5).[5]

IMPLEMENTING A STAFF GENDER POLICY: BENEFITS, COSTS, AND GOOD PRACTICES

It is extremely difficult for an organization to promote gender equity externally if it practices gender discrimination internally. A clear and agreed-on staff gender policy that promotes gender balance within the organization and fosters a culture in which women and men interact on a basis of

equality and mutual respect has important benefits, including greater work satisfaction, less stress for women and men employees, and good work relations that make it more likely that all staff members give their best.

The evidence clearly links levels of women staff in a financial services organization with women's access to services and the organization's contribution to women's empowerment. Evidence also exists that women in senior management positions provide valuable perspectives for product design and implementation, rural finance operations, business plans, marketing strategies, and policies. Gender-aware men staff members are central to contacting men within the community and changing their attitudes. When men staff members have good relations with women clients, they can increase women's confidence in dealing with men's hierarchies and break down cultural barriers.

Gender policy is likely to require quite profound changes in recruitment criteria, organizational culture, and procedures (see table 3.2). These internal changes are consistent with financial sustainability; in fact, mainstream banks are sometimes far ahead of NGOs in implementing staff gender policies (examples include Barclays in Kenya—dating back to the 1980s—and Khushali Bank in Pakistan). The promotion

Box 3.4 Checklist: Groups, Participation, and Empowerment

- Does group size increase women's collective strength? Are groups too large? Too small?
- Does group composition extend or merely replicate women's existing networks?
- Do groups discriminate against particularly disadvantaged women (very poor women, younger women, women from particular ethnic groups)?
- Are there ways for men to be involved to build support for women's initiatives but not dominate the proceedings?
- Do groups facilitate information exchange?
- Does the group structure increase women's decision-making and negotiating skills?

- Are women equally represented in group structures at all levels of the program, particularly beyond primary groups?
- Do groups undertake collective action for change (for example, collective action in relation to sexual violence or women's political representation)?
- Do savings and credit groups link with other services for women and with movements challenging gender subordination?
- In relation to all of the above, which women are participating?

Source: Linda Mayoux, "Sustainable Microfinance for Women's Empowerment: Report from International Mutual Learning Workshop, Centre for Micro-Finance Research," www.genfinance.info.

Box 3.5 Checklist: Integrating Nonfinancial Services

- What complementary nonfinancial services are needed by these particular target groups to use financial services effectively?
- What nonfinancial services are already provided by the organization or in the area? How far do women have equality of access? How far do the services empower women?
- What gender-specific services might women need? What gender-specific services might men need? Can these be mainstreamed, or do they need to be a separate intervention?
- How can nonfinancial services be provided most cost effectively? Through mutual learning and

exchange, cross-subsidy, or integration with delivery of financial services? Through interorganizational collaboration?
- What contextual factors will affect the relative costs of different levels of integration? Which, if any, needs can be most effectively and cost efficiently met by the financial service staff? Which, if any, needs can or should be met through a separate section of the same organization? Which, if any, needs can or should be met through collaboration and other means discussed above?

Source: Author.

of diversity, of which gender is one dimension, is a key element of best business practice in the West.

Many of these strategies, such as recruitment, promotion, and sexual harassment policies, cost little. Although a gender policy may entail some costs (for parental leave, for example), the cost should be compensated by high levels of staff commitment and efficiency. Unhappy and harassed staff members are inefficient and change jobs frequently, and training new staff is costly. This is not to say there are no serious challenges, potential tensions, and some costs. Mere formal change is not enough. Real change requires the following:

- A profound actual change in organizational culture and systems, requiring that the issue be raised of staff participation in decision making—a key tenet of best business practice
- A shift in the norms of behavior for women and men
- Willingness and support for change at all levels: among field staff, midlevel staff, senior management, and donors.

It is important to stress that these elements can be integrated into *all forms* of rural financial services *in some way,* including commercial and state banks as well as MFIs,

Table 3.2 Good Practices in Staff Gender Policy

Practice	Example
Recruitment and promotion	Include gender awareness in job descriptions and as key criterion for recruitment and promotion.
	Advertise employment opportunities through channels likely to reach more women.
	Adopt proactive hiring and promotion strategies to recruit women into senior management positions until gender balance is reached.
Rights at work	Review all norms and job descriptions from a gender perspective.
	Give equal pay for equal work.
	Guarantee freedom from sexual harassment (women and men).
	Establish rights and responsibilities.
	Establish structures for all staff to participate in decision making.
Family-friendly work practices	Provide flexible working arrangements: flexi-time, flexi-place, part-time work, and job sharing encouraged at all levels, including senior managers.
	Develop maternity and paternity leave policies.
	Provide childcare and dependent care leave and support.
Training	Provide ongoing training for all men and women staff in participatory gender awareness, sensitization, planning, and analysis.
	Provide follow-up training with specific tools and methodologies.
	Provide training for women to move from midlevel to senior positions.
Implementation structure and incentives	An adequately resourced gender focal point coordinates gender policy; at the same time, a mainstreaming process is implemented throughout the organization.
	Gender equality and empowerment indicators are integrated into ongoing monitoring and evaluation.
	Staff targets and incentives are established for achieving gender equality and empowerment.

Sources: Linda Mayoux, "Not Only Reaching, but Also Empowering Women: Ways Forward for the Microcredit Summit's Second Goal," www.genfinance.info; benefits of women in senior management from Cheston, "Just the Facts, Ma'am: Gender Stories from Unexpected Sources with Morals for Micro-Finance," www.microcreditsummit.org.

MBFOs, and integrated development programs. Commercial banks increasingly have gender or equal opportunity policies to encourage and retain skilled women staff. Some offer child care facilities and have implemented proactive promotion policies for women staff to attain greater diversity in the organization and better develop new market niches. In many social settings, increasing the number of women staff is essential to increasing the numbers of women clients.

Banks generally use individual rather than group-based lending and unlike NGOs cannot be expected to have participatory empowerment strategies. Some commercial banks conduct market research, however, and as an integral part of good management have been at the forefront of participatory product innovation. Some also lend to groups formed by NGOs or producer organizations over whom they have some influence (Thematic Note 2).

As noted earlier, financial institutions lacking the scope to introduce nonfinancial services can promote a vision and commitment to equality and empowerment through the questions asked during the application process (Innovative Activity Profile 1). Another way forward is to collaborate with other service providers. For example, financial institutions could provide loans to women who complete training in enterprise and business development services provided by another organization, or they could link clients with legal aid services for women or reproductive health services. This collaboration can take the form of formal partnerships or merely consist of having literature on these services available to clients while they wait to see bank staff.

Banks may or may not engage in macrolevel policy advocacy, although most are likely to make sure they are involved in policy decisions that will affect them. A clear vision and commitment to gender equality and women's empowerment should be integral to the sorts of policy changes they advocate. As mentioned earlier, their promotional materials may not only attract women clients but also change attitudes toward women's economic activities and social roles in the community.[6]

INDICATORS AND CHECKLIST

Although variation can be found in the form of gender mainstreaming and the full range of empowerment strategies, and although services must be tailored to the needs of particular groups, some common questions can be asked of all rural finance institutions to assess whether they are making their full potential contribution to gender equality and women's empowerment:[7]

- Is there a gender policy? What is its nature and scope? In other organizational documents, apart from the official gender policy—for example, in operating and staff training manuals or articles of incorporation—what are the underlying assumptions about gender difference and inequality (as expressed, for example, in the language or terminology used)?
- Are statistics on the use of different services disaggregated by gender? Do these indicate equal use of all services by women and men, or do they point to significant gender differences? Do these differences in use also indicate differences in benefits? For example, are women obtaining only small loans, or are they also obtaining large loans? Is this difference caused by implicit or even explicit discrimination in how specific services are designed, or by differences in demand?
- Are any services directed explicitly at women? What underlying assumptions are being made about gender difference and inequality? Are these strategies likely to consign women to a "women's ghetto," or will they help women to diversify and move to higher-level services?
- How far and in what ways are the needs of the poorest and most disadvantaged women taken into account?[8]
- Are any services explicitly directed at men? What underlying assumptions are being made about gender difference and inequality? Are these likely to increase or decrease gender inequality? Do any strategies targeting men explicitly attempt to redress gender imbalance?

Rural Finance Products: From Access to Empowerment

Financial products are essentially "means by which . . . people convert small sums of money into large lump sums" and may take many forms (Rutherford 1999: 1). *Loans* allow a lump sum to be enjoyed now in exchange for a series of savings to be made in the future in the form of repayment installments; these may be short-term loans or term finance. *Savings* allow a lump sum to be enjoyed in the future in exchange for a series of savings deposits made now. *Insurance* allows a lump sum to be received at some unspecified future time if needed in exchange for a series of savings deposits made both now and in the future. Insurance also involves income pooling to spread risk among individuals on the assumption that not all those who contribute will necessarily receive the equivalent of their contribution. *Pensions* allow a lump sum to be enjoyed at a specified and generally distant future date in exchange for a series of savings deposits made now.

In addition, *remittance transfer services* enable migrants to invest more household income in livelihood strategies, to build assets, and to reduce the vulnerability of families they have left behind. *Leasing arrangements* permit the leaseholder to pay a regular rent or lease for use of equipment or other property while legal title to the property remains in the hands of the renting institution. Because collateral (the leased equipment) is readily available, leasing may be an easier product for rural financial intermediaries to provide than loans to purchase larger assets.[1] Products may also be combined, for example, with combined savings and pensions, or combined loans and insurance.

The following products significantly help to improve livelihoods and make them more sustainable:

- *Increasing physical, financial, natural, and human capital assets:* Assets can be increased directly through loans, savings, pensions, or remittances used, for example, for land, housing, jewelry, education, and natural resource management, or they can be increased indirectly by generating income to purchase these assets.
- *Increasing access to markets:* Access to financial markets themselves can increase, or savings, loans, pensions, or remittances can be invested in new or existing economic activities; this makes it possible to access other financial markets or improve bargaining power in markets for inputs, products of economic activities, and labor.
- *Reducing vulnerability:* Vulnerability is reduced within the household and community when loans, savings, insurance, and pensions help to protect livelihoods; contribute to income diversification; smooth incomes for consumption; and provide a safety net in times of need, including crises within the household or community.
- *Increasing information and organization:* Information and organization increase, not only through group activity, but also through economic activities generated, application and access processes, and improved financial literacy.

The combined effects of increased assets, market access, reduced vulnerability, and improved information and organization can initiate an upward spiral of economic gain and empowerment for poor women as well as their families. In combination with the potential for groups to engage in collective action and exchange information (Thematic Note 1), the multiple effects of financial products can contribute significantly to community empowerment and local economic development.

Yet financial services do not necessarily yield these positive outcomes for the following reasons:

- *Credit is also debt.* If credit is badly designed and used, the consequences for individuals and programs can be serious. Suicides have increased in some places where farm households have become deeply indebted.

- *Savings and pension installments are foregone consumption and investment.* In many contexts, particularly in which inflation is high, depositing cash with financial institutions may not be the best use of poor peoples' resources compared with investing in other assets or directly in livelihoods.
- *Insurance premiums may be lost.* As well as representing foregone consumption and investment, insurance premiums may be lost when a crisis prevents poor people from continuing with the payments.
- *Remittance transfers reduce the funds available to migrants.* These transfers in the host country may also distort local markets in the recipient country (for example, marriage and land prices) without leading to local economic development.

KEY GENDER ISSUES

The outcomes of programs to provide financial services depend to a great extent on whether products are appropriately designed for particular client groups and contexts, on how products are delivered, and on the organization responsible for delivery. This section focuses on the details of product design, which are rarely gender neutral and which inevitably—for good or ill—affect household and community relations. Product design may either reinforce or challenge the prevailing gender inequalities that shape women's needs and priorities, women's access to different types of services, and the degree to which they benefit. For example, women have fewer and different resources to use in accessing financial products. Women's different balance of opportunities and constraints affects how and how much they benefit from different products. Finally, women's gender role and gendered expectations affect their expressed short-term practical needs as well as their longer-term strategic needs to build assets, access markets, decrease vulnerability, and increase information and organization.

An equally important point is that products targeted to men may have potentially negative impacts because they are designed without considering gender inequalities in households and communities. Products for men may reinforce or challenge gender inequalities through the implicit or explicit assumptions made about men's and women's roles and power relations within households and communities. Consequently, the products' potential contributions to poverty reduction and local economic growth are affected.

Research on women's access to finance in the 1970s and 1980s focused mainly on the lack of credit as a constraint to economic activity. In the 1990s, with the rise of microfinance, most debates on product design focused on issues of financial sustainability: interest rates on loans, the desirability of mobilizing savings, and the need for insurance products to reduce microfinance programs' risk of default. A widespread consensus, based on women's poor access to resources and power and the particular physical and social assets they could contribute to programs, developed about how to increase women's access to financial services (box 3.6). Products were very limited to simplify management for field staff, generate predictable cash flows for program managers, and be comprehensible to clients. Many programs had only one loan product, with compulsory savings as a condition for accessing loans and in some cases compulsory insurance for the assets.[2]

These measures increased women's access to financial services but often had a limited impact on incomes. Loans were too small, and repayment schedules inappropriate, for activities with a lag time between investment and returns. Although suited to trade in urban areas and small livestock, the loans were ill adapted for agriculture, large livestock enterprises, or new and more risky economic activities. Where savings and insurance payments were compulsory, problems with household financial management ensued.

Recent innovations in information and delivery technology and systems now permit greater product diversification and client-centered product development. This is particularly the case where clients also have some experience with financial services and an increasingly sophisticated understanding of their financial needs and financial management. Some of these innovations have significantly improved both the extent to which women benefit from financial services and efforts to reduce poverty and foster local economic development.

CREDIT: GOOD PRACTICES AND INNOVATIONS

As indicated by research on patterns of credit use among poor women and men and by the experience of numerous clients after many loan cycles, women's credit needs are more diverse than the initial focus on small group loans would indicate:

- Women need longer-term credit to build assets—to construct houses, buy land, and lease land, either under their own names or at least jointly. They also need credit to purchase or release from pawnbrokers and moneylenders "women's assets" such as jewelry, thereby transferring general household wealth into assets that they can easily access and control and that grow in value and provide some security.

Loans
- Offer small loans so that women can invest in small assets or in income-generating activities that yield quick returns, because of women's aversion to risk, inexperience with large-scale income generation, and time constraints
- Target loans to productive activity
- Initiate regular repayments as soon after loan disbursal as possible, to instill financial discipline
- Relax collateral requirements to include social collateral or women's property (jewelry)
- Make services accessible; locate them where women are located
- Set interest rates high enough to cover costs; such rates are still beneficial because they are lower than

rates charged by moneylenders and by women's savings and other groups

Savings
- Direct programs via savings to increase thrift and women's financial management in the household

Insurance
- Use insurance to reduce the risk from livestock and from other loans

Group-Based Delivery
- Use to reduce costs and increase empowerment

Source: Otero and Rhyne 1994.

- Women need access to credit for off-farm economic activities, but to invest in viable, profitable activities they often require larger amounts than are available. Larger sums are also needed for women to diversify out of "women's" activities or expand their range of products, especially where local markets are saturated with such products and skills.
- Households that sell their agricultural labor, as well as farming households, need consumption loans to avoid resorting to moneylenders in slack and "hungry" seasons. Providing such loans to men as well as women would reduce the alarming trend for men to take less responsibility for household well-being when they perceive that women have access to additional cash.
- Households need loans to pay for children's education and to meet social obligations that are essential for maintaining social capital and the well-being of children, particularly daughters after marriage. Again, giving men as well as women access to such loans would strengthen men's responsibility for children and not place the entire burden on women.

Gender issues in designing loan products are discussed in detail elsewhere (Mayoux 2008).[3] Box 3.7 lists specific questions to address in designing loan products for women. Some very interesting innovations in loan products have been introduced recently, but given the variation in

women's preferences and requirements, the particular product that should be offered in a given context should be decided on the basis of market research. Six examples of interesting innovations include the following:[4] (1) client-focused loans (Grameen Bank, Bangladesh), (2) loans for assets registered in women's names (Grameen Bank, Bangladesh), (3) large loans for bigger profits (South Indian Federation of Fishermen Societies, India), (4) loans for adolescent girls (Credit and Savings Household Enterprise, India), (5) consumption loans for men as well as women (Area Networking and Development Initiative, India), and (6) loans for services benefiting women (Learning for Empowerment Against Poverty, Sudan).

The loan products available in rural areas are likely to change significantly over the next few years with advances in technology and the increasing entry of commercial banks into microfinance. Banks such as ICICI in India currently aim to give universal access to loan products and other services. This strategy would consist of many elements: rolling out credit cards and ATMs in villages to give everyone individual access, building and maintaining individual credit histories through credit bureaus, basing credit decisions on scoring models (risk-based lending), moving from group-based to individual lending, and tracking clients through their life cycle to offer customized products for life-cycle needs.

These developments could significantly increase the scale of outreach. They promise credit and other services on

Eligibility and collateral requirements

Women's access questions: Do collateral requirements accept women-owned assets, such as jewelry and utensils? Do they include social collateral? Do they enable women to apply without a man's signature? Are loan histories and credit ratings based on the types of records and activities in which women are involved?

Women's empowerment question: Do collateral requirements encourage registration of assets in women's names, or at least jointly?

Gender questions in loans for men: Do collateral requirements for men make unquestioned assumptions about the control of resources within the household?: (1) Do they treat men as the household head with rights over all household assets? or (2) Do they challenge these views by, for example, requiring the wife's signature for loans for which household property is used as collateral?

Application procedures

Women's access questions: Are application forms and the location and advertising of services appropriate to women's literacy levels and normal spheres of activity? Are credit and savings disbursed by women in women's centers?

Women's empowerment question: Do application procedures encourage women to improve financial literacy and extend normal spheres of activity by increasing their understanding of how to use savings and credit or by giving experience in negotiating with men officials in men's public spaces?

Gender questions in loans for men: Do application procedures for men make unquestioned assumptions about the distribution of power within the household: (1) Do they treat men as the business owner in household enterprises with the right to make all decisions about labor and resources in the household? or (2) Do they challenge these views by devising business plans that develop and strengthen the wife's position in household enterprises?

Repayment schedules and interest rates

Women's access questions: Are repayment schedules appropriate to the income available from women's economic activities or their household cash flow patterns, thereby allowing borrowers to repay their loans on time? Can women pay the interest rates specified?

Women's empowerment question: Do repayment schedules, grace periods, and other loan characteristics allow women to maximize their productive investments from the loan?

Source: Author.

Gender question on loans for men: Do repayment schedules, grace periods, and other loan characteristics require men to divert resources from the household or their wives' incomes?

Large versus small loans

Women's access question: Are loan amounts tailored to the size of the economic activity so that women have the confidence to apply?

Women's empowerment question: Do women have equal access to loans of all sizes, particularly loan amounts large enough to enable women to increase incomes significantly or invest in key productive assets in their own names without undue risk?

Gender question in loans for men: Are men required to move up the same ladder from small to larger loans to instill financial prudence?

Loan use

Women's access question: Are loans designed for the types of economic activities in which women wish to be involved or women's human and social investment priorities?

Women's empowerment questions: Do loan packages enable women to enter nontraditional and more lucrative activities, which studies have shown to be feasible for women to pursue with existing labor allocations within the household and without excessive risk? Are loans available to increase women's ownership of assets such as houses and land?

Gender questions in loans for men: Are loans for household consumption, girls' education, and family health care available to men as well as women to allow women to use their own loans for production? Do these loans encourage housing to be registered in women's or joint names?

Individual versus group loans

Women's access questions: Are groups the only mechanism through which women can access credit, or can women obtain loans individually? Which women have access to individual versus group loans? Which do women prefer?

Women's empowerment questions: Do loan groups extend or merely replicate women's networks? Do they strengthen women's networks or weaken them? Do individual loans enable women to develop networks or prevent them from doing so?

Gender questions in loans for men: Do men have access to group loans in ways that also permit them to network? How can these networks be used to challenge and change gender inequalities, as in the Community Development Centre's work with fishery workers in Bangladesh?[5]

terms far better than any currently offered by MFIs because of economies of scale arising from their large investment in technology. The extent to which women will have equitable access to these services and benefit from them remains to be seen, however. These innovations will have to consider the gender questions mentioned earlier, particularly in relation to collateral requirements and ways in which credit histories can be built up.

Also important is ensuring that gender issues are mainstreamed in current debates about larger-scale rural finance and leasing arrangements for agricultural development and value chain upgrading. Questions similar to those in box 3.2 must be answered for all loan and leasing products. Enabling women to have equal access to such products also requires attention to women's property rights.

SAVINGS AND PENSIONS: GOOD PRACTICES AND INNOVATIONS

Debates on extending the reach of microfinance to the very poorest people increasingly focus on savings facilities. For many women, including very poor women, savings facilities are essential to increasing the amount of income under their control and building assets. In many parts of Africa, for example, where in-laws are likely to take the wife's as well as the husband's property when he dies, women's ability to have confidential savings accounts is a crucial and necessary means of security for the future. Compulsory savings systems are one of the few ways for some women to protect income against the demands of husbands and other family members. If savings are only voluntary, women may be less able to oppose the demands of other family members to withdraw them.

Nevertheless, women may already have effective ways of saving. Savings programs offered by financial service providers may be less efficient for women, particularly if savings are a condition for getting loans. Savings programs may also divert resources from indigenous savings groups, which often provide a safety net for very poor women (in Cameroon and other parts of Africa, for instance, some revolving savings associations maintain a "trouble fund" for times of crisis).[6] Savings also have to come from *somewhere*—often from foregone investment or consumption. Badly designed savings products, particularly compulsory savings, may therefore harm women's ability to increase profits and, among very poor women, may be detrimental to their nutrition and health. Savings facilities may increase women's control over household income, but, as mentioned earlier, when savings are regarded as "a women's affair," men's sense of responsibil-

ity for the household may decline. In designing savings facilities, many key issues must be considered, all of which have gender dimensions (box 3.8).

Several recent innovations in savings products can make a significant contribution to women's empowerment including Grameen Phase II in Bangladesh, flexible individual savings in Bangladesh, and children's savings cards in Mexico (Dowla and Barua 2006). Pensions—which are essentially a long-term savings product—have received far less attention than other instruments such as insurance. Pensions are potentially a key component of empowerment, however, because they offer women security for their old age and have many other implications (for example, reducing women's vulnerability in the household or influencing family size decisions). Some pension products for women exist in India, but pensions are an area in which much more thinking and work are needed.

In remote areas, mobilization and intermediation of member savings are crucial first steps before accessing external loan funds. Many studies have observed that savings-led groups perform better than credit-led groups (Allen 2005; Murray and Rosenberg 2006; Ritchie 2007). For instance, Indonesia's Agricultural Development Projects and Sri Lanka's Northeast Irrigated Agricultural Development Project have not performed as well as MBFOs using a savings-led model (examples include savings-led self-help groups and their federations in India and Gemidiriya in Sri Lanka; see also Innovative Activity Profile 1; Ritchie 2007).

Savings give poor people a buffer against unforeseen expenses, thus lowering their household risk; small, regular savings help to develop financial discipline; and intermediation of savings into loans by MBFOs enables borrowers to establish creditworthiness before external credit is introduced. Recent experience in Andhra Pradesh, India, buttresses this viewpoint that external capital can overburden the poor with debt. Over the last several years banks in India have lent considerable funds to MFIs for onlending to poor clients. The resulting stiff competition among MFIs enabled many poor women to receive loans from several lenders at the same time, often irrespective of their existing debt and repayment capacity. Many poor rural clients could not repay their loans. On the other hand, poor women who save and lend to each other in small groups in the Gemidiriya program in Sri Lanka cite easy availability of loans for emergencies as one of the main benefits of participation. The Bangladesh Rural Advancement Committee's Income Generation for Vulnerable Groups Development Program is an instructive example of how grant-based approaches

COMPULSORY SAVINGS

Access question: Do levels and conditions for compulsory savings exclude women from access to other services?

Empowerment questions: Are compulsory savings required by women themselves to increase their ability to retain control over their own income or leverage household income to put into long-term savings as an asset in their names? Or are they merely an insurance device for the institution?

VOLUNTARY SAVINGS

Minimum entry-level deposits

Access question: Are entry-level deposits low enough for poor women to take part?

Flexibility of deposits

Access question: Are deposit requirements flexible with respect to women's patterns of access to income?

Empowerment question: Do savings deposit requirements give women authority to retain control over savings in their own accounts?

Liquidity of savings and ease of withdrawal

Access question: Are withdrawal requirements flexible with respect to women's needs for income?

Empowerment question: Do withdrawal conditions protect women's savings from predation by husbands and other relatives?

Source: Author.

Confidentiality

Empowerment questions: Are women's savings confidential to protect them from predation by husbands and other relatives? Or are they public, to give women high status in the community?

Accessibility of provider and transaction costs

Access questions: Are savings providers located conveniently for women? Are transaction costs reasonable?

Empowerment question: Are savings providers located in places that enable women to visit new places and get more experience outside normally accepted "women's space"?

Returns to savings

Empowerment question: Are returns to savings sufficient to enable women to build up assets over time, or are they comparable to returns available from other savings channels? (Assessment of the level of risk needs to be included in this calculation.)

Gender questions for men

Do savings facilities for men exist to encourage them to save and provide for their families (for instance, for girls' education or marriage)? Are these products promoted by staff to reinforce men's sense of responsibility in these areas?

and financial services can be complementary (see World Bank 2003).

INSURANCE: GOOD PRACTICES AND INNOVATIONS

Most people engage in various forms of "self-insurance," such as diversifying their livelihood strategies, savings of different types, building assets, and investing in social capital that can be called upon in times of hardship. Some communities have collective forms of informal insurance such as burial societies. Although savings and loan products from financial service providers can reduce vulnerability to crises and shocks, they generally do not enable people to accumulate sufficient funds to cope with major crises. Over the last decade, an increasing number of MFIs have developed microinsurance products to address various sources of vulnerability. These products include compulsory insurance against loan defaults, health and life insurance, livestock

insurance, weather-index crop insurance, and property insurance. Microinsurance is one of the most rapidly growing, specialized, and contentious areas of innovation. Important advances have been made in agricultural and health financing as well, particularly in some MBFOs.[7]

Despite the clear need for insurance products and their great potential to contribute to the development of the rural sector, the viability and desirability of specialized microinsurance institutions for the poor have been questioned. Much concern has been expressed over badly designed microinsurance products being foisted on vulnerable people, particularly as a condition for getting a loan. In some cases microinsurance providers have collapsed, taking all the premiums with them. Several private insurers, particularly in parts of Africa, have become profitable by selling a good volume of policies to poor households. In many cases the new policyholders did not understand what they were purchasing or how to make a claim, and they did not benefit (Brown 2001).

Wider questions emerge over whether poor people can or should be expected to spend scarce resources insuring themselves against all the risks of poverty caused by bad governance, poor state health systems, and environmental disasters arising from climate change and global warming. An inevitable mismatch exists between the range of hazards against which very poor people need insurance and the level of premium they are able to pay, which undermines the potential of insurance provision (Brown 2001). Debates about insurance also have specific gender dimensions (box 3.9). Women are vulnerable in different ways, gender inequality affects how women relate to institutions of all types, and women face specific risks because of gender discrimination or cultural norms:

- Unequal control of property makes women extremely vulnerable in cases of divorce or widowhood.
- Women's lower incomes make them less able to invest in risk-reducing technology or services, such as disease-resistant strains of livestock, reliable equipment, or veterinary care.
- Women's responsibility to care for the sick means that ill health of their children and partners affects their own ability to earn.
- Women are more susceptible to certain diseases, including HIV and AIDS, and to the complications of pregnancy and childbirth.
- Women's physical vulnerability makes their property particularly vulnerable to theft and crime.
- Women's high preponderance in informal sector enterprises makes them particularly vulnerable to harassment by the authorities (for example, their property may be confiscated and market stalls destroyed).

At the same time, the following situations exist:

- Women's lower incomes make them less able to afford insurance payments. Although it may be very important for women to contribute to life and health insurance schemes for themselves and their husbands, insurance may not be the best solution where marriages are unstable. Women pay premiums—maybe out of their own consumption and investment funds, maybe to ensure loans that are used by men—and they risk forfeiting these premiums if they cannot maintain payments following divorce or if they make unsuccessful claims following the death of their former partners.
- In many cultures women are less literate and physically mobile than men, and women may therefore be less able

to understand policy conditions and pursue claims unless these factors are taken into consideration. They may be deceived into taking up policies that are not to their advantage and may be less able to take advantage even of good insurance policies without considerable follow-up by insurance providers.
- Insurance policies often explicitly exclude health concerns that apply to large numbers of women (pregnancy is one example) because they present too great a risk for insurers.

Insurance is useful only as part of a broader program to address the underlying causes of risk and vulnerability facing poor women and men. Insurance is in high demand and some programs have been successful among the better-off poor (such as LEAP [Learning for Empowerment Against Poverty] in Sudan),[8] but it is doubtful whether insurance can focus only on the needs of very poor people and remain financially sustainable. There is an inevitable trade-off between comprehensiveness of coverage and levels of premium. The keys to success are the scale of outreach and the diversity of clients and risks across the rural population. Some programs, rather than attempting to provide insurance themselves, have linked with state insurance providers and the private sector and have lobbied within the larger system for better insurance provision to women.

Box 3.9 Gender and Microinsurance: Key Questions

Access questions: Are insurance conditions sufficiently inclusive to be relevant to women's needs? For example, how do they treat women's assets, women-specific health problems and reproductive complications, divorce, and abandonment? Are the premiums within women's capacity for payment (in terms of amount and regularity)? Are payment and claims procedures accessible to women in terms of location and comprehensibility?

Empowerment questions: Do insurance conditions challenge or reinforce existing roles within the household? Do insurance providers offer financial education as part of the application process? In what ways does insurance decrease women's vulnerability? Does it increase the powers of negotiation within the household?

Question for men: Does insurance for men give their wives financial security in the case of their illness or death?

Source: Author.

REMITTANCE TRANSFER SERVICES: GOOD PRACTICES AND INNOVATIONS

Remittance transfer services can contribute very significantly to poverty reduction and livelihood development. Remittances from migrant laborers, men and women, between regions within countries as well as internationally have become a force for wealth creation, particularly in poorer regions. In 2005 it was estimated that at least $232 billion[9] would be sent home globally from approximately 200 million international migrants—a sum that is three times the amount of official development aid. Even these high figures understate the importance of remittances, because they do not capture remittances sent through informal channels, which may be twice or three times this figure, or remittances sent from migrants between regions of the same country. Nor are they an accurate predictor of potential remittances if safe and cost-effective remittance services were available.

Many observers now generally agree on the importance of developing cost-effective, formal services to transfer remittances through secure channels such as banks. The remittance industry consists of formal and informal fund transfer agents, ranging from a few global players, such as large money transfer operators (Western Union, MoneyGram) and commercial banks (Bank of America and ICICI Bank in India), to credit unions (including the World Council of Credit Unions) and hundreds of smaller agencies serving niche markets in specific geographic remittance corridors. Transfer charges vary widely and often greatly surpass actual costs in markets with little competition. A range of measures have been proposed or implemented to improve remittance services by money transfer operators, banks, and others. Microfinance and other smaller institutions generally have to enter into relationships with commercial banks because of regulatory constraints—for example, on transactions involving foreign exchange and access to national payment systems. No such constraints exist for remittances between areas in the same country, however. In India, for example, MFIs and NGOs have developed many types of remittance arrangements. Technological advances such as mobile phones also make cost-effective remittance services for the poor more of a possibility.

Remittance flows are not gender neutral. Women are an increasing proportion of migrants, and in most destination countries their numbers are growing faster than those of men. Box 3.10 lists gender issues to consider in designing remittance services. A recent study by the United Nations' International Research and Training Institute for the Advancement of Women (INSTRAW) found that women represented almost half of the international migrant population.[10] Women made up 70–80 percent of all migrants from some countries, notably the Philippines. The amount of money sent to households by migrant women and men, how it is sent, and how it is used are determined not only by the market but also by the gendered power relations within households and economies.

For migrants:

- Although this is not universally the case, women migrants (particularly independent migrants) direct most of their remittances to their families' basic needs, whereas men spend more on nonnecessities.
- Women have fewer employment options in the host country, are often limited to badly paid "women's" jobs, and therefore are likely to earn lower incomes than men and have smaller amounts of income to send.
- Some countries place considerable pressure on women to migrate to support their families, which, coupled with limited employment opportunities, can lead to abuses such as sex trafficking and domestic slavery.
- Some countries have placed remittance requirements on women migrants. For example, until recently, women migrants from the Philippines were required to remit 50 percent of their earnings.
- Even where both spouses migrate, they frequently send remittances independently and for different purposes.
- Migrant associations may seek to control women or discriminate against them.

On the more positive side, when women send remittances home, they may significantly improve their standing in their families and communities; and when migration is predominantly by women, men in the families left behind may be forced to take on women's care and work roles.

For recipients:

- Some women left behind may be highly dependent on men's earnings and face high levels of material and emotional insecurity as well as an increased workload.
- Other women become acting heads of the household, with much increased control over household resources and decisions, and assume productive roles previously carried out by men.
- Women may have a very limited voice in, or be completely excluded from, decisions about how to invest community migrant funds.

Issues for migrants: Are remittance services easily available in the locations where women migrants are working? Are the terms and conditions easily understandable, given that women migrants are likely to have lower literacy and English skills? Are services adapted to women's remittance levels and payment capacities?

Issues for recipients: Are remittance services secure? Are the offices easily accessed by women so that they can collect money securely? Are any programs in place to facilitate local investment of remittances to benefit women—for example, are there links between remittance service providers and programs promoting women's productive activities?

Source: Author.

RECENT INNOVATIONS IN PRODUCT DEVELOPMENT

Many recent innovations promise to make product development sustainable and increasingly client based. First, technological advances—mobile phones, rural information centers, computerized services, and others—promise ever-more accessible and accountable services in rural areas. To ensure that these services and technologies do not leave women behind, women's groups can manage rural information centers, communications enterprises can be set up in villages (such as Grameen's mobile phone initiatives), and computer programs and material can be made accessible to people who cannot read and write.

Second, it is now generally accepted that participatory market research and "knowing your clients" is good business practice (Woller 2002). The services provided through self-employed women's associations in India have always been based on consultation with clients. Grameen Bank has just undergone a four-year reassessment and redesign based on extensive client research, which has significantly increased outreach and sustainability. ICICI Bank in India conducts participatory market research and funds in-depth research on the needs of microfinance clients by supporting the Centre for Micro-Finance Research in Chennai. Many microfinance organizations have been trained in Microsave's market research tools and use one or more of them; the tools can be adapted to identify gender dimensions of product design.[11]

As products and competitors proliferate in the microfinance market, a third concern is consumer protection: do people know what they are signing up to do, and how can they be protected from abuse? Since at least 2003 many microfinance networks have been developing and implementing consumer protection guidelines such as the ones from Freedom from Hunger.[12] These guidelines—

especially by emphasizing privacy, ethical behavior, and treating consumers with respect—potentially offer substantial protection to women as well as men, particularly if guidelines are combined with gender training for staff within the organization.

A critical part of ensuring that these protection principles become a reality is to introduce financial literacy so that clients know their rights and understand the information given to them. Many organizations, including the Microfinance Opportunities with Freedom from Hunger, Self-Employed Women's Association (SEWA), Servicios Integrales a Mujeres Emprendedoras (SIEMBRA), and Womankind Worldwide, have developed manuals for financial literacy.[13] Other methods are being developed to help illiterate women become not only financially literate but also capable of making their own financial plans, which microfinance program staff can use to help in analyzing loan applications. Financial literacy principles and guidance can also be integrated into the application process, as indicated in the Freedom from Hunger and Acción International consumer protection guidelines.[14]

So far, financial literacy programs have been developed mostly for women. Training for men, if it were to incorporate gender-equitable household financial planning principles (for instance, if it promoted men's discussion of financial planning with their wives and equal participation in financial decisions), could contribute significantly to changing men's attitudes and behavior. If such training were a condition of access to loans, it is more likely that men would attend such courses rather than generic gender training.

None of these recent developments is necessarily gender sensitive, yet there are ways for them to take gender dimensions into account. If the current gender innovations are implemented on a wide scale, they could substantially foster sustainable gender mainstreaming in product development.

Andhra Pradesh, India: A Women-Managed Community Financial System

The vast expansion of India's banking network since the 1970s largely bypassed the rural poor, especially women. Banks did not recognize women as business clients and rarely served them beyond token participation in government-sponsored credit programs.

> **What's innovative?** A vibrant, extensive network of women's groups at the community level and higher delivered a full range of financial, social, and economic services in rural areas; engaged large numbers of the poor in the formal economy; and transformed the prospects for formal banking institutions to operate successfully in remote and underserved areas.

Poor rural women have traditionally shown good financial discipline in managing the household economy, often setting aside small sums to meet specific needs, such as schooling, weddings, and debt redemption. Poor women and men initially use credit or savings for smoothing consumption and then expand their asset base gradually before building up entrepreneurial ventures. Banks—being averse to risk—did not offer products that met poor people's needs for liquidity, ease of access, smoothing consumption, or even investing in livelihood strategies. In Andhra Pradesh, India, when savings and credit were channeled through community-based women's groups and used to meet their specific needs, rural financial services underwent a dramatic transformation and successfully catalyzed capital formation, asset accumulation, and increased market participation by the poor.

PROJECT OBJECTIVES AND DESCRIPTION

Indira Kranthi Patham (IKP) subsumes two community-driven rural poverty reduction projects supported by the World Bank and International Development Agency: the Andhra Pradesh District Poverty Initiatives Project (APDPIP) and the Andhra Pradesh Rural Poverty Reduction Project (APRPRP), implemented in South India since 2000. The IKP pursues a threefold strategy. First, it helps to create self-managed local institutions of poor women, with thrift and credit services as the core activity. Second, it helps to expand and diversify women's livelihood base. Third, it helps the poor discover and influence market mechanisms as a means of sustaining growth and equity.

By the end of March 2007, following its strategy to create a hierarchy of interdependent institutions of poor people, the IKP had mobilized 8 million women into about 630,000 self-help groups consisting of 10–15 women each from poor households in Andhra Pradesh. The groups were federated at the village level into 28,282 village organizations (VOs), which in turn formed 910 confederations at the *mandal* (subdistrict) level, called *mandal samakhyas* (MSs: subdistrict confederations). Group members deposit small amounts of money into a common pool from which loans are provided. The women take collective decisions, closely supervise how the loans are used, and pressure members to make deposits and repay loans promptly. Each VO is registered formally as a cooperative federation of self-help groups to supervise and build capacity through community professionals. By taking the initial risk for lending to the groups, VOs cultivate awareness among self-help groups on how to leverage and assimilate external resources. The core microfinance function of an MS is to lend capital over the long term to VOs and supervise microfinance activity over all tiers of the institutional hierarchy. The MSs provide seed money and venture capital to newly formed VOs, invest in VOs' new business initiatives, extend hand-holding support, and build incentive structures to encourage good performance.

INNOVATIONS IN THE PROJECT

Over the years the self-help groups and their federations have expanded the scope of their services and now offer economic and social services in addition to financial services. Services have evolved mainly through incremental innovation by community institutions. The innovative elements of community institutions and the "microfinance plus other services" approach they developed are described in the following sections.

1. A *community-managed financial system* includes elements such as the following:
- *Social mobilization,* as reinforced within the self-help groups, VOs, and MSs through their transparency, democratic governance, and inclusive decision making.
- The *thrift and credit system,* through which self-help groups direct their residual capital into the local economy. The groups prepare microcredit plans (box 3.11) as a tool for efficient fund management and to leverage external resources from the VOs and MSs.
- A *management information system* based on simple books of accounts often maintained by a paid bookkeeper such as a group member or a woman from the local community
- A *quality assessment* system for women to review their performance through a Critical Rating Index (developed in consultation with NABARD)[1]
- The *capitalization of self-help groups and their federations* as they invest interest earned and fees collected. Profits are invested in further loans, and the groups' assets increase steadily.

- *Leverage of external finance* by self-help groups from VOs (as explained in box 3.10) or from local commercial banks, based on each group's financial position determined by the Micro Credit Plan, Critical Rating Index, and group assets.
- *Monitoring* by loan recovery committees at the VO level of the end use of funds and forming a *community-based recovery mechanism* by supporting local banks in maintaining the standards of their microfinance portfolio.

2. The *"microfinance-plus" approach.* Aside from providing finance, the IKP three-tier institutional structure offers a range of other products and services (broadly summarized in table 3.3) that support the livelihoods of the poor. This livelihoods approach to reducing poverty differentiates IKP from other microfinance programs with their minimalist approaches. Following the *principle of institutional subsidiarity,* each tier specializes in the creation, aggregation, or channeling of those services that make economic sense (based on efficient delivery, economies of scale, transaction costs, and other criteria).

BENEFITS AND IMPACTS

The IKP's community-driven approaches and institutional model have catalyzed women's entrepreneurial spirit and leadership. Their self-managed rural finance system has had many impacts at the macro-, institutional, and household levels. Traditional perceptions of gender roles have also changed markedly as women's status, authority, and dignity have grown.

Box 3.11 Microcredit Plans as a Tool for Self-Help Groups

A microcredit plan is a simple list of investments that self-help group members would like to make. Microcredit planning is an iterative process with several steps:

- Engage families of group members in developing household investment plans
- Finalize parameters for determining the socioeconomic status of members
- Conduct an appraisal of socioeconomic status and participatory wealth ranking

- Exercise due diligence in assessing household investment plans
- Consolidate and order loan requests according to the priority determined by the group
- Mobilize financial resources to support the microcredit plan and to apply future cash flows (from thrift, bank loans, and other sources) to support members in order of priority
- Develop terms of partnership with borrowing members that specify how assets will be acquired, asset insurance, repayment schedule, interest rates, and penal provisions for noncompliance.

Source: Author.

Table 3.3 Financial, Economic, and Social Products and Services Created and Delivered by Self-Help Groups and Their Federations, Andhra Pradesh, India

Institution	Financial services on own account	Nonfinancial economic services on own account	Facilitation services (agent/aggregator)
Self-help group (Clients: individuals)	Compulsory thrift; short-term loans for social needs; medium-term loans for investment	n.a.	Food security; agricultural input supply
Village organization (Clients: self-help groups for financial services and individuals for nonfinancial services)	Regular thrift from self-help groups; medium-term loans to groups for onlending	Rice Credit Line; agricultural input supply; commodity marketing; fodder cultivation; milk collection	Insurance for assets, life, and health
Mandal samakhya (Clients: village organizations)	Long-term loans to VOs for onlending to self-help groups; short-term loans to VOs for seasonal operations such as agricultural input supply and commodity marketing; medium-term loans to VOs for Rice Credit Line operations	Economic infrastructure for aggregating goods and services produced by poor; bulk milk coolers; warehousing	Insurance for assets, life, and health; private/NGO partnerships; contract farming; marketing contracts; job-oriented training; retailing; labor supply

Source: Authors.

Macrolevel impact

Women make markets work for the poor in several ways:

■ *First, by building a pro-poor financial sector.* In mobilizing poor women and helping them build responsive, self-reliant, and financially sustainable institutions, the IKP project shifted long-held beliefs in the banking system. The women manage a corpus of $1 billion, which includes their own thrift of $349 million. Over six years, they leveraged a cumulative $1.2 billion from commercial banks, which made IKP one of the world's largest microfinance and financial inclusion efforts.

■ *Second, by widening and deepening access to finance.* Microfinance now figures prominently in the corporate strategy of several banks, and overall lending to women has increased multifold since the project started. A major share of this expansion can be attributed to the good credit performance of women's self-help groups:

Percentage of poor with access to financial services	90
Percentage of self-help groups linked to banks	74
Savings per group ($)	450
Bank credit accessed per group ($)	1,500
Percentage of group loans recovered	95+
Number of participating banks (100% of those having rural presence)	44
Number of partnering bank branches (90% of rural and semiurban branches)	3,850
Number of poor with access to insurance	500,000

■ *Third, by utilizing the emerging coproduction model in rural finance.* The traditional prefinance function of commercial banks in extending loans to the poor is externalized to women's self-help groups.

■ *Fourth, by bringing a livelihood focus into microfinance to promote enterprise among the poor.* The incremental asset base of the poor supported by IKP now stands at $1.3 billion. These assets cover a range of livelihoods and are expected to generate significantly higher business turnover, leading to higher incomes for the poor. Banks have become interested in introducing new products for emerging opportunities.

■ *Fifth, by making financial literacy a strategic by-product.* Perhaps the most lasting impact of the women-managed rural financial system will be financial literacy among poor women. The training has developed 98,000 bookkeepers, 3,000 microcredit planning experts, and 3,000 bank linkage experts from among these women.

Institutional impacts

Significant gains are made to women's institutions and their partners:

- *Benefits of leveraging bank finance.* Extending bulk finance to self-help groups dramatically reduced the transaction costs for financing agencies to extend credit to poor women. At the same time, self-help groups are encouraging financing agencies to make increasingly higher credit commitments—ultimately benefiting both the groups and the banks.
- *Profits for commercial banks and restraints on informal credit markets.* The recovery of loans to women's self-help groups and their federations is around 95 percent, mainly because of good community oversight and follow-up mechanisms implemented by the women. Reduced transaction costs and a good recovery climate have improved the profits of rural bank branches, and in local informal markets for credit, interest rates have softened, and unethical practices have been curbed.
- *Access to markets by the poor and stimulation of private participation.* The group structure and hierarchy helped poor women to access commodity markets and form local partnerships with the private sector, thereby improving their participation in the wider economy. The aggregation of large groups of suppliers and consumers has attracted such global partners as Olam International, ITC, Pepsico, fair trade companies, and others.
- *Women's networks as social service providers.* The diligence shown by women's networks in delivering support services to the poor has encouraged several development agencies to work with them on such programs as old age pensions, midday meals for children, and health care and ambulance services.

Household impact

Women bring home credit and gain skills and confidence in several ways:

- *By making savings productive and reducing the debt burden.* The internal accretion of capital in self-help groups accrues to all members in proportion to their individual savings. Access to credit at convenient terms has significantly lowered the cost of debt. On average, self-help groups have reduced the high cost of debt per family by $75.

- *By initiating a virtuous cycle of increasing incomes and prosperity.* Continued access to loans has helped poor women accumulate productive assets at the household level. The impressive credit histories of many women not only enhanced their creditworthiness but also increased the flow of credit for diverse purposes. Average assets per family have tripled to $2,974 between 2000 and 2006. Over the same period, growth and diversification of productive assets helped annual household incomes rise by 115 percent to $1,041. A significant share of this increment comes from the income stream attributed to women-run enterprises.
- *By being regarded as creditworthy.* Banking statistics corroborate that the overall repayment climate has improved since the women's self-help groups were established. Although banks remain reluctant to make large loans to men, women are regarded as valued clients, and banks are not averse to extending large loans to women and their families through the groups.
- *By gaining business skills and initiative.* The management of rural financial services by women not only promoted leadership but also served as good training for developing institutional management and negotiation skills. Experiential learning helped women participate in markets and negotiate market positions, which greatly enhanced their business confidence and enterprise.
- *By promoting consensual decision making at the household level.* Because men and women were both involved in microcredit planning, men came to see women as partners in earning a livelihood.
- *By helping men regain business confidence.* Women-managed interventions to provide critical livelihood support services, such as supplying agricultural inputs and marketing commodities, not only increased access to credit but also increased the direct participation of poor men in markets.

LESSONS LEARNED AND ISSUES FOR WIDER APPLICABILITY

Poverty reduction projects are generational investments and require resource commitments over extended periods. Sustained outcomes depend on the sequencing and integration of investments in social mobilization of the poor; engaging the banking system for capital formation; providing livelihood support services; and enabling the poor to participate in markets.

The astute use of human capital can greatly reduce the time and cost of institution building. Using community professionals in social mobilization and capacity building is a feasible, low-cost strategy for building strong institutions at the grassroots level (for example, engaging women group members as bookkeepers, microfinance professionals, bank linkage experts, and social auditors).

Using donor contributions as revolving funds in community institutions has strategic advantages. It encourages community ownership of donor funds, as well as transparency, vigilance, and social accountability. The initial funds encourage investment in sectors in which banks are reluctant to participate; ultimately, a record of success attracts mainstream lenders and releases capital to support the next level of innovation. The recycling of funds supports extended investment at the household level, and returns from investments help community institutions achieve financial sustainability faster.

The banking system must view the poor as coproducers of financial services and not just as credit clients. This perspective will facilitate the provision of a full range of financial products at significantly lower cost to banks and the poor.

WAYS FORWARD

Consolidate the institutional systems for expanding the products and services offered by federations through process and product innovation. Commercial banks have initiated serious efforts in this direction in partnership with women's groups as part of IKP.

Develop next-generation and alternative credit linkage models. These partnerships could take several forms: for example, the MSs could play the role of "business correspondents," extending a full range of savings, credit, and insurance products to the poor on behalf of the banks, or the VOs could act as "business facilitators" to widen and deepen the reach of bank finance.

Consolidate the women-run rural financial institutions under a state-level apex to form a community-owned, mainstream financial institution. The apex could be promoted in collaboration with NABARD, major commercial banks, and other private firms that would facilitate the integration of women-run, community-managed rural financial systems with mainstream financial markets.

Uganda: Kabarole Research and Resource Centre's, Participatory, Self-Managed Microfinance Model

The Kabarole Research and Resource Centre's (KRC's) self-managed microfinance association (MFA) model of rural finance is innovative in its promotion of independent, self-managed groups as well as its fiercely participatory decision-making structure. The KRC has successfully integrated gender into sustainable livelihood training for women and men, under a program run by the KRC and offered to MFA members. The KRC was instrumental in developing the Participatory Action Learning System methodology, which is fully integrated into MFA training and planning. By linking the MFAs with Rural Information Centres, the KRC also points to possible ways of linking rural finance for the poor with civil society development.

> **What's innovative?** Self-managed microfinance associations operate as independent, self-managed groups with a fiercely participatory decision-making structure. The associations also benefit from sustainable livelihoods training and grassroots action learning methodologies in which gender perspectives have been integrated.

ORGANIZATIONAL OBJECTIVES AND DESCRIPTION

The KRC, an NGO founded in 1996 in Uganda, has a holistic approach to civil society development. Its interlinked and mutually reinforcing program areas focus on research and information, civil peace building, microprojects, human rights, and microfinance.

The KRC started its Micro-Finance Associations Program in 2002 for rural farmers, particularly women and poorer farmers. The program's role is not simply to provide financially sustainable financial services but also to establish

sustainable organizations that help poor women and men create wealth, challenge gender inequality, and reverse environmental degradation. In the context of the KRC's wider mission of civil society development, the MFAs also aim to develop participatory and organizational skills and link with other networks for development. The program is supported by the McKnight Foundation, the Humanistisch Instituut voor Ontwikkelingssamenwerking, the Rabobank Foundation, and the Deutsche Entwicklunsdienst.

As of June 2006, the program had supported and signed contracts with 17 MFAs and was closely monitoring 17 other emerging MFAs. These associations represent more than 400 community groups in the five districts in the Rwenzori region, with total membership exceeding 10,000 people. The target is to have 35 contracted and 10 emerging MFAs, each covering a subcounty in the Rwenzori region, by the end of 2008.

ORGANIZATIONAL COMPONENTS AND IMPACTS

This section discusses the KRC program's components and impacts to date.

The MFA model

Each MFA is independent, self-managed, and member owned and is made up of 10–25 groups in a specific geographical area. Most groups had come together for savings and credit or other development projects before joining the KRC program. Internally groups are subdivided into mutual solidarity subgroups of four to seven people to act as group collateral for loan repayment to the mutual fund. Each group elects its own leaders, collects and records members' savings and shares, and compiles individual loan applications into a group application to the MFA. Regular group meetings are held to discuss issues that group leaders will take to the MFA monthly meetings and the annual general meeting. When any member of the group wishes to obtain credit, he or she applies to the group. The group leader forwards the application to the MFA and follows up on it.

The MFA membership owns, manages, and uses the services offered by the MFA. Ownership is based on purchases of shares. Each group must have a minimum of 20 shares, and no group can have more than 25 percent of the total shares of an MFA. The groups also pay annual subscription fees and deposit their savings with the MFA. Each MFA is expected to construct offices for its operations.

All key decisions regarding services are taken through member representative structures. As the MFAs develop, they are able to employ at least one full-time worker per association to coordinate the activities of all groups and mobilize new groups. Each MFA also has a board and supervisory committee composed of elected members who provide advice and service on a voluntary basis. The main decision-making forum is the annual general meeting, attended by group representatives. Ongoing discussions and management within individual MFAs occur through monthly meetings between the MFAs and group representatives. Cross-dissemination of experience and ideas between MFAs takes place at bimonthly meetings.

The money that is raised is used to provide credit to the groups and to meet operational expenses. For any group to receive a loan from an MFA, it must have deposited savings worth at least 20 percent of the loan value.

The MFAs operate under a code of conduct stipulated in the MFA rules and the cooperative by-laws of Uganda. The KRC provides initial financial support and supports training at the MFA and group levels through community trainers and community process facilitators. After a five-year contract period, the MFAs are expected to meet all of their operational costs, including training and the salary of the microfinance officer/manager.

The KRC MFAs have had a positive contribution to women's empowerment (Kasente and Hofstede 2005) and have established many innovations that contribute to women's empowerment through the MFAs and are linked to KRC's Human Rights Program: Gender Mainstreaming in Sustainable Agriculture Training, the Participatory Action Learning System, and Rural Information Centres.

Gender Mainstreaming in Sustainable Agriculture

The KRC conducts sustainable agriculture training, which many MFA members receive, usually at the request of a community. Training is provided by community process facilitators, who are mandated to train and conduct follow-up activities in the community on behalf of the KRC. These facilitators must be people of high integrity who are trusted by the community. Although most of them lack any higher education, they speak English and are willing to learn and to train others.

Gender is mainstreamed in this training on the premise that "without a sustainable household you cannot have a sustainable agriculture." Every training session includes a discussion of relations in the household, the division of labor, and access to and control of resources. This approach has contributed significantly to women's empowerment in several ways:

- *Increased confidence and sense of self-worth:* Because the training helps them earn income, women realize that they can accomplish many different tasks, including those previously considered "men" tasks.
- *Increased control over income and decision making in the household:* In general, women said they controlled the income from group activities and from assets gained through the group, such as crops and livestock. They also said there had been a positive change in decision making in the household following integration of gender awareness in sustainable agriculture training, particularly when men had also been involved in training.
- *Increased confidence and ability to participate in public discussions:* This took place as a result of the training and group activity.

There also appear to have been significant changes in men's attitudes toward women's work, helping women, women's decision making in the household, and women's capacities in general, as well as a decrease in alcoholism in men and violence after these problems were raised publicly and discussed among men and women.

These developments, in turn, had a significant positive impact on household well-being. The changes that occurred over the course of such a short training period resulted not only from the content of the training but also from the organizational context in which it occurred. What was actually learned in the training and any issues raised were subsequently followed up in group meetings and further reinforced in monitoring by the KRC (Mayoux 2005).

Participatory Action Learning System

The KRC has also spearheaded the Participatory Action Learning System (PALS), an innovative methodology to increase the effectiveness and sustainability of its core and other training.[2] PALS builds on a long-established tradition of grassroots participatory action research. However, PALS is distinctive in the way it attempts to systematically sequence use of participatory processes and diagram tools into an integrated and coherent empowerment process. PALS aims to avoid becoming another extractive participatory methodology by focusing on reflection and analysis at the individual level and helping people think through, plan, document in diagrams, and then track their own goals and strategies. Methods have been developed to help people who have never held a pen to start drawing and developing plans to achieve goals that they determine. These plans are then tracked over time on the drawing as an ongoing learning process. This individual analysis is then shared, following simple, inclusive, and participatory guidelines, in a group process for mutual learning that yields trackable plans for collective action. The individual responses, expressed in either private interviews or public meetings, are likely to be much more reliable than spontaneous responses in large group meetings. The PALS methodology is not taught in a stand-alone training session but is used as the base methodology for various types of training—for example, enterprise, gender, or organizational training—to make it more effective for people who are not literate. An independent study of three community-based KRC partner organizations concluded that PALS had resulted in impressive levels of self-confidence, full participation of all members (literate and illiterate, rich and poor, women and men) with no leadership dependency, effective self-evaluation of progress, increased collaboration, and unity in the group and within households. The methodology had also led to viable solutions being implemented for problems at the individual, household, and group levels.

A further development of PALS, the Poverty Resource Monitoring and Tracking model (PRMT), builds a Community-Based Monitoring and Information System that enables information to flow through many supportive structures at different levels in the local government, up to the national stop center (the Uganda National Bureau of Statistics, in this case), and to flow back through the same structures. The PRMT model empowers the community to participate actively in planning, implementing, and monitoring of development programs up to the macro- and policy levels.

Careful consideration needs to be given to the levels and types of decisions for which women's participation is needed for empowerment, who should participate, and the types of participation that can be most empowering (see box 3.11). It is important to be clear about the potential costs and benefits for women and to have a participatory process to identify the actual costs and benefits and the best ways forward.

Rural information centres

Information is a key tool for women as well as men farmers to improve their own enterprises, make informed decisions, and improve livelihoods through information and knowledge on human rights, gender issues, conflict management, health, hygiene, education, and democratic processes, which have strategic roles in sustaining and maximizing benefits from their agricultural enterprises.

In 2003 the KRC considered and directly implemented its first information and communications technology initiative through a pilot project, the Bwera Information Centre in Kasese District. Supporting the establishment of Rural Information Centres opens space to provide development-oriented information services to local communities in an appropriate and sustainable manner. The local community is involved not only in receiving but also in contributing information, and, just as important, it must raise the resources to make the center socially and financially sustaining. The particular information services available from Rural Information Centres depend on the farmers and the particular rural context.

The centers are legal bodies owned and managed by civil society organizations within the threshold of a political county. Representatives from civil society organizations make up the executive body with management functions; the daily running of a center is done by the caretakers, who should be knowledgeable and can be trained to deliver services.

LESSONS LEARNED, PROSPECTS FOR THE FUTURE, AND ISSUES FOR WIDER APPLICABILITY

This section sums up what can be gained from the experience of this project.

Lessons learned

The experience of the KRC has shown that people in rural communities, given appropriate support and methodologies, can develop their own financial institutions. Over time this self-managed model will be more cost effective in the context in which KRC operates than many other models, because it does not require high levels of expenditure on fuel and transport, as would be the case in programs that use credit officers. The KRC experience shows the value of mainstreaming gender in "mainstream" training efforts such as sustainable agriculture training. It also demonstrates the feasibility of setting up strong participatory learning processes to complement financial services. It points to ways in which rural finance can help strengthen civil society through the institutions it sets up—especially if rural finance is part of and linked to a wider development strategy.

Prospects for the future

The KRC is now at the point of spinning off some of the MFAs as financially sustainable and independent entities, networked with the other MFAs. It is also ready to scale up the PALS process and the Rural Information Centres.

Issues for wider applicability

The KRC model is especially viable in more remote and poor rural areas where community cohesion is sufficiently strong. It requires sufficient funding to set up the MFAs and develop the grassroots training structures, as well as patience to let them develop on a confident and participatory basis. Once this is done, however, the model promises to be more cost efficient as well as developmentally effective than other models in similar contexts.

NOTES

Overview

This Overview was written by Linda Mayoux (Consultant), and reviewed by Catherine Ragasa (Consultant); Jennifer Heney (FAO); Maria Hartl (IFAD); and Henry Bagazonzya, Renate Kloeppinger-Todd, Rekha Mehra, Meena Munshi, Ajai Nair, and Anne Ritchie (World Bank).

1. For an account of what is meant by inclusive finance, see United Nations (2006).

2. See www.grameen-info.org and www.villagebanking.org.

3. See also R. Arunachalam, "Microfinance and Innovative Financing for Gender Equality: Approaches, Challenges and Strengths," www.thecommonwealth.org; L. Mayoux, "Not Only Reaching, but Also Empowering Women: Ways Forward for the Microcredit Summit's Second Goal," paper presented at the 2006 Microcredit Summit, Halifax, Canada, www.genfinance.info.

4. M. Hussein and S. Hussain, "The Impact of Micro Finance on Poverty and Gender Equity: Approaches and Evidence from Pakistan," www.genfinance.info.

5. S. Cheston, "Just the Facts, Ma'am: Gender Stories from Unexpected Sources with Morals for Micro-finance," paper presented at the 2006 Microcredit Summit, Halifax, Canada, www.microcreditsummit.org.

6. During field research in Malawi for a World Bank study on social outcomes of rural finance, it became obvious that the number of women borrowers was vastly understated, because only single women had loans in their own right. All other loans granted to families and households were automatically in the name of the man "head of household." Officially, only 15 percent of borrowers were women, whereas household surveys indicated that for many of the loans issued to men, women still decided how the loan was to be used.

Thematic Note I

This Thematic Note was written by Linda Mayoux (Consultant) and reviewed by Catherine Ragasa (Consultant); Jennifer Heney (FAO); Maria Hartl (IFAD); and Henry Bagazonzya, Renate Kloeppinger-Todd, Rekha Mehra, Meena Munshi, Ajai Nair, and Anne Ritchie (World Bank).

1. Informal systems for pooling savings and relending to members in turn as a lump sum of credit (the rotating savings systems) or relending to savers (accumulated savings systems) vary in the size of their membership and amounts of money involved. Credit allocation may be by agreement, lottery, or auction. For details of women's use of ROSCAs in different cultures, see Ardner and Burman (1995).

2. See note 4 above.

3. For example, the wording can treat women as individuals who can make their own decisions, eliminating references to—and automatic, often erroneous assumptions about—men heads of households. Some microfinance institutions that require husbands' signatures for their wives' loans also require wives' signatures for their husbands' loans. Others do not require a spouse's signature for any loan and accept women as well as men guarantors.

4. Effective gender audits applicable across the range of rural finance providers are still to be developed, but sources that could be adapted can be accessed through www.genfinance.info.

5. Both these issues are discussed in more detail in a forthcoming IFAD report.

6. For example, these goals have been achieved for the environment and for cultural diversity in the advertising that HSBC Bank uses to convey its international image.

7. See Mayoux, note 4 above.

8. Banks and MFIs will never focus solely on the very poor. What they can do, alongside their other core business, is to develop products for these groups and develop partnerships with NGOs working with these groups. In this way, over the longer term as very poor people move up, they do not encounter barriers to further upward mobility.

Thematic Note 2

This Thematic Note was written by Linda Mayoux (Consultant) and reviewed by Catherine Ragasa (Consultant); Jennifer Heney (FAO); Maria Hartl (IFAD); and Henry Bagazonzya, Renate Kloeppinger-Todd, Rekha Mehra, Meena Munshi, Ajai Nair, and Anne Ritchie (World Bank).

1. For further general discussion on leasing, see Nair and Kloeppinger-Todd (2006); Nair, Kloeppinger-Todd, and Mulder (2004).

2. This was the case with MFIs and where NGOs were legally permitted to collect savings.

3. See also L. Mayoux, "Microfinance and the Empowerment of Women—A Review of the Key Issues," www.ilo.org.

4. List based on L. Mayoux, "Sustainable Microfinance for Women's Empowerment: Report from International Mutual Learning Workshop, Centre for Micro-Finance Research," www.genfinance.info.

5. See www.codecbd.org.

6. See note 20 above.

7. For the most recent information, see the MicroFinance Gateway (www.microfinancegateway.org) and International Labour Organization (www.ilo.org). For a compendium of case studies, see Churchill (2006).

8. See note 21 above.

9. A billion is 1,000 million.

10. C. Ramìrez, M. Garcìa Domìnguez, and J. Mìguez Morais, "Crossing Borders: Remittances, Gender, and Development" (Santo Domingo: United Nations International Research and Training Institute for the Advancement of Women, 2005), www.un-instraw.org.

11. For details of the original tools, see www.microsave.org. For gender adaptations, see L. Mayoux, "Gender Questions for Product Market Research," www.genfinance.info/MktResPALS/Gender%20Sensitive%20Product%20Market%20Research.pdf.

12. See particularly the SEEP Network's "Consumer Protection Principles in Practice: A Framework for Developing and Implementing a Pro-Client Approach to Microfinance," SEEP Progress Note 14, www.seepnetwork.org, and an overview of the October 2006 discussion on MicroLinks (www.microlinks.org).

13. For details on Womenkind Worldwide, see www.womankind.org; for Siembra, see www.siembra.org.

14. For details, see Freedom from Hunger, www.ffhtechnical.org; Accìon International, see www.microfinancegateway.org.

Innovative Activity Profile 1

This Innovative Activity Profile was written by Shweta Banerjee, Sitaramachandra Machiraju, and Parmesh Shah (World Bank); and reviewed by Catherine Ragasa (Consultant); Jennifer Heney (FAO); and Renate Kloeppinger-Todd and Anne Ritchie (World Bank).

1. The National Bank for Agriculture and Rural Development (NABARD) is an apex development bank that introduced the Self-Help Group Bank Linkage Program in India.

Innovative Activity Profile 2

This Innovative Activity Profile was written by Linda Mayoux (Consultant) and reviewed by Catherine Ragasa (Consultant); Jennifer Heney and Yianna Lambrou (FAO); Maria Hartl (IFAD); and Renate Kloeppinger-Todd, Eija Pehu, and Anne Ritchie (World Bank).

1. For details of PALS, see www.palsnetwork.info.

REFERENCES

Overview

Anderson-Saito, Katrine, Arunima Dhar, and Eija Pehu. 2004. "GENRD Operational Notes for Task Managers to Integrate Gender into Rural Projects." Operational Note 4, Gender and Rural Finance, World Bank, Washington, DC.

Burjorjee, Deena M., Rani Deshpande, and C. Jean Weidemann. 2002. *Supporting Women's Livelihoods: Microfinance That Works for the Majority.* New York: United Nations Capital Development Fund.

Cheston, Susy, and Lisa Kuhn. 2002. "Empowering Women through Microfinance." In *Pathways Out of Poverty: Innovations in Microfinance for the Poorest Families,* ed. S. Daley-Harris, 167–228. Bloomfield: Kumarian Press.

Fries, Robert, and Banu Akin. 2004. *Value Chains and Their Significance for Addressing the Rural Finance Challenge.* Washington, DC: United States Agency for International Development, Accelerated Microenterprise Advancement Project.

Hollinger, Frank. 2004. *Financing Agricultural Term Investments.* Rome: Food and Agriculture Organization.

Kabeer, Naila. 2001. "Conflicts over Credit: Re-evaluating the Empowerment Potential of Loans to Women in Rural Bangladesh." *World Development* 29: 63–84.

Kloeppinger-Todd, Renate. 2007. "Financing Small-Scale Irrigation (SSI), Water and Sanitation." Presentation for the Water Week on Water Futures: Sustainability and Growth, March. World Bank, Washington, DC.

Mayoux, Linda. 1999. "Questioning Virtuous Spirals: Micro-Finance and Women's Empowerment in Africa." *Journal of International Development* 11: 957–84.

———. 2008. *Reaching and Empowering Women: Gender Mainstreaming in Microfinance.* Rome: International Fund for Agricultural Development.

Rose, K. 1992. *Where Women Are Leaders: The SEWA Movement in India.* London: Zed Press.

United Nations. 2006. *Building Inclusive Financial Sectors for Development.* New York: United Nations.

World Bank. 2006. *Gender Equality as Smart Economics: A World Bank Group Gender Action Plan (Fiscal Years 2007–2010).* Washington, DC: World Bank.

———. 2007a. "Module 8: Investments in Rural Finance for Agriculture." In *Agricultural Investment Sourcebook.* Washington, DC: World Bank.

———. 2007b. *Gender and Economic Growth in Kenya: Unleashing the Power of Women.* Directions in Development. Washington, DC: World Bank.

Thematic Note 1

Ardener, Shirley, and Sandra Burman, eds. 1995. *Money-Go-Rounds: The Importance of Rotating Savings and Credit Associations for Women.* Washington, DC: Berg.

Ritchie, Anne. 2007. "Community-Based Financial Organizations: A Solution to Access in Remote Rural Areas." Agriculture and Rural Development Discussion Paper 34, World Bank, Washington, DC.

Rutherford, Stuart. 1999. *The Poor and Their Money.* Manchester: Institute for Development Policy Management.

Thematic Note 2

Allen, Hugh. 2005. "CARE's Village-Based Savings and Credit Programme: Successful Financial Intermediation in Rural Africa." HA Consulting.

Brown, Warren. 2001. "Microinsurance—The Risks, Perils and Opportunities." *Small Enterprise Development* 12 (1): 11–24.

Churchill, Craig, ed. 2006. *Protecting the Poor: A Microinsurance Compendium.* Geneva: International Labour Organisation.

Dowla, Asif, and Dipal Chandra Barua. 2006. *The Poor Always Pay Back: The Grameen II Story.* Bloomfield: Kumarian Press.

———. 2008. "From Access to Empowerment: Gender Mainstreaming in Microfinance." International Fund for Agricultural Development, Rome.

Murray, Jessica, and Richard Rosenberg. 2006. "Community-Managed Loan Funds: Which Ones Work?" Consultative Group to Assist the Poorest, Washington, DC.

Nair, Ajai, and Renate Kloeppinger-Todd. 2006. "Buffalo, Bakeries, and Tractors: Cases in Rural Leasing from Pakistan, Uganda, and Mexico." Agriculture and Rural Development Discussion Paper 28, World Bank, Washington, DC.

Nair, Ajai, Renate Kloeppinger-Todd, and Annabel Mulder. 2004. "Leasing: An Underutilized Tool in Rural Finance." Agriculture and Rural Development Discussion Paper 7, World Bank, Washington, DC.

Otero, Maria, and Elizabeth Rhyne, eds. 1994. *The New World of Microenterprise Finance: Building Healthy Financial Institutions for the Poor.* London: IT Publications.

Ritchie, Anne. 2007. "Community-Based Financial Organizations: A Solution to Access in Remote Rural Areas." Agriculture and Rural Development Discussion Paper 34, World Bank, Washington, DC.

Rutherford, Stuart. 1999. *The Poor and Their Money.* Manchester: Institute for Development Policy Management.

Woller, Gary. 2002. "From Market Failure to Marketing Failure: Market Orientation as the Key to Deep Outreach in Microfinance." *Journal of International Development* 14: 305–24.

World Bank. 2003. "Rural Financial Services: Implementing the Bank's Strategy to Reach the Rural Poor." ARD Report No. 26030, World Bank, Washington, DC.

FURTHER READING

Overview

Lacoste, Jean-Paul. 2002. "Livelihood Strategies of Poor Women in Zimbabwe." Ph.D. thesis, University of Geneva, Switzerland.

Mayoux, Linda, and G. Mackie. 2008. "Making Stronger Links: A Practical Guide to Mainstreaming Gender in Value Chain Development." International Labour Organization, Addis Ababa, Ethiopia.

Wenner, Mark, Sergio Navajas, Carolina Trivelli, and Alvaro Tarazona. 2007. *Managing Credit Risk in Rural Financial Institutions in Latin America.* Washington, DC: Inter-American Development Bank.

Thematic Note 1

Arunachalam, Ramesh. 2007. "Microfinance and Innovative Financing for Gender Equality: Approaches, Challenges and Strengths." Available at www.thecommonwealth.org.

Otero, Maria, and Elizabeth Rhyne, eds. 1994. *The New World of Microenterprise Finance: Building Healthy Financial Institutions for the Poor.* London: IT Publications.

Rose, Kalima. 1992. *Where Women Are Leaders: The SEWA Movement in India.* London: Zed Press.

Innovative Activity Profile 2

Kasente, Deborah, and Gerry Hofstede. 2005. "KRC Microfinance Program: Gender Sensitivity Study." Available at www.krc.or.ug.

Mayoux, Linda. 2005. "Evaluation of KRC Microfinance Program for Hivos and Rabobank." Available at www.krc.or.ug.

For more information about KRC, see www.krc.or.ug.

For more information about PALS, a copy of the original draft manual for KRC can be obtained from www.lindaswebs.org.uk or from Linda Mayoux at l.mayoux@ntlworld.com. For more about PALS diagrams, see L. Mayoux, "Thinking It Through: Using Diagrams," paper produced for the EDIAIS Web site, available at www.enterprise-impact.org.uk.

Gender Issues in Land Policy and Administration

Overview

Over the last few decades, many donor and implementing agencies, including the World Bank,[1] International Fund for Agricultural Development (IFAD),[2] and Food and Agriculture Organization (FAO),[3] have expanded their programs and activities in land policy and administration. Land policy and administration projects can contribute inadvertently not only to gender inequality but also to more general social inequality by supporting individuals who are already advantaged by wealth, power, or custom to the disadvantage of those who are poor and vulnerable. Gender inequity can be diminished when women's rights are explicitly taken into account and when women participate in designing and implementing land policy and programs. In many cases increased gender equality can also lead to increased economic equality (Meinzen-Dick and others 1997).

The World Bank, IFAD, and FAO have increasingly recognized the importance of women's land rights and the failure of land administration programs to protect them. In its recent Policy Research Report on land (Deininger 2003), the World Bank recognizes that past initiatives often failed to discern how control of assets, particularly land, is assigned within the household. The Policy Research Report argues that strengthening women's land rights is important both for potential and gains to agricultural productivity and for household-level human capital investments, such as nutrition and child schooling. It advocates legal measures, education, and capacity building, as well as preferential treatment of women in public programs, such as those dedicated to land titling and land reform. Upon request by United Nations member countries, FAO provides technical assistance for mainstreaming gender in agricultural policy and planning, usually by developing strategic policy documents in collaboration with ministries of agriculture and ministries responsible for gender issues. IFAD, as stated in its 2003–06 Plan of Action, aims to expand women's access to and control over fundamental assets (capital, land, knowledge, and technologies); strengthen women's agency, including their decision-making role in community affairs and representation in local institutions; and improve well-being and ease workloads by facilitating access to basic rural services and infrastructures.

IMPORTANCE OF GENDER IN LAND POLICY AND ADMINISTRATION

Gender is a basic determinant of social relations and rights in households and rural communities.[4] Together with class, ethnicity, and caste, gender determines to a great extent a person's opportunities, aspirations, standard of living, access to resources, status in the community, and self-perception. In addition, women's rights to resources influence their ability to produce and their behavior as producers.

In most developing countries, land is a critical asset, especially for the urban and rural poor. Land rights—whether customary or formal—act as a form of *economic access* to key markets, as well as a form of *social access* to nonmarket institutions, such as the household relations and community-level governance structures. In addition to economic and social access, rights to land also often confer rights to other local natural resources, such as trees, pasture, and water.

Depending on the norms governing intrahousehold decision making and income pooling, however, women may not fully participate in these benefits if they do not have independent or direct rights over household land. There is evidence that improvements in women's independent property rights have positive economic benefits. Comparative analysis of data from Honduras and Nicaragua, for example, suggests a positive correlation between women's land rights and their overall role in the household economy: women gain greater control over agricultural income, gain higher shares of business and labor market earnings, and more frequently receive credit (Katz and Chamorro 2003).

Land is a particularly critical resource for a woman in the event that she becomes a de facto household head as a result of migration by men, abandonment, divorce, or death. In both urban and rural settings, independent real property rights under these circumstances can mean the difference between having to depend on the natal or husband's family for support and forming a viable, self-reliant, women-headed household. Women's land rights within marriage may afford them greater claims on the disposition of assets upon divorce or death of their husband, as Fafchamps and Quisumbing (2002) found in rural Ethiopia. Moreover, for widows, control over land may be one of the few ways that elderly women can elicit economic support from their children, in the form of either labor contributions to agricultural production or cash and in-kind transfers. In the absence of other forms of social security, the elderly rural population relies heavily on intergenerational transfers for their livelihoods; children are more likely to contribute to their parents' well-being if the latter retain control over a key productive resource such as land (Deere and Leon 2001). As HIV and AIDS increase the number of women-headed households, a widow's ability to make a claim to her husband's land becomes more urgent.

Rights to land and natural resources increase a woman's bargaining power within the household, which results in increased allocation of household resources to children and women as well as increased household welfare (Katz and Chamorro 2003; Quisumbing and Maluccio 2003). Quisumbing and Maluccio also find a positive relationship between the amount of assets (including land) that a woman possesses at the time of marriage and the shares of household expenditures devoted to food, education, health care, and children's clothing. Women's rights to land and natural resources can impact women's empowerment as well, not only household welfare. Panda and Agarwal (2005) have indicated that women with property ownership are less vulnerable to domestic violence in some parts of India. However, careful program design, planning, and implementation are needed because possible responses to the empowerment process are domestic violence and community reprisal toward women who seek independent rights in many countries.

Land rights may also empower individuals to participate more effectively in their immediate communities and civil society at large. Facilitating women's greater participation in extra-household institutions diminishes men's dominance of community-level decision making and builds women's organizational skills, social networks, and social capital. Women with land rights are more likely to be active members of their communities, and, as a result, community institutions themselves are more likely to be responsive to women's needs.

GENDER EQUITY ISSUES AND LAND POLICY

The basic gender policy within the context of land administration should promote *secure access to land and other natural resources for women, independent of men relatives and independent of their civil status.* Such a policy stance is the basis for identifying and establishing instruments that eliminate, or at least decrease, gender bias with regard to natural resource tenure in land administration programs, including titling and registration, privatization, and natural resource management.

Two sets of legal framework and institutions govern access and ownership issues for community and private land: the formal and the customary systems.

Formal legal framework and institutions

Over the last few decades, many nations have reformed their constitutions and civil codes and have either incorporated gender-neutral language (favoring neither men nor women) or explicitly recognized women's rights and prohibited discrimination based on gender. Many nations have also modified land and property laws and regulations so as to guarantee women's equal property and inheritance rights.

Thus, most Latin American nations passed legal reforms during the 1980s and 1990s to remove discriminatory clauses in codes applying to family (marriage, divorce, and marital property) and inheritance.[5] They also modified land allocation laws and regulations (for example, for agrarian reform and land titling programs) to recognize and give women equal land rights explicitly. Similar movements to reform legislation occurred in Africa and Asia.

The formal institutions that establish and maintain land tenure systems (by establishing and enforcing rules for accessing, using, and controlling land) include the land registry, cadastre, titling agency, and land use agency.[6] These institutions provide information on legal norms and regulations regarding land rights and land use, as well as specific information on the holders of land rights. Institutions that issue titles and record transfers can play a particularly important role in securing women's rights to land; land stuuse agencies may become involved in natural resource management interventions.

However, passing formal legislation is usually not sufficient. Many laws recognize and protect women's rights to land (such as property and land ownership rights, equal inheritance rights for daughters and sons, and marital property rights for women), but enforcement of these laws is sporadic, and attempts by women to have the law enforced can be painfully difficult.

Reasons for this failure of enforcement include conflictive legislation, institutional weakness, and the pervasive influence of gender bias. It is not uncommon that although some laws may guarantee gender equality with regard to land rights (for example, a land law), other laws, such as family or personal laws, may be based on patriarchal norms and undermine or directly contradict the concept of equal land rights by not giving wives equal rights to marital property or daughters equal inheritance rights. On the other hand, if formal law is not culturally sensitive and does not build on local practices that are positive for women, the priority of gender equity may be ignored. Another frequent problem with land legislation and regulations is that rights and obligations may not be defined clearly.

Even where legislation is generally positive toward women's land rights, in many countries the state and its institutions, including the judiciary, exert only a weak presence beyond major urban areas. Institutional structures, capacities, internal coordination, and attitudes are also often weak. All too frequently, the state lacks, or is unwilling to commit, resources to advocating, promoting, enforcing, and protecting women's rights to land and property. In the absence of state institutions to enforce equal rights for women as well as other laws, such as land use laws, local customary norms and practices predominate.

Another difficulty with some gender-equal legislation can be traced directly to patriarchal values and attitudes that hinder the implementation of legislation and state programs in a gender-equitable manner. Most common is "gender-neutral" legislation and programs that, because they ignore the normative and practical constraints women face in obtaining land rights, are in fact biased against women. Land titling programs are a good example of this type of discrimination. Although land titling programs may have no gendered requirements, and national laws uphold gender equality, the "custom" of titling only household heads effectively discriminates against women and may actually deprive them of customary access and other rights.

Finally, even when legislation and state programs specifically address women's land rights and attempt to address constraints in programs, such as land reform and land titling, resistance from program implementers and participant populations can derail the "good intentions" of state programs, which results in token observance of women's legal land rights. Examples can be found in Bolivia (Giovarelli and others 2005) and Nicaragua (Lastarria-Cornhiel and others 2003), where, despite very positive and specific language in the land titling legislation regarding women's and men's equal land rights, the implementation of the titling program resulted in the great majority of the land being titled to men (see Thematic Note 4).

Customary norms and institutions related to land access and rights

As mentioned earlier, formal law and state institutions often have limited effectiveness beyond major urban areas. Because of the difficulties state institutions encounter when administering and managing land and other natural resources, awareness has grown that management of land and other natural resources, management of land conflicts, as well as administration of land rights may be realized more effectively by local authorities and customary institutions.[7] As a result, policy makers in some nations are formally recognizing and utilizing customary institutions and local authorities. Local authorities may be community-recognized authorities or formally appointed by government.[8] In sub-Saharan Africa, a growing number of countries explicitly recognize customary tenure systems and rules. In many Asian countries, personal or religious law, or both, is recognized and has been in effect for many years. These personal laws have a great impact on inheritance and marriage practices regarding land and property. Customary institutions have important implications for women's rights to land. Land administration programs, therefore, require a deep knowledge and clear understanding of customary tenure systems to know how they will both affect and be affected by cultural norms and practices.

Cultural or local prohibitions against women's ownership of land are often more powerful than written laws that allow women to own land. These norms may determine which rights to land a woman can exercise freely: for example, women may have the right to use a parcel of land or the right to gather fruit from it but not the right to bequeath it through inheritance, a right limited to their brothers and husbands. A woman's land-related rights are usually tied to her place in her ancestral family and her husband's family; here rights to land are viewed within the context of the distribution of wealth within the extended family. Legislative intervention alone cannot provide women with independent and effective land rights if they are not accepted and enforced culturally and socially.

Land rights in societies in which customary social structures and practices are predominant are generally determined by sociocultural and religious institutions, such as inheritance, marriage, and community land authorities. These customary tenure systems are diverse and encompass a large variety of social relations and rights related to land and other natural resources. In sub-Saharan Africa, for example, land ownership rights are often vested in a community or other corporate structure such as a lineage or clan. A significant proportion of the land is not controlled by individuals but rather by a group and managed according to community rules. Land allocated to individuals or households on a long-term basis tends to be parcels for producing food, building a home, or raising animals; rights to these parcels are generally inheritable. How this land is initially allocated to households depends on the local customary system. Most land parcels under individual or household control are transferred through inheritance, not the market.

Members of the community have different types of rights to land and natural resources depending on their lineage, ethnicity, status, gender, and marital status. In most societies, women, particularly married women, are not full and active participants in customary institutions. As secondary community members, their rights to land are generally derived from a man relative or husband. In many countries, cultural if not legal norms dictate that men are the owners of land and that women have access to land only through their relationship with a man relative, such as a father, husband, brother, or even brother-in-law.

Although customary tenure systems often do provide women with some basic security in situations when they are not living with a husband, this same system also favors men when control over land is determined (for example, through the allocation of community land for agricultural production or through inheritance practices). Because the men in the community usually control land allocation, they are able to claim individual rights when land scarcity converts the land into an asset and when family land becomes private property. In Kenya, for example, the subdivision of Maasai

group ranches caused widows to receive less-than-average parcel allocations, despite women's representation, in the statutory committee.[9] Women may not only lose the use rights to their husband's land but will also most likely be unable to claim temporary use rights to birth family land because their brothers will claim individual and private rights to the land they inherit from their fathers (see also Thematic Note 3).

Communities or lineages allocate land to their constituent families; that land, in turn, is allocated within the family and handed down to heirs through marriage and inheritance. These allocation and transfer practices are generally determined by kinship systems. Patrilineal kinship societies trace the family line through the paternal side, whereas matrilineal kinship systems trace the family line through the maternal side.

INHERITANCE PRACTICES. Inheritance practices are patrilineal, matrilineal, or bilateral. In patrilineal inheritance, land is generally handed down from father to son; if a man does not have any sons, his brother, nephew, or another man relative of his lineage often inherits his property. Daughters do not inherit land from their fathers, even though they are of the same lineage. The cultural norm is that daughters leave their birth community and family when they marry to live in their husband's community. Because wives are under the responsibility of their husband and family, it is believed that if they inherited land, their husband's family and lineage would obtain control over it.

Inheritance practices in matrilineal societies are more diverse. In matrilineal communities in South and Southeast Asia—for example, in some communities in Indiana (Agarwal 1988) and some in Malaysia (Stivens 1985)—lineage and landed property are traced through the mother's line, and land is passed on from mother to daughter. In other matrilineal communities, as in Malawi and Mozambique, although lineage and property are traced through the mother's line, normally only men can clear land, which gives them control over this resource. Once land is in the lineage, it is handed down to a young man from his maternal uncle. In other African matrilineal communities, such as those in Ghana, even though family land is usually handed down from uncle to nephew, a woman can also inherit and acquire land in her own right within her own matriliny (primarily) and her community (secondarily). A woman often inherits from a woman maternal relative (aunt, mother), although she can also inherit from her father. She retains this right even if she moves to another village (for example, if she goes to live with her husband's family).

In addition, rights to land and other resources in matrilineal communities are more diffuse.[10] Land and other wealth tend to be distributed and redistributed among lineage members through the mechanism of inheritance. This inheritance and wealth distribution pattern may be the result of the extended family nature of matrilineal societies. As the market economy exerts its influence by making production practices more labor intensive and market oriented, there is a tendency for matrilineal families to become less extended and more nuclear, for property rights to become less diffused and more concentrated, and for families to adopt patrilineal inheritance practices.

Bilateral inheritance practices, such as those found in Indonesia and the Lao People's Democratic Republic, tend to treat sons and daughters equally and sometimes to favor daughters who stay in the family home to care for elderly parents. A woman can count on inheriting part of the family assets whether or not she marries and even if she leaves her birth community. Societies with bilateral inheritance systems tend to be more gender equal with regard to land and power relations. In bilateral inheritance communities in Ecuador, for example, both wife and husband bring resources, including land, into the household, acquire resources together during marriage, and contribute their individual and joint resources to household productive and reproductive activities and goals on an equal basis. Because daughters and sons inherit land equally from their parents, women as well as men are able to enter into marriage, set up a household, and make decisions on an equal footing (Hamilton 1998).

Muslim inheritance norms are also bilateral, recognizing daughters' rights to family property (albeit a fraction of the share their brothers inherit). Where the customary tenure system is strongly patrilineal, however, Muslim norms may be ignored and strictly patrilineal inheritance practiced. In the Mossi communities of Burkina Faso, for example, although the majority of families are Muslim and in theory daughters inherit land, this practice is not observed. It would appear that the patrilineal Mossi practice of daughters not inheriting land prevails over Muslim norms. Only sons inherit land from their birth family, and daughters are given at most temporary use rights to their father's land if they leave their husband's home because of widowhood, divorce, or separation. Single daughters with children also have temporary use rights. Once women marry, their birth family relinquishes responsibility for them (Platteau and others 2000). A similar practice is found in Muslim communities in other African countries (such as Senegal) and in some countries of Eastern Europe and Central Asia (Albania, Macedonia, and Uzbekistan, for example).

MARRIAGE PRACTICES. Marriage practices in customary societies include marital residence (where the couple lives after marriage) and asset transfers (dowry and brideprice); both sets of practices determine how family land is allocated and who has rights to family land. In most patrilineal societies, residence after marriage is patrilocal (the couple and their children live in the husband's community), and family land is handed down from father to son. Women who marry into the community do not have rights to their husband's family land or community land. When a woman has the right to inherit from her birth family, the move to her husband's village reduces her ability to manage inherited land; this is one reason daughters give up their inheritance rights in favor of their brothers. Separated and divorced women leave their husband's house with no claim to any of his property. A widow, particularly if she has children, is generally permitted to stay on and work her dead husband's land until her sons can assume its management.

Customary tenure systems based on matrilineal kinship systems generally, although not always, practice matrilocal residency. A husband lives in the wife's village and is given land by her family to farm, but he has only use rights to this land. A new son-in-law is expected to pay what is often called brideservice, which normally consists of working for the bride's father, mother, or uncle for a period of time. After he has fulfilled his obligation, either a husband will stay in his wife's community—where the couple will set up their own household, and the wife's uncle or father may allocate a piece of land for the husband to cultivate[11]—or he may move back to his own matrilineal community, where he can acquire or inherit land from his matrilineage.

CURRENT TENDENCIES. As inherited family land becomes scarce, and communities are no longer able to allocate land to new households, couples are more apt to purchase land. Is this land considered jointly owned marital property? Customary societies have different practices with regard to property acquired during marriage. The exclusion of daughters and wives from rights to family or lineage land may be part of the belief that women are incapable of owning land. When land is acquired by a couple, therefore, the husband assumes sole ownership, excluding his wife from any ownership rights. This customary practice may also be applied to other noncustomary acquisition of land, such as state programs of agrarian reform and resettlements.

In those customary societies in which women and men both own land, joint ownership of marital property is more likely to be practiced. For example, in Java, where sons and daughters inherit family land, it is customary to regard land acquired during marriage as belonging to both husband and wife. If one spouse dies, half of the property remains with the surviving spouse while the other half is inherited by their children (Brown 2003).

In market economies, the question of gender equity within marital property has been a contentious issue because of prevailing patriarchal norms and values. In some market-based societies with legal systems based on common law, the recognition of both spouses' contribution to the acquisition of property during marriage has been difficult. In contrast, where legal tradition has recognized community property between spouses, the acceptance of marital property and coownership has had less opposition. Landed property acquired during marriage is generally regarded as marital property with both spouses having equal rights.

Sociocultural difficulties with women exercising land rights

Women's secondary status, lower socialization, undervalued productive work, and illiteracy in many communities often make them reluctant to claim legal rights and participate in those institutions and activities seen as men's domains.

In addition, women incur significant social costs for going against cultural norms; these costs include social ridicule and the possible loss of social benefits. In some cases a backlash of domestic violence occurs against women who claim their land rights. The extended patriarchal family generally provides a structure for the lifelong basic welfare of all family members and for assistance in times of social or economic crisis. This is particularly significant for resource-poor rural women with young children. As observed in Macedonia and Uzbekistan, daughters do not inherit any land, in spite of Muslim norms that entitle them to inherit some family land. Daughters concede their rights to brothers to avoid conflict and maintain support from the extended family. Wives and daughters may not insist on having their names included on the title to household land because of potential conflicts with husbands or their family. In Brazil, for example, few women are aware of whose name is on the land title and do not request that joint titles be issued. In Bolivia focus group discussions revealed that some men were titling land in their sons' names, stripping their daughters and wives of legal land rights (Giovarelli and others 2005). Moreover, even when women have rights under the law, such as inheritance rights, women may not claim the rights because of their preferences to have long-term social support from brothers and other family members rather than secure an asset that may not provide long-term economic security.

Women themselves may be reluctant to become publicly involved in political activities and community organizations for several reasons: inexperience in public speaking and participation, a lack of basic education and knowledge about how social and legal matters function, and domestic responsibilities that no one else will assume. Other more structural constraints include women's low literacy (including legal literacy), lack of skills in the dominant language, and lack of identity papers.

IMPLEMENTATION OF LAND ADMINISTRATION PROGRAMS

Customary norms frequently do not give equal ownership of land and other assets to women and are typically resistant to change these power equations. Legislation to address this exists in most countries, but there are several limitations to implementation, including conflicting legislation, inadequate regulatory and management systems, inadequacy of institutions to implement changes at the local level, staff and community antagonism to women's equal rights, and lack of will and resources to address gender bias. Women often do not possess the financial resources, knowledge, and capacity to go against social norms and may not exercise their legal rights. Formal land distribution and titling programs may also ignore the need for gender equity if it is not an explicit objective of the programs.

The attainment of gender equity with regard to land rights consequently depends not only on legal recognition of those rights but also on overcoming social and cultural constraints. Some useful instruments include regulations for implementing formal land, property, and family legislation in ways that address gender bias with regard to land access and land rights, legal education programs for women and men, legal assistance programs, gender training for program implementers and program beneficiaries, and, last (but most important), participation by women in designing, planning, and implementing programs. Customary biases often mean that women will not have the ability to exercise their land rights until there is a shift in the thinking, attitudes, and understanding of men and women as well as officials and local authorities (see Thematic Notes for more on specific project and program design).

Gender issues should be addressed at all phases of programs that deal with land rights and natural resource management: (1) conceptualization of the problem(s) that the program addresses, program design, and objectives; (2) implementation and program activities; and (3) monitoring and evaluation of project activities and objectives.

Although legislative reform programs, land distribution, or titling programs have a more direct impact on land ownership by women, other programs, such as community resource management, agricultural production and marketing development, and enterprise and credit development, need to use a specific gender lens to improve land ownership and access for women.

Program design and planning

It is crucial that gender analysis be incorporated (1) from the very beginning of program design, (2) in the conceptualization of the land administration issues, and (3) within the program's objectives. Otherwise, a risk exists that the different social relations determining rights to land and other natural resources will not be understood. Attempts to incorporate gender analysis once a program's design and objectives are in place often result in unproductively forcing gender issues into a framework that may not accommodate them. Throughout the process planners should examine whether women or particular groups of women are being included or excluded from the program and why. Are women excluded because of the expense and time involved in including them? Does the program target mainly men because it is simpler to deal only with heads of households? Or are men predominantly targeted because local power structures make it more difficult to approach and include women? Assumptions need to be examined and questioned: is it assumed that the household head speaks for household members and is knowledgeable about all individuals' activities and resources and that resources and benefits are equitably distributed to household members through the household head?

Given information and attitude biases and the sociocultural and time constraints faced by women, concerted efforts and imagination need to be employed in obtaining women's points of view and thoughts on their needs and in integrating them into objectives.

Much of this information, and participatory methods for acquiring it, should be incorporated into the social assessment undertaken during the design phase. Legislation and customary norms surrounding land ownership and use are usually very complex and location specific. The social assessment for any land-related project, in addition to reviewing literature on local land tenure systems, should include community-level interviews of men and women key informants as well as focus groups of potential men and women beneficiaries with respect to land tenure norms and practices. Detailed information regarding variations in, for example, multiple land-use rights, inheritance, and marital property can then be a valuable input to meeting the objective of strengthening women's land rights within the target area's sociocultural context.

Several types of training and for several populations will be critical elements in the success of gender-equity interventions—to increase the awareness and sensitivity of beneficiary populations, program staff, and land administration institution staff; to change social attitudes; to increase the participation of women in the system (in relevant institutions and support organizations); to increase the participation of women as beneficiaries; and to provide tools for implementing the interventions. Both women and men should always be included in training to prevent gender issues from being marginalized to women staff and beneficiaries.

Cambodia's land titling project provides an example of successful information campaigns that include gender issues at the local level. The educational activity includes both men and women and is careful to ensure that illiterate women are provided with appropriate information. All related materials are posted in a public place in the villages, literature on land rights and titling procedures is provided in pictorial form, meetings are held in local schools or community centers, and titles are issued locally. Involvement of both men and women field staff helps emphasize gender inclusiveness.

Apart from training of staff and beneficiaries, land administration projects would also benefit from social audit by independent NGOs so that program designers and implementers are held accountable for delivering the promised outcomes. A social audit is particularly for land distribution programs and could even be part of outside monitoring and evaluation.

Program implementation

Once the implementation of major land policies or legislation begins, the objective of including women's participation in land programs should remain a priority. Programs can reduce many of the procedural barriers women face by making program activities and benefits available at the lowest possible level and by training staff at all levels to be conscious of the obstacles women face. The increased presence of women within the system—within the relevant government institutions and boards and among project staff and support institutions (such as advocacy groups)—will go a long way in increasing access for women beneficiaries.

In addition, activities that specifically target women must be integrated into implementation. For example:

- If the project deals with improved access to land and natural resources, such as land distribution or leaseholds, do project activities *explicitly* seek out and include women as beneficiaries, whether as individuals or as a group?
- If the project deals with resource conservation or resource management, are women specifically consulted about which communal resources need to be protected and how?
- Are women targeted to participate in natural resource project activities, such as reforestation and agroforestry?
- If the project seeks to increase agricultural production, do women have secure access to land and other productive resources, participate in factor and product markets, and have access to technological assistance and credit programs?
- Are projects such as technology transfer courses and credit programs organized so that women who have access to land but may not own it are able to participate?
- If producer or other associations (such as cooperatives) are to be established, are women who may have indirect tenure rights allowed and encouraged to join?
- Is the option of women-oriented activities—such as women's cooperatives, women's credit programs, or women agricultural extension agents—considered?

At the local project level, a potential impediment to women's participation as beneficiaries is men's resistance to policies and activities that directly benefit women. This resistance is based not only on the fact that men may want the benefits of these projects for themselves and often take them over, but also because participation in the project may give women a greater sense of independence. Thus, in addition to foreseeing and avoiding differential project impacts based on gender, constraints that flow from gender norms and practices also need to be considered.

Monitoring and evaluation

The collection of appropriate gender-disaggregated data is a concern for all land administration projects and should be a priority, given the sizable investments in the land sector. Reviews of land programs and projects reveal that very little information and data are systematically collected to clarify the effects on women and their land rights. Many land titling programs, for example, do not even track the number of titles issued to men, to women, and jointly to husband and wife. The knowledge required includes information on how land rights are distributed between different groups of women and men, and what effects differentiated land rights have on gender equity and on women's capabilities. Planners should collect information such as (1) when a land administration project is being prepared, to guide project design and establish a baseline for further evaluation of program objectives; (2) when the project is implemented, to assess whether gender objectives are being attained; and (3) when the project is completed, to assess impacts. The best method to gather these data is to collect gender-relevant and gender-disaggregated data in the baseline, follow-up, and impact evaluation studies.

Detailed information gathered during project preparation regarding variations in, for example, multiple land use rights, inheritance, and marital property can be a valuable input for developing gender-specific indicators to measure the program's differential impact on men's and women's rights to land, natural resources, and other community resources.

Once a land administration program is under implementation, it is appropriate to collect gender-disaggregated information at the household level. This information can serve the dual purposes of consultation for eventual adjudication and establishing baseline data for project monitoring and evaluation. As resources allow, the baseline survey should be administered in areas targeted for intervention, as well as in similar areas not targeted.

At the project level, information on project participation and benefits should be disaggregated by gender, including such things as personnel statistics and attendance at public information and training sessions, as well as participation in other activities and events that will benefit participants. At the community level, key informant interviews and beneficiary focus groups along the lines of those recommended for the social assessment can provide qualitative feedback to project managers about the perception of project impact and men and women beneficiary satisfaction.

Finally, land projects should administer at least one midterm and one project completion household sample survey to be able to track gender-specific changes against the baseline data. If designed properly and if sufficient time has passed to permit change, such information can allow the quantitative assessment of the impact of land policy reform and land administration projects on women's economic opportunities, women's empowerment, and intrahousehold bargaining power (see also Module 16).[12] Some examples of indicators are provided in Table 4.1.

Depending on the country or region, it may be relevant to also consider ethnicity and caste alongside gender (both

Table 4.1 Monitoring and Evaluation Indicators for Gendered Access to Land and Property, Including Legal Rights and Land Dispute Resolution

Indicator	Sources of verification and tools
Percentage of women and men actively participating in land-allocation committees	• Committee meeting minutes • Interviews with stakeholders • Program or project records
Percentage of women and men actively participating in natural resource management committees	• Committee meeting minutes • Interviews with stakeholders • Local traditional authorities (such as a chief or local council) • Program or project records
Over a set period, an increase of x percent in incomes from land-based activities (such as agriculture or forestry) among women-headed and man-headed households in program areas	• Household surveys • Socioeconomic data from statistics office
Changes over x-year period of project activities in household nutrition, health, education, vulnerability to violence, and happiness, disaggregated by gender	• Household surveys, before and after • Project management information system • School records
Among surveyed women and men in target group, x percent rate their access to land, and land titling and dispute resolution procedures, as having improved during the period covered by the program or project	• Interviews with women in target groups (for instance, a sample of women in the defined area); ideally the interviews should be conducted before and after any project or program activities
Number of women with joint titles to land (either measured before and after the intervention or measured as a proportion of the total number of land titles issued over a set period)	• Land registration department records
Number of women with individual titles to land (either measured before and after the intervention or measured as a proportion of the total number of land titles issued over a set period)	• Land registration department records
Number of training sessions provided to relevant authorities for gender-sensitive land mapping and titling and for dispute resolution processes	• Land registration authority records • Project or program records
Number of women and men receiving legal literacy training	• Program or project records • Training records
Change in number of cases of women accessing legal advice regarding land claims (measured over a set period before the project intervention and compared with a set period after the project intervention)	• Legal authority records • Records of paralegals
Number and percentage of total of disputes resolved in favor of women's and men's land rights over a set period	• Interviews with stakeholders • Land registration department records • Legal Office • Local traditional authorities (such as a chief or local council)
Changes in legal norms regarding access and control of land with regard to gender over a set period	• Land registration department records • Legal Office: statistics and interviews with key informants • Local traditional authorities (such as a chief or local council)
Change in knowledge in sample group (the general community, land titling and administration staff, or legal tribunal staff) regarding women's and men's land rights and land titling and dispute resolution procedures	• Group interviews or focus groups • Interviews, before and after
Community satisfaction (disaggregated by gender and poverty ranking) with changes in land access, titling, and dispute procedures	• Group interviews or focus groups • Interviews, before and after

Source: Authors, with input from Pamela White, author of Module 16.

as comparative indicators and when collecting data), because women of lower castes or ethnic minorities are usually in the most disadvantaged situation.

NEW AND EMERGING DIRECTIONS

Based on past experiences, program evaluations, and new and modified priorities, land policy and land administration programs are attempting to focus on social equity as well as economic growth. Participation by communities, local stakeholders, ethnic minorities, and women, although not yet generally the norm, is being discussed among policy makers and program officials, and attempts to articulate policy and implement programs with such objectives are being made. Several new mechanisms to increase local participation and social equity include community-based natural resource management, joint titling, and community titling.

Participatory natural resource management (or community-based NRM) has emerged out of decentralization programs as well as efforts to increase local participation. Community-based NRM can be, and should be, a good vehicle for participation by women, who are major users and knowledgeable caretakers of natural resources.

To prevent "elite capture" of community programs by local influential persons, such programs must consciously and continuously focus on the less powerful groups, such as women, so that their interests are not ignored. For these groups to participate *actively* and *effectively*, programs should be designed to (1) include women in program activities and committees and (2) target women for gender training and education. Women should be explicitly and consciously included in the community and program activities surrounding program implementation. In this way women appropriate the program as meaningful to their lives and may be able to counteract the patriarchal and gender-biased practices that exclude them from decision-making activities. This type of local appropriation also ensures that land-related programs continue despite changes in government. In terms of monitoring and evaluation, it is important to tracking community and household dynamics, particularly conflict, because this may be an important early warning sign of potential failure of the program. Asset distribution impacts directly the power balance between classes, groups, households, and household members, and early signs or indicators would be essential to ensure that project benefits are not cornered by an elite section of the beneficiaries (see Table 4.1).

Titling programs have recently taken up the mechanism of joint titles for spouses in an effort to increase the number of women with legal land rights. When a titling program has the proper procedures and the political will to implement joint titling, the number of women holding title does increase (Giovarelli and others 2005). Joint ownership by married couples, however, is applicable only to land and property acquired by couples during marriage, such as purchased land or land acquired from the state. Many potential complexities influence whether individual or joint titling is most likely to improve and protect married women's rights to land. Where women are unlikely to acquire land on their own through inheritance or purchase, and where norms do not include marital property, the allocation of state land (under land reform or resettlement programs, for example) should include mandatory joint titling. Consideration of local inheritance and marriage institutions, agricultural production practices, and the participation of women in the design and planning of land programs will help sort out these complexities.

Community titling is a process to legalize rights to land (and other natural resources) that belongs to a community and to which community members have access rights. Community titling is often implemented where there is the risk that influential persons, corporations, or other communities may claim that land as their own. This process is innovative in that the state legally and formally recognizes a group's (a community's) communal rights to land. The boundary of the community land is defined, the community is assigned the title to that land, and the title is registered in the registration system. Parcels within the community, such as those held by individuals and families, are not generally surveyed and registered. Examples of community titling can be found in Bolivia and Mozambique. Very real concerns exist, however, that women's rights to land and other resources may not be recognized. Program officials and local authorities need to take steps to involve women fully in the community titling process.

In concluding this Overview, it is important to bring up two difficult issues—difficult because of their complexity and because they are rooted in the local context. First, when is titling of individual land parcels appropriate? At what point is a customary tenure system no longer able to allocate and administer rights to land and other natural resources fairly and efficiently? When does the legal formalization of land rights become the appropriate mechanism for improving access, and what might be lost in the process? These interrelated questions need to be approached not only from economic and legal viewpoints, but also from social and cultural viewpoints. Thematic Note 4 addresses the issue of women's rights to land within land titling programs more fully.

The second issue is related to women's rights within customary tenure systems. What can be done to improve women's access to land and to secure those rights in societies, such as patrilineal communities, that systematically deny wives and daughters property rights? Gender relations in general and land rights in particular need to be addressed simultaneously. Some mechanisms for addressing them together include campaigning for changes in customary practices through education and advocacy programs and introducing formal legislation that provides wives and daughters with rights to land that the established system does not give. An effective program will very much depend on the local context and on full participation of the local population, both women and men.

Gendered Access to Land and Property

Land tenure systems consist of the social relations that are established around natural resources, particularly land, water, and trees; they determine who can use what resources and how they are to be used. Gender, together with class, ethnicity, and caste, is one of the most important determinants of land rights in households and rural communities, including land tenure relations. It is useful to distinguish between different tenure rights, particularly between *control of* and *use of* land and other natural resources. Control of land and resources is the command an individual or group has over them and over the benefits derived from them.[1] Use rights allow a person to use land or resources for particular activities. Use rights may include some decision-making power over the production process and use of the resource but do not necessarily include enjoying the full benefits derived from the resource. Those who *control* access to land also tend to control and benefit from the labor of those who use the land.

Programs that seek to improve access to land vary from programs recognizing communal land tenure systems (with both individual and common property) to those seeking to formalize land rights into freehold ownership rights. Given these varied options, an important initial question to ask when considering land access programs is: when is legal formalization the appropriate mechanism for improving access, and what might be lost in the process?

KEY GENDER ISSUES

Women and men have three general mechanisms for obtaining rights to land: (1) through social and kinship relations at the local level, (2) on the land market, or (3) from the state. These mechanisms are embedded in institutions that create, modify, and influence land tenure systems: sociocultural institutions, state institutions, and market economy. An examination of how they influence land tenure systems is useful in understanding gendered rights to land and in proposing and implementing gender-sensitive policies and programs. Depending on a country's historical development and current socioeconomic and political conjuncture, one set of institutions is generally more important than the others in determining land rights. All three sets of institutions, however, influence and interact with each other in determining the specific tenure relations of a society. In all of these institutions, it is important to understand the gender differences in land uses and priorities, what rights men and women claim, and women's needs.

Sociocultural institutions

In societies in which customary practices and traditional social structures are predominant, rights to most land are generally determined by sociocultural and religious institutions such as inheritance, marriage, and community allocation. These customary tenure systems are diverse, with a large variety of property relations and rights. Particularly in places where land is relatively abundant, as in some areas of sub-Saharan Africa, primary land ownership rights are often vested in the community or other corporate structure such as a lineage or clan. Community authorities allocate some of this communal land to individuals and their families (generally for cultivation with long-term rights), and other land and resources are held as common property. A significant proportion of the land and the natural resources may be common land, controlled not by individuals but by the group and managed according to community rules.[2] In regions where land is quite scarce, such as Southeast Asia, very little arable land is available for allocation by community authorities; most community land is held by individuals and families.

The community determines access to communal land, forests, pastures, and water sources; generally, the basic criterion is membership in the community. Besides family or lineage considerations, gender is another membership element. Access rights to common land and its natural resources tend to be more broadly distributed throughout the community. Land-poor households make much use of resources found on common lands: for example, they may gather firewood and collect water, gather forest products, collect fodder for animals, or graze their animals. Because women in many societies depend on their husbands or a man relative for access to household land, access to common land and resources is particularly important to them.

Land allocated to individuals on a long-term basis tends to be parcels for producing food, building a home, or raising animals; rights to these parcels are generally inheritable. How this land is allocated initially to households depends on the particular customary system. In spite of individual control over these parcels, however, in many societies the community retains some rights, such as the right to gather firewood and water, or gleaning rights to gather grain or pasture animals after the harvest. These rights are important for women.

Land parcels under individual or household control are generally transferred though inheritance, not the market. With few exceptions, it is men who inherit land. For example, in The Gambia, Mandinka women, like most women in sub-Saharan Africa, do not inherit land, nor are they generally able to receive land allocations from community authorities. When a woman marries, her husband gives her cultivation rights to a plot of land; she cultivates the land to provide food and other goods for herself, her children, and husband, but she does not have other property rights to it, such as the right to pass it on to heirs. In addition, she is obligated to work her husband's crops in exchange for these cultivation rights.

Customary tenure norms provide women with some basic security in situations when they are not living with a husband, but the reality is that many customary tenure systems are no longer capable of ensuring that households and women have access to sufficient land and other resources. A number of factors, including a growing market economy, increasing poverty, and commercial agriculture, are converting land into an asset, accentuating land scarcity, and privatizing (and individualizing) land rights. Within these situations, vulnerable women such as widows and divorced, separated, or abandoned women are unable to access land. When family or lineage land becomes privatized as a result of market economy development or state action (such as titling), opportunities arise for land policy and programs to promote women's equal ownership rights. Unfortunately, privatization has often led to women losing any rights they may have had.

Allocations from the state

The state, through various agencies, allocates land to its citizens through redistributive land reform programs, resettlement programs, leasehold arrangements, market-driven land reform, land privatization programs, and antipoverty programs. These rights can range from use rights to leasehold to private individual ownership rights. Even where the legal norms for these programs do not explicitly discriminate against women, traditional norms and attitudes of program officials and participating populations work against considering women as equal participants and as property holders. For example, access and use rights to state forests are very important for women for gathering firewood, fodder, water, food, and medicinal plants. State officials, however, vary enormously in how they treat women and men. In some areas, women are harassed or denied entry. On the other hand, in the Mabiru forest in Uganda, forestry officials work with women's craft groups to identify forest products that can be sustainably harvested.

Redistributive land reform has been carried out across the globe and, recently, particularly in Latin America and Asia. The distribution of land in most cases has directly benefited men household heads by adjudicating land to them and ignoring wives and, in some cases, even single women household heads.[3] Recently, some land reform programs have attempted to integrate gender equity into their efforts. In India, for example, some states (Madhya Pradesh and West Bengal) have made concerted efforts to allocate land to women (Brown, Ananthpur, and Giovarelli 2002). In Brazil the land reform agency in August 2000 finally acknowledged the legal norm of joint property established in the 1988 constitution by announcing that it would include the names of both spouses on property documentation (Deere 2003). In South Africa, although national agrarian reform policy and offices articulate the importance of and need for gender equity, district and local level offices do not have the mechanisms and tools to implement this gender policy (Walker 2003).

The resettlement of communities and households often occurs as a result of land improvement programs such as land reclamation and water control projects (irrigation, flood control, and so forth). Land administration issues related to these projects include the allocation of previously noncultivated land or newly improved land to farming households and the conversion of customary rights to private individual rights as land is increasingly considered a productive asset. A frequently used mechanism for allocating or titling improved land is to revert such land to the state and subsequently allocate parcels to eligible farmers, either as leasehold or as private individual property (freehold). As land is improved and becomes more valuable, women may lose their traditional use rights to land. In addition, program officials and technicians generally focus their communications and beneficiary activities on men household heads.

Privatization involves changing land rights from collective or communal rights to private individual rights. In Eastern Europe mass privatization of state farms, collectives, and cooperative farms took place during the 1990s. In sub-Saharan Africa privatization of communal land has been and continues to be the result of both market forces and state efforts (such as tenure reform and land titling). As with other state programs, such as agrarian reform and resettlement, the practice has been to privatize land to men household heads. When Albania, for example, privatized and distributed collectively owned land, the state followed patriarchal norms and titled land intended for the family overwhelmingly to men household heads (Lastarria-Cornhiel and Wheeler 1998). The same pattern of granting land rights to men and ignoring women's rights can be found in state leasehold and market-assisted land reform programs.

Land market

Market economy institutions also play a significant role in allocating land rights. Market economies are generally based on private property rights and the marketability of these rights. Consequently, land rights are usually acquired through the market (for example, by buying, selling, and leasing) at market values.

Capital (either savings or access to credit) is required to purchase land on the market, and thus the ownership of assets is crucial. Women who wish to participate in the market, particularly those from landless and smallholder families, are unlikely to have such assets. If they engage in wage work, their earning power is generally insufficient to accumulate savings. The productive work they perform in their household is usually unremunerated. Men family members will most likely control the few assets that low-income households own. In addition, women often lack information on the land market, such as the availability of parcels for sale and land prices. For these reasons, women find it more difficult than men to participate in the land market and programs such as market-driven land reform.[4]

On the other hand, for those women who are able to acquire capital, the market is one mechanism for acquiring land that is generally not influenced by cultural bias or state policies. Land acquired by women on the market often escapes the restrictions and limitations placed on customary land by men-dominated family and lineages. In addition, a woman's daughters may inherit this land, because it is not considered family or lineage land.

Within the process of market formation, however, the increasing privatization of land rights generally has a negative effect on women's traditional rights to access land. Customary societies find it more difficult to enforce their rules and practices for allocating community resources, such as land, based on the need to provide resources to community households for their welfare and sustenance. During this transition period, what is regarded as customary norms and practices begins to change as social actors adapt their behavior to changing conditions, often at the cost of groups, such as women and minority ethnic groups, who are considered secondary members of the community.

POLICY AND IMPLEMENTATION ISSUES

The basic issues that affect gender-responsive outcomes in programs dealing with land access are found in two areas: program implementation and the participant population. These programs have generally tended to direct their activities and communication to men household heads in the belief that the household is a unified group whose members have the same goals and interests and that other household members and producers, such as women, will obtain benefit through the man household head.

In addition, policy makers, program planners, and project implementers are influenced by their own values and attitudes concerning women's abilities and rights. In Zimbabwe in 1998 the senior minister in charge of the land resettlement program rejected women's demands that land certificates be automatically registered in both spouses' names. He also did not permit that land earmarked for redistribution be offered to women heads of households and single unmarried women. The minister maintained that such moves would cause families to break up because they would accord women too much freedom.[5]

The norms, values, and practices of participating populations also influence how land access programs are implemented. Land allocation programs that attempt to include women may encounter resistance from community authorities and other adult men. Control over land is a significant source of status and power in rural societies, and those who hold that power are often loath to share it. Program officials and implementers may also find that women themselves are reluctant to participate because of illiteracy, inexperience, or fear of ridicule and reprisal (see Overview). Project actions to overcome these constraints on the part of both women and men include informational and training activities for the participating population (both women and men), local authorities, and local land administrators.

Where land reform programs are market based, smallholder women are constrained from participation by lower access to capital as compared to men.

GOOD PRACTICES AND LESSONS LEARNED

Although no single land-access project has had unqualified success in allocating land to women and men at equitable levels, some projects have been able to increase the number of women participants and beneficiaries. In addition to facilitating women's individual access and rights, programs that promote collective land rights for women, such as programs that help them to purchase or lease land as a group, can be a very beneficial option (Agarwal 2003).

Rice land in The Gambia

An agricultural development program in The Gambia had a land component that combined land improvement and land reform.[6] Planners made the decision to reclaim degraded lowland areas during the design phase of the project using participatory methods that involved community members and authorities. The communities that wanted to participate in the reclamation activities formally requested assistance, and community mobilization teams visited them to establish site management committees. Again, all these activities utilized participatory rural appraisal methods.

The project devolved ownership of the land from individual landowners to the community, and the community provided labor for the reclamation activities. After reclamation, the community redistributed the land, on an equal basis, to those who had provided labor for reclamation. The majority of reclamation workers were women and made up 90 percent of the land beneficiaries (22,216 women from different ethnic groups).

Leasehold of forest land in Nepal

A project in Nepal granting landless households access to forest land demonstrates successful efforts to include women. Currently, 25 percent of the participants are women; in addition, there are 74 all-women groups and 112 women group leaders. The project also employs local women group promoters to organize and attend group meetings, promote the project, organize groups, give

training, and detect problems. By working within groups, women have also been able to increase their human capacity and their ability to increase productivity both in domestic and productive work (see Innovative Activity Profile 1 for more details).

Community-based natural resource management in Namibia

Initiated in 1993, a project in Namibia sought to devolve rights over wildlife and tourism to local communities.[7] One of the project's main objectives was initially to increase benefits to Namibians from sustainable local management of natural resources. One of its specific objectives was to increase the number of women participating in officially recognized management bodies over natural resources. By 1998, 22 percent of the members of these management bodies were women. Social surveys, as well as organization and training provided by community resource monitors, provided a mechanism to integrate women into community-based management. Income generation activities based on the use of renewable natural resources also benefited women.

Unfortunately, the project lacked tools for participatory development and socioeconomic and gender analysis. As a result, gender and social equity objectives were not sustained. A midterm review found these deficiencies and recommended steps to remedy them through research and training. A gender assessment in 2005 found that great strides were made in the program's gender balance at the national level, in a greater number of women standing for election in the conservancy management committees, as well as in women's benefits from capacity development and training.

Homestead land purchase program in India

Programs that help landless families in rural India to purchase small plots are one way of providing secure housing for the rural poor and, assuming the plot is large enough, some land for home gardens or another household enterprise.[8] These productive activities provide supplemental income and may improve household nutrition and food security. They also provide space for productive activities under women's control. The experience in India has shown that participation by beneficiary communities and households in all aspects of the program, from identification of suitable land to land development plans, contributes to successful implementation and to satisfaction by beneficiary households.

An innovative feature of many of these programs in India is that the land titles (*patta*) are issued jointly to both wife and husband, sometimes with the name of the wife listed first. In some cases, land title is issued to women only. This practice is attributed to greater gender awareness and sensitivity on the part of community authorities and committees (*panchayats*).

GUIDELINES AND RECOMMENDATIONS FOR PRACTITIONERS

Guidelines for increasing women's participation in land access programs will be somewhat different for individually owned land than for common property. Women tend to have more equitable access to common property, and their rights to use common land, depending on local rules, may not be challenged. *The principal guideline is to include women's voices and interests in natural resource management programs.* For programs that allocate land as leasehold or private property, *the principal guideline is to allocate land equitably to both women and men.*

Common property

Programs that deal with common property must recognize women's access rights to common land and natural resources. Women's rights should be the same rights that other community members enjoy. When, for example, programs are established to title community land, care should be taken to recognize the women in the community (both married and unmarried) as members of the community having the same rights as men community members.

Programs that affect access to and management of common property, such as natural resource management programs, should recognize women's dependence on these resources and accommodate gender-differentiated management practices. Increasing shortages of resources, changing values (from use value to market value) for land and other natural resources, modifications in family structures, growth of commercial agriculture, and other changes are modifying social relations and cultural norms around common property. Under these conditions, women's rights to these resources may become more tenuous. Programs should seek to preserve and improve women's rights to access these resources. This objective means that programs must have an understanding of how different groups within the community relate to common property resources.

Natural resource management programs should consequently consider what role gender plays in access to and control of community resources and consider how to ensure women's participation. Issues that should be considered include the following:

- Gaining explicit awareness of women's different interests in accessing land, trees, forests, water, and other common resources, as well as of their level of control over these resources
- Ensuring that program objectives and activities do not reduce women's access to common property (for example, because of privatization or concessions)
- Recognizing, during program design, women's particular constraints (in law and norm and in practice) in accessing and managing land and other resources, and putting forward activities to reduce these constraints
- During project implementation, monitoring women's access to common property and women's involvement in managing these resources.

Allocation of land as private property

Programs that seek to facilitate access to or allocate land as private property, whether owned individually or by a group, have slightly different guidelines. Women's rights to landed property may be contested within the community and the household, and there will be a tendency to allocate land rights to men household heads (see also Thematic Note 4).

Legal Reforms and Women's Property Rights

KEY GENDER ISSUES

Joint titling and inheritance are most often cited as the main issues when considering women's legal rights to land. Do married women have a legal right to the land that is owned or used by the household? Do women have the right to inherit land from their husbands and fathers? Although these legal questions are critical, inheritance and joint titling must be considered as part of a much greater web of issues, both legal and customary, if a complete picture of women's property rights is to emerge. To paint a more accurate picture of women's property rights, the following issues are crucial:

1. Do women have the legal right to own land or hold long-term use rights to land?
2. Do women have the customary and socially accepted right to own or control land?
3. Do women's current legal property rights make sense, given the culture in which they live? That is, could or would the majority of women claim their legal rights?
4. Do the answers to these questions change if women are married, single, divorced, widowed, or in a polygamous relationship?
5. Do women know and understand their rights?
6. Do women have any means to enforce their rights?

It has become clear in the last 10 years that men's rights to land do not necessarily translate into the household's rights to land. One primary reason for this situation is that households in rural areas of developing nations are not nuclear families functioning as solitary units. Rather, these households generally include the parents of one of the spouses and operate within a larger family system, which often uses ancestral land and sometimes tribal land. Moreover, when these households break down and change, women whose property rights exist only through their husbands immediately become very vulnerable. It is at this point of change that individual legal and customary rights to land within the household become important.

This Thematic Note focuses specifically on women's legal and customary rights to land and how to effectuate them.

CONCEPTUAL FRAMEWORK

Four categories of legal rights to land affect women: (1) the rights women hold in marriage (shared tenure); (2) the right to land when the marital household changes through polygamy, divorce, or abandonment; (3) the right to receive land through inheritance; and (4) the right to purchase land. These are affected by both formal and customary law.

Scholars and service providers have taken two main approaches to these legal issues—a rights-based approach and a more gradual, institution-building approach (Tripp 2004). A rights-based approach focuses on formal legal reform as the key to women's property rights. This approach gives particular attention to the constraints imposed by customary laws and practices and to problems in implementing antidiscrimination laws. The philosophy behind the institution-building approach is that customary law and institutions should be supported. Formal law is viewed as a catalyst to expedite a process of change, but the actual ability of formal law to bring about change, especially in the household arena, is considered limited. The institution-building approach asserts that legal reforms undermine local systems of adjudication and create a rigidity in customary laws that prevents them from being modified and used flexibly (Gopal,[1] cited in Tripp 2004).

These two approaches are not as divergent as they seem at first. They differ in their starting points only; neither approach would advocate ignoring the other. Each recognizes that legal reforms must be accompanied by legal education for women, education for officials and those who implement or enforce laws and customs, and the inclusion of women in technical services, access to credit, and policy making.

POLICY AND IMPLEMENTATION ISSUES

Getting the right legislation and effective implementation and judicial enforcement are crucial. Discussed here are legislations on shared tenure, polygamy, divorce, abandonment, and inheritance and conditions in the land market that affect women's access to land and property.

Shared tenure

"Shared tenure" is a broad term that includes land co-owned within a household and may also include communal ownership of land.[2] The substantive issue for women is whether they have a right to share land tenure with their husbands or communities, and, if so, what limits are placed on that right. Formal legal rules for joint titling have to take into account the following issues:

1. Which property is jointly owned? Inherited land? Purchased land? Land distributed by the state? In many countries ancestral land is excluded from joint property (in formal law or under customary law), and most land that belongs to the household is ancestral land.
2. Who will manage the marital property? Managing the community property can be as important as formally owning it, because it may include mortgage or sale of the property. *Joint management* requires the spouses to act jointly regarding the community property; *sole management* allows one spouse the sole power to manage jointly held property; and *equal management* gives either spouse, acting alone, the power to manage the whole of the property that is jointly titled (UN–HABITAT 2005). Most countries have adopted a combination of management rules, the application of which depends on the nature of the property at issue. For example, one spouse can make all decisions except those related to the house and land, which require the agreement of both spouses (Deere and Leon 2001).[3]
3. Do consensual unions trigger the joint titling rules and protections? Do religious or customary marriages trigger them? Many women are not legally married, especially where customs and traditions predominate. Legal marriage can be expensive and time-consuming and may require residence documentation that women do not

have. In other cases, marriages are religious or customary and therefore do not include the rights reserved for marriage under the civil law.
4. Is there a mandatory registration requirement for joint titling? Even where the law presumes that married couples hold their land in joint ownership, often mandatory registration of that joint ownership is not required. Without joint registration of land, one party may have to go to court to exercise her right—a difficult and unlikely step.

Polygamy, divorce, and abandonment

In most non-Western countries, polygamy exists in one form or another, whether it is legal or illegal under formal law. Polygamic practices affect women by affecting household income; even if the two wives do not live together in one household, their husband must support two families. The livelihoods of first wives are threatened when their husbands take second wives. Additional children require more of the household income. Even without additional children, already tight resources are distributed to the second wife—and often these resources include a plot of land.

Laws against polygamy are rarely enforced and have little effect on behavior. In fact, where polygamy is illegal, women may be more vulnerable; often second wives have no rights under formal law if polygamy is not recognized.[4] Legal protections for first wives, even those who are formally married, are rare. In most instances the husband is not formally married to either wife, placing the first wife in serious economic jeopardy when her husband takes a second wife.

The existence yet illegality of polygamy is tricky when considering rules for joint titling. If a man actively supports two households, in whose name should the land be registered? If joint titling is allowed only for formal marriages, but a first wife provided resources and sweat equity for land, should that land be titled to the second wife if that marriage is formalized? What if the first marriage was formal, but the two spouses have been separated for years (although not formally divorced), and each now maintains different relationships? To whom should the land be titled?

Inheritance

A woman might inherit land in two main ways: as a daughter from a parent or as a wife from a husband. Inheritance of land by daughters or widows is often the main way through which women acquire ownership rights to land. Many pluralistic legal systems allow the marriage to determine the inheritance regime that applies. For example, if a person marries as a Muslim in India, the inheritance rules are different than if a person marries as a Hindu.

Very often, although formal law provides daughters with the right to inherit land, they will not inherit in fact, or they will not enforce their right to inherit. In patrilocal societies, daughters move from their parents' home and land to live with their husbands, so the land they may inherit is of little use to them. Often the family is responsible for a dowry or other expenses related to marrying their daughter, and those expenses are considered her share of the wealth of the family. Under customary law in many countries, inheritance of land by daughters is directly related to marital residence and to the customary means of distributing wealth.[5] In focus group interviews in rural areas of Karnataka, India, and the Kyrgyz Republic (two countries where inheritance by daughters is mandated by law), most women stated that they would not request land from their families even if they were legally entitled to it.

Inheritance of land by spouses is even less likely to occur than inheritance by daughters in patrilineal and patrilocal societies. Ancestral land is closely guarded in most communities around the world. Wives, with no blood relationship to their husband or his clan or community, are often given use rights to the house and land but not the right of ownership. Sometimes those use rights exist only if the widow has had children with the deceased partner. Depending on the depth and breadth of these use rights, they may be a worthwhile compromise. In countries such as Burundi or Rwanda, for example, where land is extremely scarce and most, if not all, communities are patrilineal, the division of ancestral land between children and their mother may not be feasible and realistic. Long-term use rights to the land, on the other hand, may be much more politically feasible. If the use rights include the right to mortgage or lease out the land, and if widows have control over how the land is used, these use rights will not differ substantially from ownership. Additionally, in many societies, although children but not mothers inherit land, the inheritance comes with the responsibility to care for the mother, an arrangement preferred by many women in the Krygyz Republic, for example. On the other hand, land grabbing of widows' land (by sons or brothers of the deceased) is a major problem in Uganda and other African countries that cannot be ignored.

Markets

Ancestral land is often not available to women, and so participation in the land market is critical to women's ability to sustain a livelihood, but this participation may be limited. Because of traditional gender roles and a lack of independent financial resources, women in many countries rarely purchase land, either independently or jointly with their husbands. Land ownership is economically empowering for women; thus, women's land ownership can be threatening to men. For example, under Muslim personal law in the Philippines, a woman must have her husband's consent to acquire any property by gift, except from her relatives (Giovarelli 2006).

It may be easier for women to lease land than to purchase land, and land market programs should not focus exclusively on ownership markets. Leasing land is less psychologically threatening than purchasing land and requires fewer entry resources. Of course, it should be noted that leasing is less psychologically threatening to the status quo for the very reason that it does *not* create long-term secure property rights in the borrower/lessee. In Burkina Faso, for example, the increased and changing market value of land has had the surprise effect of creating avenues outside traditional channels for women to lease land over the long term, anonymously (Bruce and others 2006). Men landholders who have excess land are more willing to lease to women because women cannot claim permanent rights to land. Husbands generally support this borrowing of land by their wives, and women are therefore better able to cultivate land independently, even though they do not own it (Giovarelli 2006).

Implementation

As stated earlier, legal solutions are effective only if they are socially accepted and enforced. Changing the law can be difficult, and sometimes it takes years to win one small battle. Changing people's attitudes toward a new law once it passes can also be difficult. Many examples exist of legal efforts that were ineffective in helping women gain rights to land, as well as some examples of legislation that even caused harm. At its best, legal reform is a necessary prerequisite for change, but, even then, legal reform alone is never enough. A review of two World Bank Land Titling Projects (in Bolivia and Lao PDR) found that although formal law that mandated joint titling and registration was in place, women did not gain equal rights to land. The unequal outcome was related to cultural practices and biases, lack of information, or nonenforcement of legal rules. The number of titles issued to women or in joint ownership increased only after each of these issues was addressed (Giovarelli and others 2005).

Perhaps the most critical point to be made regarding formal legal solutions is that legal solutions must be part of a larger effort to provide education, training, and other means of raising awareness about women's lack of land rights and the consequent impact on the larger economy, well-being of the family, and position and viability of women's livelihoods.

Before addressing the institutions that enforce law, two points must be made about the laws themselves. First, gender-neutral language can be gender biased in its interpretation. For land legislation to be inclusive of both men and women, at a minimum it must explicitly recognize women's and men's equal rights to land. In Bolivia, for example, the law that establishes the legal basis for the current titling program specifically states that in the distribution, administration, tenure, and use of land, equity criteria will be applied in favor of women *and independently of their civil status.*[6] The last phrase is important because it does not require that a woman be the head of the household or married to be eligible for land rights. The most useful provision to date is Article 28[g], which makes the INRA (state land agency) director (and the provincial INRA directors) responsible for ensuring that legal gender rights are observed in implementing the INRA law.

Much of the explicitness will be found in the regulations to the major laws, rather than in the laws themselves. Regulations, which lay out the details of how a law will be implemented, rarely go through the checks and balances of the legislative process. Rather, they are promulgated by state agencies and approved by one person—for example, the Minister of Lands or the prime minister. This practice can cause problems in many different ways. For instance, the law can generally or even specifically favor equal rights for women, but the regulations may not require the names of the husband and wife on the land title, as occurred in Indonesia. The registration law and accompanying regulations are silent on the issue of joint titling, and some registration officials were not certain that land could be titled jointly (Lastarria-Cornhiel and others 2003).

The registration process itself can create barriers for women to own land. In Brazil the registration regulations required that personal documents such as proof of marriage, proof of citizenship, or identity cards be presented to register land, but women lacked this documentation and were not registered. In Lao PDR women have a difficult time proving ownership of property because many families, particularly in rural areas, do not have documentation of ownership or other land rights. If documentation is required for taxation, for example, the man head of the household traditionally deals with these formal and written procedures, and his name appears on these types of documents.

Beyond what the law or custom requires and what regulations allow, for a law to be enforceable, women need legal awareness (knowledge of what is legally possible), legal information (specific and detailed knowledge of how to record land rights and engage in land transactions), and legal empowerment (the social and institutional ability to assert claims and secure land rights). Women must also understand the complexity of land issues, the relationship between different laws and practices, the options available, and the limitations of the legislation and the implementing bodies. Knowledge of both formal systems and informal systems for exercising land rights is critical in most parts of the world, and the legal situation can be quite complicated.

An important, and often missed, step toward making women's land rights secure and sustainable is providing awareness, information, and enforcement mechanisms to those who implement or enforce those land rights. Other household members, local leaders, judges, and land professionals must all understand the law and its implications and how to use and follow the law. The rule of law is more likely to have value if there are many people who understand the land law and rely on it to protect their rights.

Effectuating major legal change requires a sustained effort to implement the changes, including sensitizing the public to the changes and eventually gaining public support. Although workshops, training materials, and mass media campaigns can alert the public to new laws, they can do little to change attitudes or actions unless they are augmented by the efforts of local people who both understand and support the legal changes. Combining a mass media effort with the sustained presence of knowledgeable people at the village level will have a much more lasting effect.

Judicial enforcement of land rights is also critical and can save or harm women's property rights. In Tanzania the Land Act and constitution are progressive and mandate equality for men and women. In support of these laws, the Tanzanian High Court invalidated customary norms preventing women from selling land. In Kenya the land registration program was carried out during a time when gender was not part of the development agenda. At that time, land adjudication committees were men dominated and lacked the skills and time to carry out their duties properly, which included registering all rights (primary and secondary) to land. Women's secondary rights often went unregistered. In a later case, however, the court ruled that when the husband was registered as sole owner of property and the property was acquired during the subsistence of the marriage, evidence of co-ownership may be given under the Married Women's Property Act of 1882 and Section 126 of the Registered Land Act (Giovarelli 2006).

Uganda granted judicial capacity to local councils at the village, parish, and subcounty levels in an attempt to encourage inexpensive, expedient, and culturally appropriate justice. The local councils share concurrent jurisdiction with magistrates' courts but also are connected to customary law as they are lay judges and make their decisions based on local norms and social ties. The local councils also hear cases related to land disputes. Such courts should have been more accessible to women, but it was more difficult for women to get justice in these courts, because women could neither pay for legal service nor effectively fight against their basic position as outsiders in the men-dominated community. Women often choose to go to magistrates rather than the local councils. Informal justice does not have the legal authority and leverage of state power and has wide discretionary powers to define custom. In this instance the local councils have little ability to make dramatic pronouncements about women's rights to land, and at the same time lack authority to enforce formal laws, which may favor women's rights (Giovarelli 2006).

Legal assistance or legal aid for women is also critical to enforce their rights to land. Legal aid centers provide services to women while simultaneously feeding back information to policy makers on land issues that affect women and policy changes that are required.

GOOD PRACTICES, LESSONS LEARNED, AND GUIDELINES FOR PRACTITIONERS

Implementation efforts and changing attitudes and knowledge of beneficiaries and communities as well as institutional agents and project staff are critical for success. Participation of women in all stages of the project, as well as among institutional and project staff, is another factor. Such efforts may include the following:

Talk to women. Some legislative and social changes may be more readily accepted than others, by both men and women, and part of the process needs to involve listening to women to understand what legal rights are most valuable to them and the impact of various legal situations.

Take family law into account. Land projects that incorporate legal reform must consider family law as well as land law to have an impact on women's rights. Yet family law is rarely considered as part of land administration projects, usually owing to lack of funds for the legal review or lack of awareness of the issues.

Keep consistent gender focus through all stages of a program. In the World Bank's Land Administration Project in the Philippines, the gender-mainstreaming plan encompassed the whole project cycle, from influencing legal reforms to installing gender-sensitive monitoring and evaluation systems.

Include men and not just women. The Philippine project struggled to balance its efforts to include women and its need to include and train men as well. At one point the project focused more on women than men, also to the program's detriment. If men are to be "brought along" and included in making cultural changes, they must also be involved in training and in the design of the project.

Attend to legal regulations. Regulations have a major impact on how the more general land laws are implemented and must be considered along with formal and customary laws. For example, it is critical to understand whether the documentation required for land registration is available or common to women. If not, the requirements should be revised so that women and men have equal opportunity for registering land.

Use existing law to its best advantage, regardless of customary law. The Guayape Valley Agricultural Development Project in Honduras, funded by the Canadian International Development Agency, worked proactively with the Honduras Titling Agency to use the limited gender-related legislation that already existed to its fullest extent in order to include wives on land titles. The project was very effective in titling wives, despite strong inheritance and marital property practices that excluded women, because the project held gender training programs for project staff, government titling staff, the beneficiary population, and local authorities. The project also reviewed titling procedures to make them more accessible to and inclusive of women.

Train all implementers of the project on women's land rights. Although *beneficiaries* were trained in a World Bank land project in Panama and one in the Philippines, training of project staff was limited or lacking completely. In both projects the lack of gender training for staff led to less effective implementation of the gender strategy. On the other hand, in a U.S. Agency for International Development (USAID) Natural Resources Project in Namibia, a full-time gender trainer was hired for two years to work with staff and beneficiaries, leading to a very positive result in terms of women's involvement in the nature conservancies.

When possible, encourage the legal norms that provide women with access and control over land rights. For example:

■ Co-ownership of land and property is the presumption for land acquired during a marriage or consensual union.

- Registration regulations include specific direction as to registration of married couples and those living in consensual unions.
- Legislation requires both husband and wife to consent to a transaction involving land acquired during the marriage or cohabitation, regardless of whether the land is registered in the name of both or only one partner.
- For countries where polygamy is practiced, even if it is illegal, legislation states that when a second wife is taken all property belonging to the first marriage or consensual union will be partitioned and divided. In this case, the husband would have only his share to distribute to his new wife and children.
- Widows' rights to the use and control of land needs to be established as a priority policy issue when developing property system legislation.

Provide legal services to women to help them enforce their rights to land, once those rights are established. Enforcement of legal rights or customary rights to land often requires legal advocacy, especially where women lack information or are poorly educated.

Land Dispute Resolution

The management of land disputes involves the review of land tenure rules and the behavior of landholders with regard to these rules. As such, land dispute management is part of the justice system of any regime (whether formal or customary) and should be fair, equitable, and accessible to all. In many areas, especially rural, the formal justice system is not only inaccessible but culturally alien. Where the formal justice system is minimally present because of distance, weak state institutions, or scarce resources, customary and informal (alternative) dispute management processes are the most appropriate.

Both formal and customary tenure regimes increasingly recognize and use nonjudicial, alternative procedures for managing disputes. In reality, formal, customary, and alternative dispute resolution procedures are not exclusive.

KEY GENDER ISSUES

Women as a stakeholder group have great difficulty gaining recognition for their disputes around land rights for two reasons: status and identity. The lower status of women in many societies has already been discussed. In addition, successful mobilizations around land conflicts generally occur along class or ethnic lines, because class and ethnicity are public identities. Gender is not easily perceived as a collective identity, particularly for women in rural areas, because they have minimal power, authority, and public action. Land conflicts that involve a claim by a woman are often intrahousehold claims around divorce or inheritance. Their resolution is generally limited to intrahousehold discussion and negotiation; rarely do they transcend household boundaries to reach community and local authorities.

A further complication is that a wife is often considered an outsider in a husband's household and community. Since women's rights to land are transmitted through the men in their family or household, it is considered shameful for a woman to make a public claim for what she believes are her land rights. In the Kyrgyz Republic, for example, women have rights under formal law to the household's land and house when the household unit breaks down, yet it is shameful to assert individual rights within Kyrgyz and other Central Asian cultures. In most cases divorced or separated women no longer have access to the land, which customarily belongs to their husband's family. In addition, because women generally have no possibility of paying the fees required by the formal system, they rarely apply to court (Giovarelli and others 2001).

Given this context, the main gender issues in land dispute resolution include (1) the recognition of women's rights to land by formal judicial processes and officials and by the community and customary land authorities and (2) women's access to dispute resolution institutions. Resolving these issues involves a shift in perception, in which women's rights and claims to land cease to be regarded as a private, intrahousehold issue and are recognized as a public, societal issue. If this shift is to occur, it will require programs and actions that extend beyond legislation, including gender training and education for judicial officials as well as officials at state institutions. It will also require gender training and information dissemination for local populations involved in land programs. Finally, the facilitation of women's access to institutions that resolve land disputes (whether formal or customary institutions) will require proactive programs to overcome the barriers women face in approaching and dealing with these institutions.

Access to dispute resolution institutions is a part of democratic rights. Women's equitable participation in managing land disputes will also, in practice, improve their rights to land by setting precedents in law and by clarifying both formal and customary norms regarding daughters' and wives' rights to land and property. Success in resolving land disputes will also encourage women in general to claim and demand their rights to land and property.

In addition, women's ability to participate successfully in the process for resolving land disputes will increase women's empowerment and status in the community and within their households.

POLICY AND IMPLEMENTATION ISSUES

The principal issues for women in the resolution of land disputes are (1) access to dispute resolution institutions and (2) legal pluralism. The basic objectives for a judicial system that is both fair and gender sensitive include accessibility, transparency, efficient and timely process, predictability, and manifest impartiality.

Formal dispute management

Formal judicial systems employ a number of mechanisms and procedures to manage land disputes. These include land commissions, public advocates for agrarian issues, adjudication, and arbitration. Formal judicial systems are supposed to be transparent, unbiased, and impartial and to adhere strictly to the law; they also, however, tend to be litigious, setting one party against the other and seeking punishment and retribution rather than restoration and transformation. A notable exception is court-mandated arbitration, found in common law systems, during which court action is suspended and a mutually agreeable solution is sought.

Women's access to courts is severely limited in many countries. Practices such as seclusion of women hinder the possibilities for women to claim their rights. In many rural areas, it is shameful for a woman to appear in court to claim her rights with respect to men family members, as documented in India, for example, by Agarwal (1994). In many countries, women are underrepresented in the judiciary, and prejudices about the credibility of women witnesses are widespread. Court fees may also constitute an obstacle for rural women, who tend to have less access to cash than men. Women's access to courts may also be constrained by norms limiting their legal capacity and preventing them from bringing judicial disputes autonomously.[1] Most countries have repealed these formal norms, and some countries have granted women equal access to legal remedies—yet legal and judicial practice may be lagging.

The problem for most low-income rural residents, including women, is the distance (geographical, cultural, and social) and cost involved in resorting to formal judicial institutions. With a few exceptions—such as land reform or systematic land titling programs, which send land commissions, agrarian advocates, or arbitration teams into rural communities—rural residents are unlikely to deal with formal dispute institutions. In addition, women are less likely than men to have the preparation and legal literacy to deal with officials and opposing parties on an equal basis.

Where formal law recognizes women's equal land rights, women are able to take their cases to court, and their legal rights are likely to be upheld. In the Kyrgyz case mentioned earlier, customary law enforced at the village level does not give women access to land upon divorce. Some exceptions exist if the couple have children and the husband leaves the house. However, if a woman goes to court seeking divorce and property division, the written law is generally enforced. Women who petition the court must provide proof of their investment in the house, and they are compensated for that investment. In addition, the court generally compensates women for their portion of the household land share if their name appears on the land share certificate. Women generally consider that, in the case of divorce, written law regarding division of property is better than customary law (Giovarelli and others 2001).

Customary dispute management

Given the access difficulty with formal systems, customary or informal dispute resolution procedures may be more appropriate in some rural areas. Customary tenure regimes contain institutions and authorities to manage land conflicts. These institutions, through customary land authorities, enforce the rules mediating access to land, allocate land to community members as well as noncommunity members, and manage land conflicts. Customary systems generally adapt quickly to changing conditions that spark conflict, such as commercial agricultural production, increasing population density, and evolving land markets.

When the community regards these institutions and its authorities as legitimate, customary tenure regimes are highly successful in settling land conflicts, and community members enjoy high levels of tenure security. Functionality and legitimacy, however, do not automatically result in transparent and equitable governance. Land distribution patterns in customary systems may be highly skewed, and some community groups, such as women and ethnic minorities, may be denied access to land.

The last decade has witnessed renewed interest in the role of customary institutions in settling disputes. Niger's 1993 Rural Code requires a mandatory conciliation procedure to be undertaken before customary authorities before initiating judicial proceedings. Where communities with customary tenure regimes are linked with the formal regime, their judicial systems are embedded in the formal one. The formal regime recognizes the geographic and policy domains of the customary judiciary system. The trend toward decentralizing land administration depends strongly on embedded customary institutions to carry out state responsibilities.

For women, customary institutions have both advantages and disadvantages. On the one hand, compared to courts, customary institutions may provide more easily accessible (both geographically and economically) and speedier forums for rural women. These institutions may also enjoy greater social legitimacy. On the other hand, although their nature varies considerably from place to place, customary institutions are often gender biased in composition and orientation. Even though women may believe they have a legitimate claim in a land dispute, their secondary status within the family and the community may discourage them from approaching customary authorities. These land disputes may involve a family member, either from the woman's own family or her husband's family, who engages in intimidating actions. If women do approach customary land authorities and obtain a favorable decision, community and family members may ignore the decision. In frequently documented instances, young widows have lost their land to their husbands' parents and siblings (see, for example, Strickland 2004); this land grabbing occurs despite customary norms that guarantee a widow long-term use rights to her deceased husband's land to support herself and her children. In an ever-growing number of cases, people no longer respect these rights, and the institutions responsible for enforcing them—chiefs and elders—are either unable or unwilling to do so. Because customary institutions are constituted by men elders in most places, they may apply a men-biased interpretation of customary law. Women may even be discriminated against procedurally, because they may need a man intermediary to bring a dispute and to appear before the authority.

Some countries have attempted to improve the gender outlook of customary institutions. India's constitution, as amended in 1993, provides for direct election of members of *panchayats* (local government institutions rooted in tradition) and reserves one-third of the seats for women. South Africa's constitution recognizes the role and status of traditional institutions, although they are subject to the principles of the constitution. Similar norms are contained in Uganda's constitution. It is difficult to assess whether this type of norm is effective in reforming deeply rooted institutions. In both India and South Africa, most customary institutions reportedly continue to be dominated by men elites and to favor a gender-biased interpretation of the law.[2] Guaranteeing women's representation through quotas is an important tool, but women sitting in councils may in practice not speak, may act merely as spokespersons for their men relatives, or may otherwise face resistance to their role.

Alternative dispute resolution methods

Nonjudicial or alternative dispute resolution approaches provide another avenue for resolving conflicts in situations in which customary systems do not provide an answer and both parties are reluctant or unable to use formal dispute resolution procedures. Unlike the formal and customary approaches described earlier, alternative dispute resolution (ADR) methods emphasize decision making between the parties to the dispute rather than decision making by a third party. The parties involved agree to enter into a collaborative process of negotiation that will help them to arrive at a joint decision. The negotiations revolve around mutual interest, rather than around positions or rights, and the principal ADR procedures are negotiation, community consultation, mediation, and conciliation. A combination of these approaches, involving negotiation, advocacy, and consensus building, is often most effective, because land and natural resource disputes involve a number of stakeholders with varying interests and differing levels of economic and political power.

Although at first glance ADR methods may appear to be a less biased and more accessible means for women to resolve land disputes, these methods also assume that the parties are relatively equal in power. If women have secondary status and significantly less power than the opposing party, they will have difficulty negotiating on an equal basis and may not gain anything significant from the negotiation process.

Legal pluralism

In many countries, formal and customary land tenure regimes overlap in jurisdiction, which results in situations in which more than one institution has authority over legal rights, and multiple bodies can resolve disputes. These institutions can include customary authorities, religious leaders, and governmental bodies. Legal and institutional pluralism can give rise to contradictions and ambiguities between statutory and customary rules and legal norms. How exactly different legal orders interact and influence each other depends on power relationships between the bearers of different laws. Although legal pluralism can provide a means of coping with ecological, livelihood, social, and political uncertainty, it also exacerbates knowledge uncertainty (Meinzen-Dick and Pradhan 2002).

In the last several decades, numerous countries with vigorous customary societies have reformed their land legislation and given formal legal recognition to customary tenure regimes.[3] In some cases, as noted, the formal regime recognizes the geographic domain and policy scope of the customary judiciary system, and customary dispute resolution bodies are embedded in the formal body. This accommodation between formal and customary jurisdiction reduces ambiguities resulting from legal pluralism.

Legal pluralism enables individuals to use more than one type of law, customary or statutory, to rationalize and legitimize their decisions or their behavior. During disputes and negotiations, claims are justified by reference to legal rules. Parties will use different normative repertoires in different contexts or forums depending on which law or interpretation of law they believe is most likely to support their claims.

Legal pluralism can be disadvantageous for some groups, such as poor and uneducated women, for whom formal state institutions are distant, expensive, and conceptually foreign. It also offers opportunities for forum shopping by those whose financial and educational status enables them to operate in both customary and state legal systems. Women are often disadvantaged in the contradictions and accommodations arising between customary and statutory legal systems. Customary law often does not allow women to own land, but formal law may provide for equal rights to land ownership. State institutions and officials, however, are often reluctant to enforce women's rights to land because of lawmakers' and state officials' own patriarchal values and norms. For example, in Zimbabwe, although formal law provides for equality between men and women, customary law views women as minors. A Supreme Court decision in 1999 ruled that because under customary law women are minors, a woman could not inherit her father's property under the formal law even though she was named in his will.

Nevertheless, women also have opportunities to engage in forum shopping and appeal to different legal spheres. In some cases, when their rights are threatened by men's manipulation of custom, women call upon customary norms to retain control over their land. In other cases women appeal to statutory laws when this same system is not used against them. Women's groups and legal associations that promote and struggle for recognition of women's rights to land often prefer to present their dispute cases to the formal legal system in order to have judicial precedent,

or they may appeal to district and provincial land officials, by citing legal statutes, to recognize a property right that local customary authorities deny them.

In Ethiopia the current constitution has provided an opportunity for addressing the conflict between customary laws and the more egalitarian provisions of the civil code. The constitution revokes the abolition of customary and religious personal laws, but it allows disputants to determine which laws to apply in personal disputes. Consequently, if any disputant does not wish to apply customary or religious personal law, she or he may request that civil law provisions be applied. According to Gopal, anecdotal evidence indicates that personal law arbitrators and courts (customary bodies) are reconsidering the application of customary and religious personal laws because women disputants may prefer to transfer decisions to civil courts.[4]

GOOD PRACTICES AND LESSONS LEARNED

The Legal Assistance to Rural Citizens (LARC) project in the Kyrgyz Republic is designed to assist and teach farmers and the rural population in general how to apply the law in resolving their land disputes. In 2003 the project began to offer legal services to the rural population, to commercial and nongovernmental organizations, as well as to clients of international organizations dealing with land and agrarian law issues. The project receives support from a number of agencies, including the World Bank, the United Nations Development Programme, the Swiss Agency for Development and Cooperation, and the U.S. Agency for International Development (USAID).

The final report of the project (LARC 2006) recounts how LARC personnel helped to resolve a number of land disputes. A number of women had approached LARC for assistance with land disputes, and most of their cases resembled men's: village or local authorities had attempted to take the land the claimant had received from the land reform and assign it to someone else. It appears that in most cases local officials were attempting to reassign land to other men in the village. The report did not include any land disputes arising from divorce, which perhaps indicates that this type of dispute is uncommon or that women are reluctant to take such disputes to court.

In one case a woman who was an invalid was given the family house as a gift by her father, who used the appropriate official documentation. The woman's uncle and cousins refused to leave the house, however, and drew up a document certifying their right to the house. The woman was initially discouraged from taking the case to court by local authorities, "because it is not normal for rural people to go to law with relatives" (LARC 2006: 21). The woman took her case to the rayon and oblast courts but was unsuccessful in moving it forward. After three years she approached LARC and finally achieved a consensus with her extended family.

Clearly, the LARC project did assist women with land disputes and was successful in having their rights recognized through the judicial system. What is surprising, however, is the negligible number of intrahousehold cases (such as inheritance and divorce) brought to court by women.

GUIDELINES AND RECOMMENDATIONS FOR PRACTITIONERS

Guidelines for improving women's access to dispute resolution processes include recognition of women's legal and customary land rights by land administration, land authorities, and other land institutions; improving women's literacy regarding their land rights and legal processes; and improving access to land dispute institutions.

At the national level, beyond legislation, judicial institutions and land administration programs (such as land reform, land resettlement, and land titling) need to review their procedures for land dispute management to ensure that women as well as men can access these services and be treated fairly and equitably. These procedures begin with facilitating women's ability to approach offices and officials; this may involve bringing land dispute processes to local areas.

Other interventions are the same as have been mentioned in previous Modules: gender-responsive training for information and attitude change to national and local institutional staff, customary leaders, and beneficiary populations. Training at the local level has an additional objective: the cooperation of local authorities is essential for any program to be successful. Their cooperation in land dispute resolution is just as important, particularly because they will most likely be involved in the process.

At local levels, the gender composition of arbitration and adjudication bodies should also be considered. For example, Uganda has mandated that women be included in adjudication bodies. Their inclusion may increase women's ability and willingness to approach such public institutions.

Land administration projects should undertake specific activities to disseminate knowledge among women about their statutory and customary rights and entitlements and about dispute resolution; they should also provide legal assistance for dispute resolution. Activities should include practical application of the knowledge that is disseminated, as well as activities that improve procedures for resolving land disputes at local levels. In addition to information dissemination, projects or programs should include guidelines or mandates for including a substantial number of women in project activities and on local land boards, as indicated earlier.

Legal literacy programs are essential to teach women about their rights and about how to manage the institutions that should be protecting and enforcing their rights. In addition to training regarding land and property rights, leadership training enables women to act in a more organized and effective manner.

Numerous organizations deal with land rights and gender issues, ranging from governmental agencies to informal community organizations. A small number of organizations in each country deal with the issue of women's land and property rights; perhaps the most prominent ones are those associated with legal professions such as the women's lawyers associations found in many sub-Saharan African countries. Legal organizations are generally NGOs that provide free or low-cost legal counsel and advice to resource-poor groups and persons. One mechanism for providing legal counsel that has become quite widespread among legal organizations is the training of paralegals, who work with communities and disadvantaged groups. Many of these legal organizations also engage in advocacy for women's land rights by lobbying legislative bodies for legal reform on marital property and equal inheritance, and by pressuring land program officials to recognize women's legal land rights. These organizations also work with the public by providing education or awareness programs. Legal aid organizations can play an important role in providing legal counsel for women attempting to have their rights to marital property and inheritance recognized and in setting legal precedents.

Dispute resolution within land administration programs

Although many potential disputes can be prevented by transparent and consistent procedures, mechanisms must be developed to resolve disputes that arise either during or after adjudication. The trend in land administration is to avoid having disputes reach the court because (1) courts do not always have the expertise in land law to apply accepted principles consistently, (2) the court process is usually excessively long and costly and thus discourages all but the most economically valuable claims, and (3) disputants, particularly women, often have unequal powers to acquire legal advice and to sustain their claims.

The solutions include special tribunals that can be established not only during initial adjudication but also to settle land matters over time. Typically tribunals include land specialists and involve procedures that are less costly and time-consuming than those used by the courts. In the Bolivia titling program, for example, the titling regularization process involves resolution of disputes during titling adjudication by community members, which helps the community to become invested in the process. However, there is still a need for clearer rules and procedures on the part of the state titling agency. In areas with strong traditional laws, the involvement of recognized community elders or authorities can facilitate dispute resolution, but they may not be inclined to recognize women's land rights (Giovarelli and others 2005).

Gender-Responsive Titling

The formalization of property rights through land titling and registration guarantees state support for the landholder in his or her claims. Other positive development results may be expected from titling, including increased investment and agricultural production arising from improved access to factor markets such as credit. Not only should the formalization of land rights for women protect women's access to and control of land and facilitate access to production factor markets, but it may benefit them in other ways as well. Research suggests that property ownership increases a woman's bargaining power within the household and her status as a citizen in the community.[1]

This Thematic Note focuses almost entirely on the titling of individuals rather than on formal recognition of community rights to land. Like individual titling, community titling may fail to recognize women's rights to land by recognizing and collectively recording only adult men or household heads as community members. The titling of community land is normally an internal process conducted by community authorities, and so it is more difficult to create opportunities for recognizing women's land rights, because the process itself is based on customary norms and institutions. The challenge is to discover how to influence community authorities to recognize women as community members with equal rights to community land.

BENEFITS FROM GENDER-RESPONSIVE TITLING

The principal argument in favor of land titling programs has always been the positive effects of clear ownership rights on agricultural productivity and access to credit (Deininger 2003). From an intrahousehold perspective, this argument can be extended to advocate for greater gender equality in the distribution of property rights.

The linking of land rights and credit access, however, for smallholders and particularly for women landholders, may not always be realized. Numerous studies have shown that even with title to land, smallholders and low-income households in rural and urban areas continue to find access to commercial credit elusive (Barham, Carter, and Sigelko 1995). There is no reason to believe that this situation would be different for women with legal land titles. In addition, in the absence of insurance, low-income households are often reluctant to use their landed property as collateral, especially if they rely on agriculture, with its inherently high risks. These households prefer to use other types of collateral, such as a percentage of the harvest or other assets, to obtain credit.

Nevertheless, denying women the opportunity to participate in land programs that increase their secure rights to land may affect their ability to produce. This argument is based on the supposition that women have the capacity to farm as well as men—in other words, there are no significant intrinsic differences in the agricultural productivity of men and women farmers. Previous studies of gender differentials in farm productivity have generally supported this hypothesis (for example, Lastarria-Cornhiel 1988). Almost all of this literature, however, is plagued by methodological problems related to a lack of parcel-level, gender-disaggregated data (Quisumbing 1996). A recent parcel-based study conducted in Lao PDR in 2004–05 (financed by the World Bank) attempted to contribute to this debate (box 4.1).

Granting women legal rights to land will give wives greater power to prevent the alienation of family land needed to support the family, yet this very protection highlights the conflicting objectives of programs to formalize land rights. One principal objective of titling is to make it easy to alienate land, which is a prerequisite for a dynamic land market and a dynamic credit market based on land collateral. Another principal objective is, or should be, to

Box 4.1   Lao PDR: Land Titling, Credit, and Gender

Relationships between land ownership, farm management, and technical efficiency in rice production were examined through an analysis of data from a 2004 survey of households participating in a land titling program in Lao PDR. Parcels owned or managed by men were, on average, significantly larger than parcels owned by women or jointly with women, but the use of agricultural inputs—including irrigation, fertilizer, pesticides, and farm machinery—did not vary significantly by the gender of the parcel owner or manager. Average rice yields were also statistically identical on men- and women-managed parcels: approximately 2,000 kilograms per hectare. Taken together, the descriptive statistics suggest that women have significant formal property rights in land, as both sole and joint owners of agricultural

parcels, and that women seem equally likely to use agricultural inputs on their (smaller) fields. In addition, women appear to achieve the same (unconditional) level of productivity from their land as their men counterparts.

The data revealed some important gender differences, however. Women's parcels were a good deal smaller than men's, and they exercised effective decision-making control over only half of the parcels they owned. In addition, although men and women obtained the same average yields on parcels dedicated to rice production, the marginal returns to both land and chemical inputs were significantly lower for women, which indicates that potential differences in land quality and input application give women farmers a productivity disadvantage.

Source: Katz and Lastarria-Cornhiel 2006.

secure the assets needed for the families of rural smallholders to gain their livelihoods. This second objective would argue for protection against dispossessing vulnerable family members of their only real asset. Formal recognition of women's rights may make it more difficult for men to sell or mortgage land without their wives' permission. But land titling programs also need to take measures to secure a smallholder family's land against alienation.

Economic benefits of titling to widows, divorcees, and aged women have been enumerated earlier, as well as the empowerment benefits.

POLICY AND IMPLEMENTATION ISSUES

Numerous titling and registration programs have been implemented in Africa, Asia, Eastern Europe, and Latin America as a necessary measure to ensure the property rights of smallholders and increase their access to other production factors, particularly credit. Titling programs, in their design and implementation, have not been gender responsive for numerous reasons. Perhaps the main reason is that they are conceived as legal and technical programs, ignoring the complex sociocultural relations involved in assigning land rights to particular persons. The issues of power, social status, and cultural norms that are embedded in land tenure systems and that determine (1) the different kinds of land rights and (2) who has land rights are seldom

taken into account (see the Overview for a more detailed review of these issues). These sociocultural relations inevitably impact titling processes in determining (1) who will participate in the program and (2) whose rights are recognized. More specific issues that can influence titling and registration include legislation and regulations, institutions and staff, procedures and processes, and training. Issues of gender bias and negative sociocultural norms in legislation, regulation, procedures and processes, and institutional staff, as well as access to the system at the local level and bearable cost are critical (see Overview and Thematic Note 2).

A review of the "one title holder per household" practice has shown the following:

- Titling guidelines do not call for the identification of more than one property-right holder in the household.
- Titling procedures do not allow for inquiry into the number of property-right holders in the household.
- Titling forms do not permit the listing of more than one property-right holder.
- Titling brigades are not trained to look for and identify more than one property-right holder.
- Titling activities with communities and households (informational meetings, workshops, and so forth) focus on men heads of household and do not encourage or facilitate the participation of other persons, including women.

In addition to these explicit or implicit institutional and procedural constraints, processes associated with implementation are, at best, more difficult for women than men to traverse. Sociocultural norms do not perceive women to be full and equal participants in the community and the economy, and women sometimes lack the skills and confidence to approach institutions that have traditionally been the domain of men.

GOOD PRACTICES AND LESSONS LEARNED

Legislation and policies related to land rights and property, in language and in intent, should not mention only men as holders of land rights. Nor should they be gender neutral. Policy and legislation must explicitly assert and affirm women's equal rights to land and property, and those rights should be independent of women's (and men's) civil or marital status. In Bolivia, for example, the law that establishes the legal basis for the current titling program specifically states that in the distribution, administration, tenure, and use of land, equity criteria will be applied in favor of women *and independently of their civil status.*[2] The last phrase is important because it does not require that a woman be the head of the household or married to be eligible for land rights.

Legislation should deal with the many different household arrangements that occur in real life. Besides the nuclear family, comprising one husband and one wife who are legally married, there are couples who are married under customary rules but not civil law, couples who are in consensual unions (that is, they are not married but are in an enduring relationship), and polygamous marriages. The legitimacy of these different kinds of household arrangements and their implication for the land rights of household members should be dealt with in a gender-sensitive manner. (See Thematic Note 2 for more details regarding land rights within different types of households and changing households.)

The regulations that are drawn up to implement legislation must specifically counteract constraints to women's ownership rights. It may also be necessary to review other legislation and regulations to ensure that they do not impose such constraints. For example, in Bolivia, although the land law clearly upheld women's land rights, irrespective of civil status, legislation for the land registry required that couples be legally married to be registered as co-owners.

Formal recognition of women's rights to land involves a number of land administration agencies, including land titling agencies, land registries, and judiciary offices. Some or all of these institutions will be involved in land titling and registration projects, and their specific policies and procedures will affect whether women are granted formal legal rights to land. All of these institutions need to undertake gender-sensitivity training with respect to land and property rights and the constraints women face in asserting those rights.

A number of practices increase the likelihood that women will be included in the implementation of land titling programs. Some of the problems faced by women include traversing the geographic and social distance to program officials, lack of knowledge or information, and the interplay between statutory and customary legal systems. Programs can reduce many of the procedural barriers and some of the customary constraints by making their activities and benefits available at the lowest possible level and by training staff at all levels to be conscious of the obstacles women face.

There is growing recognition that the practice of issuing titles to just one person in the household (the head of household) often denies other persons their land rights. As mentioned, more than one person may hold rights to a particular parcel of land, or, if there is more than one parcel, different persons may have rights to different parcels. Wives, for example, often have clearly recognized and legitimate use rights to household land. One of the first determinations, therefore, that needs to be made in the identification of property holders is to clarify who, besides the household head, holds rights to household landed property. The types of titles that can be issued to individual households and parcels, depending on the number of property holders and legal options, include individual title, joint title, and co-ownership titles.

Cultural norms affecting women's land rights

Land titling and registration programs will encounter cultural norms and practices that influence who is recognized as a legitimate property holder. These may vary within project areas and may conflict with formal legal norms. Issues that most affect women's rights to land are related to marital property and inheritance. (See the Overview for more information regarding marriage and inheritance practices that affect land rights.) For example, customary inheritance rights may not be in accord with legislation regarding intestate inheritance that mandates equal inheritance rights for daughters and sons and inheritance rights for surviving spouses. Titling and registration programs should draw up guidelines and procedures for dealing with the distribution of family land to heirs in ways that conflict with the formal law.

Marriage practices are other cultural norms that may influence land rights in ways that differ from formal legislation. The customary norm and practice in both matrilineal and patrilineal societies are that land inherited or received from one's family remains the property of that person and his or her lineage—it does not become part of the conjugal couple's property.

A potential problem is how land allocated by the state is viewed by the beneficiaries and who exactly are the beneficiaries. Very often land titling programs are part of, or occur subsequent to, land allocation programs. If the allocated land is clearly state land, it should not be considered lineage or family land, and land rights should be assigned according to formal law. In that case social equity concerns would indicate that the land be allocated and titled to both spouses and to single heads of families, whether men or women. In Bolivia, for example, the land titling project adopted the procedure that land parcels titled for the first time would be titled to the couple, not only to the head of the household.

In some cases, however, the land allocated by the state may be land that the community and its families formerly owned. This practice occurred frequently in some Eastern European countries, including Albania and Latvia, during the 1990s. Families may therefore believe that the land is actually theirs and that the allocation program is simply returning the land to them. In this case the issue of lineage will most likely influence which persons are believed to be legitimate property holders. Lineage issues may become a potential problem in Lao PDR, for example, as the titling program moves from urban to rural areas. Some rural areas are patrilineal, and women do not generally acquire landed property through parents or marriage. The land administration program will need guidelines and procedures to determine whether state allocation regulations or lineage norms determine the appropriate property holder(s) for a land parcel.

Joint titling

When the importance of wives' rights to household land is recognized, one mechanism used in titling land is to issue joint titles to both spouses and not only to the household head. Where legislation recognizes marital property to include assets (such as land) acquired during marriage,[3] determining when a piece of landed property was acquired should clarify whether the property should be titled to the conjugal couple or to one of the spouses. Legislation in Bolivia and Lao PDR, for example, recognizes marital property for spouses, and the procedures of the land titling projects

in those countries also explicitly require that land acquired by a couple is titled jointly. In addition, Bolivia stipulates that land granted by the state to a family is marital property and should be jointly titled. Joint title is an important document for women in vulnerable situations such as separation, divorce, abandonment, and widowhood because they do not need to follow an administrative or judicial process to prove that the property they had with their husband or companion does belong to them.

One issue that land administration programs may encounter is informal conjugal unions. In most countries that have recently reformed legislation to be more inclusive and sensitive with respect to gender issues, the legislation explicitly states that legal marriage as well as consensual union be considered the basis for marital or community property. As mentioned, the 1996 land law in Bolivia states that men and women, regardless of civil status, have equal rights to land. The Bolivian land administration project, therefore, requires that when a legal title or regularization certificate is issued for land held by a couple—irrespective of whether they are married or in a consensual union—both names must be included in the space provided for the title holder, recording the woman's name first and then the man's.

On this point, one issue is whether to recognize consensual unions if the legislation mentions only legal marriage and does not explicitly recognize consensual unions. This issue could be dealt with in the titling regulations and procedures by suggesting that evidence of joint use rights requires the joint titling option. Social assessments on this issue should inquire as to the prevalence of consensual unions in that society and the land use rights of both spouses. The results from this social assessment should guide decisions by land administration with respect to consensual unions.

Once it has been established whether joint titles are to be issued to consensual unions as well as legally married couples, it is necessary to determine which relationships are consensual unions. Most legislation that recognizes consensual unions also has a procedure for legal recognition of consensual unions. Others may simply list some basic criteria for consensual unions. In Bolivia titling procedures indicate that field appraisals by titling brigades must verify effective possession regardless of civil status (married, divorced, separated, single, widowed) or gender. In Colombia co-ownership does not have to be proved, only stated as true. In these cases land titling procedures accept consensual unions if couples meet these criteria or possess a certificate of legal recognition. In some countries where personal identification papers are an issue, particularly for low-income and illiterate persons, undertaking any legal procedure, such as establishing a consensual union, is problematic. A land administration project in rural Peru found a solution to this problem by issuing co-property titles. Under a co-property title, a couple's marital status (formal or consensual) is not considered, and both persons own a separate share of the property rather than owning the property together as a whole (Deere and Leon 2001). Land titling guidelines and procedures could include the option of issuing co-property titles to a couple if they cannot produce a certificate of consensual union.

Marital property and polygamy

Polygamous households present another set of issues in relation to marital property.[4] Not all societies outlaw polygamy, and even if they do, the law is generally ineffective if polygamy is customary or traditional. Polygamy seriously affects women's rights to property, however, and generates much tension and anxiety over land rights in many countries. Polygamy complicates legislation requiring written consent of spouses to dispose of property; it also complicates provisions on inheritance and co-ownership of land. Legislating around polygamy is difficult, but to ignore formal or informal polygamy is to protect women's property rights inadequately. The situation is made even more difficult by the fact that many men refuse to acknowledge or discuss polygamy, and women are often hesitant to raise the issue.

No effective and gender-sensitive titling procedures have been developed for polygamous households. Several countries have attempted to legislate land rights for women in polygamous marriages. In Ethiopia, for example, the Oromiya regulations (2002) require that the husband and wife be jointly certified for their commonly held land. In a polygamous marriage a husband is allowed to get a holding right certificate with only one of his wives, and the other(s) receive an independent right certificate. The use right of a family is not affected if either the husband or the wife or both leave the area. Under Burkina Faso's 1990 Family Code, if a couple is monogamous, their property is marital property, but if there is more than one wife, all property is separate property.

Where polygamy is widely practiced but illegal, however, it is ignored in relation to land rights. Field research in the Kyrgyz Republic revealed that women were concerned that they would lose not only their husbands but also rights to their husbands' incomes if their husbands took second wives. Women state that husbands generally favor second wives, so while their husbands are living, the first wives'

incomes and security are threatened. A first wife is also vulnerable to having to divide property among all of the husband's heirs. On the other hand, second wives are also a very vulnerable group: a second wife has no legal rights to any of her husband's income or property.

Cultural differences arising from rural-urban differences and a market economy

Legal norms and practices regarding land rights in rural and urban areas differ in many societies. In Lao PDR, for example, permanent land use titles are awarded to urban landholders under the Lao Land Titling Program, whereas rural landholders are awarded land use certificates that are valid for three years. Aside from legislation, there are other urban and rural differences. For example, it appears that customary norms and practices tend to change as people move from rural to urban areas. A study of customary land tenure systems in Lao PDR mentioned that titling land to women in Hmong villages "simply would not work, despite the laws of the country," yet it observed that recently Hmong families in urban areas have not adhered strictly to this custom, and both sons and daughters inherit land (Lao PDR, Ministry of Finance 2002: 59–60). Nevertheless, as the titling program in that country extends from urban to rural areas, it will have to deal with this conflict between formal and customary legal norms. In many societies land titling programs will need to establish ways of dealing with customary property and ownership norms that do not correspond to gender-equal statutory laws.

Illiteracy and lack of access to services may have a greater impact in the implementation of land titling and registration projects in rural areas. In Bolivia, as in many Latin American countries, low-income rural women often lack the identification cards required by titling procedures. The missing papers can either slow or prevent a claim, so more flexible procedures might be considered, such as the verification of identity by community leaders or a program component that makes it easy to obtain identification.

In a market economy, rural and urban differences can also affect property rights, especially notions of individual ownership. The market economy exerts its influence in urban areas by making production practices more labor intensive and market oriented. Land rights tend to become more individualized (less communal), families tend to become more nuclear (less extended), land rights tend to be acquired through purchase (rather than inheritance), and customary practices tend to become less prevalent. These tendencies are also seen in rural areas where intensive commercial agriculture is practiced, particularly among small and medium-size farm holdings. In these situations lineage considerations may diminish in importance, and opportunities for more flexible inheritance practices may arise. As a land market develops, more opportunities exist for both wife and husband to own land they have acquired together, for women to purchase land, and for bilateral inheritance practices to develop. Legislation, regulations, and titling procedures should build on these opportunities to formalize women's rights to land. Unfortunately, the practice in the past has been to strengthen men's individual land and property rights, to the detriment of wives, daughters, and daughters-in-law.

GUIDELINES AND RECOMMENDATIONS FOR PRACTITIONERS

As the discussion throughout this Note suggests, land titling and registration guidelines should take regional differences into consideration and require procedures that accommodate different contexts. Much of this contextual information, and the participatory methods for acquiring it, should be incorporated into the social assessment undertaken during the design phase. Detailed information regarding variations in, for example, multiple land use rights, inheritance, and marital property can then be a valuable input for strengthening women's land rights within the target area's sociocultural context. Wherever possible, titling procedures should not ignore or remove any land rights women may already hold and, wherever possible, should strive for gender equity in granting land rights.

Relevant issues are the quality of legislation and regulation and, more important, effective processes that bring the law in an equitable fashion to women. At the national level, formulation of non-gender-biased legislation and regulation and effective implementation institutions are important (see Thematic Note 2 for more details).

Political will on the part of executive and legislative bodies is of prime importance in this sphere. It ensures that gender policy not only is included in legislation and regulations but also translates into (1) objectives and guidelines for titling programs and related institutions and (2) resources for gender-equity programs and activities at the local level.

In the programmatic sphere, clear and concrete implementation guidelines, and gender-sensitive training are crucial. Gender guidelines, tools, and training should include the consideration of customary local institutions and practices that largely determine who has what rights to land and how that land can be used.

Because titling programs create opportunities for land grabbing and elite capture of land, one project activity with potentially positive effects for women and men is to inform communities in advance that land is being adjudicated. This information will help communities prevent the loss of their land rights to powerful or influential persons.

In the past, titling programs have tended to be designed by national agencies with minimal consultation, discussion, and dialogue with local stakeholders with regard to local problems, program objectives, and potential solutions. When they are excluded, stakeholders generally do not identify with a program and its objectives. Nor are they invested in its success. Local stakeholders with power or authority have been able to influence program implementation for their own interests at the cost of other stakeholders who have not directly benefited from state programs. Because women usually wield little power and have minimal public influence, their interests are often ignored and their rights violated even though legal codes mandate otherwise. For example, the effort to extend land rights to women during the 1990s via joint titling in Nicaragua had unexpected outcomes: most of the joint titles were not between spouses but between men relatives, such as a father and son or a brother and brother. The proportion of joint titles issued between 1992 and 1997 was an impressive 33 percent, but only 8 percent was issued to spouses (Lastarria-Cornhiel and others 2003). It is likely that joint titling by men relatives occurred to avoid including wives on the property title.

On the positive side, programs that seek active participation by local stakeholders are more likely to achieve their objectives. Civil society organizations can be very successful at promoting gender equity by their activities on the ground. Officials in the national sphere and especially in the programmatic sphere should be aware of local conditions and the limits and opportunities they present. Consideration of these opportunities and limits often determines the success of programs and the achievement of policy objectives.

Nepal: Women Gain a Voice and Greater Access to Resources through the Hills Leasehold Project

PROJECT OBJECTIVES AND DESCRIPTION

The Hills Leasehold Forestry and Forage Development Project (HLFFDP), supported by IFAD, is unprecedented in Nepal in its commitment to transferring assets directly to the poor. The project's combined objectives are to raise living standards among the poor and to regenerate degraded forest land. The project leases users' rights to forest land (which had become degraded through common access) to groups of 5–10 poor households, who are in charge of rehabilitating the land and entitled to use the forest products. Leases are renewable after 40 years. A further objective of the project is to empower the communities concerned by forming and training groups and mobilizing savings and access to credit.

Forests were to be restored principally by banning grazing in the leasehold sites, and households were to generate income by producing livestock fodder and forage and pursuing other activities. The major inputs were the subsidized provision of high-yielding grasses, seedlings of fodder trees, improved animal breeds, veterinary services, training programs, and agricultural credit.

Until 1995 the project confined its activities to four districts and then extended gradually to six more districts. The amended project target was to form 2,040 leasehold groups of

What's innovative? Landless women and men lease degraded forest lands and obtain complementary training in sustainable land management, basic literacy, and awareness of women's legal rights. Local women group promoters are employed to ensure that women's voices are heard and that women play leadership roles. Group promoters link with professional women to build supportive networks.

14,600 poor households and to restore 13,000 hectares of degraded forest. To join a group, a household had to have less than half a hectare of land (or none) and an annual income below the poverty line, although a degree of flexibility was permitted. Priority was given to landless and near-landless groups, disadvantaged tribal groups, and women-headed households.

The project supports leasehold forestry as opposed to community forestry. Over one-third of Nepal's population participates in community forestry programs, whereas leasehold initiatives are at an early stage. Community forestry measures are directed at entire communities and concentrate on forest conservation. Leasehold forestry involves a redistribution of assets in favor of the poor by leasing degraded sites to specific groups of resource-poor farming households. The leasehold groups are smaller and more homogeneous, and their legal status remains insecure. Antagonism between the two forestry approaches has been replaced by more constructive ideas concerning their coexistence or integration.

GENDER APPROACH

When the project was designed, an explicit objective was to integrate gender and disadvantaged (ethnic) group issues and considerations in the approach and its implementation. Nine activities related to this objective were outlined within planning, training, extension, and monitoring and evaluation. Women and households headed either de jure or de facto by poor women were to receive special attention.

A key aspect of the gender agenda within the project was the leadership provided by two project leaders, one from Nepal's Department of Forests (DOF) and one from the Food and Agriculture Organization. These managers, who were both men, had the confidence and foresight to hire a three-woman gender team and grant them the autonomy to develop an innovative strategy. The team's goal was to challenge the organizational culture of the implementing agencies and make men counterparts in the DOF and the project coordination unit more aware of and responsive to the realities of rural women.

The team added an objective on gender equality to its plan; previously gender equality had not been explicitly taken up by project staff. The plan was to implement activities at the policy, district, and grassroots levels, but the team chose to focus on recruiting and developing a cadre of women group promoters throughout the project area. The promoters would mobilize rural women to participate in the leasehold groups.

Gender and leadership training was provided to the group promoters through formal training sessions and study tours to learn from other projects. Given the paucity of women staff within the implementing line agencies, the team identified gender focal persons (mostly men) within these agencies and developed the gender skills of these individuals through training, coaching, and guidance. These technical staff thus gained an awareness of gender equity issues, women's rights (including those outlined in international agreements such as the Convention on the Elimination of All Forms of Discrimination against Women), and the community work of the group promoters.

Another element of the strategy was to foster networking and communication. Two magazines were developed and distributed, one to exchange information among gender focal points in the technical agencies in the district and another created by the group promoters at the grassroots level. Articles in the group promoters' magazine boldly expressed their positions on issues related to gender and women's rights and were widely circulated throughout the DOF.

In 1999 the women group promoters began to organize group meetings, promote the project, organize groups, give training, and note problems. Training was given to couples (husbands and wives) who were prospective beneficiaries of the project. Women, mostly from ethnic minorities, were given priority in training to manage tree and plant nurseries and other relevant activities. Through these activities women have acquired technical knowledge and basic literacy and are much more aware of their legal rights. Women's participation and leadership roles were favored by the all-women group promoters. Currently, 25 percent of the participants are women, there are 74 all-women groups, and there are 112 women group leaders.

BENEFITS AND IMPACTS

The project demonstrated impacts in the areas of poverty and gender.

Project impacts

After nine years of implementation, the HLFFDP was recognized within the development community of Nepal as an innovative, unique project that achieved a significant impact on the lives of group members, especially women, as well as on the environment. Key successes are the following:

- Forty-year leases give 1,800 household groups user rights over degraded forest land totaling 7,400 hectares.
- Once restored, the forest areas are a rich source of fodder, timber, and fuel as well as trees and plants that the groups use and sell.
- Goat ownership has increased from an average of two to five per household, as has revenue from goat sales (to $100 per household per year).
- Income from grasses, grass seed, and other forest products is now significant (up to $70 per household per year), although weak market linkages and inadequate information on demand and market prices have limited sales in some areas.
- The 120 leasehold intergroups and 18 multipurpose cooperatives created during the project have been instrumental in tackling market issues because of their strong bargaining power and success in creating market outlets. Infrastructure grants made to groups and intergroups helped build culverts and bridges, renovate schools, complete 160 small drinking-water supply projects, and improve trails and footpaths.
- The women group promoters formed their own association, which continues to advocate for women's rights related to forest management and to promote women's access to livestock and forest development resources at the local and national levels.

Gender impacts

Meetings held with women participants of HLFFDP through an initiative of the International Land Coalition's Women's Resource Access Programme (WRAP) in 2001 revealed their perspectives on the project's impact.[1] (For more information in WRAP, see www.landcoalition.org.)

Saving time was the biggest benefit noted by the women, because they spent less time collecting grass, fodder, and fuelwood, which were more plentiful, closer to their homes, and located in familiar places. Many women emphasized that the substantial technical assistance, knowledge, and credit they received had better equipped them to use their new-found time.

Empowerment through group action is another benefit: regular meetings provide a forum to discuss project-related issues and general community matters. Both women's group meetings and mixed meetings are held. Women's participation is generally greater at the meetings of women-only leasehold forestry groups than at the mixed groups, and it is easier to ensure their participation in the women-only groups. In the all-women group meetings, extremely sensitive issues such as domestic violence are easily addressed. In this regard many women see the group meetings as both a "protective court"—where instances of domestic violence can be brought out into the open and challenged—and a place to confront social issues and become stronger.

Moreover, through the training program most women have acquired basic literacy skills, and the group members are much more aware of their legal rights and the importance of education and adequate health, sanitation, and nutrition for themselves and their families.

Through the workshops, training courses, and community meetings, women were progressively exposed to the world around them. Several group leaders were interviewed on television and on a weekly radio program on leasehold forestry. Young women in particular expressed a dramatic increase in their self-confidence, which they attributed to their group work, group discussions, and decision-making abilities.

Many workshop participants expressed their satisfaction at the increased amounts of food and livestock fodder that resulted from their access to leasehold forest land. With the acquisition of leasehold land, many women started cultivating mulberries and vegetables and selling *chiraito* (*Swertia* spp., a medicinal plant used to treat malaria and other health problems). The income generated from this activity is used for children's school needs, medicine, food, clothing, and group savings. Men still control most household income, but women are now more involved in household decision making.

The women interviewed about HLFFDP felt that men were more accepting of women's status and of their right to have agricultural land in their name. About 20 percent of titles are now estimated to be registered in women's names. The women also felt that men had increasingly accepted and supported this transition and the accompanying shifts in responsibility and power. Many women attributed this change to changes in their own level of confidence, which has increased over the years because they have gained access to land and received training and credit. Their husbands are willing to support these women, who have demonstrated the many benefits that can be derived from their increased responsibility and decision-making ability. Others attribute this acceptance to their husbands' belief that credit is more easily obtained by women and to the recognition that institutions (governmental and nongovernmental) increasingly favor pro-poor and pro-women schemes.

LESSONS LEARNED AND ISSUES FOR WIDER APPLICABILITY

Although the HLFFDP project is considered a success, issues are seen with security of tenure, high cost of intervention, need for increased focus on lower-cost and local technologies and knowledge, and need for increased use of support organizations.

Gender integration has contributed to successes like the following:

■ Giving women secure access to land and forestry can transform their lives.

■ Much of the project's success at producing benefits for women is due to the strategic interventions of the project's gender team and their capacity- and team-building efforts with the group promoters. The sense of trust and solidarity that evolved provided the group promoters with high levels of motivation and pride. Their status also improved through linkages with the gender team to high-level project staff and government officials.

■ Special training in gender awareness and other gender-sensitive activities can provide women with new skills and resources to challenge their traditional roles and gain secure access to natural resources.

■ Talking to poor women and men, listening to their views and perceptions, and learning from their knowledge can provide valuable insights that cannot be gained elsewhere. The method should be easily replicated, and the different needs and opportunities of the men and women reflected here could be the basis of gender-responsive actions in projects and programs.

■ The participation of women and disadvantaged groups requires more active promotion by providing appropriate sensitization training to all project staff, as well as to members of communities in which leasehold forestry is introduced. The transfer of the lease from men to women should be encouraged in cases in which the men leasehold group members are inactive.

■ One gap is related to the institutionalization of the approach. The DOF lacks a formal institutional directive for gender mainstreaming and a single structure to address the issue, so the nearly all-men department remains ignorant about the benefits that could be derived from a gender focus. One solution would be to build gender structures into the Ministry of Forests and Soil Conservation and the DOF. Although a gender cell now exists, a woman coordinator requires significantly more resources and capacity building to be effective.

Honduras: A Pilot Project Protects Women's Rights to Productive Resources

I n Honduras the Land Access Pilot Project (Proyecto Acceso a la Tierra [PACTA]), initially supported by the World Bank, promotes poor people's acquisition of land, increases the awareness of joint property rights over production resources, and implements legal alternatives to guarantee those rights regardless of whether a couple is married. The project also promotes equal participation by household members in rural enterprises, the formation of enterprises managed by women, and the development of a training process that contributes to greater gender equity.

PROJECT OBJECTIVES AND DESCRIPTION

Between 2001 and 2004 PACTA emphasized the acquisition of land and the formation of sustainable economic enterprises by self-organized landless and land-poor rural families. The pilot tested a strategy in which the private sector provided credit to buy land and the public sector provided funds for complementary investments and technical assistance to improve the land's productivity. The pilot was implemented on a larger scale in 2005–07 and then extended for another three years of implementation and evaluation from 2007 to 2009.[1]

What's innovative? Through public-private sector collaboration, a pilot project enables landless and land-poor rural families to obtain land and manage it productively. The project has devised innovative legal strategies to ensure that women, regardless of whether they are legally married, gain equal rights to the new production resources and more equal participation in new rural enterprises.

The project seeks to reach rural people with little or no access to land. Project components include technical and legal assistance to rural producers, land purchase loans, and complementary subproject grants. The project was designed with a participatory monitoring and evaluation system. PACTA also incorporated lessons from the experiences of the World Bank over the years in promoting access to land, including providing complementing services with the land purchase schemes, not imposing any models of production or association, using existing institutions where possible, encouraging stakeholder participation (PACTA's board has members from government, financial institutions, local technical units, and producer organizations), and stressing participatory project preparation.

GENDER APPROACH

The gender strategy was not formulated at the beginning of the pilot in 2001 but was deemed crucial as the pilot progressed. By the end of 2003, a gender approach was incorporated in the three-year implementation plan for the expanded pilot (2005–07). The project has implemented a number of gender-related strategies and activities (table 4.2).

BENEFITS AND IMPACTS

PACTA demonstrated impacts in the areas of both poverty and gender.

Poverty impacts

The average income of families in PACTA enterprises had increased by 130 percent as of 2004 compared to the initial levels before the project. By the end of 2004, 1,226 families that participated in the pilot were employed, and about 700–900 person-year equivalents of employment had been generated. This productive labor use is likely to increase as farms develop

Table 4.2 Gender-Related Activities and Strategies Pursued during Three Stages of the Expanded PACTA Land Access Pilot, Honduras, 2005–07

Design stage	Implementation stage	Monitoring and evaluation stage
Proposed a standard conceptual framework for rural development from the gender equity perspective in PACTA	Included a gender equity perspective in the operations and technical assistance manual	Documented experiences to systematize them
Conducted a diagnostic study to identify strategic gender equity actions that needed to be developed	Trained the local technical units so they could do their work from a gender equity perspective	Proposed indicators to be included in the project's baseline survey so that changes in gender relations within the family could be measured
Formulated a gender equity strategy	Developed a systematic training and follow-up process in one of PACTA's geographic areas	n.a.
Incorporated a gender equity approach when making up business plans, as an incentive for local technical units	Promoted the project among organized women's groups to encourage them to participate	n.a.
	Implemented legal alternatives in selected businesses to ensure that a couple has equal ownership rights over production assets	n.a.
	Incorporated gender-related components into business plans	n.a.

Source: PACTA project documents.

and consolidate. Of the 1,226 families, 980 were day laborers, sharecroppers, or other kinds of subsistence producers. The rest were poor families with access to municipal forest land or communal land.

The local support networks that coalesced around PACTA enterprises constitute a potentially important source for community economic initiatives. An example is the alliance between PACTA enterprises; a regional producer cooperative, COPRAUL (Regional Cooperative of United Farmers Ltda.); a program for marketing and processing agricultural products, PROACTA; and a local service provider that works with PACTA enterprises. In a process led by COPRAUL, these organizations cooperated to develop a purchasing and warehouse operation that enabled the 250 members of COPRAUL to sell their potato crop directly to major buyers, including a chain of supermarkets. Finally, PACTA seems to show a positive impact in reducing migration to major cities in Honduras and to the United States among families who participate in the project.

Gender impacts

Clearly, the project has helped women to own land. Among the women participating in the project in 2005, 20 percent were direct members who had acquired land and received the corresponding technical assistance and training.[2] Women who were not direct members could still obtain

funds if they actively managed business ventures. The project differentiates between women who are partners in businesses and the wives or household partners of men who are business partners. The participation of women who are household partners of men PACTA members started in 2005 (table 4.3). Previous land projects did not consider the skills, abilities, and interests of women family members and so did not include business- or work-related activities performed or managed by women in the business plan. That business plans now include the activities of women family members who are not business partners is an important innovation of this project. As of 2006, the percentage of new enterprises that assigned resources in their investment plans to income-generating activities managed by a wife or household partner of a men PACTA member was 17 percent. This figure is lower than the target of 30 percent, but it indicates that the inclusion of women family members in business plans enables services and support to reach more women.

LESSONS LEARNED AND ISSUES FOR WIDER APPLICABILITY

In its pilot phase, PACTA laid the foundation for enterprises established with its support to implement measures and actions that give husbands and wives equal access to the

Table 4.3 Measurable Impacts of PACTA

Variable	Indicator	Objective	Results
Equal access to technology	Percentage of women and percentage of men who use technology in their productive activities	50% of men and 40% of women	30% of men members and 30% of women members
Equal access to training	Percentage of women who have received training in aspects related to enterprise development and who are applying the acquired knowledge	100% of women members and 30% of wives or household partners of men members	100% of women members and 10% of wives, household partners, or both of men members
	Percentage of men who have received training in aspects related to enterprise development and who are applying the acquired knowledge	100% of men members and 20% of husbands or household partners	100% of men members and 20% of household partner of women members
Equal participation of men and women in enterprises participating in PACTA	Number of women's groups that have formed and developed enterprises	Three groups	One all-woman enterprise and four enterprises in which women are the majority
	Increase in women's participation in enterprises as direct members	20%	20%
	Percentage of new enterprises that assign resources in their investment plans to activities that generate incomes managed by the wife or household partner of men members	30%	17% of new enterprises formed between 2005 and 2006
Participation in the decision-making process	Percentage of mixed enterprises (in which both men and women are business partners) in which women are board members with decision-making power	30%	24% (mixed enterprises, 2005–06)
Rights to land and other productive resources	Percentage of enterprises that have taken legal measures to ensure that title to the land is issued to the couple, once the loan is paid off	10% of the total number of contracts	5.5% in 2005–06
	Percentage of new enterprises that stipulate rights favoring the couple regarding land and resources in their constitution document, in their rules or agreements, or in more than one of these	40% of new enterprises that began to participate in the project in 2005	9.7%
Participation in monitoring and evaluation	Percentage of men and women in families participating in monitoring and evaluation activities	50%	30%

Source: PACTA participatory evaluation and monitoring and information system.

land and other production assets. Lessons learned include the following:

- The participation of women in decision-making processes is crucial to ensure women's successful participation in business enterprises.
- To achieve the proposed objectives, it is necessary to invest in raising awareness and training staff of local technical units in gender equity.
- Developing business plans with the participation of the whole family is essential to ensure the inclusion of women in production activities.
- Providing family-oriented information and awareness encourages men to change their attitude toward their family obligations, value their wives' or partners' contribution to production activities, and recognize their wives' or partners' ownership rights over any assets they may acquire.
- Women's organization skills and experience facilitate joining the project.
- The main obstacle to women's participation in production and business activities is that they are almost exclusively responsible for raising children. Presently the enterprises that women can pursue successfully require little time and include small, profitable enterprises such as growing strawberries. An integrated development vision should foster the public institutions that rural families need to address such basic necessities as health care, education, day-care facilities, and public services so that families can increase their capacity to engage in a business venture.
- Product marketing must be strengthened, and technical assistance to make production more competitive must be guaranteed, especially for women's production activities, given that they have been excluded from acquiring such knowledge.

In its gender-related work, PACTA faces a number of challenges:

- Implementing the project's gender strategy while addressing cultural differences
- Expanding and strengthening alliances with public and private sector organizations that can help promote integrated family development and ease women's child-rearing responsibilities so that they can participate successfully in business activities
- Encouraging local support networks established with project support to adopt a gender-related perspective
- Creating awareness of the importance of gender training at all levels of PACTA staff.

NOTES

Overview

This Overview was written by Susan Lastarria-Cornhiel (University of Wisconsin-Madison) and reviewed by Nata Duvvury (Consultant); Victor Mosoti and David Palmer (FAO); Ruth Meinzen-Dick (IFPRI); Sabine Pallas (International Land Coalition); and Malcolm Childress, Edward Cook, and Indira Ekanayake (World Bank).

1. According to information from Malcolm Childress and Mukta Mahajani of the Land Policy and Administration Thematic Group, the World Bank has increased the number of land administration projects in the rural sector almost sixfold since 1995, from 4 to 23. The total loan portfolio has increased at a similar rate, from $172 million to $1,037 million. The number of rural development projects with a land administration component increased from 51 to 74.

2. For example, between 1978 and 2005, 21 percent of IFAD's projects in Latin America and the Caribbean (19 of 92 projects) had components for improving land access and tenure security (Hopkins, Carpano, and Zilveti 2005).

3. As a technical agency, FAO is currently collaborating with the World Bank on 30 land administration projects in 26 countries.

4. This Overview borrows heavily from Giovarelli and others (2005).

5. See Deere and Leon (2001) for an exhaustive review and analysis of women's rights to land in Latin America for the last few centuries and particularly since the 1950s.

6. More extensive descriptions of these land administration elements can be found in FAO (2002).

7. Customary rules and practices refer to those that are followed by communities and local groups and are not necessarily recognized by formal law; in fact, they may contradict formal legal norms.

8. Local authorities (whether formally appointed or community recognized) may not administer land and natural resources equitably or even legitimately by local norms. Experience from a number of countries has shown that oversight and supervision from a higher level of government are needed to avoid problems such as elite capture and to ensure that local authorities follow relevant formal law.

9. E. Mwangi, "Subdividing the Commons: The Politics of Property Rights Transformation in Kenya's Maasailand," CAPRI Working Paper 46 (Washington, DC: CGIAR System-Wide Program on Collective Action and Property Rights, 2006), www.capri.cgiar.org/wp/capriwp46.asp.

10. House ownership is also important in addition to land ownership. Particularly in the South Asian and Latin American context, women in a landless laborer household supplement the subsistence income from wage earning

with supplementary food from kitchen gardens on the housesites.

11. The land allocated by the woman's family to her husband is not his to alienate or pass on. If he leaves the community and leaves his wife, the land returns to the lineage.

12 See the GAL *eSourcebook* for suggested monitoring and evaluation indicators for each Thematic Note (www.world bank.org).

Thematic Note 1

This Thematic Note was written by Susan Lastarria-Cornhiel (University of Wisconsin-Madison) and reviewed by Nata Duvvury (Consultant); Victor Mosoti and David Palmer (FAO); Ruth Meinzen-Dick (IFPRI); and Malcolm Childress, Edward Cook, and Indira Ekanayake (World Bank).

1. Most tenure systems have control rights such as freehold ownership under freehold tenure, commons, family land under customary tenure, and devolution of rights of state land. These systems often coexist or overlap in an area.

2. Customary allocation and management of land and other natural resources may or may not conflict with formal legislation and regulations. Customary authorities and rules operate in situations in which state agencies are not able to enforce natural resource management rules on the ground.

3. Comprehensive reviews of land reforms by Deere and Leon (2001) for Latin America and Agarwal (2003) for India reveal how few women received land from land reform programs.

4. A recent study in Ghana, for example, has shown that women heads of households, as compared with men heads, are significantly less likely to acquire land through purchase and rental (Quisumbing and others 1999).

5. United Nations-Office for the Coordination of Humanitarian Affairs, "Zimbabwe: Focus on Women's Lack of Access to Land," OCHA and Integrated Regional Information Network, December 4, www.irinnews.org/report.aspx? repor tid=40021.

6. The Lowlands Agricultural Development Programme (LADEP) is funded by the IFAD and the government of The Gambia.

7. The LIFE Programme is a joint program between U.S. Agency for International Development (USAID) and Namibia, the World Wildlife Fund (WWF), and Namibian NGOs.

8. For a review of this type of land reform, see Nielsen, Hanstad, and Rolfes (2006).

Thematic Note 2

This Thematic Note was written by Renee Giovarelli (Consultant) and reviewed by Nata Duvvury (Consultant); Victor Mosoti and David Palmer (FAO); Ruth Meinzen-Dick

(IFPRI); and Malcolm Childress, Edward Cook, and Indira Ekanayake (World Bank).

1. G. Gopal, "Law and Legal Reforms," 2020 Focus No. 06: Brief 12 (Washington, DC: International Food Policy Research Institute, 2001), www.ifpri.org/2020/focus/ focus06/focus06_12.asp.

2. The term "owned" is used throughout this Thematic Note, but it is meant to include long-term use rights that are like ownership.

3. Civil Code of the Dominican Republic, Art. 1421, 1428; Family Code of Honduras, Article 82; Family Law in Mexican States of Aguas Calientes, Oaxaca, and Sonora; Civil Code of Ecuador; Civil Code of Guatemala.

4. Some case law from common-law African countries retroactively vests legal recognition on a polygamous (illegal) union for purposes of inheritance or divorce and maintenance.

5. On the other hand, women in matrilineal societies are often in a very powerful position in relation to land rights. For a general discussion, see Strickland (2004).

6. Article 3, Paragraph V, Servicio Nacional de Reforma Agraria, Ley No. 1715, passed in 1996 and popularly known as the "Ley INRA."

Thematic Note 3

This Thematic Note was written by Susan Lastarria-Cornhiel (University of Wisconsin-Madison) and reviewed by Nata Duvvury (Consultant); Victor Mosoti and David Palmer (FAO); Ruth Meinzen-Dick (IFPRI); and Malcolm Childress, Edward Cook, and Indira Ekanayake (World Bank).

1. In some African and Asian countries, women are still considered minors and cannot enter into transactions or initiate official procedures without an adult man.

2. See Brown, Ananthpur, and Giovarelli (2002) for India and Walker (2003) for South Africa.

3. Examples of legislative reform that recognize customary land tenure are Australia (1976), Bolivia (1995), Mozambique (1997), Niger (1993), Philippines (1997), Senegal (1964), Tanzania (1999), and Uganda (1998).

4. G. Gopal, "Law and Legal Reforms," 2020 Focus No. 06: Brief 12 (Washington, DC: International Food Policy Research Institute, 2001), www.ifpri.org/2020/focus/focus06/ focus06_12.asp.

Thematic Note 4

This Thematic Note was written by Susan Lastarria-Cornhiel (University of Wisconsin-Madison) and reviewed by Nata Duvvury (Consultant); Victor Mosoti and David

Palmer (FAO); Ruth Meinzen-Dick (IFPRI); and Malcolm Childress, Edward Cook, and Indira Ekanayake (World Bank).

1. This Thematic Note borrows heavily from Giovarelli and others (2005).

2. Article 3, Paragraph V, Servicio Nacional de Reforma Agraria, Ley No. 1715, passed in 1996 and popularly known as the "Ley INRA."

3. Most marital property laws exempt inherited property from becoming part of community property.

4. This section on marital property and polygamy is taken largely from UN-HABITAT (2005).

Innovative Activity Profile 1

This Innovative Activity Profile was prepared by Catherine Ragasa (Consultant), with input and review from Sabine Pallas (International Land Coalition) and Jeanette Gurung (WOCAN). This Profile was largely drawn from ILC (2001), IFAD (n.d.), and Gurung and Lama (n.d.).

1. This section is mainly based on ILO (2001).

Innovative Activity Profile 2

This Innovative Activity Profile was prepared by Catherine Ragasa (Consultant), with input from Aleyda Ramirez (FAO-Honduras) and Francisco Pichon (World Bank), and reviewed by Susan Lastarria-Cornhiel (University of Wisconsin-Madison). This Profile was largely drawn from the Project Appraisal Document and Implementation Completion and Results Report (World Bank 2000, 2007) and personal communication with the project team.

1. This account mainly describes impacts as of 2007.

2. Only one family member may represent a family in a business as a direct partner, to avoid duplicating nonreimbursable transfers.

REFERENCES

Overview

Agarwal, Bina. 1988. "Who Sows? Who Reaps? Women and Land Rights in India." *Journal of Peasant Studies* 15 (4): 531–81.

Brown, Jennifer. 2003. "Rural Women's Land Rights in Java, Indonesia: Strengthened by Family Law, but Weakened by Land Registration." *Pacific Rim Law and Policy Journal* 12: 631–51.

Deere, Camen Diana, and Magdalena Leon. 2001. *Empowering Women: Land and Property Rights in Latin America.* Pittsburgh: University of Pittsburgh Press.

Deininger, Klaus. 2003. *Land Policies for Growth and Poverty Reduction.* Washington, DC: World Bank and Oxford University Press.

Fafchamps, Marcel, and Agnes R. Quisumbing. 2002. "Control and Ownership of Assets within Rural Ethiopian Households." *Journal of Development Studies* 38 (6): 47–82.

Food and Agriculture Organization of the United Nations (FAO). 2002. *Gender and Access to Land.* Land Tenure Study 4. Rome: FAO.

Giovarelli, Renee, Elizabeth Katz, Susan Lastarria-Cornhiel, and Sue Nichols. 2005. "Gender Issues and Best Practices in Land Administration Projects: A Synthesis Report." Agriculture and Rural Development Department Report No. 32571-GLB, World Bank, Washington, DC.

Hamilton, Sarah. 1998. *The Two-Headed Household: Gender and Rural Development in the Ecuadorean Andes.* Pittsburgh: University of Pittsburgh Press.

Hopkins, Raul, Francesca Carpano, and Veruschka Zilveti. 2005. *The Experience of IFAD in Latin America and the Caribbean.* Rome: International Land Coalition.

Katz, Elizabeth, and Juan Sebastian Chamorro. 2003. "Gender, Land Rights, and the Household Economy in Rural Nicaragua and Honduras." Paper presented at the annual conference of the Latin American and Caribbean Economics Association, Puebla, Mexico, October 9–11.

Lastarria-Cornhiel, Susan, Sonia Agurto, Jennifer Brown, and Sara Elisa Rosales. 2003. "Joint Titling in Nicaragua, Indonesia, and Honduras: Rapid Appraisal Synthesis." Madison: Land Tenure Center, University of Wisconsin–Madison.

Meinzen-Dick, Ruth, Lynn R. Brown, Hilary Sims Feldstein, and Agnes R. Quisumbing. 1997. "Gender, Property Rights, and Natural Resources." *World Development* 25 (8): 1303–15.

Panda, Pradeep, and Bina Agarwal. 2005. "Marital Violence, Human Development and Women's Property Status in India." *World Development* 33 (5): 823–50.

Platteau Jean-Philippe, Anita Abraham, A.-S. Brasselle, F. Gaspart, A. Niang, J.-P. Sawadogo, and Luc Stevens. 2000. *Marriage System, Access to Land, and Social Protection for Women.* Namur: Centre de Recherche en Economie du Développement.

Quisumbing, Agnes, and John Maluccio. 2003. "Resources at Marriage and Intrahousehold Allocation: Evidence from Bangladesh, Ethiopia, Indonesia, and South Africa." *Oxford Bulletin of Economics and Statistics* 65 (3): 283–327.

Stivens, Maila. 1985. "The Fate of Women's Land Rights: Gender, Matriliny, and Capitalism in Rembau, Negeri Sembilan, Malaysia." In *Women, Work, and Ideology in the Third World*, ed. Haleh Afshar, 3–36. London: Tavistock Publications.

Thematic Note 1

Agarwal, Bina. 2003. "Gender and Land Rights Revisited: Exploring New Prospects via the State, Family and Markets." *Journal of Agrarian Change* 3 (1–2): 184–224.

Brown, Jennifer, Kripa Ananthpur, and Renee Giovarelli. 2002. "Women's Access and Rights to Land in Karnataka, India." Rural Development Institute Reports on Foreign Aid and Development No. 114, Rural Development Institute, Seattle.

Deere, Carmen Diana. 2003. "Women's Land Rights and Rural Social Movements in the Brazilian Agrarian Reform." *Journal of Agrarian Change* 3 (1–2): 257–88.

Deere, Carmen Diana, and Magdalena Leon. 2001. *Empowering Women: Land and Property Rights in Latin America*. Pittsburgh: University of Pittsburgh.

Lastarria-Cornhiel, Susan, and R. Wheeler. 1998. "Gender, Ethnicity, and Landed Property in Albania." LTC Working Paper No. 18, Land Tenure Center, University of Wisconsin, Madison.

Nielsen, Robin, Tim Hanstad, and Leonard Rolfes. 2006. *Implementing Homestead Plot Programmes: Experience from India*. Rome: Food and Agriculture Organization.

Quisumbing, Agnes R., Ellen Payongayong, J. B. Aidoo, and Keijiro Otsuka. 1999. "Women's Land Rights in the Transition to Individualized Ownership: Implications for the Management of Tree Resources in Western Ghana." FCND Discussion Paper 58, International Food Policy Research Institute, Washington, DC.

Walker, Cherryl. 2003. "Piety in the Sky? Gender Policy and Land Reform in South Africa." In *Agrarian Change, Gender and Land Rights*, ed. Shahra Razavi, 113–48. Oxford: Blackwell Publishing.

Thematic Note 2

Bruce, John W., Renee Giovarelli, Leonard Rolfes, Jr., David Bledsoe, and Robert Mitchell. 2006. *Land Law Reform: Achieving Development Policy Objectives*. Law, Justice, and Development Series. Washington, DC: World Bank.

Deere, Carmen Diana, and Magdalena Leon. 2001. *Empowering Women: Land and Property Rights in Latin America*. Pittsburgh: University of Pittsburgh Press.

Giovarelli, Renee. 2006. "Overcoming Gender Biases in Established and Transitional Property Rights Systems." In *Land Law Reform: Achieving Development Policy Objectives*, ed. J. W. Bruce, R. Giovarelli, L. Rolfes, Jr., D. Bledsoe, and R. Mitchell, 67–106. Law, Justice, and Development Series. Washington, DC: World Bank.

Giovarelli, Renee, Elizabeth Katz, Susan Lastarria-Cornhiel, and Sue Nichols. 2005. "Gender Issues and Best Practices in Land Administration Projects: A Synthesis Report." Agriculture and Rural Development Department Report No. 32571-GLB, World Bank, Washington, DC.

Lastarria-Cornhiel, Susan, Sonia Agurto, Jennifer Brown, and Sara Elisa Rosales. 2003. "Joint Titling in Nicaragua, Indonesia, and Honduras: Rapid Appraisal Synthesis." Madison: Land Tenure Center, University of Wisconsin–Madison.

Strickland, Richard. 2004. "To Have and to Hold: Women's Property and Inheritance Rights in the Context of HIV/AIDS in Sub-Saharan Africa." Working paper, International Center for Research on Women, Washington, DC.

Tripp, Aili Mari. 2004. "Women's Movements, Customary Law, and Land Rights in Africa: The Case of Uganda." *African Studies Quarterly* 7 (4): 1–19.

United Nations Human Settlements Programme (UN–HABITAT). 2005. *Shared Tenure Options for Women*. Nairobi: UN–HABITAT.

Thematic Note 3

Agarwal, Bina. 1994. *A Field of One's Own: Gender and Land Rights in South Asia*. Cambridge: Cambridge University Press.

Brown, Jennifer, Kripa Ananthpur, and Renee Giovarelli. 2002. "Women's Access and Rights to Land in Karnataka, India." Rural Development Institute Reports on Foreign Aid and Development No. 114, Rural Development Institute, Seattle.

Giovarelli, Renee, Chinara Aidarbekova, Jennifer Duncan, Kathryn Rasmussen, and Anara Tabyshalieva. 2001. "Women's Rights to Land in the Kyrgyz Republic." Unpublished manuscript.

Giovarelli, Renee, Elizabeth Katz, Susan Lastarria-Cornhiel, and Sue Nichols. 2005. "Gender Issues and Best Practices in Land Administration Projects: A Synthesis Report." Agriculture and Rural Development Department Report No. 32571-GLB, World Bank, Washington, DC.

Legal Assistance to Rural Citizens (LARC). 2006. *Final Report on the Activity of the Project and Public Association*. Bishkek: LARC.

Meinzen-Dick, Ruth S., and Rajendra Pradhan. 2002. "Legal Pluralism and Dynamic Property Rights." CAPRI Working

Paper 22, CGIAR System-Wide Program on Collective Action and Property Rights, Washington, DC.

Strickland, Richard. 2004. "To Have and to Hold: Women's Property and Inheritance Rights in the Context of HIV/AIDS in Sub-Saharan Africa." International Center for Research on Women, Washington, DC.

Walker, Cherryl. 2003. "Piety in the Sky? Gender Policy and Land Reform in South Africa" In *Agrarian Change, Gender and Land Rights*, ed. Shahra Razavi, 113–48. Oxford: Blackwell.

Thematic Note 4

Barham, Brad, Michael R. Carter, and Wagne Sigelko. 1995. "Agro-export Production and Peasant Land Access: Examining the Dynamic between Adoption and Accumulation." *Journal of Development Economics* 46 (1): 85–107.

Deere, Carmen Diana, and Magdalena Leon. 2001. *Empowering Women: Land and Property Rights in Latin America*. Pittsburgh: University of Pittsburgh Press.

Deininger, Klaus. 2003. *Land Policies for Growth and Poverty Reduction*. Washington, DC: World Bank and Oxford University Press.

Giovarelli, Renee, Elizabeth Katz, Susan Lastarria-Cornhiel, and Sue Nichols. 2005. "Gender Issues and Best Practices in Land Administration Projects: A Synthesis Report." Agriculture and Rural Development Department Report No. 32571-GLB, World Bank, Washington, DC.

Katz, Elizabeth, and Susan Lastarria-Cornhiel. 2006. "Land Tenure Formalization and Agricultural Productivity in Lao PDR: Exploring Gender Differences." Unpublished manuscript.

Lao PDR, Ministry of Finance, Department of Lands. 2002. *Existing Land Tenure and Forest Lands Study*. Vientiane: Ministry of Finance, Department of Lands.

Lastarria-Cornhiel, Susan. 1988. "Female Farmers and Agricultural Production in El Salvador." *Development and Change* 19: 585–615.

Lastarria-Cornhiel, Susan, Sonia Agurto, Jennifer Brown, and Sara Elisa Rosales. 2003. "Joint Titling in Nicaragua, Indonesia, and Honduras: Rapid Appraisal Synthesis." Madison: Land Tenure Center, University of Wisconsin–Madison.

Quisumbing, Agnes R. 1996. "Male–Female Differences in Agricultural Productivity: Methodological Issues and Empirical Evidence." *World Development* 24 (10): 1579–95.

United Nations Human Settlements Programme (UN–HABITAT). 2005. *Shared Tenure Options for Women*. Nairobi: UN–HABITAT.

Innovative Activity Profile 1

Gurung, Jeanette, and K. Lama. n.d. "Empowered Women and the Men behind Them: A Study of Change within the Hills Leasehold Forestry and Forage Development Project in Nepal." Rome: IFAD. Available at www.ifad.org.

International Fund for Agricultural Development (IFAD). n.d. "Nepal: Hills Leasehold Forestry and Forage Development Project (HLFFDP)." Rome: IFAD. Available at www.ifad.org.

International Land Coalition (ILC). 2001. "Nepal—Women's Resource Access Programme: Voices from the Field." Available at www.landcoalition.org.

Innovative Activity Profile 2

World Bank. 2000. "Honduras: Access to Land Pilot Project (PACTA)." Project Appraisal Document, World Bank, Washington, DC.

———. 2007. "Honduras: Access to Land Pilot Project (PACTA)." Implementation Completion and Results Report, World Bank, Washington, DC.

FURTHER READING

Overview

Agarwal, Bina. 1994. *A Field of One's Own: Gender and Land Rights in South Asia*. Cambridge: Cambridge University Press.

———. 2002. *Are We Not Peasants Too? Land Rights and Women's Claims in India*. SEEDS series. New York: Population Council.

———. 2003. "Gender and Land Rights Revisited: Exploring New Prospects via the State, Family, and Markets." *Journal of Agrarian Change* 3 (1–2): 184–224.

Barham, Brad, Michael R. Carter, and Wayne Sigelko. 1995. "Agro-export Production and Peasant Land Access: Examining the Dynamic between Adoption and Accumulation." *Journal of Development Economics* 46 (1): 85–107.

Brown, Jennifer, Kripa Ananthpur, and Renee Giovarelli. 2002. "Women's Access and Rights to Land in Karnataka, India." Rural Development Institute Reports on Foreign Aid and Development No. 114, Rural Development Institute, Seattle.

Cousins, Ben, and Aninka Claassens. 2006. "More than Simply 'Socially Embedded': Recognizing the Distinctiveness of African Land Rights." Paper presented at the Frontier of Land Issues conference, Montpellier, May.

Deere, Carmen Diana. 2003. "Women's Land Rights and Rural Social Movements in the Brazilian Agrarian Reform." *Journal of Agrarian Change* 3 (1–2): 257–88.

Food and Agriculture Organization (FAO). 2002. *Land Tenure and Rural Development.* Rome: FAO.

Giovarelli, Renee. 2006. "Overcoming Gender Biases in Established and Transitional Property Rights Systems." In *Land Law Reform: Achieving Development Policy Objectives,* ed. J. W. Bruce, 67–106. Washington, DC: World Bank.

Gopal, Gita. 2001. "Law and Legal Reforms." 2020 Focus No. 06: Brief 12. Washington, DC: International Food Policy Research Institute. Available at www.ifpri.org.

International Land Coalition. 2005. *Women's Access to Land and Other Natural Resources in Nepal.* Rome: International Land Coalition.

Katz, Elizabeth. 1997. "The Intra-Household Economics of Voice and Exit." *Feminist Economics* 3 (3): 25–46.

Katz, Elizabeth, and Susan Lastarria-Cornhiel. 2006. "Land Tenure Formalization and Agricultural Productivity in Lao PDR: Exploring Gender Differences." Unpublished manuscript.

Lao PDR, Ministry of Finance, Department of Lands. 2002. *Existing Land Tenure and Forest Lands Study.* Vientiane: Ministry of Finance, Department of Lands.

Lastarria-Cornhiel, Susan. 1988. "Female Farmers and Agricultural Production in El Salvador." *Development and Change* 19: 585–615.

———. 1997. "Impact of Privatization on Gender and Property Rights in Africa." *World Development* 25 (8): 1317–33.

———. 2006. "Women's Access and Rights to Land: Gender Relations in Tenure Issues." Paper prepared for an Advisory Group Working Meeting convened by the International Land Coalition and International Development Research Council, Rome.

Lastarria-Cornhiel, Susan, and Rachel Wheeler. 1998. "Gender, Ethnicity, and Landed Property in Albania." LTC Working Paper No. 18, Land Tenure Center, University of Wisconsin, Madison.

Legal Assistance to Rural Citizens (LARC). 2006. *Final Report on the Activity of the Project and Public Association.* Bishkek: LARC.

Lucas, Robert E. B., and Oded Stark. 1985. "Motivation to Remit: Evidence from Botswana." *Journal of Political Economy* 93: 901–18.

Meinzen-Dick, Ruth, and Rajendra Pradhan. 2002. "Legal Pluralism and Dynamic Property Rights." CAPRI Working Paper 22, CGIAR System-Wide Program on Collective Action and Property Rights, Washington, DC.

Nielsen, Robin, Tim Hanstad, and Leonard Rolfes. 2006. *Implementing Homestead Plot Programmes: Experience from India.* Rome: Food and Agriculture Organization.

Quisumbing, Agnes R. 1996. "Male–Female Differences in Agricultural Productivity: Methodological Issues and Empirical Evidence." *World Development* 24 (10): 1579–95.

Quisumbing, Agnes R., Ellen Payongayong, J. B. Aidoo, and Keijiro Otsuka. 1999. "Women's Land Rights in the Transition to Individualized Ownership: Implications for the Management of Tree Resources in Western Ghana." FCND Discussion Paper 58, International Food Policy Research Institute, Washington, DC.

Scholz, Birte, and Mayra Gomez. 2004. *Bringing Equality Home: Promoting and Protecting the Inheritance Rights of Women.* Geneva: Centre on Housing Rights and Evictions.

Strickland, Richard. 2004. *To Have and to Hold: Women's Property and Inheritance Rights in the Context of HIV/AIDS in Sub-Saharan Africa.* Washington, DC: International Center for Research on Women.

Udry, Christopher. 1996. "Gender, Agricultural Production, and the Theory of the Household." *Journal of Political Economy* 104 (5): 1010–46.

United Nations Human Settlements Programme (UN-HABITAT). 2005. *Shared Tenure Options for Women.* Nairobi: UN-HABITAT.

Thematic Note I

Alderman, Harold, Lawrence Haddad, John Hoddinott, and Ravi Kanbur. 1995. "Unitary versus Collective Models of the Household: Time to Shift the Burden of Proof?" *World Bank Research Observer* 10 (1): 1–19.

Fafchamps, Marcel, and Agnes R. Quisumbing. 2002. "Control and Ownership of Assets within Rural Ethiopian Households." *Journal of Development Studies* 38 (6): 47–82.

International Land Coalition. 2005. *Women's Access to Land and Other Natural Resources in Nepal.* Rome: International Land Coalition.

Katz, Elizabeth. 1997. "The Intra-Household Economics of Voice and Exit." *Feminist Economics* 3 (3): 25–46.

Katz, Elizabeth, and Juan Sebastian Chamorro. 2003. "Gender, Land Rights, and the Household Economy in Rural Nicaragua and Honduras." Paper presented at the annual conference of the Latin American and Caribbean Economics Association, Puebla, Mexico, October 9–11.

Razavi, Shahra, ed. 2003. *Agrarian Change, Gender and Land Rights.* Oxford: Blackwell.

Udry, Christopher. 1996. "Gender, Agricultural Production, and the Theory of the Household." *Journal of Political Economy* 104 (5): 1010–46.

Thematic Note 2

Food and Agriculture Organization of the United Nations (FAO). 2002. *Gender and Access to Land*. Land Tenure Study 4. Rome: FAO.

Katz, Elizabeth, and Juan Sebastian Chamorro. 2002. "Gender, Land Rights, and the Household Economy in Rural Nicaragua and Honduras." Paper prepared for USAID/ BASIS CRSP, University of Wisconsin–Madison.

Thematic Note 4

Katz, Elizabeth. 1997. "The Intra-Household Economics of Voice and Exit." *Feminist Economics* 3 (3): 25–46.

Katz, Elizabeth, and Juan Sebastian Chamorro. 2002. "Gender, Land Rights, and the Household Economy in Rural Nicaragua and Honduras." Paper prepared for USAID/ BASIS CRSP, University of Wisconsin–Madison.

Lastarria-Cornhiel, Susan. 1997. "Impact of Privatization on Gender and Property Rights in Africa." *World Development* 25 (8): 1317–33.

Lucas, Robert E. B., and Oded Stark. 1985. "Motivation to Remit: Evidence from Botswana." *Journal of Political Economy* 93: 901–18.

Gender and Agricultural Markets

Overview

The feminization of poverty is the tragic consequence of women's unequal access to economic opportunities.

—UNDP 1995: 36

In many part of the world, women play a major role as farmers and producers, based on materials presented in the different Modules of this *Sourcebook*. However, their access to resources and opportunities to enable them to move from subsistence agriculture to higher value chains is much lower than men's.

Women increasingly supply national and international markets with traditional and high-value produce, but compared to men, women farmers and entrepreneurs face a number of disadvantages, including lower mobility, less access to training, less access to market information, and less access to productive resources. Evidence suggests that women tend to lose income and control as a product moves from the farm to the market (Gurung 2006). Women farmers can find it hard to maintain a profitable market niche. Men may take over production and marketing—even of traditional "women's crops"—when it becomes financially lucrative to do so. Women-owned businesses face many more constraints and receive far fewer services and less support than those owned by men (Bardasi, Blackden, and Guzman 2007; Ellis, Manuel, and Blackden 2006; World Bank 2007a, 2007b). These disadvantages reduce women's effectiveness as actors in value chains and reduce overall market effectiveness. Providing women producers and entrepreneurs with the same inputs and education as men

in Burkina Faso, Kenya, and Tanzania could increase their output and incomes by an estimated 10–20 percent (World Bank 2005). Apart from efficiency gains, food security and welfare gains are also strongly linked to the provision of greater economic opportunities for women. Studies show that resources and incomes controlled by women are more likely to be used to improve family food consumption and welfare, reduce child malnutrition, and increase the overall well-being of the family (FAO 2006; see also Module 1).

Although this Module supports enabling both poor men and women to access market opportunities and resources, it focuses more on women's economic empowerment. In many societies and countries, women are excluded from more lucrative and profitable markets than men, and it is this inequality in access to resources and opportunities that is analyzed and discussed here. Bringing women into lucrative markets requires targeted analysis and program interventions. One important consideration, as presented in the Thematic Notes, is that projects and programs that aim to increase women's economic empowerment should involve both women and men as partners.

The value chain concept is a useful analytic tool to understand a series of production and postproduction activities—whether it is a basic crop, such as vegetables, or a highly processed good, such as cotton textile or canned tuna—and the enterprises and individuals who are involved. This Module uses the value chain concept as an analytic tool. A value chain incorporates the full range of activities required to bring a product or service from conception to production, delivery to consumers, and final disposal after use (Kaplinsky and Morris 2002). Gender differences are at work in the full range of activities making up value chains. A gender approach to value chain analysis makes it possible to consider the access to productive activities of men and women individually and in groups, differential gender-based opportunities for upgrading within the chain, the gender-based division of activities in a given value chain, and how gender power relations affect economic rents among actors throughout the chain.[1]

This Module suggests ways of making value chains work for smaller actors—especially women working as farmers or in micro- and small enterprises—by enabling them to capture a larger slice of the revenues. It highlights the importance of building trust and understanding among partners in a targeted value chain. It emphasizes the need to strengthen relationships between partners to open channels for the transfer of technology, information, and gains. Because men and women usually pursue distinct activities in value chains, building mutual understanding of their respective needs and responsibilities as "chain actors" ensures that product quality is maintained as it passes along the chain, which results in efficiency gains. Greater equity gains can be achieved by encouraging women to take on new roles in value chains, for example, by engaging in value-adding strategies, or to take on new roles in value chains.

REGIONAL OPPORTUNITIES AND CONSTRAINTS

As the following sections indicate, the opportunities and constraints in agribusiness vary by region, and no "one-size-fits-all" gender strategy will be appropriate to guide interventions. In-depth research and tailored support programs are required in each location.

Sub-Saharan Africa

In sub-Saharan Africa, women are largely responsible for selling and marketing traditional crops such as maize, sorghum, cassava, and leafy vegetables in local markets. In countries where urban markets for these traditional crops are expanding rapidly, such as Cameroon and Kenya, the challenge is to ensure that women retain control over their production, processing, and marketing. In Uganda strong demand for leafy vegetables (traditionally a woman's crop) in Kampala markets caused men to take over their cultivation.[2]

Women are the traditional producers and marketers of horticultural crops throughout sub-Saharan Africa.

Although horticultural production has risen steadily in most regions of the world over the past few decades, the average annual growth in per capita supply of horticultural produce was negative in sub-Saharan Africa between 1971 and 2000. Inadequate transportation infrastructure and inability to comply with international standards—especially GLOBALGAP standards[3]—limit participation in export markets. Because many producers, particularly women, lack good access even to local and regional markets, the development of cold chain, transportation, and communications infrastructure will be critical to link producers with these markets. Building capacity to manage horticultural businesses and to conduct research is a priority.

Latin America and the Caribbean

Latin American and Caribbean countries currently export a high percentage of their horticultural products, especially to the United States. Despite some notable exceptions, however, most smallholders in the region remain disenfranchised from the export market. Around one-third of the rural poor across the region are indigenous, a marked inequality can be seen in the distribution of wealth and income, and the majority of agricultural producers work small plots, usually in marginal areas with low productivity. Rural women have become one of the poorest population groups as a result of internal conflicts, migration by men both within and outside the region, natural disasters, and the consequences of structural adjustment. Women's ability to participate in markets will not improve unless they gain land ownership, access to formal financial and technical assistance, and a good level of education and training (IFAD 2002).

Assisting women farmers to access niche export markets for high-value and brand-marketed products such as fair trade and certified organic products is one way forward. Another is to conserve, research, and commercialize indigenous fruit varieties. Significant potential exists to expand production and consumption for local markets and supermarkets, but product quality and reliability must be enhanced.[4]

East and South Asia and the Pacific

The wide agroclimatic diversity of East and South Asia and the Pacific—ranging from fertile irrigated tracts to rain-fed cultivation, mountain cultivation, and coastal ecosystems—has fostered the development of indigenous species of regional interest, permits production of many different crop species, and has resulted in a very rich dietary diversity.[5] Although much of the region suffers from poor market distribution, domestic markets generally are growing strongly. Several countries, such as China, India, and Thailand, already have mature agroprocessing industries, and there are good opportunities to supply processed and other value-added products to domestic and international markets. However, in Southeast Asia, where countries remain in the early stages of moving from a centrally planned to a market-oriented economy, businesswomen generally lack entrepreneurial skills. The use of poor-quality technology and equipment is another problem; in the Lao People's Democratic Republic, only 5 percent of women-owned enterprises use electrical or motorized equipment compared with 48 percent of men-owned enterprises.[6]

Producers in the small island economies of the Pacific find it particularly difficult to compete with enterprises in industrial countries (such as in Australia and New Zealand) and with the large developing country producers of the region. The previous emphasis on cash crops grown by men, such as sugar and sandalwood, has resulted not only in a collapse of livelihoods as global markets have weakened but also in a shortage of the traditional products normally grown by women—which are now in high demand owing to tourism and the development of the export sector. Until recently no analytical work had been performed to capture women's work in farming, fishing, and natural resource management, which resulted in a lack of attention from policy makers. Today the pivotal role of Pacific Island women in ensuring rural livelihoods and food security is better understood and recognized (Booth 1999).

Central and West Asia and North Africa

Women's participation in the labor force remains significantly lower than that of men across Central and West Asia and North Africa (CWANA). Statistics for the Middle East and North Africa, a subset of the countries in the larger CWANA region, show that women labor force participation was 29.5 percent in 2006, compared to 77.3 percent for men, less than any other region in the world. Yet growing unemployment in CWANA, men's increasing inclination to train for other occupations, and rising levels of poverty in some regions suggest that men's traditional role as the sole or main breadwinner is no longer guaranteed (IFAD n.d.).

Agriculture across CWANA is becoming feminized at different rates. Women form more than 50 percent of the agricultural labor force in Egypt, Morocco, Somalia, and Turkey but just 4 percent in the United Arab Emirates. Women head more than 20 percent of rural households in Pakistan and

more than 10 percent in Cyprus, Egypt, Lebanon, Morocco, Oman, and Tunisia. More middle-aged and older women work in agriculture than younger women. Women are frequently responsible for handling livestock and for growing and processing vegetables, whereas men are generally responsible for cereal production. Women farmers across the region lack sufficient labor and appropriate energy-saving farm and household technologies. Social biases that associate machinery use with men further limit women's use of technological improvements. Not surprisingly, the output from women-dominated farms is generally low. Women are more likely to work within the family-related farm or business, often without pay, or in the informal sector. The percentage of women unpaid workers to total women agricultural workers is 79 percent in Yemen, 66 percent in Syria, 60 percent in Egypt, and 45 percent in the West Bank and Gaza. Even when remunerated, women receive salaries well below those of men; for example, on average, Syrian women are paid 41 percent of what men workers are paid (IFAD n.d.).

TRENDS IN WOMEN'S ACCESS TO MARKETS

The following section describes the constraints and opportunities facing women and men in accessing agricultural product markets and how they are impacted by the changing trends in the international and local markets.

Constraints and opportunities

As is clear from the regional picture presented above, women are significantly excluded from markets, and bringing women into markets requires targeted analysis and program interventions. Women often hold distinct rights and obligations within the household, and they often perform distinct functions with regard to market activities. These circumstances affect their ability vis-à-vis men to take up opportunities, to invest, and to take risks. Most women farmers are smallholders who cultivate traditional food crops for subsistence and sale, whereas men are more likely to own medium to large commercial farms and are better able to capitalize on the expansion of agricultural tradable goods. Farms managed by women are generally characterized by low levels of mechanization and technological inputs, which often translate into low productivity (FAO 2006). Globally integrated markets mean that international prices affect even smallholders producing only for the domestic market. The free entry of traditional agricultural products into domestic markets can hit small-scale farmers hard if they are not prepared. In the Philippines, for example, machine-sliced, ready-to-fry potatoes from the United States flooded the local market following its opening up of trade. Local prices collapsed by half, affecting around 50,000 potato farmers, most of them women (Oliveros 1997, cited in FAO 2006).

Women also have a lower presence in the formal sector and in more urbanized and developed markets. Their ability to participate in markets will not improve unless women gain land ownership, access to formal financial and technical assistance, and a higher level of education and training (IFAD 2002).

Yet there *are* opportunities for women farmers. If they use traditional production systems, they may find it relatively simple to meet some certification requirements, such as those for organic production. Many high-value crops require labor-intensive production techniques, such as pruning and trellising, which cannot be mechanized and in which women often specialize.

There is increasing demand for high-value products such as vegetables and local crops in expanding urban markets. The challenge is to ensure that women retain control over their production, processing, and marketing; product quality and reliability must be enhanced.

Impact of changing agricultural markets

Value chains are undergoing rapid change in the way they connect to local, national, and international markets. In industrialized countries, growing consumer interest in health and a consequent demand for a variety of fresh produce throughout the year have been matched by improvements in postharvest care and international cold chain logistics for the transport of fresh fish, meat, and horticultural products. High-value niche markets, such as markets for certified organic or fair trade products, are expanding. Although retailers in Europe and the United States generally dominate fresh produce chains to the frequent disadvantage of small-scale producers, farmers in developing countries can maximize their advantages in climate and labor costs to supply produce to the Northern Hemisphere seasonally or to supply traditional and exotic vegetables more cost effectively throughout the year (Jaffee 2003).

The structure, organization, and dynamics of domestic food markets are also changing rapidly in developing countries. Supermarkets are moving into middle- and working-class areas in most countries, directly affecting rural zones on the supply and demand side (Reardon and Berdegué 2002). In many countries urban demand for "traditional crops" such as leafy vegetables and cassava is increasing alongside demand for novel products. Supermarket buyers demand products of consistently high quality, yet small farmers often cannot marshal sufficient working capital to invest in improving product consistency. Smallholders' understanding of supermarket standards and of consumers also tends to be weak, unlike their knowledge of local markets and unlike the greater knowledge base of large-scale commercial farmers. Improper harvest and postharvest operations lead to short shelf-life, rejection by consumers, and contamination risks.[7] It can be difficult for small-scale farmers to deliver desired quantities at short notice or to manage the labor instability involved in "just-in-time" procurement practices (Boselie, Henson, and Weatherspoon 2003).

Thus, although agricultural commercialization is continually creating new market opportunities, much of this market is very difficult for smallholders to access because of inability to meet the requirements. Women smallholders and small enterprises face even more constraints, as seen earlier. Unless value chains are developed while keeping disadvantaged populations in mind, advantages of chain development will remain limited to larger farmers and producers, and women farmers may lose the markets, jobs, and enterprises that they currently have. These same trends open up possibilities of niche market specialization for women—in labor-intensive crops, local and traditional crops, organic farming, and fair trade.

Changing agricultural demand and supply situation. Several trends have started to emerge that will significantly influence the world food situation and food markets. Dietary patterns and the demand for food are changing rapidly in many countries in response to increased incomes, urbanization, and government policy. Rapid urbanization in low-income developing countries intensifies the pressure on food production, marketing, and processing systems. Rapidly growing demand for meat products has heightened demand for cereals to feed livestock. The increasing opportunity cost of women's time, changes in food preferences caused by changing lifestyles, and changes in relative prices associated with rural-urban migration are leading to more diversified diets. The preference for some basic staple cereals (maize, millet, and sorghum) is shifting to others (rice and wheat) that require less preparation and to milk and livestock products, fruits, vegetables, and processed food (Pinstrup-Andersen, Pandya-Lorch, and Rosegrant 1997). The growing scarcity and inappropriate allocation of water, along with diminished soil fertility in many regions of the world, are beginning to constrain food production. Climate change and demand for scarce land to use for biofuels will further affect current agricultural uses of land and water and the availability of some food crops.

For smallholders and businesses to be successful in this radically changing demand and supply situation will require considerable market linkage and business capacity—individually or in groups. These trends present important considerations in determining the most appropriate investments in women's agribusiness enterprises.

Impact of commercialization. Understanding how the commercialization of small-scale farming activities affects the gender division of labor and in turn influences resource management, income flows, expenditure patterns, food security, nutritional security, and gender relationships is essential (AGSF 2005). A gender and pro-poor analysis helps to uncover economic, organizational, and asymmetric relationships among actors in a value chain.[8]

The right to access and the ability to control key productive resources (land, labor, information)—already fostering conflict between men and women farmers—will become ever-more important. A study in Ghana to map the consequences of small-scale commercialization found that the introduction of cash crops weakened the traditional gender division of intrahousehold rights and obligations, that the gender-based division of labor broke down, and that farm women increasingly undertook tasks previously done by men (AGSF 2005).

Food security will become a major issue for women and women's enterprises. If market liberalization occurs when a large section of the population lacks access to enough food to guarantee a minimally sufficient diet, only producers of high-value cash crops may profit. Landless and near-landless people who must purchase food may suffer from its reduced availability and higher prices. If women are relatively more involved in subsistence production and men are more involved with cash crops, or if women lose their title to land as it is converted from traditional to modern cash crops, household food security may decline despite a rise in income (IFAD 2002; see also Module 1).

Reduced research focus on local and traditional crops

Private sector research concentrates on internationally traded crops, but women tend to farm locally important crops such as leafy vegetables, millet, and sorghum. Publicly funded research on these crops and growing practices may be required to improve production and meet local (and increasingly urban) market demand for these crops. Efforts to conserve traditional varieties of these and other crops grown by women will maintain important knowledge and are essential for improving those crops. Policies on traditional varieties

and food security now cover local crops important to women, including flower and handicraft crops in the Pacific.[9]

If women are to benefit from modern agricultural technologies, they need to participate in research and development. Participation will permit them to set their own priorities based on their appraisal of their needs. Key biotechnology research issues include developing a better understanding of the role of women as the guardians of traditional knowledge relevant to biotechnology applications, analyzing which crops are affected by biotechnologies, and appreciating how the introduction of genetically modified crops may affect the local valuation of "women's" and "men's" crops.[10] Several market niches are based on these local, traditional, and organic crops that could be developed as specialization areas for women farmers and entrepreneurs.

THE GENDERED NATURE OF VALUE CHAINS

The value chain approach strengthens business linkages between producer groups, service providers, and other actors, such as processors and importers, rather than focusing exclusively on farm interventions. Value chains vary in complexity and in the range of participants they draw in. Export value chains tend to be more complex than local chains in terms of the knowledge and technical facilities required, because special processing and packaging are common.

Frequently the knowledge and other information embodied in the different functions of a value chain are gender specific. In some cases women or men are entirely responsible for a whole value chain or significant aspects of it. In Madagascar, for example, men produce honey and wax, whereas women are largely responsible for silkworm production. Hives are located high in trees and harvested by night (climbing at night is not considered a suitable activity for women). On the other hand, silk production and weaving can be performed at home, enabling women to run these enterprises more easily.

Project support needs to recognize that in such cases women and men hold specific understanding of crops and livestock, their associated ecosystems, and the market. Interventions may erode the responsibilities of one gender unwittingly, and in the process it may also erode important ecological and social knowledge. For instance, in Quechua communities in Peru, the conservation and reproduction of different plant varieties, such as potatoes, are almost exclusively performed by women. Quechua women farmers are key decision makers, deciding which plant varieties meet specific nutritional needs, what crops to sell, and what crops to consume. The growing privatization and enclosure of land have circumscribed women's ability to plant "low-value," traditional crop varieties, however. Important sources of food and income for the household are being lost, along with knowledge of local plant varieties and their uses accrued by women over millennia (USAID 2006).

Women and men may also perform specific tasks along a value chain. Consequently they will have gender-specific knowledge related to that value chain—for example, knowledge of particular elements of a crop's life cycle and its requirements at that stage. The separation of tasks by gender may mean that neither men nor women possess a complete understanding of the whole value chain and of how the roles and responsibilities of different actors intersect and interact at different stages. In fishing communities in São Tome and Principe, for instance, men catch fish and maintain fishing tackle and boats. Women purchase the catch directly from the fishermen. They transport and market the catch, and in some cases transform it into dried or salted fish (IFAD n.d.).

In some cases the gender division of labor may appear to proceed harmoniously and result in a good product. In other cases, if men or women have little understanding of the requirements of the next stage in the chain, gradual losses in product quality and quantity along the chain will yield a relatively poor product. Interventions aimed at adding value through processing and marketing need to consider how to increase understanding between chain actors, identify which gender may benefit at which stage, and determine whether women can be drawn into those activities that add the most value.

Understanding the rationale behind gendered roles in value chains is useful for planning interventions. A study in Uganda,[11] based on the experience of a group of women fishers, observed that women on open water were associated with misfortune (and, indeed, women fishers were less able than men to challenge people out to steal boat engines and tackle). Based on this information, the study recommended that aquaculture, as opposed to capture fisheries, be promoted to circumvent cultural taboos and enable women to pursue a livelihood in fisheries. Women would need permission from men to build ponds, however, since women rarely own land. The study enumerates several measures that project managers could undertake to help women overcome such obstacles and become fishers themselves (see also Module 13).

Projects and programs seeking to create value chains, as opposed to supply chains, therefore, need to help men and women actors understand their specific roles in relation to those of others'. They will then learn how value is added, fulfill their particular roles more responsibly, and take on new roles.

Conducting a value chain analysis

Value chain analysis involves all or some of the following steps (adapted from Mayoux 2005): (1) market analysis, (2) chain mapping and stakeholder analysis, (3) identification of constraints and opportunities for the value chain, and (4) strategic and action plan development. These steps are summarized in box 5.1. The analytical steps (1–3) are discussed and illustrated by case studies in the sections that follow.

Market analysis. Generally a value chain analysis begins with a market study, which assesses the state of the chain relative to its competitors and explores potential gains that could be captured. In some cases a market study reveals that it is possible to add value to products that are not marketed in some locales. For example, scientists at the International Center for Research in the Dry Areas (ICARDA) and Jordan's National Center for Agricultural Research and Technology Transfer (NCARTT) heard of a tomato paste factory in the Jordan Valley that had trouble disposing of its waste without causing pollution. Scientists designed a machine to dry and grind the tomato by-product into a palatable feed and contacted the nearby Der Alla Rural Women's Cooperative Society, which started to incorporate the tomato by-product into the feed blocks it produced. Farmers were pleased with the product. Research showed that sheep and goats grew 20 percent faster and sheep fertility increased by 20 percent in animals fed with feed blocks (Rihawi 2005).

If a value chain is analyzed with gender-disaggregated understanding as an objective, the market study can be utilized to identify current niches in which women are strong, as well as potential ones in which they could compete. In developing value chains, particularly in the poorest and most marginalized areas, all of the links of a value chain may need to be constructed. Partnerships will need to be forged and considerable capacity development undertaken. Other chains may be vestigial, and the opportunities they present will need to be recognized and captured.

Chain mapping and stakeholder analysis. A gender-sensitive chain and stakeholder analysis should understand the relative position of women already in the chain—including nodes at which they are the primary actors and those where they are actors along with men.

- *Preliminary chain mapping.* Many standard research tools for mapping value chains can be made gender sensitive; for instance, a gender-sensitive questionnaire can be added to a socioeconomic survey. In other cases new tools may be needed to capture the roles and needs of women across the value chain or in particular

Box 5.1   Steps in a Value Chain Analysis

Conduct a market analysis

- Generally a value chain analysis begins with a market study to identify the potential gains that could be captured and the state of the chain relative to its competitors.

Map the chain and conduct a stakeholder analysis

- A preliminary mapping of the chain identifies the main products and their markets, as well as the kinds of activity involved, the productive unit, and the geographical location for each node in the chain. A (participatory) stakeholder analysis is then conducted to identify the different stakeholders (by function, socioeconomic category, and gender) at each node of the chain.
- The relative distribution of economic value between participants at each node is documented. Research investigates barriers to entry, the interests and power

relationships of different stakeholders, and contextual factors that explain inequalities and inefficiencies and blockages in the chain.

Identify constraints and opportunities for the value chain

- "Leverage" points are identified for upgrading the chain and redistributing values in the interests of equity and efficiency.
- The causes of ongoing change are mapped to guide decisions—not only on how to strengthen particular nodes and their associated actors, but also on how to identify any transformative actions that may be required.

Develop a strategic and action plan

- The information assembled in the previous steps forms the basis for a strategic and action plan to achieve the goals identified for the chain.

Source: Adapted from Mayoux 2005.

---

segments. Box 5.2 describes new tools developed by a project funded by the U.K. Department for International Development (DFID) to understand Ghanaian women's role in fish processing, storage, and trade and to develop multiple actor strategies to upgrade these activities.

- *Stakeholder analysis.* It is critical that project managers do not bias outcomes by subsuming women's interests to those of men's or by conflating the interests of producers with those of other stakeholders in the value chain. Tools that can help identify the interests of various actors in value chains and that minimize trade-offs between these interests are necessary. Taste panels and cooking tests have been conducted with women and men for rice (by the Africa Rice Center) and potatoes (by the International Potato Center). SWOT analysis (an assessment of strengths, weaknesses, opportunities, and threats) can take the process a step further if it is designed to create chain platforms. For example, the Papa Andina program in Latin America has been helping to organize meetings between actors in the potato value chain in Bolivia, Ecuador, and Peru in which participants discuss strengths, weaknesses, opportunities, and threats in relation to other stakeholders.

Once the linkages and stakeholder interests along the whole chain are understood, representatives of each segment come together to discuss how to improve the links and preference criteria of each stakeholder (Farnworth and Jiggins 2006).

- *Capture of the relative distribution of economic value between participants.* Calculating the value added and profit accruing to each segment of the value chain, as well as calculating employment and labor segmentation by gender, will provide the data necessary to devise interventions that increase the absolute profits reaped by women at each node in the chain.

This information can be complemented by an analysis of backward and forward linkages in the chain to determine the potential economic "spillover effects" of expanding the chain and to explore ways for low-income segments to increase participation and capture a greater percentage of value added. For example, a study of distributional gains in Peru's profitable value chain for thornless artichokes,[12] complemented by insights from a gender analysis (box 5.3), highlighted the need to incorporate producers who are less able to participate in export-oriented production and who

Box 5.2   Ghana: Tools for Understanding and Improving Women's Postharvest Roles in the Fishing Industry

The fishing industry provides an estimated 10 percent of Ghana's rural and urban population with employment. Men undertake the main fish harvesting activities in the artisanal, semi-industrial, and industrial sectors. Women are the industry's key postharvest players, responsible for fish processing, storage, and trade. Many women engage in the growing frozen fish distribution trade and in marketing fish within and outside Ghana. The "fish mummies," who informally fund many activities in the postharvest fishing industry, are among its most important actors.

These postharvest roles are crucial sources of livelihood for women who are heads of poor households, particularly in areas where many men have left in search of work. The DFID commissioned research to develop field tools for improving the understanding of poverty in the postharvest fishing industry and to develop strategies to reduce it. One tool, FishPHOM, provides a systematic analysis of the sector, which enables priority areas of activities to be identified and combined to form principles for intervention. The analysis provides a basis for formulating policy, for planning and research, and for institutional collaboration and cooperation. A Post-Harvest Livelihoods Analysis Tool (PHLAT) was also produced to help poor stakeholders clarify their circumstances and problems, examine their potential for change, and identify ways to reduce poverty by linking with macrolevel policy initiatives, such as the Ghana Poverty Reduction Strategy.

Source: www.innovation.ex.ac.uk/imm/Ghana%20PH%20flyer% 202004a.pdf.

Box 5.3   Peru: Mapping Distributional Gains in the Thornless Artichoke Chain

Mapping distributional gains

Most of the value added in Peru's artichoke industry is concentrated in the processing and export plants—an estimated 61 percent of the total value added remains in the hands of the agroexporters who process the product. Approximately 10 percent of value added stays with the small- and medium-scale farmers who grow the crop, and around 3 percent goes to those who sell seed. The distribution of costs among these actors is similar. One strategy for small and medium firms to capture a greater proportion of the final price and increase value added would be to diversify the types of processed artichokes they offer (for example, producing salads and individually frozen packets).

Adding a gender analysis

The value chain for thornless artichokes in Peru reveals consistent gender segmentation by occupation, type of activity, and level of participation in the chain. Men

Source: USAID 2007.

and women cluster in different occupations, undertake distinct activities in the fields and processing plants, and work different hours with different degrees of security. The intensity of women's labor increases in processing. Approximately 80 percent of the labor used in processing activities, such as peeling, cutting, and deleafing, is done by women, whereas men are more involved in activities related to operating and maintaining machinery. Gender wage gaps are evident throughout the chain, although they are more marked in certain segments. Women working on small and medium-size farms receive about 88 percent of men's wages. In processing plants women workers without defined job tenure make 86 percent of men's wages, and those who hold contracts for a specified period make 93 percent of men's wages. The gender analysis highlights the need to intensify efforts to guarantee labor rights for both men and women, especially in light of commitments for improving labor conditions included in the Peru Trade Promotion Agreement.

need support to overcome the deficits that limit their participation. Key strategies to foster the chain's pro-poor development would include supporting value-adding activities for smaller enterprises and intensifying efforts to guarantee labor rights for both men and women.

Identification of constraints and opportunities for the value chain.

- *Identification of "leverage" points for upgrading the chain and redistributing values in the interests of equity and efficiency:* The Thematic Notes and Innovative Activity Profiles that accompany this Module discuss suitable entry points for investment and provide case studies of good practice. The analysis must also point out women and other disadvantaged groups who may not be in the chain but whose competitive position is affected by the chain—for example, if their position in the market is being eroded. Interventions can be designed to ensure that disadvantaged groups do not suffer or are able to participate in and benefit from the value chain.
- *Mapping the causes of ongoing change:* No value chain is static. Mapping the causes of ongoing change helps to guide decisions, not only on how to strengthen particular nodes in a value chain and their associated actors, but also on which transformative actions are required. For example, dairy chains studied in Syria (Abdelali-Martini, Aw-Hassan, and Salahieh 2005) show a clear gender division of labor in production, processing, and marketing that determines the best type of technological intervention

in this value chain. Although both men and women farmers tend dairy sheep, women are more heavily represented in this activity. Among the Jabbans, women and children are mainly responsible for processing milk into cheese, whereas men handle the marketing and usually control the income. Working with this gender division of labor is important when attempting to disseminate newly developed technologies to farmers. Technologies related to milk processing need to be targeted particularly at women, among both farmers and Jabbans. Hygiene and basic animal health issues should likewise be addressed primarily to women farmers and Jabbans. The interventions suggested by researchers help maintain the feasibility of the chain, assuming an urban market for cheese continues to exist, but they do not address wider issues such as enabling women to take on new roles in the dairy chain.

ENTRY POINTS FOR SUPPORT

Once the gender dimensions of a value chain are well understood, a thorough market analysis has been performed, and a strategy and action plan have been developed, investment and support can be directed toward developing markets in ways that contribute to gender equity and reduce poverty. Entry points for support are discussed in the Thematic Notes and structured around four main areas (fig. 5.1). Thematic Note 1 explores ways of promoting a business-enabling environment to reduce structural barriers to entry by women

Figure 5.1   Entry Points of Gender Integration in Value Chains

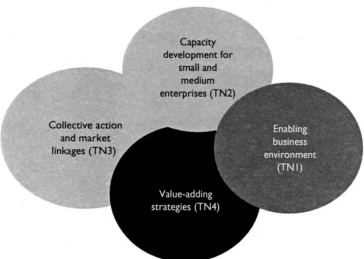

Source: Authors.

entrepreneurs. Thematic Note 2 presents a range of capacity development measures that contribute to gender equity in access to markets, Thematic Note 3 describes ways of strengthening collective action to gain access to key productive assets, and Thematic Note 4 discusses value-adding strategies.

Access to finance is crucial for accessing markets. Although finance is touched upon in this Module, readers are directed to Module 3 for a detailed discussion.

The Innovative Activity Profiles examine innovative and successful approaches to value chain development. The first one discusses the marketing extension process in Bangladesh and shows how poor women required relatively little support to begin conducting their own marketing research, organize into groups, and develop business linkages. The second Profile demonstrates how community-managed procurement centers for small-scale and marginal farmers in India enabled women to gain space in a men-dominated market.

The third Profile explores lessons from the Greater Noakhali Aquaculture Extension Project in Bangladesh, which targeted the poorest segments of the population, including women-headed households, and adopted a holistic approach to market development, from technology to training and business linkages. The approach substantially increased women's participation.

MEASURING CHANGE: GENDER-SENSITIVE MONITORING AND EVALUATION INDICATORS

Being able to measure the impact that agricultural marketing initiatives have on men and women beneficiaries, their families, and communities is important. Table 5.1 lists ideas for indicators and sources of verification, although clearly modifications are required for each program; further detail is also available from Module 16.

Table 5.1 Monitoring and Evaluation Indicators for Gender and Agricultural Markets

Indicator	Sources of Verification and Tools
Satisfaction of women and men entrepreneurs with their access to agricultural inputs, training, credit, and markets, measured annually	• Focus groups • Stakeholder interviews
Number of men and women involved in participatory technology development	• Participatory monitoring • Project records • Research organization records
Active participation of women and men in community-based rural producers' organizations, including holding leadership roles	• Bank account signatories • Organization minutes • Stakeholder interviews
Participation by women and men in small business Incubators	• Incubator records • Project records
Number of women and men small farmers trained in entrepreneurial skills and provided with market information to allow them to enter into, and manage, beneficial contract farming arrangements or businesses	• Project records • Training records
Number of newly registered businesses started per year, disaggregated by gender of owners	• Trade registration records
Gender of farmers holding supply contracts for contract farming	• Exporter or supermarket records • Sample surveys
Percentage of women and men among farmers involved in organic, fair trade, or certified marketing schemes	• Fair Trade organization records and norms • Sample surveys • Stakeholder interviews
Percentage of business owners rating their business as "successful," disaggregated by gender	• Sample surveys
Change in women's perceptions of levels of sexual harassment or violence, or need to exchange sex for products (such as fish), experienced before and after program activities	• Focus groups • Stakeholder interviews

(Table continues on the following page)

Table 5.1 Monitoring and Evaluation Indicators for Gender and Agricultural Markets (continued)

Indicator	Sources of Verification and Tools
Differences in wage and employment conditions, if any, between women and other disadvantaged groups, and men for positions of comparable content and responsibility	• Case studies • Labor audits • Project management information system or administrative records
Changes in gender of market traders per year	• Market stallholders' association records
Changes in access to food markets, before and after infrastructure development by gender	• Household surveys, before and after • Project management information system
Percentage of women and men extension workers and project staff	• Government agricultural extension and business support services records • Project records
Satisfaction of women entrepreneurs and workers with access to child care, measured before and after project activities	• Focus groups • Stakeholder interviews
Age of school leaving, disaggregated by gender	• School records
Percentage of business women and men in community using computers and Internet, and the frequency of use	• Computer center/Internet café records • Stakeholder interviews
Percentage of businesses owning motorized or electrical equipment, disaggregated by gender of owners	• Sample survey
Changes over x-year period of project activities in household nutrition, health, education, vulnerability to violence, and happiness, disaggregated by gender	• Household surveys, before and after • Project management information system • School records

Source: Authors, with inputs from Pamela White, author of Module 16.

Strengthening the Business Environment

An enabling business environment provides producers with a clear understanding of foreign and domestic demand, offers economic and political stability, facilitates low transaction costs—for example, with respect to entering into and enforcing contracts—and maintains relatively low levels of risk for business transactions. It allows for efficient business operations that embody investment, innovation, and creativity. However, a business environment that is *equitable* as well as enabling cannot be achieved without paying attention to institutional issues that reinforce gender inequalities.

Women entrepreneurs do not face a level playing field globally, nationally, or locally because they are constrained by an array of culturally specific rights and responsibilities that hamper their freedom to act in the best interests of their enterprise. National legislation in many countries intentionally or unintentionally discriminates against women. Trade liberalization typically reduces the competitive capacity of disadvantaged entrepreneurs. The local business environment depends on local enforcement of national laws and regulations, which often varies considerably from the original legislative intent and from directives provided by national implementing agencies.

The combination of gender-blind legislation and locally valid gendered norms often causes men to benefit more than women from public programs that support agriculture by providing credit, agricultural extension, and marketing services. If gender equality in entrepreneurship is to become a reality, explicit measures are required to tackle sex and gender discrimination and enable women to start and run businesses effectively. Moreover, market infrastructure, including wholesale and assembly markets and postharvest processing and storage facilities, is frequently not tailored to women's needs.

KEY GENDER ISSUES

The business climate or enabling environment for private sector development, both at global and country levels, is discussed here.

Global business environment

At the global level, trade negotiation processes generally lack transparency and mechanisms for key stakeholders to participate. The participation of civil society, including small-scale farmers, women's groups, and representatives of consumer and environmental organizations, is limited. Aside from these special considerations, developing countries often lack the personnel and organizational capacity to deal with trade negotiations and are at a great disadvantage when negotiating on behalf of their agricultural sectors. This deficiency is aggravated by pressure for rapid completion. The resulting hastily written liberalization schedules and exemption lists may not be based on informed and balanced choices between export-oriented and import-competitive products—choices that fundamentally affect the interests of women farmers. One difficulty of formulating precise objectives in support of women lies in the fact that the frameworks in which gender and trade policies are negotiated are artificially separated. Trade policies generally consider macroflows, whereas gender instruments primarily consider local actions.[1]

A growing body of evidence illustrates some of the short- and long-term impacts of regional trade agreements on women's livelihoods. A five-country study based on research conducted in Benin, Cameroon, the Dominican Republic, Ghana, and Jamaica showed that the Common Agricultural Policy in the European Union increased competition for African, Caribbean, and Pacific producers in their national and regional markets.[2] Because women in these countries have less access than men to land, capital, credit, education, and training, trade liberalization had more of an effect on women. In Benin, for example, most women's enterprises are small because they lack the economic, information, and training resources to increase profitability. In Jamaica 66 percent of poor households are headed by women. Women generally have smaller farms than men and grow a mix of crops for the domestic market rather than export crops. Women farmers and agroprocessors in countries such as these find it difficult to reap the benefits of trade liberalization and export-led growth, essentially because they do not have the resources to be competitive.

Thorough assessments of how trade liberalization may or may not affect food security, nutritional status, and access to agricultural inputs and other productive factors from a gender-differentiated perspective are required if women are to benefit. A starting point is to appreciate that food security and family well-being provide a clear rationale for protecting or enhancing women's access to, and control over, land and other productive resources. Studies show that resources controlled by women are more likely to be used to improve household food consumption and welfare, reduce child malnutrition, and increase the overall well-being of the family (FAO 2006a). Any reduction in government subsidies to social services as a consequence of trade liberalization is likely to have a significant impact on women's lives. In an extension of their "reproductive role," women would have to provide those services no longer provided by the state, and less time would be available for entrepreneurial activities. Global trade negotiations should provide an agenda that outlines welfare guidelines and includes welfare payments to facilitate access to services.[3]

National business environment

At the national level, direct discrimination may be expressed in family laws that require a woman to obtain her husband's consent before starting a business or employment (as in some Mexican states; FAO 2002). Laws in other Latin American countries limit women's ability to be self-employed by vesting family property administration exclusively in the husband. Women in Kuwait and Yemen are not permitted to work at night. In Zimbabwe married women need permission from their husbands to register land. In the Democratic Republic of Congo, where women need their husbands' consent to start a business, women run only 18 percent of small businesses. Women in neighboring Rwanda, which has no such regulations, run more than 41 percent of small

businesses (World Bank 2007b). Legal limitations may be placed on married women's capacity to act independently, as in Chile's Commercial Code (FAO 2002).

Generally, however, formal legislation in most countries rarely discriminates directly against women or mentions them explicitly. Discrimination against women entrepreneurs is largely indirect and unintended. For instance, legislation regarding membership in cooperatives and associations may not overtly exclude women but may contain conditions that many women cannot fulfill. For example, members may be required to control a key asset such as land, which women are much less likely than men to control. Another requirement that may exclude many women is that a business must be a certain minimum size. In Madagascar, where virtually all women agricultural entrepreneurs are poor and operate microenterprises with no or few salaried employees, the law recognizes only cooperatives or associations with at least five salaried employees. Women with smaller businesses are effectively excluded from the benefits of officially recognized collective association.

Research commissioned by the Deregulation Project of the Kenya Institute of Public Policy Research and Analysis suggests that the management time and cost involved in registering a business name and securing trade licenses (two basic forms of registration and licensing applicable to small businesses) together cost about 1 percent of gross domestic product each year (KIPPRA 2000). These and other barriers to entrepreneurship often present greater obstacles for women than for men. An analysis in Uganda demonstrated that women's enterprises are frequently at least as productive and efficient, as measured by value added per worker and productivity, as men's enterprises, but women face higher barriers to entry (Ellis, Manuel, and Blackden 2006). These barriers include their relative lack of time (compared to men), their relative lack of official contacts, and their less equitable access to funds. Furthermore, legal and regulatory constraints in Uganda impose a disproportionate burden on women's enterprises. The *Uganda Regulatory Cost Survey Report 2004*, which covered 241 enterprises in four regions, measured the compliance cost of registration and licensing requirements. It found that over one-quarter of all enterprises reported that government officials had interfered with their business by, for example, threatening to close it or asking for bribes. For women-headed enterprises, the figure rose to 43 percent. Forty percent of microenterprises headed by women felt that the total burden of regulation was "heavy" or "severe" (as compared with 35 percent for enterprises headed by men). Trade licenses were identified as the most burdensome regulation. Over 40 percent of women, compared to 30 percent of men, reported trade licenses procedures as an obstacle to the growth of their business (Ellis, Manuel, and Blackden 2006). Similar trends have been observed in Kenya (World Bank 2007a).

The cumulative result of structural barriers such as these is the presence of fewer formally recognized women-owned enterprises than men-owned enterprises in many countries, particularly in Africa (fig. 5.2).

Credit represents another barrier to entry for women. To obtain a loan to start and run a business, women generally have less access than men to collateral, given women's poor or nonexistent access to land titles and formal employment. Cultural factors hindering access to credit and other services include women's seclusion, other practices restricting inter-action between men and women, and normative perceptions of women's role in the family and society. Indeed, women may internalize discriminatory cultural attitudes and refrain from applying for credit (as documented in Brazil and Fiji; see FAO 2002; see also Modules 3 and 4).

Discriminatory cultural attitudes may prevent women farmers from entering value chains altogether or allow them very limited roles. Contract farming—a forward agreement between farmers and processing or marketing firms to sup-ply agricultural products—is increasingly important to modern value chains, but women in some regions cannot engage in contract farming because social norms preclude them from signing contracts. In Guatemala, for instance, women hold only 3 percent of snow pea production con-tracts but contribute more than one-third of total field labor and virtually all processing labor (World Bank 2007c).

Market infrastructure

Rural infrastructure is an important element of an enabling business environment. Market infrastructure, including postharvest processing and storage and wholesale and assembly markets, is discussed here, while the other types of rural infrastructure important for market access (for exam-ple, transport, energy, information and communication technology [ICT], water and sanitation) are discussed in Module 9.

POSTHARVEST PROCESSING AND STORAGE. Extension in developing countries often concentrates on improving the capacity to produce crops, but more attention must be given to what happens after the harvest—the handling, processing, and storage of agricultural products. All of these activities are essential to increase the effectiveness of marketing and minimize product loss.

Postharvest characteristics, such as hulling and milling quality, can be vital to processors as well as consumers. Sometimes new varieties are evaluated and selected only

Figure 5.2   Percentage of Enterprises Owned by Women in Selected African Countries

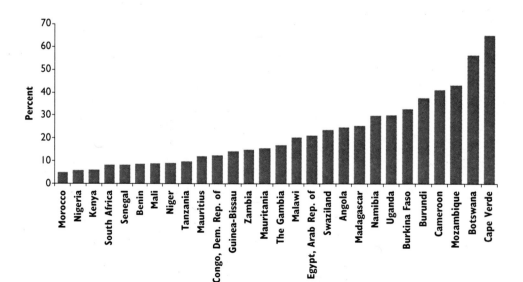

Sources: Adapted from Bardasi, Blackden, and Guzman 2007 and based on World Bank Enterprise Surveys 2002–06.
Note: The sample is restricted to individual and family firms and excludes enterprises with fewer than 10 employees and enterprises operating in the service sector.

after the postharvest characteristics can be observed. A study conducted in eastern India found a strong consumer preference for white-grained over red-grained rice because it saves women time in milling (Paris and others 2001, cited in Farnworth and Jiggins 2006). To improve a product's quality and thus add value, often consumers and other stakeholders must be brought into the evaluation process (through participation in tasting panels, for example).

Postharvest losses in developing countries can be considerable for perishables (such as fruits and vegetables) as well as staples (grains, dry beans) owing to poor product handling and processing and attacks by insects, fungi, rodents, and birds. In some areas postharvest losses reach 50 percent (Kitinoja 2002). Although it is generally recommended to harvest early in the morning to reduce the heat load on produce and make precooling faster and less expensive, in West Africa vegetables are often harvested in the late morning and endure the heat of the day while awaiting transport from the field. The women harvesters cannot come earlier because child care, cooking, carrying water, and other family responsibilities take priority (Kitinoja 2002). An integrated development approach designed to alleviate women's "reproductive" workload is necessary to address such conflicts.

Even if farmers can harvest their crops at the optimal time, they may not be able to sell them fast. The lack of a cold chain in many areas, and inadequate storage conditions more generally, lead to spoilage and reduce quality and market value. Assisting farmers and agroprocessors with proper storage not only improves product quality, but also enables produce to be marketed at times other than directly after harvest. The farmer or processor can receive a higher price, the price-depressing effects of a glut can be prevented, and the cash flow delay and costs of storage can be recouped. These benefits are as much for women farmers as for men smallholders.

Finally, transport costs are particularly important for women, who tend to trade locally in vegetables and other perishables. Remoteness increases uncertainty and reduces choice; it results in limited marketing opportunities, reduced farmgate prices, and increased input costs. Women's access to the postharvest services essential for entering the export market can be particularly problematic. Grapes, for example, depend on an elaborate cold chain from packing shed to final destination. The fruit must be refrigerated within a few hours of harvest; if the cold chain is broken afterward, the produce is damaged. A study in Brazil found that small-scale grape farmers were at a disadvantage in negotiating access to refrigerated warehouses at the point of production and on the docks, as well as to refrigerated trucks for ground transport and the refrigerated tankers that carry the fruit to Rotterdam (Collins 2000).

WHOLESALE AND ASSEMBLY MARKET. Although many wholesale and assembly markets are controlled and defined by domestic and international supermarket chains, in developing countries more than 75 percent of fresh fruits and vegetables are still sold in traditional open-air markets and in small, independent stores (Reardon and Berdegué 2002). Livestock assembly markets where producers and buyers interact directly are common. More than simply being a place to buy and sell, wholesale and assembly markets are often integral parts of the community and society.

A number of considerations may reduce women's access to wholesale and assembly markets: whether child care is provided and its cost, whether women are permitted to travel outside their community on their own or if they must travel with a chaperone (which increases their cost considerably), and whether women have access to vehicles. Women may need to pay a driver if they are not permitted to drive. Age can determine whether a woman may go to market. In Afghanistan only elderly widows without sons usually can go to the bazaar (Grace 2004).

Where women are permitted to trade in markets, and especially in cultures in which women's access to markets is limited, activities and resources must often be explicitly earmarked to include a women's section in the wholesale market.

GOOD PRACTICES AND LESSONS LEARNED

The following presents some innovative activities and synthesizes the lessons learned for future project and program design and implementation.

Global business environment

It is essential to ensure that women's defensive and offensive trade interests are part of the formulation of trade positions at the national level. One starting point is to consider the commitments to gender equality that are embedded in instruments such as the Amsterdam Treaty, the Beijing Platform for Action, the Cotonou Partnership Agreement, and the United Nations Convention on the Elimination of All Forms of Discrimination Against Women. The question, then, is to consider how such instruments can be applied in the trade context, and more broadly to consider what is needed for trade agreements to be gender sensitive. Other issues for consideration include the designation of sensitive products, trade-offs between increased production and labor conditions, and the promotion and protection of food security and the rural economy. Relating trade policy to the design, support, and funding of programs that address gender-specific supply constraints and help to increase women's economic involvement is necessary. To do this, planners may find it useful to prioritize ensuring better access for women to financial services and productive resources.[4] When framing agreements, considering indirect as well as direct effects on women as service users is important.

At the national level, support for gender sensitivity in governments' legislative systems and in the enforcement of international trade agreements is important. Support could be given to assist exporting countries to perform legal and regulatory analyses. These analyses should consider (1) whether the text of a particular trade measure reflects gender bias or could have disparate effects on women or other social groups and (2) whether the particular trade measure would conflict with or undermine the country's international commitments and domestic laws relevant to women and other social groups.[5] Box 5.4 shows that the Pacific

---

Box 5.4   Monitoring the Social and Gender Impacts of Trade Agreements in Pacific Island Countries

Pacific Island countries increasingly participate in regional and international trade agreements, but the potential social and gender impacts of these agreements have not been significantly factored into trade negotiations or closely monitored. Undoubtedly, trade liberalization will have complex and wide-ranging social and gender effects on Pacific societies, particularly among more vulnerable and marginalized groups.

Three regional organizations have developed a training package to provide Pacific Island countries with a framework and guiding methodology to monitor the social and gender impacts of trade agreements that they have signed, beginning with the Pacific Island Countries Trade Agreement. These organizations (the Pacific Islands Forum Secretariat, Pacific Foundation for the Advancement of Women, and United Nations Development Fund for Women [UNIFEM Pacific]) are using the training package to build national capacity in social and gender impact assessment.

Source: www.siyanda.org/static/Shore_picta.htm.

---

island countries are being trained to monitor the gender impacts of the Pacific Island Countries Trade Agreement.

NATIONAL BUSINESS ENVIRONMENT

Action has been taken to support and promote women agricultural entrepreneurs in several countries at various levels.

LEGISLATIVE, PROGRAM, AND INSTITUTIONAL LEVELS. At the legislative level, explicit prohibition of gender discrimination and statements of gender equality in relation to the exercise of self-employed activities are embodied in legislation, for example, in the European Union, Philippines (with regard to contractual capacity and credit), and South Africa (with regard to accessing credit and other resources). Lesotho passed a law in November 2006 allowing married women to own and transfer property and engage in legal acts without their husband's signature. Before the reform, the law classified women as legal minors (World Bank 2007b).

In a number of countries, affirmative action laws providing fiscal and other incentives for women entrepreneurs have been adopted, as in Italy (FAO 2002).

At the program level, development and gender-related plans have designed activities to promote women entrepreneurs (for instance, by improving women's access to training and credit in India and Tunisia). Public programs targeting women or reserving resources for women to obtain training, credit, and extension services have been adopted in Brazil, India, and the Philippines, for example (FAO 2002). Programs providing services through institutional devices designed to overcome the obstacles faced by women have been set up; perhaps the most well-known instance is the microcredit programs in Bangladesh.

At the institutional level, gender-related measures have been enacted with regard to the composition and activities of sectoral institutions, such as with training institutions in South Africa. Gender-specific institutions have been set up within ministries of agriculture or their departments, particularly those responsible for training and agricultural extension, such as in Burkina Faso, Italy, and Tunisia (FAO 2002).

The problem is often not the legislation and regulations but effective implementation on the ground. Social norms may prevent women from engaging in enterprise activities to which they are given access by the law. Lack of information, lack of capacity to deal with institutions, and institutional biases on the ground may stand against women farmers.

GENDER ENTREPRENEURSHIP MARKETS. A promising area of support to women's entrepreneurship has been opened up through the Gender Entrepreneurship Markets unit of the International Finance Corporation. One of its programs is developing gender and growth assessments (GGAs) to address legal and regulatory obstacles that affect men and women differently; to build the capacity of entrepreneurs, bankers, and other stakeholders; and to put in place financing mechanisms for women entrepreneurs in partnership with commercial banks (box 5.5).

IMPROVING THE BUSINESS CLIMATE. Countries with higher scores on the ease of doing business there have larger shares of women in the ranks of both entrepreneurs and workers (World Bank 2007b). A recent pilot project undertaken by the Regulatory Best Practice Program in Uganda's Ministry of Finance, Planning, and Economic Development suggests that when registration and licensing requirements are simplified, more women come into compliance and formalize their enterprises. A pilot project in Entebbe Municipality reduced the time spent by Uganda businesses in obtaining licenses by 90 percent, reduced compliance costs by 75 percent, and increased revenue collection by 40 percent. When reformers simplified business start-up procedures, business registrations shot up. The increase in first-time business owners was 33 percent higher for women than men (World Bank 2007b). The impact assessment of the first pilot at Entebbe (which recently won

---

Box 5.5   World Bank–International Finance Corporation Partnership Focuses on Women Entrepreneurs

To create an enabling business environment for women entrepreneurs, the Gender Entrepreneurship Markets unit of the International Finance Corporation (IFC), in collaboration with the Foreign Investment Advisory Service and the Africa Region of the World Bank, has developed new advisory and analytical products. At the request of governments (usually finance or trade ministries), gender and growth assessments (GGAs) have been carried out in Kenya, Tanzania, and Uganda and are underway or planned in Ethiopia, Ghana, and Rwanda. Building on the World Bank's *Doing Business* indicators, investment climate assessments, and Foreign Investment Advisory Service (FIAS) assessments, the GGAs address—through a gender lens—the legal and regulatory obstacles that affect businesses and propose concrete measures to overcome them. In Ghana, Kenya, and Tanzania, *Voices of Women Entrepreneurs* reports showcase successful women entrepreneurs as role models. Key results include the following:

- In Uganda and Kenya, GGA recommendations have been fully integrated into national strategies for private sector development.
- In Uganda a Gender Coalition has been created to support the implementation of GGA recommendations. Following lobbying from the coalition, GGA recommendations have been incorporated into four labor reform bills covering employment, occupational safety and health, labor disputes, and labor unions,

which were passed in 2006. The Ministry of Finance, acting on GGA recommendations, commissioned new legal drafts of the Companies Act, the Chattels Transfer Act, and other bills.

- GEM has worked with IFC financial markets to put in place lines of credit for onlending to women entrepreneurs through commercial banks. In Nigeria a $15 million line of credit was provided to Access Bank to lend to women entrepreneurs, and by January 2007, $4.5 million had been disbursed to 33 women-owned businesses. In Uganda $6 million has been provided to the Development Finance Company of Uganda, with $2 million set aside for women entrepreneurs. In Tanzania a $5 million line of credit for lending to women entrepreneurs has been provided to ExIm Bank, of which $1 million has been lent to a woman-owned microleasing company.
- Under a financial products and advisory services package, the IFC is helping to train bank staff in areas such as market positioning and gender sensitivity and is advising banks on new product development, such as insurance services for women. Women clients receive tailored training in how to prepare a bankable business, product development, and access to markets. To date, around 280 stakeholders in Ghana, Kenya, Tanzania, and Uganda—including government staff, lawyers, entrepreneurs, and members of civil society—have been trained in public-private dialogue, advocacy and media issues, and business management skills.

Source: Bardasi, Blackden, and Guzman 2007.

---

an International Investors award) suggested that the reforms were encouraging women-owned enterprises to obtain licenses for the first time because most of the license applications from women were first-time registrations (Bardasi, Blackden, and Guzman 2007).

Market infrastructure

Postharvest processing and storage. Innovative approaches to postharvest storage and handling can reap dividends in highly marginalized communities. In Niger women and men were able to use warehoused crops as the repayment guarantee to obtain loans (box 5.6).

Transport. Men's and women's transportation needs vary; these differences should be reflected in developing large infrastructure projects. Involving women in road maintenance management committees is one way forward. Ensuring women's participation may require modifying classic definitions of management experience and other special efforts. For example, in the Peru Rural Roads Program, the World Bank and Inter-American Development Bank aimed to address the transportation needs of men and women by consulting and

---

> ### Box 5.6   Niger: New Credit Approaches for Women
>
> A project in Niger (Project de Promotion de L'Utiliization des Intrants Agricoles par les Organisations Paysannes) introduced an innovative inventory credit approach ("warrantage") in 1999 that enables women and men to store their harvest in a warehouse until prices rise. The warehoused crops act as a guarantee, allowing farmers to access financial resources before their annual production is sold, or even without selling it. Evaluation of the warrantage project indicates that overall household well-being improved in terms of the quantity of food consumed. Because women have their own incomes, their ability to make decisions in the household has also improved, as has their standing in the wider community. The project has particularly benefited middle-aged women who are responsible for a large number of people. Social norms prevent younger women from engaging in activities that require movement within or outside the village.
>
> *Source:* FAO 2006b.

---

including women in project design and implementation. The participation of women was required in the road committees that oversaw the project's activities, as well as in the community-based microenterprises that helped maintain local roads and tracks. The criteria for membership in the microenterprises were adapted to ensure women's participation. For instance, women's household management was counted as management experience, and women from women-headed households were given priority. As a result, the project improved 3,000 kilometers of nonmotorized tracks that are largely used by women alone and often ignored in transportation projects. The benefits to women included an increased ability to participate in markets and fairs and a reduction in the time spent obtaining fuel and food. Forty-three percent of the women stated that the improved roads and tracks provided greater income opportunities.[6]

Wholesale and assembly markets. One way of enabling women to market produce successfully is to provide them with special market areas. The allotment of shops in wholesale markets and membership in market vendors' associations can significantly improve women's participation in markets. Moreover, constructing or improving wholesale markets, especially with basic facilities, will provide an efficient, safe, and hygienic trading environment for women. In India, for instance, improvements in basic facilities such as toilets and drinking water enabled market participation by women traders to increase by 18 percent (World Bank 2006). The recently opened Bagh-E-Zanana Women's Market in Kabul has begun to change the lives of many women. For the first time in decades, women have a place where they can go without men chaperones and where they can run businesses and sell their products and services to other women.[7] It may not be enough to provide market space to women, however; in the early stages, added support in the form of credit may be required if poorer women are to benefit (box 5.7).

GUIDELINES AND RECOMMENDATIONS FOR PRACTITIONERS

Legislation, regulations, policies, the business environment, and business infrastructure all need to be analyzed with a gender lens to understand the differentiated impact on women and men and to ensure an equal playing field.

Combined soft and hard investments are crucial for women's economic empowerment. Soft investments include strengthening women's access to and control over productive resources, developing women's capacity to enter markets by improving education and training, and

Box 5.7   Bangladesh: Women in Growth Center Markets

Growth center markets in Bangladesh are designated local focal points for selling rural produce and distributing agricultural inputs and consumer goods. Most rural markets are congested, muddy, dusty, and unhygienic. The Third Rural Infrastructure Development Project has constructed or improved common public facilities at 196 growth center markets to provide an efficient, safe, and hygienic trading environment.

Growth center market sites are selected through consultation with the women traders, women's union members, the market management committee, and officials. An important component of a growth center market is an exclusive area for women vendors in the open space, with shaded shops hosting a total of 120 women traders. Destitute women initially were given allotments on a lottery basis. Only women can trade; the presence of men working in a shop will lead to cancellation of the allotment. Sixty percent of the women received training before obtaining the opportunity to do business through this project. The monthly income of these traders ranges from 800 to 10,000 taka. Because these shops are located in the growth center markets, which are well connected with other nodal points, the traders can collect their tradable commodities very easily. Credit remains a major constraint, however. About 25 percent of the traders have received loans from nongovernmental organizations, but in small amounts. This experience highlights the need to provide complementary support, particularly financing, to infrastructure improvements and shop allotments.

Source: World Bank 2005.

ensuring that more extension workers are women or capable of conducting gender analyses. Hard investments include ensuring that physical infrastructure (processing and storage facilities, roads, energy, ICT, marketplaces) meets women's needs.

Legislation should explicitly prohibit gender discrimination or contain statements of gender equality in relation to self-employment. When discriminatory cultural attitudes are prevalent, affirmative action laws providing fiscal and other incentives for women entrepreneurs need to be adopted. Programs providing necessary services should be developed; and institutional arrangements leading to a more gender-equal access to these services are needed.

Processes for doing business must be eased. The most important step is to simplify registration and licensing procedures in light of international best practices. Evidence shows that the benefits of this action are sizable for women. For maximum gender impact, reform initiatives should address licensing requirements in those sectors of the economy that predominantly involve women.

Further research is needed on the likely impacts of trade arrangements on women in developing countries. Trade negotiation processes should build on the results. Statistics disaggregated by gender should be collected and gender-specific indicators developed to measure the impacts of trade arrangements on men and women.

Capacity Development for Small-Scale Women Entrepreneurs

Many women entrepreneurs in developing countries face disproportionate difficulties in accessing and competing in local markets, let alone international ones, for a number of reasons. These reasons include women's relative lack of mobility in relation to men and lower levels of use of and access to technologies that could add value to their product. Women are often concentrated in "feminized" occupations, such as handicrafts and basic food processing and sale. In these sectors, markets are often saturated and offer low returns. Furthermore, women are more likely than men to concentrate on backyard or microenterprises.

Occupational segregation by gender can impose significant costs over the long term on regional economies. These costs include rigidities in labor markets, reducing the market's ability to respond to change, the underutilization of women's labor, and lower levels of output and growth arising from suboptimal investments in early and lifelong education and capacity building for girls and women (Deutsch and others 2002). Thematic Note 1 explores the structural barriers that women entrepreneurs face; this Note considers how to improve women's skill base to help them become more competitive in markets. The focus in both Notes is on women owners and managers of small-size enterprises and the challenges they face on expanding to medium-size enterprises. Women employees in farms and agroprocessing firms and the issues they face are discussed in Module 8.

Appropriate interventions for capacity development can be devised only if some initial insight has been gained into the general opportunities and constraints that women producers and entrepreneurs typically face. This insight should be refined through an analysis of gendered constraints and opportunities in the proposed project location. Women need to be properly informed about various business options and the pros and cons of each. Prospective markets and their likely profitability should be considered in skills development and credit programs. Loan conditions and loan products

must be appropriate to the requirements of poorer women if the project hopes to reach them. The promotion of income-generating activities for women generally requires a much more practical approach than is often adopted by development programs. The bottom line is profitability.[1]

Several programs focus on capacity development of entrepreneurs—especially small entrepreneurs. Some of the issues faced by women would be common ones, but a need exists to analyze the local business environment with a specific gender lens and to develop interventions that directly respond to the issues that emerge.

KEY GENDER ISSUES

The following discussion describes the key gender issues in small enterprise development.

Identifying and characterizing women's enterprises

Women are more likely than men to manage microenterprises, often from their own home. Thus, they have the disadvantage of smaller size, higher risk aversion, local orientation, and low capacity to integrate into formal and distant markets. In some cases, they may manage several microenterprises simultaneously to spread risk or conceal the true extent of their earnings from men partners. A Zimbabwean study shows that women dispersed peanut plants throughout their plots rather than bunching them together, thus disguising the extent of their planting. Although harvesting took longer, their husbands did not realize how much money their wives were making by selling peanuts, or the significance of the social capital the women reaped through bartering and giving peanuts (Vijfhuizen 1996). Women thus may be ambivalent about expanding a particular enterprise. Any intervention needs to be alert to women's real needs and constraints and to work with them to devise a solution.

For project planners, finding the right person for capacity development can be difficult. Women may not know how to locate opportunities that might be available to them, or such opportunities may be hard to find. Poor people often do not belong to farmers' clubs because the requirements and expectations of membership can be too high. The explicit and hidden costs of membership may include fees, the need to provide food if members visit the farm, or the shame of wearing poor clothing. If development organizations choose to work with groups and clubs, or through extension workers' contacts, women who farm alone and without any man's help may be unintentionally excluded. One way of addressing this problem is to include the community in the identification and development of partner organizations and individuals (Farnworth and Jiggins 2006).

Identifying and addressing skill gaps

Women entrepreneurs are producing for increasingly competitive domestic and global markets. New skills and knowledge are required to enter export markets, such as expertise in bureaucratic procedures, national standards and requirements, marketing channels, and consumer preferences. Women wishing to enter export markets may need to acquire new skills to meet requirements that do not apply in domestic markets. Although it is demanding to develop the capacity to enter global value chains, once entry is gained, additional learning may take place through supplier-buyer interactions. Entry into global value chains can thus have a positive impact on technological capability and upgrading skills (Humphrey 2004).

In some places, however, a substantial segment of the economy has no appropriate market structures of any sort. A major challenge in such cases is to promote pro-poor strategies to include those who are truly marginalized in terms of resources and market access. Participation in these markets should aim to provide these poor men and women and their families with significant increases in income and thus contribute to food security and family welfare. However, the very poor, particularly the women, may be the most distant from potential markets and live in uniformly poor communities. A starting point may be to address generalized constraints such as illiteracy, innumeracy, low access to information, and limited levels of awareness of business opportunities. An assessment of the norms and values of the target clients and indigenous service providers might yield

alternative entry points, such as an educational focus or the promotion of awareness campaigns through the use of mass media.[2] In Kenya, for example, impoverished, geographically marginalized women's groups, whose aim is to offer support to families afflicted by HIV and AIDS, were assisted in developing a plan to buy various grains and process them into fortified flour. In so doing, they aimed to provide nutritious food to people affected by HIV and AIDS at a low price and to make a profit by selling the flour at competitive prices locally (KIT, Faida MaLi, and IIRR 2006).

Project interventions should consider how to enable women to manage risk. One method is to link poor women entrepreneurs to insurance markets to hedge against risks; another is to ensure that price information systems are prompt and effective. In some situations special capacity development programs need to be devised. The World Food Programme (WFP) has begun a program in which training focuses on *all* family members so that critical skills are not lost and a business can carry on if a family member should die (WFP, personal communication).

Devising suitable capacity development programs

Thinking through the implications of particular approaches to capacity development is important. Women may lack a clear understanding of the economic skills they require to help them upgrade their business; this may make approaches that prioritize the voice of participants problematic at times. An IFAD project in Syria found that women tended to base their choices on what they knew and liked, rather than on an understanding of markets and profitability. They usually chose what their friends had chosen, a tendency that can result in "a surplus of plastic flower arrangements on the local market and no income." Because the women knew little about nontraditional business opportunities, their choices of skills and businesses were limited.[3] This experience does not mean that participatory approaches do not work in such situations, only that they need to be coupled with other capacity development activities that assist women to develop market analysis skills.

Another issue is recognizing that women *may* have different management styles and thus different capacity development requirements than men. A study conducted in Cambodia, Lao PDR, and Vietnam showed that women typically had a more "caring" management style than men, which resulted in loyalty and high productivity among employees. They also tended to be more risk averse than men, which has implications for the product markets for which they are willing to be trained. Involvement in family-owned enterprises conferred benefits on the women entrepreneurs surveyed in terms of bargaining power and more equal relationships within the household.[4] Training programs, therefore, need to be sensitive to local management and learning styles.

REGIONALLY SPECIFIC FEATURES OF WOMEN ENTREPRENEURS AND THEIR CAPACITY DEVELOPMENT NEEDS

Capacity development programs need to be regionally and locally appropriate. Local needs assessments should be undertaken and training programs tailor made. The sections that follow summarize recent studies—including agricultural and nonagricultural sectors in all cases—undertaken in the Middle East and North Africa, sub-Saharan Africa, Indochina, and Latin America to provide a preliminary insight into women entrepreneurs and their motivations. A study from a war zone in Sri Lanka provides additional insights.

Women entrepreneurs face different opportunities and constraints according to the region they live in, although some opportunities and constraints are common across regions, such as those related to the need to meet their reproductive responsibilities. Capacity development programs need to be specifically developed to address macro-, meso- and local needs. The areas in which capacity development of women entrepreneurs may be required include basic literacy, awareness and self-confidence, market information, market management capacity, bureaucracy management, capacity to address financial and land constraints, technical capacity, and risk management capacity.

Middle East and North Africa

Participation of women in enterprise activities is very low in this region—as has been reported in the Introduction. A five-country study of women entrepreneurs across a range of small and medium-size enterprises in Bahrain, Jordan, Lebanon, Tunisia, and the United Arab Emirates found that most entrepreneurs are between 35 and 54 years of age. This finding is consistent with worldwide trends. The majority of women entrepreneurs are married, and most have children. Women identified their most difficult challenge to be achieving an appropriate work-family balance. Other key challenges include acquiring financial management skills, finding and keeping good employees, the high cost of labor, gaining access to capital, and the high cost of public services. The women expressed a strong desire for access to general

business training and support, and they wanted access to new markets for their products or services. At the same time, the women surveyed felt that women have a greater advantage than men when managing women employees. Overall they saw their gender as an asset rather than an impediment to their business.

Women entrepreneurs in all five countries use information and communications technology for their businesses at rates well above the per capita average worldwide. Many use mobile phones, computers, and the Internet (including their own Web sites) for their businesses. With respect to capital, a smaller proportion of women in the region use formal sources of credit for their businesses compared to women in other regions of the world. With very limited access to formal finance, women finance their businesses through personal sources, such as savings, friends, and family, and by reinvesting business earnings. Most entrepreneurs were interested in receiving external training and support services (CAWTAR and IFC 2007).

Sub-Saharan Africa

A three-country study (Richardson, Howarth, and Finnegan 2004) was conducted in Ethiopia, Tanzania, and Zambia. In all three countries the age range of women entrepreneurs varied from the late teens to over 50. Zambia had the oldest profile, with the largest category of women in the 41–50 age group, whereas in Tanzania the largest category was 31–40 years of age. Nearly all women entrepreneurs interviewed had an above-average level of education, having completed secondary school, compared to their contemporaries. However, some, particularly in Ethiopia, had had no schooling. The majority of entrepreneurs had gained work experience before setting up a business enterprise, either from a family business or from their own smaller business. The majority of women entrepreneurs had household and reproductive responsibilities to fulfill in addition to developing their own business. They thus experienced the typical constraints on their time and mobility associated with these responsibilities. At the same time, many of the women entrepreneurs felt they benefited positively from the support of their families by receiving financial, moral, and practical support.

The women entrepreneurs identified the chief constraints to growth as being access to credit, intense competition, and dealing with corruption among regulatory officials. Their businesses are generally labor intensive and make minimal use of new technology—whether information technology or production and process technology. These women's limited opportunities for networking reduce their ability to develop personal and business know-how and to access other physical and financial assets. Their enterprises tend to operate out of inappropriate facilities, if the women have a building separate from their home at all. This is particularly the case for food preparation and food-processing businesses, activities in which regulations require business accommodations to meet specific hygiene standards and in which women predominate. However, customary practices in the communities studied often prevent or deter women from owning or leasing premises in their own right.

Women largely confine themselves to local markets where access, mobility, and networks are easier for them to negotiate. This choice frequently results in excessive competition and underpricing. Women's ability to penetrate markets outside their local area is affected by the types of businesses in which they engage. Their locally made products are increasingly in competition with a growing range of imported goods coming into the market at all levels. Issues of quality and delivery are the same for all microenterprises, but women's relative lack of mobility, which is related to their household and community roles, limits the time they have for traveling. In some of the areas studied, women are not allowed to travel outside their communities (Richardson, Howarth, and Finnegan 2004).

Latin America and the Caribbean

A study of women entrepreneurs in Argentina, Brazil, and Mexico (Weeks and Seiler 2001) noted that, for the region as a whole, the rate of women's economic activity lags behind that of other regions. Between 1970 and 1990, however, the share of women employers and self-employed workers in Latin America and the Caribbean more than doubled and continues to grow exponentially. Women business owners are younger than their men counterparts, are relatively new to entrepreneurship, and are most likely to be in wholesale or retail trade. Their companies tend to be smaller than men-owned companies.

Key challenges identified by women entrepreneurs include insufficient access to information, training, technical assistance, technology, capital, markets, networks (women's business associations as well as broader industry or regional business organizations), and validation (in other words, being taken seriously by society at large).

Southeast Asia

A study in Cambodia, Lao PDR, and Vietnam showed that despite significant sociocultural differences between these countries, deriving partly from their historical trajectories, women in all three countries face similar constraints in the business environment.[5] Two key challenges are accessing credit and accessing markets. An overall lack of information combines with women's limited business experience to produce reactive, production-oriented business strategies—a serious problem, considering that markets in all three countries are small but competitive. The opaque and unstable legislative and regulatory environment is another constraint, particularly with regard to land law and land-use rights. Women entrepreneurs face cumbersome business procedures, ambiguity in the interpretation of legislation, and government intervention in economic activities. Lower educational levels among women, compared to men, constrain their choice of enterprise and limit their ability to take up vocational and technical training. The survey showed that women find balancing work and family responsibilities very difficult. They feel handicapped by family demands and social expectations. For example, women are expected to take the advice of relatives who are men on decisions that need to be made and how the business is run. Women feel they lack the knowledge and expertise to adapt to and master new technologies, or to innovate in developing new products and services.

The macrobusiness environment is important; these countries remain in the early stages of moving from a centrally planned to a market-oriented economy. Businesses need experience in managing quality, delivery times, and pricing before they seek to add customers. The use of outdated technology and equipment is also a problem; in Lao PDR, only 5 percent of women-owned enterprises use electrical or motorized equipment compared with 48 percent of men-owned enterprises. Although businesswomen have a general understanding of local markets and customer preferences, they lack insight into how to go about designing, making, and selling products that could be attractive outside local markets.

War Zones: An Example

A study examined Tamil women in northeastern Sri Lanka who became entrepreneurs as a result of the war (Ayadurai and Sohail 2006). A large percentage of these women are highly entrepreneurial, and their aims are to have a better life, to be self-reliant, and to support their families. Many went into business only after having lost their husbands in the war. They are educated—at a minimum, having a secondary-school education—and are involved in such businesses as livestock farming, office services, and textiles. Such businesses do not require a high capital outlay or much previous knowledge. A large majority of the women entrepreneurs are in business for the first time, and most rate their businesses as successful. Their measures of success are self-fulfillment and a balance between family and work.

GOOD PRACTICES AND LESSONS LEARNED

The following presents some innovative activities and synthesizes the lessons learned for future project and program design and implementation. Many of the examples and lessons cut across different types of rural enterprises—farm or nonfarm—whereas lessons and principles particular to a type of enterprise are specified below.

Inclusive and effective capacity development packages

Entrepreneurial training can be highly focused, or it can cover all the different aspects of creating and managing enterprises, including business and management skills. Focusing on the process of planning itself helps women to identify risks, limitations, and capital requirements and assist them in setting specific objectives useful in measuring long-term progress. Specific Modules need to be formulated around the particular needs of different groups of women, according to their background, experience, motivation, and stage in the enterprise development cycle. Training in basic literacy and numeracy may be a prerequisite to enrolling women in entrepreneurial skills programs. Moreover, all training programs should be designed to ensure access. A flexible time schedule—evenings, weekends, part time— and child care are important.

Capacity development needs to be very specific to the situation faced by the women and not general training: it should include practical guidance on how to approach and resolve the issues and needs of the entrepreneurs.

Picking effective trainers and creating partnerships

In many regions women trainers and extension workers may be more appropriate because of cultural restrictions that limit interactions between women and men who are strangers or not part of the family. Steps may need to be taken to permit women trainers to travel (box 5.8).

In some areas, however, women extension workers may not be respected by women farmers. In Vanuatu, for example, women's role in agriculture is scarcely acknowledged at

<table>
<tr><td>Box 5.8</td><td>Benefits of Ensuring the Participation of Women Trainers</td></tr>
</table>

In India, an Indian Institute of Management (IIM) project supports farmer-led participatory plant breeding and gives considerable priority to establishing links with farmer innovators. Several years into the project, it became clear to project staff that they had identified very few women innovators. It emerged that when men staff asked who was responsible for a particular innovation, women's innovations typically would be claimed by—or assigned to—the husband or another male family member. Bringing women staff on board was problematic. It was difficult to find safe places for the women to stay overnight; they needed chaperones to travel by public transport, and they would have to travel outside their own area to avoid bias. What the project did was to make arrangements for women staff to stay in a village with families known to the IIM team, women were permitted to work in their own farm, and travel was arranged so that they could be accompanied by another family member. The result was that more women innovators were located, raising the proportion of women's to men's innovations to 20:80.

Source: Farnworth and Jiggins 2006.

a policy level, although women are responsible for food production and are starting to enter the cash crop sector. Extension officers are mostly men and tend to deal with men farmers, who rarely pass on knowledge to women. Efforts to provide extension services to women through the employment of women extension officers met with resistance from women farmers who could not understand the issues being raised and were unwilling to accept advice from young women (Booth 1999). In cases like these, men extension workers trained in gender analysis may be more appropriate, at least at the outset.

Capacity development initiatives targeted at women can be very successful when they involve partnerships between men and women. For example, a World Food Programme (WFP) project in Zimbabwe involved getting women to take charge of milling in the Kala and Mwange refugee camps. Men were enrolled in training women to run the mills. Another WFP project in Tanzania provided men landowners with incentives to provide women refugees—many living with HIV and AIDS—with space to grow flowers, fruits, and vegetables.[6] In Bangladesh the Food Security for Vulnerable Group Development Women and Their Dependents (FSVGD) project provides multifaceted assistance to 110,000 women in seven districts of northwestern Bangladesh. Partner nongovernmental organizations (NGOs) deliver a comprehensive training program to FSVGD women, who in turn disseminate their learning to family members. Although women are the direct beneficiaries, men's support groups, comprising community members who are men and FSVGD spouses, have been formed. Their role is to support FSVGD women, increase their own awareness of women's empowerment and human rights issues through their meetings, and disseminate these messages to the wider community.[7]

Developing a capacity development service sector for women

Train-the-trainer approaches help to continue developing capacity over the long term. When skills are acquired and passed on by project beneficiaries themselves, a project gains momentum that endures after the project team has left. For example, community learning centers in three provinces in China provided vocational courses to women in field crops, livestock and poultry, agroprocessing technology, and gardening. Newly trained women were responsible for passing their new knowledge and skills to others; women were also provided with credit by local governments and credit cooperatives. As a consequence of the training interaction, women's social position and role in economic development increased in the communities (UNESCO 2003). Another Asian example comes from Lao PDR, where strategies for offering training in weaving have a built-in multiplying effect, with trainees required to teach others.[8]

In the Middle East and North Africa, the training-of-trainers component of "Women Get the Business Edge" (a training program sponsored by IFC's Gender Entrepreneurship Markets Unit) makes a concerted effort to target women as well as men trainers. The specific aims of the program are to develop a larger cadre of women and men trainers, to encourage businesswomen's associations to become brokers for business management training on an ongoing basis to their members through certified Business Edge partners in their countries, and to conduct focus groups and document lessons learned about women-specific business. The workshops are highly customized. In Afghanistan, for example, training was provided in marketing nontraditional businesses; in Egypt, workshop participants chose training in marketing and pricing; in Jordan, entrepreneurs requested training in pricing strategies and problem solving; and in Yemen, training was provided in financial management (www.businessedge-me.com).

Integrated and multidisciplinary approaches to capacity development

Training needs to go beyond technology focus to the entire host of skills and capacities required to run a successful enterprise. Capacity development on its own would be insufficient if other constraints faced by the women enterprises—such as credit and risk management—are not addressed in an integrated manner.

A project operated by the United Nations Industrial Development Organization (UNIDO) in Kenya provides women's groups with technical skills, basic computer literacy, business start-up assistance, and improved financial and business management skills, in addition to establishing wider marketing networks. In contrast to other projects, which focus only on improving technical skills, the UNIDO project also emphasizes confidence building to strengthen women's roles in the community. The project provides information on HIV and AIDS and offers literacy programs. By facilitating women's access to the tools and skills they need to improve, monitor, and evaluate their progress as entrepreneurs, the project enables them to set goals for themselves and to achieve their business objectives. The women are also encouraged to organize a business association. Establishing a formal association enables them to get in touch with like-minded women, exchange ideas, and take part in policy preparation processes at a variety of levels to help determine the future of micro- and small-scale enterprises (UNIDO 2003).

Establishing and training multidisciplinary teams of district-level extension and line-level agency staff can improve support to producers, particularly if they are organized into effective groups. For example, Proshika, a Bengali NGO, offers an integrated package of assistance to women's poultry groups by training women as paraveterinarians through group courses. The groups are provided with loans and technical extension services, and a compensation farm has been established to compensate for losses and therefore minimize risk for project participants. The project has caused the average weekly incomes of participating households to rise by 31 percent after becoming members.[9]

The La Carmela program in Ecuador, which instructs unemployed women in artisanal chocolate making, shows that success is possible when small-scale production units can be internationally competitive, high-quality raw materials are available, and a need can be demonstrated to integrate the work of skilled women into the production system. Crucial factors in the project's success were the interregional transfer of skills (staff training by an established Brazilian chocolate producer), the design and production of first-class marketing materials, and the creation of a fully equipped and staffed production unit for fine handmade chocolate products. The La Carmela program began when UNIDO, the government of Norway, and the nonprofit foundation Ce-Mujer saw an opportunity to increase the value added of Ecuadoran cocoa, enhance the role of women in Ecuador's industrial development, and address the problem of high women's unemployment. Women with no previous skills have now mastered the art of the artisan chocolatier and are now fully qualified to work in transnational companies or operate their own businesses.[10]

Complementary support

Preferential financial services. To kick-start women's enterprises, preferential financial services may need to be offered. For example, in Kenya, through the Growth Oriented Women Enterprise (GOWE) program, IFC and the African Development Bank are piloting an initiative to help women-owned businesses grow by providing partial guarantees that will allow them to secure loans between $20,000 and $400,000. The program, which started in 2006, also provides women entrepreneurs with customized business management skills training and mentorship support. The GOWE program plans to help up to 400 women-owned enterprises in Kenya to access credit by 2011.[11]

Business incubators. Business incubators help to extend services to small and medium-scale businesses in their critical early stages of development. Their services include assistance in drafting business plans, the introduction of new crop varieties and technologies, and improved management practices to support agricultural and rural entrepreneurship. Other services typically include providing Internet access, financial and legal advice, training, and networking.

Given the unique issues faced by women entrepreneurs, business incubators focusing specifically on women will go far in building capacities and sustainable enterprises. For example, the Village Business Incubator program in the coastal midland areas of Syria provides women in nine villages with an open learning space with a particular focus on business counseling, enterprise management training, and follow-up to monitor business performance. Several businesses have been set up.[12] In Gujarat, India, the International Centre for Entrepreneurship and Career Development (ICECD) has created the ICECD Small Business Incubator for rural women. The program provides infrastructure

(building, electricity, computer facilities, and machinery), training, and counseling to women to enhance their productivity and income opportunities. The package includes engaging assistance in conducting market surveys and drawing up business plans.[13] Business incubators are considered very useful and effective in engaging poor women entrepreneurs in productive markets.

Market intelligence. Poor women cannot afford either to undergo training or to take out loans unless a reasonable profit margin is possible. However, women often lack proper market intelligence, hindering their ability to make sound business decisions, and they require training to seek out and analyze relevant production and market information. The marketing extension component of the Livelihoods, Empowerment, and Agroforestry Project in Bangladesh is a good example of how training by extension officers on how to undertake market intelligence helped a women's group to refine their enterprise development plans to better respond to market needs. The women had been nervous and insecure about going to market. However, they used their social cohesion to support one another and—initially supported by local extension officers—were able to match supply and market demand (see Innovative Activity Profile 1 for details). Similar experiences have been documented for women's groups in Bihar (World Bank 2006).

Ensuring gender-equitable access to information and communications technology is critical. Applications relevant to the production and marketing of agricultural produce include telecenters, cellular phones, and personal digital assistants. Extension databases can track commodity prices and inform farmers. Up-to-date information on agricultural production and postharvest and processing technologies can be accessed, as can the contact details of subject matter specialists, information on plant quarantine regulations, climate records, market prices, and weather forecasts. Internet facilities can enable extension advisors and farmers to access agricultural Web sites and Web sites of universities with faculties or departments of agriculture (see also Thematic Note 4 in Module 9).

GUIDELINES AND RECOMMENDATIONS FOR PRACTITIONERS

Training and capacity development are needed to ensure that women entrepreneurs participate effectively in markets:

■ Entrepreneurial skills programs should be adapted to local cultural contexts. Although such programs may provide a broad skills base, they also need to help women develop the skills they require to access specific, identified value chains. Assisting women to understand how to make a profit is the bottom line. Training can be given in performing market surveys, accessing market intelligence, developing business plans, and other aspects of entrepreneurship.

■ In some areas training in basic literacy and numeracy may be required prior to enrolling women in entrepreneurial skills programs. Confidence-building measures may also be necessary.

■ The gender of trainers or extension workers must be considered carefully. In some cases women may be more culturally appropriate in these roles. Steps, such as providing a chaperone, may need to be taken to permit women trainers to travel. In other cases men trainers may be suitable, for example, where the gender of the trainer does not matter, or where women farmers have doubts about the competence of women extension workers or trainers. In the latter case it may be possible to introduce women trainers later.

■ Awareness should be raised in the target community about the proposed training and its purpose to gain the confidence of men relatives of women selected for training.

■ Where possible, training should have a built-in multiplication approach to ensure sustainability, with trainees required to teach others. Also in the interests of sustainability, training programs should incorporate a risk management strategy where necessary. For example, in areas where HIV and AIDS are prevalent, the continuity of business operations of the family would be threatened if the family member with the critical business competence were to die.

■ Multidisciplinary approaches to training can be very effective. Some projects have established programs run by multidisciplinary teams of district-level extension and line-agency staff, who have trained women in a variety of specialized skills.

■ Exchange or exposure visits enable entrepreneurs to view directly the successful application of income-generating activities and production techniques introduced to other programs and to share experiences. Training should use a host of practical approaches and not merely in-class instruction.

■ Developing a capacity development support sector (independent trainers) and increasing the presence of women in support services (extension, regulatory institutions, business development services) through their capacity development will lead to an increased presence of women in the system that is likely to benefit women's businesses.

Complementary support is needed in addition to training:

■ All training programs should be designed to ensure access—for example, by providing child care, considering the location of the training, and working around women's time schedules.

■ Ensuring access to, or the provision of, appropriate infrastructure (building, electricity, computer facilities, and machinery) for training may be necessary.

■ Women entrepreneurs may require regular counseling beyond business start-up to help them maintain and enhance their productivity.

■ Women's enterprises may require preferential financial services. These can be offered at start-up.

■ Training should be accompanied by an additional services and support package to ensure the sustainability of activities—for example, business development services, assistance in market intelligence, initial handholding in market management, and risk management interventions.

Collective Action and Market Linkages

Globalization has increased competition and market-related risks and uncertainties. Whether producers are supplying export markets or domestic markets, the rural organizations to which they belong have become important instruments for them to manage their assets more effectively; gain access to services, inputs, credit, and markets; and contribute more effectively to decisions made with value chain partners. Women have the most to win from collective economic action, as they often have more limited access than men to productive resources. The development of strong economic organizations can enable poor women to overcome high transaction costs, limited scale of production, poor access to a variety of resources, and lack of political and bargaining power as individuals. Quite apart from these advantages, studies show that membership in groups frequently helps members, particularly women, to improve their self-confidence and their status in the community (Dixie 2005; FAO 1995).

This Thematic Note focuses on building the capacity of rural producer organizations (RPOs) to meet the needs of women entrepreneurs. It is important to emphasize that developing capacity per se is not enough: RPOs must also learn to understand and work effectively with specific value chains that have been identified through capacity development. Effective market linkages enable women, through their organizations, to become more active in managing their roles in the value chain itself, as opposed to merely responding to the actions of other actors. The capacity development needs of RPOs include improving their access to, as well as management of, information; their knowledge of the market; their control over contracts; and their cooperation with other actors in the chain (KIT, Faida MaLi, and IIRR 2006).

One should note that the equity objective must not subsume the efficiency objectives: women RPOs must be driven by a profit motive and must be market led.

The history of RPO development is long and tortuous, with various types of groups having been created for social and economic purposes, often at the bidding of an outside agency rather than from need felt by smallholders. It is critical that RPOs developed for commercial purposes are strongly business and market oriented, and capacities developed to work effectively as partners in value chains.

Developing competitive smallholder RPOs is a long and difficult task and requires business and market orientation in the agencies providing support to the RPOs as well. As women smallholders may be even less endowed than men smallholders, this task is of an even higher complexity.

KEY GENDER ISSUES

The following discussion gives the key gender issues in rural organizations and other forms of collective action and linkages among chain actors.

Representation of women in RPOs

Formal RPOs or community-based organizations (CBOs) are membership organizations created by producers to provide themselves with technical and economic services. RPOs are not necessarily inclusive: the poorest of the poor often lack the minimum assets to take advantage of what an RPO can offer. Women, with their generally lower asset base, frequently find it more difficult to join and become active members of RPOs. For example, land ownership is a frequent criterion for membership, yet women are far less likely than men to own land.

When a household is a member of an RPO, it is usually the man who is considered to be the member and takes part in RPO activities, even though women members of the household may be active farmers.

Women who do join RPOs may find it hard to articulate their gender-related needs. Frequently the concept of *substantive* gender equality, which involves measuring and improving women's actual influence or control in value chain partnerships, is not well understood. For example, an increasingly favored approach to developing chain partnerships is fair trade. Fundamental to fair trade is the idea that producers and workers in a chain are entitled to their "fair share" of the profits. Fair trade standards include gender-specific indicators, but they do not guarantee that organizations participating in fair trade value chains fully understand, or are committed to, gender equity. Formal norms for gender equality, as expressed in fair trade standards, are generally respected. For instance, separate toilets and washing facilities for women may be provided, and women may be elected to serve on committees. Yet research in countries as disparate as Burkina Faso, Ghana, and Peru shows that women often do not participate actively in such committees (Guijt and van Walsum forthcoming). A study of women members of Coocafé (a Costa Rican Fair Trade cooperative) revealed that many women are members merely on paper to help the family unit access more credit from the cooperative or increase voting rights. Sporadic attempts by Coocafé to empower women have had limited success because they have been unfocused.[1] Because women have little voice in many RPOs, they often focus on the interests of the men's membership. Particular attention, therefore, needs to be paid to strengthening women's voice in mixed gender cooperatives.

To combat their lack of effective representation in RPOs, women are more frequently setting up their own RPOs. In the last decade, new, women-only agricultural and rural organizations have grown significantly, along with women's participation in existing cooperatives. Women's organizations outside the agricultural sector, such as social or religious groups, have also broadened their mandate to include support for agricultural income-generating activities, mainly through skills training and credit. These efforts have often required financial backing and developing collaborative links with government and private sector agencies. Despite this progress, many women's groups still lack financial resources and skills in developing and marketing products. To act effectively in value chains, women's RPOs require a step-by-step process of capacity development, with the RPOs slowly taking on more tasks as their ability to access market opportunities, services, and investments improves (box 5.9).

Weak market linkages

To begin managing value chains as partnerships of chain actors who actively cultivate and codetermine collaboration

---

Box 5.9 Bosnia and Herzegovina: Empowering Women through RPOs

A women's producer association, established in 2003 in Tesanj, Bosnia and Herzegovina, provides members with a milk collection network to help them to market surplus milk. The purpose was to secure markets for milk products and increase members' household incomes. Subsequently the producer association started to assist members in accessing credit and equipment. The women purchased more animals from the Livestock and Rural Finance Development Project credit line to increase their production. The project empowered these traditional milk producers to become more active within their communities, make greater financial contributions to their households, and thus improve their family and community positions. Women's active membership in the producer association enabled them to improve their knowledge and skills about livestock production and marketing. The marketing of milk created new jobs, increased incomes for rural men and women, and increased livestock production. The vision that the producer association has today is to expand its activities and marketing to vegetable production and processing, thus providing services to a larger number of agricultural producers.

Source: IFAD n.d.

---

with others, RPOs require the ability to cooperate with and understand the requirements of processors, traders, and retailers. Members need to be committed to continuous improvement in farm production, keep farm records, have access to independent information on market prices and trends, and obtain a good understanding of the value chain. It can take about four years or more to build a chain partnership, assuming that the farmers are already crop specialists. It can take a year or more to identify a good partner; a further year to develop trust, a shared vision, and a joint business plan; and another two years to ensure that the partnership is implemented successfully (KIT, Faida MaLi, and IIRR 2006).

Many RPOs lack a business and market orientation and an accounting system to track the progress of an economic endeavor. Many rural organizations originally were formed by governments to build social capital among farmers—for instance, to manage the seed funds of a project or run a microcredit scheme—but they were not designed to respond to market opportunities. Assisting existing or new women's groups to acquire a business orientation is therefore key to developing value chain partnerships. A business orientation requires chain partners to respond quickly and effectively to early market failures. For instance, an ultimately successful IFAD project in Tamil Nadu introduced microfinance schemes as the principal tool for empowering rural women through income-generating activities. The promotion of dynamic, cohesive women's groups, which were then formed into federations, was a major component of the project. Because the postproduction linkage of marketing was not built into the project initially, participants suffered from the lack of guaranteed marketing opportunities, nonremunerative prices, and exploitation by merchants and middlemen.[2]

Assistance to women RPOs must therefore be based on a strong profit and market orientation. The plan for capacity development must be based on a strong chain analysis with a gender lens. Capacity development efforts must be combined with complementing services essential for developing the RPO's business—be it credit, land access, or technology upgrade.

RPO development must follow from a market and value chain analysis that identifies the specific place of the RPO in the chain and the needs and requirements from it. Capacity development proceeds from this—and may focus on market, production, technology, organization, and other issues as relevant. RPOs develop as they work in tandem with other stakeholders in the chain and learn to adapt efficiently to the system. However, significant and sustained support is needed to build strong RPOs—whether this support comes from higher up the chain or from an outside development organization.

GOOD PRACTICES AND LESSONS LEARNED

The following discussion presents some innovative activities and synthesizes the lessons learned for future project and program design and implementation.

Promoting women's representation in RPOs

Gender equity is a basic founding principle of the Tamil Nadu Empowerment and Poverty Reduction (Puthu Vazhvu) project. Components include ensuring that women are represented in all project-supported village institutions. Approximately 50 percent of subcommittee members are women; in the economic activity groups one of the two leaders has to be a woman, and a quorum can be achieved at meetings only if 50 percent of the attendees are women. To ensure that project activities aimed at securing livelihoods and promoting economic activities are relevant to women, a special focus is given to providing women access to skills, information, resources, and assets. Long-term arrangements for credit, technical inputs, and markets have been set up to support women and their enterprises beyond the end of the project. Women from the poorest households, and those facing special circumstances (widows, the destitute, the deserted, and sex workers), are offered special support (World Bank 2006a).

In Tanzania the Participatory Agricultural Development and Empowerment Project advises that women make up at least 40 percent of the Community Investment Subproject Committee and the Farmer Group Investment Subproject Committee membership in each project location. Women-only subprojects are allowed. At least two signatories for subproject accounts must be women. Either the chair or the secretary of any subproject must be a woman, and village-level microplanning is done so that community members, including women, can participate in planning and prioritizing needs (World Bank 2006b).

In Chad women play a critical role in collecting fruit, fishing, cattle rearing, and processing and marketing farm produce. In response, the Agriculture Services and Producer Organizations Project seeks gender equity by requiring that subproject service providers take the viewpoints and concerns of women into account, that the departmental committees selecting subprojects prioritize women's groups and their plans, that at least 20 percent of the membership in all new committees established to implement or supervise a project must be women, and that at least 40 percent of the subprojects are to be managed by women (World Bank 2003). To date, over 3,000 subprojects have been approved, 40 percent of which have been implemented successfully by women.

Developing RPO networks

RPOs can increase their economies of scale and bargaining power by linking with other groups engaged in similar activities. "The Inter-group Resource Book: A Guide to Building Small Farmer Group Associations and Networks" (FAO 2002) describes how a participatory approach can be used to establish intergroup associations in rural areas. Key points include the following: (1) the RPO should establish a matching fund to ensure group commitment; (2) in some locations the private sector cannot deliver equity and efficiency benefits to poor people, and public support is required for RPOs to help women overcome poor access to resources and markets; and (3) an RPO does not have to offer the same services everywhere. According to need, an RPO may provide specialized services to its members, for instance, access to inputs, bulk purchase of supplies, and group marketing. In some areas separate group enterprises might be required to ensure that both women and men can be involved, whereas in other areas mixed groups might be more acceptable. Sometimes women and men may work together but on separate tasks.

The opening of community-managed procurement centers, an innovation piloted in the Andhra Pradesh Rural Poverty Reduction Project in India, successfully demonstrated ways to combat the lack of market access among poor women and men. The key innovations of the project, which have contributed to the social and economic empowerment of the rural poor, include (1) promoting of RPOs and federations, which organize the dispersed farmers to aggregate commodities; (2) localizing the value chain, bringing the market to the village level, and providing a "one-stop shop" for buyers, input suppliers, traders, and producers; and (3) promoting business expertise within the village and increasing transparency in transactions (see Innovative Activity Profile 2 for details).

Supporting women in developing chain partnerships

Box 5.10 provides examples from Nicaragua and Peru to illustrate the added value that an explicit gender focus can bring to women's associations. Nicaraguan women's coffee is marketed in the United States under a separate label from other Nicaraguan coffee. Aside from helping the women develop their technical capacity in all aspects of coffee production, the program has helped them acquire land titles, thus ensuring their control over fundamental productive assets. In Peru a dedicated marketing channel is also devoted to women's coffee. Capacity development aims to strengthen the women's self-esteem and leadership capacity. Their coffee is supplied free to homeless women in Canada, thus highlighting the brand's solidarity credentials.

Combining efficiency and equity objectives

The sheer cost of collecting produce from farmers in isolated areas means that the poorest and the most ethnically marginalized producers may not be reached. A study of Maquita

---

Box 5.10   Nicaragua and Peru: Chain Partnerships with Women's RPOs

Las Hermanas ("The Sisters") coffee, Nicaragua

Located in the Department of Jinotega, where 65 percent of Nicaragua's coffee is grown, a fair trade and organically certified coffee growers' cooperative (the Sociedad de Pequeños Productores Exportadoras y Compradores de Café SA [SOPPEXCCA]), has received special recognition for a program called Las Hermanas ("The Sisters") coffee. This coffee is grown entirely by the cooperative's 148 women (its total membership numbers 450). In 2006 Peet's Coffee featured Las Hermanas in retail stores across the United States. SOPPEXCCA is led by a woman, Fátima Ismael, and the organization has been critical to helping its affiliated women farmers gain titles to land and to produce, manage, and market their own coffee. To promote income diversification, SOPPEXCCA introduced its coffee farmers to organic honey production for sale in local markets. It has also facilitated a

primary education campaign and constructed or repaired many local schools.

Café Femenino: A Peruvian Women's Coffee Production Cooperative

Café Femenino is a women-owned brand of coffee grown in northern Peru and sold in U.S. and Canadian markets as fair trade. The coffee is also supplied free to local women's shelters in Canada through Women in Crisis. Café Femenino seeks to foster change in the prevailing socioeconomic order, and its Café Femenino Foundation helps to improve local perceptions of women's role by supporting programs and projects that generate income that women control. Forums focus on building self-esteem and leadership. With the help of organic and fair trade premiums, much progress has been made to improve conditions in coffee-growing areas, including better nutrition, improved sanitation, new wet-processing mills, and many miles of new roads.

Sources: For Nicaragua, www.ecologicfinance.org/borrow_nic.html; for Peru, www.cafefemeninofoundation.org/story.html; for Women in Crisis, www.planetbeancoffee.com/CafFem/index.html.

Cuschunchic, a fair trade initiative in Ecuador, shows that it focused very narrowly on areas of high cocoa production and on the specific ethnic groups that grew cocoa (Nelson and Galvez 2000). Isolated communities may be uniformly poor, be largely subsistence oriented, and use migration and wage labor as primary coping strategies. Can chain partnerships be developed if "economic potential" is a criterion for geographic targeting, and is "economic potential" a criterion of overriding importance when attempting to bring poor people into value chains? Equity and efficiency criteria may clash—and threaten the long-term commercial viability of a project.

The question of who pays for organizational development, and for how long, needs to be examined carefully, particularly when equity objectives are to be achieved. The case of fair trade is instructive, because it makes a deliberate choice to foster equity as well as efficiency. This commitment can mean that buyers and other intermediaries may find themselves working with poorly organized RPOs to achieve equity objectives. The question then arises as to which partner in the value chain should arrange and pay for organizational development to enable the RPO to become economically effective. In Peru, for example, Biorganika, a subsidiary banana company owned by Solidaridad (the fair trade company behind the Max Havelaar brand), works with 200 marginalized small-holder families to certify and export bananas as "fair" and "organic." Few NGOs are active in the region, so Biorganika itself—a commercial company—spends much time and money on developing capacity in RPOs. Tensions have developed among project partners because of the costs involved and the lack of clarity over which partners are actually responsible for developing capacity in the RPOs (Guijt and van Walsum forthcoming).

One way to address these issues is to combine efficiency and equity objectives by forming partnerships among a range of commercial and development actors. In Rwanda poor widows were successfully targeted by an essential oil project that enables them to sell quality produce into the international organic chain (box 5.11). The equity agenda supported the project's economic efficiency objectives by organizing women into cooperatives, providing them with good training, and providing quality technology—good plant genetic material was the key to commercial success. Several social enterprise initiatives are currently ongoing, including several funded by Care International in Africa, where a collaboration is formed between producer groups, a private marketing (and/or processing) firm, and a development organization—with the development organization supporting the unsustainable costs of initial capacity building of smallholders.

In Afghanistan a project found that it could involve women as farmers by working with, rather than challenging, existing gender roles and responsibilities. The project helped women to upgrade their poultry farming practices, and to market their products through specially designed marketing networks (box 5.12).

GUIDELINES AND RECOMMENDATIONS FOR PRACTITIONERS

■ Supporting women's RPOs to become effective chain partners is often a slow process, in part because of the social welfare origins of many RPOs and women's organizations. A step-by-step process of capacity development may be required, with the RPO taking on more tasks as its ability to access market opportunities, services, and investments improves. Although gender equity may be one of the project objectives, for success any RPO must be designed and function on completely commercial viability terms.

■ A gendered understanding of existing market linkages and the roles men and women play in specific value chains is needed before plans are developed between chain partners to upgrade or internationalize the selected value chain. Without such an analysis, women may lose out—in terms of access to and control over land and other productive assets, as managers of gene flows, and as market women in local markets.

■ Postproduction market linkages need to be strongly built into all projects. Profit is the bottom line.

■ Strengthening women's voice requires more than ensuring that women are represented on mixed-gender RPO committees, which tells us little about their levels of participation. The means of achieving substantive gender empowerment need to be discussed.

■ Project partners must clarify their respective responsibilities for organizational development of RPOs (who will do what, and when will the assistance end). This clarity is particularly important when trying to shift an RPO selected for equity reasons into an economically effective organization. Commercial RPO development is a very complex task that requires a total commercial orientation among project or program staff while keeping the social objectives intact. There is a long and sad history of unsuccessful RPOs around the world due to inadequate, non-commercial based, or misguided institutional support.

■ It is necessary to promote a conducive legal environment with laws and regulatory systems that promote growth and recognition of economic RPOs.

Agribusiness in Sustainable Natural African Plant Products (ASNAPP), a continent-wide agrienterprise, focuses on the cultivation and use of high-value natural plant products to enable African agribusinesses to compete in local, regional, and international markets. Products include herbal teas, culinary herbs and spices, and essential and pressed oils, as well as medicinal plants.

The Ikirezi Natural Products Project was initiated in 2002, when ASNAPP performed product and market assessments for agricultural products in Rwanda. ASNAPP recommended essential oils, particularly geranium and eucalyptus, as attractive agribusiness opportunities. A joint project between ASNAPP and World Relief Rwanda was established to study the viability of commercializing geranium oil. Initial funding for the pilot project was provided by the United States Agency for International Development. Following successful piloting, Ikirezi Natural Products was founded as a community-interest company in August 2005. Ikirezi's objective is to produce high-quality essential

oil for local and international markets. It works with three cooperatives with 150 members, 94 percent of whom are widows and orphans—groups that the project specifically wished to include. The cooperative farming structure was identified as a valuable social arrangement for fostering reconciliation, unity, and relationships among farmers, in addition to being an appropriate business mechanism. Ikirezi provides cooperative members with training in agribusiness management and HIV and AIDS prevention and care. Key features include the following:

- Mobilizing farmers into associations and providing technical assistance
- Constructing two 200-kilogram-capacity distillation units to produce international-quality oil in situ, thus reducing costs
- Acquiring ECOCERT organic certification
- Establishing a network of domestic and international partners with technical expertise in essential oils, and winning Rwandan government support.

Source: www.ikirezi.com.

Income generation and food security are critical concerns in Afghanistan, where women have experienced discrimination and exclusion from access to public resources for many years. Village poultry production is a culturally acceptable practice for women that addresses both the food insecurity and income generation needs of the household. Poultry provide scarce animal protein and can be sold or bartered to generate income. The Rebuilding Agricultural Markets Program and Food and Agriculture Organization sponsored a project that developed an innovative organizational structure enabling village women to receive training in poultry production, obtain production inputs, and access markets on a sustainable basis. A network of

women links village producers, through district Poultry Producer Groups, to the provincial center, where there is a technical resource base that supplies inputs and market opportunities. By November 2005 the three-year project had trained 21,364 women in poultry management and organized 850 producer groups. The training and organizational development have helped women to increase their household income; about 2,545,281 eggs are produced each month, valued at an estimated $311,032 (which comes to $20 per producer per month). Project results demonstrate that village women can be organized into an effective marketing network that links women poultry producers to urban markets.

Source: Thomas R. Fattori, "Organizing Afghan Women to Generate Income from Poultry," www.globalfoodchainpartner ships.org/cairo/papers/TomFattoriAfghanistan.pdf.

Supporting Agricultural Value-Adding Strategies

Strategies to add value that are close to the producer or district level help to ensure that more rents are captured for poverty reduction, provided that attention is paid to producers' ability to bear risk. A major challenge in market development is to ensure the equitable distribution of gains. Women historically have been excluded from gaining higher shares in value chains. Careful planning and management of interventions is required. This Thematic Note explores how the promotion of strategies to add value can help meet equity and efficiency objectives.

One approach for adding value to products and capturing higher financial benefits involves assisting women to become crop specialists while maintaining a clear market orientation. Women may need to improve their production skills, and they may need training in a set of farm management skills, such as crop and livestock production, planning, record keeping, and financial management. The time it takes to become a specialized farmer depends on the existing assets and capacities of the farmer, the type of product, and the type of market. To produce for export markets is far more demanding than to produce for local markets; it may take many years to develop the necessary skills (KIT, Faida MaLi, and IIRR 2006).

Another value-adding strategy involves helping farmers move into processing and marketing to add value to the product. This strategy also provides opportunities for landless women to enter the value chain by offering processing and marketing services to local farmers. Intervention needs to focus on marketing and market management capacity development; investments in facilities for processing, marketing, and distribution (infrastructure and professional staff); developing market outlets; designing and implementing management systems (operational procedures); and developing organizational discipline. RPOs help save costs through joint input procurement, processing, marketing, and other activities. Their key competencies should include quality grading, market outlet development, and logistics management. Thematic Note 3 discusses ways to develop the organizational capacity of RPOs to meet the needs of women members.

FINDING OPPORTUNITIES IN VALUE CHAINS

Opportunities for value adding for women may exist through an upgrade of their current role in a value chain, moving up to additional roles in value chains (for example, into processing), finding new products and becoming dominant members of a new value chain, and increasing efficiency in current interaction in the value chain. All are based on concrete analysis of the markets and value chains with a gender lens. At the minimum such an analysis should ensure that women and other disadvantaged members of chains, or women in sectors impacted by the chain, are not negatively affected by the way the chain is organized and functioning.

Chain partnerships are often highly gendered: men speak to other men when brokering agreements between producers and buyers. If this dialogue does not take into account actual and potential gender issues, women may lose out. For example, women often stand to lose when export markets are developed for local commodities. A gendered understanding of the costs and benefits to women when value chains are internationalized will not be captured if women farmers, processors, and marketers are not consulted. A gendered analysis of existing market linkages is also needed. An examination of Fair Trade mango production and marketing in Burkina Faso showed that some women gained from the new employment opportunities provided by the packing station, but other women suffered from reduced marketing opportunities. Mangoes that women used to sell locally are now marketed internationally, and women's role in the international marketing chain appears to be much smaller than it was in the local market (Guijt and van Walsum forthcoming). Not only may women lose their role as marketers in the local market, but they may also lose access to land, access to other productive assets, and their roles in managing gene flows.

GOOD PRACTICES AND LESSONS LEARNED

The following discussion presents some innovative activities and synthesizes the lessons learned for future project and program design and implementation.

Adding value to existing products

Dairy farmers, many of them women, in the Thika district of Kenya added substantial value to their products in a short time. The key to success (and project sustainability) was to involve farmers from the very beginning. They participated in the baseline survey, worked on the problem analysis, and were involved in the planning and implementation of the project. They realized that they had land and labor; they just needed to organize themselves. This knowledge gave them the capacity to take on new roles and develop their management skills. The farmers have added milk collection, transport, processing, and sale; cattle breeding; feed formulation; and feed processing to their activities. Women dairy farmers in particular capitalized on their existing skills. By baking snacks to accompany the main product they accessed a whole new market—customers who wanted a bite to eat and a drink on the spot. Women were also strongly represented on decision-making boards. The groups elected their own management committees (40 percent of the committee members are women) to take them through their plan.

A District Poverty Initiatives Project in Andhra Pradesh, India, brought landless women laborers together. They bought produce from farmers who are men, transported the produce in bulk to the market, and negotiated good prices with buyers in town. Farmers who are men were relieved of the onerous task of bringing their crop to market, and their wives were fully informed of the price that their husbands were paid, providing them with the basic information they needed to negotiate household and personal consumption budgets.[1]

A UNIDO project centering on the olive oil chain in Morocco was able to ensure that although men were trained, women were able to maintain control over the entire chain, from picking olives to selling to the final consumer. The women already knew how to make and market olive oil; upgrading and professionalizing this knowledge were critical to project success. The women were trained in improved production techniques, resulting in much-improved, more healthful, and better-tasting oil with minimum postharvest losses. As a consequence of their training in marketing skills, they went to the consumer rather than waiting to be approached. The women could risk undertaking such a steep learning curve because their efforts were backed by a strong network of local training and commercial institutions that offered complementary support (box 5.13).

Box 5.13   Morocco: Improving Olive Oil Production and Direct Marketing to Consumers

Women entrepreneurs in Chefchaouen, Morocco, used to produce olive oil using highly labor-intensive, unsafe methods that resulted in substantial losses of oil. Once the oil was bottled, the women waited for customers who came to their door. The olive oil was very acidic and posed potential long-term health risks to consumers. UNIDO introduced a mechanical olive oil production unit using locally available technology. Women producers learned to harvest the olives, produce healthful oil, and control its quality and acidity. Training sessions helped them improve their marketing skills.

The women are now building facilities where they will install new equipment. They have been assisted in purchasing packaging materials, registering trademarks,

and preparing labels and promotional materials, and they are selling their oil from kiosks in town instead of from their homes. A strong network of local support institutions has been built up with the backing of the Ministry of Industry, Commerce, and Communications, as well as a network of trainers in production technology and in business management and marketing. In total, UNIDO taught over 300 women and 50 men to produce better, safer olive oil that could command a higher price. Productivity increased by up to 40 percent. Five other groups joined the first association, resulting in a federation and the natural development of a cluster. Selling through kiosks in town has helped sales increase by at least 85 percent. Overall earnings have as much as doubled.

Source: www.unido.org/doc/27778.

Developing new products

Innovative products can be developed through pro-poor, gendered value chain analyses that meet the requirements of producers and consumers. Box 5.14 provides an example from the Philippines.

Financing value-addition strategies

Involving women in technology development is important, but poor women with weak access to markets may still struggle with financing even low-cost processing technologies designed to add value to their produce. Box 5.15 shows how this problem was addressed in South Africa.

Organizational and marketing capacity

In strongly gender-segregated, lengthier chains, it is important that women and men perform their tasks well, to ensure that maximum profits and minimum spoilage are achieved at each stage. On the northern Caribbean coast of Honduras, an initial training course (provided by the FAO Livelihoods Diversification and Enterprise Development Project) helped women understand that they would need to organize into groups. Moreover, the project helped appraise livelihood options and trained women and men in marketing skills to improve their incomes (box 5.16).

Even the poorest of women, without key productive assets like land and machinery, can enter value chains by engaging in product development, processing, and marketing services. In India a livelihood chain analysis identified commercially viable products in the informal economy. These included tissue-paper bags used by the hotel industry, shoe covers used by visitors to monuments, and incense sticks. Participatory Livelihood Plans were developed with organized groups of

---

Box 5.14   Philippines: Developing New Products

In the Philippines, rice was laborious and time-consuming for women to process by hand. The raw material was limited, because the glutinous rice varieties that women grew produced poor yields and little land was devoted to glutinous rice cultivation. Indeed, sales of glutinous rice contributed only marginally to household income, and so glutinous rice was not a high priority for plant breeders. After talking with women farmers, the Women in Rice Farming Systems project developed a study that included both formal surveys and household- and market-based action learning with women and men farmers. The results demonstrated the importance of glutinous rice sold in its processed form as a specialty product. It provided a high percentage of women's incomes, enabling them to fulfill their responsibilities for key household inputs and food management. A new, early maturing, and higher-yielding variety was developed that compared favorably in taste and eating quality with local varieties, and dehulling machinery was developed in collaboration with the women processors. This equipment improved labor efficiency and reduced the drudgery involved in hand pounding. The value-added gross returns were 70 percent.

Source: Paris 1989, cited in Farnworth and Jiggins 2006.

Box 5.15   South Africa: Financing Value Addition

In the early 1990s women's groups in South Africa's Limpopo and Gauteng Provinces started small-scale peanut butter processing and marketing to earn additional cash. Traditional processing methods were used, including labor-intensive roasting and manual stone grinding. Under these circumstances only small volumes could be processed, resulting in limited profit margins and low cash earnings. Following requests by the women's groups, a low-cost mechanized processing technology was developed jointly by the South African Agricultural Research Council and Wageningen University and Research Centre. The equipment was supplied to the groups on a loan basis, which was to be repaid from the profits of the operation. Intensive training in the use and maintenance of the equipment was provided, and the results were monitored closely. Various technical adaptations to the equipment were made, based on the groups' experiences. The technology was easily mastered by all pilot groups, and total sales and the profits of peanut processing increased. Because of better marketing opportunities, results in the periurban and urban groups were spectacular: the urban group repaid the cost of the equipment after only one year. For the rural groups, the major obstacles remain the initial investment costs and the development of marketing channels.

Source: Wanders 2003.

A majority of both women and men in the project area depend on artisanal fishing. The Livelihoods Diversification and Enterprise Development Project in Honduras offered a 30-day course to men fishers and women traders that covered theoretical and practical issues, including quality control, manufacturing best practices, basic accounting, and processing techniques. Mixing the genders led to improved understanding of each other's needs. Thanks to the training, women increased profits by 20 percent. Both women traders and men fishers now want access to technologies such as ice makers and small freezing cabinets. Men are already organized into a fishing cooperative, which makes it feasible to purchase the technology; women are now planning to form an association, recognizing that it will help them access equipment that will reduce their everyday vulnerability, improve fish storage, and thus improve market prices. Furthermore, the project leadership expects that any increase in profits from fish sales would impact positively on household nutrition and food security, given that women would control the profits. The option currently under consideration is to provide one ice production facility to the men-owned cooperative, and a second to the municipality, with open access to registered fishermen and women traders.

Source: FAO 2006.

women residents followed by sample development and establishment of marketing linkages, negotiations with the target customers, and design improvements. The Center for Urban and Regional Excellence supported the initiative through mechanisms that enabled residents to engage with the concerned agencies (USAID 2006). Box 5.17 describes how landless women were able to offer critical services to men farmers, which benefited all concerned. There are two key lessons here: (1) a step-by-step approach was taken to build the women's skills base and expand their enterprises and (2) women were already organized into a group, so training focused on developing their skills as a group.

GUIDELINES AND RECOMMENDATIONS FOR PRACTITIONERS

- Women and men need a clear understanding of their roles and responsibilities in relation to other actors in the value chain to develop vertical integration strategies aimed at providing a good quality product, minimizing postharvest losses, and meeting consumer demands. To achieve this goal, value chain analyses should be conducted (see the Overview).
- Gender analyses should be coupled with market research to obtain information on the most suitable crops or activities along the value chain, which should be prioritized for equity and efficiency gains. Women need direct access to market information, rather than obtaining this information through their husbands.
- A step-by-step approach should be adopted to build women's skills base and expand their enterprises.
- Project strategy should be based on this strong analysis—and should be very market and profit oriented if women are to compete in competitive value chains. Besides capacity development, other necessary essential elements may include technology adaptation, credit supply, and land reform. Project design must be integrative and include all of these.
- Upgrading existing activities is a relatively simple way of capitalizing on, and improving, women's current capabilities. The market already exists; the key is to supply it with an improved product and to develop a targeted marketing strategy to win customers. To do this, investments can be made in processing technology and in improving women's marketing skills.
- Other potential businesses could be niche crops or markets identified by the market assessment, in which women may have a particular advantage.
- Women may be able to increase their income by capturing additional activities within the chain—for example, by forward integrating into processing.
- Innovative approaches to product development and marketing can help poor women without key productive assets, such as land, to enter value chains.

The District Poverty Initiatives Project (DPIP) in Andhra Pradesh uses women's self-help groups as a starting point to empower the "poorest of the poor"—a group it identifies using several criteria. One of the project's activities is helping women in self-help groups to form affinity groups consisting of very poor women in a village who engage in similar economic activities. The project then helps these groups of producers move up the value chain by moving closer to consumers. Critical to this effort is an emphasis on collective (rather than individual) economic activity. Typically the first step is to help the group practice their current method of production more efficiently. For example, split-bamboo basket makers may start buying bamboo poles collectively, which lowers the price they pay.

Once an economic affinity group has developed ways of conducting their current method of production more efficiently, the project works with them to create new forms of economic activity. For example, one group began as landless agricultural laborers.

With the help of a woman agricultural specialist provided by the project, these women devised a scheme to buy from village farmers and sell it in the nearby town. The group realized that most village farmers had little to sell, paid a great deal to get their crop to town, and received poor prices because they lacked the leverage to demand a higher price. The women took out a sizable loan from the DPIP and then offered the village farmers the going price for their crop. Because the total crop that the group was brokering was quite large, they could arrange transportation at a lower price per kilo, and—with the help of the technical advisor provided by the project—they drove a good bargain with buyers in town and realized a significant profit. The profit was sufficient to repay the loan and put money into a bank account to fund a new set of activities, which first focused on learning how to grade the crop. The women then diversified into new crops. Each cycle brought further collective profits, which were put into the group's bank account to capitalize their next venture.

Source: www.rd.ap.gov.in/velugu/velugureportskaren.htm.

Bangladesh: The Six-Step Marketing Extension Tool

PROJECT OBJECTIVES AND DESCRIPTION

Marketing involves finding out what customers want and supplying it to them at a profit. The marketing extension (ME) process is about raising incomes through marketing education courses and subsequent complimentary services.

ME interventions include (1) *marketing education* (creating a better understanding of the process, the market and its demand, and terms of products and services), (2) *coordinating* (mobilizing groups, organizing events, and getting things started), and (3) *forming business linkages* (making introductions between buyers and sellers and facilitating the start of new trading relationships).

The ME process works with CBOs (community-based organizations). The six steps in the process are designed to empower community members to identify market opportunities and plan how to exploit them:

1. *Resource audit:* The analysis of resources, including embedded skills, resources and equipment, existing marketing arrangements, and knowledge.
2. *Selection of target products:* This step involves detailed cost studies, analysis of alternative markets, and the selection of location(s) for market research.
3. *Market research:* A task force holds discussions with traders on potential products in terms of prices, quantities, quality, and market opportunities.

What's innovative? Marketing extension requires relatively little development support and resources but has proven to have huge payoffs, especially where poor women have been socially and culturally constrained from exploring their opportunities in the market.

---

4. *Analysis of findings:* The market research findings and potential profitability of alternative products are analyzed.
5. *Product choice:* A strategic choice of products is made for marketing development.
6. *Planning:* An action plan clearly delineates activities, responsibilities, and timing for the selected products, setting out what will be done, when, and by whom.

PROJECT OBJECTIVES AND DESCRIPTION

The Village and Farm Forestry Project (VFFP) was implemented by Intercooperation (a Swiss international NGO) with financing from the Swiss Agency for Development and Cooperation (SDC). The project—part of SDC's larger Sustainable Land Use program—sought to support agroforestry in greater Rajshahi, in northwestern Bangladesh, by promoting quality planting material, introducing new varieties, and improving agroforestry techniques, notably in fruits, timber trees, and vegetables (mainly for homestead gardening). During the project's sixth phase, economic and market dimensions were introduced. It was obvious that poor farmers' lack of marketing knowledge was a major constraint. FAO had developed a "market education" approach, which was tailored to the project's needs in northwestern Bangladesh with assistance from missions from the United Kingdom (Accord Associates; Dixie 2005) and Switzerland (Intercooperation). The adapted approach became known as "The 6-Step Marketing Extension (ME) Tool," and in 2003 trials of the Marketing Extension Course began.

The experience had many positive outcomes. After the VFFP concluded, the course was continued and the market approach reinforced under the aegis of the Livelihood Empowerment and Agroforestry (LEAF) Project, initiated in 2004 with guidance from Intercooperation and financing from SDC. The ME tool, which is one of the components of

LEAF's market approach, is the entry point for teaching basic skills that enable community members to choose and develop the most appropriate economic activities.[1] After further development, the pilot ME process was tested with 12 CBOs. Based on this field experience and feedback from the CBOs, the methodology and tools were adapted and then implemented in 80 CBOs in 2004.

BENEFITS AND IMPACTS

Profitability at a glance. During the monitoring period (from 2004 to June 2006), 11,000 producers from 455 CBOs were active in 15 sectors, including vegetables, milk, handicrafts, minigarments, poultry, fish, and sand. At least 60 percent of the CBOs formed marketing groups to sell their products in bulk and negotiate higher prices. These groups also sought ways of improving or diversifying their output. As a result, the estimated average monthly profit increased to $55 ($2 per day per producer).

The CBOs have successfully integrated vulnerable members of the community. For example, women remain highly represented (up to 65 percent), with some even leading their CBO. Also, 25 percent of the extreme poor (landless, Adivashi-tribal communities, and women-headed households) are now running small businesses within groups in LEAF areas. The various income-generating activities developed in the CBOs have helped diversify livelihood prospects and limit income insecurity among these vulnerable groups. The field facilitators from LEAF's partner organizations have transferred their competencies to newly recruited "local service providers" to ensure that the intervention is sustained even after the project ends.

Community-based organizations develop new capabilities. Conventionally, CBO members select income-generating activities based on three criteria: known skills, proven success, and existing local markets. Rarely would their market investigations extend beyond the calculation of income (price $\times$ volume). For this reason the notion of product development, with the accompanying consideration of production costs and profits, was new and challenging for the CBOs. Selecting potential income-generating activities and then undertaking market surveys reinforced the groups' confidence and abilities to analyze market conditions.

The new skills increased the capacity of CBOs to select relevant economic opportunities and encouraged them to expand beyond traditional practices and identify diverse products and niche markets. To their benefit, they have adopted the practice of calculating production cost/profit margin to assess financial risks. Most CBOs had very limited

and unreliable information about markets. Often local traders were their only source of information. These buyers could take advantage of the villagers' limited information, knowing that they were unlikely to travel more than five kilometers beyond their homes.

Traditionally local traders have developed relationships with CBOs and villagers, sometimes even providing private loans. Such relationships can create a climate of dependency that prevents CBOs from seeking other buyers. (In their defense, it should be pointed out that the traders themselves have limited market awareness.) Through market surveys CBOs discovered how diverse and dynamic the larger market is. They became aware of the different players (middlemen, wholesalers, retailers, and others) and learned how to collaborate with them. They gained knowledge, understanding, and confidence through these interactions to communicate better and more directly with other actors in the market. Being able to compare their products to what was available in the market was a valuable experience as well. Seeing the quality, quantity, and diversity of products allowed them to make realistic assessments regarding their own production potential. After considering the limitations of their own CBOs, they could design a suitable marketing strategy without being too ambitious. The positive results of these market surveying trips persuaded many CBOs (27 percent) to make surveys a regular tactic in planning their marketing strategies. These visits also reinforce links between CBOs and traders.

Inspiring new initiatives. The lack of financial and physical assets generally has prevented the poor from expanding their production. They could sell their small surplus only to local traders. As a result of the ME process, the CBOs quickly moved to overcome this problem. They organized groups to negotiate with and sell to distant traders. By June 2006, 58 percent of 455 CBOs had done this for their existing products. Another 21 percent had established community-level collection centers to attract new traders from farther away. The results are encouraging, with 35 large traders collaborating with various CBOs.

Benefits for the extreme poor. As mentioned earlier, the extreme poor represent 25 percent of CBO members involved in marketing. At least 2,775 people (landless, Adivashi-tribal communities, and women who head households) have benefited by way of increased income and access to markets. Experience also suggests that the extreme poor have been able to raise their status in relation to traders. Half of the CBOs' action plans incorporated at least one income-generating activity specifically designed to help the extreme poor. Another innovative action taken by some CBOs was to use part of the working capital earned from savings to assist the extreme poor in starting up their own businesses.

Using professional service providers. To fulfill the targets agreed upon after the market survey, CBOs needed the help of various "experts." Notably, in the handicraft sector, skilled traders could help teach design techniques, providing training services while linking the CBOs' products to markets. LEAF helped 42 percent of CBOs find service providers to assist with quality improvement and marketing. This assistance includes identifying service providers, providing linkages with them, and even supplying financial support when necessary.

LESSONS LEARNED

- Facilitation anchors the ME process and is therefore crucial for success. The person who assumes this role is known as the "service provider ME" and must have skills in capacity development and marketing. To ensure that the service provider transfers these skills to CBO members, formal training and field training are delivered throughout the program. LEAF assists with the coaching of participants.

- A strong task force is needed to develop marketing activities in a sustainable way. The selection of the task force by members of the CBO was risky, in the sense that task force members might adopt an elite identity separate from the interests of the greater community. In fact, this has not been the case. Generally the selection of trustworthy people has reinforced social links within the CBO. Having this small committee accelerates the investigation and analysis, reducing the number of meetings. People make a point of attending decision-making sessions, especially the extreme poor, if they feel they will not be wasting time. Since the task force is made up of local people, information can be shared informally on a daily basis. LEAF has tried to ensure that the task force does not create a powerful knowledge gap, which would sabotage the community empowerment process.

- A joint approach to marketing quickly gained acceptance because of the advantages of acting as a large group. In the past, suspicion of others stealing valuable contact or product information led people to be quite secretive and solitary when selling their goods. However, after the first exercise in which people shared their marketing problems, they discovered better solutions when acting as a group. Groups with strong social bonds (from shared cultural values, land, and location, for example) were quick to select a suitable product to produce cooperatively. Interestingly, women's groups were even more

efficient than other groups in starting practical economic activities. Trust was a precondition for enacting joint strategies and establishing reliable networks with traders.

- Participants claimed that the market survey was the most powerful step in the ME process, because immediate benefits were often derived from contact with businesspeople and service providers. They valued the skills they learned, which gave them confidence that they were making informed decisions when pursuing suitable income-generating activities. Because the financial incentives are clearly linked to the market survey results, however, it is critical to involve all members at this stage, and not task force members alone.

- The ME process can be considered a formal introduction to people who need skills to become active rather than passive players in commodity transactions. The process can be expanded to select and explore one segment of the market in detail (market actors, price, designs, and other aspects). In this way the ME approach becomes a market assessment tool.

- By learning about markets and gaining initial experience at the microlevel, it has been possible to integrate the extreme poor and vulnerable groups, including women, who might otherwise have been excluded from the ME process. Shared interests and backgrounds have created a favorable environment of trust among the different categories of poor people, and these small groups have gradually raised their voices and assumed responsible roles, notably in group marketing.

- It is interesting to observe that exclusively women's groups built up their confidence to perform all of the lead roles, retaining ownership of the group even when men were invited to join for practical reasons (such as taking products to markets). The additional family income generated by the women has also earned respect and support for their endeavors from their men counterparts. Conversely, mixed groups quickly allowed men to take charge, leaving women on the fringe.

ISSUES FOR WIDER APPLICABILITY

- The quality of instruction given by the field facilitator or service provider is commensurate with the degree of success attained through ME. Because there has been a huge demand to extend ME services to CBOs, reinforcing the numbers of process "experts" has become a priority. Training resource farmers to become service providers and field facilitators has had encouraging results. The lack of proficient personnel is exacerbated in isolated communities, where the local or district network of professional services is not available to meet their business development demands. LEAF must ensure that there are enough people to give quality instruction to maintain high standards and should not expand programs prematurely.

- The extreme poor still risk exclusion from the marketing processes owing to their lack of skills. Being illiterate, with few assets and minimal spare time, means that they cannot contribute to the same degree as their counterparts. The objective is not simply to use this group as labor but to ensure that they develop the skills that enable them to participate. Smart subsidies or vocational training has been proposed as a means of supporting participation by the extreme poor in business activities. LEAF needs to explore these approaches while monitoring CBOs to see if they can maintain inclusive policies throughout ME.

- The current ME is very conservative in its targets, both for profitability and for the duration of marketing activities. The additional income generated (ranging from 20–80 taka per day) should not be overlooked, but these tiny margins will not break the cycle of poverty in a sustainable way. The economic gains from participating in weak local markets cannot compare with the substantial, sustainable gains that can be made from entering the mass markets. Although diversity has been heralded as a mark of success, managing a great number of small and medium enterprises can be a significant drain on resources. For these reasons, a more profitable strategy for advanced CBOs to pursue may be to focus on fewer promising products. Few of the groups currently have the financial clout to scale up their marketing activities, and collaboration with banks then becomes a key limiting factor. Such collaboration is not easily developed, and external support to build the capacity to attract assistance from financial institutions is essential. Given these challenges, LEAF is implementing a value chain approach based on understanding of the functioning commodity chain, enabling identifying potential leverages and constraints. Ideally, this approach will promote links between CBOs, market actors, and service providers while improving the business environment for the poor.

Andhra Pradesh, India: Making the Market Work for the Poor—Community-Managed Procurement Centers for Small and Marginal Farmers

Small and marginal farmers in rural Andhra Pradesh have been subject to intensive exploitation by moneylenders, traders, and middlemen. Lack of access to the market, lack of power to negotiate prices because of extreme poverty levels, and the daily challenge of meeting minimum subsistence needs had made them vulnerable to unfair terms of trade. Procurement was done from distant markets or through village-level traders and aggregators.

The opening of community-managed procurement centers, an innovation piloted under the Andhra Pradesh Rural Poverty Reduction Project,[1] successfully demonstrates ways to combat this inefficiency. The procurement centers are specifically defined as community-managed, decentralized units for storing, assessing, and trading agricultural commodities. Some of the unique features include management by women self-help group members and their institutions.

PROJECT OBJECTIVES AND DESCRIPTION

The Andhra Pradesh Rural Poverty Reduction Project seeks to enable the rural poor and their organizations to improve livelihoods and quality of life. The project helps to develop and empower self-managed, grassroots institutions of poor rural women, including self-help groups and their federations.

The project has mobilized 8 million women into about 630,000 self-help groups,[2] covering 90 percent of the poor. These groups have been federated into 28,282 village organizations, 910 subdistrict organizations, and 26 district

---

What's innovative? Community-managed, decentralized units for storing, assessing, and trading agricultural commodities have generated significant economic, gender equality, and other benefits, while integrating the poorest producers with the market.

---

organizations. The poor and their organizations have cumulative savings exceeding $340 million and have leveraged more than $1.2 billion of credit from commercial banks since 2000. Diversification of livelihoods and asset building has increased incomes sevenfold in six years.

PROBLEM ANALYSIS

Landholders find it difficult to transact with markets. The public and private market players also find the transaction costs of procuring from dispersed farmers prohibitive. As a result, these agencies are unable to provide low-cost and adequate extension support services to these landholders.

Therefore, state policy is to provide minimum support price operations at agricultural market yards. However, farmers from far-off villages, especially poor farmers, did not receive remunerative prices because of the long distance to the market yards, nontransparent transactions at the yards, and the increase in transaction costs for smallholders who could not aggregate their produce.

Because small-scale farmers could not access formal sources of credit, they remained indebted to traders for inputs, and even if their land produced well, nearly half of their income was devoted to the interest payments on loans and the revenue lost from accepting low unit prices for their produce from traders. In most cases, farmers ended up making distress sales of their output to traders.

Formal, large agribusinesses could not interact with smallholders because they were uninformed about quality specifications and had no local institutional arrangements for technical assistance to meet agribusiness standards.

INNOVATIVE FEATURES

To eliminate the unfair practices of local traders and enhance smallholders' bargaining power, village procurement centers, owned and operated by women's self-help group members, were opened in 2003. The village procurement center addresses the lack of credit, quality control, aggregation, and market linkage under a single umbrella. The key innovations that have helped to empower the rural poor both socially and economically are the following:

1. *Creating an institutional mechanism for aggregation:* Each procurement center, on average, aggregates produce from about 500 small-scale, dispersed producers and supplies it directly to the market yard or buyer. For private as well as public buyers, it is cost-efficient to procure directly from farmers (see box 5.18 on how to set up a community-based procurement center).

2. *Localizing the value chain, bringing the market to the village level, and providing a "one-stop shop":* Suppliers (commercial banks, input suppliers, companies trying to source raw materials) do not have to deal with a multitude of smallholders, and users (small-scale and marginal farmers) do not have to deal with different organizations for credit, inputs, and sales of their produce. A procurement center typically covers villages within a 20-mile radius, so farmers need not travel long distances to sell their produce. The centers have also adopted transparent quality control measures that enable private and cooperative agribusinesses to obtain produce of good quality and reduce the transaction costs for members.

3. *Promoting business expertise within the village and increasing transparency in transactions:* The network of grassroots functionaries in the form of trained quality controllers, bookkeepers, and storage specialists from within the community ensures transparency and efficiency in the operation of procurement centers. Market information on price and quality, displayed in the centers, is available to farmers. Now even farmers in the remote and tribal villages can access market-based information in real time by mobile phone. Quality testing and weighing are conducted by community members in a transparent manner, as opposed to profit-seeking middlemen. Farmers receive cash payment on the spot, which makes the process more efficient and favorable to the poor.

Box 5.18   How to Set Up a Community-Managed Procurement Center

A community-managed procurement center is a physical warehouse or depot at the village level, which is owned and operated by the members of the formal village organization. A typical procurement center contains weighing machines and other instruments, packing materials (gunny bags, a stitching machine, and markers, for example), tarpaulins, and moisture meters. The key design elements are the following:

■ Conducting a value chain analysis and market survey of various commodities to identify gaps and the potential for scaling up opportunities and to identify potential procurement centers at the village level.

■ Building human resource capacity at the local level. Potential community resource persons are identified and trained in bookkeeping, quality control mechanisms, and business development. Every procurement center is assisted by an organizational structure in the form of various committees, such as a purchase and sales committee, quality control committee, and village social audit committee, each of which has a clearly defined role. A committee has between three and five members, depending upon the volume of trading. Mandatory training is provided for committee members on various aspects of commodity trading and handling.

■ Developing a marketing activity calendar. Given the seasonal nature of various commodities, it is essential to prepare an activity calendar for every procurement center to plan resource needs (both human and financial, such as working capital).

■ Estimating working capital requirements in line with the marketing activity calendar prepared by the village organization. In deciding how much working capital is required, consider the seasonality of the different commodities, the estimated quantity that will be procured, and the approximate storage time needed.

■ Finalizing quality and grading parameters, including a protocol for the random inspection of stocks for various commodities before the start of procurement. Parameters used to assess the quality of produce are usually related to size, color, moisture, refraction, and free fatty acids.

Source: Authors.

4. *Innovating supply chain management enhancements:* A first innovation is *building a cadre of low-cost technical specialists drawn from the local community*—that is, members of the women's self-help group or their families. Over 100,000 grassroots functionaries participate in supply chain management by operating these centers, including bookkeepers, quality controllers, business managers, and botanists. Training this cadre of resource persons has served to demystify technical assistance and make it available at the grassroots level. "Technical sustainability"—in other words, a continuous supply of "low-cost" trained staff—is thus assured. Village botanists also engage in research and development for forest products.

A second innovation is the use of "low-cost" technology to improve efficiency and transparency. Community resource persons use mobile phones to ascertain the latest market price before entering into contracts to purchase farmers' produce.[3] Similarly, women quality controllers use digital technology to measure moisture and fat content and weigh produce.

5. *Using procurement centers to outsource or franchise services:* In the franchising partnership model, procurement centers are used by public and private agencies as forward procurement and marketing agents for community organizations. The project provides community members with working capital, which is used for small-scale infrastructure. It also trains the community resource persons in value addition, quality control, bookkeeping, and business skills. The value proposition for partners lies in the following features:

- Companies achieve scale across the state in multiple commodities. Outreach in remote areas is facilitated.
- It is a cost-effective channel, because the cost of value addition, quality control, and operation is extremely low.
- Transparency and quality assurance are provided by the women, who (being the final users) are efficient controllers. The institutions provide a strong support structure for operations.
- A responsible and traceable channel is available for products for emerging global markets, such as non-pesticide, organic, and fair trade products.

BENEFITS AND IMPACTS

Since 2003 the procurement centers have handled more than 100 commodities with a cumulative turnover in excess of $120 million and 450,000 tons. In 2007 center turnover was projected to exceed $80 million; by 2010 the procurement centers are projected to achieve an annual turnover in excess of $200 million. Apart from procuring crops, the marketing concept has been extended to milk procurement. The project has formed more than 1,200 milk procurement centers at the village level and 60 bulk milk-chilling units at the subdistrict level. The current turnover from dairying surpasses $34 million, benefiting more than 100,000 milk producers. More than 2 million self-help group members transact with the procurement centers every year, and this number is estimated to reach 5 million by 2010. Quality control and upstream value addition opportunities are now available on the ground.

Economic benefits and impact

Increase in income. The close proximity of procurement centers to farmers raised farmers' incomes by helping them to obtain better prices and reduce their marketing costs. The income gain on some commodities such as neem and lac has exceeded 200 percent. A recent impact evaluation of the partnership with APMARKFED (Andhra Pradesh State Cooperative Marketing Federation Limited) for maize procurement showed that the additional gain of decentralized marketing is highest for marginal farmers, who gained an increase of $58 in one agricultural season. Through the partnership with APMARKFED to collect maize, the cumulative additional income generated for farmers across the state in 2005–06 was $22 million.

Increase in the general market price. An evaluation conducted on the impact of maize procurement conducted by APMARKFED in 2005–06 stated that the activity increased the market price by 10 percent. For milk marketing during the same period, local market prices increased by 15 percent.[4] The procurement center's price has become a type of benchmark for the village, and local traders are compelled to offer the same rates, if not more, when they purchase in that village. The market intermediation effect has influenced other trading practices, such as proper weighing and testing for moisture, which has been favorable for small-scale producers.

Employment generation at the local level. The procurement centers, milk collection centers, and chilling units create employment for the rural poor. Dairying generated more than 5,000 new jobs at the village and subdistrict levels. The partnership with APMARKFED created 6,000 new jobs, even during a lean economic period. An impact study on maize procurement concluded that each procurement center generated an additional wage income of $400 over a three-month period for its employees.

Cash payment. Unlike traders and middlemen, who make partial payments in cash and offer the balance in the form of inputs and other supplies, the procurement center pays producers in cash at the time of purchase. This payment method gives farmers, particularly small-scale and marginal farmers, the freedom to source inputs more cheaply, and in the process it eliminates the "regressive" tied sales that were rampant in the villages. Putting cash in the hands of small-scale and marginal farmers eliminates the need to resort to informal credit to finance consumption needs.

Gender relations

Increase in participation, leadership, and technical skills of women in the rural market. Women are managing village enterprises, an activity that requires them to take on duties that were previously in the men's domain. Women are becoming active players in the rural market—negotiating with traders and representatives of the private and public sectors. They also handle such roles as quality controllers and logistics managers, and they engage in research and development for new products. They supervise *hamalis* (workers are laborers who are involved in transporting agricultural produce), organize transport, and work with district administration officials, thus proving their capacity as leaders and technical service providers.

Increase in respect from the larger community. The procurement centers benefit not only members of self-help groups but also members of the village as a whole. Owing to the benefits of their services, the women have garnered support from village elders and leaders, who in many places collaborate to provide infrastructure and logistics support to the centers.

Intrahousehold support. The maize procurement study indicates that because women work in the centers for over 10 hours, often until late at night, their families provide support. Their domestic workload is shared by other women in the family and husbands. This finding demonstrates women's increased mobility and enhanced decision-making space within the household.

Making community institutions sustainable

Collective marketing by procurement centers has strengthened village organizations in many ways. First, by generating income and adding to the institutional corpus of funds, the procurement centers serve as a business model for village organizations. In the paddy procurement season of May–June 2007, 300 centers received a commission of over $850,000 for six weeks of work from the Civil Supplies Corporation. Second, members' participation in the activities of self-help groups and village organizations has risen because of the benefits yielded by the centers. Finally, the successful operation of procurement centers as franchises for public and private partners has changed the perception of the centers' viability and potential. They are now considered profitable partners rather than mere recipients of grants. Mr. Sinha, managing director of the Andhra Pradesh Civil Supplies Corporation, observed, "At first we used to procure from agrimarket yards directly. We did not have the capacity to spread into the villages. However, this program has given us a platform by which we can bridge the gap between the government and the small/poor farmers."

LESSONS LEARNED AND ISSUES FOR WIDER APPLICABILITY

- Tremendous social capital exists in various community organizations managed by women, such as the self-help groups and other user groups. Systematic initiatives to build human capital through training in business development, quality control, and market research can enable local institutions to generate significant economic capital and other benefits, while enabling small-scale producers to integrate with the market. This kind of economic empowerment requires significant investments in market-based and management skills for women.
- Investments in community institutions, human capital, and credit should be integrated to produce a maximum impact on economic returns.
- Physical infrastructure like procurement centers can be run more efficiently by women's organizations because they are able to cultivate financial discipline and transparency, which is more difficult with traditional men's organizations.

Future directions and scaling up include the following:

- *Integrate the procurement centers operating across the state within a common trading platform, either at the district or the state level.* Integration will involve building an information technology (IT) structure to link the procurement centers, which will provide multiple benefits. Linked centers will service an "internal market"; in other words, they will be able to meet the demand and supply gaps of village organization and self-help group members across districts, will link them to the market directly, and will offer all of their products and commodities in an aggregate manner.

■ *Link with commodity exchanges and ICT-enabled procurement centers:* These centers can be linked with ICT-enabled models such as "e-choupal" (www.echoupal.com) and commodity exchanges, enabling the community-based procurement centers to engage in real-time transactions. E-choupal was initiated by a leading multinational company in India, ITC Ltd., to procure commodities directly from farmers, offering them services such as real-time information to make their choices.

■ *Integrate farmer field schools with the procurement centers:* The integration of farmer field schools and procurement centers will help to organize agricultural extension services and lead to improved production and productivity. It will help to scale up innovations such as nonpesticide technology and organically grown bioproducts, which have resulted in increased incomes for farmers in some districts.

Bangladesh: Linking Poor Women to the International Prawn Market—The Greater Noakhali Aquaculture Extension Project

PROJECT OBJECTIVES AND DESCRIPTION

The Greater Noakhali Aquaculture Extension Project (GNAEP) is one component of Danida's Agricultural Sector Programme Support in Bangladesh.[1] It was initiated in 1998 to promote improved carp polyculture in ponds through a conventional approach to technology transfer. Groups of farmers were trained in the improved technology under the "household approach" (which included men and women in the household) by young extension trainers hired through partner NGOs specifically for the project. Fifty-two percent of the pond operators were women. This program trained some 36,000 households between 2000 and 2005, and average yields in target ponds more than doubled.

Despite these positive results, GNAEP management became increasingly concerned about the project's real impact on poverty and the sustainability of that impact. Pond polyculture itself offered limited returns, and the NGOs tended to target the more creditworthy households. Moreover, the fish farmer groups tended to dissolve after training and credit were withdrawn. Thus, beginning in 2002 GNAEP began to experiment with a different approach, shifting from a technology-driven to a people-driven mode. The poorer groups in the Noakhali region were identified, and the project analyzed how it could help them out of poverty through aquaculture. The prospect of substantially improving income by introducing a low-input system for freshwater prawn culture seemed particularly promising, and local private entrepreneurs were encouraged to invest in two medium- to large-scale prawn hatcheries in the region. In the initial intervention, which introduced prawn farming in rice systems, GNAEP also moved toward a participatory learning approach, based on the Farmer Field School concept, believing that it offered greater scope for sustainability.

Some of the poorest groups targeted under GNAEP's explicitly pro-poor approach were women. The southern part of Noakhali is a charland region, an area of land subject to steady accretion over the last 50 years, and thus a focus for settlement, both planned and informal, by poor households often displaced from other areas by river erosion and other natural hazards. Up to 20 percent of such households are headed by women whose husbands died at sea or following civil strife, or who were abandoned when their husbands left in search of employment. Most attempt to make a living through agricultural labor and homestead gardening, while some resort to begging. All are subject to sociopolitical abuse from local influential people, and many have been forced to mortgage their original land holding.

BENEFITS AND IMPACTS

One of the key resources available to such households was a small backyard pond, dug when the house platform was created. Although they hold water for only six months, these ponds are suitable for nursing prawns from the post-larvae to juvenile stage for stocking in the grow-out ponds of farmers who are better off. GNAEP persuaded the prawn hatcheries to offer the women interest-free credit in kind to enable them to stock post-larvae (PL). In a typical pond, women may stock 4,000 PL at an investment of 5,000 taka (Tk). With costs of modest feed inputs and pumping for

> **What's innovative?** A holistic approach to market development, extending from technology to training to business linkages, targets the poorest segments of the population, including women-headed households, to participate in the international prawn market.

harvest, the total investment may be Tk 6,000. In less than two months, the women may expect to sell around 3,000 juveniles for a total return of Tk 12,000, or a profit of Tk 6,000. If the rains are favorable, the women can expect to take two crops a year. This represents a major improvement in income for the women, sufficient to reclaim mortgaged land or purchase large livestock (goats and cattle). Other investments are typical household improvements or children's education. The nursing technology is fundamentally simple, and the women feel confident to continue after the first year.

Another typical intervention is in community ponds in resettlement villages, typically consisting of 30–50 poor households. Here, too, the men of the community may have left in search of work, and women often dominate the pond management committee. In this case, the ponds are stocked with a prawn-carp polyculture for grow-out. Once again the hatcheries offered interest-free credit in kind, and another private sector partner provided feed from a mill promoted by the project. A typical pond may stock 5,000 PL, which may yield around 250 kilograms of good-size prawns, because such ponds have water throughout the year. Returns from the prawns alone are Tk 75,000, and total income, including the carps, may be as high as Tk 150–200,000 (or Tk 5,000–6,000 per household). In this case the project's intention is to develop a contract farming system, linking the settlement communities to a new processing plant established in Noakhali through DANIDA's Private Sector Development Programme.[2] In such a system, the hatchery and feed mill loans will be repaid through direct transfer from the processor.

Many inputs are supplied through community-based organizations, which GNAEP promoted among prawn farmers who have had positive experiences with the project, to ensure sustainability. The 87 CBOs in the area now have around 4,000 members and serve up to 11,000 households. They receive a commission on PL sales and a profit from feed sales. For the woman-headed households, CBOs are a conduit for sales of juveniles to other farmers. Channeling inputs (and in due course cultured prawns) through CBOs has created a base for the kind of traceability system that is increasingly demanded by the international market. All farmers receiving prawn seed from the hatcheries through the CBOs receive a registration card, which can also be used to record other inputs such as feed. It hoped that the registration card will then be taken to a local processing plant when prawns are sold, thus completing the chain and allowing registered farmers to obtain a premium on the normal selling price.

In some CBOs the majority of members are women; in others, as a result of their economic empowerment, women play an important role in the executive committees that run the organizations. The CBOs give members and clients a voice with local government institutions for raising social development issues, and they are a focus for government and NGO services in various sectors. As a result, the incidence of social abuse of their women clients has dropped substantially.

LESSONS LEARNED AND CHALLENGES FOR WIDER APPLICABILITY

The following discussion synthesizes the lessons learned, the challenges, and prospects for future project and program design and implementation.

Lessons learned

The GNAEP experience indicates that the promotion of small-scale commercial aquaculture can offer a basis for alleviation of poverty, even among the poorest households. By adopting a whole-system approach, based on careful analysis of livelihood potentials, GNAEP has identified niches in which poor households headed by women can be integrated into the international economy through links with local agribusiness. In this system CBOs (both rural producer and marketing organizations) act as key intermediaries, enabling farmers to access quality inputs at a reasonable cost.

The future

GNAEP is moving toward a new phase in which it plans to target a wider range of poor households—for example, women fish driers on the offshore island of Hatiya, landless women previously engaged in road construction in another DANIDA project, and women engaged in the illegal catching of wild shrimp and prawn PLs. In each case, the intervention is carefully targeted and may include income-generating activities outside aquaculture, such as making nets and handicrafts and rearing small livestock. The basic approach described here, in which the poor are linked to improved input supply and marketing opportunities, will be extended to these other sectors.

Issues for scaling up

A donor-supported project with considerable resources at its disposal, including the many highly talented individuals in the local technical assistance team, GNAEP may be seen as a special case. Although the project is nominally implemented through the Bangladesh Department of Fisheries, since 2002 the technical assistance team has largely had a free hand to experiment with the described approach. It has also had the advantage in the Noakhali region of writing on a blank page, in the sense that prawn-based aquaculture was a new enterprise there, in contrast to southwestern Bangladesh, where it had been introduced 10 years earlier. However, the approach of linking small-scale farmers with the private sector through farmers' organizations has offered real prospects of creating a sustainable farmer-to-farmer extension system in the absence of an effective government extension presence. Nevertheless, recognition exists that it will be more difficult to create the same system in areas or sectors where the supply and marketing chain are more established and competitive and that the approach will need to be adapted if it is scaled up to other areas of Bangladesh.

NOTES

Overview

This Overview was prepared by Cathy Rozel Farnworth (Consultant) and Catherine Ragasa (Consultants) and reviewed by Chitra Deshpande (Consultant); Zoraida Garcia, Siobhan Kelly, and Andrew Shepherd (FAO); Renè Frèchet and Maria Hartl (IFAD); and Rekha Mehra and Kees van der Meer (World Bank).

1. www.usaid.gov/our_work/cross-cutting_programs/wid/eg/gate_valuechain.html.

2. Kennedy M. Shiundu and Ruth K. Oniang'o, "Marketing African Leafy Vegetables: Challenges and Opportunities in the Kenyan Context," *African Journal of Food Agriculture Nutrition and Development* 7 (4), www.ajfand.net/Issue15/PDFs/8%20Shiundu-IPGR2_8.pdf.

3. The Euro-Retailer Produce Working Group's Good Agricultural Practices: www.globalgap.org/cms/front_content.php?idcat=2.

4. USAID, "Global Horticulture Assessment," www.treesforchange.org/treesandmarkets/hvc07_meet/other_materials/Global%20Hort%20Assessment.pdf.

5. See note 3 above.

6. United Nations Economic and Social Commission for the Pacific (UNESCAP), "Women in Small Business in Indochina: Issues and Key Approaches," Women in Development Discussion Paper 4, http://unescap.org/esid/GAD/Publication/DiscussionPapers/04/series4.pdf.

7. See note 3 above.

8. USAID, "Gender and Economic Value Chains: Two Case Studies from the GATE Project," www.usaid.gov/our_work/cross-cutting_programs/wid/eg/gate_valuechain.html.

9. http://gstgateway.wigsat.org/ta/gdrbiotechfinal.pdf.

10. Ibid.

11. A. Yawe, "Unleashing the Potential of Women Entrepreneurs in Export Growth: The Case of Women Fishing and Development Associations in Uganda," www.intracen.org/wedf/ef2006/Gender-Issues/Paper_Yawe.pdf.

12. G. Rebosio, S. Gammage, and C. Manfre, "A Pro-Poor Analysis of the Artichoke Value Chain in Peru,"www.microlinks.org/file_download.php/Artichoke_Peru_Research_Brief.pdf?URL_ID=18386&filename=11861594421Artichoke_Peru_Research_Brief.pdf&filetype=application%2Fpdf&filesize=299504&name=Artichoke_Peru_Research_Brief.pdf&location=user-S.

Thematic Note 1

This Thematic Note was prepared by Cathy Rozel Farnworth (Consultant) and Catherine Ragasa (Consultant) and reviewed by Chitra Deshpande (Consultant); Zoraida Garcia, Siobhan Kelly, and Andrew Shepherd (FAO); Renè Frèchet and Maria Hartl (IFAD); and Kees van der Meer and Rekha Mehra (World Bank).

1. APRODEV, "Process Report: A Gender Review of the Economic Partnership Agreements (EPAs)," paper given at the Civil Society Dialogue Meeting on Gender and the Economic Partnership Agreements, Brussels, December 6, 2006, www.aprodev.net.

2. GAWU, DHS, CIECA, ADEID, GRAPAD, and EUROSTEP, "New ACP-EU Trade Arrangements: New Barriers to Eradicating Poverty?" Brussels: European Solidarity towards Equal Participation of People, www.itssd.org/References/Think%20Tank/200406091217487864.pdf.

3. Glenys Kinnock, "Gender Review of the Economic Partnership Agreements," paper presented at the Civil Society Dialogue Meeting on Gender and the Economic Partnership Agreements, Brussels, December 6, 2006, www.aprodev.net.

4. See note 1 above.

5. Ibid.

6. United States Agency for International Development (USAID), "The New Generation of Private-Sector Development Programming: The Emerging Path to Economic Growth and Poverty Reduction," MicroREPORT No. 44, www.microlinks.org/ev_en.php?ID=10319_201&ID2=DO_TOPIC.

7. www.mercycorps.org.uk/countries/afghanistan/88.

Thematic Note 2

This Thematic Note was prepared by Cathy Rozel Farnworth (Consultant) and Catherine Ragasa (Consultant) and reviewed by Chitra Deshpande (Consultant); Zoraida Garcia, Siobhan Kelly, and Andrew Shepherd (FAO); Renè Frèchet and Maria Hartl (IFAD); and Kees van der Meer and Rekha Mehra (World Bank).

1. IFAD, "Syria: Profitability of Women's Income-Generating Activities (Syria Southern Agricultural Development Project, Phase I)," www.ifad.org/gender/learning/sector/finance/32.htm.

2. David G. Kahan, "Business Services in Support of Farm Enterprise Development: A Review of Relevant Experiences," draft for review, Agricultural Management, Marketing and Finance Service Agricultural Support Systems Division, FAO, Rome, www.fao.org/AG/ags/subjects/en/farmMgmt/pdf/business_development_services/dbs_a_reviewofCasestudies.pdf.

3. See note 1 above.

4. See note 6 on Overview Section.

5. Ibid.

6. www.wfp.org.

7. www.femconsult.org/news.php.

8. International Fund for Agricultural Development, "Lao PDR: Making Women's Weaving Activities Profitable," www.ifad.org/gender/learning/sector/finance/19.htm.

9. www.fao.org/DOCREP/004/AC154E/AC154E04.htm.

10. UNIDO, "Trade Capacity Building: Case Studies: Ecuador," www.unido.org/doc/27693.

11. International Finance Corporation, "IFC Supports Women Entrepreneurs," www.ifc.org/ifcext/africa.nsf/Content/MainStory_GOWE_August2007. See also Thematic Note 1.

12. www.vbi-lattakia.org/english/about_us.html.

13. www.icecd.org/community-development_vsc.html.

Thematic Note 3

This Thematic Note was prepared by Cathy Rozel Farnworth (Consultant) and Catherine Ragasa (Consultant) and reviewed by Chitra Deshpande (Consultant); Zoraida Garcia, Siobhan Kelly, and Andrew Shepherd (FAO); René Fréchet and Maria Hartl (IFAD); and Kees van der Meer and Rekha Mehra (World Bank).

1. Loraine Ronchi, "The Impact of Fair Trade on Producers and Their Organisations: A Case Study with Coocafé in Costa Rica," Poverty Research Unit at Sussex Working Paper No. 11, University of Sussex, Brighton, www.sussex.ac.uk/Units/PRU/wps/wp11.pdf.

2. IFAD, "INDIA-Tamil Nadu Women's Development: The Story of Sarasu," completion evaluation, April, www.ifad.org/evaluation/public_html/eksyst/doc/prj/region/pi/india/r240ince.htm.

Thematic Note 4

This Thematic Note was prepared by Cathy Rozel Farnworth (Consultant) and reviewed by Chitra Deshpande (Consultant) and Catherine Ragasa (Consultant); Zoraida Garcia, Siobhan Kelly, and Andrew Shepherd (FAO); René Fréchet and Maria Hartl (IFAD); and Rekha Mehra and Kees van der Meer (World Bank).

1. www.rd.ap.gov.in/velugu/velugureportskaren.htm.

Innovative Activity Profile 1

This Innovative Activity Profile was written by Catherine Ragasa (Consultant), with input from Grahame Dixie (World Bank), and reviewed by Siobhan Kelly and Andrew Shepherd (FAO); and Rekha Mehra (World Bank).

1. LEAF uses a value chain approach to scale up support to CBOs who are ready to engage in larger markets.

Innovative Activity Profile 2

This Innovative Activity Profile was prepared by Shweta Banerjee (World Bank), Vijaysekar Kalavakonda (World Bank), K. P. Rao (Society for Elimination of Rural Poverty, Hyderabad), and Parmesh Shah (World Bank). Comments and support were provided by Vijay Kumar (Society for Elimination of Rural Poverty, Hyderabad). This document was reviewed by Rekha Mehra and Riikka Rajalahti (World Bank).

1. The Andhra Pradesh District Poverty Initiatives Project and the Rural Poverty Reduction Project (total IDA lending: $260 million) are two statewide, community-driven rural poverty reduction projects implemented since 2000. Key investments include building institutions of the poor and developing social capital; developing financial services for the poor; promoting and expanding livelihoods through private sector partnerships; reducing vulnerability; promoting social action; and improving local governance.

2. A typical self-help group comprises 10–15 women from the poorest of the poor and the poor. The members meet once a week, collect savings, and maintain books of accounts. The groups are then federated into village organizations.

3. Community resource persons or community professionals are project participants from within the community

who have undergone training in either one or multiple facets of project implementation such as institution building, community procurement and marketing, and health services, becoming a key resource for the community and the project. Creating a cadre of such grassroots professionals has been instrumental in scaling up project activities at a low cost and will contribute to sustainability in the future. There are currently over 100,000 such resource persons.

4. S. Subrahmanyam, C. P. Nagi Reddy, and R. Nalini, "Maize Procurement by Village Organizations: An Impact Analysis," Society for Elimination of Rural Poverty (SERP), Hyderabad, www.rd.ap.gov.in/IKP/maizestudy.htm.

Innovative Activity Profile 3

This Innovative Activity Profile was written by Reshad Alam (Extension Programme Manager) and Harvey Demaine (Senior Advisor) in the Regional Fisheries and Livestock Development Component (DANIDA), the successor project to GNAEP in Phase II of ASPS, with input and review by Mona Sur (World Bank), and reviewed by Chitra Deshpande and Catherine Ragasa (Consultants); Zoraida Garcia, Siobhan Kelly, Rekha Mehra, and Andrew Shepherd (FAO); and René Fréchet and Maria Hartl (IFAD).

1. As such it is also called the Greater Noakhali Aquaculture Extension Component (GNAEC). For more details, see the project Web site: www.gnaec.org.

2. Now called B2B or "Business to Business."

REFERENCES

Overview

Abdelali-Martini, Malika, Aden Aw-Hassan, and Hisham Salahieh. 2005. "The Potential of Partnership with the Jabbans of Syria." *ICARDA Caravan* 22: 39–42.

Agricultural Management, Marketing, and Finance Service (AGSF). 2005. "Gender Impacts of Small-Farm Commercialization on Household Resource Management and Livelihoods." AGSF Working Document, Food and Agriculture Organization, Rome. Also available at www.fao.org.

Bardasi, Elena, C. Mark Blackden, and Juan Carlos Guzman. 2007. "Gender, Entrepreneurship, and Competitiveness in Africa." Chapter 1.4 of *Africa Competitiveness Report 2007*. Washington, DC: World Economic Forum, World Bank, and African Development Bank. Also available at www.weforum.org/en/initiatives/gcp/Africa%20Competitiveness%20Report/2007/index.htm.

Booth, H. 1999. "Gender Database for Agriculture and Resource Management Policies in Pacific Island Countries." RAP Publication 1999/7, FAO Regional Office for Asia and the Pacific, Bangkok.

Boselie, David, Spencer Henson, and Dave Weatherspoon. 2003. "Supermarket Procurement Practices in Developing Countries: Redefining the Roles of the Public and Private Sectors." *American Journal of Agricultural Economics* 85: 1155–61.

Ellis, Amanda, Claire Manuel, and C. Mark Blackden. 2006. *Gender and Economic Growth in Uganda: Unleashing the Power of Women*. Directions in Development. Washington, DC: World Bank.

Farnworth, Cathy Rozel, and Janice Jiggins. 2006. *Participatory Plant Breeding and Gender Analysis*. PPB Monograph 4, Systemwide Program on Participatory Research and Gender Analysis. Cali: Consultative Group on International Agricultural Research.

Food and Agriculture Organization (FAO). 2006. *Agriculture, Trade Negotiations, and Gender*. Prepared by Zoraid Garcia, with contributions from Jennifer Nyberg and Shayama Owaise Saadat. Rome: FAO. Also available at ftp://ftp.fao.org/docrep/fao/009/a0493e/a0493e.pdf.

Gurung, C. 2006. *The Role of Women in the Fruit and Vegetable Supply Chain in Maharashtra and Tamil Nadu India: The New and Expanded Social and Economic Opportunities for Vulnerable Groups Task Order under the Women in Development IQC*. Washington, DC: U.S. Agency for International Development.

International Fund for Agricultural Development (IFAD). n.d. "São Tome and Principe: Participatory Smallholder Agriculture and Artisanal Fisheries Development Program: Women Fish Traders." Internal document, IFAD, Rome.

———. 2002. "IFAD Strategy for Rural Poverty Reduction: Latin America and the Caribbean." IFAD, Rome. Also available at www.ifad.org/operations/regional/2002/pl/pl.htm.

Jaffee, Steven. 2003. "From Challenge to Opportunity: Transforming Kenya's Fresh Vegetable Trade in the Context of Emerging Food Safety and Other Standards in Europe." Agriculture Rural Development Discussion Paper, World Bank, Washington, DC.

Kaplinsky, Rafael, and Mike Morris. 2002. *A Handbook for Value Chain Research*. Brighton: Institute of Development Studies, University of Sussex.

Mayoux, Linda. 2005. "'Gender Lens' in Value Chains Analysis for Decent Work: A Practical Guide." First unpublished draft, International Labour Organisation, Geneva, November.

Pinstrup-Andersen, Per, Rajul Pandya-Lorch, and Mark Rosegrant. 1997. "The World Food Situation: Recent Developments, Emerging Issues, and Long-Term

Prospects." 2020 Vision Food Policy Report, International Food Policy Research Institute, Washington, DC. Also available at www.ifpri.org/pubs/fpr/fpr24.pdf.

Reardon, Thomas, and Julio Berdegué. 2002. "The Rapid Rise of Supermarkets in Latin America: Challenges and Opportunities for Development." *Development Policy Review* 20 (4): 371–88.

Rihawi, Safouh. 2005. "Expanding the Menu: Transforming By-products into Nutritious Feed." *ICARDA Caravan* 22: 28–30.

United Nations Development Programme (UNDP). 1995. *Human Development Report.* New York: UNDP.

United States Agency for International Development (USAID). 2006. "Pro-Poor Growth, Gender, and Markets: Creating Opportunities and Measuring Results." Greater Access to Trade Expansion (GATE) Project, Development and Training Services, Arlington, VA.

———. 2007. "A Pro-Poor Analysis of the Artichoke Value Chain in Peru." Greater Access to Trade Expansion (GATE) Project, Development and Training Services, Arlington, Virginia. www.microlinks.org/file_download.php/Artichoke_Peru_Research_Brief.pdf?URL_ID=18386&filename=11861594421Artichoke_Peru_Research_Brief.pdf&filetype=application%2Fpdf&filesize=299504&name=Artichoke_Peru_Research_Brief.pdf&location=user-S.

World Bank. 2005. "Gender and 'Shared Growth' in Sub-Saharan Africa." Briefing Notes on Critical Gender Issues in Sub-Saharan Africa 2005-1, World Bank, Washington, DC. Also available at http://siteresources.worldbank.org/EXTABOUTUS/Resources/GenderGrowth.pdf.

———. 2007a. "Cultivating Knowledge and Skills to Grow African Agriculture: A Synthesis of an Institutional, Regional, and International Review." World Bank, Washington, DC. Also available at http://siteresources.worldbank.org/INTARD/Resources/AET_Final_web.pdf.

———. 2007b. "Gender and Economic Growth in Kenya: Unleashing the Power of Women. Directions in Development." World Bank, Washington, DC. Also available at www.ifc.org/ifcext/enviro.nsf/AttachmentsByTitle/p_GEM_GenderandEconomicGrowthinKenya/$FILE/Gender+and+Economic+Growth+in+Kenya.pdf.

Thematic Note 1

Bardasi, Elena, C. Mark Blackden, and Juan Carlos Guzman. 2007. "Gender, Entrepreneurship, and Competitiveness in Africa." Chapter 1.4 of *Africa Competitiveness Report 2007*. Washington, DC: World Economic Forum, World Bank, and African Development Bank. Also available at www.weforum.org/en/initiatives/gcp/Africa%20Competitiveness%20Report/ 2007/index.htm.

Collins, Jane. 2000. "Tracing Social Relations through Commodity Chains: The Case of Brazilian Grapes." In *Commodities and Globalization: Anthropological Perspective,* ed. A. Haugerud, M. P. Stone, and P. D. Little, 97–112. Lanham, MD: Rowman and Littlefield.

Ellis, Amanda, Claire Manuel, and C. Mark Blackden. 2006. *Gender and Economic Growth in Uganda: Unleashing the Power of Women.* Directions in Development. Washington, DC: World Bank.

Farnworth, Cathy Rozel, and Janice Jiggins. 2006. *Participatory Plant Breeding and Gender Analysis.* PPB Monograph 4, Systemwide Program on Participatory Research and Gender Analysis. Cali: Consultative Group on International Agricultural Research.

Food and Agriculture Organization (FAO). 2002. *Gender and Law: Women's Rights in Agriculture.* FAO Legislative Study 76. Rome: FAO.

———. 2006a. *Agriculture, Trade Negotiations, and Gender.* Rome: FAO.

———. 2006b. "'Niger' Projet de promotion de l'utilization des intrants agricoles par les organizations paysannes." In *Gender, Markets, and Financial Services: Experiences from FAO-Supported Projects.* Rome: FAO.

Grace, Jo. 2004. "Gender Roles in Agriculture: Case Studies of Five Villages in Northern Afghanistan." Afghanistan Research and Evaluation Unit (AREU), Kabul.

Kenya Institute for Public Policy Research and Analysis (KIPPRA). 2000. *Improving the Legal and Regulatory Environment for Business through Deregulation—Trade Licensing Reform.* Nairobi: Ministry of Planning and National Development.

Kitinoja, Lisa. 2002. "Identifying Scale-Appropriate Postharvest Technology." In *Postharvest Technology of Horticultural Crops,* 3rd ed., ed. Adel A. Kader, 481–90. Oakland, CA: Division of Agriculture and Natural Resources and University of California.

Reardon, Thomas, and Julio Berdegué. 2002. "The Rapid Rise of Supermarkets in Latin America: Challenges and Opportunities for Development." *Development Policy Review* 20 (4): 371–88.

World Bank. 2005. "Bangladesh Third Rural Infrastructure Development Project." Project document, World Bank, Washington, DC.

———. 2006. "India: Taking Agriculture to the Markets." World Bank, Washington, DC.

———. 2007a. *Gender and Economic Growth in Kenya: Unleashing the Power of Women.* Directions in Development. Washington, DC: World Bank. Also available at www.ifc.org/ifcext/enviro.nsf/AttachmentsByTitle/p_GE M_GenderandEconomicGrowthinKenya/$FILE/Gen der+and+Economic+Growth+in+Kenya.pdf.

———. 2007b. *Doing Business 2008.* Washington, DC: World Bank.

———. 2007c. "Horticultural Exports from Developing Countries." In *Agriculture Investment Sourcebook,* 275–79. Washington, DC: World Bank. Also available at http://go.worldbank.org/LWEH6R38H0.

Thematic Note 2

Ayadurai, Selvamalar, and M. Sadiq Sohail. 2006. "Profile of Women Entrepreneurs in a War-Torn Area: Case Study of Northeast Sri Lanka." *Journal of Developmental Entrepreneurship* 11 (1): 1–15.

Booth, Heather. 1999. "Gender Database for Agriculture and Resource Management Policies in Pacific Island Countries." RAP Publication 1999/7, FAO Regional Office for Asia and the Pacific, Bangkok.

Center of Arab Women for Training and Research and the International Finance Corporation Gender Entrepreneurship Markets (CAWTAR and IFC). 2007. *Women Entrepreneurs in the Middle East and North Africa: Characteristics, Contributions, and Challenges.* Washington, DC, and Tunis: CAWTAR and IFC. Also available at www.ifc.org/ifcext/home.nsf/AttachmentsByTitle/MEN A_Women_Entrepreneurs_Jun07/$FILE/MENA_Wome n_Entrepreneurs_Jun07.pdf.

Deutsch, Ruthanne, Andrew Morrison, Claudia Piras, and Hugo Ñopo. 2002. "Working within Confines: Occupational Segregation by Gender in Three Latin American Countries." Technical Paper, Inter-American Development Bank, Washington, DC. Also available at www.iadb.org/sds/wid/publication/publication_7325_3544_e.htm.

Farnworth, Cathy Rozel, and Janice Jiggins. 2006. *Participatory Plant Breeding and Gender Analysis.* PPB Monograph 4, Systemwide Program on Participatory Research and Gender Analysis. Cali: Consultative Group on International Agricultural Research.

Humphrey, John. 2004. "Upgrading in Global Value Chains." Working Paper No. 28, Policy Integration Department, World Commission on the Social Dimension of Globalization, International Labour Office, Geneva.

Richardson, Pat, Rhona Howarth, and Gerry Finnegan. 2004. *The Challenges of Growing Small Businesses: Insights from Women Entrepreneurs in Africa.* Series on Women's Entrepreneurship Development and Gender Equality. Geneva: International Labour Organisation.

Royal Tropical Institute, Faida Market Link, and International Institute of Rural Reconstruction (KIT, Faida MaLi, and IIRR). 2006. *Chain Empowerment: Supporting African Farmers to Develop Markets.* Amsterdam: KIT, Faida MaLi, and IIRR. Also available at www.kit.nl/smartsite.shtml?id=SINGLEPUBLICATION&ch=FAB&ItemID=1952.

United Nations Educational, Scientific and Cultural Organization (UNESCO). 2003. "Good Practices: Gender Equality in Basic Education and Lifelong Learning through CLCS: Experiences from 15 Countries." Report, UNESCO Asia and the Pacific Regional Bureau for Education, Bangkok.

United Nations Industrial Development Organization (UNIDO). 2003. "A Path Out of Poverty: Developing Rural and Women Entrepreneurship." Brochure, UNIDO, New York.

Vijfhuizen, Carin. 1996. "Who Feeds the Children? Gender Ideology and the Practice of Plot Allocation in an Irrigation Scheme." In *The Practice of Smallholder Irrigation: Case Studies from Zimbabwe,* ed. Emmanuel Manzungu and Pieter van der Zaag, 126–50. Harare: University of Zimbabwe.

Weeks, Julie, and Danielle Seiler. 2001. "Women's Entrepreneurship in Latin America: An Exploration of Current Knowledge." Sustainable Development Department Technical Papers Series, Inter-American Development Bank, Washington, DC.

World Bank. 2006. "India: Taking Agriculture to the Markets." World Bank, Washington, DC.

Thematic Note 3

Dixie, Grahame. 2005. *Horticultural Marketing. Marketing Extension Guide,* vol. 5. Rome: Food and Agriculture Organization.

Food and Agriculture Organization (FAO). 1995. *The Group Enterprise Book: A Practical Guide for Group Promoters to Assist Groups in Setting Up and Running Successful Small Enterprises.* Rome: FAO.

———. 2002. "The Inter-Group Resource Book: A Guide to Building Small Farmer Group Associations and Networks." FAO, Rome. Also available at www.fao.org/sd/2001/pe0701_en.htm.

Guijt, Irene, and Edith van Walsum. Forthcoming. In *Fair Trade and the Food Chain,* ed. Cathy Farnworth, Janice Jiggins, and E. Thomas. London: Gower.

International Fund for Agricultural Development (IFAD). n.d. "Bosnia and Herzegovina: Women Milk Collection Network." Internal document, IFAD, Rome.

Nelson, Valerie, and Modesto Galvez. 2000. *Social Impacts of Ethical and Conventional Cocoa Trading on Forest-Dependent People in Ecuador*. Chatham: Natural Resources Institute.

Royal Tropical Institute, Faida Market Link, and International Institute of Rural Reconstruction (KIT, Faida MaLi, and IIRR). 2006. *Chain Empowerment: Supporting African Farmers to Develop Markets*. Amsterdam: KIT, Faida MaLi, and IIRR. Also available at www.kit.nl/ smartsite.shtml?id= SINGLEPUBLICATION&ch=FAB&ItemID=1952.

World Bank. 2003. "Republic of Chad—Agriculture Services and Producer Organizations Project." Project Appraisal Document, World Bank, Washington, DC.

———. 2006a. "Tamil Nadu Empowerment and Poverty Reduction 'Puthu Vazhvu' Project." Project Appraisal Document (PAD), World Bank, Washington, DC.

———. 2006b. "Tanzania Participatory Agricultural Development and Empowerment Project." Project Appraisal Document (PAD), World Bank, Washington, DC.

Thematic Note 4

Farnworth, Cathy R., and Janice Jiggins. 2006. *Participatory Plant Breeding and Gender Analysis*. PPB Monograph 4, Systemwide Program on Participatory Research and Gender Analysis. Cali: Consultative Group on International Agricultural Research.

Food and Agriculture Organization (FAO). 2006. "Honduras—Training in Marketing Skills for Women Fish Processors—Livelihoods Diversification and Enterprise Development (LDED) Project." In *Gender, Markets, and Financial Services: Experiences from FAO-Supported Projects*. Rome: FAO.

Guijt, Irene, and Edith van Walsum. Forthcoming. In *Fair Trade and the Food Chain,* ed. Cathy Farnworth, Janice Jiggins, and E. Thomas. London: Gower.

Royal Tropical Institute, Faida Market Link, and International Institute of Rural Reconstruction (KIT, Faida MaLi, and IIRR). 2006. *Chain Empowerment: Supporting African Farmers to Develop Markets*. Amsterdam: KIT, Faida MaLi, and IIRR. Also available at www.kit.nl/smartsite.shtml?id=SINGLEPUBLICATION&ch=FAB&ItemID=1952.

United States Agency for International Development (USAID). 2006. *Cross-Cutting Agra Program—Center for Urban and Regional Excellence*. New Delhi: USAID–India.

Wanders, Ab. 2003. "Small-Scale Peanut Butter Processing: Case Studies in Rural, Peri-Urban and Urban Settings in South Africa." In *Interdisciplinary Research for Sustainable Development in the South*. Annual Report, DLO Research Programme, International Cooperation.

Innovative Activity Profile 1

Dixie, Grahame. 2005. *Horticultural Marketing. Marketing Extension Guide*, vol. 5. Rome: Food and Agriculture Organization. Also available at www.fao.org/ag/ags/subjects/en/agmarket/docs/horticultural_EN.pdf.

FURTHER READING

Overview

International Fund for Agricultural Development (IFAD). 2008. "Food Security, Poverty, and Women: Lessons from Rural Asia." Available at www.ifad.org/gender/thematic/rural/rural_1.htm.

Kasnakoglu, Zehra. n.d. "Women and Agricultural Development in the Near East." Middle East Technical University, Department of Economics and Gender and Women's Studies, Ankara. Available at www.skk.uit.no/WW99/papers/Kasnakoglu_Zehra.pdf.

Lastarria-Cornhiel, Susan. 2006. "Feminization of Agriculture: Trends and Driving Forces." Contribution by RIMISP (the Latin American Center for Rural Development; www.rimisp.org) to the preparation of the *World Development Report 2008, Agriculture for Development* (Washington, DC: World Bank 2007). Available at http://asiadhrra.org/word press/wp-content/uploads/2007/11/feminization-of-agriculture-trends-and-driving-forces.pdf.

Royal Tropical Institute, Faida Market Link, and International Institute of Rural Reconstruction (KIT, Faida MaLi, and IIRR). 2006. *Chain Empowerment: Supporting African Farmers to Develop Markets*. Amsterdam: KIT, Faida MaLi, and IIRR. Available at www.kit.nl/ smartsite.shtml?id=SINGLEPUBLICATION&ch=FAB&ItemID=1952.

Thematic Note 1

Humphrey, John, and Hubert Schmitz. 2002. "Governance in Global Value Chains." *IDS Bulletin* 32 (3): 19–29.

Kader, Adel A., ed. 2002. *Postharvest Technology for Horticultural Crops*. 3rd ed. Oakland, CA: Division of Agriculture and Natural Resources and University of California.

Lodge, Junior. 2007. "Perspectives from ACP Negotiator." Paper presented at the Civil Society Dialogue Meeting on Gender and the Economic Partnership Agreements, Brussels, December 6, 2006. Available at www.aprodev.net.

Mrema, Geoffrey C., and Rosa S. Rolle. 2002. "Status of the Post-Harvest Sector and Its Contribution to Agricultural Development and Economic Growth." In *Value-Addition to Agricultural Products: Towards Increase of Farmers' Income and Vitalization of Rural Economy*, Proceedings of the 9th JIRCAS International Symposium, ed. Yutaka Mori, Toru Hayashi, and Ed Highley. Tsukuba: Japan International Research Center for Agricultural Sciences (JIRCAS), 13–20. Available at www.jircas.affrc.go.jp/english/publication/symposium/11.

United States Agency for International Development (USAID). 2005. *Global Horticulture Assessment.* Davis, CA: University of California. Available at www.treesfor change.org.

Thematic Note 2

InfoDev. 2006. "Incubators As Change Agents: Impacts and Lessons Learned from infoDev's Global Network of Incubators." Highlights, November 2. Available at http://idisc.infodev.org/en/Article.38385.html.

United Nations Economic and Social Commission for the Pacific (UNESCAP). 2000. "Utilizing Business Opportunities for Women Entrepreneurs in Asia and the Pacific, 2000." Women in Development Discussion Paper 6, UNESCAP, Bangkok. Available at http://unescap.org/esid/gad2/04widresources/05pubreport/series6.pdf.

United States Agency for International Development (USAID). 2006. "The New Generation of Private-Sector Development Programming: The Emerging Path to Economic Growth and Poverty Reduction." MicroREPORT no. 44, USAID, Washington, DC. Available at www.microlinks.org/ev_en.php?ID=10319_201&ID2=DO_TOPIC.

Thematic Note 3

Food and Agriculture Organization (FAO). 1994. *The Group Promoter's Resource Book: A Practical Guide to Building Rural Self-Help Groups.* Rome: FAO.

———. 1995. *The Group Enterprise Book: A Practical Guide for Group Promoters to Assist Groups in Setting Up and Running Successful Small Enterprises.* Rome: FAO.

Thematic Note 4

Charlier, Sophie, Isabel Yépez del Castillo, and Elisabeth Andin. 2000. "Payer un prix juste aux cultivatrices de quinoa: un éclairage 'genre et développement' sur les défies du commerce éqitable dans les Andes boliviennes." GRAIL-IED, Tournesol Conseils, Brussels.

Kader, Adel A., ed. 2002. *Postharvest Technology for Horticultural Crops.* 3rd ed. Oakland, CA: Division of Agriculture and Natural Resources and University of California.

Mrema, Goeffrey C., and Rosa S. Rolle. 2002. "Status of the Post-Harvest Sector and Its Contribution to Agricultural Development and Economic Growth." In *Value-Addition to Agricultural Products: Towards Increase of Farmers' Income and Vitalization of Rural Economy,* Proceedings of the 9th JIRCAS International Symposium, ed. Yutaka Mori, Toru Hayashi, and Ed Highley. Tsukuba: Japan International Research Center for Agricultural Sciences (JIRCAS), 13–20. Available at www.jircas.affrc.go.jp/english/publication/symposium/11.

Royal Tropical Institute, Faida Market Link, and International Institute of Rural Reconstruction (KIT, Faida MaLi, and IIRR). 2006. *Chain Empowerment: Supporting African Farmers to Develop Markets.* Amsterdam: KIT, Faida MaLi, and IIRR. Available at www.kit.nl/smartsite.shtml?id=SINGLEPUBLICATION&ch=FAB&ItemID=1952.

Sen, Amartya K. 1990. "Gender and Cooperative Conflicts." In *Persistant Inequalities,* ed. Irene Tinker, 123–50. Oxford: Oxford University Press.

United States Agency for International Development (USAID). 2005. *Global Horticulture Assessment.* Davis, CA: University of California. Available at www.treesfor change.org/treesandmarkets/hvc07_meet/other_materials/Global%20Hort%20Assessment.pdf.

Innovative Activity Profile 1

Poitevin, Bruno, and Shamim Hossain. 2006. "Marketing Extension: A Powerful Process in 6 Steps—Empowering the Poor to Exploit Market Opportunities." Report for the Livelihoods, Empowerment and Agroforestry Project (LEAF), Intercooperation in Bangladesh, Dhaka, and Swiss Agency for Development and Cooperation (SDC), Berne.

Gender Mainstreaming in Agricultural Water Management

Overview

Agriculture water management (AWM) includes irrigation and drainage, water management in rain-fed agriculture, recycled water reuse, water and land conservation, and watershed management (World Bank 2006). The approaches and technologies employed by water management projects and programs have been evolving, and change has accelerated during recent decades. The overwhelming emphasis on technical and engineering matters that was characteristic of AWM in the 1960s and 1970s has expanded outward to encompass a broader purview that incorporates social and environmental concerns. AWM is essential to food security, but it also plays a fundamental role in building human capital in rural areas. Policy and decision making regarding land and water management have traditionally been the domain of men. As a result, policies and programs do not always consider women's unique knowledge, needs, or unequal ownership rights. Women farmers need to be actively involved in the planning and implementation of land and water management programs and must be able to participate in developing the policies that affect their access and control of these resources.[1]

This overview first analyzes the principal gender issues that tend to arise in AWM projects and that need to be addressed or resolved. It then presents a number of good practices based on the experience and lessons of gender-equitable AWM projects and policies. Two Thematic Notes and two Innovative Activity Profiles examine the interface between AWM and gender issues in greater detail.[2]

KEY GENDER ISSUES

Since the Dublin Conference in 1992, policy makers have made renewed attempts to incorporate gender issues in water development projects. However, these policies have not been adequately translated into practice, and attempts in some projects to involve women in water management initiatives have met with only modest success. These disappointing results are attributable to several reasons. Policy makers and project staff often lack understanding of gender issues or of their importance. A lack of commitment and capacity to undertake gender analysis among project staff at times is evident in project design and implementation. Gender-disaggregated data are often lacking, and prevailing cultural norms can lead to serious resistance from within the affected beneficiary communities (IFAD 2007).

Women and land and water ownership and tenure. In most countries land and water rights are closely related, although water is often a public good, and therefore its use is associated with permits, concessions, and other tenure systems. Irrigated and rain-fed land is the main source of livelihood for many rural populations. Women have much less access to this essential asset than men. The distribution of this water and land is a major determinant of poverty. Even in industrial countries it is rare to have figures above 30 percent of land ownership belonging to women, and this figure tends to be much lower in developing countries. Inheritance laws that deprive women of access are often the cause. In some North African countries, women receive only half of the land or no land at all. This has been widely documented by a survey carried out by the Centre on Housing Rights and Evictions (COHRE 2006). In some societies in sub-Saharan Africa, a woman acquires land tenure rights for life. However, this right is transferred to the men members of the family after she dies. In some cases a woman may lose access to land after the death of her husband or father. Without secure land tenure, women cannot obtain access to credit (IFAD 2007).

Although proportionately fewer women own land, they may exercise many other types of tenure, such as tenant, sharecropper, or caretaker. These forms of tenure have grown more prominent with the outmigration of men. As a result there are an increasing number of women who manage farms but who do not have either de jure (that is, legal) or even de facto (that is, actual, here meaning "use") rights to natural resources (including water) or services (for example, credit or agricultural extension) that owners have. To enable more effective participation by men and women with precarious forms of tenure, it is necessary to recognize greater relevance for these types of tenure. Project design should support the actual farm managers rather than absentees or men kin who have little interest in farm affairs. Involving the "real users" will bring efficiency gains to the project because they will be the actual persons involved in project-related activities.

Labor contribution to irrigated farms. Women made up 48 percent of the global agricultural workforce in 2000 by the Food and Agriculture Organization's (FAO's) estimate.[3] In some African countries this proportion approaches 90 percent. It is evident that women's labor plays a fundamental role in agriculture and in particular in irrigated agriculture. However, a number of serious problems are associated with it:

- Although an important share of farm work is informal and undertaken by family members, access to farm income and other resources depends on how the authority to make decisions is distributed among members of the household.
- Research has shown that rural women work longer hours than men but enjoy fewer benefits.
- The access of women to wage labor is often restricted. The salaries of women who do access wage work are often lower than those of men and the working hours are longer.
- Women are generally not able to irrigate at night owing to security concerns and during the day may face other time limitations. Water distribution systems rarely provide the flexibility necessary to satisfy such needs.

- When women are owners of the farm and have adequate resources to manage it, their productivity tends to be higher than or at least equal to that of men.

Decision making at the farm level. Managing an irrigated farm means making effective decisions at the right time. How decisions are made relates to a number of factors, but principally to who within the household is responsible for what decisions. Understanding how authority and responsibilities are distributed between men and women is therefore very important in interventions that seek to target specific members of the household with services such as training and technologies such as drip irrigation. Without such understanding, some of the targeted beneficiaries may not be able to participate in the planned activity because of social restrictions imposed by family members.

Participation in water user organizations. Institution capacity is an essential element of any AWM project. Irrigation management transfer (IMT) has become an integral part of many irrigation projects and requires strong institutions (see Investment Note 10.1, World Bank forthcoming). The predominant type of organization normally established is a water user association (WUA). The participation of water users in WUAs is normally linked to the ownership of the land. Because few women formally own land, their participation and representation in WUAs are normally low. Considering the substantial proportion of women who manage but do not own irrigated farms, their exclusion from associations in which they could communicate their needs and views can result in poor technical outcomes in water management, particularly for multiple uses of water.

Access of poor women and men to irrigation benefits. In addition to small farmers in irrigated areas who may improve their living standards by using local irrigation facilities, vulnerable groups exist who are deprived of land ownership and who have low educational levels. It is widely recognized that such groups are predominantly made up of women, mostly illiterate, who rarely find work to sustain themselves. Reaching them with any AWM program is a major challenge. It is feasible, however, by involving them in the consultation process and by addressing them through specific project objectives. Expansion of irrigated agriculture enhances demand for paid agricultural labor, often predominantly women.

Domestic and other uses of water. AWM projects center on the delivery of irrigation water to farms, whereas water supply projects plan only for domestic use. However, in rural life all uses tend to concentrate around the only resource available, no matter if they were planned for irrigation or domestic use. Rural communities have diverse uses for water besides irrigated agriculture, such as fishing, livestock watering, small businesses, home gardening, and domestic tasks. Water management projects take into consideration the provision of water for different uses. The associated costs are not high if the quality of water meets the required standards, and the benefits may be significant. For instance, pipes can reduce the time required for unproductive activities such as fetching water from far distances. For instance, UNFPA (2002) estimated that women in many developing countries walk an average of 6 kilometers a day to collect water. The availability of clean water close to home saves women's and girls' time, which can be spent on other productive and human development activities, such as crop production and education (IFAD 2007).

Water quality also requires particular attention in this context. In many irrigation systems water for domestic use is taken from canals. The situation is even more difficult in areas in which nontreated wastewater is used for irrigation and the health risks are high. Understanding water quality is important not only for women but also for the whole household because family health depends upon it. Planning projects for multipurpose uses requires a thorough investigation of the nonagricultural uses and in particular of women's needs.

LESSONS LEARNED

This section discusses the lessons learned at both the project and the policy levels.

Project level

Four main issues should be considered in project planning and implementation of gender-sensitive approaches to agricultural water management:

- Genuine gender-sensitive participatory project planning and implementation will prevent elites from capturing most project benefits. The benefits will therefore extend to a much larger population base. The experience of Nepal shows that this approach is feasible and renders positive returns of women's participation (see Investment Note 10.4, World Bank forthcoming).
- Water projects should be designed to address women's and men's domestic and productive water needs. To date, many single-sector projects have been planned, for either irrigation or domestic water supply, and multiple-use needs had requirements that have been overlooked, causing particular difficulties in rural areas.

- Planners should include among project objectives specific reference to increasing women's capacity to participate in irrigation projects and plan for ways to increase their access to productive resources.
- Project planners need to have a better understanding of the social, economic, and institutional reality of the project area. In practical terms, this means that some modest incremental resources should be allocated for assessment of such realities, particularly during the planning stage.

As the points above suggest, intersectoral linkages are key in seeking gender-positive outcomes. The following specific suggestions may assist concerned planners and implementing staff:

Land tenure. Irrigation development projects often include land titling components. Opportunity exists here for expansion of women's asset base provided that new land titles are granted to women or to husbands and wives jointly, depending on the prevailing socioagricultural context. Understanding the social organization of agricultural production and the specific gender division of labor in the project area requires a thorough investigation into the gender aspects of land tenure, including the use of participatory investigations and gender-disaggregated land surveys. Land reclamation projects in particular can do much to increase women's access to and control over land. The approach used in the LADEP project (see Innovative Activity Profile 2) and the LACOSEREP project (see Innovative Activity Profile 1) provides good examples of how to overcome gender issues in land projects.

Gender division of labor. Awareness of women's sizable contributions to farm and household production is lacking among project planners. Farm models used in project design should carefully evaluate the availability of women's and men's work in the family and expected impacts of intervention on women's and men's income, time use, and social power. Labor contribution by project beneficiaries to the construction component in small projects can be very significant and reduce costs (see Investment Note 10.1, World Bank forthcoming). Few types of construction cannot be carried out by women if they are provided with suitable tools and guidance. Here again, this requires good knowledge of the available labor force (men and women) and of local traditions.

Water user organizations and other institutional arrangements. Because women are poorly represented in WUAs, careful attention is required to devise innovative ways of ensuring women's and poor men's meaningful participation in such forums. Sometimes the by-laws of an association may provide equal opportunities for all members, but then discriminatory practices are applied, leading to low participation. More often, however, the criteria for WUA membership themselves are exclusionary and primarily focused on landholding status, meaning that women and tenants are often left out. Overcoming this difficulty represents a challenge that has been successfully addressed by some projects. Approaches for tackling this issue have included the following:

Quota systems wherein a minimum number of board seats are reserved for women. This positive discrimination can increase women's participation, though quotas have also backfired in other places or been "captured" by women put up to the position by dominant men. This has also led to a focus on increasing women's participation among membership ranks as well as leadership, so that a "critical mass" of women develops. Stalker (2004) examined data from 45 villages in two World Bank–assisted projects in India and came to interesting conclusions regarding women's participation in water user committees in the domestic water supply sector. Although, in some cases, women committee members were nominal, or token, participants, evidence showed that being on a local water committee helps women develop skills and confidence.

Gender-inclusive WUAs developed by removing exclusionary membership criteria regarding land ownership. This took place in the IFAD-supported LACOSEREP project in Ghana (see Innovative Activity Profile 1) in which membership to WUAs was not limited to farmers associated with irrigation and, by doing so, opened up the opportunity to get women involved. Much depends here on how "farmer" is defined, for example, not just "irrigators" applying water to the field, which may be a man's task in many places, but also other farmers, such as those doing weeding, transplanting, harvesting, and other tasks, who are often women, and beyond crop production, those farmers using water for livestock production and other uses (often women).

Where WUAs are strictly associated with formal (often large-scale) surface irrigation systems, scope also exists to establish other water user groups at the community level that represent women's needs and interests, provided they link up formally to the WUAs so that multiple use needs are discussed. Examples of such associations are cooperatives in which membership is not limited just to owners of land but to any type of tenure. Such associations may take the place of a traditional WUA or work in parallel with them.

Recognizing organizational pluralism with various groups set up to respond to different needs is important. Turkey's Irrigation Management Transfer Programme illustrates very clearly that the management responsibility of irrigation systems can be performed by several types of organizations besides the traditional WUA model such as water cooperatives, village organizations, and municipal organizations. The important principle, again, is that larger institutional analyses and strategic forms of formal collaboration take place so that subvillage/water-point level groups, for example, are not marginalized in local planning processes for water management. The IFAD-supported LACOSEREP Project (see Innovative Activity Profile 1) illustrates a nontraditional WUA model that integrates three groups of predominant stakeholders: gardeners, livestock owners, and fishermen. The main WUA was defined as a combination of these subgroups, with an executive body comprising members from each of the three subassociations. Another interesting feature of this association was that members were put in charge and the modalities of this procedure were left to members to decide, the only condition being that plot sizes should be equal, not smaller, for women, and 40 percent should be reserved for women. The small number of women extension officers is often cited as a weak link to channeling information and knowledge to women. To change this situation, training courses for mainstreaming gender dimensions in the daily work of extension staff can be done and are effective. Many training manuals (GWA and Both ENDS 2006; Sagardoy and Hamdy 2005) and related material undertake such training courses.[4]

Designing and implementing multiple use water services. The water requirements necessary to satisfy domestic needs are a small fraction of those applied to agriculture production—usually less than 6 percent. Such small requirements rarely create conflict in terms of quantity with irrigation needs. The problems are generally posed by the quality, but proper water treatment and filtering plants provide satisfactory solutions in most cases. Thus, the question of implementing a system that satisfies the domestic water needs is essentially associated with the related costs of the system (treatment plant and water delivery) and the ability of the farmers to pay for this service. In rural areas, where houses may be erratically distributed over the land, it may not be feasible to provide them with tap water, and communal watering points may be the best solution. As women will be the main users of those watering points, planners must understand their water needs and associate them with the management of such watering point sites. A strong consultation process should take place during the planning and implementation stages, but training programs addressed to women to help them manage and maintain the points of supply will also be necessary. Implementing multiple water use projects can introduce an additional cost factor and institutional complexity in the management of the nonagricultural uses. However, the efficiency gains at the national level are much greater than if the provision of these services is done separately or not done at all (see Thematic Note 1 for details).

Reaching the poorest and most vulnerable groups. The importance of including vulnerable and often-overlooked groups such as landless workers and poor women farmers is increasingly understood but is not always included in project design. Including them in the projects means that the greatest unexploited potential to influence land and water use management will be tapped positively.

The first questions to answer are as follows: Who are the poor? How do they secure their livelihoods? Often the rural poor are women, men, and children owning little or no land and without other significant nonagricultural income. Poverty impacts of irrigation projects can include increases in demand for both agricultural labor and direct project construction, as well as the possibility of land transfers through watershed development and land reclamation efforts.

Monitoring and evaluation. Monitoring the progress made in applying gender approaches in irrigation projects is seldom undertaken. The development of gender indicators in the context of project implementation is an area that lags behind (Sagardoy and others 2007). Progress is evident, however, and a variety of gender indicators related to water are being developed by FAO and other organizations. Investment Note 10.4 (World Bank forthcoming) provides further guidance on this issue.

Policy level

The effectiveness of AWM programs is heavily affected by government policies for the sector and related sectors. Understanding government policies, the institutional environment from whence they are generated, and the priorities they reflect is an important element in designing projects that are more likely to receive support from the government.

The development community at times can have considerable leverage in promoting changes in policy. Gender issues that require active policy support include the following:

- Ensure that women enjoy de jure and de facto equality in access to land and other property, including inheritance and purchase.
- Support pro-poor development actions. Investment Note 10.3 (World Bank forthcoming) provides more detailed orientations in the interrelation between poverty-gender issues and AWM policies. The example of South Africa illustrates a relevant policy in this respect.
- Promote the participation of women in WUAs and other organizations by supporting appropriate institutional measures, such as minimum quotas, or allowing that other forms of tenure besides ownership be eligible for being a member in the association.
- Provide an equal opportunity legal framework for agricultural laborers (and others) and ensure its application, including support for gender-equitable wages.
- Provide improved coordination among concerned WUAs to facilitate the implementation of multiple-use water projects.
- Support equal employment opportunities in WUAs.
- Provide and support capacity building around gender issues in WUAs with particular attention to extension staff. The establishment of dedicated government offices to monitor gender progress and provide specialized training, technical assistance, and sometimes modest financial incentives can be most effective in providing more opportunities for women.

Some indicators to monitor the gender impact of activities in agricultural water management are provided in table 6.1.

Depending on the country or region, it may be relevant to also consider ethnicity and caste alongside gender (both as comparative indicators and when collecting data), as women of lower castes or ethnic minorities are usually in the worst situation.

Table 6.1 Monitoring and Evaluation Indicators for Gender in Agricultural Water Management

Indicator	Sources of verification and tools
Number and frequency of women, men, and other disadvantaged persons consulted during detailed design and implementation	• Community meeting minutes and records of prioritization and votes
Percentage of women and men actively participating in planning sessions for water allocation program for drinking water and agricultural irrigation	• Meeting minutes • Technical plans indicating water uses and timetable
Percentage of women and men actively participating in water user groups	• Case studies • Meeting minutes or administrative records
By year x of project operation, operational costs are covered with user fees and maintenance fees collected to agreed level	• Bank account records • Women's user group records
Percentage of women and men members of operations and management committees of irrigation projects	• Meeting minutes
Women, men, and ethnic minorities in positions of management or leadership in water user groups	• Meeting minutes • Women's user group committee records
Community satisfaction (disaggregated by gender) regarding water distribution schedules and access	• Focus groups • Interviews, before and after
x percent of women and men among total trainees receiving training in the appropriate use of irrigation for high-value crop production	• Training records
Access of women and men to support services, such as credit and extension (such as percentage of women in agricultural training and of women clients of credit institutions)	• Extension department records • Interviews with women in target groups
Access of landless women and men to water from irrigation schemes	• Community meeting minutes
Among surveyed women in target group, x percent rate their access to water for agricultural and domestic use as having improved during the period covered by the program or project	• Interviews with women in target groups (for instance, a sample of women in the defined area); ideally the interviews should be conducted before and after any project or program activities
Changes in relevant dimensions of well-being, disaggregated by gender and wealth group: food and other products, household income, labor and other costs for water conveyance, water quality for drinking, and water quantity for hygiene	• Household surveys • Water quality testing by project or local environment department

Source: Inputs from Pamela White, author of Module 16.

Gender and Multiple-Use Water Services

Multiple-use water services in poor rural and peri-urban areas are a highly effective way to use water to reduce poverty and enhance gender equity. By taking women's and men's multiple water needs as the starting point and accessing multiple sources of water in an integrated way, multiple-use water services meet a broad range of dimensions of well-being, enhance project sustainability and willingness and ability to pay, and foster more equitable water management.

It is well acknowledged that water resources are interconnected within one hydrological cycle, encompassing naturally available water resources: rainfall, groundwater, surface lakes and streams, ponds, springs, wetlands, and water and human-made storage, reservoirs, conveyance canals, pumps, reticulation networks, abstractions, and take-off points for end uses, drains, return flows, and groundwater recharge. Water from multiple and conjunctive sources is used and reused to meet multiple needs. In the past the focus has largely been at the higher aggregate basin and sub-basin levels. However, multiple-use water services approaches recognize that integrated water resources management starts within the household, especially in poor rural and periurban areas where livelihoods are highly water dependent and diversified.

Women and men tap, convey, and use water for drinking, other domestic purposes, livestock, gardening, irrigation, tree growing, fisheries, food processing and other small businesses, and cultural purposes. Multiple water sources are used simultaneously, depending on their comparative suitability for certain uses (easy accessibility, year-round availability, site, quality, or predictability). For example, more reliable, year-round, and higher-quality sources are prioritized for domestic uses; roof water and runoff are used during the rainy season; slightly organically polluted water is used for irrigation.

Multiple-use water services approaches overcome the barriers created by the way in which the water sector has structured itself. Organization was typically based around single-use sectors: a domestic sector, an irrigation sector, a fisheries sector, a livestock sector, and others. These organograms fail to fit the nature of water resources and people's multiple water needs. Conventionally, the irrigation sector, for example, prioritized productive water uses by adopting that as its mandate, even if domestic, livestock, and other more urgent water needs of their clients were not satisfied. In reality, however, users anywhere in the world made the match: they transformed single-use planned systems into de facto multiple-use systems. In response to that observation, the irrigation sector developed an "irrigation-plus" approach, for example, by adding washing steps, entry points for cattle, or special abstractions and reservoirs for domestic and livestock water supplies, especially in the dry season (box 6.1).

Usually these adaptations were seen as "add-ons" and less important than the primary mandate of water for crops. Taking people's priority water needs as the starting point instead of beginning with a bureaucratic mandate matches realities on the ground even better.

INVESTMENT AREA

Multiple-use water services bring gender to the center stage of water development, use, and management. In the past women's needs, either as providers for domestic water or as producers in their own right, were often ignored in agricultural water management projects. Yet their de facto uses of "irrigation water" for nonirrigation purposes were in reality often the most important benefit for women (Hussain 2005). Women are nowadays better recognized as producers on an equal footing with men, but irrigation and rural livelihood-oriented development investments still tend to ignore women's domestic and other water needs.

Men's responsibilities for domestic water provision, a crucial aspect of household welfare, are even more ignored.

Box 6.1	Pakistan: Socioeconomic Differences in Access to Water for Livestock Watering

An International Water Management Institute study in Pakistan found that socioeconomic level affected households' access to water for livestock watering. Better-off households living on larger properties were able to keep their animals in stalls on their home compound and bathed and watered the animals with the same domestic water the family used (that is, groundwater from hand pumps, motor pumps, and wells).

Ninety-five percent of respondents from such households found water sources sufficient for their animals. In contrast, poorer households (and those few households who lived near their fields farther from the village) had to drive their animals to canal watercourses and distributaries for watering and bathing. Only 71 percent of such respondents found such water access arrangements satisfactory.

Further, livestock use of canal water is illegal and pollutes the distributory water for downstream domestic users. The traditional livestock pond held in common in each village is now being degraded by release of wastewater and sewage from those households with private sources of water.

Source: Kuriakose, Jehangir, and ul-Hassan forthcoming.

Although the daily drudgery of fetching water is the typical gendered burden for women and girls, and to a lesser extent for boys, in many societies men do take part. Men can take the responsibility for the construction and maintenance of wells or ponds or for transport if aided by donkeys, bicycles, or cars. Domestic water provision by both women and men should be further recognized as a critical factor for household welfare from rural households and communities to national and international policy discourse. This reflects the notion of equality of men and women both in carrying out the unpaid tasks for household welfare and in generating income for the family's benefit.

Multiple-use water services also allow for pro-poor water allocation, based on a quantitative understanding of the distribution of water uses across various levels. If poverty is understood as a state of multidimensional deprivation in which basic needs are by definition broadly defined, it is an anomaly to confine "basic" water needs to one purpose only: drinking and personal hygiene. Food and income are

as critical for poor households to mitigate malnutrition and income poverty as domestic water is for drinking, hygiene, and cooking. Providing for both domestic and small-scale productive uses is estimated to require water quantities in the range of 50–200 liters per person per day (Butterworth and others 2003). Thus, in poor rural and periurban areas, such water uses all directly contribute to poverty alleviation. These quantities are minimal from the overall resource perspective from the local to the basin level and fall within the errors of hydrological models. The irrigation sector also has viewed the quantities needed for domestic uses as negligible.

BENEFITS FROM GENDER-RESPONSIVE ACTIONS

In productive-plus designs, domestic water provision is a matter of year-round provision as near as possible to the place of consumption, as is water quality for the even smaller quantities of two to four liters per person per day, depending on climate (Howard and Bartram 2003). Integrating livestock needs in irrigation design is not a quantity issue either, but a matter of protection against cattle destroying canals, soils, and crops and polluting resources. Therefore, quantities of water for such vital livelihoods hardly ever encounter environmental constraints, except perhaps in the dry seasons in areas where storage and other infrastructure development levels and natural endowments are low. The key problem is the distribution of water use among people, which can be highly skewed. This is illustrated by the Gini coefficient for water use distribution in South Africa, which was found to indicate near total inequality of 0.96 (see box 6.2).

In the domestic sector, the recognition of multiple water needs has gone along remarkably similar lines. Starting from the single-use mandate to provide water for domestic uses only and observing the reality that all "domestic" schemes are de facto used for multiple purposes, some organizations started adopting a "domestic-plus" approach. For example, they augmented the discharge of the water supply systems to allow for watering livestock and gardens also and for home-based enterprises, or they connected cattle troughs to drinking water supplies.

Some technologies, such as rainwater harvesting and wells for single or small household groups, allow for multiple uses in design. Instead of addressing drinking water quality through centralized water treatment facilities, point-of-use treatment (filtration, chemicals) has expanded significantly. This not only mitigates the inevitable pollution of domestic water projects during conveyance and

The colonial history of South Africa left a legacy of a highly skewed distribution of water resources. In the Olifants basin, the Gini coefficient for (blue) rural water uses (which constitutes 91 percent of all water uses) is 0.96. In other words, 0.5 percent of the rural population controls the access to 95 percent of the blue water resources. If the majority of the population were to double their current water use, the few large users would have to share only 6 percent of what they use now. Underlying this so-called environmental crisis in this basin, where by now most physical water resources have already been committed, is the highly inequitable socioeconomic and political distribution of water resources, which requires a redistributive water allocation reform, such as that recently launched by the government of South Africa.

Sources: Cullis and van Koppen 2005; RSA 2005.

household storage but can also solve water quality problems in "productive-plus" water services. Moreover, point-of-use treatment also applies to the millions of households that are not served by any public project. A clear example of the growing recognition of the importance of multiple-use services is the World Bank's Water and Sanitation Program. The program's vision to integrate multiple-use services fully in their approaches can be compared with the way in which sanitation has been integrated in "domestic" supplies since the 1980s.[1]

The growing dialogue between the productive and domestic water sectors to develop jointly "multiple water use services by design" integrates water services where it matters for poverty alleviation and gender equity. "It is Integrated Water Resources Management that directly advances the Millennium Development Goals.... As the water professionals created the barriers between them, it is the water professionals who have to break them down."[2]

Health impacts of a multiple-use approach

Health is also improved from multiple-use water services. In spite of strong concerns by the health and domestic water sector departments about the quality of drinking water in

"productive" schemes, many planners have realized that in areas without any domestic water supplies, the use of irrigation water for drinking purposes was an improvement over the status quo. Moreover, in the many situations in which groundwater and even surface streams are used, water quality is acceptable for domestic uses other than drinking, and in specific cases, also for drinking. Later studies confirmed that regardless of its sometimes questionable quality, the availability of any additional *quantities* of water has a beneficial impact on people's health (Esrey and others 1991; Howard and Bartram 2003; Jensen and others 2001; Van der Hoek and others 2001), especially when combined with improved hygiene behavior. Hence, within reason, water quantity is more important than water quality, and other alternatives such as various point-of-use treatments exist for the small quantities needed for actual drinking. (It should be noted, however, that for small children poor quality water remains a major risk for diarrhea; see Clasen and Cairncross 2004; Hebert 1985.)

Point-of-use treatment is increasingly seen as a more appropriate option in the domestic sector (Mahfouz and others 1995; Mintz, Reiff, and Tauxe 1995; Quick and others 1999, 2002; Reller and others 2003; Roberts 2003), particularly in dispersed or difficult-to-reach areas. Such treatment also solves the water quality concern for productive-plus schemes and, moreover, for the millions who have no access to public supplies, such as those using groundwater wells that may be contaminated with arsenic or fluoride.

KEY GENDER ISSUES

Past evidence of domestic-plus, productive-plus, and multiple-use by design approaches highlights three sets of benefits of water services that take poor women's and men's multiple water needs as the starting point.

Improving more dimensions of women's and men's well-being

Various simultaneous water uses provide a broad range of benefits: food production (crops, livestock, fish), income (from the sale of primary products and water-dependent artisanal businesses), reduced drudgery of water fetching, and enhanced health. These different benefits tend to reinforce each other into a virtuous circle out of poverty.

Women benefit in particular from dissolving the dichotomy between the domestic and productive spheres and approaches that take women's and men's water needs as equally important by design. In this way, the "productive" sectors also better recognize the priority need to alleviate the unpaid chores of women and girls for domestic water fetching, as well as the burdens of men and especially boys to take care of cattle watering at distant sources. Second, the starting point at which women are producers in need of water on an equal footing with men is effectively operationalized by stimulating productive activities around the household. In societies in which women's mobility is limited or in which women lack access to fields of their own, a situation similar to the situation of land-poor and landless households in general, homestead production offers unique opportunities for income generation. A study in Nepal confirmed how women in particular benefited from the newly installed domestic-cum-gardening water supplies and drip irrigation kits around the households (Upadhyah Samad, and Giordano 2005).

Enhancing project sustainability

Multiple-use water services enhance project sustainability in various ways. First, anticipating future "unplanned" uses prevents the problems of de facto multiple-use programs, such as damage to infrastructure, the distortion of allocations because of upstream overuse of domestic programs designed for minimum uses only, or "illegal" connections. Second, new local water management institutions for investing in and operating and maintaining new infrastructure can be grafted onto communities' existing water arrangements. The latter are invariably integrated for multiple uses and holistically govern the same water resources used by the same people. The smooth continuum between existing arrangements and new institutional elements strengthens community ownership. They also avoid the turf wars between newly imposed "domestic" WUAs and "irrigation" committees. Third, the willingness to contribute to managing new projects sustainably is higher if the programs better meet users' needs. The ability to pay for the project is enhanced by better water delivery for productive activities.

Using water more equitably

From local to basin level, the simultaneous consideration of all water uses and everybody's needs gives a human face to water development and regulation. Formal water resource allocations tend to be based on sectors, with the domestic water sector as a first priority, and agriculture, environmental needs, industrial needs, and others as the next priorities. However, this ignores the huge differences in water use

within sectors. Pro-poor and people-based allocation prioritizes all uses of water for domestic and productive needs that allow every citizen to reach at least minimum standards of well-being. Only after expanding and protecting those uses are remaining water and other resources allocated.

Keeping incremental technology costs low or none

The above-mentioned benefits come at limited incremental technology costs and even come at no incremental cost in the case of de facto multiple-use schemes. Technologies that allow for multiple uses by design reassemble the conventional technology components into a more user-friendly package. This is a matter of basic rural engineering skills, not of hardware costs per se. However, the costs that tend to increase most are the transaction costs in the early planning and design stage. A process in which women and men articulate their priority needs, which then are translated into an optimal technical and institutional design, takes time and facilitation.

POLICY AND IMPLEMENTATION ISSUES

The key actors in shifting from single-use water services to multiple-use services are national and international governmental and nongovernmental agencies. They shape the internal structuring and financing of water sector policy making, implementation, and vocational training and tertiary education. Policies and legal frameworks tend to define overall policy goals in terms of single-use water development and to set standards and quality norms, for example, for drinking water, assuming that single use is the priority use, if not the only use, of the beneficiaries of a particular program. Financing streams are also typically earmarked for one single use. Organizationally, departments are structured according to single-use mandates. In a top-down manner those mandates trickle down to lower-tier branches through job descriptions, performance evaluations, monitoring systems, technical expertise, and other ways.

These policies and legal constraints need to be transformed. In each sector sectoral mandates that are too narrow are to be expanded into multiple-use mandates. Constraining norms and standards must follow. For example, imposing unrealistically high water quality standards is now recognized to be of little use in a search for incremental improvements to deal with health hazards. The World Health Organization recently also changed its focus from fixed water quality standards to more flexible guidelines (WHO 2004).

Besides formulating and promulgating enabling policy and legal frameworks, national-level stakeholders also need to establish meaningful coordination across sectors and actors. This implies, in essence, devolution of decision-making regarding water services to the lowest appropriate level, up to clients' multiple water needs in their integrated diversified livelihoods. Bottom-up needs-based design requires poor water users to decide on the services they need. It is true that national or regional agencies will keep a role in large-scale dams and other large- or perhaps medium-scale water works and basin-level regulation. However, beyond that, national governments have a main role to play in supporting intermediate-level water services providers (local government, local nongovernmental organizations [NGOs], private water service providers, and others), so that they are enabled, in their turn, to coordinate the support for communities according to integrated needs emerging from transparent and participatory design procedures for multiple-use water services.

Long-term support by national and intermediate-level stakeholders to communities is also required for multiple-use services at any significant scale. This support is financial, institutional, and technical. Considerable financial support earmarked for multiple uses is critical for any taking multiple-use water services to scale and reaching the Millennium Development Goals. Subsidization will remain necessary for reaching the poor for decades to come. Yet cost recovery by those who can pay and earn an income from multiple-use systems should be tied into programs. National support is also needed for institution building and expanding the choice of affordable and appropriate technologies for multiple uses.

For the factual implementation of multiple-use water services, intermediate development agencies, in particular local government and other administrative structures, are pivotal, irrespective of any basin boundary. Yet Integrated Water and Resources Management institutional structures at basin or aquifer levels can strengthen cross-sectoral coordination. In fully committed basins, basin institutional arrangements would enforce water allocation that prioritizes basic domestic and productive water needs.

GOOD PRACTICES AND LESSONS LEARNED

The concept of multiple-use water services emerged in the domestic and productive water sectors alike, in response to the major lesson learned: planning and design of water services for one single use do not fit clients' needs in poor rural and periurban areas. Even productive-plus and domestic-plus approaches reproduce an implicit prioritization of water uses according to top-down defined mandates. Clients have always expressed these needs by simply transforming single-use planned systems into de facto multiple-use systems. Not surprisingly, multiple-use services tend to resonate immediately with communities and with any water professional with field experience.

In the past decade, NGOs (for example, AWARD, Catholic Relief Services, Mvuramanzi Trust Zimbabwe, Plan International, South Africa) and small-scale private sector projects (for example, Agua Tuya in Bolivia, rope pump development in Nicaragua) with a client-oriented poverty and livelihood focus swiftly started applying multiple-use water services approaches. Their mandates and internal structuring allowed them to just do it.

International research programs, in particular the Challenge Program on Water and Food of the Consultative Group of International Agricultural Research, is conducting global- and basin-level research projects on multiple water uses. International financing agencies, such as the World Bank, are also adopting multiple-use water services approaches. Wherever the political will exists, national governments have also started recognizing multiple-use services approaches. For example, the South African Department of Water Affairs and Forestry recently embarked on this road. In Colombia rural development agencies coordinate with the national government, among others, on the need for augmenting the quantity norms for rural water supplies.[3]

Early experiences also highlighted that the most challenging level is the intermediate level of service providers and WUAs. Stakeholders at this level together and in a coordinated way are to provide sustained support to investments and construction of multiple-use projects in their zone of intervention, as well as to "after care" by supporting operation and maintenance. Today, however, agencies such as local government or district irrigation agencies are typically undersourced, lack capacities, are "trapped" in ad hoc planning and trouble shooting, and divert their attention to a few "islands of success in oceans of misery." Although accountable in name to their constituencies, local officials formally report upwards to a range of typically uncoordinated bureaucracies.

Multiple-use water services are a particular form of decentralization, and their successful implementation depends upon the success of decentralization in general. Yet the main lesson of irrigation management transfer and other forms of decentralization until now is that a mere devolvement of responsibilities without the corresponding resources required to fulfill these responsibilities is bound to lead to the collapse of even the small support that previously existed (Shah and others 2002). Therefore, the most needed lessons will come from recent initiatives like the World Bank's Community Driven Development approach (Binswanger and Tuu-Van Nguyen 2005) or pilot experiments to integrate multiple-use water services into local government planning, for example, in South Africa's Integrated Development Plans (Maluleke and others 2005).

GUIDELINES AND RECOMMENDATIONS FOR PRACTITIONERS

The following recommendations apply to practitioners at the three levels (Van Koppen, Moriarty, and Boelee 2006).

At the national level:

- *Enabling policy and legislative framework.* Remove the obstacles for multiple-use water services, such as a narrow focus on one single water use only in mandates, financing streams, or standards and norms, and, instead, prioritize water development and water allocation for poor women's and men's concurrent basic domestic and productive needs.
- *Financing.* Allocate subsidies and loans to communities and to intermediate-level stakeholders for upscaling of multiple-use water services.
- *Coordination across sectors and actors.* Decentralize decision making for development to the lowest appropriate levels and shape national support according to those integrated needs.
- *Long-term institutional and technical support.* Facilitate inclusive institutional design for community-based integrated water resources management and capacity building and development and disseminate appropriate and affordable technologies and skills for multiple uses.

At the intermediate level:

- *Adaptive management.* Stimulate adaptive learning-by-doing by intermediate-level stakeholders to gradually move toward water services provision for multiple uses across increasing numbers of villages.
- *Strategic and participatory planning.* Develop transparent methodologies across a region that allow for water services planning and design based on communities' articulated multiple water needs.
- *Coordination across sectors and actors.* Organize holistic support to communities based on integrated water and livelihood needs.

- *Financing.* Establish sustainable investments and revenue collection mechanisms both for community-based schemes and water user associations and for intermediate-level support structures.
- *Long-term institutional and technical support.* Provide support to communities for community-based institution building and for a wide choice of appropriate and affordable technologies.

At the local level:

- *Livelihoods-based planning and design.* Facilitate an inclusive planning and design process in which women and men articulate their domestic water needs as shared responsibilities for household welfare and their respective productive water needs as equal opportunities for improved livelihoods.
- *Appropriate technologies.* Translate multiple water needs into affordable small- and medium-scale technical designs, in particular storage for year-round water provision.
- *Sustainable water use.* Tap synergies for more efficient water use by combining multiple sources for "more use and reuse per drop," prioritizing basic domestic and productive water needs in periods and sites of scarcity.
- *Inclusive institutions.* Graft new integrated water management institutions upon existing community-based water arrangements that already holistically govern shared water resources for multiple uses.
- *Financing.* Establish sustainable cost-recovery mechanisms at the local level, while providing smart subsidies for those who cannot afford to pay.

Project preparation

The following questions guide the preparation of projects for multiple-use water services across the various levels:

- Are project goals, mandates, and evaluation criteria constraining toward one single water use, or do they acknowledge people's multiple water needs? If constraining, what short-term strategies can be deployed to widen the mandate (such as pilot projects with intensive monitoring)? Which strategies are needed in the long term, and how can they be initiated (such as research to reexamine national standards)?
- Are technical experts in the projects sufficiently aware of clients' water needs outside their immediate focus? Are they encouraged to look outside the disciplinary box?

- Which participatory process is foreseen that allows the target group of poor women and men to express their water needs at the very beginning of a project, to identify affordable technologies, to sustainably tap multiple water sources, to design inclusive new institutions on the basis of existing water arrangements, and to establish sustainable financing mechanisms while supporting the poor and the poorest? What are the incremental costs of such a process?
- How are women's and men's mutual domestic labor and monetary responsibilities articulated and translated into the technical and institutional design?
- How are women's and men's equal needs for water for productive use considered and translated into the technical and institutional design? Which additional support is required for both women and men to make more productive use of water?
- Which incremental health benefits can be achieved for the microquantities of drinking water and for other health dimensions of water services?
- How will the capacity of the intermediate-level service providers be built to continue support to target communities and to replicate lessons learned in other communities?

Projects with a multiple-use water services focus can include the following monitoring and evaluation indicators:

- Changes in relevant dimensions of well-being by gender and wealth group: food and other products, income, reduced labor, and other costs for water conveyance, water quality for drinking, and water quantity for hygiene
- Participatory planning and design process that allows for bottom-up needs definition by women and men and articulation of gendered needs for external support
- Level of cost recovery
- Technical innovations allowing for multiple uses
- Capacity building of intermediate-level service providers to apply needs-based multiple-use water services on a larger scale
- Removal of current barriers to multiple-use water services in national policy and legislative frameworks.

Gender and Institutional Approaches to Groundwater Development and Management

Gender-sensitive approaches to groundwater development and management help secure and protect groundwater access and use for women and the rural poor. Gendered water rights determine access and control over groundwater resources. Men and women differ in their needs and technological preferences for groundwater extraction and are affected differently when groundwater development interventions are introduced. Gender analysis should thus be undertaken throughout the project cycle. Only when the needs and preference of all users are taken into account can the project objectives of poverty reduction be attained.

Recognition of gender issues in the use and management of the groundwater resource is vital to realizing the project objectives of poverty reduction and sustainable management of the resource. Groundwater has certain characteristics that make it different from surface sources. Groundwater, available in deep and shallow aquifers, provides security against drought by offering a reliable year-round natural storage of relatively good-quality water, close to the point of use, usually at a lower cost of development. It has been a crucial resource in livelihood creation programs in different parts of Asia and Africa through intervention in both deep and shallow groundwater projects. The unique characteristics of groundwater have made the provision of its services for drinking, irrigation, and other productive purposes an effective way to reduce poverty and enhance gender equity.

Investment in a gender-sensitive institutional approach to groundwater development and management brings user-preference issues to the fore and is a key part of planning for sustainable water use systems. Gender inequalities in access to and control over groundwater abound. This Note examines issues regarding access to groundwater abstraction technology and use of the resource, as well as challenges in ensuring participation of women and the poor in groundwater management activities.

Women and men have different priorities and needs with respect to water, which result from their different roles and responsibilities. Women and men also have different skills and knowledge with respect to groundwater use for domestic, agricultural, or other productive purposes and are affected differently when groundwater development initiatives are introduced. Even though groundwater offers different advantages, overexploitation of this resource through unregulated pumping as well as water quality issues poses serious threats to the well-being of rural persons, especially women and poor men and women.

GENDER AND ACCESS TO GROUNDWATER

A crucial issue in groundwater development and management is that of access to and use of the groundwater resource, including access to groundwater abstraction technology and groundwater management activities. Different rights come into play when discussing groundwater: rights to the resource either by virtue of owning the groundwater technology (individually or through a group) or by being a member of the groundwater users' group, rights to decide water allocation and distribution after water is pumped out, as well as adjudication and decision-making rights on who holds which rights (Gautam 2006; Zwarteveen 2006). Water rights are directly related to land rights in many countries. In such cases men and women without clear land titles are restricted from being members of groundwater users' group even when they may be the main decision makers on the farm or in the household (see box 6.3 for a project that overcame this constraint). In the Andean countries, Bangladesh, India, Nepal, and countries in southern Africa, migration of men from rural areas has led to an increase in women-headed households so women are overburdened with the task of maintaining the household as well as the farms.[1] The same case can be found in Yemen (box 6.3).

Box 6.3 Yemen: Women and the Water Crisis

Yemen's water crisis has affected women adversely in different ways. Groundwater irrigation for cash cropping has resulted in aquifer depletion in different agroecological regions. Traditional sources of water-harvesting structures are no longer maintained. Women and young girls travel longer distances for water in rural areas, affecting their health, safety, and literacy levels. As more men migrate to cities and other Gulf countries, women's role in irrigated agriculture has increased, although it is not always formally acknowledged because commercial cultivation was traditionally a man's preserve. In the case of urban water supply, richer households purchase water from tanks, whereas poorer women have to line up to buy water from richer neighbors, to obtain lower-quality water from wells, or periodically to get water from municipality water projects.

Source: Frédéric Pelat, "A Brief Overview of the Water and Gender Situation in Yemen," www.idrc.ca/en/ev-99527-201-1-DO_TOPIC.html.

Box 6.4 Gender and Water Quality

Naturally occurring arsenic in groundwater poses a serious threat to more than 60 million people living in South and East Asia. Almost 700,000 people have been affected by arsenicosis in the region. Skin cancer; cancer of the bladder, kidney, and lungs; diseases of the blood vessels leading to gangrene; and reproductive disorders are the main effects of arsenic poisoning. A stigma associated with arsenicosis has serious social effects on marriage prospects for men and women, as well as for job opportunities. One of the most seriously affected regions is Bangladesh in the Meghna-Brahmaputra-Ganges Delta, where arsenic has been detected in water from shallow aquifers. Women in Bangladesh prefer tubewells over surface water because these reduce their workload. However, with the rise in arsenic-contaminated groundwater, women and young girls have been disproportionately harmed.

Sources: Caldwell and others 2002; www.worldbank.org/gwmate; www.who.int/water_sanitation_health/diseases/arsenicosis/en.

Women and girls are typically responsible for collecting water for daily needs. This includes water for drinking purposes for the household, livestock, cooking, cleaning, and overall health and hygiene within the household.

Clear water rights lead to improved access to water, which is critical for maintaining good health and a sustainable livelihood. Studies from Africa show that both rural and urban women are engaged in small-scale enterprises and that improved access to water would help them to pursue these activities more effectively.[2] Experience from India has shown that when groups of landless women were provided a share of water by the members of a "land-owning" water users' association in a lift irrigation project, the women were able to work out alternative livelihood strategies. They contracted the available wasteland in the village on a long-term lease and derived an income through biomass produced from this land (Kulkarni 2005), while taking part in the restoration of the land.

GROUNDWATER OVEREXPLOITATION, WATER QUALITY, AND GENDER

Groundwater use in most developing countries is not regulated. This has led to the overexploitation of the aquifers,

causing the lowering of water tables, an increase in pumping costs, and pollution of aquifers. Continued overexploitation of groundwater reduces the availability of freshwater for use and poses challenges to health for people who are bound to live near these affected areas. Groundwater is the major source of drinking water for cities in the developing world, and demand is rising with unplanned expansion of cities. Commercial agriculture and industries are other major users.

Groundwater overabstraction negatively impacts the rural poor because they cannot afford to dig deeper wells. In water-dependent societies, this particularly impacts the lives of poor women. Industrial waste disposal, wastewater from urban areas, oil spills, and excessive use of pesticides and insecticides in agriculture are some causes of groundwater pollution. In coastal areas overexploitation causes a rise in saline intrusion. Another type of groundwater poisoning that has emerged as a serious health hazard is due to naturally occurring arsenic (box 6.4).

BENEFITS FROM GENDER-RESPONSIVE ACTIONS

An institutional approach to groundwater development and management that puts gender at the center stage:

Box 6.5   Nepal: Leadership Development of Deep Tubewell Group

The Bhairahawa Lumbini Groundwater Irrigation Project (BLGWIP-III) initiated a "demand-based participatory approach" to deep tubewell (DTW) development and management. Women and men in Durganagar village sought a DTW from the BLGWIP-III only after they were convinced of the nature of the layout of the distribution system, flow and discharge rates, expected operational costs, and the possibility of integrating DTW with the traditional spring water distribution system already in use.

After realizing the design would support their interests in vegetable cultivation, they actively participated in project planning, including the layout of the underground pipe flow distribution system. Vegetable cultiva-

tion became a lucrative business among women and smallholders who take it up on a sharecropping basis. With water in high demand, the water user group (WUG) did not face difficulties in collecting fees and has been able to hire a full-time pump operator. Both men and women actively sought out WUG leadership positions, which resulted in an overall increase in the executive board from 7 to 11 positions for the second WUG election. According to the farmers, they realized that it was "important to get a representation across all castes, ethnic lines and from women." A woman was elected to the second committee in 2004. More women were interested but were not eligible because they were not landowners.

Source: Gautam 2006.

- Helps reduce gender inequalities in water by ensuring access to groundwater for women and those without clear land titles
- Recognizes women as important water stakeholders and recognizes the class diversity and social differentiation among women
- Facilitates the representation and participation of women in aquifer management to communicate groundwater priorities of men and women for different activities (such as irrigation versus domestic supply). Consulting with men and women from the start helps improve water regulation and governance through a bottom-up process (box 6.5).

POLICY AND IMPLEMENTATION ISSUES

Livelihood support programs featuring groundwater interventions require gender-specific approaches to realize poverty reduction and gender-equity goals. Groundwater development programs should be accompanied by efforts to create an enabling environment with gender-sensitive technical and other support services and context-specific strategies to involve both women and men in decision making at the system and aquifer levels. Intravillage groups organized around water sources are particularly important mechanisms for improving women's access to water management at the local level.

Programs must improve women's access to and control over groundwater resources, including through WUA membership and leadership roles:

- Introduce and maintain a "quota" system for women and disadvantaged groups in aquifer management organizations and national organizations.
- Make social mobilization and dialogue on reforming WUA membership criteria more inclusive and not dependent on men's gender or land ownership status.
- Where women face sociocultural obstacles to interacting in public forums with men, set up separate women's groundwater users groups. Care has to be taken that such groups are then formally linked to the larger representative user associations and apex groups. In conjunctive use settings, ensure that groundwater users are also represented in the surface irrigation system WUAs.

Planners should also create an enabling environment to enhance women's participation and provide technical and support services:

- Facilitate access to credit, agricultural extension, and local commercial repair and maintenance services.
- Ensure that technical assistance programs (for example, training on pump installation, repair, and maintenance) target both men and women.

- Promote tubewells as women's collective enterprises, together with other specific income-generation and market linkage activities.
- Set up savings groups for the landless via the sustainable functioning of community organizations renting pump sets; part of the profit of renting out the pump is kept in a savings fund for repair and maintenance.
- Highlight women's rights in water management through awareness-raising and educational programs.
- Encourage interdepartmental dialogue regarding gender and groundwater undertaken by the water supply and irrigation departments to address the multiple water needs of the poor and women.

GOOD PRACTICES AND LESSONS LEARNED

Groundwater development has long focused on individual (men) "farmers'" control over technology and the resource, with less attention to organizing institutions and gender impacts. Tubewell subsidies have similarly disproportionately benefited large farmers, usually men:

- Landownership as a criterion for tubewell or pump ownership or for membership in WUAs typically excludes women, smallholders, and tenants. User association criteria need to be examined closely to prevent social exclusion.
- A single-sector approach to groundwater development (especially for irrigation) has often resulted in oversized, underused pumps. The water needs of the rural poor are diverse: if drinking water and other needs are considered, the resulting infrastructure will likely be on a smaller scale and more affordable for women and the poor.
- Maintaining quota systems helps ensure that women's interests in WUAs are represented. It also generates discussions at the local level on women's rights and roles, which can be seen as a first step in awareness raising.
- Provision to women's groups of such technologies as treadle pumps, shallow tubewells, and deep tubewells is more effective when complementary training inputs in managerial and technical skills are provided. In Bangladesh women were able to successfully manage tubewells as a collective water-selling enterprise when given management control from the start (Van Koppen 1999).
- Projects that actively included both women and men in participatory planning, design, and implementation helped generate a cadre of women leaders in formal decision-making positions.

- Providing complementary inputs (credit access, agricultural extension, and marketing support) to women farmers helps extend the impact of water infrastructure investments and overcome their institutional disadvantage in accessing services.

GUIDELINES AND RECOMMENDATIONS FOR PRACTITIONERS

- Prioritize groundwater systems to serve both domestic and productive needs of the rural poor in programs that serve to enhance agricultural livelihoods.
- Promote lightweight and portable machines in areas with high land fragmentation and a high water table.
- Provide incentives to those WUAs that combine water-saving technologies, especially in water-deficit areas.
- Support capacity building for staff with interdisciplinary approaches and gender training to enhance social analysis skills.
- Coordinate across sectors that provide technical and support services to make sure that women and the disadvantaged are appropriately targeted.
- Develop gender-specific interventions based on the local social, cultural, and agroecological context and the nature of the project. Plan and design water use systems through a participatory inclusive process.
- Allow for flexibility to incorporate innovative strategies for both the technical and institutional designs, rather than using a rigid blueprint approach. Men and women may have different choices in terms of site selection, design, and layout of groundwater structures. Differences may also exist in preferences between foldable canvas pipes, underground pipes, or open flow channels for water distribution. If wells are to serve both domestic and productive needs, a decision on the location (between homestead and field) is important to minimize walking/water-carrying distance.
- Identify existing women's groups and coordinate with women's organizations, NGOs, cooperatives, and professional women's networks for enhanced gender inclusion in countries where such provisions exist. Examples from the Licto project in Ecuador show that women wanted water titles to be in the names of both husbands and wives after a long period of awareness raising by an NGO (GWA and Both ENDS 2006).

Box 6.6 provides questions for gender-responsive project design.

Box 6.6 Sample Questions for Project Design

Institutional approaches to groundwater development and management should include gender analysis throughout the project cycle. Issues of water rights determine access and control over groundwater resources. Men and women may differ in their preferences and needs for water and are affected differently when groundwater is introduced. Some specific design questions and indicators to take into consideration are the following:

- How have rights to groundwater abstraction technology ownership been defined (in terms of landownership)? Are there asset or collateral requirements?
- How have criteria for water users' group membership been defined?
- Are there land title or groundwater technology elements that may constrain the participation of women or the poor?

- What are the access and use rights to groundwater once it has been pumped? Who defines this, and who has the right to dispose of the right or adjudicate disputes?
- Who makes decision regarding allocation and distribution of water? Are women involved? Are women members of the WUAs? Are they in leadership positions in these groups?
- Does the project design take into account user flow preferences for specific crops, from different water sources?
- Has technical training and access to complementary support services been provided to both men and women?
- What are the expected changes in workload for men and women with the introduction of groundwater infrastructure (for example, might the workload for women increase in the case of irrigation and decrease for domestic water collection?).

Source: Authors.

Ghana: Upper East Region Land Conservation and Smallholder Rehabilitation Project (LACOSREP)

The Upper East Region Land Conservation and Smallholder Rehabilitation Project (LACOSREP) was initiated in the early 1990s by the International Fund for Agricultural Development to contribute to the poverty reduction and improve livelihoods of the second poorest region of Ghana through irrigation and agricultural development.

The second phase LACOSREP (1998–2006) was aimed at addressing the shortcomings of the first phase of the project. Although WUAs were established as a precondition for small-scale dam construction and rehabilitation in the first phase, they were not considered as a key component of the project's implementation strategy. These WUAs lacked the necessary organizational skills and a clear legal status, which explain the modest achievements in some sites, with respect to collected fees, catchment area protection, and adequate operation and maintenance. The last two factors are critical to the sustainability of the small-scale dams. It was also recognized that the project in its first phase was not able to address adequately

important issues such as capacity building of the WUAs and women's access to land and water. Therefore, the second phase of the project sought to pursue rigorously and systematically granting women access to dry season irrigated plots by involving them in WUAs and establishing a quota in-plot allocation for women. WUAs thus played a greater role in the planning of the whole irrigation project and had a clear understanding on their part of their obligations to ensure the sustainability of the project (IFAD 2003).

PROJECT OBJECTIVES AND DESCRIPTION

The objectives of LACOSREP II were to (1) further develop irrigation in the Upper East Region; (2) increase productivity through farmer training and demonstrations of new technologies for increasing the productivity of crops, livestock, and fish; (3) build the capacity of government institutions that provide technical and social services at the district and subdistrict levels; and (4) construct rural infrastructure to reduce women's labor burden and take measures to mitigate the possible risks of health and negative environmental impacts.

The target group included rural people and smallholders, landless farmers, and women, in particular women-headed households. The beneficiaries were drawn from the "at risk" category that embraces both economic and social criteria and included those most at risk from malnutrition, ill health, and a generally low quality of life. They came from an area that had the highest population growth rate (3 percent) and the lowest living standards in the country. About 50 percent of the direct beneficiaries (34,400) were estimated to be from the target group.

INNOVATIVE ACTIVITIES IN THE PROJECT

The project had two innovative activities: (1) membership in WUAs was not limited to farmers associated with irrigation or to one member per household and, by doing so, opened

> **What's innovative?** The membership in water users associations (WUAs) was not limited to farmers associated with irrigation or to one member per household, and thus opened up the opportunity to get women involved in WUAs. The recognition of multiple types of users (gardeners, livestock owners and fishermen) facilitated WUA development. This also strengthened the WUAs, by avoiding possible conflicts over water use and facilitating watershed protection measures. A quota of irrigated land allocation was also established for women so that they could get access to water from the irrigation schemes and be involved in the decision-making process.

up the opportunity to get women involved in WUAs; and (2) a quota for irrigated land allocation was established for women so that they could get access to water from the irrigation projects during the dry season and be involved in the decision-making process.

The program identified three groups of predominant water users: gardeners, livestock owners (coinciding or not with gardeners), and fishermen. The apex WUA was defined as a combination of these subgroups, with an executive body comprising members from each of the three subassociations. The project offered substantial material incentives, including food rations and improved irrigation facilities, for farmers, livestock keepers, and fishermen to participate in the small-scale dam construction and rehabilitation and WUA activities. The recognition of different stakeholder groups facilitated WUA development. This also strengthened the WUA by avoiding possible conflicts over water use and facilitating watershed protection measures.

The WUAs were responsible for land allocation in the dam command areas; modalities of this procedure were left up to them to decide, the only condition being that plot sizes should be equal, not smaller, for women, and 40 percent should be reserved for women. This affirmative action was taken to give women access to productive resources because traditionally in this region women did not own land and to encourage their participation in WUAs.

Another innovative aspect of the project was the incorporation of disabled and blind farmers in the WUAs, as a form of social equity and inclusive targeting in some communities. This is a replication of the successful IFAD project in Upper West Region, where blind WUA members (a majority being women) have sustainable access to land and water. The use of community animators in tandem with extension staff was catalytic, and faciliatory mechanisms were set up for the acceptance of this category of water users.

GENDER APPROACH

WUA membership was open to all members of the target group who would benefit from the results of the project as smallholder dry season irrigators (gardeners), livestock owners, and fishermen. The percentage of women who became ordinary members was around 38 percent (and thus slightly below the 40 percent target of the project). At some dam sites, this figure, however, was much higher, up to 80 percent. Typically, general meetings were held once a month, and a quorum for decision-making authority was spelled out in the WUA bylaws. Although a woman did not become chairperson, it was common for the executive

committee's treasurer to be a woman. Furthermore, women have formed an exclusively women's group that provides a platform to discuss and form a unified opinion before any major decision is discussed in the WUA.

The main activities of the project that helped achieve the gender-mainstreaming-related objectives of the project include (1) recruitment of a gender officer, (2) farmer training demonstrations (FTDs), and (3) functional literacy groups (FLGs).

LACOSREP II employed a gender officer on a contract basis to ensure the objectives of appraisal were met; this was an effective strategy.

FTDs were conducted based on community needs assessment and planning exercises. Farmers were trained, among other things, in composting and vegetable growing. Out of 6,266 participating farmers, 40 percent (2,546) were women. This shows a considerable achievement by the project in getting a good representation of women within the groups.

FLGs, which were originally not included in the project design, were introduced during the implementation of the project to teach beneficiaries (most of them women) numeracy and literacy in indigenous languages. These groups were also aimed at establishing solidarity among groups for other purposes such as collective work and microfinance.

Other special, transitional measures taken to promote women's participation in all aspects of the project included charging slightly lower fees to women members of WUAs, although this was not applied throughout all the associations, and accepting illiterate women in community credit management committees.[1]

BENEFITS AND IMPACTS

The overall impact of LACOSREP II on beneficiary communities has been considerable in the areas of food security, income generation, cohesion, literacy, and promotion of gender issues.

Women are not traditionally land owners in this region, but the WUA system has given them direct access to dry season irrigated land. As a consequence, women play a much greater role in the management of irrigation; this is highly visible at meetings in which they speak up to represent their own views. The project has undoubtedly been influential in promoting these changes and making them sustainable. Women can grow vegetables more easily: this both contributes to food security and improved nutrition and generates cash.

Given a demonstrated, strong correlation between widowhood and extreme poverty, the inclusion of vulnerable women-headed households in at least some WUAs is an indication of the project's having been able to reach IFAD's target group.

WUAs and FLGs have also had an impact in creating modalities for increased social solidarity; the previous patterns of dispersed household settlement are changing as communities develop and perceive a need to act together more coherently in accessing key tools and input in community development.

FLGs have also provided an arena for women to cooperate and organize collective income-generating activities. The project's interim evaluation report (IFAD 2006) reported the changing dynamics of the household decision-making patterns. Husbands were reported to be listening increasingly to their wives' views on issues concerning the household and even passing on financial responsibilities to their wives, as they consider them to be financially knowledgeable. Access to greater capital and means of transport, such as bicycles, has undoubtedly accelerated women's entry into the market. The livestock component, by increasing access to investments in goats, chickens, and guinea fowl, has played a similar role.

As a contribution to institutional sustainability and empowerment, WUAs were envisaged to evolve into a "council" at the district level. Formation of district WUA councils was embedded in the project as one of the exit strategies. To date, only one council was formed with elected WUA council executives, with an operational bank account and draft by-laws. Other WUA councils are under development, and an important issue remains how to mainstream gender considerations into their operational plans systematically.

LIMITATIONS AND CONSTRAINTS

The project has successfully involved women in WUAs, but it has not been as successful on other fronts, such as providing mitigation measures for water-borne diseases. Moreover, a large number of hand-dug wells (about 40 percent of the total), which were aimed at reducing the workload of women in fetching water, are not functional (IFAD 2006). In some communities water for domestic use is fetched from the small-scale dam, which creates health and social problems.

It was also observed in some cases that plot sizes were not always equal in practice. Plot allocation differed according to, among other means, patrilineal versus matrilineal population groups; the personalities and the "morphology" of

local traditional authorities, for example, the degree of decision-making power of the traditional landowner, that is, the man descendent of the community's founding lineage—the *tindana*, earth priest, or *tigatu*—versus that of other clan heads ("headmen"), family heads, chiefs (called "skins"), and government; and the degree of "urbanization" and "politicization" (IFAD 2006).

Paradoxically, where women have access to equal (to that of men) irrigation plots, evidence suggests that these plots are overfragmented, in part because of social relations and in part because of women having limited time for agricultural labor and maximization of the output from their irrigated plot. This implies that gender-equity issues must be contextualized in project design and implementation.[2]

Another major challenge lies with ensuring effective operation and maintenance of district-level WUA councils. Line ministries responsible for the development of WUA councils have limited resources and capacities at the district level.

LESSONS LEARNED AND ISSUES FOR WIDER APPLICABILITY

- Consideration of multiple users and organizing them is a sure way to obtain beneficiaries' commitment and active participation in project activities.
- Domestic water inclusion needs to be done carefully: domestic water supply is a basic need and requires adequate technical measures to address health issues properly. Also, addressing domestic water requirements is a way to give women an opportunity to engage more in income-generating activities.
- Social equity and inclusive targeting of the marginalized and disabled rural poor can be mainstreamed into WUA activities.
- WUAs to some extent secure a "minimum platform" to ensure greater participation of women in the WUAs' decision-making processes if membership criteria are transparent and equitable.
- Bottom-up approaches to WUA formations thrive where legal and institutional frameworks exist and decentralization is advanced.
- Upscaling WUAs to district, regional, and national WUA councils will be self-empowering, but also the means for WUAs to engage in policy dialogue, advocacy, and autonomy at higher levels, where attention can be brought to women's needs.

The Gambia: Lowlands Agricultural Development Programme (LADEP)

Rice production in The Gambia is traditionally a woman's domain, with the men concentrating their farming efforts on cereals and livestock in the uplands. Rice land ownership in the traditional system is vested to men first settlers who allocate rice land to their wives and daughters. The rest of the women rice farmers (later settlers) depend on borrowing rice land on an annual basis, without the assurance of availability (renting or share cropping of farmland is not common in The Gambia). This traditional land tenure system discourages landless women rice producers (later settlers) to participate in any land reclamation efforts, because the land does not belong to them, and they have no secured access to land, even in a midterm perspective. Owners of large tracts of land cannot provide the labor required for reclamation of these lands, and therefore land reclamation is not implemented. For successful implementation of self-help (through the provision of labor and locally available materials), the issue of access to land had to be resolved.

PROJECT OBJECTIVES AND DESCRIPTION

The main objective of the IFAD-supported Lowlands Agricultural Development Programme (LADEP; 1997–2005) in

The Gambia was to involve local communities in the development process of national socioeconomic issues and to have them assume control over some activities and be empowered to make their own decisions on matters pertaining to their development.

The objectives of the innovation were as follows:

- Mobilize the beneficiaries to provide the self-help labor required to rehabilitate or develop rice fields.
- Create the environment under which landless women rice producers would permanently own land.
- Make sure that the beneficiaries take over the responsibility of repairing and maintaining the infrastructure after the project phases out.

LADEP was targeted to benefit 8,960 rice farmers under various rice-growing ecologies in the country, on 8,075 hectares of land. The intended beneficiaries were the farmers, mainly women (about 90 percent), who participated in the land reclamation efforts.

INNOVATIVE ACTIVITIES IN THE PROJECT

During the design phase of LADEP, community participation was made mandatory. The main innovative activity of the project was allocation of land in exchange for labor provided to rehabilitate swamps for rice production.

This innovation was chosen from a range of options identified by focus group discussions (part of the site management committee [SMC], itself part of the village development committee [VDC] introduced by the government):

Option 1: Use of machinery for the construction of the required infrastructure without changes in the land tenure system. Here ownership of the infrastructures, an important factor for future operation and maintenance, could not be secured.

> **What's innovative?** Community participation was made mandatory during the design phase. Land was allocated in exchange for labor provided to rehabilitate swamps for rice production. A site selection committee and intercommunity negotiations were set up to look into cross-cutting issues in the community; subsequently, a "land for labor" agreement, valued under traditional law, was reached between the program's beneficiaries and the founder settlers of the community.

Option 2: Construction of the infrastructures by the landowners. This option faced labor shortages by the landowners.

Option 3: Devolution of ownership of an equal piece of land from traditional landowners to a few men and mostly women of the communities who participated in the reclamation efforts. With the devolution of land ownership, the people had a clear incentive to contribute their labor to reclamation efforts.

The program's other innovative features included setting up site selection committee and intercommunity negotiations. Site management committees were established to look into cross-cutting issues in the community related to rice production, particularly the provision of labor and land allocation. The committees were grouped under 35 district-level farmers' associations. A legal constitution as a community-based organization was prepared for the farmers' associations and adopted in a participatory manner, before their official registration. Institutional sustainability is one of their goals, as well as an increased contribution of farmers to local decision-making processes.

Intracommunity negotiations were facilitated using the participatory rapid appraisal (PRA) method to find solutions to common community problems. The PRA method was first introduced to extension services in charge of mobilizing communities under program activities and was the foundation of the self-help approach adopted under LADEP. Through these negotiations, a "land for labor" agreement was reached between the program's beneficiaries and the founder settlers of the community. When such an agreement is made at the community level, it gains legal value under traditional law.

GENDER-RESPONSIVE ACTIVITIES

The project's innovation activity addressed the landlessness of women, traditional rice growers, and consisted of transferring the ownership of an equal piece of land from traditional landowners to the few men and mostly women of the communities who participated in the reclamation efforts. These "land against labor agreements" between landless individuals and founder settlers (landowners) were made in the presence of the whole community, which conferred a traditional legal status to the agreement. This option was chosen because of the following advantages: the allocation of land to landless women farmers who participate in reclamation efforts and the recognition of the need for women farmers to own land if they are to invest their labor in its reclamation.

The innovation of providing land ownership to landless rural people, mainly women, helped provide the long-term incentives required to mobilize beneficiaries to (1) provide the labor necessary to rehabilitate rice fields and (2) assume responsibility for infrastructure operation and maintenance after the close of the program. The innovation brought about changes in the traditional land tenure system. In the traditional system, land tenure was held by founder settlers (who were sometimes women). LADEP brought about the devolution of individually owned land to the community, and this new common land was equitably redistributed and shared among individuals, mainly women, who participated in land reclamation works.

The main factors that facilitated the innovation and played an important role in the success of the project are the following:

- The setting up of SMCs to look into the community's cross-cutting issues, especially the provision of labor and land allocation
- The facilitation of intracommunity negotiations to find solutions to common community problems.

Other actions that contributed to the success of the project include the steps taken at the design phase of the project to ensure community participation in the decision-making process:

- Public extension services sensitized communities concerned with the lowlands on LADEP.
- Public extension services collected formal requests for assistance.
- A community mobilization coordinator (belonging to the Department of Community Development, delegated to the project) visited selected communities to establish SMCs, as part of the VDCs established by the government when they existed. The process involved participatory rural appraisal, focus group discussions in which beneficiaries and the local government authorities were presented the advantages and disadvantages of each option and supported the elaboration of community action plans.

BENEFITS AND IMPACTS

The innovation brought about changes in the traditional land tenure system. In this traditional system, land tenure was held by founder settlers (women in a few instances). Yet the innovation represents the devolution of individually owned land back to the community and the sharing of this new common land property among the individuals who participated in land reclamation works.

The innovation settles the issue of land ownership in the project intervention sites. Land tenure security for the land poor has contributed to food security in no small way because of more land reclamation efforts and more land being cropped.

Planners assessed the performance of the innovation and made an impact assessment of the project. The main findings are the following:

- Poverty is streamlined as more women farmers own land and confidently work it for production. Women beneficiaries now have permanent ownership of land, and their children will inherit ownership of the land.
- Women have benefited greatly. LADEP was targeted to benefit 8,960 rice farmers in various rice-growing environments in the country, on a total area of 8,075 hectares of land. LADEP reached 24,684 farmers (90 percent of them—a total of 22,216—women) and reclaimed a total of 7,481 hectares of land.
- Community cohesion has increased.
- Beneficiaries reported a 30–100 percent increase in food production. The impact assessment found that most communities report that with upland and lowland crops they are now food secure.
- Either by water retention or swamp access, the LADEP experience resulted in an additional three months each year of rice self-sufficiency.
- Food self-reliance and household food security were improved as more land was put under cultivation. The advantage of the process followed lies in its self-regulation: communities develop the area they can actually manage to reclaim and cultivate.

LESSONS LEARNED AND ISSUES FOR WIDER APPLICABILITY

The LADEP experience provided evidence that people-led project interventions contribute to the sustainability of change. Also, the following principles or lessons were identified:

- Land reforms have to be initiated by the beneficiaries and agreed upon by mutually binding arrangements (under traditional or other law).
- Household food security can be improved if the landless are assisted in securing land permanently.

- Poverty can effectively be reduced when rice land is equitably distributed.

The key contextual elements that should be considered as prerequisites for replication outside of The Gambia are the following:

- *Social:* The communities, including the landowner minority, should be prepared to negotiate favorable land allocation systems.
- *Regulatory:* Land reforms under local government reforms (decentralization processes) should exist to support the innovation.
- *Institutional:* The village development committee concept, through which negotiations with site management committees can be jump-started, must be present.

NOTES

Overview

This Overview was prepared by Juan A. Sagardoy (Consultant) and reviewed by Chitra Deshpande Gunnar Larson, and Catherine Ragasa (Consultants); Sasha Koo (FAO); Maria Hartl (IFAD); and Nilufar Ahmad, Indira Ekanayake, and Anne Kuriakose (World Bank).

1. *FAO's Gender and Development Plan of Action 2008–2013,* conference, Thirty-fourth Session, Rome, November 17–24, ftp://ftp.fao.org/docrep/fao/meeting/012/k0721e.pdf.

2. Additional material is available at the GAL *eSourcebook* at www.worldbank.org.

3. FAO, "Gender and Food Security Statistics," www.fao.org/Gender/stats/genstats.htm.

4. See also Technical Note 3 in the GAL *eSourcebook* at www.worldbank.org.

Thematic Note I

This Thematic Note was prepared by Barbara van Koppen (Consultant) and Anne Kuriakose (World Bank) and reviewed by Robina Wahaj (Consultant); Rudolph Cleveringa, Maria Hartl, and Audrey Nepveu (IFAD); and Indira Ekanayake and Riikka Rajalahti (World Bank). Many concepts and evidence in this note are based on the findings of the action-research project "Models for Implementing Multiple-Use Water Supply Systems for Enhanced Land and Water Productivity, Rural Livelihoods and Gender Equity" (www.musproject.net), supported by the Challenge Program on Water and Food of the Consultative Group of International Agricultural Research (www.waterforfood.org). Initial findings of this research project are also synthesized in Van Koppen, Moriarty, and Boelee (2006).

1. Ede Ijjasz-Vasquez, Mexico World Water Forum, PROD-WAT 2006, www.musproject.net/content/download/810/8113/file/MUS%20Stockholm%20meeting.pdf.

2. Lenton, GWP, Mexico World Water Forum, PRODWAT 2006, www.musgroup.net/content/download/555/5690/file/Newsletter%20.

3. www.musproject.net.

Thematic Note 2

This Thematic Note was prepared by Suman Gautam (Consultant) and Anne Kuriakose (World Bank) and reviewed by Karin Kemper and Catherine Tovey (World Bank) and the GW-MATE team; and Indira Ekanayake (World Bank).

1. Both ENDS, "Effective Gender Mainstreaming in Water Management for Sustainable Livelihoods: From Guidelines to Practice," Both ENDS Working Paper Series, November 2006, www.bothends.org.

2. Eva M. Rathgeber, "Women, Men and Water-Resource Management in Africa," www.idrc.ca/en/ev-31108-201-1-DO_TOPIC.html.

Innovative Activity Profile 1

This Innovative Activity Profile was prepared by Robina Wahaj (Consultant) and reviewed by Catherine Ragasa (Consultant); Moses Abukari, Maria Hartl, and Audrey Nepveu (IFAD); and Indira Ekanayake (World Bank).

1. CCMCs assisted in group mobilization and training and were responsible for screening loan requests using local knowledge of the community and the groups, and assisted in loan recovery. The groups were required to have at least three women members out of seven.

2. IFAD and GTZ, "Knowledge Profiling: Promoting Easy Access to Knowledge and Experience Generated in Projects and Programmes: A Manual," www.ruralpovertyportal.org/english/topics/water/ifad/manual/kp.pdf.

Innovative Activity Profile 2

This Innovative Activity Profile was prepared by Robina Wahaj (IFAD) and reviewed by Catherine Ragasa (Consultant); Moses Abukari, Maria Hartl, and Audrey Nepveu (IFAD); and Indira Ekanayake (World Bank). This Profile was adopted from Nepveu, Fye, and Cleveringa (2005).

REFERENCES

Overview

Centre on Housing Rights and Evictions (COHRE). 2006. *In Search of Equality. A Survey of Law and Practice Related to Women's Inheritance Rights in the Middle East and North Africa (MENA) Region.* Geneva: COHRE.

Gender and Water Alliance (GWA) and Both ENDS. 2006. *Effective Gender Mainstreaming in Water Management for Sustainable Livelihoods: From Guidelines to Practice.* Both ENDS working paper series. Available on CD from Both ENDS, Nieuwe Keizersgracht, 45 1018 VC, Amsterdam, the Netherlands.

International Fund for Agricultural Development (IFAD). 2007. *Gender and Water Securing Water for Improved Rural Livelihoods: The Multiple-Uses System Approach.* Rome: IFAD.

Sagardoy, Juan Antonio, and Atef Hamdy. 2005. *Training of Trainers Manual on Integration of Gender Dimension in Water Resources Use and Management.* Bari, Italy: CIHEAM, MAI.

Sagardoy, Juan Antonio, Vittora Pinca, Nicola Lamaddalena, Rosanna Quagliariello, Dora Chimonidou, and Raouf Guelloubi. 2007. *Mainstreaming Gender Dimensions in Water Management for Food Security and Food Safety.* Option Méditerráeennes, Series A, No. 77. Centre International de Hautes Etudes Agronomiques Méditerranéennes. Bari, Italy: Mediterranean Agronomic Institute of Bari.

Stalker, Linda Prokopy. 2004. "Women's Participation in Rural Water Supply Projects in India: Is It Moving beyond Tokenism and Does It Matter?" *Water Policy* 2: 103–16.

United Nations Population Fund (UNFPA). 2002. *Water: A Critical Resource.* New York: UNFPA.

Van Koppen, Barbara, Patrick Moriarty, and Eline Boelee. 2006. "Multiple-Use Water Services to Advance the Millennium Development Goals." IWMI Research Report 98, International Water Management Institute, Challenge Program on Water and Food, and International Water and Sanitation Center, Colombo, Sri Lanka.

World Bank. 2006. *Reengaging in Agricultural Water Management: Challenges and Options. Series Directions in Development.* Washington, DC: World Bank.

———. Forthcoming. "Gender, Participation and Decentralization in Agricultural Water Management." Investment Note 10.1, update for *Shaping the Future of Water for Agriculture—A Sourcebook for Investment in Agricultural Water Management.* Washington, DC: World Bank.

———. Forthcoming. "Poverty-Gender Issues in Agricultural Water Management Policy." Investment Note 10.3, update for *Shaping the Future of Water for Agriculture—A Sourcebook for Investment in Agricultural Water Management.* Washington, DC: World Bank.

———. Forthcoming. "Gender-Sensitive Planning, Monitoring and Evaluation in Agricultural Water Management."

Investment Note 10.4, update for *Shaping the Future of Water for Agriculture—A Sourcebook for Investment in Agricultural Water Management.* Washington, DC: World Bank.

Thematic Note I

Binswanger, Hans P., and Tuu-Van Nguyen. 2005. "A Step by Step Guide to Scale Up Community Driven Development." In *African Water Laws: Plural Legislative Frameworks for Rural Water Management in Africa,* ed. Barbara Van Koppen, John A. Butterworth, and Ibrahima Juma, 11-1–11-20, Proceedings of a Workshop held in Johannesburg, South Africa, January 26–28. Pretoria: International Water Management Institute.

Butterworth John A., Patrick B. Moriarty, Minnie Venter Hildebrand, Barbara van Koppen, Barbara Schreiner, and Dirk Versfeld, eds. 2003. *Proceedings of the International Symposium on Water, Poverty, and Productive Uses of Water at the Household Level,* Muldersdrift, South Africa, January 21–23. Natural Resources Institute, IRC International Water and Sanitation Centre, Department of Water Affairs and Forestry, International Water Management Institute.

Clasen, Thomas, and Sandy Cairncross. 2004. "Editorial: Household Water Management: Refining the Dominant Paradigm." *Tropical Medicine and International Health* 9 (2): 187–91.

Cullis, James, and Barbara van Koppen. 2005. "Applying the Gini Coefficient to Measure Inequality of Water Use in the Olifants River Water Management Area." Unpublished paper, Pretoria: International Water Management Institute and Ninham Consulting Services.

Esrey, S. A., J. B. Potash, L. Roberts, and C. Schiff. 1991. "Effects of Improved Water Supply and Sanitation on Ascariasis, Diarrhoea, Dracunculiasis, Hookworm Infection, Schistsomiasis, and Trachoma." *Bulletin of the World Health Organization* 69 (5): 609–21.

Hebert, James R. 1985. "Effects of Water Quality and Water Quantity on Nutritional Status: Findings from a South Indian Community." *Bulletin of the World Health Organization* 63 (1): 143–55.

Howard, Guy, and Jamie Bartram. 2003. "Domestic Water Quantity, Service Level and Health." Informal paper WHO/SDE/WSH/03.02, Water Engineering and Development Centre, Loughborough University, U.K., and Water, Sanitation and Health Programme, World Health Organization, Geneva.

Hussain, Intizar. 2005. *Pro-Poor Intervention Strategies in Irrigated Agriculture in Asia: Poverty in Irrigated Agriculture. Issues, Lessons, Options and Guidelines. Bangladesh, China, India, Indonesia, Pakistan and Vietnam.* Final synthesis report. Manila: Asian Development Bank and International Water Management Institute.

Jensen, Peter K., Yutaka Matsuno, Wim van der Hoek, and Sandy Cairncross. 2001. "Limitations of Irrigation Water Quality Guidelines from a Multiple Use Perspective." *Irrigation and Drainage Systems* 15 (2): 117–28.

Kuriakose, Anne T., Waqar A. Jehangir, and Mehmood ul-Hassan. Forthcoming. "Will the Diggi Go Dry? Multiple Uses of Irrigation Water in Punjab, Pakistan." *Society and Natural Resources.*

Mahfouz, A. A. R., M. Abdel-Moneim, R. A. G. Al-Erian, and O. M. Al-Amari. 1995. "Impact of Chlorination of Water on Domestic Storage Tanks on Childhood Diarhhoea: A Community Trial in the Rural Areas of Saudi Arabia." *Journal of Tropical Medicine and Hygiene* 98: 126–20.

Maluleke, Theo, Vincent Thomas, Tessa Cousins, Stef Smits, and Patrick Moriarty. 2005. "Securing Water to Enhance Local Livelihoods (SWELL): Community-Based Planning of Multiple Uses of Water in Partnership with Service Providers." Unpublished paper, AWARD, CARE, IRC, and MUS, Bushbuckridge, South Africa.

Mintz, Eric D., Fred M. Reiff, and Robert V. Tauxe. 1995. "Safe Water Treatment and Storage in the Home: A Practical New Strategy to Prevent Waterborne Disease." *Journal of the American Medical Association* 273: 948–53.

Quick, R. E., A. Kimura, A. Thevos, M. Tembo, I. Shamputa, L. Hutwagner, and E. Mintz. 2002. "Diarrhoea Prevention through Household-level Water Disinfection and Safe Storage in Zambia." *American Journal of Tropical Medicine and Hygiene* 66 (5): 584–89.

Quick, R. E., L. Venczel, E. Mintz, L. Soleto, J. Aparicio, M. Gironaz, L. Hutwagner, K. Greene, C. Bopp, K. Maloney, D. Chavez, M. Sobsey, and R. V. Tauxe. 1999. "Diarrhoea Prevention in Bolivia through Point-of-Use Water Treatment and Safe Storage: A Promising New Strategy." *Epidemiological Infections* 122 (1): 83–90.

Reller, M. E., C. E. Mendoza, M. B. Lopes, M. Alvarez, R. Hoekstra, C. A. Olson, K. G. Baier, B. H. Keswick, and S. P. Luby. 2003. "A Randomized Controlled Trial of Household-Based Flocculant-Disinfectant Drinking Water Treatment for Diarrhoea Prevention in Rural Guatemala." *American Journal of Tropical Medicine and Hygiene* 69 (4): 411–19.

Republic of South Africa (RSA), Department of Water Affairs and Forestry. 2005. "A Draft Position Paper for Water Allocation Reform in South Africa: Towards a Framework for Water Allocation Planning." Discussion document, Directorate Water Allocations, Department of Water Affairs and Forestry, Pretoria.

Roberts, Michael. 2003. "Ceramic Water Purifier: Cambodia Field Tests. International Development Enterprise, Denver.

Shah, Tushaar, Barbara van Koppen, Douglas J. Merrey, Marna de Lange, and Madar Samad. 2002. *Institutional Alternatives in African Smallholder Irrigation: Lessons from International Experience with Irrigation Management Transfer.* Research Report 60. Colombo, Sri Lanka: IWMI.

Upadhyah, Bhawana, Madar Samad, and Mark Giordano. 2005. "Livelihoods and Gender Roles in Drip-Irrigation Technology: A Case of Nepal." IWMI Working Paper 87, International Water Management Institute, Colombo, Sri Lanka.

Van der Hoek, Wim, Flemming Konradsen, Jeroen H. J. Ensink, Muhammad Mudasser, and Peter K. Jensen. 2001. "Irrigation Water as a Source of Drinking Water: Is Safe Use Possible?" *Tropical Medicine and International Health* 6: 46–55.

Van Koppen, Barbara, Patrick Moriarty, and Eline Boelee. 2006. *Multiple Use Water Services to Advance the Millennium Development Goals.* Research Report No. 98. Colombo, Sri Lanka: International Water Management Institute.

World Health Organization (WHO). 2004. *Guidelines for Drinking-Water Quality,* 3rd ed. *Volume 1—Recommendations.* Geneva: WHO.

Thematic Note 2

Caldwell Caldwell, Bruce K., John C. Caldwell, N. Mitra, and Wayne Smith. 2002. "Tubewells and Arsenic in Bangladesh: Challenging a Public Health Success Story." Australian National University, Canberra.

Gautam, Suman Rimal. 2006. *Incorporating Groundwater Irrigation: Technology Dynamics and Conjunctive Water Management in the Nepal Terai.* Wageningen University Water Resources Series 8. Hyderabad: Orient Longman.

Gender and Water Alliance (GWA) and Both ENDS. 2006. *Effective Gender Mainstreaming in Water Management for Sustainable Livelihoods: From Guidelines to Practice.* Both ENDS working paper series. Available on CD from Both ENDS, Nieuwe Keizersgracht, 45 1018 VC, Amsterdam, the Netherlands.

Kulkarni, Semma. 2005. "Looking Back, Thinking Forward: The Khudawadi Experience with Access to Irrigation for Women and Landless." In *Flowing Upstream: Empowering Women through Water Management Initiatives in India,* ed. Sara Ahmed. Thousand Oaks, CA: Sage.

Van Koppen, Barbara. 1999. "Targeting Irrigation Support to Poor Women and Men." *International Journal of Water Resources Development* 15 (1/2): 121–40.

Zwarteveen, Margreet. 2006. "Wedlock or Deadlock: Feminists' Attempts to Engage Irrigation Engineers." Ph.D. dissertation. Wageningen University, the Netherlands.

Innovative Activity Profile 1

International Fund for Agricultural Development (IFAD). 2003. "A Brief Institutional Assessment of Water User Associations in Northern Ghana: Early Stages of Pro-Poor Local Institutional Development in Irrigated Smallholder Agriculture." Working Paper 2, Ghana design mission for Country Strategic Opportunities Programme (COSOP), IFAD, Rome, prepared by Norman M. Messer.

———. 2006. *Upper East Region Land Conservation and Smallholder Rehabilitation Project (LACOSREP)—Phase II.* Interim Evaluation Report, IFAD, Rome.

Innovative Activity Profile 2

Nepveu de Villemarceau, Audrey, John Fye, and Rudolph Cleveringa. 2005. "Rice Land for Labour Agreements Benefiting Women: the Lowlands Agricultural Development Programme (LADEP), Gambia." Case Study, IFAD, Rome.

FURTHER READING

Overview

Food and Agriculture Organization of the United Nations (FAO). 2001. *Irrigation Sector Guide. Socioeconomic Gender Analysis Programme (SEAGA).* Rome: FAO.

Thematic Note 1

Bakker Margaretha, Randolph Barker, Ruth Meinzen-Dick, and Flemming Konradsen, eds. 1999. *Multiple Uses of Water in Irrigated Areas: A Case Study from Sri Lanka.* SWIM Paper 8, International Water Management Institute, Colombo, Sri Lanka.

International Fund for Agricultural Development (IFAD). 2007. "Gender and Water: Securing Water for Improved Rural Livelihoods: The Multiple-Uses System Approach." IFAD, Rome.

Moriarty, Patrick, John Butterworth, and Barbara van Koppen, eds. 2004. "Beyond Domestic. Case Studies on Poverty and Productive Uses of Water at the Household Level." IRC Technical Papers Series 41, IRC, NRI, and IWMI, Delft.

PRODWAT Thematic Group. International Water and Sanitation Center. Available at www.prodwat.watsan.net.

Thematic Note 2

Deere, Carmen Diana, and Magdalena Leon. 1997. "Women and Land Rights in the Latin American Neo-Liberal Counter Reforms." Working Paper No. 264, Women in Development, Michigan State University.

Kuriakose, Anne, Indira Ahluwalia, Smita Malpani, Kristine Hansen, Eija Pehu, and Arunima Dhar. 2005. "Gender Mainstreaming in Water Resources Management." Agriculture and Rural Development Internal Paper, World Bank, Washington, DC.

Prakash, Anjal. 2005. *The Dark Zone: Groundwater Irrigation, Politics and Social Power in North Gujarat.* Wageningen University Water Resources Series 7. Hyderabad: Orient Longman.

Stallings, Anne Marie. 2006. "History, Cultural Knowledge, and Property Rights in the Emergence of Groundwater Irrigation in Cochabamba, Bolivia." Ph.D. dissertation. Catholic University of America, Washington, DC.

Van Koppen, Barbara, and Simeen Mahmud. 1996. *Women and Water Pumps in Bangladesh.* London: Intermediate Technology Publications.

World Bank. 1990. "Nepal: "Bhairahawa Lumbini Groundwater Irrigation Project III." Project ID: P010348, World Bank, Washington, DC.

———. 2004. "Arsenic Contamination of Groundwater in South and East Asian Countries: Toward a More Effective Operational Response." Volume 1, Policy Report No. 31303, World Bank, Washington, DC.

Innovative Activity Profile I

International Fund for Agricultural Development (IFAD). 2001. *Thematic Study on Water User Associations in IFAD Projects.* Vol. I: *Main Report.* IFAD Office of Evaluation and Studies, Rome.

Gender in Agricultural Innovation and Education

Overview

TRENDS IN GENDER ACCESS TO AGRICULTURAL INFORMATION AND TECHNOLOGY

Agricultural extension programs grew through the nineteenth and twentieth centuries as a means of making the results of agricultural research available to farmers. The demand for extension services in the United States and Europe grew as farmers adapted their practices to new geographical areas, new crops, and urban markets. During the second half of the twentieth century, research concentrated on increasing food production to feed the mushrooming world population while extension services in developing countries concentrated on encouraging farmers to shift to higher-yielding crops and breeds.

To support this effort, the World Bank supported the Training and Visit (ToT) extension in more than 70 countries between 1975 and 1995. A centralized national public extension system, it provided information to extensionists who disseminated it through (overwhelmingly men) "contact farmers" on the basis of their willingness to incorporate promoted innovations. By the mid-1990s, however, it became evident that centralized extension systems tended to promote innovations that benefited farmers with more assets and higher levels of education. As a result, the World Bank, the Food and Agriculture Organization of the United Nations (FAO), and the International Fund for Agricultural Development (IFAD) began investing in a broader range of extension approaches, including those that encouraged a larger role for nongovernmental organizations (NGOs), producer organizations, and the private sector.

By 2001 an increase in rural poverty and the number of farmers left behind became more evident, and the FAO and World Bank developed a shared vision for an integrated approach to agricultural education, research, and extension: *Agricultural Knowledge and Information Systems for Rural Development (AKIS/RD): Strategic Vision and Guiding Principles* (FAO and World Bank 2000). Knowledge and information systems, made up of farmers, agricultural educators, researchers, and extensionists, would be enhanced to better link people and organizations to promote mutual learning and to generate, share, and use agriculture-related technology, knowledge, and information for better farming and improved livelihoods (box 7.1). The concern remained for increasing the benefits of agricultural development for women and indigenous peoples in the face of an increasingly globalized food system.

Since that time the demand for high-value crops, livestock, and fisheries products has been spreading beyond the urban centers in Europe and North America to cities in countries such as China and India; this has provided new opportunities for small-scale farmers who can organize to incorporate production, packing, handling, and marketing technologies and practices so as to have a comparative

257

Box 7.1	Gender and Knowledge Systems

- Both women and men manage sectors of complex smallholder production systems.
- When gender is ignored, there is a cost to people"s well-being and sustainable growth.
- Knowledge is not transferred; it is generated and exchanged in a continuous learning process.
- Farmers, agricultural educators, researchers, extensionists, and traders form parts of knowledge and information networks.
- Rules and mechanisms governing the way different actors, organizations, enterprises, and groups interact to supply and demand knowledge and technology are critical for equitable development.

Source: Compiled by the author from various sources.

Box 7.2	The Agricultural Innovation System

An *agricultural innovation system* is "a network of organizations, enterprises, and individuals focused on bringing new products, new processes, and new forms of organization into economic use, together with the institutions and policies that affect their behavior and performance. The innovation systems concept embraces not only the science suppliers but the totality and interaction of actors involved in innovation as well. It extends beyond the creation of knowledge to encompass the factors affecting demand for and use of knowledge in novel and useful ways."

Source: World Bank 2007b: vi.

advantage in these markets. However, if women, indigenous people, and resource-limited farmers are to take advantage of this rapidly changing demand for diverse types of staple and high-value food products, then extension systems will need to focus on the organizational, technical, and management skills these groups need to be competitive. Moreover, it will be impossible for these less-advantaged groups to pay for these services, which makes it imperative to rethink the trends toward privatizing or outsourcing extension, or both, which until recently has been considered a public good.

GENDER AND THE AGRICULTURAL INNOVATION SYSTEMS FRAMEWORK

Since the Fourth World Congress on Women, held in Beijing in 1985, efforts have been made by national governments and international agencies to provide agricultural extension to women and to increase rural women's access to education. The Farming Systems perspective of the 1980s encouraged countries and organizations to look beyond the idea of a household whose members had common interests, for an understanding of the intrahousehold gender relations regarding production responsibilities in agriculture. However, the prevailing stereotype assumed that men "heads of households" made most decisions or were in charge of most aspects of the production processes in which small-scale farm units were engaged. This view impeded progress in taking women farmers into account as both key actors and stakeholders.

Since 1995 information regarding the multiple roles that women play in agricultural production and trade has been mainstreamed. It is now generally known that women and men have different roles within the household and that these roles differ in different societies and in different kinds of production units: small-scale/subsistence, medium-scale, and larger/commercial farm households. We have also learned that it is more difficult for limited-resource farmers, both men and women, to innovate because of the risks and investment required. So, although new opportunities will open up for smaller-scale women farmers to meet the demand for high-value, labor-intensive products, proposals to privatize extension services will need to be reviewed if these farmers are to benefit from them.

An attempt to rethink the way we look at agricultural systems, from farm to table globally, is the Agricultural Innovation Systems (AIS) framework that the World Bank is developing (box 7.2). This framework argues that diversity, inclusion, and participatory approaches are critical to building the quality of social capital needed for resilient and sustainable innovation systems. It focuses on strengthening the system from both the supply and demand sides of the broad spectrum of science and technology generation through the exchange activities of organizations, enterprises, and groups. The AIS framework takes into account the many actors along the value chain, as well as diverse organizational forms that can facilitate education, research, and extension systems as well as the practices, attitudes, and policies that frame agricultural production and trade. It moves the discussion from seeds and breeds to one that centers on actors and stakeholders

Table 7.1 Comparison of Approaches to Agricultural Innovation and Gender

Themes	Training and visit system	Agricultural knowledge/ information groups	AIS/Farmer organizations
General features			
Purpose	Planning capacity for agricultural research, technology development, and technology transfer	Strengthened communication and knowledge delivery services to people in the rural sector	Strengthened capacity for innovation throughout the agricultural production and marketing system
Actors	National agricultural research organizations, agricultural universities, extension services, and farmers	National agricultural research organizations, agricultural universities, extension services, farmers, NGOs, and entrepreneurs in rural areas	Potentially all actors in the public and private sectors involved in the creation, diffusion, adaptation, and use of all types of knowledge relevant to agricultural production and marketing
Organizing principle	Using science to create inventions	Access agricultural knowledge	Using knowledge in new ways for social and economic change
Nature of capacity strengthening	Infrastructure and human resource development	Strengthened communication between actors in rural areas	Strengthened interactions between actors; institutional development and change to support interaction, learning, and innovation; creation of an enabling environment
Markets	No market integration	Low market integration	High market integration
Gender dimension			
Gender inclusion	Inclusion is a problem	Improved inclusion	Full engagement of actors
Research agenda	Not gender sensitive	Becoming more gender sensitive because of greater participation of farmers	Becoming more gender sensitive because of greater engagement of farmers but must have explicit gender dimension
Role of women	Women are seen are beneficiaries of the process	Women are seen as active participants in the process	Women are seen are critical actors
Gender focus	Focus is on gender difference of access to technology and services	Focus is on gender difference of access to technology and services and on participation and representation in the research process	Focus is on gender difference in leadership and capacity to influence policy-making processes; social dimension and market linkages are made stronger but must ensure gender inclusion
Institutionalizing gender	Personnel policies and gender balance in relevant institutions are started but gender imbalance remains a major concern	Personnel policies and gender balance in relevant institutions are improved; building capacity for women scientists and farmers' organizations is the focus	Institutional development is created to support interaction and to ensure full engagement in policy-making processes but must have explicit gender dimension

Sources: General Features: World Bank 2007b; Gender Dimension: personal communication with Eija Pehu and Catherine Ragasa.

together with the rules and mechanisms that govern the way the different actors interact (World Bank 2007b: 135). Table 7.1 compares the gender dimension among different approaches to investment for agricultural innovation.

The AIS framework considers women to be critical actors in an innovation system. From this perspective, innovation is viewed as a social and economic process that draws on discovery and invention but recognizes that the most important role that these innovations have is to improve the livelihoods of all people, especially those of women and other vulnerable groups. From the perspective of the AIS framework, the active engagement of women is no longer only a right but is an imperative to future farming, processing, and marketing systems that can improve livelihoods and agribusiness development. This framework proposes that innovation involves not only new actors but also new roles and many relationships that can sustain knowledge generation and learning if technical and economic successes, together with social and environmental sustainability, are to be achieved (Spielman and Birner 2008).

From this perspective, the improvement of rural livelihoods will require nonformal education (such as Farmer Field Schools) to remain within the category of public goods. Public research and extension will have to concentrate on natural resource management, human nutrition, and support to producer organizations. Extension systems will be charged with supporting the construction of human and social capacity in rural communities so that those people who are more vulnerable can successfully pursue new crops, livestock, fisheries, or other enterprises suitable for local resources, conditions, and market opportunities. In most cases this will require the transformation of the traditional top-down, technology-driven extension model into a new approach that is more decentralized, farmer-centered, and market driven (Swanson 2008b).

Although the agricultural innovation system framework focuses on equality in access to technology, inputs, services, and markets, as well as on opportunities for participation, leadership, and equal representation as a means influencing policy-making processes, it does not make visible farmer types based on diverse asset portfolios, levels of education, and networks. So although there is a visible space for all types of actors in the system, small-scale, women, and indigenous farmers will continue to be left behind unless they receive effective support to build the organizational, technological, management, and investment capacity they will need to engage.

The AIS approach can reach its stated potential to benefit small-scale women and men farmers if it develops mechanisms to foster their organization into groups based on common interests and resources so that they can consider the economic feasibility of producing and marketing. These groups will need to sort through agroecological, market, and transport conditions to determine which products can be feasibly produced and marketed. They will need to have access to support from research so that they can fine-tune technologies to specific conditions, and they will need to develop the skills and practices needed to be able to meet export, sanitation, and certification requirements.

The challenge is to identify and develop organizations and institutions that are best suited to support these groups so that they can (1) determine their comparative advantage in producing and supplying different products for available markets, (2) gain the necessary technical and marketing skills to implement their decisions, and (3) continue diversifying into other high-value crops, products, or enterprises to both mitigate their risk and enable them to further enhance their incomes and livelihoods (Swanson 2008a).

Figure 7.1 shows how actors and organizations interact and where a sustainable agricultural innovation system incorporates equality of participation and representation of actors.

KEY GENDER ISSUES

Organizational arrangements that support women's involvement (Thematic Note 1)

Research and extension organizations have been undergoing changes since the mid-1990s in search of greater cost effectiveness and accountability. In a number of countries, such as China and India, decentralization and devolution policies have encouraged departments of central governments (including agriculture) to scale down, devolving greater responsibility for agricultural training and information services to local governments. At the same time, agricultural research has been encouraged to focus on technologies and management practices that can ensure food security and respond to the demands of resource-limited farmers rather than to those of commercial and multinational interests. The intersection of these two changes has challenged agricultural researchers, on the one hand, to dialogue with resource-limited farmers and agriculture ministries, on the other hand, to coordinate a variety of activities carried out by diverse rural agents, including private advice givers, NGOs, local governments, and commercial input suppliers. Latin America was the first region where attempts at privatizing extension took place (box 7.3 for an example in Peru) as structural adjustment and decentralization policies were put into place. In Mexico, for example, officials decided that farmers who could not pay for extension services would be assisted through the Ministry of Welfare. The void created by the closing of national extension services was filled by local NGOs financed by international organizations such as OXFAM, HIVOS, and CARITAS, who did not charge for their services.

International NGOs and funding agencies together with bilateral donors were instrumental in putting the inclusion

Figure 7.1 Interrelations among the Elements of Agricultural Innovation Systems

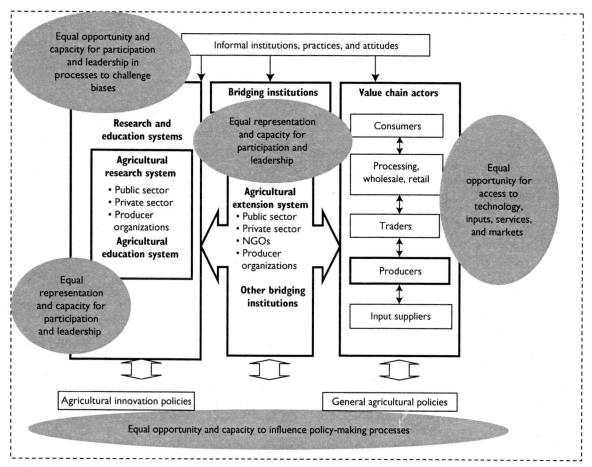

Source: Spielman and Birner 2008, modified by the author, with input from Eija Pehu and Catherine Ragasa.

> ### Box 7.3 Peru: Agro-Innovation and Competitiveness Project
>
> Through the Peruvian Agro-Innovation and Competitiveness Project (INCAGRO), for example, the government of Peru has sought to create or strengthen an agricultural advisory services market by paying up to 75 percent of project costs through competitive funds while requiring the direct beneficiaries to pay or mobilize the remainder, thereby creating a culture of payment for demanded services. Payment, at least in part, by farmers to receive advisory services will likely make services more client oriented, better identify demand, and manage quality control of services.
>
> *Source:* Roseboom and others 2006.

of women as policy makers, researchers, extensionists, and direct recipients of agricultural services on the rural development agenda. Although some strides have been made, women remain underrepresented in higher education and as scientists (see Thematic Note 3). Thematic Note 1 discusses how alternative extension models have dealt with the barriers and opportunities for involving women extensionists and farmer entrepreneurs.

Participation in research and extension (Thematic Note 2)

Participatory research efforts have been actively engaging women. Women scientists were at the forefront in 1988 when the Center for Tropical Agriculture in Colombia took on the challenge of the Participatory Research and Gender Analysis (PRGA) Program (see www.prgaprogram.org). Likewise, women scientists and technicians were actively engaged in the development of Farmer Field Schools (FFSs), especially in the Philippines (see Thematic Note 2).

As researchers began to work more closely with resource-limited farmers, the challenge of linking the technologies that agricultural research had produced to the needs of these farmers became evident. Studies done in the 1990s showed that women needed different technologies than men because their productive responsibilities were often different. These studies also brought to light the power implications of technology and showed how economic gains were often transferred from women to men when new technologies for women's spheres of production were placed in the hands of men. They also showed that women farmers are skilled in biodiversity management and marketing and are major repositories of indigenous knowledge worldwide. It became evident that women and men farmers do need information and skills but also that they can contribute to formal research processes from their own knowledge and skill banks. The unspoken challenge was how to build channels for knowledge and information exchange that could help make formal research more relevant while providing farmers with the technological knowledge they needed to negotiate agroecological changes and market demands.

Among the many participatory research experiences that had sprung up by the end of the 1980s, the CGIAR (Consultative Group on International Agricultural Research) centers mainstreamed the Participatory Plant Breeding (PPB-PRGA) initiative and the Community Agricultural Research Groups (CIAL-CIAT). Simultaneously, group extension programs supported by multilaterals included the Farmer Field Schools (FFS-FAO), Campesino a Campesino (MARENASS-IFAD) Management, and Participatory Technology Development (ILEIA-NL) (see specific examples in the Thematic Notes). Both groups of programs focused on gathering and exchanging information, testing existing and new technologies, and fostering innovation. All of these programs have been successful in involving women, most likely because the learning process takes place in the fields. There women are frequently responsible for many of the farming processes under scrutiny and can reflect upon the merits of the proposed technologies or practices and make informed decisions on whether or not to adopt them.

The financial sustainability of these programs, however, is under question because it has been difficult to show a return on investment above 50 percent. It could be argued that, especially in the case of resource-limited farmers and women, a need is present for group action programs because the increased human and social capacity resulting from these programs can be compared to that gained through other kinds of adult education programs (most often run by departments of education) qualifying them as

a public good. It should be noted that at present only a portion of agricultural research benefits from the participatory mode and that information transfer, such as daily market prices, is considered an extension activity.

Increased access for women to education and training (Thematic Note 3)

Limited agricultural education and training have been a critical factor in limiting the opportunities for women to (1) gain new technological knowledge in their areas of production, (2) occupy positions as agricultural researchers and extensions, and (3) voice their demands for research, training, and other kinds of support, including technology, policy, and financing. Initial attempts to support smallholder farm women in the South, especially in Latin America and sub-Saharan Africa, concentrated on training women researchers and extensionists in home economics. Many of these programs concentrated on preparing professionals and technicians in the skills required by farm women in the United States and Europe (food processing, nutrition based on diets high in animal products) and reinforcing the notion that men were the agriculturalists and major decision makers regarding technology and management options for the farm unit. The need for a different kind of education and training for women has become obvious because (1) women are managers in their own right, at least for part of the farm if not the entire farm, and (2) women agricultural researchers bring new ideas and insights to the table.

A need exists for girls to be encouraged during their primary and secondary school years to take up scientific subjects. In many countries this means an intentional effort to help parents and teachers to work actively to overcome the social barriers, norms, and practices that explicitly or implicitly discourage girls. Every woman in agriculture that a young girl meets in her formative years, whether she is a farm manager, extensionist, or science teacher, is a *model for the future profession that she will choose.*

Labor-saving technologies for women (Thematic Note 4)

In most developing countries, rural women's triple responsibilities of farm work, household chores, and earning cash to supplement family incomes—tasks that often add up to a 16-hour day—are well documented. Although men even from poorer families now have access to improved technologies for use in farming and nonfarm enterprise activities, most women still struggle through their days using traditional technologies that are labor intensive and time and energy consuming. Since the mid-1980s, many programs have supported the introduction of labor-saving technologies such as cleaner and more efficient cookstoves, grain grinders, and hoes of different lengths and weights. Some have been more easily adopted than others; some have resulted in a changing division of labor within the household that often benefits women but sometimes adds to their workload or even deprives them of economic opportunities.

The characteristics of technologies and processes not only set limits on who will use them but also directly influence how assets will be owned and managed. Better innovation results from more diverse perspectives on problem solving and provides one of the most important reasons for involving women in innovation processes. Innovation processes and women's livelihoods will be enhanced if a gender perspective is ensured when technologies are developed. Many examples can be noted of how technologies have both positively and negatively changed access to assets by women. Thematic Note 4 explores the complexity of the issues surrounding the design, use, and control over labor-saving technologies for women.

EMERGING TRENDS AFFECTING GENDER ROLES IN AGRICULTURAL INNOVATION

Several emerging trends are affecting the gender-responsiveness of agricultural innovations, including policies, social processes, information and communication technologies, learning and education, formal and informal organizations, and monitoring and evaluating progress.

Agricultural policies that support women's involvement in innovation systems

Gender-responsive agricultural policies have contributed to overcoming asymmetries in gender power relations, especially where they provided frameworks and mechanisms for improving women's access to assets including information, training, land, and technology. From the perspective of AIS, an increase in women's capacity to manage different aspects of a given system will enhance the capacity of that system to innovate and sustain itself as climate changes, market opportunities, and the need for alliances and networks become more and more demanding. Agricultural and social policy can enable or hinder the participation of women whether they work on farms or require education, or if they are scientists in national and international research organizations. Policies regarding farm and related labor practices, trade, and food safety, to name a few, influence gender relations far beyond the local level and throughout the system. Increased participation of women in research and extension organizations can contribute to the development of gender-sensitive

---

Box 7.4   Agricultural Policy Strategies That Help to Enable Women

Guarantee women's access to land-titling rights

- Employ women agriculturalists in research and extension posts
- Focus agricultural research on management areas for which women are responsible
- Ensure places for women in higher education
- Enact labor laws that provide equal rights to women.
- Ensure that mechanisms are in place to implement gender-sensitive policies

Source: Compiled by the author.

---

policies and practices. Box 7.4 lists some of the more effective gender-responsive strategies.

The most important policy that affects the participation of professional women in the agricultural sciences and extension is probably one that explicitly makes their contributions in national, regional, and local organizations visible. If the professional women in agriculture are not visible in newspapers, on radio and television, and in research organizations and extension offices, it is doubtful that women primary- and secondary-school students will become inspired to prepare for careers in agriculture, let alone in agricultural research.

Women extensionists need extra support throughout their scientific careers from colleagues who have "been through it" or are empathetic with them. It is not enough to motivate women to prepare for and take up positions in extension; more is needed if women are to stay involved. We require additional steps to engage women in informal networks, working groups, and teams so that they will not only be competitive but also be visible and recognized. Overcoming the hurdles women scientists face cannot be left to the individuals alone, and it will not happen with written rules alone. An effective mentoring system needs to be put into place so that women scientists can become more effective in leveraging opportunities for advancement and conditions that will make the workplace more friendly to and acceptable for them.

Informal organizations and women's access to information and services

For at least three decades awareness has been increasing that access and control are critical to inclusion and equity. We have learned much about the difficulties that women face in accessing information, extension, advisory services, and education, as well as in owning or acquiring land and technology. It is now common knowledge that women organize to learn, to support each other, and to gain recognition in their communities even when there is no direct economic benefit. However, we are only beginning to recognize the opportunities to reinforce social support systems such as community organizations, exchange labor groups (for example, you care for my animals one week, and I will care for yours the next), and extended family networks for enhancing know-how, information, and innovation systems. Potentially, exchange labor groups can become platforms for technology and management system improvement. Extended family networks provide opportunities for information exchange (increasingly via cell phones) and even for identifying and opening markets for goods and services nationally and internationally.

Women's groups provide a unique opportunity for women to build human and social capital and increase their capacity to participate fully in village and municipal governments where decisions on production and marketing strategies will be made. Unfortunately, extension services often find it easier to work with organizations controlled by men, and when women do participate they are seldom provided equal recognition for the knowledge and skills they can share. An urgent need exists to focus attention on the revitalization of women's and other disadvantaged groups' networks, as well as to link them into networks that go beyond their extended families and communities. The first step is to recognize that women (and not only men) already participate in groups and then to identify them. Whether women's groups are organized around a health center or among friends who herd on the same pasture or sell in the same marketplace, they have a store of social capital that can be built upon. Exchange visits among women's groups can reinforce the human and social capital of all involved and can be reinforced by the use of information and communication technology, especially community radio and cell phones to strengthen promising networks. However, in the case of radio and the Internet, appropriate investments will need to be made to develop content geared to groups of smallholders differentiated by gender and by scale and the kinds of agricultural processes in which particular stakeholder groups are engaged.

Social processes of communication and information exchange

Building and facilitating these processes are the principal tasks of effective extension, whether these take place in interpersonal and group situations or are mediated by technology. This *Sourcebook* discusses information and communication technology (ICT); one should keep in mind the opportunities it will open for research and extension in the future. Box 7.5 gives the viewpoint of one person on the ground. A challenge will be to link continuously the infrastructural aspects of information and communication with the social processes of communication that are critical to representation and equality. As more knowledge-intensive agriculture, fine-tuning of technologies and management systems, multifaceted negotiations, and alliance building become increasingly relevant, scientists, extensionists, and local groups will all need to gain more control over communication channels, processes, and technologies if effective dialogue is to take place.

Increased globalization and integration of markets presents both an opportunity and a threat to indigenous knowledge (IK). Local knowledge and IK, incubated over long periods of time by social practices, gendered division of labor, and cultural heritage, depend almost entirely on local media. Information and communication technologies have the potential to serve as a platform for sharing across the boundaries of IK and Western scientific knowledge if it fosters the use of many diverse expressions and reinforces cultural relevance.

As cellular telephone and Internet access become more common in marginal rural areas, networks among rural people are spreading not only from provinces to the capitals but also across continents. Community radio is an opportunity for women to build networks and to share information and experience that have been little tapped. Internet access, community radio, and cellular phones are providing opportunities

---

Box 7.5   India: Magic Boxes and Market Prices

Shankarlal does not know how the system works, or what it is called. but he knows the power of the "magic box." Every morning, together with his fellow farmers, he talks to the magic box as they check the price for potatoes at all major markets in the state. Accordingly, they decide where to take their produce. No more cheating middlemen, no more high prices.

Source: FAO, "Village User of the Gyandoot Information Kiosk in India," *SD Dimensions,* Sustainable Development Department, www.fao.org/sd/2001/KN0602a_en.htm.

to develop stronger linkages among researchers, extensionists, and farm groups. However, unless targeted investments are made to bring the technology to women and to accompany them as they take control and use the media to make their voices heard, the danger exists that gender asymmetries in knowledge among men and women farmers will increase drastically (box 7.5).

Practices that increase the commitment and empowerment of women

New information and communication technologies offer the most exciting new opportunities available to agricultural extension services if they can offer broad-based *access and control over information exchange*. One must recognize, however, that community radio has been around for a long time and has not been used as much as it could have been to bring women into the mainstream of agricultural entrepreneurship. Radio, and increasingly ICT, are available in rural areas. The challenge of the future will be *to provide content for specific user groups* of farmers and especially women to facilitate the needed shift from the "transfer of technology" to the learning mode of "innovation systems." A critical assessment criterion will be the degree to which the client or stakeholder can contribute to, give feedback on, and even generate new knowledge as a result of the information and training received through agricultural extension services. This will no doubt require the facilitation of group processes in which all involved learn and share what they know.

Strategies that engage women in agricultural innovation

The AIS perspective argues that women should be engaged not because they are in need but rather *because they are needed* if more intensified, competitive smallholder agriculture is to survive and provide sustainable livelihoods to a large percentage of presently vulnerable rural populations. Organizations and governments will need to make future investments to enhance human and social capital, and interventions will be needed to lobby research and education organizations on the importance of bringing the present and potential knowledge and skills of women farmers to bear in the construction of viable innovation systems. Groups will need to make incentives available for the technical and leadership training and employment of women scientists, technicians, and researchers, and funders will have to earmark funds for training women active in community organizations, whether they are currently in the leadership roles or not.

Innovation platforms for learning, communication, and alliance building

National and local projects and programs need to plan group activities that will allow staff to participate in learning exercises for the facilitation of innovation systems in which the benefits of *engaging a multiplicity of stakeholders* (farmers, researchers, buyers, and sellers from both public and private sectors) and *especially women* are demonstrated. Incentives such as public recognition or preferential access to information and technologies should be provided to the private sector to do contract farming with women. Competitions at local municipal and national levels should be supported where innovative management practices, products, and alliances developed by groups of farmers can be publicly recognized. Competitions can be held to award women who manage collections of germplasm, or for the design of a more efficient way of managing water, or for innovative marketing strategies, among many other possibilities.

Investment in diverse forms of research and advisory services

The overwhelming majority of smallholder men and women farmers are not presently clients for private extension services or for the kinds of advanced technologies that are currently on the market or on the shelf. If the AIS framework is to have an impact on these client groups, it will require continued social and organizational innovation in addition to new and revitalized technologies and management practices for smallholders, especially women who have a comparative disadvantage in education, mobility, and negotiating skills. If the more vulnerable members of rural communities are to benefit from that investment, groups must have careful identification of their knowledge, skills, and technology if these people are to become active contributors to resilient innovation systems. Investment in public research systems should be geared to provide incentives for multifaceted dialogue with other key actors in the innovation system from the private and NGO sectors.

Recognition for organizations that pay attention to representation by women

Many rural communities have organizational rules that operate on the basis of social inclusion and solidarity.

These values and norms are essential to rural safety nets, but they are sometimes considered to be incompatible with business-oriented organizations. Community organizations, especially those that involve a cross-section of men and women from farm households, should be recognized and rewarded for efficiency and innovation. "Rules of the game" that make it explicit that those who comply with agreements and obligations will reap the benefits should help to avoid "cultural clashes" that can occur as local organizations begin to operate high-value chains with stringent efficiency requirements. Box 7.6 provides some ideas about the direction in which existing farmer organizations need to go if they are to take on AIS challenges. Because community-based farmer organizations are usually heterogeneous due to variations in the efficiency of smallholder agriculture and to the diversified nature of smallholder agriculture, dealing with increasingly acute market competition will continue to be a challenge. Organizational settings that enable diversified smallholder producers to identify critical roles they can play in a particular AIS need to be identified and fostered. A concomitant challenge for smallholder producer organizations will be to represent the interests of a diverse membership, including those of women and younger farmers.

Box 7.6   Chile: Producer Organization for Marketing

An analysis of 410 producer organizations in Chile shows that those that succeed have developed a system of rules that (1) allocate costs and benefits to each member on the basis of his or her farming performance and market conditions, (2) enforce agreements between the organization and the individual, and (3) reduce the transaction costs of negotiating, monitoring, and enforcing agreements between the organization and its members.

Source: Berdegué 2001.

Monitoring progress of multistakeholder involvement

One of the challenges will be to track changes in the involvement of women in different aspects of innovation systems that are by nature multistakeholder and go beyond the local level. Questions that should be asked systematically include the following:

- Is the competitiveness of the activities women are engaging within the system increasing in the same measure as that of men?
- Is the activity resulting in an increase in either quality of life or income or both?
- How many of the new and adapted technologies and management strategies have been taken up by women as opposed to men, and how many by smallholders as opposed to larger farmers?
- Has some of the increased income been transformed into physical assets and human capital?
- Has local women's educational level increased?
- Have an increasing number of stakeholders at the local and national levels become involved in making decisions on the functioning of the innovation system? Among the representatives of these stakeholders, how many are women?
- Has the number of women in leadership cadres in local organizations, in research positions, and as extensionists increased? Are women involved in agricultural policy making at the national, regional, and local levels?
- Is the proportion of men to women in membership and leadership of the national, regional, and local organizations becoming more balanced?
- Are more women graduating in the fields of science that are important to agroecological management and agricultural innovation systems?

Table 7.2 provides examples of indicators for designing monitoring systems.

Depending on the country or region, it may be relevant to also consider ethnicity and caste alongside gender (both as comparative indicators and when collecting data), as women of lower castes or ethnic minorities are usually in the most disadvantaged situation.

Table 7.2 Monitoring and Evaluation Indicators for Gender and Agricultural Innovation and Education

Indicator	Sources of verification and tools
Number of women and men actively involved in participatory research and extension	• Committee meeting minutes • Program and project records
Percentage of women and men among those actively participating in agricultural committees and agricultural policy setting at the national, regional, and local levels	• Committee meeting minutes • Interviews with stakeholders • Media reports • Program and project records
Number of women and men participating in farmer field schools per quarter	• Agriculture Department records • NGO service provider records • Project records
Percentage of women and men extensionists among government, NGO, and private service providers	• Agriculture Department records • NGO and private service provider records
Number of stories on women in agriculture in media per quarter	• Print, radio, and television media surveys
Number of years of formal education of farmers, disaggregated by gender	• Household surveys • School attendance and examination records
Percentage of women among total scientists, technicians, and researchers in government agricultural institutions and universities	• Staff records
Over a set period, an increase of x percent in incomes from land-based activities (such as agriculture or forestry) among women-headed households in program areas	• Household surveys • Socioeconomic data from statistics office
Changes over x-year period of project activities in household nutrition, health, education, vulnerability to violence, and happiness, disaggregated by gender	• Household surveys, before and after • Project management information service • School records
Uptake of new and adapted technologies and management strategies, disaggregated by gender and size of land holding	• Extension records • Project records
Community satisfaction (disaggregated by gender) with access to agricultural innovations (such as seeding or processing equipment, and new seed varieties)	• Group interviews or focus groups • Interviews, before and after

Source: Authors. with inputs from Pamela White, author of Module 16.

Gender in Extension Organizations

Organizational support is critical for effective extension. Over the past 20 or 30 years, many arrangements have been tailored and reinvented to meet the needs of diverse groups of farmers, market opportunities, political situations, and funding constraints. As recently as 1996, extension was defined as "the transferring of knowledge from researchers to farmers, advising farmers in their decision making and educating farmers on how to make better decisions, enabling farmers to clarify their own goals and possibilities, and stimulating desirable agricultural developments" (Van den Ban and Hawkins 1996). but as the multinational biotechnology firms become the dominant source of crop-production technologies worldwide, the traditional role of public research and extension systems is rapidly becoming redundant. In a recent article for the *Journal of International Agricultural Research and Extension,* Burton Swanson proposes that if national agricultural extension systems in developing countries are to survive as effective organizations, they must (1) refocus on getting farmers organized (that is, build social capital), (2) increase farm income and rural employment, and (3) thereby help to alleviate rural poverty (Swanson 2006).

The services provided by extension have significant public-good attributes and are known to have a greater effect where farmers have more schooling (Anderson and Feder 2003). To date, the great majority of extension efforts have been financed by some kind of public funds, whether these take the form of international grants in aid, loans, or funds from national treasuries. Seven types of extension services are in use today (only the first two are funded entirely with private funds from farmers, their associations, or corporations):

- *Private fee-for-service programs:* In this type of program, self-employed specialists or technicians provide advice on demand to individual farmers or associations of growers. This type of extension is most common where the associations are well consolidated and have fairly high levels of human and social capital and access to credit. This is most likely the only kind of extension that is truly privately funded.

- *Private sector programs:* These are put into place by private agricultural research, input, or marketing firms to provide information, advice, and training to specific client groups who use, or wish to use, their goods and services in their agricultural enterprises. These programs often serve industry first and are often not developed in the best interests of smallholder and resource-limited producers. However, contract farming arrangements have provided an opportunity for increasing market access to smallholders and for building human and social capital among resource-limited farmers because both sides benefit more when production is efficient and of good quality.

- *Public programs that provide funds for farmers to contract services:* This type of program—such as the National Agricultural Advisory Service (NAADS) in Uganda and the Peruvian Agro-Innovation and Competitiveness Project (INCAGRO)—has shown little promise for reaching resource-limited farmers by providing them with sufficient human and social capital to design viable business plans and form alliances. With these assets at hand, groups of farmers can compete for available funds that enable them to contract needed advisory services. These programs are currently funded by international development loans (for example, from the World Bank) or loans combined with bilateral grants

- *NGO programs:* These programs are usually mandated to serve resource-limited farmers, and they became increasingly important as centralized extension programs were cut back. For many NGOs working in rural areas, support to agricultural activities is only one part of their portfolio, and they depend on research organizations and Internet-based sources for knowledge and information that they pass on to their clients and partners. They are most often supported by grants from international NGOs that receive funds from their national governments and citizens.

- *Public extension programs:* These programs organize the flow of information from research and markets to the rural constituency and are funded by governments through their own funds, international cooperation projects, or loans. These types of programs have been centrally managed and have concentrated on production issues of major cash and food crops. The programs were then decentralized, which often weakened the advisory services because they did not receive full authority to take responsibility for results and sufficient funding. Over the last decade a great majority of these programs either have been devolved to local governments or are being transformed into fee-for-service programs. In this process, most of the backup services for extension were substantially reduced, so the quality of advisory services through training and backup services remains to be addressed.

- *Farmer organizations:* These groups also have considerable, although less well documented, experiences with extension. Large or financially secure organizations can best support these efforts. The organizations Campesino a Campesino (Nicaragua) and Mviwata (Tanzania) fostered farmer-to-farmer learning. This type of organization brings together members across farmer communities or has entire rural communities as their membership. The latter situation is most common in areas with a history of tribal groups and indigenous populations in Africa, Asia (India, Lao PDR, Philippines), and Latin America (Central America, the Andes). Organizations that represent smallholder and resource-limited farmers, such as Via Campesina (http://viacampesina.org), invest a great deal of time and effort to build the human, social, and economic capital needed to generate, access, and effectively exchange knowledge and information. Other examples include marketing cooperatives that provide information and training to members to ensure high-quality products.

- *Mixed and collaborative public/private extension programs:* These programs are beginning to emerge where public funds are channeled through farmer organizations that have a controlling interest in how the funds are allocated. Uganda's National Agricultural Advisory Services (www.naads.or.ug), although facing many challenges, provides an example in which farmer organizations may

contract extension services from private providers and NGOs. In Senegal the Agence Nationale de Conseil Agricole et Rural is a mixed society whereby shares are held by government and farmer organizations. Extension services are jointly defined and evaluated by farmer organizations and their local consultation platforms. In addition, a rural services fund has been set up to make advisory services demand driven (Mercoiret 2001). Another example of this type of program can be found in Madhya Pradesh, India, where a private company and a state extension system jointly finance and provide advisory services for the use of agrochemical inputs. Table 7.3 summarizes methods of procuring funding for advisory services.

The comparative cost effectiveness of the different organizational arrangements has become of increasing concern as attempts are made to move to fee-for-service arrangements. It is hard to see, however, how the rural poor, including women, could pay for extension services, no matter how cost effective they are. Rather, it will be important to figure out how cost effectiveness should be measured and to what development goals (production goals, environmental goals, empowerment goals, and so on) it should be related, especially when increased human and social capital is more critical to the development of resilient innovation systems.

GENDER ISSUES IN NATIONAL EXTENSION PROGRAMS

Alternative organizational arrangements for future extension programs are being explored and range from the readjustment and decentralization of current systems (such as the Agricultural Technology Management Agency model in India) to the design of entirely new systems (such as NAADS in Uganda). If alternative extension systems are to contribute to improved livelihoods for women farmers, a number of simple ideas should be kept up front:

- Policy formulation and program design processes require that those groups (women and small farmers) who could be affected, either positively or negatively, have an opportunity to influence the outcome.
- Representivity and accountability contribute to sustainability. When present or potential groups of a constituency are not represented, the credibility of the organization is compromised.
- When women are active and capable extension agents, they become role models for their women associates and clients.

Table 7.3 Ways of Providing and Financing Agricultural Advisory Services

Provider of service	Source of finance for the service				
	Public sector	Farmers	Private firms	NGOs	Producer organizations (POs)
Public sector	Public sector advisory services with decentralization	Fee-based services	–	NGOs contract staff from public extension services	POs contract staff from public extension services
Private firms	Publicly funded contracts to service providers	Fee-based services or input dealers	Information provided with input sales or marketing of products	–	POs contract staff from private service providers
NGOs	Publicly funded contracts to service providers	Fee-based services	–	NGOs hire staff and provide services	–
Producer organizations	Public funds managed by farmer organizations	–	–	–	POs hire extension staff to provide services to members

Source: Birner and others 2006.

- Women bring diverse points of view to their associations or groups, their communities, development agencies, and parliament representatives. Insights and opinions can foster innovation and the quality of human and social capital.

- In many rural settings, women farmers are limited by social norms in communicating with men outside their families. In these cases extensionists can act as interlocutors, but to truly speak on behalf of women, these interlocutors need to be women.

- Because women have disproportionately fewer advantages than men (education, property, and other assets), voucher programs and other attempts to increase assets for resource-limited groups should ensure that women smallholders are adequately taken into account.

- Organizational and client confidence increases when there are greater representivity of and accountability to broader sectors of the society.

- Greater diversity of knowledge and experience contributes to more resilient and suitable technologies, farming, and management practices for more user groups.

- Many smallholder agricultural systems are extremely diversified; men and women take responsibilities for different areas of production. Therefore, the chances that overall farm productivity can be enhanced will increase if women are fully involved.

The following review of at four alternatives that are being assessed provides an idea of some of the challenges that are being faced.

ATMA farmer interest groups—India

Since 2000 the government of India's Innovations in Technology Dissemination Component has been testing new organizational arrangements and operational procedures to decentralize decision making to the district level through the creation of the Agricultural Technology Management Agency (ATMA). The goal is to increase farmer input into program planning and resource allocation and to increase accountability to stakeholders.

An ATMA is a semiautonomous organization composed of a multitude of key stakeholders involved in agricultural activities for sustainable agricultural development in the district. It is a focal point for integrating research and extension activities and decentralizing day-to-day management of the public Agricultural Technology System. An ATMA is a registered society responsible for technology dissemination at the district level. Each ATMA functions under the direction and oversight of a governing board that includes representatives of all categories of farmers in the district, including 30 percent women farmers, in addition to scheduled castes and tribal groups. As farmer interest groups became organized at the village level, their leaders were selected to serve on farmer advisory committees (FACs) at the block level, and then the chairs of these committees were selected to serve on the ATMA governing boards at the district level.

Both the FACs and governing boards quickly became "bottom-up" in terms of farmer representation on these decision-making bodies (Swanson 2008). ATMAs receive and expend public and private funds, entering into contracts and agreements and maintaining revolving accounts that can be used to collect fees and thereby recovering operating costs. ATMAs are supported by a governing board and a management committee. The governing board is a policy-making body and provides guidance and reviews the progress and functioning of the ATMA. The management committee is responsible for planning and executing the group's day-to-day activities. ATMAs promote farmer interest groups that include women in specific crop and livestock activities, farmer-to-farmer learning and knowledge sharing, and marketing partnerships.

National agricultural advisory services (NAADS)—Uganda

Despite the overwhelming participation of women in farmer groups, men still retain significant control over NAADS processes and actual decision making, even in supposedly women-only groups. Some of the factors found to undermine women's participation and control over NAADS processes include the following:

- *Literacy rates among women:* These rates are lower than among men, and the perception and experience of local community groups are that participation in NAADS and other community activities involves some form of writing or use of English. Many women-only groups co-opted men as advisors or secretaries to provide linkage to what to them appears a literate, foreign-language-speaking outside world.
- *A culture that subordinates women:* Married women in particular are oppressed by women's triple role: productive, reproductive, and community service. The need to rush home to prepare lunch for a husband or attend to children affects the level of participation in NAADS activities.
- *Ownership and control of resources:* The level of influence or control, or both, over group activities is related to the resources at one's disposal. A key resource in this case is land, because there were situations in which a women's

group chairperson has needed to beg for land for group activities from a husband or other man relative, thereby providing a window for men to exert disproportional influence underhandedly on group affairs (Stroud and others 2006). Also important in Uganda is the issue of land ownership among women-headed households (often as a result of HIV and AIDS and related illness). Despite the law protecting the woman's entitlement to the land formerly owned by her husband, lack of awareness and low literacy result in women and their children being forcefully removed from their land.

From these examples it is clear that the societal factors (literacy, women's roles, and influence) have their impact on women's participation in organizations and the way women's groups are functioning. It is up to organizations like NAADS to find appropriate mechanisms to mitigate and, where possible, change these disadvantageous situations.

National capacity-building program for rural development—Venezuela

Between 1995 and 2004, IFAD, the World Bank, and the government of Venezuela supported the CIARA Foundation to design and implement a decentralized extension service that operates at the municipal level through civic extension associations (ACEs) or grassroots producer organizations. Extension workers receive training on gender and other social aspects of community development, specifically to incorporate a gender approach in all activities. Strategies of participation, promotion, and gender equity include face-to-face contact at work and at home and the organization of dynamic and creative activities, adjusted to the needs of each group, characterized by schedule flexibility and easy access to meeting places. Extension workers design, monitor, and evaluate productive activities for families and the community that emphasize the inclusion and empowerment of women.

The new service shifted from an economic approach (aimed at improving income and production of the rural family) to a rural development approach (integral development of the family with a gender equity perspective). It facilitates the formation of rural extension networks with the participation of public and private actors, mainly through ACEs, which favor personal, organizational, regional, and interregional alliances. Experience has shown that attention to family needs, and to those of women in particular, has a high level of social relevance and is an incentive to social participation. The explicit focus on involving women responded to a recognition that women's personal growth influences family well-being, strengthens capacity for team work, and helps consolidate rural associations benefiting the family and society as a whole (Colmenares and Pereira 2004).

NERICA: feeding people, feeding minds—West Africa

The goal of the New Rice for Africa (NERICA) project is to enable rice farmers to make enough profit from their farms to send their children to school and provide them with better health care. The project, worth about $35 million, is funded by the African Development Bank. It supports the dissemination of the NERICA varieties in seven West African countries: Benin, Ghana, Guinea, Mali, Nigeria, Sierra Leone, and The Gambia. NERICA varieties have up to 30 percent higher yield than traditional varieties. In West Africa rain-fed rice is predominantly grown by women; therefore, NERICA varieties can greatly benefit them. The regional rice project aims to involve about 33,000 farm families in participatory research approaches to accelerate NERICA dissemination. Many promising new varieties have been selected by farmers using these approaches. In The Gambia, Yirima Kafo is a participating farmer organization whose membership includes 180 women and 20 men farmers. The association has made a profit of about $4,000 and has been able to open a bank account. "We are now able to send nearly all our children to school," says Oumar Bojang, secretary of the association in Jambur (WARDA 2006).

Gender issues for professionals in extension organizations

The issue of the presence of women professionals in extension organizations and their representation in decision making is critical. Although progress has been made in increasing the proportion of women in extension, difficulties continue to abound, both for women professionals and for the organizations that wish to increase their presence. Box 7.7 lists ways of addressing these difficulties.

The most important type of formal and informal policy that affects the participation of women is the strengthening of the public image of women and their identification with and activity as role models to reinforce their *visibility in leadership positions* at national, regional, and local levels. If women doing agricultural science, teaching in universities, speaking about new findings, and making decisions that affect agriculture are not visible in newspapers, on radio, and in television or in research organizations and extension offices, it is doubtful that

---

Box 7.7   Issues for Women in Extension Organizations

- Increase educational opportunities for women who wish to study in the fields of agriculture
- Identify and encourage capable women to work in the fields of agricultural extension
- Create more favorable team and residence conditions for women so that they will continue in the field
- Increase the representation of women on every rung of the career ladder
- Ensure a more effective voice for women in extension through recognition and empowerment
- Provide leadership training to increase women's capacity to leverage and negotiate
- Increase opportunities and mentoring for professional networking

Source: Fair Trade Federation, www.fairtradefederation. org.

---

women primary and secondary school students will become inspired to prepare for careers in agriculture, let alone in agricultural research and extension.

A second important policy issue is that of mentoring women who would like to become active in the field of agricultural research and extension. Although mentoring exists informally, education, research, and government organizations need to organize and support mentoring processes for their women students and staff so that they can contribute more effectively to organization building over time.

GUIDELINES AND RECOMMENDATIONS FOR PRACTITIONERS

The discussion below gives guidelines and recommendations for increasing the participation of women professionals and women producers in extension.

Increasing the participation of women professionals

- Tune in to the number of women in the active units of your organization or program—in meetings, in the laboratory, in government offices, in community meetings—and find out how they can be included.
- Incorporate personnel policies that search for qualified women candidates for research and extension positions

and for programs that mentor women in the workplace.

- Foster participatory working relationships that build mutual trust and respect across genders and generations and staff hierarchies.
- Consistently monitor to ensure that women's voices are heard in group work and meetings.
- Build on the local culture and customs of the working environment and provide physical facilities for the health, hygiene, and personal safety of women.
- Balance participation of men and women representatives of stakeholders relevant to specific undertakings of the organization or program.
- Lobby counterparts who are men to become spokespersons for gender issues at the highest level and mentor them on gender-equality issues in their sociocultural and political environments.
- Identify opportunities for scholarships and professional mentorships that women can take advantage of and share the information with women in the organization and with potential employees.
- Make the contribution of women visible at every opportunity, in multiple ways, and using as many venues as possible.
- Implement employment policies that ensure that women farmers have the opportunity to interact with women pro-

fessionals specialized in production, processing, trade, and other rural income opportunities that are of interest to them.

Increasing the participation of women producers

- Recognize women as agricultural producers and traders by clearly identifying the spheres of activity in which they have specific skills and decision-making power.
- Develop policies that guarantee that women's representation in organizational decision making is commensurate with the participation of women in agricultural production in any given nation, region, or community.
- Ensure that committees and decision-making bodies include women representatives not only of local women's organizations but also of governmental and nongovernmental partners.
- Make the participation of women visible at all levels of the organization and among the farmers who interact with extension so that it will be possible to measure advances in the future better than we can now.
- Build upon the social capital of local organizations (farmer, school, health, church), especially those in which women are already engaged.
- Engage men in the task of increasing the involvement of women on the basis of what they can offer to the innovation system.

Gender and Participatory Research

Participatory research is a perspective that emerges from the social sciences and began to be used in agricultural research in the late 1970s (see Rhoades and Booth 1982) in an attempt to understand and bridge the gap between the development of new agricultural technologies and their uptake, especially by small farmers in the South. Participatory research modes span from consultation with farmers that use technology to involvement of local groups in the identification of research issues by evaluating and adapting technologies and management practices (Probst and Hagmann 2003).

In the field of agriculture, participatory research methods were developed hand in hand with the farming systems perspective (Poats, Schmink, and Spring 1988) and followed the Green Revolution boom that had showed a limited impact on mixed (plant/animal) and diverse (multicrop) resource production systems. Both emerged as researchers and extensionists attempted to understand the complex systems that resource-limited producers, especially in ecologically diverse highland areas, were managing (for example, the Andes, Nepal, and the Philippines) and why these were not permeable to the technologies developed by the formal research institutions. Researchers observed more frequently that the Transfer of Technology model of extension was not bringing about the change envisioned for technology use by and in the management practices of the smaller-scale and resource-limited farmers. A closer look at the data on resource endowment, decision making, and management strategies used in these family agroenterprises provided by Farming Systems Research enabled researchers to begin to recognize the importance of the role of women as producers and traders worldwide (Fernandez 1994).

Although the term *participatory research* describes many kinds of farmer-researcher relationships, it is fair to say that the initial attempts to mainstream participatory research internationally were taken in 1988 (Chambers, Pacey, and Thrupp 1989). By the 1990s three streams of participatory research had taken hold. CGIAR and bilateral Collaborative Research Programs fostered the first, in which farmers contributed ideas, knowledge, and management skills to researchers' efforts to identify and select appropriate technologies (germplasm, tools, processes) that could be useful to farmers producing in more marginal settings (see box 7.8). Participatory extension came to the fore via the FAO-supported FFSs (Braun, Thiele, and Fernandez 2000), which worked in an experimental learning-by-doing group mode to help farmers reduce the quantities of harmful chemicals they were using in their fields. The third stream, termed *participatory technology development,* is a method used since the latter part of the 1990s, mostly by NGOs, to encourage groups of small farmers to test and adapt technologies, promoted by formal research, to their specific situations. The latter has been used most often by local NGOs, many of which use methods and techniques harvested and disseminated by the Center for Low External Input Agriculture in the Netherlands (www.leisa.info).

Participatory research has helped research institutions take on the questions generated by farmer organizations to overcome policy, technology, and market challenges. The National Agricultural Research Organization's Outreach Centres organized a series of multistakeholder workshops between 2001 and 2004 in which farmers, local government, researchers, and NGOs identified critical issues and planned strategies for research and action at different places within the innovation system (Fernandez and Lusembo 2002).

A recent World Bank publication indicates the kinds of changes needed to mainstream participatory research and extension in support of innovation systems:

> Taking into account the experience gained via the various modes of participatory research and the concurrent shift toward innovation systems, extension strategies face the dual challenge of supporting market competitiveness for commercial

The National Agricultural Research Organization outreach staff and farmers have appreciated the Integrated Rural Resource Management approach for the following reasons:

- Farmers identify constraints and work only with technologies they are really interested in. They are not instructed which technologies should be adopted and to what extent.
- Integrated rural resource management modifies existing technologies in a stepwise manner so that farmers become accustomed to improved farming practices and are not overwhelmed by externally introduced technology packages.
- Capacity building through participation in multistakeholder workshops helps all parties and especially women farmers become more confident to articulate their own needs and problems.
- Because of the way in which multistakeholder events are organized, farmers who are involved feel that they can freely express their concerns and that their communities are adequately represented.
- Contests among farmers are an effective way to recognize and induce innovativeness and to improve the sustainability of impacts and benefits of improved practices.
- Farmers report that the benefit of integrated rural resource management technologies can be observed in the improved condition of natural resources and higher yields. Systematic assessment still needs to be done.
- Facilitating the spread of integrated rural resource management technologies from farmer groups' trial plots to the entire farm holdings of individual farmers, together with intensification of farmer training, involvement of schools, and implementation of effective communication channels from researchers to farmers and back, remain challenges.

Source: Statement by Peter Lusembo, Centre Manager Mukono, 2004.

agriculture operating in a global market while addressing poverty in rural areas. The agenda for many extension programs will need to shift from an exclusive focus on agricultural production to a broader range of services relating to marketing, environmental conservation, poverty reduction, and off farm activities. Participation changes the roles of extension specialists—from messengers and advisers to facilitators—and may require change in organizational structures and moves toward cost sharing. Participatory approaches will change, organizational structures, facilities afforded local communities (e.g., resource centers for information and capacity building), and financing mechanisms (Alex and others 2004: 9).

GENDER EQUALITY AND PARTICIPATORY APPROACHES

The Overview of this Module explains why the construction of robust innovation systems depends on the engagement of limited-resource farmers, food processors, traders, and consumers, both men and women. When looking at agricultural innovation processes through the gender lens, participatory action research springs to the forefront because it focuses on how to identify, involve, and learn from the potential users of developing technology. More than half of resource-limited farmers, small-scale food processors, and many local traders are women, and so research and extension need to engage with them if agricultural science hopes to provide information and technology they can use. Participatory research in many of its modes not only allows for but also enables scientists to engage with women users.

Women experimenting and learning in the fields. Farmer Field Schools bring farmers together in the field to explore how to improve production by experimenting in the fields. Because women all over the world are in the field—planting, weeding, harvesting—FFSs suit women at least as much as men in many countries. The FFSs began with rice fields in the Philippines but expanded to multiple crops in the early 2000s and are now experimenting with animal production systems, crop-animal systems, and even market systems. The FFS perspective is an example of how the community takes ownership of the methodology and runs with it. Although the perspective does not specifically focus on gender equity, the FFSs meet in the fields where women work, and with their central role, they naturally become members and leaders of the FFS groups (CIP-UPWARD 2003). Figure 7.2 illustrates how the sphere of influence of the FFS methodology has broadened from integrated pest management to

Figure 7.2 Changes in the Focus of Farmer Field Schools

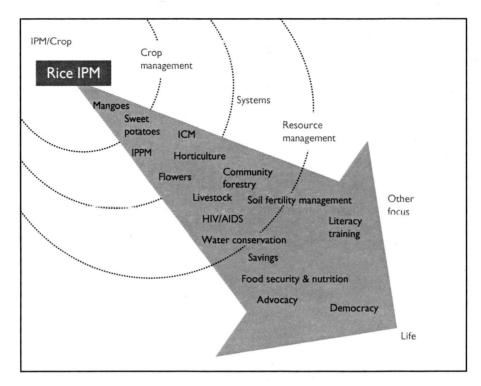

Source: CIP-UPWARD 2003.
Note: ICM = integrated crop management; IPM = integrated pest management; IPPM = integrated production and pest management.

encompass soil fertility and water conservation over time. It shows the different "waves" in adapting the FFSs.

Controversy surrounds the cost effectiveness of the forms of participatory research that engage farmers in medium- or long-term learning processes (for example, FFSs; see Quizon, Feder, and Murgai 2001), for the most part because basic and adaptive technology development and human and social capacity building are evaluated independently as research or extension, respectively. As a result, multi-institutional impacts and long-term benefits to rural communities have not been assessed to date.

Expanding research to include productive activities managed by women. One of the most tangible and visible impacts of participatory research is the way it has been able to lead researchers to focus on the productive activities that women engage in. In the Andean region until the late 1980s there was almost no information available on the health, nutrition, and production parameters of local breeds of sheep and cattle, yet Andean crops, especially potatoes, had been studied for years. It is now well documented that on farms in the high Andes, where both husband and wife are present, men make more management decisions regarding crops, while women manage livestock

(box 7.9). On the other hand, the International Livestock Research Institute chose to locate its headquarters in East Africa, where men manage cattle, and attention began to focus on labor-saving technologies for women only after research about farming systems generated data on their predominant role in crop production.

Box 7.9 Peru: Taking Care with Culture-Bound Assumptions

When the Small Ruminant CRSP (Collaborative Research Support Program)—Peru began work in indigenous communities in the highlands, it called the men together to discuss how to improve management and health practices. Although the men came to the meetings—always requesting support for cropping systems—it was only after two years, when a practice session for castration was set up, that the men stated point blank that it was the women who should be called in because they manage the animals.

Source: Fernandez 1994.

Participatory research in the Andes also brought to the fore the role of women in biodiversity management, whereas in East Africa it highlighted their role in managing indigenous vegetables. Making these lessons part of their goals, the International Potato Center research agenda has been broadened to include sweet potatoes and other indigenous tuber crops managed by women in Africa. Recognition of the role of women in genetic resource management resulted in the Participatory Plant Breeding effort, a subprogram of the Participatory Research and Gender Analysis Program, a cross-center effort of the CGIAR. The Participatory Research and Gender Analysis Program is currently being downsized, in part because of its limited impact on research geared to meet the needs of women smallholders over the last decade. This decision speaks to the size of the institutional challenges facing those who recognize the importance of women's contribution to innovation systems.

Policy issues to increase equality through participation in research. Until recently, linking processes of technology generation with those of income generation and agroenterprise development was generally left to organizations that focus on one but not both. On the one hand, agricultural research organizations have largely focused on increasing the productivity of food crops in small-scale farming systems but have neglected linking farmers to markets to diversify and increase their incomes. On the other hand, initiatives to link farmers to markets have been spearheaded by government agencies, the private sector, and to some extent nongovernmental organizations. However, these initiatives have tended to focus on export crops using top-down approaches. Few have looked at building farmers' capacity to identify and develop enterprise opportunities, to match market opportunities with investment in improving the resource base, and to build local capacity to solve problems and to generate and access technologies through farmer participatory research (Sancinga and others 2004). Research documents innumerable cases in which the introduction of new technology in small-scale farming systems has resulted in a shift in the control over the production from women to men, especially when increased cash income is involved (box 7.10). When researchers take into account the link between technology generation and income, possible shifts in control over resources from women to men can be avoided.

GOOD PRACTICES AND LESSONS LEARNED

The discussion below summarizes the experiences in project design and implication and the lessons learned.

Box 7.10 Technology Can Shift Control

In the Andes some women still shear their sheep with knives and can win a contest for speed and cleanliness against men who use shears. Hand shears were initially provided through extension programs to men. Women soon realized that once the men took over the shearing, they also took control of the wool that had previously been a product that they processed and sold.

Source: Fernandez 1994.

Enabling rural innovation

Best practices for improving women's involvement in innovation processes are those that promote equity through representation and participation. During the last few years a group of action-oriented researchers from the Center for Tropical Agriculture and the African Highland Program have developed a strategy for gender-responsive research. They have brought together many of the lessons learned over the last quarter century and have set them out as elements in a process that can foster innovation systems. In the words of the multidisciplinary team, "the strategy at the community-level seeks to eradicate gender discrimination, and promote gender equity in key areas such as participation in groups and committees, leadership positions, decision-making, asset ownership, gender differentiated enterprise options and food consumption crops" (Sancinga and others 2004).

The strategy promotes gender and equity in the access to technologies and market opportunities, as well as in the distribution of benefits and additional incomes to different categories of farmers. The researchers who have worked to pull the strategy together have chosen to encourage and sustain active participation and cooperation of both men and women while creating gender awareness at the community level through interactive adult education methods. This is easier said than done, so the following three critical gender questions must be kept on the table and revisited at each node in the process:

- Who has access to and controls resources?
- Who does what, when, and where?
- Who benefits from what and how?

When these questions are revisited often, strategic decisions can be made to ensure that gender equity is in the making.

These principles are the basis of the Participatory Learning and Action Research Project, which tracked changes in men and women farmers' knowledge regarding community by-laws. Over a five-year period, women's confidence improved, and perceptions of their status within the communities changed. Most men and women farmers interviewed (95.6 percent) indicated that women's participation in decision making and community leadership positions had improved over the last three years. On average, women represented between 34 and 50 percent of the membership in village by-law committees and policy task forces. Individual interviews and focus group discussions revealed that men's respect for and consideration of women had improved considerably. Both men (85.7 percent) and women (88.2 percent) shared the opinion that the project significantly enhanced women's self-esteem and their confidence to speak in public.[1]

Building and managing effective partnerships

Resilient innovation systems require the building and managing of effective partnerships. In the case of rural communities and small-scale farms, men and women are very strategic partners who will need to negotiate agreements for resources (loans, information resources) and negotiate with other local stakeholders (input and other traders, transport, more and less influential neighbors). A key to effective partnerships is balanced representation that can seldom benefit women unless they are empowered to recognize themselves as equal partners.

Building on community assets and opportunities

Participatory diagnosis that makes community assets and opportunities visible will facilitate the active involvement of women in realistic plans for the future that can lead to concrete action strategies for the present.[2]

In the Mafungautsi State Forest in Zimbabwe, the Center for International Forestry Research (CIFOR) began its activities with transformation training that made it possible to bring groups of people from the villages around the forest together for a series of "visioning" and action planning meetings. Natural subgroupings emerged according to the nature of the resource that people were interested in or engaged in harvesting (legally or illegally). Beekeeping and timber harvesting tended to interest only men, thatch grass harvesting cut across gender lines, whereas broom grass harvesting seemed to be of particular interest to women and especially women-headed households. Social organization

around particular resources emerged as the dominant strategy for reempowerment, and it became clear that the user groups were willing to play active roles in managing the resources they had chosen as their focus. As a result, antagonism and tensions declined, and the first steps toward a genuine partnership were taken, with two-way flows of information and active facilitation of user-group initiatives by the Forestry Commission.[3]

Identifying market opportunities and selecting community agroenterprises

Formation of farm and market research groups that include women to select, test, and evaluate marketing opportunities, technology options, and approaches to sustaining their natural resources can help ground the prioritization of opportunities and constraints.[4] In both the Andes and East Africa, women are powerful actors in the local market. Harnessing their knowledge and experience in participatory market research that identifies and evaluates market opportunities for competitive and profitable crop and livestock products is critical. Women are also key opinion makers about incentives for investment that can improve the community and family resource base to the benefit of the greatest number of members.

Increased income among resource-limited farmers has been shown where the International Center for Tropical Agriculture's (CIAT) rural agroenterprise approach has been used. In Malawi both men and women farmers earned $2.50 per day compared to the national average of less than $1.00 per day. The integration of gender in the community agroenterprise approach has resulted in more equity in the sharing of benefits for some of the enterprise crops compared to other traditional cash crops, such as tobacco. However, as the crop becomes more and more commercialized, the income share of women is becoming smaller, although the absolute amounts of money they earn increases. An example of this trend can be seen in Malawi, where the income share of women goes down as the crop shifts from a traditional subsistence bean crop managed by women to a commercial crop with formal markets.[5]

Strengthening social capital and empowering rural communities

If women are to broaden their sphere of influence beyond the household, community skills to leverage resources and to negotiate the right to control and manage them are critical.

Effective empowerment is directly related to the capacity of men and women farmers to organize to leverage information, production resources, and marketing opportunities. Prioritization and selection of agroenterprise options that ensure household food security and local safety nets make it imperative that women be present when research questions for redirecting production or increasing market share are put forward.

Participatory monitoring and evaluation

Monitoring and evaluation are critical to any innovation process and should provide for tracking the participation of women and other vulnerable groups. However, it should not be an add-on but rather an ongoing process that is born with the partnerships and activated in the preplanning stage. Monitoring and evaluation criteria need to be negotiated among all stakeholders and must take into account changes in the innovation system as a whole rather than changes in a single practice or product.

The purpose of the Sub-Saharan Africa Challenge Programme is to enhance the contribution of agriculture and natural resource systems to improved rural livelihoods, increased food and nutrition security, and sustainable natural resource management. It seeks to integrate the disciplines involved from production to consumption in integrated agricultural research for development. The integrated agricultural research for development approach emphasizes the establishment of broader partnerships and innovation platforms to strengthen participation, build linkages with policy processes, and stimulate institutional change. The program developed through a process of competitive selection of concept notes and full proposals. Research teams discussed how to identify indicators on gender, poverty, and vulnerability in a participatory manner with project beneficiaries. At the same time, basic principles of comparison were discussed and incorporated into preliminary plans for baseline studies.[6]

GUIDELINES AND RECOMMENDATIONS FOR PRACTITIONERS

- Identify research issues using participatory diagnosis involving both women and men farmers.
- Encourage producer men and women to provide information on local, indigenous, and traditional ways of dealing with the identified research issues.
- Ensure diverse gender perspectives by suggesting that initial "data collection" be done in separate groups with or by women and men.
- When issues are identified that *either* women or men find relevant, work on at least one issue of importance to each gender group.
- When building community teams for participatory research (for example, Comités de Investigación Agrícola Local, FFSs, and Participatory Technology Development [PTD]), and if the issue is of interest to *both* men and women, be sure that half the members of the group are women.
- Innovate ways of registering information and documenting processes that make findings visible to *all* group members and the wider community.
- Use methods, techniques, and tools that facilitate group analysis and information sharing (for instance, photographs, drawings, straightforward charts, and tables).
- Celebrate *each* new idea, suggestion, or way of doing something, even if it is not evident how it can be immediately incorporated into the task at hand.
- Ensure that *all* group members (women, men, young, and old) have a voice in or a contribution to *every* meeting or activity, no matter how small.
- Explore ways that group members can share information with other groups or within their own community. Beware of practices and attitudes that are exclusionary.

Gender Approaches to Agricultural Extension and Training

Despite women's importance in agricultural production, agricultural extension and training (AET) during the training and visit (T&V) period focused almost exclusively on men.[1] Women were seen primarily in their reproductive role and far less often in their productive roles in agriculture. Advisory and other services are still largely provided by men. Structural adjustment measures did not allow extension systems to recruit new staff, let alone to improve the staff gender balance, although NGOs working in extension generally have a better gender balance.

Despite the increasing involvement of women and especially women's groups in AET over the past decade, chronic underinvestment in the knowledge and skills of women is a particular handicap for agriculture, especially in agriculture-based African countries. Not surprisingly, gender inequality remains a constant theme in any analysis of agricultural development, including analysis of AET's role in development.

Each Module in this volume calls attention in various ways to opportunities for agricultural investment, growth, and income that have suffered as a result of persistent gender blindness in agricultural institutions and development projects. Within AET institutions, women remain underrepresented as students, instructors, extension agents, and researchers, and agricultural innovation processes are hardly ever directed at women. This omission continues despite evidence that farm productivity increases when women farmers receive the same advisory services as men (Bientema 2006).

TRENDS IN WOMEN'S PARTICIPATION IN AGRICULTURAL EDUCATION AND TRAINING

In tertiary education about half of the more than 22 million students enrolled in all fields of study in 57 developing countries were women in 2000–04 (fig. 7.3). Only 3 percent of these students were enrolled in agricultural sciences; of

these, 38 percent were women. The share of women students across regions ranged from 27 percent in sub-Saharan Africa to 41 percent in Asia and the Pacific.

A recent World Bank thematic study on agricultural education and training (World Bank 2007) synthesizes research from 15 African countries. In Benin, for instance, 20 percent of the students in the Colleges of Technical Agricultural Education were women. In Ethiopia's 25 agricultural technical training centers, only 11 percent of enrolled students and 9 percent of graduated students in 2005 were women. Similar gender imbalances appeared at the university level, in the College of Agriculture, Hamaraya University School of Graduate Studies, where women graduates made up less than 3 percent of graduates between 1979 and 2003. In Cameroon's University of Dchang, 22 percent of students in the Faculty of Agronomy and Agricultural Sciences were women, but almost half of these (44 percent) were concentrated in the Faculty of Economics and Sociology (that is, not in agricultural sciences). In Mozambique women within the Faculty of Agronomy and Forestry Engineering, Univerdade Eduardo Mondlane, accounted for 28 percent of undergraduates and 35 percent of graduates in 2005–06, and one-third of the teaching staff were women. Fewer than one-fifth of students at the Agrarian Institute of Boane Agricultural Collage were women.

Young women generally are not encouraged to focus on science—particularly biology and agricultural science—in secondary school, with the result that African women's participation in agricultural sciences in universities is roughly half of that in other fields. A United Nations Educational, Scientific and Cultural Organization (UNESCO) survey in 1998 found than only 8 percent of agricultural faculty members were women, compared with more than 50 percent in many European countries.

These data reflect the continuing challenges for higher education institutions to meet the needs of women who

Figure 7.3 Percentage of Women Students in Higher Education by Developing World Region, 2000–04

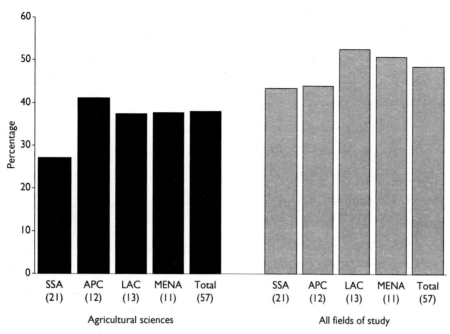

Source: Adapted from Beintema 2006.
Note: The number of countries included in regional totals is shown in parentheses. SSA = sub-Saharan Africa; APC = Asian-Pacific countries; LAC = Latin America and the Caribbean; and MENA = Middle East and North Africa.

aspire to business or scientific careers in agriculture. Some positive changes are gradually happening, however. UNESCO reported that the share of women students in the agricultural sciences increased during the 1990s (Beintema 2006). Sokoine University of Agriculture in Tanzania provides an impressive example of what can be accomplished. The university has vigorously assessed and upgraded its academic programs and surveyed graduates, employees, and private and public job markets. Ultimately it increased its graduate output of women tenfold over the last decade and raised their share in Sokoine enrollment from 17 to 29 percent. In the College of Agricultural Studies at Sudan University of Science and Technology, women student enrollment increased from 10 percent in the 1980s to 72 percent in 2007 (Gebre-Ab 1988; Idris 2007). The momentum of these successful approaches must continue for the effectiveness of AET programs to increase. In the Sudan example, the major impetus for increased enrollment of women was a policy that set the intake of women students at a minimum of 30 percent and furthered the construction of new housing for women. Enrollment by women has grown so vigorously during the last decade—not only because of new university policies but also because of rising women's literacy and secondary enrollment rates in

urban areas—that the number of women matriculating has exceeded the number of men, presenting university administrators with yet another dilemma related to the men-women student ratio.

KEY GENDER ISSUES

The mission of AET is to train people to contribute to agricultural productivity in ways that will increase economic growth and reduce poverty. In the last decades AET institutions have suffered from neglect as resources have declined and less attention has been paid in general to educational institutions, their functioning, human capital development, and facility management. Women have been increasingly underrepresented at all levels of AET institutions, from postsecondary to tertiary and higher education, although detailed gender-disaggregated data are available only very sporadically or not reported at all.

As agriculture and rural development have gained renewed attention in recent years because of globalization, trade liberalization, and changes in information and communications technology, the question of human resources in agriculture has also come to the fore. International concern over the environment, natural resource management, health care (HIV and AIDS as well as chronic ailments such as malaria and malnutrition), and women's empowerment have brought special impetus to intersecting discussions of agriculture, rural development, poverty reduction, and livelihood strategies in rural and urban spaces. Many of these discussions have cast new light on gender issues in agriculture, given women's central role in household food security, health, and nutrition. Clearly, AET institutions must address gender issues on many different levels if they are to develop human resources to address new realities in agriculture and development.[2]

The key gender issues in AET and actions to address them can be broken down under a few overarching themes.[3]

First, recognize women's roles in agriculture, and remove obstacles to fulfilling them:

- Perceptions of agriculture as a domain for men, professionally or otherwise, and the undervaluing or sheer invisibility of women's contributions to agriculture and food production must be changed through extensive research and through communication and political action using the resulting data.
- Traditions, customs, and culture hinder women from receiving agricultural extension and other support services or production inputs. Often their mobility is curtailed, especially but not exclusively in remote locations. Extension workers, facilitators, and students should be motivated and supported to reach women farmer groups and remote locations, or transport systems should be provided for the groups to reach service locations.
- Extension services often seem to follow a "man-to-man" technology transfer approach in which men extension staff work with men farmers. Not only are women neglected, but the messages and information provided to the men do not reach them. Extension support should be given directly to rural women in their multiple roles as farmers, environmental custodians, and household managers.
- Rural women's educational and training opportunities are often limited and "discriminatory" if legal measures do not mandate primary and secondary schooling for boys and girls, which is the first step toward vocational and technical training.

Second, give women better opportunities for agricultural learning:

- Literacy and secondary education of women are prerequisites for higher education. Where literacy is high, women's enrollment rates are high. National efforts to improve women's access to postsecondary, tertiary, and higher education by supporting basic literacy and secondary education are warranted.
- Offer special science courses for girls to fulfill the prerequisites for higher education. Enhance educational offerings in agriculture, food processing, preservation and preparation, and nutrition.
- Build awareness and provide career counseling for boys and girls. Young people need to be aware of professions in agriculture and rural development, such as farming, extension, teaching, agribusinesses, private sector occupations, or public service.

Third, enable women to participate in higher education:

- Establish infrastructure for women students. Provide sufficient accommodation and dormitory space, with the accompanying service, sanitary, and child care services and consideration of family obligations.
- Provide financial aid, scholarships, and grants for women.

Fourth, ensure a nondiscriminatory environment for women students and staff in agricultural education and training institutions:

- Allocate budgetary resources for gender sensitization courses for all staff and students in the training institution.
- Introduce and enforce policies to prevent discrimination, sexual harassment, and acts of violence on the basis of gender, ethnicity, or other types of diversity. Provide mechanisms for reporting such abuse confidentially and without recrimination.
- Support gender-sensitive policies and undertake initiatives that address HIV and AIDS and other sexually transmitted diseases in AET institutions for staff and students.

Fifth, revise the curriculum to reflect current and prospective needs and interests:

- Revise and modernize curricula in higher agricultural education to ensure that they include socioeconomic and gender analysis training for men and women students. Ensure that the curriculum is relevant to women's roles and contributions to agriculture, agribusiness development, and household management.
- Provide teaching materials, tools, and facilities for applied and practical training, such as facilities for developing appropriate household and farm technologies

or laboratories for food processing, preservation, and preparation.

- Introduce recent approaches, such as "livelihood diversification," into the curriculum. Identify such indigenous knowledge domains, skills, and beliefs that can serve as entry points for students to carry out action research in urban, periurban, rural, and remote locations with limited infrastructure (roads, energy, schools, and health services) and limited access to roads and markets. Provide support for faculty and students to undertake new research on livelihoods diversification activities relevant to rural women, such as gardening and trading.
- Use gender mainstreaming as a management tool in the training institution to promote equity and effectiveness in resource use and to ensure that gender-disaggregated data are collected and reported.

Sixth, promote training markets, which could serve development projects, private extension service providers, and public extension services:

- Hire women experts as consultants for situation-tailored training for staff. This will provide women with employment opportunities and, at the same time, will give them an opportunity to sell their training skills in the new markets.

GOOD PRACTICES AND LESSONS LEARNED

The following discussion summarizes the experiences in project design and implication and the lessons learned.

Achieving better gender balance in AET graduates

Targeted recruitment policies, affirmative action initiatives, academic enrichment programs, and earmarked scholarships all can increase women's enrollment. Various measures to achieve gender balance have been suggested and tested, such as developing gender-sensitive curricula, introducing new admission policies, providing adequate accommodation for women students, proposing quota systems, and recruiting more women lecturers (Abdelnour and Abdalla 1988). Other measures include monitoring dropout records by gender (to retain women students) and introducing policies against sexual harassment. These measures deserve to be tested systematically to ensure that a country's best minds are engaged in its development. Box 7.11 gives a more extended list of interventions to recruit, retain, and promote women in agricultural training institutions.

Improving women's opportunities to benefit from higher agricultural education

Access to higher agricultural education is essential for women to enter agricultural careers at all levels, from the field to research and academic organizations, to national and international institutions for agricultural policy, and to national and international development institutions. Case studies by organizations in the field in the Caribbean Community, Côte d'Ivoire, Jordan, Nigeria, and the Philippines revealed that women's completion of higher agricultural studies did not necessarily translate into an equal opportunity to benefit from that education; nor did it prevent discrimination against women in employment and public life.[4]

Box 7.11 Actions to Help Tertiary Education Institutions Recruit, Retain, and Promote Professional Women

- Establish policies that acknowledge the dual role of women (as professionals and homemakers)
- Reduce the stress of more committee work and greater non-research-track demands
- Provide mentoring (especially with regard to contract negotiation, workloads, priorities, performance, and career track)
- Recognize broader experience when appointing women and setting salaries
- Broaden and weigh the service component in promotion criteria

- Address both overt and subtle harassment of women
- Develop more practical and service-oriented curricula that appeal more to women and are more in keeping with the needs of twenty-first-century graduates
- Address the stigma attached to affirmative action appointments, and reduce the bias against women where affirmative action is not a factor
- Consider offering flexible work schedules to women and men
- Set up a crèche and after-school care facilities for staff and students

Source: Muir-Leresche 2006.

Few women were found in the top positions in agricultural institutions, whether in teaching faculties, government positions, NGOs, or the private sector. Improving opportunities for women to benefit from their agricultural education is even more of a challenge than improving women's access to higher AET (see box 7.12 for recommended measures).

Revising curricula and expanding learning options

Updated information is needed about labor market demands to revise curricula and practical competency requirements, especially for modern agribusiness management and global development issues, such as trade and markets, in industrialized and developing countries.

Teaching methods should be updated to cover information and communication technologies and problem-solving techniques. Knowing how to apply theoretical knowledge and use it creatively is critical for success. Men and women students and teachers benefit from learning how to conduct socioeconomic and gender analyses, which can be applied to various technical agricultural fields and ultimately enhance the understanding of gender roles in agriculture and rural development (FAO 2003).

At all levels—secondary, tertiary, or postgraduate—interdisciplinary approaches must be considered in developing the coursework needed to complete AET requirements. Courses on food and nutrition, food processing and preservation, water, fuel, and environmental sanitation management are equally important to men and women students. Traditional technical agricultural subjects must be complemented by courses in natural resource management, environment, and other topics that are important to smallholder agriculture, including household food security and household resource management, which are critical to all household welfare and livelihoods (Eckman 1994).

Using household resource management as an entry point allows extension workers to strengthen their understanding of different client groups' constraints, opportunities, and needs, which will enhance men and women farmers' learning and mobilization to improve their livelihoods (box 7.13). Because access to tertiary education is often limited to women from privileged families, more attention could be given to education and training contents for these professions at vocational and postsecondary levels, so that women students coming from "average" or poorer families would have opportunities to be trained for such technical jobs.

Box 7.12 Improving Opportunities for Women to Benefit from Their Agricultural Education

1. *Measures to better prepare women students for agricultural careers at all levels,* such as increasing nontraditional agricultural occupations for women and increasing practical work and skills training in management, research, extension, and specializations for which there is a job market in the country. Women also need greater opportunities to take part in postgraduate and in-service training in skills necessary for career advancement.

2. *Legislative measures* to prevent discrimination in hiring and employment and to prohibit harassment on the basis of gender.

3. *Measures to improve working conditions for women,* taking into consideration family responsibilities. These could include flexible working hours, provision of child care facilities, maternity and paternity leave, and flexibility in posting women with family responsibilities in the field.

4. *Measures to provide financial aid and services to women* to set themselves up in agricultural enterprises or to become established as farmers. These measures could also include assistance to women agriculturists and extensionists to provide their clients with inputs, credit, and other services.

5. *Measures to professionalize agricultural occupations* to make them more attractive.

6. *Measures to improve salaries and emoluments,* especially for those working in rural areas, and to eliminate disparities in salaries of men and women.

7. *Organization of women agriculturists in professional associations,* which can act as pressure groups to promote women's access to agricultural education and occupational opportunities.

8. *Gender sensitization at all levels* of national and international governmental and nongovernmental bodies dealing with agricultural development policies and planning, including research institutes.

Source: Marilee Karl, "Higher Agricultural Education and Opportunities in Rural Development for Women: An Overview and Summary of Five Case Studies," Report No. 40997-AFR, FAO, Rome, www.fao.org.

Box 7.13   Revitalizing the Dialogue on Household Resource Management

"Household resource management" has been defined by Engberg as the "process of making decisions about how to maximize the use of resources, such as land, water, labor, capital, inputs—whether purchased or produced on-farm—cash, agricultural credit, and agricultural extension" (Enberg 1993: 2). Each of these resources is accessed and managed by women and men differently, based on the gender division of responsibilities and management.

Curriculum reorientation and relevant training in agriculture and home economics have been a concern for FAO, other "food and nutrition" agencies (such as the World Health Organization, International Fund for Agricultural Development, and the World Food Program), bilateral development partners (Canadian International Development Agency and the Finnish International Development Agency), and national and international professional organizations (International Federation for Home Economics) since the 1980s, when rural development agendas increased their attention to rural poor and smallholder farm families. It was recognized that the roles of household members (men, women, the elderly, and youths) in managing farm and household resources and production activities needed to be considered in developing training units and curricula, so that students would graduate with the skills to improve rural livelihoods. Several approaches to teaching about household resource allocation and management have been reconceptualized. Corresponding training units have been developed, tested, and evaluated in various institutional settings, in both English- and French-speaking countries and cultures (Eckman 1994; Engberg 1993; FAO 2002, 2004).

Source: Author.

The major challenge has been to develop learning and research activities that enhance problem-solving approaches for typical tasks in rural households, which can be grouped as follows:

1. *Subsistence production:* crop production/gardening, livestock and poultry, forestry, hunting and gathering, home manufacturing, food processing, home construction and maintenance, and domestic/household activities
2. *Home production:* intrahousehold reproduction: caring for, rearing, and educating children; attending to the elderly, sick, dependents, and visitors; interhousehold obligations such as rituals and ceremonies; and community service
3. *Market production:* participation in the local economy—wage labor, services, trading, and business; participation in the larger economy—commercial farming, business, or industry
4. *Social activities and personal needs:* recreation, sports, family relations, and personal care.

Within this approach, the AET graduates as future development practitioners, policy makers, and planners are able to better understand, analyze, and address farm household needs and gender roles in task allocation, time and financial management, household food security and nutrition, decision-making dynamics, and communication to meet the changing development demands of rural households (Hamada, Kirjavainen, and Gapasin 2002).

Strengthening outreach, linkage, and partnership programs

A recent Kellogg Foundation study on AET programs in African countries has documented various partnering strategies undertaken by donors, NGOs, educational institutions, and bilateral organizations (Kingslow 2007). These include formal, informal, and in-service AET programs that benefit small-scale farmers and rural communities. For instance, Sokoine University of Agriculture in Tanzania provides outreach programs in which agricultural researchers and tertiary-level faculty work in rural communities. Their

multiple technical expertise in agricultural production, postharvest crop handling, rural processing, value-added agriculture, agroforestry, enterprise development, and credit serve smallholders, including women farmers.

Sokoine University also "produces" highly employable men and women graduates. A recent tracer study was done to review programs offered by various university departments in relation to the current and future job market and determine which labor market demands should be reflected in courses and skill sets. The assessment revealed that 28.2 percent of tracked economics and agribusiness graduates were women and were employed not only in government but also in banking institutions and local and international NGOs working in agriculture (SUA 2005). Sokoine University also has expertise and degree programs in food science and technology and in home economics and nutrition (www.worldagroforestry.org), which give graduates additional competencies to work with household food security issues in nutrition research and training institutions in multiple workplaces.

Furthermore, Sokoine University has a strong commitment to strengthening linkages across the agricultural research, education, and extension systems, with active men and women farmer participation. It also offers a "sandwich" partnership program with U.S. universities in which students study abroad and then undertake applied research in their home country (which also helps to ensure that students return to work in their home country or region; Kingslow 2007). Many U.S. universities are looking to rebuild and revive the tertiary training programs offered in the 1980s to students from developing country universities.

Universities in the Nordic countries have also implemented partnership programs between research faculties and AET institutions in developing countries. For more than 20 years the University of Helsinki has conducted partnership programs in farming systems and agroforestry research and supported long-term tertiary and higher education programs for both men and women students and professionals with Sudanese universities (two major universities involved in this program are the Faculty of Agriculture and Forestry of Khartoum University and the Shambat College of Agriculture of the University of Science and Technology, Khartoum).

Promoting scholarships, grants, and mentoring programs for women

Recent initiatives to strengthen gender integration in AET include the provision of scholarships earmarked for women to attend technical and higher educational institutions for degree and exchange programs in agriculture and life sciences. These scholarships have been provided by various foundations, including Winrock International, African Women Leaders in Agriculture and Environment (AWLAE), the Rockefeller Foundation, and the Carnegie Corporation. Carnegie stipulates that the study or research program must be "partnered" regionally among at least three universities. Some professional organizations have also introduced professional mentoring programs on postgraduate career advancement opportunities for women agriculturalists, scientists, and managers.

The Bill and Melinda Gates Foundation recently provided $13 million for educating and training African women in the agricultural sciences under a four-year grant to the CGIAR Gender and Diversity Program. The grant will directly benefit 360 women in agricultural research and development, along with some 40 institutions in sub-Saharan Africa (specifically in Ethiopia, Ghana, Kenya, Malawi, Mozambique, Nigeria, Tanzania, Uganda, and Zambia). Competitive fellowships with three capacity-building cornerstones (mentoring, science skills, and leadership development) will be provided. The AWARD program will operate in close partnership with several of Africa's agricultural research networks and universities as well as CGIAR agricultural research centers (www.genderdiversity.cgiar.org).

Monitoring a gender perspective in tracer studies

Tracer studies that survey graduates of institutions of higher education are often seen as an important tool of institutional development, especially when employment markets are changing rapidly. Knowledge of graduates' whereabouts and working conditions and retrospective assessment of their course of study might stimulate debate on revising and initiating programs. Many tracer studies have remained gender blind, however, beyond disaggregating respondents by gender, and they have lacked gender-aware reporting. Systematic gender monitoring is needed in tracer studies, from their design to final reporting, to ensure that gender-relevant information is collected and analyzed and thus useful for policy making, AET planning, curriculum development, and human resource management.

Between 1996 and 2000, 15 tracer studies were done in seven African countries (Cameroon, Ghana, Kenya, Malawi, Nigeria, Tanzania, and Uganda), sponsored mainly by the Association of American Universities (AAU) Study Program on Higher Education Management at the Universität Kassel in Germany. About 8,000 graduates participated in the studies. They answered a lengthy questionnaire about the transition from higher education to work, job search, employment conditions, use of knowledge and skills, appropriate position and job satisfaction, and retrospective assessment of study conditions. Because all studies used nearly the same questionnaire, the resulting data offer an extraordinary opportunity for a comparative analysis.[5]

In the United States, a Food and Agriculture Education Information System (FAESIS) has been set up to explore and analyze data on employment opportunities for college graduates between 2005 and 2010 (CREES 2005). FAESIS data are collected from institutions offering courses in food, agriculture, natural resources, and human sciences in specific areas. Gender and ethnicity of the graduates are also analyzed.

Engendering training components in agricultural development projects

Training is increasingly a component of many agricultural development projects. Training often omits gender perspectives, however, unless gender training is explicitly included in the project's human resources development plan and specific gender criteria are used to nominate students for advanced study, in-service training, or short courses to upgrade skills.

A good example is the World Bank's Land Administration Project in the Lao People's Democratic Republic, which systematically monitored gender perspectives and analyzed best practices. The gender dimension of its training components has become visible and made a notable impact, because the development of educational and training programs included both men and women, which eventually led increasing numbers of women to become involved in implementing project activities. An institutional liaison with the Lao Women's Union strengthened the project's capacity to address gender issues at local levels (World Bank 2005).

FAO has developed and extensively disseminated an instructional tool for extension advisers working with rural women that contains various checklists and training tools designed for use at various levels in formal and less formal educational settings and in a range of cultural settings.[6] The six instructional units cover (1) the rationale for working with rural women; (2) information on rural women; (3) contacting rural women; (4) time and location of extension activities; (5) access to credit, inputs, and technology; and (6) communication methods and techniques. Another learning Module, produced by the World Bank, provides a checklist of strategies to consider when addressing gender issues in the education and training components of agricultural development projects (box 7.14).

GUIDELINES AND RECOMMENDATIONS FOR PRACTITIONERS

- *Admission and recruitment policies.* Revisit the admission policies in AET institutions. Advise and initiate negotiations with AET administrators and policy makers to introduce aggressive recruitment policies with affirmative action for women (for example, a minimum intake quota for women of 30 percent). Discuss the develop-

ment and provision of supportive and preparatory training courses for men and women in science, mathematics, or related subject areas to facilitate admission to secondary and higher agricultural education.

- *Gender statistics.* Introduce gender statistics and gender-sensitive indicators to decision makers in line ministries and institutions to justify and facilitate the increase of women's opportunities to be trained in agriculture at all levels (vocational, technical, and tertiary). Carry out gender-disaggregated human power surveys in various sectors to obtain data to guide decisions, and if needed include an admission quota for women to narrow the gender gap.

- *Institutional partnerships.* Link with national institutions, professional associations, private sector allies, and women's political action networks to obtain support and infrastructure for women's advanced education, including dormitories, practical training laboratories, classrooms, and appropriate technology facilities. Such facilities will enhance the integration of household-focused practical training and entrepreneurial activities in the curriculum.

- *Incentives and retention.* Enhance women staff retention in training institutions and higher education establishments through job creation, recruitment policies, benefit sharing, and a working environment with defined sexual harassment policies. The alternative is the continuing loss of women to overseas employment.

- *Donor and lender dialogue.* Initiate dialogue with the donor community to enhance awareness and mobilize resources for reviewing, assessing, and strengthening the management of education for agriculture (including forestry, fisheries, livestock, and home economics) and rural development at postsecondary, tertiary, and postgraduate institutions. Establish liaisons with national policy makers to raise awareness and enhance their political will and interest in ensuring equal opportunities for women and men students and staff to advance and work for agricultural education and extension. Link financial support to AET institutions to increasing numbers of women trainees and women trainers and to successful integration into the labor market.

- *Partnership in implementation.* Seek partnerships with international agencies with mandates in food, agriculture, and natural resources and invite gender specialists to train a cadre of men and women trainers in agricultural colleges in basic socioeconomic and gender analysis skills. Introduce instructional approaches and build capacity to raise awareness of gender roles in family

Increase women's enrollment in agricultural courses

- Conduct campaigns in secondary schools to promote agriculture as a career for women
- Increase girls' enrollment in secondary schools and particularly in science courses
- Provide scholarships for women to attend agricultural courses at colleges or universities
- Provide supplementary, precollege courses in science and other subjects as needed
- Provide separate boarding facilities for women or a completely separate college if necessary
- Encourage parents' visits to training colleges to help them ascertain that the facilities are suitable for their daughters

Increase training in gender issues for everyone

- Appoint a staff person with gender expertise as a teaching/training coordinator to review gender issues in all training modules
- Insert modules on gender issues in agricultural college and university courses
- Include gender issues in in-service training and use information from gender studies to prepare training sessions
- Send teachers on short-term training courses in gender issues

Source: World Bank 2002.

- Engage agricultural college staff and students in gathering project preparation data on gender issues

Increase training for women in projects

- Include minimum targets for training of women agricultural technicians
- Make study tours and training abroad accessible to women staff
- Set minimum targets for training of women farmers
- Consider conducting agricultural training with literacy activities
- Include a functional literacy component in agricultural training courses
- Include specific targets for women and men participants in agricultural training, depending on their literacy levels
- Collaborate with other ministries, agencies, or NGOs on functional literacy
- Include a grassroots management training component to train rural women farmers in business management techniques, financial management, human resource management, marketing, and running small businesses, for example, as in the World Bank's pilot projects in Burkina Faso, India, Malawi, Nigeria, and Senegal, developed by the Economic Development Institute (EDI) and in FAO's numeracy projects for women entrepreneurs in West African countries (Benin, Côte d'Ivoire, and Ghana).

relations, health management, and nutritional wellbeing in HIV and AIDS care, operating a farm enterprise, and fostering community participation. Use external expertise to develop training course content in organiza-

tion, leadership, negotiation, and mitigation and to train staff to analyze such current issues as the impact of environmental degradation, rural-urban migration, resettlement, demographic trends, and conflict resolution.

Labor-Saving Technologies and Practices

In most developing countries, rural women's triple responsibilities of farm work, household chores, and earning cash to supplement family incomes—tasks that often add up to a 16-hour day—are well documented. Although even men from poorer families now have access to improved technologies for use in farming and nonfarm enterprise activities, most women still struggle through their day using traditional technologies that are labor intensive and time and energy consuming.

Domestic chores such as collection of water and fuelwood divert women's use of time from farming tasks and nonfarm enterprise activities. This is a particular problem in areas of labor scarcity such as sub-Saharan Africa, where women's time-poverty and lack of access to improved technologies lead to low agricultural yields and low levels of food security.

A wide range of technologies could help address some of women's labor constraints. Over the last 30 years many development projects and programs have aimed at reducing women's time-poverty by increasing their access to these technologies. Many barriers remain to the adoption and sustained use of these technologies, however, and women are still overburdened. In fact, women's workload is increasing in some regions as a result of deforestation, droughts, rural-urban migration, and the spread of HIV and AIDS (Bishop-Sambrook 2003).

KEY GENDER ISSUES

Rural women in developing countries divide their time among farming, domestic, and nonfarm activities, with the focus varying among regions, type of household, and farming systems.

On-farm activities

The roles of men and women in farming are well defined, with men responsible for land clearing and preparation and women responsible for planting, weeding, harvesting, and postharvest activities such as threshing, winnowing, and grinding. All these tasks take up a great deal of time and energy, a burden that can be reduced in one of two ways:

- Making existing tasks easier and increasing productivity of existing labor and draft power
- Changing farming practices to methods that use less farm power.

Increasing farm power

Improved technologies can increase labor productivity in farming, but they have mostly been adopted in relation to men's tasks, often with negative consequences for women. For example, tractors and animal-drawn plows have been used by men to increase the acreage under cultivation, leaving women to struggle with an increase in weeding and harvesting using only handheld tools. This adds to women's workload but can also result in major crop losses if weeding is done late or with insufficient care. Although many women now undertake men's tasks because of migration by men or death from HIV and AIDS, manufacturers and suppliers of farming equipment seem to be unaware of this changing division of labor and continue to distribute ploughs that are too heavy for women or have handles they cannot reach (IFAD 1998).

Tools and equipment appropriate for women's tasks (for example, planting, weeding, and grinding) do exist, but many barriers block their adoption. Of all women's land-related tasks, weeding with handheld hoes is the most punishing and time consuming, causing fatigue and backache. Long-handled hoes are available that could reduce the strain of squatting using traditional short-handled hoes, but in many parts of Africa these are rejected for cultural reasons. Manufacturers of farm implements make different weights of hoes, including very light ones that are better suited to women's needs, but most women continue to use heavier hoes because they are unaware of the full range of available tools. Lighter implements suitable for use with donkeys are available, and, unlike with oxen, no taboos exist for women working with donkeys. A donkey-drawn intercrop cultivator could reduce weeding time per acre from two to four weeks to two to four days, but women lack the cash to purchase such equipment, and men see no need to purchase donkeys and equipment for their wives when the work can be done manually at no cost. In addition, animal-draft technologies are seen as being men's domain, and animal traction training courses tend to be restricted to men (IFAD 1998). Even when donkeys and equipment are distributed to women through development projects, constraints on sustained use arise. For example, in one project in Uganda, women lost their donkeys through lack of cash to pay for drugs to keep their animals healthy (GRTI 2006).

Plastic drum seeders, which have been widely promoted through the International Rice Research Institute (IRRI) and other organizations in Southeast and South Asia, enable farmers to sow rice seeds directly instead of broadcasting or transplanting rice seedlings. These seeders have proved very popular with farmers because they lower production costs through reduced use of seeds and labor and because they give higher yields. Data from an IRRI-supported project in Vietnam show that the time spent by women on tasks such as gap filling and hand weeding is vastly reduced. This has proved popular with women from better-off households who now have more time to spend on child care, income-generating activities, and community activities, but it has resulted in the loss of livelihoods for the many women from

poorer and landless households who used to be hired by farmers to undertake these tasks. In addition, extension agents interacted only with men. Because women had no knowledge of the drum seeders and were not involved in decisions to adopt them, they had no opportunities to acquire them on a cooperative basis as a way of earning income through providing hire services to farmers (Paris and Truong Thi Ngoc Chi 2005). The drum seeders are now being transferred through an IFAD/IRRI program to Bangladesh. Without any transfer of lessons on gender learned from the Vietnam experience, the same outcomes can be expected, with only men owning the seeders and the poorest rural women losing jobs and experiencing an increase in poverty (IFAD 2006).

Grinding mills, cassava graters, and oil expellers are now to be found in almost every village in the developing world. Some are owned by community organizations and women's groups, but most are owned by individual entrepreneurs, who are mainly men. The rapid spread of these processing technologies has been fueled by the increasing availability of energy supplies in rural areas and by the significant profits that can be made from operating rural processing enterprises. Rural mills cut the time involved in hand pounding or grating from several hours to only minutes and undoubtedly have improved the lives of millions of women (box 7.15).

Two problems exist, however. First, the mills have opened up investment opportunities for men rather than for women, who cannot afford to buy them. They also exclude women from the poorest farm households, who cannot afford to pay for milling services. Second, as with drum seeders, when large numbers of women have earned their

---

Box 7.15 Nepal and Botswana: Labor- and Time-Saving Crop-Processing Technologies

In Nepal mechanized mills were found to reduce the time needed to process one kilogram of rice from 19 minutes to 0.8 minute, but women were walking for 10 to 180 minutes to reach the mill and waiting an average of 30 minutes for their turn. Such behavior has been noted in many parts of Asia and Africa and suggests that women are more concerned with the energy savings than the time savings connected to mechanical crop processing.

Sources: ITDG 1986; Spence 1986.

In Botswana sorghum mills have reduced the time needed to process 20 kilograms of sorghum from two to four hours to two to four minutes. Pounding traditionally takes place in the evening, whereas the mills operate only in the mornings. Women have solved this problem by sending grain to the mill with their children on the way to and from school.

living by manually processing crops for local farmers, rural mills can result in the loss of a valuable source of income with dire consequences if no alternative remunerative work can be found. Such women can be assisted in various ways. In Bangladesh in the 1980s, mechanized rice mills were leading to the displacement of about 100,000 women per year. The Bangladesh Rural Advancement Committee (BRAC), a large NGO, introduced a program to organize these women into cooperative groups and provided them with loans so that they could purchase their own mills and share in the benefits of the new technology (Ahmad and Jenkins 1989).

Changing farming practices

Increasing access to farm power, including access to mechanized equipment, is one way of solving women's time and energy constraints related to on-farm activities, but it is also possible to reduce the demand for power by changing farming practices. A good example is the adoption of conservation agriculture or zero/minimum tillage agriculture, which overcomes the critical labor peaks of land preparation and weeding by planting directly into mulch or cover crops, with weed control being done through cover crops and mulch as well as by hand with the use of herbicides.

Although IFAD, FAO, and others have implemented projects to introduce such practices, results have been mixed. For example, in the FAO-supported Conservation Agriculture and Sustainable Agriculture Development Project in Kenya and Tanzania, yields increased and time spent on land preparation, planting, and weeding was much reduced. Women in poor farm households benefited from a decrease in labor pressure, but women in landless households received fewer opportunities to work in planting and seeding, although this effect could be cushioned by higher labor requirements in harvesting if yields were sufficiently increased (Maguzu and others 2007).

Increased yields are an incentive to the adoption of conservation agriculture, which still faces numerous challenges. One of these challenges is cultural resistance to a farming system that keeps crop residues as soil cover and involves no-till practices, both of which are considered signs of laziness because a plot that is not thoroughly prepared with a clean seedbed looks "dirty." However, it is the dirty soil cover and trash that prevent the weeds from growing. Conservation agriculture is no more expensive than conventional agriculture, but it can involve the need for cash to purchase inputs up front and to purchase tools suitable for direct planting. In addition, the use of herbicides in conservation agriculture can be a health hazard to the women who apply them if the wrong products or equipment is used and no training in application methods is provided (Bishop-Sambrook 2003).

Domestic chores

Tasks such as water and firewood collection, cooking, cleaning, child rearing, and health care take up inordinate amounts of women's time and divert their labor from farming and income-generating activities. Numerous programs and projects have been introduced with the aim of improving access of rural populations to water and energy supplies and providing infrastructure such as rural roads and rural health clinics aimed at increasing mobility and access.

Interventions to reduce time spent by women on domestic chores fall into two categories: (1) integration of women's needs in mainstream infrastructure projects and (2) projects aimed at delivering time- and energy-saving technologies directly to women. Infrastructure projects aimed at supplying piped water, electricity, and rural roads are dealt with in Module 9 and are potentially important ways of reducing the time women spend collecting water and firewood and transporting crops from fields and to markets. However, it will take decades for piped water and the grid to reach the majority of poor rural communities. In the meantime labor-saving technologies and practices such as rainwater harvesting projects, protected springs, and improved stoves have a significant role to play. In a similar fashion, even where rural roads have been built, women still need access to appropriate transport technologies such as wheelbarrows, bicycles, and donkey carts to assist with carrying loads along these roads.

LOW-COST WATER TECHNIQUES

Women's involvement in community-based water schemes has been significant, and women have benefited from them both practically, in terms of time savings and improved hygiene, and strategically in terms of increased voice and control (box 7.16).

Improved stoves

Fuelwood is collected free from surrounding forest or scrub areas and used by women in traditional open fires or in improved biomass stoves to cook meals and provide space heating. The collection of fuelwood is one of the most time-consuming tasks undertaken by rural women, with the

The nine-year IFAD-supported Central Dry Area Smallholder and Community Services Development Project started operation in Kenya in 2001 with the objective of reducing severe poverty. The water programs introduced through the project involve community-based action to ensure sustainability. Water user associations have been established that own, operate, and maintain the water supply facilities. Women represent only 29 percent of the members of the water user associations, mainly because membership is registered in the name of the man head of household who owns the land. However, the women who do participate have made their voices heard and gained respect in the community. The time spent by women in collecting water has been significantly reduced from half a day to only minutes through projects such as construction of protected access to springs close to the village. Water quality is also much improved. Time is spent instead on tending kitchen gardens and rearing cows and goats for milk to be sold for cash, and women no longer need to withdraw their daughters from school to help them fetch water.

Source: Matuschke 2007.

amount of time increasing as supplies become scarcer as a result of deforestation. The provision of fuel encompasses time spent not only in actual travel, cutting, and carrying but also in the preparation of fuel for burning and use, which can take more time than the actual collection itself. In addition, cooking on traditional stoves is time consuming and requires constant attention, so it prevents women from engaging more fully in other tasks.[1]

After three decades of projects aimed at introducing improved stoves, millions of women still prepare meals using traditional open fires, and continued attempts by development agencies to introduce improvements still face difficulties (Bishop-Sambrook 2003). Major obstacles include women's lack of access to cash and the unwillingness of their husbands to contribute when cooking can be undertaken free of charge on an open fire. Attempts by development projects to solve this problem by distributing stoves free of charge have rarely proved successful and often have been counterproductive (Ghertner 2006). Widespread uptake of improved stoves requires that women have control of their own source of income or that their husbands see sufficient economic benefits from the use of the stoves to warrant investing in them.

An increasing number of projects are introducing stoves that use alternative fuels such as biogas, ethanol, and liquid petroleum gas, which have many benefits in addition to saving time for women (box 7.17). A detailed review of the range of energy technology options that could assist women can be found in the recent FAO publication *Energy and Gender Issues in Rural Sustainable Development* (Lambrou and Piana 2006) and from ENERGIA, the International Network on Gender and Sustainable Development (www.energia.org).

Rural transport technologies

One way of easing the burden of women's work is to increase their access to carrying devices, such as donkeys, wheelbarrows, and carts. In addition to helping with the collection of water and fuelwood, such technologies can also help women with a range of other transport tasks related to carrying tools to and from the fields, carrying crops from fields to grinding mills and markets, and transporting children and the elderly to health clinics. Many studies undertaken over the years show that African women typically spend up to 2,000 hours each year on transportation tasks, which is three to four times greater than the time spent by men (Barwell and Calvo 1987; Blackden and Wodon 2006). Despite their heavier transport burden, women have fewer opportunities than men to use transport technologies to alleviate it (Fernando and Porter 2002).

Carrying heavy loads along a road may be better than struggling along a rough path, but only marginally so. Particularly in Africa, women have had very few alternatives between head-loading/walking and movement by conventional car, bus, or truck. Where public transport systems exist, they provide a reasonably cheap way for women to travel to market or to health clinics, but they are not without their difficulties. Women often are left behind or stranded along the route when preference is given to men customers or to those traveling a longer distance. Harassment and safety are major concerns for women traveling long distances alone. One group of women in Kenya solved this problem by registering as a cooperative to obtain a loan and then buying their own bus, which operates successfully as a profit-making enterprise and gives preference to women cooperative members (Kneerim 1980).

Box 7.17   China and Sudan: Alternative Fuels for Domestic Cooking

The IFAD-supported West Guangxi Poverty Alleviation Project in China has involved the introduction of 2.73 million biogas tanks that have been built by villagers. An estimated 7.65 million tons of standard coal and 13.40 million tons of firewood are saved annually. Similar IFAD-supported projects implemented elsewhere in China save women time for more agricultural production as well as improving the living environment and producing high-quality organic fertilizer. The Wulin Mountains Minority Areas Development Project includes a credit component aimed directly at women's income-generating activities so that they can use released time to earn extra cash.

In Sudan, after initial fears about the safety of liquid propane gas (LPG), women now like the new LPG stoves because they are cleaner and quicker than fuel-wood stoves and easier to tend. However, many women stop using their LPG stoves after a while and revert to charcoal stoves, even though the cost of fuel per month is more expensive. One explanation is that currently LPG is available only in large containers that last for a full month. With no tradition of saving money, women have a cash flow problem when their containers are empty and revert to buying small amounts of charcoal on a daily basis. Efforts are now being made to promote a savings culture to overcome this problem. In addition, the private company that supplies LPG in Sudan has realized there is a potentially large market for its product in rural areas and is planning many innovations, including better distribution systems, smaller containers, and provision of credit to assist with stove purchase.

Sources: Bates 2007; Dianzheng 2007; IFAD 2007.

Improved roads make it possible to use a range of intermediate means of transport that would not be appropriate for use on rough rural paths and that, in theory, can result in a significant reduction in the time and effort spent by women on transportation tasks. For instance, the use of a wheelbarrow with a payload of 50 kilograms compared with head loading (20-kilogram capacity) can reduce the time spent on water transport by 60 percent (Mwankusye 2002). However, there is a range of sociocultural and economic barriers to women's access to such intermediate means of transport. Wheelbarrows often are rejected by women who are used to standing straight while head loading and find it physically discomforting to bend and push these devices. Carts are expensive and often owned by men who use them for their own purposes and do not provide their wives with access, even when they have been distributed through development projects aimed at assisting entire rural households. As seen earlier, using draft animals for farm activities and transport is often seen as a men's activity, and training is given only to men.

An interesting aspect of intermediate means of transport is that they often result in a changing division of labor within the household. Sometimes this is to women's advantage, but it can also add to their workload or deprive them of new economic opportunities. In one project in South Africa, in which donkey carts were distributed to help with fuelwood collection, the carts were monopolized by men who used them to collect and sell wood from resources closest to the homestead, leaving women to travel even farther to get fuelwood for domestic use (Venter and Mashiri 2007). In India, when bicycles were introduced through a literacy program, women learned to ride and had limited access to their husband's bicycle. This increased women's self-confidence and increased their involvement in community activities, but it also meant that they had to undertake work such as marketing that was not expected of them when they were less mobile (Rao 2002).

Off-farm activities

A major objective of projects that introduce labor-saving technologies and practices is to help women divert time from subsistence farming activities and domestic chores into more productive, income-generating enterprises. Often the most remunerative of these enterprises are intensive in their use of water, fuelwood, or both, and involve laborious production and processing methods using traditional techniques and technologies. This can require quantities of women's time that simply may not be available to them. In some circumstances increasingly scarce water supplies and rising costs of fuel can threaten the existence of women's traditional food-processing industries unless they can gain access to improved technologies and practices.

Brewing is a major source of income for most women in sub-Saharan Africa but accounts for up to 25 percent of total wood fuel consumed by the average household and requires time-consuming energy management. Interventions include design and dissemination of improved stoves for home brewing in the expectation that women will invest in the stoves if they lower costs of production. but continuous fire management affects fuel efficiency more than technology design, a fact often missed in development projects that have failed to consult with women entrepreneurs.[2] Innovative practices that break with tradition and establish cooperative brewing enterprises using larger-scale technologies could provide a more satisfactory solution.

The examples in box 7.18 show that when women are properly consulted and involved in the design and adaptation process, there can be significant benefits for rural women involved in food-processing enterprises and for rural artisans involved in the production and sale of the improved technologies on which they are based.

Finally, the increasing demand for time- and energy-saving technologies can in itself form the basis for income-generating activities for women. In India illiterate women from eight states have been trained as "barefoot solar engineers" to establish solar energy systems in areas where the electricity supply is either nonexistent or highly erratic.[3] Other examples of women's involvement in energy production include earning money through manufacturing lamps in Bangladesh, manufacturing and marketing clay liners for improved stoves in Kenya, making biomass briquettes for sale in Malawi, and operating diesel generators as businesses and selling energy services in Mali (UNDP 2001). One benefit from the provision of rural electricity is the ability to work on income-generating activities, such as crafts in the evenings, which effectively "extends" as opposed to saves time. While this increases earning opportunities, it also increases women's workload (Clancy and Kooijman 2006).

GOOD PRACTICES AND LESSONS LEARNED

Findings are divided into two major groups:

- Those that relate to the *dissemination* of labor-saving technologies and practices in terms of appropriateness, acceptability, and fit with priority needs
- Those that relate to the *impact* of these technologies on different types of women in terms of meeting practical and strategic needs and sustainability.

Dissemination

Many of the labor-saving technologies introduced through development projects or available through commercial

---

Box 7.18   West Africa: Women's Role in Innovation

Most women in the coastal areas of West Africa make a living through smoking and selling fish. In collaboration with women users, a local technology institute developed an improved oven that is now widely used throughout the region. The new oven enables women to undertake three smoking cycles a day, whereas only one cycle was possible with the traditional technology. Most women spend the same time processing more fish, but some time savings still exist because the new technology is easier to operate and allows women to tend to other household tasks while the fish is being smoked. One unexpected consequence of this profitable technology is that men are beginning to take over what has traditionally been a women's industry and compete with them.

In Nigeria, the most time-consuming aspect of preparing *gari,* a convenience food made from cassava, is grating the tubers, which can take a whole day using traditional manual technologies. A mechanized grater was developed by an artisan carpenter in Benin State at the behest of his three wives, and the original prototype has been adapted by local artisans over time in response to the suggestions of women users of the graters. Time spent on grating is reduced from one day to around 15 minutes, but women cannot afford to own the graters they have helped to design. Most are owned by men who hire women operators. Thus, although the graters lead to a reduction in the time women spend on grating cassava (time that they divert mainly to other economic activities such as making more *gari* and engaging in retail trade), they do not benefit from profits on the grating process, and the profit made from *gari* processing (as opposed to grating) is very small.

Sources: Adjebeng-Asem 1990; ILO/Netherlands government 1985; Sandhu 1989.

---

channels have not found widespread acceptance among rural women. Several reasons account for this. Sometimes, as is the case with many semimechanized crop-processing technologies, they are not much more efficient than traditional technologies and so do not merit the extra investment involved. In other cases the technologies have been imported from other countries and introduced without adaptation or have been adapted by local manufacturers and artisans without proper consultation with proposed users. When, as a result, these do not meet the specific needs of the users, they tend to be rejected. When research and development institutions, local manufacturers, and artisans have been able to find a way to relate to women users and to incorporate their ideas into the design and adaptation process, as was the case with smoking ovens and cassava graters in West Africa, then improved technologies have been successfully disseminated. Ways need to be found to replicate such experiences in other developing countries such as those in East and Southern Africa, where there is very little interaction between blacksmiths who produce farm equipment and rural women who are their potential clients.

In some cases, women reject labor-saving technologies for sociocultural reasons, such as taboos on working with oxen or using long-handled hoes. Although it is important to be sensitive to cultural issues, they can represent a major constraint on economic development. Sometimes taboos have been overcome as a matter of necessity as with African women using oxen when they are forced to take over men's farming tasks as a result of increased migration and the spread of HIV and AIDS. In other cases, such as Senegalese women using long-handled hoes and Indian women riding bicycles, communities have simply accepted change in response to external stimuli. Examples such as these can be used as role models for women and men in other parts of the world.

Even when labor-saving technologies are appropriate, culturally acceptable, and meet a priority need, many factors limit women's access to these. As seen with farm implements in East Africa, women often do not know the range of technologies that are available. Traditional government extension services provide a narrow range of information that, in the case of agriculture, is normally restricted to seeds and fertilizers rather than tools (IFAD 1998), and extension workers tend to relate to men rather than women. Commercial companies rarely do market research or supply information to potential clients, and local blacksmiths are rarely linked to outside sources of information. Box 7.19 lists some good practices for dissemination.

Although many programs such as IFAD's First Mile Project promote the use of new information and communications technologies to get information to women and men farmers about market prices, they have not gone far enough in using these as a way of supplying information about the range of available labor-saving technologies.[4] Some NGO initiatives are moving ahead on this front. One such initiative is the network of village kiosks and coordinating hubs that has been set up by the M. S. Swaminathan Research Foundation in India to link rural women virtually with scientists and technologists, who can respond to their problems and requests for information (Fairless 2007). Other examples include the various initiatives of Women of Uganda Network (WOUGNET) in Uganda that seek (in collaboration with government programs) to use the Internet to bridge the gap between researchers, extension workers, and women farmers (various WOUGNET newsletters at www.wougnet.org).

Another major barrier to women's access to labor-saving technologies is their lack of access to cash and reluctance on the part of their husbands to contribute toward such technologies when they feel that the work can be done (as it

---

Box 7.19   Good Practices for Dissemination

- Involve women users in the development and adaptation of labor-saving technologies and practices
- Disseminate examples of women overcoming cultural barriers to use of labor-saving technologies and practices and encourage exchange visits
- Strengthen and develop programs to spread information on labor-saving technologies and practices

through information and communication technologies
- Disseminate information on the value of women's time in subsistence activities
- Enable women to use time saved by labor-saving technologies and practices in income-generating activities through credit, training, and access to markets

Source: Authors.

always has) free of expense by women. As long as women's labor is perceived as having little or no value, then little progress can be expected. However, experience shows that two strategies can be effective. First, research findings that put an economic value on women's time spent on survival tasks can be more widely disseminated to decision makers and rural communities as a tool for advocating for the introduction of labor-saving technologies on economic grounds. Second, strategies can be introduced that increase the chances of the time saved by women being redeployed in economically productive ways so that they are better able to cover the costs of labor-saving devices. This was the case with the IFAD biogas project in China that provided loans for women's income-generating activities as an integral part of the project (box 7.17).

Access to training and technical skills has also proved to be a barrier to women's use of technologies because it is often men rather than women who are targeted for training opportunities. When women are given the chance to learn new skills, as with the women barefoot solar engineers in India (see above), they show that they are well able to put this to good use. Experience also shows that women are extremely good at sharing new knowledge with each other and that peer training and exchange are often more effective tools in spreading improved technologies than formal training courses.

Impact

Reaching women with labor-saving technologies is only half of the battle. Experience shows that outcomes are not always as expected and that any short-term practical benefits can sometimes be lost if the use of the technologies does not lead to longer-term strategic changes. Measuring impact is a difficult task. Although it is easy to put a figure on the amount of time that women can save through using a particular technology, it is much more difficult to trace how women make use of this time. Sometimes the time is simply used to collect more water or fuelwood, farm more land than was possible before, or reduce the amount of time that children must spend on such activities. Sometimes it is used to earn more income. And sometimes it is put into social and community activities such as visiting friends and family or attending literacy classes and committee meetings. Often it is split among all such uses. All are important, but policy makers and development planners can and do influence choices through changing taxes on imported tools and equipment, subsidizing water or electricity provision, and providing credit and training related to income-generating

activities. Ministries of agriculture, industry, and rural development can also assist through support to rural blacksmiths and artisans who produce appropriate tools and equipment for agricultural production and processing and through ensuring that commercial distributors are better informed about the needs of rural producers.

Any one technology can have a differential impact on women in different regions and levels of household status. Generally women in poor and landless households living in areas of labor surplus such as Asia are more likely to be displaced by labor-saving on-farm technologies than helped by them. In these circumstances, more programs such as those introduced by BRAC in Bangladesh are needed if the poorest women are to share more equally in the benefits associated with modern farm machinery. Even in conditions of labor scarcity, rural women are not always able to benefit fully from the mechanization of their more arduous tasks. In most of Africa the majority of rural mills and oil presses are owned by men entrepreneurs. Thus, although most women have access to these technologies, they do not own them or control the significant profits to be made from their operation. Attempts have been made to promote cooperative ownership with mixed results. However, experience shows that when the need and the benefits are great enough, as with the case of the women's bus cooperative in Kenya, women can take control of their lives through ownership of a modern technology.

This issue of access versus ownership and control relates directly to the distinction between meeting practical and strategic needs. Many projects result in practical benefits, such as reduced time spent in collecting water or fuelwood, but fewer of them meet strategic needs in terms of changing the balance of power within the household or increasing women's ability to negotiate effectively with local decision makers. An effective way of increasing women's status within the household and community is to increase their earning capacity, thus strengthening the argument for labor-saving technologies that provide women time to engage in income-generating activities.

Finally, labor-saving technologies can have some unexpected results. For example, they can lead to changes in the division of labor within the household or to men taking over women's traditional industries when they become more profitable. To the extent these changes deprive women of income-earning opportunities, they need to be addressed through measures that support women's ownership and control of the technologies involved. In addition, short-term gains that women derive from some labor-saving technologies can be lost if there is no system in place to maintain and repair them. Training women to undertake such tasks can serve the double purpose of keeping systems in operation and providing a useful source of income.

GUIDELINES AND RECOMMENDATIONS FOR PRACTITIONERS

Different aspects of women's work and lives are so intertwined that it makes little sense to try to deal with one aspect in isolation. Thus, rural transport projects should not be dealt with separately from water supply, rural energy supply, and health provision projects. Furthermore, programs that incorporate measures to reduce the time women spend in subsistence activities should have components that facilitate women's increased involvement in income-generating activities. Integrated approaches are needed if women's strategic and practical needs are to be met effectively.

Programs and projects should reduce emphasis on imported technologies and support local blacksmiths and artisans instead. This will increase women's voices in the design and adaptation process and better ensure that tools and equipment can be maintained and repaired in a timely and cost-effective manner. Support measures include training, assistance with commercialization of technologies, and fostering linkages with women clients and outside sources of information. The use of information and communication technologies can play an important role in building linkages between women clients, artisans, research and development institutions, and the private commercial sector, both locally and globally.

When one group of women benefits from labor-saving technologies and practices at the expense of another, measures are needed to assist the losers in diversifying into alternative ways of earning an income. This can involve various organizing strategies and provision of credit, skills training, and information on new economic opportunities. In general, women's access to credit and rural finance facilities is essential in situations in which women have little or no cash or assets and their subsistence activities are given no value. More attention also needs to be given to ensuring women's equal access to training and extension services and to linking women with local artisans, technologists, and commercial distributors through information and communication technologies and other channels.

Peru: Natural Resource Management in the Southern Highlands

The Management of Natural Resources project in the southern highlands of Peru—known by its acronym, MARENASS—uses a highly innovative methodology developed with 13 rural communities in Chumbivilcas, Cusco, during the 1980s.[1] The methodology, called Pachamama Raymi, assists rural communities to mobilize funds and knowledge to manage locally developed natural resources in ways that suit the organizational and cultural strengths of rural communities in the Andes. The MARENASS project, funded by a loan from IFAD to the government of Peru, began operations in 1997 (table 7.4). It scaled up the work initiated with the original 13 communities to reach 360 communities, with the assistance of a small technical support unit and farmer specialists/knowledge sharers. The project involved entire communities—men, women, children, and elders—in a series of contests to recover, adapt, and innovate technologies for sustainable natural resource management.

Although the project ended in 2005, the government of Peru continues to monitor the impact of the methodology and has found that many communities continue to use it on their own. In 2002 the World Bank's Agriculture and Rural Development (ARD) Division supported the use of the methodology for the Rural Resource Management Project

> **What's innovative?** Natural resources are locally developed and managed in ways that mesh with and support the organizational and cultural strengths of Andean communities. Women are the major actors in the management of these resources.

executed by the Mukono Agricultural Development Centre of Uganda's National Agriculture Research Organisation (NARO). During the four years of the project, rural communities in a number of districts enthusiastically received and adapted the Pachamama Raymi methodology (Fernandez and Lusembo 2002).

The following sections of this Innovative Activity Profile on the MARENASS project are excerpted from the IFAD Web site (www.ifad.org).

PACHA MAMA RAYMI AND THE MARENASS PROJECT

The literal meaning of "Pacha Mama Raymi" is Festival of Mother Earth. The methodology draws upon the cultural, mythological, and religious traditions of Andean communities in relation to the cultivation of "Mother Earth." These

Table 7.4 Marenass Project Data	
Project cost	$15.2 million
IFAD loan	$12.3 million
Borrower's contribution	$2.9 million
Percentage transferred to communities	80% of total project cost
Project cost per community	$40,000 per community; average of $350 per family. Capital formation in the communities very quickly surpassed that amount.
Number of participants	20,015 families in 360 communities (average 55 families/community)

Source: Compiled from "Plan de Trabajo Institucional Proyecto de Recursos Naturales en la Sierra Sur del Peru 'Pacha Mama Raymi,'" Abancay, Peru, 2003.

traditions allow productive natural resources to be managed while still respecting the vision and needs of local farmers. Pacha Mama Raymi uses competitions to promote new technological practices among villagers to improve natural resource management, agricultural production, and living conditions. The families or communities that best apply the advice provided by technical staff and that achieve the top results earn a cash prize presented at a Mother Earth festival. The competitions are a catalyst—an efficient and effective means of sharing, disseminating, and replicating local technological innovation throughout the entire project area.

Farmer-to-farmer training

MARENASS provides technical services based on the transfer of resources to communities. The funds enable communities to hire, supervise, and evaluate technical staff directly. The communities themselves select people who are to participate in farmer-to-farmer training. This approach has kept service costs low and encouraged the broad-based acceptance and adoption of new technologies by the communities. Continued support (in the form of stronger training programs and adequate funding) will be important to develop local service markets and ensure that supply meets farmers' demands.

Economic outlook

MARENASS has shown that the key to overcoming poverty in the harsh conditions of the southern highlands of Peru is to rehabilitate and conserve productive natural resources. The surplus generated by agricultural production and small businesses, as well as the prizes won by villagers in the competitions, have increased beneficiaries' financial and fixed assets, such as housing, corrals, terraces, irrigation infrastructure, and pastureland. Further substantial increases in production are expected, and farmers will need to enhance their links to markets and diversify production to ensure that they can sell surplus produce.

Women as key decision makers

Women's groups were entrusted with the administration of small funds providing small amounts of credit for the development of microbusinesses such as agricultural production and livestock breeding and fattening. Some groups are also working to preserve biodiversity through the recovery of seeds of native species and the development of small nurseries. The fund has been successful: average capitalization is around 50 percent. The women's groups have invested in activities that showed large enough returns for the enterprises to grow after paying back the credit. Ideas about social and family equity disseminated through gender and other types of training, combined with the increased empowerment of villagers, have led to a more equitable distribution of benefits among the poorest. Women in particular enjoy improved status because of the training and their increased ability to manage funds. The greater visibility and prestige of women with respect to their productive and reproductive roles and contribution to the family have also led to a more equitable sharing of responsibility within families, further enhancing women's status and position. Women and children have more time to improve their living conditions and concentrate on education. To continue supporting women's roles as key decision makers, women will need access to further training in managing microcredit and microbusinesses.

BENEFITS AND IMPACTS

The project and the community use "talking maps" to establish goals and a plan of action that begins with training and dissemination activities within the community. Talking maps portray the community graphically at three levels: the past (30 years before the project), the current situation (as of the project start-up date), and the future (in 20 or 30 years). Based on these maps, each year communities develop a community plan of action. This instrument enjoys wide social acceptance (bolstered by the competitions between communities) and is the true basis for "real and participatory" planning in the community.

Activities in resource management and conservation are organized and executed by the communities themselves, using their own means: families or communities make investments beforehand (mainly in labor but also materials), and although they may later win an award, it will never equal the value of the investment.

The competitions between communities are the instrument that has made it possible to achieve two objectives: first, community cohesion, and second, mass dissemination of resource management techniques and their subsequent application. Although the level of participation in the competitions between families is quite variable (averaging 40 percent of families in each community), by decision of the assembly, the competitions between communities necessarily involve all families in each community. The competition and the award provide the strong initial impetus. Later, concrete results become the incentive to continue with the practices introduced: production improvements that translate into higher earnings for the farmers, thanks to more effective use of their productive natural resources and the consequent appreciation in the value of those resources, which constitute their main asset.

The funds for organized groups of women have helped to finance the microbusinesses they manage. In several communities mixed groups of men, women, and young people have formed. Most groups have their own bank accounts; the others use the community account. The MARENASS funds are transferred into these accounts, as are the revenues of the microbusinesses. The businesses managed by the women run the gamut from agricultural production and livestock breeding and fattening to micromarketing and microcredit operations, which extend loans directly to users under agreements established by the group itself, stipulating the form of repayment. As mentioned, some groups also recover seeds of native species and develop small nurseries. This fund has achieved remarkable success. About 50 percent of the women's groups have been able to begin a process of capitalization. The project has been remarkably successful in fostering widespread use of technologies for land management such as terracing and crop rotation that are part of farmers' shared cultural heritage but had been abandoned (farmers say they were "forgotten," although it is likely that they were supplanted by technologies such as external input use that were suitable only for capital-intensive farming on high-potential land). The most positive results are seen in the practices employed in the environment nearest to and worked most intensively by families, where the quantity and quality of produce for home consumption have improved.

The impact of MARENASS on human capital is directly related to the improvement in living conditions as a result of (1) lightening the burden of everyday tasks for the family, especially women; (2) greater, more varied, and more stable production throughout the year (with a consequent reduction in vulnerability); (3) refurbishment of physical assets and improvement of homes; and (4) acquisition of new goods (increased family economic activity). These improvements are behind the optimism expressed by all those interviewed. Security about their potential for growth utilizing the resources at their disposal forms the basis for their claims.

The ideas about social and family equity disseminated through the gender and citizenship training for both women and men, combined with the empowerment of participants and groups under MARENASS, have fostered increased attention to and better—that is, more equitable, effective, and representative—distribution of benefits among the poorest sectors of the community. As noted, the improvement in women's status within the family and community has been due to better training for women, their capacity to manage funds, and firm encouragement of their participation.

The most immediate impact of the improved practices has been to reduce women's workload, because women have traditionally been responsible for feeding and herding animals and for small-scale sales of small livestock and agricultural products. Improvements in the quantity, quality, and diversity of family production are making it possible for women not only to cover the basic needs of their families but also to contribute financially (sometimes for the first time) to family income through retail sales of small surpluses. Feeling more secure about their families' well-being has given the women a new sense of self-assuredness.

MARENASS project activities have emphasized "capacity-building," recognizing that local stakeholders are pivotal to facilitating its interventions. The project thus has had a very great impact on stakeholders' proficiency in all three dimensions of "capacity": knowledge, know-how, and the ability to take action.

The management of funds has enhanced the capacity of women's group members to engage in commerce in addition to enhancing their prestige. In most cases women's groups have mastered the theory and practice of teamwork (pooling and joint marketing of goods; mutual support among participating families) and avoided the individualistic attitudes that result from the break-up of communities.

The families and communities participating in MARENASS have taken ownership of the project and, with it, of something that they felt was already theirs: the terraces, the houses, the water, the pastures, a technology with a high labor content that produces high returns with little or no external input. But, above all, they have taken ownership of a "friendly" project that has offered technologies within their reach and rooted in their culture and ancestral practices. The project's sustainability depends largely on this concept of "regaining ownership" and on acceptance of the idea, often repeated by community members: "We are MARENASS."

LESSONS LEARNED AND ISSUES FOR WIDER APPLICABILITY

- The successful methodology used by MARENASS was based on the transfer of decision making and responsibility for planning and financial resources to the communities, privatized services of technical assistance and farmer-to-farmer training, and the supply of low-external-input technology to farmers.

■ In strengthening the social fabric of the communities, the project has succeeded in respecting and maintaining local values and culture.

■ Providing training in management of funds has been key to women's engagement in business ventures and, in turn, in providing them with economic empowerment.

■ An innovative aspect of the project is the use of competitions to evaluate and reward the best approaches devised by communities to manage natural resources.

■ Twenty-five thousand families have moved from a subsistence existence and are now producing a surplus and enjoying greater physical and financial assets and food security.

■ It is estimated that the return on project investments in terms of increased value of beneficiaries' assets ranges between $3 and $5 for every dollar spent by the project on the communities.

■ A high level of participation exists in community activities. People identify closely with MARENASS and have endorsed the methodologies that seek the best alternatives and adopt the most relevant technologies.

■ The communities say: "We are MARENASS. We do the work, we make the decisions, we irrigate and we improve our homes, our farms, our pastures. . . . What we do, we do for ourselves and it remains here for us."

Tanzania: Conservation Agriculture for Sustainable Development

PROJECT OBJECTIVES AND DESCRIPTION

The Sustainable Agriculture and Rural Development (SARD) initiative was launched at the World Summit on Sustainable Development as a multistakeholder umbrella framework designed to support the transition to people-centered sustainable agriculture and rural development and to strengthen participation in program and policy development. A major objective of the project on Conservation Agriculture for Sustainable Agriculture and Rural Development is to derive lessons about the feasibility of conservation agriculture (CA) for small-scale and resource-poor farmers.[1]

The project, which started in 2004, aims to facilitate and accelerate the adoption of profitable CA practices by small-scale farmers in five districts in Tanzania and five districts in Kenya. The project builds on CA pilot activities in both countries. Over the long term the project will contribute to improved food security and rural livelihoods and lay the foundation for CA to expand and support sustainable agriculture and rural development.

What's innovative? Energy-efficient agricultural production technologies, combined with participatory methodologies, enable farmers to adopt farming practices that reduce labor and raise yields and incomes. Women, the main providers of agricultural labor, benefit most from the reduced labor needed for conservation agriculture. Equal training and extension opportunities are offered to women and men.

Aside from fostering environmental sustainability through soil and water conservation, the CA project aims to contribute to the social and economic pillars of sustainable agriculture and rural development through the following:

- Reducing the workload and time spent for agricultural production, therefore enabling people to diversify their livelihoods, develop businesses, and gain time for education, family care, community development, and political empowerment
- Increasing crop yields, especially by reducing drought sensitivity and dependence upon purchased fertilizers (with their widely fluctuating prices)
- Increasing production and agricultural earnings
- Enhancing crop biodiversity and diversifying food intake
- Fostering the development of secure livelihoods for other rural actors such as rural artisans and small-scale entrepreneurs.

Two main concepts inform the project and its intended approach:

- The *technical concept of conservation agriculture (CA),* which combines minimal soil disturbance (reduced tillage, minimum tillage, direct planting); permanent soil cover with the crop itself or with the utilization of cover crops, residues, or mulch; and crop rotations/associations, through crop sequences, intercropping, relay cropping, and/or mixed crops.
- *The methodological concept of using participatory extension approaches to introduce the CA concept.* Both FAO and IFAD have good experience with FFSs, which emphasize farmer-driven and farmer-first methodologies. A major challenge of the project was to combine this participatory methodology with a clear technical farming concept. The project, now in its second phase, has more than 120 FFSs operating in 10 districts and directly involving 3,000 farmers. In addition to farmers, the project also aimed to involve extension workers, researchers, and, most important, the

private sector. The private sector was emphasized as a way of ensuring that farmers would have agricultural inputs and services, specialized CA tools and equipment, and farm power by the end of the project.

The project is funded by the German Ministry of Agriculture and Consumer Protection. The main implementing agencies include FAO, the African Conservation Tillage Network (ACT), the Ministry of Agriculture (Kenya), the Kenya Agricultural Research Institute (KARI), the Ministry of Agriculture and Food Security (Tanzania), and the Selian Agricultural Research Institute (SARI) (Tanzania).

BENEFITS AND IMPACTS

The following summary of benefits and impacts is drawn from a study undertaken in Arumeru District of Tanzania by ACT (Maguzu and others 2007) and from an IFAD/FAO study in Tanzania in 2002 (Bishop-Sambrook and others 2004). Particular emphasis is given to the role of women and the reduction in their workloads as a result of adopting CA practices.

Arumeru District is located in the Arusha region of Tanzania. Farming is rain fed, and 90 percent of the population relies on agricultural activities for a living. Sixty to seventy percent of arable land is cultivated using tractor-drawn discs and draft animals. The remaining 30–40 percent of land is cultivated by hand hoes. The quality and effectiveness of these methods, as well as their suitability for women, vary widely. The main staple food crop is maize, which is intercropped with beans or pigeon peas.

Traditionally rural women in Tanzania are marginalized. The man household head makes all decisions concerning agricultural production. In addition, agricultural equipment is owned by men, even though women are responsible for most agricultural work. The prevalence of HIV and AIDS in the district is high. As a result, families have had to sell their assets, the availability of family farm labor has decreased, and children have left school to help their families' farm. The labor shortages have reduced agricultural production and food security. Women have been especially affected by these developments, because their workloads have increased considerably as they care for HIV sufferers, attend to household chores, and manage farm operations simultaneously. The adoption of CA practices that reduce labor requirements was therefore expected to benefit women significantly.

By 2006 the project had established 11 FFSs involving 325 farmers (148 men and 177 women). Gender was con-sidered when forming all FFSs to ensure that women could learn about CA and extension services to the same extent as men. Each FFS runs experiments on a test plot, and each farmer is obliged to dedicate part of his or her own land to one or more CA techniques.

Animal-drawn instruments such as rippers and manually operated instruments such as the jab planter, as well as seed for staple and cover crops, are supplied by the project. The animal-drawn ripper allows for reduced tillage because it cuts furrows into the soil rather than inverting it completely.

The manually operated jab planter allows for planting operations to be done through the soil cover with no tillage. By using the jab planter, the farmer does not have to prepare the field before planting, thereby saving time. Farmers have to share these instruments because they are expensive. If the equipment is unavailable, farmers must revert to conventional farming or adapt practices using traditional tools, such as the planting stick or the hands. Table 7.5 shows that jab planters are, on average, five times less costly than a no-till ripper and four times less costly than the conventional ripper. This price differential, in addition to the fact that they are easier to use, makes the jab planter popular with smallholders.

The adoption of CA has had three main impacts, discussed in the sections that follow: it has reduced the demand for household labor, increased food security by achieving higher yields, and increased household income.

Reduced labor requirements

Farmers in the district depend mainly on family labor but may also hire labor for certain tasks such as weeding. Women and children are traditionally responsible for planting and weeding, while men are responsible for preparing the land. With conventional agriculture, men guide the animals and the plow as women walk behind to place seeds in the ridge and cover them with their feet. Weeding is particularly tedious and may take up to 28 days per hectare. In addition, hoes often tend to be obsolete or not adapted to women's use. With the adoption of CA practices, labor requirements are not only greatly reduced (table 7.6), but the workload

Table 7.5	Cost of Conservation Agriculture Implements	
Implement	**Price ($)**
No-till ripper	195.00
Conventional ripper	136.50
Jab planter	35.10

Source: Adapted from Maguzu and others 2007.

Table 7.6 Labor Requirements with Conservation and Conventional Agricultural Practices

Farming activity	Conservation agriculture			Conventional agriculture		
	Labor/acre (no. people)	Implement	Time/acre (days)	Labor/acre (no. people)	Implement	Time/acre (days)
Land preparation	2–3	Ripper and slashers	3	2–4	Plow	3–4
Planting	2	Jab planter	2	3	Draft animals	3–4
Weeding	8–10 performed once	Hand hoe	1	8–10 performed twice	Hand hoe	1

Source: Adapted from Maguzu and others 2007.

shifts to some extent, because men work alongside women in planting operations once a jab planter is available.

Lower labor requirements associated with CA practices affect women and other family members differently. Poor women-headed households benefit from lower labor demands, because a decrease in labor pressures frees family members from the requirement of working in the field. Children can pursue their education uninterrupted by sudden labor shortages. Women in landless households have fewer opportunities to sell their labor, but higher crop yields—and thus higher labor requirements for harvesting—could cushion the reduction in hired labor opportunities. Additional employment opportunities for rural women laborers as a result of higher yields would have an immediate effect on household livelihoods, as additional income is used for schooling and medical care.

Women in farm households spend time released by CA on household chores and income-generating activities, such as raising chickens, tending vegetable plots, or selling crops at local markets. More time is also spent participating in communal activities or simply taking more rest.

Increased yields and incomes

Farmers who adopted CA practices reported higher yields. Yields of maize rose by 40 to 70 percent, and increased yields were also reported for the cover crops, some of which bring higher returns than maize in the market. Yield increases lead directly to greater household food security and, if surpluses are sold, to higher incomes.

LESSONS LEARNED AND ISSUES FOR WIDER APPLICABILITY

Although CA obviously has yielded some benefits, barriers to adoption remain. Another concern is that not everyone

has benefited equally from CA. A number of issues must be considered in developing plans to encourage wider dissemination of CA techniques.

Attitudes toward CA can present strong, deep-rooted challenges. Farmers are considered good and hard-working by their peers if they keep their fields clean and plow them. Farmers who keep crop residues as soil cover on their fields and use no-till practices are considered lazy. Grazing rights are another concern. The practice of allowing community livestock (particularly cattle) to graze on harvested fields endangers the soil cover used in CA. Grazing rights should be addressed through community laws or codes of practice.

As mentioned, women in poor households are likely to benefit from the reduced labor requirement of CA, but women from landless households may simply lose their source of income unless alternative jobs are created in harvesting increased yields of maize and cover crops. Careful attention should be given to analyzing the potential impact of CA on all categories of women, and plans must be made to provide income-generating alternatives for those who may lose their source of livelihood.

A major consideration in the adoption, sustainability, and diffusion of these practices is the cost of inputs and specific tools. At the moment, these are available through the project at a subsidized rate, but their cost and limited availability may represent major constraints if farmers have to rely on commercial distributors, because commercial supply channels have yet to be built up. Commercial channels are expected to open when demand rises. Demand is created through farmers' success stories, demonstrations, and promotional activities. Women (who have less access to cash and credit than men) will be most affected by the cost of inputs and tools. Special rural finance mechanisms to deal with this problem will need to be built into dissemination strategies.

Junior Farmer Field and Life Schools: Empowering Orphans and Vulnerable Youth Living in a World with HIV and AIDS

In 2007 an estimated 33.2 million people worldwide were living with the human immunodeficiency virus (HIV), which may lead to acquired immunodeficiency syndrome (AIDS) (UNAIDS 2007). The HIV and AIDS pandemic has had devastating impacts on food security and rural development within households, communities, nations, and regions, and these impacts will endure long into the future. Because HIV and AIDS affect people's physical ability to work, their spread in rural areas has negative repercussions for agricultural production and therefore food security. The quality of life in households affected by the disease can decline drastically, and their vulnerability—physical, economic, and social— may rise commensurately.[1] For biological and sociocultural reasons, HIV and AIDS have a greater effect on women and girls than on men and boys. The level of infection can be three to five times greater among women.[2]

The pandemic may lead to an increase in women's work burden, as women are often the primary carers for the sick. They are also likely to take on new roles in agricultural production and in caring when other members of their household can no longer work because of illness. Given the major role women play in household food security, HIV and AIDS are likely to affect household food security by reducing the time women spend in securing and preparing food and in generating income (thus reducing their purchasing power for food). The sale of assets to cover medical costs further erodes households' resilience to the impact of HIV. To accommodate these burdens, girls are removed from school more often than boys to help with caring for the sick, agricultural production activities, and household tasks. In sub-Saharan Africa, HIV and AIDS have exacerbated women's and children's vulnerability with respect to property rights because of the growing incidence of "land grabbing," which occurs when a deceased husband's relatives take land and other productive assets away from the surviving woman and her children.

What's innovative? The Junior Farmer Field and Life Schools (JFFLSs) have a unique learning methodology and curriculum, which combine both agricultural and life skills. The JFFLSs' dual focus on life and agricultural skills creates a double impact, strengthening life skills and protecting rural young people from shocks such as HIV and other diseases in the immediate term, while creating long-term food security and livelihood opportunities that empower rural young people over the long term, thus minimizing their vulnerability to destitution and coping strategies.

An innovative aspect of the JFFLSs is the way children are encouraged to develop as people; a school timetable includes cultural activities such as singing, dancing, and theater. This allows the children to grow in confidence while keeping local cultural traditions alive.

Consequently, women and children are often forced into high-risk activities to secure food and/or income for themselves or their families (Izumi 2006). As the disease wipes out entire generations of parents, their indigenous agricultural knowledge is disappearing, and the mentoring and apprenticeship opportunities for teaching children about livelihood strategies have vanished as well.

HIV and AIDS have left an estimated 143 million orphans worldwide. Research on HIV and AIDS, gender, and food security by FAO has highlighted the urgent need to work with boys and girls who have lost one or both parents to the disease, as well as with other vulnerable young people, to help them develop the agricultural and livelihood skills and knowledge they will need to sustain themselves and their families in the future and to forge a place for themselves in their society. To assist them, the Gender, Equity and Rural Employment Division of FAO, in collaboration with the World Food Programme (WFP) and other partners, supports the creation and development of Junior Farmer Field and Life Schools (JFFLSs) in countries where the prevalence of AIDS is highest: Cameroon, Kenya, Malawi, Mozambique, Namibia, Sudan, Swaziland, Tanzania, Uganda, Zambia, and Zimbabwe.[3]

PROJECT OBJECTIVES AND DESCRIPTION

The JFFLS program seeks to improve the livelihoods of vulnerable youths, give them opportunities for long-term food security, and minimize their vulnerability to malnutrition, abuse, and high-risk activities. The program aims to achieve these goals by increasing vulnerable and orphaned youths and children's knowledge of improved agricultural practices for sustainable local development and working toward greater gender equality and empowerment.[4]

The JFFLS methodology is an adaptation of two successful participatory learning approaches: the Farmer Field Schools developed for adult farmers in Cambodia and the Farmer Life Schools (FLSs). In JFFLSs the FFS and FLS approaches have been adapted to the needs and situations of orphans, vulnerable children, and youths. Experience has shown that JFFLSs tend to be more effective when they are connected to adult FFSs implemented in the same area. For example, since FFSs in Mozambique have been included in the National Ministry of Agriculture Work Plan, the integration of JFFLS graduates into existing farmers' associations has been strongly encouraged.

The program provides boys and girls with training in traditional and modern agricultural techniques and in the life skills that will foster their capacity to solve problems, build social relationships, take responsibility, and acquire a range of practical survival skills.

Children learn practical agricultural skills by doing practical agricultural tasks in an allocated plot or field. The children, who are 12–18 years of age, are trained for periods from 6 to 12 months (depending on where the schools are set up) following the local cropping cycle. Children learn about local agroecological conditions, field preparation, sowing and transplanting, weeding, irrigation, integrated pest management, utilization and conservation of available resources, utilization and processing of food crops, harvesting, storage, and marketing skills. The choice of agriculture-related activities varies, as it depends on the agroecological location of the school.

The emphasis on life skills is there because many of the children attending the JFFLSs do not have parents who can share those socializing skills that we all need to live a healthy and balanced life. The JFFLSs address such issues as HIV and AIDS awareness and prevention, sensitization on gender equality, child protection, nutritional education, good hygiene, and the prevention of human, crop, and livestock diseases and their treatment. Efforts are made to ensure that the different needs of boys and girls are identified and met when covering the life skills components. Emphasis is placed on participatory educational theater and social animation to explore sensitive issues such as sexuality, sexual health, children's rights, gender roles, and HIV and AIDS.

For 12 months, a multidisciplinary team of facilitators leads participatory sessions with a group of about 30 girls and boys who range in age from 12 to 18. These sessions are given two to three times a week in the field and classroom, after regular school hours.

INNOVATIVE FEATURES

The learning methods and content of the JFFLSs break with classical approaches to education and apprenticeship in several ways. Boys and girls have equal access to learning, and school resources are distributed fairly among them. Equal distribution of school meals to boys and girls presents an alternative to local practices in many communities, where more food is often allocated to boys, resulting in higher levels of malnutrition among girls.

Food support is important for a successful JFFLS program because it provides an initial incentive for the JFFLS participants to enroll, attend sessions, and have enough energy to participate in the learning process. In general, all children who attend a JFFLS receive some type of school meal.

One of the objectives of the JFFLS program is to promote the creation of gender-equal attitudes, not only through the equal exercise of roles and responsibilities, but also through the development of the capacity to critically assess relationships and links (box 7.20).

The schools stress the active participation and independence of all participants in an effort to build their confidence and self-esteem and help them take charge of their own lives. Experiential learning methods are emphasized. Facilitators strongly encourage participants to express themselves freely, to engage actively in discussions, and to find their own answers to the problems identified.[5] Initiative, creativity, and innovation are rewarded.

Through the Junior Farmer Field and Life Schools, girls and boys learn to question unhealthy gender norms and to participate in agriculture—and life—in a gender-equitable manner. The curriculum in the JFFLSs includes exercises that address gender issues. The "Planning for the Future" module introduces the daily clock exercise, which amply illustrates how women, men, girls, and boys spend their time differently because of socially imposed expectations. The cropping calendars exercise emphasizes the different roles men and women play in producing different crops and livestock, and it illustrates their use and control of resources. Girls and boys also discuss why these differences exist and whether they really must exist.

Girls and boys share tasks in the JFFLSs. For example, they weed and water, and girls as well as boys present agroecological systems analyses. Ultimately, transmitting gender-equitable attitudes to students depends very much on gender-equitable attitudes among the facilitators. In the training course for facilitators, participants usually are asked to present two theatrical scenarios: a classroom with a gender-aware teacher and one with a teacher who reinforces traditional gender norms. Through humor, the theatrical session effectively demonstrates how girls and boys are treated differently in many classrooms, which leads to a more general discussion of customs and what the community might do to address injustices.

Source: FAO 2007.

The activities cover a range of topics and are based on a standard program with Modules that follow the agricultural calendar:

- *Life cycles,* in which participants get acquainted with the learning field and each other and explore the similarities between plant and human life cycles
- *Planning for the future,* in which participants undertake initial agricultural planning and explore future aspirations
- *Growing up healthy,* in which participants explore what it takes to grow a healthy crop, and how good hygiene and nutrition can help them grow up healthy
- *Diversity,* in which participants explore how diversity in food production helps support food security, and how gender equity and respect for diversity help strengthen the community
- *Protection,* in which participants learn how to protect the crop from pests and disease, and learn how to protect themselves from threats such as HIV, violence, and exploitation
- *Water for life,* a short Module that coincides with the rainy season, exploring crop water management and revisiting the issue of hygiene
- *Care and loss,* which coincides with the harvest: participants learn how to maximize output in the face of agricultural losses and how to conserve and store food for the future and, at the same time, explore how to care for their own psychosocial health and plan for their own futures.

- *Business skills and entrepreneurship,* the focus of the second year/agricultural cycle of the JFFLS, in which participants explore how to take everything they learned about agriculture and life and transform it into livelihood opportunities.

BENEFITS AND IMPACTS

Women and girls, for a number of socioeconomic reasons, often have limited access to productive resources, technology, and information, resulting in lower agricultural productivity. By providing skills that can help women attain the same degree of access to these resources, the program can have a positive impact on agricultural and food production. Nutrition education is also likely to have a positive impact on the nutritional well-being of community members. The training on gender issues,[6] children's rights, and human rights has the potential to change perceptions of the role and status of women and children in households and communities, which may eventually lead to long-term behavioral changes that favor gender equality.

More specifically, preliminary assessments indicate that the JFFLSs are already producing benefits, such as the following:

- Building women's and girls' confidence and providing them with the skills that lead to their empowerment
- Offering new role models for girls through innovative education

- Markedly improving self-esteem, as seen in students' increased self-confidence, satisfaction, pride in school performance, and capacity to share their newly acquired knowledge with others in their communities
- Improving academic performance: anecdotal evidence suggests that the academic performance of JFFLS participants surpasses that of students attending standard schools because of the participatory approaches used in the JFFLSs
- Improving both individual and community farming knowledge and skills. The JFFLS participants have more practical skills, greater expertise, and higher prestige within their home communities. Once perceived as a burden, the students are now regarded as valuable resources for their households and communities.

LESSONS LEARNED AND ISSUES FOR WIDER APPLICABILITY

The JFFLS approach addresses basic issues of access to appropriate education and skills for rural communities, particularly for young people and especially in communities affected by HIV and AIDS, where farm livelihoods must be sustained despite the lack of adult labor and tutelage. By addressing gender-equality issues during the adolescent years, when attitudes and behaviors are more flexible and open to change, JFFLSs give participants the opportunity to narrow gender gaps and transform gender relations. JFFLSs are also proving to be a valuable instrument at the local level for meeting the nutritional, food security, and livelihood needs of orphans and vulnerable children, in ways that are consistent with national strategies, policies, and operations.

Experience has shown that school feeding programs are critical for attracting children in the JFFLSs, especially children from food-insecure and vulnerable households. The WFP's assistance in the pilot schools was crucial in this respect.

The selection of an appropriate host institution is of crucial importance and has immediate and long-term implications for the implementation and potential up-scaling strategy of the JFFLS approach.

In Mozambique and Uganda, JFFLS sites were implemented in conjunction with faith-based organizations or local NGOs, or were linked to formal primary schools. In Mozambique the institutional link to formal schools provides more practical entry points. Several models have been tested. To date, excellent results have been attained when a formal link is created between the JFFLSs and formal schools, or between the JFFLSs and Farmer Field Schools.

The work of the JFFLSs should be strongly linked with sectoral activities and other sector-wide approaches. Identification of an appropriate host institution (such as the Ministry of Agriculture, Education, or Social Development) has also proved crucial. The growing popularity and initial success of the JFFLSs have led to more requests for enrollment. A potential solution to this problem, which would also strengthen links between the JFFLSs, local schools, and other relevant institutions, is the progressive integration of some of the program's content and methods into national school curricula.[7]

If students who complete the JFFLSs are to put their knowledge to use, they will require secure access to land and other vital resources. This issue is especially serious among youths, single-parent families, and households led by orphans, but in the long term all participants in the program require better access to resources, credit, and other facilities to use their skills, stimulate economic activity, increase incomes, and ultimately eliminate the need for the JFFLS program. Changes in national policies of investment and action will also be necessary. The JFFLS approach shows that educational and training goals (including the promotion of gender equity) can be linked effectively, at the local level, with the goals of health and agricultural extension services in combating the multifaceted impacts of HIV and AIDS—directly and indirectly, immediately and in the long term—on individuals, households, and communities.

NOTES

Overview

This Overview was prepared by Maria E. Fernandez (Center for Integrating Research and Action, University of North Carolina-Chapel Hill) and reviewed by Marilyn Carr, Ira Matuschke, Catherine Ragasa, and Mary Hill Rojas (Consultants); Magdalena Blum, Rosalia Garcia, Josef Kienzle, Clare O'Farrell, and Florence Tartanac (FAO); Maria Hartl (IFAD); Nienke Bientema (IFPRI); Burt Swanson (University of Illinois); and Eija Pehu (World Bank).

Thematic Note I

This Thematic Note was prepared by Maria E. Fernandez (Center for Integrating Research and Action, University of North Carolina-Chapel Hill) and reviewed by Rupert Best (CIAT); Marilyn Carr, Ira Matuschke, Catherine Ragasa, and Mary Hill Rojas (Consultants); Magdalena Blum, Rosalia Garcia, Josef Kienzle, Clare O'Farrell, and Florence Tartanac (FAO); Maria Hartl (IFAD); Nienke Bientema (IFPRI); Burt Swanson (University of Illinois); and Eija Pehu (World Bank).

Thematic Note 2

This Thematic Note was prepared by Maria E. Fernandez (Center for Integrating Research and Action, University of North Carolina-Chapel Hill) and reviewed by Rupert Best (CIAT); Marilyn Carr, Ira Matuschke, Catherine Ragasa, and Mary Hill Rojas (Consultants); Magdalena Blum, Rosalia Garcia, Josef Kienzle, Clare O'Farrell, and Florence Tartanac (FAO); Maria Hartl (IFAD); Nienke Bientema (IFPRI); Burt Swanson (University of Illinois); and Eija Pehu (World Bank).

1. Pascal Sanginga, Annet Abenakyo, Rick Kamugisha, Adrienne Martin, and Robert Muzira, "Tracking Outcomes of Participatory Policy Learning and Action Research: Methodological Issues and Empirical Evidence from Participatory Bylaw Reforms in Uganda," paper prepared for Farmer First Revisited, Institute of Development Studies, Sussex, www.farmer-first.org.

2. Articles on participatory diagnosis can be found at www.idrc.ca/en, www.fao.org/participation and www.iied.org.

3. Ravi Prabhu, Carol Colfer, Chimere Diaw, Cynthia McDougall, and Robert Fisher, "Action Research with Local Forest Users and Managers: Lessons from CIFOR's Research on Adaptive Collaborative Management," paper prepared for Farmer First Revisited, Institute of Development Studies, Sussex, www.farmer-first.org.

4. Examples can be found at www.ciat.cgiar.org/ipra.

5. Jeremiah Njuki, Susan Kaaria, Pascal Sanginga, Elly Kaganzi, and Tennyson Magombo, "Empowering Communities through Market Led Development: Community Agro-Enterprise Experiences from Uganda and Malawi," paper prepared for Farmer First Revisited, Institute of Development Studies, Sussex, www.farmer-first.org.

6. Adrienne Martin, "So What Difference Does It Make? Assessing the Outcomes and Impacts of Farmer Participatory Research," paper prepared for Farmer First Revisited, Institute of Development Studies, Sussex, www.farmer-first.org.

Thematic Note 3

This Thematic Note was written by Leena Kirjavainen (Consultant) and reviewed by Marilyn Carr, Mary Hill Rojas, and Bill Saint (Consultants); Magdalena Blum and Clare O'Farrell (FAO); Maria Hartl (IFAD); Nienke Beintema (IFPRI); and Eija Pehu (World Bank).

1. The introduction and data are drawn from the recent research synthesis by World Bank (2007) and from Beintema (2006).

2. Marilee Karl, "Higher Agricultural Education and Opportunities in Rural Development for Women: An Overview and Summary of Five Case Studies," Report No. 40997-AFR, FAO, Rome, www.fao.org.

3. Much of the discussion draws on Karl (ibid.).

4. Ibid.

5. Harald Schomburg, "Tracer Studies in Africa: Comparative Analysis," www.uni-kassel.de.

6. See note 2 above.

Thematic Note 4

This Thematic Note was prepared by Marilyn Carr (Consultant) and reviewed by Ira Matuschke, Catherine Ragasa, and Mary Hill Rojas (Consultants); Theodor Friedrich, Josef Kienzle, and Florence Tartanac (FAO); Maria Hartl (IFAD); and Eija Pehu (World Bank).

1. Elizabeth Cecelski, "Re-Thinking Gender and Energy: Old and New Directions," ENERGIA/EASE Discussion Paper, May, www.energia.org.

2. Mike McCall, "Brewing Rural Beer Should Be a Hotter Issue," *Boiling Point* No. 47, HEDON Household Energy Network, www.hedon.info.

3. Shruti Gupta, "Barefoot, Female and a Solar Engineer," *India Together* (Oct. 19), www.indiatogether.org.

4. The First Mile Project is supported by the government of Switzerland and implemented in collaboration with the Agricultural Marketing Systems Development Programme of the government of Tanzania. It aims at using information and communications technologies to build linkages between producers and consumers. See www.ifad.org/newsletter/update/2/6.htm for more information on the First Mile Project.

Innovative Activity Profile 1

This Innovative Activity Profile was prepared by Maria E. Fernandez (Center for Integrating Research and Action, University of North Carolina-Chapel Hill) and reviewed by Catherine Ragasa and Mary Hill Rojas (Consultants); Maria Hartl (IFAD); and Eija Pehu (World Bank).

1. Javier Cabero and Willem van Immerzeel, "Building Learning Networks for Small-Scale Farmers: Pachamama Raymi as an Innovative Knowledge Management System," *Knowledge Management for Development Journal* 3 (2): 52–63, www.km4dev.org/journal.

2. Vargas-Lundius, Rosemary, in collaboration with Annelou Ypeij. 2007. *Polishing the Stone. A Journey through the Promotion of Gender Equality in Development Projects*. Rome: International Fund for Agricultural Development.

Innovative Activity Profile 2

This Innovative Activity Profile was written by Marilyn Carr (Consultant), Ira Matuschke (Consultant), and Marietha

Owenya (IFAD) and reviewed by Catherine Ragasa and Mary Hill Rojas (Consultants); Theodor Friedrich, Josef Kienzle, and Florence Tartanac (FAO); Maria Hartl (IFAD); and Eija Pehu (World Bank).

1. Sustainable Agriculture and Rural Development/Food and Agriculture Organization, "Conservation Agriculture (CA) for Sustainable Agriculture and Rural Development (SARD)," www.fao.org.

Innovative Activity Profile 3

This Innovative Activity Profile was written by Hadiza Djibo (FAO) and Marina Laudazi (Consultant), with inputs from Carol Djeddah, Patricia Colbert, Francesca Dalla Valle, Brian Griffin, and John Hourihan (FAO), and reviewed by Catherine Ragasa and Mary Hill Rojas (Consultants); Maria Hartl and Annina Lubbock (IFAD); and Eija Pehu (World Bank).

1. From 2005 to 2007, the number of people dying from HIV and AIDS-related illnesses has declined in part because of the life-prolonging effects of antiretroviral therapy. HIV and AIDS remain the primary cause of death in Africa (UNAIDS 2007).

2. A variety of factors, such as lesser socioeconomic status, can jeopardize women's and girls' ability to choose safer and healthier life strategies and place them at greater risk of infection.

3. The JFFLS approach may also prove effective in regions hosting refugees or afflicted by conflict. Schools have been set up for young refugees in northern Kenya at the Kakuma refugee camp and are being established for former child soldiers in South Kordofan (Sudan). FAO's ESW will be piloting the approach toward the end of 2008 in the Dadaab refugee camp (Kenya) and Darfur (Sudan).

4. Situation where men and women benefit equally from what the world has to offer and can contribute equally to society.

5. Local facilitators always include at least one extension worker, a teacher, a nurse and/or community animator (dealing with health, youth, and sports). Volunteers identified by the community also are part of the team. Strategic partners such as WFP and UNICEF provide technical expertise and learning materials.

6. Extension workers and facilitators receive training in gender issues through the Socio-Economic and Gender Analysis (SEAGA) Programme.

7. The institutional framework of the program can be strengthened, in relation to local stakeholders (community-based organizations, NGOs), as well as with governments and international partners. Communities and local stakeholders (particularly faith-based organizations and primary schools) can be involved in the management of the program, eventually leading to the local ownership of many of the JFFLSs. In addition, governmental structures from the Ministries of Agriculture and Education are increasingly taking over key roles in the management and conceptualization of the program (such as monitoring, training, and impact assessment).

REFERENCES

Overview

Berdegué, Julio. 2001. "Cooperating to Compete: Associative Peasant Business Firms in Chile." Department of Communication and Innovation Studies, Wageningen University and Research Centre, the Netherlands.

Food and Agriculture Organization and World Bank. 2000. *Agricultural Knowledge and Information Systems for Rural Development (AKIS/RD): Strategic Vision and Guiding Principles.* Rome: FAO and World Bank.

Roseboom, Johannes, Matthew McMahon, Indira Ekanayake, and Indu John-Abraham. 2006. "Institutional Reform of Agricultural Research and Extension in Latin America and the Caribbean." *en breve* Newsletter No. 90, May, Latin America and the Caribbean, World Bank, Washington, DC.

Spielman, David J., and Regina Birner. 2008. "How Innovative Is Your Agriculture? Using Innovation Indicators and Benchmarks to Strengthen National Agricultural Innovation Systems." Discussion Paper, World Bank, Washington, DC.

Swanson, Burton. 2008a. "Global Review of Good Agricultural Extension and Advisory Service Practices." Draft, Food and Agriculture Organization, Rome.

———. 2008b. "Module 1: Basic Concepts Relating to the Development and Evolution of Agricultural Extension and Advisory Systems." Part of E-Learning Course on Agricultural Extension, draft, World Bank-ARD, Washington, DC.

World Bank. 2007a. *Enhancing Agricultural Innovation: How to Go beyond the Strengthening of Research Systems.* Washington, DC: World Bank.

———. 2007b. *The World Development Report 2008: Agriculture for Development.* Washington, DC: World Bank.

Thematic Note 1

Anderson, Jock, and Gershon Feder. 2003. "Rural Extension Services." Policy Research Working Paper 1976, World Bank, Washington, DC.

Birner, Regina, Kristin Davis, John Pender, Ephraim Nkonya, Ponniah Anandajayasekeram, Javier Ekboir, Adiel Mbabu, David Spielman, Daniela Horna, Samuel Benin, and Marc J. Cohen. 2006. "From 'Best Practice' to 'Best Fit': A Framework for Analyzing Pluralistic Agricultural Advisory Services Worldwide." Development Strategy and Governance Division Discussion Paper Series 37, International Food Policy Research Institute, Washington, DC.

Center for Rice Development in Sub-Saharan Africa (WARDA). 2006. News release, Africa Rice Center.

Colmenares, Maria Magdalena, and Andrea Pereira. 2004. "Rural Women as Axis of Family and Community Empowerment in the Agricultural Extension Project of Venezuela." Draft paper for ICR Report No. 29081, World Bank, Washington, DC.

Mercoiret, Marie-Rose. 2001. "Enhancing the Capacities of Rural Producer Organisations: The Case of Agricultural Services and Producer Organisations Support Programme (PSAOP)—Senegal." Working Paper, World Bank, Washington, DC.

Stroud, Ann, Engerok Obin, Rajiv Kandelwahl, Francis Byekwaso, Chris Opondo, Laura German, Joseph Tanui, Olive Kyampaire, Beda Mbwesa, Alex Ariho, and Africare and Kabale District Farmers' Association. 2006. "Managing Change: Institutional Development under NAADS." Working Paper No. 22, African Highlands Initiative, Kampala.

Swanson, Burton. 2006. "The Changing Role of Agricultural Extension in a Global Economy." *Journal of Agricultural International Extension and Education* 11 (3): 5–17.

———. 2008. "Global Review of Good Agricultural Extension/Advisory Service Practices." Draft, Food and Agriculture Organization (FAO), Rome.

Van den Ban, Anne W., and Helen S. Hawkins. 1996. *Agricultural Extension*, 2nd ed. Oxford: Blackwell Science.

World Bank. 2006. "Module 3: Investments in Agricultural Extension and Information Services." In *Agriculture Investment Sourcebook,* 105–50. Washington, DC: World Bank.

Thematic Note 2

Alex, Gary, Derek Byerlee, Marie-Helene Collion, and William Rivera. 2004. "Extension and Rural Development: Converging Views on Institutional Approaches?" Agriculture and Rural Development Paper No. 4, World Bank, Washington, DC.

Braun, Ann R., Graham Thiele, and Maria Fernandez. 2000. "Farmer Field Schools and Local Agricultural Research Committees: Complementary Platforms for Integrated Decision-Making in Sustainable Agriculture." Agricultural Research and Extension Network Paper No. 105, Overseas Development Institute, London.

Chambers, Robert, Arnold Pacey, and Lori Ann Thrupp, eds. 1989. *Farmer First: Farmer Innovation and Agricultural Research.* London: Intermediate Technology Publications.

CIP-UPWARD. 2003. "Farmer Field Schools: from IPM to Platforms for Learning and Empowerment." In International Potato Center, *Users' Perspectives with Agricultural Research and Development.* Los Baños, Laguna, Philippines.

Fernandez, Maria E. 1994. "Women's Agricultural Production Committees and the Participative-Research-Action Approach." In *Tools for the Field: Methodologies Handbook for Gender Analysis and Agriculture,* ed. Hilary Sims Feldstein and Janice Jiggins, 239–43. West Hartford: Kumarian Press.

Fernandez, Maria E., and P. Lusembo. 2002. "Farmers Leading Change: A Learning Approach to Involving Small-Holders in Agroecosystem Revitalization Management Strategies." National Agricultural Organization of Uganda, Kampala.

Poats, Susan, Marianne Schmink, and Anita Spring, eds. 1988. *Gender Issues in Farming Systems Research and Extension.* Boulder: Westview Press.

Probst, Kirsten, and Jürgen Hagmann. 2003. "Understanding Participatory Research in the Context of Risk Prone Environments." AGREN Network Paper 130, Overseas Development Institute, London.

Quizon, Jaime, Gershon Feder, and Rinku Murgai. 2001. "Fiscal Sustainability of Agricultural Extension: the Case of the Farmer Field School Approach." Working Paper, Development Research Group, World Bank, Washington, DC.

Rhoades, Robert E., and Robert H. Booth. 1982. "Farmer Back to Farmer: A Model for Generating Acceptable Agricultural Technology." *Agricultural Administration* 11: 127–37.

Sanginga, Pascal, Rupert Best, Colletah Chitsike, Robert Delve, Susan Kaaria, and Roger Kirkby. 2004. "Enabling Rural Innovation in Africa: An Approach for Integrating Farmer Participatory Research and Market Orientation for Building the Assets of Rural Communities." *Uganda Journal of Agricultural Sciences* 9: 942–57.

Thematic Note 3

Abdelnour, H. O., and A. W. Abdalla. 1988. "Junior Colleges/ Institutes of Agriculture in the Sudan: Review and Analysis of Current Curricula and Means of Orienting Them to the Needs of Rural Development." Food and Agriculture Organization (FAO) Project (GCP/SUD/030/FIN), Workshop Paper, College of Agricultural Studies, Khartoum Polytechnic, Khartoum North, Sudan.

Beintema, Nienke M. 2006. "Participation of Female Agricultural Scientists in Developing Countries." Brief prepared for Women in Science: Meeting the Challenge, adjunct to the CGIAR Annual General Meeting, Washington, DC, December 4.

Cooperative State Research, Education, and Extension Service of the United States Department of Agriculture (CREES). 2005. *Employment Opportunities for College Graduates in the U.S. Food, Agricultural, and Natural Resources System, 2005–2010.* CREES and Purdue University College of Agriculture.

Eckman, Karlyn. 1994. "Rural Households and Sustainability: Integrating Environmental and Gender Concerns into Home Economics Curricula." Working Paper, Food and Agriculture Organization, Rome.

Engberg, L. 1993. *Rural Households, Resource Allocation and Management: An Ecosystems Perspective.* Handbook with Case Studies. Rome: Food and Agriculture Organization.

Food and Agriculture Organization (FAO). 2002. *FAO Gender and Development Plan of Action 2002–2007.* Rome: FAO. Also available at www.fao.org.

———. 2003. *Socio-Economic and Gender Analysis (SEAGA) Macro Level Handbook: Gender Analysis in Macro-Economic and Agricultural Sector Policies and Programmes.* Rome: FAO. Also available at www.fao.org.

———. 2004. *Socio-Economic and Gender Analysis (SEAGA)—Rural Households and Resources: A Guide for Extension Workers.* Rome: FAO. Also available at www.fao.org.

Gebre-Ab, N. 1988. "Agricultural Manpower Utilization and Training at Intermediate Level in Northern Sudan." Survey and Analysis Report for Training Agricultural Technicians for Rural Development Project (GCP/SUD/030/FIN), Food and Agriculture Organization, Rome.

Hamada, Dorothy, Leena Kirjavainen, and Dely Gapasin. 2002. "Gender Issues in Household Resource Management: A Pilot Study." Indonesia: Summary Report, World Bank, Washington, DC.

Idris, Yousif Mohamed Ahmed. 2007. *Personal Communication.* Dean College of Agricultural Studies, Sudan University of Science and Technology, Khartoum, Sudan.

Kingslow, M. E. 2007. *Agricultural Education and Training in Africa; A Survey of Programs.* Battle Creek, MI: W. K. Kellogg Foundation.

Marilee, Karl. 1997. "Higher Agricultural Education and Opportunities in Rural Development for Women: An Overview and Summary of Five Case Studies." Food and Agriculture and Organization (FAO), Rome. Available at www.fao.org.

Muir-Leresche, K. 2006. *Improving Approaches to Effective Teaching and Learning: Tertiary Agricultural Education.* Nairobi: World Agroforestry Center.

Sokoine University of Agriculture (SUA). 2005. *Training Needs Assessment, Job Markets, and Tracer Studies for SUA Degree Programmes.* Final consultant reports of K-Rep Advisory Services Limited, Development Associates Ltd., and Afrozone. Morogoro, Tanzania: Sokoine University.

World Bank. 2004. "Agricultural Education and Training," Gender in Agriculture: A World Bank Learning Module. Washington, DC: World Bank. Available at http://web.worldbank.org/WBSITE/EXTERNAL/TOPICS/EXTGENDER/0,,contentMDK:20208195~pagePK:210058~piPK:210062~theSitePK:336868,00.html.

———. 2005. *Gender Issues and Best Practices in Land Administration Projects: A Synthesis Report.* Washington, DC: World Bank.

———. 2007. *Cultivating Knowledge and Skills to Grow African Agriculture. A Synthesis of an Institutional, Regional, and International Review.* Washington, DC: World Bank.

Thematic Note 4

Adjebeng-Asem, Selina. 1990. "The Nigerian Cassava Grater." In *Tinker, Tiller, Technical Change,* ed. Matthew Gamser, Helen Appleton, and Nicola Carter, 80–96. London: IT Publications.

Ahmad, M., and A. Jenkins. 1989. "Traditional Paddy Husking: An Appropriate Technology under Pressure." In *Women and the Food Cycle,* ed. Marilyn Carr, 11–16. London: IT Publications.

Barwell, Ian, and Christina Malmberg Calvo. 1987. *Makete Integrated Transport Project.* Oxford: IT Transport.

Bates, L., ed. 2007. *Smoke, Health and Household Energy:* Vol. 2. Rugby, U.K.: Practical Action.

Bishop-Sambrook, Clare. 2003. "Labour-Saving Technologies and Practices for Farming and Household Activities in Eastern and Southern Africa." Joint study by International Fund for Agricultural Development and Food and Agriculture Organization, Rome.

Blackden, C. Mark, and Quentin Wodon. 2006. "Gender, Time Use and Poverty." Introduction in *Gender, Time Use and Poverty in Sub-Saharan Africa,* ed. C. Mark Blackden and Quentin Wodon, Working Paper 17, World Bank, Washington, DC.

Clancy, Joy, and Annemarije Kooijman. 2006. "Enabling Access to Sustainable Energy: A Synthesis of Research Findings in Bolivia, Tanzania and Vietnam." Final draft, University of Twente, Enschede, the Netherlands.

Dianzheng, Liu. 2007. "Bringing 'Natural' Light to Remote Households in China." *Making a Difference in Asia and the Pacific,* Newsletter 15 (March/April 2007). Also available at www.fao.org.

Fairless, Daemon. 2007. "From Wheat to Web: Children of the Revolution." *Nature News* (Oct. 22).

Fernando, Priyanthi, and Gina Porter, eds. 2002. *Introduction in Balancing the Load: Women, Gender and Transport.* London: Zed Books.

Gender and Rural Transport Initiative (GRTI). 2006. "Donkey Project in Uganda." GRTI Country Report 14, World Bank, Washington, DC.

Ghertner, D. Asher. 2006. "Technology and Tricks: Intra-Household Technology Improvements and Gender Studies." *Gender, Technology and Development* 10 (3): 281–311.

Intermediate Technology Development Group (ITDG). 1986. Internal Report on Nepal.

International Fund for Agricultural Development (IFAD). 1998. "Agricultural Implements Used by Women Farmers in Africa." IFAD/FAO, Technical Advisory Division.

———. 2006. "Agricultural Technology and Transfer to Poor Farmers in Bangladesh." *Making a Difference in Asia and the Pacific* Newsletter 8 (January/February 2006). Also available at www.fao.org.

———. 2007. "Wulin Mountains Minority-Areas Development Project, China." Supervision Mission Report: Crosscutting Issues (May 2007).

International Labour Organization (ILO) and Government of the Netherlands. 1985. *Field Report on Post Adoption Studies, Technologies for Rural Women.* Geneva: ILO.

Kneerim, Jill. 1980. *Village Women Organize: The Mraru Bus Service.* New York: Population Council.

Lambrou, Yianna, and Grazia Piana. 2006. "Energy and Gender Issues in Rural Sustainable Development." Gender and Population Division, Food and Agriculture Organization, Rome.

Maguzu, Catherine W., Dominick Ringo, Wilfred Mariki, Marietha Owenya, Flora Kola, and Charles Leseyo. 2007. "Arumeru District." In *Conservation Agriculture as Practised in Tanzania: Three Case Studies,* ed. Richard Shetto and Marietha Owenya, 1–48. Nairobi: African Conservation Tillage Network.

Matuschke, Ira. 2007. "Case Study: The Central Dry Area Smallholder and Community Services Development Project (CKDAP), Kenya." International Fund for Agricultural Development, Rome.

Mwankusye, Josephine. 2002. "Do Intermediate Means of Transport Reach Rural Women?" In *Balancing the Load: Women, Gender and Transport,* ed. Priyanthi Fernando and Gina Porter, 39–49. London: ZED Books.

Paris, Thelma, and Troung Thi Ngoc Chi. 2005. "The Impact of Row Seeder Technology on Women Labour: A Case Study of the Mekong Delta, Vietnam." *Gender, Technology and Development* 9: 158–84.

Rao, Nitya. 2002. "Cycling into the Future: the Pudukkottai Experience." In *Balancing the Load: Women, Gender and Transport,* ed. Priyanthi Fernando and Gina Porter, 151–68. London: ZED Books.

Sandhu, R. 1989. "Women and Fish Smoking." In *Women and the Food Cycle,* ed. Marilyn Carr, 71–78. London: IT Publications.

Spence, Nancy. 1986. "Impact of Technology on Women in Crop Processing." CIDA.

United Nations Development Programme (UNDP). 2001. "Generating Opportunities: Case Studies on Energy and Women." UNDP, New York.

Venter, Christo J., and Mac Mashiri. 2007. "Gender and Transport: Towards a Practical Analysis Framework for Improved Planning." Paper prepared for 26th Annual South Africa Transport Conference, Pretoria, July.

Innovative Activity Profile 1

Fernandez, Maria E., and P. Lusembo. 2002. "Farmers Leading Change: A Learning Approach to Involving Small-Holders in Agroecosystem Revitalization Management Strategies." National Agricultural Research Organisation, Kampala.

Innovative Activity Profile 2

Bishop-Sambrook, Clare, Josef Kienzle, Wilfred Mariki, Marietha Owenya, and Fatima Ribeiro. 2004. *Conservation Agriculture as a Labor Saving Practice for Vulnerable Households.* Rome: International Fund for Agricultural Development and Food and Agriculture Organization.

Maguzu, Catherine W., Dominick Ringo, Wilfred Mariki, Marietha Owenya, Flora Kola, and Charles Leseyo. 2007. "Arumeru District." In *Conservation Agriculture as Practised in Tanzania: Three Case Studies,* ed. Richard Shetto and Marietha Owenya, 1–48. Nairobi: African Conservation Tillage Network.

Innovative Activity Profile 3

Food and Agriculture Organization (FAO). 2007. "Getting Started: Running a Junior Farmer Field and Life School." FAO, Rome.

Izumi, Kaori, ed. 2006. *Reclaiming Our Lives: HIV and AIDS, Women's Land and Property Rights and Livelihoods in East and Southern Africa—Narratives and Responses.* Cape Town: HSRC Press.

Joint United Nations Programme on HIV/AIDS (UNAIDS). 2007. *2007 AIDS Epidemic Update*. Geneva: UNAIDS.

FURTHER READING

Overview

Swanson, Burton. 2007. *Enhancing Agricultural Innovation: How to Go beyond the Strengthening of Research Systems*. Washington, DC: World Bank.

Thematic Note 1

National Institute of Agricultural Extension Management (MANAGE). n.d. "Agricultural Technology Management Agency (ATMA)." Available at www.manage.gov.in.

Innovative Activity Profile 3

Djeddah, Carol, Rogério Mavanaga, and Laurence Hendrickx. 2006. "Junior Farmer Field and Life Schools: Experience from Mozambique." In *AIDS, Poverty, and Hunger: Challenges and Responses*, ed. Stuart Gillespie, 325–39. Washington, DC: International Food Policy Research Institute. Available at www.ifpri.org.

See also the GAL *eSourcebook* for additional case studies at www.worldbank.org:

Innovative Activity Profile 4—First Mile Project.

Innovative Activity Profile 5—Sudan: Strengthening Agricultural Technical Training Using a Gender Lens.

Gender Issues in Agricultural Labor

Overview

Making the rural labor market a more effective pathway out of poverty is . . . a major policy challenge that remains poorly understood and sorely neglected in policy making.

—World Bank 2007

Total labor in agriculture has declined in most countries, and this trend will continue as countries industrialize. Over half of all laborers worldwide, however, rely on the agricultural sector. In sub-Saharan Africa and South Asia, 70 percent or more of the labor force works in agriculture. In many regions more women than men are employed in agriculture. In the Middle East more than twice as many women work in agriculture as men, and in South Asia close to one-third more women are working in the sector than men (fig. 8.1). Most work in agriculture is onerous, and the returns are lower than in other sectors. Improving the quality and quantity of jobs in rural areas, and in agriculture, for both women and men, has been identified as a means of promoting economic growth and reducing poverty (Heintz 2006; World Bank 2007). The most significant positive impact on agricultural labor will come through creating a dynamic rural economy in both the agriculture and the nonfarm sectors, focusing primarily on creating a good investment climate (World Bank 2007). This dynamism will assist poor men and women laborers, who both face many constraints in terms of lack of access to resources and power.

An extensive literature exists on labor issues in general and agricultural labor issues in particular. This Module focuses specifically on the gender equalities in the agricultural labor market and the implications to project and program design.

Gender inequalities in all labor markets are pervasive. Gender inequalities in the agricultural sector are more difficult to quantify but are equally extensive. Reducing labor inequalities makes good development sense. Reducing labor market segmentation and wage inequalities improves the mobility of labor and increases employment. Simulations of Latin American economies show both a reduction of poverty and an increase in economic growth by increasing women's labor force participation; a 6 percent expansion of growth was shown to be possible if men's and women's wages were equal (Tzannatos 1999).

Increasing labor opportunities and returns for poor women in rural areas is pro-poor and improves family and social welfare as increasingly evidenced in literature. Increasing women's earnings and share of family income has been shown to empower women by strengthening their bargaining power in the household. Empirical evidence shows that women invest more than men in the development of children;[1] thus, higher levels of employment and earnings for women not only contribute to current economic growth but also have intergenerational implications (see relationships in fig. 8.2). A global increase in women-headed households, which are asset-poor, heightens the importance of improving employment opportunities to reduce poverty.

The contribution of women's work to family and society is significant, through their productive and reproductive

Figure 8.1   Percentage of Women and Men in Agriculture by Region, 2007

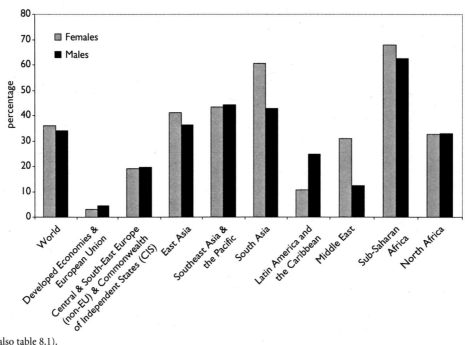

Source: ILO 2006 (see also table 8.1).

Figure 8.2   Relationship between Women Labor Force Participation (LFP), Poverty, and Economic Growth

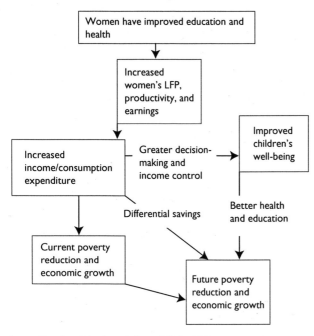

Source: Based on Morrison, Raju, and Sinha 2007.

roles; however, if the quantity and quality of that work are poor, or if they reinforce patriarchal gender practices, the negative effects on their health and that of their children can attenuate the development impact. Yet, to the extent that the empowerment of women is an end in and of itself, responsible

employment for rural women can increase confidence, promote participation in community activities, and contribute to a perception on the part of women of a better life (Vargas-Lundius 2007).

DEFINITIONS AND TRENDS

This section defines and discusses the trends in agricultural labor.

Definitions of agricultural labor

Agriculture in this Module entails all production, marketing, and processing activities related to agricultural products, including crops, livestock, agroforestry, and aquaculture. *Agricultural labor* means human efforts in these areas; *agricultural wage labor* consists of those activities that are remunerated. Agricultural labor, given this definition, can take place on-farm (for example, agricultural production activities such as planting, weeding, harvesting, milking, or fishing) or off-farm (for example, agroprocessing activities such as cleaning, cutting, packaging, labeling, or marketing). Agriculture is not synonymous with the rural sector, although most agricultural activities take place in rural areas. Increasingly, however, agroprocessing activities take place in factories that may be located in semiurban areas closer to marketing or export sites. Agricultural labor can be unpaid (such as on-farm family labor), paid-in-kind (such as barter or labor exchange), self-employed (such as marketing of one's own produce), or wage labor. Given the coexistence of these forms of labor across crop and noncrop products, the measurement of agricultural labor is challenging, as will be discussed below.

This Module focuses largely on on-farm agricultural labor and agricultural wage labor, with the emphasis on wage labor. The constraints based on gender differences facing agricultural entrepreneurs (self-employed producers, farmers, and business owners), such as access to land, markets, and technology, are detailed in other Modules (see Modules 4, 5, 7, and 12). Strong linkages exist between these different agricultural categories: these economic activities can all be conducted by the same person. A small business owner may also be working on a farm or in another business as a laborer. The Module focuses on agricultural wage labor but recognizes that improvements in labor conditions are dependent on other subsectors (for example, finance, marketing, and rural infrastructure).

Wage laborers may work in formal markets, where workers make individual agreements, or bargain collectively with employers to secure contractual agreements about wage and benefits. But the majority of agricultural wage laborers in many countries, particularly women, either are working on land owned by spouses, families, or neighbors or are hired in informal markets. Most women working in agriculture thus typically do not have contracts that provide them direct control over the returns to their labor or that legally oblige employers to provide benefits or adhere to existing labor laws. This Module provides a detailed analysis of several areas of intervention designed to promote decent work in agriculture throughout developing countries, focusing largely on issues related to women's employment. The Innovative Activity Profile in this Module provides a best practice example from Thailand.

Trends in gender and agricultural labor

The agricultural workforce is estimated at around 1.1 billion, of which 450 million are estimated to be hired farm workers (Hurst, Termine, and Karl 2005). The number of waged workers, including women wage workers, is growing even though the agricultural workforce as a whole is shrinking. Migrant labor in agriculture is increasing. As agriculture industrializes and global competition increases, downward pressure on the costs of employment leads to more informal and flexible employment contracts, termed the "casualization" of labor. Independent smallholder farmers increasingly supplement their earnings with wage labor. These trends have important gender implications.

The growing proportion of women in the labor force has been one of the most striking trends of recent times. A large body of literature has debated the "feminization" of labor markets.[2] This discussion has, however, been for the most part based on analyses of data on urban employment statistics for industrial or middle-income countries. Assessing levels and trends in agricultural labor, particularly by gender in poor countries, is far more difficult. To the extent that women are concentrated in both unpaid and casual labor, their efforts in agriculture are grossly underrepresented. The *2008 World Development Report* estimated agricultural labor from multiple country surveys and identified key trends; some of these trends are summarized below.

There is declining agricultural labor. Labor in the agricultural sector is declining for both men and women, with the exception of women in the Middle East and North Africa (see table 8.1). Although men are migrating out of agriculture faster in some areas, the declines in women's agricultural employment are also significant. Over the long run, migration out of agriculture is necessary. Migration poses opportunities and risks for both men and women. Young women who migrate from rural areas for work are particularly vulnerable to abusive contracts and work situations. Underage Khmer, Lao, and Myanmar girls migrate to work in agriculture in Thailand, where some are held captive working under poor conditions (Pearson and others 2006).

More women than men work in agriculture. Data show that when both self-employment and wage labor are considered, women provide more employment in agriculture than men in many regions (see tables 8.1 and 8.2). Women represent a larger proportion of laborers than men in the agricultural sectors of Asia, sub-Saharan Africa, and the Middle East and North Africa. Women also dominate in some Caribbean and Central American countries, especially in economies with low per capita income. And women's proportion in agricultural wage labor markets has increased, although it still lags behind that of men in all regions. Further regional data are also presented in table 8.3.

The number of waged women workers in agriculture is rapidly increasing because of globalization, high-value agricultural production, and the "casualization" of labor. One stimulus for the growth in women's agricultural wage labor has been the "industrialization" of agriculture, particularly the growth of high-value agriculture production and agroprocessing for export. Vegetable production can require up to five times more labor than cereal production. Between 1986 and 1994 in Chile, women agricultural workers in the fruit export industry increased by more than 20 percent, and men agricultural workers declined by 20 percent (Lastarria-Cornhiel 2006). Table 8.4 shows the high proportion of women workers for some of these crops. These trends and the implications for labor conditions for women

Table 8.1 Men's and Women's Share in Total Employment by Sector, 1997 and 2007

	Employment in agriculture (%)		Employment in industry (%)		Employment in services (%)	
	1997	**2007**	**1997**	**2007**	**1997**	**2007**
Women						
World	43.5	36.1	16.8	17.6	39.6	46.3
Central and Southeast Europe (non-EU) and CIS	26.9	19.2	22.2	17.9	50.8	62.8
Developed Economies and European Union	5.3	3.2	16.7	12.5	78.1	84.3
East Asia	51.9	41.0	22.8	25.5	25.3	33.5
Latin America and the Caribbean	14.6	10.7	13.6	14.5	71.9	74.8
Middle East	28.4	31.0	20.0	18.8	51.5	50.2
North Africa	31.2	32.6	19.1	15.2	49.7	52.2
South Asia	74.0	60.5	11.2	18.4	14.7	21.1
Southeast Asia and the Pacific	50.3	43.4	13.9	16.3	35.8	40.3
Sub-Saharan Africa	74.8	67.9	5.9	5.8	19.2	26.4
Men						
World	40.0	34.0	24.0	25.6	36.1	40.4
Central and Southeast Europe (non-EU) and CIS	27.0	19.8	33.2	32.6	39.8	47.6
Developed Economies and European Union	6.7	4.6	37.1	34.3	56.1	61.1
East Asia	44.6	36.3	25.6	28.0	29.8	35.7
Latin America and the Caribbean	28.6	24.7	24.8	27.1	46.5	48.2
Middle East	19.6	12.5	27.2	28.0	53.3	59.4
North Africa	36.6	32.9	20.1	22.3	43.3	44.8
South Asia	53.5	42.9	17.0	23.0	29.5	34.1
Southeast Asia and the Pacific	47.7	44.3	19.4	21.0	32.9	34.7
Sub-Saharan Africa	70.0	62.4	10.4	12.4	19.6	25.2

Source: ILO 2006.

Note: CIS = Commonwealth of Independent States.

are documented in Thematic Note 3 on Labor-Intensive Export Agriculture.

Growth in agricultural employment has come in areas such as horticulture, floriculture, aquaculture, pigs, and poultry, in which factory-style operations are possible and economical. Economies of scale apply, so the bulk of the work is carried out by paid employees (ODI 2007). Women figure prominently in these sectors, such as shrimp-processing plants in Argentina, Bangladesh, India, and the Pacific Islands and poultry processing in Brazil. An increasing number of these industries employ labor under temporary conditions or through third parties.

A rapid expansion in the use of contract labor has been seen, with labor provided on a third-party basis to producers. In India men casual workers increased from 65 percent in 1972 to 80 percent in 2002; women casual workers increased from 89 percent to 92 percent over the same period (World

Bank 2007). Between 25 and 50 percent of labor in the Chilean fruit export market is contracted. Casualization in Chile, and many other countries, has a distinct gender bias: Between 52 and 70 percent of temporary workers are women, whereas permanent workers are mostly men (Barrientos and Barrientos 2002). Under these temporary employment conditions, women are subject to low levels of protection in terms of wage levels, employment security, health and safety, and environmental standards and social protection.

Representation of women in traditional labor institutions is weak. The deregulation, globalization, and competitive pressure described above have also been influential in, or have accompanied, the erosion of trade unionism and traditional forms of collective action, although, for example, foreign direct investment is not necessarily detrimental to rights to association and collective action (Brown 2007). Where collective bargaining functions, it can play a role in protection

Table 8.2 Rural Employment by Sector of Activity and Type of Employment, Selected Countries

Sector of Activity	East Asia and the Pacific (excl. China) (%)	Europe and Central Asia (%)	Latin America and the Caribbean (%)	Middle East and North Africa (%)	South Asia (%)	Sub-Saharan Africa (%)
Men						
Agriculture, self-employed	46.8	8.5	38.4	24.6	33.1	56.6
Agriculture, wage earner	9.4	10.1	20.9	9.4	21.8	4.0
Nonagriculture, self-employed	11.5	7.4	9.2	8.8	11.8	6.9
Nonagriculture, wage earner	17.4	31.4	17.2	30.9	15.4	8.6
Nonactive or not reported	14.4	27.5	13.4	26.0	14.6	21.7
Women						
Agriculture, self-employed	38.4	6.9	22.8	38.6	12.7	53.5
Agriculture, wage earner	5.7	5.4	2.3	1.0	11.4	1.4
Nonagriculture, self-employed	11.3	1.6	11.7	2.8	2.9	6.8
Nonagriculture, wage earner	8.4	18.1	11.5	3.9	2.7	2.8
Nonactive or not reported	35.5	46.9	51.2	53.3	64.3	32.7

Source: World Bank 2007, table 9.2.

wages. New forms of national and transnational movements have emerged, including women's associations such as the Self-Employed Women's Association (see Thematic Note 1) and international movements, such as those against child labor or toward fair trade.[3] These movements increasingly have the power to influence labor conditions.(see Thematic Note 3).

KEY GENDER ISSUES

This section discusses the gender issues specific to agricultural labor markets.

Women's time allocation

Worldwide, women are the primary workers in the "reproductive economy": maintaining households, raising children, preparing food, and taking care of sick and indigent relatives, including parents. In rural areas where these activities are more onerous because of the paucity of basic services such as electricity and water, women are more constrained. In the Middle East and North Africa, IFAD found that solutions to water and fuel supply freed women to participate in income-earning activities.[4] Concomitantly, practitioners must avoid interventions (such as new technologies) that increase women's labor without corresponding financial benefits (Deutsch, Duryea, and Piras 2001).

Parental care for children consumes a significant proportion of women's time. Lack of adequate child care represents one of the principal barriers to women's employment and may be a principal reason for the larger proportion of women in agricultural activities. In labor markets women pay for the inflexibility by being consigned to the informal sector or to jobs with lower wages. Studies demonstrate that the provision of affordable child care increases women's labor force participation and earnings (Deutsche, Duryea, and Piras 2001).

Unemployment and the casualization of labor

More women than men as a proportion of their labor force are seeking work but unable to find it in almost all regions of the world. In 2003 the global women's unemployment rate was 6.4 percent compared to 6.1 percent for men (Elder and Schmidt 2004). Women living in rural areas are more likely than men to be unemployed or underemployed and without access to a cash income. Men are more able to migrate for employment, whereas women have primary responsibilities for households. The proportion of women among categories of nonpermanent workers is increasing (ILO 2003). Women are the first to be laid off, because casual and seasonal laborers have little security.

Wage gaps

Women represent the largest group of "unpaid" workers in both rural and urban areas. Globally the proportion of women who are "contributing family workers" is 34.5 percent,

Table 8.3 Regional Characteristics and Key Issues of Women's Agricultural Labor

Region	Characteristics of women's agricultural labor force	Key issues for women's agricultural labor
Central and Southeast Europe (non-EU) and Commonwealth of Independent States (CIS) Employment to population ratios: Women: 45.6%; men: 63.8% Working women in agriculture (2007): 19.2% Working women in wage jobs (2007): 78.5%	Low percentage of men and women in agriculture, but high percentage of women vs. men Formal market stronger in most countries Wage inequities in formal market Young women's employment to population ratio higher than for young men	Rural productivity low Labor legislation not enforced Women not included in agricultural productivity-enhancing programs, such as training
Latin America and the Caribbean Employment to population ratios: Women: 47.1%; men: 73.7% Working women in agriculture (2007): 10.7% Working women wage and salaried jobs (2007): 64.6%	Considerable variability across countries High on-farm labor (some countries) Low ratio of participation in agriculture in comparison to men's participation Growing women's informal labor market participation Highest rates of occupational segregation	Women's employment opportunities in rural and urban areas low Occupational segregation Social protection for women in growing informal agricultural labor markets
North Africa Employment to population ratios: Women: 21.9%; men: 69.1% Working women in agriculture (2007): 32.6% Working women in wage and salaried jobs (2007): 58.4%	Lowest women's employment levels of all regions Only region where women's employment in agriculture increased Wage labor concentrated in urban areas More women in rural areas than men due to migration High percentage of women as on-farm labor Women responsible for small livestock	Low productivity of on-farm labor Heavy household labor burdens Social constraints to market work Limited access to nonagricultural employment
South Asia Employment to population ratios: Women: 31.4%; men: 78.1% Working women in agriculture (2007): 60.5% Working women in wage and salaried jobs (2007): 15.5%	High percentage of informal agricultural labor Higher percentage of women in agriculture (60.5% of women vs. 42.9% men) High percentage of self-employment Overlap of culture and caste with gender in discrimination Occupational segregation in wage market	Unequal access for women in formal sector employment Few legal protections Undeveloped labor market institutions
Southeast Asia and the Pacific Employment to population ratios: Women: 62.5%; men: 78.4% Working women in agriculture (2007): 43.4% Working women in wage and salaried jobs (2007): 39.2%	Highest women's labor participation High percentage in agriculture High involvement in fisheries Overlap of culture and race with gender in discrimination Large gender wage gap	Improvement in work conditions in agroprocessing and agricultural wage markets needed Discrimination in all forms to be addressed
Sub-Saharan Africa Employment to population ratios: Women: 56.9%; men: 79.7% Working women in agriculture (2007): 67.9% Working women in wage and salaried jobs (2007): 15.5%	High percentage of on-farm labor Gender-specific on-farm tasks and crops Occupational segregation in wage market Large involvement in informal sector (processing) Growth in women's labor in high-value crops Unskilled labor force	Limited employment opportunities for women in rural areas Unequal access for women in informal sector development Few legal protections, especially for informal workers Undeveloped labor market institutions Productivity levels of women's labor low

Sources: ILO 2008; World Bank 2007.

Note: Data for North Africa exclude Middle East data, but Middle East data are similar; data exclude East Asia.

Table 8.4	Proportion of Women Wage Laborers in High-Value Crops	
Country	Crop	Women as share of workers
Northeast Brazil	Vineyards	65% of field workers
Chile	Fruit	50% of temporary workers
Colombia/ Mexico	Flowers	60–80% of workers
Kenya	Horticulture	70–80% of packing, labeling, and bar coding
Sinaloa, Mexico	Vegetables	40% of field workers 90% of packers
South Africa	Deciduous fruit	69% of temporary workers
Uganda	Flowers	85% of workers

Sources: Dolan and Sorby 2003; ILO 2003.

compared to 24.9 percent of men (ILO 2008). In agriculture women labor on family farms but rarely control farm income. When women are employed, they are usually paid less than men, even for the same tasks. In India the average wage for agricultural casual work is 30 percent lower for women than for men, 20 percent lower for the same task (World Bank 2007). Studies indicate that wage gaps between men and women in many sectors have narrowed over time, but they persist in many countries. Recent studies in agroprocessing show large wage gaps. For example, in Bangladesh women fry catchers and sorters earn about 64 percent of what men fry catchers and sorters earn (USAID/GATE Project 2006).

Occupational segregation

In general, women and men work in distinct activities that offer different rewards and career opportunities, even when they have similar education and labor market skills. In agricultural production, women usually produce the food crops for the household, whereas the men are responsible for crops that will be marketed or sold. Some tasks are "feminized," such as weeding on the farm, or poultry processing and flower packing in the factory, despite evidence of the ability of men to perform these tasks equally well in other companies or countries. The reverse also holds, and generally men run equipment and handle tools, jobs that usually require training and elicit higher wages. Occupational segregation is particularly strong in some countries in South

Asia, Southeast Asia, and Latin America. The high-value agricultural export industry is highly segmented and gender segregated, as discussed in Thematic Note 3.

Stereotyping of gender roles is ubiquitous. For example, a manager in a cut-flower-processing plant in Kenya said that "women are more dexterous, which is good for flowers" (Collinson 2001). Confining women to a limited number of occupations has high equity and efficiency costs, and it contributes to misallocation of labor and suboptimal investments in women's education because girls' potential is usually gauged through current market opportunities (Tzannatos 1999).

Violence, health, and safety

The high prevalence of women in casual, low-paid employment with limited security leads to other abuses. Violence and sexual harassment in the workplace are more frequent under these conditions. Men supervisors control decisions concerning work performance and hence remuneration for the "task." Studies have shown that women must trade sex for job security, markets, and other employment benefits that should be part of the labor contract. In studies of the cut flower industry in Kenya, women reported that supervisors required sexual favors for job security, and refusal could lead to dismissal (Dolan, Opondo, and Smith 2002). This harassment occurs in spite of company codes of conduct that prohibit such behavior. An example cited in Module 13 of this volume indicates that the increasing competition between local fish traders, who are generally women, and external buyers is resulting in risky fish-for-sex exchanges that have negative social consequences for local fishing communities.

The prevalence of HIV and AIDS rises in communities where unequal labor relations leads to increased sexual activity in the workplace. An additional safety risk for women arises under shift work that entails traveling at night. However, regulations controlling women's access to different jobs can be discriminatory (see Thematic Note 2).

Women face health hazards in the cultivation of many crops reporting back pain and pelvic problems in rice cultivation and weeding. Agricultural work can be arduous for both sexes, but to the extent that women are concentrated in specific activities, they will experience greater exposure to some risks. Occupational safety risks can be high in factories and agroprocessing plants, including equipment accidents, exposure to unsafe conditions, and contact with chemicals and toxic substances. Women who work in fish- and shrimp-processing experience arthritis and other negative health effects of standing or sitting in wet, cold environments for

10 to 12 hours a day (USAID/GATE Project 2006). In a recent study of the fish and shrimp industry in Argentina, the majority of the women interviewed held temporary jobs and therefore had no medical or social coverage. More than two-thirds of the women interviewed work more than five days a week, and 63 percent work more than eight hours a day (Josupeit 2004).

Health risks in the growing horticulture industry include exposure to toxic products through inadequate training and protective clothing, poor hygienic conditions, and physical demands and long hours. Every year at least 170,000 agricultural workers are killed as a result of workplace accidents, and some 40,000 of these are from exposure to pesticides (ILO 2003). To the extent that women predominate in some of these activities, they have greater exposure. See Thematic Note 3 for a more detailed discussion.

Under conditions of temporary, seasonal, or limited contracts, no health insurance is provided. Where there are no on-site medical facilities, these women, in greater proportion than men, bear the cost of medical services. In factories or on plantations, such as in fruit-producing areas in South Africa, medical facilities may be few or lacking, and workers may even be dependent on employers for transport to medical facilities.

Gender and child labor

In certain areas the issues of gender and child labor overlap. The International Labour Organization (ILO) estimates that some 70 percent of child labor occurs in agriculture (ILO 2003). Studies of the fisheries industry in India indicate that 60 percent of workers in the factories are young women and girls under the age of 25 and as young as 14.[5] A recent study of the cotton industry in India estimated that 450,000 children under the age of 14 are working in hybrid cotton fields, mostly in Andhra Pradesh, under conditions of "bonded labor" (Ventkateswarlu n.d.). Girls may be particularly at risk in some countries because they are the least likely to get schooling. A study in Ghana showed that children between the ages of 12 and 16 frequently quit school to work on agricultural farms and plantations.[6] In Ecuador children between the ages of 9 and 11 work in the flower plantations (ILO 2000). The hazards for working young girls are great: physical abuse, no protective gear, and exposure to chemicals that may increase risks to reproductive capacity, little information on hazards, and no medical services. However, surveys also indicate that families would prefer to send their children to school but need the income additional family members provide (ILO 2004).

KEY CONSIDERATIONS FOR PROGRAM AND PROJECT DESIGN

The following summarizes the key principles and guidelines in designing gender-responsive projects and programs. Details and concrete examples are presented in Thematic Notes 1–3 and Innovative Activity Profile 1.

Ensuring equitable agricultural labor impacts when designing policies and programs

Remarkably, gender impact is still frequently ignored in the design of policies and programs. Most, if not all, policies and programs designed to impact economic growth in urban or rural areas, agriculture, or industry will have gender impacts on agricultural labor. These impacts can result in a positive change in the gender distribution of participation and returns on labor, as industrial growth in China has promoted opportunities for young women, but in each case the earnings, productivity, and employment impacts must be examined.

A gender analysis is important for development policies and programs directed at agriculture. A review of the gender effects of trade agreements shown in box 8.1 demonstrates

---

Box 8.1   Gender Impact of Trade Agreements

Labor demand: Relative prices of factors change demand for labor, and sectors expand and contract. If women are located in sectors with comparative advantage for trade, they will benefit from employment, and, if not, they will be displaced. In Zimbabwe a reduction in tariffs on imported clothing closed the domestic industry, which employed predominantly women.

Wages: The convergence of factor prices as a result of liberalizing trade is postulated to benefit both consumers and producers. But in regions where unions are weak or nonexistent, workers may not be able to capture these benefits. In Mauritius, following liberalization in the 1970s and declines in wages, between 1985 and 1995 wages rose and women benefited from employment in the growing textile sector. But in the *maquila* sector in Mexico, with a very elastic supply of labor, wages fell between 1980 and 1999.

Source: Gammage, Jorgensen, and McGill 2002.

---

the price, employment, wage, and consumption effects and differing impact on men and women.

Designing gender-equitable agricultural labor programs and projects

Given that agriculture is a declining sector, expanding agricultural labor markets is not a policy objective on its own, for men or women. Other policies must complement policies targeted at improving the quantity and quality of rural labor. Facilitating migration out of the rural sector may be more urgent in some countries. An increase in nonfarm opportunities implies a potential reduction in the supply of agricultural laborers, which would increase agricultural wages.

Generating more rural employment opportunities, on- and off-farm

The *World Development Report 2008* argues that the most significant positive impact on agricultural labor will come through creating a dynamic rural economy in both the agriculture and the nonfarm sectors, focusing primarily on creating a good investment climate. Key government actions should be taken to "secure property rights; invest in roads, electricity, and other infrastructure; remove price interventions adverse to rural products; develop innovative approaches to credit and financial services; and aid in the coordination of private and public actors to encourage agro-based industry clusters" (World Bank 2007).

The promotion of dynamic regional towns and small cities is crucial to improve conditions for rural laborers through spillover effects. In Indonesia, even within rural areas, wage employment as a percentage of total nonfarm employment increases with village size (World Bank 2007). Many rural workers migrate to try to find better jobs, often in urban areas or manufacturing industries. Many poor households in developing countries now combine farm and off-farm activities seasonally. Improvements in communications and transport have created conditions for the large-scale internal movement of people. In India up to 40 percent of some villages commute daily to urban areas. Patterns in China are similar. Policies that support development in semirural areas will reduce the burden of migration on households. Active labor market programs, described below, can be instrumental in facilitating the successful migration from rural to urban areas. The challenge is to ensure that these programs and policies remain gender-neutral or reduce gender inequalities where they exist.

Extending legal rights frameworks for women agricultural laborers to increase decent work

Agricultural labor rights are mainly determined by *labor law*, and particularly by two broad groups of norms: those concerning all workers, both men and women (minimum wage, safety and health, trade union rights, and others), and those specifically concerning women (nondiscrimination, maternity benefits, "protective" legislation) (FAO 2006). International legislative frameworks exist largely through UN and ILO forums. The promotion of these international conventions has assisted in improving labor conditions in adopting countries, although not all are implemented to the same extent. Most of the conventions and recommendations are outlined in Thematic Note 2.

Even if international conventions have been ratified, national legislative frameworks may be inadequate. For example, Kenya does not have explicit provisions against sex discrimination (FAO 2006). And, where legislation exists, an *affirmative action strategy* is usually necessary to implement the legislation. Beyond labor law, other norms such as family law and case law are also relevant. For instance, in some countries family law allows the husband to demand his consent for his wife's signature on an employment contract or allows him to terminate the contract. Case law can establish a basis for women's employment rights. See Thematic Note 2 for a more detailed discussion.

Labor contracts also function as a legal framework regulating women's labor rights and responsibilities. Recently *corporate social responsibility (CSR) codes,* established by companies (often under pressure of international and national nongovernmental organizations [NGOs]), have become important instruments for establishing standards of decent work. Although many definitions of CSR can be found, most of the codes have grown out of demand from social groups and consumers that corporations "treat stakeholders in an ethical or responsible manner" (Hopkins 2004). The Fair Trade and Ethical Trading Initiatives are two groups of stakeholders that have established standards, institutions, and infrastructure to bring about change in corporate behavior. Not all codes of conduct (or codes of practice) benefit women and men equally, and greater attention needs to be paid to gender impacts of these codes. Codes of conduct and their application in the horticulture industry are discussed in Thematic Note 3.

Multilateral organizations are in a position to encourage national government actions on promotion of ratification of international labor conventions, support for development of national legislation and implementation frameworks, and promotion of affirmative action strategies. One example is external support for the integration of gender into Chile's legal framework. Presenting the economic arguments to governments and companies for improvements in labor conditions is a cost-effective component of a strategy. Overall arguments for improved labor allocation as well as research in areas such as productivity enhancement and social protection should be presented.

Increasing employment opportunities and active labor market programs

Rural wage employment has the potential to provide an escape route from poverty for many women. Increasing employment is best achieved through sound economic policies to stimulate the private sector. However, governments and other organizations can facilitate the process under conditions of market failures or instability, such as economic downturns, and, in the case of agricultural laborers, seasonal fluctuation and periodic market volatility.

Affirmative action programs address discrimination in the market where social factors create barriers to full market information. Affirmative action employment programs can promote gender equality in the formal sector in countries with fairly well-developed labor markets and reasonable law enforcement. Despite concerns about reverse discrimination and productivity costs, recent studies from the United States find little empirical evidence that affirmative action hires are less productive than other workers (Holzer and Neumark 1999). Programs do not have to be restricted to quotas but can include special recruitment efforts, broader screening practices, and special assistance programs, such as training and changes in hiring, pay, or promotion standards (World Bank 2001).

In cases of downsizing, governments and other organizations can provide employment information and networking, unemployment insurance systems, small start-up loans, and legal aid and can develop training capacity and new venture services (USAID/GATE Project 2005).

In an economic downturn or under other economic or sector-specific changes, a wide range of programs have been attempted to lower unemployment rates: these programs have been termed *active labor market programs* (ALMPs). ALMPs, used in Europe to reduce unemployment, have been implemented in many countries, but their application in agriculture has been largely to support migration out of the sector. For example, a job-matching program for migrants in China provided off-farm employment to about 200,000 upland laborers over six years. Women made up 25 percent of these laborers and reported more confidence,

reduced work burdens when returning home, and greater economic independence (World Bank 2007). ALMPs have been successfully implemented in Organisation for Economic Co-operation and Development (OECD) countries to reduce the risk of unemployment and to increase the earnings capacity of workers. Particular interventions include employment services, training, public works, wage and employment subsidies, and self-employment assistance. A recent evaluation indicated that although ALMPs were not a panacea for unemployment, some types of interventions, properly designed, could be effective for some workers (Betcherman, Olivas, and Dar 2004). Many findings from industrialized countries seem to apply broadly to transition countries, but this is not always true in the case of developing countries (on the basis of what is still a small sample of studies). The ingredients for successful interventions, however, do seem to apply for all countries. Good design features include comprehensive packages of services, programs that are oriented to labor demand and linked to real workplaces, and careful targeting. Nevertheless, it should not be assumed that women will be automatic beneficiaries of these programs. To ensure that women benefit as much as men in ALMPs, gender analysis should be included in the design.

The most effective set of ALMPs were employment-based training (Betcherman, Olivas, and Dar 2004). The interventions that are successful often feature an integrated package of services (education, employment, social as needed) to complement the training. Employment services are generally the most cost effective of the ALMPs.

Public works programs have variable success rates at short-term income transfer and even more uncertain effects on long-term employment. Longer-term employment effects are more often found where these programs generate viable infrastructure. In India the Maharashtra Employment Guarantee Scheme, designed in large part to fill the seasonal employment gap due to seasonal fluctuations, famines, and natural disasters, has been able to provide significant amounts of work, leading to increased wages in the economy, although other rural employment generation projects have not been as successful (ODI 2007). Public works programs in South Africa with the objective of contributing to long-term employment, including the popular Work for Water program, have generated interest among planners. Although the infrastructure and social impacts are positive, few studies document whether skills development in equipment use or financial management has succeeded in increasing rural employment. In any type of public works program, the design must consider gender roles to avoid excluding women.[7]

Reducing wage gaps and strengthening institutions

Women must be able to recognize the wage differential, understand the legal context, and organize within institutions or create new ones to negotiate equal wages and engage with employers, and employers must also comply with legislation. Stronger community organizations, including unions and women's organizations, can raise the issues.

One of the means of raising awareness of women's rights among workers has been to strengthen local organizations by training on alliance formation and networks. The ILO has developed a program with Danish and Norwegian support (Women's Education for Integrating Women Members in Rural Workers' Organizations) with the objective of increasing empowerment of rural women in Tamil Nadu and Madhya Pradesh. The program has two objectives: increasing awareness in trade unions of ILO standards as applied to gender and promoting the involvement and representation of women in trade unions. Small grants were provided by USAID to assist Latin American organizations working to improve women's labor conditions (WID TECH 2003b). These grants facilitated training in worker's rights and the sponsoring of community awareness events. The role of unions is discussed in Thematic Note 2.

Diversifying occupational choice

To achieve the full economic benefit from employment, women need to have greater choice over their occupations. Education programs can help through scholarships and mentoring programs and through ensuring curricula are not biased toward segregation by theme and occupation lines. Affirmative action programs have been successfully implemented in some countries.

One of the most effective ways of ensuring gender balance is to increase the number of women among "front-line staff" (IFAD 2000). Programs and projects can hire qualified women candidates or train women for occupations associated with "segregated" occupations, such as hiring women extension staff (for example, in Sudan) or by giving extension responsibilities to women's group promoters. In Ghana community-selected women extension volunteers have proved effective as an interface between women's groups and government extension services. In other countries, such as Cambodia and Indonesia, women volunteers have been trained as auxiliaries for animal vaccination (IFAD 2000). Women can be trained in workplace safety programs (WID TECH 2003b) as agricultural or fisheries extension workers or fishnet weavers trained to become fisherwomen. The "Projoven" program in Peru is noted to have reduced

occupational segregation during 1996–2000 through supplying semiskilled training and work experience to urban, low-income, young people in specific trades that are in demand in the productive sector (Betcherman and others 2004).

Improving social protection

The disproportionate number of women in casual and seasonal jobs and the attendant risks for women and children have heightened the need to increase social protection for women in all sectors of the labor market. Social protection can focus on reducing risks or on maintaining assets.[8] In the context of agricultural labor, social protection refers mainly to medical and unemployment benefits and pension provision.

The extension of public social protection programs to temporary, casual, and seasonal laborers will address some of the issues of gender inequity in agricultural labor. (Box 8.2 provides several brief examples of social protection programs.) Unemployment insurance, health insurance, and pension programs are all inaccessible to temporary and casual workers in most developing countries. General agreement holds that the private sector should not have to bear the full cost of these programs, but the balance between private and social costs and benefits needs to be evaluated. Barrientos and Barrientos (2002) develop a social responsibility matrix and discuss the roles of each stakeholder (see Thematic Note 3).

Box 8.2 Social Protection Programs

Turkey has taken steps to establish public social security schemes for agricultural workers. A voluntary program was established in 1983. Contributions paid at a prescribed level for at least 15 working days each month provide entitlement to old-age, invalidity, or survivor's pensions. A number of trade union initiatives have evolved from pressure from workers' organizations. In Argentina, Union Argentina Trabajadores Rurales y Estibadores (UATRE: Union of Rural Labourers and Dock Workers) operates a health and unemployment fund, and the union's initiative to extend protection to large numbers of unregistered and unprotected workers was recently formalized in national legislation. A national registry of agricultural workers and employers (RENATRE) was an important first step to the development of an unemployment fund and benefit system.

Source: ILO 2003.

Programs to extend social protection to workers in the informal sector in India and temporary agricultural workers in Chile present an opportunity to assess the costs and benefits of these programs (see Thematic Note 1).

A recent approach to extending social protection can be found through private sector codes of conduct. These codes are increasingly being applied along the global value chain in horticulture. Building the business case for improving labor standards performance is critical to engage the private sector (see Thematic Note 3). The role of social dialogue should not be neglected because collective bargaining is instrumental in improving social protection.

Improving health, security, and safety

Providing a healthy workplace and maintaining the health of workers should be good business, but managers of companies may have to be convinced of the economic benefits of, or be forced into, applying basic standards. Health concerns for women include violence and sexual harassment in the workplace, exposure to HIV and AIDS, as well as occupational safety issues surrounding, for example, accidents and exposure to unsafe conditions, chemicals, and substances. Overtime and night shifts can also create safety concerns for women, although these can also be used to restrict women from employment categories.

Improved information and data provided by laborers and labor organizations concerning a perceived problem can help lead to its resolution (see box 8.3). Dissemination of policies is important, and the implementation of training programs is necessary.

The workplace is an extremely effective center for HIV and AIDS awareness campaigns. Plantations in Uganda were experiencing extremely high rates of mortality, but as government campaigns were complemented by company information and condom distribution, the mortality rate has fallen significantly. Human rights work in some regions has been expanded to domestic violence and its social and economic repercussions. Some companies have recognized the cost of violence and facilitated support for abused women.

Increasing the information base

Integral to convincing governments, businesses, and civil society of the efficacy of change is accurate, up-to-date analysis based on reliable statistics. The quality of agricultural labor data is weak, and for the women agricultural

---

> **Box 8.3 Nicaragua and Guatemala: Improving Information for Health, Security, and Safety**
>
> A representative sample survey was introduced by the Maria Elena Cuadro Women's Movement in Nicaragua, which represents over 7,000 women members. As the influence of the organization has grown through publicity campaigns and increased membership, information from the survey supports arguments for better work conditions. The publication of the results has been influential.
>
> In Guatemala organizations for women in *maquilas* supported occupational health workshops and formation of health and hygiene committees; women represented workers to lobby companies for compliance with environmental health standards (Izabal Labor Union).
>
> *Source:* WID TECH 2003a.

---

labor force, it is even worse. Estimates of temporary women workers in horticulture in Chile alone vary from a low of 57,000 to a high of 162,500. Each program, project, or activity should have gender-disaggregated data to support it, or the means to collect the data built into the initiative. Efforts should be made to integrate gender-disaggregated variables into international, national, and local statistical databases on labor markets. UNIFEM has supported redefinitions of work and labor to ensure that data on unpaid and informal sector workers, much of which would be in agriculture, are included in employment databases (Chen and others 2005). Detailed and accurate costs are also required to convince governments and employers of the efficiency and effectiveness of programs that promote women's labor market participation.

MONITORING AND EVALUATION

Table 8.5 gives some ideas for indicators and sources of verification, though clearly modifications are required for each specific program. Further information is provided in Module 16 Monitoring and Evaluation.

Depending on the country or region, it may also be relevant to consider ethnicity and caste alongside gender (both as comparative indicators and when collecting data), because women of lower castes or ethnic minorities are usually in the most disadvantaged situation.

Table 8.5 Monitoring and Evaluation Indicators for Gender and Agricultural Labor

Indicator	Sources of verification and tools
Number of entrepreneurs or business operators trained in occupational health and safety issues and corporate social responsibility	• Program records
Incidence of occupational health and safety incidents, and measures taken to prevent future incidents	• Administrative records • Review of procedures as against local and national regulations training records
Spread of HIV and AIDS, prostitution, alcoholism, and other problems from in-migrant workers, compared with baseline	• Community health surveillance • Health records • Local authority reports
Differences in wage and employment conditions, if any, between women and other disadvantaged groups, and men for positions of comparable content and responsibility	• Case studies • Labor audits • Project management information system or administrative records
Percentage of time spent daily in household on paid and nonpaid activities, disaggregated by gender and age	• Gender analysis • Time use studies
Age of school leaving, disaggregated by gender	• School records
Percentage of women and men in activist or leadership positions in labor unions	• Union records
Membership of unions or informal labor networks, by gender and compared with number of men and women in workforce	• Stakeholder interviews • Union or labor group records
Number of women and men receiving training on labor standards, social clauses, and employment rights per quarter	• Program records • Training records • Union records
Access of women and men to social security and unemployment insurance	• Government social security records • Stakeholder interviews • Union or other insurance scheme records
Change in number of cases of women and men accessing legal advice regarding labor rights (measured over a set period before the project intervention and compared with a set period after the project intervention)	• Legal authority records • Records of paralegals
Change in knowledge in sample group (the general community, employers, or legal tribunal staff) regarding labor rights and dispute resolution procedures	• Group interviews or focus groups • Interviews, before and after
Change in women's and men's perceptions of levels of sexual harassment experienced before and after program activities	• Focus groups • Stakeholder interviews
Number of women and men from district employed in agricultural enterprises, annually	• Administrative records
Over a set period, an increase of x percent in household incomes from agriculture or forest enterprise-based activities among women-headed households and poor households in program areas	• Household surveys • Project management information system Socioeconomic data from statistics office
Changes over x-year period of project activities in household nutrition, health, education, vulnerability to violence, and happiness, disaggregated by gender	• Household surveys, before and after • Project management information system • School records
Proportion of household income coming from women and girls versus men and boys	• Household surveys

Source: Authors, with inputs from Pamela White, author of Module 16.

Gender and Informal Labor

The term *informal economy* is widely used and can refer to such disparate economic activities as shoeshine workers in Calcutta, garbage collectors in Cairo, or street cassava sellers in East Africa. The important characteristics of activities in the informal economy are a mode of organization different from a firm or corporation, unregulated by the state, and excluded from national income accounts (Swaminathan 1991). Chen and others (2005) add that "the workers in these activities are not likely to be protected by labor legislation or organized by formal trade unions." The ILO defines informal work as self-employment in small unregistered businesses and wage employment in unregulated and unprotected jobs (ILO 2002).[1]

Informal workers include those for whom marginal, risky, and low-paid work is better than no work. Such workers do not have any safety net and earn low income or benefits provided by an uncertain or dangerous job. There is also a clear gender dimension to such employment: in general, women are less likely than men to have formal jobs, more likely to work in the informal economy, and, within the informal economy, more likely to work in the lowest-paid and most precarious forms of employment.

The largest number of informal workers is in the developing world, where institutions providing regulation and support to business and labor are the weakest. Although informal work does provide income, it does not necessarily provide a wage sufficient to meet household needs. In the short run such employment provides a means of livelihood to a majority of women workers. However, income gaps between formal and informal workers remain, and so there is a concentration of poverty and related antisocial activities and a degradation of the environment. A poor and deprived women's labor force leads to unhealthy future generations and wide income disparities.

INFORMAL WORK IN AGRICULTURE

The following categories of agricultural labor are considered part of the informal sector: (1) agricultural laborer—spouse or other family members, generally unpaid; (2) wage laborer, for cash or in-kind compensation, on small, family-owned agricultural land; (3) casual wage laborers on registered agribusiness; and (4) seasonal wage laborer on registered agribusiness. In developing countries, and in some industrial countries, almost all agricultural labor could be considered informal.

In general, rural women are the main producers of the world's staple crops—maize, rice, and wheat—which provide up to 90 percent of the rural poor's food intake. Women are involved in sowing, weeding, applying fertilizer and pesticides, and harvesting and threshing of crops. Moreover, in many countries they are responsible for the household's legumes and vegetables and participate in the livestock sector, feeding and milking larger animals and raising poultry and small animals, such as goats, guinea pigs, rabbits, and sheep. Furthermore, rural women provide most postharvest labor, arrange storage, and take care of handling, stocking, processing, and marketing of the produce. Studies have shown that rural women in particular are responsible for half of the world's food production and produce between 60 and 80 percent of the food in most developing countries. However, women generally do not own the land on which they labor, and in many cases they remain unremunerated for their family labor.

As agriculture becomes industrialized with globalization, women remain concentrated in the labor-intensive parts of the agricultural value chains, without contracts and with low wages and limited benefits. In horticultural enterprises one of the growth areas in developing countries, women are concentrated in the "cool chain" distribution and the retail end, both of which are more labor intensive and dominated by women's employment (Lund and Nicholson 2003). The horticultural sector is discussed in Thematic Note 3. Fisheries and poultry are other agricultural industries in which women represent a significant part of the informal labor force. Women assist spouses in artisanal fishing, net preparation, and fish cleaning and marketing (see Module 13). In the growing fish and shellfish industries, women work in the labor-intensive parts of the value chain, as in the horticultural industry. Women are also involved in the growing poultry processing industry as casual and seasonal laborers and dominate informal food preparation and street vending in many areas, such as sub-Saharan Africa. In Nigeria, for example, all informal cowpea processors and street vendors are women.

CHARACTERISTICS OF LABOR IN THE INFORMAL SECTOR

Informal employment is particularly important in developing countries, where it constitutes one-half to three-quarters of nonagricultural employment, and for the year 2000 the shares specifically are 78 percent in Africa, in the range of 45 to 85 percent in Asia, and 57 percent in Latin America (see table 8.6). Women's collaborative, self-help, and traditional practices and initiatives in the informal sector are a vital economic resource (Chen 2004).

Within the informal economy, women are concentrated in work that is insecure and badly paid, with high risks of poverty. A gender gap in earnings exists across almost all employment categories, including informal wage employment and self-employment. Therefore, a hierarchy of earnings is found in different types of informal employment, ranging from employers and self-employed workers, mainly men, at the top to home-based workers, mainly women, at the bottom. This corresponds to a hierarchy of poverty risk among households, depending on whether they have some formal sources of employment income or are limited to informal

sources and depending on what type of employment provides the main source of employment income.

Today in India as in many other developing countries, the informal or the unorganized economy accounts for an overwhelming proportion of the poor and vulnerable population (table 8.7). In 1990–2000, informal women workers in India made up 85 percent of all workers, most of whom were employed in agriculture. The wage gap is significant globally between women and men workers. Women tend to be employed in a wider variety of levels compared to men, so their earnings can be more fragmented.

In the 1960s and 1970s it was widely assumed that, worldwide, development of the modern economy would shrink and absorb informal sector employment. Instead, the global economy has shown a tendency to encourage precarious forms of work. The modern industrial system has not expanded as fully in developing countries as it did at an earlier period in industrial countries. Informal production more typically takes place in family businesses or in single-person units, whereas traditional, more personalized systems of production and exchange still exist in agricultural and artisan production. But in today's global economy, both traditional and semi-industrial relations of production and exchange are being inserted into the global system of production. Also, women are highly involved in traditional and home-based work, which is on the rise because of shrinking overhead costs of formal employment.

LESSONS LEARNED AND GUIDELINES FOR PRACTITIONERS

Understanding the gendered impact of economic and social policies is critical. The impact of policies on men and women is not the same because men and women are involved in different types of activities, have different ownership of resources, and have different needs in relation to health and education. Recognizing that a single policy prescription for the informal economy would not be able to help improve the conditions of such workers is very important. A good practice should be *participatory and inclusive* and allow for policies to be developed through consultation with informal workers themselves and through consensus of relevant government departments and other appropriate social actors.

Labor laws need to govern informal sector work

A legal framework is an important prerequisite to improve labor conditions; however, it is not sufficient to change

Table 8.6	Informal Employment in Developing Countries		
Informal employment as a percentage of	Africa (%)	Asia (%)	Latin America and the Caribbean (%)
New jobs	93	n.a.	83
Nonagricultural employment	78	45–85	57
Urban employment	61	40–60	40

Source: Charmes 1998 (updated 2000).

Type of Worker	Gender	Share of Workers, 1999–2000 (%)		
		Rural Sector	Urban Sector	All India
Casual worker	Men	45.98	24.28	37.77
	Women	78.55	38.79	68.54
Self-employed worker	Men	42.01	33.64	38.84
	Women	15.53	21.03	16.92
Employer	Men	1.50	1.45	1.48
	Women	0.49	0.41	0.47
Regular wage/salary earner	Men	10.52	40.63	21.91
	Women	5.42	39.77	14.07
Total	Total men	72.25	82.48	75.81
	Total women	27.75	17.52	24.19
Total	All	100.00	100.00	100.00

Source: Various rounds of National Sample Survey Organisation (NSSO) survey data.

conditions. Thematic Note 2 discusses international, national, and other legal frameworks in detail. Experience in Ghana demonstrates how laws can affect the informal sector. Labor laws there were outdated and fragmented and did not fit with the work conditions guaranteed in Ghana's constitution. However, in 2003 the New Labour Act was negotiated through a tripartite process, involving the government, trade unions, and employers. The act applies to all workers (excluding the armed forces, police, and others). The major objective of the act was to extend important protective elements secured by formal workers to informal workers. It contains special provisions relating to temporary and casual workers that allow them to benefit from the provisions of collective agreements, such as equal pay for work of equal value, access to the same medical provisions available to permanent workers, full minimum wage for all days in attendance, and public holidays (Government of Ghana 2003). Such laws can be examples for other developing countries with growing informal labor forces.

Information technology and skills training for informal workers

In Africa many women entrepreneurs who are traders—ranging from those microtrading in foodstuffs to those doing large-scale import-export trade—are in need of market information and are beginning to use information and communications technologies (ICTs). In Senegal the Grand Coast Fishing Operators Union, an organization of women who market fish and are fish producers, uses ICTs to exchange information on supply and demand between their different locations along the Atlantic coast. The women feel that this tool has improved their competitiveness in the local market. They have a Web site to enable the nearly 7,500 members to promote their produce, monitor export markets, and negotiate prices with overseas buyers before they arrive in Senegal (Hafkin and Taggart 2001).

The Centre for Mass Education in Science, an NGO founded in Bangladesh in 1978, uses a flexible skills training program that leads to immediate income generation. The program is directed at adolescents and youth who cannot afford school and must work. It serves about 20,000 students in 17 rural areas and has a specific gender empowerment program aimed at helping young women fight discrimination and stereotypes and obtain more skilled employment. It identifies and pilots small, untried income-generating activities in villages, including soap and candle making, solar electrification, and computer use (ILO 2002).

ICTs can also be used by informal producers to increase productivity and competitiveness. The National Development Dairy Cooperative in India, whose 10.7 million member-owners produce the major share of processed liquid milk, introduced a computerized system to measure and test the milk that small producers delivered to their local collection centers, reducing perceptions of malfeasance and underpayment. In Samoa, through a computerized system, dairy farmers, many of whom are women, receive immediate payment by using an identification card and save considerable time. In many centers the entire transaction takes no more than 30 seconds from delivery to payment. The system is currently installed at 2,500 milk collection centers, benefiting more than 50,000 dairy farmers (Jhabvala and Kanbur 2002).

Social protection for the informal sector

South Africa has a healthy private pension regime for its population of 40 million. The pension is a vitally important source of household security, plays a role in the promotion of small enterprises, and has a household income-smoothing function: families spend it on "social" items such as children's schooling and transport to health services and use it for agricultural inputs and for small enterprise development. A number of signs of its importance in local and rural economies are visible: major hire purchase firms have changed their collection schedules to coincide with pension days, and clients of a microfinance organization have asked for coordination between pension payment dates and dates of microfinance loan repayments (Chen, Vanek, and Carr 2004).

Although most of the labor force in Costa Rica is not covered by occupationally related social insurance, a voluntary insurance is available for independent workers, own-account workers, and unpaid workers (family workers, housewives, and students). It is aimed at those either who have never contributed to a health or pension plan or who did not do so for long enough to accumulate adequate benefits. To join, families must have a per capita family income that is lower than the basic basket of food products determined by the Statistics Institute. The insurance is funded by the contributions of the state and the individuals who join. This is an interesting example of where a country with a good history of social provision is attempting to adjust in flexible ways to changes in the labor market—in this case the increasing numbers of informal workers (Martínez Franzoni and Mesa-Lago 2003).

Over 90 percent of India's workers are in the informal economy (including agricultural workers), with little, if any, statutory social security (see box 8.4). Most are casual laborers, contract and piece-rate workers, and self-employed, own-account workers. The government of India recently launched the Unorganised Sector Workers' Social Security Scheme on a pilot basis in 50 districts. The scheme provides for three basic protections: old age pension, personal accident insurance, and medical insurance (Lund and Srinivas 2000).

The ILO Work Improvement in Neighbourhood Development (WIND)[2] project in Vietnam is an example for improving health conditions for rural people. ILO WIND is a voluntary, participatory and action-oriented training program that promotes practical improvements in agricultural households through the initiatives of village families. It is currently being adapted to local conditions, translated and pilot-tested in Ethiopia, the Kyrgyz Republic, Moldova, and Senegal.

In Bolivia the Mutual Health Insurance Scheme covers basic health services for its members, half of whom are

---

Box 8.4   India: National Commission for Enterprises in the Unorganized Sector (NCEUS)

One of the major highlights of the Fourth Report of NCEUS (2007) was the official quantification of unorganized or informal workers, defined as those who do not have employment security, work security, and social security. These workers are engaged not only in the unorganized sector but in the organized sector as well.

Examination of the regulatory framework for ensuring minimum conditions of work for unorganized wage workers shows that (1) there is a lack of comprehensive and appropriate regulations in India and (2) even where regulation exists, inadequate and ineffective implementation mechanisms exist. The commission reviewed and analyzed the various perspectives on a comprehensive legislative framework for unorganized wage workers and made appropriate recommendations. The commission established at a very high government practice level the need to make separate policies for informal workers and women workers.

Source: NCEUS 2007.

---

informal economy workers excluded from other social security systems. The program is run by an NGO and financed through member contributions and grants from development agencies.

In Brazil the Rural Social Insurance Program is a rare Latin American example of state-sponsored social protection for those outside the formal sector. The program is a noncontributory pension and disability program for the rural poor, instituted by the 1988 constitution, which extended basic pension benefits to elderly and disabled people in informal rural employment. It has not only alleviated poverty but has also led to recipients moving from subsistence agriculture to sustainable household production. Ancillary social benefits include increased school enrollment among children in beneficiary households (Lund and Srinivas 2000).

India's welfare funds, many of which are sponsored in the state of Kerala, are also good examples of effective social protection for informal workers. Many funds have been started for informal workers in both agricultural and nonagricultural enterprises, including head-load workers, in 1981; fishermen, 1986; cashew workers, 1988; coir workers and khadi workers,

1989; agricultural workers, 1990; tailors, 1995; beedi workers, 1996; and bamboo workers, 1998. Welfare funds may be contributory or tax based, or a combination thereof. In the tax-based programs, a tax is levied on the production or export of goods. Workers have access through the funds to different types of coverage, some of which may be medical care, education of children, housing expenditures, and other forms of assistance. Coverage varies across the projects; some require cards to access benefits (Subrahmanya 2000).

Approaches have also been developed to address health care for the informal sector. The Indian government has started a health initiative as described in box 8.5. In Chile the Ministry of Health's national program of Occupational Health Surveillance has been underway since 2001 in nine regions of the country, covering basic health, risk prevention, protection of personnel, handling and control of agrochemicals, hazardous waste containers, and expired pesticides. The work is based on a set of standards issued by the ministry that includes suggestions from businesses in the sector. The results from the inspection of 770 farms were delivered in March 2002.

The Occupational Health Commission in Chile has promoted a special program for women seasonal workers that covers five aspects: supervision of occupational health conditions, supervision of pesticide use, health examinations, information on health rights, and training. In the fisheries sector tripartite roundtables have been established in three regions of the country where most women fishery workers are concentrated to reach consensus on measures for improving their working conditions. In this context information workshops have been conducted on occupational health, firms have been inspected, child care centers have been opened, and meetings of women fishery workers have been held.

Networks, organizing, and institutional support

Three networks of informal workers have established good practice standards for organizing and providing support to these workers: Streetnet, Women in Informal Employment: Globalizing and Organizing (WIEGO), and HomeNet. Box 8.6 summarizes relevant information on these groups. These networks have been effective in providing training to informal workers in finance and leadership skills. The organizations disseminate relevant information to members and have had input into legislative processes in various countries. WIEGO has been effective in working with international organizations to raise the profile of workers in the informal sector.

Develop better targeting mechanisms

Women also tend to be concentrated in more vulnerable types of informal employment, in which earnings are very low and unreliable. The average earnings from these types of informal employment are too low, in the absence of other sources of income, to raise households out of poverty (UNIFEM 2005). Identifying households by types is important, between those with primary income from informal work and those with primary income from formal work. In a study conducted for India, poor households were defined by examining household member-level data (National Sample Survey Organisation 1993–94, 1999–2000, 2004–05). The study found that more women belong to poor households with earnings from the informal sector (Sinha and Sangeeta 2000). Targeting such households for specific welfare benefits would benefit poor informal women workers.

Box 8.5   India: Health Insurance Plan for Workers in the Unorganized Sector

The government of India has designed a Health Insurance Scheme for the Unorganized Sector Workers to be implemented by the Ministry of Labor and Employment. The eligibility criteria for getting benefits in the program are being planned so that informal workers living below the poverty line would be beneficiaries. Innovatively for India, the beneficiaries will be issued smart cards for the purpose of identification. The in-patient health care insurance benefits would be designed by the respective state governments based on the requirements of the people and geographical area. The regional governments have to incorporate at least the following minimum benefits: coverage of the informal workers and their families (units of five); total sum insured Rs. 30,000 per family per year on a family floater basis; cashless attendance to all covered ailments; hospitalization expenses, taking care of most common illnesses with as few exclusions as possible; all preexisting diseases to be covered; and transportation cost (actual with a maximum limit of Rs. 100 per visit) within an overall limit of Rs. 1,000. The program is not specific to women workers, but the criteria of workers below the poverty line would ensure that many women workers would be covered under this plan.

Source: National Advisory Council, "Draft, The Unorganized Sector Workers' Social Security Bill," Government of India, New Delhi, http://pmindia.nic.in/nac/communication/Draft_Unorganized_Sector_Workers_Bill.pdf.

Box 8.6 Informal Worker Networks

"At the first international meeting on street vendors, held in Bellagio, Italy in 1995, a group of activists from 11 countries adopted an International Declaration that set forth a plan to promote local and national policies to support and protect the rights of street vendors" (Chen, Vanek, and Carr 2004). For the next several years, they organized regional meetings of street vendors in Asia, Africa, and Latin America and provided support to newly emerging local and national associations of street vendors in several countries. "StreetNet International was formally established in November 2002 and held its first International Congress in March 2004, attended by 58 delegates from 15 organisations, at which an International Council was elected for a three-year term" (Chen, Vanek, and Carr 2004).

WIEGO: Women in Informal Employment: Globalizing and Organizing was established in early 1997 with India's well-known Self-Employed Women's Association (SEWA) as a founding member. Through a consultative planning process, WIEGO identified five priorities for its work: (1) urban policies to promote

and protect street vendors, (2) global trade and investment policies to maximize opportunities (and minimize threats) associated with globalization for home-based workers, (3) social protection measures for women informal sector workers, (4) organization of women informal sector workers and their representation in relevant policy-making bodies at all levels, and (5) statistics on the size and contribution of the informal economy. WIEGO now has affiliates in over 25 countries, as well as project partners and activities in more than 12 countries. At the international level WIEGO has been effective at raising the visibility of the informal economy in public policy forums and at working with the ILO and the United Nations (Chen 2004).

HomeNet: Recently the government of India asked representatives of SEWA to participate in the formulation of a national policy on home-based work. HomeNet now has active member organizations in over 25 countries and publishes a newsletter that reaches organizations in more than 130 countries (Chen 2004).

Labor Rights and Decent Work for Women Agricultural Laborers

Promoting gender equality in legal entitlements relating to agriculture is crucial for two main reasons: first, the empowerment of women is a highly important end in itself, and second, the legal empowerment of women is "essential for the achievement of sustainable development" (Cairo Programme of Action on Population and Development, para. 4.1).

LABOR RIGHTS LEGISLATION: INTERNATIONAL, NATIONAL, AND CUSTOMARY[1]

Agricultural labor rights are mainly determined by labor law, and in particular by two broad groups of norms: those concerning all workers, both men and women (for example, minimum wage, safety and hygiene, and trade union rights), and those specifically concerning women (for example, nondiscrimination, maternity leave, and "protective" legislation).

One of the important challenges for agricultural labor workers has been ensuring the coverage of labor law in the sector. In some countries agricultural workers have been deliberately omitted from the law. For example, in Brazil labor law was differentiated for agricultural and nonagricultural workers, to the considerable disadvantage of agricultural workers, until the dualistic laws were completely repealed in 1988 (FAO 2006). Although in many countries labor laws should extend to agricultural workers, in practice little motivation is present for compliance by many of the agricultural organizations and agribusiness companies. Where there is pressure for compliance, means have frequently been found to circumvent compliance—for example, through third-party contracts. The following sections outline the existing international frameworks, with reference to some national examples.

Relevant international law

The United Nations and ILO have adopted a series of international instruments that provide an international legal framework for the realization of human and labor rights relevant to women agricultural laborers. The right to work without discrimination is recognized in the Universal Declaration on Human Rights (UNDHR, articles 2 and 23), as well as in the International Covenant on Economic, Social and Cultural Rights (ICESCR, articles 2(2) and 6–8) and the Convention on the Elimination of All Forms of Discrimination against Women (CEDAW, article 11). The rights included in these documents are the right to choose freely an occupation, to enjoy a just and favorable remuneration, to work in safe and healthy conditions, and to form and join trade unions. Women have a right to employment opportunities and treatment equal to men, including equal pay for work of equal value. Women also have the right to enjoy special protection during pregnancy and paid maternity leave and the right not to be dismissed on grounds of pregnancy or maternity leave. Among the ILO's conventions, the core labor standards dealing with freedom of association and collective bargaining, nondiscrimination in employment and occupation, and the elimination of forced labor and child labor are recognized internationally as a minimum floor of principles and rights that all countries must respect. In addition, a number of other ILO conventions are relevant for women agricultural laborers. (See table 8.8 for a more complete description of international conventions and covenants.)

Some countries, unfortunately, have not ratified these conventions, and the challenge remains for those that have to implement the adopted legal frameworks through enacting national legislation and appropriate regulations and enforcement mechanisms. Ratified ILO conventions are supervised, and the ILO Committee of Experts plays a role in revealing and removing gender inequalities. These issues are discussed in greater detail below.

Another deficit in the legislative framework is that temporary and casual workers are not explicitly covered by most legislation. Recent changes in approach at the ILO stress

Table 8.8 International Law Governing Rights for Women Agricultural Laborers

International Law	Dates and Articles	Provision
C89 Night Work (Women) Convention (Revised)[a]	1948	Makes provision that women without distinction of age shall not be employed during the night in any public or private industrial undertaking, or in any branch thereof, other than an undertaking in which only members of the same family are employed
ILO Convention 95—Protection of Wages[a]	1949	Makes provision of the partial payment of wages in the form of allowances in kind, considering that such allowances are appropriate for the personal use and benefit of the worker and his family; and the value attributed to such allowances is fair and reasonable
ILO Migration for Employment (Revised) Convention 97	1949	Provides guarantees for lawfully migrant workers, without discrimination on the basis of sex
ILO Equal Remuneration Convention 100	1951	Equal pay for men and women for equal work or work of equal value
ILO Convention 99 Minimum Wage Fixing Machinery (Agriculture) Convention[a]	1951	Creates adequate machinery whereby minimum rates of wages can be fixed for workers employed in the agricultural sector
ILO Maternity Protection (Revised) Convention 183 (103 remains in force in the countries that have ratified it)	1952	Entitles pregnant workers to a maternity leave of at least 12 weeks (with no fewer than 6 weeks after childbirth); allows additional leave in case of late delivery or pregnancy-related illness; prohibits dismissal while on maternity leave; entitles women to medical and cash payments, provided through either compulsory social insurance or public funds; and allows work interruptions for nursing purposes
ILO Discrimination (Employment and Occupation) Convention 111	1958	Prohibits discrimination in both opportunity and treatment and provides for affirmative action
C129 Labour Inspection (Agriculture) Convention[a]	1969	Maintains a system of labor inspection in agriculture
Universal Declaration on Human Rights (UNDHR)	1948, Arts. 2, 23	Right to employment opportunities and treatment equal to men, including equal pay for work of equal value Right to social security in cases of retirement, unemployment sickness, invalidity, and old age
ILO Termination of Employment Convention 158	1982	Prohibits dismissal on grounds of sex, marital status, and absence during maternity leave
Convention on the Elimination of All Forms of Discrimination against Women (CEDAW)	1979, Art. 11	Right to employment opportunities and treatment equal to that of men, including equal pay for work of equal value; principle of nondiscrimination explicitly envisages the elimination of discrimination against women "by any person, organization, or enterprise" Right to social security in cases of retirement, unemployment sickness, invalidity, and old age
International Covenant on Economic, Social and Cultural Rights (ICESCR)	1976, Arts. 2(2), 6–8	Right to employment opportunities and treatment equal to that of men, including equal pay for work of equal value Right to social security in cases of retirement, unemployment sickness, invalidity, and old age
C171 Night Work Convention, 1990[a]	1990	Takes measures to ensure that an alternative to night work is available to women workers, and that the income of the woman worker shall be maintained at a level sufficient for the upkeep of herself and her child in accordance with a suitable standard of living

(Table continues on the following page)

International Law	Dates and Articles	Provision
ILO Night Work (Women) (Revised) Convention 89 and Protocol	1948, 1990	Prohibits women's work at night (defined) for some industrial occupations (not for agricultural work; this convention is increasingly seen as discriminatory and not promoted)
ILO Plantations Convention 110 and Protocol	1958, 1982	Protects the labor rights of plantation workers, without discrimination on the basis of sex. *Plantation* is defined, and specific crops are listed, excluding small-scale production Contains guarantees as to recruitment, annual paid leave and weekly rest, compensation for injury, trade unions, and maternity protection

Source: FAO 2006.
[a]Additions from ILO 2006.

that the spirit of the regulations applies to all workers, and particular attention is currently being paid to informal economy workers, implicit in the Decent Work for All declaration. The ILO has developed methods for constructing country profiles based on normative indicators as a tool for progress toward decent work. Country profiles on occupational safety and health are available for many countries (Zarka-Martres and Guichard-Kelly 2005). A recent study of Ethiopia's Poverty Reduction Strategy paper shows that the framework for decent work standards can be applied even to least developed countries (Buckley 2004). Signs are encouraging that some governments, such as Chile and South Africa, are taking steps to incorporate informal workers under labor legislation. Chile established the Program for Women Seasonal Workers in Export Agriculture.[2]

National legal systems, and women's legal status within them, differ greatly from country to country. However, similarities are appearing more and more often across countries. Most constitutions prohibit discrimination based on gender, although the principle might be qualified in some cases to exempt family and customary law. For example, the Kenyan constitution exempts family law and customary law, areas of law that are crucial in shaping women's rights in agriculture. Some constitutions contain an affirmative action clause, and attempts to promote gender equality may be embodied in legislation. In South Africa the Promotion of Equality and Prevention of Unfair Discrimination Act 2000 prohibits unfair discrimination on grounds of gender and sex in both public and private life and envisages affirmative action.

Legislation other than that which directly addresses gender equality can have an impact on women's labor conditions as well. In 1973 the military government of Chile restricted collective bargaining to firm-level unions. Temporary workers are excluded from these unions; as a result, women who are largely employed in these positions have no access to union organizational skills or bargaining power (Barrientos and Barrientos 2002).

Moreover, some national legal systems include plans of action and/or institutional machinery to promote gender equality and the advancement of women. In many cases these instruments were adopted in the aftermath of the Beijing Declaration and Platform for Action. These plans of action have been useful in promoting an institutional framework to negotiate public-private partnerships and support more localized measures to ensure gender equality. In Brazil Councils for Women's Conditions have been established. In Mexico several states have established commissions for the advancement of women. South Africa formed the Commission for Gender Equality to monitor and evaluate laws and make recommendations and established the Equality Review Committee through the Promotion of Equality and Prevention of Unfair Discrimination Act 2000 to monitor the operation of that act.

Customary law

In many developing countries, national laws and policies are little implemented in rural areas. This limited implementation results, on one hand, from a lack of institutional capacity for enforcement, entrenched sociocultural practices, a lack of financial resources, inadequate knowledge of legal rights, and a lack of perceived legitimacy of official rules and institutions. On the other hand, customary legal systems are commonly applied in much of Africa, in many parts of Asia, and by indigenous communities in Latin America. Customary law is a body of rules basing its legitimacy on "tradition" (FAO 2006). Great diversity is found in customary law resulting from a range of cultural, ecological, social, economic, and political factors. These traditional legal systems may contain rules disadvantageous to women in areas such as income control or asset disposition. The practice of signing wives' wages over to husbands has been largely removed, but other practices may persist. In Latin America women often must ask for their husband's authorization before undertaking a job and quit if their husband tells them to (FAO 1994). On the other hand, some customary law may be more advantageous to women and provide them access to specific rights not protected under civil laws. Customary legal systems evolve over time and can be changed.

Beyond labor law, other norms such as family law and case law are also relevant. For instance, in some countries, family law allows the husband to demand consent for his wife's signature on an employment contract or allows him to terminate the contract (FAO 2006). Women may also be affected by norms founded on religious principles or interpretations. These norms may be applied in countries because they are recognized in the legislation or followed in practice. These norms frequently govern matters such as family relations and inheritance and may affect the existence or exercise of women's rights. However, as with customary law, these norms vary significantly from locality to locality and country to country. These norms are also flexible and change over time.

KEY GENDER ISSUES IN LABOR RIGHTS OF AGRICULTURAL WORKERS

The legal and extralegal frameworks providing social protection and promoting gender equity and decent work conditions for women are proliferating and improving. More countries are enacting legislation, and more forces are creating a demand for better legislative frameworks. However, some issues remain and require continued attention.

Women's access to employment may be restricted by family law norms requiring authorization of the husband. Some of these norms have been challenged through courts and at the local level, but many are still applied in practice. The legal case *Maria Eugenia Morales de Sierra v. Guatemala* challenged the civil code in Guatemala that allowed a husband to oppose the employment of his wife. The case, initiated in 1995, was raised to the Inter-American Commission in 2001

before the state was called to fully comply with international human rights obligations (FAO 2006).

Labor law does not prohibit sex discrimination in all countries. For example, neither Fiji nor Kenya has explicit provisions against sex discrimination (FAO 2006). Frequently where there is a provision, no sanction is recommended. Affirmative action measures are envisaged only in some cases.

Only some countries have adopted legislation addressing sexual harassment in the workplace. Field studies document that this is a major problem affecting women working in plantations and in factories, as in many other workplaces. Discrimination in the workplace or in employment based on sexual orientation is also rarely addressed in developing countries. The prevalence of HIV and AIDS has important labor market implications, some of which may be gender specific. With the growth of HIV prevalence in many countries, particularly in sub-Saharan Africa, the average age of the active labor force is declining, and girls as well as boys are forced into working earlier. Workplace discrimination in the face of HIV and AIDS is a major challenge for labor law (Fenwick, Kalula, and Landau 2007). Southern African Development Community has developed a Code on HIV and AIDS and Employment, which was introduced in 1992. The code emphasizes human rights principles regarding nondiscrimination and confidentiality and provides a series of specific recommendations about how to manage HIV and AIDS in the workplace. In 2001 the ILO developed the Code of Practice on HIV and AIDS and The World of Work.

Provisions exist for maternity protection in many countries. However, the requirements for application of the protection may be very demanding and de jure or de facto exclude women agricultural workers (who are concentrated in seasonal and temporary labor force). Considerable variation is also found in the provisions of maternity leave. In cases where maternity leave is paid by the employer, the cost of women's labor is higher, creating an economic disincentive for their employment.

Most laws and standards apply only to permanent laborers in agricultural and other sectors. Seasonal and temporary laborers, many of them women, are omitted and suffer the worst of labor conditions. Large-scale migration also poses a challenge to the protective capacity of labor law in many countries (Fenwick, Kalula, and Landau 2007). Documented migrants, those who enter a country legally, likely work under favorable conditions; undocumented migrants, the majority, are vulnerable to exploitation and abuse and do not have recourse to the protection afforded by labor laws. The informalization or casualization of work has increased, resulting in a reduction in the number of permanent full-time employees. In Namibia casualization is most predominant in the construction industry, followed by the fishing, retail, and manufacturing sectors (Klerck 2002). Although casual labor is not new in agriculture, as the agricultural sector matures, the potential for decent work, which increases with the development of most sectors, diminishes with an increase in informal contracts.

Workplace safety and exposure to chemicals are two of the most important areas that require stronger legal protections for all workers within the sector. Although strong international standards have been set, most of which are supported at the national level, these are generally not applied in the agricultural sector. Regulations in these areas are applicable to all persons regardless of age or gender, but recent concern over the potential for increasing birth defects has an added gender dimension to exposure to toxins (see Thematic Note 3 for a more in-depth discussion).

Not all laws support the rights of women to decent work. For example, women's access to some agricultural work may be hindered by "protective" legislation prohibiting women's night work in the agricultural sector. Prohibitions may reduce women's choices while attempting to protect them. Cargill's Sun Valley poultry factory in Thailand has chosen to provide all workers with transport, which enables both men and women to work night shifts and overtime and reduces the risk of nighttime travel. Although this is clearly in the interest of the company, it also provides those employees who desire to work more with safe transit (see Innovative Activity Profile 1). In Yemen laws that protect women from working late hours or require employers to provide child care centers if they employ a certain number of women make it more costly for the private sector to hire women rather than men (World Bank 2005). The ILO Committee of Experts has raised this point with the government of Yemen.

LESSONS LEARNED AND GUIDELINES FOR PRACTITIONERS

Many actors are involved in the process of ensuring gender equity and decent work for men and women in agricultural labor markets. Government plays an important role by enacting laws, extending information and training on laws, and establishing structures for enforcing the laws. National and international NGOs can provide information, train NGOs, and act as watchdogs. Private sector entities such as buyers can assist by developing codes and ensuring that they are applied and that compliance is monitored. Trade unions can negotiate terms of codes and advocate for compliance to existing codes within the country and with firms.

Supporting legal reform

In some countries information about and analysis of labor laws are limited. A recent study of labor laws in southern Africa noted that the very limited information made an evaluation of the coverage difficult (Fenwick, Kalula, and Landau 2007). The lack of information is particularly relevant to sub-Saharan Africa.

Legal reform can be promoted by international organizations, particularly with regard to international conventions and covenants. Dialogue with national leaders on the economic benefits of gender equity in labor markets should be initiated.

In Uganda a Gender Coalition has been created to support the implementation of the International Finance Corporation and World Bank–supported Gender and Growth Assessment (GGA) recommendations. Following lobbying from the coalition, GGA recommendations have been incorporated into four labor reform bills covering employment, occupational safety and health, labor disputes, and labor unions, which were passed in 2006. The Ministry of Finance, acting on GGA recommendations, commissioned new legal drafts of the Companies Act, the Chattels Transfer Act, and other bills (Cutura 2006). The GGA is a tool that can be used to bring information on gender and labor to government, the private sector, and labor organizations. By documenting links to economic growth, the GGA becomes a persuasive tool for change.

Recently legislators in various countries have paid greater attention to gender aspects of labor relevant to agriculture. In South Africa, women farm workers until recently had very little protection. In 1993 legislation on minimum labor standards was extended to agricultural workers. Moreover, the Employment Equity Act of 1998 prohibits direct and indirect unfair discrimination in access and treatment on grounds of gender, sex, pregnancy, marital status, and family responsibility. Where discrimination is alleged, the burden of proof is placed on the employer. The act also provides for affirmative action, including preferential treatment and numerical goals, in establishments employing 50 or more workers (including agricultural employers) (FAO 2006).

Some countries have tackled specific issues that typically concern women workers, especially on plantations. Brazilian Laws 9029 (enacted in 1995) and 9799 (enacted in 1999) prohibit employers from requiring sterilization or pregnancy certifications or examinations as a condition for employment, and bar employers from conducting intimate examinations of employees. Several countries have adopted specific norms on sexual harassment in the workplace (such as the 1995 Anti-Sexual Harassment Act of the Philippines) that apply equally to farms and plantations. (FAO 2006).

Developments have also come through judicial decisions. In India guidelines on sexual harassment in the workplace were developed by the Supreme Court in *Vishaka v. Rajasthan and Others* (AIR 1997 SC 3011), building on the Indian constitution and the CEDAW. Lawsuits have also been brought by women agricultural workers, although the overall number of these cases remains low. In South Africa case law has been developed under the Extension of Security of Tenure Act of 1997, which protects from eviction persons occupying land with the consent of the land owner, including farm workers. A particularly important case is *Conradie v. Hanekom and Another* (1999 (4) SA 491 [LCC]), in which the South African Land Claims Court set aside an eviction order against two farm workers, husband and wife, employed on the same farm. Having dismissed the husband, the landowner had sought to evict both. The court held that the wife had a right as an employee not to be evicted under the 1997 act, and her eviction order was set aside. The court also held that the act guaranteed to her the right to family life, so that her husband (who after his dismissal was no longer a protected "occupier") had a right to reside on the land as a family member (FAO 2006).

In addition to its traditional strategies for adopting regulations and supervision and providing information about rights, the government of Chile has adopted a program to improve access and working conditions for women, known as Good Labour Practices for Equal Opportunity between Men and Women. This has involved developing a strategy for ongoing dialogue with the private sector. The initiative includes activities for sensitizing the business sector; recognizing firms that adopt good labor practices to promote equal opportunity between men and women; establishing standards for good labor practices; and conducting studies and producing practical guidance for implementing these policies, the contents of which relate to measures inherent to the work process, the reconciliation of occupational and family life, economic measures, and health coverage. Activities include the preparation of model codes of good labor practices in two of the country's major firms; the sponsoring of seminars and joint work with the Foreign Investment Committee, the Chile-United States Chamber of Commerce, and Acción Empresarial, a body that advises its member companies on socially responsible business policies (Government of Chile 2004).

Raising awareness of conditions and rights

Increasing the availability of resources in communities on legal rights and documenting labor conditions that violate existing standards are important avenues for combating gender inequities in the sector. In Latin America examples exist of advocacy and public awareness to increase the awareness of women's issues within the community and nationally. An annual campaign, "Work, yes—but with dignity!" is run by the Maria Elena Cuadro Women's Movement in Nicaragua. The movement also conducted a representative survey of 20 percent of women in the factories to identify actual labor conditions. The results have been effective when used in dialogues with business and government (WID TECH 2003).

Increasing the monitoring of labor conditions can also contribute to an increased awareness of conditions and establish the conditions for change. COVERCO (Commission for the Verification of Corporate Codes of Conduct), an NGO based in Guatemala, has pioneered the effort in advancing independent monitoring of working conditions in Guatemala's garment factories and agricultural export industries. COVERCO monitors conditions and evaluates compliance with standards established in codes of conduct and national and international law. COVERCO has also built a coalition of NGOs engaged in monitoring and assists in the capacity building of these NGOs. A study of conditions of women working in coffee plantations, funded by USAID, was relevant in developing Starbuck's code of conduct for coffee purchases. The government of Chile has engaged private sector companies in several activities to promote the development and adoption of good codes of labor practices. Thematic Note 3 discusses codes of conduct.

Increasing access to legal advice

Increasing women's access to reliable, affordable legal advice is another means of improving their capacity to achieve legislative support. The Beijing Platform for Action called on governments "to ensure access to free or low-cost legal services including legal literacy, especially designed to reach women living in poverty" (para. 61[a]). Legal support might be as simple as locating documentation of marriage in the case of the death of a spouse or facilitating access to identification cards, as was determined in Brazil (in the case of land transfer, but this could apply to pension access) (Guivant 2001). A movement of legal and paralegal NGOs is integral to improving access to the legal system through training and awareness raising, counseling and legal assistance, individual and public litigation, and representation and advocacy (FAO 2006).

Promoting role of women in institutions that govern women's labor rights

Women need to be involved in areas of government that have control over labor law. Although ministries devoted to women's and children's affairs have been notably marginalized and ineffective in many countries, examples may be identified of change when specific issues are addressed (such as Chile).

Where unions exist, a need is present to promote gender awareness. CEMUJER, an NGO in El Salvador, used a small USAID-funded grant to help women in unions develop leadership skills, assist women already in leadership positions, train women union members in legal rights, and provide legal advice for women (WID TECH 2003).

Where there are no unions, or existing unions do not meet women's needs, other organizations have been instrumental in raising specific issues for action. Women's organizations in Central America have implemented education and capacity-building programs for women working in *maquilas* (factories) (see WID TECH 2003 for examples). The National Fishworkers Forum in southern India has been effective in raising the conditions of migrant women workers in fish-processing plants (Nayak 2005). Both international and national NGOs have become instrumental in raising awareness of gender inequalities and workplace conditions in developing countries. For effective change, development of civil society organizations within relevant countries is a prerequisite.

Gender and Employment in Labor-Intensive Export Agriculture

Agricultural exports are significant to foreign exchange earnings, employment, and government revenues of the poorest countries. Agriculture accounts for 61 percent of employment and 14 percent of gross domestic product (GDP) in developing countries and an even higher proportion in the least developed countries (85 percent of employment and 36 percent of GDP). Trade in traditional agricultural commodities (such as bananas, coffee, grains, and tea), on which developing countries largely depend, has been beset by adverse world market conditions, restrictive macroeconomic policies, excessive market controls, and political instability. The decline of revenues from these classic export commodities, coupled with trade liberalization and structural adjustment reforms, has prompted many countries to diversify their export portfolios into specialty crops and higher-value agriculture products (floriculture, high-protein meats, horticulture, and processed food products). By 2000 high-value agricultural exports were estimated to account for approximately two-thirds of total agricultural trade (Dolan and Sorby 2003).

The wage labor force in agriculture is highly concentrated in the export sector: large labor forces still exist on plantations growing traditional commodity exports, and in recent years rising numbers of laborers are involved in the production or agroprocessing of high-value commodities. Participation in commodity chains for high-value commodities provides considerable opportunities for growth and poverty reduction. Yet labor conditions under the new export markets echo the frequently degrading conditions found on plantations.

This Thematic Note addresses the labor issues of gender and identifies some of the main features and conditions of work in traditional plantation production and in high-value agriculture export production. Women face similar issues of discrimination in both these areas of employment. Participating in high-value export industries can bring positive consequences for gender equality, but specific challenges such as occupational segregation and environmental health must be addressed to achieve positive outcomes.[1] The Thematic Note also includes a presentation of governance structures that affect export markets including corporate social responsibility, fair trade, and codes of conduct.

TRADITIONAL EXPORT COMMODITIES: PLANTATION AGRICULTURE

Conditions for laborers on plantations remain dire in spite of years of publicity and awareness. Permanent employees have better conditions and wage rates, but the increasingly high proportion of temporary and seasonal labor implies that most laborers are working under poor conditions. As has been highlighted throughout the discussions of the agricultural labor force, women are concentrated in these less stable employment positions and thus suffer the worst conditions.

The concern about child labor has recently brought work conditions on plantations back under scrutiny. Studies on plantation banana production in Ecuador and sugarcane in the Philippines, among others, have highlighted the scale of child labor and the hazards these children face at work, including heat, heavy work, long hours, wounds, and risk of poisoning from pesticides (de Boer 2005; Pier 2002). Gender inequities also persist. Women face violence and sexual harassment. Box 8.7 provides an overview of problems faced by women working on plantations.

Although initiatives by governments, private companies, and NGOs have addressed labor conditions, one of the most serious problems facing companies and their labor forces on these large-scale agricultural plantations is the decline in prices over recent years as demand has stabilized and production has increased. Coffee is one of the most important examples: prices have declined because of new technology that uses lower-quality beans and increased coffee production

Box 8.7 Gender Issues on Plantations

- Discrimination in access to employment, with women concentrated in subordinate and lower-paid jobs in the fields and men in higher positions, particularly as supervisors and headmen
- Discrimination in access to training and vocational courses
- Discrimination in allocation of benefits, such as housing
- Discrimination within trade unions (regarding participation and access to leadership positions)
- Sexual harassment
- Wage differentials, with higher wages for positions typically held by men (such as sugarcane cutters) than for women's positions (such as weeders)

Source: Mbilinyi and Semkafu 1995.

with the entry of Vietnam and growth from crops in Brazil. Coffee prices reached their lowest level in 30 years in 2001. The declining prices limit producers' capacity to improve workers' conditions and cause workers to lose what little negotiating power they had. The world market conditions for tea are similar, although not as drastic as those for coffee.

One of the strategies used to raise the prices of the primary product has been to focus on specialty markets; however, these products count for only a small part of the market. For example, currently the specialty coffee sector accounts for only about 6 to 8 percent of production (World Bank 2007). No studies exist that show whether or not companies entering into specialty production have passed on any of the price premium to workers. See Module 5 for a further discussion of marketing of traditional export crops.

HIGH-VALUE AGRICULTURAL COMMODITIES: AGROPROCESSING INDUSTRIES

For many developing countries, declining revenues from traditional commodities and the opportunities of a globalized market have led to the adoption of high-value agricultural exports. Over the last decade, these exports have generated significant amounts of foreign exchange, contributed to the upgrade of agricultural production skills, and created substantial opportunities for waged employment and self-employment. Women in particular have been able to profit from these new labor market opportunities both as smallholders and as wage employees. However, although high-value

agriculture can be an engine of growth for developing countries, and the employment it generates is empowering for women, it is characterized by several shortcomings (Dolan and Sorby 2003).

GOVERNANCE STRUCTURES: CORPORATE SOCIAL RESPONSIBILITY, FAIR TRADE, AND CODE OF CONDUCT

The following sections describe corporate social responsibility, fair trade organizations, codes of conduct, and their gender dimensions.

Corporate social responsibility

The concept of corporate social responsibility is still evolving. However, CSR increasingly refers to the ethical treatment of stakeholders by corporations (Hopkins 2004). CSR covers actions in areas as broad as the environment, health, human rights, governance, corruption, and labor practices. Because CSR has largely grown "up" from stakeholder concerns into corporate actions, the number of international, multinational, and national principles, charters, and codes has proliferated.

CSR initiatives have led to the development of several sets of standards on which companies base codes of conduct (many of these are listed in table 8.9). Some codes have received attention in the development field because of their focus on agricultural producers. The Ethical Trading Initiative, established in the United Kingdom in 1998 as a tripartite forum of NGOs, companies, and trade unions, is one of the largest initiatives. The Fair-Trade Labelling Organisations (FLO) International was established in 1997 as an umbrella organization of 17 national fair trade labeling initiatives.

Fair trade organizations

Fair trade initiatives try to provide better market access and better trading conditions to small-scale farmers. This includes a price premium for producers to be invested in social and environmental improvements and sometimes improved conditions for workers. Fair trade products represent only a small percentage of world agricultural trade; however, in the last 10 years fair trade has emerged as an increasingly popular tool to create markets. In 2005 alone an estimated $100 million was provided to producers and their communities above the conventional price for these goods (Farnworth and Goodman 2006). The yearly growth of fair

Table 8.9 Principles, Charters, and Codes of Practice for Fair Trade, Ethical Trade, and Corporate Social Responsibility Efforts

Initiatives	Date	Main Issues
Governmental- or intergovernmental-led:		
Ethical Trading Initiative (U.K. government and NGO)	London, 1998	Labor practices in trade
European Union Principles	Brussels, 2001; revised 2002	Multistakeholder
International Labour Organization Tripartite Declaration on Transnational Corporations	Geneva, 1977; revised 2000	Employment
Organisation for Economic Co-operation and Development Guidelines	Paris, 1976; revised 1977	Employment, triple bottom line (financial, social, and environmental indicators) indicators
U.S. Model Business Practices	Washington, DC, 1996	Community, corruption, environment, health and safety, labor, law
UN Global Compact	New York, 2000	Human rights, labor, environment
NGO-led:		
Account Ability 1000	London, 1999	Social and ethical "assurance"
Amnesty International HR Guidelines	London, 1998	Human rights and security
Fairtrade Labelling Initiative	FLO established 1997	Market access and trading conditions for small farmers
Global Reporting Initiative	Boston, 1997; revised 2002	Multistakeholder, triple bottom line indicators
ICFTU Code of Practice	Brussels/Geneva, 1997	Labor and trade union issues
SA8000	London, 1998; revised 2002	CSR and labor
Company-led:		
Caux Principles	Minnesota, 1994	Multistakeholder
Fair Labor Association (FLA), United States	California, 1998	Labor practices
Global Sullivan Principles	United States, 1999	External stakeholders
ICC Business Charter for Sustainable Development	Brussels, 1991	Environment, health, and safety
World Economic Forum	Davos/Geneva, 2002	Corporate governance
Trade-union-led:		
ICFTU/ITS Basic Code of Labor Practice	ICFTU/ITS Working Party on MNCs, December 1997	Labor practices

Source: Based on Hopkins 2004.

trade volume has been around 20 percent since 2000, although the products represent only a small percentage of world agricultural trade. The biggest volumes have been reached for bananas and coffee.

The FINE criteria, presented in box 8.8, represent the goals of the fair trade coordination platform. FINE is the informal coordination platform composed of the following representative bodies: FLO (Fair-Trade Labelling Organisations International), IFAT (International Federation for Alternative Trade), NEWS (Network of European World Shops), and EFTA (European Fair-Trade Association) (Develtere and Pollet 2005).

Note that product-specific fair trade standards exist for bananas, cane sugar, coffee, cocoa, cut flowers, fresh fruit, fruit juices, honey, rice, sports balls, tea, and wine. In general, gender issues have been underrepresented in the codes and agreements.

Codes of conduct, gender, and labor conditions

Codes of conduct covering employment conditions of southern producers exporting to European markets mushroomed throughout the 1990s. Over 200 codes related to worker welfare specifically were identified at the beginning

The key criteria:

- For workers, fair wages, good housing, health and safety standards, and the right to join trade unions
- No child or forced labor
- Programs for environmental sustainability
- For small farmers' cooperatives, a democratic structure that allows members to participate in the cooperative's decision-making process.

Moreover, the trading terms must include the following:

- A price that covers the cost of production
- A social premium to improve the living and working conditions
- Partial advance payment to prevent small producer organizations from falling into debt
- Contracts that allow long-term production planning.

Source: Develtere and Pollet 2005.

of this decade, with over 20 codes applying to agriculture in developing countries (Blowfield 2000). Many companies adopt codes to reduce the risk of negative exposure related to poor employment practices within their supply chain. The large number of codes implies great variability in content: some codes integrate international conventions relating to gender discrimination and inequality, yet other codes make no mention of gender at all. The variability extends to the auditing of codes (Barrientos, Dolan, and Tallontire 2001).

Barrientos, Dolan, and Tallontire (2001) developed a three-level framework for analyzing the gender sensitivity of codes in labor practices. The levels range from those that both men and women confront in employment (for example, collective bargaining, contracts, discrimination, freedom of association, safety and hygiene, wages, and work hours) to broader socioeconomic issues that affect women's ability to access employment types (for example, domestic responsibility, education, gender relations, and social norms and practice). An evaluation of two relevant codes, SA 8000 and ETI, within this framework reveals that although both effectively address issues at Level A, neither is strong in extending coverage to Levels B and C. Neither covers repro-

ductive rights, maternity or paternity leave, or protection for pregnant women or child care.

KEY GENDER ISSUES

The following sections discuss the key gender issues in export agriculture industries.

The informalization of labor in high-value agricultural industries

Labor relationships in these new industries vary considerably. Global poultry production generally employs a permanent labor force. In the cut flower industry, the proportion of the permanent labor force can be as low as 35 percent, although companies in Kenya and Zimbabwe have up to 50 percent permanent workers. However, these examples are exceptional, and great variability exists across companies and countries. In the Colombian cut flower industry, only 16 percent of the workforce is temporary, and workers are generally hired for the full year. But in Ecuador, the temporary labor force is hired on a short-term basis, and contracts are often terminated prior to the date of conversion to permanent status (Dolan and Sorby 2003).

Subcontracting is a dominant feature of the labor force in high-value export crop production. In Colombia companies contract with former supervisors to provide labor for piecework. These laborers are hired for periods as short as two weeks or as long as several months. The lack of a direct relationship between company and employee makes the employee more vulnerable. Across many of the countries recently studied, women are concentrated in the temporary, casual, and seasonal labor forces. In the Chilean fruit industry, women represent 50 percent of temporary laborers but only 5 percent of permanent laborers.

Occupational segregation and wage discrimination

Occupational segregation in plantation agriculture is standard practice. Many of the tasks are divided according to physical strength, but another division is related to the use of equipment. Men are usually accorded jobs that involve training and use of light or heavy equipment. This segregation leaves women in lower-paying positions and provides them with limited upward mobility. Women form the majority of the tea pickers on plantations in Sri Lanka and rarely participate in other occupations. Prior to 1978 women's wages for picking were lower, but now a uniform wage is applied. But women work longer hours for the same wage, and tradition in the areas studied showed that wages are still frequently turned over to the husband (Wickramasinghe and Cameron n.d.).

Wage disparity results as well from discriminatory undervaluation of the work in occupations in which women are concentrated. Occupational segregation is prevalent in horticultural industries as well, and women are frequently placed in work categories based on perceptions of "women's" attributes and tasks related to domestic work. For example, a strong gender division of labor prevails in production of high-value crops on smallholder farms such as vanilla producers (Kasente and others 2000), the cut flower industry, and poultry production. Women are responsible for the highly labor-intensive tasks of harvesting, planting, processing, and weeding, while men perform activities related to feed production, fumigation, irrigation, precultivation, and slaughter houses. The occupational sectors in which women are concentrated are usually accompanied by the poorest benefit packages and lowest wages, as illustrated in table 8.10, which shows the gap for wage earners in the Kenyan horticulture industry. The wage differences largely reflect job segregation as described earlier. Wage gaps for similar jobs are difficult to calculate with such extreme occupational segregation.

Costs versus benefits

The employment versus empowerment debate is difficult to resolve in the context of high-value agriculture industries. On the one hand, employment can (and does) engender some tangible gains for women, who often obtain access to an independent income stream, increased autonomy, and new social networks. Data also show that certain employment benefits, such as education, health care, and training, bolster women's "human capital" and further women's empowerment. In contrast to their informal income-generating activities, which have long been overlooked, women's participation in waged work also makes them more visible in the economy.

However, women also experience clear costs by working in agroprocessing industries. One set of costs arises from the often poor working conditions and flexible and insecure employment. A second set has to do with the social and economic consequences of the increase in women's time burdens, an increase that affects the health and well-being of women and their families. The extent of these implications varies considerably across industries and countries, but they do signal cause for concern. Nevertheless jobs in these industries provide many women with the best chance they have for improving their lives in a context of limited to nonexistent alternatives.

Occupational health and safety and sexual harassment

One of the most serious problems on large plantations is the lack of adequate protective measures and training related to the use of fertilizers, insecticides, and pesticides. Aerial spraying of bananas in Ecuador exposes all workers, but in activities in which either men or women are concentrated, one gender may be more affected than the other. Crowded conditions in housing, poor sanitation, and drinking water in fields or factories are all cited in studies of plantations.

In the flower, poultry, and vegetable industries, women are most vulnerable to repetitive stress and joint injuries. Rotation of jobs can reduce these injuries, and the poultry industry has introduced this practice (Dolan and Sorby 2003).

Exposure to chemicals during storage, mixing, and spraying is far too common in these industries. Problems arise in particular from the use of pesticides and other chemicals in confined spaces, such as greenhouses and packinghouses, where exposure tends to be high and the workforce is largely women. Effects of chemical exposure can include skin irritation, respiratory problems, nausea, and dizziness. The longer-term effects can be more serious. Some health concerns are specific to women: damage of reproductive organs and damage to unborn children (malformed fetuses, higher instances of miscarriage). Although most countries have established occupational health standards, compliance is variable in the horticulture industries. Some of the harmful exposure is due to inadequate training.

Table 8.10   Kenya: Wages in Horticulture by Skill Level and Gender

Type of Labor	Packinghouse		Farm		All	
	Men	Women	Men	Women	Men	Women
Unskilled	21.00	17.80	12.80	12.60	15.00	14.70
Semiskilled	22.00	23.30	17.00	14.10	17.40	19.40
Skilled	49.00	n.a.	15.30	n.a.	23.80	n.a.

Source: Dolan and Sorby 2003.

Note: Figures in Kenyan shillings; on April 16, 2001, 10 Kenyan shillings equaled $0.12912.

In Uganda evidence suggests that spraying is conducted when workers are unprotected in greenhouses (Dikjstra 2001 in Dolan and Sorby 2003).

Child labor is still evident in many traditional export crop production systems. Children as young as 11 years old work on banana plantations in Ecuador, sugarcane plantations in the Philippines, and tea plantations in Sri Lanka (de Boer 2005; Pier 2002).

Sexual harassment on plantations is widespread. Women are frequently concentrated in menial tasks, such as tea leaf picking, with men supervisors who abuse their positions by requesting sexual favors in exchange for job security, bonuses, or lighter workloads. Studies in many countries have found evidence of sexual harassment in many factories and fields (Dolan and Sorby 2003). Its prevalence is mediated by local gender norms.

GOOD PRACTICES AND LESSONS LEARNED

Several methods may extend social protection to informal workers. A social responsibility matrix outlines the roles of various stakeholders in a global value chain. The social responsibility matrix for the horticulture sectors in Chile and South Africa provided in table 8.11, which was developed by Barrientos and Barrientos (2002), outlines international and state actors, market actors, community actors, and household resources.

International and state actors, such as the ILO and national labor laws, set the legislative framework (details are discussed in Thematic Note 2). For example, Chile has developed a strategy for mainstreaming the gender perspec-

tive in the country's major agricultural business organizations through the Public-Private Committee on Women Seasonal Farm Workers.

Social protection from market actors generally protects only workers in the formal market. In Chile social protection is government mandated but privately provided. In both Chile and South Africa low coverage is provided for temporary workers in agriculture from these sources. However, roles are in place for both corporations and unions at this level. One of the significant differences between traditional plantation export crop production and the relatively newer industries focused on high-value export crops is the degree of unionization. Workers on large-scale plantations for crops such as tea and coffee are more likely to have union representation than those companies in cut flowers or vegetables. Several explanations may be given for this imbalance, including the differing ages of the industries, the deliberate sabotage of unions by multinational and national companies, and the predominance of casual, temporary, and seasonal labor in the industry, which is a result of both the nature of the products and management decisions.

A more recent approach can be found through private sector codes of conduct. Initiatives in developed countries—for example, the Fair Trade Initiative and the Equitable Trading Initiative—have raised premiums on prices of commodities for companies that are willing and able to comply with the prescribed standards. Pressure from civil groups and NGOs in industrial countries on buyers has increased the demand for these products.

Codes of conduct have been particularly important in the high-value crops area. The initiative on the part of the

Table 8.11	Chile and South Africa: Social Responsibility Matrix for Informal Workers in Horticulture	
Domain	**Domestic**	**International**
State	Labor inspectorate Ministries National government	Economic Commission of Latin America and the Caribbean, European Union, International Labour Organization, International Social Security Association, World Health Organization, World Bank
Market	Employers/producers Exporters Labor contractors Private insurance and welfare providers (pensions, health, etc.) Trade unions	Ethical trade initiative Importers Multinational enterprises Supermarkets
Community	Church organizations Community organizations Domestic NGOs Political parties Trade unions	Consumer organizations International NGOs
Household	Extended household	Migrant relatives

Source: Barrientos and Barrientos 2002.

The Uganda Code of Practice for the Horticulture Sector, finalized in 2002, sets down strict guidelines for farmers and managers in occupational safety, worker welfare, discrimination, and equal pay. The code puts the industry ahead of other agricultural sectors in labor standards, while bringing Uganda in line with other flower exporters in the region. An ILO report released in 2000 found that flower farms provided workers accommodation, free tea and lunch, medical care, adequate leave, prompt payment of salaries and salary advances, and the right to leave for the day at 5 P.M.

A study conducted in 2006 by the Canadian International Development Research Centre found that most women employees are hired as permanent workers with full benefits. The report claimed that all workers have contracts and get 60 days of paid maternity leave. They also have a doctor and dispensary where drugs are distributed at very low cost to workers and their families with money raised for a medical fund for operations or for family members who suffer complications. The study also indicated that a fully equipped lab for HIV and malaria testing was being established for floricultural workers.

Source: Asea and Kaija 2000.

horticulture industry in Uganda to provide consistent labor practices through a code of practice is described in box 8.9.

A recent multicountry review of codes of conduct by the Ethical Trading Initiative concluded that the overall impact of these codes was positive, particularly on health and safety, but the effect on important gender issues such as discrimination was minimal (Institute of Development Studies 2007). The greatest concern was that few codes cover temporary workers, and therefore the codes exclude a large proportion of women in many industries (see box 8.10). Codes of conduct are frequently less relevant to informal employment conditions, and they are weak or negligible in their coverage of issues such as equal pay and sex discrimination. Few codes extend to employment-related issues such as reproductive rights, child care provision, or sexual harassment. Reasons for the deficiencies in the application of codes center on the inability of the buyers to enforce principles. Many companies operate in complex value chains, in which suppliers deal with multiple buyers and agents, so any one buyer has limited influence. Communication and monitoring weaknesses also limit the application of the codes of conduct.

Another major problem with codes of conduct is compliance. External and independent monitoring is the surest way of evaluating adherence to the codes, but few industries have initiated these procedures. This has been highlighted in a case study of South Africa that identifies that the labor inspectorate is poorly resourced and lacks the capacity to monitor widely dispersed, isolated farms (Barrientos, Kritzinger, and Roussouw 2004). Private or nonprofit organizations also play an important role in monitoring codes of conduct.[2] Codes of conduct can be advantageous to companies, but a code of conduct is not necessary to motivate a company to implement good labor practices. The case of Cargill's Sun Valley poultry factory in Thailand indicates that good policies lead to high productivity (see Innovative Activity Profile 1).

Access to the fair trade market is also an incentive for corporations to enact equitable labor practices. An example involving a large banana plantation in Ghana shows how a traditional plantation can provide better conditions for the workforce (see box 8.11).

Better work environments can also be achieved through partnerships between private companies, NGOs, and governments. One such example is a cashew nut factory in Mozambique. Established by a private entrepreneur, the government cashew institute and other organizations contributed to the development of a guaranteed loan. A USAID-financed NGO assisted in the design of the factory, and a Dutch NGO, SNV, has assisted with marketing. In 2002 the factory had two cashew plantations with 50 tons of production per year. Workers receive a free meal at work, and according to their contracts they have access to health assistance, paid annual holidays, and severance pay in case of professional illness or work accidents. A trade union has been set up, and a child care facility has been constructed, where women can leave their children if they bring a child care provider with them (Kanji 2004).

GUIDELINES AND RECOMMENDATIONS FOR PRACTITIONERS

Ultimately, standards for decent work and gender equity need to be enacted at the national level, as presented in Thematic Note 2, but initiatives organized by multiple stakeholders within industries, preferably including labor as well as suppliers and buyers, can be an effective intermediate

Box 8.10 Ethical Trading Initiative

The *Ethical Trading Initiative Impact Assessment*, implemented by the Institute of Development Studies in Sussex, found that codes of labor practice were having a positive effect on improving certain "visual issues." The biggest impact was on health and safety, with positive changes found on 20 out of 25 sites. This led to improvements in the lives of workers' families through observance of health and safety at home. For example, banana workers no longer hugged their children while wearing overalls used for pesticide spraying. Other changes were in better adherence to legal minimum wages and documented employment benefits for regular workers. On a Costa Rican banana plantation, women had seen some decline in occupational segregation, although they were not better represented at management levels.

Codes are helping to raise supplier awareness of the need to comply with national regulation. But codes have had little impact on the improvement of "less visual issues," such as freedom of association and no discrimination. No workers at the sites felt more able to join a trade union as a result of codes (although unions had already existed before codes on some sites in the study). Codes had little effect on discrimination in the hiring, training, and promotion of women and migrant workers. Another important finding was that regular and permanent workers were most likely to have benefited from changes resulting from codes. Casual and migrant workers (international or internal) were found in all case study countries, and the use of third-party labor contractors was found in most countries except Vietnam. These workers were least likely to have benefited from the implementation of codes of labor practice, and on many sites they faced significant discrimination.

Source: Institute of Development Studies 2007.

Box 8.11 Access to the Fair Trade Market Can Significantly Improve Working Conditions

The Volta River Estates, Ltd. (VREL) is a Ghanaian-registered commercial plantation that has been producing bananas for the European fair trade market under the Oke label (marketed by Agrofair) since 1996. VREL is the only exporter of bananas from Ghana, in the top 40 Ghanaian companies for both turnover and number of employees, and one of only two initiatives in Ghana serving the fair trade market. The company has 900 full-time workers. VREL meets the social and labor standards established by the Fair Trade Organization and Max Havelaar, and it has increased wages to 30 percent above Ghana's minimum wage. One-third of the fair trade premium is allocated toward meeting environmental standards, and two-thirds is given directly to workers, who choose investments through a premium committee, consisting of two management members and eight worker representatives, all chosen through elections. Bicycles were a recent investment by the company when workers received a particularly large premium. Permanent employees get paid annual and sick leave as well as maternity leave. Only 16 percent of VREL employees are women, partly because of the nature of the work, but mainly because of social and economic constraints. VREL, however, has established a development project and has focused on increasing gender participation. Health care is provided for workers through an on-site clinic, and the company is considering building a hospital.

Source: Mick Blowfield and Stephanie Gallet, "Volta River Estates Fairtrade Bananas Case Study," www.nri.org; www.vrelorganic.com/fairtrade.htm.

step, particularly where multinational companies operate in countries with weak governance. National and intermediate initiatives include the following:

Raise the gender implications of the growth of agroprocessing and production of high-value agricultural exports in global discussions. Multilateral organizations have the opportunity to articulate a strong policy position in international conventions and debates, securing the rights of women working in these industries. The gender implications of high-value agricultural export production could be highlighted and disseminated in a variety of forums, raising the profile of these issues in policy circles.

Support ratification of international conventions. Following the recommendations in Thematic Note 2, national governments need to be encouraged to ratify ILO conventions. International standards are binding to all countries. The economic and social arguments for applying these standards should be presented at the national level to relevant policy makers. Incorporating informal workers fully under existing labor legislation must be given top priority.

Identify appropriate institutions to educate women on their employment rights, the content of codes, and relevant national regulations. In high-value agriculture women's empowerment requires education and training and must be based on participatory approaches to development. The development community could advocate for the provision of training and educational programs to workers. These programs also could disseminate information on labor standards, social clauses, employment rights, and the content of codes of conduct. Supporting the entry of temporary, casual, and seasonal laborers into labor unions will eventually bring greater awareness of their issues.

Expand codes of conduct. In general, retailers in the United Kingdom and continental Europe have progressed much further than the United States in the application of labor codes. Consequently companies supplying retailers in European markets are more likely to provide better employment conditions and more equitable opportunities to men and women. A wider range of agribusiness companies and large retailers, in the United States and in other major demand markets, could be encouraged to support the introduction and monitoring of codes throughout their supply chains, thereby extending the coverage of labor standards.

Support the inclusion of gender issues in codes of conduct. Several gender issues are not adequately covered in codes of conduct addressing labor conditions in developing countries. Policies against sexual harassment must be given more importance, especially training across companies. Codes are not effective if workers are not aware of the principles in the codes.

Ensure temporary workers are covered under codes of conduct. Suppliers are more willing to respond when a critical mass of buyers request codes of labor practices. Collaboration between buyers can help to enforce the message of inclusion of temporary workers. Social auditors need to include casual migrant and contract workers in monitoring and engaging with trade unions and NGOs who are aware of these workers. Local multistakeholder initiatives can play an important role, such as that of the Wine Industry Ethical Trade Association (WIETA) in South Africa. Bringing labor contractors into the dialogue is a more effective means of ensuring improved labor conditions.

Enable local organizations to participate in monitoring of codes of conducts relevant to labor standards. Involvement of civil society organizations should be encouraged in monitoring and auditing labor standards and the social aspects of codes of conduct. This involvement is essential to protect and enhance the working conditions and employment rights of all workers in these industries. A need is also present to establish mechanisms for ongoing and confidential reporting of violations of the code by all groups of workers, including those in less secure and temporary work. For example, Kenya stakeholders in the flower export industry developed their own participatory auditing methodology.[3]

The entry of rural women in developing countries into the industrializing agricultural labor market can expose them to new risks and poor employment conditions, but these jobs can also create new opportunities to raise living standards for the rural poor. Additional work is required in more countries, particularly in Asia, to better understand the role that national and international organizations can have in improving labor relations and reducing gender inequalities. For example, the East Africa Business Summit from Kenya, Tanzania, and Uganda has been held annually since 2002. In 2003 participants resolved to increase their sourcing of inputs from small- and medium-size enterprises, with a target of 25 percent of total inputs (Kivuitu, Yambayamba, and Fox 2005). Gender equity and the links to improved productivity should be raised on the agendas of these and similar meetings.

Thailand: Cargill's Labor Improvement Program for Sun Valley Foods

Thailand's relatively low wages afford considerable competitive advantage in labor-intensive industries with low skill requirements. A large number of Western companies have established labor-intensive factories in poultry, shrimp, and other agroprocessing industries. In 1995 Cargill's Thailand division, Sun Valley Foods—the third-largest poultry processor in Thailand, accounting for about 10 percent of the country's exports—began to evaluate human resource management problems. Chief among these was a high voluntary turnover rate among its largely women workforce. In 1995 turnover was 100 percent. There was also a high rate of absenteeism, and although accident and injury rates were low for the industry, room for improvement was identified. In a study for the Gender

Agriculture Project for USAID, John Lawler described the strategy Cargill implemented to improve productivity in its Thai poultry business (Lawler and Atmiyanandana 2000). Cargill's strategy was not radical, but it was equitable and family friendly, and it yielded important lessons about the potential of company-led gender-sensitive policies in an industry dominated by women laborers.

Thailand has one of the highest proportions of women working outside the household (47 percent). The Thai government has implemented policies to improve working conditions for women. The current constitution prohibits discrimination, including employment discrimination based on gender. However, legislation to prohibit gender discrimination in the private sector has not been enacted. For example, employers in Thailand often advertise job openings specifically restricted to men or women, depending on the type of job.

Cargill has operated in Thailand since the early 1960s through two companies in addition to Sun Valley. Sun Valley, with a workforce of about 3,900, is a fully integrated poultry business that produces raw chicken that is further processed (skinned, deboned, and so on) before sale. Almost all of the company's output is exported. The processing plant, located in Saraburi, employed 1,500 or more when operating at peak capacity. In the processing plant supervision and work activities were regulated, with teams of 40 to 50 workers headed by a supervisor and one or more assistant supervisors. Employees wore uniforms that were color coded to indicate general job category. Job and work pace were highly routinized, requiring manual dexterity. Because of the care required in production work, individual workers and work groups had a significant impact on productivity, despite the work pace set by assembly line technology. Base pay for production workers was the local minimum wage.

Jobs were highly segregated. Almost all the workers in the feed mill were men, as well as most of the workers involved in

---

What's innovative? Sun Valley management developed a series of initiatives in human resource management, including a range of family-friendly policies as well as cultural and gender-sensitive incentives such as the following:

- Promoting a culture of community and family through training on company values
- Providing some supplementary assistance, such as payment toward hospitalization fees, and reassigning pregnant women to work that was not physically taxing and did not normally require them to work overtime
- Giving financial assistance for the schooling of employees' children, along with some scholarships for students with particularly good grades
- Providing free bus service to and from work, which women particularly viewed as a friendly policy.

slaughtering animals. In contrast, the vast majority of workers who processed the chickens after slaughter were women.

An analysis of the production facility identified several sources of turnover. Job dissatisfaction led to employees quitting and absenteeism. Family responsibilities were a second cause. Day care did not seem to be such a problem because of the availability of extended family members, but medical care required more time off, and employees frequently ended up quitting to care for family members. Turnover meant that the company was not recovering the training costs of employees. Sun Valley management knew that employees with more than a year of service had double the productivity of employees with only six months of service.

PROGRAM DESCRIPTION AND SPECIFIC ACTIVITIES

Between 1995 and 2000 Sun Valley management determined to turn the employment record around for the company and developed a series of initiatives in human resource management. Those initiatives included a range of family-friendly policies as well as cultural- and gender-sensitive incentives.

The company introduced several programs that linked pay to performance. It initiated performance appraisals to determine annual pay increments and promotion opportunities. Employees were given bonuses for length of service. Annual bonuses were paid to employees based on overall company performance and were larger for longer-term employees. Bonuses were attached to specific indications, such as chicken mortality rates in barns of the grow-out farms. Other bonuses were specifically linked to daily attendance, and Sun Valley paid a special award annually to those with perfect attendance.

The company also promoted a culture of community and family through training on company values. Supervisors were most often women, who were promoted from within the ranks of production workers, which worked well in Thailand's culture. These supervisors could arrange short or even extended leaves of absence without pay to allow an employee to handle family emergencies, such as a sick child or family member; and short-term leave without pay was allowed during the harvest season. These policies enabled employees to take time off for medical and family emergencies but encouraged them to return.

Although maternity leave with pay is required by Thai law, interviewees indicated that other companies and employers discourage workers from using it. Medical care for pregnant workers was covered under the Thai Social Security Act, but Sun Valley provided some supplementary assistance, such as payment toward hospitalization fees. In addition, Sun Valley reassigned pregnant women to work that was not physically taxing and did not normally require them to work overtime.

Sun Valley also provided financial assistance for the schooling of employees' children, along with some scholarships for students with particularly good grades. The company also implemented an educational program to improve literacy and made provisions to allow employees to attend classes several hours per week outside of normal work hours and receive pay. The program served to build ties to the company.

Free bus service was provided to and from work; other companies provided buses but charged for their use. Women in particular viewed this as a friendly policy. Many lived far from the plant and were concerned about their safety traveling alone, particularly at night. Sexual harassment was prohibited in company policies that were widely disseminated, and in interviews women indicated that there were far fewer problems than they had experienced in other companies.

BENEFITS AND IMPACTS

The benefits from the program accrue to both the company and the employees.

Company costs and benefits

Data are not available on the additional costs of these improved human resource programs, but the main categories of costs included wage-related costs, such as bonuses and costs for education programs, transport, and health and safety improvements. The benefits of the programs in terms of increased productivity clearly exceeded the cost outlay.

During and following the period of implementation of these policies, the company continuously met or exceeded its financial performance goals. In 2000 Sun Valley embarked on an ambitious expansion program to increase production capacity by 30 percent. In 2001 the company received Thailand's National Health and Safety Award.

Employee benefits

Employees cited an improved work environment at the company. Sun Valley's policies provided significant economic benefit at the individual and household levels by reducing the cost of unemployment and the costs of employment search for women who needed to take leave. The education program had both direct and indirect benefits: women expressed considerable benefit from the education program, both as an example to their children and in terms of personal accomplishment. The safety programs and improved transport increased safety and likely reduced the risk of violence for women, benefits that are not easily quantified but are important for well-being.

LESSONS LEARNED AND ISSUES FOR WIDER APPLICABILITY

Several of the lessons learned by Sun Valley can be applied more widely.

The private sector can independently contribute to improved working conditions. The management of Sun Valley was seeking means to address problems affecting the profitability of the company and identified several policies to solve problems of absenteeism and turnover. These strategies might now work in all industries. In fact, in studies of the costs of applying codes of conduct, researchers have indicated that for some companies, especially small companies, compliance costs are onerous (Collinson 2001a, 2001b). The most significant costs tend to be health and safety costs, due to equipment, and the costs of auditing and management systems. Ironically, improving working conditions without certification may be the best option for some companies in which these practices can increase productivity, or in which companies can benefit from the CSR publicity without certification.

Improved work conditions can benefit the corporate bottom line. Improved work conditions can benefit corporations in several ways. The Sun Valley examples illustrate that productivity increases can be substantial. Declines in health expenditures, and a reduction in turnover and absenteeism, are more easily measurable than good worker morale and a positive workplace environment, but all of these factors increase worker productivity. Improved working conditions at Sun Valley increased business sustainability through raising the company's profile within the country. More qualified workers are likely to be drawn to a company with a good reputation, and the national and local business environment should be improved.

There are challenges in relying on voluntary labor standards. Labor market regulation is a blend of specific rules negotiated by parties (either individually or collectively) to an employment relationship and general legislative imperatives that establish baseline entitlements for workers. Voluntary

company codes of conduct or employment practices do not rely on an employment contract, legislation, collective agreement, or common law. When the corporation is responsible for the production of norms governing the workplace, there is no minimum standard, no guarantee of consistency, and no monitoring or compliance mechanisms. The current proliferation of company codes of conduct has been criticized for these deficiencies. Where national employment legislation and collective action organizations are weak, however, multinational and transnational corporations may be instrumental in setting standards. These companies, as the Cargill example shows, can establish the economic, financial, and social value of these standards. In addition, in a competitive environment as labor markets tighten, such standards may create additional social benefits as other companies adopt labor standards in order to compete.

NOTES

Overview

The Overview was written by Kristy Cook (Consultant) and reviewed by Nata Duvvury and Catherine Ragasa (Consultants); Eve Crowley, Libor Stloukal, and Paola Termine (FAO); Maria Hartl (IFAD); Sriani Ameratunga, Peter Hurst, Mary Kawar, Susan Maybud, Martin Oelz, and George Politakis (ILO); Ratna M. Sudarshan (Institute of Social Studies Trust); Steve Wiggins (ODI); and Elena Bardasi and Rekha Mehra (World Bank).

1. A summary of these studies is presented in World Bank (2001), appendix 4.

2. See World Bank (2007), articles by D. Elson, G. Standing, and S. Horton, among others.

3. Both of these movements are well documented by nongovernmental and international organizations, including NGOs, research organizations, the United Nations, and trade unions.

4. IFAD, "Experience Sharing from the Rural Development Project for Taourirt-Taforalt in Morocco: Coping with Constraints to Reach Women," www.ifad.org.

5. In India it is legally permissible for children over the age of 14 to work. However, large numbers of children under this age work full time.

6. Guy Blaise Nkamleu, "Children at Risk in the Agricultural Sector in Sub-Saharan Africa: Determinants of Child Labor Participation in the Cocoa Farming of Côte d'Ivoire," paper presented at Sixth Annual Global Development Network Conference, Dakar, Senegal, www.gdnet.org.

7. Cecilia Luttrell and Caroline Moser, "Gender and Social Protection," draft paper for Department for International Development, www.eldis.org/go/topics/resource-guides/

gender/key-issues/gender-and-social-protection&id=22475&type=Document.

8. Specialists at the World Bank define *social protection* as consisting of public interventions "to assist individuals, households and communities in better managing income risks" (Holzmann and Jorgensen 1999). The ILO, on the other hand, sees social protection as defined by basic rights: "Entitlement to benefits that society provides to individuals and households—through public and collective measures—to protect against low or declining living standards arising out of a number of basic risks and deeds" (von Ginneken 2000 as quoted in Barrientos and Barrientos 2002).

Thematic Note 1

This Thematic Note was written by Anushree Sinha (National Council for Applied Research [NCAER]), and Kristy Cook (Consultants), with inputs from Catherine Ragasa (Consultant), and reviewed by Nata Duvvury (Consultant); Maria Hartl (IFAD); Eve Crowley, Libor Stloukal, and Paola Termine (FAO); Sriani Ameratunga, Peter Hurst, Mary Kawar, Susan Maybud, Martin Oelz, and George Politakis (ILO); Ratna M. Sudarshan (Institute of Social Studies Trust); Steve Wiggins (ODI); and Elena Bardasi and Rekha Mehra (World Bank).

1. ILO popularized the notion of the informal sector in the early 1970s and has a long history of contributing to the conceptual and policy debates about the informal economy. Various expert groups, such as the Delhi Group on Informal Sector Statistics, have sought to distinguish between the informal sector and informal employment. The concept of informal employment refers specifically to the activity undertaken by a person as the unit of observation. The term informal employment is used by the ILO Task Force (2002) to mean employment that has no secure contracts, worker benefits, or social protection. The major component of such employment is (a) self-employment in the informal sector and (b) paid employment in informal occupations. The latter could also be in the formal sector, and certain evidence can be found of such employment. Informal workers employed in the formal sector do not get similar wages/benefits as formal workers.

2. See also www.ilo.org/public/english/protection/cond trav/pdf/agri_wind.pdf and www.ilo.org/public/english/protection/condtrav/workcond/agriwork/agricult.htm.

Thematic Note 2

This Thematic Note was written by Kristy Cook (Consultant) and reviewed by Nata Duvvury and Catherine Ragasa (Consultants); Maria Hartl (IFAD); Eve Crowley, Libor Stloukal, and Paola Termine (FAO); Sriani Ameratunga, Peter Hurst, Mary Kawar, Susan Maybud, Martin Oelz, and

George Politakis (ILO); Ratna M. Sudarshan (Institute of Social Studies Trust); Steve Wiggins (ODI); and Elena Bardasi and Rekha Mehra (World Bank).

1. This section is drawn largely from FAO's "Gender and Law: Women's Rights in Agriculture" (FAO 2006).

2. Government of Chile, "Report on the Implementation of the Beijing Platform of Action Presented by the Government of Chile to the United Nations Division for the Advancement of Women. Response to the Questionnaire," April, www.un.org.

Thematic Note 3

This Thematic Note was written by Kristy Cook (Consultant), with inputs from Catherine Ragasa (Consultant) and Hild Rygnestad (World Bank), and reviewed by Nata Duvvury (Consultant); Maria Hartl (IFAD); Eve Crowley, Libor Stloukal, and Paola Termine (FAO); Sriani Ameratunga, Peter Hurst, Mary Kawar, Susan Maybud, Martin Oelz, and George Politakis (ILO); Ratna M. Sudarshan (Institute of Social Studies Trust); Steve Wiggins (ODI); and Elena Bardasi and Rekha Mehra (World Bank).

1. This discussion draws heavily on research by recent authors on nontraditional agricultural exports (see Barrientos, Kabeer, and Hossain 2004; Dolan and Sorby 2003; Tallontire 1999).

2. In England a group of NGOs organized by Christian AID has worked with supermarket chains to ensure that the African women who pick and pack fruits and vegetables are being fairly treated.

3. Ethical Trading Initiative, "Final Report of the ETI Multi-Stakeholder Seminar on Colombia Flower Industry," www.ethicaltrade.org.

Innovative Activity Profile 1

This Innovative Activity Profile was written by Kristy Cook (Consultant) and reviewed by Catherine Ragasa (Consultant); Maria Hartl (IFAD); and Eija Pehu (World Bank). This Profile draws heavily from Lawler and Atmiyanandana (2000).

REFERENCES

Overview

Barrientos, Armando, and Stephanie Ware Barrientos. 2002. "Extending Social Protection to Informal Workers in the Horticulture Global Value Chain." Social Protection Discussion Paper 0216, Human Development Network, World Bank, Washington, DC, June.

Betcherman, Gordon, Karina Olivas, and Amit Dar. 2004. "Impacts of Active Labor Market Programs: New Evidence from Evaluations with Particular Attention to Developing and Transition Countries." Social Protection Discussion Paper 0402, World Bank, Washington, DC. Also available at www.worldbank.org.

Brown, Drusilla K. 2007. "Globalization and Employment Conditions Study." Social Protection Discussion Paper 0708, World Bank, Washington, DC, April.

Chen, Martha Alter, Joann Vanek, Francie Lund, James Heintz, Renana Jhabvala, and Christine Bonner. 2005. *Progress of the World's Women 2005: Women, Work and Poverty.* New York: United Nations Development Fund for Women.

Collinson, Chris. 2001. "The Business Costs of Ethical Supply Chain Management: Kenya Flower Industry Case Study. Final Report." NRI Report 2607, Natural Resources Institute, Chatham, U.K., May.

Deutsch, Ruthanne, Suzanne Duryea, and Claudia Piras. 2001. "Labor Markets and Employment, in Empowering Women to Achieve Food Security." 2020 Focus No. 06, Brief 07. Also available at www.ifpri.org.

Dolan, Catherine, Maggie Opondo, and Sally Smith. 2002. "Gender, Rights and Participation in the Kenya Cut Flower Industry." NRI Report No. 2768, Natural Resources Institute, Chatham, U.K.

Dolan, Catherine, and Kristina Sorby. 2003. "Gender and Employment in High-Value Agriculture." Agriculture and Rural Development Working Paper 7, World Bank, Washington, DC, May.

Elder, Sara, and Dorotea Schmidt. 2004. "Global Employment Trends for Women, 2004." Employment Trends Unit, Employment Strategy Department, International Labour Organization, Geneva.

Food and Agriculture Organization (FAO). 2006. "Gender and Law. Women's Rights in Agriculture." FAO Legislative Study 76, Rev. 1, FAO Legal Office, FAO, Rome.

Gammage, Sarah, Helene Jorgensen, Eugenia McGill, with Marceline White. 2002. "Trade Impact Review." Women's Edge, Global Trade Program, Washington, DC, April.

Heintz, James. 2006. "Globalization, Economic Policy and Employment: Poverty and Gender Implications." Employment Policy Unit, Employment Strategy Department, International Labour Organization, Geneva.

Holzer, Harry J., and David Neumark. 1999. "Assessing Affirmative Action." NBER Working Paper W7323, National Bureau for Economic Research, Cambridge, MA, August.

Holzmann, Robert, and Steen Jorgensen. 1999. "Social Protection as Social Risk Management: Conceptual Underpinnings for the Social Protection Sector Strategy Paper." Social Protection Discussion Paper Series No. 9904, Social Protection Unit, Human Development Network, World Bank, Washington, DC.

Hopkins, Michael. 2004. "Corporate Social Responsibility: An Issues Paper." Working Paper No. 27, Policy Integration Department, World Commission on the Social Dimension of Globalization, International Labour Organization, Geneva, May.

Hurst, P., P. Termine, and M. Karl. 2005. "Agricultural Workers and Their Contribution to Sustainable Agriculture and Rural Development." Sustainable Development Department, Food and Agriculture Organization SD Dimensions, Rome.

International Fund for Agricultural Development (IFAD). 2000. *An Overview of Gender Issues in IFAD-Assisted Projects.* Gender Perspective, Focus on the Rural Poor. Rome: IFAD. Also available at www.ifad.org/pub/gender/engl_1.pdf.

International Labour Organization (ILO). 2000. *ABC of Women's Workers' Rights and Gender Equality.* Geneva: ILO.

————. 2003. "Decent Work in Agriculture." Background Paper for International Worker's Symposium on Decent Work in Agriculture, Geneva, September 15–18.

————. 2004. *Girl Child Labour in Agriculture, Domestic Work and Sexual Exploitation. Rapid Assessments on the Cases of Philippines, Ghana and Ecuador.* Volume 1. Geneva: International Programme on the Elimination of Child Labour Headquarters.

————. 2006. "Global Employment Trends Model." ILO, Geneva.

————. 2008. "Global Employment Trends for Women, March 2008." ILO, Geneva.

Josupeit, Helga. 2004. "Women in the Fisheries Sector in Argentina, Uruguay, and Southern Brazil." FAO Fisheries Circular No. 992, Food and Agriculture Organization, Rome.

Lastarria-Cornhiel, Susan. 2006. "Feminization of Agriculture: Trends and Driving Forces." RIMISP–Latin American Center for Rural Development, Santiago, Chile, November.

Morrison, Andrew, Dhushyanth Raju, and Nistha Sinha. 2007. "Gender-Equality, Poverty and Economic Growth." World Bank Policy Research Working Paper No. 4349, Gender and Development Group, Poverty Reduction and Economic Management Network, World Bank, Washington, DC, September.

Overseas Development Institute (ODI). 2007. "Rural Employment and Migration: In Search of Decent Work." Briefing Paper No. 27, ODI, London, October.

Pearson, Elaine, Sureeporn Punpuing, Aree Jampaklay, Sirinan Kittisuksathit, and Aree Prohmmo. 2006. "The

Mekong Challenge. Underpaid, Overworked and Overlooked: The Realities of Young Migrants in Thailand. Vol. 1." Mekong Sub-regional Project to Combat Trafficking in Children and Women, International Labour Organization, Bangkok.

Tzannatos, Zafiris. 1999. "Women and Labor Market Changes in the Global Economy: Growth Helps, Inequalities Hurt and Public Policy Matters." *World Development* 27 (3): 551–69.

USAID/GATE Project. 2005. "Enhancing Women's Access to Markets: An Overview of Donor Programs and Best Practices." Report prepared for the Greater Access to Trade Expansion (GATE) Project, Development & Training Services, Arlington, VA, October.

———. 2006. "A Pro-Poor Analysis of the Shrimp Sector in Bangladesh." Report prepared for the Greater Access to Trade Expansion (GATE) Project, Development & Training Services, Arlington, VA, February.

Vargas-Lundius, Rosemary, with Annelou Ypeij. 2007. *Polishing the Stone—A Journey through the Promotion of Gender Equality in Development Projects.* Rome: International Fund for Agricultural Development.

Ventkateswarlu, D. n.d. "Child Labour and Trans-National Seed Companies in Hybrid Cottonseed Production in Andhra Pradesh." India Committee of the Netherlands, the Netherlands.

WID TECH. 2003a. "Economic Opportunities and Labor Market Conditions for Women: Perspectives from Latin America: Bolivia, Ecuador, Peru, and Brazil." Paper prepared for USAID by WID TECH, Development Alternatives, April.

———. 2003b. "Economic Opportunities and Labor Market Conditions for Women. Perspectives from Latin America: Guatemala, El Salvador, Honduras." Paper prepared for USAID by WID TECH, Development Alternatives, Washington, DC, April.

World Bank. 2001. "Engendering Development through Gender Equality in Rights, Resources and Voice." Policy Research Report, World Bank, Washington, DC.

———. 2007. *World Development Report 2008: Agriculture for Development.* Washington, DC: World Bank.

Thematic Note I

Charmes, Jacques. 1998. "Informal Sector, Poverty and Gender: A Review of Empirical Evidence." Background paper for *World Development Report 2001: Attacking Poverty.* Washington, DC: World Bank.

Chen, Martha Alter. 2004. "Women in the Informal Sector: A Global Picture, the Global Movement." *SAIS Review* 21 (1): 71–82.

Chen, Martha Alter, Joann Vanek, and Marilyn Carr. 2004. *Mainstreaming Informal Employment and Gender in Poverty Reduction: A Handbook for Policy-Makers and Other Stakeholders.* Ottawa: Commonwealth Secretariat/IDRC.

Chen, Martha Alter, Joann Vanek, Francie Lund, James Heintz, Renana Jhabvala, and Christine Bonner. 2005. *Progress of the World's Women 2005: Women, Work and Poverty.* New York: United Nations Development Fund for Women.

Government of Ghana, Ministry of Labour. 2003. "New Labour Act, 2003 (Act No. 651)." Official Gazette, 2003-10-10, 1–69.

Hafkin, Nancy, and Nancy Taggart. 2001. "Gender, Information Technology and Developing Countries." Academy for Education Development, Washington, DC.

International Labour Office (ILO). 2002. "Women and Men in the Informal Economy: A Statistical Picture." ILO Report, Geneva.

Jhabvala, Renana, and Ravi Kanbur. 2002. "Globalization and Economic Reform as Seen from the Ground: SEWA's Experience in India." Revised version published in *India's Emerging Economy: Performance and Prospects in the 1990s and Beyond,* ed. Kaushik Basu, 293–312. New York: Oxford University Press.

Lund, Francie, and Jillian Nicholson. 2003. "Chains of Production, Ladders of Protection: Social Protection for Workers in the Informal Economy." School of Development Studies, Durban, South Africa.

Lund, Francie, and Smita Srinivas. 2000. "Learning from Experience: A Gendered Approach to Social Protection for Workers in the Informal Economy." International Labour Organization, Geneva.

Martínez Franzoni, Juliana, and Carmelo Mesa-Lago. 2003. *Las Reformas Inconclusas: Pensionesy Salud en Costa Rica.* San José: Friedrich Ebert Stiftung.

National Commission for Enterprises in the Unorganized Sector (NCEUS). 2007. "Report on Conditions of Work and Promotion of Livelihoods in the Unorganized Sector." Fourth Report of NCEUS, New Delhi. Also available at http://nceus.gov.in/Condition_of_workers_sep_2007.pdf.

National Sample Survey Organisation. 1993–94. Report No. 4.9 of 50th Round Survey of "Employment and Unemployment." Central Statistical Organisation, government of India.

———. 1999–2000. 55th Round, Schedule 10.0 on "Employment and Unemployment." Central Statistical Organisation, government of India.

———. 2004–05. 61st Round, Schedule 10.0 on "Employment and Unemployment." Central Statistical Organisation, government of India.

Sinha, Anushree, and N. Sangeeta. 2000. "Gender in a Macroeconomic Framework: A CGE Model Analysis." Paper presented at the Second Annual Meeting of the Gender Planning Network, Kathmandu, November 22–24.

Subrahmanya, R. K. A. 2000. "Welfare Funds." In *The Unorganized Sector: Work Security and Social Protection*, ed. Renana Jhabvala and R. K. A. Subrahmanya, 38–73. New Delhi: Sage.

Swaminathan, Madhura. 1991. "Understanding the Informal Sector: A Survey." WIDER WP 95, Helsinki.

United Nations Fund for Women (UNIFEM). 2005. *Women's Informal Employment in Efforts to Combat Poverty and Gender Inequality.* New York: UN.

Thematic Note 2

Barrientos, Armando, and Stephanie Ware Barrientos. 2002. "Extending Social Protection to Informal Workers in the Horticulture Global Value Chain." Social Protection Discussion Paper 0216, Human Development Network, World Bank, Washington, DC, June.

Buckley, Graeme J. 2004. "Decent Work in a Least Developing Country: A Critical Assessment of the Ethiopia PRSP." Working Paper No. 42, Policy Integration Department, National Policy Group, International Labour Organization, Geneva, July.

Cutura, Jozefina. 2006. "Making the Investment Climate Work for Women." Uganda Gender and Growth Assessment Project, Smart Lessons in Advisory Services, International Finance Corporation, Washington, DC, August.

Fenwick, C., E. Kalula, and I. Landau. 2007. "Labour Law: A Southern African Perspective." Discussion Paper Series No. 180, International Institute for Labour Studies, Geneva.

Food and Agriculture Organization (FAO). 1994. "The Legal Status of Rural Women in Nineteen Latin American Countries." FAO, Rome.

———. 2006. "Gender and Law. Women's Rights in Agriculture." FAO Legal Office, FAO, Rome.

Government of Chile. 2004. "Report on the Implementation of the Beijing Platform of Action Presented by the Government of Chile to the United Nations Division for the Advancement of Women. Response to the Questionnaire." April. Available at www.un.org.

Guivant, Julia S. 2001. "Gender and Land Rights in Brazil." Paper prepared for the UNRISD Project on Agrarian Change, Gender and Land Rights, Social Policy and Development Programme Paper No. 14, United Nations Research Institute for Social Development, June.

International Labour Organization (ILO). 2006. "Gender Equality and Decent Work: Selected ILO Conventions and Reccommendations Promoting Gender Equality." ILO, Geneva.

Klerck, Gilton. 2002. "Trade Union Responses to the 'Flexible' Workforce in Namibia." *African Sociological Review* 6 (2): 98–129.

Nayak, Nalini. 2005. "Sharpening the Interlinkages: Towards Feminist Perspectives of Livelihoods in Coastal Communities." Institute of Social Studies Trust, Ecumenical Resource Center, United Theological College, Bangalore, June 6.

United Nations Population Fund (UNFPA) and the Population Division of the UN Department for Economic and Social Information and Policy Analysis. 1994. "Cairo Programme of Action." General agreement on the Programme of Action during International Conference on Population and Development (ICPD), Cairo, Egypt, September 5–13, 1994. Available at http://www.dirittiumani.donne.aidos.it/bibl_2_testi/d_impegni_pol_internaz/a_conf_mondiali_onu/c_conf_cairo_e+5/a_cairo_poa_engl_X_pdf/cairo_dich+pda_engl.pdf.

WID TECH. 2003. "Economic Opportunities and Labor Market Conditions for Women. Perspectives from Latin America: Guatemala, El Salvador, Honduras." Paper prepared for USAID by WID TECH, Development Alternatives, Washington, DC, April.

World Bank. 2005. "Republic of Yemen. Women in Local Economic Development." Water, Environment, Social and Rural Development Department, Middle East and North Africa Region, Report 332259-YEM, Aden, December 6.

Zarka-Martres, Monique, and Monique Guichard-Kelly. 2005. "Decent Work, Standards and Indicators." International Labour Organization Working Paper No. 58, ILO, Geneva, August.

Thematic Note 3

Asea, Patrick K., and Darlison Kaija. 2000. "Impact of the Flower Industry in Uganda." Working Paper No. 148, International Labour Organization, Geneva.

Barrientos, Armando, and Stephanie Ware Barrientos. 2002. "Extending Social Protection to Informal Workers in the Horticulture Global Value Chain." Social Protection Discussion Paper 0216, Human Development Network, World Bank, Washington, DC, June.

Barrientos, Stephanie Ware, Catherine Dolan, and Anne Tallontire. 2001. "Gender and Ethical Trade: A Mapping of the Issues in African Horticulture." Working Paper for Department for International Development, ESCOR Research Report. Also available at www.nri.org.

Barrientos, Stephanie Ware, Naila Kabeer, and Naomi Hossain. 2004. "The Gender Dimensions of the Globalization of Production." Working Paper No. 17, Policy Integration Department, International Labour Organization, Geneva, May.

Barrientos, Stephanie Ware, Andrienetta Kritzinger, and Hester Rossouw. 2004. "National Labor Legislation in an Informal Context: Women Workers in Export Horticulture in South Africa." In *Chains of Fortune: Linking Women Producers and Workers with Global Markets*, 103–32. London: Commonwealth Secretariat.

Blowfield, Mick. 2000. "Ethical Sourcing: A Contribution to Sustainability or a Diversion?" *Sustainable Development* 8 (4): 191–200.

de Boer, Jennifer. 2005. "Sweet Hazards: Child Labour on Sugar Cane Plantations in the Philippines." Terre des Hommes, the Netherlands.

Develtere, Patrick, and Ignace Pollet. 2005. "Co-operatives and Fair-Trade." Background Paper commissioned by the Committee for the Promotion and Advancement of Cooperatives (COPAC) for the COPAC Open Forum on Fair Trade and Cooperatives, Berlin, Catholic University Leuven and Higher Institute of Labor, Leuven, February.

Dolan, Catherine, and Kristina Sorby. 2003. "Gender and Employment in High-Value Agriculture." Agriculture and Rural Development Working Paper 7, World Bank, Washington, DC, May.

Farnworth, Cathy, and Michael Goodman. 2006. "Growing Ethical Networks: The Fair Trade Market for Raw and Processed Agricultural Products (in Five Parts) with Associated Case Studies on Africa and Latin America by Nabs Suma (Africa) and Sarah Lyon (Latin America)." RIMISP-Latin American Center for Rural Development, Santiago, Chile.

Hopkins, Michael. 2004. "Corporate Social Responsibility: An Issues Paper." Working Paper 27, Policy Integration Department, World Commission on the Social Dimension of Globalization, International Labour Organization, Geneva, May.

Institute of Development Studies (IDS). 2007. "Corporate Codes of Labour Practice: Can the Most Vulnerable Workers Benefit?" IDS Policy Briefing, Issue 35, Brighton, U.K., April. Also available at www.ids.ac.U.K.

Kanji, Nazneedn. 2004. "Corporate Responsibility and Women's Employment: The Cashew Nut Case." Perspectives on Corporate Responsibility for Environment and Development No. 02, International Institute for Environment and Development, London.

Kasente, Deborah, Matthew Lockwood, Jessica Vivian, and Ann Whitehead. 2000. "Gender and the Expansion of Agricultural Exports in Uganda." Occasional Paper No. 12, UNRISD, Geneva.

Kivuitu, Mumo, Kavwanga Yambayamba, and Tom Fox. 2005. "How Can Corporate Social Responsibility Deliver in Africa? Insights from Kenya and Zambia." Perspectives on Corporate Responsibility for Environment and Development No. 3, International Institute for Environment and Development, London, July.

Mbilinyi, Marjorie, and Ave Maria Semakafu. 1995. "Gender and Employment in Sugar Cane Plantations in Tanzania." Sectoral and Working Discussions Papers, Agriculture, SAP 2.44/WP.85, International Labour Organization, Geneva.

Pier, Carol. 2002. "Tainted Harvest: Child Labor and Obstacles to Organization on Ecuador's Banana Plantations." Human Rights Watch, New York.

Tallontire, Anne. 1999. "Gender Issues in Export Horticulture." NRET Working Paper 3, February.

Wickramasinghe, Ananda, and Donald Cameron. n.d. "Human and Social Capital in Sri Lankan Tea Plantations: A Note of Dissent, Culture beyond Universal and National Cultural Dimensions." Department of Business Administration, University of Sri Jayewardenepura, Sri Lanka. Also available at www.management.ac.nz.

World Bank. 2007. *World Development Report 2008: Agriculture for Development*. Washington, DC: World Bank.

Innovative Activity Profile 1

Lawler, John, and Vinita Atmiyanandana. 2000. "Gender and Agribusiness Project (GAP) Case Study. Cargill Sun Valley, Thailand." International Program and Studies, University of Illinois at Urbana-Champaign, September.

Collinson, Chris. 2001a. "The Business Costs of Ethical Supply Chain Management: Kenya Flower Industry Case Study. Final Report." NRI Report 2607, Natural Resources Institute, Chatham, U.K., May.

———. 2001b. "The Business Costs of Ethical Supply Chain Management: South African Wine Industry Case Study. Final Report." NRI Report 2606, Natural Resources Institute, Chatham, U.K., May.

FURTHER READING

Overview

Department of International Development (DFID). 2004. "Labour Standards and Poverty Reduction." U.K. Department of International Development, May.

International Center for Research on Women (ICRW). 2005. "Toward Achieving Gender Equality and Empowering Women," ICRW, Washington, DC.

International Labour Organization (ILO). 2002. "Women and Men in the Informal Economy: A Statistical Picture." ILO, Geneva.

Kabeer, Naila. 2008. "Gender, Labour Markets and Poverty: An Overview." Poverty in Focus Number 13, International Poverty Centre, Brasilia, January.

Kanji, Nazneedn. 2004. "Corporate Responsibility and Women's Employment: The Cashew Nut Case." Perspectives on Corporate Responsibility for Environment and Development No. 02, International Institute for Environment and Development, London.

University of Illinois. n.d. Gender in Agribusiness Project, www.ips.uiuc.edu.

USAID/GATE Project. 2005. "Enhancing Women's Market Access and Promoting Pro-Poor Growth." Report prepared for the Greater Access to Trade Expansion (GATE) Project, Development & Training Services, Arlington, VA, January.

Wiggins, Steve, and Priya Deshingkar. 2007. "Rural Employment and Migration: In Search of Decent Work." ODI Briefing Paper No. 27, London, October.

World Bank. 2005. "Improving Women's Lives. World Bank Actions since Beijing." World Bank Gender and Development Group, Washington, DC, January.

———. 2007. "Kyrgyz Republic. Poverty Assessment. Vol. II: Labor Market Dimensions of Poverty." Report 40864-KG, World Bank, Washington, DC, October 19.

Zhang, L., A. De Brauw, and C. Rozelle. 2004. "China's Rural Labor Market Development and Its Gender Implications." *China Economic Review* 15 (2): 230–47.

Thematic Note 1

Barrientos, Stephanie Ware, Catherine Dolan, and Anne Tallontire. 2001. "Gender and Ethical Trade: A Mapping of the Issues in African Horticulture." Report 2624, Natural Resources Institute, Chatham, U.K., July.

Barrientos, Stephanie Ware, S. McClenaghan, and L. Orton. 1999. "Gender and Codes of Conduct: A Case Study from Horticulture in South Africa." Research Report to the U.K. Department for International Development, Christian Aid, London.

Basu, Kaushik. 2004. *Emerging Economy: Performance and Prospects in the 1990s and Beyond.* Cambridge, MA: MIT Press.

Charmes, Jacques. 1998. "Informal Sector, Poverty and Gender: A Review of Empirical Evidence." Background paper for *World Development Report 2001: Attacking Poverty.* Washington, DC: World Bank.

Government of India, Ministry of Rural Development. 2005. *The National Rural Employment Act: NREGA Operational Guidelines.* 2nd ed. New Delhi.

Government of India, National Commission for Enterprises in the Unorganised Sector. 2007. "Report on Condition of Work and Promotion of Livelihoods in the Unorganised Sector." Government of India, Delhi.

Government of India, National Common Minimum Program. "Unorganized Sector Workers Social Security Bill, 2005," www.nac.nic.in.

Harriss-White, Barbara, and Anushree Sinha, eds. 2007. *Trade Liberalization and India's Informal Economy.* Delhi: Oxford University Press.

International Labour Organization (ILO). 2007. The Informal Economy: Enabling Transition to Formalization." Background document for the Tripartite Interregional Symposium on the Informal Economy: Enabling Transition to Formalization, ILO, Geneva, November 27–29. Available at www.ilo.org/public/english/employment/pol icy/events/informal/download/back-en.pdf.

Kritzinger, Andrienetta, Heidi Prozesky, and Jan Vorster. 1995. "Die Arbeidsopset in die Suid Afrikaanse Sagtevrugte-uitvoerbedryf, Plaaswerkers." Werkopset Deel III, University of Stellenbosch, Stellenbosch.

Nikolic, Irina A., and Harald Maikisch. 2006. "Public-Private Partnerships and Collaboration in the Health Sector: An Overview with Case Studies from Recent European Experience." Health, Nutrition, and Population Discussion Paper, World Bank, Washington, DC, October.

Sinha, Anushree, and N. Sangeeta. 2003. "Gender in a Macroeconomic: A CGE Model Analysis." In *Tracking Gender Equity under Economic Reforms: Continuity and Change in South Asia,* ed. Swapna Mukhopadhyay and Ratna M. Sudarshan, 321–63. www.idrc.ca/en/ev-58060-201-1-DO_TOPIC.html.

Skinner, Caroline. 2002. "Understanding Formal and Informal Economy Labour Market Dynamics: A Conceptual and Statistical Review with Reference to South Africa." Research Report No. 50, School of Development Studies (Incorporating CSDS), University of Natal, Durban.

Thematic Note 2

Barrientos, Stephanie Ware, Andrienetta Kritzinger, and Hester Rossouw. 2004. "National Labour Legislation in an Informal Context: Women Workers in Export Horticulture in South Africa." In *Chains of Fortune: Linking Women Producers and Workers with Global Markets,* 103–32. London: Commonwealth Secretariat.

INSTRAW. 2000. "Engendering the Political Agenda: The Role of the State, Women's Organizations and the International Community." INSTRAW, Santo Domingo.

International Labour Organization (ILO). 2000. "ABC of Women Workers' Rights and Gender Equality." ILO, Geneva.

_____. n.d. "Database of International Labour Standards." ILO, Geneva. Available at www.ilo.org/ilolex/english/con vdisp1.htm.

United Nations International Research and Training Institute for the Advancement of Women (INSTRAW). 2000. "Engendering the Political Agenda: The Role of the State, Women's Organizations and the International Community." INSTRAW, Santo Domingo.

Thematic Note 3

Barrientos, Stephanie Ware. 2002. "Extending Social Protection to Informal Workers in the Horticulture Global Value Chain." Social Protection Unit, Human Development Network, World Bank, Washington, DC, June.

Barrientos, Stephanie Ware, and Sally Smith. 2006. "The ETI Code of Labour Practice. Do Workers Really Benefit?" Report on the ETI Impact Assessment 2006, Institute of Development Studies (IDS), Sussex. Available at www.ethicaltrade.org.

Bertelsmann Stiftung and GTZ. 2007. *The CSR Navigator. Public Policies in Africa, the Americas, Asia and Europe.* Gütersloh and Eschborn: Bertelsmann Stiftung and GTZ.

Brown, Drusilla K. 2007. "Globalisation and Employment Conditions Study." Social Protection Discussion Paper 0708, World Bank, Washington, DC, April.

Collinson, Chris. 2001a. "The Business Costs of Ethical Supply Chain Management: South African Wine Industry Case Study—Final Report." NRI Report No. 2606, Natural Resources Institute, Chatham, U.K., May.

———. 2001b. "The Business Costs of Ethical Supply Chain Management: Kenyan Flower Industry Case Study." NRI Report No. 2607, Natural Resources Institute, Chatham, U.K., May.

Dankers, Cora. 2003. "Environmental and Social Standards Certification and Labelling for Cash Crops." Raw Materials, Tropical and Horticultural Products Service, Commodities and Trade Division, Food and Agriculture Organization, Rome.

Dolan, Catherine, Maggie Opondo, and Sally Smith. 2002. "Gender, Rights & Participation in the Kenya Cut Flower Industry." NRI Report 2768, Natural Resources Institute, Chatham, U.K.

Id21. 2001a. "Fresh Off the Shelf. Gender and Horticulture in Africa," Id21 *Insights* Issue 36, March. Available at www.id21.org.

———. 2001b. "Raising Gender Sensitivity: Ethical Trade in African Horticulture." Id21 Research Highlight, October 9. Available at www.id21.org.

Institute for Development Studies (IDS). 2007. "Corporate Codes of Labour Practice: Can the Most Vulnerable Workers Benefit?" IDS Policy Briefing, Issue 35, Brighton, U.K., April. Available at www.ids.ac.uk.

Krier, Jean-Marie. 2005. "Fair Trade in Europe 2005 Facts and Figures on Fair Trade in 25 European Countries." Fair Trade Advocacy Office, Brussels, December. Available at www.fairtrade.net.

Nelson, Valerie, Joachim Ewert, and Adrienne Martin. 2002. "Assessing the Impact of Adoption of Codes of Practice in the South African Wine Industry and Kenyan Cut Flower Industry. Phase 1." Natural Resources and Ethical Trade Programme, IDS, Sussex, June.

Tallontire, Anne, Sally Smith, and Chosani Njobvu. 2004. "Ethical Trade in African Horticulture: Gender, Rights and Participation. Final Report on Zambia Study." NRI Report 2775, Natural Resources Institute, Chatham, U.K., May.

Gender in Rural Infrastructure for Agricultural Livelihoods

Overview

The provision of rural infrastructure has been a core priority of governments for many decades to improve the welfare of rural populations and increase the productivity and value added from agriculture and other economic activities in rural areas.[1] The recognition that gender equity should be an important aspect of rural infrastructure policies and programs is more recent. Various studies have increasingly documented four major differences between men and women with respect to rural infrastructure: (1) differences of needs for the type and location of physical infrastructure; (2) differences in priorities for infrastructure services; (3) unequal opportunities to participate in decision making on the choice of infrastructure services, both within the households and within the communities, or to participate in the implementation of the infrastructure programs and the delivery of services; and (4) significant disparities in access to infrastructure services.

Rural infrastructure covers a wide range of physical infrastructure and derived infrastructure services. In this Module, the emphasis is on energy, transport, information and communication technologies (ICTs), sanitation and hygiene services, and potable water. Other types of rural infrastructure, such as irrigation, schools, health centers, administrative buildings, and markets, are not included. Irrigation is covered in Module 6, markets are covered in Module 5, and social and administrative infrastructures will be referred to only briefly. Each of these sectors has many different services, modes of delivery, variation in coverage, and range of users as well as technical parameters for construction, rehabilitation, and maintenance, thus making it difficult to generalize about gender and infrastructure issues. The distinction between the physical infrastructure and services is critical because the provision of the physical infrastructure will not suffice to achieve improvements in rural livelihoods if the technology or the services that enable the use of the infrastructure are absent or deficient. In addition, significant regional and country variation exists in gender issues and the economic, political, institutional, and sociocultural context of infrastructure that needs to be taken into account (Clarke 2007).

This Overview provides the framework for developing gender-equitable rural infrastructure policies, programs, and projects and illustrates the significance and merits of integrating gender equity for the sustainability of rural infrastructure investments and services.

THE FRAMEWORK AND SIGNIFICANCE OF GENDER FOR SUSTAINABLE RURAL INFRASTRUCTURE

Recognition of gender in the design, implementation, and use of rural infrastructure policies, programs, and projects is vital for achieving poverty reduction and sustainable agricultural livelihoods. Rural infrastructure plays not only a significant *economic* role but also a critical role in the *human capital* development of rural populations and a fundamental *social* role as a factor of change in the economic and social fabric of rural communities. Rural infrastructure and infrastructure services impact rural populations in many ways, ranging from self-respect (in the case of sanitation and hygiene), to accessing health and education, to enabling rural populations to increase their productivity, access markets, improve their welfare, and emerge from isolation. Understanding those impacts on men and women as well as the gender disparities in *risks and vulnerabilities* should guide the work on rural infrastructure.

It is important to note that the relationship between social empowerment, human capital development, and economic empowerment is not linear; it is more akin to a positive spiral (see fig. 9.1). A complex interrelationship exists between them, and the change process is iterative. A certain amount of social empowerment is needed to get women out of the domestic sphere into economic endeavors that lead to economic empowerment. Full-blown social empowerment takes a long time to achieve, such that opportunities leading to women's economic empowerment frequently also provide opportunities for their social empowerment. Increased human capital is needed to achieve economic empowerment and, in turn, economic empowerment enables human capital development. Furthermore, different risks and vulnerabilities affect each gender group in each sphere.

The significance of gender for sustainable rural infrastructure: key characteristics and differential impact

Integrating gender in sustainable rural infrastructure policies, programs, and projects is a matter of development effectiveness. Understanding the linkages between gender equity and development effectiveness is essential: what are the gains, in terms of outcomes, and what are the essential characteristics of rural infrastructure and derived services that must be taken into account when designing policies and programs.

Time saving

At the heart of gender inequalities is the gendered division of labor, access, and control of resources embedded in the household economy and the household economy's interdependence with the market economy. Although men focus on market income, women juggle multiple roles supporting the household economy, community services, and market income, when possible. The household economy is "invisible" and uncounted in national accounts, yet the market economy depends on it.

Time is an economic good. The time costs associated with a heavy domestic labor burden place constraints on women's labor time as both family and hired labor. In the absence of physical infrastructure to support the household

Figure 9.1 The Four Dimensions for Infrastructure Services

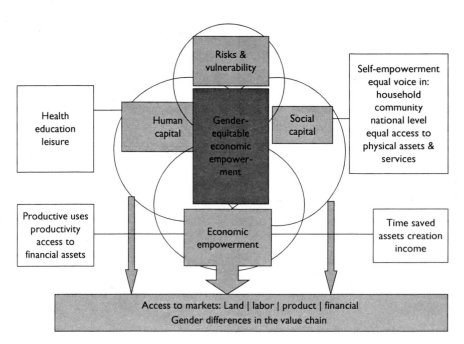

Source: Author.

economy, "such as pipeborne water and electrification the tasks performed by pipes and wires in the developed world are performed by women and girls—they become the *living infrastructure*. They carry water and fuel to the home and take the excrement and rubbish away with a crossing of 'clean' and 'dirty' functions—cooking food on animal excrement or preparing food after disposing of garbage" (Grieco 2002). These activities have time and opportunity costs for women and girls, for households, and for the economy at large.

The disparity in time poverty between women and men is the single most important economic factor that justifies integrating gender equity into rural infrastructure policies, programs, and projects. Because of the greater time burden linked to the tasks traditionally assigned to women, rural infrastructure services facilitate time savings, which in turn increase women's productivity and leisure time, and therefore the welfare of the whole household and community. Time saved thanks to infrastructure services can be used for rest for improved health and quality of life, for girls to attend school, and for women to expand their knowledge and develop skills. Understanding the respective time endowment or time poverty of women and men linked to the roles and responsibilities assigned to women and men is critical to selecting processes that enable both women and

men to access, design, or deliver infrastructure services (Blackden and Wodon 2006). Because they are important inputs to the agricultural value chain, better access to infrastructure facilities and services can also substantially improve agricultural productivity, value added, and incomes. For example, in rural Mali provision of diesel-powered multifunctional platforms that supplied not only electricity for lighting but also motive power for labor-intensive work such as agroprocessing (milling and dehusking) and pumping water resulted in considerable time saving, fostered the development of processed products, and increased women's daily earnings by $0.47.[2]

Heterogeneity and differential impact

Rural infrastructure and derived services are heterogeneous, and their specificity needs to be understood. Although they have common characteristics, and at times common institutional solutions, the provision of transport, energy, ICT, water and sanitation, and market infrastructure requires sector-specific policies, competencies, and technical solutions. An attempt to identify the differential impacts of rural infrastructure services on women and men is summarized in table 9.1; examples illustrating most of these impacts are given in the discussion that follows.

Table 9.1 How Infrastructure Services Affect Rural Populations

Type of impact	Transport	Energy	ICT	Sanitation and hygiene	Potable water	Markets[a]
Social empowerment:						
Access to administrative, financial, and technical services	√	√	√	√	√	√
Dignity	√	..	..	√	√	..
Equal voice: individual, household, community	√	√	√	√	√	√
Mobility within or outside the community	√	√	√	√	..	√
Economic empowerment:						
Income	√	√	√	..	√	√
Productivity	√	√	√	..	√	√
Time saved	√	√	√	√	√	√
Human capital development:						
Access to education	√	√	√	√	√	..
Access to health	√	√	√	√	√	√
Basic needs	..	√	..	√	√	√
Leisure	√	√	√	..	..	√
Risks and vulnerabilities:						
Security	√	√	√	√	√	√

Source: Author.

Note: A check mark indicates the contribution of the sector to a specific impact. .. indicates no or limited contribution.

[a]Discussed in Module 5.

Conjunctive development

The provision of one type of rural infrastructure and its derived services may not suffice to achieve the expected benefits of human capital development or social or economic empowerment; the complementary development of several infrastructure services may be needed. For example, it may not be sufficient to improve the transport infrastructure and services to facilitate access to schools and administrative services, because separate latrines for men and boys and women and girls also need to be provided. In addition, men and women teachers or administrative staff need to be available or trained to address women's and men's needs. The Peru Rural Infrastructure Program is a good example of such a multiple infrastructure development approach (see Innovative Activity Profile 1).

Complementarity and sequencing of infrastructure interventions

Integrating gender equity may entail different *sequencing* of rural infrastructure interventions from gender-indifferent approaches. For example, improving household fuel supplies first rather than starting first with electrification, which is not as high of a priority for women, might lead to higher welfare and economic benefits to the household and to the whole community. Similarly, improving the water supply and sanitation to benefit women first might yield greater returns than starting with the improvement of an access road to a main market. These questions need to be raised and debated at the time of program or project formulation and design through consultations with the various groups in the community.

Finally, it must be recognized that issues of social empowerment of both women and men, quality of life improvements, and human capital development are *preconditions* for the economic empowerment to be generated by rural infrastructure services, be it at the individual, household, or community level. This has implications both for the design of project processes and for the sequencing of infrastructure interventions. For example, unless processes are in place to facilitate the social empowerment and human development of both genders first, the economic outcomes are not likely to be gender equitable.

GENDER-EQUITABLE SOCIAL EMPOWERMENT

Given the wide range of women's and men's needs for infrastructure and infrastructure services, it is critical to ensure gender equity in the planning, decision making, and management processes lest the development of the infrastructure and services cause or aggravate gender disparities. The following sections give key issues to consider.

Gender equity in planning and decision making

Women and men rarely have an equal voice in the planning and decision making for rural infrastructure. At the household level, men most often decide alone on the priorities for the family. Men also participate predominantly in community meetings at which decisions are made on the selection of priorities for, and on the location of, infrastructure investments. As a result, it is not uncommon that water wells and adjacent washing facilities, for instance, are located in areas where women are unwilling to go, or that the road between the farmstead and the market is improved before the footpath used by women to collect water or fuelwood. Another striking illustration is the attention given to electrification versus improved woodlots or improved stoves: men favor power to listen to the radio or watch television over women's need for cooking fuels and reduced indoor air pollution. The experience of the Uruguay Rural Water Program argues that women's involvement in decision making increased the viability of the rural water program by locating and designing the new water facilities to reflect women's needs. It also increased women's social empowerment through their participation in water association boards (Sotomayor 2007).

Gender equity in access to rural infrastructure assets

Experience from projects suggests that the equitable enhancement of women's and men's social capital is not automatic; it depends upon whether the design and placement of infrastructure was explicitly designed to develop social capital. For example, the Peru Rural Roads Program worked with men and women of the Andean region to improve main roads and smaller roads and tracks, and it involved rural women in its design and implementation. After project completion, 77 percent of the women reported that the rehabilitated roads and tracks enabled them to travel farther, 67 percent felt that the improvements enabled them to travel more safely, and 43 percent felt that the improvements enabled them to obtain additional income. The percentage of women participating in and leading road committees has increased slowly, and the percentage of women voting in local elections, another way of having their voice heard, increased significantly (see Innovative Activity Profile 1, this Module).

Gender equity in the management of services

Women can also participate in the management of the infrastructure services. This is the case when women participate in water user associations, in road maintenance committees, or on the boards of rural power utilities. Such participation is often an opportunity for improving their self-esteem and developing their decision-making capabilities. In the Peru and Bangladesh Rural Road Projects, 20 percent of the members of the road committees that were set up were required to be women. Proactive initiatives to mandate such participation in program and project design give the best results, but the implementation of these initiatives requires sensitivity to and understanding of the local culture, economic activities, social realities, and more important, it requires trust (Sotomayor 2007).

RURAL INFRASTRUCTURE AND GENDER EQUITABLE ECONOMIC EMPOWERMENT

Rural infrastructure and derived infrastructure services are essential for the economic empowerment of the rural population through access to key markets: financial, labor, and product markets, as well as other services that contribute to improving the value chain, especially information and training and administrative and legal services. Ensuring gender-equitable access to all these economic opportunities is therefore essential to maximize the economic returns and development impact of rural infrastructure programs and projects. The following sections summarize selected key issues.

Gender equity in business creation

Given the range of works involved, the development of rural infrastructure and related services lends itself well to the participation of small and medium-size enterprises. Although the majority of such enterprises continue to be owned, managed, and staffed mostly with men, recent efforts to integrate women in the development of such businesses has given very positive results. In the Peru Rural Road Project, which set a target of 10 percent of the members of road maintenance microenterprises being women, women's participation increased from 3.5 percent in 2001 to 24 percent in 2006 (Gutiérrez 2007). Some infrastructure sectors lend themselves more easily than others to entry by women. ICT, for example, has seen extensive women's participation, especially where ICT-based enterprise creation is supported with microcredit—for example, for the purchase of a telephone, which becomes the main asset of the enterprise. However, in most countries one of the challenges facing women in creating infrastructure microenterprises is their higher rate of illiteracy and their more limited access to credit for start-ups. Women's associations are a successful alternative to individual enterprises, such as the women's energy microenterprise of Char Montaz, Bangladesh, in its early years (see Thematic Note 2).

Gender equity in employment

The construction and maintenance of rural infrastructure generate a significant demand for labor and therefore provide significant opportunities for employment and income creation for the rural population. Providing for gender equity in the labor market and ensuring equal pay are therefore essential. This is not easily achieved because of numerous constraints: women's lack of time to engage in nonagricultural activities, taboos about women engaging in certain labor markets such as road construction, and men's perceptions that women cannot handle certain "heavy tasks" or equipment such as chain saws and driving machinery even though women have always done heavy agricultural work. The integration of women in road rehabilitation programs in Liberia is a good example of how this can be accomplished. The program recruits labor at the community level and proactively encourages women to join the labor force. Some (albeit few) of the labor recruiters and road technicians are women, which facilitates demystifying the work on the road. However, as women have lower literacy rates and lack high school diplomas and formal technical skills, their participation in the labor force is still only one-quarter to one-third that of men, and men's share of the wage bill generated by these road works is three times that of women's (Lallement 2007).

Gender equity in accessing product markets

Both women and men are very active in product markets, although it appears that men predominantly procure commercial inputs (seeds, commercial fertilizers, and pesticides) and market higher-value commercial crops, whereas women tend to market lower-value traditional crops (cereals, tubers, fruit, and vegetables). Experiential evidence points to significant gender disparities in access to product markets, although this is not very well documented. These disparities are correlated to gender disparities in access to transport services; women have less access to bulk and motorized transport (see Thematic Note 2). Significant opportunities occur when women organize to market food crops and share transport costs to more distant but higher-value markets, including cities, which in turn enables them to earn higher incomes. Similar benefits are generated when women organize to store or partially process food crops, which raises the issue of gender equity in access to storage facilities and in the availability of energy infrastructure to sustain the cold chain. This has been achieved in Senegal with string bean growers, who are predominantly women (ESMAP-GVEP 2003; see also Module 5).

Additional constraints for women to access higher-value product markets include the lack of facilities for women to stay overnight or several days, lack of child care facilities, lack of separate latrines at marketplaces, and other risks associated with their physical security. ICT services have proved effective in bringing product market information to both men and women. Women are benefiting more from ICT services because they have lesser mobility and literacy than men. In India, for example, telephony has enabled rural women to obtain direct information on the price of food crops, empowering them to better negotiate prices with middlemen.

Gender equity in accessing financial markets

Rural infrastructure services, in particular ICT, are improving gender equity in access to rural financial markets. Many factors have constrained access to commercial rural finance (lack of land titles and other collateral, distance to banks) by both men and women, but women have been at a particular disadvantage in most developing countries (see also Module 3). ICT, however, breaks some of these barriers by providing information to both women and men on requirements for obtaining credit and on managing income and savings, information that previously would have required going to a bank. In this respect, ICT saves on transport costs, helps overcome the barriers linked to illiteracy by providing auditory information, and removes the obstacle of women's inability to go to a bank because of lack of time, money for transport, or approval from their husbands. ICT also now more often enables women to make financial transactions and empowers them to develop rural businesses. A significant aspect of ICT is the facilitation of migrant remittances, on which many rural families depend (see Thematic Note 3).

Gender equity in access to labor markets

Improving access to nonrural labor markets is critical to improving rural livelihoods and incomes. Rural infrastructure, particularly ICT and transport, is a powerful means of enabling the rural population to access nonrural labor

markets. ICT services facilitate the flow of information on employment opportunities, and transport infrastructure and services facilitate the movement of people. Aspects of gender equity include ensuring that broadcast information on employment opportunities be tailored to both women and men's employment opportunities, and ensuring safe and affordable transport between urban markets and rural areas, in particular for women and girls, who are usually at greater risk of some form of harassment or violence. Well-lit bus stops have proven very effective in enabling women to safely travel to and from jobs that require periodic shuttling to and from the village, such as housekeeping jobs in South Africa or textile factory work in Bangladesh (see also Module 8).

Gender equity in accessing other services

Access to social services, not only schools and health facilities but also administrative services (civil and land registration, legal services), is also highly dependent on the availability, reliability, and cost of rural infrastructure services. Transport infrastructure and services are possibly the most important to facilitate geographical access, but one must also consider whether the on-site infrastructure of these other services caters to the respective needs of women and men (for example, whether there are separate toilets or waiting rooms).

GENDER-EQUITABLE HUMAN DEVELOPMENT

All rural infrastructure and derived services affect human development, albeit to different degrees. Understanding these impacts is critical to gauging the potential economic impact of infrastructure. If rural populations are in poor health, uninformed, or uneducated, they are unable to take advantage of the benefits that other infrastructure services can provide. The following sections summarize five key variable impacts.

Basic needs

Potable water and energy are the two most important infrastructure services for human survival. The importance of potable water is easily illustrated by the UNICEF (2006) report "Progress for Children: A Report Card on Water and Sanitation," which found that 88 percent of the deaths of children under age five from diarrheal diseases are caused by unsafe water (combined with poor sanitation and lack of hygiene). This is equivalent to about 4,000 children under five dying every day. By contrast, it is not yet sufficiently well known that 95 percent of basic staple foods must be cooked to be transformed into human energy (DFID 2002); as a result, energy services are not yet recognized among the Millennium Development Goals (MDGs) for poverty eradication. The gender dimension of these services relates to the primary role traditionally assigned to rural women and girls for the collection of water and fuelwood, child care, and family cooking and to the time use, drudgery, and health effects of the related tasks. Both genders equally benefit or suffer from the availability or quality of water and fuel supplies.

Access to information

ICT provides information and access to product markets, credit, and other information that permit rural communities and households to integrate into the local, regional, national, and world economies. In rural areas ICTs are crucial for economic and social development and, when used appropriately, provide a platform for communities to debate and to advocate for issues important to them. In many rural areas the shortwave radio becomes the community telephone, making announcements and conveying messages between dispersed community members. It also serves as the early warning system for emergencies.

Access to health

The link between rural infrastructure and health is very strong. The impact of sanitation, hygiene, and potable water on human health is well documented and accepted. In recent years researchers have recognized the significant health effects of indoor air pollution (IAP) caused by the burning of traditional biomass fuels (wood, charcoal, animal dung) and other smoky fuels (coal, kerosene). In 2000 premature deaths from IAP were estimated by the World Health Organization at 1.6 million people, accounting for 3 percent of the global burden of disease. In some countries IAP is the second- or third-leading cause of disease. It is responsible for a range of respiratory and other diseases among the 3 billion people who still rely on traditional fuels and burning methods for heating and cooking. Women and young children are disproportionately affected by IAP, again because of the role assigned to them by society for cooking and child care. The 2000–01 Uganda Domestic Household Survey data indicate that children aged 6 to 11 months experienced a rate of symptoms of acute respiratory infections of 33 percent (Blackden 2006).

Access to transport to emergency obstetrical care can reduce maternal and newborn mortality and reduce the loss of productive capacity. Improved paths to water points or fuelwood locations can save women's and girls' hardship and time. Nonmotorized transport alleviates women's and men's carrying burdens and can contribute to reducing bone and muscular diseases. ICT is used more and more often to provide rural health services, in particular for diagnostic work, and in more advanced rural settings for supervised surgical treatment (Infodev 2006).

Access to education

Energy, transport, and ICT are three key rural infrastructure services for improving access to education. Schools equipped with lighting and power are more effective, and when they incorporate ICT infrastructure they can benefit from accessing educational information from around the world (Lallement and Siegel 2002). ICT also can provide further teacher training and can enable rural students, girls in particular, to pursue secondary school education. Radio is a critical source of information and means of lifelong learning. Lighting in teachers' homes improves security and the retention of teachers in rural areas, especially women teachers. Children from electricity-lit homes versus those from homes with candles or kerosene lamps gain two to three years compared to their peers (ESMAP 2001). Girls benefit most because their household chores usually occupy the hours of daylight after school.

Access to leisure

The time saved thanks to rural infrastructure services, in particular from energy and transport, is reallocated by rural people for productive activities or leisure. Asymmetries in time poverty by gender are well documented. For example, in Uganda, if woodlots were within 30 minutes of the homestead and if the water source were within 400 meters, households would save more than 900 hours each year, with the benefits going primarily to women and girls. This is close to 0.5 person-years of work (Barwell 1996).

Radio is often perceived primarily as a source of leisure for men. In reality, rural radio is a communication tool that can benefit both women and men with information and education, and it can be listened to while people work. Many health education and agricultural radio programs are targeted toward rural people.

RISKS AND VULNERABILITIES

The development of rural infrastructure is not without risks and vulnerabilities, and it is important to be aware of how these risks and vulnerabilities affect men and women differently. The following issues should be taken into account in the development of rural infrastructure initiatives:

Security

Rural infrastructure services enhance the security of households and communities in many ways. In November 2007, when a cyclone hit the most remote areas of Bangladesh, the solar power and telephone infrastructure enabled authorities to activate warning systems and deploy emergency assistance within less than 24 hours. However, various infrastructure services do have gender-differentiated effects. Where roads are in poor condition and road transport is limited, pregnant women hesitate to go to the clinic for delivery for fear of dying on the way (Potgieter, Pillay, and Rama 2006). For women and girls, the risks of rape and harassment are reduced when safe basic sanitation is provided close to their households and when paths to water sources and woodlots are improved and maintained.

It is also critical to be aware of increased risks in some areas and to provide the needed education, information, and government regulation. For example, accidents occur with the improper use of bottles of liquid propane gas. Acid from discarded batteries has been used for violence against women. Although ICT has facilitated labor movements, it has also led to increased labor-trade misconduct and human rights violations (a key issue for household employees from East and South Asia who migrate to the Middle East without any social protection). Transport infrastructure can also bring risk. Improvements in rural roads can lead to increases in the number of injuries and fatalities related to transportation (see Thematic Note 2).

HIV and AIDS

Transport, mobility, and gender inequality increase the spread of HIV and AIDS, which along with other infectious diseases, follow transport and construction workers on transport networks and other infrastructure into rural areas, causing serious economic impacts. The evidence overall of risk-taking behavior by transport workers, and their relatively higher HIV and AIDS prevalence rate compared to the general population, is overwhelming (see Thematic Note 1). The World Bank requires that bidders for construction contracts in the transport sector provide HIV and AIDS education for their workforce and supply free condoms; this is best practice and should be implemented in all sectors and infrastructure development assistance programs.

Resettlement and displacement

Women, children, and the elderly are most negatively affected by loss of land or access to income resources from land due to displacement or resettlement for transport and other infrastructure. Payment of resettlement compensation to those with legal title is intrinsically gender biased because land and property are usually registered in men's names. Women are usually excluded from receiving compensation. Furthermore, they see their dependency on men increase because of the loss of income from common property resources, and changes in resource use patterns increase their workload to collect fuelwood and water. Widows and deserted women when displaced are particularly vulnerable. Displacement and resettlement often lead to the breakdown of community networks, destroying an important source of help for women in hard times (see Thematic Note 1).

The rural-urban divide

With increasing urbanization, the competition between rural and urban residents for scarce resources and services is increasing. This is already an acute problem in many dry areas. For example, to provide Chennai, India, with water, a fleet of over 13,000 water tankers plies between the rural sources and the city. Private trucks collect water from farms and villages, where wells are the main source, competing with village women for the resource, with little attention paid to the added time burden waiting for their turn.[3] Many areas face similar problems supplying fuelwood and charcoal for cities. Programs for rural infrastructure services such as water and energy, therefore, need to take a more comprehensive approach and assess the risks inherent to the competition with urban demands, as well as the potential gender impact. The Household Energy Project in Hyderabad, India, is a good illustration of how a comprehensive rural-urban household energy policy that includes both traditional biomass fuels and fuel switching can be designed and implemented, with a positive impact on the supply of energy services and on women, in both rural and urban areas (ESMAP 1999).

Environmental degradation and climate change

For many years the effects of environmental degradation on rural infrastructure services have been focal points for policy makers and development practitioners. Environmental degradation can have significant gender impacts, such as an increase in women's time burden. In the hill villages of

Nepal, where women perform 82 percent of the firewood collection, extensive deforestation increases the time they take to complete this task by 75 percent per load of firewood. For women in deforested areas, this translates to an additional 1.13 hour each day collecting firewood (Kumar and Hotchkiss 1988). On the Central Plateau in Burkina Faso, where population density is high, women spend between 32 and 35 hours each week collecting firewood (Monimart 1989 in Saito, Mekonnen, and Spurling 1994). Studies in Pakistan find that as women's access to potable water deteriorates, their time spent collecting water increases (Ilahi and Grimard 2000). Many programs have aimed at addressing these issues with the rural communities. For example, the Village Land Management Program in Burkina Faso has implemented large-scale land, water, and biomass conservation measures for over 15 years.

Awareness of the impact of climate change on rural infrastructure is increasing, especially in disaster-prone areas, such as the lowlands of Bangladesh. The reforestation of coastal areas and the construction of dikes are deemed to have lessened the impact of the November 2007 cyclone. In these areas the majority of solar home systems withstood the cyclone well because they are designed to be quickly dismounted, and the warning systems gave owners the time to dismount them. Risk assessment and management will need to play a greater role in the design and management of rural infrastructure, which will require the training of infrastructure engineers. A recent study in Canada documented that fewer than 50 percent of water, transport, energy, and construction engineers strongly agreed that climate change considerations would affect their engineering decisions in the near future. More than 80 percent agreed they needed more information to understand the various aspects of climate change (Canada Standards Association 2007) (see also Module 10).

PRACTICAL ISSUES FOR INTEGRATING GENDER INTO POLICIES, PROGRAMS, AND PROJECTS

Gender equity is a matter of development effectiveness and should therefore be addressed throughout the project cycle. Numerous factors facilitate and ensure systematic analysis and adequate responses to gender concerns in rural infrastructure projects. These factors for incorporating best practices can be summarized as follows:

- Adopt well-defined donor and government gender-equity policies with adequate political and bureaucratic support to ensure the proper analysis of gender-equitable outcomes of rural infrastructure programs.

- Use gender audits and gender budgets to identify gaps in gender balance and to analyze infrastructure budget allocations to monitor who is benefiting from services. These tools also help increase accountability and transparency.

- Use participatory approaches consistently throughout the policy formulation and project cycle to design, implement, supervise, and evaluate the gender-disaggregated effects of investments. Such approaches are critical to build ownership of the policies and programs.

- Include gender and poverty issues in project objectives and design to prevent marginalization or delays in the implementation of special activities, which are essential for analyzing and addressing gender and poverty concerns. Identify well-defined targets that can be achieved through step-by-step progress.

- Address women's time poverty with appropriate labor- and time-saving technology. Investment aimed at reducing the domestic burden of women, given the effect on productivity and labor, will substantially increase the benefits of other investments. For the energy sector, improving traditional fuel use (through fuel-efficient stoves and alternative fuels) is important.

- Include labor and business opportunities for women and men during project implementation so that they can equally benefit from the market expansion resulting from rural infrastructure programs.

- Include gender-sensitive experts in all design and review teams to ensure that both women and men are equally consulted and that the relevant components can be reviewed carefully and the necessary revisions proposed. Structure capacity-building opportunities for project stakeholders (team members and other partners) to promote ownership and commitment to the objectives of gender equity in rural infrastructure as a matter of development effectiveness for achieving the goals of improved agricultural livelihoods.

- Use gender-disaggregated monitoring and evaluation indicators to measure gender equity in all aspects of policy, program, and project implementation and outcomes. To do so, use available tools, such as household surveys and sectoral surveys. When routine measures do not exist or are not sex disaggregated, it is important to assist in building systems that do so.

Addressing gender and poverty concerns and improving rural livelihoods necessitate changes in how business is conducted. Achieving any degree of success in processes for policy, program, and project design, implementation, and monitoring and evaluation requires more time and resources and relevant institutional changes. Furthermore, it is important to continue action-research by learning as experience is gained.

MONITORING AND EVALUATION

Specific indicators relevant to transport are mentioned in the Thematic Notes, but some general indicators are provided in Table 9.2 regarding rural infrastructure as examples of issues that should be monitored.

Depending on the country or region, it may be relevant also to consider ethnicity and caste alongside gender (both as comparative indicators and when collecting data), because women of lower castes or ethnic minorities are usually in the most disadvantaged situation.

Table 9.2	Monitoring and Evaluation Indicators for Gender and Rural Infrastructure
Indicator	**Sources of verification and tools**
Active participation by women and men in infrastructure planning and siting, and decision making regarding levels of local contribution	• Community meeting minutes • Project records
Functioning participatory monitoring and evaluation system recording community involvement in planning, construction, and monitoring of rural infrastructure, including gender-disaggregated data	• Community meeting minutes • Records of interviews • Records of monitoring visits by community monitors and follow-up
Number of women and men trained and participating in user groups and operations and management committees (including bank account signatory roles)	• Bank records • Committee meeting minutes • Interviews with stakeholders • Local traditional authorities (such as a chief or local council) • Program and project records
Participation in training in specific construction skills, disaggregated by gender and age	• Training records
Employment in infrastructure construction, disaggregated by gender, age, and ethnicity	• Infrastructure committee records • Local contractor administrative records
Differences in wage and employment conditions, if any, between women and other disadvantaged groups, and men for positions of comparable content and responsibility	• Case studies • Labor audits • Project management information system or administrative records
Changes in percentage of women in local maintenance crews, before and after program activities	• Infrastructure maintenance committees and user group maintenance records • Local contractor administrative records
Restoration or replacement of livelihoods of affected people (including women and ethnic minorities) following resettlement, including measurement of number of households or persons affected; extent of loss, and replacement of homesteads and agricultural lands	• Case studies • Census • Community monitoring committees • Project management information system • Resettlement plans: existence and monitoring • Sample surveys
Changes to livelihood sources (on-farm and nonfarm employment) among resettled men, women (especially woman-headed households), and other disadvantaged groups	• Case studies • Community monitoring committees • Participatory rural appraisal (PRA) • Sample surveys
Access to services and facilities (irrigation, electrification, water supply, and sanitation), disaggregated by gender and ethnicity	• Administrative records • Infrastructure maintenance committees/user group records/PRA • Sample surveys
Satisfaction levels with water allocation among various users (such as irrigation and domestic water supply), disaggregated by gender	• Focus groups • Sample surveys
Satisfaction levels among community with quality and usefulness of infrastructure constructed, disaggregated by gender and age	• Focus groups • Stakeholder interviews • User surveys

(Table continues on the following page)

Table 9.2 Monitoring and Evaluation Indicators for Gender and Rural Infrastructure (*continued*)

Indicator	Sources of verification and tools
Time spent or distance walked by household members to collect potable water, disaggregated by gender and age	• Household surveys • PRA
Percentage of time spent daily in household on paid and nonpaid activities, disaggregated by gender and age	• Gender analysis • Time use studies
Age of school leaving, disaggregated by gender	• School records
Access to public and private sanitation, before and after project activities, disaggregated by gender	• PRA • Sample surveys
Uptake of new technologies such as low-fuel stoves, pumps, new forms of transport, and use of ICT, disaggregated by gender and education level	• Sample surveys • Stakeholder interviews
Changes to transport, handling, and storage costs for disadvantaged groups involved in marketing surplus produce, measured by cost or time spent in marketing, before and after infrastructure construction	• Case studies • Sample surveys
Number of women and men participating in training on higher-value crop production or small enterprise development	• Training records
Number of women and men receiving training in ICT	• Training records
Percentage of women and men in community using computers and the Internet, and the frequency of use	• Computer center and Internet café records • Stakeholder interviews
Changes over *x*-year period of project activities in household nutrition, health, education, vulnerability to violence, and happiness, disaggregated by gender	• Household surveys, before and after • Project management information system • School records
Spread of HIV and AIDS, prostitution, alcoholism, and other problems from in-migrant workers involved in rural infrastructure construction or using roads, compared with baseline, disaggregated by gender	• Community health surveillance • Health records • Local authority reports

Source: Authors, with inputs from Pamela White, author of Module 16.

Rural Transport

Rural transport contributes to rural livelihoods by increasing the mobility of people and goods and facilitating access to resources that serve basic needs as well as labor and commodity markets, services (health, education, and financial), and information. Rural transport infrastructure often opens the way for the development of water, energy, and other infrastructure. Rural transport includes motorized and nonmotorized rural transport services for passengers and freight (such as public and private trucks, buses, trains, and boats as well as bicycles, animals, and other intermediate means of transport) and rural transport infrastructure (rural roads, bridges, tracks, trails, paths, and waterways).

The rapid growth of urban centers and periurban sprawl in developing countries has blurred the boundaries of rural and urban and increased nonfarm income opportunities for rural men and women. The globalization of food production, distribution, and retailing based on integrated global value chains and the adoption of high-value agricultural export production (for example, flowers, tropical fruit, and vegetables) in many developing countries, facilitated by transport linking paths and roads to airports and railroads, have increased options for women and men in labor-intensive crop production and processing (Barrientos, Kabeer, and Hossain 2004; Dolan and Sorby 2003).

Conventional rural transport planning has focused on road networks and the long-distance transport of produce, neglecting transport solutions for the many rural women and men who lack access to motorized transport and travel by foot on feeder roads, foot bridges, and tracks. Upgrading a rural road can increase the flow of motorized traffic without directly benefiting local rural people and often creates safety risks for them. There are conflicting local and through-traffic needs and impacts for national and state highways that pass through rural villages. Local people want safety and access; pass-through travelers want rapid traffic flow (Tiwari 2001). A road investment alone does not guarantee that adequate transport services will meet the needs of local women and men, particularly in areas with low population density (Plessis-Fraissard 2007; World Bank n.d.).

Although recognition is growing that transport can make significant contributions to achieving the MDGs and extensive research has been conducted on gender differentials in access, mobility, and patterns of rural transport use, as well as many successful transport pilots and activities that address women's needs and priorities, the integration of gender and other social dimensions has not become an established part of doing business in the rural transport sector. Many decision makers still assume that transport is "gender neutral," that is, it benefits men and women equally. Rural transport policy rarely incorporates national gender policies or social and gender assessments. Conversely, country gender assessments and strategies seldom address infrastructure issues.

A rural livelihoods approach to transport planning goes beyond conventional cost-benefit analysis to examine environmental and social impacts as well as gender disparities. Transport is approached in the wider context of individual, household, and community development, as a *means* of enhancing rural economic growth and reducing poverty and responding to women's and men's needs, not an end in itself (Fouracre 2001; Starkey and others 2003).

KEY GENDER ISSUES

Gender inequality is now recognized as a serious obstacle to poverty reduction and economic growth, particularly in rural areas where women play significant roles in agriculture and food security (World Bank 2001). In most instances rural women have more limited access to land, labor, financial, and product markets (agricultural inputs and outputs). Women have more limited opportunities than their men counterparts to secure employment outside of agriculture, to increase nonfarm income, and to access education, training, and transportation services that will facilitate their livelihood (both domestic and income earning). They have fewer assets with which to pursue their livelihood strategies and have more vulnerabilities. This affects women's mobility, access, and transportation needs and results in gender differences in the impact of transport interventions (Graeco 2002; Peters 2002).

Gender inequality in transport burdens

Transport takes up a large amount of time and physical effort in rural areas, and women bear most of that burden[1] Rural men and women play multiple roles (productive, reproductive, and community management), but men generally are able to focus on a single productive role and play their other roles sequentially. Because rural women need to play these roles simultaneously and balance competing claims on limited time, women's labor time and flexibility are much more constrained and inelastic than men's. In addition to their prominence in agriculture and the informal sector, women and girls bear nearly all of the "invisible" domestic tasks of processing food crops, providing firewood and water, and caring for the elderly and the sick. Women's heavy domestic burden limits the time they can spend on economic activities and restricts them to activities compatible with domestic responsibilities. Thus, rural women face trade-offs in time allocation between different productive activities, between market and household tasks, and between meeting short-term economic and household needs and long-term investment in capacity and human capital. Women's time poverty and income poverty often reinforce each other with negative impacts. As long as the household economy is invisible, rural transport policy makers and planners are unlikely to attempt to address the trade-offs among different productive and domestic tasks (Blackden 2003; Blackden and Wodon 2006; Quisumbing 2003; World Bank n.d.).

For example, a UNDP time allocation study in Benin found that women worked 67.2 hours per week and men worked 50 hours. Men spent 24 hours on production, and women spent 17.5. Women spent 9.6 hours gathering wood and water, whereas men spent only 1.4 hour. Women spent 13.3 hours processing agricultural products and preparing meals; men spent 1 hour (Blackden 2003). In Zimbabwe, in an average family of six persons, 90 percent of the transport burden is headloaded, primarily by women. Women and girls collect and carry 95 percent of the water for household

use and 85 to 90 percent of the fuelwood (Tichagwa 2000). In areas where water or firewood is scarce, this time and effort can be substantially more. In Tanzania Masaai women walk up to 30 kilometers to the next water hole during the dry season (World Bank n.d.).

Headloading and backloading transport activity has direct costs in human energy and time as well as health and opportunity costs. Headloading adds an estimated 20 percent to women's travel time. Women's heavy transport burden reduces their agricultural productivity, diminishes their ability to grow and market cash crops, and limits their access to farm and nonfarm employment as well as local community decision making. Headloading also causes back and neck injuries (Peters 2002).

Gender differentials in access to transport

In many developing countries men's control of household cash and intermediate means of transport (IMTs), such as draft animals, bicycles, and carts, and social and cultural constraints on women's mobility limit women's access to transport opportunities that could reduce their transport burdens (Edmonds 1998). Men's control also creates differential access to markets, inputs, training, extension services, grain mills, and financial and health services for women and men. A multidonor report, "Can Africa Claim the 21st Century?" concluded that in Tanzania reducing time burdens of women could increase household cash incomes for smallholder coffee and banana growers by 10 percent, labor productivity by 15 percent, and capital productivity by 44 percent; in Kenya, giving women farmers the same level of agricultural inputs and education as men could increase yields obtained by women by more than 20 percent (World Bank 2000).

Rural transport services are often infrequent and expensive. Schedules and frequency of service are based on peak periods of travel to and from work rather than the multiple travel tasks of women who often "trip-chain," combining various domestic and caretaking responsibilities with wage-earning trips that occur throughout the day when services are limited (Peters 2002). The high cost of providing transport in areas with low population density often translates into high tariffs unless government subsidies are provided to service operators and users. Many rural men and most rural women lack the resources to pay these tariffs or to purchase intermediate means of transport. Thus, if the distance is too great to headload crops to market, farmers must sell to middlemen, who take a large share of the profit. For women and men who can afford rural transport services, only limited amounts of produce can be accommodated, making the transport costs high in relation to profits from sales (Plessis-Fraissard 2007).

Limited access to transport has serious human costs as well. Every minute around the world a woman dies in childbirth, and most of these deaths are preventable. Transportation delay to emergency obstetrical care because of lack of roads, transport services, and money to pay for transport is one of three types of delays that can lead to medical complications, including obstetric fistula,[2] which can result in maternal and newborn deaths (Babinard and Roberts 2006; Riverson and others 2005). These losses reduce labor and production capacity and threaten family welfare.

Unequal access to rural transport-related employment and income

Employment in rural transport that is dominated by men includes construction labor; provision of public or private transport services, such as driving and maintaining buses, trucks, and cars; and work in public sector institutions that plan for and manage transport services. Barriers to rural women's access to transport jobs and enterprises include information networks that bypass women, perceptions of "appropriate" work for women, differential pay rates for women and men, and gender inequalities in access to schooling that leave women without the necessary qualifications (Lallement 2007; SIDA 1997). Although labor-based construction has provided an entry point for women, even projects with gender inclusion provisions face serious challenges in institutionalizing these approaches (Tanzarn and others 2007). Redundancy resulting from privatization of transport services is also gender differentiated; women are almost universally the first to lose jobs.

Inadequate safety and security measures

Safety and security issues are seldom adequately addressed in rural transport projects even though increased road connectivity also brings increased injuries and deaths, most often among the poorest. Pedestrians with headloads, nonmotorized transport, and motorized vehicles move at very different paces on the same road, which often has little or no shoulder. The most vulnerable road users are pedestrians and people riding on nonmotorized vehicles and motorcycles. People living in rural areas are more likely to be killed or seriously injured if they are involved in road accidents because motor vehicles tend to travel faster there and trauma care is extremely limited (World Health Organization 2004). Men are involved in more fatal accidents than women, and women are involved in more nonfatal accidents. Less motorized countries account for 86 percent of global fatalities (TRL and DFID 2000). The economic impact of road accident fatalities and injuries represents an estimated annual $53 billion in lost production in developing countries. In India road accident costs account for an estimated 2 percent of gross domestic product (Tiwari 2001).

Rural transport services are often dangerous. Drivers speed and overload vehicles and seldom give passengers enough time to safely board or exit. Women are often harassed, and their goods are poorly handled (Plessis-Fraissard 2007). Limited transport service availability often means that rural women going to markets or to work in agroprocessing must wait for buses or trucks before dawn and return after dusk, placing them at risk for assault (Dolan and Sorby 2003).[3] In addition, the trafficking of girls and women increases with greater road connectivity, especially near major roads and in cross-border corridors. Risk is greatest where women have low status and there is widespread poverty, such as in rural Nepal (Latif 2005).

Transport, mobility, and gender inequality and the spread of HIV and AIDS

HIV and AIDS and other infectious diseases follow transport and construction workers on road and other transport networks into rural areas, causing serious economic impacts on human capital and agricultural productivity. Mobility and long absences from home make transport workers particularly vulnerable to HIV and AIDS, whether they work on land, sea, or air routes. The evidence overall of risk-taking behavior by transport workers and of their relatively higher HIV and AIDS prevalence rate compared to general populations is overwhelming (International Transport Workers Federation 2007). In regions where HIV and AIDS are entrenched, more women are now infected than men, and in countries where epidemics are just beginning, new infections among women outnumber those among men. Unequal gender relationships force millions of women, already biologically much more vulnerable to infection than men, to submit to demands for unprotected sex and prevent them from learning about the casual sexual encounters of their partners. Gender differences in risk factors, vulnerability, and the impact of HIV and AIDS have implications for prevention, care, treatment, and coping mechanisms. HIV and AIDS have been particularly devastating in sub-Saharan Africa, where women play a major role in agriculture and food security and bear the burden of care for HIV-positive family members and AIDS orphans (Cook 2003; ITF 2007; Lema and others 2003; Mutemba and Blackden 2000).

The disproportionate effect of resettlement and displacement by transport infrastructure on women

Women, children, and the elderly are most negatively affected by loss of land or access to land because of displacement or resettlement for transport and other infrastructure. Payment of resettlement compensation to those with legal title is intrinsically gender biased because land and property are usually registered in men's names. Thus, women are usually excluded from receiving compensation. Negative impacts of resettlement and displacement can include the increasing economic dependence of women on men due to the loss of their income from common property resources, the increasing vulnerability of widows and deserted women when displaced, and the added burden for women and girls due to changes in resource use patterns, particularly the loss of familiar sources of fuelwood and water. In addition, the breakdown of community networks destroys an important source of help for women in hard times (Asian Development Bank 2004; Cernea 2000).

BENEFITS OF GENDER-RESPONSIVE ACTIONS

The discussion addresses the key benefits of gender mainstreaming into rural transport projects and programs.

Increased agricultural production, economic growth, and economic empowerment

Construction and rehabilitation of feeder roads, tracks, and bridges and more affordable access to road and water transport services and intermediate means of transport increase the productivity and incomes of men and in particular women farmers who rely on them more heavily, by reducing time and opportunity costs and expanding their access to markets and inputs. For example, in Peru the rehabilitation of nonmotorized tracks in isolated communities reduced poverty from 83 percent to 74 percent, and 77 percent of the women traveled more frequently. Routine road maintenance created 6,000 jobs, 24 percent of which were held by women (World Bank 2007b). Boats carry consumer products and medicines to remote communities and serve as shops for their owners, who are often women. Floating markets are widespread in the Mekong Delta, where rural women and men also depend on water transport to take fertilizer or seed to their fields and carry the crops for consumption and sale (IFRTD 2003).

Increased infrastructure cost effectiveness, accountability, and sustainability

Participatory, gender-inclusive assessment of transport needs and transport planning identifies local needs of women and men and identifies problems and resources that can affect the outcomes of a project, thus increasing the efficiency and outcome benefits. It builds a local sense of local ownership of the road and commitment to repair and maintenance, which increases sustainability. It also reduces conflicts and tensions and thus prevents construction delays that increase costs. This process increases local-level planning capacity, accountability, and transparency in use of local resources and more gender-equitable distribution of benefits. Also, it reduces the risks of adverse effects on intended beneficiaries. Involvement of local women in rural transport planning often provides more pragmatic inputs on road selection and design that more directly reflect local economic and safety needs. For example, separate consultations with women in the Yemen Rural Access project resulted in safety features such as speed signs and speed bumps near schools. The women working on road maintenance in the Second Peru Rural Roads project improved the quality of road work because men drank less and worked more regularly with women on the team. Women were responsible for ensuring the quality of roadwork and handling payments because they were viewed as incorruptible. The economic rate of return for the project was over 30 percent (Caballero 2007; World Bank 2007b).

Increased human capital

Access to transport to emergency obstetrical care can help reduce maternal and newborn mortality and reduce the loss of productive capacity. Access to IMTs such as donkeys for carrying water and wood can reduce domestic transport time burdens and free up time for girls to attend school and for women to participate in literacy and farming and business skills training. Road access and dedicated transport services for girls can also facilitate safe access to school for girls and boys and increase school attendance. Research in Nepal, a landlocked country with severe accessibility problems, showed that road access affects girls' school enrollment more than boys'. When the school is a four-hour walk from the road, boys' enrollment is 56 percent and girls' is 31 percent. When the school is a 30-minute walk from the road, enrollment increases to 67 percent for boys and 51 percent for girls (Shyam 2007). In Morocco improved, all-weather roads increased access to butane gas for heating and cooking. This reduced women's and girls' domestic burden and tripled girls' primary school enrollment (Levy 2004). Vietnam, a country with great dependence on water transport, uses boats to carry children to and from school (IFRTD 2003).

Reduced risks and vulnerability

Improved rural road safety—particularly for pedestrians, nonmotorized transport, and school areas—through safety education and public awareness raising, traffic management (for example, safety bumps, signs, separate paths for non-motorized traffic), and enforcement can reduce unnecessary disabilities, injuries, and deaths that otherwise diminish rural human capacity and productivity.

Information, education, and mobilization programs linked to transport projects can raise awareness and change behavior to reduce transmission of HIV and AIDS, combat sex trafficking in rural areas where it is prevalent, and reduce harassment and gender violence on routes to school, transport to wage labor, or on paths around villages.

Equitable relocation and resettlement mitigation strategies can reconstruct the basis for rural livelihoods for women and their children through compensation transfers directly to women's bank accounts, access to communal land, livelihood training and employment opportunities, health and education facilities and services, and food security programs (Asian Development Bank 2003; Cernea 2000).

POLICY AND IMPLEMENTATION ISSUES

The sections discuss the key policy and implementation issues in gender integration into transport projects and programs.

Gender-sensitive rural transport policies

Transport policies should be informed by social and gender analysis to address rural women's and men's needs and constraints, including women's domestic labor burden. The consultation process for transport strategy development needs to engage a wide range of stakeholders, including women. The rural transport strategy needs to spell out the key institutional arrangements for the three principal areas of rural accessibility and mobility in gender-equitable terms: (1) infrastructure, (2) rural transport service, and (3) location of physical facilities such as markets, schools, and clinics (Essakali 2005; Malmberg-Calvo 1998; Starkey and others 2003).

Balancing economic efficiency, engineering standards, and socioeconomic transport needs

On the one hand, community-driven development projects are often very effective in social and gender inclusion and responding to local women's and men's needs but less effective in meeting engineering standards or cost effectiveness and may fail to link to the larger transport grid. This can result in roads that do not link to markets and that deteriorate quickly (Ishihara 2007). On the other hand, large, centrally managed rural road projects are usually technically sound and cost effective but seldom address gender and other social issues. This can result in negative impacts on local people and in poor maintenance due to lack of local sense of ownership, and in some instances conflict can delay road construction. To achieve a balance between transport social "software" and construction "hardware," transport program designers and managers need the capacity to formulate and analyze questions about the socioeconomic and gender aspects of transport requirements and the implications of transport interventions. Integrating social scientists with gender and transport expertise into rural transport project teams and transport agencies is one way to achieve this. The most effective integration of gender in transport projects has included concerted efforts to build social and gender analysis capacity and awareness in transport agencies. The Feeder Road Prioritization Approach, developed in Ghana, combines attention to women's and men's transport needs with technical rigor and cost effectiveness in a participatory process that builds local ownership (Hine, Ellis, and Done 2002).

Transport governance issues

Weak governance reduces the efficiency, sustainability, and equitable distribution of benefits of rural transport interventions, particularly for women who generally have little voice in community decision making. One common issue is exclusive, ineffective local governments that are fragmented, lack planning and coordination, and have little or no transparency and accountability. Another common issue is a lack of clarity on who (national, local, or private entity) owns and is responsible for maintenance of roads and tracks. Resolution of these issues within a gender-sensitive framework requires aggressive interventions to improve management, accountability, and equity. Rural roads need to be planned and managed as a pivotal network in the entire transport chain, a network that relates to all other modes or transport subsectors and in which women are prime movers (Graeco 2002; Rankin 1999; Starkey and others 2003).

Financing also needs to be gender sensitive and transparent, whether this includes locally raised revenues, central-to-local fiscal transfers, road maintenance funds, or donor, community, government, and road fund financing (Rankin 1999). Road funds are among the more popular forms for filling road sector financing gaps by pooling fuel taxes, tolls, and other resources under various institutional arrangements and oversight rules. The establishment of road funds has increased road maintenance funding and its stability throughout Africa. It is very important to ensure representation of women's interests on the boards that govern the road funds.

Gender-responsive monitoring and evaluation systems

Creating a gender-responsive monitoring and evaluation system requires appropriate baseline data, relevant sex-disaggregated indicators, and sustainable mechanisms for data management and evaluation. It is important to measure gender differences in social and economic impacts to determine the extent to which transport is contributing to the MDGs, equitable poverty reduction, and women's empowerment (Maramba and Bamberger 2001). Monitoring and evaluation systems are essential for guiding planning and midterm adjustments, tracking the distributional effects, establishing accountability, and ensuring commitment to achieving gender-specific priorities (see also Module 16).

GOOD PRACTICES AND LESSONS LEARNED

Recognizing significant regional and country variation in gender and rural transport issues is important, as well as the institutional frameworks in which rural transport operates. Differences must also be examined among rural women based on livelihood strategies, age, ethnic and religious affiliations, disabilities, and other factors. No one-size-fits-all solution may be found. Good practices must be adapted to respond to different and changing contexts based on social analysis that takes gender into account. Very few projects have integrated gender throughout the project. Many use innovative approaches to one or two aspects of a project, such as consultation or monitoring and evaluation.

Raising gender awareness for rural transport decision makers

Mainstreaming gender in rural transport policy, strategy, and the design and delivery of infrastructure and services requires a high level of sustained political and managerial commitment, which can be facilitated through awareness raising, using evidence of positive outcomes to foster high-level champions for gender issues in transport. The World Bank conducted regional and country-specific training for transport sector staff, including engineers, and as a result, the engineers became advocates for social dimensions of transport planning.[4] The Gender and Rural Transport Initiative (GRTI) in Africa conducted numerous training activities, such as the training for principal secretaries in Malawi (box 9.1). (See other examples of gender sensitization in Module 2.)

Accessibility planning

Optimal accessibility is crucial to reducing rural gender-based exclusion (Graeco 2002). Access is a key element in providing opportunities for economic and social development and thus an entry point for local-level planning (Edmonds 1998).[5]

Box 9.1 Malawi Forum: High-Level Officials Address Gender Imbalances in Rural Travel and Transport

The principal secretaries in Malawi have a significant impact on policy formation. On April 8, 1999, they signed the Makokola Declaration on Gender, which supports the need to integrate gender issues into all areas of development. Because transport was not explicitly mentioned, GRTI conducted a workshop to increase awareness of the gender and rural transport issues and gain the secretaries' support for needed changes. The principal secretaries developed a gender action plan for Rural Travel and Transport (RTT) with the aim to (1) ensure that the transport policy adequately addresses gender issues in the transport sector and RTT subsector, (2) build the capacity for gender analysis of gender focal points in all ministries, (3) involve gender focal points in decision making, (4) formulate an effective coordinating committee among ministries to ensure progress in gender mainstreaming, and (5) develop a project to facilitate rural women's access to IMTs through, among other things, the provision of credit facilities.

Source: Gender and Rural Transport Initiative 2002.

The Rural Access Index for roads measures the percentage of the rural population that lives within 2 kilometers of an all-season road.[6] Typically this is equivalent to a walk of 20 to 24 minutes. The World Bank Transport Sector Board has established the Rural Access Index as one of the key diagnostic measures for the sector. It is also part of the results measurement system launched for the 81 countries that receive International Development Association assistance. In the 48 countries for which the index has been calculated, only 56 percent of the population had access to an all-season road in 2006, leaving an estimated 1 billion people without access. The Rural Access Index provides a measure of the need for improved accessibility to achieve the MDGs. For example, a high correlation has been found between low access and high maternal mortality ratios as well as low school enrollment, particularly for girls (Roberts, Shyam, and Rastogi 2006).

Integrated rural accessibility planning (IRAP) is a tool developed by transport planners in the International Labour Organization for district-level integrated planning of facilities (water sources, schools, clinics, hospitals, markets, shops, woodlots, and government offices) in conjunction with roads, tracks, and other transport links. IRAP is based on mapping the location of households, facilities, and transport links, and women and men in local communities are encouraged to participate in the mapping exercise. IRAP has been successfully adopted in a range of countries in Africa and Asia (Donnges 2003). Efforts to incorporate gender issues in IRAP include analysis of the social and gender aspects of accessibility and travel patterns, origin and destination studies using sex-disaggregated data, integration of gender issues and indicators into data-collection manuals, women's representation among key informants and in community-level planning, inclusion of women's nongovernmental organizations (NGOs) in decision makers' pools, sex disaggregation of data, and use of gender indicators.[7] A geographic-information-system-based IRAP map of settlements and facilities in a district can be a powerful tool for planning. A similar approach has been adopted by the Ministry of Public Works in Lesotho (box 9.2).

Gender-sensitive intermediate means of transport

IMTs can increase women's mobility, independence, productivity, entrepreneurship, and empowerment and reduce domestic burdens. For example, in Tamil Nadu, India, bicycles introduced in a literacy program in the 1990s have increased women's mobility, independence, and empowerment in a sustainable way. Large numbers of girls bike to school daily (Rao 2002). Bicycles with carrier

---

Box 9.2   Lesotho: Mapping Mobility and Access in Rural Areas

A pilot project focused on the potential of using a geographic information system (GIS) and participatory digital mapping as tools to analyze differential impacts of existing and proposed infrastructure and services on access and mobility of men and women in two remote river valleys in Lesotho. Participatory mobility and access mapping was integrated into the GIS using a Global Positioning System (GPS) device. Mobility and access maps to emergency transport, health centers, schools, grinding mills, and other services were generated for men, women, children, and the elderly in different villages. Mapping and interviews revealed significant gender and locality differences in mobility patterns with implications for differential impacts of transport investments. For example, women's lack of access to IMTs results in fewer opportunities than men have to access health services in the region. Elderly women in particular are adversely affected by poor transport to access their pension payments in the district capital. The study also revealed a fragmentation of services that increases the number of trips required to access them.

Source: Walker and others 2005.

---

baskets reduce travel time to fields and markets and increase the amount of produce or other goods that women farmers and entrepreneurs can carry.

One effective way of enhancing women's access to IMTs has been the provision of credit to women for IMT purchases. Another has been to encourage joint business ventures by women using IMTs. It is also important to work closely with women's organizations to avoid sociocultural barriers to women's access and use of IMTs and to involve community leaders (men and women) and get their support of women's use of IMTs. It is important to ensure that IMTs are designed for women's size and strength. Facilitating local production of IMTs has produced the most sustainable use in sub-Saharan Africa. Training rural women how to maintain and repair IMTs can provide entrepreneurship opportunities for women. It is also important to coordinate IMT initiatives with road design to ensure safety. IMT projects designed to benefit the entire family help ensure that women's participation does not create domestic conflict (Edmonds 1998; Peters 2002; Rankin 1999; Starkey 2001).

Multisectoral approaches

A multisectoral approach to rural transport for rural liveli-hoods can address key access issues and contribute to achievement of the MDGs.

Multisectoral strategies: The World Bank Africa Travel and Transport Project concluded that providing water was an important way of addressing transport needs. Africa trans-port programs in several countries are engaged in the prepa-ration of integrated rural development plans that include the provision of basic services. Similarly, Economic and Sector Work on "Rural Infrastructure in Peru" recommends adopt-ing a territorial perspective that links rural economies to sur-rounding towns and avoids separate sectoral interventions and provides infrastructure services with stronger links to local realities and participation (World Bank 2006).

Labor-saving technology: Nontransport interventions sometimes provide more cost-effective solutions to reduc-ing transport burdens than transport options. Nearby access to grain mills, wells, pumps, and wood lots and the use of alternative fuels and fuel-efficient stoves can significantly reduce domestic transport burdens (Edmonds 1998; Starkey 2001). A study of time saved by use of a new water supply closer to the household found savings of 120 minutes for each household per day in Chad, 17–86 in Kenya, 60 in Lesotho, 106 in Mozambique, and 100 in Zaire. In Zambia transport efficiency more than doubled when wells were used. However, in a number of projects, the failure to involve women in planning for the source and location of new water supplies has resulted in limited or even negative impacts (Malmberg-Calvo 1994).

Fuel-efficient wood-burning stoves can also reduce trans-port burden. Assuming that firewood consumption and the distance to collect firewood are equal to that of the average household in the Makete, Tanzania, the time spent on fire-wood collection would be reduced by 73 to 145 hours per year (1.4 to 2.8 hours per week) through the use of an improved wood-burning stove. The corresponding reduc-tion in energy would be 6 to 12.2 tonne-kilometers each year. In Asia improved stoves also reduce cooking time by 20 to 30 percent. The estimated total average annual time saving is 250 hours (4.7 hours per week) (Malmberg-Calvo 1994). (See also Module 7 and Thematic Note 4.)

Rural markets: Increasing the density of rural markets reduces transport time and cost and increases market access, particularly for women, given their domestic burden and limited resources. Efficient, affordable transport ser-vices and access to IMTs can also lower the time and cost required to get to markets and reduce postharvest loss

(Starkey and others 2003). The Bangladesh Second Rural Roads and Markets Project combines these benefits with women's empowerment outcomes (box 9.3). (See also Module 5 and Thematic Note 1.)

Transport employment and enterprises: Inclusive employ-ment policies in labor-based construction, repair and maintenance, and other transport employment with fair wages can increase economic and social empowerment, particularly for women. Targets and contract requirements with specific clauses in bidding documents for construc-

---

Box 9.3 Bangladesh: Second Rural Roads and Markets Project

The Bangladesh Second Rural Roads and Market Project (1996–2003) provided women the oppor-tunity to access labor, product, and financial markets for their own economic empowerment, where previously women had to remain within their households without any income. A social and gender assessment revealed a demand for mecha-nisms to provide women access to labor and product markets, equal wages, participation, and decision making. In response, the project reserved 30 percent of the road construction jobs, 30 percent of the mar-ket management committee positions, 30 percent of the shops, and 100 percent of the tree plantation and maintenance work for women. The project also facilitated the formation of women's contract-ing societies, traders' associations, self-help groups with savings and revolving loan funds, and microenterprises for road rehabilitation. Partner-ships were established with local government institutions for scaling up and strengthening the activities. Gender was also mainstreamed in the government agency to ensure sustainability after the completion of the project and to scale up the approach in other sectors, such as water manage-ment, urban development, and flood protection. There was a 50 percent increase in women's employment and equal wages. Girls' and boys' enrollment in schools has increased dramatically as well. The World Bank, Asian Development Bank, U.K. Department for International Development, and German Gesellschaft für Technische Zusam-menarbeit have scaled up this approach to cover the entire country.

Sources: Ahmad 2007; Pulley, Lateef, and Begum 2003.

---

tion companies addressing equal opportunities for women combined with accountability through monitoring and evaluation are generally needed to ensure that women are hired and are paid equal wages. For example, contractors for the World Bank Mozambique Rural Roads and Bridges project are required to hire 100 percent local labor, 25 percent of which must be women. They are also required to provide HIV and AIDS awareness raising, testing, and treatment for men and women construction workers and communities near the roads.

Grants and access to reasonable credit may be needed to enable poor women and men to establish transport-related enterprises. For example, rural road rehabilitation and maintenance projects in Bangladesh, Mozambique, and Peru set quotas for women's employment. In Peru it was necessary to modify the criteria for participation in roadwork, to accept women's agricultural experience as relevant for the road tasks. The projects in Bangladesh and Peru also provided road-rehabilitation skills training. In Peru women's participation in road work increased from 3.5 percent in 2001 to 24 percent in 2006 (Ahmad 2007; Caballero 2007). These projects enabled illiterate women to become entrepreneurs, establish businesses, and earn income for the first time.

Emergency medical transport: Motorcycle ambulances have been operating in several African countries since 1998 to reduce delay in access to emergency care. The largest number of these is in eastern South Africa with a dozen units each covering a 50-kilometer radius. (Babinard and Roberts 2006). Ethiopia's transport agency is planning innovative pilots, such as the introduction of emergency access cards, to enable the rapid transport of women in obstructed labor to the nearest capable health facility. Work with NGOs, the Red Cross, and technical schools will introduce IMTs to help transport emergency patients. Communities will receive tools for labor-based construction activities, including culvert and bridge construction and maintenance, to help ensure year-round access for emergency transport. These transport activities will complement health and social activities (Clarke 2007; Riverson and others 2005). In Vietnam boats serve as water ambulances (IFRTD 2003).

Information and communication technology for transport: The rapid expansion of mobile telephones in developing countries can facilitate road improvement schemes and efficient use of transport services. ICT can enable pooling of resources among a wider set of communities in joint operation of a vehicle or vehicles and enables multiuse of public transport facilities (Graeco 2002; Starkey

and others 2003). It also provides a means of coordinating access to emergency obstetrical care, accessing information on market prices, and conducting business. A project in Sierra Leone provided radios to summon vehicles to take women to hospitals. Another project in Uganda provided VHF radios and walkie-talkies to health posts, ambulances, medical officer vehicles, traditional birth attendants, and midwives to improve the referral system (Babinard and Roberts 2006).

HIV and AIDS prevention: Contract clauses on HIV and AIDS prevention and treatment for construction contracts were proposed by World Bank engineers in the Africa region as a practical approach to address the increased incidence of HIV and AIDS where roads were constructed. These contract requirements are now applied in the general health and safety conditions in standard bidding documents of major works contracts (more than $10 million) under World Bank lending projects for transport. The Asian Development Bank has similar requirements.

The Western Africa HIV and AIDS project for the Abidjan-Lagos transport corridor aims to increase access to HIV and AIDS prevention, treatment, support, and care services for underserved vulnerable groups (truck drivers, women traders, and sex workers). The project distributes information about HIV and AIDs as well as condoms for men and women, trains health officers, and promotes free movement of people and goods by reducing cumbersome border-crossing procedures. The project informs women traders of their rights and the documentation required for crossing borders to avoid harassment at border checkpoints. It also trains women sex workers about HIV and AIDS prevention; provides free condoms; and gives financial grants to help them find alternative employment. The project also helps strengthen women's organizations' capacity-raising awareness of the rights and needs of people living with HIV and AIDS (World Bank 2007a).

GUIDELINES AND RECOMMENDATIONS FOR PRACTITIONERS

The following guidelines provide crucial actions needed to increase development effectiveness and sustainability of rural transport infrastructure and services by taking into account the different constraints, opportunities, and needs of women and men and engaging them in the entire development process. Monitoring and evaluation of investment outcomes and impacts using sex-disaggregated beneficiary indicators and gender indicators of progress toward gender equality are also essential (box 9.4).

Access

- Increased number of women and men within two kilometers of an all-weather road
- Reduced time required for transfer of a woman with obstructed labor to emergency care
- Reduced time required for girls and boys to travel to school
- Increased school enrollment and completion for girls and boys
- Women's and men's access to IMT for agriculture and domestic tasks

Employment and entrepreneurship

- Number of women and men employed in transport construction, transport services, and government transport agencies
- Number of men and women operating transport-related services

Income

- Increased women's and men's income from produce marketed using transport services

- Increased women's and men's income from transport employment and enterprises

Time

- Women's and men's time reduced for domestic transport tasks (water, fuelwood, food crop collection, food processing)
- Women's and men's time reduced for marketing transport tasks
- Women's and men's time reduced for travel to non-farm employment

Affordability

- Percentage of income spent by women and men on transport tariffs

Voice in transport decision making

- Number of women and men participating in road committees
- Number of women and men leading road committees
- Number of women and men managers in rural transport agencies

Sources: Kunieda and Gauthier 2007; Maramba and Bamberger 2001; Rankin 1999.

Policy dialogue:

- Increase awareness of government officials and communities that rural transport policies and projects are not gender neutral and specific interventions are needed to ensure that women benefit.
- Ensure that rural transport policy and strategy are owned by the beneficiaries through participatory planning, implementation, and monitoring and evaluation that includes women as well as men.
- Inform rural transport policies, strategies, projects, and project adjustments with social and gender analysis. It is essential to understand and address gender differences in transport needs, constraints, and potential impacts.
- Ensure that adequate human and financial resources are allocated to addressing gender and other social dimensions of rural transport at institutional, community, and project levels.

Operations:

- Embed transport-knowledgeable social or gender staff in the implementing agency with terms of reference that include gender integration. The gender sensitivity of the implementing agency is a critical factor in achieving positive outcomes.
- Develop gender action plans as roadmaps for integrating gender in transport projects. Developing a gender action plan with stakeholder participation ensures community and institutional support and accountability for the implementation of the activities.
- Use gender-inclusive mechanisms. Participatory approaches do not automatically include women. Mechanisms are needed to increase women's participation, such as inclusive consultations with women by women, quotas for road construction and road committees, outreach and mobilization, socially responsible contract clauses, formation

of women producers and processors groups, and training for women to level the playing field with men in transport work.

■ Work with local women's organizations, NGOs, and networks. NGOs with strong institutional capacity and a government willing to partner with NGOs can mobilize local support, increase women's participation and decision making, and provide training. Not all NGOs have the human, organizational, or financial capacity to provide the necessary assistance.

■ Provide awareness raising and technical assistance on gender and other social dimensions of rural transport at all levels.

■ Use gender-sensitive results-based monitoring and evaluation to guide rural transport planning and investment, as well as supervision of project implementation and impact evaluation. Gendered measures of impact need to be integrated into specific and routine monitoring processes, such as passenger and household surveys on transport issues. All routine measures related to beneficiaries should be disaggregated by sex and, where appropriate, age and other social characteristics. Where routine measures are not established or sex disaggregated, these need to be developed to assist in building the systems and capacity needed for routine application.

Energy

Taking into consideration men's and women's different constraints, needs, and potential contributions when designing rural energy policies, programs, and projects can significantly enhance economic and social development in rural areas and promote the sustainability of rural energy investments and services. At present, about 2 billion people do not have access to electricity for lighting and power, and 3 billion rely on traditional biomass for their basic cooking and heating needs. Providing women and men with access to energy helps them meet their basic nutritional needs; 95 percent of staple foods need to be cooked to be transformed into human energy (DFID 2002). Providing energy also makes access to clean water possible (through pumping or purification). Gender disparities in access to rural energy are significant. Women and girls bear the greatest time and health burdens of providing and using energy in rural areas, spending as much as three hours a day collecting traditional fuels, and 1 million to 2 million of them die prematurely every year from fume inhalation. Men make most of the decisions on the priorities and choice of energy technologies. Because women contribute 70 to 80 percent of the labor for agricultural production and household work, energy equipment that can enhance their productivity would considerably enhance household and community welfare.

A substantive amount of work has been done on gender in energy over the last 20 years, both in academia and among development agencies.[1] However, most of the development assistance with a gender dimension benefited fairly small projects, mostly for improved household fuels production and use, as well as research projects that documented either the issues or the development benefits of including gender in energy projects or programs. In the World Bank the work on gender in energy has been fairly limited and mostly done through the Energy Sector Management Assistance Program, Regional Program for the Traditional Energy Sector, and Asia Alternative Energy Program. Some of the knowledge generated through this work was integrated into the Bank's 1996 Rural Energy Strategy policy paper and into recent projects in Burkina Faso, Lao, Mali, and Senegal.

Energy has been identified as a major input for achieving the MDGs, particularly in rural areas:

- Lighting and clean water (which requires energy) can help reduce maternal mortality.
- Safe water can help reduce the incidence of water-borne diseases and mortality for infants and children under five years old.
- Lighting and power provide higher returns to investments in schools and education (longer use of facilities, higher teacher retention rate, longer study time for children).
- Lighting and power are needed to create businesses and generate income and employment, in particular for women who have less access to labor markets and income-earning opportunities.

This Thematic Note reviews selected issues and does not pretend to be exhaustive. It also offers suggestions for practitioners on how to reflect women's and men's needs and opportunities regularly in the design of energy policies, programs, and projects and on how to monitor results.

KEY GENDER ISSUES

The following discussion looks at the key gender issues to consider in energy projects and programs.

Gender equity and the domestic energy crisis

Although it is a core priority for meeting people's basic needs, *domestic energy* for household needs— such as cooking, heating and cooling, lighting, and food processing— until fairly recently has stayed as invisible in energy sector policies, programs, and projects as household tasks are to the economy: not counted in GDP, not considered important. For example, in Uganda, although 90 percent of energy consumption is traditional biomass for basic needs and only 1 percent is electricity, 90 percent of investments have gone to the electricity sector and 1 percent for domestic energy, according to 2003 data (Blackden 2007).

Domestic energy tasks in rural areas are disproportionately women's responsibilities, especially when the main sources of energy are collected fuelwood and animal wastes, and where women and girls do most of the cooking. One of the main characteristics of these gender disparities is the time burden on women and girls and, to some extent, young children of both sexes. Another example from Uganda illustrates the problem: there the transport burden of women is four times that of men in time spent, it is five times greater in volume, and a significant share of this burden consists of fuelwood and water. In Nepal women can walk over 20 kilometers on each trip, and the time spent collecting fuelwood is at the expense of income-earning activities or rest. By contrast, when wood sources are significantly closer to homesteads, the time gains and therefore the potential economic improvement to the household and the economy are significant. In Zambia about 600 hours per household could be saved annually if wood sources were within a 30-minute walk from the homesteads. Where modern fuels (kerosene, liquid propane gas) are available and affordable, men's share of time spent on procuring energy on markets increases, as documented in an Integrated Research and Action for Development (IRAD) study (Parikh and Sharma 2006) in Himachal Pradesh, India (table 9.3).

Another major characteristic of gender disparities in domestic energy is the impact on women's and children's health. In Himachal Pradesh 19 percent of the people reported symptoms such as backaches (50 percent), neck aches,

headaches, and bruises every week (80 percent). In addition, the unsafe use of traditional biomass fuels causing indoor air pollution is now recognized as a major public health issue. Children under five years of age account for 56 percent of total deaths from indoor air pollution, the main cause being acute lower respiratory infections. The World Health Organization (2002) estimates that 50 percent of the 2.1 million deaths of children under five annually from respiratory infections are attributable to indoor air pollution, lack of adequate heating, and other precarious conditions. Women are also more at risk than men, not just from more acute lower respiratory infection due to smoke inhalation but also from chronic obstructive pulmonary disease, lung cancer, pulmonary tuberculosis, eye damage, and having low-birth-weight babies. Finally, women are more at risk of violence (rape, beating, and injuries), and girls often miss school to assist in wood collection and other food-processing-related chores, at the expense of furthering their education.

Gender-sensitive solutions to the domestic fuel crisis are available, even if they are difficult to implement. They imply a whole range of sociological and behavioral changes, as well as economic and financial incentives to broaden technical options. Solutions range from reforestation with a specific focus on establishing conveniently located fuelwood sources that will reduce the transport burden for women, helping households obtain better stoves and switch to modern fuels, and developing indigenous renewable energy resources for electricity generation:

- Where efficient stoves and fuels other than biomass are available, women save 2 to 3 hours a day, which they can use for alternative productive activities or leisure.[2]
- Where mechanical energy is available to draw water, till, and transport crops, girls' school attendance and performance increase by the equivalent of one or two

Table 9.3 India: Difference in Gender Responsibilities Due to Difference in Need and Uses

Fuel type	Gender (%)		Age (Average)	
	Men	Women	Men	Women
Agricultural residue	24.5	75.5	19.0	32.5
Cooking gas (liquid propane)	100.0	0.0	29.0	n.a.
Dung cake	4.0	96.0	57.0	34.0
Kerosene	58.5	41.5	21.5	36.0
Wood	38.0	62.0	53.5	29.0
Others	60.0	40.0	51.5	41.5

Source: Parikh and Sharma 2006.
Note: Young and senior women—biomass; Young men—kerosene and liquid propane gas (LPG).

grades, and when girls are educated, they can enter the job market (UNDP 2001).

- When electric power is available for women to have access to telephones, radio, Internet, and television, they develop businesses, get better prices for their crops, and enjoy a bit of leisure (ESMAP 2003b).
- When women develop commercial energy businesses, regardless of the primary source of energy, the economic value of their labor is recognized, gender relationships change in the community—as seen, for example, in the Char Montaz project in Bangladesh (ESMAP 2004) and the World Bank PROGEDE Project (World Bank 2003)—and women's economic power increases.

The selection of the solutions, therefore, requires the equitable participation of women and men in decision making, as discussed in the following section.

Gender equity in decision making

Given their traditional household responsibilities, rural women are the main decision makers regarding fuelwood collection: when, where, and with which group of women to do it. Rural women also manage biomass use and adjust to growing biomass fuel shortages by changing food-processing techniques, cooking fewer meals, and changing the types of food eaten, where possible.[3] By contrast, rural women traditionally tend to have limited decision-making power about household purchases of energy commodities (candles, batteries), including priorities in energy expenditures and investments, and choice of technologies. When it comes to community decisions, men for the most part attend community-level meetings at which community investments are discussed and decided, and they rarely report to women on those decisions (Agarwal 2001). At the national level few women are among the energy policy makers, either in relevant ministries or in parliaments. However, because rural women are the main suppliers and consumers of energy, associating women with energy would benefit individual households, whole communities, and whole countries. Educating women about energy options and technologies can increase women's abilities to contribute to energy solutions. Table 9.4 lists the areas and range of issues in which the participation of women, not only men, in decision making is essential.

Empirical research shows that households' transition to modern fuels changes when women's and men's labor is valued as a function of income opportunities from the time saved through using modern fuels, including when wood becomes a commodity rather than being collected.[4] Consequently the integration of gender into the decision-making process toward the transition to safer and more efficient fuels for cooking, lighting, and power could be accelerated if both women and men participated in income-generating activities. This, in turn, would mean introducing energy solutions that free women's labor for higher income-earning opportunities and providing women with opportunities to be more effective energy suppliers, regardless of the fuel source: improved wood or charcoal production, liquid propane gas or kerosene marketing, and any other energy supply enterprise.

Gender equity in accessing rural energy assets and services

Traditional energy assets include woodlots or community forestry as well as collection rights over animal waste. Modern energy assets range from individual household energy systems—solar home systems, biogas systems, on-farm windmills, dual-purpose diesel engines (for irrigation during the day and electricity generation at night)—to community systems, such as microhydro or diesel plants and community wind farms. Individual households and communities rarely have access to grid electricity generation assets, but communities or farmers' associations can be the owners of electricity distribution assets (for example, rural electricity cooperatives in Bangladesh, the Dominican Republic, and the Philippines).

Access to energy assets tends to be gender biased to women's detriment because of traditional land rights, the greater participation of men in community infrastructure decisions, and women's greater difficulty in accessing credit to acquire assets or services for lack of collateral. The frequent argument that women are reluctant to change does not hold. For example, the study done in Himachal Pradesh (Parikh and Sharma 2006), documented that 71 percent of women there were willing to pay to install a window to improve ventilation and reduce indoor air pollution, and 82 percent were willing to use clean fuel (table 9.5). Informing women about energy solutions and encouraging them to organize to develop their own energy assets is one well-tested way to correct the gender disparities in access to energy assets and services. An example of this is found in a photovoltaic pump project in Brazil, where the system reduces women's drudgery and contributes to increased economic activity, better health, and improved living conditions (Branco 1997).

Table 9.4   Energy Issues Demanding Gender-Balanced Participation

Energy choice	Issues	Gender perspective
Woodlots	Plantation, location, and choice of trees for their calorific value; conditions of utilization; whether to continue fuelwood collection from natural forest or wasteland or establish a plantation.	Proximity of woodlots saves family labor, mostly women's and girls', reduces risks of harassment, diminishes transport burden; selection of trees with higher calorific value reduces volume to be transported.
Fuel switching	Whether to move from wood to more costly but higher calorific value, fuels such as kerosene and liquid propane gas (LPG; when available) for cooking; limited LPG-distribution networks, high cost of first canister; women's time collecting, transporting, and preparing fuelwood and other biomass fuels is not given any economic or financial value; when the price of modern cooking fuels increases, the poor revert to traditional fuels or women cook and eat less.	Redistribution of time allocated to fuel procurement between men and women; time saved by women can be reallocated to other activities (leisure, learning, child care, productive activities); higher calorific value of modern fuels saves women's household expenditures.
Cooking fuels versus electricity	Whether to invest in cleaner and more efficient cooking fuels versus electricity	Women, girls, and small children are the main beneficiaries of cleaner and more efficient fuels in terms of time saved, reduced health risks.
Cooking and other household appliances	Improved stoves needed for more efficient use of biomass and to reduce health risks; radio and television provide information and leisure	Health gains from improved stoves may provide higher benefits to the family than investing in a radio or a television, although women and girls will initially benefit more than men.
Use of household energy	When and for what to use power and lighting.	Women will optimize the use of power and electricity to household chores, children's studying time, and nighttime productive uses before using leisure-oriented appliances. Men tend to be more sensitive to the latter use.
Individual household versus community energy services	Investing in energy to serve community facilities rather than individual households	Women tend to give higher priority than men to investing in energy to serve a community clinic, school, or a center for productive services where they can work outside the homestead (food grinding, productive activities, telecenters).
Off-grid versus grid extension	Off-grid electricity solutions may be provided faster than grid-extension when infrastructure is limited	Women are inclined to see the immediate benefits of off-grid solutions rather than waiting indefinitely for the grid.
Institutional arrangement for energy service provision	Privately owned versus cooperative or community-owned energy enterprises	Women more easily see the opportunity from cooperative or community ownership for personal empowerment as well as meeting the needs of the whole community.
Technical options	Limited number of women managers, engineers, and technicians in energy enterprises	Women managers, engineers, and technicians tend to be more sensitive to designing technical options that meet women's constraints (location of the Solar Home Systems, electrical boxes, weight of improved stoves, and others).
Policy making and choices	Targeting of subsidies, determination of priorities for investing in energy infrastructure and services, tailoring of programs to meet women's as well as men's needs	At the national level, women decision makers will weigh the pros and cons of targeting subsidies for cooking fuels, which benefit women more directly versus for electricity connections, and will give stronger consideration to domestic and productive use of energy issues.

Source: Author.

Table 9.5 India: Women Willing to Use Clean Fuels in Shimla, Himachal Pradesh			
Yes (82.5%)		No (17.5%)	
Reason	Response (%)	Reason	Response (%)
Easy accessibility	7.0	The place is too far away	5.0
Convenient (to turn on/off)	18.0	Supply is inadequate	7.5
Cleaner household	36.0	We forgo our share of rations	12.5
Time saving	39.0	We do not need it	26.0
		It is expensive	49.0
Total	100.0	Total	100.0

Source: Parikh and Sharma 2006.

Gender equity in accessing rural energy business opportunities

The supply of rural energy services can be a significant business in rural areas, creating income and employment. The participation of women and men in various energy supply businesses tends to be technology driven, with a higher participation of men in such activities as electricity generation based on diesel, microhydro, modern biogas, and solar power, whereas women's businesses are based on traditional biomass (charcoal and dung cakes). Providing women with opportunities to create modern energy businesses is therefore important to correct disparities, and successful examples are now emerging from many countries (box 9.5).

Improved availability of energy services provides opportunities for creating new businesses. In the Philippines and Vietnam, households with electricity have two or more times as many businesses as households without electricity (fig. 9.2). Studies also document that rural women even more than rural men become entrepreneurs as soon as lighting and power becomes available, starting home-based or community-center-based businesses. In the Philippines the majority of home-based microbusinesses have been started by women (ESMAP 2002). In addition, lessons from experience highlight that rural energy programs need to include a "productive uses" component to couple the development of the energy services with the development of income-earning opportunities that can generate enough income and thus revenues to pay for the service. In Bolivia the rural electrification program also includes a rural ICT and business development program, including microcredit for the development of new businesses. It is critical, therefore, to ensure that both women and men participate in such income-generating programs. For women, such programs enable progress toward meeting a major set of their strategic economic and welfare needs.

GUIDELINES AND RECOMMENDATIONS FOR PRACTITIONERS

The bias of rural energy programs toward rural electrification, noted earlier in the discussion of issues in this Module, causes women's energy needs and solutions to be neglected. Correcting for this bias requires a shift from the supply-driven approach that has dominated numerous rural energy development programs to a demand-oriented approach. Some suggestions for addressing these problems and others related to gender in energy follow.

Undertake gender audits. The gender audit is a tool developed by ENERGIA.[5] Gender audits look at energy policies, government practices, and institutions. They identify gaps in energy and gender approaches and formulate recommendations to fill the gaps. Many governments—for example, in Cambodia and Uganda—have now elected to have gender focal points in all the technical ministries to work closely with the ministry of gender and social affairs. Practical suggestions to ensure gender-equitable rural energy policies include the following:

- Ensure the participation of women's groups in policy formulation.
- Systematically question the impact of rural energy policy interventions not only on women's and men's time and work profiles but also on the control over the resources and on their social and economic empowerment.
- Collect and use sex-disaggregated data to monitor progress. For example, monitoring the results of a policy intended to expand access to off-grid electricity services might reveal that women's uptake is less than men's because they lack access to credit and collateral such as land titles. Pricing and financing mechanisms should be analyzed for differential impacts on women and men.

Figure 9.2   **Rural Philippines and Vietnam: Households with Business Income**

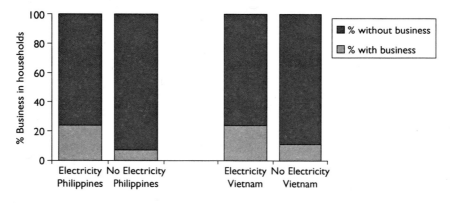

Source: ESMAP 2002.

Provide gender-awareness and sensitivity training for policy makers and program and project designers, including those in financing agencies, such as the World Bank. Gender sensitivity in national rural energy policies is most likely to be advanced in cases where government policies related to gender equity are already in place.

Adopt a demand-oriented approach. The demand-oriented approach starts with the assumption that understanding gender and poverty issues is an important part of the development and implementation of rural energy projects and will eventually impact the viability and effectiveness of the projects. The needs assessment provides information to project designers, households, and communities to make informed decisions on the choice of rural energy technologies and services, institutional arrangements, and financing

mechanisms that will best respond to the needs of all the members of the community. The needs assessment provides the foundations for longer-term programs.

Integrate gender monitoring and evaluation into the full project cycle. Implementation of rural energy programs is usually done in a series of projects that span four distinct phases: preparation, design, implementation, and postproject impact assessments (Dayal 2007). Mirroring the recommendation to inform the gender dimension and impact of rural energy policies, a need is present to integrate monitoring and evaluation parameters for projects at the preparation stage, so that the input of the potential beneficiaries and participants helps shape the design of the project.

Use gender-assessment tools. Numerous tools have been designed over time to conduct gender assessments,[6] but two distinct tools are recommended here: participatory assessments and socioeconomic impact surveys (ESMAP 2003a). The types of activities in *participatory assessments* include community mapping, stakeholder meetings, focus group discussions, and other participatory techniques. *Socioeconomic surveys* provide baseline data for the people living in the project area, and when conducted at periodic intervals, they allow the tracking of progress and the long-term impact of rural energy projects. The surveys involve collecting quantitative data through questionnaires (box 9.6), random samples of populations, and formal interviews. Participatory assessments are more focused on local conditions, whereas surveys have the merits of generating information that can be generalized to a broader population. A good example of a project where these tools have been used is the Lao PDR Rural Electrification Project financed by the World Bank (World Bank 2007).

Box 9.6   Topics for Survey Questionnaires

- Socioeconomic profile of actual and potential beneficiaries and customers
- Fuel and energy use before improved electricity services, including energy from all sources, such as candles, biomass, batteries, electric grid, and diesel generator sets
- Monthly expenditures on fuels and energy, by source
- Potential and actual willingness to pay for energy services, by application
- Energy use as it relates to substitutes for improved electricity services (kerosene, candles, and others)
- Energy use as it relates to substitutes for improved cooking/heating/cooling services (biomass, kerosene, paraffin, and ice)

- Reasons for not connecting to the grid or purchasing improved energy services
- Barriers to the adoption of improved electricity or other technologies and services
- Incentives to overcome barriers to adoption of improved electricity or other technologies and services
- Appliances in households and small businesses, including those with and without electricity
- Time use (men and women) as it relates to existing energy use and appliances.

Source: ESMAP 2003a.

Information and Communication Technologies

In an increasingly globalized and networked world, rural women and men should have access to a range of information to enable them to make informed choices concerning their livelihoods, management of resources, community health, and development, and to understand and influence the policy decisions that impact them. The role of ICTs in enabling women and men to access and compile this kind of information cannot be overestimated. Despite much support for the diffusion of ICTs in rural areas, gender disparity in access to ICT services continues, much to women's detriment. A widespread assumption that rural women have no real use for or interest in ICTs persists. Examples from around the world prove otherwise.

ICTs are commonly referred to as comprising the converging modern-day technologies of phone, wireless, and Internet. ICTs in a rural context, however, must also include traditional technologies, such as radio, satellite radio, and television. Over time, we can expect these distinctions to blur as the technologies converge further. The three defining characteristics of modern ICTs are their *convergence,* their *speed,* and, increasingly, their comparatively *low operating costs.* These characteristics offer a broad range of possibilities for information collection, manipulation, transfer and transmission, storage, and presentation, which can be effectively applied in rural contexts. As technologies and software applications improve and their diffusion spreads, ICTs offer rural populations new ways of networking and communicating. ICTs complement other forms of communication that are indispensable to improving rural livelihoods (box 9.7).

At the time of writing, the technology of choice in terms of bridging the information gap between rich and poor is the *cellular telephone* and not the personal computer: "emerging markets will be wireless-centric, not PC-centric."[1] Mobile telephone subscriptions will continue to increase at a very dramatic pace, rising from an estimated 15 million in 2004 to 191.8 million by 2014—raising the penetration level from

---

Box 9.7 Communication for Development

Communication for Development is based on the premise that successful rural development calls for the conscious and active participation of the intended beneficiaries at every stage of the development process. Rural development cannot take place without changes in attitudes and behavior among the people concerned. Communication for Development is defined as the planned and systematic use of communication, through interpersonal channels, ICTs, audiovisuals, and mass media in an effort to accomplish the following:

- Collect and exchange information among all those concerned in planning a development initiative

with the aim of reaching a consensus on the development problems being faced and the options for their solution.

- Mobilize people for development action and assist in solving problems and misunderstandings that may arise during plan implementation.
- Enhance the pedagogical and communication skills of development agents (at all levels) so that they may have a more effective dialogue with their audience.
- Apply communication technology to training and extension programs, particularly at the grassroots level, to improve their quality and impact.

Source: FAO and GTZ 2006: 3–7.

2.2 percent to 19.4 percent in all least developed countries.[2] Wireless phones allow farmers to check prices in different markets before selling their produce, they make it easier for people to find work, they can be shared by a village, they pose fewer problems for the illiterate, and the content is in the local dialect and instantly shared.

One limitation to ICT access is its dependence on a dependable source of energy. Radios may run on batteries, but cell phones and computers are ultimately dependent on a supply of electricity. In other words, the physical access to ICTs in rural areas (including community connectivity points such as telecenters or Internet cafés) is reliant on a dependable energy infrastructure.[3]

At the core of ICTs is the range of interactive communication tools that have the potential to support *participatory mechanisms,* enabling those with access *direct* engagement around the decisions that affect them. The connectivity factor, whether phone-to-phone or computer-to-computer, changes the mode and immediacy of communications and, in the process, fosters different organizational relationships between different stakeholders. The continuing momentum in the development of mobile connectivity has important implications for men and women in terms of their own mobility, security, privacy, and the time it takes to access information.

WHY GENDER PERSPECTIVES MATTER IN IMPROVING ICT POLICIES AND PROJECTS

Gender perspective is critical in ICT for three main reasons:

- Rural women face significant disadvantages in information, communication, transactions, access to services, access to skills and education, access to earning and employment opportunities, and "voice."
- ICTs (the full range, including everything from radio to mobile phones) can be highly effective tools in addressing these disadvantages.
- However, for ICT interventions to be effective (and, indeed, to avoid making women's disadvantages worse), they must be designed and implemented in a gender-sensitive way from the start.

Although gender-differentiated data are difficult to find, reports indicate gender differences—in particular that women's rates of Internet access and use do not automatically rise with national rates of Internet penetration (Hafkin 2007). An awareness of gender differences between men's and women's socioeconomic contexts is important in determining how to deliver ICT programs that meet these differentiated needs. Broadly speaking, these gender differences in a rural context include the facets listed in table 9.6.

The Warana Wired Village Project in India serves to illustrate the unintended implications of *not* including women. Warana lies in the sugarcane belt of the most prosperous regions in Maharashtra. Kiosks were set up in 70 villages and equipped with a computer and printer, which were networked to the Central Administration Building via wireless telephony. Looking back, project staff pinpointed weaknesses of the project, many of which were attributed to the omission of women as beneficiaries. Warana neither assessed the information needs of the community nor promoted local ownership and participation. Because Warana did not attend to women and poor people's ICT access, these groups were marginalized. Women were not encouraged to become information kiosk operators, and the resulting increase in men's digital literacy exacerbated the men-women digital divide. The poorest, landless laborers and tribal groups did not use the kiosks, even though these groups would benefit the most from the available information about employment and educational opportunities.[4]

There are a number of sociocultural factors common to women's access to and use of ICTs in rural areas worldwide:

- Cultural attitudes discriminate against women's access to technology and technology education: what would a woman farmer want with a computer?
- Compared to men, rural women are less likely to own communication assets, such as a radio or cell phone.
- Rural women are less likely to allocate their income to use in public communications facilities, except when they need to communicate with family or to arrange for income transfers.
- Rural women are often reluctant to visit "cyber cafés" or public Internet centers, which are often owned by men and visited by men. The café culture often excludes girls and women from frequenting them.
- Rural women's multiple roles and heavy domestic responsibilities limit the time they can allocate to learning and using ICTs, until and unless they realize the potential information benefits (and time-saving elements) of using these technologies.

Unless gender considerations are incorporated into employment policies, ICT diffusion strategies, or national policies, strategies may inadvertently result in negative consequences that compound gender and income disparities. Many developing countries are turning to the ICT sector as a new means of attracting foreign direct investment,

Table 9.6 Major Factors Regarding Gender Differences in Rural Populations

Gender differences	Major factors
Higher information paucity for and among women compared to men	Rural women face narrow choices of information and low perceptions of the value of indigenous knowledge. The negative effects of this poverty of information in terms of health, agriculture and livestock farming systems, harvesting and marketing, and environmental resource management put the typical rural woman at a distinct disadvantage.
Women's relative lower access to and control over resources	Lack of access to and control over land, water, and energy resources is a key factor of economic poverty, social exclusion, political subordination, and cultural marginalization. Relative to men, women are more likely to suffer the consequence of systemic loss of control over resources, and this also applies to their control over ICT assets.
Imbalances in education and training between men and women	Rural girls and women face a challenging set of circumstances in which the school system and the social structure reinforce each other and work against women's equal access to training, from primary education to higher qualifications to lifelong learning.
Lack of balance in representation of women's and men's needs and interests	Whether through intermediary agencies, local government bodies, farmers, associations, microcredit institutions, or capacity-building organizations, rural women lack a voice in determining or negotiating their strategic needs, and again, compared to men, are more likely to be left behind in articulating their specific interests. Communication media also play a dual role in reinforcing and challenging gender stereotypes.
Different gender roles in food production	In many regions of the world, women play a vital, if underrecognized and unsupported, role in food production. They have less access to extension training, affordable credit, and loans than do men. This works against their access to ICTs as well. By implication, women have less opportunity to articulate, negotiate, or act upon their concerns in the food production sector at the policy level. At the same time, research indicates that women make up to 65 percent of day-to-day on-farm decisions and 80 percent of marketing decisions.
Women's greater dependence on environmental income	Rural women derive a significant portion of their total income from ecosystem goods and services (forests, grasslands, lakes, and marine waters provide resources, such as building materials, fuel, fish, medicinal plants) and from small-scale agriculture. Because of this dependence on environmental income, the poor are especially vulnerable to ecosystem degradation and to physical disasters brought on by climate change, such as increased hurricanes, droughts, erosion, and flooding.

Source: Author.

primarily in data entry and call center facilities. These facilities, however, are currently located in a handful of countries: China, India, Ireland, Israel, Mexico, and the Philippines. The projected development of this aspect of labor-intensive, low-skilled ICT work seems to be no different from the route followed by the long-established garment and electronics industries: poor wages, poor work conditions, the absence of workers' representation, little to no skill or technology transfer, absence of career growth, and feminization of the low-end, low-paying jobs. Some e-commerce–based initiatives in which women are producing crafts or handmade products to market online do not in fact provide women with direct control over ICTs. They are quite far removed from the decisions and the applications around ICTs. In contrast, initiatives exist in which ICTs are integrated comprehensively throughout

an existing institution, such as in Self-Employed Women´s Associations, in which women learn to apply different kinds of ICTs to a wide range of activities.

ICTS RELEVANT TO RURAL WOMEN

ICTs have an increasingly important role in the *delivery of services and infrastructure* to women in rural areas. In many countries ICTs are an integral part, if not *the* underlying platform, in the delivery of municipal services. This includes software applications in the budgeting and forecasting, monitoring, and planning, and increasingly the delivery of a wide array of critical services in rural areas. ICT software can be applied to monitor systemic infrastructural issues, such as water and sanitation services, energy, and transport.

A growing aspect of ICTs is their potential to provide a *secure and mobile platform for commercial engagement and financial transactions,* with its related income, credit, and savings implications. ICTs can supplement or support financial services through applications that extend and manage credit support to women-run rural enterprises. Migrant and other income remittances that many rural families depend upon are also facilitated through SMS (short message system) or e-mails to request money from relatives or to receive notice of a transfer waiting for pickup at the local post office outlet. Debit or stored-value "smart" cards are other technologies that facilitate remittances. The all-women Dhoblai Milk Cooperative Society of Naila village in Rajasthan, India, has pioneered a business accounting and payment system, using smart cards for its members. The system helps maintain accurate milk supply records as well as secure payment transactions. SMART money in the Philippines allows remittance senders in 17 countries to transfer money electronically to their subscribers' home accounts and smart cards (see Module 3).

Rural women often supplement their income from agricultural activities through engaging in a wide range of other activities. ICTs and the digitization of information enable businesses and companies to locate and manage production away from the main site (for example, Bangladeshi village girls sewing shoes for a local shoe-exporting company). This has implications both for the individual employment of women and for the growth of clusters of small enterprises and their ICT investments. ICTs offer women the possibilities of both flexible locations and flexible hours through telecommuting or self-employment. Conversely, women's "flexibility" may also result in casual, part-time, piece-rate, and seasonal employment.

GOOD PRACTICES AND LESSONS LEARNED

Innovative Activity Profile 2 describes the gender approach of Community e-Centers established in Malaysia. Other examples from the African Great Lakes Region, Armenia, Brazil, Fiji, India, Nepal, Somalia, Sri Lanka, Uganda, and Uruguay are presented below.

Addressing rural women's illiteracy issues

Radio and mobile telephony can jump-start women's access to information without literacy. Simple and effective applications have been developed and applied in the field to enable illiterate users to access information critical to their socioeconomic welfare. *Macallinka Raddiyaha* (the Radio

Teacher) in Somalia was launched in 2002 by the Africa Educational Trust with the BBC World Service Trust.[5] This education project teaches rural Somali women and men to read and write through radio programming and training. The program includes three teaching elements: a half-hour weekly radio program broadcast by the BBC World Service, print materials, and face-to-face teaching. The radio programs use materials almost entirely from Somalia that look at human rights issues, ways of sustaining the environment, and strategies people can use to be healthy. Literacy teaching is based on key words that emerge from the radio programs. The radio programs are heard all over Somalia and in neighboring countries, including Djibouti, Ethiopia, Kenya, and Yemen. In this instance, ICTs supplement and enhance more traditional learning methods.[6]

In Bolivia, AGRECOL initiated a documentation methodology project to help farmers share local knowledge and develop local capabilities through multimedia presentations.[7] Earlier methods of information exchange were costly, and minimal sharing of information took place between those people who did and did not attend. Moreover, few women could leave their houses to participate, thus confining the benefits of information exchange to men farmers. Recognizing these limitations and the interest of farmers to record the farmer visits (some farmers would bring tape recorders or cameras to the exchanges), AGRECOL made ICTs available to the rural farmers. Now the Quechua-speaking farmers use digital cameras, laptop computers, and multimedia projectors to record and share their local knowledge, particularly about organic agriculture and resource management. The local facilitators and farmers are the ones who choose a topic, solicit experiences, develop a storyline and script, select appropriate technologies, carry out the documentation, edit material, create a presentation, screen the presentation with the community, and revise the product until it is an accurate portrayal. Local appropriation of ICTs is evident in the ways in which local groups have broadened the scope of their presentations. Women have benefited from the documentation process through increased access to information, which improves planning for farming and natural resource management, which in turn can increase crop yields and income.

Certain features of the project are indicative of the First Mile Principles outlined at the end of this Thematic Note. The selected ICTs emphasize oral and visual communication, which not only is in keeping with local culture but also strengthens the processes of local knowledge that can disappear through migration and the undervaluing of local culture. The documentation process can be used to build relationships with local authorities and other development organizations, thereby improving the collective capacity of the community. The presentations have created new learning opportunities for rural households, and women farmers who had been excluded can now be reached effectively (Piepenstock, Arratia, and Aguilar 2006).

Developing content relevant to rural women

The Kubere Centre in Uganda aims at improving access to information for rural women on the basis of the outcomes of information needs assessments. Women indicated that their main interest was in farming techniques, market prices for farmer produce, and health and education issues. The information center has newspapers and magazines and distributes leaflets and brochures on a variety of topics, many of which are agriculture and health related. It has Internet connectivity and makes use of World Satellite Radio as a source of external information. A reporter seeks out rural communities and collects local information, which is repackaged to suit the needs and capacities of the recipients. This results in folders and leaflets and in special radio programs, produced by women for women, which are then broadcast on community radio. Women in rural communities have established listener groups and will gather to listen to the radio. Each of these groups has a mobile phone through which they receive information on market prices and with which they can phone into radio shows during question-and-answer sessions. The women were very enthusiastic about both the radio and the mobile phone because the devices were easy to use, created a sense of community, and did not require them to travel or to acquire complex technical skills.

Enabling women to access resources more effectively

ICTs are becoming an integral platform for the delivery of critical services to the poor. As government social and education services such as land ownership databases, registration for health support, and information on legal rights are diffused, women are better able to tap into these information channels for their economic and strategic needs. The Well Women Media Project in the Horn of Africa and African Great Lakes Region was launched by Health Unlimited,[8] a United Kingdom–based NGO that supports communities affected by war or conflict to achieve better health and well-being. The Well Women Media Project works with local audiences in Rwanda and Somalia to develop interactive radio and television programs that promote "positive" attitudes toward women's reproductive and sexual health. Programs include soap operas and phone-in shows dealing with issues such as HIV and AIDS, domestic violence, genital mutilation of women, and birth spacing.

Addressing imbalances in education and training

Women's digital literacy can be supported through a range of ICTs, which are an important interactive tool of education. Good examples can be identified of applied forms of formal and informal peer learning. Planners can introduce women to the concept of lifelong learning and provide them with the tools to create their own teaching materials for other women. Distance education through ICTs also presents an important opportunity for the otherwise isolated or time-constrained woman.

Many rural dwellers in developing countries do not perceive domestic violence and the lack of access to education, information, and social services as violations of basic human rights. To redress such injustices, the Digital Broadcast Initiative provided access to locally produced, high-quality information on topics that assist communities in advancing their social and economic development efforts. From 2001 to 2006 the initiative distributed vital information, education, and leadership training to remote rural communities through satellite and AM/FM radio. The project was piloted in Nepal and was later implemented in Afghanistan, Cambodia, India, the Lao People's Democratic Republic, and Tajikistan. Tackling issues such as agriculture, HIV and AIDS prevention, women's empowerment, law and justice, and landmine awareness, programming was distributed through a combination of satellite and FM/AM radio and multimedia and solar technologies selected to meet local needs and infrastructure. Because many remote listening communities lack sufficient energy resources, Equal Access distributed car batteries and solar panels to fuel satellite receivers. In Nepal a rural women's listening group spearheaded a program against the social ills of drinking alcohol and gambling. Following a program on safe migration, a young Cambodian woman decided against migration after following the program's advice on checking the specifics of her potential job, fearing she would be trafficked into the sex trade.[9]

The e-Lanka Development Project in Sri Lanka uses e-government applications in education services that are tailored to promote women's skills training.[10] Telecenters are set up around the country to provide access to ICT services, including Internet, e-mail, and computer classes for poor rural communities that would not otherwise have access. The centers are run by rural businesswomen and men (women form the majority of owner-operators). A voucher scheme initially grants women and rural youth free access to rural telecenters. This is phased out once they understand the potential uses of ICT and the value of the facilities and services; then they pay a few cents per hour to make the centers financially sustainable. The World Bank currently lends an estimated $1 billion per year to various e-government projects. Services such as online access to land, voter registration, and license applications can benefit women and youth, especially when such services would otherwise be available only in the capital.

Representing rural women's needs and interests

As women use ICTs (including radio and video) for communications and information purposes, they are able to relay direct messages to policy makers and initiate change in their interests. The Rural Outreach Programme in Uganda uses a variety of information and communication strategies and tools to raise women's awareness about their rights. Women journalists visit 10 rural districts four times a year to conduct participatory workshops on issues ranging from reproductive rights to constitutional rights to political and economic rights. Issues raised are often adapted into plays that are staged within the communities and tickets are sold. Between visits, communities organize into radio listening clubs to discuss programs developed for rural populations. During field visits that last four or five days, women journalists record participants' experiences, which are aired on Radio Uganda or published in local newspapers.

In 1994 the Dimitra Project was launched by the European Commission as a unique tool for women and their organizations to make their voices heard at the national and international levels. The Dimitra network acts as a two-way communication channel by bringing information from the grassroots level up to decision makers and vice versa. Dimitra's main goal is to empower rural women and to improve their living conditions and status by highlighting the extent and value of their contributions to food security and sustainable development. The network operates on three basic principles: (1) working closely with its 10 local partners in Africa and the Near East to highlight local knowledge, (2) encouraging the active commitment of civil society organizations, and (3) networking to promote and support the exchange of good practices, ideas, and experiences using traditional and new communication technologies and tools and local languages. The information

collection and dissemination capacities of the partners are developed through linkages with rural community radio stations and the development of local content by the rural women themselves. Various technologies support the Dimitra network. The FAO-Dimitra Web site contains an online database in English and French with information on over 1,420 organizations, 3,000 projects, and almost 1,000 publications. In addition, Dimitra has provided information at all levels using different media (television and radio broadcasts, films, press articles, demonstrations, newsletters, databases, and CD-ROMs).[11]

Fiji's Foundation for Rural Integrated Enterprises N Development (FRIEND) is recognized for its creative and effective efforts to alleviate poverty by creating opportunities for communities using existing skills and resources in a meaningful manner that benefit rural women. FRIEND uses a variety of ICTs: the organization's Web site and newsletter advertise their projects, initiatives, and products; e-mails are one of the primary means of communicating and exchanging information; mobile phones are used to reach rural areas; a partnership with *Femlink* facilitates the broadcasting of community initiatives on radio programs; and some of the projects have been televised. FRIEND has three programs—income generation, savings program, and governance—that are targeted in rural contexts. Almost three-quarters of the participants in the income generation and savings programs are women. Women are encouraged to use their traditional skills and locally available resources, and so a clear message is given that local (indigenous) knowledge and those who use it are valuable. FRIEND addresses gender and rural-urban disparities in unequal access to education and training by offering diverse trainings to participants *and* their families. Training courses range from leadership, production, and packaging regulations to business planning, budgeting, marketing, and savings options. FRIEND is committed to ensuring that rural women and men articulate their own ideas for economic empowerment and to following up with the necessary support to make the ideas a reality. In doing so, FRIEND is challenging the lack of representation of rural women.[12]

Supporting women as food producers and natural resource managers

The AGRECOL Andes Foundation in Brazil uses participatory learning settings to teach the processes of recording and cataloguing sustainable agricultural practices using ICTs. Local facilitators are trained to use a combination of digital camera and computer presentation software to produce animated presentations. As a result, farmers are articulating their local knowledge and contributing to the construction of new knowledge. For instance, a group of women working with medicinal plants and a group of beekeepers generated new group knowledge out of their individual experiences. The beekeeping group went on to use ICTs to generate materials for project management, fundraising, and marketing. In other words, communities will find new applications of ICTs for their own benefit (as opposed to ICTs creating communities for ICT benefits) (Burch 2007: 40–41).

The Network of Groups of Rural Women of Uruguay coordinates women's groups from rural areas in south and central Uruguay. In 1991 rural women began organizing into self-help groups, and by 1994 the network was formalized. The network has five goals: (1) minimize gender e-exclusion, which is particularly prevalent in rural communities; (2) develop access to information for activities in rural areas; (3) facilitate access of rural people to the work market in equal conditions to the people with formal education on ICTs; (4) disseminate ICT training to rural communities so they can develop social and productive activities; and (5) develop a knowledge base about on-demand ICT training for rural women. Member groups have various areas of focus—some are business oriented, focusing on their canning, cheese-making, apiculture, or woodworking activities, whereas others concentrate on improving community life in health and education. For one of its projects the network has collaborated with the "Women for Democracy, Equity and Citizenship" and the Universitario Autonomo del Sur. The strategic partnership is aimed at strengthening linkages among universities, research centers, gender organizations, and women's organizations to develop networking and e-learning strategies for women's digital literacy. The project also aims to increase the visibility of rural women's contributions to society. Updates of this and other gender issues and news are featured on one of the country's popular Web sites, Montevideo.com.[13]

Raising awareness and boosting livelihoods for rural women

International institutions such as the Food and Agriculture Organization (FAO) have developed content, participatory training methodologies, and partnerships that use rural radio to raise awareness about issues critical to rural development. The FAO's rural radio program focuses on establishing community radio stations owned and managed by the community, connecting these stations to the Internet, and training broadcasters to carry out participatory

content development. In addition to providing resources, the rural radio Web site supports an online community of radio practitioners around the world. A dedicated portal also provides specialized content, including a warning service on food security from Simbani Africa and a news service that focuses on human rights and democracy, gender and development, environment, HIV and AIDS, and food security.[14]

The Network and Capacity Building for Rural Women in Armenia project's aims were to improve the livelihoods and status of rural women and to support gender equality in the local community through teaching them ICT and its use, to contribute to the establishment of a women's club that would promote information exchange among rural women and disseminate up-to-date information, and to strengthen existing ties among various agencies and rural women through improving women's access to ICTs. The project design reflects the First Mile Principles (outlined in the following section of this Thematic Note), in particular through its solicitation of local women's problems and needs. Not only has the initiative improved the lives of the women participants, but it has also brought innovations and valuable skills to the villages. However, its exclusive focus on women may alienate men and further increase women's burden to support household and community life. Rural men also need the skills and knowledge to enter the information age and to work alongside women to fight against discrimination, social injustice, and gender inequality.[15]

More than 15,000 rural artisans from the desert districts of North Gujarat, India, have joined the SEWA Trade Facilitation Centre (STFC; www.sewa.org) in hopes of overcoming their poverty through enhanced trade. STFC is a unique grassroots commercial enterprise that connects rural craftswomen in the informal sector to computer operators, who sell their textile and handicraft products online. STFC shareholders gain socioeconomic security and full employment through the efficient integration of the design, production, and marketing of their products and services in mainstream national and international markets. Previously women's craft activity was done on a project basis with limited market access. Building producer-buyer relationships was difficult because different stages of production, such as designing, cutting, stitching, and finishing, were outsourced to many women. As a result of scattered production, rejection rates frequently rose above 25 percent. After STFC worked to coordinate the supply chain and standardize production, rejection rates decreased to 11 percent, and the length of the production cycle dropped from six months to two and a half months.

GUIDELINES AND RECOMMENDATIONS FOR PRACTITIONERS

ICTs can reinforce gender differentials or help overcome them. Enabling marginalized groups to appropriate ICTs is as much about overcoming the "information divide" as it is about pushing forward the processes of social inclusion. In other words, *closing the information and communications divide is one aspect to closing the economic and social divide between men and women.*

There are good reasons for optimism about the development of ICTs and the benefits that may accrue to women, and especially to poor women. This optimism, however, is conditional on countries' and regions' ability to support effective, proactive, and deliberate policies that push for the social inclusion of women in all spheres of economic and social activity and decision making. In the absence of deliberate policies, the diffusion and use of ICTs and their intended benefits can actually exacerbate existing income and economic divides, with the poorer sections of the population being further marginalized, exploited, and impoverished as a result. ICT programs and policies must be developed to increase poor people's access to information, to enhance the transfer of these technologies to resource-poor areas so that people can learn how to use these tools, and to improve the quality and delivery of education and other public services.

The following First Mile Principles are five key recommendations for practitioners put forward by the Intermediate Technology Development Group in its report "Connecting the First Mile: A Framework for Best Practice in ICT Projects for Knowledge Sharing in Development" (Talyarkhan 2004):

Assess ICT capacity needs among men, women, and different social groups, and build this into project planning, budget allocation, and capacity building toward ICT. Be cognizant, in any aspect of capacity building, training, or outreach to rural women, that there may be a role for ICTs. Incorporate a range of interactive audiovisual and digital tools to enable men and women to gravitate toward different tools for different purposes. In Uganda village women were given a simple microphone and tape recorder to share their stories about the abuses they faced during the long civil war during Idi Amin's regime. Personal stories from the war were being heard and shared for the first time as a result, with significant outcomes for both individuals and the broader community alike.

Poor women and men are most effectively reached not as individuals but as distinct gender groups, and this requires both leadership at the community level and individual participation. Set aside time and space for rural women to familiarize themselves with both the technology and content relevant to their needs. Breaking this "virtual wall" that

many rural women face is an important first step. The activity of e-mailing each other or finding local sources of information on the Web can immediately improve women's regard for the potential use of ICTs. Service and training delivery to rural women should be a group exercise so as to build community endorsement and interaction.

Use ICTs to connect the first mile, and work with "infomediaries" who are reaching women in a dynamic and learning-oriented approach. This is probably the most important project design factor of all. Consolidate and build on the work of existing activities and outreach of NGOs, women's groups, and associations that are already approaching their activities in a gender-sensitive manner. Applying an ICT platform to their main activities not only encourages ICT familiarity among both men and women, but also promotes transparency and accountability. A Cameroonian organization for women entrepreneurs, for instance, began to offer computer training classes to students, ensuring that equal numbers of girls and boys had access to the classes. It continued to run the microcredit arm of its activities, however, using traditional paper accounting methods instead of converting to computerization and mobile banking processes, which would have taken its ICT capacity up a notch and promoted accountability and accuracy within its microcredit program.

Conduct research into existing gender information systems and design ICT initiatives that build on these networks and that involve local participation. Don't assume that just because women are using ICTs, it means that they are empowered. There are numerous examples of women who earn income from selling cell phone services in a rural setting but who remain uneducated and do not access ICTs for lifelong learning. Be on the lookout for promoting ICT-related activities that increase women's household burden or that place them in debt. It cannot be assumed that community-based ICT initiatives will necessarily include women in the net of beneficiaries. In Sri Lanka, for instance, one pilot project was located next to a garage so that those who came to the garage for vehicle repairs would use the multipurpose telecenter; however, those who patronize the garage are men.[16] Careful planning, an ongoing commitment to addressing gendered barriers to access, and the collection of benchmark data from which to begin monitoring progress are critical.

Build local people's capacity to use technologies and information to improve their livelihoods (rather than focus on identifying uses for new technologies). Encourage community-driven initiatives that value indigenous information and promote local decision making. A danger exists that supply-side ICT solutions driven by donor expectations can exacerbate development problems and gender differentials. Where ICTs have been successfully appropriated at the local level, one is likely to find a strong existing social network of users with similar interests or contexts or goals. Another way of looking at this is that individual access to ICTs does not ensure that the technology will be used by women for their empowerment. Rather, ICTs become advantageous to women when women are able to organize themselves around information that meets or addresses their specific needs.

In conclusion, technological and financial solutions to development problems are secondary to social solutions. The core solutions lie in building alliances, supporting dialogue, and enabling women to determine their choices, priorities, and "ways of doing and being." While incremental changes are being made, these changes are still patchy and not systemic. Women continue to be left out of key decisions concerning resource allocation and rural livelihoods.

Sanitation, Hygiene, and Potable Water

Sanitation usually refers to the disposal of human excreta, but it may also involve wastewater and solid waste. Safe sanitation, better hygiene, and better access to potable water can greatly improve health and reduce health costs of families and nations. Diarrhea and acute respiratory infections are the two main causes of death of children. Hand washing can reduce the former by 40 percent, and research indicates that hand washing also prevents respiratory infections from spreading (Fung and Cairncross 2006; Shordt 2006). Other significant reductions in infections from improved sanitation, hygiene, and water supply include dracunculiasis, or guinea worm, disease (75–81 percent), schistosomiasis (59–87 percent), trachoma (up to 79 percent), and the worm loads from hookworm (26 percent) and ascariasis (60 percent) (Cairncross and Valdmanis 2006). Half of patients with HIV or AIDS get chronic diarrhea. Having access to a toilet, hygiene promotion, and enough water for hygiene enables patients to stay healthy and productive longer and lowers the work burden and negative development impacts (such as reduced school attendance) for the caregivers (Kgalushi, Smits, and Eales 2004).

Good sanitation, hygiene, and water supply are also priorities for women and girls because of harassment and the risk of rape linked to open defecation and the collection of water and firewood and because of their challenges in observing menstrual hygiene. Finally, improvements can also reduce time and energy spent walking long distances, especially for women and girls. Women often use time gains for economic work in agriculture, food processing, education, and community development. Improvements provide girls more time for schooling, especially when separate toilets for girls are also available (FRESH n.d.). The reductions in time and energy spent give women involved in agriculture and the informal sector more time for child care, rest, and social relations.

An improved water supply can further make it easier to use larger quantities of water, not only for domestic hygiene but also for domestic production: for example, vegetable gardening and food processing (usually by women), brick making (often by men), and animal raising (by both sexes, often with a gender division by animal type, type of work, and control over products and income). Higher levels of education and economic productivity are linked to improvements of women's status and gender relations (see, for example, Verhagen and others 2004), lower population growth, and more rapid economic development.

Despite the social and economic benefits they provide, investments in sanitation and hygiene still have a low priority, whereas the urgency to invest in safe water is now widely accepted. Investments in these three subsectors are still predominantly seen as social investments and not as critical for economic development because many international financial institutions do not perceive the opportunities to receive a return on investments in these areas. With the exception of some countries, the world is on track to meet the drinking water Millennium Development Goals target of halving the number of those without access by 2015, but the world is likely to miss the sanitation target by half a billion people (WHO-UNICEF Joint Monitoring Program 2006).

Initially, water and sanitation programs focused on women as beneficiaries and overlooked the necessity of their participation in the planning, management, and maintenance of community services. In contrast, men and boys were left out of hygiene programs. However, either sex has its own tasks, needs, and areas of decision making and control regarding water, sanitation, and hygiene. These vary with age, socioeconomic status, and family positions and culture and are subject to change over time. Lessons on effectiveness and sustainability have taught that both women and men must be involved in the planning, maintenance, and management of services and be involved in program agencies, and that men must also be involved in hygiene promotion to gain a better understanding of its importance.

KEY GENDER ISSUES

Equity issues come into play in important areas related to sanitation, hygiene, and potable water.

Equity in decision making

At the domestic level, men and women have different tasks, responsibilities, and authority in water supply, sanitation, and hygiene. Women household heads decide where and how domestic water is collected, stored, drawn, and used and also manage most of the waste, although some of the work may be done by daughters-in-law or children. Men family heads decide on larger domestic investments (such as a pump, tap, or toilet), and men household members handle men's work-related issues, for example, in construction. Both men and women often use potable water also for domestic production: women use it for horticulture, animal and small livestock keeping, brewing, and food processing, and men use it for large livestock keeping, brick making, and cash-crop processing. Sexes and classes may compete for water and waste as productive resources if these commodities are in short supply. Culturally, women and adolescent girls have the highest needs for improved excreta disposal facilities because of their greater demands for privacy and safety, their requirements for menstrual hygiene, and their greater safety risks. However, for health purposes, men, adolescent boys, and children should use toilets hygienically and consistently, and infants' excreta should be disposed of safely—aspects that often require special promotional efforts.

Gender and gender relations also affect management decisions at the community level. Both men and women generally ascribe existing community-level management of water and waste only to leaders who are men, often from the local elite. Women in general, poor women and men, and people from minority groups are less often represented on decision-making bodies, have less time and freedom to attend meetings, are under pressure to keep silent, and generally have less power to influence the ensuing decisions, their implementation, and their effects. Having women and poor people on local management bodies can be mere window dressing if they do not actually participate in meetings, make decisions, and see decisions carried out as intended.

Influenced by middle-class concepts of women as housewives and mothers who manage hygiene as an exclusive women's domain, hygiene improvement programs initially focused only on women and adolescent girls and bypassed men and young men. This led to an increase in women's workloads, whereas men's responsibilities for family health and hygiene—in construction and financing and in setting examples for and educating boys—were left out. Prevailing gender relations often made it impossible for wives and daughters to correct men's practices and for daughters (and daughters-in-law) to correct any beliefs, knowledge, or practices of their mothers (and mothers-in-law).

Addressing these constraints and involving the different groups in decision making ensure that the differences in knowledge, skills, and needs of the different types of actors are taken into account in planning and management decisions. Quantitative evidence from 18 completed water and sanitation projects in 15 countries revealed that more equitable participation in planning and management was positively and significantly associated with better sustained and used services (Gross, van Wijk and Mukherjee 2001; van Wijk-Sijbesma 2002). A review of the evaluation reports of 121 large rural water supply projects supported by multilateral agencies (26 percent), bilateral agencies (26 percent), and international and national NGOs (15 percent) showed that where women had been informed and participated in decision making, 12 out of 14 scores on project performance and impacts were higher (Narayan cited in van Wijk-Sijbesma 2002). However, very few evaluations have investigated the linkages between approaches for gender equity on the ground and the institutional changes and supportive policies that determine whether gender and development benefits will be sustained (Hunt 2004).

Equity in access to assets and opportunities

In four general areas of sanitation, hygiene, and potable water programs, equity of access is important for women and men: (1) information, education, and training; (2) infrastructure technologies, facilities, resources, and products; (3) finances and credit; and (4) functions and jobs.

Information, communication, and education are important elements in water, sanitation, and hygiene programs. For effective communication, a gender strategy is required because men and women differ in the type of information in which they are interested and in the information channels they use. Both women and men need information on and a choice of the various technologies and designs, because they deal with different technology-related aspects. Women, for example, have an interest in and knowledge of access and ease of use for women's needs, ease of cleaning, and children's use and safety, whereas men are interested in costs and appropriateness for men's uses. Furthermore, programs must take into account that men are more literate than women and that women and men with a higher status are more often literate than poor women and men. Men and elite men and women also speak and read the national language more often, not just the indigenous language. People's access to mass media (newspapers, radio, tabloids, and TV) and the time they spend consuming these media also differ by, for example, sex, age, and class. In personal contacts, men tend to communicate with men and women with women on aspects related to their roles, responsibilities, and interests. Because water supply and sanitation projects are carried out by men technicians, who contact primarily leaders who are men, information and communication remain often limited to the elite who are men. However, with special strategies, poor men and women may also learn about plans, opportunities, and options and take part in decisions in planning and decision making. Hygiene promotion may especially reach better-off women and girls, although they need it least because of their better living conditions, education, and information access. Without equality on gender and for the poor, older men and adolescents, out-of-school children, the elderly, and poor women and girls may be reached least, even though young and adult men, children under 12, and the elderly are the groups with the lowest toilet use and frequency of hand washing.

Gender and other social constraints similarly affect access to training. Requirements to speak the national language, be literate, have time for training, and be able to travel make that training go mostly to men or to elite men and women. Because of gender stereotypes in communities and among program planners, managers, and staff, most often men (and often the more educated and younger men) are the people trained for technical, financial, and managerial tasks, whereas training on health and hygiene goes to women and adolescent girls, thus limiting equality in access, results, and benefits. Training only young men in maintenance and repair of water distribution points is, for example, not necessarily the best solution, because they do not routinely visit these points, have no personal interest in keeping them working, may only want full-time jobs and salaries, and, without specific arrangements, are not accountable to women users. However, it may be equally the case that not all women who live near water points and use them daily are suitable to receive the training, because they need enough time, freedom, recognition, capacity building, and compensation to do a proper job. The best experiences and results have been obtained with carefully selected, trained, and equipped women from low-income urban and rural households who as licensed plumbers and masons promote and install water connections, toilets, and rainwater reservoirs and work in latrine production centers. Trained local women have also been generally successful as

financial managers. Training builds on their need for and commitment to paid work in their direct environment, contacts with other women, and the preference of both sexes to deal with women workers at times when men are away from home (van Wijk-Sijbesma 1998).

Access to physical facilities is not necessarily equitably distributed. Influence from the elite often results in water facilities being located on their land or near their houses. This gives them easier access to more water for consumption and hygiene and thus to better health. Their greater access to land, livestock, seed, credit, labor, implements, markets, extension services, and so on further gives better-off men and women better opportunities than poor people to use potable water and time and energy gains productively. In addition, such families can often make extra money by selling the cheap (often subsidized) water and products made from the water to the poor.

Ownership of toilets is also higher among higher-income groups, reflecting more space, higher education and incomes, and better access to information, credit, and subsidies. Self-construction with low-cost and free materials is an option for the poor but is hard for some groups, such as women household heads, people with physical disabilities, and the elderly. There are good examples of participatory allocation of subsidies with public transparency and accountability and of neighborhood and women-managed shared toilet and washing and bathing facilities, however. Biowaste that was once a free fuel and compost resource for the poor is increasingly lost due to recycling in biogas plants and eco-toilets. Improved hygiene also requires resources: more water, time for cleaning, new implements such as safe water-storage vessels, and soap for personal and domestic hygiene. This makes practicing good hygiene harder for the poor.

If gender constraints can be overcome, sanitation, hygiene, and water supply interventions offer good opportunities for women to become members and functionaries on planning and management committees, local maintenance workers and latrine masons, retail vendors of water, waste collectors and recyclers, hygiene educators, and program staff. The work often fits the existing gender-specific work of women, such as dealing with health and hygiene aspects, paying home visits, and communicating with other women. Women also already pay daily visits to water distribution facilities and with proper training are highly committed to keep them working through proper maintenance and sound financial management. Moreover, both women and men household members appreciate when women latrine masons work within homes and compounds in the absence of men, especially if high-quality work is delivered.

One final category requiring equitable access to sanitation, hygiene, and potable water is children and teachers in schools. Schools are places where many children gather. Risks of infection are therefore great and increase when children and teachers have no toilets or unhygienic ones, no safe drinking water, and no water and soap for washing hands after defecation and before eating. Schools offer opportunities for participatory hygiene promotion activities to instill hygienic habits in children and create links with hygiene improvements in children's and teacher's homes. Separate sanitation provisions for boys and girls in schools have encouraged parents to allow girls to continue attending school after the onset of puberty.[1] School programs further offer opportunities to discuss gender and poverty perspectives of sanitation, hygiene, and water supply and equitably share hygiene work among children and teachers without discrimination based on age, sex, ethnicity, caste, or class.

Equity in economic empowerment

Bringing potable water close to homes not only has important health benefits but also enhances opportunities for the economic use of water and time gains. This is especially the case in dry rural areas and seasons when women and children must spend long hours collecting water, and in poor urban and periurban areas with opportunities for related home industries, such as food processing, and urban forms of agriculture, such as market gardening and small-livestock raising. To ensure that especially poor women and men can use such opportunities requires careful planning. Additional resources and inputs are required for optimal benefits and to avoid conflicts between women and men and between different groups of women over sharing the available water. Water vending to homes is generally done only by young men and, other than for women and children who collect water for the household, always involves some form of transport. If these vendors are not taken into account, a water project may lead to the loss of such work and provoke vandalism against the new systems, especially when alternative employment opportunities are rare.

In sanitation, the recycling of excreta, various types of solid waste, and waste also provide opportunities for economic empowerment of women and men. For example, one year of urine from one person can support agriculture over an area of between 300 and 400 square meters. Calculations from the Stockholm Environment Institute (SEI) and the Centre for Low-Cost Drinking Water Supply and Sanitation (CREPA) in Burkina Faso show that poor rural women could save 7 euros per year in the cost of fertilizers by recycling urine (IFAD 2008). Some types of work related to recycling are done mostly by women at home, such as composting and productively using biodegradable waste, whereas in the collection and recycling of other resources, such as paper and plastics and scavenging of solid waste dumps, both sexes participate (see box 9.8).

The degree to which women and adolescent girls benefit from economic opportunities is highly dependent on the prevailing gender relations. Others in households, such as relatives who are men and mothers-in-law, may control how the women and girls in the family use their time and the products and income that they generate. In such cases, (younger) women may do the work but not share in the decision making about and the use of the resources they generate. Labor equality issues in the sanitation, hygiene, and water sector are common. Often, men most often get paid functions and jobs, whereas women are not involved or are expected to work as volunteers, or the women do the same work or work more hours for lower pay. Being more tied to the home, women are also more commonly found in the lowest-level committees and functions, whereas men have functions and jobs at higher levels with the accompanying power, income, and control.

An important effect of sanitation, hygiene, and water improvements is the reduction of risks and vulnerability. Well-planned and executed interventions can greatly reduce morbidity and mortality and the involved costs (Cairncross and Valdmanis 2006). Some of these risks are gender specific because they relate to types and places of work of women and men. For example, 75 percent of those blinded by trachoma are women because as main caregivers they are infected by infected children and have less access to health care than men (O'Connor and others 2004). Health and safety risks in informal solid waste collection and recycling can also be reduced while consolidating the economic benefits of the work (Cointreau 2006). Economic products and earnings also reduce risk and vulnerability by helping families endure the lean times of the year when income from cash crops dries up (Verhagen and others 2004). Improved water and sanitation further increase socioeconomic development because they enable children, and especially girls, to start and complete school. Reducing their water collection and excreta disposal burdens makes it possible for girls to go to school, and separate toilets for girls allow them to remain in school when they reach the ages of prepuberty and puberty (Burrows, Acton, and Maunder 2004).

Recife has 1.3 million inhabitants and the highest unemployment rate of urban Brazil. Poor drainage is aggravated by poor management of solid waste. Contamination of water by waste and incidence of WASH (water supply, sanitation, and hygiene)-related diseases are high, entailing high costs to households and the city. Through an innovative municipal partnership that provides gender-sensitive environmental and hygiene education, people learn to separate recyclable materials at the source and to donate them to groups, cooperatives, and community-based organizations (CBOs) of men, women, youth, and children, who collect, sort, and sell waste for a living. Four interdependent projects operate in an integrated manner: (1) the Voluntary Delivery Spots project, with 40 containers for the segregated collection of recyclable goods in high-income neighborhoods; (2) the Communal Selective Collection project, in which women in households and women's groups in middle-to-low and low-income neighborhoods exchange separated waste for food, meal tickets, or construction material for a communal

building; (3) the project Support to Selective Collection by the Informal Sector for the street pickers, cart pullers, and rag pickers at the main city dump, in which CBOs helped establish four pickers/pullers cooperatives in an effort to promote more hygienic collection and sorting methods; and (4) a project to upgrade the 60 hectares around the main city dump in the municipality of Jaboatao dos Guararapes.

Positive effects of the dump pickers' project are an increased number of participants, reduced direct contacts with contaminated garbage, a reduced number of dump sites, an improved urban environment, and cost savings in waste collection. The projects gave a 73 percent increase in recycled materials in two years, a 62 percent annual increase in the volume of material for recycling, a 482 tons/month reduction of solid waste, a 56.5 percent reduction in special operations for solid waste collection, a reduction in the number of dump sites from 285 to 124 (a 43.5 percent reduction), a reduction in the amount of garbage collected by 5,796 tons/month, and an extension of 5 to 20 years of the life of the dump site.

Sources: Arrais 1996.

LESSONS LEARNED AND GUIDELINES FOR PRACTITIONERS

In national and international policies and programs, expanding the supply of potable water services still receives a much higher priority than the improvement of sanitation and hygiene. Yet the three are very complementary. Improved sanitation and hygiene are even more important than improved water supply, except when the old source of water is more than a 30-minute round trip away or when connections to the home are provided. The choice also fails to reflect that women have a higher priority for improved sanitation than men and that well-planned and executed investments in hygiene promotion are highly cost effective for achieving better public health (Cairncross and Valdmanis 2006). Therefore, it is crucial to raise the priority level of sanitation and hygiene improvement in national policies and investment programs (see box 9.9 for an example of best practices).

Within the human aspects, gender and gender-equity aspects in policy and strategy documents are still often limited to a few paragraphs on women and their involvement

(Appleton and Smout 2003). The remaining text contains gender-neutral language, such as *people, users, committee members, staff,* and *leaders* whenever referring to people. Gender mainstreaming means being specific on the "who" question, distinguishing not only between women and men but also between women and women and between men and men of different ages, economic, racial, ethnic, and cultural categories to end exclusion and discrimination of the disadvantaged. A simplified gender analysis tool (see box 9.10) has been instrumental in distinguishing and detailing gender and poverty in policies and strategies and in monitoring and evaluation.

Qualitative and quantitative research has shown that, along with good facilitation and support, the following characteristics are important for successful community water supply and sanitation: a more informed and democratic say for the different groups of women and men in the kinds of facilities that they will use and are able and willing to support; a greater and informed choice of the different interest groups in the local types of maintenance,

Box 9.9   India: Best Practice—Policy

Few countries have a special policy on sanitation and hygiene. India is one exception. In 2001, it published the "Guidelines for the Central Rural Sanitation Programme Total Sanitation Campaign." With regard to gender division, women are mainly seen in their traditional roles as housekeepers and mothers and not as, for example, trained and paid latrine masons and solid waste recyclers. The latter functions would relate closely to the already common daily labor of poor women as mason helpers and waste collectors. The guidelines do, however, allocate funds for separate school toilets for girls and for women's sanitation blocks (for example, when space for household toilets is lacking). It also states that "it is essential to train the community, particularly *all the members* of the family in the proper upkeep and maintenance of the sanitation facilities" (emphasis added; Government

of India, Ministry of Rural Development, Department of Drinking Water Supply 2001). Implicitly, the guideline stresses that hygiene work in the home, which increases after toilet installation and hygiene education, should be shared between women and men, boys and girls. Not addressed are (1) how lower rates of literacy among women and gender differences in responsibilities, interests, concerns, and communication channels affect information, education, and communication (which gets 15 percent of program funds); (2) training for women (technical and social); (3) health and hygiene education for men; (4) giving women an informed choice in choices of technologies and design of facilities; and (5) gender balance in community management of sanitation and hygiene. See also www.genderandwater.org/content/download/307/3228/file/ GWA_Annual_Report.pdf.

Source: Government of India, Ministry of Rural Development, Department of Drinking Water Supply (2001).

Box 9.10   Simplified Gender and Poverty Analysis—the "Who" Question

- *Work:* Who does which work (such as physical, organizational, and intellectual): men, women, both? Poor women, men? Any patterns of discrimination?
- *Resources:* Who gets resources (such as water, waste, information, training, and credit): men, women, or both? Poor men, women? Any patterns of discrimination?
- *Decision making:* Who makes decisions at which levels: men, women, both? Poor men, women? Any patterns of discrimination?
- *Control:* Who has control over choices, resources, products, and income: men, women, both? Poor men, women? Any patterns of discrimination?
- *Benefits:* Who gets which benefits (such as facilities, services, jobs, and payments): men, women, both? Poor women, men? Any patterns of discrimination?
- *Losses:* Who loses work, resources, influence, control, benefits: men, women, both? Poor women, men? What are or may be the impacts for the people and the services?

Source: Indonesian Sanitation Sector Development Program, internal document.

management, and financing systems; and locally chosen and trained representatives of the different stakeholder groups dealing with management, including accountability to users (van Wijk-Sijbesma 2002).

Typical participatory planning issues requiring consultation and informed and joint decisions include the type of technology and, in the case of a water supply or sewerage system, the level of service (private, shared, or neighborhood facilities); the numbers, designs, and locations of the facilities; local arrangements for maintenance, management, and financing; needs and arrangements for capacity building; and arrangements for accountability and prevention of corruption (Mathew 2006). Practical measures (see table 9.7) help give local women more equitable participation and influence in environments in which gender inequalities and technical bias favor men's participation to the exclusion and subordination of women (Coates 1999).

For effective promotion of hygienic conditions and practices, different strategies can be adopted. Social marketing is one option to promote one particular product or practice, such as the installation and use of an affordable toilet, washing hands with soap at critical moments, or the solar disinfection of drinking water. It is also possible to develop programs for more comprehensive behavior change and to build capacities in communities to plan, implement, and manage their own hygiene and sanitation program, for example, for total sanitation (Austin and others 2005, Kar and Pasteur 2005). In each, strategy measures are needed to

Table 9.7	Ten Steps to Enhance Women's Participation in Projects at the Community Level
1	Contact men's leadership for understanding and support
2	Use information channels that reach women
3	Facilitate women's participation in project meetings: • Help women speak out (use vernacular language, discussion breaks, and spokeswomen) • Hold meetings at times and places suitable for women • Hold separate meetings with women when necessary • Inform women and men and invite both to attend (for example, as couples) • Make seating arrangements appropriate to women (to avoid having them sit in the back)
4	Involve women in local planning and design decisions about the following issues: • Capacity building, including for innovative jobs and positions • Choice of committee members and their tasks and accountability • Choice of local caretakers, operators, mechanics, and their tasks and accountability • Choice of technologies and designs and locations of facilities • Local financing system • Local management system
5	Enable women to choose their own representatives for trust, ease of contacts, leadership capacities, and feasibility
6	Ensure representation of women on higher-level committees and bodies
7	Help create new roles and jobs for women related to their gender interests and tasks: • Comanagers of water, sanitation, and hygiene services and programs • Construction of facilities in the home environment • Maintenance and repair of facilities • Promotion of hygiene among women (men promoting hygiene and hygiene support by men) • Tariff collection and financial management
8	Link water, sanitation, and hygiene projects and programs with income generation opportunities, especially for poor women (and men)
9	Train women in technology and management, and train men in hygiene and hygiene promotion and ensure that they can apply the training
10	Have mixed women-men project teams for technical and social aspects and train teams and management on reasons for and modalities of gender equality

Source: Based on Wakeman 1995: 77.

ensure that the gender and gender-equity aspects of hygiene and hygiene promotion are incorporated for effectiveness and sustainability and as a human right.

At the agency support level, a first condition for mainstreaming gender equality is understanding and recognizing gender and gender factors in the broader sense: looking at positions, roles, and relations differentiated not only by sex but also by age, ethnicity, race, caste, class, religion, and marital status. Work toward gender equality should be one of the explicit objectives of all sector agencies. Because of the multidimensional nature of the sector, having a mix of men and women technical and social specialists is essential, either within single implementing agencies or through cooperation between technical and social organizations, such as engineering firms and NGOs. However, mixed staffing is not enough by itself. To be effective, both technical and social workers (and, where relevant, environmental and other specialists) should have a basic knowledge about each other's working areas and their gender and

gender-equity aspects, operate as teams and not in parallel, and have managers who demand, appreciate, and reward gender-equity approaches.

Gender training and gender specialists and consultants can be helpful but can also make others think that the issue has been taken care of and that mainstreaming has been achieved. In practice, mainstreaming is an ongoing way of thinking and a continuing process for which all are responsible. The investigation of gender knowledge, skills, and practices, therefore, deserves to be part of the job descriptions, recruitment processes, and performance assessments of all staff and managers. For an example of best practices in human and organizational capacities, see Innovative Activity Profile 1 on sanitation in Kerala, India.

Mainstreaming also involves making gender and gender-equity aspects part of the organization's documentation and reporting and part of the development, testing, institutionalization, and periodic upgrading of project and program procedures. Budgets should contain clear evidence of gender inclusiveness by including funds not only for gender training and consultancies but also for designing, implementing, monitoring, and evaluating new and more equitable gender roles for women and men in projects and programs. In-house gender equality is further reflected by a balance in men and women staff and career paths, equal salaries and benefits for equal work, and working conditions that make taking care of family responsibilities easier for both sexes.

MONITORING AND EVALUATION

Which indicators and sources of verification are chosen depend on the level of the work (for example, policy, support organization, or implementation), the stages of the project cycle, and the type of projects and programs (sanitation, hygiene, water supply). Table 9.8 gives a number of possible indicators and their means of verification. Ideally there should be a mix of quantitative and qualitative indicators. Depending on the country or region and the aspects considered, it will be relevant to look especially at particularly sensitive categories, such as the poorest women and men, members of minority groups, and daughters-in-law and single women and men, because of their less acceptable situations and opportunities regarding workloads, resources, influence, control, and so on.

Because numbers do not indicate actual participation in processes and decisions, a sliding-scale system may be used to assess the degree of gender mainstreaming, for example, in decision-making bodies and meetings: only men are members; women are members but do not attend decision-making meetings; women attend but keep silent; women attend and express themselves but are not heard; women attend, express themselves, and influence at least one decision; women attend, express themselves, and influence most and finally all decisions (Mukherjee and van Wijk 2003).

Table 9.8 Monitoring and Evaluation Indicators for Gender Equity in Sanitation, Hygiene, and Water	
Indicator	**Sources of verification and tools**
Participation of the national women's institutional framework, women NGOs, and/or gender specialists in the formulation and review of sector policies	• Interviews with policy makers • Minutes of policy planning meetings
Presence (incidental or systematic) and nature of gender (women's participation or gender equality) in policies	• Review of policy documents
Percentages, cooperation, and working relations of women and men technical, social, and support staff in agencies and projects, by level	• Interviews • Staff data
Percentage of budgets earmarked for gender capacity building and for activities related to gender, and the actual expenditures	• Financial records • Project/program budgets
Percentage of women and men active on planning and management committees at different levels, including disadvantaged women/men, over time	• Participatory survey • Program and project records
Distribution of projects over poorest, poor, less-, and least-poor communities in project or program area	• Ranking of communities by welfare mix • Welfare classification (Participatory Rapid Appraisal [PRA]) technique by community
Distribution of access over time to improved water supply, waste disposal, and hygiene education/facilities over poorest, poor, less-, and least-poor households in project communities	• Participatory survey with welfare classification and access mapping (PRA) • Program and project record
Functionality of facilities and services over time and degree and purposes of use by sex and age in the different user groups	• Group interviews and focus group discussions • (Participatory) household survey • Project/program data
Percentage of women and men trained over time in agencies and communities for technical, social, managerial, financing, and hygiene work, including disadvantaged women and men, and experiences with application	• Interviews with stakeholders • Participatory survey with matrix counting • Program and project records
Measured or perceived positive and negative impacts of the interventions on time and water use, hygiene conditions and practices, work, positions, knowledge, skills, resources, capacities, incomes, and health of women and men in different age, socioeconomic, and cultural groups	• Changes according to group interviews and focus group discussions • Prestudies and poststudies
Community satisfaction (disaggregated by gender, class, caste, and so on) with project and program processes, implementers, and changes	• Group interviews and focus group discussions • Interviews, before and after

Source: Author.

Peru: Rural Roads Project, Second Phase

The first phase of the Peru Rural Roads Project was implemented between 1995 and 1999 in 12 departments that ranked highest in rural poverty, primarily in the highlands and in one jungle area. Among the poorest are indigenous people, the majority of whom live in the highlands.[1] The second phase, implemented in 2001–06, focused on the same 12 departments and emphasized creating development opportunities with an emphasis on inclusion and equity, particularly for indigenous women (World Bank 2007). The third phase, the Decentralized Rural Transport Project (2007–12), will scale up the program to the entire country, with an emphasis on social inclusion and participatory democracy.

The focus of this Innovative Activity Profile is the second phase, which was assessed by the World Bank Quality Assurance Group and the Independent Evaluation Group as a highly satisfactory and highly efficient project[2] that establishes a "new demand-led paradigm for transport planning and development" (World Bank 2007: 39) and is a "pioneer" in developing performance indicators. The project also received awards for excellence from the World Bank and the NGO community in Peru (World Bank 2007). Recognizing that "women are a driving force in poverty reduction," the project used innovative, participatory approaches to mainstream gender in ways that increased the impact and sustainability of the investment and empowered poor rural women (World Bank 2007). The project is supported by loans from the World Bank and the Inter-American Development Bank (IADB). Phase two investments include $50 million each from the World Bank and the IADB and $51.21 million from the government of Peru.

PROJECT OBJECTIVES AND DESCRIPTION

The project development objective for phase two was to "improve the access of rural poor to basis social services,

market integrating infrastructure, and income-generating activities with gender equity to help alleviate rural poverty and raise the living standards of rural communities" (World Bank 2001: 2). The specific objectives were to integrate poorly accessible zones to social services and regional economic centers, generate employment in rural areas, and strengthen local institutional capacity to manage rural roads on a sustainable basis and launch community-based development objectives. The project used local labor for road and nonmotorized transport track rehabilitation and established local microenterprises for road maintenance, with oversight by community-based road committees. A local development window (LDW) assisted communities in planning, skill development, and seeking funding to support local development projects once road or track access was established.[3]

The project design responded to the important economic roles played by rural women and the need to help them overcome constraints on their productivity and mobility, including heavy domestic and time burdens (accessing fuel and water), low literacy, language barriers,[4] cultural barriers to their use of public transport, limited control of household resources, and limited voice in planning of previous transport initiatives, as well as isolation due to lack of adequate transport infrastructure (World Bank 2001). Combined with these factors are high rates of woman-headed households and migration by men (Gutiérrez 2007; JICA 2007).

> **What's innovative?** Key to the success of the project was the participatory, inclusive design and implementation with interconnected, complementary, gender-informed initiatives: microenterprises for road rehabilitation, the development window, and strengthening local governance.

Although gender was not incorporated in the project design for the first phase, a study of gender-differentiated impacts of road rehabilitation was commissioned and revealed differences that spurred a gender focus in the second phase. A gender training workshop for staff of the implementing agency, carried out during the interface between phases one and two, used the study findings to illustrate how gender issues cut across road rehabilitation activities in the project. The social assessment for phase two addressed gender issues; the stakeholder analysis and outreach strategy identified women as a vulnerable group and called attention to the risk of low participation of women in road maintenance microenterprises and rural road committees.

Technical assistance missions from the World Bank assisted the project implementation unit in developing a matrix defining specific gender targets and follow-up actions for the implementation phase. Assistance was also provided to conduct a gender analysis of the project's operational procedures and develop a gender action plan. The key elements of the gender action plan included equal opportunities for selection of women and men as microenterprise workers (revision of selection criteria to avoid exclusion of women), promoting gender equity in operational procedures (revision of the operational handbook), creation of rural committees that included women's group representatives, definition and monitoring of gender indicators and gender focal points in central and field staff, and gender training. No specific human or financial resources were allocated to gender in the project design, but there was flexibility to rearrange budget lines to target money and staff time for gender actions.

The implementing agency, Provias Descentralizado, hired a Peruvian gender consultant to guide the institutionalization of gender in Provias's operations. Under her guidance, Provias created a structure to address gender issues, including a gender coordinator and regional focal points, and developed a gender training program for managers and field staff, evaluated barriers to women's involvement in microenterprises for road maintenance, and developed and monitored gender-related indicators throughout the project cycle.[5] Gender equity was part of Provias's policy. Training for road operators on rehabilitation and maintenance of roads reached 1,018 participants, 35 percent of whom were women, and reached 11 percent of the direct beneficiaries.[6] Engineer monitors assisted in the nonmotorized transport and road rehabilitation (Caballaro and Alcahuasi 2007a; Forte and Menedez 2005; Gutiérrez 2006).

Community consultation workshops were organized in villages affected by the project. Separate sessions for women and men were convened to ensure that women were able to talk freely about transport needs and constraints. In response to local needs, particularly women's, the project rehabilitated 3,465 kilometers of nonmotorized transport tracks. The nonmotorized track rehabilitation involved the most vulnerable and excluded parts of the rural population in the planning process. These tracks proved to have a greater impact on economic growth and the roads, in part because they connected previously isolated communities with markets.

The LDW implemented a rapid rural poll, differentiated by sex, age, and economic status, to help ensure the inclusiveness of the participatory process, particularly for women. The LDW developed a network of strategic partnerships between civil society, government, and donors, built planning and fund-raising capacity and initiatives at the local level, and empowered women and communities to improve their lives (Dasso 2005). The LDW took into account women's needs, which resulted in the strong participation of women in the identification and implementation of entrepreneurial activities, as well as rural roads committees and cooperatives. Examples of projects include fish farming in Sauce Lake, benefiting 150 families, and production of organic, aromatic medicinal plants (Caballero 2007b; World Bank 2007).

GENDER APPROACH

Through a learning process over 10 years, the Peru Rural Roads Project has established a new, inclusive, demand-driven paradigm for transport planning and economic development (World Bank 2007: 39). Critical elements of this paradigm include participatory, inclusive project design and implementation; gender-informed project activities; the design of a set of interconnected, synergistic elements (rural road rehabilitation and maintenance, local microenterprise; LDW, and strengthening local governance capacity); and gender-sensitive monitoring and evaluation that informs the project. Involvement of the NGO Caritas and its local affiliates was very important in the inclusion of women in the project.

Gender equity in road maintenance

Gender equity in the performance-based contracting microenterprises for road and track maintenance was accomplished by modifications in the project operating manual requirements that recognized women's agricultural experience and roles as household managers and leaders of women's organizations as qualifying criteria and that dropped the literacy requirement. Gender awareness and quality of work were incorporated into the training. The participation of women in road maintenance was resisted at first, but the project prompted social change. After five years of women's participation, they proved themselves to be efficient and were able to overcome the initial gender stereotypes.[7] A new perception of women characterizes them as valiant, hard working, entrepreneurial, honest, and not corruptible (World Bank 2006b). Women's membership in these enterprises (24 percent) exceeded the requirement for 10 percent women.

Gender equity in the local development window

The LDW enhanced social capital and fostered community participation with a clear gender focus, which empowered women through 40 percent women's participation in local development initiatives (IBRD/IADB 2005). The LDW can serve as a coordination model that facilitates decentralization. It has established a decision-making mechanism from the bottom up that stimulates the empowerment of local men and women producers to decide their own future (Dasso 2005: 72).

Inclusive strengthening of local governance

Local Road Institutes worked with municipalities to develop strategies for road rehabilitation. Road committees approved the roads and tracks for rehabilitation, assigned tasks, paid wages, and organized the contribution of labor. The project required 20 percent of the members of road committees to be women. Thirty percent of the members elected by their communities, with Caritas guidance, were women.

Gender-sensitive monitoring and evaluation

Provias, the project-implementing agency, has continued to be a learning organization, based on performance monitoring. A social and impact monitoring system clarified the expected gender-differentiated outcomes and how different local realities might affect women's participation in project activities. The project team also developed gender-related indicators that were tracked throughout by the gender coordinator in Provias. Women's participation in maintenance microenterprises was monitored to ensure there was no bias against them. A gender impact assessment was conducted at the end of phase two.

BENEFITS AND IMPACTS

The project has increased income and household food security from roadwork and other microenterprise initiatives for women and men. It reduced travel time for women and men by up to one-half; rehabilitation of nonmotorized tracks significantly reduced the multitask burden of women, which reduced the opportunity cost of their time and increased their productivity and mobility choices. Seventy-seven percent of the women surveyed said they traveled more, and 67 percent said they felt they traveled more safely. Cleaner, safer tracks encouraged them to travel to sell agricultural products, obtain name registration,[8] deliver their babies in health centers, and participate in community meetings. Girl's access to primary education increased by 7 percent.

As a result of the project, 100 community organizations engaged in local development activities, and 500 microenterprises performed routine maintenance on roads. This created 6,000 one-year-equivalent unskilled jobs, 24 percent of which were held by women, which exceeded the 10 percent quota established in the gender action plan. Twenty-four percent of the members of rural roads committees were women, and 42 percent of the rural roads committee treasurers were women.

Women provided pragmatic input into project design, such as the request for rehabilitation of tracks, which had more impact on poverty alleviation than on the road rehabilitation. Women's participation has increased the efficiency, quality, and transparency of road maintenance microenterprises (World Bank 2007: 86). Women were more trusted because they were viewed as "incorruptible." They were more reliable in managing income because they were more transparent in accounts management and viewed corrupt practices more negatively than did men. They were more effective at negotiating payments and trusted to ensure that the quality of the work met the agreed technical standards. Women gained trust among their colleagues by doing a reliable job in managing funds, and they gained respect by motivating the team to achieve quality in road maintenance. Men stopped drinking during roadwork and took fewer breaks. Women also served as treasurers in 42 percent of the road committees, ensuring transparency.

Women's increased productivity contributes to overall economic growth. Women's income improves nutrition and increases education of children. The participation of women also had a positive impact on the efficiency of entrepreneurship activities generated through the local development window (Caballero and Alcahuasi 2007a; World Bank 2007: 84).

LESSONS LEARNED AND ISSUES FOR WIDER APPLICABILITY

- *Including gender equity within the project development objective* was the single most important element to justify the allocation of human and financial resources for gender activities.
- *Institutionalizing gender mainstreaming in the implementing agency is important.* The inclusion of the gender perspective in the agency was one of the keys to the success of the project. Building on existing human and institutional resources enhanced capacity to carry out sustainable gender actions. Social scientists in the project were eager to take on the gender work as a way of gaining leverage within the project. Participation of this staff in the design of the gender action plan enhanced their capacity to conduct gender analysis and established their ownership of the plan.
- *Institutional support for gender from donor agencies and the project implementation unit was crucial.* The World Bank missions sent a clear message that gender was important and allocated resources for gender activities. In the project implementation unit, the director supported the efforts of the gender focal points to put in place mechanisms to implement the gender action plan.
- *Gender champions are crucial for raising awareness of gender issues over time and contributing to sustained gender work.* Gender expertise was developed by the gender focal point in agency headquarters and the consultant hired to design and monitor the project's gender agenda. Staff and beneficiaries also helped mainstream gender in Provias's operations (Caballero and Alcahuasi 2007a). The Social Development Staff member in the World Bank Resident Mission played a key advocacy role throughout the life of the project, maintaining the momentum on the gender work by raising the gender issue to task managers and project implementation unit staff (Ruiz-Abril 2005).
- *Coordination of road rehabilitation with local productive activities can stimulate development and improve the efficiency and effectiveness of the rural roads project.* The local development window, implemented by a large national NGO, helped identify synergies between areas for productive growth, create linkages between local service providers, and coordinate access to key financial services in areas where the transport conditions were improved (Valdivia 2007; World Bank 2006a, 2007: 41).
- *Participation of the local population at all stages of the project is key to increase impacts and ensure the sustainability of investments* (Provias comment; World Bank 2007: 44). Community participation played an important role in the development of the project by providing guidance and advancing local development goals. Ensuring that women have an opportunity to express their needs during the participatory planning process is particularly important. This often requires separate discussion groups for women and meetings held in indigenous languages (Dasso 2005).
- *Management capacity building is crucial to guarantee a long-term impact on gender equity and the sustainability of gender know-how.* Identifying women leaders and ensuring their participation in training workshops could have been further developed (World Bank 2007: 89).
- *Local women's organizations can be excellent allies in fostering rural development and women's empowerment.*
- *Selecting a good partner is essential.* Building partnerships is not an easy task. It requires rules of engagement; standards for agreement; clear objectives; precise conditions, roles, and functions; a balance of contributions from the parties; and, most of all, trust.
- *The local development window requires systematization to expand and replicate it elsewhere in Peru.* Guidelines are needed on the contents, methodology, and process for implementing the LDW, combined with training workshops (Dasso 2005). An organized project funding logic is needed as well. A need is present for diversification and use of local productivity chains (IBRD/IADB 2005).
- *Gender-sensitive monitoring is very important to ensure that the gender action plan is implemented and to inform and improve the next phase of the project.* Comprehensive measures of direct and indirect effects of rural transport services and induced economic activities on women's welfare and access to income-generating activities are important. It is also important to measure the value added from women's participation. If performance measures for road maintenance activities had taken the quality of work more into account, it would have provided more evidence of the value added by women's participation (World Bank 2007).

Malaysia: Community E-Centers

Malaysia provides an interesting example of overall rural telecommunications access. The United Nations Economic and Social Commission for Asia and the Pacific (UNESCAP) and Malaysia's Institut Tadbiran Awam Negara (INTAN) have compiled an online how-to guidebook on setting up and running a community e-center (UNESCAP 2006). The guidebook chronicles the experiences of three rural projects in Malaysia (Rural Internet Centre, Medan InfoDesa, and eBario Project),[1] using their successes and failures to inform community groups interested in setting up their own center. Community e-centers (CeCs) are public-access facilities that provide electronic communication and multimedia services. The long-term goal is to reduce poverty through increased digital literacy and greater control and access to ICTs.

Telecommunications access in rural areas is best provided in a community center that is open equally to men and women. In recent years, a number of CeCs have been piloted worldwide, but very few are successful, because most of them are not financially sustainable and do not really engage directly with the community. The community e-centers case studies presented here have some good practice guidelines because they address sustainability issues from the standpoints both of financial viability and of community engagement and participation.

CeCs can have several functions. They will enable the communities to access new knowledge and information that can be incorporated into their local knowledge and context, such as information on employment opportunities, educational resources, government services (for example, providing links to e-government), and technical information on agriculture for their daily lives, such as information on new varieties of crops, planting techniques, and disease prevention. The CeCs may also be used as training centers for local people to learn and practice their computer and ICT skills, to provide access to distance education (e-learning), for human resource training, and for business ventures. The CeCs can also allow entrepreneurs to plan and prepare their business arrangements and to communicate with partners and potential clients from a distance (e-commerce).

Through the Internet students and educators can register with educational institutions at any location in the world, access archival materials, or receive online instruction. CeCs can also serve distance education to students by providing educational software packages on site and upgrading them as new educational packages are produced.

Specialized services can also be offered to health care workers, enabling them to use telediagnostics programs, order supplies, convey public health information, and obtain specialist advice for complex health problems. In this respect CeCs serve as "virtual roads" or communication highways that can benefit the society.

GENDER APPROACH

The online *eSourcebook* has mainstreamed gender considerations throughout. It lists equity-oriented questions that should be answered in the planning, monitoring, and evaluation stages. Questions challenge communities to articulate

---

What's innovative? Community e-centers provide electronic communication services, especially in marginalized or remote areas where ICTs are not prevalent. The centers serve as avenues for providing universal-access communications and multimedia services to rural communities, including telephones, faxes, computers, the Internet, photocopiers, and other equipment and services. One of the innovations is the focus on people and not just on technology.

the different groups' needs and constraints so that they can be met and mitigated, to identify which groups will be empowered by the CeC, to outline how gender equity can be achieved through hiring and hours of operation, and to assess which types of technologies are most appropriate. The guidebook suggests not only monitoring ICT use on an ongoing basis but also keeping records of the distance people traveled to the CeC and their mode of transportation. Evaluation of the CeC's contribution to the overall socioeconomic development of the community is recommended. Such gender mainstreaming increases the potential for benefits accrued to rural women and minimizes the constraints they face.

BENEFITS AND IMPACTS

The short-term benefits of the three CeC case studies included the provision of ubiquitous, affordable, equitable, and quality access to ICTs. Before the eBario project began in 1999, 90 percent of villagers had never used a computer. Now the community is world renowned as an innovative community en route to bridging the digital divide. The project has spurred a local tourist industry, resulting in the creation of new job opportunities. These new opportunities have encouraged youth and young families to remain in Bario and consequently have decreased the rates of rural-urban migration. The project's Web site enabled local producers to sell their food products and handicrafts online. There are broader political ramifications: the Malaysian government has become sensitized to the potential of ICT-induced rural development and is supporting other villages to set up CeCs.

LESSONS LEARNED AND ISSUES FOR WIDER APPLICABILITY

Based on the case studies, the following factors are essential to the success of the CeCs:

■ *Focus on people, organization, contents, and processes rather than technology.* The key to success is very much a focus on the very people the CeCs are targeting. For CeCs to work, a proper organizational structure needs to be put in place. Technology implementation is generally the easiest component to implement.
■ *Relevant to local needs.* The CeC's existence and sustainability are tied to the capacity of CeCs in meeting the actual needs of the community. Applications and services of CeCs should be driven by the needs of communities (demand driven).

■ *Community participation. The* members of the target community of the CeCs must participate in the whole process of setting up the CeCs. They are not only the ones who are aware of the needs of the community, but also the ones who will be managing the CeCs in the long run because NGOs, government bodies, and sponsors may be able to assist for only one or two years.
■ *Roles of local champions.* In the Malaysian context local champions of the case studies are a key component in the success of the CeC. These local champions are passionate about helping their community to improve. These local champions act as catalysts and motivators to the project and persevere through setbacks.
■ *Smart partnerships.* Partnerships among various stakeholders are required throughout the process of the development of a CeC. Stakeholders include governmental bodies (which provide approvals, funds, and advice to NGOs), NGOs (which provide human resources and training to private companies and the community), private companies (which may assist in the forms of sponsorship), and the community that will be affected by the project, to name a few. In the case of eBario, in addition to Universiti Malaysia Sarawak (UNIMAS) and the Bario community, which were the main organizers of the project, other partners included the Marudi District Council (which provided approvals and the premises), government ministries, NGOs, and private companies (Comserv and Telekom Malaysia).
■ *Training programs.* As the community will be using and running the CeCs, the community must be prepared to be able to use and run the CeCs effectively and efficiently. Skills, such as management skills, computer literacy, and maintenance skills, are essential to the continued operation of the CeCs.
■ *Business plan.* CeCs that intend to be financially independent must have a business plan. The business plan provides a description of the organization, the objectives of the CeC, how the objectives are to be achieved, the market of the business, financial forecasts, and earnings targets.

Although CeCs may start out with external donor funding or a grant and may rely to a large extent on volunteer support, their goal is always to be able to generate adequate revenue through the provision of services and, eventually, to become self-sustainable. To achieve this goal, the multipurpose CeCs need to be managed well and provide services that are in demand, because even CeCs that are nonprofit entities need to be financially viable to be successful. Key factors that have enabled successful CeCs to become sustainable include the following:

- *Community ownership is crucial:* organizational structures should provide authority, responsibility, and management of resources to the community.
- *Locally relevant content/services should be designed and implemented to suit the needs of the community.*
- *Technology options that provide affordable and universal local connectivity, including the use of multimedia (radio, video, TV, and the like), must be carefully examined.*
- *Financial and operational sustainability needs to be obtained over a period of time.* Sustainability has other dimensions beyond self-financing, such as the social, cultural, political, and technological arenas. Social and cultural sustainability is measured by whether it empowers people in the community, meets the needs of various groups (men and women, young and old), and allows for community ownership and engagement. Political sustainability is measured in terms of whether a stable regulatory framework to promote and support CeCs has been secured. Technological sustainability is measured in terms of whether appropriate technology options were chosen for the community. Financial sustainability indicates whether a CeC is fully or partially viable, whether it can recover its capital investment, operational expenses, and replace equipment as needed or can recover only operational expenses but not the initial and future capital investments.

NOTES

Overview

This Overview was written by Dominique Lallement (World Bank) and reviewed by Mari H. Clarke, Rekha Dayal, Catherine Ragasa, Christine Sijbesma, and Nidhi Tandon (Consultants); Clare O'Farrell (FAO); Moses Abukari, Rudolph Cleveringa, Maria Hartl, and Audrey Nepveu (IFAD); and Nilufar Ahmad, Indira Ekanayake, and Eija Pehu (World Bank).

1. This Module uses the term *agricultural development* to include crops, forestry, livestock, fisheries, land and water, agroindustries, and the environment (see *Sourcebook Overview*).

2. According to a UNIDO and International Fund for Agricultural Development project cited in Blackden and Wodon (2006).

3. R. Srinivasan, "Stealing Farmers' Water to Quench Chennai's Thirst," InfoChangeAgenda, March, www.infochangeindia.org.

Thematic Note 1

This Thematic Note was written by Mari H. Clarke (Consultant) and reviewed by Dominique Lallement and Catherine Ragasa (Consultants); Moses Abukari, Rudolph Cleveringa, Maria Hartl, and Audrey Nepveu (IFAD); and Indira Ekanayake and Eija Pehu (World Bank).

1. The specific nature of men's and women's transport tasks varies by country, socioeconomic status, age, ethnic group, location, household livelihood strategies, and other factors.

2. Obstetric fistula is a hole that forms between the vagina and the bladder or the rectum as a result of prolonged (an average of 3.8 days) and obstructed labor of young, often teenage, mothers. This is prevalent where teenage marriage is the cultural norm and access to emergency obstetrical care is limited (Riverson and others 2005).

3. For example, because of safety issues related to women's travel after long hours in agroprocessing work in Guatemala, a company provided dormitory housing for women during peak processing periods (Dolan and Sorby 2003).

4. Reidar Kvam, personal communication, 2007.

5. Access has two components: (a) mobility, meaning the a ease or difficulty of travel to a service or facility and (b) proximity of the services and facilities.

6. An all-season road is passable year-round by the prevailing means of transport (typically a truck or four-wheel-drive). Occasional interruptions of short duration are accepted. All-season access is less than 40 percent in sub-Saharan Africa and the Middle East and North Africa (Roberts, Shyam, and Rastogi 2006).

7. International Labour Organization (ILO), "Asia Pacific Integrated Rural Accessibility Planning," Second Expert Group Meeting, September 5–6, 2000, Bangkok, www.ilo.org/public/english/employment/recon/eiip/download/ratp/ratp08.pdf.

Thematic Note 2

This Thematic Note was written by Dominique Lallement (World Bank) and reviewed by Elizabeth Cecelski (Consultant); Moses Abukari, Rudolph Cleveringa, Maria Hartl, and Audrey Nepveu (IFAD); Tanja Winther (Oslo University); and Douglas Barnes and Indira Ekanayake (World Bank).

1. In particular through UN organizations (UNIFEM, FAO, and UNDP) and bilateral agencies—namely, DFID (U.K.), the Netherlands, SIDA (Sweden), USAID (U.S.), and, more recently, GTZ (Germany)—that have included gender as one of the main pillars of their energy assistance programs.

2. Winrock, "Grameen Shakti & Winrock Show the Way: Biogas Offers Fuel, Health and Income Solutions in Bangladesh," Solution Story, South Asia Energy Initiative

Grants Project, Winrock International, Little Rock, AR, www.winrock.org.

3. Joy Clancy, Margaret Skutsch, and Simon Batchelor, "The Gender-Energy-Poverty Nexus: Finding the Energy to Address Gender Concerns in Development," project funded by U.K. Department for International Development, www.sarpn.org.za.

4. Because labor is considered a factor of production, only when women's labor is valued above men's labor do households move from collecting fuelwood to purchasing fuelwood or another fuel commodity, so that the time saved from fuel collection can be invested in other women's income-generating activities.

5. See http://energia-africa.org/GenderAudits.

6. A summary of these tools is provided in ESMAP (2003a).

Thematic Note 3

This Thematic Note was written by Nidhi Tandon (Consultant) and reviewed by Dominique Lallement, Kerry McNamara, and Catherine Ragasa (Consultants); Clare O'Farrell (FAO); Maria Hartl (IFAD); and Indira Ekanayake, Kayoko Chibata Medlin, and Samia Melhem (World Bank).

1. C. K. Pralahad, quoted in *The Economist*, July 9–15, 2005: "Calling an End to Poverty."

2. Andersson et al. 2007.

3. "Sixty to 70 percent of Africa's population live in rural areas and rely heavily on traditional and unprocessed biomass (for example, wood, animal dung, agricultural waste) for their daily domestic energy needs, with limited choice and options of fuels for their productive activities. The rate of access to modern energy in these areas has dropped to as low as 1 percent, in some countries" (UNECA 2005: 9).

4. Simone Cecchini, and Monica Raina, "Village Information Kiosks for the Warana Cooperatives in India," Success/Failure Case Study No. 1 eGovernment for Development, University of Manchester, www.egov4dev.org/warana. htm; National Informatics Centre, "Project Proposal for Wired Village Project at Warana Nagar, Maharashtra," National Informatics Centre, Pune, India, www.mah.nic.in/warana.

5. BBC World Service Trust, "Building Basic Education in Somalia," www.bbc.co.uk.

6. www.comminit.com/en/node/118505;"Building Basic Education in Somalia" (February 22, 2007), www.bbc.co.uk.

7. www.apcob.org.bo.

8. www.healthunlimited.org.

9. www.equalaccess.org; "Equal Access-Making Digital Broadcast Work for Development," www.un.org.

10. "e Lanka Development," www.worldbank.org.

11. www.fao.org/dimitra; "Dimitra Project, Rural Women and Development," www.itu.int/net/home/index.aspx.

12. www.fijifriend.com; www.genderawards.net.

13. www.genderawards.net.

14. www.fao.org/sd/ruralradio; www.simbani.amarc.org.

15. www.hra.am/eng/?page=organization&id=70; www.genderawards.net.

16. Leelangi Wanasundera, "Expanding Women's Capacities through Access to ICT: An Overview from Sri Lanka," paper presented at Gender Perspectives on the Information Society South Asia Pre-WSIS Seminar, Bangalore, India, April 18–19, www.itforchange.net.

Thematic Note 4

This Thematic Note was written by Christine Sijbesma (Consultant) and reviewed by Dominique Lallement and Catherine Ragasa (Consultants); Maria Hartl and Laurent Stravato (IFAD); and Indira Ekanayake (World Bank).

1. See, for example, www.freshschools.org/water&sanitation.htm.

Innovative Activity Profile I

This Innovative Activity Profile was written by Mari H. Clarke (Consultant) and reviewed by Dominique Lallement (Consultant); Moses Abukari, Rudolph Cleveringa, Maria Hartl, and Audrey Nepveu (IFAD); and Luz Caballero (World Bank).

1. A national household survey in 2001 found that indigenous people represent over 45 percent of the Peruvian population. Nearly 64 percent of these households are poor, and more than 35 percent are extremely poor. A small proportion of the indigenous people live in the Amazon region (World Bank 2006a: 86).

2. The net economic rate of return was 31 percent (World Bank 2007: 26).

3. "Local development window" reflects opening a window of opportunity through which rural communities could translate their expectations into actions and realities (World Bank 2001: 72). This approach builds on indigenous traditions of reciprocity, solidarity, and community work (Dasso 2005: 65; World Bank 2006b: 131).

4. Seventy percent of the illiterate population is Peru consists of monolingual rural indigenous women (World Bank 2006b: 132).

5. Examples of indicators include the number of women involved in the maintenance of rural roads, the number of women attending community meetings related to transport, and the percentage of women attending training workshops on transport and gender (World Bank 2006b: 134–35).

6. Training on gender and road management for project operators (Project Implementation Unit personnel, Rural Roads Institutes, and external consultants) and rural road

operators (microenterprises and members of road committees) in three phases: sensitization on gender, gender in the project cycle, and decentralization and road network management with a gender approach (Gutiérrez 2007).

7. The most common reason given for excluding women from road maintenance was the assumption that the work was too physically demanding. Husbands were also reluctant to authorize their wives' work on the road because men are supposed to be the breadwinners, and both men and women were concerned about what others would think of families whose women worked on the road (World Bank 2007).

8. About 25 percent of the Peruvian population is undocumented because of limited access to name registration, home birthing, and other factors. Most of the undocumented people are rural, indigenous, illiterate, and women (Caballero and Alcahuasi 2007a: 4).

Innovative Activity Profile 2

This Innovative Activity Profile was written by Nidhi Tandon (Consultant) and reviewed by Dominique Lallement and Catherine Ragasa (Consultants); Maria Hartl (IFAD); and Eija Pehu (World Bank). This Profile was largely drawn from UNESCAP (2006).

1. The eBario project has been internationally recognized for its innovativeness and effectiveness and has won several awards, including the Mondialogo Award (2005, Berlin), eAsia Award (2004, Taipei), Anugerah Perdana Teknologi Maklumat (2003, Kuala Lumpur), Industry Innovators Award for Systems Development & Applications from the Society of Satellite Professionals International (March 2002, Washington, DC), Top Seven Intelligent Communities by the World Teleport Association in 2001, and, recently, the Gold Medal of the Commonwealth Association of Public Administration and Management (CAPAM) International Innovations Awards in Sydney, Australia, on October 25, 2006 (see www.researchsea.com).

REFERENCES

Overview

Barwell, Ian. 1996. "Rural Transport in Developing Countries." In *Engendering Development,* Policy Research Report. Washington, DC: World Bank.

Blackden, C. Mark. 2006. "Gender and Energy in Uganda." Background Note for Country Assistance Strategy, World Bank, Washington, DC.

Blackden, C. Mark, and Quentin Wodon, eds. 2006. "Gender, Time Use, and Poverty in Sub-Saharan Africa." World Bank Working Paper No. 73, World Bank, Washington, DC.

Canadian Standards Association. 2007. *Climate Change and Infrastructure Engineering: Towards a New Curriculum.* Ottawa: IHS Publisher.

Clarke, M. 2007. "Background Paper on Gender, Enterprise, and Infrastructure." Pre-conference on Enterprise Development, African and Global Lessons for More Effective Donor Practices from Women's Perspective, GTZ, October 15.

Department for International Development (DFID). 2002. "Energy for the Poor: Underpinning the Millennium Development Goals." U.K. Government, London, August.

Energy Sector Management Assistance Program (ESMAP). 1999. "Household Energy Strategies for Urban India: The Case of Hyderabad." Report 214/99, World Bank, Washington, DC. Also available at www.esmap.org.

———. 2001. "Rural Electrification and Development in the Philippines: Measuring the Social and Economic Benefits." Report 243/01, World Bank, Washington, DC.

ESMAP-Global Village Energy Partnership (GVEP). 2003. "Energy-Poverty Reduction Workshop." Dakar, Senegal, Field Visit, February, World Bank, Washington, DC.

Grieco, Margaret. 2002. "Gender, Social Inclusion, and Rural Infrastructure." Final Report for the World Bank, World Bank, Washington, DC.

Gutiérrez, María. 2007. "Peru: Benefits from Gender Sensitive Approach to Rural Roads." Paper presented at workshop on transport and gender, World Bank, Washington, DC, March 22.

Ilahi, Nadeem, and Franque Grimard. 2000. *Public Infrastructure and Private Costs: Water Supply and Time Allocation of Women in Rural Pakistan.* Economic Development and Cultural Change. Chicago: University of Chicago Press.

Infodev. 2006. "Improving Health, Connecting People." Draft Report, World Bank, Washington, DC.

Kumar, Shubh K., and David Hotchkiss. 1988. *Consequences of Deforestation for Women's Time.* Washington, DC: IFPRI.

Lallement, Dominique. 2007. "Opportunities for Women's Participation in Infrastructure Labor Market in Liberia." Draft Report, World Bank, Washington, DC, June.

Lallement, Dominique, and Judy Siegel. 2002. "Energy and Poverty Reduction." PowerPoint presentation at World Summit Sustainable Development–WSSD, World Bank and Global Village Energy Partnership, Johannesburg, September.

Potgieter, Cheryl-Ann, Renay Pillay, and Sharmla Rama. 2006. *Women, Development and Transport in Rural Eastern Cape, South Africa.* South Africa National Roads Agency. Cape Town: HSRC Press.

Saito, Katrine, Hailu Mekonnen, and Daphne Spurling. 1994. "Raising the Productivity of Women Farmers in

Sub-Saharan Africa." Discussion Paper 230, World Bank, Washington, DC.

Sotomayor, Maria Angelica. 2007. "Mainstreaming Gender in Water and Sanitation: Lessons from Paraguay." Power-Point presentation, Water Week, World Bank, Washington, DC, March.

UNICEF. 2006. "Progress for Children: A Report Card on Water and Sanitation." Report, United Nations, New York.

Thematic Note I

Ahmad, Nilufar. 2007. "Bangladesh: Women's Empowerment through Rural Transport and Markets." Paper presented at the World Bank Roundtable on Mainstreaming Gender in Transport, Washington, DC, June 20.

Asian Development Bank (ADB). 2003. "Gender Checklist: Resettlement." ADB, Manila.

———. 2004. "LAO PDR: Gender, Poverty and the MDGs." Mekong and Regional Sustainable Development Departments, ADB, Manila.

Babinard, Julie, and Peter Roberts. 2006. "Maternal and Child Mortality Development Goals: What Can the Transport Sector Do?" World Bank Transport Sector Board Transport Papers TP-12, World Bank, Washington, DC.

Barrientos, Stephanie, Naila Kabeer, and Naomi Hossain. 2004. "The Gender Dimensions of Global Production." Working Paper 17, Policy Integration Department, World Commission on Social Dimension of Globalization, International Labour Organization, Geneva.

Blackden, C. Mark. 2003. "Too Much Work and Too Little Time: Gender Dimensions of Transport, Water and Energy." Paper presented at a World Bank–sponsored training event, Arusha, Tanzania, February 3–7.

Blackden, C. Mark, and Quentin Wodon, eds. 2006. "Gender, Time Use, and Poverty in Sub-Saharan Africa." World Bank, Washington, DC.

Caballero, Luz. 2007. "Peru Second Rural Roads Project: Gender Mainstreaming along the Road: Walking towards Women's Empowerment and Democracy." PowerPoint presentation for World Bank Roundtable on Mainstreaming Gender and Social Dimensions in Transport Programs, World Bank, Washington, DC, June.

Cernea, Michael. 2000. "Risks, Safeguards, and Reconstruction: A Model for Population Displacement and Resettlement." In Risks and Reconstruction: Experiences of Resettlers and Refugees, ed. Michael Cernea and Chris McDowell, 11–55. Washington, DC: World Bank.

Clarke, Mari H. 2007. "Progress Report on the Dissemination of Gender and Transport Good Practices." Paper prepared for the World Bank, Energy Transport & Water Department–Transport Unit (ETWTR), Washington, DC, October.

Cook, Cynthia. 2003. "Multisectoral HIV/AIDs Projects in Africa: A Social Analysis Perspective." Social Development Paper 43, World Bank, Washington, DC.

Dolan, Catherine, and Kristina Sorby. 2003. "Gender and Employment in High-Value Agricultural Industries." Agriculture and Rural Development Working Paper 7, World Bank, Washington, DC.

Donnges, Chris. 2003. "Improving Access in Rural Areas: Guidelines for Rural Accessibility Planning." International Labour Organization, Geneva.

Edmonds, Geoff. 1998. "Wasted Time: the Price of Poor Access." International Labour Organization, Geneva.

Essakali, Mohammed Dalil. 2005. "Rural Access and Mobility in Pakistan: A Policy Note." Transport Note 28, Roads, Highways and Rural Transport Thematic Group, World Bank, Washington, DC.

Fouracre, Phil. 2001. "Transport and Sustainable Livelihoods." Rural Transport Knowledge Base. Module 5:3:a. World Bank, Washington, DC, and Department for International Development (DFID), London. Also available at www4.worldbank.org/afr/ssatp/Resources/HTML/rural_transport/ knowledge_base/English/Con tents.htm.

Gender and Rural Transport Initiative. 2002. "Ghana and Malawi Country Reports." In Gender and Transport Resource Guide, Module 4, Country Reports 5 and 9. Washington, DC: Africa Region Transport Group, World Bank.

Graeco, Margaret. 2002. "Gender, Social Inclusion and Rural Infrastructure Services." Report, World Bank, Washington, DC, June 14.

Hine, J., S. Ellis, and S. Done. 2002. "Ghana Feeder Road Prioritization." International Labour Organization Conference, Maputo, May.

International Forum for Rural Transport and Development (IFRTD). 2003. "Waterway Livelihoods: Improving Rural Access and Mobility through the Development of Rural Water Transport." Toolkit, IFRTD, London. Also available at www.ruralwaterways.org.

International Transport Workers Federation (ITF). 2007. "Agenda: Challenging HIV/AIDS in Transport." Agenda, Issue 1. London: ITF.

Ishihara, Satoshi. 2007. "CDD and Transport: the Azerbaijan Experience." Presentation at World Bank Roundtable on Mainstreaming Gender in Transport, Washington, DC, June 20.

Kunieda, Mika, and Aimée Gauthier. 2007. "Gender and Urban Transport: Smart and Affordable." In Sustainable Transport: A Sourcebook for Policy-Makers in Developing Cities, Module 7a. Eschborn: German Federal Ministry for Economic Cooperation and Development.

Lallement, Dominique. 2007. "Women's Economic Empowerment through Participation in Labor Markets Created by Bank-Financed Infrastructure Projects." World Bank, Washington, DC, June.

Latif, Shireen. 2005. "Gender in Road Infrastructure." Presentation at Transport Infrastructure and Poverty Reduction Workshop, Asian Development Bank, Manila, July 18–20.

Lema, Antoine, Stephen Brushett, Negede Lewi, John Riverson, and Silue Siele. 2003. "Taming HIV/AIDS on Africa's Roads." Sub-Saharan Africa Transport Policy Program (SSATP) Technical Note 35, May, World Bank, Washington, DC.

Levy, Hernan. 2004. "Rural Roads and Poverty Alleviation in Morocco." Paper presented at the Scaling Up Poverty Reduction Conference, Shanghai, May 25–27, Session C1, Case 2, World Bank, Washington, DC.

Malmberg-Calvo, Christina. 1994. "Case Study on the Role of Women in Rural Transport: Access of Women to Domestic Facilities." Sub-Saharan Africa Transport Policy Program (SSATP) Working Paper 11, World Bank, Washington, DC.

———. 1998. "Options for Managing and Financing Rural Transport Infrastructure." Technical Paper 411, World Bank, Washington, DC.

Maramba, Petronella, and Michael Bamberger. 2001. "A Gender Responsive Monitoring and Evaluation System for Rural Travel and Transport Programs in Africa: A Handbook for Planners, Managers and Evaluators." Sub-Saharan Africa Transport Policy Program (SSATP) Working Paper 55, World Bank, Washington, DC.

Mutemba, Shimwaayi, and C. Mark Blackden. 2000. "The Gender Dimensions of HIV/AIDS: Putting Gender on the MAP." Technical Note, World Bank, Washington, DC, December.

Peters, Deike. 2002. "Gender and Transport in Less Developed Countries." Paper commissioned by UNED Forum for expert workshop on "Gender Perspectives for the Earth Summit 2002," Berlin, January 20.

Plessis-Fraissard, Maryvonne. 2007. "Planning Roads for Rural Communities." Paper presented at the Low Volume Roads Conference, Austin, June 24–27.

Pulley, Tülin Akin, Shireen Lateef, and Ferdousi Sultana Begum. 2003. "Making Infrastructure Work for Women in Bangladesh." Asian Development Bank, Manila.

Quisumbing, Agnes. 2003. "What Have We Learned from Research on Intrahousehold Allocation." In *Household Decision, Gender and Development: A Synthesis of Recent Research,* ed. Agnes Quisumbing, 1–16. Washington, DC: International Food Policy Research Institute.

Rankin, Elizabeth. 1999. "Gender and Transport: A Strategy for Africa." World Bank, Washington, DC.

Rao, Nitya. 2002. "Cycling into the Future: The Experience of Women in Pudukkottai Tamil Nadu." In *Balancing the Load: Women, Gender and Transport,* eds. Priyanthi Fernando and Gina Porter, 186–205. London: Zed Books.

Riverson, John, Mika Kunieda, Peter Roberts, Negede Lewi, and Wendy Walker. 2005. "The Challenges in Addressing Gender Dimensions of Transport in Developing Countries: Lessons from the World Bank's Projects." World Bank, Washington, DC.

Roberts, Peter, K. C. Shyam, and Cordula Rastogi. 2006. "Rural Access Index: Key Development Indicators." Transport Sector Board Transport Paper 10, World Bank, Washington, DC.

Shyam, K. C. 2007. "Rural Accessibility and Gender Differences in School Enrollment in Nepal." Paper presented at the World Bank Roundtable on Mainstreaming Gender in Transport, Washington, DC, June 20.

Starkey, Paul. 2001. "Local Transport Solutions: People, Paradoxes and Progress: Lessons Arising from the Spread of Intermediate Means of Transport." Sub-Saharan Africa Transport Policy Program (SSATP) Working Paper 56, World Bank, Washington, DC.

———. 2002. *Local Transport Solutions for Rural Development.* London: Department for International Development.

Starkey, Paul, Simon Ellis, John Hine, and Anna Ternell. 2003. "Improving Rural Mobility: Options for Developing Motorized and Non-Motorized Transport in Rural Areas." Technical Paper 525, World Bank, Washington, DC.

Swedish International Development Cooperation Agency (SIDA). 1997. *Handbook for Mainstreaming a Gender Perspective in the Rural Transport Sector.* Stockholm: SIDA.

Tanzarn, Nite, Jeff Turner, Meike Spitzner, and Rolf Hennes. 2007. "Labor-Based Methods: A Key Area for Mainstreaming Gender in the Road Infrastructure Sector." Paper presented at the 12th Regional Seminar for Labor Intensive Construction, Kwa Zulu Natal, South Africa, October.

Tichagwa, Wilfred. 2000. "Gender and Rural Travel and Transport: Zimbabwe." Report prepared for the World Bank Gender and Rural Transport Initiative, World Bank, Washington, DC.

Tiwari, Geetam. 2001. "Social Dimensions of Transport Planning." Transport Research and Injury Prevention Programme, Indian Institute of Technology, Delhi, February.

Transport Research Laboratory (TRL) and Department for International Development (DFID). 2000. "Estimating Global Road Fatalities." TRL Report 445, TRL, Berkshire, U.K.

Walker, Wendy, Shalini Vajjhala, Thasi Phomane, Nonkuleleko Zaly, Senate Moonyane, and M. Mokhoro. 2005. "Ground Truthing: Mobility Mapping and Access in Rural Lesotho." World Bank and Lesotho Ministry of Public Works, April.

World Bank. 2000. "Can Africa Claim the 21st Century?" Report prepared jointly by the African Development Bank, African Economic Research Consortium, Global Coalition for Africa, Economic Commission for Africa, and World Bank, Washington, DC.

———. 2001. "Gender Inequality Hinders Development." In *Engendering Development: through Gender Equality in Rights, Resources, and Voice,* 73–106. Policy Research Report. Washington, DC: World Bank.

———. 2006. "Rural Infrastructure in Peru: Effectively Underpinning Local Development and Fostering Complementarities." Finance, Private Sector and Infrastructure Unit, Latin America and the Caribbean, World Bank, Washington, DC, January 26.

———. 2007a. "A Decade of Action in Transport: An Evaluation of World Bank Assistance to the Transport Sector 1995–2005." World Bank, Washington, DC.

———. 2007b. "The Second Peru Rural Roads Transport Project Implementation Completion Report." World Bank, Washington, DC.

———. n.d. "Case Study 8: Gender Mainstreaming: Rural Roads and the Transport Sector. Module III. Integrating Gender into Transport Projects." World Bank Institute, Washington, DC.

World Health Organization. 2004. "World Report on Safety and Injury Prevention." World Health Organization, Geneva.

———. 2003a. "Monitoring and Evaluation in Rural Electrification Projects: A Demand-Oriented Approach." Technical Paper 037, World Bank, Washington, DC.

———. 2003b. *The Impact of Energy in Women's Lives in Rural India.* ESMAP Formal Report 276, World Bank, Washington, DC.

———. 2004. "Opportunities for Women in Renewable Energy Technology Use in Bangladesh (Phase 1)." World Bank, Washington, DC, April.

Lallement, Dominique. 2008. "Evaluation of Women's Energy Cooperative in Char Montaz." World Bank, Washington, DC.

Parikh, Jyoti, and Saudamini Sharma. 2006. "Energy Poverty and the Gender Nexus in Himachal Pradesh." ENERGIA International Network on Gender and Sustainable Energy, Leusden, the Netherlands.

United Nations Development Programme (UNDP). 2001. "Generating Opportunities: Case Studies on Energy and Women." UNDP, New York.

World Bank. 2003. "Senegal: Sustainable and Participatory Energy Management." World Bank, Washington, DC.

———. 2007. "Lao PDR. Making Infrastructure Responsible to Women's Needs." World Bank, Washington, DC.

World Health Organization. 2002. "Healthy Environments for Children: Initiating an Alliance for Action." World Health Organization, Geneva, Switzerland.

Thematic Note 2

Agarwal, Bina. 2001. "Participatory Exclusions, Community Forestry, and Gender: An Analysis for South Asia and a Conceptual Framework." *World Development* 29 (10): 1623–48.

Blackden, Marc. 2007. *Gender and Energy: Issues for the PEAP Revisions.* Washington, DC: World Bank.

Branco, Adelia de Melo. 1997. "Women of the Drought: A Study of Employment, Mobilization and Change in Northeastern Brazil." University of Manitoba, Manitoba, Canada.

Dayal, Rekha. 2007. "Learning from Best Practices." Background Paper for Rural Infrastructure Module, World Bank, Washington, DC.

Department for International Development (DFID). 2002. "Energy for the Poor: Underpinning the Millennium Development Goals." U.K. government, London, August.

ESMAP. 2002. "The Development of Rural Electrification in the Philippines: Measuring the Socio and Economic Impact." Report 255/02, World Bank, Washington, DC.

Thematic Note 3

Andersson, Ingrid, Ananya Raihan, Milagros Rivera, Idris Sulaiman, Nidhi Tandon, and Friederike Welter. 2007. *Handbook on Women-owned SMEs: Challenges and Opportunities in Policies and Programmes.* Sponsored by International Organisation of Knowledge Economy and Enterprise Development and Global Knowledge Partnership. Malmö, Sweden: IKED. Available at www.iked.org.

Burch, Sally. 2007. "Knowledge Sharing for Rural Development: Challenges, Experiences and Methods." Latin American Information Agency, Quito.

FAO and GTZ. 2006. *Framework on Effective Rural Communication for Development,* ed. Riccardo Del Castello and Paul Mathias Braun. Rome: FAO.

Hafkin, Nancy. 2007. "Critical Issues and Approaches for Designing Policy Relevant Research on Strengthening Women's Control of ICTs as Development Assets." Paper presented during the Consultation on Strengthening Women's Control of Assets, International Food Policy Research Institute, Washington, DC, November 14.

Piepenstock, Anne, Orlando Arratia, and Luis Carlos Aguilar. 2006. "New Technologies Support Farmers'

Documentation." *LEISA Magazine on Low External Input and Sustainable Agriculture* 22 (1): 28–29.

Talyarkhan, Surmaya, with David J. Grimshaw and Lucky Lowe. 2004. "Connecting the First Mile: A Framework for Best Practice in ICT Projects for Knowledge Sharing in Development." Intermediate Technology Development Group (ITDG, now Practical Action), Rugby U.K. Also available at www.itdg.org.

United Nations Economic Commission for Africa (UNECA). 2005. "African Regional Implementation Review for the 14th Session of the Commission on Sustainable Development (CSD-14)," Report on Energy for Sustainable Development in Africa. Also available at www.uneca. org/csd/CSD4_Report_on_Energy_for_Sustainaible_ Development.htm.

Thematic Note 4

Appleton, Brian, and Ian Smout, eds. 2003. "The Gender and Water Development Report: Gender Perspectives on Policies in the Water Sector." Water Engineering Development Centre (WEDC), Loughborough, U.K. Also available at www.genderandwater.org/content/download/307/3228/file/GWA_Annual_Report.pdf.

Arrais, Silvia Cavalcanti. 1996. "Selective Solid Waste Collection and Recycling in Recife, Brazil." In *Best Practices: Water Supply, Sanitation and Solid Waste Collection Services in Low Income Urban Areas* (Summaries prepared by IRC and partners for the Habitat II conference), 21–23. The Hague, Netherlands: IRC International Water and Sanitation Centre.

Austin, John, Lizette Burgers, Sandy Cairncross, Andrew Cotton, Val Curtis, Barbara Evans, and others. 2005. "Sanitation and Hygiene Promotion: Programming Guidance." Water Supply and Sanitation Collaborative Council, Geneva, Switzerland. Also available at www.wsscc.org/pdf/publication/Sani_Hygiene_Promo.pdf.

Burrows, Gideon, Jules Acton, and Tamsin Maunder. 2004. "Water and Sanitation: The Education Drain," Education Media Report 3, WaterAid, London. Also available at www.wateraid.org/documents/education20report.pdf.

Cairncross, Sandy, and Vivian Valdmanis. 2006. "Water Supply, Sanitation and Hygiene Promotion." In *Disease Control Priorities in Developing Countries,* ed. Dean Jamison and others. Washington, DC: World Bank. Also available at www.dcp2.org/pubs/DCP.

Coates, Sue. 1999. "A Gender and Development Approach to Water, Sanitation and Hygiene Programmes." A WaterAid Briefing Paper, WED, Loughbourough, U.K. Also available at www.wateraid.org/documents/plugin_documents/genderdevelopmentapproach.pdf.

Cointreau, Sandra. 2006. "Occupational and Environmental Health Issues of Solid Waste Management: Special Emphasis on Middle- and Lower-Income Countries." Urban Paper No. 2, World Bank, Washington, DC. Also available at http://siteresources.worldbank.org/ INTUSWM/ Resources/up-2.pdf.

FRESH. n.d. "Core Intervention 2: Provision of Safe Water and Sanitation." Partnership for Health Development, Focusing Resources on Effective School Health (FRESH) program, London. Also available at www.freshschools. org/water&sanitation.htm.

Fung, Isaac Chun-Hai, and Sandy Cairncross. 2006. "Effectiveness of Handwashing in Preventing SARS: A Review." *Tropical Medicine and International Health* 11 (11): 1–10. Also available at www.sibs.ac.cn/sars/file/wenxian/051415.pdf.

Government of India, Ministry of Rural Development, Department of Drinking Water Supply. 2001. *Central Rural Sanitation Programme Total Sanitation Campaign:* Guidelines 2001. New Delhi: Government of India, Ministry of Rural Development, Department of Drinking Water.

Gross, Bruce, Christine van Wijk, and Nilanjana Mukherjee. 2001. "Linking Sustainability with Demand, Gender and Poverty: A Study in Community-Managed Water Supply Projects in 15 Countries." World Bank Water and Sanitation Program, Washington, DC. Also available at http://lnweb18.worldbank.org/ESSD/sdvext.nsf/07ByDoc Name/StrengtheningOperationalSkillsinCommunity- DrivenDevelopmentOpenSessionsEmpowermentand- Gender.

Hunt, Juliet. 2004. "Effective Strategies for Promoting Gender Equality." Organisation for Economic Co-operation and Development (OECD)/DAC Network on Gender Equality, Paris. Also available at www.oecd.org/dataoecd/59/2/ 32126577.pdf.

International Fund for Agricultural Development (IFAD). 2008. "Safe and Sustainable Livelihoods in Agricultural Communities: Optimizing the Recycling of Human Waste." Seminar of IFAD and the Stockholm Environment Institute, Rome, Italy, January 29. Also available at www.ifad.org/events/lectures/sei/index.htm.

Kar, Kamal, and Katherine Pasteur. 2005. "Subsidy or Self-Respect? Community Led Total Sanitation. An Update on Recent Developments." IDS Working Paper 257. Institute of Development Studies, Brighton, U.K. Also available at www.livelihoods.org/hot_topics/CLTS.html.

Kgalushi, Rudzani, Stef Smits, and Kathy Eales. 2004. "People Living with HIV/AIDS in a Context of Rural Poverty: The Importance of Water and Sanitation Services and Hygiene Education." Mvula Trust and Delft, IRC, Johannesburg, South Africa. Also available at www.irc.nl/ page/10382.

Mathew, Kochurani. 2006. "Preventing Corruption in a Sanitation Programme in India—Process and Tools." Paper presented at the Stockholm Water Week, Water Integrity Network, August 20–26. Also available at www.waterintegritynetwork.net/page/200.

Mukherjee, Nilanjana, and Christine van Wijk. 2003. "Sustainability Planning and Monitoring in Community Water Supply and Sanitation." World Bank Water and Sanitation Program and IRC, Washington, DC. Also available at www.wsp.org/publications/mpa% 202003 .pdf.

O'Connor, S., S. K. West, B. Lorntz, F. Vinicor, and C. Jorgensen. 2004. "Women and Infectious Disease—Chronic Disease Interactions [conference summary]." *Emerging Infectious Diseases Journal.* Also available at www.cdc.gov/ncidod/EID/vol10no11/04-0623_14.htm.

Shordt, Kathy. 2006. "Review of Handwashing Programs." Study for the HIP Project, IRC International Water and Sanitation Centre, Delft, Netherlands. Also available at www.irc.nl/content/download/28336/298224/file/ Hand%20Washing%20HIP%2020Jan06.pdf.

van Wijk-Sijbesma, Christine. 1998. "Gender in Water Resources Management, Water Supply and Sanitation: Roles and Realities Revisited." Technical Paper No. 33, IRC International Water and Sanitation Centre, the Hague, Netherlands.

————. 2002. "The Best of Two Worlds? Methodology for Quantifying Participatory Measurement of Sustainability, Use and Gender and Poverty-Sensitive Participation in Community-Managed Domestic Water Services." University of Wageningen, Department of Communication and Innovations, and IRC, Delft, Netherlands.

Verhagen, Joep, A. J. James, Christine van Wijk, Reema Nanavatty, Mita Parikh, and Mihir Bhatt. 2004. "Linking Water Supply and Poverty Alleviation: The Impact of Women's Productive Use of Water and Time on Household Economy and Gender Relations in Banaskantha District, Gujarat, India." Occasional Paper OP_36E. IRC, Delft, Netherlands. Also available at www.irc.nl/page/5980.

Wakeman, Wendy. 1995. *Gender Issues Sourcebook for Water and Sanitation Projects.* Washington, DC: UNDP-World Bank Water and Sanitation Program/PROWWESS Working Group on Gender Issues of the Water and Sanitation Collaborative Council.

WHO-UNICEF Joint Monitoring Program. 2006. "Meeting the MDG Drinking Water and Sanitation Targets: The Urban and Rural Challenge for the Decade." WHO-UNICEF Joint Monitoring Program, Geneva, Switzerland. Also available at www.who.int/water_sanitation_ health/ monitoring/jmpfinal.pdf.

Innovative Activity Profile 1

Caballero, Luz, and Nerida Alcahuasi. 2007a. "Gender in Peru: Can Women Be Integrated into Transport Projects?" *En Breve* Analytical Note Series No. 112. World Bank Latin America and Caribbean Region, Washington, DC, October.

————. 2007b. "Peru Second Rural Roads Project: Gender Mainstreaming along the Road: Walking towards Women's Empowerment and Democracy." PowerPoint presentation for World Bank Roundtable on Mainstreaming Gender and Social Dimensions in Transport Programs, World Bank, Washington, DC, June.

Dasso, Elizabeth. 2005. "Roads Toward Local Development." In *Thinking Out Loud VI: Innovative Case Studies on Participatory Instruments,* World Bank Civil Society Team, Latin America and the Caribbean Region (summer), 61–76.

Forte, Lucia, and Aurelio Menendez. 2005. "Making Rural Roads Work for Both Women and Men: The Example of Peru's Rural Roads Program." In *Promising Approaches to Engendering Development,* 1–2. Washington, DC: World Bank.

Gutiérrez, María. 2006. "I Didn't Know That I Had Rights: The Process of Training Workers in the Peruvian Rural Roads Infrastructure Project." Paper presented at the International Forum for Rural Transport and Development, London.

————. 2007. "The Process of Training Workers in the Peruvian Rural Roads Infrastructure Project." Paper presented at the World Bank Workshop on Gender and Transport, World Bank, Washington, DC, March.

International Bank for Reconstruction and Development and Inter-American Development Bank (IBRD/IADB). 2005. "Results of the Evaluation of the Local Development Window Program in the Peru Second Rural Roads Project." Joint assessment team presentation, IBRD, Washington, DC, April.

Japanese International Cooperation Agency (JICA). 2007. "Peru Country Gender Profile." JICA, Tokyo, January.

Ruiz-Abril, Maria Elena. 2005. "Mainstreaming Gender in Rural Roads Projects: The Case of the Rural Roads of Peru." World Bank, Washington, DC.

Valdivia, M. 2007. "Peru Rural Roads Program Impact Evaluation 2006." Paper presented at World Bank Brown Bag Luncheon on the Second Peru Rural Roads Project, World Bank, Washington, DC, June.

World Bank. 2001. "Project Appraisal Document on Proposed Load for Second Peru Rural Roads Project." World Bank, Washington, DC.

————. 2006a. "Rural Infrastructure in Peru: Effectively Underpinning Local Development and Fostering Complementarities." World Bank, Washington, DC, January.

————. 2006b. "Project Appraisal Document on Proposed Loan for a Decentralized Rural Transport Project." World Bank, Washington, DC, November.

————. 2007. "Implementation Completion and Results Report for the Second Peru Rural Roads Project." World Bank, Washington, DC, June.

Innovative Activity Profile 2

UNESCAP. 2006. "Guidebook on Developing Community E-Centres in Rural Areas: Based on the Malaysian Experience." United Nations Economic and Social Commission for Asia and the Pacific (UNESCAP), New York. Also available at www.unescap.org.

FURTHER READING

Overview

Davis, Jenna. 2007. "Failure to Meet United Nations Sanitation Target Could Affect Millions of the World's Poorest." Press Release, Stanford University, March.

International Center for Research on Women (ICRW). 2005. "Infrastructure Shortfalls Cost: Women Time and Opportunity." Report, ICRW, Washington, DC.

Organisation for Economic Cooperation and Development (OECD). 2004. "Development Assistance Committee's Network on Gender Equality: Why Gender Matters in Infrastructure." Report, Paris, October.

World Bank. 2002. "Gender, Social Inclusion and Rural Infrastructure." Report, World Bank, Washington, DC.

Thematic Note 1

WEB SITES

Gender and Transport Network (GATNET): http://ifrtd.gn.apc.org/new/gender_gat/about.htm.

Global Road Safety Partnership (GRSP): www.grsproadsafety.org.

Global Transport Knowledge Partnership: www.gtkp.com.

International Forum for Rural Transport and Development (IFRTD): http://ifrtd.gn.apc.org.

International Labour Organization Advisory, Support Information Services and Training (ILO ASIST), "Mainstreaming Poverty Alleviation Strategies through Sustainable Infrastructure Development": www.iloasist.org.

International Labour Organization Gender Equality Tools: www.ilo.org/dyn/gender/gender.home.

Rural Transport Knowledgebase: Sponsored by SSATP, the World Bank, and Department for International Development: www.transport-links.org/rtkb/ rtkb.htm.

Waterways and Livelihoods: www.ruralwaterways.org.

World Bank Gender and Transport Resource Guide: www.worldbank.org.

World Bank Transport and Social Responsibility: www.worldbank.org.

DOCUMENTS

Department for International Development (DFID), IDL Group, and World Bank. 2004. Rural Transport Training CD-ROM.

Fernando, Priyanthi, and Gina Porter, eds. 2002. *Balancing the Load: Women, Gender and Transport.* London: Zed Books.

Leyvigne, Jerome. 2007. "Rural Roads in Yemen." Presentation at the Roundtable on Mainstreaming Gender in Transport. World Bank, Washington, DC, June 20.

Ventner, Christo, Mac Mashiri, and Denise Buiten. 2006. *Engendering Mobility: Towards Improved Analysis in the Transport Sector.* Gender Studies. Pretoria: University of Pretoria Law Press.

Walker, Wendy, and Cheikh Sagna. 2002. "Social and Poverty Issues/Impacts in the Africa Transport Sector." World Bank, Washington, DC, December.

World Bank. 2003. "AIDS and Transport in Africa: A Framework for Meeting the Challenge." World Bank, Washington, DC.

————. 2006. "Social Analysis in Transport Projects: Guidelines for Incorporating Social Dimensions into Bank-Supported Projects." Social Analysis Sector Guidance Notes, World Bank, Washington, DC.

————. n.d. "Case Study 9: Gender, HIV/AIDS and Transport: West Africa. Module III. Integrating Gender into Development Projects." World Bank Institute, Washington, DC.

Thematic Note 2

Energia and United Nations Development Programme. "Gender and Energy for Sustainable Development: A Toolkit and Resource Guide." Available at www.undp.org.

ESMAP. 2002. "Energy Strategies for Rural India: Evidence from Six States." Report 258.02, World Bank, Washington, DC, August.

————. 2004. "Supporting Gender and Sustainable Energy Initiatives in Central America, Volume II." Technical Paper 62, Annex 4, World Bank, Washington, DC.

Lambrou, Yianna, and Grazia Piana. 2006. "Energy and Gender in Rural Sustainable Development." FAO, Rome.

Ramani, K., and Enno Heijndermans. 2003. "Energy, Poverty, and Gender." Synthesis Report, World Bank, Washington, DC.

Republic of Kenya, Ministry of Energy. 2007. "Updating the Rural Electrification Master Plan." Internal report, Nairobi.

World Bank. 2007. "Making Infrastructure Projects Responsible to the Needs of Women in Rural and Remote Areas: Access to Rural Electrification in Lao PDR." World Bank Discussion Paper (Draft), East Asia and Pacific Region Gender Program, World Bank, Washington, DC.

Thematic Note 3

Batchelor, Simon, and Nigel Scott. 2005. "Good Practice Paper on ICTs for Economic Growth and Poverty Reduction." *DAC Journal* 6 (3). Available at www.oecd.org.

Chen, Derek H. C. 2004. "Gender Equality and Economic Development: the Role for Information and Communication Technologies." Policy Research Paper 3285, World Bank, Washington, DC.

Food and Agriculture Organization (FAO). 1996. "The First Mile of Connectivity." FAO, Rome.

Gurumuthy, Anita. 2004 "Gender and ICTs: Overview Report." BRIDGE, Institute for Development Studies; University of Sussex, Brighton, England.

Harris, Roger W. 2004. "Information and Communication Technologies for Poverty Alleviation." UNDP Asia-Pacific Development Information Programme (UNDP-APDIP), Kuala Lumpur, Malaysia.

One World South Asia (OWSA). 2005. "Rural Livelihoods, the Key to Development." *Mainstreaming ICTs*, March–April, OWSA, New Delhi.

Tandon, Nidhi. 2002. "Women Take on Digital Economics: Sustainable Livelihoods and Small-Scale Enterprise." Paper presented at Post-Johannesburg: New Strategies for Sustainable Livelihoods, York University, York, U.K., September 27. Available at www.yorku.ca.

UNESCAP. 2006. "Guidebook on Developing Community E-Centres in Rural Areas: Based on the Malaysian Experience." United Nations Economic and Social Commission for Asia and the Pacific (UNESCAP), New York. Available at www.unescap.org.

Warschauer, Mark. 2004. *Technology and Social Inclusion: Rethinking the Digital Divide*. Cambridge, MA: MIT Press.

World Bank. 2005. "Engendering Rural Information Systems in Indonesia: Rural Development and Natural Resources Sector Unit East Asia and the Pacific Region." World Bank, Washington, DC.

———. 2006. "Information and Communications for Development: Global Trends and Policies." World Bank, Washington, DC.

Thematic Note 4

Borba, Maria-Lúcia, Jo Smet, and Christine Sijbesma. 2007. "Enhancing Livelihoods through Sanitation." Thematic Review Paper, IRC International Water and Sanitation Centre, Delft, the Netherlands. Available at www.irc.nl/page/36080.

Butterworth, John, and Patrick Moriarty. 2003. "The Productive Use of Domestic Water Supplies: How Water Supplies Can Play a Wider Role in Livelihood Improvement and Poverty Reduction." Thematic Overview Paper, IRC International Water and Sanitation Centre, Delft, the Netherlands. Available at www.irc.nl/page.php/256.

Fong, Monica S., Wendy Wakeman, and Anjana Bhushan. 1996. "Toolkit on Gender in Water and Sanitation." World Bank, Washington, DC. Available at http://go.worldbank.org/6KG607ZRK0.

Hunt, Caroline. 2001. "A Review of the Health Hazards Associated with the Occupation of Waste Picking for Children." *International Journal of Adolescent Medical Health* 13 (3): 177–89.

Khosla, Prabha, and Sara Ahmed. 2006. *Gender and IWRM Resource Guide*. Dieren, the Netherlands: Gender and Water Alliance. Available at www.genderandwater.org/page/2414.

Mbugua, Wariara, Dana Peebles, and Nadine Jubb. 2006. "Gender, Water and Sanitation: Case Studies on Best Practices." United Nations, New York. Available at www.unwater.org/downloads/unwpolbrief230606.pdf.

Nicol, Alan. 2000. "Adopting a Sustainable Livelihoods Approach to Water Projects: Implications for Policy and Practice." Sustainable Livelihoods Working Paper 133, Overseas Development Institute, London. Available at www.odi.org.uk/publications/wp133.pdf.

Strand, Arne, and Gunnar Olesen, eds. 2005. "Afghanistan: Findings on Education, Environment, Gender, Health, Livelihood and Water and Sanitation from Multidonor Evaluation of Emergency and Reconstruction Assistance from Denmark, Ireland, the Netherlands, Sweden and the United Kingdom." Chr. Michelsen Institute, Bergen, Norway. Available at www.cmi.no/publications/file/?2125=afghanistan-findings-on-education-environment.

Woroniuk, Beth, and J. Schalkwyk. 1998. "Waste Disposal and Equality between Women and Men." SIDA Equality Prompt No. 7, SIDA, Stockholm, Sweden. Available at www.oecd.org/dataoecd/3/30/1896568.pdf.

Innovative Activity Profile I

Inter-American Development Bank (IADB). 2006. "Local Development Window Technical Cooperation." Profile, IADB, Washington, DC.

Gender and Natural Resources Management

Overview

I n the future, the natural resources needed to sustain the human population will exceed available resources at current consumption levels.[1] Unsustainable and uneven consumption levels have resulted in an increasingly stressed environment, where natural disasters, desertification, and biodiversity loss endanger humans as well as plant and animal species. The challenge of reversing the degradation of natural resources while meeting increasing demands for them involves significant changes in policies, institutions, and practices (FAO 2007a). Effective programming and policies require understanding and addressing the gender-specific relationships to natural resources use and management and highlighting the linkages between natural resources, cultural values, and local knowledge. Addressing the gender-specific aspects of natural resources will provide policy makers with information for more effective natural resource use and conservation policies and will provide guidance for equitable access to natural resources. Here, one must assess the gender-differentiated impacts of environmental changes, including biodiversity loss, climate change, desertification, natural disasters, and energy development.

KEY ISSUES IN NATURAL RESOURCES MANAGEMENT

Natural resources provide a range of goods and services—food, fuel, medicines, fresh water, fisheries, and air and water regulation—that support life on Earth. The rural poor in developing countries remain the most directly dependent on

natural resources for their food and livelihood security. Subsistence farmers, fishers, hunters and gatherers, and agricultural wage workers (more than 1.3 billion people) depend on the availability of usable land, water, and plant and animal species for their livelihoods (FAO 2004). Thus, the agricultural livelihoods of poor rural women and men depend on the condition of natural resources, particularly livelihoods of people living on fragile lands (World Bank 2005).

Over the past 50 years, ecosystems have changed more rapidly than in any comparable period of time in human history, largely because of the need to meet rapidly growing demands for food, water, timber, fiber, and fuel (MEA 2005). Now climate change, caused largely by fossil fuel use, further threatens ecosystems. One strategy to mitigate climate change and reduce fossil fuel dependence emphasizes increased use of bioenergy from crops, which is likely to put more pressure on land, water, and species diversity. These changes contribute to the degradation of natural resources, which exacerbates poverty for some groups of people, especially people living in marginal environments (box 10.1). This Module identifies and addresses five major challenges facing sustainable natural resource management and gender:

- Biodiversity conservation and adaptation
- Mitigation of and adaptation to the effects of climate change and variability
- Bioenergy
- Natural disasters
- Land and water degradation and desertification.

Current changes in biodiversity are the fastest in human history, with species becoming extinct 100 times as fast as the rate in the fossil record; 12 percent of birds, 23 percent of mammals, and 30 percent of amphibians are threatened with extinction.

- The expected increase in biofuel feedstock production may lead to increased rates of genetic erosion.
- Global fish stocks classed as collapsed have roughly doubled to 30 percent over the last 20 years.
- An increase in so-called dead zones, where marine life can no longer live because of the depletion of oxygen caused by pollutants like fertilizers is expected.
- Annual emissions of CO_2 from fossil fuels have risen by about one-third since 1987.
- Eleven of the warmest years since records have been kept occurred during the last 12 years.
- In the twentieth century the average temperature increased by 0.74°C, sea level increased by 17 centimeters, and a large part of the Northern Hemisphere snow cover vanished.

- There are 20 to 30 percent of plant and animal species that are in danger of extinction if the temperature increases 1.5 to 2.5°C.
- Only very large cuts in greenhouse gases of 60 to 80 percent can stop irreversible change.
- Globally more than 2 million people die prematurely every year because of outdoor and indoor air pollution.
- If present trends continue, 1.8 billion people will live in countries or regions with absolute water scarcity by 2025, and two-thirds of the people in the world could be subject to water stress.
- Unsustainable land use and climate change drive land degradation, including soil erosion, nutrient depletion, water scarcity, salinity, desertification, and the disruption of biological cycles.
- In the first half of 2006, 174 disaster events occurred in 68 countries, affecting 28 million people and damaging property and assets valued at more than $6 billion. Annual economic losses associated with such disasters averaged $75.5 billion in the 1960s, $138.4 billion in the 1970s, $213.9 billion in the 1980s, and $659.9 billion in the 1990s.

Sources: IPCC 2007; MEA 2005; www.unep.org.

Addressing these natural resource challenges requires an understanding of their underlying causes. According to the Millennium Ecosystem Assessment (MEA), the main drivers of change include the following:

- Climate change led by the burning of fossil fuels
- Habitat and land-use change, primarily due to the expansion of agriculture
- Overexploitation of resources, especially overfishing
- Deliberate and accidental introduction of invasive alien species
- Pollution, particularly nutrient loading, leading to a loss of biodiversity, agricultural productivity, and increased human health problems.

Understanding and changing natural resource tenure and governance as well as unequal patterns of access to and control over natural resources lie at the heart of reversing natural resource degradation. These issues are crucial to addressing the gender dimension of natural resources.

In addition, efforts aimed at reversing natural resources degradation must consider other factors, including the following:

- Sociodemographic trends, including growth, migration, and diseases such as HIV and AIDS
- Economic trends, including economic growth, disparities, and trade patterns
- Sociopolitical factors, ranging from equal participation in decision-making processes to conflicts
- Technological change that leads to increases in crop yields and agricultural intensification practices, with severe consequences for natural resources.

Climate change, biodiversity loss, land and water degradation and desertification, and natural disasters share many common causes. Because a worldwide consensus recognizes the acceleration of climate change, efforts to mitigate and adapt to climate change promise to have major consequences for natural resource availability and use. Many of the solutions and problems of natural resources degradation lie in agriculture. Agriculture, heavily dependent on natural resources, also provides environmental services such as carbon sequestration. Agriculture occupies 40 percent of the land surface, consumes 70 percent of global water resources, and manages biodiversity at the genetic, species, and ecosystem levels (FAO 2007a). Agriculture contributes to soil erosion, agrochemical pollution, and climate change, accounting for about one-third of greenhouse gas emissions (World Bank 2007). Land and water degradation, shrinking biodiversity, and climate change threaten the viability of farming in various settings. Because of gender-differentiated roles and responsibilities in natural resources management, interventions must address the specific needs and opportunities of rural women and men, particularly the poorest, to reduce inequalities, stimulate growth, and reverse environmental degradation.

KEY GENDER ISSUES

Improving natural resource management practices and protecting the environment require reducing poverty and achieving livelihood and food security among rural women and men. The following are some of the key gender issues in natural resources management interventions.

Rural women and men have different roles, responsibilities, and knowledge in managing natural resources

Rural women's and men's different tasks and responsibilities in food production and provision result in different needs, priorities, and concerns. Although rural women's and men's roles and responsibilities vary across regions and cultures, they often follow similar gender divisions of labor. In most regions men use natural resources in agriculture, logging, and fishing for commercial purposes more than women. In crop production in many regions of the developing world, men tend to focus on market-oriented or cash crop production, whereas women often work with subsistence crops, minor crops, and vegetable gardens. Women often grow a wider diversity of crops. In some cases men and women perform complementary roles—for example, men clear land, women plant and tend crops, and men harvest and market crops. However, observers have come to learn that these gender patterns are neither simplistic nor static. For example, women often work with their husbands in producing cash crops. In Kenya women grow green beans for the European market, and in regions where men migrate, women

take over household cash crop production. Also, gender divisions of labor vary substantially by age, race, ethnicity, and marital status. Consequently, their water use and management will vary accordingly. For example, men use water for irrigation systems, whereas women may not have access to irrigation systems for vegetable gardens and subsistence crops. In livestock management men often care for cattle and larger animals, and women care for smaller animals such as poultry and small ruminants. In many instances women also have responsibility for collecting fodder for animals, often depending on common property resources that are threatened in many cases.

Because women (and sometimes girls) are often responsible for providing their households with the basic necessities of life—food, fuel, and water—they rely heavily on natural resources. Men seldom have responsibility for collecting and using natural resources for household use. Earlier development efforts assumed that women's fuelwood collection and use led to deforestation, but it is now known that the major problems related to biomass collection include women's and children's exposure to indoor air pollution and heavy workloads for women and girls. Environmental degradation increases women's time for labor-intensive household tasks, such as having to walk longer distances for the collection of fuelwood and water. Decreases in agricultural production and household food security create additional health problems related to their increasing workload. Although both rural women and men play a critical role in natural resources management, women's use, conservation, and knowledge of resources play a key role in shaping local biodiversity. Also degradation of natural resources can alter gender responsibilities and relations in households and communities.

Gender differences exist in rights and access to natural resources, including land, trees, water, and animals

In most societies women typically have fewer ownership rights than men (Rocheleau 1996). Women frequently have de facto or land-use rights as compared to men's de jure or ownership rights. Women often have use rights that are mediated by their relationships with men. Thus, when women are widowed or divorced, they may lose these rights, as in recent cases of land grabbing from AIDS widows in southern Africa. How men and women use resources reflects gendered access. For example, women may collect branches and limbs from trees, whereas men may have rights to harvest trees, but for both men and women, insecure land tenure reduces incentives to make the improvements in farming practices necessary to cope with environmental degradation. Without secure land rights, women and men farmers have little or no access to credit to make investments in improved natural resource management and conservation practices. Poor rural women lacking secure land tenure often depend on common property resources for fuelwood, fodder, and food and, therefore, for the well-being of their households. The depletion of common property resources poses a severe threat to the livelihoods and food security of poor rural women and men. Women household heads remain at a particular disadvantage in terms of access to land, water, and other natural resources. A key point is that gendered relations and responsibilities in terms of natural resources are dynamic and subject to change.

Access to new technology, information, and training related to natural resource management remains highly gendered, with most of the related initiatives targeted to men

Despite numerous efforts to mainstream gender, many governments, nongovernmental organizations (NGOs), and development agencies find these efforts particularly difficult in the agriculture and natural resource arenas. For example, extension personnel in agriculture and natural resources frequently speak only to men, often erroneously expecting that the men will convey information to their wives. Until gender is successfully mainstreamed, women's groups, organizations, and networks can increase women's access to knowledge, information, and technologies (Agarwal 2003; Enarson and Meyreles 2004; Sachs 2007).

Degradation of the natural resource base can result in new forms of cooperation, conflict, or controversy between men and women or different ethnic groups

When natural resources become insufficient to support the livelihoods of the population, drastic measures result, such as men's or women's out-migration. Men's out-migration leaves women to assume men's traditional roles and responsibilities, increasing their work burden, but leaving them without equal or direct access to financial, social, and technological resources (Lambrou and Laub 2004). In some instances of severe drought, women migrate to secure extra income for their families (Alston 2006). The intrahousehold reallocation of labor can lead to a decline in agricultural production and in turn result in food insecurity and an overall decrease in financial assets (FAO 2005).

Women are still absent from the climate change and natural resource-related decision-making processes at all levels

Equal participation in community-based decision making remains a complex and difficult goal to achieve, especially in the contexts of highly unequal gender and class relations. At the local level, more natural resource projects and interventions emphasize community-level participation. Careful and thoughtful planning in relation to gender must be exercised in the design of participatory projects. Community-level participation often leaves women's voices and concerns unacknowledged. Even when women attend meetings or events, they may not feel free to voice their opinions, or their opinions and needs may not be taken seriously (Agarwal 2003; Prokopy 2004). Community participation often favors local elites, usually men, but sometimes elite women's concerns directly conflict with and override poor women's access to resources such as fuel and water (Singh 2006; Sultana 2006). Despite attempts to mainstream gender at the national and international levels, few women participate. Gender is rarely a central issue in policy initiatives. Men tend to dominate in the newly emerging decision-making and policy arenas of climate change and bioenergy. Women's limited participation in decision-making processes at international and local levels restricts their capacity to engage in political decisions that can impact their specific needs and vulnerabilities (Denton 2002; Masika 2002).

GENDER IN SUSTAINABLE LIVELIHOODS FRAMEWORK

The Module applies a gender in sustainable livelihoods (SL) framework (see the *Sourcebook* Overview for more details on this framework). This framework conceptualizes the following elements as key in the livelihood strategies of the rural poor: assets, markets, information and organizations, risk and vulnerability, and policies and institutions.

The framework adopts a *people-centered approach* that places at the center the agricultural livelihoods of rural women and men and the natural resources management strategies they adopt. The SL framework also requires a *holistic approach* that integrates scientific, technical, and economic aspects with social and human dimensions. This Module applies the SL framework to natural resources management to highlight key gender concerns in programs and projects, and aspects of the framework will be applied in the different Thematic Notes as appropriate. To refrain from repetition, each component of the framework— assets, markets, information and organizations, risk and vulnerability, and policies and institutions—will not be discussed in detail in each Thematic Note.

Assets

Rural women and men combine a range of assets to achieve their agricultural livelihood outcomes. Assets critical to rural women and men—not only for securing food and a livelihood for their household but also for the conservation and sustainable use and management of natural resources—include the following:

- *Natural resource assets:* land, water, forests, biodiversity
- *Financial assets:* credit, capital, and income
- *Physical assets:* technology, in particular labor-saving technologies
- *Information assets:* local knowledge, formal education, access to information.

A rural household with a large range of assets at its disposal will better cope with shocks and stresses, such as droughts. Poor rural women and men have very limited access to assets. Socially constructed gender roles and relations also influence women's and men's access to assets and the benefits obtained from these assets. Gender-based inequalities often result in women's and girls' limited access to assets, which generates implications for natural resources management conservation. Women face a variety of gender-based constraints as farmers and managers of natural resources. In many societies discriminatory customary and social practices curtail women's rights to land; women generally receive the most marginal lands. Insecure land tenure reduces rural women's and men's incentives to improve natural resources management practices and conservation. Without secure land rights, women and men farmers have little or no access to credit, which is essential for making investments in improved natural resources management and conservation practices. Consequently the technological advances yielding substantial gains in agricultural productivity over the last few decades have often bypassed women farmers and reduced their productivity.

Markets

Access to markets varies by gender and location. Women tend to sell in local markets where they find demand for traditional varieties of crops. Men tend to sell uniform and exotic varieties in export markets. These gender differences in market access vary by location. Local trade can improve rural women's and men's livelihoods by providing them with a source of income and, at the same time, an incentive to manage, use, and conserve a variety of local indigenous plants.

However, women, in comparison to men, continue to face many challenges in accessing and benefiting from markets. They face illiteracy, lack of market information, and transport to markets. At the national and global levels, unfair terms of trade still disadvantage poor farmers, including women. For instance, the World Trade Organization's Trade Related Intellectual Property Rights Agreement (see Thematic Note 1) poses direct challenges for poor farmers, particularly women, in accessing seeds for food production. Trade negotiations rarely consider women's and men's different knowledge and skills. They often neglect their use of assets in determining their livelihoods, and they overlook the potentially differential impact of their provisions on poor rural women and men.[2]

Information and organizations

Evidence from different regions shows that women often face more obstacles than men in accessing agricultural services and information as well as in participating in organizations. Men relatives often mediate women's access to information, markets, and credit. Fewer women than men participate in farmers' organizations and commercial networks. Furthermore, agricultural extension services and technology development frequently target men, wrongly assuming men will convey information to women (Lambrou and Laub 2004). Because few women own land in their own names, they rely heavily on common property resources. As women and men use and manage natural resources in different ways, their full and equal participation in community-based decision-making processes remains critical for safeguarding local natural resources.

Risk and vulnerability

Degradation of natural resources disproportionately harms poor rural women and men and sometimes is the principal cause of poverty. In turn, poverty can lead to the overexploitation of natural resources. Rural poor people rely the most directly on natural resources and are the most vulnerable to changes in ecosystems. Significant differences between the roles and rights of women and men in many societies lead to increased vulnerability of women with the deterioration of natural resources. In some instances deterioration of natural resources results in the renegotiation of gender roles. To design ways to mitigate the negative impacts on rural women and men, one must understand the context of their vulnerability.

Vulnerability depends on the types of resources women and men rely on and their entitlement to mobilize these resources. (Those with limited access to resources will have the least capacity to cope with the impacts of natural resources degradation and are thus the most vulnerable.) Natural resources degradation and natural disasters impact rural peoples' ability to manage and conserve natural resources. These have differential impacts on rural women's and men's livelihood strategies, which also vary according to age, ethnicity, and socioeconomic status.

Policies and institutions

To understand the agricultural livelihood and natural resources management strategies of women and men at the household level, these strategies must be placed within the broader political, socioeconomic, and environmental context. This involves analyzing the current and potential impacts of policies, processes, and institutions on rural women's and men's livelihood strategies and outcomes. The political and institutional context includes the following:

- *Policies:* environmental, economic, energy/bioenergy, and trade agreements
- *Legislation:* such as land rights and intellectual property rights
- *Incentives:* such as for growing cash crops or improved varieties that could replace local varieties or for growing biofuel feedstock
- *Institutions:* extension services that promote technology developments and external innovations
- *Culture:* such as cultural norms and practices that may influence women's and men's access rights and cultural values that may influence gender-based decision making on crop, livestock, and fish selection and management.

Policies and institutional changes in sectors other than natural resources and agriculture include economic and energy development, demographic trends and migration patterns, incidence and impact of disease, and conflicts. Policies, processes, and institutions *have different impacts* on women and men's access to and control over livelihood assets.

BENEFITS FROM GENDER-RESPONSIVE ACTIONS

Benefits from gender-responsive actions can be placed in several overarching categories.
General:

- Overall improvement is seen in natural resources management, use, and conservation and increased agricultural productivity.

- Rural women and men maximize their contributions to household food security.
- Understanding and addressing the gender dimensions of environment and energy programs ensure effective use of development resources.
- Gender relations improve and the social acceptance of women in decision-making positions increases.
- By identifying gender-differentiated opportunities and constraints, project implementers make better-informed decisions and develop more effective environmental and biodiversity conservation interventions.
- Intrahousehold relations improve with an increase in women's control over household resources.
- Women's market participation increases as they become more active and successful in negotiations and trade.

Biodiversity:

- Understanding rural women's and men's roles and traditional knowledge of local biodiversity management, practices, and uses results in the development of innovations that meet farmers' real needs and priorities.
- Development interventions that recognize property rights of rural women and men over their knowledge systems and practices lead to the equal sharing of project benefits as well as increased biodiversity conservation.
- More effective biodiversity conservation interventions result from attention to gender-differentiated opportunities and constraints in agrobiodiversity management.
- Biodiversity conservation increases through recognizing the intellectual property rights of rural women and men.

Climate change:

- Households that are better equipped to cope with the impacts of climate change or extreme weather events can better use, manage, and conserve natural resources.
- Efficient, cost-effective, and relevant interventions take place.
- Gender analysis helps clarify the specific and often different needs, vulnerabilities, and coping strategies of women and men, so that they can be more adequately addressed in response to the impacts of climate change and variability.
- Programs create opportunities to transform gender relations and empower women.

Bioenergy:

- Access to more efficient technologies and modern energy sources reduces the health and safety problems associated with energy acquisition and use. Such access lifts rural women and men out of poverty and enables women and girls to live more productive and healthy lives.

■ The time burden of women and girls of walking long distances, carrying heavy loads, and collecting fuel in dangerous areas is reduced.

■ Access to more efficient technologies for household use can reduce health and safety problems associated with indoor air pollution (UN-Energy 2007).

■ Women who have access to modern fuels face a lighter cooking burden, which frees up time for educational, social, and economic opportunities.

■ Involving both men and women smallholders in bioenergy production offers the possibility of improved incomes and livelihoods.

Natural disasters:

■ Gender analysis helps to clarify the specific and often different needs, vulnerabilities, and coping strategies of women and men to better respond to the impacts of disasters.

■ Gender-responsive actions better equip households to cope with and recover earlier from the impacts of disasters.

■ Postdisaster recovery efforts present opportunities to transform gender relations and empower women.

Land and water degradation and desertification:

■ Affected households cope better with the impacts of desertification and more effectively manage and conserve natural resources.

■ Promoting the participation of women and men farmers in restoring ecosystem health facilitates the reestablishment of soil and land productivity.

■ Strengthening the capacity of rural women and men in dryland management enhances management of local

natural resources and protects the environment from further stresses.

■ Increasing women's access to information and extension services strengthens their ability to cope with and recover from dryland degradation.

MONITORING AND EVALUATION

Monitoring and evaluation of natural resources management projects provide means for learning from past experience, improving project formulation and implementation, planning and allocating resources, and demonstrating results as part of accountability to key stakeholders (World Bank 2004).[3] By measuring change in the status of women and men over a period of time, gender-sensitive indicators assess progress in achieving gender equality. Researchers have little experience in the area of gender-sensitive indicators in the management of natural resources. To select an indicator, the cost of collecting and analyzing data against the quality and usefulness of the information in decision making must be weighed. The indicator should be relevant to the needs of the users, clearly defined, sex disaggregated, and easy to understand and use (FAO 2007b). Both quantitative and qualitative indicators prove useful (see also Module 16). Examples of gender-sensitive indicators appear in the Thematic Notes in this Module on biodiversity, climate change, bioenergy, natural disasters, and land and water. However, Table 10.1 provides some example indicators across the range of topics.

Depending on the country or region, it may also be relevant to consider ethnicity and caste alongside gender (both as comparative indicators and when collecting data), because women of lower castes or ethnic minorities are usually in the most disadvantaged situation.

Table 10.1 Monitoring and Evaluation Indicators for Gender and Natural Resources Management

Indicator	Sources of verification and tools
Percentage of women and men actively participating in natural resource management committees (including bank account signatory roles)	• Bank records • Committee meeting minutes • Interviews with stakeholders • Local traditional authorities (such as a chief or local council) • Program and project records
Over a set period, an increase of x percent in incomes from land-based activities (such as agriculture or forestry) among women-headed households in program areas	• Household surveys • Socioeconomic data from statistics office
Number of women and men in climate change planning institutions, processes, and research (including disaster preparedness and management) at the professional and lay-community levels	• Institutional and university staff records
Average number of hectares of land owned by women- and men-headed households	• Land registration department records
Changes in productive hours spent by, or earnings of women and men, from, household-level agroprocessing, fisheries-, or forest-based enterprises in comparison with baseline (or as percentage of household income)	• Case studies • Sample surveys
Community satisfaction (disaggregated by gender) with changes in natural resources management	• Interviews, before and after • Group interviews or focus groups
Number of women and men receiving training in natural resources management or innovative agroforestry techniques	• Program and project records • Training records
Number of men and women producing bioenergy crops	• Agricultural department statistics • Agricultural extension records • Cooperative records • Household surveys
Percentage of men and women farmers who have access to high-quality, locally adapted planting material	• Agricultural extension records • Interviews with stakeholders
Number of households headed by men, women, or couples benefiting from intellectual property rights	• Natural resources management committee records and meeting minutes
Number of women and men receiving environmental services payments for protecting watersheds or areas of high biodiversity	• Forestry or Natural Resources Management Department records • Global Environmental Facility records • Protected area management committee records and meeting minutes • Protected area management contracts
Percentage of men and women owning and using energy-efficient technologies and low-carbon practices	• Household surveys • Interviews with stakeholders

Source: Authors, with inputs from Pamela White, author of Module 16.

Gender and Biodiversity

Biodiversity provides the basis for ecosystems and ecosystem services upon which all people depend.[1] Biodiversity in agriculture, forestry, and fisheries underpins agricultural and bioenergy production (FAO 2007a; MEA 2005). Sustainable use and management of biodiversity result in global food security, environmental conservation, and viable livelihoods for the rural poor. For poor rural households, in particular, biodiversity remains a key livelihood asset, because these households are the most reliant on local ecosystems and often live in places most vulnerable to ecosystem degradation. A wide portfolio of genetic resources proves crucial to adapting and developing agricultural production systems and for regulating local ecosystems to meet the food needs of future generations. The challenges of environmental degradation, including desertification and climate change, underscore the need to

retain this adaptive capacity. Today the fundamental cause-and-effect relationship between biodiversity degradation and poverty has been recognized. Indeed, biodiversity makes a vital contribution to meeting the UN Millennium Development Goals and will increase in significance in the coming decades (FAO 2007a).

Yet genetic resources are being depleted at unprecedented rates. As mentioned in box 10.1, species extinction is happening 100 times as fast as the rate in the fossil record: 12 percent of birds are threatened with extinction, as are 23 percent of mammals and 30 percent of amphibians (www.unep.org; box 10.2). The main factors contributing to biodiversity loss include unsustainable technologies, destructive land-use practices, invasive species, overexploitation, and pollution (FAO 2005).[2] Climate change, driven by fossil fuel use, changes species ranges and behavior

---

Box 10.2   Current Trends in Biodiversity Loss

- Biomes with the highest rates of biodiversity loss in the last half of the twentieth century are the following: temperate, tropical, and flooded grasslands and tropical dry forests (more than 14 percent lost between 1950 and 1990).
- Wide-ranging areas have seen particularly rapid change over the last two decades: the Amazon basin and Southeast Asia (deforestation and expansion of croplands); Asia (land degradation in drylands); Bangladesh and parts of the Middle East and Central Asia, and the Great Lakes region of Eastern Africa.
- Based on recorded extinctions of known species over the past 100 years, extinction rates are approximately

100 times greater than those characteristic of the fossil record.
- Genetic diversity has declined globally, particularly among domestic species. A third of the 6,500 breeds of domesticated animals are threatened with extinction because of small population sizes.
- Globally approximately 474 livestock breeds are classified as rare, and about 617 have become extinct.
- Roughly 20 percent of the world's coral reefs have been destroyed, and an additional 20 percent have been degraded.
- Some 35 percent of mangroves have been lost in the last two decades in countries where we have adequate data.

Sources: FAO 2003, 2005; MEA 2005.

(www.unep.org). Unfortunately, one key solution to climate change, the replacement of fossil fuel use with bioenergy, also threatens genetic diversity (see Thematic Note 3). Additional influential forces include agricultural development approaches that favor high-yield and uniform varieties of crops, the heavy use of agrochemicals, and the depreciation and devaluation of diversity and accumulated local knowledge (FAO 2003, 2007a; MEA 2005).

Poor rural households that depend heavily on biodiversity in forests, on common lands, and on their farms use diverse domesticated and wild plants for fuel, food, and building materials. Current policies and economic systems often fail to incorporate the values of biodiversity effectively (www.unep.org). To limit these losses and address the multidimensional problems of biodiversity loss and ecosystem degradation, we need policies and programs that cut across sectors and encompass the technical, economic, and social spheres. The human and social dimension of biodiversity loss requires an understanding of its relation to poverty, as well as the gender-specific relationship to natural resources management.

KEY GENDER ISSUES

Rural women and men play important roles in biodiversity management, use, and conservation through their different tasks and responsibilities in food production and provision. Consequently they have different needs, priorities, and knowledge about diverse crops, plants, and animals. As natural resource managers, they influence the total amount of genetic diversity conserved and used. Women are typically involved in the selection, improvement, and adaptation of local plant varieties, as well as seed exchange, management, and saving. They often keep home gardens where they grow traditional varieties of vegetables, herbs, and spices selected for their nutritious, medicinal, and culinary advantages (box 10.3). Women, therefore, play an important role in maintaining biodiversity, working against the decrease in biodiversity caused in part by men favoring cash-oriented monocultures, as in the Mexican Yucatan (Lope Alzina 2007). Women are also the primary collectors of wild foods that provide important micronutrients in diets, are vital for the survival of their households during food shortages, and may also provide income. In the Kalahari Desert, fruits, gums, berries, and roots gathered by the Kung women provide 60 percent of the daily calorie intake. In the Lao People's Democratic Republic, women gather 141 different types of forest products (Momsen 2007). Women possess extensive, often unrecognized, knowledge of the location

Box 10.3   Cameroon and Uganda: Indigenous Vegetables

In Cameroon and Uganda, indigenous vegetables play an important role in both income generation and subsistence production. Indigenous vegetables offer a significant opportunity for poor women and men to earn a living, as producers and traders, without requiring a large capital investment. The indigenous vegetable market provides one of the few opportunities for poor unemployed women to secure a livelihood. Despite the growth in exotic vegetables, indigenous vegetables remain popular in rural areas, where people consider them more tasty and nutritious.

Source: FAO 2005.

stock, and wild plants for achieving household food security and nutritional well-being, especially among the rural poor. However, women's roles and knowledge are often overlooked or underestimated in natural resource management and related policies and programs (Howard 2003).

Local knowledge serves as a critical livelihood asset for poor rural women and men for securing food, shelter, and medicines.[3] The different tasks and responsibilities of rural women and men have enabled them to accumulate different types of local knowledge and skills (FAO 2005). Some studies have expressed concern that local knowledge is disappearing; women do not pass this information on to their daughters, and men no longer pass it down to their sons. Especially in women-headed households (because of HIV and AIDS and migration), changing dietary habits lead to the erosion of women's knowledge of processing, preparation, and storage and lead to the erosion of plant diversity, family food security, and nutritional well-being (Howard 2003).

The type of knowledge farmers possess varies by age, gender, roles and responsibilities, socioeconomic status, and environment. Access to or control over resources as well as education, training, information, and control over the benefits of production also influence the type of knowledge rural women and men have. Experience-based local knowledge interweaves with cultural values and develops and adapts continuously to a gradually changing environment. Rural women's and men's local knowledge, skills, and innovations raise the issue of recognition and protection of farmers' rights.

Markets

Men tend to sell their crops in national or export markets (for uniform, exotic varieties), whereas women tend to sell in local markets where they find demand for traditional varieties (box 10.3). Trade can improve rural women's and men's livelihoods by providing them with income and, at the same time, an incentive to manage, use, and conserve a variety of local indigenous plants. However, women, in contrast to men, face challenges in accessing and benefiting from markets. For example, in the Bamana region of Mali, men have appropriated women's vegetable gardens to establish market-gardening enterprises based on nontraditional foods (box 10.4), which has led to a decline in nutritional well-being.

At the national and global levels, unfair trade disadvantages poor farmers, many of whom are women. New agreements under the World Trade Organization influence biodiversity and have gendered impacts. Gender-based inequalities in access to and control over productive resources have concrete consequences (Randriamaro 2006). Trade negotiations rarely consider women's and men's different knowledge, skills, and

---

Box 10.4   Mali: Changes in Agricultural Production, Gender Relations, and Biodiversity Loss

A case study of the Bamana region in Mali shows how men dismissed agrobiodiversity and the local knowledge held by women. The introduction of exotic vegetables for market production, mainly a men-driven enterprise, led to a shift from subsistence production of a wide variety of indigenous food plants to market gardening of a limited number of exotic food varieties. This process has led to a change in gender roles, with men taking over women's traditional vegetable gardens to establish commercial enterprises. Although traditionally responsible for growing local plant varieties for direct consumption, women were displaced to marginal lands. This has implications for women's contribution to the food security of their household (reduced income and food production for household consumption) and their social standing in the community. Moreover, women's exclusion from the garden realm may lead to changes in culinary patterns, a possible decline in nutritional status, and a reduction in local plant diversity and overall environmental stability.

Source: Wooten 2003.

---

uses of agrobiodiversity. The agreement on Trade-Related Aspects of Intellectual Property Rights (TRIPS) poses direct challenges for poor farmers, particularly women, to access seeds for food production, food security, and nutritional well-being.[4] Moreover, on the one hand, a shift toward production for the global market may be at the expense of local crop varieties for domestic consumption. On the other hand, globalization can give women and men small-producers the opportunity to target niche markets for fair trade or organic products and may go far toward protecting biodiversity (Momsen 2007).

Risk and vulnerability

The impact of biodiversity loss, particularly within common property resources, threatens household food security and livelihoods. These resources prove particularly important for poor rural women, who lack secure land tenure and depend on these common resources for fuelwood, fodder, and food and, therefore, the well-being of their households.

Commercialized agriculture often relies on the replacement of a wide range of locally adapted plant and livestock varieties with a relatively small number of uniform, high-yielding varieties, causing the erosion of local plant and animal genetic resources (FAO 1996).[5] With the increased commercialization of agriculture, technological improvements have created farming systems that are highly dependent on external inputs such as agrochemicals, and these systems often bypass women. Because of their limited access to financial resources, women may have difficulty acquiring seeds, technology, and fertilizers as well as information and training. These processes have negative impacts on small farmers, especially women, who rely on a wide variety of genetic diversity as part of their environmental risk management strategy. In turn, this erosion of resources can also lead to the loss of local knowledge and sometimes to changes in gender roles (box 10.4).

Clearly, biodiversity loss entails different consequences for women and men in the performance of their productive, reproductive, and community roles (Lambrou and Laub 2004). Coping strategies such as the improved management of biodiversity should give options for poor rural women and men to reduce their vulnerability to the effects of biodiversity loss and to build the potential to react to further changes (box 10.5).[6] Poor rural women and men farmers often spread risk by growing a wide variety of locally adapted crops, some of which will be resistant to drought or pests, and livestock breeds that have adapted to the local agroecological zone (FAO/IPGRI 1996). Diversification, an important

Millions of households across Africa have been affected by HIV and AIDS. Rural women and men may respond with a range of coping strategies. For example, in Uganda rural households change the mix of farm products, focusing first on subsistence production and then on growing a surplus to sell in markets (Armstrong 1993). Another strategy is to reduce land under cultivation, resulting in reduced outputs (FAO 2003). In Uganda women-headed households cultivate only 1.3 acre, on average, compared with affected men-headed households, which cultivate 2.5 acres, on average (FAO 2003). Some HIV- and AIDS-affected households have turned to livestock production as an alternative to crop production. Other households sell livestock to pay for medical bills and funeral expenses. A trend has been identified where households raise smaller livestock (such as pigs and poultry) because they are less labor-intensive and often readily available to women.

Source: White and Robinson 2000.

coping strategy adopted by poor rural households, will protect them against climate change, desertification, and other environmental stresses. Women, in comparison to men, are often more vulnerable to the erosion of biodiversity, because they experience gender-based inequalities in accessing assets critical to livelihood security (Lambrou and Laub 2004).

Women and men farmers' full and equal participation in programs and projects dealing with biodiversity conservation, management, and use affects gender-responsive outcomes. Researchers and breeders often work in isolation from women and men farmers and are sometimes unaware of their needs and priorities beyond yield and resistance to pests and diseases.[7] Moreover, extension agents and research organizations tend to consider many local varieties and breeds to be low-performing and inferior. National policies that provide incentives such as loans and direct payments for the use of modern varieties and breeds contribute to the loss of genetic diversity and affect traditional gender roles.

POLICY AND IMPLEMENTATION ISSUES

International policies and agreements regulate the management and use of biodiversity and agrobiodiversity.[8] The

majority of these instruments do not highlight the potential gender-differentiated impacts of their provisions. Only the Convention on Biological Diversity (CBD) and the Global Plans of Action (box 10.6) recognize the key roles played by both women and men, especially in the developing world, in the management and use of biodiversity (Lambrou and Laub 2004).[9] Unfamiliar with these policy instruments, extension workers, development agents, and farmers working on biodiversity and environmental conservation will find it challenging to understand their impact and to implement the relevant provisions in their daily work (FAO 2005).

The CBD advocates the fair and equitable sharing of genetic resource benefits. It also establishes a connection between sustainable conservation and development and the rights of indigenous peoples and local communities[10] (FAO 2005; Lambrou and Laub 2004). The International Treaty on Plant Genetic Resources responds to the outstanding issues not covered by the CBD and formally endorses farmers' rights (box 10.7) through a legally binding instrument at the global level. Observers have noted a growing trend toward the recognition and creation of indigenous rights over genetic resources and related knowledge (FAO 2005).

Despite the increased recognition of the linkages between gender dynamics and biodiversity management and use, little progress has been shown in translating these into programs and projects for agrobiodiversity management and conservation at the local level (FAO 2005). Rural women's vital contribution to the management of biodiversity, agricultural production, and household food security remains misunderstood, ignored, or underestimated (Howard 2003).

GOOD PRACTICES AND LESSONS LEARNED

Experience shows that agricultural biodiversity management and related policies and programs have often failed to recognize the differences between rural women's and men's labor, knowledge, needs, and priorities. This negatively affects biodiversity, local knowledge, and household food security.

Community seed fairs in Tanzania

As part of the LinKS project, the Food and Agriculture Organization (FAO) organized community seed fairs in Tanzania to raise awareness about local crop diversity. The FAO provided learning opportunities for the rural communities (including the younger generations), researchers, extension

The Global Environment Facility (GEF), the financial mechanism for the Convention on Biological Diversity, helps countries fulfill their obligations under the CBD. Since 1991 the GEF has invested nearly $7.6 billion in grants and cofinancing for biodiversity conservation in developing countries. The biodiversity portfolio supports initiatives that promote in situ and sustainable biodiversity conservation in protected areas and production landscapes as well as capacity building and knowledge dissemination (www.gefweb.org).

The Global Plan of Action on Plant Genetic Resources, adopted in 1996, provides a coherent framework, identifying priority activities in the field of in situ and ex situ conservation, sustainable utilization, and capacity building (FAO 1996). It develops activities and measures to strengthen women's capacity to sustainably manage these resources (FAO 2005).

The Global Plan of Action for Animal Genetic Resources, adopted in 2007, presents the first internationally agreed-to framework to halt the erosion of livestock diversity and support the sustainable use, development, and conservation of animal genetic resources. The plan supports indigenous and local production systems and associated knowledge systems. In this context, the plan calls for the provision of veterinary and extension services, delivery of microcredit for women in rural areas, appropriate access to natural resources and to the market, the resolution of land tenure issues, the recognition of cultural practices and values, and the addition of value to specialty products (FAO 2007c).

After exchanging seed varieties, community members discussed local practices. Seed fairs increased local networks, the appreciation of local knowledge, and the roles and responsibilities of farmers in managing agrobiodiversity. (See other examples in Module 12, in particular Thematic Note 2.)

Agroforestry domestication program

A program in Africa supported by the International Fund for Agricultural Development (IFAD) has helped women and men in the domestication, cultivation, and sale of indigenous fruit and medicinal trees. The first phase of the program ran from 1999 to 2003 in Cameroon, the Democratic Republic of Congo, Equatorial Guinea, Gabon, and Nigeria. Training on vegetative propagation techniques enabled many farmers to establish their own nurseries. As a result of project, average household incomes increased, and women and men farmers acquired new skills in propagation techniques, such as grafting and the rooting of cuttings. The program has been particularly effective in improving the livelihoods and status of women. Women's groups have established nurseries, enabling women to participate in income-generating activities. This has led to an increase in school attendance among children. The tree domestication program has also contributed to increased nutritional well-being at the household level, because the women also produce a variety of food for household consumption previously unavailable to them (IFAD n.d.).

staff, and organizations about the importance of crop diversity and local knowledge in food security. Women were the key collectors and savers of seeds. Seed fairs provided farmers with a meeting place where they could buy, sell, and barter seed, thus encouraging the conservation of crop diversity and the spreading of local seed varieties among women and men farmers. The seed fairs were organized on a local scale to make them accessible and affordable for the rural communities.

Guidelines for policy development on farm animal genetic resources management

A joint FAO, South African Development Community (SADC), and United Nations Development Programme (UNDP) project in the SADC region developed policy guidelines that recognize women's roles in livestock management. Those guidelines assist SADC member states in designing policies and a legal framework for the conservation, sustainable use, and management of farm animal genetic resources. The guidelines stress the need for the effective participation of all stakeholders, with a particular focus on women who own or manage a substantial amount of the genetic resources. In highlighting the vital role that women play, the guidelines call for their full and equal participation at all levels of policy making and implementation. Furthermore, the project encourages the development of policies that provide incentives to farmers for the conservation and sustainable use of indigenous animal genetic resources, as well as for the protection of farmers' rights and indigenous knowledge.

The Philippines: indigenous knowledge systems and intellectual property rights

Funded by IFAD and implemented by the International Research Centre for Agroforestry between 2003 and 2004, this project aimed to provide technical assistance in documenting the ethnobotanical knowledge of the Subanen indigenous communities, especially that of women. The objectives included identifying and documenting traditional rice varieties and wild plants and animals, facilitating local participatory planning of natural resource management, and establishing property rights of local communities over their knowledge systems and practices. Men and women participated equally in learning new skills of technical documentation. The technical expertise of the Subanen members of the ethnobotanical documentation team, as well as of concerned women, was enhanced significantly. Technical assistance helped the communities ensure that documentation material that was produced guaranteed their intellectual property rights. A memorandum of understanding signed by the government on behalf of the communities and based on their specific requests and stipulations secured their intellectual property rights and options for obtaining benefits from any future commercial or beneficial use of their knowledge. The project also awakened a strong interest in local women in continuing the reproduction of threatened rice varieties for in situ conservation and documentation (IFAD 2004).

Nepal and India: gender, genetic resources, and indigenous minorities

The International Development Research Centre (IDRC) carried out an action research project on agrobiodiversity management among three ethnic groups in the eastern Himalayas, with a special focus on gender. The three groups were the Rai of east Nepal, the Lepchas of Sikkim and Kalimpong, and the Chekasang and Angami of Nagaland, India. All three research teams received training workshops in gender analysis and writing skills. In Nepal the team built on six years of community development experience in participatory plant breeding to undertake an action research project to develop seed technologies for maize. The IDRC provided interested farmers with rudimentary plant-breeding skills (field isolation, plant selection, cob selection, storage practices). The organization provided timely technical action for maintaining seed purity in the course of the crop cycle and was successful in generating new seeds for the coming season. The organization also initiated similar activities with 50 farmers in an adjacent community. After a visit to eastern Nepal, two agricultural scientists from neighboring Sikkim and Kalimpong started a similar initiative with 20 farmers in Kalimpong, focusing mainly on the development of a disease management strategy for ginger, based on best practices from farmers.

GUIDELINES AND RECOMMENDATIONS FOR PRACTITIONERS

Rural women's and men's vulnerability to biodiversity loss must be understood, so planners can design ways to mitigate the effects of decreasing biodiversity. This implies an understanding of the following issues:

- Rural women's and men's different local knowledge of indigenous plant, fish, and livestock biodiversity uses and practices, including their cultural values and belief systems that influence their traditional knowledge and biodiversity management practices
- The livelihood constraints and opportunities of rural women and men who are managers and users of biodiversity and, in particular, the gender-based inequalities in accessing and controlling critical livelihood assets such as land, credit, technology, and information, as well as participation in farmers' organizations and other decision-making processes
- The different ways rural women and men use biodiversity management practices to secure a livelihood in the

face of environmental stresses such as floods and droughts and other shocks such as HIV and AIDS

- Strategies to improve farmers' involvement and benefit sharing, in particular, the issues of farmers' rights and obtaining prior informed consent, which should be considered within a legal and ethical context[11]
- Eliminating incentives for uniform varieties and supporting rural women and men in accessing information about their rights to plant genetic resources (FAO 2005)
- Gender-sensitive participatory plant breeding, which contributes to the conservation and sustainable use of plant and animal genetic resources;[12] as women and men use and manage agrobiodiversity in different ways, their full and equal participation in decision-making processes is critical for safeguarding local biodiversity.

Often the most appropriate solutions to local problems and needs combine traditional and scientific methods. This fusion enhances the adoption and acceptance of the new methods by the local community and provides methods that reflect the actual needs of women and men.

MONITORING AND EVALUATION

The following are examples of gender-sensitive indicators for biodiversity (FAO 2007b):

- Percentage of men and women farmers who have access to high-quality, locally adapted planting material
- Number of households headed by men, women, or couples benefiting from intellectual property rights
- Ratio of men's and women's income from production of high-value horticultural crops
- Ratio of the number of livestock owned by men and women
- Amount of credit and microcredit available to women and men for improving livestock enterprises.

Gender Dimensions of Climate Change

Global climate change is one of the greatest environmental challenges facing the world today. In the twentieth century the increase in global average temperature reached 0.74°C, the average sea level increased by 17 centimeters, and the Northern Hemisphere experienced a considerable decrease in snow cover (IPCC 2007). Eleven of the warmest years since records have been kept have occurred during the last 12 years, representing an accelerating warming trend. The Intergovernmental Panel on Climate Change (IPCC)[1] projects additional global warming over the twenty-first century from 1.8 to 4.0°C.[2] According to the IPCC's Fourth Assessment Report, climate warming is unequivocal, evident from observations of increases in global average air and ocean temperatures, widespread melting of snow and ice, and rising sea levels. Long-term changes in climate include widespread changes in precipitation, ocean salinity, wind patterns, and extreme weather events. Extreme weather events resulting from climate change include droughts, heavy precipitation, heat waves, and the intensity of tropical cyclones (IPCC 2007).

The increase in greenhouse gas[3] concentrations accounts for most of the observed increase in global average temperatures since the mid-twentieth century.[4] The international response to climate change focuses on mitigation measures that aim to reduce greenhouse gases and enhance carbon sinks. Carbon sinks are the natural ability of trees, other plants, and the soil to soak up carbon dioxide and temporarily store the carbon in wood, roots, leaves, and the soil. However, in recent years many observers recognize adaptation strategies as critical elements in reducing the vulnerabilities to climate-induced change to protect and enhance the livelihoods of poor women and men (Soussain, Burton, and Hammil 2003). Even if we stabilize greenhouse gas concentrations, climate change will continue for centuries, and the ability of the most vulnerable to adapt will remain a serious issue (IPCC 2007).

Climate change poses a serious risk to poverty reduction and development, with adverse impacts expected on the environment, human health, food security, economic activity, natural resources, and infrastructure.[5] Global warming will have profound effects on agriculture, forestry, grasslands, livestock, and fisheries and, thus, on food security (FAO 2007). The IPCC assesses that 20 to 30 percent of plant and animal species are in danger of extinction if the rise in global average temperature exceeds 1.5 to 2.5°C. The sharpest impact of a changing climate will be the rise in incidence and severity of climate-related disasters such as increased flooding, particularly in Asia, as well as fiercer storms and prolonged droughts (see Thematic Note 4). The IPCC's Fourth Assessment Report warned that global warming would cause widespread food shortages in the developing world (Harvey 2007; IPCC 2007).[6]

Although industrial countries' use of fossil fuel and industrial processes contributes inordinately to greenhouse gas concentrations, people living in developing countries are most likely to suffer the consequences of climate change (box 10.8). This uneven distribution of the impacts of climate change occurs both between and within countries. Least-developed countries prove the most reliant on rain-fed agriculture and natural resources and are the most vulnerable to climate change. These countries generally lack the necessary adaptive capacities, such as a stable economy, infrastructure, technology, information dissemination system, and equitable access to resources. Poor people tend to live on marginal lands that are most subject to droughts or floods and are most likely to be affected by small changes in climate variability. Because of gender-based inequalities in accessing critical livelihood assets such as land, credit, technology, information, markets, and organizations, women have more exposure to these risks.[7]

KEY GENDER ISSUES

Until recently, international climate change policy makers have neglected the gender dimension of climate change (Lambrou and Piana 2006a). A focus on technical solutions has ignored social and political factors (Masika 2002). The successful implementation of climate change policies and projects requires an understanding of the gender-based roles and relationships vis-à-vis natural resources, as well as the gender-differentiated impacts of climate change and the different risks and vulnerabilities of women and men. This includes the structural constraints that curtail women's access, control, and ownership over assets (Denton 2002). Research must also identify who is responsible for CO_2 emissions and how social, political, and planning conditions might affect emission reduction (Lambrou and Piana 2006b). A discussion of some gender issues related to climate change follows.

Climate change impacts

Climate change could alter the tasks people perform and their time use, affecting men and women differently. For example, rural women, and girls to some extent, frequently provide households with water and fuelwood for heating and cooking. The time needed for their work in gathering water and fuel will likely increase with water shortages and depletion of forests. Decreasing the time available to women for food production and preparation as well as participation in income-generating activities will likely affect household food security and nutritional well-being (see also Module 1).

Another example of climate change that directly impacts men and women differently is the effect of climate change on water quality and supply. Children and pregnant women are physically vulnerable to waterborne diseases, and their role in supplying household water and performing domestic chores makes them more vulnerable to diseases, such as diarrhea and cholera, that thrive in conditions of degraded water.[8] Decreased water resources may also cause women's health to suffer as a result of the increased work burden and reduced nutritional status. For instance, in Peru following the 1997–98 El Niño events, malnutrition among women was a major cause of peripartum illness.

Adaptation

At the local level, farmers continuously adapt to climate variability. They change crops or varieties, choose different harvest and sowing dates, alter land management, and employ water efficiency techniques (FAO 2007). Long-term climate change poses a new set of challenges to farmers dependent on natural resources, and so at the national and international levels, governments and development agencies play a fundamental role in building the capacity of farmers to cope with and adapt to a changing environment (Soussain, Burton, and Hammil 2003).

The adaptive capacity of people depends on how they can draw from resources to maximize their livelihood outcomes (Masika 2002), so adaptation depends on factors such as economic status, technology, health, education, information, skills, infrastructure, access to assets, and management capabilities (IPCC 2001). Differentiated power relations between men and women and unequal access to and control over assets mean that men and women do not have the same adaptive capacity; instead, women have distinct vulnerability, exposure to risk, coping capacity, and ability to recover from climate change impacts (Masika 2002). Although women are generally more vulnerable to the impacts of climate change, they play an active role in adapting to its impacts to secure food and a livelihood for their household.[9]

Gender components determine adaptation strategies in terms of how men and women can contribute. For example, as a result of gender-differentiated roles in agrobiodiversity management, women often have greater knowledge of indigenous plant varieties with important nutritional and medicinal values (FAO 2005). As the keepers of seeds, women often possess knowledge of a variety of genetic resources to adapt to varying climatic conditions such as resistance to drought or pests. However, because men have more secure access to land or land tenure, they have more incentive to contribute to effective natural resources management, use, and contributions necessary for adaptation.[10]

Gender also often determines who receives inputs for adaptation strategies. Frequently new agricultural technologies bypass women farmers, despite women's knowledge. For example, extension personnel introducing new varieties intended for higher drought or heat tolerance rarely speak directly with women farmers (Kurukulasuriya and Rosenthal 2003).

Finally, a gender component exists for the adaptive strategies that are pursued and the consequences of adaptation. For example, in New South Wales, Australia, women migrate away from farms for work, which enables men to remain in agriculture. In other regions impacted by drought, men migrate, leaving women, who have fewer resources, to perform agriculture. In either case, the drought strains traditional gendered relationships (Alston 2006).

Mitigation

Mitigation has revolved around the reduction of greenhouse gases and the enhancement of carbon sinks to absorb them (Boyd 2002).[11] Although responsibility for carbon emissions resides primarily in industrial countries, fossil fuel use and industrial processes, rural poverty, and subsistence agriculture account for a portion of emissions of carbon dioxide that stem from deforestation and land-use change.[12] In addition, rural poor women and men generally lack access to energy-efficient services that do not degrade the ecosystem or contribute to environmental change. Rural households typically rely on biomass for cooking and heating. Because women usually prepare food, their decisions about cooking fuels and efficiency can reduce carbon emissions. Households with lower average income and level of education generate lower emissions; however, they also have a lower mitigation and adaptive capacity. Low educational levels of women and men household members limit awareness of mitigation options, such as the use of energy-efficient devices (Lambrou and Piana 2006a). Therefore, as issues of

sustainable energy development (renewable energy and energy efficiency) and sustainable transportation receive more attention, it is important to encourage and improve the active involvement of key stakeholders. Women's active involvement in agriculture, and their dependence on biomass energy, make them key stakeholders in effective environmental management related to mitigation (Denton 2002).

GOOD PRACTICES AND LESSONS LEARNED

Programs in Bolivia, Costa Rica, and India contribute to good practices and lessons learned.

Bolivia: Noel Kempff Climate Action Project

Unfortunately, many climate change projects fail to take gender into account. For example, in 1996, in the region of Santa Cruz in the Bolivian Amazon, the Noel Kempff Climate Action Project's primary objective involved purchasing logging concessions and expanding the Noel Kempff National Park to 1.5 million hectares for conservation and increased carbon credits. However, the project failed to take into account a gender perspective that recognized the different power relations and cultural practices as well as the gender bias in institutions (Boyd 2002). The project also aimed to improve local agricultural and forest management practices, stimulate employment, and obtain 400,000 hectares of communal land for three key local communities. The project provided opportunities for the participation of both women and men, who successfully participated in some aspects of the project. The participants met some basic necessities, such as trying new varieties of crops and accessing credit. With a majority of men local and technical staff, women had little chance to join decision-making processes relating to the future of the park, land title, and other project activities. Men dominated public meetings, overlooking women's needs and concerns, which ultimately were not reflected in the project activities. Boyd (2002) stresses that the project did not challenge existing gender relations and division of labor, nor did it empower women. The project's enforcement of existing social structures and wide reliance on traditional norms in decision making weakened women's ability to participate.

Costa Rica: Carbon emission mitigation through Payment for Environmental Services Programme

Since 1996 Costa Rica's government has implemented the Payment for Environmental Services Programme (Programa de Pago por Servicios Ambientales) to promote and encourage conservation, reforestation, carbon emission mitigation, and sustainable management of Costa Rica's natural resources.[13] The program offers economic rewards to landowners who conserve the forests on their land. However, most landowners are men, and women have little access to the economic rewards. To help resolve this problem, FONAFIFO (National Fund for Forestry Finance), the national institution in charge of implementing the program and promoting gender equity, imposes a fee. This fee goes into a fund to support women who want to become landowners.[14]

India: carbon sequestration project

An innovative agroforestry project in Gudibanda Taluk, Karnataka, India (implemented by the NGO Women For Sustainable Development [WSD]), supports local women and men farmers in planting mango, tamarind, and jackfruit tree orchards for harvest and carbon sequestration.[15] The project supports women's participation in decision-making processes. One way in which the project does this is by taking into account women's time and cultural constraints when establishing public forums. The project set up a prototype carbon marketing facility to sell the certified emissions reduction of the global environmental services that the participants (poor rural women and men) provide.[16] Because farmers have an average annual income of less than $100, they cannot afford to plant fruit trees without financial assistance. Success requires expensive irrigation changes and planting tools. Farmers will live on the carbon sales from their mango plantations for the first few years, until they harvest their crop. Fruit production should start about four years after planting, and one acre of crop will at least triple their annual income. The program anticipates sustainable incomes for women and men farmers, as well as the additional benefits derived from the ecofriendly farming techniques. The project lifetime is 35 years, with an estimated CO_2 benefit of 23 tons of carbon sequestration per acre. The project target is 35,000 acres, for a total sequestration of 575,000 tons of carbon.

POLICY AND IMPLEMENTATION ISSUES

The United Nations Framework Convention on Climate Change (UNFCCC), the main international policy instrument to address climate change, aims to stabilize the concentrations of greenhouse gases in the atmosphere within a time frame sufficient to allow ecosystems to adapt naturally to climate change. The UNFCCC, supported by the 1997

Kyoto Protocol, contains legally binding targets that dictate that industrialized countries must reduce by 2008–12 combined emissions of six key greenhouse gases by at least 5 percent in relation to 1990 levels.[17] The Global Environment Facility and the Clean Development Mechanism (box 10.9) of the Kyoto Protocol play a role in climate change mitigation and adaptation strategies.[18]

GUIDELINES AND RECOMMENDATIONS FOR PRACTITIONERS

Awareness and understanding of the complex links between gender roles and relations, the environment, and livelihood security will aid in the design of climate change mitigation and adaptation projects. To ensure women's participation in climate change mitigation and adaptation projects, we must incorporate women's needs and concerns in the design of relevant and successful climate change policies. Pinpointing specific goals within the main climate policies and developing corresponding indicators for monitoring and evaluation will help mainstream gender issues into climate change policies. Ways of incorporating women's needs and concerns relating to mitigation include the following:

- Analyze women's and men's energy use, transport use, and other consumption patterns impacting climate.
- Introduce more formal and informal education about the environmental impacts of their current life styles to increase men's and women's mitigation capacity (Lambrou and Piana 2006b).
- Promote cleaner-burning fuel for household use to reduce harmful emissions, cut household energy costs, and reduce women's and girls' work burdens.
- Increase poor women's and men's access to payments for environmental services.

Goals and issues related to adaptation include the following:

- Many women prove to be proactive at local levels in mitigating hazards and strengthening the disaster resilience of households and communities.
- Make available to both men and women usable, science-based climate prediction information and incorporate existing local knowledge (FAO 2007).
- Strengthen the capacity of rural institutions such as extension services to use appropriate tools and strategies, including participatory identification of current vulnerabilities and risk reduction measures, implementation of prioritized community-based disaster risk reduction

In the Kyoto Protocol the Clean Development Mechanism allows for and addresses divergent objectives and priorities between the North and South. A bilateral agreement between an industrialized country and a developing country mandates reduced greenhouse gas emissions under the convention. Under the CDM industrialized countries invest in projects that increase economic productivity and may reduce local environmental problems in developing countries (Denton 2002).

Those projects that focus on technologies relating to household energy, food processing, forest management, and water pumping must target both rural women and men and take into account their different roles and responsibilities. However, extension services that convey this technology typically target men, who are perceived as the principal decision makers and users of these technologies (for a more detailed discussion, see Denton 2002; Wamukonya and Skutsch 2001).

activities, and increased capacity of communities to manage their resources (FAO 2007).

MONITORING AND EVALUATION

Examples of gender-sensitive indicators in climate change include (indicators are from Aguilar 2007; FAO 2007) the following:

- Proportion of men and women who own and use non-motorized transport and use public transport

- Number of women owning and using energy-efficient technologies, using renewable energy, and involved in sustainable forest management (climate change mitigation)
- Number of women and women-headed households receiving training and assistance related to disasters (such as the number of women who know how to swim)
- Participation of women in climate change–planning institutions, processes, and research (including disaster preparedness and management) at the professional and lay-community levels.

Gender and Bioenergy

Over one-third of the world's population, 2.4 billion people, rely on traditional biomass in the form of fuelwood, agricultural residues, and animal wastes for their primary energy needs (Sagar and Kartha 2007). Use of traditional biomass poses many problems: poor health, heavy workloads, land degradation, deforestation, biodiversity loss, and climate change. New forms of bioenergy, primarily liquid biofuels, are rapidly being developed as replacements for fossil fuels. Global interest in modern bioenergy—which includes liquid biofuels, biogas, and solid biomass—has grown rapidly in recent years.[1] (This Thematic Note focuses on modern bioenergy; for a detailed discussion on the wider issues of gender and energy, refer to Modules 9 and 15.)

At a time when energy analysts anticipate a period of unpredictable oil markets, fossil fuel dependence poses a major risk for many developing economies. Oil imports now consume a large and unsustainable share of the meager foreign exchange earnings of many poor nations, offsetting any gains from recent foreign debt elimination agreements. Unstable and unpredictable oil prices have complicated economic planning around the world and are further damaging poor economies (UN-Energy 2007).

Available energy services currently fail to meet the needs of the world's poor. Four out of five people without electricity live in the rural areas of developing countries (UNDP 2004; UN-Energy 2007). Extending an electricity supply grid to remote households in rural areas is unlikely to occur quickly because of costs that are seven times the cost of providing electricity in an urban area (FAO 2006).

Given plausible economic and institutional assumptions, this century could see a significant switch from fossil fuels to bioenergy, with agriculture and forestry as the leading sources of biomass for biofuels (FAO 2005).[2] Although increased production of, and access to, bioenergy offers only one of the possible answers to climate change and energy

security challenges,[3] a number of features make it an interesting but complicated option (FAO 2007). Locally produced bioenergy can supply energy for local agricultural, industrial, and household uses, in some instances at a lower cost than fossil fuels (UN-Energy 2007). Modern bioenergy, with appropriate policies, could help meet the needs of poor women and men who lack access to electricity, while generating income and creating jobs in poorer areas of the world.

Although the rapid development of modern bioenergy presents a broad range of opportunities for achieving sustainable energy, it also entails multiple trade-offs and risks. The first concern relates to the impact of bioenergy on food markets, food prices, and food security. Current biofuels depend on food crops, including corn, sugarcane, soybeans, rapeseed, and palm oil. The boom in bioenergy has already resulted in some rises in food prices.[4]

A second concern is the impact of modern bioenergy production on sustainable livelihoods for rural households. If production and processing of biofuels occur through large-scale, vertically integrated commodity chains, small farmers will be unlikely to benefit. Efforts to use biofuels to promote sustainable development must include strategies to incorporate small producers (Sagar and Kartha 2007).

The rapid development of modern bioenergy requires careful handling of key social, economic, and environmental sustainability (UN-Energy 2007). New crops, farming techniques, and second-generation technologies (for example, fuels made from lignocellulosic biomass feedstock using advanced technical processes) now under development may mitigate some of the social, environmental, and economic costs associated with large-scale production of liquid biofuels and increase their potential and environmental benefits.[5] Where we grow crops for energy purposes, use of large-scale monocropping could lead to significant biodiversity loss, soil erosion, and nutrient leaching, with negative consequences for local rural women's and men's ability to secure food and their livelihoods.

Most likely, new bioenergy production will involve large-scale biomass production that does not necessarily benefit the rural poor. The challenge is to develop small-scale bioenergy concepts and technologies that local people can use and sustain. A transitional solution uses improved cook stoves, which reduce indoor pollution and burn fuel much more efficiently. Bioenergy options, such as small- and medium-scale biogas or gasifiers and power generators, operate with locally available biomass resources. They may become the most economical and reliable providers of energy services for poor rural women and men (UN-Energy 2007).

KEY GENDER ISSUES

Gender-differentiated issues related to bioenergy differ substantially among traditional biomass, small-scale biofuel production, and large-scale biofuel production.

Gender and traditional bioenergy

Rural women shoulder the burden of traditional biomass (fuelwood, manure, agricultural residues) collection. Many women spend up to three to four hours a day collecting fuel for household use, sometimes traveling 5 to 10 kilometers a day (WHO 2006). Women in women-headed households report water and fuelwood collection as their most time-consuming tasks (FAO/IFAD 2003). In many African, Asian, and Latin American countries, rural women carry approximately 20 kilograms of fuelwood every day (FAO 2006). Increasing pressure on and degradation of these resources result in women walking longer distances from the safety of their communities. This increases their work burden, limiting time available for food production and preparation, household-related duties, and their participation in income-generating activities and educational opportunities.

Women's limited access to fuelwood relates to the heavily gendered nature of rights and responsibilities with respect to trees. Mearns (1995) reports that in Kenya women are expected to provide their households with daily supplies of wood, but they lack access to tree farms. Men dominate tree planting, and trees planted in woodlots typically fall under men's control. Rights to trees are tied to land ownership, which falls almost exclusively to men. Thus, although trees may be nearby, women may lack access to them and therefore walk long distances to gather wood or switch to other types of biomass for fuel, such as maize stalks or dung.

Reliance on traditional biomass further entrenches gender disparities. When women spend many hours collecting traditional fuels, they do not receive education and training for productive income-generating activities. When withdrawn from school to gather fuel and attend to other domestic chores, girls lose literacy opportunities and suffer lifelong harm. They also have less time to participate in organizations and learn to negotiate in decision-making processes. Household use of traditional bioenergy locks people in the developing world, women in particular, into a cycle of poverty and ill health (UN-Energy 2007).

The most dramatic gender-differentiated and health benefits from the use of modern bioenergy relate to household applications. Traditional bioenergy uses affect the health of women more severely than men, because women traditionally bear responsibility for household-related duties, including food preparation (UN-Energy 2007). Rural people rely heavily on biomass as their primary cooking fuel: 93 percent in sub-Saharan Africa, 87 percent in India, and 93 percent in Indonesia (Sagar and Kartha 2007). Open fires in the household produce unventilated smoke and expose women and children, who are most often indoors, to high concentrations of carbon monoxide, nitrogen oxides, and other pollutants (Lambrou and Piana 2006). Smoke inhalation from cooking indoors with traditional biomass increases the risk of major diseases and is the sixth largest health risk in developing countries. The rural poor in Southeast Asia and sub-Saharan Africa suffer the highest death toll (Schirnding and others 2000; UN-Energy 2007).

Many early efforts to reduce use of traditional biomass involved the development and introduction of improved cook stoves. These efforts had limited success. Some of the improved stoves were less efficient than claimed and were relatively expensive. Women were reluctant to give up traditional cook stoves because they preferred cooking with them, and the stoves offered additional benefits of heating and repelling insects. More recent cook stoves have achieved more success, especially in China and India, with estimates of 220 million improved cook stoves worldwide (Sagar and Kartha 2007).

Gender and modern biofuels

Shifting basic energy uses from traditional bioenergy (when used in unsustainable and health-damaging forms) to modern fuels and electricity poses difficult challenges (UN-Energy 2007). When household income increases, people typically switch to more fuel-efficient technologies. The push to modern bioenergy offers both possibilities and challenges for enhancing gender equity. Poor rural women and men often lack the economic resources to use different bioenergy options.[6] The rural poor, a disproportionate number of whom are women, do not have the means to purchase modern energy services. The cost and efficiency of a stove or other systems such as biogas or small gasifiers often deter women more than the actual cost of fuel (UN-Energy 2007).

Modern bioenergy may take the form of small-scale production or large-scale plantation production. Small-scale biofuel use has the potential to reduce women's health risks from wood fires and reduce their work collecting fuelwood. Biofuels have the potential to reduce women's work burden, but they may also generate additional work if women produce the biomass to make the fuel (such as for biogas) (UN-Energy 2007).

The transition to liquid biofuels may especially harm women and men farmers who do not own their land and the rural and urban poor who are net buyers of food. "At their best," according to UN-Energy (2007: 24), "liquid biofuel programs can enrich farmers by helping to add value to their products. But at their worst, biofuel programs can result in concentration of ownership that could drive the world's poorest farmers off their land and into deeper poverty." The rural poor, women in particular, typically do not have official title to their land. Driving small farmers without clear land titles from their land will destroy their livelihoods (UN-Energy 2007).

Large-scale bioenergy production

Several key gender issues that may result from the production of large-scale biofuels include the following:

- Biofuels require the intensive use of resources including land, water, chemical fertilizers, and pesticides, to which small farmers have limited access. Women, and particularly women in women-headed households, will face greater barriers acquiring these resources and participating in biofuel production (Rossi and Lambrou 2008).
- The large amount of land required for biofuel production will put pressure on marginal land and common property resources. Marginal lands are particularly important for women who raise food crops, collect fodder and fuel, and graze livestock. The conversion of these lands to biofuel crops might result in the displacement of women's agricultural activities toward lands that are even more marginal, thus decreasing household food security (Rossi and Lambrou 2008).

- The potential loss of biodiversity from large-scale mono-culture plantations may affect women and men differently. The establishment of plantations on previously uncultivated land may threaten wild edible plant species. Women often rely on the collection and preparation of wild plant species for food, fodder, and medicine.
- Livestock farmers will be particularly affected by biofuel production with the conversion of grazing land to crop land and the higher price of livestock feed. Livestock is especially important for the food security of poor farmers. The potential reduction in the number of animals, especially ruminants (cattle, sheep, and goats), raised by small farmers, will reduce their livelihood strategies. In many regions men are primarily responsible for managing cattle and buffalo, and their ability to raise these animals will be affected (Rossi and Lambrou 2008).

POLICY AND IMPLEMENTATION ISSUES

The Earth Summit in Rio de Janeiro in 1992 and the Fourth World Conference on Women in Beijing in 1995 recognized the need to design environmental and energy programs with a gender focus (Salazar 1999). In 2001 the Ninth Session of the Commission on Sustainable Development urged governments to address the health and safety concerns of women and children in rural areas related to the impacts of carrying loads of fuelwood over long distances and exposure to smoke from indoor open fires. In addition, the commission recommended international cooperation to promote equal access to energy through energy policy decision-making processes (Lambrou and Piana 2006).

In 2006 FAO launched the International Bioenergy Platform as a framework for bioenergy cooperation. This program aims to enhance access to energy services from sustainable bioenergy systems, emphasizing the provision of modern, gender-sensitive bioenergy services for local communities and the most vulnerable and poor.

In many developing countries, small-scale bioenergy projects could face challenges obtaining financing from traditional financing institutions. Although these projects could provide modern energy services to rural women and men currently lacking access, they will likely require credit mechanisms at all stages of production.

GOOD PRACTICES AND LESSONS LEARNED

Some observers have suggested that the rural poor, who have a small environmental footprint, gained positive experiences with the decentralized and small-scale production and use of fuel crops. The production and use of liquid biofuels from local feedstock improve access to sustainable and affordable energy for poor rural women and men (DESA 2007).

Zambia: Small-scale production of liquid biofuels

For the last seven years a group of Zambian women with the support from German Technical Cooperation (GTZ) have developed a soap-making enterprise using jatropha oil. Between 2000 and 2001 the National Oilseeds Development Program, under the Ministry of Agriculture and Cooperatives of Zambia, carried out demonstrations on the various uses of jatropha oil through national agricultural and commercial shows. This project used a bottom-up approach, promoting women's participation and ownership. In 2006 the Biofuels Association of Zambia mounted an awareness campaign on the potential of *Jatropha curcas* to provide practical substitutes for fossil fuels and its important implications for meeting the demand for rural energy services. In its 2007 budget the Zambian government allocated $150,000 for research on *J. curcas* and other biofuels. Biofuels predominate in new energy policies, which often set standards for a specified minimum proportion of biofuels in blends for all consumers. In this project rural women and men are improving their livelihoods and generating income through activities related to the production of jatropha oil.

Tanzania and Mali: Small-scale biofuel production

In Tanzania a project has sought to introduce and expand production of jatropha as a cash crop for raw material for plant-oil industries. They demonstrated its potential in reforestation, erosion control, and reclamation of degraded land. Working with local women's groups, the grantee (KAKUTE Ltd.) trained over 1,500 women and men in jatropha management techniques and planted more than 400 hectares of jatropha on marginal lands donated by the communities. The project successfully demonstrated the livelihood benefits of the crop, helping launch jatropha farming as a cash crop, while assisting others to begin soap-making businesses. Seventeen different village-based women's groups coordinated the project. Women produced the seedlings and cuttings for planting. In the first four years of the pilot project, they sold 52,000 kilograms of seeds to oil processors for approximately $7,800, producing 5,125 liters of oil, worth about $10,250 on the local market, and 3.5 tons of soap, worth $20,533. Although the amount of oil and soap produced does not approximate the capacity of the land to produce jatropha seeds, it goes a long way toward demonstrating the potential profitability of the crop. The project aimed to improve rural women's and men's livelihoods and income-generating activities using bottom-up approaches and promoting women's participation and ownership.

The Mali Folke Center in Mali works with local rural women and men in developing plantations of jatropha.[7] Working with the GTZ, they use a UNDP-led technology, a multifunctional apparatus called the Mali platform, which can run on crude jatropha oil. The platform generates electricity for the whole community and powers water pumps, crushes the oil seeds, and provides energy for a welding and carpentry shop. The Mali Folke Center converted its Toyota pickup truck to run on jatropha oil. Women, the main beneficiaries of the project, have cited the ability to use jatropha oil for soap making as more of an economic benefit than the energy.

Nepal: Biogas program

The World Bank's biogas project in Nepal aims to develop biogas use as a commercially viable, market-oriented industry by bringing fuel for cooking and lighting to rural households. Subsidies provide a key element in making these biogas plants accessible to poor households. Between 2004 and 2009 the project will install 162,000 quality-controlled, small-size biogas plants in the Terai, hill, and mountain regions of Nepal. Revenue from the Community Development Carbon Fund will reduce the dependency on large government and external donor subsidies and will help expand the biogas installation to more remote and poorer areas. These biogas plants displace traditional fuel sources for cooking—fuelwood, kerosene, and agricultural waste. Each biogas plant can reduce 4.6 tons of carbon dioxide equivalent annually. The project will generate approximately 6.5 million tons of carbon dioxide equivalent during the 10-year crediting period. The Community Development Carbon Fund expects to purchase a minimum of 1 million tons of carbon dioxide equivalent with the potential of additional purchase. The project engages household members to understand their needs, the possibilities of the technology, and where to locate it. The project estimates that women will save three hours daily per household using biogas for cooking versus cooking with collected fuelwood. Women use this time for child care, literacy training, and participation in community organizations. Biogas-fueled stoves also dramatically reduce indoor air pollution.

Costa Rica: Solar-powered cookers

The focus of a project implemented by the Fundación Sol de Vida (Foundation of Sun and Life) in the Santa Cruz and Nicoya counties of the Guanacaste region of Costa Rica is to promote the use of solar power for cooking and to build women's capacity for other activities through constructing and using solar cookers. Over 130 households have switched from wood, electricity, or gas to solar cooking, thereby reducing greenhouse gas emissions. The project has reduced the health risks associated with wood burning and reduced women's workload because they no longer collect fuelwood. The project, led almost completely by women, has supported and built women's ability to take action, particularly regarding the environment and livelihood issues. Its work illustrates how women's solar energy can open up new opportunities for women and improve their standing in the community. Because women build the stoves themselves, the project covers only the costs of materials, in addition to small amounts for transportation and instructors for the workshops. After women learn how to build these cookers, they teach others to do the same. Sol de Vida has exported this model to Guatemala, Honduras, and Nicaragua.

India: Large-scale biofuel production

India's National Mission on Biofuels plans to bring 400,000 hectares of marginal land under cultivation of jatropha for biodiesel production (Rajagopal 2007). The biofuels plan considers these marginal lands to be of little ecological or economic benefit. However, these lands, which are common property resources, provide essential food, fuel, fodder, and building materials for the rural poor, especially the most vulnerable (Rajagopal 2007). In India common property resources contribute between 12 and 25 percent of a poor household's income. The poorest households, often headed by women, rely most heavily on these common property resources. Thus, without specific interventions to benefit and include poor men- and women-headed households in the benefits of jatropha production, the livelihoods of the rural poor are likely to decline (Rossi and Lambrou 2008).

GUIDELINES AND RECOMMENDATIONS FOR PRACTITIONERS

Understanding and addressing the linkages among gender, environment, and energy undergird the success of bioenergy project development and implementation (UNDP 2007).

- Rural women and men possess different needs and priorities vis-à-vis energy services. Multiple strategies for providing energy to the rural poor are needed, including promoting more efficient and sustainable use of traditional biomass and enabling poor women and men to switch to modern fuels and technologies. The appropriate strategy will depend on local circumstances.
- We must reduce harmful emissions where dependency on traditional fuels will likely continue—for example, in the next two to three decades in Africa (UN-Energy 2007).
- Additional measures may be necessary for small-scale women and men farmers to be included in medium- or large-scale biofuel crop production, such as policies supporting decentralized production, local use of the energy produced, and organization of cooperatives or other forms of participation.
- Subsistence farmers, women in particular, remain less likely to shift their production to bioenergy, particularly if they live in marginal areas and have fewer options to counteract risks and higher discount rates. Organizing small-scale women and men producers' groups can enhance local benefits. Cooperatives can play a useful role in linking large firms to independent growers (as in Brazil and Mauritius). However, projects require rural women's participation in these cooperatives to ensure attention to their needs and concerns.

MONITORING AND EVALUATION

Examples of gender-sensitive indicators in bioenergy include the following (FAO 2007; see also the Monitoring and Evaluation section in the Overview):

- Percentage of women-headed and men-headed rural households with access to electricity, water, markets, and adequate storage facilities
- Percentage of men and women owning and using energy-efficient technologies and low-carbon practices
- Percentage of men and women who participate in decisions about biomass use for energy
- Number of hours spent by men and women in obtaining biomass for household consumption and small-scale enterprises
- Number of men and women producing bioenergy crops.

Gender and Natural Disasters

The incidence of natural disasters and related environmental disasters has escalated since the 1990s (UN 2001; UNDP 2004).[1] In the first half of 2006 alone, 174 disaster events occurred in 68 countries, affecting 28 million people and damaging property and assets valued at more than $6 billion (UNDP 2007). The effects of earthquakes, landslides, drought, floods, storms, and tropical cyclones severely threaten human survival and sustainable livelihoods and pose a challenge to achieving the UN Millennium Development Goals (FAO/WFP 2005). Disasters cause major loss of human lives and livelihoods and destroy economic and social infrastructure (UN 2002). Climate change, environmental mismanagement, and degradation (including unsustainable exploitation of natural resources) as well as unplanned urbanization and uneven distribution of assets cause increased risk and vulnerability to natural disasters (UN 2002). (The focus of this Thematic Note is on natural disasters; for a wider discussion on crises relating to conflicts and wars, see Module 11. For more on climate change, see Thematic Note 2.)

Natural disasters, often exacerbated by environmental degradation and mismanagement, adversely impact the environment. With sound management, the reverse proves true, thus establishing a direct link between disaster mitigation and environmental management (King 2002). Natural resource degradation leads to an increased frequency of small- or medium-impact disasters, such as recurrent floods or minor landslides, as well as slow-onset disasters, such as land degradation and drought. Human activity has altered ecosystems. The ability to recover from natural disturbance has diminished considerably. For instance, deforestation impairs watersheds; raises the risk of fires, landslides, and floods; exacerbates droughts; and contributes to climate change. Destruction of coastal wetlands, dunes, and mangroves diminishes the environmental buffer system for coastal storms. All these contribute to making at-risk areas such as low-lying islands more vulnerable to extreme weather events (Abromovitz 2001). Although often excluded from databases evaluating disaster impacts, small-scale disasters often account for more aggregate suffering than major ones (UN 2001). Scientists project that these will continue to increase as a result of climate change (Abromovitz 2001).

A growing body of evidence links environmental degradation and competition for natural resources to many of the internal and international conflicts that contribute to many complex emergencies (McNeely 2000). For example, desertification exacerbated the conflict in Darfur because it forced people to migrate from their homes into areas where they competed with others for scarce land and water (Harvey 2007). Severe environmental stress—when accompanied by underlying social or ethnic conflict, poverty, and weak governance—contributes to violent conflict and complex emergencies (UN 2001, 2002).

Although natural disasters strike in the industrialized and developing worlds, developing countries remain the most vulnerable to these risks and sustain greater losses. Countries that face similar patterns of natural hazards—from floods to droughts—often experience widely differing impacts when disasters occur. The impact depends in large part on previous investment in appropriate infrastructure, urban planning, and disaster risk management and reduction policies (UNDP 2004).[2] Within developing countries, the poor and socially disadvantaged remain the most vulnerable. Often the rural poor occupy the most marginal lands, relying on areas prone to drought, flooding, and other hazards for precarious livelihoods. They also face greater exposure to hazards resulting from poor-quality construction material and lack of access to information (Kumar-Range 2001). Rural poverty frequently determines risk for disasters such as flooding or drought (UNDP 2004).

Gender-based inequalities in access to livelihood assets, division of labor, and participation in decision-making processes result in women's and girls' increased vulnerability to the risks of natural disasters.[3] Disaster risk reduction and management interventions must take gender into account to reduce vulnerability effectively. The impacts of natural disasters can be mitigated by using a gender perspective to address their root causes, including social, political, economic, and cultural vulnerabilities (UN 2002).

KEY GENDER ISSUES

Key gender issues include risk and vulnerability to disasters, postdisaster vulnerability, and disaster mitigation, response, and recovery.

Risk and vulnerability to disasters

Natural disasters affect rural women and men differently. Women and girls have limited access to and control over critical assets that provide livelihood security, protection, and recovery, and thus they remain most vulnerable to the impacts of natural disasters. Understanding their different roles and responsibilities—in agriculture, fisheries, and forestry, both within the household and at the community level—can reveal women's and men's different vulnerabilities (Cannon 2002).

Disaster statistics, for which sex-disaggregated data exist, show that women are more likely to die or be injured when disaster unfolds.[4] Women and children are 14 times more likely than men to die as a result of disasters (Aguilar 2008). Women's disaster exposure results from their overrepresentation in highly vulnerable social groups, including the poor and elderly, that are less able to prepare for, survive, and cope with disaster (UN 2004). Additionally for, women do not receive timely warnings or other information about hazards and risks (Fothergill 1998; UN 2001). Mobility restrictions, dress codes, and culturally ascribed roles and behaviors disadvantage women. A disproportionate number of women died in the 1991 cyclone in Bangladesh because of cultural norms restricting their mobility outside the household. Less likely than men to know how to swim, women had few chances of escaping from the affected areas. More women than men died in the tsunami in Sri Lanka because they did not know how to swim or climb trees (Sachs 2007). Recent evidence also suggests that many women who drowned in the tsunami were looking for their children. Existing gender-based inequalities in the allocation of food within the household put women at risk (see also Module 1). For

instance, in Bangladesh women's lower nutritional status in predisaster situations worsened during crises (Cannon 2002; Masika 2002). Because they lack mobility and resources, elderly women, those with disabilities, pregnant and nursing women, and those with small children remain most at risk in cases of emergency.

Postdisaster vulnerability

In postdisaster situations women remain more vulnerable than men. Women's responsibilities in caring for household members increase after a disaster, as access to resources for recovery decreases. The daily work involved in providing food, water, and fuel for households after a disaster requires intensive labor. In the aftermath of Hurricane Mitch in Honduras and Nicaragua, women's household and care responsibilities increased, making it difficult for them to return to work (Nelson and others 2002).

In many parts of the developing world, discriminatory customary and social practices curtail women's rights to land. This situation deteriorates after natural disasters. Natural disasters such as hurricanes, tsunamis, and earthquakes damage and destroy land vital to women's and men's livelihoods. Disasters disrupt land ownership and use patterns by killing land titleholders, destroying land records, and erasing boundaries. Other efforts delay and impede the equitable redistribution of land, including the location of refugee camps, the relocation of affected communities, and measures to increase future resilience such as no-construction zones (Brown and Crawford 2006). Poor and marginalized women and men often have little alternative but to remain in or return to disaster-prone areas (Masika 2002).

Natural disasters frequently result in the degradation of water sources. Children and pregnant women are particularly susceptible to diseases such as diarrhea and cholera that thrive in such conditions. Because of their roles in managing household water supply and domestic chores, women take greater risks.[5] Women's health may also suffer as a result of reduced nutritional status when their workload increases. For instance, in Peru following the 1997–98 El Niño events, malnutrition among women caused peripartum illness. Flooding or rise in temperature in highland areas can extend the range of vector-borne diseases, such as malaria. Also, HIV and AIDS and other diseases can exacerbate the disaster risks brought on by climate change, urbanization, marginalization, and conflict (UNDP 2004). Health problems during disasters have psychological components as well as physical ones. Rural women and men victims of disasters may suffer from a variety of psychological problems related to loss of family members, trauma, unemployment, and identity (Graham 2001).

To cope with small- and medium-scale, and slow-onset disasters, women (and girls to some extent) often take on additional roles and responsibilities. With water shortages and depletion of forests (as a result of wildfires, droughts, desertification, land degradation, and other occurrences), women and girls walk longer distances to collect water and fuelwood, sometimes far from the safety of their households. This decreases the time available for food production and preparation, with consequences for household food security and nutritional well-being. Girls sometimes leave school to help with the increased work burden. Food distribution in refugee camps has resulted in a significant drop in girls' schooling rates.

As a result of slow-onset disasters such as land degradation and drought, men's out-migration has increased in some parts of the developing world. In Brazil, for example, people call women household heads "widows of the drought" (Branco 1995). Women left behind take on men's traditional roles and responsibilities, increasing their work burdens, but without having equal access to financial, technological, and social resources (Lambrou and Laub 2004). In some regions women's out-migration accompanies drought, such as in Australia, where women migrate to urban areas to seek additional income while their husbands remain on the farm (Alston 2006).

According to some estimates, 25 million environmental refugees have lost their homes because of environmental degradation or localized conflicts related to competition for resources (Tickell 2001). Uprooted populations generally encounter problems of protection and safety, with women in particular suffering sexual and physical abuse. Areas outside camps where women gather fuelwood and water can present dangers. Families frequently select girls to collect fuelwood used for the preparation of food inside refugee camps, and girls receive food in return. Women experience more violence while displaced than in normal circumstances, and violence against women increases in postconflict situations (FAO/WFP 2005). When displaced, women in particular frequently find themselves stateless and dependent on external assistance (Graham 2001). Gender and age determine entitlements to relief supplies, and access to food based on household registration procedures favors men in some settings.

Disaster mitigation, response, and recovery

People regularly cope with all kinds of "daily" disasters and have developed local strategies for reducing risk and responding to natural disasters (UN 2001).[6] Although women and children remain most vulnerable, many women at local levels mitigate hazards and strengthen the disaster resilience of households and communities. In Central America, the Caribbean, and other regions where the proportion of women-headed households is high and women actively engage in economic activities, women assume leadership roles in situations such as food distribution that require organizational and administrative capacities, impartial judgment, and social commitment (Toscani 1998).

Responses by men and women before, during, and after disasters relate to their status, roles, and position in society (Kumar-Range 2001). Most studies show that women's and men's responses to a disaster follow traditional gender lines (Fothergill 1998). Women take responsibility for child care, household, and supportive tasks, whereas men take leadership positions. Men usually participate in the public sphere in formal emergency and planning operations, and they discourage women from participation in critical planning and preparedness decisions.

Household organization also affects resilience. In responding to and recovering from disasters, social and kin networks determine available strategies (Kumar-Range 2001). Women-headed households remain the most economically and politically disadvantaged in gaining access to these networks (Graham 2001). In addition, rural poor women and men often lack savings or assets to ensure them against external shocks (Masika 2002).

Emergency decision-making processes after disasters often exclude women. Women's limited participation restricts their engagement in political decisions that impact their specific needs and vulnerabilities. Relief workers view women as victims rather than potential agents of change, which leads to the reconstruction of gender inequalities. For example, failure to recognize women's informal sector work may reduce their access to economic recovery assistance and undermine perceptions of women as full contributors to the recovery process. To take an active part in shaping projects that meet their needs, women must participate. Men are also at risk. Failure to recognize men's socioeconomic and emotional needs may delay men's long-term recovery (UN 2001, 2002).

POLICY AND IMPLEMENTATION ISSUES

Natural disasters and environmental management appeared on the international agenda throughout the International Decade for Natural Disaster Reduction (1990–2000). The Yokohama Conference in 1994 strongly emphasized the links between disaster reduction and sustainable development. It also recognized the need to stimulate community involvement and the empowerment of women at all stages of disaster management programs. Additionally, the Beijing Platform for Action (1995) and the twenty-third special session of the United Nations General Assembly (2000) viewed a gender perspective as integral to natural disaster mitigation (Enarson and Meyreles 2004). In 1999 the United Nations Inter-Agency Standing Committee issued a policy statement that requires all member organizations to mainstream gender when providing humanitarian assistance in emergencies. In 2005 the World Conference on Disaster Reduction emphasized integrating a gender perspective into all disaster risk management policies, plans, and decision-making processes.

A recognition of the social dimensions of disasters has resulted in increased attention to community involvement and ownership. However, gender perspectives in policies and strategies to prevent and respond to natural disasters (CSW 2002) have not yet received adequate attention.

Postdisaster reconstruction presents the opportunity to challenge existing gender relations and empower women to better respond to this challenge. Immediately following a disaster, the political climate lends itself to much-needed legal, economic, and social change in such areas as governance, land reform, skills development, employment, housing, and social solidarity (UN 2002). However, an excessive focus on relief assistance may obscure or compromise efforts to challenge these roles. Emergency relief used inappropriately may discourage independence and undermine local coping strategies. These strategies result in the reconstruction of vulnerability rather than the promotion of more equitable and sustainable conditions during the postdisaster window of opportunity for social change (UN 2001).

Major research gaps exist on the linkages among gender, environmental management, and disaster risk reduction at all levels—from climate change to local, small emergencies. Further work must examine gender-based differences in vulnerability, livelihood impacts, and specific needs during disasters (UN 2001).

GOOD PRACTICES AND LESSONS LEARNED

Interventions and life-saving strategies may succeed when gender differences have been properly understood and addressed (FAO/WFP 2005). The following examples of good practices and lessons learned from relevant projects take gender issues into account.

Safe access to fuelwood and alternative energy in humanitarian settings

An interagency program aims to promote safe access to fuelwood and alternative energy in humanitarian camps.[7] When women leave camps to collect wood, they often experience gender-based violence. In Chad all humanitarian efforts include efforts to reduce gender-based violence. In Rwanda and Tanzania programs support safety improvements. In Sudan some women have successfully transitioned to the use of mud-based fuel-efficient stoves in the camps. In Indonesia policies promote access to sustainable timber and minimize illegal logging caused by demand for shelter. Large concentrations of displaced populations in camps place excessive pressure on already degraded natural resources. This endangers the food security and livelihood of nearby local communities and fosters resentment and controversial relations with the host population. People compete for charcoal and wood for fuel and timber for shelter construction. Alternative sources of energy have had a positive impact on the livelihoods of women and men. These alternative sources have reduced women's and girls' time and workload for fuelwood collection and have reduced the risk of gender-based violence.

Nepal: Community-based disaster management project

The UNDP currently implements a community-based disaster management project in Nepal aimed at disaster risk reduction. It represents a clear shift from postdisaster rescue and relief to predisaster mitigation and preparedness and mainstreaming disaster risk reduction. The main goals of the community-based disaster management project are to enhance the safety of women and men vulnerable to natural disasters and to protect common property and community resources in select disaster-prone districts. The project uses participatory approaches and capacity-building measures and aims to enhance the capacities of stakeholders at the community, district, and national levels in different aspects of disaster management. Additionally, the project focuses on supporting specific disaster mitigation measures to reduce the vulnerability of women-headed, displaced, and poor households. Activities include 50 percent women's participation in training and education on HIV and AIDS, violence against women, and trafficking related to vulnerability during natural disasters.

Pakistan: Building capacity to cope with disasters

Pattan, a local NGO in Pakistan, increases community capacity to cope with disasters through supporting social organizations and developing local institutions. Previously Pattan worked in flood-prone areas that have unrepresentative community organizations dominated by local power elites, usually men. The NGO worked with the community to organize representative, democratic forums called Pattan Dehi Tanzeems (PDTs) that made collective decisions. Barred by local tradition from joining the PDTs, women formed separate PDTs and overcame resistance to their participation. Pattan used the disruptive nature of floods to develop institutions enabling women to make key decisions. The 1992 floods completely destroyed many villages, and so the NGO initiated a project to rehabilitate houses in which women participated in the PDTs. In Pakistan women maintain traditional (*kacha*) housing. The project involved women in the design and construction of improved (*pakka*) housing. Households received loans, and women took responsibility for collecting money to repay loan installments. Initially, men objected to giving women this responsibility, but the NGO developed an easy-to-use monitoring system. The NGO introduced the concept of joint ownership of the new *pakka* housing. It took time for the concept to take hold, but men eventually saw the value in joint ownership. The experience of the housing project has given women confidence to take collective action in many other projects (Bari 1998).

GUIDELINES AND RECOMMENDATIONS FOR PRACTITIONERS

Understanding the gender dimension in disaster-related development processes requires addressing root causes and ensuring equitable and efficient risk reduction measures (UN 2002). A gendered approach considers (1) the specific roles and responsibilities of men and women in food security and agriculture, (2) their main constraints and needs, and (3) their ability to carry out activities under emergency situations and early rehabilitation (FAO/WFP 2005). The following are important principles of disaster management (see box 10.10 for additional guidelines):

■ Understand gender-based differences in vulnerability and in livelihood impacts in natural disasters, including small- and medium-scale and slow-onset disasters.
■ Consider gender divisions of labor, time-use patterns, additional workload, and gender-based asymmetries in accessing and controlling livelihood assets (FAO/WFP 2005).
■ Recognize that community-based preparedness and response must consider women's and men's different physical and socioeconomic vulnerabilities to reduce their exposure to the adverse effects of climate change

---

Box 10.10   General Guidelines for Disaster Management

■ Create and implement, with the involvement of community groups and women's groups, comprehensive rural and urban development strategies and land-use plans that provide opportunities to mitigate damages caused by hazards.
■ Include gender-based hazard mapping and social and environmental risk assessment at the appraisal stage of all development projects, involving women and men equally at all levels of the assessment.
■ Systematically include hazard proneness and gender-based vulnerabilities in environmental impact assessments and formulate disaster reduction measures where appropriate, with particular regard to the protection of lifeline infrastructure and critical facilities.
■ Promote agricultural technologies and give specific regard to addressing, from a gender perspective, environmental degradation hazards that threaten food security.
■ Recognize the expertise and local knowledge of women and men disaster survivors and empower

them in the management of social and environmental hazards and prevention of disasters.
■ Target disadvantaged groups and households, and raise their awareness of women's human rights and the critical role women play in coping with natural disasters.
■ Increase women's access to risk management information through gender-sensitive early warning systems and target specific social groups for warning information to address gender-specific needs and circumstances.
■ Collaborate in the creation of networks that promote community access to gender-sensitive information and communication technologies that support information exchange on environmental management and disaster risk reduction.
■ Establish appropriate channels and mechanisms for information flow and dialogue that women and men in disaster-affected areas may access.

Source: UN 2001.

(Lambrou and Piana 2006). The participation and involvement of local women and men are essential.

- Create early warning systems and monitoring based on detailed information to minimize exposure to vulnerabilities and ensure preparedness. One strategy to increase preparedness is the creation of risk maps, including gender-based hazard maps (UN 2002).
- Factor the effects of food aid, subsidies, and rehabilitation programs on women as the principal providers of food for the household. In documentation and registration procedures, women should have the right to register in their own names. Devote attention to ensuring that women household heads receive benefits (FAO/WFP 2005).

MONITORING AND EVALUATION

Monitoring and evaluation processes enable staff to analyze the performance of emergency operations. Indicators include the following (FAO/WFP 2005):

- Percentage of aid targeted to the different needs of affected men and women
- Percentage of women elected and appointed to village committees
- Roles of women members in distribution committees (for example, weighing, rebagging, and monitoring that people actually got their entitlements) and whether this made the distribution fairer
- Percentage and number of women and men who benefited from the relief project
- Percentage of women and men who migrate and the impact of migration on the recovery pace within the village
- Impact on women's income and livelihood options (for example, income-generating activities and new employment opportunities)
- Ratio of the number of women to men who received emergency project relief and distributed food rations to their families.

Gender Dimensions of Land and Water Degradation and Desertification

Land degradation affects more than 900 million people worldwide and as much as two-thirds of the world's agricultural land (UNDP 2007a). Unsustainable land use and climate change drive land degradation, including soil erosion, nutrient depletion, water scarcity, and desertification.[1] Land degradation leads to the loss of plant and livestock genetic and species diversity, important sources of food, medicine, and commercial products (UNDP 2007a). Increased irrigation and expansion of agricultural land into former dry-season grazing areas exacerbate land degradation (FAO 2002). In Africa, 36 countries face dryland degradation or desertification (GEF 2003).

If present trends continue, 1.8 billion people will live in countries or regions with absolute water scarcity by 2025, and two-thirds of the people in the world could be subject to water stress.[2] The decline in quantity and quality of water leads to overexploitation of surface and groundwater resources and magnifies problems related to desertification. Water crises raise political tensions in many parts of the world, particularly where people share rivers and lakes across borders. Africans have the least access to clean water; the largest numbers of people with no access to basic sanitation live in Asia (UNDP 2005). Competition for increasingly precious water resources has intensified dramatically over the past decades. Water shortages, water quality degradation, and aquatic ecosystem destruction seriously affect economic and social development, political stability, and ecosystem integrity (UNDP 2005).

Desertification has emerged as one of the most pressing global environmental challenges facing the world today.[3] Drylands occupy 41 percent of the Earth's land area and are home to more than 2 billion people, 90 percent of whom live in developing countries.[4] Dry and subhumid lands present unique landscapes containing a wide variety of biodiversity well adapted to the often harsh conditions that characterize these areas (CBD 2007). Some 10 to 20 percent of drylands have already degraded, with a much larger number under threat from further desertification (MEA 2005). Desertification, which leads to loss of production capacity, reduces the land's resilience to natural climate variability and may temporarily affect climate change (UNCCD 2005). It results in persistent reductions in the capacity of ecosystems to provide services such as water, fuel, nutrients, soil fertility, and other necessities. Observers have seen a major decline in the well-being of women and men living in drylands (MEA 2005). Desertification contributes significantly to food insecurity and famine, the internal displacement of people, and international migration, and it creates environmental refugees who add stress to areas that may not yet have degraded.[5]

Pastoralists and farmers in drylands try to maximize herd size and crop production during good periods and to minimize losses and obtain some yield during periods of drought. Pastoralists may follow seasonal variations in vegetation by moving their livestock, sometimes over long distances. Resilience against fluctuations may mean bridging drought periods by drawing on local reserves, such as using different types of seeds or other adaptable genetic resources. Knowledge of local biodiversity minimizes risks in the face of land and water degradation. Rural women and men's reliance on a variety of genetic resources, including plant varieties and livestock breeds, allows them to adapt their agricultural systems to changing environmental, economic, and social conditions. For instance, livestock helps provide a safety net when other sources of income are no longer available.

Desertification causes rural poverty, just as rural poverty contributes to desertification. Poverty induces women and men to increase pressure on deteriorating drylands and to exploit the natural resource base in unsustainable ways. This accelerates land degradation, leading to a reduction in productivity and incomes while decreasing the livelihood options for poor rural women and men. The result is food scarcity, malnutrition, and economic and social instability, which increase poverty and further exacerbate pressure on the natural resource base.

Policies, programs, and projects implemented at the local, international, and national levels often fail to account for land and water degradation and desertification when addressing poverty and sustainable development.[6] Land degradation and desertification cannot be addressed in isolation from other efforts to protect biodiversity, water resources, food security, and energy security and to combat climate change.

KEY GENDER ISSUES

Combating desertification and reversing land and water degradation will help secure the livelihoods and overall well-being of women and men farmers and pastoralists. Land and water degradation impacts poor rural women and men most severely, because they directly depend on these resources for securing food and livelihoods (Lambrou and Laub 2004). When drylands become degraded, rural women and men become vulnerable to food insecurity, malnutrition, disease, and loss of livelihoods (FAO 2003). Gender-based inequalities make rural women and girls more vulnerable than men. Caste, ethnicity, and other socioeconomic considerations interact with gender to make certain groups of women and men particularly vulnerable.

Rural women and men have different roles, responsibilities, and knowledge in managing natural resources. Consequently, the impact of land and water degradation on rural household members will vary according to gender. This division of labor results in women's and men's different priorities for water use and management. Men typically use water for agricultural production, principally for irrigating cash crops. Women play an important role in water management as collectors, users, and managers of water (FAO 2007a), and they use water for both agricultural and household purposes. As previously discussed, the task of providing domestic water almost always falls to women and girls. Women also water some subsistence crops and vegetable gardens and spend considerable time collecting water for household use (for example, food preparation, drinking, and sanitation). Water collection makes up a large part of rural women's work in Asia and Africa. In Senegal women spend 17.5 hours each week collecting water, whereas in Mozambique they spend 15.3 hours in the dry season. In Nepal girls play an important role collecting water, averaging five hours per week (Crow and Sultana 2002). In rural Africa and India, 30 percent of women's daily energy intake is spent in carrying water (Ray 2007).

Depletion of land and water resources may place additional burdens on women's labor and health as they struggle to seek their livelihoods in a changing environment. Land degradation, water degradation and scarcity, desertification, and deforestation often cause women and girls to walk longer distances to collect fuelwood and water, with consequences for their health and sometimes exposing them to violence. In some cases, such as in Bangladesh, extraction of groundwater for irrigation has made drinking water pumps dry up (Crow and Sultana 2002).

Through their different tasks and responsibilities, rural women and men have accumulated knowledge and skills concerning the management and use of biodiversity in dryland ecosystems. This includes knowledge of local crop varieties, animal breeds, tree species, agricultural systems, and the medicinal and nutritional values of plants. Adept at managing their own scarce resources, rural women and men living in drylands have developed coping strategies to deal with periods of scarcity. Local knowledge provides a wide range of accumulated experience on how to manage natural resources in farming and grazing (UNCCD 2005). Rural women's and men's local knowledge proves crucial to the conservation, use, and management of drylands, including its biodiversity.

In southern and eastern Africa, some HIV- and AIDS-affected households have turned to livestock production as an alternative to crop production. People adopted this strategy when soils became infertile and crop management practices too demanding for the available labor. Other households sell cattle to pay for medical bills and funeral expenses. In pastoral societies, in which milk provides a major component of nutrition, selling cattle can contribute to malnutrition. Some households raise small livestock, such as poultry, which is a less labor-intensive practice and is often the responsibility of women (White and Robinson 2000).

Insecure land tenure reduces rural women's and men's incentives to make long-term investments in soil rehabilitation and conservation, which are crucial to drylands management. A reduction of agricultural productivity and more competition for relatively productive land leave women with the more marginal, fragile lands. The impact of environmental degradation on common property resources in drylands threatens household food security and livelihoods. Poor rural women who lack secure land tenure depend on these common resources for fuelwood, fodder, and food—and, therefore, the well-being of their households.

The projected increase in freshwater scarcity will cause greater stresses in drylands. Water shortages not only undermine agricultural production but also threaten the health of affected households. Local norms and customary practices can limit women's rights to water resources (Gender and Water Alliance 2003). Access to water depends on land rights, control over resources, and social networks, all of which more severely restrict women than men (IFAD 2006).

Excluding women's roles and perspectives in water and land management interventions will have adverse effects. For instance, an inappropriate design or location of tap stands or wells may increase the time women spend collecting water (FAO 2007a). Many projects emphasize participation of men and women in water management associations. A study in India found that (1) even when women are on water management boards, they choose not to attend meetings and send men relatives instead, and (2) women in different castes often have different needs for water, with elite women's preferences determining the placing of hand pumps and thus decreasing poor women's access to water (Singh 2006).

In southern and East Africa, HIV and AIDS have led to increased tenure insecurity for women and children. As women become widows and children lose their parents to AIDS, the incidence of "property grabbing" increases. The perpetrators are not always women; in some regions of Namibia and Zambia, sisters-in-laws are the main perpetrators (Izumi 2007). Most often, a husband's relatives take land and other productive assets from the deceased's widow or children.

POLICY AND IMPLEMENTATION ISSUES

The international community has long recognized that desertification presents a major economic, social, and environmental concern to many countries in all regions of the world. In 1977 the United Nations Conference on Desertification adopted its "Plan of Action to Combat Desertification." The United Nations Environment Programme concluded in 1991 that the problem of land degradation in arid, semiarid, and dry subhumid areas had intensified (UNCCD 2005). To tackle the problem of desertification with renewed efforts, the international community adopted the United Nations Convention to Combat Desertification (UNCCD) in 1994. The convention stresses the importance of a bottom-up participatory approach in identifying, implementing, monitoring, and evaluating projects that combat desertification and mitigate the effects of drought. The UNCCD recognizes the role of women in rural livelihoods,

explicitly encouraging the equal participation of women and men (Lambrou and Laub 2004).

The Convention on Biological Diversity (CBD) also acknowledges the importance and uniqueness of the biodiversity of dry and subhumid lands.[7] In 2000 the CBD Conference of the Parties emphasized the importance of increasing the knowledge base and supporting best management practices on dry and subhumid lands; the CBD also recognized the need for the full participation of women at all levels of policy making and implementation.[8] The World Summit on Sustainable Development reaffirmed land degradation as one of the major global environment and sustainable development challenges of the twenty-first century, calling for action to address causes of desertification and land degradation and to restore land and address poverty resulting from land degradation (GEF 2003).

Linkages among biodiversity, poverty alleviation, and gender issues remain intertwined with land and water degradation and desertification. Because they consider it "nonscientific" or inferior, practitioners overlook or ignore rural women's and men's local knowledge on the conservation and sustainable use of natural resources.

GOOD PRACTICES AND LESSONS LEARNED

Involving women in participatory land and water management promotes more sustainable land and water use, reversal of desertification, and improved socioeconomic conditions (Aswani and Weiant 2004; Nyssen and others 2004). Projects that adopt a bottom-up participatory approach create an "enabling environment," designed to support local women and men in achieving livelihood security.

Asia: Farmer-Centered Agricultural Resource Management

Supported by the UNDP and implemented by FAO, the Farmer-Centered Agricultural Resource Management (FARM) program was implemented in China, India, Indonesia, Nepal, the Philippines, Sri Lanka, Thailand, and Vietnam.[9] Between 1993 and 1998, the program aimed to promote sustainable use and management of natural resources in agriculture and household food security in ecologically fragile, rain-fed areas. Recognizing that women farmers contribute significantly to agriculture, the program promoted women's participation in decision-making processes and other activities at all levels. FARM adopted a participatory assessment planning (PAP) approach that incorporated a gender analysis tool—a practical tool for examining activities, problems, knowledge, and access to natural resources of both women and men. The output of the PAP approach resulted in greater accountability and equitable sharing of benefits and ownership of assets. FARM also carried out training of trainers under FAO's Socio-economic and Gender Analysis Program (SEAGA). The emphasis on gender has created awareness and improved understanding of social-equity issues among community members. Women have begun to play important roles in decision making and leadership management.

China: Wulin mountains minority-areas development project

This joint IFAD–World Food Programme project aimed to increase food and cash crop production through a range of land-improvement activities. These included the conversion of dryland to paddies, improvement of livestock and fish production, and literacy and numeracy training for women. Improved drinking water supply systems and the introduction of labor- and time-saving technologies reduced women's workloads. Small livestock husbandry provided additional income for food, school fees, and clothing, and drinking water systems and training improved hygiene and health. Women gained self-esteem and social position with their entrepreneurial success.

Egypt: Matruh Resources Management Project

The Matruh Resources Management Project, funded by the World Bank, seeks to break the cycle of natural resource degradation and poverty in the fragile ecosystem of Matruh, Egypt, in which Bedouin women play a critical role in rural production and environmental management. The project works closely with community groups to define the needs of women and men and ensure participation in preparing and implementing local resource management plans. To fulfill these objectives and enable the community groups to address gender issues effectively, project staff received early gender training. In addition, women extension agents based in each subproject area work directly with women.

The Gambia: Partial participation by women in irrigation program

Efforts undertaken through development initiatives have rarely succeeded in providing women farmers with secure access to irrigated assets.[10] Sometimes women obtain access indirectly or acquire irregular or seasonal access, but even when they do obtain use of irrigated land, they may end up losing this access. When IFAD-funded drylands projects attempted to ensure better access for women to irrigated land (for example, by designating the land only for women's crops), men sometimes took over the crops, as in a rice irrigation project in The Gambia. However, "partial participation" by women in irrigation projects may still benefit women. Women's consumption of water improved, even though their control of assets and status did not increase. Women may also use water for their livestock or their domestic needs, even though they cannot use it for their crops. Indirect or limited access to irrigation water may somewhat improve their livelihoods in the short term.

Mauritius and Rodrigues: Capacity-building for sustainable land management

The UNDP implemented this three-year, $1.38-million project (including a Global Environmental Facility grant of $600,000) to design sustainable land management capacities in appropriate government and civil society institutions and user groups.[11] The project's long-term goal was to ensure that agricultural, pasture, forest, and other land management efforts in Mauritius and Rodrigues consist of sustainable, productive systems that maintain ecosystem productivity and ecological functions while contributing directly to economic and social well-being. Women participated actively in stakeholder consultations during the project's formulation. Women represented 31 percent of overall participation at the inception workshop, where they voiced their needs and contributed their perspectives. Since that time, the project has ensured a good balance of women and men in training courses and other activities. A gender specialist conducts capacity-building exercises to ensure that the project takes gender issues into consideration in all UNDP-supported projects, including sustainable land management.

Niger: The Keita Project

The Keita Project, financed by the Italian Government and implemented by FAO with support from the World Food Programme, aimed at combating desertification in the Keita region of Niger. The project adopted a gender-sensitive participatory approach that led to better understanding of local land-use systems and husbandry. Its aim was to facilitate women's access to income-generating activities (garden and fruit production, sheep production) and promote their participation in local and national-level organizations and activities. Time-saving technologies introduced by the project alleviated women's work burden.

GUIDELINES AND RECOMMENDATIONS FOR PRACTITIONERS

An assessment of gender-specific relationships to natural resources and of gender-differentiated impacts of land and water degradation and desertification will facilitate the development of effective projects related to land and water degradation and desertification. The following guidelines are of particular importance:

- Understanding the gender-based inequalities in accessing livelihood assets, in the division of labor, and in participation in resource planning and management provides a sound basis for the sustainable management of land and water.
- To understand the gender-differentiated vulnerabilities and coping strategies in relation to land and water degradation and desertification, we must identify changes in land use, land scarcity, and the economy that affect the ability of women and men to meet their livelihood needs.
- The success of sustainable land and water management requires women's and men's full and equal participation, through incorporating local women's and men's perspectives, needs, and priorities. In some cases, women can benefit from partial participation. Efforts to encourage women's participation in decision-making processes and organizations should take into account women's time and mobility restrictions. Serious efforts should ensure that women's participation goes beyond tokenism. In addition, these efforts must acknowledge that women from different castes and classes may have different interests and power in making natural resource management decisions such as where to locate pumps.

- Strengthening the capacity of women and men users and managers of drylands resources remains one of the most important factors in reversing land and water degradation. Participatory processes and innovations in community-based planning and decision making work best to build capacity. Women must gain leadership positions, participate in organizations, and gain access to technology. Strengthening women's group-based lending has sometimes enabled women to overcome requirements for collateral. Credit activities served as entry points for organizing women for broader activities (IFAD 2006).

MONITORING AND EVALUATION

Examples of gender-sensitive indicators include the following (FAO 2007b):[12]
Land:

- Average number of hectares of land owned by women-headed and men-headed households
- Percentage of women and men with de facto and de jure land rights
- Number of women and men with decision-making authority in cooperatives and marketing associations
- Ratio of number of men and women with access to credit based on land rights.

Water:

- Ratio of women and men who are members of water users associations
- Ratio of number of irrigated farms managed by women and men
- Change in the number of hours of labor required by men and women with the introduction of irrigation projects.

Gender, Biodiversity, and Local Indigenous Knowledge Systems (LinKS) for Food Security

PROJECT OBJECTIVES AND DESCRIPTION

The goal of the LinKS project was to improve rural women's and men's food security and promote the sustainable management of agrobiodiversity.[1] To achieve this goal, the organizers raised awareness of how rural men and women use and manage agrobiodiversity and promoted the importance of local knowledge for food security and sustainable agrobiodiversity at local, institutional, and policy levels. They worked with a range of stakeholders—development agents, researchers, and extension services—to strengthen their ability to recognize and value women and men farmers' knowledge and use gender-sensitive and participatory approaches in their policies, programs, and interventions.

Launched in 1997, the project, funded by the government of Norway and administered by FAO, operated in Mozambique, Tanzania, and Zimbabwe. Activities in Swaziland began in 2000 and continued until the end of September 2005.

The main strategy of the project was to support, build on, and strengthen the efforts of other groups already working on food security, indigenous knowledge, and agrobiodiversity issues in the four countries. These other groups included NGOs, research, training, and academic institutions; government agencies; and policy institutions. The project teams and management used participatory approaches in project design, formulation, and implementation activities.

The project operated through three central areas of activities:

- *Capacity building and training* to raise awareness and develop tools and methods to enhance capacity, change development practitioners' attitudes about rural women and men's local knowledge, and stress the importance of this knowledge for sustainable management of biodiversity and food security
- *Research on gender-based differences* in farmers' knowledge and management of biodiversity, highlighting the role of agrobiodiversity management for food security, and the different roles and responsibilities of rural women and men in the use and management of agrobiodiversity
- *Communication and advocacy* to enhance the exchange of information about the value of local knowledge in agriculture between communities, as well as with institutions that work with farmers and policy makers.

INNOVATIVE FEATURES

The LinKS project was conceived in response to the emerging international debates on the sustainable management of natural resources and participatory approaches during the early 1990s culminating in the 1996 International Technical Conference on Plant Genetic Resources for Food and Agriculture. In the period leading up to 1996, the understanding of gender and local knowledge systems and the rich source of information embodied in the knowledge, skills, and practices of women and men as managers and users of biodiversity were not very clear. Agricultural and rural development programs and policies, in particular those related to natural resources management, often failed to take into account

---

What's innovative? The LinKS project played an important role in shedding light on how food security will have to build much more on local knowledge and agrobiodiversity with a clear understanding of gender implications, keeping in mind the continuously changing global socioeconomic and political conditions. The participatory management style, together with a holistic approach, represented a new and innovative approach for FAO in project implementation.

---

rural women's and men's local knowledge systems in farming activities (Rocheleau 1996; Shiva 1996). Furthermore, research, science, and national policies tend to undermine the value of local knowledge, capacities, skills, and innovations of local farming communities to sustain and manage agrobiodiversity and secure food. The misconception that local knowledge proves inferior to scientific and technical approaches leads to a marginalization and loss of local practices and knowledge.

The LinKS project evolved with the aim to bridge this gap between local and scientific knowledge (box 10.11).

BENEFITS AND IMPACTS

The project enhanced the capacity of participants in understanding the linkages between local knowledge, gender, and agrobiodiversity and incorporating these issues in their work through the use of gender-sensitive participatory approaches. Workshops organized to document traditional practices emphasized, first, the potential benefits and risks of sharing such knowledge, and, second, the responsibilities of researchers and development agents to record and document local knowledge. Several specific training workshops were organized to strengthen knowledge and skills in implementing gender-sensitive participatory agricultural and livestock research and training. Other capacity-building activities included the following:

■ About 1,125 people participated in the training workshops on gender, local knowledge, and biodiversity and the application of gender analysis and participatory methods.

■ A training manual, *Building on Local Knowledge, Gender and Biodiversity,* highlighted the specific concepts and links between these issues from the perspective of sustainable livelihoods.

■ A local pool of experienced trainers was built up to facilitate with the training workshops on LinKS issues and gender-sensitive participatory approaches.

■ Integration of local knowledge, gender, and agrobiodiversity issues in the educational curriculum of local training colleges, universities, and other institutions of higher learning (such as the Sokoine University of Agriculture).

■ Visits provided farmers, researchers, NGO representatives, and development workers an opportunity to exchange ideas and experiences, and to take part in mutual learning experiences. In Tanzania, as part of a research project focusing on the management of animal genetic resources by the Maasai, pastoralists from various study areas exchanged visits to share experiences and views.

The project also supported 28 research activities that documented and increased understanding of the linkages between local knowledge, gender, and agrobiodiversity; reinforced collaboration between researchers and rural communities; demonstrated the complementarities between the local and scientific systems of knowledge; and enhanced the potential of developing approaches to increase food security and agrobiodiversity. The stakeholders identified three broad topics as particularly important: (1) traditional seed systems (box 10.12), (2) animal production and genetic diversity (box 10.13), and (3) the relation between HIV and AIDS and local knowledge systems (box 10.14).

Box 10.11   Linkages between Local Knowledge, Biodiversity, Food Security, and Gender Issues

Biodiversity serves as one of the most important natural assets for poor rural women and men. They rely on a diverse range of natural resources—crops, trees, livestock, fish—for subsistence production and sale. Yet, because of environmental stresses, introduction of new improved varieties and marginalization of local knowledge, biodiversity is lost at a rapid rate, posing a grave threat to long-term food security.

The different tasks and responsibilities of rural women and men result in accumulation of different types of local knowledge and skills. This local knowledge

shapes and influences plant and animal diversity at both the gene and species levels. It also provides an important coping strategy for poor rural women and men vulnerable to the risk of environmental degradation and natural disasters. For instance, poor rural women and men farmers often spread risk by growing a wide variety of locally adapted crops, some of which will be resistant to drought or pests.

Thus, local knowledge, gender, and agrobiodiversity are closely interrelated.

Source: FAO 2005.

Box 10.12 Tanzania: Traditional Seed Systems

Research activity on gender and biodiversity was set up in the southern highlands of Tanzania, a region heavily exposed to improved seed varieties. The goal was to improve the availability and accessibility of high-quality seeds of crop varieties preferred by farmers to enhance household food security. The main findings at the end of the project were the following: (1) some crop species had disappeared because of changes in weather, migration, government policies and interventions, or farmers' preferences; (2) many varieties had been introduced; (3) in general, agrobiodiversity increased over the years; (4) levels of food consumption and their composition varied within the different socioeconomic groups; (5) food-secure households relied more on staple food and less on natural and collected crops; and (6) the informal system provided a better source of seeds and information for many farmers than the formal seed system.

Source: Author.

Box 10.13 Tanzania: Animal Production and Genetic Diversity

In the Mbarali district, a study was conducted to gauge local knowledge on breeding and selection of livestock in the Maasai community. The study examined the types of animals (cattle, sheep, goats) preferred and the criteria used to achieve the desired traits. These preferences were analyzed in relation to gender and age, roles and responsibilities, decision making, and goals of food security and herd survival. The objective was to let the Maasai pastoralists identify the gaps and make corrections. The threats or constraints to the pastoralists' local knowledge for the sustainable management of indigenous livestock were identified, and possible solutions offered. The decreasing grazing land and water for livestock in the Mbarali district and livestock diseases were major constraints. (See also Module 14.)

Box 10.14 The Relation between HIV and AIDS and Local Knowledge Systems

A study on the impact of HIV and AIDS on local seed systems in both Mozambique and Tanzania showed the gender specificity of local knowledge. Men and women are responsible for different crops; for example, a widower would not necessarily know or be able to produce, after his wife's demise, the local crops she had planted. Her specific knowledge about local seed varieties would be lost. HIV and AIDS constitute a severe threat to agrobiodiversity. At the request of four communities in Tanzania, several local seed fairs enabled farmers to share and exchange their local knowledge and local seed varieties.

Source: FAO 2005.

The project's communication strategy increased the visibility of women's and men's knowledge among communities, development workers, and policy makers. Communication activities conducted through participatory processes included the following:

- A total of 787 researchers, policy makers, and development workers participated in workshops and seminars organized to raise awareness and facilitate discussion of the issues.
- Small workshops explored farmers' rights and intellectual property rights. Through these workshops, the project fostered discussion of local knowledge and its link to biodiversity conservation and food security in each of the project countries.
- Twenty short case-studies, 33 research reports, and two videos were disseminated to project partners through training workshops, seminars, and the LinKS project mailing list.
- Agricultural fairs, contributions to national television and radio programs, national newspapers, and specialist magazines were given support.
- A Web site (www.fao.org/sd/links/gebio.htm) provides useful resources and links to information sources.

LESSONS LEARNED AND ISSUES FOR WIDER APPLICABILITY

The project's thematic focus and the scope of its activities, as well as the number of countries involved, made it a complex project to implement. Addressing and linking the main themes of gender, local knowledge, and agrobiodiversity brought conceptual and analytical challenges as well. *Gender-sensitive participatory approaches* proved to be the most valid approach to achieve the project objectives.

The project adopted a *holistic, interdisciplinary approach* for understanding the linkages between gender, local knowledge systems, and agrobiodiversity management for food security. Research activities were designed in a process-oriented way to include the active involvement of all disciplines in planning, implementation, analysis, and interpretation. Because ministries, universities, and most NGOs traditionally work within a sectoral approach, such a multidisciplinary approach proved extremely challenging.

Project partners experienced difficulties grasping the conceptual themes and applying them to their work. Despite intensive training, the application of concepts to field work and data analysis remained unclear to researchers. Consequently, researchers participated in pre-field training to ensure that they were able to document local knowledge in such a way that local communities benefited. Training workshops focused on the application of gender-sensitive participatory tools. It became clear that workshops were not sufficient to increase understanding of the concepts and their linkages; thus, a training manual was developed to address this gap.

The participatory management style of the project presented limitations due to existing institutional frameworks and bureaucracy. To mitigate these limitations, LinKS set up a special project structure that entailed national coordination teams with managerial responsibility for project activities in each project country. National team offices within the hosting institutions facilitated a closer collaboration with partner institutions.

A major lesson learned was that training prior to undertaking research, although important, was not sufficient. Participants often stressed the need for postworkshop follow-up, monitoring, and mentoring. LinKS tried to address this through intensive technical support throughout the research process, from research design, data collection, and analysis to interpretation and presentation. Furthermore, many researchers found analyzing socioeconomic data challenging and consequently failed to report research results in a coherent and eloquent manner, thus, pointing to the need for capacity building and developing appropriate training materials.

Research activities were closely linked to capacity building and advocacy. Government officers, researchers, and NGO staff who participated in the training and awareness workshops often developed research proposals for increasing recognition of the knowledge of men and women, documenting experiences, community-to-community exchanges, or follow-up action. All research activities explored the hypothesis that women are important custodians of knowledge in the management of biodiversity. Communication at the rural community level, conducted through participatory research processes, encouraged dialogue, feedback to communities, and follow-up action that further enhanced learning and empowerment. Research reports were shared with the local communities and stakeholders for feedback. Such feedback sessions were also important to identify follow-up action with the local communities and stakeholders to ensure that they benefited from the studies.

India: Karnataka Watershed Development Project

PROJECT OBJECTIVES AND DESCRIPTION

The aim of the Karnataka Watershed Development Project (KWDP) is to improve the productive potential of selected watersheds; the steps involved include the following actions:

- Enhance production and livelihood systems.
- Strengthen community and institutional arrangements for natural resource management.
- Promote participatory involvement of primary stakeholders/beneficiaries.
- Offer assistance to women, the landless, and other vulnerable groups by supporting investments in income generation activities.

The project also aims to strengthen the capacity of communities to participate in planning, implementation, social and environmental management, and maintenance of assets. They will operate in a more socially inclusive manner within the framework of a watershed development plan implemented through community groups.

The KWDP, initiated in 2001 and scheduled to end in 2009, is being implemented in seven districts of Karnataka by the Watershed Development Department of the government of Karnataka and funded by the World Bank. The

target districts are drought prone and dominated by rainfed agriculture. High soil erosion leads to declining productivity. Groundwater from existing tubewells is only for three to four months after monsoon rains. Deterioration of common lands results from poor management.

The project addresses (1) social mobilization and institution building to help plan and implement participatory watershed treatments, (2) farming system intensification and participatory research, (3) income generation activities to benefit socially vulnerable and landless groups, and (4) capacity building, monitoring, and evaluation. The project is being implemented in a phased manner: phase 1 consists of 10 subwatersheds, phase 2 covers 20 subwatersheds, and phase 3 covers the final 47 subwatersheds. The project is now working mainly on the phase 3 subwatershed.

The project uses a complex institutional structure to develop critical partnerships between government technical specialists, NGOs, communities, local authorities, and research organizations, for instance, through the formation of community-based organizations such as self-help groups (largely women and landless), area groups (mainly landowning farmers), and a community-level executive committee. Self-help groups, the basic units of planning for income generation activities, are consolidated at the microwatershed level.

What's innovative? Program design promotes greater local participation and encompasses traditional soil and water conservation as well as rural livelihood development. The gender dimension of KWDP aims at creating opportunities for vulnerable groups, including women's economic activity, access to basic resources, and participation in decision-making processes.

BENEFITS AND IMPACTS

On over 270,000 hectares, soil and water conservation improved average crop yields to between 525 and 1,136 kilograms per hectare. Crop diversity, especially cash crops, increased to four to nine crops. Groundwater availability following monsoon rains improved to four to six months.

The project established 4,300 farmer groups and 6,600 new self-help groups to sustain participatory watershed management across 7,000 communities in 742 microwatersheds.

The KWDP significantly impacts the lives of women. Visible impacts include increased self-esteem, confidence, and decision-making ability; improved livelihoods; and economic empowerment.

Annual household income increased to approximately $373. Self-help groups flourished with project support. Taking into account member savings, project revolving funds, and leveraged commercial loans, the total potential capital base in these community groups is almost $13 million, which is being used to help establish small businesses, particularly among women and the landless. The majority of members are women. More than 60 percent of the self-help groups are linked to commercial financial institutions. Moneylenders are no longer a major force in these communities.

The success of self-help groups in creating savings resulted in women's economic empowerment. Women in self-help groups better articulate their needs and plan their livelihood strategies. The majority of women feel that the project has offered several new opportunities, such as a teleconference, a satellite-based training program, and demonstrations.

Approximately 70 percent of the women and landless participating in the income-generating activity component preferred to enhance their incomes through livestock and poultry production. The project partners agreed to introduce village-based private veterinary service providers, "Gopal Mitras," to promote effective and low-cost service to people. Field visits and monitoring and evaluation data confirm the important role that the Gopal Mitras now play in many communities. All Gopal Mitras use mobile phones to make it easier for people in more distant villages to call via a community call box. Earnings by the Gopal Mitras range from $75 to $375 per month, with an average of $125.

Women's role in decision making has improved considerably at both the family and the community/institution levels. More than 70 percent of women reported that their life has changed for the better with respect to education, financial matters, marriages, and other social issues. At the institutional level, about 70 percent of women feel that their status has improved, their views are respected, and their social acceptance level has increased.

LESSONS LEARNED

The discussion below surveys some of the lessons learned from past experiences.

■ Specific emphasis on women's participation in capacity building includes training programs and exposure visits. Group formation, leadership, conducting meetings, and

skill development modules stress women's participation. This project strives to improve the status of women, increase their participation, and empower them to be more self-reliant and self-confident. The project facilitated women and vulnerable groups to participate and express their views freely. Thus, the project addresses community empowerment, social justice, and gender equality.

■ The training provided by the project created a high level of awareness and confidence among the executive committee and self-help groups, but relatively less among the area groups. The training knowledge is utilized primarily for microcredit management and income-generating activity rather than for watershed activity. Women view access to credit as vital to their ability to earn income and to control their status and autonomy.

■ Marginal and landless people are the major beneficiaries of demonstrations in the project (81 percent). However, the spread of knowledge about watersheds remains limited. People conceive of the project as more of an income-earning enterprise rather than spreading knowledge about watershed management.

■ The increased financial stability through savings and employment generation (at the self-help group level) has substantially reduced people's dependency on moneylenders. The extra earnings and employment opportunities have decreased out-migration, especially in the Haveri district and, to a lesser extent, in Chitradurga, Kolar, and Tumkur. Families now experience the opportunity to live together with family members. However, long-term employment generation is yet to be realized.

■ The Haveri and Kolar districts report slightly improved access to fodder and fuel, and a few districts report improved drinking water facilities. However, these issues largely depend on natural resource development and increased biomass, which require a longer period to show results.

■ Reasons for the limited participation of women include the nonsupportive social environment, cultural taboos, the presence of dominant caste and politically influential members, illiteracy, and a lack of clarity of benefits.

CHALLENGES FOR WIDER APPLICABILITY

■ Self-help groups should develop a sense of identity, cohesiveness, and competence in areas such as managing their finances, taking up group income-generating activities (IGAs), and involvement in community affairs. IGA products produced under the project can be branded as "KWDP" as a unified marketing label.

- Women are usually unable to participate in community activities without the consent and support of men in their families and in the community. Men, therefore, need to be more aware of the importance of the contribution of women to the project and to the development of the village.

- Women field guides can work effectively with women, and it is easier for women staff to interact with them in the community. More women field guides are needed, and they need to be trained in facilitating women's participation and technical aspects of the project.

- The involvement of women in project planning should be ensured, especially with respect to how they are treated, participation in productive work, and benefits of production. Open-house meetings at regular intervals ensure better transparency and participation.

- Women committee members must be given specific responsibilities and made signatories to the bank accounts to emphasize the importance of their role.

- Equal opportunities in employment and equal wages for men and women commensurate with the nature of work must be ensured.

- Women should be given rights over village common property land to access the resources for their livelihood, and benefit-sharing mechanisms should be developed for wider participation.

- Common property resources must meet daily household needs for fuel and fodder and provide livelihood options for women. Social fencing creates hardships for vulnerable groups. To circumvent the long gestation period for realizing the benefits, a buffer zone approach should be used to develop common property land.

NOTES

Overview

This Overview was prepared by Carolyn Sachs (Pennsylvania State University) and Marina Laudazi (Consultant), with inputs from David Boerma, Dominique Lantieri, Regina Laub, Sibyl Nelson, Andrea Rossi, and Reuben Sessa (FAO), and reviewed by Mary Hill Rojas (Consultant); Yianna Lambrou (FAO); Ilaria Firmian, Maria Hartl, and Sheila Mwanundu (IFAD); and Erick Fernandes, Robin Mearns, and Daniel Sellen (World Bank).

1. "Global Environment Outlook 4," www.unep.org.

2. Commonwealth/International Labour Organization, WTO TRIPS Agreement, Globalisation and Gender Briefs, Series 2, July, www.ilo.org/dyn/empent/docs/F1599852333/No%202%20-%20TRIPS.pdf.

3. For a full discussion on monitoring and evaluation, refer to Module 16.

Thematic Note 1

This Thematic Note was prepared by Carolyn Sachs (Pennsylvania State University) and Marina Laudazi (Consultant), with inputs from David Boerma, Dominique Lantieri, Regina Laub, Sibyl Nelson, Andrea Rossi, and Reuben Sessa (FAO), and reviewed by Mary Hill Rojas (Consultant); Yianna Lambrou (FAO); Ilaria Firmian, Maria Hartl, and Sheila Mwanundu (IFAD); and Erick Fernandes, Robin Mearns, and Daniel Sellen (World Bank).

1. "Global Environment Outlook 4," www.unep.org. The Convention on Biological Diversity defines *biodiversity* as the variability among living organisms from all sources, including terrestrial, marine, and other aquatic ecosystems and the ecological complexes they are part of; this includes diversity within species, between species, and of ecosystems. The convention defines *sustainable use* as the use of components of biological diversity in a way and at a rate that does not lead to the long-term decline of biological diversity, thereby maintaining its potential to meet the needs and aspirations of present and future generations.

2. Over the last few decades, agricultural development has been characterized by agricultural intensification and expansion, achieved mainly through technological advancements and the replacement of local plant or livestock varieties with improved, high-yielding, uniform varieties, as well as large-scale conversion of forests or other natural habitats to monocultural farming systems (FAO 2005).

3. *Local knowledge* is a collection of facts and relates to the entire system of concepts, beliefs, and perceptions that people hold about the world around them. This includes the way people observe and measure their surroundings, how they solve problems, and how they validate new information (FAO 2004; Warburton and Martin 1999).

4. Note that there is some contention between TRIPS and the CBD. TRIPS allows for the privatization of biological resources, but the CBD acknowledges that local communities have rights over these resources and the indigenous knowledge involved in their usage (Sahai 2003).

5. High-yielding exotic crops are often less nutritious than indigenous varieties. FAO's 1996 *State of the World's Plant Genetic Resources for Food and Agriculture* report states that the main cause of genetic erosion, reported by almost all countries, is the replacement of local varieties by improved or exotic varieties and species (FAO 2005).

6. "Poverty and Climate Change: Reducing the Vulnerability of the Poor through Adaptation," www.oecd.org/dataoecd/60/27/2502872.pdf.

7. Gerry Toomey, "Farmers as Researchers: The Rise of Participatory Plant Breeding," International Development Research Centre (IDRC), Ottawa, Project No. 950019, www.idrc.ca/en/ev-5559-201-1-DO_TOPIC.html.

8. In addition to the ones listed here, the legal instruments relating to biodiversity include the International Undertaking on Plant Genetic Resources adopted by FAO in the early 1980s to protect plant genetic resources; the International Treaty on Plant Genetic Resources for Food and Agriculture, which promotes conservation and sustainable use of plant genetic resources for food and agriculture; and the Global Strategy for the Management of Farm Animal Genetic Resources, which provides a technical and operational framework for assisting countries. Further information on these aspects is highlighted in Bragdon and others (2003).

9. Because of space limitations, the relevant policy instruments will not be discussed in detail here. For a discussion on these instruments from a gender-sensitive perspective, see Bragdon and others (2003); FAO (2005); Lambrou and Laub (2004).

10. For a full discussion on the intellectual property rights of indigenous and local communities, see FAO (2005); Lambrou and Laub (2006).

11. For a full discussion on these issues, see FAO (2005).

12. Cathy Rozel Farnworth and Janice Jiggins, "Gender and Participatory Plant Breeding," CGIAR, Program on Participatory Research and Gender Analysis, www.prgaprogram. org/modules/DownloadsPlus/uploads/PRGA_Publications/General/Reports/PPBMonograph4.pdf. Conventional breeding programs are recognized to have brought little benefit to some marginalized groups of farmers. However, encouraging examples can be found of projects in which women and men farmers are involved in crop improvement and breeding programs.

Thematic Note 2

This Thematic Note was prepared by Carolyn Sachs (Pennsylvania State University) and Marina Laudazi (Consultant), with inputs from David Boerma, Dominique Lantieri, Regina Laub, Sibyl Nelson, Andrea Rossi, and Reuben Sessa (FAO), and reviewed by Mary Hill Rojas (Consultant); Yianna Lambrou (FAO); Ilaria Firmian, Maria Hartl, and Sheila Mwanundu (IFAD); and Erick Fernandes, Robin Mearns, and Daniel Sellen (World Bank).

1. The IPCC is a body of the world's leading scientists convened by the United Nations. It has been established to assess scientific, technical, and socioeconomic information relevant for the understanding of climate change, its potential impacts, and options for adaptation and mitigation. The IPCC won the Nobel Peace Prize in 2007.

2. Continued greenhouse gas emissions at or above current rates would cause further warming and induce many changes in the global climate system during the twenty-first century that would very likely be larger than those observed during the twentieth century.

3. The main human-produced greenhouse gases are carbon dioxide, methane, nitrous oxide, and chloroflurocarbons. Because of space limitations, this Thematic Note will not explore the scientific basis of climate change. For information, see the IPCC's assessment reports at www.ipcc.ch.

4. This is an advance since the IPCC Third Assessment Report (2001), which concluded that "most of the observed warming over the last 50 years is *likely* to have been due to the increase in greenhouse gas concentrations."

5. See also "Poverty and Climate Change: Reducing the Vulnerability of the Poor through Adaptation," www.oecd. org/dataoecd/60/27/2502872.pdf.

6. In this context, climate change was brought before the UN Security Council for the first time in April 2007, as the issue was identified as one of the key factors behind the conflict in Darfur, because desertification had forced people from their homes and into areas where they competed with others for scarce resources such as water (Harvey 2007).

7. See the Overview for this Module and the Key Gender Issues section in this Note.

8. See "Poverty and Climate Change: Reducing the Vulnerability of the Poor through Adaptation," www.oecd. org/dataoecd/60/27/2502872.pdf.

9. FAO, IFAD, and the World Bank have provided evidence through a number of their studies and lessons learned. See also Thematic Notes 1 and 4 and Module 11.

10. Human activity has altered ecosystems so extensively that their ability to bounce back from natural disturbance has diminished considerably. For instance, deforestation impairs watersheds; raises the risk of fires, landslides, and floods; exacerbates droughts; and contributes to climate change. Destruction of coastal wetlands, dunes, and mangroves diminishes the environmental buffer system for coastal storms. All these contribute to making at-risk areas (such as low-lying islands) more vulnerable to extreme weather events (Abramovitz 2001); see also Thematic Note 4.

11. For a detailed discussion on mitigation policies aimed at reducing or avoiding greenhouse gas emissions in the areas of renewable energy and energy efficiency, see Thematic Note 3 and Module 15. The causes of global warming can be reduced either by reducing the emissions of greenhouse gases or by subtracting carbon dioxide from the atmosphere (www.fao.org/clim).

12. www.fao.org/clim/mitigation_en.htm.

13. Payments for environmental services are a market-based conservation tool in which land users are paid for the

environmental services they generate. The central principles of this approach are that those who provide environmental services should be compensated for doing so and that those who receive these services should pay for their provision (see the Overview for more details).

14. www.fonafifo.com/index.htm.

15. For examples of best practices and lessons learned relating to sustainable energy development (energy efficiency and renewable energy), see Thematic Note 3 and Module 15. For natural disaster projects, see Thematic Note 4 and Module 11.

16. For more information on this mechanism, see ftp://ftp.fao.org/agl/agll/docs/misc37 or www.climateindia.com.

17. "United Nations Framework Convention on Climate Change," http://unfccc.int/resource/docs/convkp/conveng.pdf.

18. For a full discussion on the Clean Development Mechanism and gender issues, see Denton (2002); Lambrou and Piana (2006a).

Thematic Note 3

This Thematic Note was prepared by Carolyn Sachs (Pennsylvania State University) and Marina Laudazi (Consultant), with inputs from David Boerma, Dominique Lantieri, Regina Laub, Sibyl Nelson, Andrea Rossi, and Reuben Sessa (FAO), and reviewed by Mary Hill Rojas (Consultant); Yianna Lambrou (FAO); Ilaria Firmian, Maria Hartl, and Sheila Mwanundu (IFAD); and Erick Fernandes, Robin Mearns, and Daniel Sellen (World Bank).

1. This Thematic Note uses the following definitions: *Bioenergy:* energy produced from organic matter or biomass. Bioenergy includes all wood energy and all agroenergy resources (FAO 2006; UN-Energy 2007). *Biomass:* material of biological origin (excluding material embedded in geological formations and transformed to fossils), such as energy crops, agricultural and forestry wastes, and by-products, manure, or microbial biomass. *Biofuel:* fuel produced directly or indirectly from biomass, such as fuelwood, charcoal, bioethanol, biodiesel, biogas (methane), or biohydrogen. *Modern bioenergy:* biomass that may be burned directly, further processed into densified and dried solid fuel, or converted into liquid or gaseous fuels using so-called first- or second-generation technologies, depending on their level of development.

2. For a discussion on the plausible institutional and economic assumptions necessary for bioenergy development, see UN-Energy (2007). Projections to 2050 suggest that bioenergy sources could supply 10 to 25 percent of total energy demand (FAO 2005, 2007).

3. As a low-carbon or carbon-neutral source of energy, biofuel systems with low-energy inputs into the production process are already significantly contributing to climate change mitigation by replacing fossil fuels and through carbon sequestration in plants and soil biomass in perennial energy plantations (FAO 2006).

4. The demand for corn for ethanol in the United States doubled or tripled the price of corn in Mexico between 2006 and 2007, which led to a tortilla crisis. Poor Mexicans receive more than 40 percent of their protein from tortillas. In the United States, chicken feed costs increased 40 percent between 2006 and 2007 because of rising corn prices (Sagar and Kartha 2007).

5. The full cycle of greenhouse gas emissions of bioenergy varies widely based on land-use changes, choice of feedstock, agricultural practices, refining or conversion processes, and end-use practice. If, for example, forest is converted into sugarcane, treated with chemical fertilizers and pesticides, and refined with coal and natural gas, the resulting biofuel could have a greater impact on climate over its life cycle than fossil fuels (UN-Energy 2007). A recent study estimates that when the amount of land cleared to grow corn, sugarcane, and soybeans for fuel crops is taken into account, biofuels will have higher greenhouse gas emissions than fossil fuels (Fargione and others 2008).

6. Modern forms of energy such as electricity and petroleum-based fuels account for only a fraction of the energy use of poor rural communities. The expansion of the electricity grid is costly and often not affordable for poor communities, particularly those in sub-Saharan Africa. Electricity from renewable energy sources such as small hydro, solar, and wind energy systems also has high capital costs. See United Nations Department of Economic and Social Affairs (DESA), "Small-Scale Production and Use of Liquid Biofuels in Sub-Saharan Africa: Perspectives for Sustainable Development," Background Paper No. 2 for Commission on Sustainable Development, Fifteenth Session, www.un.org/esa/sustdev/csd/csd15/documents/csd15_bp2.pdf.

7. www.malifolkecenter.org.

Thematic Note 4

This Thematic Note was prepared by Carolyn Sachs (Pennsylvania State University) and Marina Laudazi (Consultant), with inputs from David Boerma, Dominique Lantieri, Regina Laub, Sibyl Nelson, Andrea Rossi, and Reuben Sessa (FAO), and reviewed by Mary Hill Rojas (Consultant); Yianna Lambrou (FAO); Ilaria Firmian, Maria Hartl, and Sheila Mwanundu (IFAD); and Erick Fernandes, Robin Mearns, and Daniel Sellen (World Bank).

1. Annual economic losses associated with such disasters averaged $75.5 billion in the 1960s, $138.4 billion in the 1970s, $213.9 billion in the 1980s, and $659.9 billion in the 1990s (UNDP 2004; a billion is 1,000 million).

2. The level of risk in relation to natural disasters in a society is determined by the levels of vulnerability combined with the level of probability of the occurrence of a natural hazard (flood, drought, landslide, earthquake, volcanic eruptions, storm, cyclone) as well as the level and intensity of such a hazard. See United Nations Division for the Advancement of Women (DAW), "Environmental Management and the Mitigation of Natural Disasters: A Gender Perspective," Report of the Expert Group Meeting, Ankara, Turkey, November 6–9, www.un.org/womenwatch/daw/csw/env_manage/documents/EGM-Turkey-final-report.pdf.

3. Social vulnerability to disasters is a function of human action and behavior. It describes the degree to which a socioeconomic system or physical assets are either susceptible or resilient to the impact of natural hazards and environmental changes (ibid.).

4. Whether it is a drought in Malawi (Vaughan 1987), a cyclone in Bangladesh (Ikeda 1995), or an earthquake in Mexico (Dufka 1988).

5. "Poverty and Climate Change: Reducing the Vulnerability of the Poor through Adaptation," www.oecd.org/dataoecd/60/27/2502872.pdf.

6. For a full discussion on disaster mitigation, response, and recovery, see Module 11.

7. The agencies taking part are the DPKO, FAO, IFRC, IOM, OCHA, OHCHR, UNDP, UNFPA, UNHCR, UNICEF, UNIDO, WFP, and WHO.

Thematic Note 5

This Thematic Note was prepared by Carolyn Sachs (Pennsylvania State University) and Marina Laudazi (Consultant), with inputs from David Boerma, Dominique Lantieri, Regina Laub, Sibyl Nelson, Andrea Rossi, and Reuben Sessa (FAO), and reviewed by Mary Hill Rojas (Consultant); Yianna Lambrou (FAO); Ilaria Firmian, Maria Hartl, and Sheila Mwanundu (IFAD); and Erick Fernandes, Robin Mearns, and Daniel Sellen (World Bank).

1. "Global Environment Outlook 4," www.unep.org/geo/geo4/media.

2. Ibid.

3. United Nations University, "Experts Advise World Policies to Cope with Causes, Rising Consequences of Creeping Desertification," www.inweh.unu.edu/inweh/drylands/Algiers_news_release-Final.pdf.

4. Ibid. According to the Millennium Ecosystem Assessment (2005), *drylands* include all terrestrial regions where the production of crops, forage, wood, and other ecosystem services is limited by water. Formally, the definition encompasses all lands where the climate is classified as dry

subhumid, semiarid, arid, or hyperarid. This classification is based on Aridity Index values.

5. See note 56 above.

6. Ibid.

7. See Thematic Note 1 for details on the CBD.

8. "What Is Dry and Sub-humid Lands Biodiversity?" www.cbd.int/drylands/what.shtml.

9. FARM Programme, http://dbtindia.nic.in/FARM/page1.htm.

10. IFAD (2006).

11. UNDP (2007b).

12. For more on monitoring and evaluation of natural resources management projects, see the Overview. For a full discussion on monitoring and evaluation in general, see Module 16.

Innovative Activity Profile 1

This Innovative Activity Profile was written by Marina Laudazi (FAO), based largely on Lambrou and Laub (2006), and reviewed by Catherine Ragasa and Mary Hill Rojas (Consultants) and Maria Hartl (IFAD).

1. Agrobiodiversity comprises the variety and variability of animals, plants, and microorganisms that are used directly or indirectly for food and agriculture, including crops, livestock, forestry, and fisheries. It comprises the diversity of genetic resources (varieties, breeds) and species used for food, fodder, fiber, fuel, and pharmaceuticals. It also includes the diversity of nonharvested species that support production (soil microorganisms, predators, pollinators) and those in the wider environment that support agroecosystems (agricultural, pastoral, forest, and aquatic) as well as the diversity of the agroecosystems. Local knowledge and culture can therefore be considered as integral parts of agrobiodiversity, because it is the human activity of agriculture that shapes and conserves this biodiversity.

Innovative Activity Profile 2

This Innovative Activity Profile was written by Marina Laudazi (FAO), based largely on project documents, and reviewed by Catherine Ragasa and Mary Hill Rojas (Consultants) and Maria Hartl (IFAD).

REFERENCES

Overview

Agarwal, Bina. 2003. "Gender and Land Rights Revisited: Exploring New Prospects via the State, Family, and Market." *Journal of Agrarian Change* 3 (1/2): 184–224.

Alston, Margaret. 2006. "The Gendered Impact of Drought." In *Rural Gender Relations*, ed. B. Bock and S. Shortall, 165–80. London: CABI.

Denton, Fatma. 2002. "Climate Change Vulnerability, Impacts, and Adaptation: Why Does Gender Matter?" *Gender and Development Journal* 10 (2): 10–20.

Enarson, Elaine, and Lourdes Meyreles. 2004. "International Perspectives on Gender and Disaster: Differences and Possibilities." *International Journal of Sociology and Social Policy* 24 (10/11): 49–63.

Food and Agriculture Organization (FAO). 2004. *The State of Food and Agriculture 2003–2004*. Rome: FAO.

———. 2005. *Building on Gender, Agrobiodiversity and Local Knowledge*. Rome: FAO.

———. 2007a. "Environment and Agriculture." Committee on Agriculture, 20th Session, Rome, April.

———. 2007b. "Gender-Sensitive Indicators." Draft, FAO, Rome.

Intergovernmental Panel on Climate Change (IPCC). 2007. "Climate Change 2007: Synthesis Report. Contribution of Working Groups I, II and III to the Fourth Assessment Report of the Intergovernmental Panel on Climate Change." IPCC, Geneva.

Lambrou, Yianna, and Regina Laub. 2004. *Gender Perspectives on the Conventions on Biodiversity, Climate Change and Desertification*. Rome: Food and Agriculture Organization.

Masika, Rachel. 2002. "Gender and Climate Change." *Gender and Development Journal* 10 (2): 2–9.

Millennium Ecosystem Assessment (MEA). 2005. *Millennium Ecosystem Assessment*. Washington, DC: Island Press. Also available at www.millenniumassessment.org/en/index.aspx.

Prokopy, Linda Stalker. 2004. "Women's Participation in Rural Water Supply Projects in India: Is It Moving beyond Tokenism and Does It Matter?" *Water Policy* 6: 103–16.

Rocheleau, Dianne. 1996. "Gender and Environment: A Feminist Political Ecology Perspective." In *Feminist Political Ecology: Global Issues and Local Experiences*, ed. Dianne Rocheleau, Barbara Thomas-Slayter, and Esther Wangari, 3–23. New York: Routledge.

Sachs, Carolyn. 2007. "Going Public: Networking Globally and Locally." *Rural Sociology* 72 (1): 2–24.

Singh, Nandita. 2006. "Women's Participation in Local Water Governance: Understanding Institutional Contradictions." *Gender Technology and Development* 10 (1): 61–76.

Sultana, Farhana. 2006. "Gendered Waters, Poisoned Wells: Political Ecology of the Arsenic Crisis in Bangladesh." In *Fluid Bonds: Views on Gender and Water*, ed. Kuntala Lahiri-Dutt, 362–87. Kolkata: STREE.

UN-Energy. 2007. *Sustainable Bioenergy: A Framework for Decision-Makers*. New York: United Nations.

World Bank. 2004. *Monitoring and Evaluation: Some Tools, Methods, and Approaches*. Washington, DC: World Bank.

———. 2005. *Agriculture Investment Sourcebook*. Washington, DC: World Bank.

———. 2007. *World Development Report 2008: Agriculture for Development*. Washington, DC: World Bank.

Thematic Note I

Armstrong, S. 1993. "The Last Taboo." *World AIDS* 29: 2.

Bragdon, Susan, Cary Fowler, Zenete Franca, and Elizabeth Goldberg, eds. 2003. *Law and Policy of Relevance to the Management of Plant Genetic Rresources*. The Hague: International Service for National Agricultural Research.

Food and Agriculture Organization (FAO). 1996. *State of the World's Plant Genetic Resources for Food and Agriculture*. Rome: FAO.

———. 2003. *HIV/AIDS and Agriculture: Impacts and Responses. Case Studies from Namibia, Uganda and Zambia*. Rome: FAO.

———. 2004. "What Is Local Knowledge." Module 1, fact sheet in *Building on Gender, Agrobiodiversity and Local Knowledge*. Rome: FAO. Also available at www.fao.org/sd/links/documents_download/Manual.pdf.

———. 2005. *Building on Gender, Agrobiodiversity and Local Knowledge*. Rome: FAO.

———. 2007a. "Environment and Agriculture." Committee on Agriculture, 20th Session, FAO, Rome, April.

———. 2007b. "Gender-Sensitive Indicators." Draft, FAO, Rome.

———. 2007c. "Global Plan of Action for Animal Genetic Resources" Draft, FAO, Rome.

Food and Agriculture Organization (FAO)/International Plant Genetic Resources Institute (IPGRI). 1996. "Working Group Meeting," International Plant Genetic Resources Institute, Rome, October 1–4.

Howard, Patricia. 2003. *Women and Plants, Gender Relations in Biodiversity Management and Conservation*. London: ZED Books.

International Fund for Agricultural Development (IFAD). 2004. "Enhancing the Role of Indigenous Women in Sustainable Development: IFAD Experience with Indigenous Women in Latin America and Asia." Third Session of the Permanent Forum on Indigenous Issues, IFAD, Rome. Also available at www.ifad.org/english/indigenous/pub/documents/indigenouswomenReport.pdf.

———. n.d. "Tree Domestic Programs in Africa Help Families Out of Poverty." IFAD, Rome. Also available at www.ruralpovertyportal.org/.

Lambrou, Yianna, and Regina Laub. 2004. *Gender Perspectives on the Conventions on Biodiversity, Climate Change and Desertification*. Rome: Food and Agriculture Organization.

———. 2006. "Gender, Local Knowledge and Lessons Learnt in Documenting and Conserving Agrobiodiversity." United Nations University (UNU) Research Paper No. 2006/69, UNU, Helsinki.

Lope Alzina, Diana Gabriela. 2007. "Gendered Production Spaces and Crop Varietal Selection: Case Study in Yucatan, Mexico." *Journal of Tropical Geogaphy* 28 (1): 21–38.

Millennium Ecosystem Assessment (MEA). 2005. *Millennium Ecosystem Assessment*. Washington, DC: Island Press. Also available at www.millenniumassessment.org/en/index. aspx.

Momsen, Janet. 2007. "Gender and Biodiversity: A New Approach to Linking Environment and Development." *Geography Compass* 1 (2): 149–62.

Randriamaro, Zo. 2006. *Gender and Trade*. Brighton, U.K.: BRIDGE/Institute of Development Studies. Also available at www.bridge.ids.ac.uk/reports/CEP-Trade-OR.pdf.

Sahai, Suman. 2003. "India's Plant Variety Protection and Farmers' Rights Act." *Current Science* 84 (3): 407–11.

Warburton, Hilary, and Adrienne Martin. 1999. "Local People's Knowledge in Natural Resources Research." In *Socio-Economic Methodologies for Natural Resources Research*. Chatham, U.K.: Natural Resources Institute. Also available at www.nri.org/publications/bpg/bpg05. pdf.

White, Joanna, and Elizabeth Robinson. 2000. *HIV/AIDS and Rural Livelihoods in Sub-Saharan Africa*. Greenwich, England: Natural Resources Institute, University of Greenwich.

Wooten, Stephen. 2003. "Losing Ground: Gender Relations, Commercial Horticulture, and Threats to Local Plant Diversity in Rural Mali." In *Women and Plants, Gender Relations in Biodiversity Management and Conservation*, ed. Patricia Howard, 229–42. London: ZED Books.

Thematic Note 2

Abramovitz, Janet. 2001. "Unnatural Disasters." Worldwatch Papers 158, October, Worldwatch Institute, Washington, DC.

Aguilar, Lorena. 2007. *Gender Indicators*. Geneva: World Conservation Union.

Alston, Margaret. 2006. "The Gendered Impact of Drought." In *Rural Gender Relations*, eds. Bettina Bock and Sally Shortall, 165–80. London: CABI.

Boyd, Emily. 2002. "The Noel Kempff Project in Bolivia: Gender, Power and Decision-Making in Climate Mitigation." *Gender and Development* 10 (2): 70–77.

Denton, Fatma. 2002. "Climate Change Vulnerability, Impacts, and Adaptation: Why Does Gender Matter?" *Gender and Development* 10 (2): 10–20.

Food and Agriculture Organization (FAO). 2005. *Building on Gender, Agrobiodiversity and Local Knowledge*. Rome: FAO.

———. 2007. *Adaptation to Climate Change in Agriculture, Forestry and Fisheries. Perspectives, Framework and Priorities*. Rome: FAO.

Harvey, Fiona. 2007. "UN Climate Panel Detailed Potential for Global Conflict." *Financial Times*, October 13.

Intergovernmental Panel on Climate Change (IPCC). 2001. *Climate Change 2001: Impacts, Adaptation and Vulnerability. Contribution of Working Group II of the IPCC to the Third Assessment Report of the Intergovernmental Panel on Climate Change*. Cambridge: Cambridge University Press.

———. 2007. *Climate Change 2007: Synthesis Report. Contribution of Working Groups I, II and III to the Fourth Assessment Report of the Intergovernmental Panel on Climate Change*. Geneva: IPCC.

Kurukulasuriya, Pradeep, and Shane Rosenthal. 2003. "Climate Change and Agriculture: A Review of Impacts and Adaptations." Climate Change Series 91, Agriculture and Rural Development Department and Environment Department, World Bank, Washington, DC.

Lambrou, Yianna, and Grazia Piana. 2006a. *Energy and Gender Issues in Rural Sustainable Development*. Rome: Food and Agriculture Organization.

———. 2006b. *Gender: The Missing Component of the Response to Climate Change*. Rome: Food and Agriculture Organization.

Martens, P. 1998. *Health and Climate Change: Modeling the Impacts of Global Warming and Ozone Depletion*. London: Earthscan.

Masika, Rachel. 2002. "Gender and Climate Change." *Gender and Development* 10 (2): 2–9.

Soussain, J., Ian Burton, and Anne Hammil. 2003. "Livelihoods and Climate Change: Combining Disaster Risk Reduction, Natural Resource Management and Climate Change Adaptation in a New Approach to the Reduction of Vulnerability and Poverty." Winnipeg: International Institute for Sustainable Development.

Wamukonya, Njeri, and Margaret Skutsch. 2001. "Is There a Gender Angle to the Climate Change Negotiations?" Paper prepared for ENERGIA for the Commission on Sustainable Development, Session 9, New York, April 16–27.

Thematic Note 3

Fargione, Joseph, Jason Hill, David Tilman, Stephen Polasky, and Peter Hawthorn. 2008. "Land Clearing and

Biofuel Carbon." *Science Express Paper,* 319 (5867) February 7: 1235–38.

Food and Agriculture Organization (FAO)/International Fund for Agricultural Development (IFAD)/International Land Coalition. 2003. "Rural Women's Access to Land and Property in Selected Countries." FAO Report, FAO, Rome. Also available at www.fao.org/sd/2003/PE07033_en.htm.

Food and Agriculture Organization (FAO). 2005. "Bioenergy—Committee on Agriculture," 19th Session, Rome, April.

———. 2006. *Introducing the International Bioenergy Platform.* Rome: FAO.

———. 2007. *Adaptation to Climate Change in Agriculture, Forestry and Fisheries. Perspectives, Framework and Priorities.* Rome: FAO.

Lambrou, Yianna, and Grazia Piana. 2006. *Energy and Gender Issues in Rural Sustainable Development.* Rome: Food and Agriculture Organization.

Mearns, Robin. 1995. *Institutions and Natural Resource Management: Access to and Control over Woodfuel in East Africa, in People and Environment in Africa,* ed. T. Binns. New York: John Wiley.

Rajagopal, Deepak. 2007. *Rethinking Current Strategies for Biofuel Production in India.* Paper presented at the International Conference "Linkages between Energy and Water Management for Agriculture in Developing Countries," Hyderabad, India, January 29–30.

Rossi, Andrea, and Yianna Lambrou. 2008. *Gender and Equity Issues in Liquid Biofuels Production: Minimizing the Risks to Maximize the Opportunities.* Rome: Food and Agriculture Organization.

Sagar, Ambuj, and Sivan Kartha. 2007. "Bioenergy and Sustainable Development?" *Annual Review of Environmental Resources* 32: 131–67.

Salazar, R. H. 1999. "Mujer, medio ambiente: acuerdos internacionales." In *Género, sustentabilidad y cambio social en el México rural.* Verónica Vázquez, ed. Mexico: Colegio de Posgraduados.

Schirnding, Yasmin von, Nigel Bruce, Kirk Smith, Grant Ballard-Tremeer, and Majid Ezzati. 2000. "Addressing the Impact of Household Energy and Indoor Air Pollution on the Health of the Poor: Implications for Policy Action and Intervention Measures." Meeting Report, World Health Organization, Geneva.

United Nations Department of Economic and Social Affairs (DESA). 2007. "Small-Scale Production and Use of Liquid Biofuels in Sub-Saharan Africa: Perspectives for Sustainable Development." Prepared by Energy and Transport Branch Division for Sustainable Development, UN DESA. Commission on Sustainable Development, Fifteenth Session, Background Paper Number 2, April

30–May 11, New York. Available at http://www.un.org/esa/sustdev/csd/csd15/documents/csd15_bp2.pdf.

United Nations Development Programme (UNDP). 2004. *Gender and Energy for Sustainable Development: A Toolkit and Resource Guide.* New York: UN.

———. 2007. *Gender Mainstreaming a Key Driver of Development in Environment and Energy.* New York: United Nations.

UN-Energy. 2007. *Sustainable Bioenergy: A Framework for Decision-Makers.* New York: United Nations.

World Health Organization (WHO). 2006. *Fuel for Life: Household Energy and Health.* Geneva: WHO.

Thematic Note 4

Abramovitz, Janet. 2001. "Unnatural Disasters." Worldwatch Papers 158, October, Worldwatch Institute, Washington, DC.

Aguilar, Lorena. 2008. "Acknowledging the Linkages: Gender and Climate Change." Paper presented at Social Dimensions of Climate Change Conference, World Bank, Washington, DC, March 5.

Alston, Margaret. 2006. "The Gendered Impact of Drought." In *Rural Gender Relations,* ed. Bettina Bock and Sally Shortall, 165–80. London: CABI.

Bari, Farzana. 1998. " Gender, Disaster and Empowerment: A Case Study from Pakistan." In *The Gendered Terrain of Disaster: Through Women's Eyes,* ed. Elaine Enarson and Betty Hearn Morrow, 125–32. Westport, CT: Praeger.

Branco, Adelia de Melo. 1995. "Organizadas para Sobrevivir: El Caso de un Grupo de Mujeres del Sertao de Araripe." In *Sociedad y Disastres,* vol. 5. Lima: LARED.

Brown, Oli, and Alec Crawford. 2006. "Addressing Land Ownership after Natural Disasters: An Agency Survey." International Institute for Sustainable Development, Winnipeg, Canada.

Cannon, T. 2002. "Gender and Climate Hazards in Bangladesh." *Gender and Development* 10 (2): 45–50.

Commission on the Status of Women (CSW). 2002. "Women's Commission Adopts Agreed Conclusions on Poverty and Natural Disasters." Press release, United Nations,www.un.org/News/Press/docs/2002/ WOM1333.doc.htm.

Dufka, Corrine. 1988. "The Mexico City Earthquake Disaster, Social Casework." *Journal of Contemporary Social Work* 69: 162–70.

Enarson, Elaine, and Lourdes Meyreles. 2004. "International Perspectives on Gender and Disaster: Differences and Possibilities." *International Journal of Sociology and Social Policy* 24 (10/11): 49–63.

Food and Agriculture Organization (FAO)/World Food Programme (WFP). 2005. *SEAGA for Emergency and Rehabilitation Programmes.* Rome: FAO.

Fothergill, Alice. 1998. "The Neglect of Gender in Disaster Work: An Overview of the Literature." In *The Gendered Terrain of Disaster: Through Women's Eyes,* ed. Elaine Enarson and Betty Hearn Morrow, 11–25. Westport, CT: Praeger.

Graham, Angus. 2001. "Gender Mainstreaming Guidelines for Disasters Management Programmes—Principled SEAGA Approach." Document EGM/NATDIS/2001/EP.1, United Nations Division for the Advancement of Women, UN, New York.

Harvey, Fiona. 2007. "UN Climate Panel Detailed Potential for Global Conflict." *Financial Times,* October 13.

Ikeda, Keiko. 1995. "Gender Differences in Human Loss and Vulnerability in Natural Disasters: A Case Study from Bangladesh." *Indian Journal of Gender Studies* 2 (2): 171–93.

King, Angela. 2002. Introductory Statement. Commission on the Status of Women. 46th Session, UN, New York.

Kumar-Range, S. 2001. "Environmental Management and Disaster Risk Reduction: A Gender Perspective." Document EGM/NATDIS/2001/BP.1, United Nations Division for the Advancement of Women, UN, New York.

Lambrou, Yianna, and Grazia Piana. 2006. *Gender: The Missing Component of the Response to Climate Change.* Rome: FAO (Food and Agriculture Organization).

Lambrou, Yianna, and Regina Laub. 2004. *Gender Perspectives on the Conventions on Biodiversity, Climate Change and Desertification.* Rome: Food and Agriculture Organization.

Masika, Rachel. 2002. "Gender and Climate Change." *Gender and Development* 10 (2): 2–9.

McNeely, Jeffrey. 2000. "Biodiversity, War, and Tropical Forests." Paper presented to Conference on War and Tropical Forests: New Perspectives on Conservation in Areas of Armed Conflict, Yale School of Forestry and Environmental Studies, New Haven, CT, March 30–April 3.

Nelson, Valerie, Kate Meadows, Terry Cannon, John Morton, and Adrienne Martin. 2002. "Uncertain Predictions, Invisible Impacts, and the Need to Mainstream Gender in Climate Change Adaptations." *Gender and Development* 10 (2): 51–59.

Sachs, Carolyn. 2007. "Going Public: Networking Globally and Locally." *Rural Sociology* 72 (1): 2–24.

Tickell, Crispin. 2001. "Risks of Conflict: Resource and Population Pressures." In *Environmental Change and Security Project Report,* Issue No. 7, Woodrow Wilson International Center, Princeton, NJ.

Toscani, Letizia. 1998. "Women's Roles in Natural Disaster Preparation and Aid: A Central American View." In *The Gendered Terrain of Disaster: Through Women's Eyes,* ed. Elaine Enarson and Betty Hearn Morrow, 207–12. Westport, CT: Praeger.

United Nations (UN). 2001. "Environmental Management and the Mitigation of Natural Disasters: A Gender Perspective." Document UN/ISDR, EGM/NATDIS/2001/Rep.1, United Nations Division for the Advancement of Women, UN, New York.

———. 2002. *Commission on the Status of Women (CSW).* Report of the 46th Session. E/2002/27, Economic and Social Council, UN, New York.

———. 2004. *Making Risky Environments Safer: Women Building Sustainable and Disaster-Resilient Communities.* New York: UN.

United Nations Development Programme (UNDP). 2004. *Reducing Disaster Risk. A Challenge for Development.* New York: Swift.

———. 2007. "Natural Disaster Preparedness and Opportunities." Paper prepared for Joint Meeting of the Executive Boards of UNDP/UNFPA, UNICEF, and WFP, January 19 and 22, New York: United Nations.

Vaughan, Megan. 1987. *The Story of an African Famine: Gender and Famine in Twentieth Century Malawi.* Cambridge: Cambridge University Press.

Thematic Note 5

Aswani, Shankar, and Pamela Weiant. 2004. "Scientific Evaluation in Women's Participatory Management." *Human Organization* 63 (3): 301–19.

Convention on Biological Diversity (CBD). 2007. "What is Dry and Sub-humid Lands Biodiversity?" Available at http://www.cbd.int/drylands/what.shtml.

Crow, Ben, and Farhana Sultana. 2002. "Gender, Class, and Access to Water: Three Cases in a Poor and Crowded Delta." *Society and Natural Resources* 15 (8): 709–24.

Food and Agriculture Organization (FAO). 2002. *Land Degradation Assessment in Drylands (LADA).* Rome: FAO.

———. 2003. *Gender and Sustainable Development in Drylands: An Analysis of Field Experiences.* Rome: FAO.

———. 2007a. "Gender Mainstreaming in Water Management—A Pocket Guide." Draft, FAO, Rome.

———. 2007b. "Gender-Sensitive Indicators." Draft, FAO, Rome.

Gender and Water Alliance. 2003. *The Gender and Water Development Report: Gender Perspectives on Policies in the Water Ssector.* The Netherlands: Gender and Water Alliance Secretariat.

Global Environment Facility (GEF). 2003. *Operational Programme on Sustainable Land Management.* Washington, DC: GEF.

International Fund for Agricultural Development (IFAD). 2006. *Gender and Desertification—Expanding Roles for Women to Restore Drylands.* Rome: IFAD.

Izumi, Kaori. 2007. "Gender-Based Violence and Property Grabbing in Africa: A Denial of Women's Liberty and Security." *Gender and Development* 15 (1): 11–23.

Lambrou, Yianna, and Regina Laub. 2004. *Gender Perspectives on the Conventions on Biodiversity, Climate Change and Desertification.* Rome: Food and Agriculture Organization.

Millennium Ecosystem Assessment. 2005. *Millennium Ecosystem Assessment.* Washington, DC: Island Press.

Nyssen, Jan, Jean Poesen, Jan Moeyersons, Jozef Deckers, Mitiku Haile, and Andreas Lang. 2004. "Human Impact on the Environment in the Ethiopian and Eritrean Highlands: A State of the Art." *Earth Science Reviews* 64 (3–4): 273–320.

Ray, Isla. 2007. "Women, Water, and Development." *Annual Review of Environmental Resources* 32: 421–49.

Singh, Nandita. 2006. "Women's Participation in Local Water Governance: Understanding Institutional Contradictions." *Gender, Technology and Development* 10 (1): 61–76.

United Nations Convention to Combat Desertification (UNCCD). 2005. *Promotions of Traditional Knowledge. A Compilation of UNCCD Documents and Reports from 1997–2003.* Bonn: UNCCD.

United Nations Development Programme (UNDP). 2005. "Water Governance—The Gender Dimension." Fact sheet, UNDP, New York.

———. 2007a. *Sustainable Land Management: The Why and How of Mainstreaming Gender in Sustainable Land Management.* New York: UNDP/GEF.

———. 2007b. *Women and Sustainable Land Management.* Gender Mainstreaming Guidance Series. New York: United Nations.

White, Joanna, and Elizabeth Robinson. 2000. *HIV/AIDS and Rural Livelihoods in Sub-Saharan Africa.* Greenwich, England: Natural Resources Institute, University of Greenwich.

Innovative Activity Profile I

Food and Agriculture Organization (FAO). 2005. *Building on Gender, Agrobiodiversity and Local Knowledge.* Rome: FAO.

Rocheleau, Dianne. 1996. "Gender and Environment: A Feminist Political Ecology Perspective." In *Feminist Political Ecology: Global Issues and Local Experiences,* ed. Dianne Rocheleau, Barbara Thomas Slayter, and Esther Wangari, 3–23. New York: Routledge.

Shiva, Vandana. 1996. *Biopiracy: The Plunder of Nature and Knowledge.* Cambridge, MA: South End Press.

FURTHER READING

Overview

Alix, Jennifer, Alain De Janvry, and Elisabeth Sadoulet. 2003. "Partial Cooperation Political Economy and Common Property Resource Management: The Case of Deforestation in Mexico." University of California, Berkeley.

Convention on Biological Diversity: www.cbd.int.

Convention on the Elimination of All Forms of Discrimination against Women: www.un.org.

Food and Agriculture Organization (FAO). 2001. *Socio-Economic and Gender Analysis Programme (SEAGA).* Rome: FAO. Also available at www.fao.org.

Landell-Mills, N., and I. Porras. 2002. "Silver Bullet or Fools' Gold? A Global Review of Markets for Forest Environmental Services and Their Impact on the Poor." International Institute for Environment and Development, London.

Pagiola, Stefano, Agustin Arcenas, and Gunars Platais. 2005. "Can Payments for Environmental Services Help Reduce Poverty? An Exploration of the Issues and the Evidence to Date from Latin America." *World Development* 33 (2): 237–53.

United Nations Convention to Combat Desertification: www.unccd.int.

United Nations Framework Convention on Climate Change: www.unfccc.int.

Thematic Note I

Berg, Trygve, Ruth Haug, and Kjersti Larsen. 2000. "Research Guidelines: Gender Local Knowledge and Plant Genetic Resource Management." Oslo: Agricultural University of Norway. Available at www.fao.org/sd/LINKS/resources/resources.html.

Garí, Josep. 2003. "Local Agricultural Knowledge Key to Fighting HIV-AIDS and Food Security." United Nations Office for the Coordination of Humanitarian Affairs–Integrated Regional Information Networks, PlusNews, September.

International Development Research Centre (IDRC). 1998. *Gender and Biodiversity: Research Guidelines.* Ottawa: IDRC.

International Institute for Rural Reconstruction (IIRR). 1996. *Recording and Using Indigenous Knowledge: A Manual.* Silang, Philippines: IIRR.

Sachs, C., K. Gajurel, and M. Bianco. 1996. "Gender, Seeds, and Biodiversity." In *Women Working in the Environment,* ed. C. Sachs, 177–92. Washington, DC: Taylor and Francis.

Thematic Note 3

Lambrou, Yianna, and Grazia Piana. 2006. *Gender: The Missing Component of the Response to Climate Change.* Rome: Food and Agriculture Organization.

Swedish International Development Cooperation Authority (SIDA). 2003. "Energy Policy and Equality between Women and Men." *Equality Prompt* No. 9, SIDA, Stockholm.

United Nations Development Programme (UNDP). 2007. *Sustainable Land Management: The Why and How of Mainstreaming Gender in Sustainable Land Management.* New York: UN.

UN-Energy. 2005. *The Energy Challenge for Achieving the MDGs.* New York: UN.

Thematic Note 4

Food and Agriculture Organization (FAO). 2005. *Building on Gender, Agrobiodiversity and Local Knowledge.* Rome: FAO.

Kumar, Shubh K., and David Hotchkiss. 1998. "Consequences of Deforestation for Women's Time Allocation, Agricultural Production and Nutrition in Hill Areas of Nepal." Research Report 69, International Food Policy Research Institute, Washington, DC.

Innovative Activity Profile I

Lambrou, Yianna, and Regina Laub. 2006. "Gender, Local Knowledge and Lessons Learnt in Documenting and Conserving Agrobiodiversity." Research Paper No. 2006/69, Helsinki: United Nations University–World Institute for Development Economics Research.

LinKS training manual: www.fao.org/sd/LINKS/resources/resources.html.

LinKS Web site: www.fao.org/sd/links/gebio.htm.

Gender and Crises: Implications for Agriculture

Overview

This Module examines the nexus between agriculture and crisis brought on by conflicts and natural disasters from a gender perspective. The focus here is on the exceptional circumstances, needs, and opportunities that arise for women and men in the aftermath of crises. Although in many instances the impacts of conflicts and natural disasters are similar, the underlying conditions and environment that humanitarian and development actors encounter can be profoundly different as a result of political and security conditions. In situations involving armed conflict, the politically charged atmosphere affects every aspect of the economy, including agricultural production. By contrast, where natural disasters occur, conditions are not necessarily further exacerbated by military actions or political impasse. These differences can have significant effects on the agricultural sector, but the primary goal in all instances is to ensure basic food security and the protection or recovery of livelihood strategies.

Natural disasters and violent conflict can have severe effects on every aspect of agricultural production. When conflicts break out, the destruction of fields, roads, and markets through the placing of landmines or use of other weapons; the looting of food stores and plantations; and the displacement of local populations are often strategies used by warring parties. In this context women and men are also targeted deliberately and affected differently. Men are at higher risk of being killed or imprisoned and either flee to generate income elsewhere or are forced to fight. Women are

at high risk of sexual violence and displacement and of shouldering the full burden of productive work. The net impact on agriculture is significant. Studies from the 1990s indicate that for every year of conflict, agricultural production can drop by 12.3 percent; in the case of Angola, between 1975 and 1993 there was a 44.5 percent reduction (Zaur 2006). Natural disasters also have a heavy toll. In Asia alone, the 2004 tsunami and the 2005 earthquake in Pakistan caused an estimated $1.81 billion in damage to the agricultural sector, including livestock, crops, fisheries, and related infrastructure (Kryspin-Watson, Arkedis, and Zakout 2006). The gender dimensions were most starkly evident in the disproportionate number of deaths of women as a result of the tsunami in many places.

AGRICULTURE AND CRISES

Agriculture and related environmental resources can also be the source, cause, catalyst, or fuel of crises. The issues are often interrelated, but three dimensions must be considered:

■ *Scarcity of resources:* Scarcity is caused by population growth such that resources have to be divided between more people, or it is caused by increased per capita activity, resulting in increased demand. The combination can cause significant degradation of the needed resources. In Africa scarcity of land and continued environmental degradation are the main ecological dimensions associated with several conflicts. In Rwanda land scarcity was politicized and helped fuel the ethnic tensions that resulted in the 1994 genocide. In Somalia much of the fighting has concentrated in the agriculturally rich Jubaland region, where factions are vying for control.[1] The 2007 "Sudan Post-Conflict Environmental Assessment" by the United Nations Environment Programme (UNEP) points to severe environmental degradation and its effects on agriculture as causes of the conflict (box 11.1).

- *Abundance of resources:* If scarcity catalyzes conflict, then the abundance of resources (agricultural, mineral, or otherwise) can fuel and sustain conflict. The poppy fields of Afghanistan and coca plantations of Colombia are key sources of income, fueling the drug trade and guerrilla warfare that plague each country. In Colombia the Revolutionary Armed Forces of Colombia (FARC) formed in the 1960s as a Marxist movement fighting against unequal distribution of wealth, land, and power. FARC turned to drug trafficking as its main source of income in the 1990s. With other armed groups (right-wing paramilitary units) and drug traffickers, FARC has militarized the countryside, caused mass displacement of rural populations, and disrupted agriculture and livelihoods, particularly among indigenous communities and jungle-based tribes. An estimated 1.85 million people have been displaced. The U.S. government estimates that FARC supplies 50 percent of the world's cocaine.[2]

- *Meeting demand, ensuring supply:* The April 2008 food riots in Egypt, Haiti, and other parts of Africa rang alarm bells globally. Price hikes in agriculture are not uncommon.

But, as the UN Task Force on the "Global Food Security Crisis" states, "the world food situation is rapidly being redefined.... The recent trend of unprecedented increases in the price of food and overall import bills for the poorest countries, coupled with diminishing food stocks and difficulties accessing food by some communities, has created a host of humanitarian, socio-economic, developmental, political and security-related challenges." The main driver of price hikes is the increase in demand, notably from China and India, but many other factors have contributed to create the "perfect storm." The United Nations points to short-term causes, such as 30-year-low levels of wheat stock, combined with medium-term causes, including climate change and harvest failure due to extreme weather conditions. These factors are exacerbated by long-term resource scarcity, including water shortage, diminishing land for agriculture, and limited sources of energy and oil, which affect food supplies and prices. Speculative financial activities on the part of hedge funds, including investments in commodity futures, national tax and tariff policies, and lack of investment in agriculture development and research are also contributing to the crisis. The poorest people in the poorest of nations are at the frontlines of this crisis. From an international standpoint, this is perhaps the first time in modern history that food insecurity and hunger are igniting violent protests simultaneously in many parts of the world. As the Task Force states, "This risk is particularly high in countries emerging from violent conflict, where fragile security, political and economic progress is easily derailed."[3]

Box 11.1   Sudan: Environmental Degradation Causes Conflict

The UNEP study "Sudan Post-Conflict Environmental Assessment" notes that deserts have spread southward by an estimated 50 to 200 kilometers since the 1930s. This land degradation is a result of different developments relating in part to Darfur's increased population, which has grown sixfold over the last four decades to about 6.5 million. In turn there has been an explosion of livestock (from 27 million animals to around 135 million), which has caused overgrazing of the fragile soils. In addition, a "deforestation crisis" has led to a loss of almost 12 percent of Sudan's forest cover in just 15 years, and some areas may lose their remaining forest cover within the next decade. At the same time, average annual rainfall in El Fasher in northern Darfur has dropped nearly by half since data were first gathered in 1917. Increasing scarcity has also led to rising tribal antagonism over the last 20 years. These issues, together with increased banditry and political and economic neglect, catalyzed rebellion in February 2003 and have fanned ethnic conflict. Internally displaced persons and refugees are exacerbating the underlying conditions by cutting down trees, which depletes underground water supplies and thus adversely affects local populations.

Source: UNEP 2007.

- *Structural conditions:* The unequal distribution of resources is often rooted in colonial legacies, political struggles, and cultural practices. Tremendous gender inequity may also be embedded in the structural issues. For example, in many instances colonial rulers ignored matrilineal land inheritance practices and excluded women from control over property. In modern times women face legal, political, and cultural barriers to the ownership and control of resources. Structural conditions result in the concentration of resources in the hands of a few, while a vast population is subject to shortages and scarcity, which can trigger and fuel conflict over time. In Burundi, for example, 80 percent of the country's foreign exchange comes from coffee production. Government control over the sector helped finance the conflict against rebels in the 1990s. A government monopoly over exports at one end of the commodity chain was matched with fixing lower prices for producers at the other end. This inequity of resource distribution contributed to the mounting tensions.[4] In Palestine (box 11.2), inequitable access to water has been a contributor to conflict (Homer-Dixon and Kelly 1995).

After a war or conflict has ended, the return of refugees and internally displaced persons and their claims to land can be a source of increased tension. In Burundi, which covers just 27,830 square kilometers, an estimated 115,000 internally displaced persons and 17,000 refugees were waiting to resettle in 2007. In Afghanistan refugees are returning to reclaim land after two decades, often confronting their own relatives in their effort to get it back.

An increase in the value of resources, particularly shared land, can also trigger conflict. Where markets develop and farmers intensify production or population pressures increase, the value of resources goes up and competition may heighten. In some instances existing customary practices and informal processes of adjudication may quell tensions but can also fuel them if the access and rights to property rights of all stakeholders are not secure. This is pertinent in the aftermath of conflicts or natural disasters in which traditional practices and leadership structures may no longer exist.

Increased demand and production are also leading to the depletion of resources and destruction of ecological systems that have helped prevent or mitigate the impact of natural disasters. Most notably, clear-cut logging and road building result in a reduction of natural protection against landslides and soil erosion. Similarly, the destruction of coastal wetlands not only affects fisheries but also increases the risk of flooding. The negative impact can be seen in many ways.

MULTIDIMENSIONAL ISSUES OF AGRICULTURE IN TIMES OF CRISIS

To address basic survival, food security, and longer-term livelihood issues, early recovery strategies must fully integrate agricultural sector issues. The approaches needed vary considerably, however, depending on the conditions in each

Box 11.2 Gaza: Structural Inequity and Access to Water

In Gaza, following the signing of the Oslo Peace Accord in 1993, a study revealed the inequitable access to water among Palestinians, Jewish settlers, and the Israeli population. Beginning in 1967, strict quotas were placed on the Arabs' rights to pump water. Over the years, quota levels were maintained by banning the drilling of new wells or the rehabilitation of old wells, blocking springs, or uprooting citrus trees. In contrast, Israelis had no limits placed on them, which resulted in waste and overuse. Pricing structures were also disadvantageous to the Palestinians. Settlers received significant subsidies, paying $0.10 per cubic meter for water that costs $0.34 per cubic meter; Palestinians, who received no subsidies, could pay up to $1.20 per cubic meter for water from local Arab authorities. Relative to per capita income, Palestinians were thus paying as much as 20 times the amount Israeli settlers paid for water. Water scarcity also led to increased salinity and thus a decline in crop yields for Gaza-based farmers. Without extensive support to the agricultural sector and increased access to water, Palestinian agriculture went into decline. The consumption restrictions and water gap contributed to the friction between the populations.

Source: Homer-Dixon and Kelly 1995.

case. Although there are common features to take into account, significant differences also exist:

- In any given country, an emergency or conflict can be unfolding in one area, while elsewhere in the same country the impact may not be as significant. For example, the effect of an earthquake decreases farther from the epicenter, and the conflict in northern Uganda is less visible in effect in other parts of the country.
- An overlapping of events may occur (for example, Aceh and Sri Lanka were already struggling with the effects of conflict when the tsunami hit). This has implications for the type of actions possible (or constraints relating to security issues) and opportunities for addressing the agricultural sector.
- Conflict situations increase the flow of arms and weaponry, thus creating greater insecurity for local populations and international actors.
- In many postconflict states, opportunities present themselves for redressing structural and legal inequalities that have affected portions of the population. For example, land reform may be on the agenda. Legislation to end discrimination based on identity may be addressed. These are key moments for tackling issues of gender discrimination as well. In the aftermath of disasters, such opportunities can also exist, and interventions designed with prevention in mind can tackle root causes.
- Natural disasters can have either quick or slow onsets (such as earthquakes versus droughts), so the opportunities vary to prepare for, mitigate, or prevent the onset of a crisis. The type of identified hazard determines the necessary nature and type of intervention. For example, droughts can be predicted in advance and the effects mitigated to some degree at a lesser cost, whereas protection from earthquakes and mudslides is structural and costly, and these events can be less predictable. Nonetheless, emergency and early warning systems can be established for sudden-onset events.
- Human-caused and natural emergencies can have both short and protracted effects in terms of displacement, as well as access to and usability of resources.
- Response strategies can be significantly affected if conflict and political tensions are at play (for example, humanitarian relief in Tamil-controlled areas in Sri Lanka was more challenging than in other areas of the country after the tsunami).
- In situations in which humanitarian emergencies are largely the result of conflict or political struggles, the options for effective response can be severely constrained and curtailed by political and military leaders.

These phases should also be considered.

- *Precrisis:* As a drought sets in or conflict escalates, the potential impact on agriculture can be determined. Strategies to prevent and mitigate crises have been developed. Good early warning systems together with effective preparedness and emergency measures can considerably lessen the impact of a natural hazard. Often, however, where natural disasters hit randomly, no effective warning is given, as in the Asian tsunami of 2004 and the 2003 Bam earthquake in Iran. Similarly, although conflict early warning systems exist, the information may not be conveyed effectively to those involved in the agricultural sector, and thus the opportunity for preventive measures or preparedness is limited. Effective communication and emergency preparedness planning to at-risk populations are central to the prevention and mitigation of crises.
- *During the crisis:* Responding during the unfolding of a crisis is also challenging. Typically, natural disasters have a shorter time span than conflicts. Where conflict is the cause of a crisis, the international community may have less access to the affected areas. A danger also exists that external assistance and provisions are at risk of being exploited by partisans in the conflict and thus inadvertently fueling the violence. Moreover, it may not be economically viable to provide agricultural or related infrastructural support if it is at risk of being targeted during the conflict.
- *Immediately postcrisis/transition period:* International assistance and presence increase dramatically in the immediate aftermath of conflict or natural disaster. The transition period is an important time for identifying and addressing root causes of crises and developing alternative preventive strategies for agricultural development.

These phases are not necessarily chronological or consecutive. In other words, even in the midst of a crisis or conflict it is necessary to consider means of mitigating and preventing further damage. This can help limit the negative impact of crisis on a given population. Where protective measures can be put in place, local resilience increases, and recovery processes will also be quicker. In 1999 in Sri Lanka, for example, the International Development Association (IDA) developed a community-based program to rebuild the irrigation systems that had been damaged by the ongoing conflict between the government of Sri Lanka and the Liberation Tamil Tigers of Eelam in the agriculture-rich North East Province. The IDA project focused on rebuilding roads and irrigation systems. Despite the ongoing conflict, the project ensured food security for 33,250 people and enabled the cultivation of 212,944 hectares of prewar farmland (World Bank 2007; see also Innovative Activity Profile 1).

Although the postconflict or emergency period is rife with difficulties, it is also a time of great opportunity. In Rwanda, for example, after the genocide the national Rwandan Demobilization and Reintegration Commission offered a choice of livelihoods to former fighters. Some returned to agriculture, and others were given skills training to enter other sectors (UN 2005).

Particularly in postconflict settings, long-standing structural issues can be addressed. Land tenure, inheritance, and property ownership issues that create significant inequities and result in long-term food insecurity and livelihood challenges can be redressed. Opportunities also are present for promoting economic (including agricultural) diversification to decrease livelihood dependency on land or cash crops.

There is also a clear need and opportunity to reach out and draw on the resources and expertise of both the public and private sectors. Community-based resources must also be harnessed. The extent of damage requires a full division of labor, and the different skills and capacities of women and men must be included.

The arrival and presence of external actors, in particular those providing food aid, can have a tremendous impact on local producers, men, and increasingly women. Situation analyses and consultative processes are important not only for minimizing damage but also for understanding how local capacities can be strengthened.

Recovery and reconstruction programs, therefore, should be seen not only simply for replacing losses but also for redressing conditions that in the past heightened vulnerability. These programs provide a chance to make improvements and, in particular, to address the needs of underprivileged groups and inequalities, including on the basis of gender, that profoundly impact women's and men's access to food security and livelihoods.

GENDER DIMENSIONS OF AGRICULTURE DURING CRISES

Women, men, boys, and girls can have profoundly different experiences and face different risks in conflict situations and natural disasters. These experiences are shaped by and have a direct effect on their capacity to sustain livelihoods, ensure food security, and engage in the agricultural sector. In designing interventions, organizations must understand the social capital (gained and lost) as a result of a crisis and must recognize the gender differences in skills, knowledge, access,

and participation in agricultural activities. It is important to acknowledge that conflict and crisis tend to push women into the productive sphere (as men migrate or are embroiled in conflict). This shift can mean prompt empowerment, but it can also result in women becoming overburdened. External interventions can be helpful and harmful. The challenge is to understand the context and realities of people's lives so that the assistance provided is beneficial to men and women.

Different physical risks and vulnerabilities faced by women and men

Natural disasters can be disproportionately deadly for women. In the Kobe earthquake of 1995, 1.5 times more women died than men, and in the 2004 Southeast Asia tsunami, death rates for women across the region averaged three to four times that of men.[5] By contrast, conflicts are more deadly for men. In Iraq 90 percent of the dead are reportedly men. Following the 1994 Rwandan genocide, 70 percent of the surviving population was women. Men, particularly younger men, are also more vulnerable to military recruitment and arrest than women in conflict-affected situations. Women (and their dependents) are at greater risk of forced displacement and exposure to insecurity in public spaces and camps for internally displaced persons and refugees.

Women's exposure to sexual violence escalates during times of crisis. In conflict situations, rape is increasingly used as a weapon of war and ethnic cleansing. In the aftermath of natural disasters such as the tsunami, the breakdown of security and social structures fuels the incidence of rape. Within 10 days of the tsunami, the United Nations was receiving reports of sexual exploitation and rape of women, including as payment for being pulled out of the ocean (Lalasz 2005).

Although physiology accounts for some of the differences in mortality rates between women and men, other sociocultural norms also come into play. A 2005 Oxfam report notes that, on average, women and girls did not know how to swim or climb trees as well as their men counterparts; they were not taught these skills and thus were unable to rescue themselves.[6] Women's dress codes can restrict their mobility. Cultural norms that prevent women from leaving their homes unaccompanied (such as in Afghanistan and rural Bangladesh) increase the risks they face. In many earthquake-prone areas, women working in poorly constructed homes are at greater risk than men, who may be working outside in fields or in well-built public buildings. In India men survived an earthquake by virtue of sleeping on rooftops on warm nights. Local culture there forbids such behavior among women.

Barriers to immediate relief

Women's and girls' access to relief can be inadvertently obstructed. In many societies women have subordinate public positions but still control resources and have power through informal networks and social ties. During crises and relief efforts, during which the process is heavily dominated by men, women are often systematically excluded. Women's marginalization can be compounded by a lack of physical security, increases in their domestic duties that prevent their participation in public efforts, and actions by external actors who may unwittingly empower self-designated men "leaders" to distribute relief.

There are also gender dimensions to food security and nutrition during crises. In many instances in which a food crisis takes place, women and girls reduce their intake in favor of other household members, particularly men and boys. This increases incidence of malnutrition among women. However, men are at greater risk during famines because they have a higher nutritional requirement. As a result, in many recorded famines mortality rates are higher among men than women.

Dangerous security conditions can limit women's mobility and access to humanitarian aid or markets. Pregnant and lactating women in particular are at greater risk of malnutrition as a result of their physiological condition and limited mobility. Households led by men can also be at risk. Often men do not know how to cook or care for younger children, thereby exposing them to increased malnutrition. Similarly, single men and boys separated from their families are vulnerable to malnutrition. In camps in southern Kenya, for example, it was noted that the young men received food rations but did not know how to cook (UN IASC 2006).

Different structural barriers

In addition to physical and psychological vulnerability, women and men can experience different structural barriers that affect their access to and control of assets. This includes the strength or weakness of institutions (formal and informal) and policies to address food security and agricultural needs and recognize the differential needs and changed circumstances of women and men. For example, land and property ownership and inheritance laws that are gender discriminatory pose significant risks to women's livelihoods. This is partly compounded by higher illiteracy rates among women in many poor countries. Other barriers include the following:

- *Access to assets:* Cultural and legal barriers to accessing credit and physical infrastructure (such as transportation) needed for agricultural production can affect women more than men. Women tend to work more out of the home and in the informal sector. The destruction wrought by natural disasters can trigger "decapitalization" and a reduction in women's share of productive activities, formal or informal. They sustain direct losses (homes and production) and indirect losses as their share of unpaid emergency domestic tasks rises (for example, care for children who cannot attend school, the elderly, and the injured).

- *Access to markets:* In crises, women's small-scale trading networks can also be damaged, thus reducing a key source of income. Conflict situations, however, can limit men's and open women's access to markets. Men may flee, join armed groups, face imprisonment, or be killed during conflicts, which puts women under greater pressure. Women take on responsibilities in public spaces, including in markets, and formal and informal employment.[7] But they are at greater risk than men from physical infrastructure or external conditions (such as state of housing or public safety) and from sociocultural conditions, such as the acceptance of women's entry in public forums and labor markets, sectors traditionally occupied by men. Many women are forced out of these social spaces when conditions "normalize."

- *Information flows to and about women and men:* Women and men access different sources of information. Women's vulnerability is exacerbated by their subordinate position in traditional patriarchal societies and often lack access to information that men may have. In Peru fishermen were warned about El Niño and its negative impact on fishing. Women did not receive this information and thus had no chance to plan household budgets or save funds to withstand the crisis. In South Africa women farmers wanted seasonal climate forecasts to be available through community-based channels such as schools and not just over the radio. In attempting to balance their domestic, child care, and farming duties, they had no time to listen to the radio. Data and information (including sex-disaggregated data) are critical for ensuring accurate assessment. Where formal assessments cannot be undertaken, informal consultations are still valuable.

Opportunity in crisis: women's empowerment and confidence building

For men, protracted crises, displacement, loss of income, and the associated sense of lost status and inability to protect their families can be profoundly disempowering. Women are often forced into the public sphere. Although the burdens of care and responsibility mount, they also gain experiences, exposure, and confidence. Where there is protracted conflict and women are either in communities or in refugee camps, they often develop new skills to sustain livelihoods. By contrast, returning fighters (men or women) may have little or no skills relating to agriculture or production.

In situations in which natural disasters have destroyed their livelihood, men tend to migrate more quickly than women in search of employment and resources. They are less physically vulnerable and less culturally burdened with child care and other daily domestic responsibilities. Women are thus left to carry the family burden alone. Their limited and localized coping strategies can be critical for their own and their family's survival. They also tend to work more communally. Ignorance of gender issues can also exacerbate women's situation. Gains they may have made as a result of their activities and mobilization during the crisis are often lost because of external interventions. At a minimum, external actions must not harm local populations. To ensure this and sustain positive impacts, therefore, the gender dimensions of poverty and insecurity must be understood and addressed (box 11.3).

Box 11.3 Key Principles for Effective Intervention

■ *Interventions should "do no harm" and should not perpetuate existing harm.* Gender analysis helps to understand the different obstacles that potential beneficiaries face, their varying capacities to mobilize resources, and their different social and economic responsibilities and skills. Without this basic understanding, we risk ignoring some sectors of the population, which may do damage and fuel the root causes of a crisis.

■ *Identifying baseline conditions enables the provision of targeted and more effective programming to improve livelihoods over the long term.* Without gender perspectives, existing local capacities can be squandered.

■ *Ending gender-based poverty and food insecurity contributes to future, long-term prevention and survival strategies.* Integrating gender perspectives is one means of reducing people's vulnerabilities and building on their strengths and social capital. It can help identify tactics and strategies to increase their ability to prevent and withstand the effects of crises.

Sources: Anderson 1999; Naraghi-Anderlini 2007.

Although common patterns exist, no one-size-fits-all approach can be seized upon. The context is a key determinant of the risks and opportunities facing people in crisis-affected areas, a point made clear in the following quotation from an International Labour Organization document (Enarson 2000: vii):

While tornadoes, volcanic eruptions, earthquakes and floods may occur with regularity, their social, political, and economic effects are neither inevitable nor "natural." People's relative risk of harm is a function of their exposure to hazards (e.g., residing in a seismic zone), their capacity to mitigate the effects of these disasters (e.g., seismic-zone construction standards, earthquake preparedness), and their social vulnerability (e.g., lack of income to retrofit housing, restricted social/physical mobility). Vulnerability, in turn, has physical and social dimensions, but is ... a function of relative access to, and control over, key survival and recovery resources. Risk is differentially distributed between and within societies. The root causes [of] social vulnerability are deeply embedded, reflecting political choices made in the course of human settlement and political-economic and social development. ... [D]isaster vulnerability is not synonymous with poverty or social class. Within societies, people's relative ability to access or control key resources is shaped ... by age ... physical ability, citizenship status, racial/ethnic ... cultural group, and gender.

CONCEPTUAL FRAMEWORK FOR GENDER-SENSITIVE AGRICULTURAL PROGRAMMING IN CRISES

Addressing food security, livelihood, and agricultural developments in crises requires preparation and programming in phases: precrisis, during the crisis, early recovery, and postcrisis/recovery. The early recovery phase overlaps the during-the-crisis and postcrisis/recovery phases (see fig. 11.1).

At each phase the full spectrum of the population and their differing needs, situations, and conditions should be considered. This includes the following groups:

■ Traditional rural communities directly affected by the crisis
■ Rural communities indirectly affected
■ Temporary displaced populations in rural areas
■ Displaced populations in urban areas
■ Urban populations and the related markets.

Figure 11.1   Gendered Impacts of External Factors

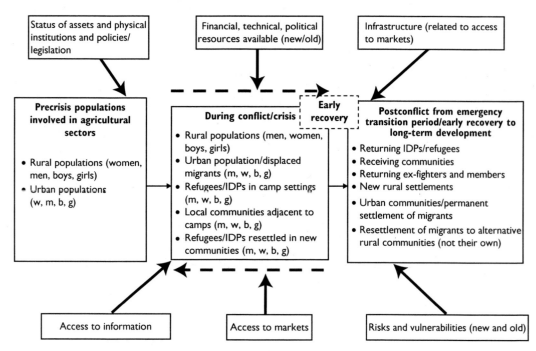

Source: Author.

These populations are not static. Over time, as the crisis continues or subsides, the makeup of the population also changes. For example, in the aftermath of crises the following are often found:

■ Returning internally displaced persons and refugees into rural and urban settings
■ Returning former fighters (opposition or state actors)
■ New long-term settlements in rural areas
■ Long-term settlers in urban areas.

External factors ranging from access to assets and markets to institutional conditions and policies can help or hinder people at each stage. Typically, a gender dimension contributes to the impact of such factors, with women facing greater barriers than men.

INTEGRATING GENDER PERSPECTIVES

Gender differences exist within each subgroup. Widows, single mothers, and women-headed households typically face greater hardships than married women. Dependents (children or the elderly) in *men only*–headed households also may be more vulnerable than other household members,

because single men may not have needed care-giving skills (such as cooking).

The World Bank, like many organizations, has institutional policies and commitments to ending discrimination against women, including the realization of the third Millennium Development Goal (MDG) of promoting gender equality. These policies could and should be used tactically at the country level to prompt dialogue and ensure the equal and equitable treatment of and attention to women alongside men. Three approaches to gender mainstreaming can be undertaken to ensure effective outreach and benefit to women and men (Greenberg and Zuckerman 2004). These strategies can be undertaken simultaneously, as part of a menu of options, or consecutively in a program:

■ *Targeted projects:* Agricultural initiatives can be specifically targeted at either women only or men only to redress inequalities, lack of access or skills, and other issues. Even in broader programs women-only or men-only groups are important in order to gather information, build confidence, and address gender-specific needs before working with mixed groups.
■ *Mainstreaming of gender perspectives:* In designing interventions, planners will find it essential to identify

and address factors that could obstruct women's and men's equal access and benefit. This process ensures the inclusion of women and men as equal beneficiaries so that discrimination is not perpetuated and programming is targeted correctly. Mainstreaming includes recognition of the different roles and contributions that women and men can make in communities and agricultural work. Mainstreaming also relates to external actors. For example, the presence of women staff increases access to women in traditional societies and allows for better understanding of their needs, capacities, and solutions.

■ *Transformative programs:* These programs are designed to transform or recalibrate gender relations by tackling the underlying structural causes and effects of inequality and food insecurity. For example, initiatives to change inheritance laws and practices (at the community level) can significantly alter the status and access of women to assets, particularly land.

The challenges for agricultural interventions in crisis situations include the following:

■ Reducing the vulnerabilities and risks to livelihood faced by women and men
■ Strengthening existing capacities and social capital (and ensuring that interventions do not squander or crush these resources)
■ Ensuring sustainable, long-term, equal access to opportunities, including to assets and resources and to information and markets
■ Helping redress structural factors to reduce vulnerability in the future.

Crises and conflicts not only affect women and men differently but also have a profound impact on gender roles and relations. For women, the heightened physical vulnerability comes with exposure to public space and use of their survival strategies. They are often exposed to new skills and, although overly burdened with the trauma of displacement, also gain new confidence in their own abilities to cope and care for their dependents. For men, it can be a period of disempowerment and profound socioeconomic change as they struggle to rebuild their lives and provide for their families. It is also a time when they garner new respect for women. Interventions must seek to reach all those affected and address their needs and sustain and strengthen their newfound capacities.

The Thematic Notes that follow explore the practical implications of gender perspectives in precrisis, midcrisis, and postcrisis settings:

■ *Thematic Note 1* highlights the nexus between agricultural practices and the relevance of gender to preventive action and disaster risk reduction. It frames the discussion around the provisions of UN Security Council Resolution 1325 (2000), specifically the demand for increasing women's participation in conflict prevention, and the Hyogo Framework's five priorities regarding risk reduction, notably, (1) governance, organizational, legal, and policy frameworks; (2) risk identification, assessment, monitoring, and early warning; (3) knowledge management and education; (4) the reduction of underlying risk factors; and (5) preparedness for effective response and recovery.
■ *Thematic Note 2* examines the links between food, agricultural aid, and development during crises. It identifies the gender dimensions and highlights effective means of balancing this aid so that the specific needs of women and men in local communities are addressed and they benefit equitably.
■ *Thematic Note 3* focuses on critical land issues, including tenure and inheritance rights, education, information, and outreach issues in the postcrisis setting from a gendered perspective. It highlights critical issues and lessons drawn from current and past crises.

Table 11.1 provides ideas for the monitoring of gender issues in crisis situations (although obviously the nature of the crisis may require very environment-specific monitoring).

Depending on the country or region, considering ethnicity and caste alongside gender (both as comparative indicators and when collecting data) may also be relevant, because women of lower castes or ethnic minorities are usually in the most disadvantaged situation.

Table 11.1	Monitoring and Evaluation Indicators for Crisis and Agriculture
Indicator	**Sources of verification and tools**
Number of deaths, disaggregated by gender, age, location	• Government records
Percentage of women and men receiving weather information—regular bulletins or extreme weather warnings—in accordance with their area of work or location	• Focus groups • Household surveys • Media • National-level NGOs, particularly women's groups • Networks of health workers, community organizers, and human rights defenders
Percentage of women and men members of community-based disaster preparedness committees	• Community meeting minutes • Women's community-based groups and NGOs
Balanced level of participation of women and men in decision making (at the local and national levels)	• Community meeting minutes
Number of men, women, and ethnic minorities who receive extension advice per month	• Agricultural extension records • Training records
Percentage of women and men actively participating as members of postdisaster reconstruction committees	• Committee meeting minutes • Interviews with stakeholders
Number and percentage of women and men receiving gender-specific disaster training	• Training records
Sex-disaggregated assessment of impact of disasters on men and women, girls and boys	• Project monitoring • Refugee camp management records
Percentage of women and men receiving land, emergency rations, replacement stock, seed, or loans	• Agricultural extension records • Refugee camp management records • Regional land department records
Satisfaction levels of women and men with postemergency management and reconstruction	• Focus groups • Interviews with stakeholders
Number and percentage of women reporting violence per month (such as threats, beatings, and rape)	• Interviews with community leadership • Interviews with stakeholders • Police records • Refugee camp management records
Percentage of women and men with access to insurance packages	• Household surveys
Changes at start and end of emergency support in household nutrition, health, education, vulnerability to violence, and happiness, disaggregated by gender	• Household surveys, before and after • Project management information system • School records

Source: Authors, with input from Pamela White, Module 16 author.

Risk Management and Preventive Action

In agriculture, as in other sectors, preventing natural disasters and conflict-induced crises is better than needing to cure them. This principle is easily grasped, but the practice has been harder to undertake because there is still a tendency to address crises through an after-the-fact humanitarian response. Prevention and risk-management strategies are still evolving. The challenge to development actors, including those working in agriculture, is to implement programs that not only provide the stated benefits of improving livelihood and food security but also can help prevent or mitigate the effects of crises in the lives of women and men. This entails recognizing the following points:

- Development can exacerbate conflicts and natural disasters. Therefore, existing practices must be reassessed to ensure that they do not inadvertently expose people to greater risk, diminish their coping capacities, or exacerbate the impact of natural disasters and conflict.
- Disasters can be highly detrimental to developmental gains, and the impact of disasters can vary significantly between women and men.
- A shift toward a culture of prevention and crisis-sensitive development programming may and often does require a change in the way work is done, a deep understanding of local culture and practices, and the inclusion of all sectors of society. Women and men have different capacities and strengths that should be drawn upon in making the shift toward prevention.

PROACTIVE PREVENTION

In 2005 governments participating in the World Conference on Disaster Reduction in Hyogo, Japan, recognized the "importance of disaster risk reduction being underpinned by a more pro-active approach to informing, motivating and involving people in all aspects of disaster risk reduction in their own local communities" (www.unisdr.org). The resulting 2005–15 Hyogo Framework for Action identifies five key areas requiring attention to prompt the shift toward proactive preventive actions:

- Governance: organizational, legal, and policy frameworks
- Risk identification, assessment, monitoring, and early warning
- Knowledge management and education
- Reducing underlying risk factors
- Preparedness for effective response and recovery.

These issues are also related to the climate change debate. Many now contend that global warming cannot be prevented in the short term, and so responses to the effects of climate change (including increased risks of natural disasters, such as flooding and drought) must be integrated into risk reduction and coping strategies.

Similar issues have been identified in the field of conflict prevention. Conflict early warning and response systems have evolved over the last 15 years, with an emerging discourse on gendered indicators and differential information that women and men may possess. Frameworks for conflict-sensitive analysis and programming exist. Preliminary steps toward proactive prevention have been initiated by the UN system in West Africa and Central America, where they have worked with women's groups. Because conflict is political, however, questions of state sovereignty continue to hamper external interventions aimed at conflict prevention and transformation. In the 1990s the "Responsibility to Protect" (R2P) principle emerged out of the discourse on addressing the needs of internally displaced persons (IDPs). Part of the approach was to point out that states not only have rights but also have a responsibility to provide protection and security for their citizens. When such responsibility is abrogated, according to the R2P advocates, the international community has a right to intervene to minimize the loss of life and insecurity.

Despite the conceptual advances, the practice of conflict prevention is still limited, especially in states in which violence is impending. It has gained credence in postconflict situations in which the risk of resurgence (and the memory of violence) exists, and thus the desire for and commitment to preventive initiatives and peace building are stronger. In 2000 the UN Security Council passed resolution 1325 on women, peace, and security, a key development in the realm of conflict prevention and peace building. It was the first major international legislative document calling on states, multilateral organizations, and nonstate actors to ensure the participation and contributions of women in conflict prevention and to address women's protection needs during conflict and in the recovery processes.

This Thematic Note highlights the nexus between agricultural practices and the relevance of gender to preventive action and disaster risk reduction. It frames the discussion around the provisions of resolution 1325, specifically the demand for increasing women's participation in conflict prevention, and the Hyogo Framework's five priorities regarding risk reduction.

PRIORITY 1. GOVERNANCE: ORGANIZATIONAL, LEGAL, AND POLICY FRAMEWORKS

Generating a culture of prevention is perhaps the most important and challenging issue. This involves raising awareness, building political will, and leadership. It further requires effective legislation, the establishment of an overarching national framework, and effective multilateral approaches, including mechanisms that do the following:

- Link national to local actors.
- Ensure inclusion of the different needs and capacities of different stakeholders in overall assessments and analytical frameworks.
- Enable coordination between sectors.
- Integrate risk reduction and conflict sensitivity into ongoing development policies and programs.
- Prompt the development and implementation of strict compliance and regulation standards for infrastructural work.

Conflict and natural disasters affect societies in different ways. Typically, those who are most vulnerable under "normal" conditions are most affected when a crisis hits. Given that women represent 70 percent of the world's poor and their unequal social status in most societies, they are often at greater risk than men. However, women are not passive actors. They are often proactive in their efforts to minimize risks and adapt to evolving conditions.

To be effective, state or multilateral initiatives must acknowledge and draw upon this duality of experience—vulnerability and ability to adapt—to guide and develop the policy frameworks and macrolevel initiatives that they establish. Drawing on research conducted among village women in Bangladesh, India, and Nepal, a 2007 ActionAid report offers a set of policy recommendations with a view to mitigating the risks faced by communities, as well as means of assisting communities in adapting to the heightened risk and prevalence of natural disasters arising from climate change (Mitchell, Tanner, and Lussier 2007). They include the following:

1. At the bilateral or multilateral level, ensuring that adaptation funds under the UN Framework Convention on Climate Change have clear guidance and targeted measures for the inclusion of women in adaptation assistance projects and as beneficiaries. For mechanisms that are not directly operational, gender and poverty must be included as central guidance measures for negotiators. Recipient countries must have gender-sensitive approaches in place and measurable outcomes specifically regarding the impact and inclusion of women as beneficiaries.
2. At the state level, policies and mechanisms relating to adaptation must ensure the following:
   - Women's full participation in adaptation financing discussions and decisions
   - That women's needs are considered and addressed in livelihood adaptation programming
   - That regressive sociocultural practices do not hinder women's capacity to adapt
   - That the most vulnerable sectors are provided with insurance packages to prevent complete devastation. The Self-Employed Women's Association (SEWA) in India has initiated such a program (box 11.4).
3. Legislative guarantees are needed that promote and protect women's equal rights to the following:
   - Relevant knowledge and information
   - Land and property ownership: laws that mandate joint titling of land and property can help reduce women's vulnerability and risk of losing property or being evicted in the aftermath of disaster or conflict
   - Equal participation in decision making (at the local and national levels)
   - Access services such as agricultural extension and veterinarians.

SEWA represents low-income women workers in India's vast informal sector. Under a basic program that asks for a fixed deposit of $22 and an annual premium of $1.85, its members can secure insurance against hospitalization (up to $43), house and asset insurance (up to $110), and insurance against accidental death ($870). Higher-priced schemes providing more protection also are available. Over a 10-year period, 2,000 women received benefits amounting to $327,400.

Source: UN ISDR, review of the relevance of eight MDGs to disaster risk reduction and vice versa, quoting SEWA, Jivika: Livelihood Security Project for Earthquake Affected Rural Households in Gujarat, www.sewa.org and www.sewainsurance.org.

Following the 2004 tsunami, Caritas India's Relief and Reconstruction Programme aimed at assisting the marginalized communities and vulnerable sectors of the population. The program shifted priorities following the intervention and inclusion of grassroots women in the decision making. The women prioritized the reconstruction of shelter and housing and the establishment of a community-based disaster preparedness (CBDP) initiative with some capacity building. Women's committees were formed to monitor the CBPD and shelter program. The CBPD enhanced the knowledge of local actors—women, men, and children—in responding to crises. Each community devised and implemented its own local solutions to crises. These solutions include organizing a village emergency fund (composed of handfuls of rice and kitchen utensils) for flood-affected families, forming self-help groups and community task forces trained in firefighting, converting and controlling waste to rid villages of disease-carrying mosquitoes, and providing housing to widows and orphans and other vulnerable community members.

Source: UN ISDR 2007.

4. Coordination mechanisms are needed to link national and local actors and empower grassroots communities in disaster mitigation. Experiences from Latin America and Asia illustrate the positive impact of women's participation on the community's well-being. The initiatives (box 11.5) have reduced communities' dependence on external interventions while strengthening rapport and ties and transforming attitudes toward women and other marginalized groups.

PRIORITY 2. RISK IDENTIFICATION, ASSESSMENT MONITORING, AND EARLY WARNING

Risk identification, monitoring, assessments, and early warning systems are among the range of tools being developed and used to inform policies and programs focusing on risk reduction. Numerous obstacles remain to be overcome, however, including the need to shift institutional practices and business-as-usual approaches in development practice. Assessments and analytical frameworks often highlight gaps in existing practice and require significant changes in the formulation of projects and programs. But bureaucratic inertia and lack of familiarity with new initiatives can hinder the full integration of risk reduction and conflict sensitivity into program planning. Consequently, one-time projects are often initiated alongside existing programs, but this can result in no significant change in practice. In other words, conflict and risk

reduction is not yet being effectively mainstreamed into development initiatives.

The issues are further complicated by the range and variability of risks that need to be considered. In Afghanistan, for instance, schools and clinics were built with light, flexible roofing to meet seismic standards as part of a $73 million program, but the roofs could not withstand the heavy snowfalls that are common in the region. In the winter many children were left without a school (Kryspin-Watson, Arkedis, and Zakout 2006).

In principle, gender perspectives should already be fully integrated into development planning. In reality, confusion and lack of understanding and awareness of gender differences have meant that gender perspectives remain marginal. Often practitioners are unaware of the value that gender perspectives can bring to their work and how it can enhance the impact of their initiatives. If baseline assessments overlook the different needs and contributions of women and men, programs can be poorly targeted. Existing social capital can be overlooked, and negative consequences may be present.

For example, with regard to early warning about environmental change in Peru, women in fishing communities complained that state officials informed the men of an impending El Niño (and its negative effect on fish stock), but women, who were responsible for household resources, were not informed. Similarly, in 1991 in Bangladesh, warnings about an impending cyclone were posted in public places. But because women were more restricted than men in their movements, many were not aware of the risks. This contributed to the disproportionate rate of death among women versus men (71 per 1,000 versus 15 per 1,000) (Seager and Hartmann 2005).

Various frameworks and initiatives do exist. The Food and Agriculture Organization's (FAO) Socio-Economic and Gender Analysis Programme provides extensive resources illustrating the relevance and means of integrating gender analysis to macro-, meso-, and microlevel agricultural programs. The World Bank and the United Nations Development Programme have taken preliminary steps toward integrating gender perspectives and indicators into their conflict and development analysis frameworks. Oxfam and other international nongovernmental organizations (NGOs) have developed tools and guidelines. In Nepal the NGO Center for Population and Development Action provided basic training in gender and social inclusion to government ministries as part of the peace-building process as a means of building state capacities to assess and integrate the differential needs of women and men in all sectors, notably agriculture, where women represent the majority of workers.[1]

Still, much of the existing information is not entering mainstream frameworks. This is reflected in a 2005 UNEP Division for Early Warning and Assessment (DEWA) report "Mainstreaming Gender in Environmental Assessment and Early Warning" (Seager and Hartmann 2005). The authors conclude that "neither DEWA nor UNEP has been proactive in bringing gender analysis to its work". In highlighting the challenges, they also point to the following:

- A lack of research directed at the early warning, environment, and gender nexus
- The importance but lack of sex-disaggregated data relevant to early warning climate assessment
- The inherent problem of using an aggregated "household unit" as the level of analysis, which obscures the gender differences (sometimes profound) that exist within households
- The fact that "the field of disaster management is highly [men dominated] which typically results in the actions and knowledge of women being marginalized, unrecognized

and undervalued. Women are still poorly represented in planning and decision-making processes in disaster mitigation and protection planning" (Seager and Hartmann 2005: 30).

A shift in practice requires a preliminary attitudinal shift among analysts and practitioners. As long as gender analysis is perceived as a burden and a nonessential issue, it will not be fully integrated into assessments or early warning systems. Yet, given the differential roles, experience, knowledge, commitment, and capacities of women and men, it is clearly a fundamental aspect of risk reduction.

PRIORITY 3. KNOWLEDGE MANAGEMENT AND EDUCATION

The Hyogo Framework also calls on states to "ensure equal access to appropriate training and educational opportunities for women and vulnerable constituencies; promote gender and cultural sensitivity training as integral components of education and training for disaster risk reduction" (www.unisdr.org).

Knowledge management, like early warning, must be a two-way system. On the one hand, national or international policies, practices, and strategies must be made available to local communities so that they benefit from the progress being made, lessons being learned, and information being acquired. On the other hand, at the local level, people (women, men, boys, and girls) have access to information and knowledge that are often needed to develop national responses and preventive strategies. Depending on their function in the household or community and their familiarity with their local environment, they may be the first to notice changes that are indicative of a larger phenomenon. They may also be the first responders to famine or other crises.

In rural Ethiopia, for example, FAO documents the use of wild-food and famine-food plants that are typically collected by children and women. When food shortages arise, "able-bodied men migrate to find work. ... Women and children are left behind to manage as best they can" (FAO 2005: 1). Often women have better knowledge of local wild fruits and plants, their nutritional and curative values, and means of improving them. National strategies must incorporate methods of accessing specialized knowledge in a timely manner and ensuring that the stakeholders, particularly women, are included in the development of all aspects of risk-reduction strategies.

In many societies women and men access information through different channels. In rural communities women and men often work in separate spaces and sectors; thus, in the event of a natural disaster, it is essential that they are equally informed about risk-reduction strategies and that the information given to them is tailored to their environment. For example, if men engage in fishing and water-related activities, they need to know how best to survive potential earthquakes and tidal waves. For women, on the other hand, if they tend to work inside homes or in fields, the risks they face (such as a roof collapsing) and related survival strategies may be different.

They also need to be educated regarding the preparation of emergency kits or materials to take with them in the event of a natural disaster or conflict.[2] Information and education regarding the maintenance of livestock and produce are another gender issue. In Nepal women expressed interest in the importance of skills training and exposure visits that could help them diversify their income-generation pool. Where monsoon crops are at risk of flooding, for example, they mentioned goat and poultry rearing as alternative activities (Mitchell, Tanner, and Lussier 2007).

In some instances, culture and traditional practices can appear to be obstacles to the sharing of knowledge and can contribute to the subservience of women. However, cultural practices are not static, and sensitive interventions can yield results. A 2004 study in India revealed that women performed 50 to 90 percent of all day-to-day care and management activities of domestic livestock and poultry (Ramdas and others 2004). Yet women were denied access to specialized knowledge relating to the healing of animals because for generations this knowledge was transferred from father to son. However, when traditional healers were told of the roles and responsibilities of women, they took a pragmatic approach, agreeing that it was important to share the information with women as well.

Another critical aspect of knowledge and information sharing is the integration of resource management into education curricula. Gender issues and the particular roles of women and men in communities can be a tremendous asset. This was exemplified in northeastern Brazil as part of a groundwater management project in 2003. The project's goal was to empower women, men, and children in sustainable and collective management of scarce water resources, as a means of reducing drought risk. The program integrated gender perspectives by acknowledging the different and important roles of women and men in water use and management. For example, it brought farmers (mainly men) together with teachers and health workers (mainly women) for capacity-building workshops, training and information exchange, and the collective development of educational

material. It also targeted younger community members, the future guardians of the land and environment, in an effort to educate them about resources and engage them in material development.

The social roles and responsibilities ascribed to men and women in each cultural context can and often do determine the education they have, the information they can access, and the limits they face in sharing their knowledge. Yet, as indicated above, ensuring the full inclusion of women and men in risk-reduction strategies is integral to the success of such efforts. Women need to be included because they have different information and skill sets that can help reduce vulnerability. They need to be included because crises often force them to cope with the consequences alone. They need to know because they, more than any external entity, are committed to ensuring food security and sustainable livelihoods for their families and dependents in the long run.

PRIORITY 4. REDUCING UNDERLYING RISK FACTORS

Reducing the underlying risk factors as much as possible is fundamental to prevention. In conflict prevention new initiatives that integrate peace building into development programming are emerging. This includes training community members in conflict resolution and mediation skills to enable more effective negotiations when tensions arise. In Cambodia, for example, village women are known as the "backbone of the forestry network" and are a strong presence in the environmental movement. In 2002 they led demonstrations against major logging interests and the abuse of people's land rights. Trained in nonviolent action and mediation skills, they often intervene within and on behalf of communities to dispel tensions (McGrew, Frieson, and Chan 2004).

The international debate over natural disasters and climate change has evolved in recent years, with many experts asserting that efforts to curb global warming or reduce greenhouse emissions are not enough to protect the most vulnerable populations in the near term. Measures to adapt to climate change and reduce the risks of crises must be put in place. Typically such efforts are highly localized, and to be effective they must be tailored not only to the local environment but also to the sociocultural context. Once again, gender comes into play, as women and men use and manage different resources and have differing roles depending on the context and immense potential for contributing to risk reduction.

In Bangladesh, for example, women use a variety of strategies to withstand the impact of flooding. They take livestock to higher ground, store seeds in higher places, seek refuge with relatives, or raise the levels of their homes using a plinth. To reduce losses from rotting crops, some have changed to crops that can be harvested before the flood season. Evidence of diversification is also seen. Recognizing the effect of the floods, women have switched to running fisheries alongside their vegetable farms. The women are frequently alone, because their husbands migrate to find work, and so they need (and many are demanding) skills training to enable a scaling up of their ventures and more effective access to markets (Mitchell, Tanner, and Lussier 2007).

In Nepal women are also developing asset-sharing strategies, including group saving programs and self-help groups to avoid private lenders and high interest rates. Many have also expressed interest in adopting labor-reducing technologies, multicropping strategies, and adopting more-marketable, drought-resistant crops, but typically women lack access to the necessary financial and technical resources (Mitchell, Tanner, and Lussier 2007).

In El Salvador, as well, there are community-based initiatives. During the rainy season, landslides are a regular occurrence, creating environmental hazards for the communities of Lake Coatepeque. Throughout a series of community meetings conducted in 2007, community members identified measures to prepare for natural disasters, including planting fruit trees and shrubs that require little water but can mitigate the effects of landslides, developing emergency evacuation plans and training women (who are more likely to be at home) to prepare basic necessities, making retention walls using chicken wire, and engaging church and community leaders to encourage people's participation in disaster preparedness and planning (Morehead 2007).

Men and women living with the threat of crisis are committed to reducing risks wherever possible. They devise their own strategies but can benefit significantly from external guidance and support. Because of women's traditional absence from public spaces, and particularly from decision making, women's initiatives are often less formal and less visible but are essential and effective nonetheless. Acknowledging women's roles and engaging with them is an essential aspect of any external intervention. No risk-reduction initiative can afford to overlook the capacity and needs of 50 percent of the population.

PRIORITY 5. PREPARING FOR EFFECTIVE RESPONSE AND RECOVERY

The steps noted in the preceding sections contribute immensely toward effective response and early recovery, as they help to limit the damage done. Nonetheless, the loss of life and destruction of property and livelihoods can be devastating with long-term effects. Gender issues are again central to recovery strategies as women's and men's survival strategies and needs often vary. The UN Inter-Agency Standing Committee (IASC) produced a gender handbook for humanitarian action (2006) that provides a comprehensive and practical approach to the integration of gender perspectives in all emergency response processes. The handbook notes the following three basic steps:

- Ask the difference between women's and men's experiences.
- Undertake participatory assessments including women, men, boys, and girls together and separately.
- Use the information to guide programming.

A critical first step toward effective response is knowing the demographics and profile of the target population and determining its specific needs and capacities. The collection of sex-disaggregated data is essential, as is analysis of the data to understand the implications. Where this is not done, the potential exists for compounding the existing vulnerability of sectors of the population, particularly women.

Understanding the division of labor and coping strategies of women and men is also important to effective recovery. In Sierra Leone, for example, a World Bank study noted that agricultural rehabilitation was hindered by the fact that seeds were distributed to households, and the household heads, who were typically men, were the source of information on what resources were needed. Yet women and men in Sierra Leone farm different crops and thus require different sets of tools and seeds (UN IASC 2006). Care International adopted an alternative approach of distributing seeds to all adults. In this way women obtained groundnut seeds (a crop typically planted by women), and this contributed to their income generation and empowerment alongside men. Care's approach was effectively gender mainstreaming with the benefit of empowering women as part of the process.

The IASC handbook provides a series of checklists and guidelines for a full range of issues (registration, shelter, provision of food and nonfood items, support to livelihoods, and health care). Its key message is that interventions should identify beneficiaries, work with them collaboratively, and adapt programming as needed. The framework for gender-sensitive emergency response and early recovery programming is summed up by the acronyms ADAPT and ACT collectively (box 11.6).

Over the last decade, reams of documents, policies, resolutions, and reports have been produced by states, multilateral

> **Box 11.6   IASC Framework for Emergency Response**
>
> **ADAPT and ACT collectively:**
>
> Analyze gender differences
> Design services to meet needs of all
> Access women, men, boys, and girls
> Participate equally
> Train women and men equally
> and
> Address gender-based violence in sectoral programs
> Collect, analyze, and report sex- and age-disaggregated data
> Target actions based on analysis
> Coordinate actions with all partners
>
> *Source:* UN IASC 2006.

organizations, and NGOs addressing the relevance of gender perspective to development, agriculture, conflict prevention, and disaster mitigation. Nonetheless, gender analysis is still an add-on or afterthought in the daily business of risk identification, assessments, warnings, and program implementation. Misconceptions about gender issues and confusion among agency personnel (across many entities on the international and national levels) are compounded by limited data and analysis. Despite the evidence of their effectiveness, gender-equitable approaches are not being embraced and implemented often enough. As a result, the practices are ad hoc, documentation is weak, and people remain vulnerable and excluded. Risk reduction and conflict sensitivity are increasingly being recognized as necessary ingredients for sustainable development. If gender sensitivity is not acknowledged and prioritized in the same way and across the five priority areas of the Hyogo Framework, the chances of effective action are diminished.

From Relief to Recovery and Self-Reliance: The Relationship between Food Aid and Agriculture in Complex Emergencies

When disaster strikes or conflict erupts, emergency food aid becomes a critical component of international aid. It saves lives and is generally recognized as being effective in containing the extent of suffering and damage caused by crises, but it is not a neutral entity. Conventional wisdom suggests that food aid is detrimental to agricultural development and creates a culture of dependency and even exacerbates conflict. Yet when crises disrupt agricultural production and distribution, displace populations, and render land unusable, food aid is of critical importance in the short term. The question, however, is when and how agricultural assistance should be provided. How can it be provided given physical insecurity and potential for violence in many of the places where humanitarian emergencies persist?

This Thematic Note examines the links between food, agricultural aid, and development during crises. It highlights effective means of balancing this aid so that local communities benefit most. It also identifies the gender dimensions of this work. The Note draws on key findings emerging from recent studies undertaken by the Organization for Economic Co-operation and Development (OECD), the World Food Programme (WFP), the United Kingdom's Overseas Development Institute (ODI), Oxfam, the Food and Agriculture Organization (FAO), and others.

EMERGENCY FOOD AID, SHOCKS AND CRISES

Although it is commonly believed that local agriculture is damaged by the arrival of food aid and relief, according to the OECD, in natural disaster situations, the impact on agricultural development—"either direct disincentive impacts on markets and production or indirect effects through policy"—varies (OECD 2006: 33). One factor that determines the likelihood of negative impacts is the type of food aid given. Bilateral food aid—from governments to government, or from government to NGOs—is generally monetized to provide resources for development activities. The monetization process—timing and choice of market—can have negative impacts on local markets. Food aid delivered to multilateral agencies such as the WFP is generally not monetized and is used in targeted project interventions resulting in a far lower likelihood of negative impacts.

In some instances, particularly where the food aid is significant, the positive economic impact can include indirect effects of growth in consumer demand for food and local products. Although studies on the long-term impact of food aid are relatively new, the OECD quotes a 2004 report on sub-Saharan Africa that concludes "large-scale food aid operations to meet short-term deficits in drought affected countries in sub-Saharan Africa in the early 1980s and early 1990s were important in preventing destabilizing effects of covariant shocks on largely agricultural economies" (OECD 2006: 31). These positive effects are nonetheless contrasted against negative consequences, including the following:

- The scramble to provide emergency relief often results in funds being diverted away from long-term projects designed to bolster self-reliance and recovery. According to Oxfam, for example, in May 2006, a month after its launch, the UN's Consolidated Appeal for Somalia was just over one-quarter funded (27 percent). The majority was directed at immediate relief. In the same year, the appeal for Ethiopia had generated 78 percent of its funding requirement for food and 64 percent needed for water and sanitation, but projects aimed at longer-term solutions had received just 1 percent of the requested funds.[1]
- Late-arriving, inflexible relief that does not allow a switch from imports to local purchases hampers the recovery of local economies affected by natural disaster.

It can also contribute to changes in consumer preferences and increased demand for imported foods.

- The restricted basket of commodities available as emergency aid creates difficulties in providing socially and nutritionally appropriate rations.
- Preexisting development-oriented food aid programs can be helpful in times of crisis because the aid can be delivered more rapidly. The effect should not be overstated, however, because there can be significant targeting problems resulting from the inflexibility of geographical coverage and beneficiary selection at a household level. Typically the poorest and most vulnerable can be left out, particularly women and children. Some food aid implementers have explicit requirements, such as targeting women as recipients of food aid and seeking 50 percent representation of women in local food aid committees.
- Political sensitivities can be exacerbated. For example, U.S.-sourced genetically modified maize in southern Africa in 2002 caused controversy and highlighted the political sensitivities in recipient countries—even in crisis—that can disrupt distribution plans and raise costs because of donor inflexibility on sourcing.
- A culture of dependency can arise with no space or opportunity to nurture self-reliance.
- Although "vulnerable" groups may be targeted as recipients, at times less attention and fewer resources are directed to addressing the causes of vulnerability or diversifying the agricultural sector or livelihoods to enable communities to withstand crises in the long term. The WFP and others do engage in a variety of development-oriented programs, including watershed management.
- Governments that are reliant on revenue generated through bilateral food aid programming and sales may have no incentive to support long-term programs that bolster domestic food production.
- Local procurement of food aid, as increasingly done by WFP, can foster market development. A risk of market collapse exists, however, if WFP no longer requires food after several years of procurement.

The potential negative effects of food aid are more notable in conflict-affected states. Government and opposition forces can exploit food aid provision for their own benefits and hold local populations hostage to their own demands. This violates the right to food as enshrined in the Universal Declaration of Human Rights. Moreover, food and other forms of humanitarian aid have fueled conflict. The links between war, famine, and humanitarian aid became most evident in Ethiopia and Sudan during the 1980s and conflicts that emerged in the 1990s. With the end of the Cold War, humanitarian agencies were able to expand relief operations into war zones and areas controlled by insurgents, but the assistance provided was exploited by warring factions. In some instances the food and clothes designed to reach the most vulnerable populations became a source of competition between factions. In the Democratic Republic of Congo following the Rwandan genocide, international aid literally fed the perpetrators and enabled them to continue the sporadic cross-border violence and fueled ongoing conflict in neighboring Burundi (Barber 1997). Conflicts in Liberia and Sierra Leone were among cases in which civilian populations were seen to be deliberately targeted as a means of creating displacement and ensuring an influx of international aid that was then used to fuel the violence.

Thus, on average, internationally procured food aid is seen as a second best option for responding to emergency situations. Where markets function and effective trade links exist, the OECD suggests that "financing of public imports through the commercial sector, and allowing the private sector to respond to rapidly changing market conditions" is more effective (OECD 2006: 32). The WFP procures its food aid locally where donor resources provide flexibility and local markets can support the demand without causing price rises, which would affect non-food-aid recipients. In some cases, for example, the WFP procures food and grains locally, even though some stocks have been imported commercially. The international response, says the OECD,

"should be sensitive to the specifics of the options that are practically available, the social and economic environment and governance in the affected country. For example, in the 1991–93 drought crises in Southern Africa large-scale commercial imports were organized and arrived more quickly than food aid and so played the key role in averting a regional crisis. Allowing the private sector to respond to rapidly changing market conditions through commercial imports and stock adjustments, as in Bangladesh after the floods in 1998, limits the need for potentially destabilizing increases in public expenditure" (OECD 2006: 31).

Moving from food aid to agricultural assistance

The real challenge, however, is how and when to initiate assistance for local agricultural production. This is critical for food aid beneficiaries who may sacrifice food consumption in order to save food aid given as whole grain for planting. Recent years have seen a growing consensus on the need to shift toward early recovery and self-reliance as soon as possible. In part this is a means of mitigating the negative impact of food and humanitarian relief on conflict, but it is also recognition of the chronic and long-term nature of many of the crises that exist today. For example, the average length of displacement is now 17 years (taken globally among displaced populations; UNFPA 2007: 6). Affected populations cannot and should not be reliant on an ongoing cycle of short-term humanitarian relief. The situation is complex, however, as allowing displaced populations to settle can itself be a source of conflict with host communities and contribute to land and resource degradation. In addition, displacement can result in the loss of skills and knowledge in food production from one generation to the next, as household heads, typically women alone, have to develop alternative copying and livelihood strategies in the new environments in which they find themselves.

In 1997 the international humanitarian community produced the Sphere Humanitarian Charter and Minimum Standards in Disaster Response (Sphere Standards) as a means of setting a standard for the provision of aid to people affected by crisis and conflict. The guidelines touch on all aspects of humanitarian assistance, including the need to ensure food security and livelihoods. The standards address the full range of issues from conducting nutritional assessments to protecting production mechanisms, ensuring sustainable and diverse agricultural practice, and guaranteeing access to markets for producers and consumers in crisis situations.

Taking a step back and focusing on preventive measures, the World Bank report *Mainstreaming Hazard Risk Management in Rural Projects* (2006: 9) draws attention to the actors and stakeholders that need to be included. Consensus is emerging "on the best way to organize the components of national systems for hazard risk management has begun to converge around several key points." First, the report notes that regardless of whether existing systems are centralized or decentralized, risk management involves multiple stakeholders, including representatives from a range of national-level institutions or sectors, including land-use planning, environment, infrastructure, communications, utilities, and health. Second, the report points to the importance of local level capacity and participation in comprehensive risk management. Reasons for this include the following:

- The effect of disaster is first felt by the community, and they are the first to respond.
- Failure to understand the behavior and culture of the community can result in badly designed early warning systems.

- Involvement of local people builds self-reliance.
- Reconstruction efforts are more effective if the community is actively involved and feels a sense of ownership.
- Many communities are remote and rely on their own resources to cope with crises.
- Preparation at the community level is a building block toward improving national capacities to respond and cope.
- Increased community participation can lead to increased local pressure on governments to address disaster risk issues adequately.
- Community-level focus allows for targeted identification of access, and engagement with a full cross-section of society, including the elderly, the disabled, the young, women, and minority groups who are often excluded (World Bank 2006).

Theory and realities on the ground, therefore, emphasize the need to shift from relief to interventions that aid early recovery and self-reliance. Yet international practice lags behind. A decade after Sphere, neither the standards set for protection of agricultural production nor those regarding access to markets are being fully met. Multiple challenges remain to be overcome:

1. The lack of security, particularly in conflict-affected areas, can be a major obstacle to the provision and implementation of agricultural programming. Access can be hazardous, land may be mined and unusable, and the presence of armed groups and the proliferation of weapons contribute to insecurity.
2. The lack of effective institutions and the collapse and loss in many cases of social capital are profound obstacles to any sustainable development effort.
3. Tensions exist between short-term relief efforts and long-term rehabilitation and development programming. In theory, early recovery and rehabilitation initiatives conducted during or after conflict or crises are meant to promote self-reliance and resilience and help transition societies from relief to development. In practice, however, the processes are at odds with one another. For example, relief efforts often operate on short-term (sometimes six months) budgeting cycles. Thus, the support provided is often piecemeal, as opposed to being comprehensive and infrastructural with longer-term durability.
4. Lack of coordination between donors contributes to the ad hoc and at times duplicative nature of the support provided.

A 2007 ODI study (Longley and others 2007) offers further insight into the current gaps relating to agricultural programming in "fragile states"—those prone to, or affected by, conflict and those with limited ability to provide basic services (including guaranteeing food security) to their citizens. It critiques existing agricultural programming in such situations for being piecemeal and not tackling underlying structural and institutional issues that affect agriculture. It also notes that insufficient links still exist between agricultural programming and social protection. Reflecting on seed aid programs in Afghanistan, Sierra Leone, and southern Sudan, for example, the study highlights the following:

- In Afghanistan seed distribution was used to promote "new variants" to farmers without providing the requisite training to inform them about the seeds or activities such as trials and demonstrations to allow them to learn more. No systems are in place here for ensuring that aid agencies are accountable to their beneficiaries.
- In Sierra Leone "lack of regulation in the procurement and distribution of seeds led to efforts to promote the local production of these inputs . . . involving community seed banks." Yet observers noted few incidences of sustained and successful programs, "raising questions about the appropriateness" (Longley and others 2007: 2) of the initiatives.
- In southern Sudan local seed production systems were formed in the 1990s. Yet they were overly reliant on NGOs, and when the NGOs were forced to pull out of the region, many farmers were unable to market their seeds. Concerns about dependency on NGOs and external actors remain.

The study calls for consideration of four overarching issues (Longley and others 2007):

- *Addressing vulnerability and livelihood strategies:* Agriculture may not be a source of livelihood for many of the poorest people, and it is necessary to assess and understand the structural causes of vulnerability, including sociocultural issues that affect equity and discrimination.
- *Coordinating a comprehensive approach:* A more coordinated and comprehensive program of assistance to farmers is required that includes a diverse range of inputs and services.
- *Promoting markets:* Private sector involvement is needed in the provision of agricultural services and inputs, and the strategy of stimulating demand through the provision of resources (cash or vouchers) to beneficiaries.

- *Strengthening institutions:* The paper advocates attention and enhancement of institutions as a means of supporting rural livelihoods and agriculture. In many instances significant reform of such institutions is needed to ensure that the root causes of conflict are addressed.

In addition, greater understanding of and respect for local coping mechanisms and traditional knowledge are needed, including understanding the gendered division of labor, so that interventions are appropriately targeted. An understanding of traditional knowledge and means of coping in crisis situations is also needed. Outsiders need to grasp the sociocultural context, while also drawing on their mandates to ensure that marginalized groups are not doubly victimized.

The link between agricultural assistance and institutional structures is of particular importance. For responders, however, a need exists to acknowledge the differential circumstances wrought by conflict and natural disasters. In conflict situations, relief aid is typically provided by external actors outside the confines of the state structures. Sometimes this is important because the state has no actual capacity to deliver the aid. At other times the key is to access communities directly without hindrance from the state. With the end of conflict, a noticeable shift occurs as rehabilitation and reconstruction aid is channeled to the state.

Transformative recovery

An overarching goal of international reconstruction efforts is to enhance state capacities to move reconstruction away from fragility toward sustainability. The dilemma, however, is that re-creating past status quos and systems can also mean re-creating the conditions that led to conflict in the first place. In other words, not only should outsiders avoid doing no harm with interventions, but they should also avoid perpetuating harm or discrimination that existed and contributed to the crisis. Thus, in postconflict situations the goal should not be simple recovery, but actual transformation and tackling of root causes to limit future vulnerability. From the perspective of the agricultural sector, this touches on issues ranging from redressing land ownership and tenure, to rural governance structures, to policies relating to diversification of products and skills and market and infrastructure development.

In the case of natural disasters, however (where there is no violent conflict), the state and its armed forces are often the first responders. Donors and humanitarian agencies typically coordinate with the state to ensure the delivery of relief. In the aftermath, however, programming aimed at building up national capacities to manage and withstand crises is not focused on building state capacities per se. Recognition and inclusion of the multiple stakeholders, at all levels, as the World Bank (2006) study says, are thus essential.

KEY GENDER ISSUES

Men and women must be recognized among the "multiple stakeholders" noted by the 2006 *Mainstreaming Hazard Risk Management in Rural Projects* World Bank study. Interventions must build on the local knowledge and responsibilities of women and men in agricultural processes. For example, in Afghanistan and Pakistan, women play a central role in animal husbandry. In some areas in Pakistan they also manage the finances and resources. Practices vary across cultures. If interventions are planned based on assumptions or with disregard for the gendered dimensions of agricultural work, they can fail or do harm.

Emergencies and disasters affect people differently depending on their gender, stage of life, socioeconomic status, and cultural practices. Even within the same family or household unit, the impact and capacity to respond can vary. For example, in many instances women will eat less and share their portion with their boy children. Pregnant and lactating women can be at acute risk of malnutrition in crises. Similarly young men or men-only-headed families are also vulnerable because they often do not have the necessary cooking and food preparation skills. Recognition of these issues creates indicators of who the most vulnerable may be and can ensure more targeted, relevant, and early responses for those groups.

Crises: challenges and opportunities for redressing gender inequality

Crises—conflict or natural disaster, short or long term—can affect the composition of households with extended family members, widows, unmarried women, and others joining together. Often men are absent (because of death or migration), leaving women with multiple burdens in the public and private spheres. Changes in these situations are related to and affected by sociocultural norms, which in turn should inform relief and recovery programming. For example, even in a traditionally men-dominated society such as that of Nepal, it cannot be assumed that, in times of crisis, households are led by men and relief can be distributed through them. Elsewhere, past practices that favored the distribution of food and relief to men proved to be not

only highly inequitable toward women but also contributed to the cycle of violence, for example:

- Sale of relief aid in exchange for alcohol or other substances
- Sale or exchange of relief aid for weapons
- Common practices of polygamy so that distribution of family rations to one man results in lack of rations for other wives and children
- Malnutrition among young men in a displaced camp due to lack of cooking skills (and inability to use the rations provided).

The changes, while difficult, also create opportunities for addressing longstanding discrimination against women. For example, the WFP has initiated procedures to distribute relief primarily through and to women. This can benefit them in the short term and prompt greater empowerment over the longer term. Similarly, targeted efforts to allocate land and assistance to women in postconflict and crisis situations can be initiated. In postwar Cambodia and El Salvador in the 1990s women were recipients of land. Yet for the effect to be sustainable, equal access must be matched with equitable treatment and understanding of the underlying factors that could affect women detrimentally.

In the case of food aid, for example, local conditions (such as corruption, loss of food aid to local militia, distances that goods need to be carried, and weight of packages) can prevent equal access and expose women to further insecurity. In the case of land allocation, in Cambodia often the tracts given to women were of the poorest quality and in areas that were difficult to access. Moreover, women heading households required the assistance of men in their communities to undertake the hard physical work. For many women, simple ownership of the land was not enough to enable them to sustain a livelihood. In Rwanda after the genocide, changes in legislation to enable women's inheritance of their husband's property were not readily implemented at local levels, where they went against culture and historic norms. In effect, although opportunities exist, to avoid a backlash, intervention must be designed with sensitivity to the cultural norms. A key aspect of program design is to understand the differing roles, responsibilities, capacities, and constraints of women and men in the region in question. This includes understanding their traditional division of labor in the agricultural sphere, as well as the changes that have resulted from the crisis. Although formal needs assessments can be difficult to undertake in the midst of crises or where insecurity is rife, informal and ongoing consultations with different sectors can provide the necessary information and ensure gender-sensitive programming as in the case of the Sri Lankan irrigation project (see Innovative Activity Profile 1).

Where the issues are addressed and integrated into programming, the positive impact is not felt by the individual beneficiaries but by the community as a whole. A 2004 study in El Salvador documents that in communities where women received basic support such as child care, they were able to participate in community development initiatives, whereas they were absent in areas where such support was not provided. The study indicates that where women were involved, the community's overall development and economic standing were greater than in communities where they were not (Pampell-Conaway and Martinez 2004).

GUIDELINES AND RECOMMENDATIONS FOR PRACTITIONERS

Food aid and agricultural assistance are both necessary components of effective interventions in most crisis situations. The key to sustainability, however, is to ensure that the aid provided is not perpetuating or harming the communities and stakeholders it aims to assist. This requires substantial knowledge of the ways in which the agricultural sector works, as well as the existing sociocultural underpinnings. If information is gathered during "normal" times, it can assist in planning for crisis response. Establishing networks of local communities and organizations can be a means through which information is gathered and shared. The capacities built locally can also be a critical aspect of early recovery.

The FAO (2003) and the UN's IASC (2006) have developed frameworks for conducting needs assessments and establishing contact groups to inform external actors of the changing nature and conditions of affected populations. Similar approaches can be taken in formulating agricultural initiatives. IASC guidelines on food security, for example, offer advice on gathering information about the following issues disaggregated by sex:

1. *Demographic factors,* including numbers of landless poor, herdless pastoralists, poorest in caste or ethnic groups, most marginalized communities (by composition and sex), migrants (long and short term)
2. *Local capacities,* including
   - Understanding the local division of labor between women and men
   - Identification of preexisting community structures (formal and informal) and how or by whom they are led; in

many cases women have structured networks of support that may not be overtly visible but are essential for effective food production, storage, and sales
   - Understanding the importance of local and household-based power structures relating to use of food, land, livestock, tools, finances, conservation, storage, and other productive resources, to ensure that interventions are tailored to each group and are culturally appropriate
   - Understanding the skills needed by women and men (particularly those returning from conflict)
3. *Changes in social factors,* including
   - Household composition
   - Division of labor
   - Needs (including of the sick, elderly, the young, and their caretakers)
   - Different needs and coping strategies of women and men (for example, dislocation and the loss of jobs and social standing can traumatize and disempower men, whereas for women, taking on new responsibilities, while difficult, can also be a source of empowerment)
4. *Changes in economic factors,* including
   - Incidences and nature of poverty (for example, it is typically high among widowed women)
   - Identification (through consultation) of forms of intervention that are most targeted and beneficial to the full cross-section of the population (for example, for many of the very poorest with no land or livestock, cash or vouchers are a means of generating a livelihood)
   - Ensuring equitable access to markets for food procurement and the sale of goods (for example, in Bangladesh a "ladies' corner" was established in one local market to provide a culturally accepted space for women to sell their goods)
   - Ensuring that subsidies do not inadvertently harm women's and men's food and crop production and incomes
5. *Political conditions that can affect women and men differently,* including
   - Discrimination based on group identity
   - National and customary practices and laws that limit equal access to agricultural resources, particularly land and access to agricultural services (including training, equipment, seeds, and support)
   - Changes in legislation to promote gender equality (and the potential backlash locally or among select groups)
   - Access and involvement in consultation processes and decision making, ability, and constraints related to engaging with external actors and donors

6. *Institutional and security factors,* including

- Mechanisms and arrangements to enable full participation of community members (men, women, differentiated by age, economic status, and so on) in consultative processes
- Physical security threats facing women (and men) in traveling to and participating in markets and accessing support
- Impact of landmines and weapons on women's and men's ability to work fields and reach markets
- Impact and incidences of sexual- and gender-based violence that threatens women's security and negatively affects their capacity to engage in agricultural work

7. *Information gathering and dissemination,* including

- Ensuring effective outreach to women and men in rural communities through use of special measures (for example, partnership with community radio and networks of rural health workers) where necessary to inform most excluded groups (for example, widows in Afghanistan or Dalit women in rural Nepal with no literacy skills and knowledge of dialect languages)
- Ongoing consultative processes or forums (such as village-level councils) to enable all stakeholders to provide feedback on the impact of the interventions and participate in problem solving and decision making.

Managing Land and Promoting Recovery in Postcrisis Situations

L and issues—from tenure to usage, ownership, reform, and redistribution—are a critical feature in crises and emergencies. "The relationship," states a 2004 USAID study, "is stark, whether we are talking about how land issues function as causal or aggravating factors in conflict, or whether we are thinking about land-related issues that arise in post-conflict settings."[1] Access and usage are not only a question of immediate survival but have sociocultural implications tied to issues of history and identity. The Israeli Palestinian conflict is a case in point. On the Palestinian side, the incursion of Israel into the "Occupied Territories" is not just a military issue, it also has meant the destruction of homes and orchards and their replacement with modern housing, erasing the identity of their owners.

Land is also a cause of and can fall victim to natural disasters. Overuse, deforestation, and desertification can lead to landslides and flooding. Earthquakes and tsunamis can wreak devastation on a massive scale, sometimes causing irreparable damage.

As a crisis or conflict continues, the issues become even more intertwined.[2] Displacement and resettlement among new communities can ignite new tensions. The destruction of traditional social networks and family structures, the increase in women heads of household and widows, and the inevitable reformulation of relations give rise to disputes, as people from diverse communities (or identity groups) often have differing approaches and practices relating to land management and usage. These changes spill over into the postconflict and crisis setting, and if they are not addressed, they can cause a resurgence of violence.

This Thematic Note focuses on key land issues in the postcrisis setting from a gendered perspective. It highlights critical issues and lessons drawn from current and past crises. Additional gender analysis related to land can be found in other Modules in this *Sourcebook*. The Rural Development Institute (RDI) identifies the following linkages between women, land, and improving livelihoods:

- Women represent over 50 percent of the world's population and provide 60–80 percent of the world's agricultural labor, yet research indicates they own less than 5 percent of the world's land.
- Assets and income in the hands of women result in higher caloric intake, better nutrition, and food security for the household than when they are in the hands of men.
- Women's property rights increase women's status and bargaining power within the household and community.
- Secure land rights provide women with greater incentives to adopt sustainable farming practices and invest in their land. More than 80 percent of farmers in Africa are women, yet women in most African countries do not have secure rights to the land they farm.
- Providing women with secure rights to land has the potential to mitigate the impact of HIV and AIDS on food security and reduce high-risk behaviors.

POSTCRISIS ISSUES

Physical recovery from crisis (manmade or natural) is complicated by practical issues such as weakened local management structures; the loss, destruction, or falsification of records; and the return of IDPs and refugees who make claims on land or have it allocated to them. As noted in a 2004 FAO publication, governments and donors rarely consult, coordinate with, or compensate local communities with regard to the resettlement of refugees and IDPs (Unruh 2004).

Differing interpretations and implementation of international laws and norms pertaining to land access can also cause difficulties. Sometimes the confusion arises among donors themselves with "disagreement . . . as to the direction that the development of the property rights system should take after a conflict, with differences often tied to the economic and foreign policies of the donor countries involved" (Unruh 2004: 3). The drive toward private property ownership can clash with traditional communal tenure and ownership practices, as well as demands for social justice and equitable distribution of resources. This can be particularly stark in the case of widowed or single women claiming the right to live on their family property while the law prohibits women ownership.

Security plays a role as well. In postconflict settings, mined land is useless for cultivation and is a drain on limited resources because demining is slow and expensive. In Afghanistan and Mozambique, for instance, much of the most fertile lands was mined. It is also a public health issue. Farmers are often driven (or need) to cultivate mined land that has lain fallow but expose themselves and their family to great risk, as landmine victims require long-term care and assistance. Women in particular are more vulnerable if harmed because in many societies men may shun them if they can no long perform household duties. Lack of effective security structures is another challenge. Criminal gangs and splintered armed groups can emerge in the vacuum created by a weakened state. Extortion can become commonplace, as in Nepal, where it emerged during the Marxist-led conflict. Sexual violence is a common feature and can debilitate women's productivity and movement. State-sponsored confiscation or expropriation also occurs, fueling tensions and stifling economic growth.

Time is another key factor. Immediately after the crisis need and demand exist to move quickly to resettle people and regenerate the economy and livelihoods. Many states emerging from conflict may not have the personnel or technical capacities to address the issues. As stated by FAO, "in post conflict situations a land rush can occur after a conflict, which very quickly outruns the ability of a re-establishing formal tenure system, and the best intentions of government and donors to manage. This can take community and household land tenure, resettlement, eviction, restitution and disputing in directions that are largely outside of the control of a slowly reformulating formal tenure system" (Unruh 2004). Inevitably, the combination of traditional practices, the lack of women in decision making, and the lack of sensitivity among policy makers and international actors to the differential experiences and needs of women and men results in the inadvertent exclusion of women as beneficiaries.

Yet the difficulties that emerge in postcrisis environments come with new opportunities to review and redress long-standing or root causes of conflict and discrimination. Just as there are conflicts that arise over land issues, so too can peace agreements set into motion land reform and reallocation. The recovery period can also be a time for national institutions to review and revise legislation that discriminated against one group or sector of the population. In South Africa, for example, the changes in legislation were directed at benefiting the majority black population that had endured decades of discrimination. The influx of international aid and technical support can help establish alternative livelihood opportunities. Mechanisms for resolving disputes and ensuring more equitable access to land can be put in place. After experiencing a crisis—especially a natural disaster—national and community leaders and stakeholders may be more amenable to embracing more sustainable livelihood methods as a means of reducing risk and future vulnerability.

LAND AND TRANSFORMATIVE RECOVERY: THE CHALLENGES FACING WOMEN

The challenges and opportunities present in postcrisis environments affect women and men. In most instances, however, the challenges facing women are greater than those faced by men. The reasons vary according to region and culture. On the one hand, women, more than men, are engaged in agricultural production and the cultivation of land. On the other hand, women farmers' literacy and educational skills are more limited than those of men. Often they have little or no legal protection or ownership rights. Cambodia in the aftermath of the Khmer Rouge regime and the 1991 peace agreement is a case in point. Women are responsible for 80 percent of the food production, yet most have no control or ownership of the land they work. Nearly 50 percent of women farmers are either illiterate or have basic primary school education (World Bank 2004).

The situation is exacerbated by natural disasters or conflict, as men migrate for waged employment, join armed groups, or are targeted by them, leaving women alone in rural settings. In Honduras, for example, the proportion of women-headed households doubled in the aftermath of Hurricane Mitch in 1998 (Bradshaw 2004). In effect, the vulnerability and disparity that exist for women under "normal" situations (for example, lower skills and education, less access to decision making, no formal ownership rights) are exacerbated when crises emerge and livelihoods and traditional social systems are destroyed. Initiatives aimed at promoting recovery must therefore aim to address and resolve some of the baseline criteria that contribute to the gendered disparity and vulnerability.

The key issues facing women in postcrisis settings have been noted in a range of reports, including a 1999 UN Center for Human Settlement (Habitat) study (UN Habitat 1999), and are summarized in the following five sections.

Legal barriers

In many instances women's rights to land, housing, or property are limited during times of peace. Their rights are circumscribed by customary practices whereby access is determined by men relatives. In many societies women have no right to own, rent, or inherit property in their own name. Across Asia and Africa women often need their husband's permission to access credit or acquire titles independently (Farha 2000). Conflict and crises can exacerbate this. As refugees and IDPs they lose access to their homes and properties. Once the crisis subsides, the situation does not improve. As widows (or with spouses missing), as women heading households (caring for siblings or elderly relatives), as daughters or sisters, they often have no legal protection or claim on their homes or properties, yet often they are the sole caretakers of families. In Rwanda, for example, a decade after the genocide women led some 30 percent of households (Brown and Uvuza 2006). In Aceh, after the tsunami, women have been caught in disputes with in-laws or men family members laying claim to land and property (Fitzpatrick 2007). In Palestine women are subjected to not only the confiscation of land by Israeli forces but also social pressures to renounce inheritance rights when husband or fathers are killed (Farha 2000).

Registration and recordkeeping

Recordkeeping and documentation can also have significantly different implications for women and men in postcrisis periods. Customary practices and the protection afforded by clan elders are often destroyed during crises, making women more vulnerable. In many cases only the men head of household is recorded, and property, whether or not it is jointly owned, is recorded under men's names. Sometimes it is inadvertent. In Java, Indonesia, for instance, customary practices dictate joint ownership by husbands and wives. Yet when registration was put in place, the registration forms provided space to register only a single owner, and typically men's names were recorded. This minor bureaucratic oversight had significant implications for people's lives (Brown and Uvuza 2006: 25).

Often during conflicts, administrative offices and records are deliberately destroyed in looting and property ownership becomes a disputed issue. In natural disasters the destruction of records is among the many consequences. In the recovery period, systems are put in place to handle claims. But with men absent or dead, women may face challenges to their claims of joint ownership. Even where state laws give men and women equal rights, without proactive efforts to realize and protect women's rights, they can be neglected or abused. In a 2007 Oxfam study in Aceh (Fitzpatrick 2007), the issues women raised regarding their ability to claim property included the following:

- Their access was limited, because only the men members of their families were registered on property titles.
- They were too traumatized to venture into the public sphere and make their claims.
- With their primary responsibilities as caregivers and providers for their families, they had neither the time nor the resources to mobilize and assert their rights.

Other factors that affect women include the following:

- Their traditional social networks are destroyed, and they have less access or capacity to influence local leaders, who are often charged with decision making.
- They face entrenched sociocultural barriers, so decisions are often made against them and in favor of men.
- They lack information or knowledge about their legal rights or where to get assistance.

Land allocation and reform

Peace processes or political transitions often catalyze land and property reform, liberalization, or reallocation programs. Such programs, however, are often hampered by a lack of sufficient resources from the outset. For example, in Guatemala prior to the civil war, 2 percent of the population owned 70 percent of the land. The 1996 peace accords included a provision for land reform. Land taxes and a land fund associated with an autonomous government agency (Fontierras) were among the mechanisms established to enable the reform, but the costs of undertaking land reform far outweighed the allocated budget. By 2006 it was estimated that only 2 percent of the demand had been met.[3]

The purchase of the land amounts to only 30–40 percent of the total costs associated with sustainable land reform, according to one Africa-focused 2006 World Bank Study (Van den Brink and others 2006). Other costs associated with resettlement, housing, start-up grants, agricultural inputs, training, and advisory services are also critical to success, yet they are rarely accounted for. South Africa, for example, has allocated a realistic budget toward land purchases but underfunded the nonland costs (Van den Brink and others 2006).

Women, especially widows or women heading households, are often losers in land reform programs. Before the conflict in Cambodia, for example, women's rights to ownership were recognized. They had equal access to land through inheritance, and acquisition through cultivation. However, the postwar period coupled with liberalization policies has marginalized women, making them more vulnerable to market forces, debt, and landlessness. Close to 50 percent of war widows have no access to land. Of those who do, some 84 percent have less than 0.05 hectare of often poor quality land, making it difficult to sustain a livelihood (World Bank 2004).

The reasons for disparity vary. One reason is lower literacy levels among women and less knowledge of land titles, tenure requirements, or new land laws. In family disputes (or divorce) women do not have knowledge of their legal rights. Another reason is that in many places women are also socialized to care for elderly and sick parents and are thus more likely than men to spend savings, go into debt, or sell assets to provide care. Yet another reason is that social stigma is attached to women engaging directly with men regarding legal issues or local authorities. This can impact their inheritance rights, because their men relatives may keep the certificates of entitlement and directly (or indirectly) pressure women to conform to societal norms (McGrew, Frieson, and Chan 2004).

Equality but not equity: the multiple burdens of women

As noted above, although the law may often offer some protection or rights to women, in practice societal forces present obstacles to the realization and implementation of the law. In effect, there is legal equality, but in practice, the situation is not fair or equitable.

As heads of households in postcrisis situations, women have the combined burden of domestic and agricultural responsibility. Many cannot make full use of their land or maximize their production and revenue with limited literacy skills and an overwhelming combination of domestic and productive duties. They often have no knowledge of or time to seek out information regarding their rights or the nature of titling procedures. Their exclusion from the men-dominated bodies that administer land issues and are an integral aspect of social and political networks compounds the problem.

Compared to men, women farmers also tend to have less access to high-quality inputs or information about improved techniques. Often agricultural extension staff are predominantly men. As such, in many traditional societies they cannot engage in face-to-face contact with women farmers. Moreover, little attention is given to the fact that women and men specialize in different tasks. Research and outreach to women's specialized tasks are limited.

Women typically have less access to credit. According to FAO, where data are available, only 10 percent of credit allowances are extended to women.[4] Their access to markets is also more circumscribed. Security concerns and domestic duties prevent women from engaging in market-related activities and accessing basic services (including health or education regarding land management). Thus, even where land laws may espouse equality or be progressive (such as the one passed in Cambodia in 2001), the differences between women's and men's access and opportunities remain stark.

International financing: helping or harming?

International aid comes rushing in after crises, but the impact on women and men can vary deeply. Women can be inadvertently negatively affected. Issues that arise include the following.

Location and resettlement of refugees and IDPs. At times, international actors do not consult, compensate, or coordinate sufficiently with local communities regarding the settlement of refugee or IDP populations. Differences in customary tenure practices versus government practices can cause increased tensions and fuel conflict between the two communities.

Competing ideologies and lack of coordination between donors. Donors can have differing interpretations of or priorities relating to international laws and norms and how they affect land tenure issues in postcrisis settings. Donors' policies can be contradictory. Many may support gender-equality measures but unwittingly undermine equality as they call for a shift toward a market economy and privatization as a precondition for the provision of financial assistance. This means a shift away from customary titling practices toward private ownership. Where customary practices hold sway and are the only safety net available to women, the move toward privatization can be devastating. Widows (who traditionally were permitted to remain in their homes until death or remarriage) find themselves evicted by men heirs keen on generating an income or benefiting from increased land prices that are a common feature of postcrisis countries.

Ad hoc approach to international laws especially women's rights. Within the framework of international laws and conventions, numerous provisions articulate women's rights to property ownership (see summary in box 11.7). The World Bank, like other entities, has its own policies and guidelines. In many postcrisis settings, women's rights advocates rely on such provisions to further their demands and ensure protection for women. Yet support provided by international actors—bilateral or multilateral entities—is at best ad hoc.

UN Convention on the Elimination of Discrimination against Women (CEDAW) (1980), adopted by 191 UN member states, includes the following:

- Article 15: "State parties . . . accord to women equality with men before the law"; "they shall give women equal rights . . . to administer property."
- Article 16: "the same rights for both spouses in respect of the ownership, acquisition, management, administration, enjoyment and disposition of property."

The Habitat Agenda (1996), adopted by all UN member states, commits governments to "providing legal security of tenure and equal access to land to all people including women . . . and undertaking legislative and administrative reforms to give women full and equal access to economic resources including the right to inheritance and to ownership of land and other property."

UN Sub-Commission on the Prevention of Discrimination and Protection of Minorities, Resolution 15 (1998), urges all governments "to take all necessary measures . . . to amend and/or repeal laws and policies pertaining to land, property, housing which deny women security of tenure and equal access and rights to land, property and housing, to encourage the transformation of customs and traditions which deny women [this] security, and to adopt and enforce legislation which protects and promotes women's rights to own, inherit, lease or rent land, property and housing."

UN Security Council Resolution 1325 (2000): "Calls on all actors involved, when negotiating and implementing peace agreements, to adopt a gender perspective, including . . . the special needs of women and girls during repatriation, resettlement and for rehabilitation, reintegration and post conflict reconstruction."

Source: Author.

Cultural relativism is often used as an excuse to avoid the pursuit of measures that can protect women, despite the fact that the demands for such changes are often emerging from grassroots communities themselves. Inconsistency, apathy, or ignorance of institutional policies can heighten women's vulnerability at a time when they are struggling to survive and maintain their households and communities.

USEFUL LESSONS AND OPPORTUNITIES FOR ADDRESSING GENDER DISPARITIES

Despite the difficulties that arise, major crises also create new opportunities for tackling gender-based disparities regarding land ownership, tenure, and use. Most important, perhaps, is that many women come to the fore as a result of the effects of crises. As refugees and IDPs, they often have an opportunity to mobilize, gain awareness of their rights, and assert their demands. Support from international entities can strengthen their capacities while still ensuring that the demands are locally driven and homegrown. Moreover, women themselves are the best navigators of their cultural terrain. If informed of the international policies and norms, they can be effective in bridging the purported divisions between the policies and traditional practices without

prompting a backlash or accusations of cultural insensitivity. Opportunities include the following:

Peace accords as a key entry point. Peace accords can be a key entry point for addressing land reform. As in Guatemala, in the Israeli-Palestinian conflict, land ownership and occupation are clearly among the most contentious yet critical issues to be resolved. Just as marginalized ethnic or indigenous groups may demand their rights to land, specific discrimination against women can also be highlighted. In Sri Lanka in 2002, a women's coalition comprising local and international women's rights advocates held lengthy community-based consultations to identify women's concerns around the then-emerging peace process. Land issues were among the issues noted (box 11.8).[5] The recommendations they developed were aimed at national parties to the conflict as well as international entities involved with supporting the implementation of agreements or assisting recovery.

New constitution and legislations. Eritrea, Ethiopia, Mozambique, and South Africa are just some of the countries where women's mobilization, political pressure, and public demands enshrined their rights to property ownership in the constitution and legislation. In South Africa, the land reform legislation introduced following the end of the apartheid era explicitly addresses gender equality. Within

Box 11.8 Sri Lanka: Women's Concerns and the Peace

"Land rights appear to be one of the most difficult and contentious issues throughout the northeast. The displaced [people] need to reclaim their land and property and receive compensation for loss and damage. Those who cannot return must be resettled elsewhere. Those occupying land and property abandoned by the displaced or evicted must vacate such property and be re-settled. Women and, in particular, widows and women heads of household must be given title to land and property. Issues of inheritance for women must be clarified and women's right to land & property protected."

Source: Excerpts from Women and Media Collective (2002).

Recommendations made by the Mission:

1. Land laws must be reformed to ensure equal rights of women to inherit and dispose of land and property.
2. Where necessary, lands must be surveyed to establish boundaries.
3. Ownership rights should be respected, and persons living in houses owned by others should be provided with alternative accommodation.
4. Widows and relatives of the disappeared need assistance in accessing the documentation they require to prove their rights to property and inheritance.

---

the Land Affairs Department a Sub-Directorate on Gender Affairs was also established. In Rwanda, in the aftermath of the genocide, inheritance laws were changed in 1999 to allow equal inheritance rights for sons and daughters and to protect women's joint property rights in formally registered marriages. In 2005 parliament adopted a new Land Law to establish rights to land and leaseholds, resolve uncertainty in land holdings, and encourage consolidated use as a means of promoting productivity. The law will be implemented through a series of more issue-specific legislation and regulations.

Such legislative changes provide a new normative framework through which the issues affecting women can be addressed. However, they are often neither sufficient nor comprehensive. For example, the 1999 inheritance law does not provide protection to women in consensual unions (or other customary practices) and has been interpreted to limit a widow's claims on her husband's properties. Typically local women's organizations are among the first to identify such gaps. To address them, they require assistance and support from a variety of actors, including international agencies.

In any context, effective and equitable implementation of new land laws requires a number of other measures to inform the cross-section of stakeholders at national and community levels and ensure their support and adherence. Nepal offers an example of an opportunity to implement legal change. As the peace process began there in 2007, local NGOs identified some 103 laws that discriminated against women. The state must take a lead in repealing or striking down such laws and drafting new provisions that explicitly recognize and protect the independent and equal right to property ownership and inheritance for women and men. NGOs and international agencies can provide technical and financial support to local actors. They can lead research and analysis to provide the necessary information. They can lead by example, incorporating existing international norms and standards in their own practices.

Protecting women's rights in registration.[6] As noted earlier, registration procedures are critical to ensuring equal and fair access and ownership of land:

- In Vietnam, when it was discovered that only men were being registered on land titles, new certificates were issued that included space for the names of both spouses.
- In Cambodia, at the time of registration, an assistant is nominated at the village level with responsibility to inform women and the most vulnerable members of the community of their rights and to assist them in making land claims or objecting to existing claims.
- In Aceh recommendations for more equitable practice include making joint titling mandatory. Registration forms could include questions about existing spouses or others who are co-owners of the land (for example, men or women siblings).
- In addition, as noted by the Sri Lankan women (box 11.8), land must be surveyed, and all stakeholders (with special outreach to women) should be included in community mapping, consultative, and adjudication processes.

Inclusive consultations. Direct interaction and consultation between the makers and implementers of land policy and women's rights groups are essential for understanding the specific issues facing women and the contributions women can make toward effective resolution and implementation of land reform policies.

In 2006 the Rural Development Institute (RDI) and Women Waging Peace (renamed the Initiative for Inclusive Security) cosponsored a workshop for Rwandan government personnel and women's civil society groups with the goal of enabling direct discussions about the implementation of the new land laws and remaining gaps regarding women's protection and needs. The women's groups formed a policy and law task force to comment on forthcoming legislation and provide lawmakers and government officials with recommendations to better protect women's land rights. Similar initiatives could be sponsored in other settings. The effect is beneficial to all stakeholders.

Outreach and education programs with special attention to women. Informing land administration officials, the judiciary, and others involved in land adjudication and communities about upcoming changes is fundamental. As part of the officials' training, there is an opportunity to alert them to and highlight the specific needs of women. Ensuring targeted outreach to women to inform them of their rights (and the processes being put in place) is also a key dimension of many initiatives aimed at improving laws and practices:

- In Cambodia government initiatives included targeted outreach and education programs for women and other groups at risk of being harmed by reform processes. The interventions were scheduled for times and located in places that were easily accessible to women.
- In Rwanda the National Women's Council, a governmental body with representatives at the community level, was interested in taking a leading educational role in the implementation of new land laws in 2006.
- In Nepal, *ASMITA*, a magazine owned and run by women journalists with a focus on women's rights, has been a key conduit of information about and for Nepalese women. The magazine's target audience is semiliterate rural women; thus, it is picture heavy. The publishers also produce booklets and posters addressing issues such as women's land rights and other legislative changes.[7]

Data, research, monitoring, and impact. In many postcrisis settings, little documentation and analysis exist regarding the impact of legislation or customary marital property and inheritance practices. In Nepal, for example, the direct impact of conflict on women and the related migration of men are not fully understood in the context of land ownership. Yet land reform is a key element of the 2007 peace accord. Without this information, new laws, policies, and programs can inadvertently do harm or exclude the majority of women, as in the Rwandan 1999 Inheritance Law.

A paucity of sex-disaggregated data and analysis in terms of the impact of crises on women and the effects of provided aid or assistance also exists. Reflecting on responses to Hurricane Mitch, a 2004 study by the Economic Commission of Latin America and the Caribbean (ECLAC) states that "There are still not many statistics on impact differentiated by gender. Most of the agencies interviewed indicated that they did not explicitly take gender into account and did not break down their data on the disaster by sex nor analyze their results from a gender perspective" (Bradshaw 2004: 19). A review and revision of existing data collection methods and frameworks are needed to enable sex-disaggregated data gathering at the household and other basic levels.

Finally, implementation needs to be monitored and adjusted to address the needs of all sectors of the community. RDI's recommendations for Rwanda's 2005 Land Law resonate in other instances:

- The implementation of new laws should be piloted and assessed from a gender perspective. Women and men should be directly targeted regarding their experiences of the different dimensions of the program, ranging from their exposure to the public education efforts to registration. Comparative case studies should be conducted to highlight the differential experiences and needs of women and men (for example, widows, women heading households, and married women and men). Monitoring and evaluation of the pilots, including consultations with the target groups, should inform and be addressed in the draft legislation and related regulations, programs, and budgets.
- Resources should be dedicated to the development of a specialized monitoring and evaluation process and technique that can be applied nationwide once the legislation is being implemented. The process can include and inform policy makers as well as civil society actors and other stakeholders, with a view to identifying gaps and obstacles at an early stage and enabling their resolution.
- Existing assessment frameworks and questionnaires, such as those developed by FAO, ECLAC, and other entities,[8] can be adapted and tailored to each case.

CONCLUSIONS

To be sustainable and to reduce vulnerability, recovery has to be transformative. Crises present the opportunity to initiate new practices and systems. The challenge is to balance the drive toward returning to a status quo and recognized past practices with the need to address the practices that contributed to the vulnerability. External interventions must seek to raise awareness among local leaders of the existing gender disparity and the consequences for the community as a whole. Local populations and leadership are often open to change in the aftermath of a crisis. They also are often conscious of the extreme vulnerability of women and are ready to seek solutions. External actors should prioritize the provision of technical assistance and support to enable this shift.

Food Aid versus Agricultural Support and Sustenance of Social Capital

SRI LANKA: NORTH-EAST IRRIGATED AGRICULTURAL PROJECT

In 1983 war broke out between the government of Sri Lanka (GoSL) and the Liberation Tamil Tigers of Eelam (LTTE).[1] Over the years the North East Province of Sri Lanka, where the conflict has been most violent, has been devastated. Before the war nearly two-thirds of the population depended on farming, fishing, and livestock as their main source of livelihood. The conflict destroyed much of the irrigation system and road infrastructure. It also caused mass displacement and the collapse of social institutions such as farmers' organizations. Gender-based disparities in income and occupation resulting in higher poverty rates among women were further exacerbated by war, as women were burdened with traditional men's tasks as well. War-affected communities and displaced populations in the region have been exploited by both sides. The conflict hampered international humanitarian efforts. According to a 1999 British Refugee Council briefing document, "the restrictions and delays in agricultural inputs [were] in part . . . responsible for a substantial reduction in agricultural production with resulting decrease in jobs and income."[2]

> **What's innovative?** The recognition and inclusion of the Women's Rural Development Societies in this project was a significant achievement. Before the project, these groups had not been given the chance to play such a central role in the well-being of their communities. The project gave them the chance to build their institutional strength, as well as demonstrate their capacities to contribute to and gain the respect of the community as a whole.

PROJECT OBJECTIVES AND DESCRIPTION

Amid these difficult political, human, security, and logistical conditions, the International Development Association in collaboration with the GoSL initiated a community-focused project to (1) help conflict-affected communities in the northeast and adjoining areas reestablish at least a subsistence level of production and community-based services through assistance for jump-starting agricultural and small-scale reconstruction activities, and (2) build the capacity of such communities for sustainable social and economic reintegration. Initially, 398 villages were included in the program, of which 30 were in the Jaffna district (Wanasundera 2006).

The project was the first large-scale development project funded by any major donor in the area after the outbreak of war in 1983. It was thus a pioneering initiative for the restoration of livelihoods among the internally displaced population and conflict-affected people. Its proactive outreach to ensure the full and equal inclusion of women and men was also innovative. The successful implementation of the project in the first two years paved the way for other major donors, such as the Asian Development Bank and Japanese Bank for International Cooperation, to plan and implement similar complementary operations in the North East Province targeting the conflict-affected people.

Typically, irrigation tanks provide water for irrigation and drinking water for rural villages in Sri Lanka.[3] The project focused on the revival of agricultural production in conflict-affected villages through the restoration of irrigation tanks damaged by the war or abandoned by people fleeing the villages. The irrigation tank restoration was complemented by the rehabilitation and provision of essential village facilities, such as village access roads, drinking water facilities, construction of community buildings, and support for income-generating activities to enable the displaced people who returned and were returning to the villages to revive their livelihoods. To plan and implement these interventions and ensure care of the rehabilitated facilities at the end of the intervention, the project facilitated the revival of community organizations, such as farmers' organizations and women's community-based organizations (CBOs) that existed in the villages before the outbreak of the war but were weakened or fell apart because of the war.

The project's development focus was therefore appropriate and timely to provide sustainable livelihoods for conflict-affected people and encourage the return of the IDP. At its start, the project had four major components. A fifth component, the livelihood support activities (LSAs), was added halfway on the basis of the experiences emerging from the initial implementation and the priorities identified by the target population.

- *The rehabilitation of irrigation projects.* The project sought to rehabilitate 400 irrigation projects, including refilling breached sections of embankments, raising low spots on embankments, repairing or replacing sluices, fixing and improving spillways, repairing scheme access roads, and cleaning and desalting main canals and irrigation tanks.
- *Community capacity building and small-scale reconstruction.* The project financed community capacity building, including support and partnership with *Madar Sangam,* the women's rural development societies (WRDSs); support for social mobilization, including repaired rural roads and drinking water facilities; and technical assistance to community-level organizations.
- *Feasibility studies.* Feasibility studies were done for rehabilitation of the 10 most dilapidated major irrigation schemes in the North East Province and in the border villages of the four neighboring provinces.
- *Provision of technical and financial management auditors.* Given the limited banking facilities available, the project financed independent technical and financial auditors to ensure transparency and accountability.
- *Livelihood Support Activities.* The LSA was added in 2002 to make the project more inclusive. It provided an opportunity for the landless and the most vulnerable families, as well as women, who could not benefit from irrigation tank rehabilitation to access project support. The Development Credit Agreement was amended in December 2002 to permit (1) livelihood support grants to WRDSs and (2) WRDSs to provide repayable loans to members for undertaking small individual household income-generating activities related to (a) agriculture

and allied activities, (b) improved production and marketing of commodities, (c) promotion of various microenterprises, and (d) construction of common assets such as community buildings.

Although security conditions and the mobility of people in the project area slowly improved after the signing of the ceasefire agreement in February 2002, the situation in the project area remained precarious following the LTTE's withdrawal from the peace talks in April 2003, the LTTE's internal conflicts in March 2004, and the tsunami disaster in December 2004. Despite these constraints, the project successfully achieved its development objectives and completed its physical targets, as is evident from the Implementation Completion Report.

KEY ELEMENTS

The following section discusses key elements of the project.

Community consultations. When the project was initiated, the conflict between the GoSL and LTTE was raging. Because of the consequent security constraints, conventional project preparation activities (social assessments, institutional analysis, baseline surveys, and beneficiary consultations) could not be undertaken. However, wide consultation was undertaken with the main stakeholders, including the North East Provincial Council, district secretaries and government agents in the project area, the United Nations High Commission for Refugees (UNHCR), the International Committee of the Red Cross (ICRC), commanders of the Sri Lanka army (SLA) in the project area, and the political wing of the LTTE.

The project director, a woman, was based in the region and had in-depth knowledge of the active communities and organizations. According to external assessments, other project officials were not as sensitized to the gender issues, but she was and selected *Madar Sangam* (WRDSs) as an implementing partner because of their efficiency (Wanasundera 2006).

Lessons drawn from past experiences, including a previous World Bank irrigation project, demonstrated that a simple operation focused on irrigation rehabilitation through community participation was possible in the North East Province.

Active participation of conflict-affected communities. The project design also recognized the need for active participation of the conflict-affected communities in the planning and implementation of the project interventions.

Inclusion of and support to women. From the outset within the community capacity-building component, specific attention was given to the inclusion of WRDSs. The project director knew the groups' work and integrated them into the project implementation. The idea was embraced by project officials, other local partners, and the community, as they experienced the "dynamism" that the WRDSs brought.[4] Additional adjustments were made later to ensure that women and landless people could benefit from the project.

Pragmatic and tailored project design. The implementation design was simple and pragmatic and recognized the unique context of the conflict situation and the related constraints. Interventions were planned in both "cleared areas" (areas under the military control of the SLA) and "uncleared areas" (areas controlled by the LTTE), the division of which changed continually at first. The difficulties that the project team faced included (1) working staff of line ministries and departments based in Colombo (capital of Sri Lanka), who were reluctant to travel to the North East; (2) requiring clearance from the SLA and the LTTE before moving any government and Bank staff, vehicles, and construction materials into uncleared areas; (3) developing monitoring mechanisms for project funds needed in the uncleared areas that were acceptable to the SLA and the GoSL; and (4) working in areas where there were no formal banking facilities. To address these difficulties, the project design included developing strong partners and consulting with them to determine pragmatic and simple solutions. The partners include the SLA, NGOs, UNHCR, ICRC, and independent technical and financial auditors.

Localized responsibility and accountability. The project management responsibility was fully devolved to the North East Provincial Council (NEPC), despite claims by several central government ministries based in Colombo to become the lead ministry for project implementation. However, the Ministry of Provincial Councils and Local Government was appointed as the anchor ministry for the project, but its role was limited to a facilitative role for matters that could not be resolved at the NEPC level but required the attention of high levels of the government, including the Treasury and Ministry of Defense.

The NEPC devolved implementation responsibility to the participating districts to enable transparent and consultative selection of focal villages and beneficiaries, close liaison with other development partners at the district level, and better supervision and monitoring. The implementation at the district level relied upon collaborative working partnerships between relevant provincial council agencies and the district wings of the central government departments. This arrangement promoted collaborative working partnerships between the agencies of the provincial council and the central government within the districts. The design included NGOs as implementing partners. This was appropriate because the NEPC lacked capacity and prior experience in

community mobilization, and the partnering CBOs and NGOs (including *Madar Sangam*) had already been engaged in community-based activities in the project area.

Key role of partnerships. The inclusion of SLA, ICRC, and UNHCR as formal members of the project steering committee proved to be invaluable in identifying and targeting focal villages, coordinating and monitoring project activities, enhancing accountability and transparency in the use of project resources in uncleared areas, and facilitating security clearances to ensure speedy and timely mobility of staff, vehicles, and construction materials to project sites.

Independent auditing. The inclusion of both independent technical auditors and financial auditors, carried out by private sector agencies for the first time in a Bank-funded project in the country, was important to GoSL, particularly to SLA. The engagement of audits not only satisfied their concerns about transparency and accountability in the use of development funds in the prevailing risky environment, but also helped the Project Management Unit in enhancing the diligence in financial management and engineering quality of the design of subprojects during the implementation.

BENEFITS AND IMPACTS

An estimated 55,000 families benefited from the project (31,000 farm and 24,000 nonfarm families). The project, centered around 378 small and medium irrigation schemes, reached more than double the anticipated targeted families and total population, totaling 275,000 people, of whom 123,750 were men and 151,250 were women. At the time of project's conclusion:

- 369 irrigation schemes had been rehabilitated (others were near completion), enabling the cultivation of 24,980 hectares of prewar farmland.
- 1,294 kilometers of roads were rehabilitated.
- The original target of rehabilitating 300 drinking wells was increased to 775 (to address needs), of which 754 were completed.
- 379 village-level multipurpose buildings were completed (as planned). Of these, 291 were taken over by rural development societies (RDSs) and WRDSs. The buildings serve as meeting places, shelter for kindergartens, mobile clinics, and other purposes.
- Women were given access to credit through the LSA to start microenterprises, including poultry raising and grinding mills.
- The project, recognizing the women's groups' commitments, also prioritized women's organizations in several village/field assessments (Wanasundera 2006).

The project successfully reactivated, created, or strengthened a total of 1,057 CBOs—371 farmers organizations, 369 RDSs, and 317 WRDSs—in all focal villages. These CBOs engaged in planning and implementing project-supported activities satisfactorily in their respective areas of responsibilities. The project contributed to community capacity building through (1) introducing and supporting bottom-up planning processes of developing Village Social Profiles and Village Development Plans facilitated by NGOs; (2) providing training on procurement, financial management, and technical aspects of project-related civil works; and (3) creating linkages between CBOs and government offices, such as the Irrigation Department, Agrarian Service Department, Provincial Road Development Authority, and the Rural Development Department.

The WRDSs and the resultant empowerment of women were one of the project's most important achievements. Prior to the intervention, institutionalized groups of women did not exist in the focal villages. The WRDSs included the majority of women in the villages targeted, and their representatives demonstrated strong leadership. The WRDSs were seen by many as being the most robust village-level CBOs, catering not only to women but also to the poor and the vulnerable.

Although the LSA component was added later, the impact was significant. The WRDSs administered loans to a total of 18,975 households. The LSA was new to project staff, but by reaching poor households, it boosted the overall impact of the project. All loan recipients were women, and the activities undertaken were in most cases geared to their economic empowerment (microcredit enterprises) and household food security (as noted above). The success of the LSA was largely attributable to effective management of the loans by WRDSs. By and large, the capacities of the WRDSs for financial management increased, although more systematic support would have enhanced them further and should be included in future projects.

The project design did not specifically provide for an institutional or implementation arrangement for ensuring construction quality of civil works, nor did it provide for developing practical management information and monitoring and evaluation systems.

The successful implementation of the project led to the preparation of a follow-up operation. The Bank's board approved the Second North East Irrigated Agriculture Project in 2004. By 2007, progress had been slow. The project was restructured to be more demand driven, flexible, and resilient in light of the reescalation of the conflict.[5] However, the impact of increased levels of violence in the region was not known fully at the time of writing.

GENDER-SENSITIVITY APPROACHES

From a gendered perspective, the project was somewhat inclusive and sensitive to the differential experience and capacities of women and men, but this was partly ad hoc. The woman local project director was the key to identifying and integrating the WRDSs into the process. According to FAO, other "officials implementing this project understood little of gender issues" (Wanasundera 2006: 21).

The project documents do not provide detailed information on the processes and approaches taken to ensure equitable inclusion of women and men in the consultative processes and as beneficiaries. Nonetheless, they do refer to the work done and achievements relating to women. No analysis or reflection on the impact of the project on men per se is included as well, or why the farmers' organizations (run by men) were not as effective as the WRDSs.

At the outset, the project consciously adopted two strategies: *mainstreaming* and *transformative* approaches. Recognizing that this still excluded a significant portion of the women's population, the project added a third strategy halfway through that was directly *targeted* at women: the LSA component. These three strategies are summarized in the following:

- *Mainstreaming:* The selection of a woman project leader was a key step. Her knowledge of and selection of the WRDSs as implementing partners was a good example of mainstreaming. From the outset, the project leaders included women in the consultative processes and as beneficiaries. Although the project could have integrated women into the RDSs, there was recognition of the efficacy of enabling women to operate in new parallel structures, as opposed to trying to find their voice and leadership in preexisting (and perhaps entrenched structures). The approach taken from the outset was very pragmatic. The goal was to assist conflict-affected populations, and this naturally included attention to women. The selection of the WRDSs was also pragmatic in part because they were known to be effective, committed, and able to reach all affected populations. Their selection was not perceived as an overt focus on women only, which could have caused a backlash among the community and landowners.

- *Transformative:* A key goal and achievement of the WRDSs was to empower women and increase their roles in local decision making and management. The selection of the WRDSs by the project director was itself transformative because it brought their work (and commitment) to the attention of the project officials. The FAO also notes that in programs (run by other agencies) in which men-dominated NGOs were selected as project partners, women remained marginal beneficiaries with access only through small entities. The partnership with the project also increased the WRDSs' status (and women's status) in the communities. As stated, the project did not highlight this as an overt goal but implicitly wove this dimension through the practical initiatives. This enabled women to demonstrate their leadership at the community level alongside men, without creating a backlash or being seen as the sole beneficiaries of the intervention. That women's organizations were prioritized in field and village assessments is indicative of how the project staff became aware of (or changed their attitudes) toward the relevance and potential of women in recovery programming.

■ *Targeted:* The project realized that despite its efforts to integrate women in the community structures, many women (particularly the very poor and landless) were still not benefiting from the intervention. The LSA component sought to redress this by targeting loans to women specifically. Giving implementation responsibility (and technical support) to the WRDSs was also a means of enhancing their management capacities. Interestingly, the introduction of the LSA late in the process could be a positive technique for providing targeted support to women. If others are already benefiting from the intervention, they may be more willing to acknowledge that the very poor are still excluded and thus be supportive of (or at least not against) targeted efforts to reach them.

LESSONS LEARNED AND ISSUES FOR WIDER APPLICABILITY

The degree of gender sensitivity that emerged in this project was not overtly planned at the outset. It was a positive and somewhat unanticipated outcome, but one that does indicate that gender-sensitive assessment and analysis are critical to a program's overall effectiveness. The lessons and issues that emerge for future projects include the following:

■ Women-run CBOs are often the most effective partners in supporting the poor and the most vulnerable. Where women's organizations are not included as project partners, women typically do not benefit from the resources available and remain marginalized and more vulnerable (Wanasundera 2006).

■ Delivering assistance directly to communities and forming strategic alliances between key stakeholders are critical determinants of project success in conflict-affected situations.

■ Anchoring a project at the provincial level can increase ownership at the local level and facilitate project implementation, particularly in "pause-in-conflict" and post-conflict situations in which institutions have become weaker but need to revive their lost capacity quickly to engage in broader reconstruction programs, as was the case with this project.

■ Innovation and flexibility in project design, initial piloting of project activities, and close and competent supervision are important if projects are prepared quickly in conflict-affected situations.

■ In a conflict situation, securing technical assistance to build local capacity is critical. The changes wrought by conflict and the impact in every sector are overwhelming for states and grassroots communities. These impacts are exacerbated over time as education and skill-building opportunities diminish (because of violence), technocrats or other skilled citizens migrate, and the violence forces isolation on those left in rural areas. Communities (and governments) often need support to assess and understand the changed conditions, the needs that exist, and means to work when basic infrastructure is weakened or destroyed (such as no banking systems).

■ Selecting villages in poorer areas and activities targeted at poor and landless people ensures that the benefits of irrigation-led projects reach communities and families most in need of assistance.

■ The full inclusion of women's structures at the village level can be an effective means of drawing upon and strengthening women's leadership.

■ Livelihood support to women can make a project more inclusive and has tremendous potential for alleviating poverty. It would be necessary, however, to ensure that every sector in society is benefiting equitably and that "traditional" community leaders are informed and consulted about targeted support to women. Otherwise a risk of backlash exists.

■ CBOs need sufficient training and technical backup to sustain project-created assets. This can range from training in maintenance of the new infrastructure to management of resources and funds to monitoring and accountability methods and consultative decision-making practices.

■ Continuous monitoring and assessing of project processes and impacts with beneficiary participation should be part of project monitoring and evaluation systems. It is not sufficient to have technical auditing without a clearly defined practical quality management system in place. Such monitoring should include collection and analysis of sex-disaggregated data at the outset, mid-point, and end of the project to assess if and how women and men have benefited. It could also include consultations with beneficiary groups (or individuals) to determine whether needs were met and how processes can be improved.

■ The project reports and documentation should provide more information and analysis of the strategies and tactics adopted to ensure women's inclusion. This should include analysis of the reactions of and interactions with the traditional leadership in the community. In addition to the quantitative data needed, a description and analysis of processes undertaken would be helpful for future efforts. For example, the project should document how men and women were consulted (as groups, individuals, together, separately) and what differences the approaches made. The impact of the interventions (such as grants to landless women) should also be documented.

Niger: Taking Preventive Action with Food Banks

Niger, one of the poorest nations in the world, is a landlocked Sahelian country with a predominantly agrarian society. Eighty percent of the population lives in rural areas characterized by subsistence crop production and livestock keeping. Sixty-three percent of Niger's population lives below the poverty line, and the country's policy makers are confronted with high illiteracy and child mortality rates. Women and women-headed households constitute the country's poorest and most vulnerable social group.

Niger's agricultural production is hampered by insufficient and irregular rains, which lead to frequent droughts. Low soil fertility, parasite attacks, and a high population growth rate aggravate the pressure on agricultural production. As a consequence, the country is faced with chronic food insecurities, particularly during the so-called hunger season, which is the season before the harvest. In 2004 Niger experienced insufficient rains and locust attacks, which caused a severe food crisis in 2005. The Maradi region and women and children were hit especially hard. The crisis was described as a situation in which food was either not available or not accessible to the population.

As a reaction to this situation, the government of Niger, with the support of foreign donors, established an emergency program in 2005 to distribute free food, emergency seeds, and fodder. In 2006 IFAD and the Belgian Survival Fund started a second emergency program, which established food banks to ensure sustainable supplies of food and, ultimately, to relieve food insecurities of vulnerable households. The program targeted the most vulnerable women in the Maradi region.

The program was implemented in several steps:

- Villages in the Maradi region with a food deficit of more than 50 percent were identified as target villages. Selected communities were informed extensively about the setup of food banks.
- Within the target villages, the most vulnerable women were identified according to predetermined criteria. These included the possession of land and livestock assets as well as the income and food security situation of the household. According to these criteria, women were classified as extremely vulnerable, very vulnerable, vulnerable, and slightly vulnerable.
- In every village, management committees consisting of a president, treasurer, and secretary were appointed by a general assembly of food bank beneficiaries. The members were selected on the basis of their displayed commitment. Most of the committees were composed entirely of women. In villages with very low women's literacy rates, a literate man was appointed secretary. Committee members were then trained at the regional level on how to manage food banks and were provided with management manuals to be used on a day-to-day basis.
- After the establishment and training of the management committees, food was purchased and a storage place (the food bank building) was arranged. The initial food stock financed by the project was about six tons per bank.

What's innovative?

- The most vulnerable in the population, women in a particular region in this case, are exclusively targeted.
- Food bank beneficiaries elect and control the management committees, which results in high commitment to the operations of the food bank.
- Management committees are intensively trained on the regional level to ensure efficient operations of the bank.

Food distribution (of mainly cereals) takes place weekly during the hunger season, which generally runs from July through September. Only women may take a food loan from the bank. After the harvest, recipients have to repay the bank in kind the amount of food taken out plus 25 percent interest. The interest rate is determined by the management committee and may be lowered in times of bad harvests. Stocks are thus recovered and stored for the next hunger season. The allocation and recovery of the food stock are managed entirely by the elected committee member. Finally, a follow-up and evaluation process at the regional and governmental levels was established to assess clearly which households benefited and in what ways. The evaluation process is carried out jointly by the management committees and the project managers. Because the food banks started in 2006, no quantifiable impacts on beneficiaries are yet available.

Over the period of one year (2006–07), 111 food banks in 111 villages were set up. About 683 tons of cereals were distributed, which benefited 26,000 households in the Maradi region, or approximately 200,000 persons. Census data that quantify how many women, apart from the woman loan holder, live in a beneficiary household are not currently available. Eighty percent of the beneficiaries were food secure for less than six months a year. Repayment rates for the loans are 97 percent, which is unusually high. Consequently, the increase in food stocks varies between 10 and 25 percent in the target villages. Part of this success is attributable to the fact that beneficiaries of the bank are actively involved in the bank's management. This kind of empowerment gives rise to a close personal identification with the food bank and consequently results in high repayment rates.

GENDER APPROACH

The project targets and deals with women directly in all its stages, which is unusual for the men-dominated society that prevails in Niger. The project targets the most vulnerable women in the Maradi region, and only they are allowed to take out food from the food banks. Remarkably, the management committees of the food banks are predominantly composed of women, who are actively involved in the establishment of the bank. In addition, the management committee controls the allocation and recovery of the food stock. Committee members and beneficiaries meet regularly to discuss problems and needs associated with the food bank and decide upon the potential solutions. Placing the project management and control into the hands of beneficiaries is unique in this context and has

empowered rural women in a positive way, as illustrated in the following section.

BENEFITS AND IMPACTS

The impacts of the project have yet to be quantified because the project began so recently, in 2006. Still, it is reported that the food banks allowed the beneficiaries to cover most of their food needs during the hunger season. The increase in food availability led to a reduction in malnutrition, particularly for women and children, who were able to increase the number of meals available to them. For example, children received two to three meals, on average, during the hunger season. With a larger availability of food, the number of meals increased to three to five meals each day.

Other direct impacts of food banks are related to the coping strategies that rural households employ during a crisis. For example, agricultural productivity of the target households improved because farm households were no longer forced to redirect household labor off-farm to earn additional income for food purchases. Productivity also rose because the physical capacities of farmers increased because of regular food intake. In addition, farmers were no longer forced to harvest their crops prematurely, which often leads to lower yields.

The higher availability of food, supplied by food banks, also resulted in lower rates of livestock sold to raise income for food supplies. Livestock usually belong to women in Niger. Therefore, the higher food availability led to a higher retainment of women's assets. Similarly, households took out fewer loans, which they often resort to in response to a crisis, resulting in lower household debts.

Interestingly, indirect impacts have also been reported. Through their active involvement in the formation and management of the food banks, women raised their organizational capacities in areas that are traditionally men dominated. Moreover, closer social networks evolved among women, who started to share a common goal. Most importantly, by targeting and involving the most vulnerable women, the project helped them improve their social position and decision-making power within the household and the village.

To ensure the continued success of food banks, further steps have to be taken. The stock of food should be increased to about 10 tons per bank to allow for the coverage of food needs during the whole hunger season. Moreover, upgrading of storage facilities and further strengthening of management capacities are necessary to improve the performance of the food banks.

LESSONS LEARNED AND ISSUES FOR WIDER APPLICABILITY

Establishing food banks where food is taken as a loan and repaid in kind is an approach not frequently followed in Niger and other developing economies. Yet the project illustrated that food banks can serve (1) to act as an efficient tool to ease a food crisis, (2) to prevent sustainably future food crises, and (3) to avoid having the most vulnerable households be hit hardest by food shortages. Food banks may also act as an instrument to relieve household debt and to prevent the out-migration of young men to earn off-farm income. Placing the management and control of the bank into the hands of the beneficiaries is a unique element of this project that resulted in a high commitment to the project and thereby may cement its success and sustainability. The empowerment of vulnerable groups, particularly women, in the management of the bank may be a channel for improving these groups' social position in the village and in the household.

NOTES

Overview

The Overview was written by Sanam Naraghi-Anderlini (Consultant) and reviewed by Nata Duvvury and Catherine Ragasa (Consultants); Deborah Rubin (Cultural Practice); Kaori Abe, Suzanne Raswant, Ilaria Sisto, and Richard Trenchard (FAO); Katuscia Fara, Maria Hartl, and Sheila Mwanundu (IFAD); and Ian Bannon, Lynn Brown, and Eija Pehu (World Bank).

1. "Ecological Sources of Conflict," *Somaliland Times*, March 15, 2003, www.somalilandtimes.net.

2. "Colombia Displacement," May 3, 2007, www.alertnet. org.

3. "Background Information," The UN Secretary General's High Level Task Force on the Global Food Security Crisis," www.un.org/issues/food/taskforce/background.shtml.

4 "Burundi: Land Tops List of Challenges for Returnees," June 14, 2007, www.irinnews.org.

5. See S. Gabizon, "Natural Disasters and Gender," Women in Europe for a Common Future, www.wecf.de.

6. Eric Neumayer and Thomas Plumper, "The Gendered Nature of Natural Disasters: The Impact of Catastrophic Events on the Gender Gap in Life Expectancy, 1981–2002," Social Science Research Network, January, www.ssrn.com.

7. In the Occupied Palestinian Territories men have left the agricultural sector for better-paying jobs, but as men's unemployment has risen, increased pressure has been put on women to generate incomes through their agricultural work and informal employment (Esim and Kuttab 2002). See www.erf.org.eg.

Thematic Note 1

This Thematic Note was prepared by Sanam Naraghi-Anderlini (Consultant) and reviewed by Nata Duvvury and Catherine Ragasa (Consultants); Deborah Rubin (Cultural Practice); Kaori Abe, Suzanne Raswant, Ilaria Sisto, and Richard Trenchard (FAO); Katuscia Fara, Maria Hartl, and Sheila Mwanundu (IFAD); and Ian Bannon, Lynn Brown, and Eija Pehu (World Bank).

1. Author involved in the program, December 2007.

2. In Liberia and Timor-Leste, community activists noted that in the rush to flee the onslaught of violence, women tend to carry mattresses with them, not cooking pots or other utensils needed for food preparation. (The author of this Note participated in a UNFPA workshop in which the issues were raised, in Tunis in June 2007.)

Thematic Note 2

This Thematic Note was prepared by Sanam Naraghi-Anderlini (Consultant) and reviewed by Nata Duvvury and Catherine Ragasa (Consultants); Deborah Rubin (Cultural Practice); Kaori Abe, Suzanne Raswant, Ilaria Sisto, and Richard Trenchard (FAO); Katuscia Fara, Maria Hartl, and Sheila Mwanundu (IFAD); and Ian Bannon, Lynn Brown, and Eija Pehu (World Bank).

1. "Long Term Recovery Sidelined in East Africa Food Crisis," press release, May 2006, www.oxfam.org.

Thematic Note 3

This Thematic Note was prepared by Sanam Naraghi-Anderlini (Consultant) and reviewed by Nata Duvvury and Catherine Ragasa (Consultants); Deborah Rubin (Cultural Practice); Kaori Abe, Suzanne Raswant, Ilaria Sisto, and Richard Trenchard (FAO); Katuscia Fara, Maria Hartl, and Sheila Mwanundu (IFAD); and Ian Bannon, Lynn Brown, and Eija Pehu (World Bank).

1. David Bledsoe and Michael Brown, "Land and Conflict, A Toolkit for Intervention," USAID, www.usaid.gov.

2. John Unruh, "Post Conflict Land Tenure, Using a Sustainable Livelihoods Approach," LSP Working Paper No. 18, www.fao.org.

3. Estimate by IDRC, available at www.idrc.ca.

4. "Women and Sustainable Food Security," www.fao.org.

5. The full report is available at www.lines-magazine. org/Art_Feb03/WomenMission.htm.

6. As documented in Brown and Uvuza (2006).

7. Women's News Network, "Nepal's ASMITA Brings Women Powerful Advocacy," January 10, 2008, women news-network.net.

8. ECLAC 2004, FAO/SEAGA program.

Innovative Activity Profile 1

This Innovative Activity Profile was prepared by Sanam Naraghi-Anderlini (Consultant) and reviewed by Nata Duvvury and Catherine Ragasa (Consultants); Deborah Rubin (Cultural Practice); Kaori Abe, Suzanne Raswant, Ilaria Sisto, and Richard Trenchard (FAO); Katuscia Fara, Maria Hartl, and Sheila Mwanundu (IFAD); and Ian Bannon, Lynn Brown, and Eija Pehu (World Bank).

1. The descriptions and assessment provided here are predominantly drawn and largely directly quoted from the official project documents available at www.worldbank.org.

2. The British Refugee Council, Sri Lanka Monitor Briefing, October 1999, "The Food Aid Weapon," www.brcslproject.gn.apc.org.

3. *Irrigation tank* is the name used in Sri Lanka to describe a lake or reservoir of water constructed to capture and store seasonal rainfall for use in irrigation during the dry season and for domestic use in the villages. Most of the rural human settlements (villages) have typically evolved and located near irrigation tanks.

4. In a communication with the author, the World Bank project director stated that the idea was introduced and welcomed. The FAO document points to the "dynamism" that the WRDSs brought.

5. Available from www.worldbank.org.

Innovative Activity Profile 2

This Innovative Activity Profile was prepared by Ira Matuschke (Consultant) and reviewed by Nata Duvvury, Sanam Naraghi-Anderlini, and Catherine Ragasa (Consultants); Deborah Rubin (Cultural Practice); and Hubert Boirard and Maria Hartl (IFAD). This was heavily from the author's experience and from several sources: Government of Niger (2007), IFAD (2007a, 2007b); Roumanatou and others (2007); and UNOPS (2007).

REFERENCES

Overview

Anderson, Mary. 1999. *Do No Harm, How Aid Can Support Peace or War.* Boulder: Lynne Rienner.

Enarson, Elaine. 2000. "Gender and Natural Disasters." Working Paper No. 1, IFP/CRISIS, Recovery and Reconstruction Department, September, International Labour Organization (ILO), Geneva.

Esim, Simel, and Eileen Kuttab. 2002. "Women's Informal Employment: Securing a Livelihood against All Odds." Working Paper 0213, Economic Research Forum, Cairo.

Greenberg, Marcia, and Elaine Zuckerman. 2004. "The Gender Dimensions of Post Conflict Reconstruction." *Gender and Development* 12 (3): 70–82.

Homer-Dixon, Thomas, and Kimberley Kelly. 1995. "Environmental Scarcity and Violent Conflict, The Case of Gaza." Part 1, Occasional Paper, Project on Environment, Population and Scarcity, June, American Association for the Advancement of Science and the University of Toronto, Washington, DC.

Kryspin-Watson, Jolanta, Jean Arkedis, and Wael Zakout. 2006. "Mainstreaming Hazard Risk Management into Rural Projects." Disaster Risk Management Working Paper No. 13, April, World Bank, Washington, DC.

Lalasz, Robert. 2005. "The Indian Ocean Tsunami, Special Challenges for Women Survivors." January, Population Reference Bureau, Washington, DC.

Naraghi-Anderlini, Sanam. 2007. *Women Building Peace: What They Do, Why It Matters.* Boulder: Lynne Rienner.

United Nations (UN). 2005. "Disarmament, Demobilization, Reintegration (DDR), and Stability in Africa." Conference Report, UN, New York.

United Nations Environment Programme (UNEP). 2007. "Sudan Post-Conflict Environmental Assessment," June, UNEP, Geneva.

United Nations Inter-Agency Standing Committee (UN IASC). 2006. *Women, Men, Boys and Girls, Different Needs, Equal Opportunities.* Gender Handbook in Humanitarian Aid. New York: UN.

World Bank. 2007. "Restarting Irrigation in Sri Lanka's Farming Zone." "IDA at Work," May, World Bank, Washington, DC. Also available at www.worldbank.org.

Zaur, Ian. 2006. "Agriculture and Conflict: A Conceptual Framework for Development." Master's thesis, Tufts University.

Thematic Note 1

Food and Agriculture Organization (FAO). 2005. "Building on Gender, Agrobiodiversity and Local Knowledge." FAO, Rome.

Kryspin-Watson, Jolanta, Jean Arkedis, and Wael Zakout. 2006. "Mainstreaming Hazard Risk Management into Rural Projects." Disaster Risk Management Working Paper No. 13, April, World Bank, Washington, DC.

McGrew, Laura, Kate Frieson, and Sambath Chan. 2004. *Good Governance from the Ground Up: Women's Roles in Post Conflict Cambodia.* Washington, DC: Hunt Alternatives.

Mitchell, Tom, Thomas Tanner, and Kattie Lussier. 2007. "We Know What We Need: South Asian Women Speak Out on Climate Change Adaptation." ActionAid/Institute for Development Studies, London.

Morehead, J. 2007. *Risk Diagnostic and Needs Assessment of the Coatepeque Caldera, El Salvador.* San Salvador, El Salvador: International Organization New Acropolis.

Ramdas, Sagari, Nithya Ghotge, Nandini Mathur Ashalatha, M. L. Sanyasi Rao, N. Madhusudhan, S. Seethalakshmi, N. Pandu. Dora, N. Kantham, E. Venkatesh, and J. Savithri. 2004. "Overcoming Gender Barriers: Local Knowledge Systems and Animal Health Healing in Andrha Pradesh and Maharashtra." In *Livelihood and Gender: Equity in Community Resource Management,* ed. Sumi Krishna, 67–91. Thousand Oaks, CA: Sage.

Seager, Joni, and Betsy Hartmann. 2005. *Mainstreaming Gender in Environmental Assessment and Early Warning.* Nairobi: United Nations Environmental Programme.

United Nations Fund for Population Action (UNFPA). 2007. *Global Review of Challenges and Good Practices in Support of Women in Conflict and Post-conflict Situations.* New York: UNFPA.

United Nations Inter-Agency Standing Committee (UN IASC). 2006. *Women, Girls, Boys and Men: Different Needs—Equal Opportunities.* Gender Handbook in Humanitarian Action. New York: UN.

United Nations International Strategy for Disaster Reduction (UN ISDR). 2007. "Gender Perspectives: Working Together for Disaster Risk Reduction." ISDR, Geneva.

Thematic Note 2

Barber, Ben. 1997. "Feeding Refugees or War? The Dilemmas of Humanitarian Aid." *Foreign Affairs* 76 (July/August 1997): 8–14.

Food and Agriculture Organization (FAO). 2003. *Socio-Economic and Gender Analysis (SEAGA) Programme Handbooks.* Rome: FAO.

Longley, Catherine, Ian Christoplos, Tom Slaymaker, and Silvestro Meseka. 2007. "Rural Recovery in Fragile States: Agricultural Support in Countries Emerging from Conflict." Natural Resource Perspectives No. 105, February, ODI, London.

Organisation for Economic Co-operation and Development (OECD). 2006. "The Development Effectiveness of Food Aid: Does Tying Matter?" OECD, Paris.

Pampell-Conaway, Camille, and Salomé Martinez. 2004. "Adding Value, Women's Contribution to Reintegration and Reconstruction in El Salvador." Women Waging Peace, Washington, DC.

United Nations Fund for Population Action (UNFPA), 2007. *Global Review of Challenges and Good Practices in Support of Women in Conflict and Post-conflict Situations.* New York: UNFPA.

United Nations Inter-Agency Standing Committee (UN IASC). 2006. *Women, Girls, Boys and Men: Different*

Needs—Equal Opportunities. Gender Handbook in Humanitarian Action. New York: UN.

World Bank. 2006. *Mainstreaming Hazard Risk Management in Rural Projects.* Washington, DC: World Bank.

Thematic Note 3

Bradshaw, Sarah. 2004. "Socio-Economic Impact of Natural Disasters: A Gender Analysis." UN ECLAC, Santiago, Chile.

Brown, Jennifer, and Justine Uvuza. 2006. "Women's Land Rights in Rwanda." Rural Development Institute, Seattle.

Farha, Leilani. 2000. "Women's Rights to Land, Property and Housing." *Forced Migration Review* (April 7): 23–26.

Fitzpatrick, Daniel. 2007. "Women's Rights to Land and Housing in Tsunami-Affected Indonesia." Oxfam International Policy Paper, Asia Research Institute, Singapore.

McGrew, Laura, Kate Frieson, and Sambath Chan. 2004. "Good Governance from the Ground Up: Women's Roles in Post Conflict Cambodia." Initiative for Inclusive Security, Washington, DC.

United Nations Habitat. 1999. "Women's Rights to Land, Housing and Property in Post Conflict Settings. A Global Overview." Land Management Series No. 9, United Nations Centre for Human Settlements (Habitat), Nairobi.

Unruh, Van. 2004. "Post-Conflict Land Tenure Using A Sustainable Livelihoods Approach." Livelihood Support Programme (LSP), Working Paper 18, Food and Agriculture Organization (FAO), Rome.

Van den Brink, Rogier, Hans Binswanger, John Bruce, Glen Thomas, Frank Byamugisha, and Natasha Mukherjee. 2006. "Consensus, Confusion, and Controversy: Selected Land Reform Issues in Sub-Saharan Africa." Working Paper No. 71, World Bank, Washington, DC.

Women and Media Collective. 2002. "Women's Concerns and the Peace Process: Findings and Recommendations." Report of the International Women's Mission to the North East of Sri Lanka, October 12-17, 2002. Women and Media Collective, Colombo.

World Bank. 2004. "A Fair Share for Women, Cambodia Gender Assessment." World Bank, Phnom Penh.

Innovative Activity Profile I

Wanasundera, Leelangi. 2006. *Rural Women in Sri Lanka's Post-Conflict Rural Economy.* Bangkok: Food and Agriculture Organization.

Innovative Activity Profile 2

Government of Niger. 2007. "Rapport d'Achèvement du Programme d'Urgence 2006 Financé sur Don FIDA No. SUPPL-IT-52-NE." Niamey.

International Fund for Agricultural Development. 2007a. "Niger—L'Experience du PPILDA/AGUIE dans le Renforcement de la Sécurité Alimentaire. des Actions á Soutenir." IFAD, Rome.

———. 2007b. "Oeuvrer pour que les Ruraux Pauvres se Libèrent de la Pauvreté au Niger." IFAD, Rome.

Roumanatou, E., D. Hamado, and A. Aboubacar. 2007. "Expériences des Banques des Soudure au PPILDA." Niamey.

United Nations Office for Project Services (UNOPS). 2007. "Projet de Promotion de l'Initiative Locale pour le Développement á Aguié. Rapport de la Mission de Supervision." Dakar, Senegal.

FURTHER READING

Thematic Note 1

Fordham, Maureen. 2001. "Challenging Boundaries: A Gender Perspective on Early Warning in Disaster and Environmental Management." United Nations Division for the Advancement of Women, United Nations, New York.

Macdonald, Mott. 2007. "Brazil Working with Both Women and Men to Promote Gender Balance." In *Gender Perspectives: Working Together for Disaster Risk Reduction*, ed. R. Alain Valency, 3–6. Geneva: UN International Strategy for Disaster Reduction.

Pusch, Christoph. 2004. *Preventable Losses: Saving Lives and Property through Hazard Risk Management. A Comprehensive Risk Management Framework for Europe and Central Asia.* Washington, DC: World Bank.

Thematic Note 2

Kryspin-Watson, Jolanta, Jean Arkedis, and Wael Zakout. 2006. "Mainstreaming Hazard Risk Management in Rural Project," Disaster Risk Management Working Paper No. 13, April, World Bank, Washington, DC.

Gender in Crop Agriculture

Overview

CROP AGRICULTURE, GENDER, AND PATHWAYS FROM POVERTY

The proposition that *agriculture, including crop production, is the only realistic driver for mass poverty reduction and rural development in most of the developing world,* and perhaps particularly in sub-Saharan Africa, is now accepted by many academics, international development organizations, and national governments (Lipton 2005; World Bank 2007) (box 12.1).

A further proposition, emphasized in a recent *World Development Report* (World Bank 2007), is that *farming is a key pathway out of poverty for women,* and that women's prospects for taking this path improve when they have better access to resources. Because of their limited access to essential production resources, such as land, labor, and inputs, women's role in crop agriculture is often restricted to producing subsistence food crops with low potential to generate income. The prospects for women to expand their incomes through alternatives such as seasonal migration or labor markets outside agriculture are limited. Women's mobility is usually more constrained by social and cultural norms, and women play a central role in raising and caring for children.

An important element of development strategies that rely on agriculture is to enable women to improve food production and—depending on the context—to move beyond subsistence production into higher-value and market-oriented production (World Bank 2007). Women, more than men, spend their incomes on food, with consequent improvements in household food security, nutritional security, and especially the development of children. In Guatemala the amount spent on food in households whose profits from nontraditional agricultural exports were controlled by women was double that of households in which men controlled the profits (World Bank 2007).

As a means of understanding agriculture's present and prospective role in development and poverty reduction, developing countries can be grouped into three broad categories: agricultural-based economies, transforming economies, and urbanized economies (World Bank 2007). Farmers (including women) in each category face different challenges in improving their living conditions. This Module focuses on agricultural-based economies, in which many poor women rely on agriculture for their livelihoods and in which improvements in crop agriculture can yield the greatest impact. This Module and accompanying Thematic Notes also examine the role of gender in high-value and organic crop production.[1]

CROP AGRICULTURE AND EARLIER DEVELOPMENT TRENDS

To understand changing perceptions of crop agriculture and its role in development, a review of earlier development trends and policies is important. A major principle in the development of crop agriculture has been to raise the yields of a selected number of staple food crops. This effort,

Food and Agriculture Organization: "There has been a shift in the general trend of giving low priority to agriculture as compared to industrialization. A new recognition is growing in many parts of the world of the crucial role of the agricultural sector for increasing export earnings, generating employment and improving food security."

World Bank: "Rural poverty is as diverse as are the rural poor in their livelihood strategies, but in most of the poorest developing countries agriculture is the main source of rural economic growth. That is why improved agricultural productivity and growth are central to the Bank's strategy."

International Fund for Agricultural Development: "Investment in agriculture is the key to meeting the MDGs [Millennium Development Goals] given that 75 percent of the world's poorest people, living on less than a dollar a day, live in rural areas and depend on agriculture and related activities for their livelihoods."

Department for International Development, United Kingdom: "Agriculture should be placed at the heart of efforts to reduce poverty . . . [as] there is a mass of evidence that increasing agricultural productivity has benefited millions through higher incomes, more plentiful and cheaper food, and by generating patterns of development that are employment intensive and benefit both rural and urban areas."

Sources: DFID 2005: 1; FAO 2007a; IFAD 2007; World Bank 2003: xv.

originating on a wide scale for developing countries in the middle of the twentieth century, led to vast increases in food supplies in many Asian countries (Tripp 2006).

The 1960s represented a time of great hope for agriculture in developing countries. This decade marked the beginning of what became known as the Green Revolution in Asia, the principal manifestation of which was the distribution of short-strawed, fertilizer-responsive varieties of wheat and rice. For a few years it looked as if the strategy of supplying appropriate varieties and complementary fertilizers, pesticides, and other inputs could end rural poverty and chronic food shortages (Tripp 2006). Eventually it became

evident that these new packages of technology were not spreading evenly among farmers; they mostly benefited farmers in favored environments with access to productive soil and irrigation facilities. Evidence emerged that widespread adoption took place in countries and regions that invested in infrastructure development and input and credit supply while supporting and stabilizing the prices of cereal crops (Gabre-Madhin, Barrett, and Dorosh 2003).

Attempts to address this imbalance and replicate Green Revolution experiences in less-favored regions led to the conclusion that farmers in "complex and risk-prone" areas (Chambers 1997) were unable to benefit from standardized technology packages and that alternative processes of technology development were required. The poverty levels of many farm households precluded any reasonable hope that they could take advantage of technologies requiring a significant financial investment (Tripp 2006).

Market orientation was and remains another important driver for crop agriculture development, resulting in improved crop varieties (notably hybrids) with uniform yields and crop characteristics and a dependence on external inputs and technologies. In market-oriented crop production systems, access to production resources is crucial, which poses potential gender inequalities. These inequalities are widened even further because very few improvements in farm technology have been devised to overcome women's constraints. Efforts to intensify agriculture by promoting large-scale farming and commercial crop production for export, farm mechanization, improved seed, fertilizer, and pesticides have been linked mostly to cash crop production, from which men are more likely to benefit. On the other hand, where surplus staple crop production is sold, local food and seed markets are flourishing. These types of markets are often dominated by women (Smale and others 2008).

RETHINKING CROP AGRICULTURE DEVELOPMENT STRATEGIES

Crop agriculture faces a new set of challenges. The persistence of poverty reveals the need to reconsider development strategies to improve equity and access. The environmental costs of previous crop production strategies are another important consideration. So-called second-generation problems with Green Revolution technologies have been observed. For example, evidence is at hand that rice yields in Asia are reaching a plateau (Horie and others 2005). Serious questions are being asked about natural resource degradation and the long-term sustainability of some intensive cropping systems (Murgai 2001; Oluoch-Kosura and Karugia 2005).[2] The use of agricultural methods that rely heavily on external inputs has caused 38 percent of agricultural land to be lost to soil erosion and depletion. Although soil erosion is a common effect of various land-use practices, 70 percent of annual erosion is estimated to occur on land used for agricultural purposes (Crucefix 1998).

The recent Millennium Ecosystem Assessment (2005) delineated the negative impact of intensive agriculture on vital ecosystem services and biodiversity—outcomes that were not considered sufficiently in the past. A growing body of evidence shows that the poor depend and will continue to depend on biodiversity as an important livelihood resource (Ash and Jenkins 2007), whereas modern crop production is based on only a few plant species (Gruère, Giuliani, and Smale 2006).

Climate change and its potential consequences for agricultural production also require urgent attention in strategies for crop agriculture development. The role of crop diversity is an important element to consider in developing such strategies.

New methods of plant breeding have also affected current crop production strategies, and their impact on gender in crop production is not yet established. For example, the private sector has invested substantially in developing genetically modified (GM) crops, such as Bt maize, with a clear commercial focus. Bt maize contains an endotoxin from *Bacillus thuringiensis* that protects plants from insect pests such as corn borers. Disease-resistant crops, herbicide-tolerant crops, biofortified crops,[3] and renewable energy crops are just a few additional examples of new technologies that are available or under development.

All of these factors make it important to reconsider how and why crop production technologies are developed. Although market orientation remains an important driver of new crop technologies, new niche markets are emerging for organic and fair trade products, among others, which could offer an opportunity for women to participate.

Innovation in agriculture now gives greater emphasis to processes that depend on local resources, including knowledge and skills, natural resources, and social structures. The realization that most technologies need to be adapted not only to local agroecological conditions but also to individual socioeconomic farm circumstances is an additional justification for promoting innovations based on local resources and skills, and the development of such resources and skills certainly offers an opportunity for empowering women as well as men farmers and their communities (Tripp 2006). It

is important to recognize that this strategy does not entail a wholesale rejection of external inputs to improve productivity, but rather the increased recognition and reinforcement of complementarities and a thorough analysis of resource availability and needs in subsistence and commercial production systems.

The Thematic Notes that accompany this Module demonstrate the extent to which using local resources is vital for improving crop agriculture. The first two Thematic Notes focus on gender in relation to soil and seed, two of the primary natural resources essential to crop production. A central theme of these Notes is the role of human and social capital in the knowledge-intensive management of agricultural technology. The Notes also identify potential complementarities between (1) local and external inputs and (2) knowledge and institutions. The third Thematic Note focuses on gender and crop protection, because crop protection is another knowledge-intensive area with high potential to improve crop productivity.

WHY IS GENDER A VITAL CONSIDERATION IN CROP AGRICULTURE?

Addressing gender is crucial in crop agriculture for reasons discussed in the following sections.

Women play vital but unrecognized roles in crop production, household food security, and household nutrition

The need to increase food production is clear. Growing populations and declining agricultural productivity are leaving millions without secure sources of food. Yet advances in food production are constrained by the "invisibility factor"—in other words, by women's major but largely unrecognized roles in agriculture.

Although detailed statistics are not available and figures vary depending on the geographical context, it is fair to say that women supply a large proportion of the agricultural labor and in some societies produce up to 80 percent of the food crops (FAO 2007b). Failure to recognize this contribution is costly. It results in misguided policies and programs, forgone agricultural output and associated income flows, higher levels of poverty, and food and nutritional insecurity (World Bank 2007).

It is widely understood that gender and household food security are fundamentally linked. Many cultural and regional differences exist in women's involvement in crop production, but rural women are the main producers of the world's staple crops—rice, wheat, and maize—which provide up to 90 percent of the food consumed by the rural poor. Women sow, weed, apply fertilizer and pesticides, and harvest and thresh crops. Their contribution to growing secondary crops such as legumes and vegetables is even greater. Grown mainly in home gardens, these crops provide essential nutrients and are often the only food available during the lean seasons or when major crops fail (FAO 2007b). Yet women often have the least access to means for significantly increasing output and yields.

Women's contributions to crop production are not just qualitatively but quantitatively invisible as well. Statistics on women's yields, women's technology adoption rates, and women's uses of inputs are rarely reported, which proved problematic in developing this Module (the importance of gender-disaggregated data is discussed in Module 16).

Women manage complex, species-rich production systems

Women tend to manage complex production systems with multiple functions, purposes, and species. These systems are not designed to maximize the productivity of any single crop but to ensure overall stability and resilience among the crops that are produced. This agricultural reality is often overlooked when yields of a single crop are taken as a criterion for evaluating the performance of crop production. Given the increasingly severe weather events caused by climate change, criteria such as crop stability and resistance may be valued more highly in the future.

Women have limited access to agricultural services and inputs, are more likely to lack assets, and grow more subsistence crops

Women farmers are more likely to be asset-poor subsistence farmers. In sub-Saharan Africa it has been calculated that agricultural productivity could increase by up to 20 percent if women's access to such resources as land, seed, and fertilizer were equal to men's (DFID 2007), yet women still face serious constraints in obtaining essential support for most productive resources, such as land, fertilizer, knowledge, infrastructure, and market organization (these issues are discussed in detail in other Modules). The ease of obtaining agricultural services and inputs is even more important in light of women's heavy workloads and time constraints outside of agriculture.

Although rightly contending that the effectiveness of development strategies hinges on reaching African smallholders,

agricultural experts seldom recognize that most of Africa's smallholders are women (World Bank 2007)—as seen by the costly errors that have arisen from ignoring the fact that women smallholders may face different constraints than men do, and that such constraints are therefore an important part of the problem. The Agriculture for Development Policy Brief (World Bank 2008: 1) states, "The design of many development policies continues to assume wrongly that farmers and rural workers are men. The important role of women in agriculture in many parts of the world calls for urgent attention to gender-specific constraints in agricultural production and marketing. Mainstreaming gender in agricultural policies and programs is essential for development success."

Beware narrow assumptions about women's "food security first" agenda

Women's engagement in farming is commonly associated first and foremost with a food security agenda. Although this statement is certainly true, such a narrow view will limit women's engagement with commercially oriented crop production and will do nothing to help women achieve their broader livelihood goals (NEF 2006). In many situations, women combine both food production and commercial agriculture, although often on a small scale. The gender division of activities in crop cultivation can be quite complicated, with different fields being cultivated for different purposes by men and women or family groups, especially in sub-Saharan Africa. Women often manage the home gardens, and small-scale crop production can contribute significantly to women's incomes as well as to household food security. Women often grow "minor" crops with limited or no market value. However, it is important to realize that women have the potential and the right to participate in more commercially oriented crop production. Local markets offer a good opportunity to earn income through small-scale sales of staple crops and vegetables. Often these opportunities are only seasonal.

Crop production is the primary employer of women in most countries

Crop production is still the primary source of employment for women in most developing countries, particularly in sub-Saharan Africa and Asia. Almost two-thirds of rural women are from low-income households. Women-headed households are the poorest among these, making up more than 35–40 percent of all heads of household in some parts of Asia (Balakrishnan and Fairbairn-Dunlop 2005). Box 12.2

presents some indicative statistics on women's importance in agriculture and crop production.

Women are not only vitally involved in crop production—their role is expanding. Development strategies will be compelled to address gender concerns very explicitly because the number of women involved in and responsible for crop production in developing countries appears to be growing so rapidly. Known as the "feminization" of agriculture, this sociodemographic trend is causing temporary as well as permanent shifts in women's responsibilities and tasks. An important factor behind this trend is the migration of young men in search of more lucrative employment off of the farm. The depredations of HIV and AIDS in sub-Saharan Africa have also encouraged this trend. In some areas the feminization of agriculture has altered the availability of labor for producing crops, which in turn may alter cropping patterns, tasks, and crop technology preferences (see Thematic Note 4, Module 7). An example from Bolivia (box 12.3) gives indications of these trade-offs.

A potential advantage of migration is that it provides additional cash to invest in crop agriculture and facilitate a move from subsistence to more commercially oriented agricultural systems. These shifts can offer new opportunities for women but can also imply cultural changes and a redefinition of gender roles in crop production. Gladwin and others (2001) observe that in "most parts of Africa, women consider farming for food as part of what makes them women and gives them a gender identity." In other situations women themselves are the ones who migrate in search of employment, which again has significant consequences for crop production. These intrahousehold socioeconomic changes are important to understand and consider in any crop production intervention.

KEY GENDER ISSUES

The following discussion describes the key gender issues in crop agriculture and the potential benefits of addressing them.

Gender and crop choice

As pointed out earlier, cash and export crops are frequently regarded as "men's" crops and subsistence crops as "women's" crops.[4] The standard explanation for this division of crops by gender is that women are responsible for feeding the family and thus prefer to grow subsistence crops for the household, whereas men are responsible for providing cash income and thus raise cash and export crops.

In general, however, it is difficult to tell whether women grow lower-value subsistence crops because they have different preferences and concerns or because they cannot access the land, inputs, credit, information, and markets that would permit them to do otherwise (Doss 1999). In Ghana, for instance, women farmers view maize production as a productive, income-generating activity yet refrain from growing maize because they lack the capital to purchase the required inputs (fertilizer, herbicide) or hire someone to plow the fields. Instead they continue cultivating cassava and yams, which require fewer external inputs. Moreover, the majority of women consider maize cultivation to be a risky enterprise because the crop is sensitive to drought (Adjei-Nsiah and others 2007; see also Thematic Notes 1 and 2).

Cultivation not only of different crops but also of different *varieties* of the *same* crop may also vary by gender. Maize, for instance, may be grown as a cash or subsistence crop. High-yielding maize varieties were introduced in many areas to generate a marketable surplus, but many of these varieties had different processing, cooking, and storage characteristics than the local varieties. The high-yielding varieties were often promoted as cash crops. Consequently in many places local varieties are considered "women's" crops, and high-yielding varieties are considered "men's" crops (Badstue and others 2007). To the extent that high-yielding varieties are grown for cash and local varieties for food, this gender-variety pattern may persist. However, as high-yielding varieties that meet the consumption preferences of smallholder farmers are developed, the distinctions between subsistence and cash varieties may become blurred. For instance, both hybrid maize and local maize can be viewed as either subsistence or cash crops, depending on a farmer's circumstances and market opportunities. A case study in Tanzania (FAO 2008) showed that groundnut yields would determine whether the crop was controlled by men or women. If the groundnut harvest was good, men sold the produce in the market; if it was not, control would remain with the women.

Gender differentiation also occurs with respect to combinations of crop species and varieties. Commercial systems feature homogeneous varieties of a single crop species, whereas traditional cropping patterns are much more diverse. As noted, women tend to manage complex and species-rich production systems designed to ensure overall production stability and resilience. Some traditional crops determine the social status of men and women and are linked closely to traditional knowledge and culture. They are also integral to social capital because of their important roles in ceremonies and traditional meals. In this sense,

changes in crop diversity can alter social capital formation and power relations (Howard 2003).

The loss of crop diversity could also threaten poor people's ability to adapt their agricultural enterprises to climate change. A recent study by Cline (2007), which reinforces the likely negative impact of global warming on crop agriculture, indicates that the combined effects on agriculture are likely to be seriously unfavorable in developing countries, with the most severe losses occurring in Africa, India, and Latin America. These rapidly emerging issues need to be taken into account in designing interventions in crop agriculture. Understanding women farmers' production strategies with respect to crop stability and resilience will enable agricultural research and development interventions to strengthen farmers' capabilities to adapt to climate change and improve family food security.

Gender and crop management tasks

In most parts of the world, men and women tend to work at different tasks. Numerous time allocation studies have examined which household members perform which farm tasks (for example, see Hirschmann and Vaughan 1984; McSweeney 1979; Pala 1983). These studies often identify some tasks as men's tasks and others as women's tasks. For example, in Kenya women reported that men were responsible for building the granary, and women were clearly responsible for hand digging, harvesting, and transporting the crops (Pala 1983). Although many tasks may be viewed as exclusively women's or men's, in practice the divisions are blurred, and both men and women are involved. Relatively few tasks are done only by men or only by women (Doss 1999).

That women throughout Africa tend to provide more labor for agriculture than men—and almost always provide more total labor—has implications for technology adoption. Even if they know they can increase productivity, women may be unable to increase the number of hours that they spend working. Simple comparisons of hours worked do not capture issues related to the type of work being done and the energy expended. The value of time will vary by season and task; thus, people will be interested in saving the time that is the most costly (Levi 1987). However, to the extent that the tasks vary by gender and the value of women's time is lower, farmers may be more inclined to adopt technologies that save men's time.

The gender division of labor appears to change in response to changing economic opportunities. As noted, when men leave agricultural communities in search of higher earnings, women assume many traditionally "men's" tasks. Men usually move into traditionally "women's" crop activities when those activities are perceived as having become more productive or profitable. Women in Burkina Faso traditionally picked shea nuts, for example, but now that sales of shea nuts are profitable, men are becoming involved, often with the assistance of their wives. Another factor behind changes in labor allocation for different tasks is the adoption of new technologies. For instance, the mechanization of "women's" tasks may cause men to take greater control of those tasks. The extent to which these changes benefit or disadvantage women and men is not always clear, and it is difficult to predict a priori what changes will occur (Doss 1999).

Seasonality further influences labor allocations. Compared to Asia, where irrigated agriculture is much more common, in Africa the seasonal demands for labor are more pronounced, because crop agriculture is mainly rain fed and the growing season is relatively short. In Africa, 50–70 percent of the labor is required within a four-month period; comparable figures for Asia are 40–50 percent (Delgado and Ranade 1987). If this seasonal demand coincides with migration by men, women's burden of labor becomes even higher and negatively affects overall crop production, because women will have to prioritize labor allocation between food and cash crops.

Research and extension systems can become more effective in developing sustainable crop production systems if they adopt a gender perspective that heightens their understanding of the distinct roles, needs, and opportunities of different household members (see also Module 7).

Gender and knowledge differences

Men and women can accumulate very distinct and rich sets of agricultural knowledge and skills as a result of gender divisions in the tasks they undertake, such as seed management and conservation and pest and disease management. Many studies show that men and women have different preferences and criteria for choosing among crops and varieties and performing such activities as selecting seed, cultivating, harvesting, and processing (Howard 2003). Because women tend to manage complex farming systems, they have developed multiple assessment criteria for crop system performance, encompassing risk minimization, vulnerability, and other objectives that must be considered in promoting innovations.

Local knowledge of men and women farmers is an important asset in innovation and technology development,

especially for such key crop production issues as seed management, plant breeding, crop protection, and soil fertility management. Understanding gender differences in local knowledge and recognizing the contribution women can make in this field are important, because women are more frequently involved in traditional farming practices. Knowledge difference can reveal important opportunities to contribute to crop improvement or crop and variety selection (see the discussion of farmer innovation in Thematic Note 1 and seed management in Thematic Note 2). Knowledge differences must also be understood to improve the effectiveness of any technology dissemination or extension process (see the discussion of integrated pest management in Thematic Note 3).

Gender and access to information, organizations, and markets

Information—appropriate information, given and received on a timely basis—is critical to the development and use of technical innovations and improvements, yet women frequently cannot obtain such information. Agricultural research and development, including extension services, have been dominated by men and have largely ignored women's role in crop production (Jiggins, Samanta, and Olawoye 1997) and have not focused on women's needs for technology and information. Social norms and cultural practices can prevent women from participating in development interventions or information campaigns. Using more appropriate information channels is one way to address this situation (see Thematic Note 3). Another strategy is to provide more relevant information by specifically addressing gender aspects of crop production.

Over the last two centuries, societies have invested considerably in complex institutional arrangements to advance technological innovation in agriculture. Many of these institutions have overlooked women and have marginalized women farmers in terms of technology adoption. Gender-responsive actions should enable women farmers to take greater advantage of extension systems and increase the accessibility of new agricultural technologies and innovations. Organizational innovations, such as participatory research, farmer-extension linkages, and strengthening the linkages between formal and local seed systems, can improve women's livelihood outcomes by ensuring that technologies meet their needs. These issues are discussed in greater detail in Thematic Notes 1 and 2, which describe potential complementarities between formal and informal organizations (see also Module 7).

Markets will continue to influence the choice of crop species and varieties in important ways. Markets can offer opportunities for women as well as men, and crop interventions must not fail to consider this point (examples include assessing the export potential for women's crops or facilitating women's participation in niche markets for organic or fair trade produce). Markets are also important for providing agricultural inputs. Because women so often lack the economic resources or mobility to reach input markets, improving access to local markets can be particularly important for them (see also Modules 5 and 8). For example, as discussed in Thematic Note 2, local seed markets are an increasingly important means for women to obtain improved crop species and varieties and exchange knowledge. Flourishing food markets for local consumption can render distinctions between cash and subsistence crops less obvious, and local markets give women an opportunity to become involved in crop commercialization.

KEY AREAS FOR INTERVENTION

Soil—specifically *soil productivity* and *fertility*—is a key asset for resource-poor women and men. The degradation of soil through overuse and erosion can severely limit people's livelihoods. Because sustainable soil management is fundamental to the future of crop agriculture, Thematic Note 1 discusses interventions specifically designed to help women sustain soil productivity.

Diversity—both in the types of crops grown and in the *genetic makeup of specific crops*—is another important asset, especially for resource-poor farmers. Farmers may select crops and varieties of crops that make it possible to pursue a greater range of livelihood strategies (which may vary by gender among household members), enhance household food security, and minimize risk. For example, the failure of one variety or crop may be mitigated by the survival of others. Strategies to understand and conserve genetic diversity must not overlook the fact that women often have different means of accessing and exchanging seed (Thematic Note 2).

Women and children are often directly or indirectly involved in *crop protection,* and their limited access to information about safe pesticide use imperils human health and poses an environmental hazard. Twenty to forty percent of the world's potential crop production is lost annually to weeds, pests, and diseases (CropLife International 2007). Crop protection strategies that may be particularly relevant to women are discussed in Thematic Note 3.

For each of these key areas for intervention, the following points should be kept in mind:

- Women and men, depending on their cultural and social backgrounds, perform different roles and have varying responsibilities in agriculture—in crop production as well as crop management. A better understanding of these differences will help to address the prevailing gender issues.
- In making decisions about their livelihoods, men and women have different perceptions of what is important. Men and women base their decisions on information from different sources.
- The unequal power relationships between rich and poor, men and women, must be understood to achieve equitable development and full participation of women.
- Interventions must be developed based on a comprehensive understanding of the needs that women and men identify to improve their situations. The strategic interests of women and the most disadvantaged groups need to be addressed to improve overall crop production and reduce poverty.

The adoption and use of new technologies and inputs are strongly affected by who controls and owns a given crop. Failure to understand and address these and other socioeconomic dimensions of crop production means that interventions are bound to fail. All interventions that aim to enhance the productivity of crop agriculture must take explicit account of gender. The principal concerns are well known; many are discussed specifically in this volume. As a matter of course, women farmers must have access to information, credit, and other inputs, as well as the organizations through which markets are accessed and policies are influenced. Years of experience confirm that these things are still easier said than done. At the same time, it is critical to acknowledge the "feminization" of agriculture (particularly in sub-Saharan Africa) and overcome the bias of associating women's farming exclusively with a food security agenda. Recognizing women's involvement in commercial crop production and ensuring that they benefit from research, extension, credit, land tenure rights, market access, and other elements of production, innovation, and participation still requires a significant organizational shift in many agricultural services. Without such a shift, it will be difficult to broaden the base of women farmers who can adopt crop technologies, and thus it will be difficult for agriculture to contribute to poverty reduction, environmental sustainability, and economic growth as envisioned in many countries.

MEASURING CHANGE: GENDER-SENSITIVE MONITORING AND EVALUATION INDICATORS

It is important to be able to measure the impact that crop and soil initiatives have on men and women beneficiaries, their families, and communities. Table 12.1 gives some ideas for indicators and sources of verification, though clearly modifications are required for each program.

Depending on the country or region, it may be relevant to also consider ethnicity and caste alongside gender (both as comparative indicators and when collecting data), because women of lower castes or ethnic minorities are usually in the most disadvantaged situation.

Table 12.1 Monitoring and Evaluation Indicators for Gender and Crops	
Indicator	**Sources of verification and tools**
Over a set period, an increase of *x* percent in household incomes from crop-based activities among women-headed households and poor households in program areas	• Household surveys • Project management information system • Socioeconomic data from statistics office
Changes over *x*-year period of project activities in household nutrition, health, education, vulnerability to violence, and happiness, disaggregated by gender	• Household surveys, before and after • Project management information system • School records
Number of local farmers involved in fair trade production and marketing groups, disaggregated by gender	• Sales records of group
Number of women and men holding management or treasurer positions in natural resource management groups	• Bank account records • Committee meeting minutes
Number of farmers using zero tillage, mulch, cover crops, and new innovations to decrease labor needs and increase soil fertility, disaggregated by gender	• Agricultural extension records • Interviews with stakeholders • Observation
Changes in soil condition in farmland, before and after program activities (such as nutrient levels, percentage of ground cover)	• Department of Agriculture surveys • Farm records • Participatory monitoring by villagers or herders
Number of women and men actively involved in participatory research and innovations	• Agricultural extension records • Interviews with stakeholders • Observation • Participatory monitoring
Percentage of men and women farmers who have access to high-quality, locally adapted seed	• Agricultural extension records • Interviews with stakeholders
Percentage of men and women farmers who implement seed saving and participate in local seed supply systems	• Agricultural extension records • Interviews with stakeholders • Program records
Seed type preferences, disaggregated by gender and ethnicity	• Agricultural extension records • Interviews with stakeholders • Seed sales records
Number of men and women participating in community seed bank management	• Committee meeting minutes • Program and project records
Number of women and men participating in training on integrated pest management	• Training records
Awareness of safe practices for handling agricultural chemicals and access to appropriate protective equipment, disaggregated by gender and ethnicity	• Focus groups • Observation • Posttraining assessment • Stakeholder interviews
Adoption of recommended practices and technologies among men and women farmers, before and after program activity	• Case studies • Interviews of farmers • Sample surveys

(Table continues on the following page)

Indicator	Sources of verification and tools
Gender differences in workload as a result of introduced practices or new technology for crop production	• Case studies • Gender analysis (such as comparative time clocks of men's and women's activities) • Participatory rapid appraisal • Sample surveys
Percentage of women and men community extension workers and professional agricultural extensionists	• Department of agriculture records • Project records
Numbers of years of formal education of farmers, disaggregated by gender	• Household surveys • School attendance and examination records
Level of satisfaction among women and men with access to and quality of extension and training services	• Interviews of farmers • Sample surveys
Women or other disadvantaged groups actively participating in management committees and boards of producer groups and cooperatives	• Committee meeting minutes • Interviews with stakeholders • Local traditional authorities (such as a chief or local council) • Program and project records

Source: Authors, with inputs from Pamela White, author of Module 16.

Gender and Soil Productivity Management

WHY CONSIDER SOIL PRODUCTIVITY FROM A GENDER PERSPECTIVE?

Healthy, fertile soils are integral to the goals of sustaining agricultural livelihoods, attaining food security, and fostering agricultural development. Because most high-quality agricultural land is already in production, the marginal benefit of converting new land diminishes. In West Asia and North Africa, at least 87 percent of suitable land is already farmed; in South Asia, the corresponding figure is 94 percent (FAO 2006). Natural resources such as land and water are increasingly scarce, and their quality is declining. Growth in food production will depend primarily on further intensification of agriculture, mostly in high-potential areas (FAO 2005a). Yet unless considerable care is taken, intensification can exact a heavy toll on soil health, fertility, and productivity.

A recent report on how to meet the first Millennium Development Goal of halving hunger by 2015 argues that *improving soil health is the first entry point* for correcting soil nutrient imbalances, improving agricultural productivity, and thus reducing hunger, particularly in Africa (UN Millennium Project 2005: 13). Soil fertility is an important component of soil health, along with organic matter content and microorganism populations. Another critical entry point for improving soil productivity and reducing hunger is *the adequate, location-specific choice of crops and crop management practices.*

As population pressure increases in many areas, especially sub-Saharan Africa, traditional fallow and crop rotation systems no longer maintain and restore soil fertility. When soils become less productive, crop yields stagnate or decline, and farmers become more dependent on external inputs to maintain crop productivity. Although soil fertility losses are particularly worrisome in Africa (box 12.4), they are also severe in tropical Asia and Latin America, where soil nutrient losses are high in agricultural systems compared to

natural ecosystems (Hartemink 2004). Other factors, such as soil erosion and climate change (leading to more severe weather events), have further depleted soils and heighten the need for more holistic soil management approaches.

Women—especially if they are the main providers of staple food crops—are particularly affected by declining soil fertility. Men often control the best land with the best soil to produce commercial crops, and women more often farm marginal land. They have limited or no access to external inputs such as fertilizer. Often they have less access to land itself, because inheritance laws and other legal and cultural norms favor men (see also Module 4). When women own farmland, their plots are generally smaller than those owned by men. In Mexico, for example, women own less than 20 percent of all farmland (Korinek 2005), and in 2000, 56 percent of women farmers owned less than 2 hectares, compared to 35 percent of male farmers (White, Salas, and

---

Box 12.4   Africa: Consequences of Unproductive Soils

Agricultural production is the main source of economic activity in sub-Saharan Africa, where the declining health and productivity of the soil indicate that it is rapidly losing its value as a critical agricultural asset. Not only can less food be grown on unproductive soils, but the production of cash crops for export is endangered. It is essential that agricultural production and soils be managed in sustainable ways, so that the present generation is fed and soil conditions can improve to support future generations.

Source: "Sustainable Land Management and Soil Productivity Improvement in Support of Food Security in Sub-Saharan Africa," www.fao.org.

Gammage 2003). In this respect women face a complex challenge: they have to produce their crops on poorer soil, often on smaller areas, and with fewer or no inputs.

EVOLVING APPROACHES TO GENDER-RESPONSIVE SOIL FERTILITY MANAGEMENT

Developing countries' approach to soil fertility management has evolved considerably over the last 50 years. Researchers have shifted from an almost exclusive focus on inorganic (chemical) fertilizer toward a broader range of approaches and nutrient sources (NEF 2006). At least in the research community, the value of integrated nutrient management—"the judicious manipulation of nutrient stocks and flows" (de Jager, Nandwa, and Okoth 1998: 37)—is now widely accepted.

The high climatic risks, uncertain markets, and poor infrastructure characteristic of many low-potential, isolated zones have challenged the economic wisdom of using high levels of external inputs and placed a premium on technologies that rely relatively little on such inputs (IFAD 2002). Many recognized alternatives to inorganic fertilizer are available. The use of animal manure, agroforestry, legumes, living mulch, compost, and other technologies that enhance soil fertility is traditional in many farming systems, especially systems that are managed and controlled by women. In other contexts, such technologies have been promoted actively (Uphoff 2002). The value of conservation agriculture has been established in many locations, with important lessons to be drawn (FAO 2005b).

Low-external-input strategies to improve soil fertility are often labor and knowledge intensive, however. Consequently they may be difficult for resource-poor farmers to adopt, given their limited access to labor and information, especially in remote areas where few formal institutions exist to strengthen human and social capital.

Despite the recognized importance of low-external-input strategies, chemical fertilizer remains the basis of soil fertility management in many farming systems and most intensification trajectories (NEF 2006). Chemical fertilizer is central to most extension messages, and the use of nitrogenous fertilizer continues to increase rapidly in the developing world (van Dam 2005). For a host of economic and logistical reasons, however, resource-poor farmers, including women, cannot apply fertilizer at high rates. The cost of fertilizer can represent a high proportion of the total variable cost of production, an investment that poor farmers can ill afford where there is a risk of crop failure (FAO 2006). Fertilizer is often sold in quantities too large for poor women to buy. Fertilizer may be considered too risky to buy, especially when it will be used to produce food crops with little possibility of generating cash income. Even when farmers can afford fertilizer, they cannot always obtain it. Access is often directly limited by inadequate infrastructure and transport facilities.

Conventional soil improvement technologies based solely on the use of external inputs have widened the divide between better-off and resource-poor farmers. External inputs require cash and access to markets, so women engaged in subsistence agriculture have benefited least from their introduction. The vulnerability of resource-poor households often makes them averse to risk and discourages them from pursuing new activities or adopting new practices and technologies (ICAD 2004). The introduction and promotion of low-external-input technologies, which would rely on resources that are more easily available to women in small-scale production systems, could improve their soil fertility management capacities and address disparities between better-off and less-favored households, because these technologies are better suited to the latter.

As mentioned earlier, improving soil productivity is a key to improving food security. Women may benefit from improved crop production by selling surplus in the local market. Enhanced crop productivity could thus be a starting point for livelihood diversification. Increased soil productivity also increases returns to labor, which is especially important for labor-constrained women, because it may free time for additional activities. Zero-tillage systems, cover crops, and mulches, for example, can significantly improve soil productivity and at the same time reduce labor for weeding. These alternatives are often context specific; mulching, for instance, is more appropriate for small-scale farming.

Women farmers often apply different criteria to assess soil productivity, because they are more concerned with the overall output of the cropping system (often a mixed cropping system). Mixed cropping systems may yield as much or more food as monoculture systems, and often they are designed to foster overall crop stability and system resilience. Agricultural research and development interventions can be better targeted if they take these local strategies for managing soil productivity into account. Combining fertilizer use with other soil productivity management strategies, such as mulches, cover crops, or intercropping, could further improve the stability and resilience of cropping systems, characteristics that are gaining importance in light of the potential negative effects of climate change.

POLICY AND IMPLEMENTATION ISSUES

It takes time to improve soil productivity. The results of investments in soil productivity are usually not seen in the first years. The lag time between investment and results means that farmers may face a trade-off between meeting their immediate needs (which may lead to nutrient mining) and ensuring the longer-term sustainability of their land (DFID 2002). It also means that land tenure is a major influence, both on the maintenance of soil fertility and on the ability to intensify farming sustainably. Because women so frequently lack secure access to land, they may be reluctant to invest in soil improvement. "Secure access" to land refers not only to having legal title to the land but also to having the power within the household to make and influence decisions about how the land will be used. A possible scenario, for instance, is that men household members will start managing a formerly unproductive field once the women have invested labor and resources to enhance its soil productivity.

Extension systems continue to direct information on soil improvement largely to men (see also Module 7). The imbalance between men and women extension staff reduces the effectiveness of extension services for women farmers, and the apparent failure to focus on women's crops and production systems renders many extension messages meaningless for them. Because fertilizer recommendations are usually designed for monoculture systems, they are difficult for women to apply in mixed cropping systems.

Extension systems supply limited information on alternatives to chemical fertilizers, partly because research systems still have limited capacity for studying the synergistic effects of soil amendments (such as manure and compost) and inorganic fertilizers (DFID 2002).

In some countries the withdrawal of subsidies for inorganic fertilizer has reduced its availability for resource-poor farmers, including women. An alternative policy could be to adopt "smart" (targeted and time-bound) subsidies that increase the possibility that poorer farmers will use fertilizer, especially by making small packages of fertilizer available at a reasonable price (DFID 2002).

GOOD PRACTICES AND LESSONS LEARNED

Actions to address key gender issues in managing soil productivity can be clustered into three categories: (1) the use of chemical fertilizer; (2) the use of low-external-input technologies, including synergistic effects of fertilizer and other practices; and (3) the appropriate choice of crops and crop management practices to enhance soil productivity. The actions and corresponding lessons are discussed in the sections that follow.

Chemical fertilizer use in gendered crop agriculture

The use of chemical fertilizer needs to be considered from a regional perspective (table 12.2). The African continent (including North African countries and South Africa) has consistently represented only 2–3 percent of world fertilizer consumption; the share for sub-Saharan Africa (excluding South Africa) is generally less than 1 percent (FAO 2005a).

Table 12.2   Regional Disparities in Chemical Nutrient Consumption, 2002/03–2003/04

Region	Nutrients (000 tons)		Change (%)	Percentage of world total
	2002/03	2003/04		
Africa	4,278	2,924	−0.7	**2.1**
Central Europe	4,086	3,528	−0.9	2.5
East Asia	50,612	51,751	1.0	**36.3**
Eastern Europe and Central Asia	3,660	3,887	1.1	2.7
Latin America	13,230	13,191	−1.0	9.3
North America	22,022	22,024	1.0	15.4
Oceania	3,162	3,233	1.0	2.3
South Asia	20,882	20,937	1.0	**14.7**
West Asia	4,607	5,678	1.2	4.0
Western Europe	15,142	15,436	1.0	10.8
World	141,681	142,589	1.0	100.0

Source: "IFADATA Statistics," www.fertilizer.org.
Note: Bold faced entries are regional totals.

The regional averages hide considerable variation among countries. Whereas fertilizer use is increasing rapidly in southern Africa (Crawford, Jayne, and Kelly 2005), it is stagnant or declining elsewhere in Africa. The majority of Africa's farmers (many of them women) are smallholders with less than 2 hectares (Altieri 2002), and they grow most of their basic food crops with virtually no or minimal fertilizer. For example, 72 percent of millet, approximately half of all food legumes, and nearly all yams and cocoyams are produced in this way (Altieri 2002). In Tanzania and Uganda, the average use of chemical fertilizers is less than 1 kilogram per hectare per year, which implies that most land is never fertilized (Wynen and Vanzetti 2002).

Overall trends in fertilizer consumption can be summarized as follows (FAO 2006):

- Fertilizer consumption has increased substantially, although not consistently, in countries with rapidly increasing exports of agricultural commodities, such as Argentina and Brazil.
- Structural adjustment programs implemented to correct financial imbalances in certain developing countries in the 1980s and 1990s negatively affected fertilizer use among small-scale farmers.
- In countries where centrally planned systems, with their heavy support to agriculture and planned allocations of fertilizer, were superseded around 1990 by market-oriented systems, fertilizer consumption fell abruptly.
- In the few developing countries where governments continued to support fertilizer use, sometimes despite pressure to the contrary, fertilizer consumption continued to increase.

Unfortunately, no systematic national or global data sets compare fertilizer use by gender. Indirect evidence for the unequal use of inorganic fertilizer can be obtained by analyzing fertilizer use by crop species where data are available. According to FAO:

> In Latin America seven crops (maize, soybean, sugar cane, beans, wheat, coffee and rice), plus vegetables and fruits, account for 88 percent of the total fertilizer consumption. A substantial proportion of the fertilizer is used on agricultural cash and commodity crops for the domestic commercial market and export. Although statistics are not available, it seems that little fertilizer is used in the subsistence/small-scale farming sector. In SSA the main crops to receive fertilizer include maize, millet and sorghum. In South Asia and Southeast Asia about 60 percent of fertilizers are used on cereals. In South Asia, crop production is oriented towards supplying domestic demand, whereas Indonesia, Malaysia, Thailand and Viet Nam are also important exporters.
>
> FAO (2006: 55)

The data suggest that the larger share of fertilizer is applied to commercial crops, which indicates that women use only a small proportion on their staple crops.

Many reasons account for women's limited use of fertilizer. As mentioned earlier, because fertilizer is mainly sold in large quantities, it is a big investment, especially for cash-constrained women. Women usually have less access to transport and find it more difficult to carry bags of fertilizer home. In remote rural areas, fertilizer is not usually readily available, and thus it is especially difficult for women, who have fewer opportunities to leave the village, to obtain. All of these constraints reveal strategic entry points for interventions that could improve women's use of fertilizer.

It is also important to emphasize that fertilizer is usually promoted in conjunction with other technologies, especially improved crop varieties. The long-term sustainability of such "packages" depends on the continued availability of their components. Box 12.5 illustrates the problems inherent in this approach and demonstrates why it is vital to address gender inequality in access to assets and services.

Alternative crop management practices for improved soil productivity

For resource-poor farmers engaged mainly in subsistence production, low-external-input technologies are usually a more affordable way to improve soil productivity. Crop rotations, improved fallows, agroforestry systems, integrated soil and water management practices, and the choice of suitable crops are some of the options. It is important to emphasize that the crop management practices described in this section as a means to enhance soil productivity *do not exclude* the use of external inputs. The use of these practices and the use of external inputs can be complementary, depending upon the resources and socioeconomic situation of each farmer.

As mentioned, low-external-input technologies are often based on local practices that have been adapted in light of additional knowledge and skills. Recognizing the beneficial effects of legumes on soil productivity, women farmers often grow legumes in combination with other crops such as tubers and cereals, but this practice requires, among other resources, farmers' time and knowledge. Because the lack of labor is often cited as a major constraint to the adoption of low-external-input technologies, it is essential to match the

Box 12.5   Ghana: Nuances of Success among Men and Women Farmers

The Ghana Grains Development Project is one of the few African success stories of long-term donor support to strengthen national research and extension for food production. Ghana is also one of the few African countries with sustained increases in per capita food production. The Ghana Grains Project focused primarily on increasing the output of maize and cowpeas through the development and adoption of well-adapted varieties and management practices for each of Ghana's agroecological zones. Graduate-level training was provided to about 50 scientists, nearly all of whom returned to the project. Annual maize production rose from 380,000 tons in 1979, when the project started, to more than 1 million tons by the project's end in 1998. Maize yields increased by 40 percent, from 1.1

tons per hectare to 1.5 tons. The project's bottom-up approach integrated farmers in all stages of the research and included a socioeconomic assessment of the technology. Large-scale extension programs to promote the varieties and practices, supported by Sasakawa Global 2000 (a nongovernmental organization [NGO]), enabled more than half of all maize farmers in Ghana to adopt improved varieties, fertilizer, and planting methods by 1998. After fertilizer subsidies were removed, fertilizer use dropped to 25 percent, challenging the approach's sustainability. Adoption was significantly lower among women farmers (39 percent) than men (59 percent), reflecting differences in access to assets and services, and especially the biases in extension.

Source: Canadian International Development Agency, personal communication 2006, cited in World Bank 2007.

labor demands of such technologies carefully with household labor availability. These issues are especially important for women farmers who have specific seasonal labor-use patterns and who have no recourse to assets and services (World Bank 2007).

Some low-external-input technologies require no more labor than current practices. Others, such as conservation tillage, are attractive precisely because they save labor. In some cases (such as stone bunds for soil conservation), the initial labor investment for establishing the technology is high, which can limit adoption if the work coincides with peak labor periods. In Burkina Faso, for example, stone bunds contribute to soil and water conservation, promoting higher yields and, eventually, higher returns to labor. Nevertheless, 48 percent of women involved in their construction claimed that the bunds added to their workload, and only 12 percent said the bunds lightened their work (Atampugre 1993).

A further criticism of the application of low-external-input technologies is their highly context-specific nature, which means that they must be adapted to particular agroecological and socioeconomic conditions. Although much of the responsibility for local adaptation is ultimately borne by farmers themselves, these technologies clearly imply an even greater burden for national agricultural research systems (Sumberg, Okali, and Reece 2003). A shift to participatory innovation development—a process that combines local and external knowledge and skills—is required, supported

by training and capacity building among researchers, extension staff, and participating farmers. The shift to participatory development of innovations has important positive consequences for the development of human and social capital, as seen in the following examples. For a range of cultural and socioeconomic reasons, women often must be specifically approached and encouraged to participate in such initiatives.

The examples also indicate the wide range of options available for integrated soil fertility management. Farmer-led research initiatives (Budelman and DeFoer 2000; DeFoer and Scoones 2001) have demonstrated the promise of complex responses to nutrient scarcities that include organic as well as inorganic nutrient sources. Rather than favoring one approach over the other, observations in the field indicate that farmers are interested in experimenting with organic and chemical fertilizers to better attune responses to local needs, a process that inevitably requires an integrated approach.

Involving women in soil fertility management innovations. It is widely acknowledged that the sustainability of projects and programs to develop technology is linked closely to the participation of the target audience. Such participation is especially important in projects that rely on the traditional knowledge of women farmers to develop soil fertility management innovations. Many promising experiences in promoting farmers' innovations in soil management have been described, but two projects funded by the Netherlands offer examples that are especially pertinent for working with women farmers: (1) Promoting Farmer Innovations (PFI) and (2) Indigenous Soil and Water Conservation in Africa (ISWC). These projects, which operate in several African countries—including Burkina Faso, Ethiopia, Tanzania, and Uganda—aim to establish multistakeholder platforms for technology development and encourage women's participation.

For instance, in all of Ethiopia, research and development related to land husbandry have usually ignored the potential of women's knowledge and innovation. Women's domestic work has low status in Ethiopian society, and their productive work in agriculture is seldom acknowledged. As a rule, women in rural families do not regard themselves as farmers and would not present themselves as innovators in land husbandry. This situation is not unique to Ethiopia. Among farm families in Kenya, Tanzania, and Uganda, the PFI also found that women did not come forward to show and explain their own innovations; instead, men household members assumed this task, even though they did not understand the innovations as well as the women did (Critchley, Ong'ayo, and Njoroge 2001).

Many factors can explain women's lack of self-esteem with respect to their farming activities: traditional beliefs and attitudes regarding women's role in rural society; women's low levels of formal education; the limited mobility of women compared to men, who often migrate to towns or other countries to seek work; and women's poor access to external information. In Ethiopia ISWC endeavored to recognize women's innovation in land husbandry as a means of changing perceptions of this activity, including the perceptions of the women themselves, and of increasing the women's self-confidence and capacity to contribute to development. The first steps were to gather evidence of innovation by women farmers (box 12.6) and to make these accomplishments more widely known through training, tours, and exchange visits.

Promoting the use of legumes as mulch and cover crops. The use of legumes to improve soil productivity is well established in traditional agricultural systems and in technologies developed more recently by researchers. Projects promoting the use of legumes as green manure have often achieved limited impact, however, because they ignored farmers' multiple criteria for selecting suitable legume species. Women in particular resisted adopting species that people could not eat, even if they were the best choice for improving soils. Failing to involve men and women farmers in the selection of appropriate legume species may limit a project's impact. An example from Malawi (box 12.7)

emphasizes the importance of placing farmers at the center of research and extension to improve the adoption of legume-based technologies.

Choosing new and more profitable crops

Soil fertility is only one component of overall soil productivity. Many more possibilities are available to enhance soil productivity. The selection of appropriate crops, in combination with soil-improving practices, is one alternative, as seen in Bangladesh (box 12.8).

The Bangladesh case highlights the importance of promoting innovations that mesh with the livelihood strategies of women across wealth categories, especially poorer and landless women whose prospects for participation may

initially appear bleak (Adato and Meinzen-Dick 2007). It
also shows the potential for empowering women beyond the
initial bounds of a project. In areas where market infrastructure is available, vegetable sales could empower women
in the sense that earning money could increase their decision-making power within the household. In some areas it
could create opportunities for women to move into public
space, such as the market, to sell produce themselves.
Women who become members of groups involved in NGO-
sponsored development projects gain self-confidence from
their solidarity with the group and the added status of being
part of an outside organization.

Although the rapid expansion of horticultural crop production appears to hold considerable promise for poor
people who depend on agriculture, including women, the
experience in Bangladesh shows that if interventions based
on new and more profitable crops are to succeed among
women, the interventions must operate on a scale that is
accessible to them. Experiences from large-scale vegetable
production, for example, are not only different but are
probably more suited to (men) farmers with far greater
resources. The production of horticultural crops increases
the returns on land about 10-fold compared to returns for
cereal crops (World Bank 2007). It generates considerable
employment in the field—horticultural crops require
about twice the labor input per hectare of cereal crops—
and generates more off-farm jobs in processing, packaging,
and marketing. Women hold many of these new jobs,
although they often work under unfavorable conditions
(see also Module 8).

Yet the possibilities for resource-poor farmers to invest in large-scale production of horticultural crops are limited. Horticultural crops are management intensive, a variety of crops are grown, the cash outlay is large, and the use of chemicals is heavy (inflicting considerable harm on the environment; horticultural crops account for 28 percent of global pesticide consumption; World Bank 2007). Horticultural enterprises are risky because of pest outbreaks and volatile prices. Fruit production requires an investment of several years to recoup costs. The production of high-value horticultural crops for export leads to labor shortages, which force women to reduce the time devoted to independent income-producing activities or crops under their own control, with potentially negative impacts on food security.

Organic production, with the corresponding practices to maintain soil fertility and soil health, may be a potentially more benign alternative to conventional, high-value horticulture. The organic food movement has been endorsed by FAO, which maintains in a recent report (FAO 2007) that organic farming fights hunger, tackles climate change, and is good for farmers, consumers, and the environment. Organic farming is now regarded less as a niche market within industrial countries and more as a vibrant commercial agricultural system practiced in 120 countries on 31 million hectares of cultivated land and 62 million hectares of certified wild harvested areas. The organic market was worth $40 billion in 2006 and is expected to reach $70 billion by 2012. The strongest benefits of organic agriculture are its use of resources that are independent of fossil fuels, are locally available, incur minimal agroecological stresses, and are cost effective (FAO 2007). Some have argued that women farmers, who already rely on few external inputs, may be well positioned to become organic producers and benefit from the rising interest in organic produce.

A report from the International Institute for Environment and Development in the United Kingdom (Datta and Kar 2006) examined 14 NGOs promoting ecological agriculture in Bangladesh. Most of the NGOs ran programs that encouraged poor women to grow vegetables using organic fertilizers and pesticides on homestead land. This practice was extended to larger farms, generally controlled by men landowners. Farmers received environmental education and training along with financial and technical support. The training in organic agriculture had a significant impact on homestead farming and commercial farming. The awareness of organic agriculture rose significantly, particularly among women, who used organic fertilizer and actively promoted these technologies outside the project boundaries.

Despite the promise of organic production practices, it must be remembered that organic agriculture shares many of the attributes of low-external-input agriculture. It is labor intensive and knowledge intensive and requires a range of local inputs, such as manure and compost, which are not always available. Yields of organic crops are often lower than yields of nonorganic crops. Conventional farming inputs, such as chemical fertilizers and pesticides, are easily available, and farmers can use credit to purchase them. Landless and smallholder farmers depend on sharecropping, which forces them to maximize short-term benefits from conventional farming, depend on the immediate returns gained from using chemical inputs, and forego the longer-term benefits from organic farming.

Finally, obtaining organic certification is a costly process that requires a good amount of organization, even among farmers with considerable assets. The successful establishment of organic production systems will therefore require targeted services and infrastructure, including transport and markets, especially if women and the poor are to benefit.

GUIDELINES AND RECOMMENDATIONS FOR PRACTITIONERS

The following guidelines and recommendations apply to practitioners:

- The lack of gender-disaggregated data on the use of fertilizer and other soil productivity technologies mirrors the lack of attention given to this subject and makes it difficult to analyze the impact of interventions from a gender perspective.
- Experiences thus far have focused either on using fertilizer to address short-term soil fertility problems or on the development and promotion of low-external-input technologies. Although the complementarity of these approaches is mentioned in the literature, there is little evidence of their combined use in farmers' fields. The judicious use of affordable doses of inorganic fertilizer, combined with other soil fertility technologies, may offer good prospects for women to improve overall crop production. A better understanding of the synergistic effects of soil amendments (such as manure and compost) and inorganic fertilizers is essential—along with improvements in research and extension capacity to develop and promote combined technologies.
- Support is needed for research to adapt existing methods of fertility management to specific agroecological zones and to cropping systems managed by women in those

zones, and for extension to promote these techniques in ways that include women. Research on fertility management technologies that specifically addresses women's resource constraints and livelihood strategies has been limited.

- Land tenure is a major influence on the maintenance of soil fertility and on the ability to intensify farming in a sustainable way. Given that farmers must have secure access to land if they are to invest in it, soil productivity initiatives must be accompanied by initiatives to secure women's access to land (see Module 4).
- Women's empowerment through participatory approaches to technology development is critical. Although projects seek to involve men and women, in practice women's participation in soil improvement projects is often limited. A systematic effort is often needed to increase women's participation.

A final lesson is that more holistic soil productivity indicators are needed for monitoring and evaluation, especially with respect to the gender effects of soil management interventions. Until soil productivity management interventions are monitored and evaluated in a gender-disaggregated way, meaningful conclusions on the gender equality of interventions will be extremely challenging to obtain (see also Module 16). Men's biases in adoption do not necessarily mean that a particular technology is inappropriate

for women; better targeting and institutional and policy support may be needed to make the technology more accessible for women.

Soil productivity management interventions need to be monitored and evaluated within a wider livelihood context. Measuring short-term, single-crop productivity gains will not capture the full picture. Direct and indirect impacts of interventions, both quantifiable (such as yields, incomes, and labor requirements) and qualitative (such as system resilience and stability or women's empowerment), need to be taken into account. Productivity gains in one crop do not translate directly into increased household income, and benefits are not equally shared between men and women household members.

Furthermore, a need is present to develop monitoring and evaluation criteria that measure the contribution of soil productivity technologies to minimizing the risk of adoption for women farmers. Questions that elicit information on women's reliance on and contribution to different livelihood assets, such as labor, knowledge, and local natural resources, are important for understanding the potential impact on women. This list, although certainly not comprehensive, nevertheless indicates the importance of assessing technologies on the basis of criteria that extend beyond simple production data and of relinquishing the "one-size-fits-all" approach in developing and promoting soil management technologies.

Gender in Seed Production and Distribution

Seed is one of the most crucial elements in the livelihoods of agricultural communities. It is the repository of knowledge passed from generation to generation, and the result of continual adaptation and innovation in the face of ever-greater challenges for survival. The potential benefits from the use of good quality seed of adapted varieties by farmers can be enormous, and the availability of quality seed of a wide-range of varieties and crops to farmers can increase productivity, reduce risks from pest, drought and disease pressure, and increase incomes. Production increases through the use of adapted varieties in a given area can create employment opportunities related to processing, marketing, and other activities generated through quality seed production.

ASBP (2006: 6)

A farming community's food security depends heavily on its seed security. Women's need to ensure good supplies of their preferred varieties of seed can be particularly acute, because women are often the main growers of food to feed the family. Although both men and women farmers regard seed as a key resource for food and livelihood security, it is crucial to remember that *important socioeconomic and gender differences in seed diversity, seed security, and food security must be understood to target any seed interventions effectively* (FAO 2008b).

Farmers participate in multiple seed systems that help them produce and obtain the seed they need. These systems (box 12.9) can be divided broadly into formal and local (sometimes called "informal," "traditional," or "farmer") systems. Commercial farmers rely mostly on formal systems, which are responsible for the flow of improved and hybrid seed. Subsistence farmers tend to rely more on local systems. Local systems are responsible for flows of seed of traditional as well as modern varieties, which enter the system through different processes (Sperling and Cooper 2003). Farmers may mix seed from different sources if they lack sufficient seed or if they wish to experiment with or

modify a traditional variety. Farmers may incorporate improved varieties and expose them to local conditions and management, fostering their local adaptation. Local knowledge of men and women farmers is important because they manage different crop species and varieties and may participate in different seed systems for different purposes.

Although much attention has been paid to the development of formal, national seed systems, their contribution to noncommercial production systems remains limited. One widely recognized problem in many countries is the extended time between the initial identification of new varieties and their eventual release, seed production, and sale, which considerably delays adoption. In many countries local seed systems provide by far the largest share of seed for noncommercial crops. An estimated 80 to 90 percent of all seed used to produce staple food crops in subsistence systems comes from local seed systems (FAO 2008b; GTZ and CGN 2000).[1] In local seed systems, farmers themselves produce, disseminate, and obtain seed directly through their own harvested crops or through sale, exchange, or barter with others in the local area (ASBP 2006; Sperling and others 2004).

For resource-poor farmers, especially women, the local seed system is not surprisingly the main and most reliable source of seed (FAO 2008b; Pionetti 2006; Smale and others 2007), but medium-scale and better-off farmers also rely on seed from this source (FAO 2008b). An important reason for relying on local seed systems is that small-scale farmers, especially women, often grow a diversity of crops to minimize the risk of total crop failure and food insecurity (box 12.10). Another reason is that women in many societies are in charge of selecting and storing seed of many traditional food crops. Often these crops are valued for specific attributes: they are cheaper, available in small quantities, better adapted to local conditions, and easier to obtain, and they possess other qualities (for food preparation, ceremonies, or

Seed systems are often large and complex. A seed system generally encompasses a large number of individuals, organizations, and institutions involved in different functions related to seed, such as plant breeding research and the subsequent multiplication, processing, storage, distribution, and marketing of seed. Seed systems, very broadly defined, can be categorized as informal (or traditional) or formal seed systems.

Individual farm households are the foundation for informal seed systems, in which each household performs numerous seed system functions on its own. The formal sector, by contrast, consists of public and private organizations with specialized roles in supplying seed of new varieties. Different types of seed from organizations and individuals in one stage of the seed chain will flow to the next stage through informal and formal channels. Rules and regulations, such as procedures for releasing new varieties of seed to the public, intellectual property rights regimes, seed certification programs, seed standards, and contract law influence the structure, coordination, and performance of the seed system.

Source: Maredia and Howard 1998.

Women farmers in South India frequently point out that they could not grow such a wide range of crops if they did not have the seeds "in their hands." One farmer articulated the issues as follows: "Where would we get small amounts of seeds for our traditional crops if we did not save them ourselves?"

Small-scale farmers need relatively *small amounts of seed for a large number of crop varieties:* 100 grams of sesame, 500 grams of black gram, 1 kilogram of finger millet, and a handful of roselle seeds. Women farmers also want to grow very specific crops in addition to staples such as sorghum or maize. There is no guarantee that formal seed agencies can provide seed for all of these crops. Thanks to their carefully maintained seed stocks, the women can maximize the number of crops grown on their land and achieve a varied and nutritious diet.

Source: Pionetti 2006.

other uses) that are integral to cultural traditions. Seed of most of these crops and varieties is not developed or supplied through formal channels.

Although the local seed systems are well adapted to farmers' specific production environments, they often face numerous constraints. Traditional varieties have been and continue to be lost for a variety of reasons (including conflict, drought, change in preferences, and research and extension campaigns promoting modern varieties). Interventions to strengthen local seed supply systems, such as establishing seed banks and breeding and multiplying seed, are gaining popularity among NGOs and public institutions that supply seed. Often such initiatives enable formal and informal systems to work in complementary ways. Farmers also express demand for seed of new and improved crops and crop varieties and for improved seed management and processing technologies, which can be supplied by the formal seed system.

Small commercial seed enterprises might be a good means of serving these markets, which may not be attractive

to large private seed companies and poorly served by public seed agencies. Partnerships between public and private agencies (for example, a public research organization could supply seed for multiplication and sale to small, private entrepreneurs) may be another means of catering to these markets. Because women are responsible for selecting and saving seed in many traditional farming systems, commercial seed production presents good opportunities for including them as entrepreneurs, as contract farmers to multiply seed, and as marketers as well as employees.

KEY GENDER ISSUES

The following sections describe the key gender issues in crop agriculture and the potential benefits of addressing them.

Seed sources and access to information differ by socioeconomic group and gender

As mentioned earlier, an apparent gender bias exists in access to formal seed systems. Men, who are generally more involved in growing commercial crops, seem to access and benefit more easily from formal systems. Women, in turn, rely more heavily on local systems to obtain seed for staple and minor crops. A resource endowment bias has also been observed. Resource-poor farmers—men or women—generally lack the cash to purchase seed of modern varieties from formal seed suppliers. In Bangladesh access to irrigation was a significant determinant of whether a farmer would adopt modern rice varieties (Hossain 1988). A study in Ghana revealed that farmers preferred different rice varieties depending on whether they would be grown under high-input or low-input conditions (Stirling and Witcombe 2004). Gender-responsive action in the local seed sector should increase the availability of adequate seed and thus increase food and livelihood security for resource-poor farmers—especially for crops that are less interesting to commercial seed suppliers.[2] Encouraging local seed banks, establishing small-scale seed enterprises, and facilitating local seed exchange through an enabling policy environment are some measures to consider.

Based on their different portfolios of crop species and varieties, men and women can contribute different knowledge of seed characteristics

Aside from multiplying and distributing seed, local seed systems are important sources of knowledge of seed characteristics and management. Gender differences in local seed knowledge and skills are an important asset for strengthening links between the local and formal seed systems. Given women's traditional roles in selecting and saving seed, they can be strategic partners for forming liaisons between formal and informal seed systems. The formal system can play a more significant part in developing and supplying seed if it adopts a gender perspective—in other words, if it succeeds in understanding and addressing the seed needs of different household members.

Women's role in local markets and small seed enterprises

Local markets are often a crucial link in local seed systems. Local markets bring in grain, which farmers can subsequently sort and use for seed. These local "seed-grain markets" differ from formal outlets selling seed that is specially produced as seed, on specialized fields, within the framework of a seed business enterprise.[3] In many African and Latin American contexts, vendors of local seed and grain are to a large extent rural women. Farmers are sourcing less and less seed from their "classic" informal source (their own stocks) and depending more on local seed and grain markets (Smale and others 2007).[4]

Women increasingly participate in the formation and management of small seed enterprises (World Bank 2005). These more recent experiences need to be monitored and evaluated carefully to better understand their contributions and impacts on improved seed security and overall livelihood security. Applying a gender perspective to analyze and improve seed systems will help to overcome or at least reduce existing biases in access to, availability of, and use of adequate seed.

POLICY AND IMPLEMENTATION ISSUES

The following sections detail critical policy and implementation issues.

Public versus private seed enterprises

Seed provision is at an important crossroads in many developing countries. Donor support to public seed enterprises has diminished because these enterprises have been inefficient. Strategies for supporting the private seed sector are still evolving. A major challenge for public and private seed enterprises is to ensure repeated seed sales, because farmers may purchase seed once and then save it from their harvest. The emergence of a private seed industry is almost always based on sales of hybrid seed, which must be purchased anew each season or yields will decline, or on seed that farmers find difficult to save, such as vegetable seed. Seed of many other crops (particularly self-fertilizing crops with a low seed multiplication factor that are grown mainly for home consumption) is less likely to be available through a nascent private seed industry based on large, centralized seed enterprises—a vision that shows the formal seed sector's bias toward men and commercial farmers. Opportunities may present themselves for including such crops in small, locally operating seed enterprises with lower transport and overhead costs, however. The development of small, local enterprises could be a means for women to break into seed markets and supply the local and improved seed of crops and varieties that are neglected by large commercial seed companies.

Seed regulations and crop and variety protection

Numerous national and international policies influence the development and operation of formal and local seed systems. In many countries the regulatory and legal framework for the national formal seed system limits the development of local seed systems and directly affects women's position within them.

National seed regulations are usually based on international standards that are often incompatible with the reality of farmers' lives.[5] They restrict the free exchange and marketing of seed. The combination of compulsory variety registration and seed certification, as practiced in countries in Europe and elsewhere, heavily constrains the efficient functioning of the formal seed sector (notably the development of small-scale seed enterprises) and the development of alternative seed systems (GTZ and CGN 2000). The same constraint arises from the implementation of strong intellectual property rights regimes (World Bank 2006) and arrangements restricting access to genetic resources (Louwaars 2007).

The development of small-scale seed enterprises and local seed markets requires an enabling policy environment. A clear recognition of the roles and contributions of men and women farmers to seed development and management will necessitate a review of farmer's rights, access and benefit-sharing regulations, and intellectual property rights.

GOOD PRACTICES AND LESSONS LEARNED

Past experiences highlight the need to look at both local and formal seed systems, their linkages, and the policy environment that affects them.

Interventions focusing on the local seed system

An analysis of the local system is the starting point for any strategy that aims to strengthen and build on the existing system. A blueprint approach to seed system development will not work; a thorough analysis of the limiting factors of each existing system is vital. Within a household, for example, interests or priorities with respect to seed management may vary by gender and age group. Within a community or region, wealth status or ethnocultural differences can affect knowledge, preferences, and access to critical resources such as seed (FAO 2008b). Projects operating at the community level must be aware that stakeholders are likely to have different needs and priorities (GTZ and CGN 2000). The identification of weaknesses or gaps in seed security will help to define activities that can improve household and community seed security. For example, community seed banks (box 12.11) and community seed fairs (box 12.12) both help to strengthen local seed systems. Managed successfully, they can foster seed exchange networks and establish local institutional mechanisms to supply seed, especially of traditional varieties, within a community. National seed security will improve when local seed security is increased.

Interventions strengthening the formal seed system

The formal seed sector's achievements have been summarized as follows:

> Since the 1960s, scientific plant breeding that developed improved varieties suited to smallholders in subtropical and tropical areas—the green revolution—has been one of the major success stories of development. Initially spearheaded by semi-dwarf varieties of rice and wheat and improved varieties of maize from international agricultural research centers of the Consultative Group on International Agricultural Research (CGIAR), public breeding programs in developing countries have released more than 8,000 improved crop varieties over the past 40 years. In the 1980s and 1990s, improved varieties are estimated to have accounted for as much as 50 percent of yield growth, compared with 21 percent in the preceding two decades.
>
> World Bank (2007: 160)

Because these achievements have not been uniform across regions or socioeconomic groups, formal seed systems must develop better strategies for developing and disseminating seed of improved varieties to reach resource-poor farmers.

Plant breeding interventions. Countless breeding interventions aim to address the nutritional and production constraints of resource-poor farmers and significantly improve household food security. Perhaps the most controversial of these interventions is the development of GM crops. Even more than conventional hybrids and other modern varieties, GM crops face significant barriers to dissemination and adoption. Most GM crops in developing countries are currently produced in large, commercial production systems, as they require inputs, knowledge, and management skills that are not available to all farmers. The private sector is the main force behind the development of these crops, and many questions arise about their suitability for poor, small-scale producers.

Attempts are being made—often by public organizations in collaboration with private enterprises—to develop GM crops that tolerate unfavorable crop production conditions common in developing countries, such as poor soils or drought. Vitamin- and micronutrient-enhanced crops, as well as crops that produce vaccines and other pharmacological products, are also envisioned in plant-breeding strategies to improve health and reduce poverty. Despite these efforts, numerous challenges remain in developing and approving GM crops that can be considered to benefit poor people. The accessibility and suitability of such crops, including the potential ecological and socioeconomic risks for resource-poor households, must be assessed further (see Thematic Note 3).

Box 12.11   Enhancing Local Seed Systems through Community Seed Banks

Community seed banks help to meet the complementary goals of improving local food security and recognizing and maintaining the contributions of local crop diversity. Seed of traditional varieties frequently cannot be obtained in the market. Instead, rural people exchange seed within their villages or with people from neighboring villages. This kind of seed exchange is an important instrument for seed supply and diffusion; it is usually based on kinship, traditional relationships, and cultural practices. The establishment of a community seed bank empowers local people to select and multiply seed of traditional crops and varieties of their choice. By facilitating access to seed, especially among women, seed banks often encourage and sustain cultivation of traditional varieties and household seed security. The banks also help farmers to contribute and communicate their knowledge of seed storage technologies. Two examples of community seed banks follow.

- In *Paraiba, Brazil,* frequent droughts and farmers' small landholdings mean that families often cannot produce enough grain to use as food and to save as seed for the next year's crop. Genetic diversity has also been eroded by the preference for seed of commercial rather than local varieties. Commercial varieties are grown to meet market demands and are also used for distribution in government seed programs. Community seed banks help to reverse this trend through participatory, collective efforts to grow and supply seed. In addition to conserving biodiversity, the banks enable

farmers to be self-reliant by supporting the timely provision of seed.

- In *Jeypore, India,* interested households contribute a specific quantity of seed to the community seed bank. Seed is mixed with powdered neem (*Azadirachta indica*) and karanja (*Pongamia pinnata*) leaves to preserve it from storage pests. The village committee (*palli samithi*) forms the seed bank management committee, which consists of three men and women who share the responsibility of managing the bank. The bank records the names and quantities of seed required by needy farm families, and it distributes the seed. The involvement of women has strengthened the seed bank and the seed exchange system. The women perform vital tasks such as periodically monitoring seed quality. About 200 farmers (men and women) are actively involved in the program. The seed bank primarily stores seed of 15 traditional paddy cultivars, along with some millet, oilseed, and vegetable varieties. In 2000 about 700 kilograms of seed were handled.

Apart from their impact on food security, seed banks can improve socioeconomic conditions in rural communities, especially the status of women. By establishing self-help groups to operate seed banks, women can become more active in decision making and more self-confident, and can communicate more easily with government officials or outsiders. Men can become more supportive of women, and conflict between men and women can be reduced.

Sources: Authors; FAO 2002 (India example); FAO 2008a (Brazil).

Seed distribution interventions. Farmers like to experiment with new crops and varieties, and innovative distribution strategies could facilitate poor women's access to improved seed. Packaging seed in small and affordable quantities could be one way of increasing women's access. It is also important to recognize that seed of improved varieties and hybrids often gives the best yields when grown in conjunction with fertilizer and improved crop management strategies (following specific spacing, irrigation, and weeding practices, for example). The availability of these additional resources can be a crucial precondition for successful adoption of improved seed, yet many women lack access to cash and irrigated land.

A detailed analysis of available resources is therefore necessary before promoting such varieties among women.

Interventions strengthening links between local and formal seed systems

In developing countries, farmers' demand for seed is complex and diverse. It would be unrealistic or inefficient for the public, formal seed sector to attempt to meet total seed demand; nor would private, commercial seed providers be able to address all of the seed requirements of resource-poor farmers (Almekinders, Louwaars, and de Bruijn 1994).[6]

Increasing Seed Diversity and Local
Knowledge through Community
Seed Fairs

Community seed fairs have shown positive results, especially for women farmers. Community seed fairs offer a venue for displaying and freely sharing seed of different crops and varieties. Seed fairs also offer a good opportunity for knowledge to be shared across generations, between farmers, between communities, and with research and extension staff, thus contributing to expanding farmers' social networks (FAO 2006). Experiences from a range of organizations indicate that these informal settings encourage women's participation.

In China, for example, participants in seed fairs promoted by the Center for Biodiversity and Indigenous Knowledge (CBIK) included 80–150 farmers, local agricultural technicians, officials, scientists from the Yunnan Academy of Agricultural Sciences, CBIK staff, and other guests. Often the share of women participants was as high as 70 percent, because women are closely involved in farming and are the key decision makers when it comes to choosing new varieties. Farmers in each area have their own seed exchange networks but rarely have access to new species and varieties from outside their network. The seed fairs, which were relatively new for participating farmers, served to improve the flow of seed and information within and among communities and to promote the conservation of a wide crop genetic resource base. Experts were invited to give speeches on topics of interest, such as marketing organic produce. Yao and Hani traditional healers took the opportunity to exchange knowledge about medicinal plants.

Sources: Authors; CBIK (China example): www.cbik.org.

Box 12.13 Decentralized Participatory Plant
Breeding

Decentralized and participatory plant breeding approaches allow farmers to select and adapt technologies to local soil and rainfall patterns and to social and economic conditions, using indigenous knowledge as well. Participatory plant breeding and varietal selection have reduced the development and dissemination of new varieties in some cases by 5 to 7 years, which is half the time (10–15 years) taken by conventional plant-breeding programs.

In very poor areas of South Asia where rice is produced without irrigation (and where the Green Revolution never took hold), participatory plant breeding is now paying off, with strong, early adoption of farmer-selected varieties that yield 40 percent more grain in farmers' fields. The approach must be tested more widely in the more heterogeneous rain-fed environments of Africa, where involving farmers, especially women, in selecting varieties has shown early success for beans, maize, and rice. The cost effectiveness of the approach for wider use also needs to be evaluated.

Source: Adapted from World Bank 2007: 160–61.

A recent World Bank evaluation of the Seed Systems Development Project (SSDP) in Ethiopia, a project ongoing for over 10 years, rated its outcome as moderately unsatisfactory (DEReC 2007). The SSDP achieved its main objective of decentralizing and strengthening the government seed-producing agency (the Ethiopian Seed Enterprise), but it failed to achieve its secondary objective of promoting seed production by private firms and fostering local seed production by farmers.

Recognition is growing that stronger links between local and formal seed systems can lead to the development of an integrated seed system in which formal and local actors each play a role. This approach does, however, require collaboration between the many actors involved—breeders, genebanks, and seed projects operated by the formal sector; farmers; and NGOs. Experience with participatory plant breeding initiatives offers some insight into the potential for fostering an integrated approach (box 12.13).

Traditional breeding approaches tend to focus on one characteristic (such as higher yields, more stable yields, or disease resistance). Although the results may be impressive with respect to that particular characteristic, farmers, especially women, may not like the accompanying changes in other characteristics (such as grain color, taste, and ease of processing). In this instance, the knowledge and criteria that men and women use in selecting seed and in their other crop improvement efforts offer the opportunity to strengthen links between local and formal seed systems.

Enhancing communication between local and formal seed systems. Food and livelihood security can increase significantly when shortcomings in local seed systems are resolved. For example, in areas of Bangladesh where CABI's Good

Seed Initiative used videos to outline techniques to improve rice seed quality, seed yield rose an estimated 10 percent. This initiative (supported by the Swiss Agency for Development and Cooperation) aims to strengthen farmers' ability to guarantee food security and improve their livelihoods. The approach, which combines local technologies with those developed by formal research organizations to help women produce quality seed, is now being tested in Africa. CABI, WARDA (Africa Rice Center), and their partner organizations in West Africa and Uganda seek to reach as many as 10,000 farmers. Additional videos will be produced locally as the value of the approach spreads.

Introducing new varieties into the local seed system. Farmers' experimentation with new varieties and the subsequent introduction of adapted and accepted varieties can potentially strengthen cropping systems by increasing yields, improving drought resilience, boosting resistance to pests and diseases, and capturing new market opportunities (Sperling and Remington with Haugen 2006), all of which could widen women's livelihood options. It is important to realize, nevertheless, that not all "improved" varieties will benefit farmers in all agroecological and socioeconomic situations. A careful gender-disaggregated analysis of demand for particular varieties is warranted. Sperling and Remington (2006) discuss key steps for ensuring that characteristics demanded by farmers are considered in introducing new varieties.

Local seed and grain markets, discussed earlier, can offer a good venue for introducing new varieties. These markets, which are frequently visited by rural women, have virtually no formal access to new varieties, to basic (foundation) seed as an input, or to seed quality control services. Even so, there are dramatic examples of how quickly new varieties (including beans in western Kenya and green gram varieties in eastern Kenya) can move through local markets, as farmers spread the word that the new varieties on offer really do perform.[7]

Because the buyers and sellers in local markets are frequently women, the opportunity to support both groups of women by linking new varieties to local seed and grain markets appears substantial. The following actions are necessary to further strengthen women's capacity and access in this context:

- Greater support needs to be given to increasing the quality of seed for the crops and varieties in greatest demand in the markets (these may be local varieties or new ones). Suppliers of large quantities of seed and grain to the market require training to produce better seed

(which does not need to be certified). Most training is concentrated in small community-based groups, often funded by development projects, but general knowledge on how to improve seed quality must be mainstreamed in farming communities.

- The capacity to produce high-quality seed is not enough; farmers and farmer groups require much more training in agroenterprise development. Seed enterprises need to yield profits on a continual basis. The commercial sector has shied away from selling seed of subsistence and open-pollinated crops because the profits are limited. To stimulate consistent demand for this kind of seed, communities must diversify seed production by crop and variety and, crucially, ensure that they have a sustained supply of new and appreciated seed.

- In reference to the point above, direct links need to be forged between those who breed new varieties and those who can multiply and distribute seed at a decent price. Right now, new varieties filter through to communities at an unacceptably slow rate. Research systems have to deliver new materials not only to seed parastatals and commercial producers but directly to important community-based nodes throughout a country.

- Traders and farmer groups need continued access to advice on quality control that is enabling and not threatening. A trader who becomes known for truly good seed should eventually be able to garner worthwhile price margins.

Encouraging the formation of small-scale seed enterprises. The formation of small-scale seed enterprises—that is, farmer seed enterprises—meets dual objectives: to distribute and promote sustainably modern crop varieties and to establish a regular source of "clean" seed of local or modern varieties. Yet experience indicates that a certain level of resources (such as labor and land) is required to manage farmer seed enterprises successfully; the resource requirement could exclude or discourage women from participating. Some alternative strategies may be better suited to the limited resources controlled by poor people.

For example, the Malawi Smallholder Seed Development Project established by ActionAid in 1995 uses two seed production strategies. The less-poor farmers are encouraged to produce certified seed and operate independently, although they still face marketing problems, for which new approaches, such as the use of stockists, are being investigated. The poorer farmers (many of whom are women) are organized into community groups to produce and distribute seed on a communal basis using group revolving funds (box 12.14). The second strategy has provided encouraging

Box 12.14	Malawi: Community-Based Seed Production

Through the Malawi Smallholder Seed Development Project, groups of smallholders produce improved seed as a means of enhancing household food security. The project has organized 5,405 smallholders into 235 community-based groups to produce seed. Group members are selected through a participatory rural appraisal to identify and assess needs of poor households. The project's concentration on the poorest households has ensured that many more group participants are women, who also perceive greater advantages in belonging to groups than men do. About 70 percent of group members are women, and over 80 percent of the seed-producing groups are composed entirely of women. Women's groups are better organized and their revolving grants for seed production have higher repayment rates than those of men's groups. Women get higher seed yields, generate better savings, and sustain more cohesive groups.

Source: Musopole 2000.

Box 12.15	Southern India: The Role of Gender-Sensitive Policies for Plant Variety Protection and Farmers' Rights

In the dryland farming systems of South India's Deccan Plateau, women's roles in maintaining seed and crop diversity enable rural families to cope with the region's many environmental demands. Here seeds and their management form an economy all of their own, whereby self-reliance in seed, crop diversity, and nutrition are closely intertwined.

But as seed increasingly becomes the "property" of private seed-producing enterprises, this self-reliance is undermined. Plant variety protection enables private companies to cover the cost of breeding new varieties, but it can restrict the scope for farmers to save their own seed through a mix of technological, legal, and economic strategies. These strategies include reducing the genetic variability of new crop varieties through pure line breeding methods; intellectual property rights regimes, such as breeders' rights and patents, which make it illegal for farmers to reuse seed; variety registration and seed certification schemes backed by economic rules; and gender-blind laws that provide no scope for enhancing women farmers' practices, choices, and concerns in the realms of biodiversity and seed production.

Source: Pionetti 2006.

evidence that women's skills and scarce resources can be mobilized to strengthen seed systems and enhance family seed and food security.

Interventions to foster an enabling policy environment

All of the initiatives discussed earlier could benefit from complementary efforts to foster a favorable policy environment, such as the development of seed legislation that protects breeders' rights, interventions that strengthen farmers' rights, and more flexible interpretation of seed laws to support local seed systems. To stimulate the private sector and at the same time support local seed systems for crops that are often ignored by the private sector, well-designed seed and intellectual property rights laws will need to go hand in hand with the recognition of farmers' rights—a balance that is not necessarily easy to attain. Policies for plant variety protection and intellectual property rights must also be gender sensitive. In some instances formal seed interventions and policies can be counterproductive, especially for women's participation in the seed system (box 12.15).

KEY IMPLEMENTATION ISSUES

The guiding principle in any seed intervention is that seed security is a key component of food security. Women are the main food producers in farm households, and so their seed security—in other words, their access to reliable supplies of good seed—is of the highest priority.

A clear assessment of seed demand should be the first step in designing any seed-related intervention. The precise nature of the demand for seed will significantly determine the appropriate seed supply response. It is important to understand exactly why farmers seek seed off the farm:

- Are farmers (men and women) searching for new varieties (which may simply require an initial introduction of seed)?
- Are men and women farmers purchasing hybrids (which can be supplied by a commercial enterprise)?

- Do farmers have seed quality or management problems (which require specialized seed enterprises or extension advice to improve farm-level seed management)?
- Do seed purchases indicate a poverty-induced seed shortage (which will not be addressed by conventional seed provision)?

As formal and informal seed systems focus on different crop species and varieties and seem to serve different clienteles, they should be considered complementary. Both systems have strengths and weaknesses on which development interventions can be based. As seen earlier, women farmers are already active in local seed markets and informal seed systems, and they could make important contributions to emerging small-scale seed enterprises.

The formal seed system can enhance the quality and functioning of the informal seed system by, for example, implementing capacity-building activities addressing both men and women, strengthening community seed banks, and improving seed selection and storage.

These activities require multistakeholder interventions targeting the following actors (GTZ and CGN 2000):

- Individual farmers and farmers' groups, especially women farmers
- Small seed enterprises
- NGOs and development agencies
- Researchers and technicians of national systems
- Policy makers
- Public and private seed companies.

Seed policy should create a framework that enables public and private resources to be used to meet gender-specific demand for seed and that fosters an enabling environment for the synergistic development of the formal and informal seed system. This enabling policy environment will take into account such issues as secure tenure rights for women farmers and improved access to resources, such as inputs or irrigation.

Gender and Crop Protection

Some 20–40 percent of the world's potential crop production is lost annually because of the effects of weeds, pests, and diseases (CropLife International 2007). New pest problems continue to develop. Attempts to control agricultural pests have been dominated by chemical control strategies, but the overuse of chemicals has adversely affected human health, the environment, international trade, and farm budgets. All of these concerns justify giving high priority to crop protection in development interventions.

Agriculture ranks among the three most hazardous occupations in developing and industrial countries, alongside mining and construction (World Bank 2007). The leading cause of injury on the farm is the improper use of chemicals. Poor awareness of safe practices for handling chemicals and a lack of appropriate protective equipment also contribute to injuries.

Crop protection strategies—the management of pests, diseases, and weeds—have changed dramatically over time. The intensification of agriculture alters agricultural practices significantly. For example, in intensive agricultural systems, more traditional and labor-intensive physical and biological crop protection measures are superseded by pest-resistant varieties and more capital-intensive use of pesticides.[1] In marginal areas, the generally small returns to these expensive chemical inputs make them difficult for farmers to use (IFAD 2002). The recent development of crops that are genetically modified to resist specific pests and diseases presents yet another crop protection alternative to farmers, but the benefits and risks of this technology are still poorly understood in many settings, especially with respect to gender differences.

Pesticides can increase agricultural productivity, but when handled improperly, they are toxic to humans and other species. Aside from the health concerns posed by pesticide residues in food, unintentional poisoning from exposure kills an estimated 355,000 people each year, two-thirds

of them in developing countries.[2] The costs of medical treatment, lost labor, and reduced long-term productivity can be high. Many farmers in developing countries overuse pesticides and do not take proper safety precautions because they do not understand the risks and fear smaller harvests. Making matters worse, developing countries seldom have strong regulatory systems for dangerous chemicals: pesticides banned or restricted in industrialized countries are used widely in developing countries. Farmers' perceptions of appropriate pesticide use vary by setting and culture.

Additional negative environmental effects and socioeconomic costs include the debt incurred by farmers to purchase these inputs, the loss of local knowledge and practices once used to protect crops, and dependence on external sources of inputs.

As with so many capital-intensive technologies, the poor, including women and children, are the ones least able to benefit from their use. Recent research in India, for example, shows that small-scale and marginal farmers take loans from private finance corporations to purchase inputs and then, unable to pay their debts, become answerable to moneylenders (Mancini and others 2005). Ultimately farmers may be forced to sell their land to cover their debts, thereby losing their only economic asset. The same study also found marginal farmers to have a 10 times greater risk of severe pesticide poisoning than large-scale farmers.

A study by FAO, WHO, and UNEP (2004) broadly estimates that between 1 million and 5 million cases of pesticide poisoning occur each year, resulting in several thousand fatalities. Pesticide fatalities are overwhelmingly a developing country phenomenon. Although developing countries use just 25 percent of all pesticides produced, 99 percent of deaths from pesticide poisoning occur in developing countries. Children and women are especially at risk. In Egypt, for example, more than 1 million children who help to manage cotton pests are exposed to pesticides.

An agricultural production model is urgently needed that starts to internalize the external costs of pesticide use and incorporates the prevention of ill health, environmental contamination, and the conservation of biological capital into production processes and markets. This goal is specified in the Rio Declaration on Environment and Development. Agenda 21, Chapter 14, deals with promoting sustainable agriculture and rural development, and section I covers "Integrated pest management and control in agriculture" (UN 1992). The Agenda explicitly mentions women as a specific target group for interventions.

KEY GENDER ISSUES

The following sections detail the key gender issues in crop protection and potential benefits of addressing them.

Gender and pesticide exposure

It is important to gain a better understanding of how women are exposed to pesticides in agricultural production, as well as the differential patterns of pesticide use between women and men. Marginal farmers are often engaged in professional pesticide spraying and therefore subject to continuous exposure. Women and children are specifically at risk because they are frequently employed in mixing pesticides and refilling pesticide tanks (Rother 2000). Women and children also perform secondary activities that have been neglected in studies dealing with direct exposure. Extremely time-consuming operations such as weeding are often performed by women and children during the peak spraying season, when residue levels in fields are high (Mancini and others 2005) and can cause secondary poisoning. Women are also exposed to pesticides in the home, for example, by washing pesticide-soaked clothing and disposing of (or using) empty chemical containers.

Women's involvement in piecework and seasonal labor, and the unfavorable conditions associated with such work (such as less training and protective equipment), increase their risk of pesticide exposure. Women are particularly vulnerable to pesticides at certain times of their lives, especially when they are pregnant. Growing evidence of associations between pesticide exposure, women's reproductive health problems, and health problems passed on to offspring adds to the concern over pesticide poisoning in women (London and Bailie 2001).

Gender and knowledge of pesticide risks

Compared to men, women are usually less informed about safe pesticide practices and the dangerous side effects of pesticide use. High levels of pesticide poisoning among resource-poor farmers, especially women, are often reported to be linked to low levels of literacy and education. In many cases, the husband is responsible for buying pesticide from the cooperative, market, or storekeeper, and no information is passed between the husband and wife about safe use—with the result, for example, that women reuse pesticide containers for storing or transporting their crops or cooking supplies. Often pesticide products are not labeled, but even if they are, many women cannot read the information. Although educating people in proper pesticide management is extremely important, education alone will not prevent poisoning. Other factors also require attention, including difficulties in obtaining protective gear, which may be costly, may not be supplied by employers, or may be inappropriately designed for hot climates (London and Bailie 2001; Mancini and others 2005).

Pesticide use is costly and unsuited to women's cropping strategies

Pesticide use is capital intensive: the pesticide, sprayer, and protective gear all must be purchased. Women's limited access to productive resources often makes them more reluctant than men to purchase inputs such as pesticides to use on their crops (which are usually food crops). The blanket recommendations commonly provided by extension units or displayed on pesticide labels may be inappropriate for women's complex mixed-cropping systems. To benefit women, pest control mechanisms must be tailored to the pests encountered in staple and minor crop production.

Inconsistent benefits of alternative pest control technologies across socioeconomic groups

"The distribution of benefits from commercial genetically modified crops is uneven. Although these crops are now grown more widely in developing than in developed countries, to date the benefits have been uneven, concentrated in developed countries and a few commercial crops."[3] The challenge remains to develop and win approval for GM crops that are suited to the agricultural preferences and constraints of poor women and men. In the near term, the application of new molecular biotechnologies and new breeding strategies to crops that are specifically relevant to smallholder production systems in developing countries will probably be constrained for a number of reasons: the lack of reliable longer-term research funding, inadequate technical and operational capacity, the low commercial value of the crops, the lack of adequate conventional breeding programs, and the need to select the relevant production environments (FAO 2004: 24).

POLICY AND IMPLEMENTATION ISSUES

Many governments have inadequate legislation overseeing problematic pesticides and herbicides. Where the legislative framework is in place, enforcement capability is often weak. The viability of occupational health and safety structures and functions in developing countries is also a primary concern. Agriculture tends to be excluded from many national labor laws and is not subject to any comprehensive international standard. Where regulations exist, they are often sporadically applied because of inadequate legal provisions, low levels of unionization, and insufficient labor inspection. As women form a large percentage of agricultural laborers, they are directly affected by this lack of oversight (see also Module 8).

The chemical industry heavily promotes the use of pesticides for crop protection. In developed countries, on the one hand, the industry markets "new-generation" pesticides that have high efficiency ratios (small doses achieve maximum results) and limited adverse effects on people and the environment. In developing countries, on the other hand, significant quantities of outdated pesticides remain in circulation, and extension agencies and pesticide sellers may not necessarily promote "new-generation" pesticides, which in any case are expensive. Instead, farmers buy older, cheaper, and more hazardous products. As much as 30 percent of the pesticides sold in developing countries do not meet international quality standards. FAO has recently expressed concern about the proliferation of cheap unlabelled pesticides in Africa (FAO/WHO 2001). Many are adulterated, unauthorized, or illegal.

The current drive for economic growth and agricultural trade promotes an approach to food production that emphasizes agribusiness, land consolidation, and contract farming (IIED 2003), in which pesticides play an established role. Although these production systems are important in some segments of the farming community, they do not address the specific circumstances and priorities of resource-poor women farmers, who risk becoming even more marginalized if agriculture increasingly presents alternatives that they cannot adopt. The discussion of GM crops needs to take this issue into account.

Experiences with crop protection in developing countries suggest policies and other interventions that could support crop protection strategies that do not further exclude and endanger the poor, especially women and children.

These strategies include promoting alternatives to hazardous chemicals; improving training and information for women and others in agriculture; and reducing access to dangerous agrochemicals.

Promoting alternative to hazardous chemicals

Crops can be protected from pests in ways that preclude the use of hazardous chemicals, including integrated pest management (IPM), organic crop production, the use of less toxic chemical products, and the promotion of GM crops (although the risks, costs, and benefits of this last option are still imperfectly understood in many settings).

Integrated pest management. IPM (box 12.16) has been implemented successfully across a wide range of crops and agroclimatic zones. Many aid and development agencies have adopted IPM as the model for the agricultural development they support, and the OECD Development Assistance Committee encourages its member states to support IPM.

IPM should go hand in hand with appropriate pesticide management to allow for pesticide regulation and control, including trade, and for the safe handling and disposal of pesticides, particularly those that are toxic and persistent. Cumulative evidence shows that farmers trained

---

Box 12.16 Integrated Pest Management Defined

The Systemwide Program on Integrated Pest Management of the Consultative Group on International Agricultural Research offers a concise synthesis of IPM principles:

> Integrated Pest Management is an approach to enhancing crop and livestock production, based on an understanding of ecological principles, that empowers farmers to promote the health of crops and animals within a well-balanced agro-ecosystem, making full use of available technologies, especially host resistance, biological control and cultural control methods. Chemical pesticides are used only when the above measures fail to keep pests below acceptable levels, and when assessment of associated risks and benefits (considering effects on human and environmental health, as well as profitability) indicates that the benefits of their use outweigh the costs. All interventions are need-based and are applied in ways that minimize undesirable side-effects.

Source: SP-IPM In Brief, www.spipm.cgiar.org/Brief/spIPMbrif.htm.

in appropriate methods of pesticide use suffer lower exposure and can achieve higher net returns than those who are not trained.

IPM has shown positive results in a wide range of socioeconomic and ecological conditions (FAO 1999, 2000; FAO and World Bank 2000; Tripp, Wijeratne, and Piyadasa 2005). An important advantage of IPM is that it *builds on the knowledge of women and men farmers* about crop, pest, and predator ecology to increase the use of pest-resistant varieties, beneficial insects, crop rotations, and improved soil management. It combines local knowledge with external knowledge in the search for improved management strategies. The success of IPM depends largely on how well farmers understand and combine knowledge of biological and ecological processes with their farming experience to develop and select options that reduce losses to pests, increase agricultural productivity, manage risk, and meet the demands of local and global markets. As men and women often possess different types of knowledge, applying a gender perspective to IPM is integral for understanding farmers' perceived pest management needs.

IPM is thus knowledge intensive and builds on available human and social capital. By addressing women as well as men, IPM programs and projects can help to invest more equitably in developing human and social capital—two crucial assets for sustainable livelihoods. When women attended farmer field schools to learn about IPM, they reported that the schools helped them gain recognition of their personal skills and abilities. Mancini, van Bruggen, and Jiggins (2007) showed that the personal growth stimulated by participation in field schools was particularly relevant to women and confirmed the importance of increasing women' access to these and other educational programs.

Because IPM is not capital intensive, it is suited to family food production systems, including the production of traditional crops and varieties. Whereas pesticides are more commonly used in commercial production systems, IPM, if developed from a gender perspective, can contribute to increased food security.

Even in these cases, the wider promotion of IPM practices must overcome a number of limitations. IPM can be a time- and labor-intensive strategy, with potential constraints for women, who often lack surplus labor to invest in such initiatives. These factors are highly context specific and must be understood thoroughly before making any decision to promote IPM. For example, in some cases women have had to walk long distances to fetch water to prepare pesticides for cotton production, and switching to IPM based on biological pest control lightened women's labor.

Because IPM is knowledge intensive, it requires an intensive educational approach, which is more challenging to scale up (as farmer field schools and training-the-trainer approaches have shown) as well as demanding of human and financial resources (Feder, Murgai, and Quizon 2004).

The policy environment can also constrain expansion of IPM programs. Policies inhibiting the expansion of community IPM (Fakih, Rahardjo, and Pimbert 2003) include inequitable property rights over land and other natural resources (see also Modules 4 and 10), which commonly affect women more than men.

An important lesson of IPM projects in various countries is that women have continued to be underrepresented (Fakih, Rahardjo, and Pimbert 2003). Often IPM projects rigidly impose criteria for selecting participating farmers, which include the completion of lower secondary school, some farming experience, and the ability to communicate knowledge to others. Although useful in themselves—especially where ensuring the dissemination of knowledge is concerned—these criteria, if formally and rigidly applied, restrict women's access. Other external constraints on women's full participation in farmer field schools and training-of-trainer courses, as well as on their ability to be active farmer trainers, include the following (Nhat Tuyen 1997):

- In many cultures women need permission from their husbands or fathers to attend schools and courses, especially if all or most participants are men. In some cultures it is simply unacceptable for women to participate in group activities with men who are not their husbands or close relatives.
- It may be difficult to schedule activities so that they do not clash with the wide range of family support tasks for which women bear primary responsibility.
- The extent to which men farmers accept having women as part of a group or as trainers must be determined.
- Village leadership, including village administration and cooperative management, plays an important if not essential role in organizing IPM training courses. These leaders interpret and apply the selection criteria. If men dominate village leadership, as is often the case, this domination can easily lead to men's bias in selection.
- The trainers' role is critical in organizing training events in ways that meet the requirements of men and women farmers. When introducing a training course to local leaders, trainers often lack information about how gender operates in the local division of labor. For this reason, they do not have the capacity to negotiate fair representation of women in field schools or other training events, and

often trainers themselves are not convinced that equality of representation is important. The degree to which women have participated in field schools, until now, has depended on the perceptions and initiatives of individual staff and trainers.

■ For these newer training approaches to succeed among men and women, a shift in attitudes must occur. The customary preference for working with men farmers must not be transferred from conventional research and extension approaches to new training approaches.

These constraints should be taken into account in future interventions. The IPM farmer field school literature provides a good starting point for reviewing ways of overcoming gender bias.

Other approaches to reduce hazardous chemicals. Other approaches to reduce pesticide use are the promotion of less toxic pesticides, the promotion of organic farming (discussed in Thematic Note 1), and the development of pest- and disease-resistant crops, including GM crops. Scientists, development practitioners, civil society organizations, and politicians have long debated the benefits and constraints of genetically modified crops. Recent conclusions with respect to these issues have been summarized as follows:

> The scientific consensus is that the use of transgenic insect-resistant Bt crops is reducing the volume and frequency of insecticide use on maize, cotton and soybean (ICSU [International Council for Science]). These results have been especially significant for cotton in Australia, China, Mexico, South Africa and the United States. The environmental benefits include less contamination of water supplies and less damage to non-target insects (ICSU) ... As a result of less chemical pesticide spraying on cotton, demonstrable health benefits for farm workers have been documented in China. ... and South Africa. ... Herbicide use is changing as a result of the rapid adoption of HT [herbicide-tolerant] crops (ICSU). There has been a marked shift away from more toxic herbicides to less toxic forms, but total herbicide use has increased. ... Scientists agree that HT crops are encouraging the adoption of low-till crops with resulting benefits for soil conservation (ICSU). There may be potential benefits for biodiversity if changes in herbicide use allow weeds to emerge and remain longer in farmers' fields, thereby providing habitats for farmland birds and other species, although these benefits are speculative and have not been strongly supported by field trials to date. ... There is concern, however, that greater use of herbicides—even less toxic herbicides—will further erode habitats for farmland birds and other species (ICSU). ... Scientists agree that extensive long-term use of Bt crops and glyphosate and gluphosinate, the herbicides associated with HT crops, can promote the development of resistant insect pests and weeds.
>
> FAO (2004, Section B, Chapter 4: 68–71)

Aside from their environmental consequences, GM crops have important socioeconomic consequences. The adoption of Bt cotton can be cited as an overall success for increasing yields, improving farm incomes, and significantly reducing pesticide applications, but these effects have varied depending on the context (World Bank 2007). Some farmers in India experienced losses following the adoption of Bt cotton. In some parts of India, Bt cotton yields less than traditional cotton varieties. The reduced yields, together with rising seed costs, increased farmers' indebtedness.[4]

The distribution of benefits from commercial GM crops has been uneven, concentrated in industrial countries and a few crops. The largest share of GM crops is found in highly commercial production systems (FAO 2004), and the strong commercial interest of the private sector largely determines the kinds of GM crops and traits that are developed. A few promising initiatives aim to develop and promote GM crops with traits that are relevant for developing countries. New Rice for Africa (NERICA), a high-yielding, drought- and pest-resistant type of rice developed specifically for African conditions, is one example. IFAD has provided $2 million to WARDA to promote the use of NERICA in West Africa and is now designing a series of grants to accelerate NERICA seed multiplication activities in Côte d'Ivoire, the Democratic Republic of Congo, and Guinea (IFAD 2007). The lack of gender-disaggregated data on the adoption and benefits of GM crops makes it impossible to draw gender-specific conclusions, apart from pointing out the gender-specific constraints encountered with other interventions in crop protection and in plant breeding more generally (see Thematic Note 2 on seed systems, for example).

Improving training and information for women in agriculture

Only safe, correct management will minimize the negative consequences of pesticides for human and environmental health and foster their sustained, positive impact on crop production and farmers' overall livelihoods. Given rural women's generally poor access to information and extension exposure, it remains a challenge to convey messages about safe pesticide use to them. Government, the chemical industry, and NGOs have undertaken various campaigns to promote safe pesticide use, but their lasting impact on women's knowledge and on resulting levels of pesticide poisoning is not well documented.

Some of the innovative communication strategies developed in IPM projects could help to convey this important message to rural communities, specifically to women. Aside from the farmer field schools and training-of-trainers initiatives described earlier, these strategies have included radio programs, audio cassettes, and local "resource centers" with exhibits and educational material, including videos of local people's experiences with IPM, comic books, leaflets, and posters. These alternatives might be better alternatives for reaching women.

Important subjects for an awareness campaign include the following:

- *Delineating the links between chemical exposures, the effects on human health and the environment, and gender differences in risks and impacts.* In most communities, people are unaware of their routine, even daily, exposure to toxic chemicals in the workplace, at home, and in the general environment. Raising awareness of the immediate health risks of toxic chemicals used in agriculture in developing countries is an intervention that informs work at all subsequent stages of the policy process.
- *Explaining the different toxicity classes of pesticides and the meaning of their corresponding labels.*
- *Describing the physiological effects of pesticide poisoning (short and long term).* Interesting lessons may be learned from participatory self-assessments of pesticide poisoning among men and women farmers (box 12.17).

Providing access to information, knowledge, and technology that promote new and less hazardous methods of using pesticides is another approach that has shown benefits. Box 12.18 describes how the development of appropriate equipment for applying seed dressings helped to reduce pesticide exposure and its ill effects among women in eastern and southern Africa.

One must emphasize that educational strategies alone cannot protect farmers from the harmful effects of pesticides. Sherwood, Cole, and Murray (2007) note that research financed by the Novartis Foundation—the single largest study ever conducted on pesticide safety concerns—concluded that it was unrealistic to expect poor people in developing countries to manage pesticides safely. Major causes of poisoning in developing countries are the improper labeling, storage, and use of chemicals. Unintentional poisonings account for an estimated 50,000 deaths of children aged 0–14 every year.[5] Sherwood, Cole, and Murray (2007) report that the Novartis Foundation study concluded that "any pesticide manufacturer that cannot guarantee the safe handling and use of its products should withdraw those products from the market"—a scenario difficult to envision in countries where government and industry capacity to enforce standards is severely limited (see the next section). Other factors, including the lack of appropriate protective gear (discussed earlier), the lack of facilities for washing, and the lack of health services, favor the continued unsafe use of pesticides (London and Bailie 2001; Mancini and others 2005).

Reducing access to hazardous chemicals through regulation and enforcement

Access to the more dangerous agrochemicals could be reduced by strengthening and enforcing laws against exposure to hazardous chemicals. Although regulation and

---

Box 12.17   Farmer Self-Monitoring of Pesticide Use in Cotton in India: A Tool to Create Awareness

In 2003 the Integrated Pest Management Program for Cotton in Asia (a joint effort by the European Union and Food and Agriculture Organization) designed a participatory project to assess the frequency and severity of acute pesticide poisoning among cotton growers in Andhra Pradesh, India. Through farmer field schools, the program educated farmers about the adverse effects of pesticides on human health and the environment and presented sustainable alternatives to pesticide use. The assessment of acute pesticide poisoning was conceived as a complementary activity to be undertaken in three villages that had farmer field schools. The idea was to measure the health effects of pesticide exposures in real time (over the course of the cropping season) through direct documentation by farmers. Because previous studies focused on men farmers who applied chemical products, this effort concentrated on women as respondents (for themselves and for their men relatives). The assessment's primary aim was to raise farmers' awareness of the seriousness of the pesticide poisoning occurring in the villages. It also aimed to quantify the problem through direct reporting by farmers.

Source: Mancini and others 2005.

> **Box 12.18 Tanzania and Zambia: Testing a Seed Dressing to Reduce Pesticide Problems**
>
> Women in small- and medium-scale farming suffer the worst health problems from pesticide use because they spray the fields themselves, usually without safety precautions. To assist them, the United Nations Industrial Development Organization (UNIDO) has developed a new way to coat seed with a minimal amount of pesticide ("seed dressing"). Seed dressing has proved to be one of the most effective and economic forms of protection. It can control a wide variety of fungal and bacterial diseases, in addition to soil-borne insects and nematodes. The much lower amount of pesticide used also greatly reduces the environmental and human health impacts.
>
> Seed dressing is already used in many areas, but it is usually restricted to large-scale farmers who can afford the large, expensive, imported machines that are required. UNIDO developed a mobile seed dressing applicator to meet the needs of women in small-scale farming, initially focusing on Arusha in Tanzania and Lusaka in Zambia. Men and women were trained to use the seed dressing equipment and to handle treated seed safely. Trials of the technology were conducted from 1992 to 1994, and the groundwork was laid for commercial implementation. Farming women were very pleased with the new approach, which would not only enable them to increase their yields, food supply, and incomes, but would also dramatically reduce their exposure to pesticides and reduce pollution in the local environment.
>
> *Source:* UNIDO 1995.

enforcement have no explicit gender component, men, women, and children alike would benefit if countries strengthened and enforced the pesticide regulatory framework to conform to best practice as laid out in the FAO Code of Conduct on the Distribution and Use of Pesticides (FAO 2003). The cooperation of the private sector is crucial to the success of such efforts.

Highly hazardous pesticides (Class I) are still common in many smallholder farming systems. Because patents on many of these products expired long ago, chemical companies can market them at bargain prices, which are attractive to farmers. Farmers are also reluctant to stop using them because the pesticides are often highly efficient, and farmers do not know about their serious health and environmental risks. Farmers may also believe that yields will fall if they stop using these chemicals, especially if no alternatives are introduced. Restricting access to highly hazardous pesticides appears to have no measurable negative effect on rural economies, aside from a decline in pesticide sales (Sherwood, Cole, and Murray 2007). Farmers identify alternatives, "proving that these pesticides can be substituted by switching to non-chemical pest control or less toxic pesticides. The latter are usually more expensive than highly toxics, but judicious use leads farmers to use them economically" (Sherwood, Cole, and Murray 2007: 32). Sherwood and coworkers also report that knowledge-based methodologies, including farmer field schools, successfully assisted growers

in abandoning highly hazardous chemicals without suffering reduced yields. They conclude that "despite the claims of governments and industry, the problem with eliminating highly toxics never has been a lack of alternatives, but rather the political will to place the interest of the public over those of influential private actors" (Sherwood, Cole, and Murray 2007: 33).

There is growing recognition, based on ever-more evidence, that Class I pesticides negatively affect health, especially of women and their unborn babies. The rapid physiological changes experienced by women during pregnancy, lactation, and menopause render them more vulnerable to toxins. Exposure to pesticides can cause miscarriage, premature birth, birth defects, and low birth weight (WHO 2006). A substantial portion (up to 33 percent) of a woman's chemical burden can be passed on to an unborn child during gestation and to a baby through breastfeeding.

In light of this and other evidence, FAO encourages the early withdrawal of highly toxic pesticides (FAO 2006). Use of such pesticides is prohibited or severely restricted in OECD countries, and in line with the International Code of Conduct, FAO would like to see them banned at the earliest date in developing countries, where it is virtually impossible to guarantee their safe use. A growing number of developing countries, including China, Thailand, and Vietnam, have are already prohibited the use of methyl parathion, monocrotophos, and several other Class I pesticides.

GUIDELINES AND RECOMMENDATIONS FOR PRACTITIONERS

Pest control is undoubtedly essential for commercial and subsistence farming systems to meet the growing demand for food and contribute to other development goals, but evidence is mounting that the sole reliance on pesticides to achieve such objectives is unsustainable. The high environmental and human costs of pesticide use must now be taken into account, along with the considerable gender effects of pesticide use, which despite their seriousness have been largely ignored.

The strategies discussed in this Module to reduce the use of harmful pesticides can be promoted in parallel. To succeed, they will need supportive policies, and they will also need to be devised with a full understanding of women's circumstances. Several actions must be considered:

- *Government and institutional support:* Alternatives to pesticide use must be promoted actively. Structural factors that encourage the inappropriate and unnecessary use of pesticides—including direct or indirect subsidies; pro-pesticide biases in research, extension, and training; or credit linked to pesticide use—should be removed. Research and extension services require institutional support to conduct work with a clear gender focus.
- *Technical solutions:* Farmers require solutions to their crop protection problems that take account of gender-specific needs. Researchers must work with farmers, recognizing gender divisions of labor, to develop appropriate solutions. This collaboration is particularly important in the promotion of genetically modified crops, because no gender-disaggregated data on risks and benefits are currently available.
- *Farmer participation:* Participatory field schools or their equivalents are good channels for providing information on safe crop protection strategies to farmers, for strengthening many good farmer practices, and for recognizing farmers' expertise. A focus on the gender differences in expertise for different crops and production systems is important. Farmers who use pesticides need to acquire the knowledge and confidence to use sustainable alternatives.
- *Explicit inclusion of women:* Unless women are specifically identified and included in project planning and implementation, and encouraged to assume leadership roles, they are likely to remain invisible. Training, information, and extension to reach these women are essential, or else they will continue to bear many of the consequences of unsafe pesticide use.
- *Messages developed to reach women:* Pest control messages have conventionally been targeted at men farmers, a bias that must be addressed to ensure that women benefit from information campaigns. Messages designed to improve women's awareness, knowledge, and skills with respect to safe pesticide use must be designed to overcome the barriers that are often raised by women's lower socioeconomic status, more limited education, and other constraints. The use of alternative communication channels should be explored.

NOTES

Overview

This Overview was written by Sabine Gündel (Consultant) and reviewed by Ira Matuschke, Mary Hill Rojas, and Catherine Ragasa (Consultants); Regina Laub (FAO); Maria Hartl (IFAD); Robert Tripp (ODI); Eija Pehu (World Bank); and Niels Louwaars (WUR).

1. Although there is not scope in this Module to discuss urban agriculture, recent studies document its benefits among women who are responsible for family food provision (Anosike and Fasona 2004; Ba Diao 2004). Women use urban agriculture as a primary strategy to maintain livelihoods and protect household income through subsistence production. Urban agriculture requires an investment of household resources, such as land, labor, and capital, that can motivate women to go beyond acquiring food for domestic use. Urban food enterprises represent an avenue through which unskilled and uneducated women potentially gain entry into the business milieu (Hovorka and Lee-Smith 2006).

2. For a discussion of broader natural resource management issues in relation to gender, see Module 10.

3. For example, crops with greater amounts of micronutrients that promote human health, such as betacarotene, iron, and zinc.

4. Among many examples, see Adato and Meinzen-Dick (2007).

Thematic Note 1

This Thematic Note was written by Sabine Gündel (Consultant) and reviewed by Ira Matuschke, Mary Hill Rojas, and Catherine Ragasa (Consultants); Regina Laub (FAO); Maria Hartl (IFAD); Robert Tripp (ODI); Eija Pehu (World Bank); and Niels Louwaars (WUR).

Thematic Note 2

This Thematic Note was written by Sabine Gündel (Consultant) and reviewed by Ira Matuschke, Mary Hill Rojas, and

Catherine Ragasa (Consultants); Regina Laub (FAO); Maria Hartl (IFAD); Robert Tripp (ODI); Eija Pehu (World Bank); and Niels Louwaars (WUR).

1. See also International Center for Agricultural Research in the Dry Areas, "Contributions from Seed Programs and Projects," *Seed Info: Official Newsletter of the WANA Seed Network* 33, www.icarda.org.

2. Examples of such crops include self-pollinating crops (common beans, groundnuts, rice), vegetatively propagated crops (potatoes, sweet potatoes, cassava), and crops with limited seed demand (indigenous vegetables, forages, open-pollinated maize) (Scott and others 2003).

3. Louise Sperling, "Finding the Seeds of Recovery Close to Home," *CGIAR News* (March), www.cgiar.org.

4. See also ibid.

5. N. P. Louwaars, "Seed Laws: Biases and Bottlenecks," www.grain.org/seedling_files/seed-05-07-2.pdf.

6. Niels P. Louwaars, "Seed Laws: Biases and Bottlenecks," *Grain* (July): 3–7, www.grain.org/seedling_files/seed-05-07-2.pdf.

7. See note 3 above.

Thematic Note 3

This Thematic Note was written by Sabine Gündel (Consultant) and reviewed by Ira Matuschke, Mary Hill Rojas, and Catherine Ragasa (Consultants); Regina Laub (FAO); Maria Hartl (IFAD); Robert Tripp (ODI); Eija Pehu (World Bank); and Niels Louwaars (WUR).

1. Pesticides are chemicals, including insecticides, herbicides, and fungicides, that are used to control insects, weeds, and other pests and diseases.

2. "Global Occupational Health," http://globalhealthedu.org/Pages/Default.aspx.

3. "Brief 37-2007: Executive Summary Global Status of Commercialized Biotech/GM Crops: 2007," www.isaaa.org.

4. "Indian Cotton Farmers Betrayed," press release, www.i-sis.org.uk.

5. World Health Organization, "What Happens When Children Live in Unhealthy Environments?" Fact Sheet 272, www.who.int/mediacentre/factsheets/fs272/en.

REFERENCES

Overview

Adato, Michelle, and Ruth Meinzen-Dick, eds. 2007. *Agricultural Research, Livelihoods, and Poverty: Studies of Economic and Social Impacts in Six Countries.* Washington, DC: International Food Policy Research Institute.

Adjei-Nsiah, Samuel, Thomas W. Kuyper, Cees Leeuwis, Mark K. Abekoe, and Ken E. Giller. 2007. "Evaluating Sustainable and Profitable Cropping Sequences with Cassava and Four Legume Crops: Effects on Soil Fertility and Maize Yields in the Forest/Savannah Transitional Agroecological Zone of Ghana." *Field Crop Research* 103 (2): 87–97.

Anosike, Vide, and Mayowa Fasona. 2004. "Gender Dimensions of Urban Commercial Farming in Lagos, Nigeria." *Urban Agriculture Magazine* 12: 27–28.

Ash, Neville, and Martin Jenkins. 2007. "Biodiversity and Poverty Reduction: The Importance of Biodiversity for Ecosystem Services." Cambridge: United Nations Environment Programme World Conservation Monitoring Centre.

Ba Diao, Maty. 2004. "Women and Periurban Agriculture in the Niayes Zone of Senegal." *Urban Agriculture Magazine* 12: 23–24.

Badstue, Lone B., Mauricio R. Bellon, Julien Berthaud, Alejandro Ramírez, Dagoberto Flores, and Xochitl Juárez. 2007. "The Dynamics of Farmers' Maize Seed Supply Practices in the Central Valleys of Oaxaca, Mexico." *World Development* 35 (9): 1579–93.

Balakrishnan, Revathi, and Peggy Fairbairn-Dunlop. 2005. "Rural Women and Food Security in Asia and the Pacific: Prospects and Paradoxes." FAO, Regional Office for Asia and the Pacific, Bangkok.

Chambers, Robert. 1997. *Whose Reality Counts? Putting the First Last.* London: Intermediate Technology Publications.

Cline, William R. 2007. "Global Warming and Agriculture." Brief, September, Centre for Global Development, Washington, DC.

CropLife International. 2007. *CropLife International Annual Report, 2006–2007.* Brussels: CropLife International.

Crucefix, David. 1998. *Organic Agriculture and Sustainable Rural Livelihoods in Developing Countries.* Chatham: Natural Resources and Ethical Trade Programme, Natural Resources Institute.

Delgado, Christopher L., and Chandrashekhar G. Ranade. 1987. "Technological Change and Agricultural Labor Use." In *Accelerating Food Production in Sub-Saharan Africa*, ed. John W. Mellor, Christopher L. Delgado, and Malcolm Blackie, 118–35. Baltimore: Johns Hopkins University Press.

Department for International Development (DFID). 2005. *Growth and Poverty Reduction: The Role of Agriculture.* London: DFID.

———. 2007. *Gender Equality at the Heart of Development: Why the Role of Women Is Crucial to Ending World Poverty.* London: DFID.

Doss, Cheryl R. 1999. "Twenty-five Years of Research on Women Farmers in Africa: Lessons and Implications for Agricultural Research Institutions." With an Annotated Bibliography. CIMMYT (International Maize and Wheat Improvement Center) Economics Program Paper No. 99-02, International Maize and Wheat Improvement Center, Mexico, DF.

Food and Agriculture Organization (FAO). 2007a. "Gender and Food Security. Synthesis Report of Regional Documents: Africa, Asia and Pacific, Europe, Near East, Latin America." FAO, Rome.

———. 2007b. "Women and Food Security." FAO, Rome.

———. 2007c. "Gender and Food Security: Facts and Figures." FAO, Rome.

———. 2008. "Improving Seed Management Interventions: Lessons Learned from the Field: A Review of Selected LinKS Studies." FAO, Rome.

Gabre-Madhin, Eleni, Christopher Barrett, and Paul Dorosh. 2003. "Technological Change and Price Effects in Agriculture: Conceptual and Comparative Perspectives." MTID Discussion Paper 62, International Food Policy Research Institute, Washington, DC.

Gladwin, Christina H., Anne M. Thomson, Jennifer S. Peterson, and Andrea S. Anderson. 2001. "Addressing Food Security in Africa via Multiple Livelihood Strategies of Women Farmers." *Food Policy* 26: 177–207.

Gruère, Guillaume P., Alessandra Giuliani, and Melinda Smale. 2006. "Marketing Underutilized Plant Species for the Benefit of the Poor: A Conceptual Framework." IFPRI Environmental and Protection Technology Discussion Paper No. 154, International Food Policy Research Institute, Washington, DC.

Hirschmann, David, and Megan Vaughan. 1984. *Women Farmers of Malawi: Food Production in the Zomba District.* Berkeley: Institute of International Studies.

Horie, Takeshi, Tatsuhiko Shiraiwa, Koki Homma, Keisuke Katsura, Yohei Maeda, and Hiroe Yoshida. 2005. "Can Yields of Lowland Rice Resume the Increases That They Showed in the 1980s?" *Plant Production Science* 8 (3): 259–74.

Hovorka, Alice J., and Diana Lee-Smith. 2006. "Gendering the Urban Agriculture Agenda." In *Cities Farming for the Future: Urban Agriculture for Green and Productive Cities,* ed. R. van Veenhuizen. Leusden: RUAF Foundation, International Institute of Rural Reconstruction, and International Development Research Centre.

Howard, Patricia, ed. 2003. *Women and Plants: Gender Relations in Biodiversity Management and Conservation.* London: Zed Books.

International Fund for Agricultural Development (IFAD). 2007. "European Commission and IFAD Commit to Increased Investment in Agriculture for Rural Poverty Eradication." Press release.

Jiggins, Janice, R. K. Samanta, and Janice E. Olawoye. 1997. "Improving Women Farmers' Access to Extension Services." In *Improving Agricultural Extension: A Reference Manual,* ed. Burton E. Swanson, Robert P. Bentz, and Andrew J. Sofranko, chapter 9. Rome: Food and Agriculture Organization.

Levi, Michael. 1987. 'Weapons of the Strong: and How the Weak Resist Them." Paper presented at the Midwest Political Science Association Meeting, Chicago.

Lipton, Michael. 2005. "The Family Farm in a Globalizing World: The Role of Crop Science in Alleviating Poverty." 2020 Policy Brief No. 74, International Food Policy Research Institute, Washington, DC.

McSweeney, Brenda G. 1979. "Collection and Analysis of Data on Rural Women's Time Use." *Studies in Family Planning* 10 (11/12): 379–83.

Millennium Ecosystem Assessment. 2005. *Ecosystems and Human Well-Being: Synthesis.* Washington, DC: Island Press.

Murgai, Rinku. 2001. "The Green Revolution and the Productivity Paradox: Evidence from Indian Punjab." *Agricultural Economics* 25: 199–209.

New Economic Foundation (NEF). 2006. *A Long Row to Hoe: Family Farming and Rural Poverty in Developing Countries.* London: NEF.

Oluoch-Kosura, Willis, and Joseph T. Karugia. 2005. "Why the Early Promise for Rapid Increases in Maize Productivity in Kenya Was Not Sustained: Lessons for Sustainable Investment in Agriculture." In *The African Food Crisis,* ed. Goran Djurfeldt, Hans Holmen, Magnus Jirstrom, and Rolf Larsson, 181–96. Wallington: CABI.

Pala, Achola O. 1983. "Women's Access to Land and Their Role in Agriculture and Decision-Making on the Farm: Experiences of the Joluo of Kenya." *Journal of Eastern African Research and Development* 13: 69–85.

Smale, Melinda, Lamissa Diakité, Brahima Dembélé, Issa Seni Traoré, Oumar Guindo, and Bouréma Konta. 2008. "Trading Millet and Sorghum Genetic Resources: Women Vendors in the Village Fairs of San and Douentza, Mali." IFPRI Discussion Paper No. 746, International Food Policy Research Institute, Washington, DC.

Tripp, Robert. 2006. *Self-Sufficient Agriculture: Labor and Knowledge in Small-Scale Farming.* London: Earthscan.

World Bank. 2003. *Reaching the Rural Poor: a Renewed Strategy for Rural Development.* Washington, DC: World Bank.

———. 2007. *World Development Report 2008: Agriculture for Development.* Washington, DC: World Bank.

————. 2008. "Agriculture for Development: The Gender Dimensions." Agriculture for Development Policy Brief for the *World Development Report 2008*, World Bank, Washington, DC.

Thematic Note I

Adato, Michelle, and Ruth Meinzen-Dick, eds. 2007. *Agricultural Research, Livelihoods, and Poverty: Studies of Economic and Social Impacts in Six Countries.* Washington, DC: International Food Policy Research Institute.

Altieri, Miguel A. 2002. "Non-Certified Organic Agriculture in Developing Countries." In *Organic Agriculture, Environment and Food Security,* ed. Nadia El-Hage Scialabba and Caroline Hattam, chapter 4. Rome: Food and Agriculture Organization.

Atampugre, Nick. 1993. *Behind the Stone Lines.* Oxford: Oxfam.

Budelman, Arnoud, and Toon DeFoer. 2000. "Not by Nutrients Alone: A Call to Broaden the Soil Fertility Initiative." *Natural Resources Forum* 24: 173–84.

Crawford, Eric, Thomas. S. Jayne, and Valerie Kelly. 2005. "Alternative Approaches for Promoting Fertilizer Use in Africa, with Particular Reference to the Role of Fertilizer Subsidies." Department of Agricultural Economics, Michigan State University, East Lansing.

Critchley, Will, Milcah Ong'ayo, and Janet Njoroge. 2001. "Women and Innovation: Experiences from Promoting Farmer Innovation in East Afria." In *Farmer Innovation in Africa,* ed. Chris Reij and Ann Waters-Bayer, 110–21. London: Earthscan.

Datta, Dipankar, and Kamal Kar. 2006. "Getting the Message Across: Promoting Ecological Agriculture in Bangladesh." Gatekeeper Series 122, International Institute for Environment and Development, London.

DeFoer, Toon, and Ian Scoones. 2001. "Participatory Approaches to Integrated Soil Fertility Management." In *Dynamics and Diversity: Soil Fertility and Farming Livelihoods in Africa,* ed. Ian Scoones, 164–75. London: Earthscan.

de Jager, André, Stephen M. Nandwa, and Peter F. Okoth. 1998. "Monitoring Nutrient Flows and Economic Performance in African Farming Systems (NUTMON). I. Concepts and Methodologies." *Agriculture, Ecosystems, and Environment* 71 (1–3): 37–48.

Department for International Development (DFID). 2002. "Soil Fertility and Nutrient Management." Key Sheets for Sustainable Livelihoods, DFID, London.

Food and Agriculture Organization (FAO). 2005a. *Current World Fertilizer Trends and Outlook to 2009/10.* Rome: FAO.

————. 2005b. "The Importance of Soil Organic Matter: Key to Drought-Resistant Soil and Sustained Food and Production." *FAO Soils Bulletin* 80, FAO, Rome.

————. 2006. "Fertilizer Use by Country." *FAO Fertilizer and Plant Nutrition Bulletin* 17, FAO, Rome.

————. 2007. "Organic Agriculture and Food Security." FAO, Rome.

Haile, Mitiku, Fetien Abay, and Ann Waters-Bayer. 2001. "Joining Forces to Discover and Celebrate Local Innovations in Land Husbandry in Tigray, Ethiopia." In *Farmer Innovation in Africa: A Source of Inspiration for Agricultural Development,* ed. Chris Reij and Ann Waters-Bayer, 58–73. London: Earthscan.

Hallman, Kelly, David Lewis, and Suraiya Begum. 2003. "An Integrated Economic and Social Analysis to Assess the Impact of Vegetable and Fishpond Technologies on Poverty in Rural Bangladesh." EPTD (Environmental and Production Technology Div.) Discussion Paper No. 112, International Food Policy Research Institute, Washington, DC.

Hartemink, Alfred E. 2004. "Soil Fertility Decline on Agricultural Plantations in the Tropics." Paper presented at the IFA Regional Conference for Asia and the Pacific, Auckland, New Zealand, December 14–16.

Interagency Coalition on AIDS and Development (ICAD). 2004. *HIV/AIDS, Gender Inequality, and the Agricultural Sector: Guidelines for Incorporating HIV/AIDS and Gender Considerations into Agricultural Programming in High Incidence Countries.* Ottawa: ICAD.

International Fund for Agricultural Development (IFAD). 2002. "The Rural Poor: Survival or a Better Life? The Choice between Destruction of Resources and Sustainable Development." Paper submitted to the World Summit on Sustainable Development, Johannesburg, September.

Kerr, Rachel Bezner, Sieglinde Snapp, Marko Chirwa, Lizzie Shumba, and Rodgers Msachi. 2007. "Participatory Research on Legume Diversification with Malawian Smallholder Farmers for Improved Human Nutrition and Soil Fertility." *Experimental Agriculture* 43: 437–53.

Korinek, Jane. 2005. "Trade and Gender: Issues and Interactions." OECD Trade Policy Working Paper No. 24. Organization for Economic Co-operation and Development, Paris.

New Economic Foundation (NEF). 2006. *A Long Row to Hoe: Family Farming and Rural Poverty in Developing Countries.* London: NEF.

Sumberg, James, Christine Okali, and David Reece. 2003. "Agricultural Research in the Face of Diversity, Local Knowledge, and the Participation Imperative: Theoretical Considerations." *Agricultural Systems* 76: 739–53.

UN Millennium Project. 2005. "Investing in Development: A Practical Plan to Achieve the Millennium Development Goals." United Nations Development Programme, New York.

Uphoff, Norman. 2002. *Agroecological Innovations.* London: Earthscan.

van Dam, A. A. 2005. "The Future of Oil and Agriculture in Developing Countries." Master's thesis, School of Development Studies, University of East Anglia, Norwich.

White, Marceline, Carlos Salas, and Sarah Gammage. 2003. "Trade Impact Review: Mexico Case Study. NAFTA and the FTAA: A Gender Analysis of Employment and Poverty Impacts in Agriculture." Women's Edge Coalition, Washington, DC.

World Bank. 2007. *World Development Report 2008: Agriculture for Development.* Washington, DC: World Bank.

Wynen, Els, and David Vanzetti. 2002. "Certified Organic Agriculture: Situation and Outlook." In *Organic Agriculture, Environment and Food Security,* ed. Nadia El-Hage Sciallaba and Caroline Hattam, chapter 3. Rome: FAO.

Thematic Note 2

African Seed and Biotechnology Programme (ASBP). 2006. "African Seed and Biotechnology Programme: Twenty-fourth Regional Conference for Africa." Conference Proceedings. Bamako, Mali, January 30–February 3.

Almekinders, Conny J. M., Niels P. Louwaars, and G. H. de Bruijn. 1994. "Local Seed Systems and Their Importance for Improved Seed Supply in Developing Countries." *Euphytica* 78: 207–16.

DAC Evaluation Resource Centre (DEReC). 2007. "Ethiopia Seed System Development Project (SSDP)." Report No. 40124, DEReC, World Bank, Washington, DC.

Deutsche Gesellschaft für Technische Zusammenarbeit (GTZ) and Center for Genetic Resources, the Netherlands (CGN). 2000. *Support for the Informal Seed Sector in Development Cooperation: Conceptual Issues.* Eschborn, Germany: GTZ and CGN.

Food and Agriculture Organization (FAO). 2002. "Rural and Tribal Women in Agrobiodiversity Conservation: An Indian Case Study." RAP Publication 2002/08, FAO Regional Office for Asia and the Pacific, FAO, Bangkok, and M. S. Swaminathan Research Foundation.

———. 2006. "Community Diversity Seed Fairs in Tanzania: Guidelines for Seed Fairs." Report No. 51, FAO, Rome.

———. 2008a. "Brazil: Community Seed Banks, Paraiba." Sustainable Agriculture and Rural Development, FAO, Rome.

———. 2008b. "Improving Seed Management Interventions. Lessons Learned from the Field: A Review of Selected LinKS Studies." FAO, Rome.

Hossain, Mahabub. 1988. "Natures and Impact of the Green Revolution in Bangladesh." IFPRI Research Report No. 67, International Food Policy Research Institute, Washington, DC.

Louwaars, Niels P. 1994. "Integrated Seed Supply: Institutional Linkages in Relation to System Efficiency, Biodiversity, and Gender." In *Alternative Approaches to Bean Seed Production and Distribution in Eastern and Southern Africa: Proceedings of a Working Group Meeting, Kampala: International Center for Tropical Agriculture (CIAT),* ed. Soniia David. Kampala: CIAT.

———. 2007. "Seeds of Confusion: The Impact of Policies on Seed Systems." Ph.D. dissertation. Wageningen University, the Netherlands.

Maredia, Mywish, and Julie A. Howard. 1998. "Facilitating Seed Sector Transformation in Africa: Key Findings from the Literature." Policy Synthesis No. 33, United States Agency for International Development (USAID) Bureau for Africa, Washington, DC.

Musopole, Edson. 2000. "Small-Scale Seed Production and Marketing in Malawi: The Case of a Smallholder Seed Development Project." In *Finance and Management of Small-Scale Seed Enterprises,* ed. Sam Kugbei, Michael Turner, and Peter Witthaut, 78–83. Proceedings of a Workshop on Finance and Management of Small-Scale Seed Enterprises, October 26–30, 1998, Addis Ababa, Ethiopia. Aleppo, Syria: ICARDA (International Center for Agricultural Research in the Dry Areas).

Pionetti, Carine. 2006. "Seed Diversity in the Drylands: Women and Farming in South India." Gatekeeper 126, International Institute for Environment and Development, London.

Scott, Jason, Patrick Kambewa, Rowland Chirwa, and Vas Aggarwal. 2003. "Local Seed Systems for Beans in Malawi." CIAT Africa Occasional Publication Series, No. 40. CIAT (International Center for Tropical Agriculture), Kampala.

Smale, Melissa, Brahima Dembélé, Issa Seni Traoré, Oumar Guindo, and Bouréma Konta. 2007. "Trading Millet and Sorghum Genetic Resources: Women Vendors in the Village Fairs of San and Douentza, Mali." Discussion Paper, International Food Policy Research Institute, Washington, DC.

Sperling, Louise, and H. David Cooper. 2003. "Understanding Seed Systems and Strengthening Seed Security." Background paper for Effective and Sustainable Seed Relief: A Stakeholder Workshop, FAO, Rome, May 26–28.

Sperling, Louise, and Tom Remington, with Jon M. Haugen. 2006. "Seed Aid for Seed Security: Advice for Practitioners."

Practice Briefs 1–10, International Center for Tropical Agriculture and Catholic Relief Services, Rome.

Sperling, Louise, Tom Remington, Jon M. Haugen, and Sigrid Nagoda, eds. 2004. *Addressing Seed Security in Disaster Response: Linking Relief with Development*. Cali: International Center for Tropical Agriculture.

Stirling, Clare M., and John R. Witcombe. 2004. *Farmers and Plant Breeders in Partnership*. 2nd ed. London: Department for International Development.

World Bank. 2005. *Agricultural Investment Sourcebook*. Washington, DC: World Bank.

———. 2006. "Intellectual Property Rights: Designing Regimes to Support Plant Breeding in Developing Countries." Agriculture and Rural Development. Report No. 35517, World Bank, Washington, DC.

———. 2007. *World Development Report 2008: Agriculture for Development*. Washington, DC: World Bank.

Thematic Note 3

CropLife International. 2007. "This Is Agriculture." *CropLife International Annual Report, 2006–2007*. Brussels: CropLife International.

Fakih, Mansour, Toto Rahardjo, and Michel P. Pimbert. 2003. *Community Integrated Pest Management in Indonesia*. London: International Institute for Environment and Development.

Feder, Gershon, Rinku Murgai, and Jaime B. Quizon. 2004. "Sending Farmers Back to School: The Impact of Farmer Field Schools in Indonesia." *Review of Agricultural Economics* 26 (1): 45–62.

Food and Agriculture Organization (FAO). 1999. "Technical Assistance to the Integrated Pest Management Training Project: Indonesia." Report No. AG: UTF/INS/072/INS, FAO, Rome.

———. 2000. "Inter-Country Programme for Community IPM in Asia: Phase IV Mid Term Review." FAO, Rome.

———. 2003. *International Code of Conduct on the Distribution and Use of Pesticides*. Rome: FAO.

———. 2004. *Agricultural Biotechnology: Meeting the Needs of the Poor? The State of Food and Agriculture 2003–2004*. Rome: FAO.

———. 2006. "FAO Encourages Early Withdrawal of Highly Toxic Pesticides." News release, December.

Food and Agriculture Organization (FAO), United Nations Environment Programme (UNEP), and World Health Organization (WHO). 2004. "Childhood Pesticide Poisoning: Information for Advocacy and Action." UNEP, New York.

Food and Agriculture Organization (FAO)/World Health Organization (WHO). 2001. "Amount of Poor-Quality Pesticides Sold in Developing Countries Alarmingly High." FAO/WHO press release, February 1.

Food and Agriculture Organization (FAO) and World Bank. 2000. "Agricultural Knowledge and Information Systems for Rural Development (AKIS/RD): Strategic Vision and Guiding Principles." FAO, Rome.

International Fund for Agricultural Development (IFAD). 2002. "The Rural Poor: Survival or a Better Life? The Choice between Destruction of Resources and Sustainable Development." World Summit on Sustainable Development, Johannesburg, South Africa, August 26–September 4.

———. 2007. "Climate Change, Biofuel Markets, and Migration to Feature in African Green Revolution Conference." Press release.

International Institute for Environment and Development (IIED). 2003. "The Millennium Development Goals and Local Processes: Hitting the Target or Missing the Point?" IIED, London.

London, Leslie, and Ross Bailie. 2001. "Challenges for Improving Surveillance for Pesticide Poisoning: Policy Implications for Developing Countries." *International Journal of Epidemiology* 30 (3): 564–70.

Mancini, Francesca, Ariena van Bruggen, and Janice Jiggins. 2007. "Evaluating Cotton Integrated Pest Management (IPM) Farmer Field School Outcomes Using the Sustainable Livelihoods Approach in India." *Experimental Agriculture* 43: 97–112.

Mancini, Francesca, Ariena van Bruggen, Janice Jiggins, Arun Ambatipudi, and Helen Murphy. 2005. "Acute Pesticide Poisoning among Female and Male Cotton Growers in India." *International Journal of Occupational and Environmental Health* 11 (3): 221–32.

Nhat Tuyen, Nguyen. 1997. "Women Farmers and IPM Farmer Field Schools in Viet Nam." *ILEIA Newsletter* 13 (4): 20.

Rother, Hanna Andrea. 2000. "Influences of Pesticide Risk Perception on the Health of Rural South African Women and Children." *African Newsletter on Occupational Safety and Health* 2: 42–46.

Sherwood, Stephen, Donald Cole, and Douglas Murray. 2007. "It's Time to Ban Highly Hazardous Pesticides." *LEISA Magazine* (September): 32–33.

Systemwide Program on Integrated Pest Management (SP-IPM). 2006. "Biological Alternatives to Harmful Chemical Pesticides." IPM Research Brief No. 4, SP-IPM Secretariat, International Institute of Tropical Agriculture, Cotonou.

Tripp, Robert, Mahinda Wijeratne, and V. Hiroshini Piyadasa. 2005. "What Should We Expect from Farmer Field Schools? A Sri Lanka Case Study." *World Development* 33 (10): 1705–20.

United Nations. 1992. "Agenda 21." UN Department of Economics and Social Affairs, Rome.

United Nations Industrial Development Organization (UNIDO). 1995. "Women, Industry, and Environment: Sample Cases." Women in Industry Series, UNIDO, Vienna.

World Bank. 2007. *World Development Report 2008: Agriculture for Development.* Washington, DC: World Bank.

World Health Organization (WHO). 2006. "Gender Equality, Work and Health: A Review of the Evidence." WHO, Geneva.

FURTHER READING

Thematic Note 1

Food and Agriculture Organization. n.d. "Sustainable Land Management and Soil Productivity Improvement in Support of Food Security in Sub-Saharan Africa." Available at www.fao.org/ag/agl/agll/farmspi/spi.stm.

Muzira, Robert N., Pamela N. Pali, Pascal C. Sanginga, and Robert J. Delve. 2007. "Farmers' Participation in Soil Fertility Management Research Process: Dilemma in Rehabilitating Degraded Hilltops in Kabale, Uganda." In *Advances in Integrated Soil Fertility Management in Sub-Saharan Africa: Challenges and Opportunities,* ed. Andre Bationo, Boaz S. Waswa, Job Kihara, and Joseph Kimetu, 1051–59. Dordrecht: Springer.

Thematic Note 3

Chandrasekar, K., and G. T. Gujar. 2004. "Bt Cotton Benefits Short-Lived—Study." Indian Agricultural Research Institute. *Financial Express* (India), February 11.

van den Berg, Henk, and Janice Jiggins. 2007. "Investing in Farmers: The Impact of Farmer Field Schools in Relation to Integrated Pest Management." *World Development* 35 (4): 663–86.

Wilson, Clevo, and Clem Tisdell. 2001. "Why Farmers Continue to Use Pesticides Despite Environmental, Health and Sustainability Costs." *Ecological Economics* 39: 449–62.

Gender in Fisheries and Aquaculture

Overview

The fisheries and aquaculture sector is estimated to provide direct employment and revenue to 200 million people. The increasing demand on the sector is met by both large-scale and industrial production systems and small-scale and artisanal production systems. Small-scale fisheries of all kinds are a major source of animal protein in many parts of the world. Facing declining fish stocks in capture fisheries, aquaculture has been the focus of development investment since the 1980s and is now the fastest-growing food sector in the world. It is expected to contribute more than 50 percent of total fish consumption by 2020. Although just over 90 percent of this production originates in Asia, and nearly 70 percent in China alone, efforts continue to expand its production into new areas, such as sub-Saharan Africa and Latin America. Aquaculture is promoted as an alternative and sustainable income source to those involved in capture fisheries and agriculture, as long as environmental and disease issues are addressed (Belton and Little 2008; World Bank 2006). It is also viewed as being especially attractive to rural women because it can be carried out with minimal investment and close to homesteads and can be integrated into existing food systems.

This Module details investments that address livelihood problems arising from the ongoing changes in production systems, marketing, and technology in the fisheries and aquaculture sector and examines investments that reflect gender inequities that exist in many societies.[1] These gender inequities include the comparatively low value attached to work done by women, and women's limited access to essential resources such as ponds, new technology, education, and information and skills. These inequities reflect societal norms of masculinity and femininity that determine who can and should do what and are visible in local communities, in institutions serving these communities, and in the way many national and international organizations operate. The investments include the following:

- The formation at the community level of gender-responsive resource management bodies and small groups for accessing resources needed for aquaculture development (see Thematic Note 1 and Innovative Activity Profile 1)
- The provision of gender-responsive advisory services that address systematic bias in essential services providing information and skills if small-scale family production systems are to remain competitive and everyone is to benefit (see Thematic Note 2 and Innovative Activity Profile 2)
- Action to enable marginalized groups of fishers, processors, and traders to access new national and international markets and to obtain improvements in work conditions in new labor markets (processing and packaging factories at sea or on land) that are largely unregulated (see Thematic Note 3)
- Support to marginalized groups, including poor women, in identifying and sustaining alternative livelihoods to reduce

reliance on their fishing activities, which put pressure on the fragile and constricted marine resources and coastal ecosystems (see Thematic Note 4).

All these investments are concerned with protecting livelihoods at risk and supporting strategic changes in gender relations that will enable everyone to gain.

GENDER ROLES, POWER, AND THE DISTRIBUTION OF PROFITS

Fisheries and aquaculture value chains are diverse and often complex and dynamic systems, with men and women often undertaking different and changing roles depending on local norms about resource access and control and mobility, type of technology involved, the extent of commercialization, and the product involved. Table 13.1 illustrates some of this diversity for capture fisheries. As indicated in the table, many small-scale fisheries operate with the men investing in fishing vessels, nets, and other gear and doing the fishing and with the women investing in processing equipment and being responsible for fish purchasing, processing, and sales, but this pattern is not followed everywhere. In terms of boat investments, in some situations women use the proceeds from their trading to invest in boats and gear—for example, in Ghana, West Africa, described by Walker (2001), and in the Lake Victoria fisheries bordering Uganda, described by Allison (2003). These women may not enter the water to fish but may hire crews for their own boats, thus securing their incomes from fresh or processed fish. In Cambodia, the Democratic Republic of Congo, and Thailand and in indigenous fisheries in Latin America, women are involved in boat fishing, and in a number of other countries (Benin, the Democratic Republic of Congo, and a number of countries in Asia, including Bangladesh and India) women collect shellfish, including crabs, and produce shellfish seed. Women's involvement in fish processing is widespread and, along with the collection activities described here, is regarded as an appropriate activity for women given their domestic tasks and responsibilities.

In small-scale systems, although it is possible to detail the divisions of labor by sex, often whole families are involved.[2] Therefore, even though it is largely men who fish and women who purchase the fish, the women may include wives and other women relatives, especially those who have helped the fisher in the past, and traders who have provided credit, who may also be relatives. Jul-Larsen and others (2003) describe the multiplicity and complexity of the relationships that men fishers working on Lake Victoria have with their women

buyers and how these relationships influence how much fish they are allowed to buy. Consequently, even if one sex faces greater business risks than the other, without detailed, context-specific intrahousehold information on roles and responsibilities, it is difficult to predict the impact on household livelihoods.

Regardless of gender-role differences, wealthier groups of women and men play dominant roles in the parts of the chains where they operate. Poor members of the chain have weak bargaining power and little control over others in the chain and prices paid for goods and services, and they are more vulnerable than wealthier groups to decreases in catch and poor services because they are unable to accumulate assets. For example, in capture fisheries not all men own boats. The majority work as crew and may never accumulate enough assets to own a boat (Allison 2003). The same is true of processors and traders. In parts of West Africa a hierarchy of traders and processors exist, with younger and poorer women working for wealthier ones and depending on them for their livelihoods. The situation of these poorer women involved in fish processing is demonstrated in the following description from the Sustainable Fisheries Livelihoods Programme (SFLP 2006: 6) of women fish processors in West Africa:

> Their activities are less profitable; they access poor quality fish and are unable to keep fish fresh thereby attracting higher prices, since they have no information on marketing or ice. Loans from micro-finance institutions serve more as revolving funds for marketing than investment loans for fishing and processing equipment. Informal and formal credit is risky because profits are minimal. Poorer women use revolving funds to meet household expenses in periods of poor catch which reduces funds available for business. Most female-owned fishery enterprises are therefore small, and grow slowly, if at all (Benin, Niger and The Gambia in West Africa).

The distribution of power and therefore of profits is similar in aquaculture chains and can be demonstrated by looking at the shrimp value chain, which is dominated by China, Ecuador, Indonesia, and Thailand. A considerable part of this market is almost entirely in the hands of large producers, supported by external capital, and destined for the international market. In Bangladesh, which is also one of the major players in the market for shrimp, most shrimp production is in the hands of small producers, although processing is completed in factories (Gammage and others 2006).[3] Figure 13.1 indicates the various stakeholders and resources involved.

As many as 1.2 million individuals are reported to be directly involved in the shrimp value chain in Bangladesh,

Table 13.1 Gender Roles in the Capture Fisheries Value Chain

Scale	Region	Investment	Catch	Processing	Sales
Small	Sub-Saharan Africa	• Capital for boats and gear from processing and fish sales • Community management groups invest in landing sites and refrigeration • Women invest in processing and drying	• Boat owners: wealthy and older women and men • Crew: young men and boys • Nets: young boys • Mending nets: women of all ages • Women collect shellfish, for example, Benin and Congo	Women smoke and dry fish and cook for sale	• Fresh fish purchase by women for drying/processing and sale • Fresh fish sales depend on ice plants managed by local committees and private owners (especially fishers). Sales are to long-distance traders and to women for local sales. Women transport fish and act as middlemen.
Small	Asia	• Savings: women • China: women and men invest	• Boat owners: wealthy and older men • Crew: adult and young men • Women and men mend nets • Women collect shellfish, for example, Cambodia and Thailand	Women smoke and dry fish	• Women and men sell in local markets, and to contractors for international and national markets • Sales are more likely to be controlled by men in "conservative" locations
Small	Latin America	Especially indigenous community fisheries	• Boat owners: women in Wayuu indigenous communities • Women and men fish in Brazil and Mexico • Crew: young men	Women and young men	• Women and young men in local sales. Colombia: women and young men in Wayuu communities; Honduras: indigenous Garifuna fish traders. • Supermarkets buy through contractors
Large	National/ global	International and national capital	Industrial fishing fleets dominate in some countries in Latin America but are also significant in other locations	Factories: • Women clean, resize, control quality • Men fillet and supervise	• Large local and international buyers, including supermarkets, especially in Latin America, southern Africa, and parts of Asia control marketing

Source: Personal communication with Chitra Deshpande. Analysis based on various sources.
Note: The men and women involed in small-scale production systems may be family members. In Latin America artisanal or small-scale fishers have larger boats (are semi-industrial) than in similar systems in other regions.

with a further 4.8 million household members indirectly dependent on it for their livelihoods. Nevertheless, profits generated from shrimp exports are not shared equally throughout the chain, and middlemen and exporters realize more profits than farmers and fry catchers. Fry catchers are the most vulnerable workers along the chain. They are often locked in a cycle of debt with others higher up in the chain, although this is not to say that indebtedness does not appear elsewhere in the chain. The chain is also a highly sex-segmented labor market, with women and men receiving different wages along the chain for the work they do. Women fry catchers and sorters earn about 64 percent of

Figure 13.1   Flow Diagram of the Shrimp Value Chain in Bangladesh

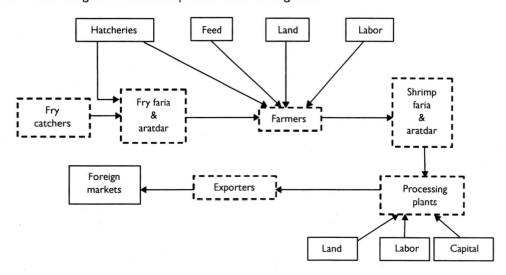

Source: Gammage and others 2006.

Note: Faria are intermediaries who buy and sell products in Bangladesh. *Aratdar* are commission agents or intermediaries who buy and sell products in Bangladesh.

what men fry catchers and sorters earn, for example, and these differences are linked directly with women's domestic roles. Women are also found in the most insecure nodes of the shrimp chain—working as fry catchers and laborers, and undertaking various low-paid tasks in the shrimp-processing plants.

With increased mechanization in production and even a reported influx of newcomers into the sector as other sectors decline, the pressure on resources increases, and many of the existing actors struggle to maintain their position. Women are frequently the first to lose their role in the sector. The following quotation from Tietze and others (2007: 3) about capture fisheries in the states of Maharashtra and Orissa in India is typical of what is detailed for many countries as systems become more commercialized: "Motorization and mechanization of fishing vessels led to a concentration of fish landings at fewer harbours and landing sites and, in some cases, resulted in the takeover of fish trade by fish merchants [who were men]. This process displaced many women from the retailing of fish."

Reports from a few locations tell of women engaging in sex-for-fish exchanges to ensure their access to fish (SFLP 2006), and others may seek employment in industrial processing factories. In Latin America these factories serve local supermarkets as well as the North American export market. Elsewhere, processing factories are more likely to be exclu-

sively serving the export market, although this may be changing rapidly. Both women and men are reported to be benefiting from employment in these factories even though conditions may be poor, but women are frequently reported as benefiting least. For example, women from fishing communities in Orissa State (India) become wage earners in the growing seafood export processing industry, but at a cost—they have to stay away from their homes for longer periods, which makes it more difficult for them to fulfill their domestic roles, their wages are lower than those of men doing the same work, and they experience poorer working conditions (Tietze and others 2007). In Bangladesh women are also paid less than men, and their employment is casual and temporary (Gammage and others 2006). Women find themselves in similar situations in processing factories in Kenya (Markussen 2002), Latin America (Josupeit 2004), and Sri Lanka (de Silva and Yamao 2006) (see also Module 8).

GENDER PLANNING

From this Overview of the fisheries and aquaculture sector, it is evident that asset access and control is vital for enabling those involved not only to survive but also to gain from ongoing changes in the sector. These assets include everything from financial capital and ovens to knowledge about new production systems and skills and collective organizing to enable less-powerful actors to deal with powerful players in the value chains. Although the Sustainable Livelihoods framework points to the need for strategic investments to be made to challenge policies and social attitudes that limit the choices and options available to less powerful individuals and groups, various development programs using livelihood approaches give the sense that targeting asset provision to achieve these strategic changes is a straightforward process. However, asset provision has been shown to be easily subverted in the face of existing norms and values about what different categories of women and men can and should do under certain circumstances, including when they are in the presence of more powerful players (see Thematic Note 1).

Although many women and men have benefited from ongoing changes in this sector, in a number of programs women's reproductive roles (their caring responsibilities for both children and adults) and their current economic roles have been used to justify limiting their role in new aquaculture systems (in northeastern Thailand and in Bangladesh, reported by Kelkar 2001 and Barman 2001, respectively). They can also be subverted by implementing organizations that argue that it is too expensive to include both women and men in training programs and that it is too difficult to justify organizationally given the interest in supporting small-scale family production systems (see Thematic Note 2 for a more detailed discussion on family approaches). The outcomes of these kinds of decisions reinforce gender inequities that already exist or even introduce inequity where it did not previously exist; women may be left in the position of helpers to others, possibly weakening their bargaining positions over the allocation of benefits produced. Alternatively, they might be placed in less-valued jobs.[4] These issues of exclusion are addressed in the interventions detailed in Thematic Notes 1 and 2.

The rapidly changing marketing situation for fish products and the growth of inequalities within fisheries and marketing chains also point to the need for some kind of protection against livelihood threats.[5] These are explored in gender analysis but not in livelihoods. What might be referred to as social protection investment might include directly supporting women's entry into new markets and more profitable enterprises, working to raise the awareness of the dangers of fish-for-sex transactions, and seeking regulatory mechanisms for factories operating in the sector. Meso-level gender-responsive organizations have a particular role to play in these investments. In their role in advocating for gender-responsive regulatory mechanisms, they will seek to secure agreements that will enhance the value of women's labor contribution, thereby increasing women's self-esteem and contributing to the achievement of gender equity.

Investments such as these are innovative and reflect the sense of urgency that has entered into the documentation on fisheries and aquaculture to move beyond only seeking outcomes of increased production and technical efficiency and including women in these, to addressing social relational issues that are causing major problems in this sector.

The following are central elements of any gender analysis for planning in the fisheries sector:

- Investigate ongoing changes in livelihoods (at the community, household, and individual levels) and related gender issues.
- Use an analysis that begins with gender roles, moves to gender relations, and includes local understandings about what women and men are able to be and do with their resources, rather than what resources they do or do not have.
- Focus interventions on addressing changes that are increasing the vulnerability of the men and women involved and seek improvements that will address the need for strategic changes in their lives and will ensure gender equity.

BENEFITS FROM GENDER-RESPONSIVE ACTIONS

Several important benefits result from actions that are responsive to gender issues:

- Securing the position of postharvest activities in natural resource planning processes will enhance the position of women and enable improvements in the sector as a whole.
- Supporting women's independent rights to resources will enhance their capacity to strengthen their livelihoods and cope with change.
- Using an investment approach that aims to increase the capacity of women to engage in all aspects of new aquaculture systems technology and moves away from linking their involvement in aquaculture with their domestic responsibilities will help achieve women's empowerment and social advancement and help improve the livelihoods of women, their households, and their communities.

- Protecting women's incomes and preventing the deterioration of their status and position in a context of changing political, social, and economic circumstances are essential for achieving the objective of creating responsible fisheries and aquaculture systems. The loss of local employment affects the money flows in local communities and therefore their economic security and survival (NEF 2002). Local job losses also can potentially destroy the social fabric of the community as people maneuver to maintain their positions. Women and men in weaker bargaining positions are unlikely to gain in these processes.
- A focus on enabling women and men to benefit from new (for them) markets will provide them with skills and networks that they can use in other situations, and changes that involve women and men simply engaging in low-paid, low-status, and risky activities can lead only to increased livelihood insecurity and overall welfare losses.

MONITORING AND EVALUATION

Table 13.2 provides indicators that might be used when monitoring gender issues in fisheries and aquaculture.

Depending on the country or region, it may be relevant to also consider ethnicity and caste alongside gender (both as comparative indicators and when collecting data), because women of lower castes or ethnic minorities are usually in the most disadvantaged situation.

Table 13.2 Monitoring and Evaluation Indicators for Gender in Fisheries and Aquaculture

Indicator	Sources of verification and tools
Number of women and men actively participating in established and well-functioning fishers groups, fishing boats, fish marketing and processing enterprises, or marketing cooperatives	• Committee meeting minutes • Interviews with stakeholders • Program and project records
Women or other disadvantaged groups actively participating in management committees and boards	• Committee meeting minutes • Interviews with stakeholders • Local traditional authorities (such as a chief or local council) • Program and project records
Number of women and men holding management or treasurer positions in natural resource management groups	• Bank account records • Committee meeting minutes
Gender differences in workload as a result of introduced practices or new technology	• Case studies • Participatory rapid appraisal • Sample surveys
New and total employment or paid labor generated in fish-processing factories for the local population, disaggregated by gender (with or without ethnicity)	• Administrative records of firms
Over a set period, an increase of x percent in household incomes from fish-based activities (such as fisheries or aquaculture or processing) among women-headed households and poor households in program areas	• Household surveys • Project management information system • Socioeconomic data from statistics office
Among surveyed women in target group, x percent rate that their access to income from fish (either via fishing or aquaculture) has improved during the period covered by the program or project	• Interviews with women in target groups (for instance, a sample of women in the defined area); ideally the interviews should be conducted before and after any project and program activities
Number of women and men participating in training in new methods of fishing or fish cultivation	• Program and project records • Training records
Number of women and men starting new small enterprises in fish processing or marketing	• Household surveys • Project records • Socioeconomic data from statistics office
Change in attitudes of women and men about changed roles of women in fisheries or aquaculture	• Group interviews or focus groups • Interviews, before and after
Change in attitudes of women and men about access to credit and satisfaction with repayments	• Group interviews or focus groups • Interviews, before and after

(Table continues on the following page)

Table 13.2 Monitoring and Evaluation Indicators for Gender in Fisheries and Aquaculture (continued)

Indicator	Sources of verification and tools
Number of women and men participating in training in alternative income-generating topics	• Program and project records • Training records
Number of women and men starting new small enterprises in alternative, nonfishing livelihoods	• Household surveys • Project records • Socioeconomic data from statistics office
Community opinions (disaggregated by gender) with changes in level of conflicts over gender	• Group interviews or focus groups • Interviews, before and after
Community opinions (disaggregated by gender) with changes in level of conflicts over fisheries exploitation	• Group interviews or focus groups • Interviews, before and after
Improved health of fisheries stocks or aquatic habitats, measured by total numbers of each species and the number of different species, measured before and after program	• Fisheries Department records • Participatory monitoring by villagers • Program records
Changes over x-year period of project activities in household nutrition, health, education, vulnerability to violence, and happiness, disaggregated by gender	• Household surveys, before and after • Project management information system • School records

Source: Authors, with inputs from Pamela White, author of Module 16.

Gender-Responsive Institutions for Accessing and Managing Resources

The creation of gender-responsive institutions at all levels has been recognized as necessary for achieving gender equity since the 1980s. As a gender-mainstreaming process, it has been at the core of gender planning since the mid-1970s and responds to the evidence assembled during the United Nations International Women's Decade from 1976 to 1985 from many countries (Dixon-Mueller 1989) that women are disadvantaged in relation to men in their resource access and control over decision making in a range of institutions, including the international community, the state, the marketplace and communities, families, and kinship groups. This Thematic Note is concerned with the formation of gender-responsive user groups in fisheries and aquaculture[1]—community-based natural resource management (CBNRM) groups and small groups of women for accessing resources where previously they had none—for achieving strategic changes in the status and position of women.

The major premise of community management is that sustainable resource management is best achieved when driven by those who rely on the resource for their survival. Within CBNRM, the need for gender-responsive action is based on the understanding that women who may have a direct or an indirect stake in the sector are more often than not excluded from participating in the activities of these groups or have only token representation, are perceived by themselves and others as having no right to speak, and have no presence on major decision-making bodies (for fisheries, see Bennett 2005). The exclusion of women is justified on a number of grounds by local and nonlocal stakeholders: that women's interests are taken care of by men, that benefits are shared equitably within households, and that challenging local norms that constrain women's public action is culturally insensitive and politically unacceptable.

The problem of women's visibility also presents itself, for even though numerous documents describe the roles of both men and women in fisheries and aquaculture, the "catching sector" (Bennett 2005) is the one largely dominated by men and determines policy agendas while the "processing and marketing sector" is ignored. The invisibility of production activities dominated by women in fisheries and aquaculture is linked with the domestic roles of women and associated social and cultural understandings about the value of these activities (Mowla and Kibria 2006, among others).

The formation of women's user groups to enhance their resource access rights and for receiving targeted services is well established as good gender practice. Although both poor men and poor women have been organized into groups to access resources, it is women who are more commonly formed into small groups, and for whom this practice is regarded as ideal given their socially weaker positions and limited mobility in public spaces in many societies. The following brief examples illustrate the kinds of actions involved in both fisheries and aquaculture:

The Bangladesh Meghna-Dhanagoda Command Area Development Project (Asian Development Bank Financing): Under this program, nongovernmental organizations (NGOs) were engaged to organize the poor (2,590 landless and marginal people, of whom 96 percent were women) into groups, provide them with access to ponds for fish farming through private lease arrangements, assist them with acquiring skills in fish farming and marketing, and provide them with microfinance services, including microcredit and savings facilities.

The Oxbow Lakes Small-Scale Fishermen's Project (supported by International Fund for Agricultural Development, the government of Bangladesh, Danish International Development Assistance, and the Bangladesh Rural Advancement Committee): The primary work of this program involved providing men from villages surrounding government-owned lakes with long-term access leases and forming them into lake management groups. The groups were large and experienced problems of conflict and lack of social cohesion.

Women were not initially considered as recipients of publicly owned resources, and mixed groups in any case were not considered to be socially acceptable. When women were targeted, they were formed into small pond farming groups to access ponds on similar lease arrangements. These groups included widowed and divorced women, who were considered to be especially vulnerable and socially weak. None of the women's groups experienced problems of social cohesion, largely because of their size and the fact that members of each group came from the same community (Nathan and Apu 2004).

The Oxbow Lakes Project, implemented in 1990, was unique in its attempt to give poor women group rights over public water bodies, and its success demonstrates how action to support women and poorer community members can easily be sabotaged. During the project, powerful men attempted to sabotage the work of the project and acquire the long-term leases for themselves, taking over selling fish and making purchases, especially of fingerlings, which are central to effective pool management. There were even reports of husbands who had earlier deserted their wives returning to seek benefits from them, as well as of husbands reducing their own contributions to meeting household requirements once wives or other women household members began to earn income from the sales of their products (Nathan and Apu 1998, 2004). Of the ten pond farming groups formed, five were retained by the women themselves, two were taken over by men, and three were leased to men by the women.

BENEFITS FROM SUPPORTING GENDER-RESPONSIVE LOCAL INSTITUTIONS

Ensuring the inclusion of women in decision making over resources and enabling them to directly access resources and their benefits will lead to women's social and economic empowerment. The Coral Reef Rehabilitation and Management Program (COREMAP) II program, detailed in Innovative Activity Profile 1, also demonstrates the link between these empowerment objectives and other gains—in this case, improvements in the condition of the coral reef. Reports also tell of improved solidarity and conflict resolution in natural resource management groups in which both women and men are involved (reported by Westermann, Ashby, and Pretty 2005, but not for fisheries).[2] The main practical benefits expected from this action are the protection of women's incomes and, therefore, their ability to contribute to the survival of their households, families, and communities.

Community-level action, such as within CBNRM groups, that takes into account the interests of all local stakeholders leads to a whole-sector approach in addressing resource management problems and planning solutions. This approach will result in gains in social and economic well-being for the community as a whole (see rural community evidence reported by NEF 2002). Within communities where men migrate away to fish, the inclusion of women in these groups will increase the viability of households in which both husbands and wives must be presumed to have a joint interest.

A central understanding behind the formation of groups of women and poorer members of communities is that these members often access resources through social relationships based on dependency, relationships in which they have to trade in their autonomy for security. As shown by the Oxbow Lakes example, the women's groups formed are expected to provide relationships based on solidarity and reciprocity and to build autonomy.

POLICY AND IMPLEMENTATION ISSUES

CBNRM groups, with or without direct government involvement, have a poor record of being gender responsive. This reflects the technical agenda that inspired the formation of the groups and that is the main concern of the ministries involved in their implementation. In response to the demand, by donors and others, that these groups become gender sensitive, it is tempting for these public organizations to take administrative action by appointing individual women to fill quotas. As experience has shown from outside fisheries and aquaculture, such women are unable to speak directly, influence decision making, or use their membership to protect their livelihoods or achieve other development goals. In fisheries and aquaculture, the major policy challenge is to ensure that plans for community-level resource management take into account all linked activities in the value chains and that all stakeholder groups are able to influence decision making. The COREMAP II program (see Innovative Activity Profile 1) demonstrates the level of commitment required to making this happen.

The information from fishing communities in Benin, Burkina Faso, the Democratic Republic of Congo, Gabon, and The Gambia presented in box 13.1 demonstrates the problem of attendance for women in community-level groups, as well as the issue of them having a voice in important matters.

All marginal groups experience some inequities, but the African women reporting here noted that men perceive that women's participation and increased access to know-how and information will make them less submissive, more independent, and better able to challenge them. As a result, although women may attend meetings, they may hesitate to take on leadership positions, to follow up on decisions, and to practice newly acquired skills. Addressing these issues requires relevant strategies and budget allocations.

Mowla and Kibria (2006), among others, provide some insight into the well-known problems associated with focusing on women's participation in user groups. They begin by noting that the purpose of the Patuakhali Barguna Aquaculture Extension Project (PBAEP) implemented between 1997 and 2004 was to strengthen the socioeconomic status of women and men and increase their participation in integrated pond farming: "Women expressed satisfaction with their ability to *meet their practical needs*—access to fish— and noted that they were able to do the work because of the *location of the ponds close to their homesteads.* Nevertheless, this was achieved at a *cost*—their *labor burdens* had increased and because they were too busy with the new activity plus their domestic work, they expressed *reluctance to attend training* sessions, thus disadvantaging themselves" (pp. 21 and 26; emphasis added).

The issue of labor burdens on women who are largely, if not entirely, responsible for domestic work is rarely mentioned in the documentation on fisheries and aquaculture projects. This short note on the PBAEP points to the dilemma for women. They may wish to be involved, but the gains from their participation are often costly in terms of time and in terms of their ability to access skills and information.

The women who gained most from the Oxbow Lake Project were reported to be divorcées, widows, or women household heads, and for them aquaculture had become a main source of cash income. Indeed, by 1998 a number of the women's groups were already recording a range of benefits: a higher per capita income from their aquaculture investments than from their small livestock activities, increased knowledge of new production methods, interaction with traders and officials, and enhanced social and family positions (Nathan and Apu 1998). In spite of these reported positive outcomes, the reports from this project also point out that the change process is often long and will demand considerable commitment on the part of all those involved to maintain their independent right (claims) to productive resources (IFAD Oxbow Lakes documentation). Finally, action for married women is possibly more difficult to implement than for other categories of women because they must negotiate what they do with spouses, in-laws, and others.

LESSONS LEARNED AND GUIDELINES FOR PRACTITIONERS

The following three sections offer advice and practical knowledge gleaned from the experience of fisheries and aquaculture projects.

Ensuring participation

All efforts must be made to ensure that the different stakeholders attend meetings and participate in decision making. This is especially important for postharvest stakeholder groups who in large part are women. The programs of CARE Bangladesh and PROFOUND in Vietnam (see Thematic

Note 2), COREMAP II (see Innovative Activity Profile 1), and PBAEP in Bangladesh (reported in Mowla and Kibria 2006) provide practical guidance when seeking the participation of women:

- Meetings must be held at a convenient time and place because of the limits on women's mobility and because of their domestic roles.
- Women must be present in sufficient numbers within a stakeholder group if the group is to have influence.
- Postharvest stakeholder groups must be acknowledged as having rights equal to those of other stakeholder groups.
- Women must occupy some important decision-making positions in order to be in a position to press for action in line with their interests.

Facilitating production group formation

The formation of production groups for allocating valuable and therefore scarce resources to women and poorer groups will face significant opposition at all levels—donors, governments, and local communities—where this conflicts with customary practice. Strategies need to be identified at the outset for dealing with these. In the Bangladesh case of the Oxbow Lakes Project, where groups of unmarried, widowed, divorced, and married women were organized for receiving long-term user rights in public water bodies for aquaculture production, documentation by Nathan and Apu (1998; 2004) provides some unique information on project outcomes and useful best practices for partnership formation (highlighted in the following excerpts from various sections of the paper by Nathan and Apu 1998 and Barman 2001):[3]

> With the *support of the national government,* and in collaboration with BRAC and DANIDA as *gender responsive funders,* collective investments in aquaculture were made in Jessore in the SW of Bangladesh where women are not commonly involved in aquaculture. Here landless women (and men) who formed themselves into Fish Farming Groups (FFGs) and Lake Fishing Teams (LFTs) obtained *long-term user rights in public water bodies* (20 years in the first instance), which for the purpose of this activity were treated as common pool resources with access rights restricted to the FFGs and LFTs, and some other fishing groups around the lake. The project was documented as *commercial* with the desired outcome predicted on the strength of the incentive derived from acquiring long-term user rights in common pool resources, of strengthening women's participation in fish culture. To make this happen, *women extension agents* were provided under the equally innovative Mymensingh Aquaculture Extension Project (MAEP 1999) to deliver inputs required. (emphasis added)

Gaining control of management tasks

While meeting household needs might be interesting to women, they are unlikely to take on additional work burdens over a long period if the work does not result in sufficient cash income. To achieve this, they must also control the tasks that are essential to effective enterprise management, such as selling fish and making purchases of fingerlings, in the case of aquaculture pond management.

Using monitoring and evaluation indicators

From the various program examples referenced in this Module, it is clear that there are always at least two concerns: (1) how the group or project is functioning and (2) how group members or project participants are using their membership to serve their own interests and the interest of others for whom they are responsible. This second focus is essential, given the interest of this *Sourcebook* in achieving broader desirable development outcomes beyond economic growth and improved productivity.

Creating and strengthening institution and group focus

From the outset, a clear gender objective must be negotiated with local people and included in project objectives. To achieve its gender-equality objective, the SFLP conducted gender-analysis training with its local collaborators and reached agreements with them about desirable changes and how to get them. In cases like this, indicators will be developed by the groups themselves.

The creation and strengthening of local institutions represent the development of substantial resources at the group level—decision making, information flow and awareness, skill learning, and so on. All these areas address how well the group is doing in terms of its objectives. The indicators should enable everyone to answer the question, How well does the institution draw on and invest in members for the ongoing institutional development? It is useful to divide these into social, human, natural, financial, and physical resources. For example, social and human resource development enables members to act collectively to manage the defined resources.

Focusing on members

A second set of indicators is needed to answer the question, How are the management arrangements or group processes affecting members' lives? Again, it is useful to divide these into social, human, natural, financial, and physical resources. For example, women's membership has affected their wider social and gender relations, their ability to access fish, their ability to negotiate with others, and so on.

Family-Based Systems for Aquaculture Development in Asia

The World Bank (2006) describes aquaculture in Asia as having taken three distinct development pathways that have sometimes merged and overlapped as social and economic conditions have changed in different countries. The first is described as a static model rather than a pathway because the system is vulnerable and lacking in growth potential. The second is described as a transition pathway, depicting the more advantaged farmer or small enterprise with access to the knowledge, markets, and capital necessary for increasing the scale of production and offering a way out of poverty for the household. The last is referred to as a consolidation pathway, which covers both corporate and community enterprises, in which corporate enterprises operate as vertically integrated farms and community enterprises include a group of organized small farmers benefiting from economies of scale by engaging in joint activities. The World Bank (2006) argues that all three pathways have contributed to poverty reduction in the region and gives the example of the growth of catfish culture in the Mekong Delta from a subsistence family-based system through the Vietnamese integrated farming system, VAC (vuong/ao/chuong or garden/pond/animal husbandry) system, to more commercialized agribusiness.[1]

The focus of this Thematic Note lies in the first two models that describe small farms or family-based systems that are found to a greater or lesser extent in all the countries in the region and are critical for sustaining livelihoods in a number of countries such as Bangladesh, India, Indonesia, and Vietnam, where they are the most common type of aquaculture system. Like the VAC system found in Vietnam, they are often intensive systems that rely on the labor of family members for their success, although where they are successful, households may employ a small number of casual laborers.

KEY GENDER ISSUES

Although both men and women are involved in small-scale aquaculture systems in Asia, the extent of the involvement of women varies considerably, even if their involvement has increased substantially over the last decade or more. Frequently, women are described as lacking in knowledge and skills that are regarded today as critical for engaging in modern aquaculture systems described by the World Bank as being knowledge based. This lack of skills and capacity on the part of women was raised as early as 1995–96 in reference to the Training of Trainers to Promote Women's Small-Scale Aquaculture Enterprises program in rural areas of northern Vietnam (Voeten and Ottens 1997)[2] and was found to be a critical issue in the five-country study reported on by Brugère and others in 2001, as well as in a review paper by Nandeesha (2007) covering most countries in the region. Although this neglect of women's capacity-building needs is understood to be a reflection of the way service-delivery organizations operate—employing largely men staff to deliver information to the main decision makers in households who may or may not pass the information to others in the household—it is also seen to reflect the kind of society in which project implementation organizations work. Debashish and others (2001: 149) describe the way in which training is often delivered in the promotion and improvement of small-scale aquaculture systems as follows:

> The successful management of aquaculture systems relies on several household members working together and yet the need for a household approach in training is often overlooked as an explicit strategy. Training sessions often target only one member of the household, either the husband or the wife. In the management of ponds, rice-fish or cage system roles are separated along gender lines. This means that there is a reliance on the trained participant to pass along all that she/he has learnt to the other family members. Even when information is transmitted

to others in the family, there is often a significant loss or transformation of the information as it passes from one person to another. In addition, the majority of extension workers are men. This has implications for the training. For example, during training sessions, the men often dominate the discussion and women's views or needs can be dismissed or ignored. In addition, male trainers often have little empathy with the women and their specific requirements.

Debashish and others also note that organizations frequently ignore the need for women's and men's different learning styles. At least in Bangladesh, women's lack of familiarity with formal learning environments and their lower level of literacy can also result in their particular learning needs and requirements being overlooked. Based on its experience in addressing these concerns in its aquaculture projects, CARE Bangladesh adopted a three-tiered approach:

■ Having specific goals for the participation of women stated in project logical frameworks
■ Using extension approaches and promoting interventions that facilitate increased benefits for women in agriculture and aquaculture systems
■ Promoting changes, including staff development activities that result in a more gender-sensitive organization.

At the same time, CARE and other organizations are aware of the impact of culture on the ability of extension systems to build the capacity of both women and men to work

in aquaculture, and the need, therefore, to adapt programs to different situations. Distinctions have been made between what are described as conservative and less conservative locations (Zaman 1998); data from interviews with women and men in locations covered by the New Options for Pest Management (NOPEST) program of CARE Bangladesh suggest what these differences entail (table 13.3).

Factors supporting the ability of women to become and continue to be involved in aquaculture include geographic location, local traditions and outlook, the historical mobility of women, family support and interest, community and peer group support, the age of the women, and the effectiveness of the NGO support (Debashish and others 2001 based on the CARE Bangladesh experience).

In addition to this concern about information and skills being accessible to both women and men, women are frequently described as lacking access to other resources necessary for engaging in aquaculture and as lacking control over the benefits of improved household incomes and, therefore, as being more vulnerable than men in families. Critical for control over income is the involvement in marketing, and in this respect considerable variation exists within the region. Women in Cambodia and China are described as undertaking a range of tasks in different aquaculture systems (more and less commercial and including the ornamental fish industry), including marketing the products. Women in Bangladesh, Malaysia, and India are described as having more limited (if growing) involvement, and only in "subsistence aquaculture"

Table 13.3 Perceptions about Women Working in Conservative and Less Conservative Areas

Perceptions of men and women in conservative areas	Perceptions of men and women in less conservative areas
Men's perceptions:	Men's perceptions:
• Women should not work outside the homestead for social and religious reasons. • It is superstitiously believed that having women working in the fields will result in a poor harvest. • Women have no time to work outside the home. • Women are unable to do all kinds of work. • Women should stay within the homestead, as that is the way it has always been.	• Women learn from working outside. • It is all right for women to work outside the home. • Men value women's work and skills. • Both men and women are needed to manage a household. • Men appreciate women's work.
Women's perceptions:	Women's perceptions:
• Women sometimes want to work outside the home, but there are no opportunities. • Women cannot get permission from their husbands to work outside the home. • Women are unable to work outside. • Women do not have time to work outside. • Women do not want to work outside.	• Husbands are supportive. • Husbands appreciate women's work. • Women can work near the home with the men. • Women want to improve family welfare. • Women want to work outside the home.

Source: Debashish and others 2001: 150.

(Nandeesha 2007). In these three countries, in general men are more likely to be involved in marketing than women. In Indonesia, small-scale aquaculture (on farms of less than half a hectare) is largely undertaken as a family activity, but it is unclear to what extent women engage in marketing. Men are reported to control aquaculture production in the Philippines, where small-scale systems are less widespread, whereas the opposite is true in Thailand, where marketing is dominated by women. Both cultural and practical reasons are given to account for this variation, including the more significant out-migration of men from rural areas in the case of Thailand and Vietnam.

BENEFITS FROM A FAMILY-BASED APPROACH

Bangladesh has been a focus of activities to improve the position and status of women in society since the country's war of liberation from Pakistan in 1971 and the famine in 1972. At that time international development assistance was considered critical, and NGOs began their work. These NGOs were both international and national, and many specifically targeted women and were supported in their activities by the national government. This activity partly reflects the role that women have in allocating food within the family, but it also reflects the levels of poverty in the country and the constraints placed by customary norms on the use of public space and on women's ability to engage in production activities outside the home. Interventions covering a wide spectrum of welfare needs such as health and family-planning provisions, as well as resources for economic development such as microcredit and training for income-generating activities, have focused on women. Projects promoting integrated aquaculture systems in Bangladesh have tried to focus on women specifically. This is justified on the following grounds:

- Women are often responsible for managing homestead vegetable gardens and livestock.
- Although the nutritional needs of all family members are often not met in lean seasons and in times of hardship, women are likely to be especially disadvantaged by an understanding that they have a lesser claim on household resources.

Among the various options available, aquaculture is recognized as ideal for meeting the protein requirements and fish consumption needs of the population; if it is successful, it can contribute significantly to the livelihood security of rural households and the economic status of the family.

Integrated aquaculture systems, which can be located close to homesteads, were seen as an ideal intervention for enabling women to access directly some of these benefits and thus contribute directly to improving their own welfare as well as the welfare of their families and thereby to changing their status in the home.

Programs have also sought to change customary norms that limit women's ability to access the knowledge and skills, water, and financial resources required to participate effectively (to use aquaculture as a way out of poverty and for livelihood growth as discussed by the World Bank 2006). Reports on the use of a gender-responsive family approach in integrated aquaculture programs suggest that women can, for example, acquire new skills in breeding common carp or culturing fish in cages, ponds, and rice paddies and that, as a consequence, their mobility increases and their status improves (Debashish and others 2001).

POLICY AND IMPLEMENTATION ISSUES

Although widespread recognition exists of the benefits of adopting a family approach within integrated aquaculture systems, the donors and implementing agencies in Bangladesh, where this production system has been especially promoted, have not found this approach straightforward. Issues of cost for training both women and men in a family are often raised, and project time frames are short for achieving sustainable social and economic change in what is considered to be a conservative social environment. For more than a decade, the Agriculture and Natural Resources sector of CARE Bangladesh has piloted such a family approach in its aquaculture programs. This approach has involved taking into account the social and cultural context within which the program is being implemented from the outset and has provided both men and women, husbands and wives, with information and skills. To facilitate effective learning, and again considering the cultural context, men and women are preferably trained separately in groups, although staff working in the field indicate that forming groups of women is more difficult in conservative areas.

In terms of policy and implementation, one of the most important issues in adopting this approach is the need for organizations involved to develop a clear strategy for achieving changes in the role and position of women in families and communities. CARE Bangladesh and PROFOUND in Vietnam both adopted a gender-mainstreaming strategy that involved, in the first instance, an affirmative action policy in staff hiring and a large commitment to staff training to change their behavior, followed by the involvement of both men and women staff in working with family members of both sexes. Implementation issues that are raised in many programs—whether to form single-sex or mixed groups, for instance, or to restrict engagement with women to women staff—gradually disappeared as a result of implementing this strategy.

LESSONS LEARNED AND GUIDELINES FOR PRACTITIONERS

To achieve the desired changes, implementing agencies must have gender-balanced field staff with interests in both technical and social issues. As the prevailing social circumstances pose many challenges to achieving a balanced staff composition, an organizational policy with a vision is essential to overcome those challenges. To accomplish this, gender sensitization of the staff or others involved in implementation is the first essential step to be taken. Voeten and Ottens (1997: 417, 424) detail the PROFOUND approach to implementing gender-responsive training in the training of trainers program in Vietnam in which they were involved:

> Trainers who were trained to pass information and skills to others included members of the 4 communities in which the programme was being piloted, and representatives from the Vietnamese Women's Union (VWU), trained 120 women, from 120 households in the 4 communities. The training was organized to fit into the women's existing time schedule and took place within the communities, thus enabling women [to] attend with minimum disruption to their regular work. Both the trainers and the women trained received practical skill-based information and were made aware of a central gender question that the project was asking: Does an increase in fish production mean an improvement in the economic and social position of women? The two key organizations involved in this project, VWU and PROFOUND, saw raising women's consciousness on this issue as the first step in moving from increased production to increased income and higher social position, a shift that was considered to be essential for ensuring women's active participation in their own development . . . . The starting point for the on-farm research undertaken in this project addressed the invisibility of women's contribution to VAC. . . . Detailed data on time use, access and control over resources involved, cost/benefit analyses and decision-making on management were all collected and discussed. Men in local power structures and husbands of women in training, participated.

In the programs of CARE Bangladesh and PROFOUND in Vietnam, the involvement of both men and women in the activities was found to have a great impact on the sustainability of changes. In the case of CARE Bangladesh, studies have shown that in areas where the rice-fish culture activity was sustained after the withdrawal of the project, this sustainability was attributed to the active participation of women in the program. Likewise, the education of women on aquaculture and their involvement in the activity have produced improvements in family nutrition as well as in the family economy. In the case of the PROFOUND project in Vietnam—which was, among other things, designed to make women's contribution visible—after the training, women's position improved, they valued the technical knowledge acquired, and men considered their training to be a valuable investment. No gender conflicts were reported, and some husbands started to assist their wives with domestic work.

The use of gender analysis tools is mentioned in most programs in fisheries and aquaculture that adopt a gender-responsive approach. The Food and Agriculture Organization (FAO)/Sustainable Fisheries Livelihood Programme (SFLP) started all its community interventions by undertaking gender and poverty analysis/profiling with community members. PROFOUND introduced what it refers to as *gender mapping*,[3] and all programs are very clear about the need to make community members, especially those directly involved in the program, aware of possible gender issues. PROFOUND points to the significance of gender mapping for challenging established views about equality, for instance, and what this mapping might mean for individuals and their families.

Instead of aiming to transfer technology from laboratory to farmers, organizers' efforts to educate farmers on the basic principles of the new technology and encouraging them to innovate further and adapt the technology to their farm conditions based on their capacity will contribute to increasing productivity immensely. However, here again, it is critical to involve both men and women and allow them to discuss and decide on the strategy to be evolved in such an adaptation process to suit their family economy and farm environment.

Paddy cultivation and pest management processes were not taught to women in the early stages of the CARE project. However, practical sessions that dealt with pesticides and their impact on health and environment, sessions that involved both women and men, had a dramatic effect on pesticide use. Such practical aspects of the programs of CARE and PROFOUND have made these projects attractive to local authorities because they help the local economy. In the case of CARE, this resulted in local authorities providing physical infrastructure and logistical support. In the case of PROFOUND, the rural women's union was supportive because its own prestige was increased as a result of the training activities.

MONITORING AND EVALUATION INDICATORS

Broad examples of indicators to measure improvements at the household and community levels include the following:

- Benefit distribution from the improved VAC system—by sex
- Improved health and nutrition of women and children
- Positive attitude of husbands and other men toward women's training
- More involvement of women in decision making in aquaculture management, especially stocking density, which is critical for farm productivity.

CARE emphasizes the need for a participatory approach to monitoring and evaluation, with families involved in the program determining indicators of change of value to them.

As is clear from the activities detailed in this Thematic Note, participation is costly in terms of time, and although an incentive is always present to provide positive reports, the pressure on time, especially that of women, needs to be monitored. Voeten and Ottens (1997) note that knowing more and being more involved in decision making result in more time being spent in management. Although they report that this was not regarded as a problem by the women involved in the PROFOUND pilot project, the authors argue that it must be monitored because it can lead to costs in welfare.

Associations for Protecting the Livelihoods of Fishers, Processors, and Traders

Many examples exist of locations where the livelihoods of small-scale local fishers, processors, and traders are threatened by ongoing changes in the fisheries and aquaculture sector. These changes reflect both the impact of the globalization of markets for fish and fish products, as well as economic shifts at the national and local levels.

The massive growth in the international demand for fish and aquaculture products since the 1980s has led to a situation in which powerful international and local firms now play significant roles in this sector, at times competing with local fishermen for the same species but with more sophisticated equipment and at other times purchasing directly from small-scale fishermen and excluding local traders and processors. Shifts to industrial processing and packaging, either on fishing vessels or on land, have meant that local postharvest workers, a large proportion of whom are women, have been bypassed. Some of the small-scale local players have found employment in the new factories, and although this employment has provided income-earning possibilities for men and women, the conditions of work for many are poor, the hours are long, and work is frequently casual and low paying in many parts of the world. Shifts in local economies in some locations have resulted in better returns to fishing and aquaculture, compared with alternatives such as food crop production. This has resulted in more people entering the sector and competing for fish and other products with small-scale operators.

Fish stocks are also reported to be declining and the natural resource base is deteriorating. Comanagement strategies to achieve more responsible fisheries, sustain local livelihoods, and protect the resource base have been introduced and can be effective (see Innovative Activity Profile 1) but may also lead to a higher-quality catch suitable for more distant and remunerative markets and exclude local processors and traders. As competition for fish increases at local levels,

some local fish buyers, frequently men, may gain direct access to fish by becoming licensed fishing operators, possibly even purchasing fish directly from vessels before the fish is landed and excluding other local members of the value chain. Reports also tell of increases in the incidence of sexually transmitted diseases, which have been linked with local women buyers engaging in risky fish-for-sex relations with fishers, who are largely men, to maintain their access to the fish that they depend on for their livelihoods.

This Thematic Note is mainly concerned with interventions to protect threatened livelihoods in the sector by enabling those already involved to enter new markets with new or value-added products. This action is linked with others that seek to provide alternative income sources for those engaged in fish-for-sex transactions, as described by WorldFish in Malawi (2007), and that seek to prevent any further spread of disease, provide care services for those in high-risk situations (such as migrant fishers), and provide mitigation for families and communities already affected (as detailed in SFLP 2005). It is also concerned with seeking protection for workers in processing factories, making this a more valuable alternative income source that can serve for livelihood building as well as for food security.

ACCESSING NEW MARKETS

The challenge in successfully creating access to new markets for small-scale fishers, processors, and traders is enormous, regardless of the sex of the sellers. This is a risky venture, and few examples exist in the fisheries and aquaculture sector where this has been attempted. In general, these suppliers are less organized and have fewer business and negotiating skills than buyers such as wholesalers, contractors acting on behalf of supermarkets, and exporters, who are regarded as the more powerful players in the marketing chain. This, along with the small-scale suppliers' minimal access to capital, input supplies, and advisory services, constrains their ability to establish and maintain a reliable supply of high-quality products that meet all health and safety regulations. Specific action that is required includes organizing groups of small-scale fishers, processors, and traders; providing these groups with training in business, management, and negotiating skills and training in improved product development practices that meet the international and national standards as well as the standards of individual buyers; ensuring their access to credit, which takes into consideration the level of risk involved in meeting the delivery conditions of large buyers; and ensuring they have horizontal links with associations, federations, and cooperatives that are in a position to support smaller groups and that have links with vertical institutions.[1]

PROTECTING WORKERS IN PROCESSING FACTORIES

Reports of poor working conditions in fish-processing and packaging factories are now available for every continent. However, despite the growing emphasis among some donors, governments, and private sector business on the need to adopt socially responsible practices, the link between pervasive social injustice and the food system has not generally been made. When it has, although exceptions exist, the dominant picture is one of women occupying most, if not all, of the posts regarded as requiring minimum skills, working in exceptionally poor conditions with no health or safety protection, and working on a casual basis with no job security or benefits (De Silva and Yamao 2006; Gammage and others 2006; Josupeit 2004; Markussen 2002; Swanrangsi 2003; Tiesze and others 2007). At the same time, women continue to shoulder virtually all the domestic work in their homes. Little information is available about precisely who these women are. For parts of India, Sharma (2003) describes them as being mostly younger, educated women who have been drawn into paid work for the first time and who may be subject to sexual harassment. Where factories are close to large towns or cities, the workforce may be drawn from the cities rather than from communities directly affected by changes in the sector. Gammage and others (2006) provide a little more information beyond work conditions and note that very few of the women employed at any level in factories in Bangladesh are key decision makers or active in trade unions. Reports from Latin America, sub-Saharan Africa, and South Asia suggest that women's livelihoods often become more vulnerable when they take on work in these new processing factories; their employment simply serves to maintain their poor economic circumstances and that of their dependents.

Addressing this problem will involve engaging in advocacy and drawing on existing international and national legislation to support the demands for change. Although successful initiatives to change this situation have not been reported in this sector, organizations such as INFOPESCA operating in Latin America and the Caribbean have undertaken work to expose poor work practices (Josupeit 2004). At least one company, Aqua Fish in Honduras, has, on its own initiative, chosen to follow socially responsible practices.

BENEFITS FROM ADDRESSING LIVELIHOOD THREATS

Highlighting the threats to those involved in the sector is an issue addressed in the 1995 FAO Code of Conduct for Responsible Fisheries. Protecting livelihoods is a major issue for all small-scale fishers, processors, and traders as well as for the welfare of their communities because income loss from increased competition and changes in the distribution of benefits in the marketing chains affect everyone involved. Nevertheless, it is women who play the most significant role in the postharvest sector and who are often reported to be the first to be displaced by ongoing changes but who at the same time lack the resources (social, economic, and political) to enter easily into alternative income-earning activities.

In many locations women are confined to low-status activities already rejected by others and are unsupported by services. Furthermore, incomes supporting livelihoods beyond simple survival are gained by these women only through a significant increase in work burdens or, as in the reported cases of their engagement in fish-for-sex activities, at significant risk to themselves and their dependents. The weak bargaining position of women is pinpointed in studies of the spread of HIV and AIDS in fishing communities in parts of sub-Saharan Africa, studies that also show how women's comparative lack of knowledge and skills (apart from their reported interests in meeting household food security needs) is used, for example, to justify their exclusion from new commercial activities in aquaculture (Kusabe and Kelkar 2001; Nandeesha 2007). In the case of factory workers, although all involved workers may be considered to be in a weak bargaining position in the sense that few alternative sources of employment may be available, sufficient evidence exists to demonstrate that women are most likely to be placed at the bottom of the workforce, working under conditions that make it difficult for them to combine this work with their domestic labor. Addressing women's specific needs means seeking enforcement of codes of conduct that will lead to gender equality.

POLICY AND IMPLEMENTATION ISSUES

To enable access to new markets (or existing markets not yet reached) with new or improved existing products, both suppliers and buyers need to be sure that their work is supported by appropriate economic policies. Public bodies must provide a policy environment that promotes mutually beneficial partnerships between buyers such as supermarkets and small producers and that promotes a legal framework that protects all partners involved and ensures the maintenance of good business practices.

The central issues to be addressed at the implementation level are the constraints on women and men entering these marketing chains. Although women and men may share the same disadvantages of illiteracy and lack of collateral for taking a large loan, women are frequently more disadvantaged by their gender-specific constraints—such as in social settings where their physical movement is restricted, including their meeting in groups—and ideologies about men breadwinners and the lower value attached to women's work (Kabeer and Subrahmanian 1996). Given these gender-specific disadvantages, care must be taken to resist adopting assumptions about women's lack of interest in engaging in commercial activities and about the appropriateness of microcredit programs to meet their practical needs, which might include small enterprise development.

Growing international concerns about labor exploitation are placing pressure on governments to set standards and systems for enforcing these standards. Even though evidence from individual company reports suggests that the companies themselves can introduce changes, it is not clear that the sector can bring pressure to bear on its members.

A useful tool for clarifying what might be regarded as the ideal outcomes of any interventions in the practice of private firms involved in processing and packaging in this sector is the "gender pyramid" conceptualized by Barrientos (2001) and Barrientos, Dolan, and Tallontire (2003). This tool consists of three interlinked segments that cover the key issues relating to conditions of employment. Segment A covers issues of employment regulation relating to formal employment (predominantly the International Labour Organization conventions and national legislation). Segment B refers to employment-related issues that facilitate women's employment (meeting practical gender needs such as child care provision, maternity and paternity leave, transport, and housing). These issues are particularly relevant to gender equality because they address the factors that enable women to combine paid productive employment with their reproductive tasks. Segment C encompasses the socioeconomic

circumstances that affect women's ability to access particular types of employment. These circumstances are shaped by cultural norms, education, reproductive work, and gender relations. Reporting on their study, Barrientos, Dolan, and Tallontire (2003) note that none of the codes of conduct they reviewed cover segment C of the pyramid, even though precisely these issues maintain women's subordinate and exploited position. They argue that because the wider social circumstances are what maintain women's subordinate and secondary status in society and underpin the gender division of labor within paid employment, codes can have only a very limited impact in addressing women's labor exploitation if they fail to address segments B and C of the pyramid fully.

The codes serve a dual purpose: (1) to provide a clear objective or target that civil society organizations and governments, for example, can use to monitor performance and (2) to inform different categories of workers, including women, of their rights. The codes can help them understand the meaning of their rights and serve to engage them in discussions of the issues that need to be addressed. This is essential if programs are supporting the associations of suppliers to bargain collectively for their rights because the success of this action will depend on all stakeholders being involved.

Although addressing these threats to lives and livelihoods is not the core business of most implementing institutions in fisheries and aquaculture, all programs must have some commitment to the creation of greater social and economic equality in addition to their main objectives of increasing production while protecting the resource base. This commitment will involve working with organizations with expertise in these areas; working with fishers, processors, and traders who need support for their continued involvement in the sector; and working with their associations, who need to be able to act on their behalf beyond the life of individual programs.

Civil society organizations of various kinds are essential for achieving the strategic changes being sought in this action because the transformation of existing norms is not an individual matter, even though at the individual and household levels changes may be sought and achieved (Kelkar, Nathan, and Rownok 2003). However, civil society organizations, including women's organizations, are facing financial difficulties, although the Organization for Economic Co-operation and Development has recently introduced changes to cover the financing of these organizations specifically (OECD/DAC 2006). As in the case of the producer groups discussed in Thematic Note 1 (which covers the creation of gender-responsive local institutions), if these organizations are well structured, they are the means by which members will be able to exercise collective agency, support weaker members or members in need, advocate for policy support, and challenge norms of behavior that limit their capacity to participate in alternative livelihood-building activities. Changing the position of donors on funding for these civil society organizations is one of the expected benefits from these interventions.

LESSONS LEARNED AND GUIDELINES FOR PRACTITIONERS

Recent examples of good practice within fisheries and aquaculture on any or all of the actions covered in this Thematic Note are difficult to find. An early report refers to a shrimp farmers association in Tamil Nadu, India, that successfully used World Bank support (the India Shrimp and Fish Culture Project, 1992–2000) to introduce a voluntary code of conduct among its members, control the quality of inputs, monitor ponds, and use collective-bargaining skills to market their product (Kumaran and others 2003). One of the most recent and comprehensive programs to address a range of social issues is the SFLP, supported by FAO and the Department for International Development (DFID) in small-scale artisanal fisheries in West and Central Africa. Although program achievements are still in the process of being documented, the program has integrated gender analysis along with poverty profiling at the community level for intervention planning, has taken on the challenge of working with associations of suppliers to enter new markets (see the FAO Web site for SFLP documentation: www.sflp.org), and has assisted in the creation of a policy environment conducive to guaranteeing investments on action to address HIV and AIDS in fishing communities in the countries covered by the program. The donors for this program have been especially concerned with influencing policy on all the issues covered in this Thematic Note, and the SFLP policy briefs are examples of good practice in this regard.

Although it is common in reporting on good practice to focus on technical outcomes such as incomes, the good practice interventions noted in the next two sections all focus on social and economic empowerment. Together they demonstrate that enabling groups of disadvantaged suppliers to access new markets is a long process that must be supported by other action if the threats to their lives and livelihoods in existing markets are to be addressed. In addition, processes that are put in place to secure their social and economic empowerment will need to be monitored to ensure that the interests of the most vulnerable members are protected.

In many **locations** both young women and adult women are especially **vulnerable**.

Lake Chad pilot project

The following **note** reports briefly on a pilot project to improve **local fish** supplies from Lake Chad and the Chari River by **working** with groups of fishers, processors, and traders:

Strengthening the national capacity for fish health inspection and improvements in the quality of fisheries products from Lake Chad and the Chari River: Pilot project 3 of the DFID/SFLP (Period: April 2005–October 2006; Budget: $300,000).

> The objectives of this project were to build local capacity in fish safety **and the responsible** handling of fish and fishery products in order **to improve** food security and increase incomes of fishing communities along Lake Chad and the River Chari.
>
> The **project had** two components: to improve national fish inspection **services**, and to support training in the use of technology **designed** to improve fish preservation and processing, as well **as in** accessing marketing niches in small-scale fishing communities within the project area.
>
> The benefits/impact and lessons learnt: The groups set up and strengthened in gender-sensitive organizational development by the SFLP were trained in the use of improved postharvest equipment made available in what are referred to in the documentation as "community technological platforms" and at the same time were made gender aware. Economic returns from the fish products increased by 30–50 percent, and women were not marginalized in the use of the equipment provided. Nevertheless, problems arose with the competition for access to the platforms by wealthy processors, and by the end of the project in October 2006, the extension officers were asked by FAO to work with the beneficiaries to set up a rotation for use by different groups in the community, and to periodically monitor the process. The national government has been involved in the program from the outset and acknowledged both the technical effectiveness of the platforms as well as the ability of the poverty profiling process, along with the strengthening of socioprofessional groups, to enable access to these facilities by poorer community members. A national strategy was formulated at the end of the project to allow up-scaling of this approach.
>
> Communication with Yvette Diei Ouadi (FAO and SFLP)

In a separate note from the same source, it is made clear that although poor men and women were more vulnerable, women processors and traders also faced competition from men in accessing fresh fish. Although the men are described as being engaged only in fishing, when the technology was made available, they began to compete with the women for access to the fish preservation and processing facility. They were able to access the fish directly or to meet other fishermen on the lake itself, which the women were not able to do. In addition, the women were more constrained in accessing remote and more lucrative markets. The group focus of this activity made it easier for the women to address these constraints, even though the groups often had both men and women members.

Ethical fish processing in Honduras

Although factory managers may be reluctant to provide the data needed for improving poor working conditions, the large increase in the number of codes of conduct developed since the 1990s suggests considerable incentives now encourage companies to adopt good practices—to increase sales and profits from ethical trade, for example—and therefore to respond to pressure that they demonstrate corporate social responsibility. The case of Aqua Finca's operations is the best-known example in fisheries and aquaculture of a company that has been motivated to adopt ethical operational principles, including principles around working conditions and labor contracts. Some of its environmental ethical practices are covered in the following short communication from Helga Josupeit (FAO GLOBEFISH):

> Aqua Finca has the largest tilapia farm in Honduras, with 30 tons of daily fresh fillet exports mainly to the United States. In 2006 Aqua Finca Saint Peter Fish opened a brand new fish meal plant and a biodiesel plant based on tilapia oil. Total investment totaled $20 million, which included fish meal, biodiesel, processing, and production. All the vehicles and the machines of the farm are running on biodiesel. The company is now venturing into organic aquaculture and has just received the organic seal of approval by Naturland and the Bio Swiss. Aqua Finca just started to transport fresh fillets using a technology called OceanChill to its overseas market in the United States by boat, which reduces both the energy spent for transport as well as operating costs.

> Aqua Finca also has a huge interest in supporting social infrastructure activities in communities where it operates (reforestation, education, health centers, community-owned fish cages), which are entitled by the company owner to receive 10 percent of company production capacity, and this enables the communities to produce alongside Aqua Finca.

Some of the first studies of company practices in the fisheries and aquaculture sectors were undertaken by the Centre for Marketing Information and Advisory Services for Fishery Products in Latin America and the Caribbean (INFOPESCA) and are reported in Josupeit (2004).

MONITORING AND EVALUATION INDICATORS

In large part the focus of monitoring and therefore of the evaluation of marketing programs already initiated in this sector has centered on the returns on the fish and fish products marketed. However, the main benefit sought through the actions covered in this Thematic Note is the social and economic empowerment of those involved, and especially of women, who have been identified in many locations as especially disadvantaged by ongoing changes. Indicators are needed that will demonstrate changes in empowerment—changes that may result from improved economic circumstances of the women and men involved as well as their households, but may also result from the processes of capacity building and other factors that are essential to enabling these women and men to engage in the new marketing chains.

Gender and Alternative Livelihoods for Fishing Communities

People in rural fishing communities depend heavily on aquatic resources as a source of protein and livelihoods. The open-access nature of marine resources and coastal ecosystems drives a large number of people to fish as an occupation of last resort when other sectors, such as agriculture, decline. Groups of fishers often have limited alternative livelihood options, and this makes them particularly vulnerable to changes in the condition of and access to the aquatic resources on which they depend. Environmental degradation, habitat destruction, and overfishing have led to the point at which many fishers find it progressively harder to make a living from traditional fishing practices.

In general, livelihood diversification activities available for fisheries communities can be grouped into two categories: (1) fishing and fishing-related activities (such as fish trading, marketing, and processing) and (2) activities unrelated to fishing, including aquaculture. In several contexts, migration and mobility are also parts of the diversification practices in fishing communities. The latter group of nonfishing-related activities is referred to as *alternative livelihoods* (ALs) in this Thematic Note (see the comprehensive list and specific examples in Brugère and Allison, in preparation, and FAO 2007). The term *alternative* refers to the diversification of sources of household income rather than the dependence on a single economic activity that is heavily based on scarce natural resources. In the context of fragile and constricted marine resources and coastal ecosystems, assisting fishing communities in identifying and achieving sustainable AL to their fishing activities bears much importance.

Including AL components in projects related to conservation and sustainable use of aquatic resources is an integral approach in project planning. For instance, the policy of limiting fishing efforts in marine protected areas or the closure of traditional fishing grounds will have an impact on the fishing community, so steps need to be considered to provide fishers with ALs. Moreover, without effective development assistance and intervention, the increasing competition, natural resource restrictions, and other rapid changes in the sector have forced many poor women to work as agricultural laborers and construction workers and to take on other types of unskilled employment in addition to their already heavy workload. Although AL activities and components can serve as special entry points for including gender dimensions in projects, AL activities also have the potential to reinforce and worsen gender inequalities.

KEY GENDER ISSUES AND BENEFITS OF GENDER-INTEGRATED FISHERIES MANAGEMENT

Fishing has been understood to be predominantly men's work, but awareness is growing that women play critical roles in the fisheries sector in developing countries, particularly on the postharvest level (see Overview and Thematic Note 3). In coastal villages in West African countries, the main activity of women is the processing and marketing of fishery products (FAO 1997), whereas in Manipur, India, fisheries activities are largely dominated by women—they are involved in capture fisheries, aquaculture, fish processing, fish marketing, and fish transporting (Gurumayum, Devi, and Nandeesha 2004). In the Pacific Island countries, near-shore fishing activities, such as harvesting of fish, shellfish, crabs, and seaweeds for family consumption, is frequently the work of women and children, whereas men traditionally concentrate on fishing in deeper waters (FAO 1996).

Gender division of labor in the fisheries sector varies largely among region and country, but women typically have a different social and economic role in the community than men and hold different kinds of information about aquatic resources. However, because the involvement of women in the fisheries sector often tends to be at the small-scale, artisanal level,[1] activities by women such as the harvesting of fish and shellfish for household consumption were not construed as fishing in some traditional cultures. As a result, women's contribution to the sector has often been overlooked, and this has affected the way the fisheries sector has been supported.

Although project developments that focus on the improvement on governance of fisheries management have been emphasized in recent years, the author's review of the World Bank's fisheries and aquaculture portfolio indicates that less attention has been paid to the gender aspect in the fisheries sector than in the agricultural sector.[2] Development activities affect men and women differently, and specific steps are often needed to make sure that vulnerable groups such as women and youth are included. Moreover, fisheries conservation measures such as banning of certain types of gear may have unforeseen gender impacts, because some types of fishing gear may be used by only one of the sexes.

ALs as an entry point to address gender issues

Identifying and developing sustainable ALs can be an entry point for investments to address the above gender inequalities in the sector. Many examples can be identified of the promotion of ALs for fishing communities and small-scale fishers with different policy objectives. In many cases ALs provide an opportunity to empower women groups through increased income. Despite offering an entry point or special opportunity to address gender issues, AL activity may not automatically be gender sensitive. As such, explicit efforts to integrate gender issues in projects and programs that promote ALs are warranted.

Examples of ALs

Various forms of aquaculture have been promoted as part of livelihood diversification in several tropical countries, such as Indonesia, the Philippines, and Tanzania (see Thematic Note 2). In the Pacific Islands, the search for ALs was initiated by coastal communities with support from international NGOs to complement the recovery and rehabilitation of resources taking place in their locally managed marine areas.[3] The AL activities include the opening of a women's souvenir shop in the Solomon Islands, and the setting up of a mat-buying venture and the establishment of a honey-making venture by women and youth in Fiji. In Pohnpei in the Federated States of Micronesia, sponge culture was identified as a potential income-generating activity for women that does not conflict with traditional roles.[4]

Studies in Orissa and Maharashtra in India have identified possible livelihood opportunities for women in coastal fishing communities: coastal horticulture and forestry (such as cultivation of coconuts and cashew nuts); production of shellcraft items; weaving of fishing nets; production of palm leaf and bamboo products; retail activities; small-scale collection of wild sea bass, mullet fry, and prawn seed to be sold to fish farmers; livestock production and processing; crop production and processing; and agrotourism (FAO 2007).

GOOD PRACTICES AND LESSONS LEARNED

AL options for fishing communities are diverse, and no single approach or organizational structure is suitable for all situations. Therefore, it must be kept in mind that good practices and lessons learned must be adopted and applied to reflect local needs.

AL covers a wide range of sources of household income, and so most of the discussion and recommendations in other modules in this *Sourcebook* (particularly Crops, Labor, Livestock, Markets, Rural Finance, and Rural Infrastructure) are applicable to this Thematic Note. For instance, key elements of sustainable AL development include "capability building of fisherfolk organizations such as cooperatives and associations to implement livelihood projects, the preparation of feasibility studies and business plans, technical skills development, sound financial management practices, development of innovative and high quality products, access to new markets including urban and regional markets and the full participation of fisherfolk in the identification of livelihood activities and micro-enterprises" (FAO 2006: v).

This section presents concrete examples and more relevant types of development support in the fisheries sector.

Community-based initiatives backed up by technical and credit assistance

Applicable to both aquaculture and other AL activities, technical assistance is an important tool to help fishing community organizations identify suitable livelihood activities. In many cases, credit assistance is needed as starting sources of funds for the community. In the coastal communities of Zanzibar Island in Tanzania, where most women had no major source of income, the introduction of seaweed farming has generated income for women and enabled them to take a greater part in the decision making at home because they were now making a significant financial contribution

Box 13.2 Tanzania: Strengthening Technical and Marketing Assistance

Seaweed farming in Tanzania has been practiced almost exclusively by women. Seaweed farming was introduced in Tanzania in the early 1980s, and seaweed culture on a commercial scale was started in Zanzibar in 1989 by two private seaweed farming companies on the east coast of the island. Soon commercial seaweed farming flourished there, and many coastal villagers, particularly women, have benefited from this practice, but seaweed farmers are now facing challenges. Currently two *Eucheuma* species are cultured in Tanzania: *E. spinosum* and *E. cottoni*. The traded price for *E. cottoni* is significantly higher than that of *E. spinosum*, but because *E. cottoni* is more difficult to grow, a need exists for technical support. Farmers are depending on their buyer company for the supply of seed, stakes, and ropes, so they have no negotiating power on price. The

World Bank's Marine and Coastal Environment Management Project (MACEMP) in Tanzania has paid special attention to the gender aspects in the fisheries sector, particularly through assistance for ALs for women. In the planning phase, the project has identified a variety of AL opportunities (for example, crop farming, seaweed farming, solar salt ponds, aquaculture, and crafts), but women are often restricted by the availability of capital, training, or market access. For example, gender roles exist in marine resource use activities (for example, women collect shellfish, fish, octopus, and farm seaweed), and this may restrict the feasibility of certain AL activities. MACEMP is providing seaweed farmers technical assistance and exploring the possibility of developing value-added seaweed products to improve market access.

Source: FAO 1991, MACEMP Project Appraisal Document.

---

to the household (box 13.2). A similar success story of community initiative based on seaweed farming can be found in Kojadoi Village of Eastern Indonesia. The COREMAP team provided a range of assistance that included information, training, organizational expertise, and funding (see also Innovative Activity Profile 1).

A mariculture project in the state of Kerala in India also gives an example of how community-based initiatives could be supported by the government and financial institutions with credit assistance. The project was initiated in 1994 as a pilot field test of the culture of oysters and mussels under the guidance of Central Marine Fisheries Research Institute scientists. The pilot initiative has grown into a lucrative business activity and AL for over 250 families in about 15 villages of the northern Malabar coast of Kerala (FAO 2003). With an initial production of a few kilograms involving a few women, mariculture production increased to 1,300 metric tons involving more than 1,000 women and 250 men in 2002. The demonstration effect of this activity turned commercial venture has now spread to the neighboring states of Goa, Karnataka, and Maharashtra (FAO 2003).

The major gender impacts are the contribution of women to household income and the freedom in economic decision making at the household level, which have given them a measure of economic independence. Moreover, women gained more self-confidence and self-esteem, more important than

their economic gains from the project. The experience of working in groups and shouldering collective responsibilities has enhanced women's skills in interpersonal relationships as well as in microenterprise management (FAO 2003).

The Kerala initiative has provided some valuable lessons related to technology development and transfer to end users. For instance, the gap between technology development and adoption could be bridged more successfully through participatory action plans where all stakeholders form part of the decision-making process. The initiative also illustrated the importance of providing a package of services and interventions to assist women's self-help groups (SHGs) that includes technological assistance, credit, capability building, stakeholder participation, and support for community organization. The follow-up studies on livelihood opportunities and microfinance support for women in coastal fishing communities in the states of Orissa and Maharashtra[5] found that although many women SHGs and cooperatives have been formed and training had been provided through NGOs, government agencies, and banks themselves, only a few women have received bank loans (FAO 2007). To link SHGs with financial institutions, bank staff must be sensitized as to the concept of SHGs and familiarized with operational guidelines on lending to SHGs. A need for sensitizing women fish workers was also identified because many are presently not aware of the SHG movement.

Critical aspects of the success of the Kerala project include the following:

- The initiative started out as a pilot activity to assess the feasibility and potential of the ALs venture.
- The technology for the culture of the bivalves was simple and user friendly.
- A close partnership existed between the women's group and the men's group in pilot farming activities: for mussel farming, the women's SHGs procured the seed and prepared the seed ropes while men were hired to erect poles in the estuary. Women saw to the routine upkeep of the seeded ropes. For oyster farming, women took charge of the upkeep and marketing activities while men constructed racks and harvested the oysters.
- The project incorporated all key players, such as village elders, interested village people, bank officials, village extension workers, and district administrators into the interactive sessions to promote technology.
- Constant technical support was provided to community organizations, such as help setting up demonstration farms and detailed training and interactive sessions to promote the technology.

- The initiatives supported by community groups were backed up by credit assistance from financial institutions and local government.
- Information campaigns and awareness building programs were carried out.

Empowering fisherwomen through a multisectoral approach

The following example shows how multisectoral ALs (outside of the fisheries sector) can empower poor rural fishing communities.[6] Coastal communities in Bangladesh, where the primary livelihood activity is artisanal fishing, are home to the country's poorest inhabitants. These communities face a number of challenges, including declining fish stocks due to overfishing. The Empowerment of Coastal Fishing Communities for Sustainable Livelihoods Project (box 13.3) emphasized empowering highly disadvantaged groups of rural poor, primarily in Cox's Bazar, Bangladesh, and on creating and sustaining livelihood security.[7] The project considered a holistic view of development and attempted to assist the target communities through a gender-sensitive development approach.

Box 13.3   Bangladesh: Empowerment through Multisectoral Alternative Livelihoods

The Empowerment of Coastal Fishing Communities for Sustainable Livelihoods Project (Government of Bangladesh/UNDP/FAO: 2000–06) was designed to facilitate the empowerment of poor rural Bangladesh fishing communities. The project had seven components (themes): mobilization, health, education, income generation, disaster preparedness, legal assistance, and coastal fisheries resource management. Emphasis was placed on gender for the development of alternative income-generating activities.

Within the first two years of project implementation, need-based community-level skill training was provided. The project also conducted a series of field-level result demonstrations for the target beneficiaries, and 1,753 community members (both men and women) were trained during the second year of project implementation.

Based on the participatory rapid appraisals conducted to identify and prioritize resources and income-generating opportunities in 37 villages, poultry rearing was considered a top priority area for community members, especially for women and for improving nutrition and income. In the second year 167 women community members were trained in livestock and poultry rearing. Selected women members were also trained to vaccinate poultry. Additionally, training in homestead vegetable farming was conducted, and 196 women in 11 village organizations benefited from this training and adopted the recommended vegetable farming. The project took a participatory process involving communities, government personnel, and NGOs and helped communities to orient and understand the project objectives. As a follow-up to the participatory rapid appraisals, need-based training was organized for the communities, which led them to undertake appropriate income-generating activities.

Source: DiPasquale 2005.

The project evaluation report indicated that the movement of women has increased through participation in village organization meetings, parents' meetings in schools, government offices, NGO offices, and other marketplaces. Social bonding has also increased, as has participation of women in various income and nonincome activities other than household work. Income-generating activities have shifted from shrimp-catching activities to other activities largely related to livestock rearing, kitchen gardening, and fish drying. Additionally, and perhaps most important, the project generated a considerable level of economic freedom among women members of the community.

Critical for success are (1) village-organization-based participatory exercises, such as participatory rapid appraisals, which enabled communities to identify and plan for potential nontraditional income-generating activities, both farm and nonfarm based, and prioritize activities based on the analysis of attributes, including their limitations, and (2) taking a multisectoral approach to ALs, which enabled communities to move away from destructive fishing practices.

Linking marine conservation and ALs

Environmental NGOs and development agencies have attempted more often to provide ALs as a means of reducing pressure on degraded marine resources and coastal ecosystems. However, the effectiveness of such interventions was found to be very mixed (Perera 2002).

A study that reviewed different interventions to generate ALs for people dependent on mangrove and coral reef ecosystems in Sri Lanka found that initiatives aiming at the promotion of alternatives have suffered from several common failings.[8] In particular, conflicts arose between the desire to reduce the exploitation of natural resources and the needs and priorities of the poor themselves (Perera 2002). The study also found that community-based organizations should be identified and strengthened before an AL program is introduced.

The experiences from the Fourth Fisheries Project in Bangladesh (2000–07)[9] provided valuable lessons about the problems caused by (1) the lack of support to strengthen both men and women groups and their consultation before the introduction of AL program and (2) the lack of government's willingness to provide ALs with gender-specific focus.

Coastal migration and mobility

Mobility and migration are also an important part of the livelihood diversification strategies used by poor coastal communities to reduce vulnerability and as an alternative to their fishing activity. These activities take several forms: traditional seasonal migrations, temporary mobility to find employment opportunities and business ventures elsewhere, and permanent or long-term migration. Although mobility and migration usually offer an important opportunity for greater gender equalities, they often involve some increased vulnerability for those who left and those left behind, and particularly for poor women and men.[10] The old, disabled, and single women heads of households and poor women often find it more costly and more risky to migrate. These people generally have disproportionately less access to information, rural infrastructure, and favorable labor markets and thus are at higher risk to migrate. IMM (n.d.) points to potential pressures on family structure caused by migration:

- Women who themselves migrate in search of work are particularly susceptible to exploitation and insecurity.
- Those able to migrate permanently face considerable risk because they lose contact with the networks of social support, patronage, and kinship that are often so important in their livelihoods.
- High transaction costs and the risk or cost of loss of social safety nets and decision-making power are higher for women because of related cultural and structural factors perpetuating gender inequalities.

Limited studies exist on gender dimensions of migration and mobility, especially in the context of fishing communities. More studies could be devoted to better understanding the impact of migration and mobility on the livelihoods of migrants and those left behind and on gender inequalities.

GUIDELINES AND RECOMMENDATIONS FOR PRACTITIONERS

Projects that promote alternative livelihoods and facilitate migration and mobility have the potential to reduce gender inequalities, but they also have the potential to reinforce or worsen gender inequalities. Projects must make explicit provisions to include gender dimensions in these strategies to ensure positive equity impacts.

The examples in this Thematic Note and other studies suggest that a *participatory approach* in decision making throughout all project phases is crucial to the long-term success of AL projects. If the AL options are identified and discussed among *all stakeholders,* it is more likely that the activities for women will be supported by the entire community. Several studies suggest that a *close link between ALs and traditional fishing occupations* can make it easier for the activities to be accepted by communities and avoid conflicts with traditional gender roles.

Community organizations, such as fishers' organizations and women's groups, play vital roles in decision making and voicing their particular interests to obtain support from the project. Thus, it is important to *identify and strengthen community organizations* before introducing alternative income-generating activities. Targeting women as special beneficiaries could be counterproductive or at least insufficient to improve their contributions to as well as benefits from development. It is important to take overall structural factors into consideration, including the rules and practices of households and community, market behavior, and the particular characteristics of the relationship between men and women in each society.

As highlighted in the Sri Lanka review study, the AL projects driven by the desire to reduce the exploitation of natural resources tend to overlook the needs and priorities of poor people. As a result, they often fail to gain community interest and support. In designing AL programs for conservation purposes, task team leaders need to pay special attention to the local needs and division of labor between men and women.

Finally, *feasibility studies* and *capacity building through training and basic education* are important. These are necessary not only for beneficiary groups but also for implementing agencies, such as fisheries departments, in order to raise gender awareness and so that agencies can provide the continuous support required by fishing communities.

MONITORING AND EVALUATION INDICATORS

- Human resource capacity built by the project
- Community organizations identified and strengthened
- Improved involvement of stakeholders in decision making
- Conflicts over gender roles minimized or resolved
- Improved living conditions in coastal communities (evidence of socioeconomic benefits)
- Participation of women and youth in both non-income- and income-generating activities
- Improved health of fisheries stocks or aquatic habitats.

Indonesia: Coral Reef Rehabilitation and Management Program

PROJECT OBJECTIVES AND DESCRIPTION

The Coral Reef Rehabilitation and Management Program, Phase II (COREMAP II), aims to increase family welfare from fisheries and aquaculture in 250 coastal villages located in seven districts spread across eastern Indonesia (Biak, Buton, Pangkep, Raja Ampat, Selayar, Sikka, and Wakatobi). Districts included in the project have significant coral resources, totaling 3,300 square kilometers. Village residents are poor with an average per capita monthly income of $25 and depend on reef fish to supply about 90 percent of their protein intake. Like other coral reefs throughout the nation, the condition of these reefs has deteriorated, with only about 30 percent now in good health.

About 60 percent of the Indonesian population lives within 120 kilometers of the coast, and 80 percent of these people engage in activities that depend on marine activities, including fishing and mariculture. Coral reefs are able to meet the needs of the local population for marine food, but the reefs have deteriorated as a result of unhealthy practices such as overfishing, destructive fishing using bombs and poisons, and coral mining. Economic problems are one of the main reasons behind these negative practices.

The deterioration of this resource base has had a major impact on fisher households. Fishers, who are largely men, are faced with a declining catch, and women find difficulties taking care of the family, because they commonly control

---

What's innovative? COREMAP II seeks to transform women's economic and social status and foster change in household and community welfare and coral reef management. Women have also been encouraged to work through community groups and to take up leadership roles in the administration and management of COREMAP.

---

the household budget. Women also engage directly in fisheries and aquaculture activities, although their specific roles vary in accordance with local customs. In Papua, Raja Ampat District, for example, many women work full time in fisheries, whereas women in other districts, such as Sikka, cultivate seaweed. In Matiro Kanja village in Pangkep District, South Sulawesi, women engage in processing and in producing fish cakes and shredded meat, among other products. In other COREMAP areas, women often collect fish and sell it in the marketplace. In general, women in COREMAP villages fill a wide range of roles, from catching and collecting fish and aquaculture products to processing and marketing.

Field analysis undertaken by COREMAP II determined that women who work in fisheries and aquaculture face various constraints on their ability to contribute to household livelihoods and community development. These constraints include low educational status, poor economic status of the family, undervaluation of their lives, and the expectation that they will stay home to care for children and the house.

GENDER APPROACH

COREMAP II specifically aims to improve coastal and fisher women's capacity to engage in coral reef management and community development. The project seeks to (1) increase the total number of women managing and implementing the program and (2) increase women's economic and social empowerment. If these objectives are achieved, women will play a more significant role in improving the welfare of their households and communities. This will thereby change fishing practices linked with the deterioration of coral reefs.

COREMAP II has highlighted gender throughout the planning, design, policy development, implementation, and monitoring and evaluation processes. After thorough discussions, the government was convinced of its value, and minimum gender participation percentages were incorporated into the project's legal documents. With clear guidelines set, the project has worked hard to meet, and even exceed, the goals. Gender issues are reflected at every level of implementation, from the national to village levels. These goals are constantly monitored by both the government through internal meetings and the Bank at the time of its missions. For example, the 2006 World Bank Second Supervision Mission made detailed recommendations as to the numbers of women to be included in the project management units (PMUs) and on the community-based management teams. It was recommended that all PMUs should prioritize recruitment of women senior extension and training officers and community facilitators to reach a 30 percent target by 2007; and all PMUs were required to recruit equal numbers of men and women village motivators. In addition, the project has established community groups (Kelompok Masyarakat, or POKMAS [self-help group]) consisting of three subgroups, one of which focuses on gender concerns (POKMAS Gender). The remaining two groups focus on production and conservation issues.

COREMAP II is innovative in its gender approach in a number of ways. First, at a time when most programs subsume gender issues under poverty objectives and when gender objectives commonly focus on meeting practical gender needs, COREMAP II explicitly seeks to foster strategic shifts in women's economic and social positions within the project. Second, the project is clear in its understanding that such a transformation in women's status and position will lead to changes in household and community welfare and ultimately to improvements in the condition of the coral reefs. Third, the project has demonstrated practical ways of achieving these structural changes. Women's community groups have been given key roles in promoting messages on the core program objective of protecting the coral reefs through community-based management, and in addition, women are managing village and district funds.

Although the program has yet to demonstrate clear long-range outcome impacts, it has demonstrated good practice by (1) adopting specific targets to be achieved within a specific timeframe, (2) ensuring that sufficient numbers of women are involved in the project to make their presence visible, (3) ensuring that women occupy a number of key positions to demonstrate the value of their work, and (4) engaging women directly in the main program activities and providing them with technical as well as gender training.

BENEFITS AND IMPACTS

Progress to date is significant. At the central level, the national coordination unit (NCU) coordinates national planning, implementation, monitoring, and evaluation. By 2007 women's participation at this level reached 16 percent at the NCU, 43 percent at the national project implementation unit (NPIU) of the Indonesian Institute of Sciences (Lembaga Ilmu Pengatauan Indonesia), and 13 percent at the NPIU of the Ministry of Forestry's Forest Protection and Conservation Section (Perlindungan Hutan dan Konservasi Alam). The regional coordination units (RCUs) participate in implementation at the provincial level and coordinate, monitor, and evaluate progress with gender objectives at the district level. Total women's participation at the provincial level has varied from a low of 18 percent to a high of 27 percent; at the district level, women's participation varied from 11 percent to 33 percent. The 50 percent target for village motivators was fully met by 2007. Efforts continue to boost the numbers of women at the project's operating units.

An additional, and perhaps more telling, indication of impact, is that women hold positions of major significance, especially at the national and provincial levels. Examples include the project's Senior Contracts Officer, the Monitoring, Evaluation, and Feedback Coordinator, the assistant director of the PHKA program, primary budgeting staff, and key consultants.

At the village level, women play a leading role in implementing the planned activities by becoming members of the POKMAS for gender, production, and conservation. Women's membership in the gender POKMAS has reached 87 percent of the target. Women's membership in the production and conservation POKMAS, although existent, is as yet limited.

Training offered to members of women's community groups (such as prayer and social groups) has enabled them to become the primary communicators of key messages on coral reef management and community participation to family members and others in their community. Among the women working in the RCUs and PMUs, 167 have been trained on gender and a range of technical issues relating to the project (table 13.4).

LESSONS LEARNED AND ISSUES FOR WIDER APPLICABILITY

COREMAP II, although still in the midst of implementation, has already demonstrated some useful lessons learned.

Table 13.4 Training Related to Gender Issues in COREMAP II's Regional and Project Management Units

Participating Units	Type of training	Aims of training	Time and place	Attendees (Total = 167)
RCU South Sulawesi	Capacity building for coastal and fisheries women	To increase women's capacity in fisheries entrepreneurship	Hotel Cokelat Makassar, July 25–28, 2007	30
RCU Nusa Tenggara Timar (NTT)	Fisheries women training	To increase women's capacity in fisheries	Kupang, December 4–6, 2007	30
PMU Pangkep	Gender training	To transfer gender knowledge to participants; to increase participation in public campaigns to ensure coral reef sustainability; to increase skills in regard to family economic development	Gedung APTISI Jl. Perintis Kemerdekaan Kotamadya Makassar, South Sulawesi Province, December 11–12, 2006	47
PMU Wakatobi	Gender training	To increase women's participation in COREMAP II publicity activities	Gedung Dharmawanita, Wangi-Wangi Kab. Wakatobi, October 15–16, 2006	30
PMU Biak	Gender training	To train communities, especially POKMAS gender groups, in using fisheries resource to increase family incomes	Hotel Mapia Biak, 24–28 November 2006	30

Sources: PMU 2007; RCU 2007.

Four steps, which can be taken in different contexts, are central to achieving gender objectives in COREMAP II:

- Set clear, defined gender targets.
- Socialize the targets so that all stakeholders are aware of the program's gender objectives. COREMAP II seeks to create a sense of program ownership among women. When women understand that they have abilities and opportunities equal to those of men, they can develop their skills themselves and contribute to their own welfare and that of their communities.
- Develop the understanding of the contribution that everyone makes to development. This process of understanding is achieved through individuals and organizations and by examining their value systems.
- Give women the opportunity to develop themselves.

CARE Bangladesh: Family Approaches in Integrated Aquaculture

The Agriculture and Natural Resources sector of CARE Bangladesh operates five major projects that centered on improving livelihoods and promoting integrated aquaculture and agriculture over the last 15 years.

Two projects—Integrated Rice and Fish and New Options for Pest Management—aim to reduce or eliminate pesticides in paddy cultivation and to promote rice-fish culture wherever possible. Other objectives are to raise paddy yields through efficient use of inputs and increase farmers' income by using dike space in paddy fields to grow vegetables.

The Greater Options for Local Development through Aquaculture (GOLDA) project in southwestern Bangladesh was operated to improve prawn production practices and reduce the risk to poor farmers in producing this high-value but high-risk activity.

The Cage Aquaculture for Greater Economic Security (CAGES) project introduced new technology for the poor and poorest farmers with limited or no access to ponds and land. The technology consists of small cages of one to two cubic meters for the culture of fish in ponds or open water bodies.

The Locally Intensified Farming Enterprises (LIFE) project has relied on farmer participatory research to increase the productivity of farm families by improving farming practices; rice-fish culture and fish culture in ponds formed the major aquaculture component.

What's innovative? This program is almost unique among fisheries and aquaculture programs in successfully implementing a gender-mainstreaming strategy to achieve its gender objectives. The mainstreaming strategy—which helped women and men engage in aquaculture development for the benefit of their families as well as themselves—challenges orthodox perceptions of the financial value of family approaches.

All five projects operated for three to five years through farmer groups, except for CAGES, which worked largely through partner NGOs. Their success attracted additional funds—mainly from DFID and the European Union—for exploring new ideas through new projects or in new areas. The projects, which operated in different parts of Bangladesh, employed more than 700 staff. Each project had a central technical team that provided support to field-based staff, all of whom had bicycles to enable easy movement. Field staff organized several thousands of men and women into groups, and the projects' strategic interventions helped to improve livelihoods, as well as the local environment in which the projects operated. The projects offered no material support. They shared knowledge and skills and guided participants to appropriate credit organizations whenever they needed such support.

GENDER OBJECTIVES AND INNOVATIVE FEATURES OF CARE'S PROGRAM

CARE Bangladesh has explored ways to (1) enhance women's participation in integrated aquaculture and (2) empower women through aquaculture programs. Family approaches, which have involved including women and men in extension activities, farmer field schools, participatory monitoring and evaluation, and action research, have been found to be effective in achieving these objectives in a sustainable way.

This program successfully implemented a gender-mainstreaming strategy to achieve its gender objectives, and this success is almost unique in fisheries and aquaculture programs. The main component of the gender-mainstreaming strategy (to hire, train, and use men and women staff to address social as well as technical issues) was essential for working in Bangladesh. This strategy provided an enabling environment for women and men, especially husbands and wives, to engage in aquaculture development to benefit themselves and their families. The success of this approach challenges orthodox beliefs about its value in financial terms.

BENEFITS AND IMPACTS

This CARE approach reflects the understanding within gender analysis that existing norms and behavior within communities and development organizations may need to be challenged directly to transform gender relations and achieve sustainable gender-equitable outcomes. These are the kinds of benefits and impacts sought in all programs but are frequently not achieved because of program time frames and the priority placed on production outcomes over the distribution of benefits.

Gender-balanced teams

CARE evolved its own organizational gender policy, which guided the organization in undertaking gender-sensitive activities. In recruiting staff for the projects described earlier, efforts were made to hire gender-balanced teams, particularly for field operations. In all of the projects, women constituted 30–50 percent of the teams. In some projects, such as GOLDA, the ratio was almost 1:1. The recruitment process had an electrifying effect, contributing to many positive developments while presenting new challenges to a conservative society resisting change. Although women staff initially experienced many difficulties in working in the field, constant support from the organization and continuous interaction with the community created an environment in which the staff could contribute productively.

Staff participated in practical technical and social training. Social training covered issues such as organizing farmer groups, raising gender awareness, and building community networks to sustain activities after the projects ended. The GOLDA project placed the staff in farm families for a week so that they could witness the conditions in which the families lived, learn how to address issues in fish and prawn culture as they arose, and focus on meeting practical needs.

Gender-responsive participatory processes

CARE targeted both men and women family members in all of its agricultural projects out of a conviction that the empowerment of women should begin with building their knowledge about the technology and providing skills to undertake activities that would bring economic benefits to the family. If either the husband or wife could not take part in program activities, they were replaced by other family members. Although efforts were made to form mixed-sex groups, separate groups of 20–30 men or women were formed. Participants preferred the single-sex groups, even though they were sometimes difficult to form. In forming groups of women, special care had to be taken, and greater flexibility was needed until the community understood the project interventions.

Management of gender-based farmer groups

Though in the beginning men trainers managed the men's group and the women trainers focused on women, once the community recognized the commitment of the trainers, the gender of the trainer became irrelevant. Trainers trained groups but also provided follow-up support to each of the farm families involved in carrying out the activities on their own farms.

Economic, social, and environmental impacts

With the addition of women's labor to the workforce, the area under rice-fish production in different areas increased by one-third, but the biggest benefit by far was the dramatic reduction in pesticide use. Productivity increased by 20 to 40 percent. The prawn farming lessons had impressive positive effects that helped to increase incomes by almost 50 percent. Using small cages of one cubic meter, women demonstrated the possibility of growing 20–30 kilograms of fish in six months. A woman managing three to four cages could earn enough to sustain herself and improve the nutrition of her children as well.

Empowered men and women not only improved their livelihoods from aquaculture and agriculture but also made progress in breaking gender and social barriers more generally. Aside from field days, which increased participants' experience and confidence, Farmer Science Congresses were organized to share results. Women dominated the presentations.

Days were also devoted to discussing gender issues and setting goals and a timeframe for meeting them. Gender issues confronting each area were identified, and short learning sessions developed. Field trainers were trained to discuss the issues with men's and women's groups. Discussions on children's education focused on girls. Adequate food provision was emphasized as essential for both boys and girls. Issues of dowry, work distribution patterns, work sharing, and family decision-making processes all provided material for learning sessions. The discussion and learning days were very well received and appreciated as a step in the right direction to bring change.

LESSONS LEARNED AND ISSUES FOR THE WIDER APPLICABILITY OF FAMILY APPROACHES

The family approach is highly effective but expensive. Funding agencies are often more interested in increasing the number of families covered by the program than in ensuring that everyone in a family receives the necessary information. For this reason it is essential to convince donors that both the husband and wife must be trained if the lives of all household members are to improve and if they are all to achieve higher productivity.

Development projects should allocate resources to invest in building knowledge and skills through adequate numbers of gender-balanced field staff. Building a gender-balanced staff of sufficient strength is a task that can be accomplished only when there is an organizational policy that will ensure gender-balanced staff recruitment and that sets out definite strategies to attain this balance within a given time. Once a balanced team is built, the impact on project outcomes is far reaching.

NOTES

Overview

The Overview was prepared by Christine Okali (Consultant), with inputs from M. C. Nandeesha (Central Agricultural University, Tripura); Chitra Deshpande (Consultant); and Katrien Holvoet, Helga Josupeit, and Melba Reantaso (FAO); and was reviewed by Eriko Hoshino, Catherine Ragasa, and Mary Hill Rojas (Consultants); Yvette Diei Ouadi, Ib Kollavick-Jensen, Rebecca Metzner, Susana Siar, Ilaria Sisto, and Rohana Subasinghe (FAO); Maria Hartl and Antonio Rota (IFAD); and Kieran Kelleher and Eija Pehu (World Bank).

1. Considerable variation exists in the position and status of women in society. In China and Southeast Asian countries (for example, Cambodia, Lao People's Democratic Republic, Thailand, and Vietnam), for instance, women are often able to play more independent economic roles and have at least some, if not total, control over benefits, whereas in South Asian countries (for example, Bangladesh, India, and Pakistan) women are more constrained, especially in their ability to market produce that is viewed as central to achieving control over income. (However, for India see Busby 1999 and Prahdan and Flaherty 2008.)

2. Gammage and others (2006) stated in their part of the Bangladesh shrimp production report to USAID that women who are self-employed are likely to be accompanied by dependent children and that this accounts for some of the reports of child labor being used in small-scale fisheries.

3. Shrimp production was selected as the example for aquaculture because there is more information available on the social implications of shrimp production and because it is largely the boom in shrimp production that has driven the global market in aquaculture products. Other species have led to or preceded the boom in aquaculture in more regional or local products (for example, catfish, tilapia, grouper, scallops, or lobster culture).

4. These are the intangible elements of knowledge and skills in the sense that what is seen to be required can vary depending on who is being trained or who is applying for employment. Training programs always contain tangible and intangible elements.

5. More recent thinking on social protection includes the use of interventions that are transformative in purpose (see Devereux 2001; Devereux and Sebates-Wheeler 2004).

Thematic Note 1

This Thematic Note was written by Christine Okali (Consultant) and was reviewed by Eriko Hoshino, Catherine Ragasa, and Mary Hill Rojas (Consultants); Yvette Diei Ouadi, Ib Kollavick-Jensen, Rebecca Metzner, Susana Siar, Ilaria Sisto, and Rohana Subasinghe (FAO); Maria Hartl and Antonio Rota (IFAD); and Kieran Kelleher and Eija Pehu (World Bank).

1. The term *gender-responsive user groups* is used here in preference to the term *self-help groups*, which describes groups that are not making claims on government or have no expectations of service delivery but rather rely on bottom-up processes for their development. Rubinoff (1999) refers to them as *small cooperative groups.*

2. This study analyzed data from 46 rural programs in 20 countries in Africa, Asia, and Latin America.

3. Examples of the different possible roles that can be expected to be performed by different partners are given in SFLP (2006).

Thematic Note 2

This Thematic Note was written by M. C. Nandeesha (Central Agricultural University, Tripura) and Christine Okali (Consultant), with inputs from Melba Reantaso (FAO), and was reviewed by Chitra Deshpande, Eriko Hoshino, and Mary Hill Rojas (Consultants); Susana Siar, Ilaria Sisto, and Rohana Subasinghe (FAO); Maria Hartl (IFAD); and Kieran Kelleher (World Bank).

1. The Vietnam VAC system is a system with a mix of annual and perennial crops, including fruits and vegetables, small livestock and poultry, and several species of Chinese and Indian carps grown in ponds. Since 1989 the Vietnamese government has distributed land to farmers and encouraged the development of the family economy through such diversified farming systems. The system is labor intensive and protects the environment.

2. This was a pilot project involving the Vietnamese Women's Union plus PROFOUND, a Dutch development organization, in consultation with the Asia Institute of Technology and the Vietnamese Research Institute for Aquaculture. The project was funded by the Commission of the European Communities. For ease of reference in this document, the project is referred to as PROFOUND.

3. PROFOUND uses this gender tool to make women's position in the household and society visible. It involves mapping resources and institutions in the community, adding male and female signs for access to and control over these, and decision making.

Thematic Note 3

This Thematic Note was written by Christine Okali (Consultant) and Katrien Holvoet, Helga Josupeit, and Yvette Diei Ouadi (FAO), and was reviewed by Chitra Deshpande, Eriko Hoshino, Catherine Ragasa, and Mary Hill Rojas (Consultants); Susana Siar and Ilaria Sisto (FAO); Maria Hartl (IFAD); and Kieran Kelleher (World Bank).

1. These horizontal links include associations such as the Latin American Network of Women in Fisheries, or Red Mujer, the South Indian Federation of Fishermen, and the Fisherfolk Association in Gabon.

Thematic Note 4

This Thematic Note was prepared by Eriko Hoshino (Consultant), with inputs from Catherine Ragasa (Consultant), and reviewed by Christine Okali and Mary Hill Rojas (Consultants); Katrien Holvoet, Rebecca Metzner, and Susana Siar (FAO); Maria Hartl (IFAD); and Kieran Kelleher and Eija Pehu (World Bank).

1. *Artisanal fisheries* are traditional fisheries involving fishing households (as opposed to commercial companies), using relatively small amounts of capital and energy, relatively small fishing vessels (if any), making short fishing trips, close to shore, mainly for local consumption (definition based on FAO fisheries glossary).

2. Implementation completion reports for 26 completed Bank projects and project appraisal documents for 15 ongoing projects (in 2007) that had at least one component related to fisheries, aquatic resource management, or aquaculture were reviewed to extract examples of positive or negative impacts on gender.

3. Secretariat of the Pacific Community, *Women in Fisheries Information Bulletin* (March 16), www.spc.int.

4. "An Assessment of the Role of Women in Fisheries in Pohnpei, Federated States of Micronesia," www.spc.int.

5. The studies were carried out as a follow-up to the national workshop on best practices in microfinance programs for women in coastal fishing communities in India, held in 2003.

6. This discussion was mainly taken from the various project documents available at www.livelihoods.org.

7. See also Sustainable Fisheries Livelihoods Programme, "Gender Credit Study in Tanji and Albreda Fishing Communities," www.sflp.org.

8. This refers to the South Asia Cooperative Environment Programme (SACEP) review of different interventions to generate alternative livelihoods for people dependent on mangrove and coral reef ecosystems in Sri Lanka. The project was initiated in April 2002 at the inaugural session of the Sri Lanka Coral Reef Forum, a joint venture of SACEP, CORDIO (Coral Reef Degradation in the Indian Ocean) and GCRMN (Global Coral Reef Monitoring Network), at which more than 40 stakeholders gave their initial inputs.

9. This section was drawn heavily from project documents.

10. Integrated Marine Management, "The Sustainable Coastal Livelihoods," www.ex.ac.uk/imm.

Innovative Activity Profile 1

This Innovative Activity Profile was written by Dian Fiana (COREMAP II Consultant), with inputs from Charles Greenwald (COREMAP II), and reviewed by Chitra Deshpande, Christine Okali, Catherina Ragasa, and Mary Hill Rojas (Consultants); Melba Reantaso, Susana Siar, Ilaria Sisto, and Rohana Subasinghe (FAO); Maria Hartl (IFAD); and Pawan Patil (World Bank). This Profile was largely drawn from the author's own experiences from being involved in the program. Other references used were Fiana (2007); NCU (2005, 2006, 2007a, 2007b); PMU (2007); RCU (2007); and World Bank (2006).

Innovative Activity Profile 2

This Innovative Activity Profile was written by M. C. Nandeesha (Central Agricultural University, Tripura) and Christine Okali (Consultant); and reviewed by Chitra Deshpande, Catherine Ragasa, and Mary Hill Rojas (Consultants); Melba

Reantaso, Susana Siar, Ilaria Sisto, and Rohana Subasinghe (FAO); Maria Hartl (IFAD); and Pawan Patil (World Bank). This Profile is based in large part on Debashish and others (2001).

REFERENCES

Overview

Allison, Edward H. 2003. "Linking National Fisheries Policy to Livelihoods on the Shores of Lake Kyoga, Uganda." LADDER Working Paper No. 9, Overseas Development Group, University of East Anglia, Norwich.

Barman, Benoy K. 2001. "Women in Small-Scale Aquaculture in North-West Bangladesh." *Gender and Technology Development* 5 (2): 267–87.

Belton, Ben, and David Little. 2008. "The Development of Aquaculture in Central Thailand: Domestic versus Export-Led Production." *Journal of Agrarian Change* 8 (1): 123–43.

Busby, Cecilia. 1999. "Agency, Power and Personhood: Discourses on Gender and Violence in a Fishing Community in South India." *Critique of Anthropology* 19 (3): 227–48.

De Silva, D. A. M., and Masahiro Yamao. 2006. "The Involvement of Female Labour in Seafood Processing in Sri Lanka: The Impact of Organizational Fairness and Supervisor Evaluation on Employee Commitment." In *Global Symposium on Gender and Fisheries: Seventh Asian Fisheries Forum, 2004,* ed. Poh-Sze Choo, Stephen J. Hall, and Meryl J. Williams, 103–14. Penang, Malaysia: World Fish Center.

Devereux, Stephen. 2001. "Livelihood Insecurity and Social Protection: A Re-Emerging Issue in Rural Development." *Development Policy Review* 19 (4): 507–19.

Devereux, Stephen, and Rachel Sebates-Wheeler. 2004. "Transformative Social Protection." IDS Working Paper 232, Institute of Development Studies, Brighton, U.K.

Gammage, Sarah, Kenneth Swanberg, Mubina Khandkar, Md. Zahidul Hassan, Md. Zobair, and Abureza M. Muzareba. 2006. *A Pro-Poor Analysis of the Shrimp Sector in Bangladesh.* Report prepared for the Office of Women in Development of the U.S. Agency for International Development, Dhaka, Bangladesh.

Josupeit, Helga. 2004. "Women in the Fisheries Sector of Argentina, Uruguay and Southern Brazil." FAO Fisheries Circular, No. 992, Food and Agriculture Organization, Rome.

Jul-Larsen, Eyolf, Jeppe Kolding, Ragnhild Overå, Jesper R. Nielsen, and Paul van Zwieten, eds. 2003. "Management, Co-management or No Management? Major Dilemmas in Southern African Freshwater Fisheries." FAO Fisheries

Technical Paper 426/1 and 2, Food and Agriculture Organization, Rome.

Kelkar, Govind. 2001. "Gender Concerns in Aquaculture: Women's Roles and Capabilities." In *Gender Concerns in Aquaculture in Southeast Asia,* Gender Studies, Monograph 12, ed. K. Kusakabe and G. Kelkar, 1–10. Bangkok: Asian Institute of Technology.

Markussen, Marith. 2002. "Women in the Informal Fish Processing and Marketing Sectors of Lake Victoria." Norwegian Institute for Urban and Regional Research Working Paper 115, Oslo.

New Economics Foundation (NEF). 2002. "Plugging the Leaks: Making the Most of Every Pound That Enters Your Local Economy." NEF, London.

Pradhan, Dolagobinda, and Mark Flaherty. 2008. "National Initiatives, Local Effects: Trade Liberalization, Shrimp Aquaculture, and Coastal Communities in Orissa, India." *Society & Natural Resources* 21: 63–76.

Sustainable Fisheries Livelihoods Programme (SFLP). 2006. "Gender Policies for Responsible Fisheries—Policies to Support Gender Equity and Livelihoods in Small-Scale Fisheries." *New Directions in Fisheries—A Series of Policy Briefs on Development Issues.* Rome: Food and Agriculture Organization.

Tietze, U., Susana Siar, Suchitra M. Upare, and Maroti A. Upare. 2007. "Livelihood and Micro-Enterprise Development Opportunities for Women in Coastal Fishing Communities in India: Case Studies of Orissa and Maharashtra." FAO Fisheries Circular No. 1021, Food and Agriculture Organization, Rome.

Walker, Barbara Louise Endemaño. 2001. "Sisterhood and Seine-Nets: Engendering Development and Conservation in Ghana's Marine Fishery." *Professional Geographer* 53 (2): 160–77.

World Bank. 2006. *Aquaculture Review: Changing the Face of the Waters. Meeting the Promise and Challenge of Sustainable Aquaculture.* Report 36622-GLB. Washington, DC: IBRD/World Bank.

Thematic Note 1

Barman, Benoy K. 2001. "Women in Small-Scale Aquaculture in North-West Bangladesh." *Gender and Technology Development* 5 (2): 267–87.

Bennett, Elizabeth. 2005. "Gender, Fisheries and Development." *Marine Policy* 29: 451–59.

Dixon-Mueller, Ruth. 1989. *Women's Work in Third World Agriculture.* Geneva: International Labour Organization.

Mowla, Runia, and Md. Ghulam Kibria. 2006. "An Integrated Approach on Gender Issues in Coastal Fisheries." In *Global Symposium on Gender and Fisheries: Seventh*

Asian Fisheries Forum, 2004, ed. Poh-Sze Choo, Stephen J. Hall, and Meryl J. Williams, 21–28. Penang, Malaysia: World Fish Center.

Mymensingh Aquaculture Extension Project. 1999. "Female Involvement in Different Activities of Women in Mymensingh Aquaculture Extension Project." Paper presented at Workshop on Women's Involvement in Fisheries, NFEP, Parbatipur, Dinajpur, Bangladesh, July.

Nathan, Dev, and Niaz Ahmed Apu. 1998. "Women's Independent Access to Productive Resources: Fish Ponds in the Oxbow Lakes Project, Bangladesh." *Gender Technology and Development* 2 (3): 397–413.

———. 2004. "Case Study of the Oxbow Lakes Small-Scale Fishermen's Project (OLSSFP) IFAD Innovation Mainstreaming Initiative, Bangladesh—1990–1997." Draft document submitted to International Fund for Agricultural Development, Rome.

New Economics Foundation (NEF). 2002. *Plugging the Leaks: Making the Most of Every Pound That Enters Your Local Economy.* London: NEF.

Rubinoff, Janet Ahner. 1999. "Fishing for Status: Impact of Development on Goa's Fisherwomen." *Women Studies International Forum* 22 (6): 631–44.

Sustainable Fisheries Livelihoods Programme (SFLP). 2006. "Gender Policies for Responsible Fisheries—Policies to Support Gender Equity and Livelihoods in Small-Scale Fisheries." FAO Policy Brief on New Directions in Fisheries No. 6, Food and Agriculture Organization, Rome.

Westermann, Olaf, Jacqueline Ashby, and Jules Pretty. 2005. "Gender and Social Capital: The Importance of Gender Differences for the Maturity and Effectiveness of Natural Resource Management Groups." *World Development* 33 (11): 1783–99.

Thematic Note 2

Brugère, Cecile, Malene Felsing, Kyoko Kusabe, and Govind Kelkar. 2001. "Women in Aquaculture." Final Report, Asia Pacific Economic Cooperation Project, FWG 03/99, Asian Institute of Technology, Pathumthani, Thailand and Institute of Aquaculture, Stirling, U.K.

Commission of European Communities (CEC). 1993. *Women and Development, Cooperation with Latin America, Asian and Mediterranean Countries, Management of the Project Cycle.* Brussels: CEC.

Debashish, K. S., M. Shirin, F. Zaman, M. Ireland, G. Chapman, and M. C. Nandeesha. 2001. "Strategies for Addressing Gender Issues through Aquaculture Programs: Approaches by CARE Bangladesh." In *Proceedings of the International Symposium on Women in Asian*

Fisheries, ICLARM Contribution No. 1587, ed. M. J. Williams, M. C. Nandeesha, V. P. Corral, E.Tech, and P. S. Choo, 147–56. Penang, Malaysia.

Nandeesha, M. C. 2007. "Asian Experience on Farmer's Innovation in Freshwater Fish Seed Production and Nursing and the Role of Women." In "Assessment of Freshwater Fish Seed Resources for Sustainable Aquaculture," FAO Fisheries Technical Paper No. 501, Food and Agriculture Organization, Rome.

Voeten, Jaap, and Bert-Jan Ottens. 1997. "Gender Training in Aquaculture in Northern Vietnam: A Report." *Gender, Technology and Development* 1: 413–32.

World Bank. 2006. "Aquaculture Review: Changing the Face of the Waters. Meeting the Promise and Challenge of Sustainable Aquaculture." GLB Report No. 36622, IBRD/World Bank, Washington, DC.

Zaman, F. 1998. *Dissemination of NOPEST Activities Study and Sustainability Study.* Dhaka: CARE Bangladesh.

Thematic Note 3

Barrientos, Stephanie. 2001. "Gender Flexibility and Global Value Chains." *IDS Bulletin* 32 (3): 83–93.

Barrientos, Stephanie, Catherine Dolan, and Anne Tallontire. 2003. "Gendered Value Chain Approach to Codes of Conduct in African Horticulture." *World Development* 31 (9): 1511–26.

De Silva, D. A. M., and Masahiro Yamao. 2006. "The Involvement of Female Labour in Seafood Processing in Sri Lanka: The Impact of Organizational Fairness and Supervisor Evaluation on Employee Commitment." In *Global Symposium on Gender and Fisheries: Seventh Asian Fisheries Forum, 2004,* ed. Poh-Sze Choo, Stephen J. Hall, and Meryl J. Williams, 103–14. Penang, Malaysia: World Fish Center.

Gammage, Sarah, Kenneth Swanberg, Mubina Khandkar, Md. Zahidul Hassan, Md. Zobair, and Abureza M. Muzareba. 2006. "A Pro-Poor Analysis of the Shrimp Sector in Bangladesh." Report prepared for the Office of Women in Development of the U.S. Agency for International Development, Dhaka, Bangladesh.

Josupeit, Helga. 2004. "Women in the Fisheries Sector of Argentina, Uruguay and Southern Brazil." FAO Fisheries Circular No. 992, Food and Agriculture Organization, Rome.

Kabeer, Naila, and Ramya Subrahmanian. 1996. "Institutions, Relations and Outcomes: Framework and Tools for Gender-Aware Planning." Discussion Paper 357, Institute of Development Studies, Sussex, U.K.

Kelkar, Govind, Dev A. Nathan, and Jahan I. Rownok. 2003. "We Were in Fire, Now We Are in Water: Micro-Credit and

Gender Relations in Rural Bangladesh." Consultant report, International Fund for Agricultural Development, Rome.

Kumaran, M., N. Kalaimani, K. Ponnusamy, V. S. Chandrasekaran, and D. Deboral Vimala. 2003. "A Case of Informal Shrimp Farmers Association and Its Role in Sustainable Shrimp Farming in Tamil Nadu, India." *Aquaculture Asia* 8 (2): 10–12.

Kusakabe, Kyoko, and Govind Kelkar, eds. 2001. *Gender Concerns in Aquaculture in Southeast Asia.* Gender Studies Monograph 12, Gender and Development Studies. Bangkok: School of Environment Resources and Development, Asian Institute of Technology.

Markussen, Marith. 2002. "Women in the Informal Fish Processing and Marketing Sectors of Lake Victoria." Norwegian Institute for Urban and Regional Research Working Paper 115, Oslo.

Nandeesha, M. C. 2007. "Asian Experience on Farmer's Innovation in Freshwater Fish Seed Production and Nursing and the Role of Women." In "Assessment of Freshwater Fish Seed Resources for Sustainable Aquaculture," FAO Fisheries Technical Paper No. 501, Food and Agriculture Organization, Rome.

Organisation for Economic Co-operation and Development/Development Assistance Committee (OECD/DAC). 2006. "Summary Record of the Fourth Meeting of the DAC Network on Gender Equality, Paris 5–7 July 2006," Paris, September.

Sharma, Chandrika. 2003. "The Impact of Fisheries Development and Globalization Processes on Women of Fishing Communities in the Asian Region." *Asia-Pacific Resource Network Journal* 8: 1–12.

Sustainable Fisheries Livelihoods Programme (SFLP). 2005. "Impact of HIV/AIDS on Fishing Communities: Policies to Support Livelihoods, Rural Development and Public Health." In *New Directions in Fisheries—A Series of Policy Briefs on Development Issues.* Rome: Food and Agriculture Organization.

Swanrangsi, Sirlak. 2003. "Technological Changes and Their Implications for Women in Fisheries." Fish Inspection and Quality Control Division, Department of Fisheries, Bangkok.

Tietze, Uwe, Susana Siar, Suchitra M. Upare, and Maroti A. Upare. 2007. "Livelihood and Micro-Enterprise Development Opportunities for Women in Coastal Fishing Communities in India: Case Studies of Orissa and Maharashtra." FAO Fisheries Circular No. 1021, Food and Agriculture Organization, Rome.

WorldFish. 2007. "Innovative Fish Farming Project for HIV-Affected African Families Doubles Incomes and Boosts Household Nutrition in Malawi." Press release, August.

Thematic Note 4

Brugère, Cecile, and Edward Allison. Forthcoming. "Livelihood Diversification in Coastal and Inland Fishing Communities: Misconceptions, Evidence and Implications for Fisheries Management." Working Paper, Food and Agriculture Organization, Rome.

DiPasquale Brandi M. 2005. "Empowerment of Coastal Fishing Communities for Livelihood Security Literature Synthesis Report." UNDP, FAO, and government of Bangladesh. Available at: www.livelihoods.org.

Food and Agriculture Organization (FAO). 1991. "Seaweed Collection and Culture in Tanzania." Aquaculture for Local Community Development Programme. GCP/INT/436/SWE.14. Rome: FAO. Also available at www.fao.org.

———. 1996. Vanuatu—Technical Report: "An Assessment of the Role of Women in Fisheries in Vanuatu." Mechanical Report, FAO, Rome.

———. 1997. "Workshop on Gender Roles and Issues in Artisanal Fisheries in West Africa. Lomé, Togo, 11–13 December 1996." Technical Report 97, January, ed. Benoit W. Horemans and Alhaji M. Jallow. Rome: FAO. Also available at www.fao.org.

———. 2003. "Report of the National Workshop on Best Practices in Microfinace Programmes for Women in Coastal Fishing Communities in India. Panaji, Goa, India, 1–4 July 2003." FAO Fisheries Report No. 724, FAO, Rome. Also available at www.fao.org.

———. 2006. "Report of the National Workshop on Micro-Enterprise Development in Coastal Communities in the Philippines: Sharing of Experiences and Lessons Learned." FAO Fisheries Report No. 850, FAO, Rome. Also available at www.fao.org.

———. 2007. "Livelihood and Micro-Enterprise Development Opportunities for Women in Coastal Fishing Communities in India—Case Studies of Orissa and Maharashtra." FAO Fisheries Circular 1021, FAO, Rome. Also available at www.fao.org.

Gurumayum S. D., G. A. Devi, and M. C. Nandeesha. 2004. "Women's Participation in Fisheries Activities in Manipur Valley in India with Traditional Fish-Based Beliefs and Customs." In *Global Symposium on Gender and Fisheries: Seventh Asian Fisheries Forum.* Penang, Malaysia: World Fish Center.

Integrated Marine Management (IMM). n.d. "The Sustainable Coastal Livelihoods." Available at www.ex.ac.uk/imm.

Lyn, L. 2000. "An Assessment of the Role of Women in Fisheries in Pohnpei, Federated States of Micronesia." Available at www.spc.int.

Perera, Nishanthi. 2002. "Alternative Livelihood through Income Diversification: As Management Options for Sustainable Coral Reef and Associated Ecosystem Management in Sri Lanka." South Asia Co-Operative Environment Programme (58), Colombo, Sri Lanka. Summary available at www.icriforum.org.

Secretariat of the Pacific Community (SPC). 2007. "Women in Fisheries Information Bulletin." Issue of March 16. Available at www.spc.int.

Sustainable Fisheries Livelihoods Programme (SFLP). 2004. "Gender Credit Study in Tanji and Albreda Fishing Communities." Available at www.sflp.org.

Innovative Activity Profile 1

Fiana, D. 2007. "COREMAP II and Gender Dimensions: Recent Progress and Challenges." Report submitted to the Executive Secretary and Project Management Advisor of the World Bank, World Bank, Washington, DC.

National Coordination Unit (NCU). 2005. "World Bank 1st Supervision Mission Aide Memoire Action Items." Unpublished Project Report.

———. 2006. "World Bank 2nd Supervision Mission Aide Memoire Action Items." Unpublished Project Report.

———. 2007a. "Project Quarterly and Annual Reports, 2005–2007." Unpublished Project Report.

———. 2007b. "Progress Review Action Items." Unpublished Project Report.

Project Management Unit (PMU). 2007. "Project Quarterly and Annual Reports, 2005–2007." Unpublished Project Report.

Regional Coordination Unit (RCU). 2007. "Project Quarterly and Annual Reports, 2005–2007." Unpublished Project Report.

World Bank. 2006. "Final Aide Memoire on COREMAP II: Second Supervision Mission." World Bank, Washington, DC.

Innovative Activity Profile 2

Debashish, K. S., M. Shirin, F. Zaman, M. Ireland, G. Chapman, and M. C. Nandeesha. 2001. "Strategies for Addressing Gender Issues through Aquaculture Programs: Approaches by CARE Bangladesh." In *Proceedings of the International Symposium on Women in Asian Fisheries*, ICLARM Contribution No. 1587, ed. M. J. Williams, M. C. Nandeesha, V. P. Corral, E.Tech, and P. S. Choo, 147–56. Penang, Malaysia.

FURTHER READING

Overview

Allison, Edward, and Janet Seeley. 2004. "HIV and AIDS among Fisherfolks: A Threat to 'Responsible Fisheries'?" *Fish and Fisheries* 5: 215–34.

Bennett, Elizabeth. 2005. "Gender, Fisheries and Development." *Marine Policy* 29: 451–59.

Brugère, Cecile, Malene Felsing, Kyoko Kusakabe, and Govind Kelkar. 2001. "Women in Aquaculture." Final Report, Asia Pacific Economic Cooperation Project, FWG 03/99. Asian Institute of Technology, Pathumthani, Thailand, and Institute of Aquaculture, Stirling U.K.

Food and Agriculture Organization (FAO). 2005. "Increasing the Contribution of Small-Scale Fisheries to Poverty Alleviation and Food Security." Technical Guidelines for Responsible Fisheries No. 10, FAO, Rome.

Harrison, Elizabeth. 1997. "Fish, Feminists and the FAO: Translating 'Gender' through Different Institutions in the Development Process." In *Getting Institutions Right for Women in Development*, ed. Anne Marie Goetz, 61–74. London: Zed Books.

Sustainable Fisheries Livelihoods Programme. 2005. "Impact of HIV/AIDS on Fishing Communities: Policies to Support Livelihoods, Rural Development and Public Health." *New Directions in Fisheries—A Series of Policy Briefs on Development Issues*. Rome: Food and Agriculture Organization.

Thematic Note 1

Allison, Edward, and Frank Ellis. 2001. "The Livelihoods Approach and Management of Small-Scale Fisheries." *Marine Policy* 25: 377–88.

Ferrer, Elmer, Lenore de la Cruz, and Marife Domingo, eds. 1996. *Seeds of Hope: A Collection of Case Studies on Community-Based Coastal Resources Management in the Philippines*. Manila, Philippines: CBCRM Resource Center.

Kusakabe, Kyoko. 2003. "Women's Involvement in Small-Scale Aquaculture in Northeast Thailand." *Development in Practice* 13 (4): 333–45.

Kusakabe, Kyoko, and Govind Kelkar, eds. 2001. *Gender Concerns in Aquaculture in Southeast Asia*. Gender Studies Monograph 12, Gender and Development Studies, School of Environment Resources and Development, Asian Institute of Technology, Bangkok.

Leach, Melissa, Robin Mearns, and Ian Scoones. 1997. "Environmental Entitlements: A Framework for Understanding the Institutional Dynamics of Environmental

Change." IDS Discussion Paper 359, Institute of Development Studies, Sussex, Brighton, U.K.

Locke, Catherine. 1999. "Constructing a Gender Policy for Joint Forest Management in India." *Development and Change* 30: 265–85.

Nandeesha, M. C. 2007. "Asian Experience on Farmer's Innovation in Freshwater Fish Seed Production and Nursing and the Role of Women." In "Assessment of Freshwater Fish Seed Resources for Sustainable Aquaculture," FAO Fisheries Technical Paper 501, Rome, Food and Agriculture Organization.

Sullivan, L. 2006. "The Impacts of Aquaculture Development in Relation to Gender in Northeastern Thailand." In *Global Symposium on Gender and Fisheries: Seventh Asian Fisheries Forum, 2004,* ed. Poh-Sze Choo, Stephen J. Hall, and Meryl J. Williams, 29–42. Penang, Malaysia: World Fish Center.

Thematic Note 4

Assisting Coastal Communities in the Pacific Islands with Alternative Sources of Livelihood and Income: www.spc.int.

Environment and Development in Coastal Regions and in Small Islands: Developing Alternative Livelihoods: www.unesco.org.

JFPR Grant to Develop Alternative Livelihoods for Poor Fishers in Indonesia's Coastal Communities: www.adb.org.

Livelihood and Micro-Enterprise Development Opportunities for Women in Coastal Fishing Communities in India: Case Studies of Orissa and Maharashtra: www.fao.org.

Seaweed Farming: An Alternative Livelihood for Small-Scale Fishers?: www.crc.uri.edu.

Semporna Islands Darwin Project—Alternative Livelihoods: www.sempornaislandsproject.com.

Trends in Poverty and Livelihoods in Coastal Fishing Communities of Orissa State, India: www.fao.org.

Innovative Activity Profile 1

Cesar, Herman. 1996. "Economic Analysis of Indonesian Coral Reefs." Working Paper Series "Work in Progress," World Bank, Washington, DC.

Ministry of Marine Affairs and Fisheries. 2007. "Quarterly Progress Report: Implementation Status of COREMAP II. Period April–June 2007." Coral Reef Rehabilitation and Management Program II, Directorate General of Marine, Coastal, and Small Islands, Indonesia.

World Bank. 2004. "Technical Appraisal." In "Project Appraisal Document for the Coral Reef Rehabilitation and Management Project (Phase II), Indonesia," World Bank, Washington, DC.

Innovative Activity Profile 2

Nandeesha, M. C. 1994. "Aquaculture in Cambodia." *Infofish International* 2: 42–48.

———. 2007. "Asian Experience on Farmer's Innovation in Freshwater Fish Seed Production and Nursing and the Role of Women." In "Assessment of Freshwater Fish Seed Resources for Sustainable Aquaculture," FAO Fisheries Technical Paper No. 501, Food and Agriculture Organization, Rome.

Gender and Livestock

Overview

D emands for meat and milk are growing because of population increases, economic growth, and consumer preference. The projected demand for meat alone is expected to increase by 6 to 23 kilograms per person worldwide by 2050.[1] This draws attention to the potential benefits that can be gained from livestock production. Livestock provides income generation, employment creation, and improved food and nutrition security across different production systems (table 14.1) and along different value chains (such as meat, dairy, live animals, hides, and eggs).[2] In some countries, livestock now accounts for up to 80 percent of the agricultural gross domestic product (World Bank 2007). A number of challenges face the livestock sector, including ensuring food, resource, and livelihood security for poor smallholder producers and processors. The challenges demand innovative and sustainable approaches, particularly given that more than 200 million smallholder farmers in Asia, Africa, and Latin America rely on livestock as the main source of income (FAO 2006b). Applying a "gender lens" to identify and address women's and men's different needs and constraints related to relevant livestock production systems and value chains is important for determining the most optimal outcomes as well as the most effective use of resources.

This Module is intended to support efforts to strengthen the design and implementation of livestock initiatives. It applies a Gender in Sustainable Livelihoods approach to livestock sector programming (see also *Sourcebook Overview*). In so doing, it highlights a range of gender issues to consider—from intrahousehold roles and relations to institutional supports and barriers and beyond to policy considerations. As the range of issues is broad, the Module suggests a number of references that can provide the reader with more in-depth coverage on particular issues.

OVERVIEW OF THE SECTOR

The livestock sector continues to grow globally. On the one hand, extensive rangeland systems face potentially dramatic changes to grazing lands, feed, and water availability. On the other, a rapidly industrializing sector based on more intensive systems depends on high-performing livestock breeds,[3] greater inputs, waste management, and food safety and biosecurity measures. As such, the livestock sector faces numerous challenges and poses challenges to other sectors, including finance and trade, water and land, education, and health. Furthermore, current concerns around the social, economic, and health-related impacts of transboundary animal diseases, such as avian influenza, highlight a number of other issues facing the livestock sector (FAO 2006a), including the following:

- Ensuring safe trade in livestock and animal products
- Safeguarding environmental sustainability and biodiversity, which is paramount to the sector
- Finding effective prevention and control of major animal diseases to safeguard animal and public health.

Table 14.1	General Characteristics of Different Livestock Production Systems
Production system	**Characteristics**
Landless industrialized systems	• Industrial, market-driven production systems • Detached from their original land base, commercially oriented, and specialize in specific products • Generally associated with large-scale enterprises • Small-scale urban-based production units also important in developing countries *Potential areas for gender concern:* labor conditions, mobility, control over production, decision-making power
Small-scale landless systems	• Small-scale landless livestock keepers typically not owning croplands or with access to large communal grazing areas • Typically found in urban and periurban areas and in rural areas of high population density *Potential areas for gender concern:* access to water, fodder, decision-making control, control over benefits, access to information on disease prevention, control
Grassland-based or grazing systems	• Typical of areas unsuitable or marginal for growing crops • Most often found in arid and semiarid areas • Adaptive management practices needed for challenging environmental conditions *Potential areas for gender concern* (depends on scale): *large-scale* ranches: labor conditions, living conditions such as accommodation, control over decision making; *small-scale:* intrahousehold decision making, control over benefits, decision making, local knowledge, and gendered roles in animal husbandry, disease prevention, and control
Mixed farming systems	• Most of the world's ruminants kept within crop-livestock systems • Characterized by relatively low levels of external inputs • Products of one part of the system used as inputs for the other *Potential areas for gender concern:* access to and control of inputs (land, water, credit); intrahousehold decision making; access to extension, veterinary services; capacities for scaling up

Sources: FAO 1997, 2007.

Most notable, perhaps, is the increasing demand by the sector for *natural* capital (land, water, fodder, fuelwood), *physical* capital (transport, abattoirs, market and home refrigeration) (based on FAO 2006a, 2006b; World Bank 2005b), and *human* capital (labor, knowledge, public-private partnerships in research and extension).

KEY GENDER ISSUES

A number of gender issues are central to discussions of agricultural livelihoods. These include, but are not limited to, access to and control of assets and gendered divisions of labor (IFAD 2004). Within the Sustainable Livelihoods framework, gender issues must also be considered in the wider political, economic, institutional, environmental, social, cultural, and demographic context. This means considering related factors, such as age, vulnerability, and socioeconomic status. The following sections discuss some of the key gender issues currently facing the livestock sector.

Access to and control of livestock and other assets

Controlling assets such as land, water, livestock, and agricultural implements has a direct impact on whether men, women, boys, and girls can forge life-enhancing livelihood strategies. For example, Namibia has implemented legislation to prevent property and asset confiscation, yet it is still common practice for a husband's family to take livestock and other assets from a widow and her children upon the husband's death. This has immediate impacts on a woman and her children in terms of loss of food security insurance, potential income, draft power, and fertilizer.[4] Moreover, land tenure is often required to establish access to other inputs such as credit, an often essential ingredient for improving livestock productivity and food security and livelihood improvement.[5] Because of a number of factors that relate particularly to a lack of *human* capital (for example, knowledge, capacity, political commitment) and *financial* capital (for example, lack of funds, decentralization constraints), many countries still face challenges in translating legislation related to women's access to and control of resources into action at the community and household levels (IFAD 2004). This impacts women's capacity to control and benefit from livestock. Poultry pose an almost universal exception; around the world, women tend to have more control over the poultry they produce and market.

Roles, responsibilities, and decision making

In general, women, men, boys, and girls provide labor for different livestock-related tasks. However, gendered roles are not set in stone and are open to change for different social, economic, environmental, and health-related reasons. For instance, in a case from Tanzania, the pastoralist groups of Morogoro and Tanga showed a clear division in gender roles. Yet in times of labor shortages, women could and did perform "men's" tasks, such as herding and watering animals. On the other hand, men seldom performed "women's" tasks, except in cases where there was potential to gain control over assets (Hill 2003).

Although differences, of course, exist within and between different livestock production systems and across regions, women are almost universally recognized for their role as the main actors in poultry, small ruminant, and microlivestock production as well as dairying, including the processing and marketing of milk and milk products.[6] Increasingly, experience shows (Bravo-Baumann 2000; Niamir-Fuller 1994) that women's labor and responsibilities in animal production remain underrecognized and underappreciated by those designing and implementing livestock policies and plans (IFAD 2004). Further, women and girls may or may not control, or be part of, household decision-making processes, especially in relation to the disposal of animals and animal products.[7] In the agropastoral systems of Iringa, Mara, and Mwanza in Tanzania, women could not sell or slaughter their animals without consulting their husbands, but they could decide to use their money from the sale of surplus food crops to buy livestock. They could also sell or exchange their poultry without seeking their husband's permission. In the intensive systems of Kilimanjaro, milk, which was once under women's control, came under women's and men's control as it became a key source of household income (Hill 2003).

Women and men as custodians of local knowledge and domestic animal diversity

As keepers of local knowledge, women and men contribute to the enhancement of gene flow and domestic animal diversity (FAO 2002). They also hold knowledge useful in the prevention and treatment of livestock illness. Men, women, boys, and girls will often have differing livestock knowledge and skills depending on their roles and responsibilities in animal husbandry. Women who process wool may have far different criteria for breed selection than men. Men herding cattle may have different knowledge of fodder and disease prevention than others in their household. Men's and women's reasons for keeping livestock may differ, as shown in a study conducted in Bolivia, India, and Kenya (Heffernan, Nielsen and Misturelli 2001 in IFAD 2004). In Kenya women thought of livestock as primarily contributing to food

security, whereas men saw livestock as a way to meet needs such as school fees, food, and a way to invest.

Livestock services and a restructuring sector

Gendered asymmetries in access to and delivery of livestock and veterinary services not only do a great disservice to women and men livestock producers and processors, but they also stifle the potential for more sustainable and effective actions along a given livestock value chain. With a restructuring of the livestock sector has come the restructuring of services. As services are increasingly privatized, women face disproportionate challenges compared to men in accessing livestock services and information for reasons mentioned above and in other sources. Women's poor access to markets, services, technologies, information, and credit decreases their ability to improve productivity and benefit from a growing livestock sector (for more on different constraints faced by poor smallholders in general, see FAO 2006a).

WHY MAINSTREAM GENDER?

Mainstreaming gender can benefit both beneficiaries and project implementers and other stakeholders. Some of the key benefits that can be gained from mainstreaming gender in livestock initiatives follow.

Key benefits: beneficiaries

Improve individual and household well-being. Understanding men's and women's different decision-making powers and negotiating strategies can inform livestock initiatives of the dynamics within and between households that need to be addressed in developing more viable livestock options and, in turn, improving the livelihoods and overall well-being of all household members. Addressing gender in livestock projects means identifying, understanding the relevance of, and addressing the different livelihood needs, priorities, interests, and constraints of men and women along lines of age, ethnicity, socioeconomic status, and ability (among others). It means maximizing the available *social capital* through engaging all household members as agents of poverty reduction. Women and men are far more likely to participate in efforts to improve their livestock initiatives if they can see that the benefits (for example, improved productivity, food security, income generation, less disease) outweigh the costs (for example, time, labor, social commitment).

Address women's and men's needs and interests. Mainstreaming gender in livestock initiatives means addressing the perceived needs and interests of women, men, boys, and girls involved in livestock production. Women may have very different interests and criteria for selecting livestock, as shown in the example from the study from Bolivia, India, and Kenya noted above. Addressing gender issues in livestock production can contribute to women's and men's economic and social empowerment, particularly for those who are vulnerable or living in marginalized areas. This empowerment can contribute significantly to meeting commitments agreed upon in international conventions (such as the Committee on the Elimination of the Discrimination against Women, Article 14; World Food Summit) as well as the Millennium Development Goals, particularly Goal 1 (Eradicating extreme poverty and hunger) and Goal 3 (Promoting gender equality and empowering women).

Improve social protection. Addressing gender in livestock programs and projects is important as a social protection measure. Doing so builds assets at the individual, household, and community levels through reducing vulnerability and increasing the opportunities of men, women, boys, and girls. Women in many areas around the world use income generated from poultry and dairy production—for instance, to pay for social goods such as children's school fees, medical fees—and other assets to provide for their families. This is particularly relevant to protect those in vulnerable situations from being forced to take risks to secure food, income, shelter, clothing, and other necessities. In sub-Saharan Africa, preventing confiscation of livestock upon the death of a husband is an important social protection mechanism. Heifer Zambia, an NGO, recognized the constraints women faced in owning and inheriting property, including livestock. Heifer worked with households and communities to establish joint ownership of livestock by the husband and the wife. A signed contract also allowed for a woman to inherit the livestock if her spouse died,[8] which provided a form of social protection.

Key benefits: program implementers

Use programming resources effectively and ensure more optimal outcomes. Understanding women's and men's livelihood-related roles and responsibilities can lead to more effective design and implementation of livestock programs. An approach that considers the gender and equity dimensions from within the household as well as across the spectrum of relevant livestock value chains works best. An example of a project from Nepal highlights the consequences of ignoring gender in project design and the subsequent suboptimal outcome. The project sought to transform buffalo milk production from subsistence to integration into the cash economy. The strategy focused on supporting the production of buffalo milk for the Kathmandu market. Although many households benefited from improved income to cash and food security, benefits were distorted along gender lines. Women and girls' labor grew because of the increased needs for fodder and fuelwood collection, stall cleaning, feed preparation, milking, and buffalo bathing. Women and girls faced restricted mobility and decreased leisure time, and, furthermore, girls also dropped out of school. Even though women were the primary buffalo caretakers, none of them seemed to gain any extra income or other personal assets. On the other hand, men were more concerned with the investment in, rather than the management of, the buffalo (Thomas-Slayter and Bhatt 1994).

Monitor changes in livestock-related livestock strategies and overall well-being more effectively. National- and project-level agricultural and livestock surveys *may* collect age and sex of head-of-household data, yet the researchers rarely use these data to analyze and interpret what is really happening with people's agricultural livelihoods. However, experience shows that collecting data along these lines can greatly inform livestock program initiatives, improve implementation (working with the most appropriate beneficiaries), and lead to a more effective monitoring and evaluation process (for example, defining gender-sensitive indicators to assess who is benefiting or not benefiting, how, and why).[9]

Promote better livestock technology development and adoption. Involving adult men and women—and where appropriate, boys and girls or elder women and men[10]—in livestock technology development is more likely to lead to more relevant technologies and greater adoption rates. As discussed, different household members typically hold different livestock responsibilities; they also may have different livestock priorities and constraints. Over time, extension services in Chiapas, Mexico, tried to improve wool production through cross-breeding Chiapas sheep with exotic breeds. However, the animals they introduced either died or produced little. This was in great part because of the difficult environment in the mountains. Then the Institute of Indigenous Studies at the University of Chiapas began to work with women Tzotzil shepherds to select breeding animals based on the women's own criteria, which included evaluating fleece quality. The selection program showed results through significant increases in the quality and quantity of wool. The Tzotzil women showed high acceptance of the "improved Chiapas sheep," to a great extent because of their involvement throughout all project phases as well as the animals' quick adaptation to local conditions (GRAIN n.d.). The project showed that women will be reluctant to adopt an improved breed if it means they must allocate an unreasonable amount of time and labor because the costs to them will far outweigh any benefits that might be gained. Similarly, they may value certain breeds far differently than men based on their priorities and interests. Women benefit most when they have decision-making authority over the animals they manage, even if they do not hold the legal ownership (Miller 2001).

The next section provides an overview of the SL framework as it pertains to livestock production. The framework can be used to help assess the gender issues facing different production systems and inform subsequent planning and implementation of livestock-related initiatives.

THE SL FRAMEWORK AND LIVESTOCK

Understanding the significance of mainstreaming gender is an important step in redressing the lack of attention to women's and men's different roles, responsibilities, needs, interests, and constraints in the planning of livestock initiatives. However, *translating* this understanding into action poses the greatest challenge to livestock officers, planners, and implementers at all levels and across regions. This section provides an overview of the SL framework in the context of the livestock sector. The framework and the issues therein can be adapted to different production strategies, livestock value chains, and situations.

SL framework: elements

The key defining elements of the SL framework as they pertain to the livestock sector are described in the following paragraphs. Box 14.1 provides a SL checklist for livestock initiatives to help guide the mainstreaming of gender in livestock programs.

Assets. Livestock acts as a *financial, social,* and *natural* asset, contributing to smallholder livelihood portfolios of an estimated 70 percent of the world's rural poor women and men. For many of these women and men, livestock acts as a primary form of savings, as well as insurance against accidents, illness, and death. Few other resources can match livestock as a means of investment. Livestock acts as collateral for accessing other inputs, such as agricultural credit—usually with large animals (Dorward and others 2005). In a comparative study of poor livestock keepers in Bolivia, India, and Kenya, Heffernan, Nielsen, and Misturelli (2001)

asked households to rank the best form of investment. In all three countries, livestock outranked business and housing (IFAD 2004). Women and men who raise livestock may gain income quickly by selling animals during times of need: for example, when women need medicine for their children or sick relatives. Regular income from the sale of milk, eggs, manure, livestock transport, or breeding sires can provide money for other household goods and services (for example, school fees, implements, livestock services) or for "trading up" (for example, acquiring larger or greater numbers of livestock). Finally, livestock may also act as a social asset. As such, livestock may confer status on its owners and build social capital through the exchange of animals or their use in ceremonies (de Haan 2001). Thematic Note 3 highlights the importance of livestock as women's and men's assets in relation to livestock technology development.

Markets. Trade can improve food security and well-being for poor, vulnerable women and men. Specifically, trade can support women's and men's rise out of poverty and provide income for food and other goods. However, women and men face gender biases in livestock-marketing systems and infrastructure (Baden 1998). For example, women typically face more constraints in accessing livestock markets than do men for various reasons, including gendered asymmetries in intrahousehold decision-making powers and access to transport (for example, access to money for transport, control over household transport, safety while traveling, and lack of mobility though limited impositions on overnight stays). Examples from Nepal and Tanzania provided in this Module suggest that when livestock are produced to generate income, men often take over the decision-making matters related to the sale of animals or products and the distribution of income benefits within the household.

As the livestock sector restructures, women as well as men increasingly find themselves working in situations in which they have less control over production and processing (such as industrial factory operations). Moreover, poor livestock producers, particularly women, typically face disproportionate barriers in meeting a growing number of regulations (for example, phytosanitary standards) required by more structured markets. They also find it more difficult to compete when barriers such as tariffs are in place.

Women, more than men, may also face an increased risk of harassment and abuse as they move into working situations in which they do not control their own labor, as is found in industrial livestock systems.

Finally, market "shocks" may affect women and men in different ways, particularly in terms of their access to

Box 14.1   Sustainable Livelihoods Checklist for Livestock Initiatives

The following checklist draws on the SL framework and provides a number of issues that may be relevant to the design and implementation of livestock initiatives. Note that differences may exist based on region, production system, and locally specific concerns. The framework and checklist can be used to guide initial assessments or to reflect on implementation midway through a project. They are also useful for informing a monitoring and evaluation framework and developing appropriate gender-sensitive indicators to measure impact and results.

Livelihoods development context: Livestock policies and institutions

■ Examine the different policies and regulations that guide the livestock sector. Consider how the policies might support or constrain women producers and processors as compared to men. Consider sanitary measures and tariffs.

■ Consider how relevant institutions address gender in their organizational and programming efforts. Look for a guiding gender policy, strategy, or plan. Look at how policies translate into action in communities and with women producers and processors as compared to men.

■ Consider that relevant institutions may have gender-differential implications for the livestock sector; these include line ministries of agriculture, district veterinary and livestock extension offices, community customs and institutions, livestock research offices, and, on a more regional and global scale, the World Trade Organization and similar bodies and district and community customs and institutions.

Assets

■ Examine the differences in women's and men's property rights around livestock, land, and water. Consider how these might impact women's and men's capacity to improve their livestock-related activities and livelihoods.

■ See women and men as important custodians of local knowledge for domestic animal diversity, disease prevention and control, processing, and so on. Explore with them their roles and responsibilities, and build on their custodianship.

■ Consider livestock-related roles and responsibilities along gender, age, caste, and ethnicity lines as different age groups as well as different castes or classes

may have different livestock knowledge, needs, interests, and priorities. Avoid "elite capture," where resources are deflected into the hands of dominant community groups or other stakeholders.

■ Identify and build on women's and men's different livestock interests, priorities, and needs (such as food security, income generation, and status).

■ Consider the costs and benefits to women and men from proposed livestock interventions (for example, labor inputs and diversion from other activities, time, income generated, food security, and social impacts).

Markets

■ Consider how and to what extent women and men participate in and have decision-making power in
   – Land designation mechanisms and markets
   – Livestock and livestock product markets (such as dairy, hides, and live animals)
   – Finance markets that support livestock production.

■ Look at how these differences might impact women as compared to men in initiatives to strengthen livestock-related livelihood strategies. Explore whether other factors come into play, such as age, ethnicity, caste, and socioeconomic class.

If relevant (that is, beyond subsistence production), consider the distribution of risks and gains for women and men along a particular livestock value chain (such as dairy, poultry, and eggs) as

■ Producers (for example, in terms of income generated and food security gained from livestock)

■ Processors (for example, in access to processing technologies and information)

■ Marketers (for example, access to transport, safe overnight accommodation, potential abuse and harassment from others at markets—women may expect demands for sexual transaction in exchange for buying a product)

■ Economies of scale (for example, bringing women together to improve marketing position).

Risk and vulnerability
Different communities and the women and men therein may face different risks associated with livestock. Consider the following points and think about which may be relevant to the particular situation. Look

at women's and men's different experiences in and capacities for responding to the following:

- Livestock sector trends (for example, policy biases and changes, supermarketization, lengthening livestock value chains, and vertical integration)
- Regional shocks affecting livestock (for example, climate and ecosystem change, drought, flooding, political upheaval, conflict, animal disease, demographic shifts)
- Household shocks (for example, illness or death of family member, "distress sales" of livestock to pay for medical treatment, and livestock confiscation upon the death of a husband).

Information and organization
Where relevant, consider women's and men's access to, participation in, decision making in, and contributions to the following:

- Livestock extension and veterinary information and services and artificial insemination services
- Participating in developing livestock programs and policies (for example, vaccination, culling, compensation, and restocking programs)
- Developing livestock and related technologies (for example, fodder, breeding, disease prevention, biosecurity, livelihood decision-making tools)
- Training and engagement as community animal health workers/paraveterinarians.

Consider how these differences might impact women as compared to men in initiatives to strengthen livestock-related livelihood strategies. Explore whether other factors come into play such as age, ethnicity, caste, socioeconomic class, and so on.

Source: Author; Questions adapted from SL Framework, *Sourcebook* Overview.

---

compensation and restocking schemes (for example, market shocks and responses around avian influenza). Thematic Note 2 addresses the relationships between gender and different aspects of livestock markets and proposes areas for action.

Information and organization. Addressing the challenges faced by the livestock sector depends increasingly on an effective and efficient flow of information. This is crucial to addressing the production, economic, environmental, and health aspects, among others, of the sector. Whether on a small or a large scale, women and men producers and processors depend on information related to markets, consumer demands, and disease patterns to help them plan their enterprises. For example, it is crucial that all involved along a poultry value chain (from producers to consumers) have up-to-date access to information on the status of avian influenza in their area so that they can take effective (farmer and other) biosecurity or biocontainment measures and respond to any market shocks (through, for example, diversification, compensation, and restocking). Women and men leverage social capital and collective action (such as women's groups and neighbors) around livestock activities to strengthen their livelihoods and resilience against possible shocks (for example, market, environmental, and health).

Along with traditional veterinary and extension services, women's networks and groups have been proven to be useful "organizational" pathways for passing information on livestock to women. A study on Heifer Project International's efforts to disseminate improved goat breeds through a village group process in Tanzania showed that social capital influenced people's ability to access a goat. Their ability to access and manage information was also crucial (de Haan 2001). This study showed that women's groups help women access other resources they may not otherwise be able to access.

It is equally important for information to be passed from women and men producers and processors to those regulating the livestock sector, developing improved breeds and other technologies, and monitoring livestock diseases. Innovative Activity Profile 2 in this Module discusses the importance of recognizing local gender and age-based knowledge in prioritizing breeding criteria in two different regions of Tanzania.

Risk and vulnerability. Women and men keep livestock, in part, as a means of livelihood diversification and important capital in savings, insurance, and the management of risk, and the livestock can be disposed of in times of need or emergency (FAO 2006a; SDC 2007; Upton 2004). At the same time, these aspects of their livelihood are vulnerable to animal disease (see Thematic Note 1), market trends and shocks, overall restructuring of the livestock sector, and environmental factors, including climate change. Women often have less access to information on sanitary measures in more intensive, industrial systems, potentially putting them at greater risk. In part because of a lack of information and other resources, women in Vietnam face risks to their own health where they are often on the frontlines with poultry and are at most risk of becoming exposed to avian influenza.

Similarly, because women are not seen as "owners" and their roles and responsibilities are often neglected by decision makers and planners, they risk being left out in vaccination, compensation, and restocking schemes. On the other hand, livestock also provide a certain degree of resilience to those owning or benefiting from them because they can be sold in times of distress (such as for medicines or funerals). This is not ideal, but selling their livestock is often the only way that women can access money to pay for treatment for a family member or themselves. Gender-differentiated knowledge is important to risk aversion, particularly in transhumant pastoralist systems. Thematic Note 1 looks at some of the key gender and livelihood issues related to livestock disease control and biosecurity and provides examples of good practices and lessons learned.

Policies and institutions. Effective policies and programs are required to respond effectively to the many challenges faced by the livestock sector, particularly in the face of global warming and economic globalization. Improving livestock productivity depends on the maintenance of the primary *natural* capital of livestock development: domestic animal genetic resources. Examples from Mexico and Tanzania outlined in Innovative Activity Profiles 1 and 2 point to the importance of *human* and *social* capital in this process because smallholder women's and men's custodianship of local husbandry knowledge and skills maintains and improves domestic animal diversity and productivity. Yet institutional mechanisms and policy frameworks across regions tend to favor large-scale production of fewer breeds over small-scale production based on a diversity of breeds. At the household level, the claims that women can make in relation to land access have eroded, which undermines their capacity to provide for the family and invest in their own assets including livestock (Diarra and Monimart 2006 in Trench and others 2007). Clearly, policies and institutions impact the processes that affect livelihood outcomes; they impact markets, information, risk and vulnerability, and assets. Because of policies intended to ensure safe animal

products for the consumer and an increase in returns to the producer, small-scale livestock producers and processors, particularly women, face great challenges entering wider markets because of different sanitary restrictions, tariffs, and concentrated distribution channels imposed under different political and legal frameworks (FAO 2006a; SDC 2007). Innovative Activity Profile 1 looks at the social, economic, scientific, and other benefits of collaboration between formal and informal researchers on improving local sheep in Chiapas, Mexico.

MEASURING CHANGE: GENDER-SENSITIVE MONITORING AND EVALUATION INDICATORS

It is important to be able to measure the impact that livestock initiatives have on men and women beneficiaries, their families, and communities. The SL framework is useful for identifying areas in which change should be measured and for developing gender-sensitive indicators to assess change. Because the livestock sector covers many issues and includes several levels, it is not possible or advisable to prescribe gender-sensitive indicators across the board. Ideally, such indicators are best developed with the participation of those concerned—for example, men and women smallholder livestock keepers, abattoir workers, marketers, and consumers (see table 14.2 for examples of indicators). Beneficiaries are best placed to identify their livestock and livelihood priorities. The following areas are examples of issues to consider at different levels:

- *Establish a baseline.* What is the situation like now? How do livestock planners see the situation? How do men and women producers, processors, and laborers view the situation?
- *Establish a target or different targets.* Women and men may have different priorities, needs, and concerns depending on their gendered roles and relations, their livelihood strategies, and their roles with different livestock. It is important to consider not only the economic factors in identifying targets (and indeed baselines), but also the targets in relation to human and social capital. How are the targets entwined with information and market needs and constraints? What vulnerabilities face women as compared to men, youth as compared to adults and elders? What different risks do women potentially face as compared to men?
- *Define target results.* After identifying a baseline and targets, women and men, livestock planners, and others can then define "success" or "benefits" from meeting those targets. This will help identify and develop effective

Table 14.2 Examples of Monitoring and Evaluation Indicators for Gender and Livestock

Indicator	Sources of verification and tools
Change in sales by *x* percent per month of livestock products (such as milk, eggs, meat, and fiber)	• Participatory monitoring by producer or herder groups • Project records
Over a set period, an increase of *x* percent in household incomes from livestock-based activities among women-headed households and poor households in program areas	• Household surveys • Project management information system • Socioeconomic data from statistics office
Changes over *x*-year period of project activities in household nutrition, health, education, vulnerability to violence, and happiness, disaggregated by gender	• Household surveys, before and after • Project management information system • School records
Change in amount of milk and animal protein consumed by household family members	• Child health records • Household surveys • Rapid nutrition surveys
Change in nutritional status of children under five years old, before and after program activities	• Child health records • Household surveys • Rapid nutrition surveys
Changes in soil and pasture condition in farmland, before and after program activities (such as nutrient levels and percentage of ground cover)	• Department of Agriculture surveys • Farm records • Participatory monitoring by villagers and herders
Number of women and men participating in training in new methods or types of livestock raising per quarter	• Program and project records • Training records
Level of satisfaction among women and men with veterinary and training services	• Interviews of farmers • Sample surveys
Adoption of recommended practices and technologies among men and women farmers, before and after program activity	• Case studies • Interviews of farmers • Sample surveys
Percentage of women and men farmers practicing proper use and management of veterinary chemicals	• Farm records • Interviews of farmers
Number of women and men who have accessed credit and training from the project and are engaged in livestock production	• Case studies • Project management information system or administrative records • Sample surveys
Percentage of women community animal health workers, livestock extension agents, and paravets	• Department of agriculture records • Project records
Access to extension services (animal production, artificial insemination, marketing, and health): number of contacts, disaggregated by gender	• Department of agriculture records • Project records
Percentage of men and women farmers who have access to high-quality, locally adapted livestock	• Agricultural extension records • Interviews with stakeholders
Morbidity and mortality of livestock per quarter, disaggregated by gender of owner	• Household surveys • Project management information system • Veterinary department records
Women or other disadvantaged groups actively participating in management committees and boards of producer groups and cooperatives	• Committee meeting minutes • Interviews with stakeholders • Local traditional authorities (such as a chief or local council) • Program and project records
Number of women and men holding management or treasurer positions in natural resource management groups	• Bank account records • Committee meeting minutes
Gender differences in workload as a result of introduced practices or new technology for livestock production	• Case studies • Gender analysis • Participatory rapid appraisal • Sample surveys
New and total employment or paid labor generated in livestock population for the local population, disaggregated by gender (with and without ethnicity)	• Administrative records of enterprises
Number of women and men starting new small enterprises in animal product processing or marketing (such as milk, eggs, meat, or fiber products)	• Household surveys • Project records • Socioeconomic data from statistics office

Source: Authors, with inputs from Pamela White, author of Module 16.

gender-responsive indicators to monitor change. Quantitative and qualitative indicators are both important and need to be measured in different ways. Participatory approaches are useful for looking at different stakeholders' perceptions and views.

Depending on the country or region, it may be relevant to also consider ethnicity and caste alongside gender (both as comparative indicators and when collecting data), as women of lower castes or ethnic minorities are usually in the most disadvantaged situation.

Livestock Disease Control and Biosecurity

ivestock acts as natural and economic capital, contributing to women's and men's diets and livelihoods through income generation and home consumption, acting as live banks, imparting social status, and providing draft, transport, and fertilizer, especially for resource-poor men and women farmers. Yet an estimated 30 percent of livestock production in developing countries is lost because of disease (Upton 2004). Animal diseases, particularly *transboundary animal diseases,*[1] including zoonoses (diseases that can be spread from animals to humans), are an ongoing threat to women and men livestock producers and processors as well as to markets and consumers (Otte, Nugent, and McLeod 2004). The impact of livestock disease on the livelihoods and food security of poor livestock producers and processors, particularly women, is of great concern because they are less resilient to disease-related shocks such as market loss, loss of animals, and domestic animal diversity, and because they have less access to compensation and restocking programs (World Bank 2005).

Zoonotic diseases have captured global concern because of their potentially far-reaching impact on both human health and markets, livelihoods, and food security. The economic losses alone due to highly pathogenic avian influenza (HPAI) are estimated to be at least $1 billion worldwide (World Bank 2005). In a study conducted in Vietnam, all of the communities surveyed had suffered losses due to avian influenza outbreaks; 96 percent of those surveyed were poultry producers, and 78 percent of them (smallholders) had not received compensation.[2]

This Thematic Note addresses some of the key gender and livelihoods issues related to livestock disease control and biosecurity and provides examples of good practices and lessons learned as well as suggestions for ways to move forward.

KEY GENDER ISSUES

Engaging women and men producers, processors, traders, researchers, and service providers in livestock disease prevention and control can promote more sustainable livelihoods along livestock value chains (from farmer to market) and beyond. The following paragraphs discuss some of the key gender issues associated with this subsector.

"By knowing who does what, one can discover who is in the best position to observe clinical signs signalling animal health problems" (Curry and others 1996). Knowing this can also help expose possible biosecurity risks along livestock value chains—for example, movement of hatching eggs, birds, and poultry products before retail (Lucas 2007 in Otte and others 2007). Adult and older women and men as well as younger boys and girls may all hold different human capital associated with their livestock health and production roles (for example, women's groups, grazing groups, knowledgeable elders, and healers). In a study conducted in India (Geerlings, Mathias, and Köhler-Rollefson 2002), researchers found that, for the most part, women mentioned different plants than men in terms of their ethnoveterinary applications. Women and men may also access social capital that supports their livelihoods and livestock-related activities, as in the case of exchanging goats in Tanzania (de Haan 2001). In Uasin Gishu, Kenya, both adult women and older men and adult men had daily responsibilities caring for the cattle. Both men and women respondents knew nearly half of the 65 unique syndromes. Women volunteered only about one-quarter of these, as did men. Except for rinderpest, which was not present in the district at the time of the study, women respondents were familiar with the terms that described diseases across categories. Women's knowledge of local disease terms was comparable to that of men. The study showed that veterinary extension activities also need to be geared toward adult women and older men to improve diagnostic capabilities on farms (Curry and others 1996). Elsewhere, in a study conducted by Anthra in India, out of 316 traditional healers interviewed, 293, or 93 percent, were men, and only 23, or 7 percent, were women (Ghotge and Ramdas 2002). Researchers found the low number of women surprising; they suggested that it could be due to a highly gendered flow of information from fathers or grandfathers to sons.

Women, as well as men, may be well placed to identify disease, yet they may not have direct access to veterinary or epidemiological services for various reasons. All too often, those working formally on livestock disease prevention and control perceive adult men to be the ones raising livestock.[3] Yet adult women, girls and boys, and often elder men and women, may be responsible for diverse production and health activities. Men often have greater access to physical capital (such as transport) than women to travel to disease prevention and control offices or training. They likely hold better access to financial assets to pay for services and information. In Vietnam women have less access to important human capital than men, and they are less informed than men about poultry production issues, particularly in terms of HPAI prevention and control. Women who lack access to information are also the ones at greater risk of being exposed to HPAI because of the roles they play in poultry production (FAO/MARD/ACI 2007).

Furthermore, finding ways of preventing and responding effectively to animal disease requires a certain type of social capital—the active involvement and participation of men and women—at the household, community, and national levels. Yet at the household level, disease prevention or control measures may actually add to women's workloads, reducing their capacity to participate in community meetings related to animal health.

Gendered asymmetries in capacity development affect livestock disease prevention and control. Women are increasingly entering into, and practicing in, fields related to livestock disease prevention and control, including veterinary medicine, epidemiology, lab technology, and research. Elsewhere, however, it is estimated that only 15 percent of the world's agricultural extension agents are women.[4] At the community level, women are still less present in general in the roles of formally trained community animal health workers or paraveterinaries. In many areas, cultural or religious factors bar men from meeting or talking to women to whom they are not related. In these areas women need to be trained and supported in other ways (such as adequate and safe housing and transport) to work with other women producers and processors.

BENEFITS FROM GENDER-RESPONSIVE ACTIONS

The following benefits may be gained from gender-responsive actions:

■ Working with local women and men (including elders and ethnoveterinary practitioners) and sharing their knowledge can be helpful in identifying disease patterns and identifying more technically effective and cost-effective ways to prevent outbreaks or transmission. Finding out who does what (for example, milking, raising chicks, grazing cattle), who controls what (income, draft implements, donkey transport, grazing lands), who knows what (disease patterns, availability and quality of water, grazing lands, market trends), and who is affected by what helps health care officers design more effective processes of prevention, diagnosis, and treatment of livestock disease.

■ Knowing who has decision-making power over livestock in the household and community can enable animal health practitioners to identify ways of building on valuable human capital (for example, men may make the decisions, but women may have specific knowledge). Women and men may be active in a number of roles (production, slaughtering, marketing, consuming) along livestock value chains (such as poultry and dairying). In Vietnam women control their poultry in operations in which there are only a few chickens, but men tend to control larger poultry operations even though women provide the labor.

■ Gender-responsive remedial action can provide more cost-effective and technically effective responses to disease fallouts such as those experienced from market shocks such as those witnessed in a number of countries affected by avian influenza.

■ Health care officers can help improve the livelihoods of rural men, women, and children by ensuring that improved veterinary technology and knowledge are provided directly to those members of the household responsible for livestock health care and production. A more proactive and interactive system of working with clients, including interaction with adult women and younger boys and girls, can facilitate the improvement of overall livelihoods through more effective disease diagnosis and overall health maintenance (Curry and others 1996).

Some of the preceding issues were addressed in an initiative undertaken in India. The gendered livestock roles in India are changing rapidly for many reasons: an urbanizing environment, migration of men for jobs, industrialization of agriculture and postharvest activities, and the impact of HIV and AIDS on rural households and labor. Despite women's involvement in day-to-day care, livestock management is still considered a man's role by livestock planners and decision makers because the work that women do is seldom recognized. Women are also kept out of decision-making processes. Anthra, a local nongovernmental organization (NGO), found that although women in different communities were knowledgeable about local remedies, cures, and medicines for treating small ruminants, they had, for the most part, been kept out of professional healing. Women expressed a desire to gain this knowledge, and they wanted to learn how to recognize conditions that were not treatable with local remedies. To rectify this, Anthra ensured that 75 percent of all new animal health workers were women. Apart from focusing on animal health issues, training also focused on women's health and gender in sustainable development and natural resource use. The project encouraged the animal health workers to work closely with other women in the village to share their knowledge with them (Ghotge and Ramdas 2002).

POLICY AND IMPLEMENTATION ISSUES

To address livestock disease control and biosecurity measures, action is required at all levels and across different livestock value chains (from producers to markets to consumers). Increasingly, initiatives to prevent or stop the spread of livestock disease recognize the importance of considering the different socioeconomic and gender factors involved—for example, malignant catarrhal fever in Kenya, trypanosomiasis in Uganda (Mugisha 2004), and HPAI in Vietnam (Kariuki 2003). Yet addressing the challenges of transboundary diseases becomes more complex in a global environment increasingly contextualized in longer market chains and wider geographical sourcing of products (FAO 2005). The global strategy for the progressive control of HPAI (FAO/OIE/WHO 2005) points to several key policy and implementation issues in which gender is relevant in livestock disease control and biosecurity, including the following:

Controlling livestock disease, particularly transboundary animal disease, is a public good requiring both public and private intervention in prevention, diagnosis, and response. Rapid response to disease outbreaks calls for increases of biosecurity, containment, culling of infected animals, and disinfection and the use of vaccination when appropriate (Brushke, Thiermann, and Vallat 2007). Key actors in

disease intelligence and biosecurity strategies include women and men from the household level to the global level. Yet women's involvement as livestock managers, producers, processors, researchers, and policy makers comes into question. Women have difficulty accessing resources and information essential to meeting government-regulated standards.[5] A lack of effective incentives (such as well-designed compensation packages that benefit women and men producers and processors) also hinders disease intelligence and reporting. Further, preventive vaccination campaigns that do not consider women's and men's abilities to pay, or that do not include training for those involved in the actual production responsibilities, are unlikely to succeed.

The provision of infrastructure and services to prevent and combat livestock diseases is a public good, which is more efficiently offered by governments rather than by communities of farmers in many cases (Otte, Nugent, and McLeod 2004). However, it has been well established that women have less access to public and private livestock services than men. It is important that governments must address cost-effective incentives to participate in control efforts (for example, for women, men producers and processors; Otte, Nugent, and McLeod 2004). This cost effectiveness needs to be addressed in terms of economic and social costs (for example, labor reduction, time reduction, improved income generation, food security, lower cost inputs) to women and men livestock producers and processors.

Effective prevention and progressive control of major animal diseases depend on strong capacity across a number of levels. Involving men and women in both formal and informal capacity building is an effective and cost-efficient way of capitalizing on what can be costly training. Men and women who are trained in disease prevention and control and the design and application of effective biosecurity measures can have a better chance at ensuring wider outreach to women and men raising and processing livestock. Useful policy changes affecting tertiary education include promoting the strengthening of curricula to include gender-sensitive participatory methods in disease diagnosis, treatment, and biocontainment.

In southern Sudan, Vétérinaires sans Frontières—Belgium's community-based animal health program—aimed at increasing household food security in pastoralist communities through improving the supply of milk, blood, meat, and livestock for sale and barter. Women were not involved in the community dialogue in developing the animal health program, and the program implementers realized that very few women were seizing the opportunity to be trained as community animal health workers. The program managers conducted an assessment to look at the program's expected impact on women as opposed to men. They assessed the extent to which the program responded to the specific needs and interests of women and identified opportunities for women's involvement. They believed that understanding the roles that different household members play as animal health care providers is essential to the program. Many observers had assumed that men alone care for the animals. Yet women play very important roles in animal care, roles that are not acknowledged because the women do not own animals; these roles include cleaning, collecting cow dung, releasing and bringing in the cattle, milking, observing ill health in animals and reporting this to men, and caring for calves, goats, and chickens (Amuguni 2000).

GOOD PRACTICES AND LESSONS LEARNED

Over the last 15 years or so, women and men have received growing attention as custodians of animal health and managers of livestock in their own right. Yet, for the most part, national plans and strategies to develop biosecurity measures and prevent and control livestock disease have not recognized and employed this knowledge to the fullest extent. The following discussion presents a number of examples and lessons learned regarding the improvement of disease prevention, control, and response strategies.

Recent studies on malignant catarrhal fever in Kenya (Kariuki 2003), Newcastle disease in southern Africa (Alders and others 2005), and vector-borne diseases in Uganda (Mugisha and others n.d.) confirm the importance to animal health planning of recognizing and understanding the linkages between gender and animal health across production systems and in different areas.

Addressing gender in tertiary curricula supports animal health practices in communities. For years, men, more than women, have been viewed as the "livestock raiser" by animal health workers and others. This is changing slowly, however, as lessons emerge from the practices of tertiary education institutes such as Makerere University in Uganda. In the early 2000s, the university's veterinary faculty sought to change its curriculum in ways that would address gender concerns. Currently there is a course unit of veterinary sociology (with a large focus on gender) in the veterinary curriculum. Other programs including gender issues are the Bachelor's in Animal Production Technology and Management program and the Master of Sciences in Livestock Development Planning and Management program.[6] Such

emerging practices have the capacity to improve and better support animal health practices in general.

Studies on avian influenza from Vietnam and Egypt have shown that initiatives to mitigate impacts related to animal disease, such as compensation mechanisms (Geerlings 2007), need to identify gendered needs, interests, and constraints and respond accordingly. Vouchers for school fees or medical costs may be more appropriate for women in cases where they do not control household income.

Involving women in developing communication messages and interventions is important in effectively controlling animal disease and/or developing rehabilitation strategies, as lessons emerging from Egypt indicate.[7] Because they are often on the front line of disease diagnosis, women are important conduits for information on the prevention, control, and responses to livestock disease, as demonstrated in the case of avian influenza in Vietnam. To this end, the Southern Africa Newcastle Disease Programme worked with women as community vaccinators and as income providers. Controlling Newcastle disease also allowed the women's groups to further develop their village poultry enterprises (AusVet 2006).

Lessons from Egypt suggest that in cases where restocking is not feasible (for example, because of ongoing outbreaks), it is important to develop alternative income-generating activities (Geerlings 2007). As part of this, it is important to consider women's constraints, particularly those of women who are illiterate or who face restricted mobility.

Although it is often promoted as a way of averting risk, livestock microinsurance may pose several gender-based questions that need to be answered before engaging in widespread promotion. Women, more so than men, and particularly those in marginal populations (poor and vulnerable) and areas (arid and semiarid) likely face particular difficulties in investing in livestock microinsurance; they must divert scarce resources (perhaps from school fees or other foodstuffs) for such insurance. There is no guarantee that they can continue to pay the premiums should a serious difficulty arise, such as an ill or dying household member or lost income.[8] Moreover, because women are often more likely to be illiterate than men in communities, they may face difficulties in reading and understanding policies. Finally, "the whole thrust behind [promoting] micro-finance has been the search for a self-help strategy for poverty reduction which has limited costs for donors and avoids difficult questions about wealth redistribution and basic service provision. Microinsurance, like micro-finance in general, is only useful as part of a broader programme to address the underlying causes of risk and vulnerability facing poor women and men."

Strategic research that builds on women's and men's knowledge and experience in disease diagnosis, prevention, and local biosecurity measures is useful for informing strategies to address animal disease and adapting practices elsewhere. For example, experiences such as those of working with the Vietnam Women's Union on HPAI can be useful for informing strategic prevention and response interventions elsewhere in the region.

GUIDELINES AND RECOMMENDATIONS FOR PRACTITIONERS

The following recommendations apply to practitioners at the three levels.

Macro- (policy/strategy) level

Evaluate proposed solutions for transboundary disease and control/biosecurity using gender-sensitive criteria.[9] Improve the evaluation of proposed technical solutions and costs of transboundary animal diseases and various control efforts and biosecurity to address socioeconomic, gender, age, and livelihoods concerns (for example, impact on women's and men's labor, time, livestock management roles, men's and women's different capacities to pay for preventive vaccinations).

Consider women's and men's differential abilities to benefit from insurance (including microinsurance) programs. When considering the cost effectiveness of insurance as opposed to the control of transboundary animal disease directly, it is important to consider women's and men's differential abilities to contribute to, and benefit from, insurance programs. In many cases, group rather than individual programs may be more appropriate and enable more women to leverage assets collectively to benefit. Consider the potentially different impacts of insurance programs on men and women beneficiaries.

Ensure terms of reference call for addressing gender and livelihoods concerns and identifying gender-sensitive indicators in collective agreements, funding, and management of global, regional, and national responses. This should consider gender-sensitive compensation packages.

In establishing intelligence-gathering strategies for disease, ensure that incentives for reporting benefit both women and men producers and processors. Incentives might include compensation, capacity strengthening, improved access to information, and strengthening social networks.

Enhance countries' capacities to undertake national action that considers gender-responsive participation in efforts toward livestock disease control and biosecurity. This may include promoting women, as well as men, in relevant fields at the tertiary education level and providing incentives for pursuing relevant career paths.

Intermediate (institutional) level

Ensure women and men are provided with the opportunities to train as community animal health workers. Training for women, and perhaps some men, may need to be broader in terms of confidence building, literacy, numeracy, advocacy, and other factors. Provide gender support to community-based institutions, such as those supporting the training and support of community animal health workers. Engage men in dialogue (both animal health workers and community members) to support women community animal health workers.

Schedule vaccination campaigns, training, and information campaigns for times and places that meet women's and men's needs, such as at women's group meetings, at mobile clinics in the fields with the women, and in households.

Promote the understanding of animal health and other staff in this field of the socioeconomic, gender, and age-based linkages to disease prevention and control. Campaign for staff to work on animal health and biosecurity issues more closely with women, as well as with men in livestock-keeping households.

Collect and use data disaggregated by gender and age to support animal health policy and planning. As shown, women and men are often responsible for different aspects of livestock production and animal health. Moreover, younger boys or girls may hold specific knowledge useful for informing animal health policy and planning because of their specific roles (such as grazing and dairying).

Local level

Plan for disease prevention, control, and response issues, needs, and constraints along gender, age, and socioeconomic lines.[10] As noted above, it is important to identify adult men and women, elder men and women, and boys' and girls' roles in, and knowledge of, different aspects of animal husbandry and livestock production. Understanding women's and men's different use of labor and time can be important to ensuring sustainability and success of any animal health initiative.

Consider the social and economic costs and benefits of biosecurity measures (including farmer biosecurity) to women and men. Ensure local (household) social and economic cost effectiveness of bioexclusion and biocontainment measures in terms of (1) financial costs—poor rural women raising livestock typically lack access to money or credit (financial assets) in many areas—and (2) costs to human and social capital—women's use of time differs from that of men and also differs along lines of age.

Ensure that women, as well as men, are involved in information sharing in outreach related to disease control, biosecurity, and animal health in general.

MONITORING AND EVALUATION INDICATORS

Indicators to monitor changes in numbers of livestock lost, culled, or restocked and general economic impacts of livestock disease and biosecurity measures should be developed in a way that considers gender- and age-differentiated impacts. Such indicators should be developed with women and men in a participatory manner to look at the impact of proposed or ongoing initiatives on women's and men's livelihood strategies, their income, labor, and differentiated access to knowledge and training. Indicators should consider both the economic and social impacts on women's and men's livelihoods and well-being, including the impacts on their social networks, local knowledge and skills, and means of exchanging information.[11] See examples in table 14.2.

Livestock Marketing, Market Integration, and Value Chains

The livestock sector supports the livelihoods of an estimated 600 million rural poor people around the world. The volume of livestock production in developing countries has steadily increased since the 1980s, in terms of both internal consumption and regional and international exports (World Bank 2005).[1] Improved access to livestock markets can play a significant role in increasing women's and men's income and livelihoods. However, with the restructuring of the livestock sector and subsequent lengthening of value chains to meet the growing demands of a globalizing economy, poor producers and processors, particularly women, face numerous challenges in benefiting from these changes. One challenge is dealing with the effects of trade agreements and regulations that favor large producers and processors, because women tend to be more actively engaged in the smallholder sector. Another challenge is finding effective means of averting risk and responding to extreme events and market shocks (such as flooding, drought, and avian influenza). Women also face a lack of access to market information, education (numeracy and literacy), and enterprise training that would provide them with a solid foundation for commercializing their livestock activities.

This Thematic Note addresses the relationships between gender and livestock marketing, market integration, and value chains from a gender and livelihoods perspective. Module 5 in this volume addresses the issues of gender and markets in greater detail, focusing on the challenges facing the sector (see also Module 1, which covers food security and value chains).

KEY GENDER ISSUES

A number of gender differential impacts arise from the restructuring of the livestock sector and are present at different points along different value chains. Trade agreements and related mechanisms tend to favor large producers and processors over small ones, many of whom are women (such as meeting sanitary regulations). The restructuring of the sector brings opportunities for generating income, but it also brings the risks of unregulated and gender-insensitive employment (sexual harassment, insecure contracts, dependence upon suppliers). Following structural changes, women may face different challenges than men in working with (1) different kinds of livestock (such as changes in labor, skills, and information); (2) different livestock management systems (such as time and information); (3) new technology for housing, health, and processing (such as information, skills, and education); (4) changes in transport arrangements (such as infrastructure); and (5) changes in institutional arrangements to enable vertical integration in the market (Okali 2004). A study in Kenya in the 1990s showed how the economic changes eroded women's positions in negotiations with their husbands over cattle "ownership" (Oboler 1996).

For the Nandi people in Kenya, cattle have been part of traditional household property. Men traditionally inherited and controlled livestock. Women accessed livestock products through being food providers and household managers. A woman had cattle assigned to her house to provide milk for her family when she married. Men and boys received the morning milk, and women and girls the evening milk. As dairy production become increasingly commercialized, cross-bred cattle began to replace the Zebu cattle. Husbands usually bought these cross-breeds and considered them their property. As a result, women's rights to milk from specific cattle have been disappearing. Because morning milk is being sold more often, the evening milk must now be shared among the entire household (Huss-Ashmore 1996 in IFAD 2004).

Figure 14.1   Kenya: Dairy Market Chains, 2004

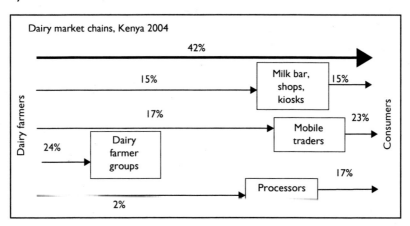

Source: FAO 2006.

The Kenyan market chain in figure 14.1 (FAO 2006) highlights key points at which gender issues can be addressed, including the following:

- Access to, control of, and use of resources
- Access to production, market, and veterinary information and services
- Participation in decision making
- Change in labor and time use
- Mobility and access to markets
- Benefits and costs (social, economic, environmental).

Women and men have different access to markets, infrastructures, and related services. Expanding supermarketization in developing countries since the 1990s has meant the rise of wholesalers, large-format stores, national and multinational chains, and the consolidation of national chains (FAO 2005). For the most part, women producers, more than men, face greater constraints in *accessing* different points along these chains, as well as the related *technologies, infrastructures,* and *information* about livestock markets. A study undertaken by the International Food Policy Research Institute in Ethiopia showed that an increase of 10 kilometers in the distance from the rural village to the closest market town reduces the likelihood of sales of livestock and livestock products and decreases the likelihood that women engage in and sell processed foods (Dercon and Hoddinott 2005). Women who lack the financial capital also have a more difficult time accessing privatized veterinary and extension services that are often essential in helping producers meet phytosanitary standards. One example of how this could happen comes from a study in Orissa, India

(IFAD 2004). Although the dairy cooperatives were established in the wives' names, a committee of men actually managed the group. By extension, it is assumed they could more easily access information and services as they made the decisions.

Market shocks can affect women and men differently. There are different types of shocks to livestock markets—from natural disasters (drought, flooding) to human-induced shocks (conflict, policy, media and consumer reactions to disease) to disease-related shocks (animal deaths, culling). The impacts of, as well as the responses to, market shocks can differ along gender, age, and socioeconomic lines. Droughts in arid parts of Africa can polarize the wealth in pastoralist communities, such as when smallholders sell their livestock to large herd owners (White 1990). In Egypt women raising ducks were left out of the campaign to raise awareness about HPAI because the focus was on chickens.[2]

BENEFITS FROM GENDER-RESPONSIVE ACTIONS

Gender-responsive actions in livestock market and value chain initiatives can convey a number of benefits to both women and men beneficiaries as well as other stakeholders. The following are a few of these benefits (see also box 14.2):

- Opportunities to narrow gender-based gaps and transform women's and men's livelihoods and overall well-being. In India the NGO Anthra trained village women as community animal health workers. Not only did they gain the skills to deal more effectively with their animals,

"Cui, a 40-year-old woman, has been married for 16 years and is the family breadwinner. The family has been facing hard times because of poor production from their land. When she heard about the project, she decided to apply for credit to raise pigs. She was able to raise and sell a sufficient number of pigs to repay the loan in one year. Having started with one pig, today she has 12. The piglets are sold for CNY 150 when they are two months old. She is pleased with this new income and has used the extra cash to open a shop that stocks items for daily use. She earns on average CNY 200–300 per month from the shop and plans to expand the business. Her two sons go to school. 'We were very poor and when my sons were in primary school we found it hard to keep them in school as there was no money to buy food. Now it is different.' She laughs and adds, 'Now there is no shortage of food and I can also say there is no shortage of money. Today I have the same standard of living as people who are better off in this area.' The neighbours admire her and would like to follow her example. She is in fact known as the star of the village.'"

Source: IFAD 2002: 24.

but they gained the confidence to become more involved in community decision making and conflict resolution (Ghotge and Ramdas 2002).

- Improved identification of relevant responses to potential or real market shocks. A recent initiative in Vietnam set out to ensure that women, as well as men, were compensated after the culling of their poultry.
- More effective restructuring of subsectors when women and men are included in decision making. When women were left out in efforts to transform the buffalo dairy sector from subsistence to commercial enterprises in Nepal, their labor inputs increased, yet they gained no visible financial or social benefits.
- Greater participation of women when they can see the benefits and assess the costs.

POLICY AND IMPLEMENTATION ISSUES

Various policy and implementation issues that must be addressed are discussed in this section.

Women and men smallholders are often neglected in livestock and trade policies. In recent years trade liberalization strategies have emphasized the need for an export-driven economy. To this end a number of developing countries have responded by developing domestic agricultural policies in line with this thinking. Yet many developing countries have become net importers, rather than exporters, of agricultural produce. Milk is the most imported item by weight, and imports of poultry and pigs are growing fast (Upton 2004). A gap clearly exists in meeting the need of domestic markets for livestock products. With trade liberalization geared toward increased production of export-oriented produce and goods, women smallholders keeping livestock and growing crops are often neglected or merely given lip-service (Garcia and others 2006) in the development of agriculture, livestock, and general trade-related policies. Yet, as shown in this Module, women play active roles in livestock production across production systems, across regions, and along value chains.

Policies increasingly promote intensification to landless systems, creating greater gaps in women's access to, and control over, livestock-related resources. As the urban demand for livestock products grows, policies increasingly promote intensification to landless systems, creating ever-widening gaps in terms of women's access to and control of the natural, social, and human capital around them and affecting their capacity to make decisions about their livestock. With the intensification of livestock production systems, poor women stand to face even greater challenges in terms of being able to access guaranteed favorable employment conditions that pay and treat them fairly without discrimination or abuse.

Policies promoting intensified landless production may force employment migration, affecting women's and men's livestock roles, relations, control, and income. In cases in which greater control of intensified landless production is assumed closer to the urban market, women and men may increasingly be forced to migrate away for employment. This leads to their suspending or abandoning their role as custodians of local production systems and knowledge of local breeding and animal husbandry practices, as well as methods of disease surveillance, prevention, and control. These are all crucial to the sustenance of domestic (local) animal diversity and, ironically, to the livestock sector in general. Moreover, jobs such as those in big livestock sheds or in large-scale processing may not always result in improved living conditions for women or their families. Implications can be drawn from across sectors in terms of increased demand for women's labor. When men migrate, women are often left behind to take up the agricultural labor shortage. Women may also migrate away for labor, working in abattoirs, dairies, meat-packing facilities, and other placed. This "heightened demand for female labour is not usually associated with higher wages, but is associated with an increase in flexibility of the labour market. This generally goes hand in hand with low wages, a lack of social protection, and poor contractual conditions such as very short-term contracts with reduced benefits, long working hours, and no rights of association, all of which exacerbate the exploitation of women and child labour" (Garcia and others 2006: 39).

GOOD PRACTICES AND LESSONS LEARNED

Lessons learned from previous projects as well as good practices are addressed in this section.

Building women's, as well as men's, assets in other areas such as credit and information is likely to promote more sustainable outcomes around livestock initiatives for all. The Asian Development Bank funded the Second Participatory Livestock Development Program 2003 in Bangladesh. The program sought to raise women's employment and incomes by addressing gender *in all components*; increasing women's involvement at all stages of project planning and implementation; building women's assets through increased access to and control over assets like credit, information, training, and livestock support services; and increasing women's employment in livestock rearing and in marketing livestock products, such as feed. An IFAD-funded initiative in Bangladesh identified the need to consider different aspects of women's poultry production, from microcredit to the appropriate development and use of hatchery technology, to the use of income generated.[3]

In Dukana, Kenya, women lacked collateral security as compared to men because they rarely owned livestock or owned or controlled other tangible assets. Microfinance for women was limited. FARM (Food and Agriculture Research Management) Africa considered these concerns and initiated a program that provided credit to women without collateral (assets). FARM Africa began a savings and credit system based on the Grameen Bank system and worked with 23 women to form a pilot group. The women were mostly single mothers or widows and women who

were already engaged in a small business. They were able to expand their businesses, which included processing and selling hides and skins, running butcheries and kiosks, and trading livestock. The women benefited financially and gained confidence. With greater assets, they began to borrow from other lending institutions. The project realized its effectiveness and expanded to other groups and districts (FARM Africa 2002).

USAID-funded research was carried out under the Global Livestock Collaborative Research Support Program (http://glcrsp.ucdavis.edu). In particular, the work of the "Improving Pastoral Risk Management on East African Rangelands" (PARIMA) project in Kenya and Ethiopia and of the "Enhancing Child Nutrition through Animal Source Food Management" (ENAM) project in Ghana has had a thematic focus on gender issues. The PARIMA project studied collective action by women's groups and identified their efforts to combat the effects of drought by successfully and sustainably managing cooperative microfinance efforts, range management, and destocking. These Ethiopian women's groups were also involved in cross-border exchanges with Kenyan women's groups, and the activities of both sets of groups were enhanced through the process. The ENAM project, still under way, is also building strong women's groups and providing them with microfinance and nutrition education to promote the establishment of enterprises that provide income to be used for the purchase of animal source foods to improve children's nutrition. These efforts link household-level improvements to expanding enterprises with benefits to the wider community.[4]

Livestock market initiatives are more likely to be successful when they are developed in a participatory, gender-responsive manner. Lessons from a number of experiences in different countries show that failing to consider women's and men's needs, priorities, and constraints can have disastrous consequences. For example, the government of India developed a goat distribution project for women living in poverty in Maharashtra. The project failed because the women beneficiaries, most of whom had never raised goats, were not consulted or trained before the goats were distributed. Within six months, most of the animals had died (Ghotge and Ramdas 2002). Lessons point to the importance of the need to also assess employment protection specifically for women working in the informal and formal livestock sectors (Okali 2004).

Continual monitoring at points along a livestock value chain using sex- and age-disaggregated data helps highlight areas of success or concern. This allows for midcourse corrections to promote equitable benefits. As shown by projects that did not consider gender in the design or implementation stage, the cost of *not* establishing a baseline along gender (and age, socioeconomic, and ethnicity) lines means higher costs and potential failure over time. For example, in Nepal the Asian Development Bank supported the Department of Livestock Services' (DLS) reorientation of its approach to the livestock sector and to developing the capacity of rural communities to plan and manage livestock development with improved access to inputs, markets, and services provided by NGOs and the private sector. Although Nepali women are responsible for 70 percent of the livestock-related work, the project had neglected women in terms of their participation and access to benefits. The lack of women technical assistants and a lack of men project staffs' awareness of the gender-differentiated roles led to limited outreach to women farmers. A series of midproject corrections were identified and put in place:

- Developing a gender action plan to promote meaningful participation of men and women farmers
- Conducting an assessment of women's roles, constraints, and opportunities in livestock development
- Conducting a two-day regional gender training program for DLS management, field staff, men and women farmers, district women in development offices, and NGOs
- Focusing on gender-differentiated roles in the livestock subsector and women's constraints to access training, credit, and participation in mixed farmers' groups
- Focusing on constraints and opportunities in processing and marketing livestock and livestock products.

As the Third Livestock Development Project came to a close in 2003, project staff agreed that the gender action plan had significant impacts, including women's increased capacity to access credit without collateral and an increase in share of agroprocessing activities. The gender-mainstreaming approach was incorporated into the Community Livestock Development Project in Nepal in 2003.

Building women's and men's capacities around production, processing, and marketing is key to promoting successful transitions to market economies. In an IFAD-funded project intended to empower women dairy producers in Bosnia and Herzegovina, training included topics characteristic of livestock activities carried out by women, including cattle breeding and milk production. Training also included a focus on the new European Union standards for the milk sector and guidance on how to apply these. However, capacity at another level was shown to be needed. Men, who were typically in the decision-making bodies of the producers' associations, felt threatened and were not ready to accept women on management boards or generally in the management structure. Lessons pointed to the need to work with women and men, particularly in the need for changing perceptions of roles and decision making as well as related behaviors.[5] Another IFAD project in Vietnam also points to the need for livestock projects to engage with men, particularly husbands, to support the goals of women's empowerment and gender equity.[6]

GUIDELINES AND RECOMMENDATIONS FOR PRACTITIONERS

The following recommendations apply to practitioners at the three levels.

Macro- (policy/strategy) level

Address, in a gender-responsive manner, the constraints to smallholder livestock raisers and producers along livestock value chains. Consider potential impacts on women's and men's livelihoods as they are forced to migrate away from rural areas because of unfavorable policies. What employment policies are in place? Do they support or discriminate against women in the labor force?

Look at the different and interlinked livelihood issues related to livestock production systems in developing and implementing livestock policies.[7] Consider the opportunities and constraints that men and women producers, laborers, and processors face in accessing other important assets, such as information, labor, land, water, infrastructure, and transport.

Identify the different constraints that smallholder women and men livestock producers may have to meet in terms of required government regulations and phytosanitary standards to compete in the market. Facilitate processes and capacity building for women and men producers and processors to meet these standards and provide necessary capital to help them integrate.

Consider the different needs of men and women producers and processors in accessing and benefiting from the design and implementation of infrastructure related to livestock markets (such as abattoirs, transport, and market routes).

Plan proactively to identify and avert potentially different risks for smallholder women and men producers. Understanding the roles that women and men play in the particular livelihood strategy and livestock production system is crucial to identifying and developing appropriate compensation and restocking schemes or finding other appropriate means of responding to market shocks.

Intermediate (institutional) level

Seek ways to facilitate more equitable access by women and men to services. Women, as well as men, need access to marketing services and information. In some cases, for religious or cultural reasons, this may mean training more women on service delivery and information (government regulations, marketing information, changes in prices, livelihood risk diversification, marketing rules, and others) so that they can reach women in rural areas.

Find innovative ways to make capital more accessible to women, as well as men, producing, processing, or marketing livestock. In most areas women still face more constraints than men in accessing credit, particularly those living in remote or marginal areas and lacking other collateral. Often women's groups are more effective at leveraging loans than individual women. Credit facilities need to be made more accessible to women also so that they can benefit from emerging livestock markets.

Local level

Support women livestock entrepreneurs through strengthening their capacity in numeracy, literacy, negotiation, and business management. Without such skills, it is difficult for women to benefit from a rapidly restructuring livestock sector. Support is also effective when provided to groups of women so that they can work collectively to improve their livelihoods and identify and benefit from appropriate markets.

Support women's, as well as men's, diversification into feasible livestock enterprises. Local women can benefit from diversifying their livelihoods to include adding value to their products. In some places drying, smoking, or canning meat may be appropriate to ensure a longer life of the product. This may best be done through a women's processing collective or another context-specific and appropriate way.

Promote women's participation in agricultural fairs and farmers' days. Local women may benefit from participating in local agricultural fairs or farmers' days to "advertise" their livestock or livestock goods. They can use these opportunities to market their livestock services (such as a hatchery or breeding ram).

Promote women's, as well as men's, involvement in producers' decision-making bodies. Efforts should be made to work with both men and women on effective ways of changing their perceptions and behaviors to encourage and support the active involvement of men and women in decision-making bodies.

GENDER-SENSITIVE VALUE CHAINS ANALYSIS FOR IMPROVING LIVESTOCK MARKETING

The first step of conducting gender analysis is identifying appropriate interventions for different aspects related to livestock markets and value chains. A "recipe-book" approach to prescribing interventions has little effect in a complex subsector, contextualized in a rapidly globalizing economy (see Mayoux 2005). A useful model to adapt to the livestock sector for such an analysis is that developed by the International Labour Organization's gender-sensitive value chains analysis:

1. Identify the main questions facing the livestock value chain.
2. Conduct a stakeholder analysis to identify the different actors and their interests and roles along the livestock value chain (such as farmers, abattoirs, markets, and consumers). (Remember to consider adult men, women, elder men, women, and boys and girls in this analysis because different considerations may exist, particularly in areas that are affected by conflict, migration, or HIV and AIDS, for example.)
3. Map the following:

   ■ Supply, production, marketing, or consumption chains related to the particular livestock subsector
   ■ Main types of products and markets (for example, milk, meat, live animals, hides, or manure) and different types of activity (herding, collecting milk, value addition, marketing, consumption)
   ■ Productive units and geographical locations.

4. Look at the relative distribution of "values" to different stakeholders at different points of the chain (poor men and women smallholders, women and men marketing live animals or livestock products). Consider the numbers of women and men involved and the different proportions of "value" going to them. Remember: "Values" may be attributed for the following reasons: economic, social—for example, the status gained, the relationships built through livestock—and natural—capacity for offspring or manure for women's and men's crops. Men and women may attribute different values to livestock all along the value chain, including marketing and consumption, and factors such as taste and cooking quality.
5. Investigate the following:

   ■ The barriers to women's and men's entry into the livestock value chain (for example, women's lack of collateral to obtain inputs, poor men's and women's lack of access to transport and markets, and lack of market information)

- Women's and men's different interests and power relations in the value chain (for example, socioeconomic conditions influence ability to engage in the value chain, and men may have greater decision-making power along particular value chains, such as those related to the meat and live cattle trade)
- The contextual factors explaining inequalities (based on gender, socioeconomic status, caste, and others) and inefficiencies and blockages in the livestock value chain.

6. Identify potential "leverage" points for upgrading the chain as a whole and redistributing values in ways that benefit both men and women, particularly poorer smallholders based on the preceding analysis. (For example, consider things such as income and employment generation and spin-offs to promote empowerment of women in community decision making.)

The chain for commercial chicken production and supply shown in figure 14.2 highlights the increasing super-marketization of poultry in Thailand. The preceding value chains analysis can be used to consider what kinds of gender issues might be present and how they can be addressed.

MONITORING AND EVALUATION INDICATORS

The process of developing a livestock marketing initiative should include the development of a monitoring framework that addresses who and what is to be measured, as well as why, where, and when. Ideally, *gender-sensitive indicators* should be developed in participation with the men and women producers, processors, laborers, and traders at different points along the livestock market chains. This may include extension workers, health care practitioners, those developing livestock market infrastructures, and these promoting livestock market integration. Increasingly, particularly in cases in which there is vertical integration, the livestock producer may also be the processor and trader. Lessons learned show that it is important to monitor the following issues:

- *Whether* men and women are benefiting along the particular livestock value chain

Figure 14.2 Thailand: Commercial Chicken Production and Supply Chain, 2003

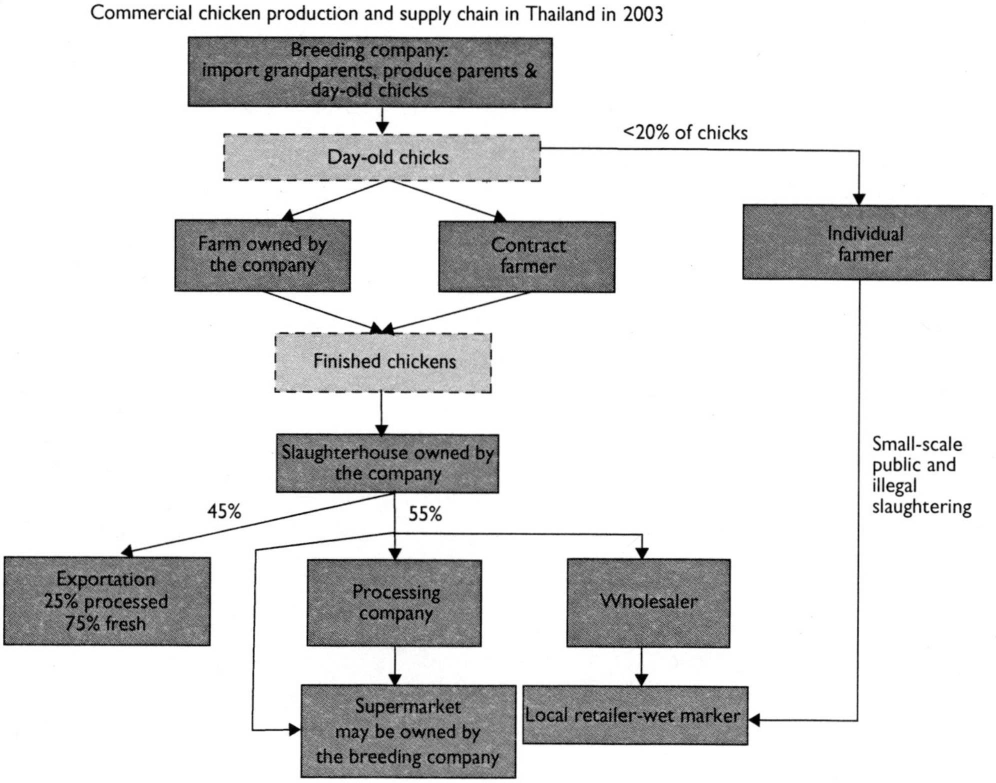

Commercial chicken production and supply chain in Thailand in 2003

Source: FAO 2006.

- *How* men and women are benefiting, or not (note that this should consider age as well because adult men may benefit more than young men or boys and adult women) along the value chain
- The reasons *why* women and men are benefiting, or not.

It may be important to develop indicators that also consider factors such as age and socioeconomic class, particularly in rural areas experiencing fast-changing demographics due to the HIV and AIDS epidemic, out-migration, or emergency situations, such as conflict or environmental disaster. It is important to develop qualitative, gender-sensitive indicators that capture women's and men's different perceptions of priorities, constraints, and benefits. Focus groups, interviews, participant observation, and the use of other participatory learning approaches are all useful methods for collecting such qualitative information. See examples in table 14.2.

The Development and Use of Livestock Technologies to Improve Agricultural Livelihoods

Livestock technology development applies to a wide range of activities across livestock production systems and value chains, including feed and fodder development, breed improvement, dairy mechanization, disease prevention and control, and draft power and transport. If livestock technologies are developed in ways that consider the needs, interests, and concerns of poor women and men, they can reduce women's and men's workloads, increase productivity and improve food security, provide important information to producers and markets, and contribute to the generation of income. Yet the development and delivery of livestock technologies have often been biased toward larger, better-off producers and intensive industrial (landless) systems, areas in which men have tended to benefit more than women. Women tend to have more presence in the smallholder sector, a segment of the population that tends to benefit less from technology development.[1] This Thematic Note addresses the relationships between gender and the development and use of different livestock technologies to improve agricultural livelihoods.

KEY GENDER ISSUES

Many gender issues are specific to discrete factors in the subsector, such as production system, livelihood strategy, socioeconomic class, caste, ethnicity, and environmental constraints. However, some gender issues cut across regions and production systems. These issues are outlined in the following paragraphs and are summarized in a hypothetical example in table 14.3.

Men and women have different needs, interests, and constraints related to livestock technology development and delivery. Many examples may be pointed to of new technologies that have not been adopted because the technology did not suit women's sociocultural, physical, or economic needs, interests, or constraints (FAO n.d.). A study in Kenya

showed that the majority of women viewed livestock primarily as a means of ensuring food security for the family, whereas men perceived livestock as a means of meeting present needs, such as food and school fees and as a form of investment. In Bolivia both men and women considered livestock a source of income and a guarantee of future food security. In India both men and women highlighted the role of livestock in income generation and food security (IFAD 2004). Women and men living in arid areas may need breeds that are adaptable under extreme climatic conditions. They may also have other criteria specific to their own needs (for example, in terms of meat or milk production). Younger women and increasingly older women and men (as in cases in which grandparents take in orphaned grandchildren) who may have to pay school fees on an ongoing basis or who require protein for sick household members may need fast-producing poultry that provide a continuous source of income and nutrition security through egg production. Finally, women, more than men, may be constrained by a lack of access to other productive resources, such as land and water, and other inputs, such as credit.

Men and women are custodians of livestock knowledge and skills that are important in strengthening technology development and adoption. Women and men have different knowledge and skills about different livestock breeds and animal husbandry practices. This can form a solid foundation for informing the development or strengthening of livestock production or disease prevention and control (IFAD n.d. [b]). In part because of their role in milking cows, Maasai women have an intimate knowledge of the character and qualities of their cattle. They also hold knowledge on their animals' bloodlines (FAO 2007). Women know whether or not a cow is docile, fertile, a good milk producer, or a good mother. This information is critical because it is believed that these kinds of traits are passed

625

Table 14.3 Key Gender Issues in Livestock Technology Development

Points to consider for a hypothetical community	Issues related to technology, interests, and needs	Issues related to technology knowledge and skills	Issues related to access to and participation in technology development
Women: consider, for example, age, ethnicity, and socioeconomic status	• Food security • Income generation for school fees or cooking utensils • Mobility • Improved poultry production	• All aspects of poultry production • Egg marketing • Prevention of disease in larger stock (goats and cattle) • Dairying (goats)	• Mobility to local market • Access to extension and veterinary services • Women have shown that they work well in groups
Men: consider, for example, age, ethnicity, and socioeconomic status	• Food security • Income generation for farming implements or larger stock • Status	• Little involvement in poultry production • Younger men and boys graze cattle • Adult men market cattle	• Control cattle and goats • Land tenure in men's name • Mobility provides access to extension and veterinary services through use of bikes or road transport (trucks or buses)

Source: Author.

on in the women's line. In selecting a breeding bull, the Maasai also look at the performance of its dam. Women, with their extensive knowledge in this area, are crucial in this process.

Women and men may have different access to technology development and extension. Experiences from Afghanistan show the importance of training women in technology research and development. Village women play important roles in cattle management yet cannot be approached by men extension workers or technology developers. In a German-supported dairy project in the Kabul, Kunduz, and Mazar regions, women extension staff are employed and used for fieldwork.[2] A case from Senegal shows the importance of working with both women and men to inform technology development. Doing so can also expose cultural biases that can affect the use of draft technologies, for example. The case shows that "even where taboos [against women working with cattle] do not exist, men tend to monopolize animal traction when they are present in the community, because, traditionally it is a man's technology. The same applies to animal traction with horses in Senegal, where men justify the prohibition against women by saying that the implements are too heavy and that the women have not been suitably trained. In point of fact, however, the implements for inter-row work are much lighter in Senegal than in other parts of Africa and even small boys use them. It seems, therefore, that the men's arguments are unfounded" (IFAD/FAO 1998: 7–8).

BENEFITS FROM GENDER-RESPONSIVE ACTIONS

Some observers have suggested that women tend to adopt technologies earlier than men and are therefore well placed to act as catalysts for technology change (IFAD 2004). Other benefits from engaging in gender-responsive actions in the development and delivery of livestock technologies include the following:

■ More effective use of financial, human, social, physical, and natural assets, at both the household and institutional levels
■ Better, more relevant technology design in line with men and women's priorities, interests, and needs
■ Improved chances of technology adaptation and sustainability by those responsible for particular aspects of livestock production and processing
■ Improved livelihoods and overall well-being of women, men, boys, and girls
■ Better use of women's and men's labor and time.

POLICY AND IMPLEMENTATION ISSUES

Women and men depend on other resources for livestock production. Livestock production depends on other productive resources, including land and water. The development of different livestock technologies such as those related to improving fodders, zero grazing, and dairying are therefore strongly linked to women's and men's capacity to access and use other productive resources. Any livestock technology development—such as the development and introduction of improved breeds and poultry intensification—must therefore consider possible gender-based constraints to these resources.

Curricular changes are required at the tertiary level of agricultural education. A need exists to broaden the focus of agricultural education at the tertiary level to include a focus on the development context in which livestock technologies are designed and introduced. In the early 2000s, Makerere University worked to engender the veterinary curriculum in Uganda through engaging in research, developing materials, and changing course requirements and course material.

Local breeds of livestock are often more adaptable to context-specific environmental and weather changes, food availability and quality, and desired characteristics. Women often place great value in local breeds because they are often more likely to help them divert risk and ensure greater food and income security. As Geerlings, Mathias, and Köhler-Rollefson (2002: 1) point out, "The development of high-performing livestock and poultry breeds has no doubt greatly contributed to the increase of food production, especially in temperate climates. But their indiscriminate export into tropical countries has often ended in failure, as the animals cannot stand the heat, need optimal inputs, and readily succumb to disease."

Using a gender-in-livelihoods focus in the research and development of livestock technology can be useful for identifying environmentally sustainable practices for use by women and men producers and processors—for example, in waste management and fodder improvement. Understanding how women's and men's production strategies differ, the types of resources they use, and the management of products such as manure, skins, and feathers is important for determining sustainable environmental practices.

Diverse perspectives are important for effective livestock technology development. Men's and women's different perspectives as producers and as more formal researchers and practitioners are important in technology development. Governments need to look at ways to attract women in livestock sciences and related fields (such as water and land management) and develop incentives to ensure they remain in these fields. This also means supporting girls in primary and secondary education to develop the skills necessary for furthering their studies in the area of livestock technology development.

GOOD PRACTICES AND LESSONS LEARNED

A number of goals must be linked to identify opportunities in developing technological innovations intended to benefit poor rural women (Kaaria and Ashby 2001). These also can be applied to the livestock sector and include the following:

- Increasing returns to women's labor and their independent income through the integration of women's production and processing activities related to livestock through developing or adapting labor-saving technologies (for example, improvement of local breeds, donkey transport), particularly for low-return activities where women do not control the products.
- Considering the linkages between technology development, intensification, and women's capacity to rehabilitate the natural resource base on which this intensification depends (such as scaling up of cashmere goat production in China).
- Considering both production and processing activities because the opportunities and constraints to technology development and adoption need to be seen along the livestock market chain (for example, women may be involved in production but not in the marketing or obtaining the benefits from a particular technology).

Technology research and adoption need to evolve with local women and men over a period of time to encourage adoption and "carry" consensus affecting changes to traditional practices (IFAD n.d. [a]). Innovative Activity Profile 1, which focuses on Chiapas, Mexico, highlights the importance of long-term technology innovation strategies.

Comprehensive approaches are needed for developing livestock technology, including linking feed, disease prevention, water points, shelter, and waste management. In Ethiopia a study on urban livestock production showed that women are involved in feeding large animals, cleaning barns, milking dairy cattle, processing milk, and marketing livestock products. It also noted the role of women in managing confined animals and their critical role in managing manure, which is often made into cakes for sale or fuel. Involving women in livestock technology development within the urban environment is crucial because they have a major role in minimizing environmental pollution and public health problems (Tegegne 2004). See box 14.3 for a good-practice example in Jordan.

Livestock technology development has typically been biased toward the promotion of exotic breeds and cross-breeding rather than the improvement of local breeds. Such efforts have often neglected poor or marginal households and women

The DFID-funded Badia Livestock Extension Project grew out of a livestock research project with Bedouins in an area difficult to access by vehicle. Political (borders), environmental (declining oases and increased piped water), economic and market (grain subsidies), and social (schooling) factors have all played a part in the Bedouins' increasing move to establishing permanent settlements and migrating only seasonally. The project forged links to the Ministry of Agriculture and made progress on improving livestock extension by addressing the needs and interests of both women and men in a difficult institutional context that assumed most clients were mobile and largely men. Their strategy included the following:

- Recruiting a local woman with experience in gender and participation to work closely with expatriate men livestock specialists.
- Providing gender awareness training for two of the men extension staff.
- Including the need to conduct gender training in the terms of reference of short-term consultants.

- Applying participatory rural appraisal tools to analyze gender differences in livestock production. The project worked with women and men farmers in a range of communities, and women from local NGOs and the Ministry of Agriculture worked with men in the project.
- Developing an impact assessment framework and gender-sensitive framework that helped them identify livestock interventions that would have the most impact for women and men.
- Forming women's farmers groups. Once the woman extension specialist was in place, the team was able to form women's farmers groups, and attendance of women was high. Notably, the women's groups stated they also wanted to address women's strategic interests, such as literacy as well as livestock production.
- Recruiting a woman veterinarian and a local woman extension specialist. This helped the project influence the institutional acceptance of women as "technical specialists" and highlighted the benefits of hiring women.

Source: "Rural Livelihoods: Gender Issues in Livestock," case studies, June 1999, www.siyanda.org/docs_gem/index_sectors/natural/ nr_case9.htm.

and have often led to the disappearance of local breeds that are important for minimizing farmers' risks and strengthening livelihoods (Gura and League for Pastoralist Peoples 2003).

Training women in specific livestock technologies is not enough. A study of the Integrated Livestock Development Program in Orissa, India (IFAD 2004), showed that training women in specific technologies is not enough. Women were trained as Community Link Workers on particular veterinary livestock technologies (poultry vaccination, deworming of sheep and goats, and castration of bucks and rams). Yet the women had little education, and their role as Community Link Workers broke with tradition. The experience suggests that women also need related training and confidence-building measures to function effectively as technology users and providers and help them challenge traditional norms. Working with the rest of the community or community leaders to raise their awareness of the need for women to work in new roles related to livestock is also helpful.

Information and communication technologies offer possibilities for helping poor men and women livestock keepers. Recently, the field of information and communication technologies has shown promising developments to help poor livestock keepers. Notably, the University of Reading's Livestock Development Group has developed software called the Livestock Guru to help farmers diagnose, present, and, where possible, treat specific livestock diseases. Even farmers unable to read can use the touch-sensitive computer screen to help them with their livestock health questions.

Insurance programs are helpful for mitigating women's risks, or perceived risks, in adopting technologies. One interesting proposal for mitigating women's risks, or perceived risks, in adopting technologies is the use of insurance schemes for livestock purchases (IFAD n.d. [a]). For example, in India women opted to buy cows and goats on the basis of repaying the loans from milk yields, but inadequate fodder proved to be available for the cross-bred cows, which led to low milk yields (IFAD n.d. [a]).

GUIDELINES AND RECOMMENDATIONS FOR PRACTITIONERS

The following recommendations apply to practitioners at the three levels.

Macro- (policy/strategy) level

Engage men and women in civil society in identifying and defining livestock technology research policies. Include those whose livelihoods are dependent, in part or in whole, on livestock and consider the needs and constraints of those living in marginal or remote rural areas. This may identify areas of concern that were not previously considered (for example, issues of rural smallholders as opposed to larger producers) or identify local technologies that can be strengthened (such as Chiapas sheep). Give higher priority to women's and men's knowledge systems related to livestock (husbandry practices, breeding management, and ethnoveterinary knowledge) and protect these through regimes such as farmers' rights or similar appropriate mechanisms in use or under proposal under different international agreements.

Link women's and men's smallholder technologies with consumer demands. In defining livestock technology research, consumer preferences should be identified and ways found for smallholder women and men to look at their livestock production to identify possible technology needs.

Link gender-responsive approaches to developing livestock technology to other pressing concerns and related sectors to respond better to issues such as global warming, as well as smallholder risk aversion in cases of drought, flooding, food shortages, and disease outbreaks.

Promote women's property rights through translating international and national commitments into tangible action at the local level. Women have more chances to be involved in the process of technology definition and development when they can leverage capital (including, above all, land, water, livestock) to influence technology decisions.

Intermediate (institutional) level

Keep women and men beneficiaries in mind when defining livestock technology research and development agendas. Experience shows that it is important to include technology users in the research and development of new technologies. Women and men (as well as boys and girls) may all be useful in developing different livestock technologies, as experiences from Bangladesh, Mexico, and Tanzania demonstrate.

Recognize men's and women's different spaces and schedules when developing livestock research. The research and develop-

ment of livestock technologies must be built on the lives and livelihoods of women and men. Although some research must necessarily take place in laboratories or similar places, much research is best done in the communities, particularly with the men and women involved in working with livestock.

Local level

Link technology development and use to women's and men's different assets.[3] Look at who uses the different assets related to livestock production and who has access to and controls the different assets (assets including knowledge and information, grazing lands and other land, water, money). What implications does this have for promoting sustainable livestock production and improving the livelihoods and overall well-being of all household members?

Consider technology-related gendered roles and responsibilities. In researching and developing livestock technologies, look at who is responsible for different aspects of animal husbandry and how these relate to other aspects of the livelihood strategy. Consider, where relevant, selection and breeding, care, cleaning, fodder, water collection, disease diagnosis, treatment, prevention, herding, marketing, and value addition. Think about adult women, adult men, boys, girls, elder men, and elder women. Consider how the introduction of the proposed technology may change the existing division of labor. Whom will it affect? How? What sorts of impacts will this have on other parts of their livelihood strategy? How will it affect their well-being?

Understand and build on women's and men's existing livestock and related technologies. Work with local women and men to understand the livestock and related technologies they currently use and get their inputs on how these can be improved. This may lead to better adoption and more sustainable application over the long run.

Identify potential gendered technology benefits and costs. Working with those involved with the particular livestock technology will help identify potential benefits or negative impacts. It is important to consider how women and men measure these benefits. This may be in terms of income generated, social networks formed or strengthened, knowledge gained, local practices validated, and confidence strengthened. It may also open up women's options in other ways or raise their status. On the other hand, the opposite may happen, in which case mitigation strategies must be identified.

MONITORING AND EVALUATION INDICATORS

Although adoption rates of technologies are important to the technology developers, it is equally important to monitor the perceptions of women and men around technologies. Whether monitoring initiatives focused on improving breeds, waste management, fodder, or information and communication technologies, it is important to avoid using the general categories "women" and "men." Rather, it is useful to identify specific groups of women and men to monitor technology adoption and use as well as *elite capture*.[4] It is also important to monitor whether the ownership, control, use, and benefits move from one group to another. For example, there may be a move from poor women to poor men or to better-off women or men depending on the technology introduced and the sociocultural, political, and economic context in which it is introduced. Livestock technologies may have adverse effects; gender and age-based labor and time-use patterns may actually increase with a new technology, which should be monitored.

The first step in developing gender-sensitive indicators should be to work with the women and men (this may also include elder and younger women and men) in the identification of technology priorities related to their livestock and livelihoods:

- One useful way of developing gender-sensitive indicators is to ask participants to draw a picture to describe the current status of their livestock and related livelihood activities.

This helps establish a baseline. For example, women might draw a sick cow, three chickens, and little feed.

- From there, asking participants to draw how they would like the situation to be in the future helps establish a target or different targets. This should be done separately with women and men to compare priorities, needs, and constraints. Here, women might draw two healthy cows, chickens and eggs, and increased access to feed for their animals.

- From there, participants can be asked to think about how they would define success or benefits from meeting those targets. This can help identify gender responsive indicators to monitor change. Quantitative indicators may arise, such as "increase in number of eggs sold by participating women" or "women's income generated by eggs sold increased by *x* percent." Qualitative indicators might also be noted, such as "women's sense of well-being increased." These types of qualitative indicators are best measured using participatory approaches to discuss women's perceptions and views (for example, focus groups or participatory learning approaches).

- Although these examples all focus on men, the indicators should look at the situation in comparison to men in the household and community. See examples in table 14.2.

Chiapas, Mexico: Indigenous Women in Sheep Improvement Research

In the early 1990s, the Institute of Indigenous Studies at the University of Chiapas in Chiapas, Mexico, set out to improve sheep by involving those responsible for sheep husbandry: the women Tzotzil shepherds. The process continues today and shows the value of long-term collaboration and of approaches that value women's local experience, expertise, knowledge, and interests.

Animal extension approaches that introduced cross-breeding intervention and exotic genes for sheep improvement have failed in the past because of high-performance breeds' lack of ability to adapt to local conditions. Government programs in Mexico had tried to introduce exotic breeds such as Rambouillet and Merino to Chiapas to increase wool production in the area. These breeds were known to produce several kilograms of wool every year, compared to the local sheep that barely produced 1 kilogram of wool during the same amount of time. However, several problems presented themselves: the sheep did not adapt to the climate, could not thrive on the poor forage, and could not fight parasitic illnesses without depending on supplements of commercial foods (Gomez, Castro, and Perezgrovas 2001).

INNOVATIVE FEATURES

About 36 percent of the income of the Tzotzil ethnic group comes from sheep husbandry and weaving. Past government efforts tried to substitute local wool sheep with high-producing breeds but had no success. Then the Institute of Indigenous Studies began to collaborate with Tzotzil women on a sheep-improvement plan. The institute worked to improve sheep based on the women's own needs, as well as their criteria for fleece quality. The local women's direct participation in sheep husbandry and weaving is considered a key factor in the success of this program (Castro-Gámez and others n.d.).

The initiative focused on breeding improvement, animal health, and management. The institute used an ethnoveterinary approach to look deeper into the local indigenous knowledge to understand the possibilities for learning about animal management and health (box 14.4). They learned to "listen carefully and respectfully to those who, educated or not, know better" (Perezgrovas, Peralta, and Pedraza 2002: 1).

The project is also one of the only initiatives that has recognized and respected (at least partly) local women's and men's property rights. The project helped maintain property rights by

- Developing the flock from the local population and managing it in a way that agreed with local traditions and customs
- Working with the breeding and culling decisions of the Tzotzil women who worked with the sheep
- Ensuring that local (Tzotzil) communities got first choice of the progeny of the nucleus flock (Anderson and Centonze 2006).

BENEFITS AND IMPACTS

The list of benefits and impacts over the many years of collaboration between researchers and shepherds is extensive:

- A demonstrated genetic gain was seen in those traits selected by the local women.
- A high demand exists for and by the Tzotzil communities for the breeding rams produced by the programs (Anderson and Centonze 2006).

What's innovative? By involving Tzotzil women in the decisions about which traits should be improved in the sheep, the initiative helped the women bring about demonstrable gains in the sheep characteristics that they had deemed desirable.

- Researchers underwent a change in attitude (they became the learners, and the shepherds became the teachers) and learned to observe carefully and respect opinions.
- Improved rams from the nucleus flock have been introduced within community flocks, and their offspring have inherited superior fleece-quality traits.

- Direct participation in the program by local experts in sheep husbandry and weaving has been a key factor in the success of the research approach.

LESSONS LEARNED AND ISSUES FOR WIDER APPLICABILITY

According to the Food and Agriculture Organization, poor people need animal genetic diversity that is suitable to their needs and livelihoods, particularly because they often face a number of production challenges posed by difficult environmental, climatic, and economic conditions. Breeds used for intensive production systems have been found to be inappropriate for livelihoods of many smallholder livestock producers, particularly those living in remote or marginal areas (Anderson 2004). This was shown to be the case in Chiapas.

The original approach employed by government staff failed, mainly because they did not have close contact with the women shepherds, who were the key users and beneficiaries. Their recommendations were not only out of context, but were also at cross-purposes with the culture of the Tzotzil people, for whom sheep are "sacred animals" that are named, cared for, and respected as integral members of the family (Perezgrovas, Peralta, and Pedraza 2002).

"Improved" traditional management systems stand a better chance of being adopted by local communities when they build on the communities' existing systems and are designed within the cultural context of the people.

TIME FRAME

The work with the Tzotzil women has been proceeding for more than a decade. The experience shows the value of long-term commitment to working with women and men raising livestock.

Maasai Men's and Women's Knowledge in Cattle Breeding

Under the LinKS ("gender, biodiversity, and local knowledge systems for food security") project, many key researchers, scientists, policy makers, and extension experts from different institutions were invited to work together on a field study among women and men Maasai livestock keepers in two areas of Tanzania. The study focused on women's and men's management of livestock genetic resources. Designing and conducting the study brought the researchers into direct contact with local women and men and their knowledge and technologies. The study used informal, participatory research methods to enhance the exchange of information and mutual learning.

Initially, the project objectives were to enhance knowledge and increase awareness among policy makers, researchers, and extension agents on the role of women's and men's local knowledge in the sustainable use and management of animal genetic resources. Later the objectives were amended to focus on improving the capacity of agricultural sector institutions to work efficiently at the village level. It was felt that a better understanding of women's and men's knowledge among representatives of such institutions would contribute significantly to achieving this objective. To

this end, the project aimed to enhance insights into the relationship between local knowledge, biodiversity, gender roles, and sustainable agricultural production. It also intended to strengthen agricultural and rural development in southern and eastern Africa.

The study specifically focused on Maasai women's and men's local knowledge of breeding and selecting cattle and, to a lesser extent, sheep and goats. It also focused on the relationship of their knowledge and practices in relation to the goals of food security and herd survival. The study was carried out in three phases:

- Phase 1 was conducted in Simanjiro in northern Tanzania, a presumed area of origin of Maasai livestock keepers.
- Phase 2 was carried out in Mbarali in southern Tanzania, an area to which Maasai livestock keepers have migrated over the last 50 years.
- Phase 3 included an exchange visit organized for northern Maasai people to visit the southern study area, and for southern Maasai to visit the northern study area.

INNOVATIVE FEATURES

There were at least *three innovative aspects* to the project. Although not all of these were planned to address gender specifically, all were relevant to addressing research in ways that took into account a gender (and broader livelihoods) perspective.

Multidisciplinary, interinstitutional collaboration. The research team was composed of people from different institutions: the central government, an extension field service, and two different universities. The team was not interdisciplinary per se, because all team members had livestock-related backgrounds (for example, veterinary medicine, animal production, animal nutrition, animal husbandry, range management, farming systems research),

---

What's innovative?

- The project drew on the expertise of researchers from many disciplines related to livestock and relied on the collaboration of multiple institutions.
- The study associated with the project used gender-sensitive informal research methods to yield a more accurate picture of the situation.
- The project organized exchange visits between two groups of Maasai people who lived 1,200 kilometers apart.

but it was clear that this kind of interinstitutional collaboration was a novelty. Team members received fairly general training on the principles of gender analysis at the beginning of the study. The training was not specifically on Maasai women or on the role of women in livestock. This helped to some extent in strengthening the understanding of those involved of the importance of gender concerns in the research.

Use of informal research methods. The study used informal gender-sensitive research methods. Such methods were new to the researchers because they came from a thoroughly formal and technical background. At the inception of LinKS, team members received training in informal and participatory research methods. This included training on some of the basic principles of gender. However, this was far from providing a sufficient basis on which to conduct a proper informal and gender-sensitive field study. It has been suggested that the quality of the study suffered because of the disdain that some researchers felt for the "unscientific" research methods. Some of the team members worked hard to apply the informal research methods, while others kept opposing them throughout the process.

Inclusion of a farmer exchange visit. The most innovative element was the (unplanned and rather accidental) decision to dedicate Phase 3 to a farmer exchange visit. Four women were included in each of the two groups of 12 Maasai who participated in the exchange. The researchers had to be persuaded to agree to the idea because in the original plans, Phase 3 was meant to be a conventional sort of seminar to "present the research results" to the usual stakeholders, including relevant authorities, heads of services, politicians, university scientists, and some farmers' representatives. The exchange visit turned out to be a much more useful activity. It was extremely interesting for the 24 Maasai who took part in the exchange visit to see how other Maasai 1,200 kilometers away managed their livestock and dealt with different constraints. Even more interesting was to see that despite different circumstances, the constraints faced by women and men in both groups were so similar and that the two distant communities shared a common base of local knowledge on the management of animal genetic resources.

BENEFITS AND IMPACTS

It is not yet clear to what extent the Maasai women or men benefited from the study. Clearly, participating in the exchange provided the women and men with an *opportunity to explore other experiences, skills, and knowledge.* Still, differing perceptions exist about the impact of the study on

scientists, policy makers, and extension officers. Without further investigation, it is not clear to what extent their *views of the Maasai* have changed as a result of this activity. In Kenya and Tanzania, the Maasai are still discriminated against and are seen as "backward" or "primitive." Much work is still needed to change the attitudes of researchers, extension workers, and politicians and their attitudes toward Maasai women and men in terms of their views that they should "give up their traditional ways of life and start being serious [sic] about livestock-keeping. 'Serious' in this respect means using 'improved' breeds, stall-feeding the animals, selling more animals . . . to pay for modern veterinary drugs."[1] Researchers have been trained in "formal" institutes that value, above all, "modern" technology. In most cases, their training leaves them with a lack of respect for or understanding of the value of women's and men's local knowledge and ways.

Compared to conventional methods, gender-sensitive participatory research methods are meant to be less extractive, less top-down, and more egalitarian. To have positive effects all around, it is essential for those involved to have adequate training in gender and participatory research methods. An extended process of strengthening capacity is needed; such a process should provide participants the opportunity to question their own formal training and to explore the value of women's and men's local knowledge and skills. A participatory study is supposed to have positive effects on the studied population, such as active involvement in the research process, the analysis and interpretation of the results, ownership, awareness, and emancipation. In this particular case, mainly because of lack of experience with this (still seemingly innovative) research method, these effects have been minimal.

LESSONS LEARNED AND ISSUES FOR WIDER APPLICABILITY

Informal research methods, like formal methods, provide serious ways of exploring livestock technology development and other issues. Over the past 20 years, they have been increasingly recognized by many disciplines. To make the best use of informal research methods, researchers working on livestock-related issues should do the following:

- Prepare thoroughly for research and become familiar and conversant with the methodology.
- Collect relevant information about the area to be studied *before* going to the field—for example, demographics,

livestock population, prevailing livestock and agricultural production system, livelihood strategies, and socioeconomic aspects. "Relevant" information should be of a certain scientific level and quality and not simply agricultural statistics. It is important to leave behind preconceived ideas about, for example, livelihood strategies and women's and men's knowledge and skills.

- Prepare guiding gender- and age-sensitive questions and checklists with care.
- Conduct interviews with men and women (including elders and youth where relevant) in a serious and respectful way.
- Document gender- and age-disaggregated data meticulously.

More important, participatory learning or informal research methods are not to be taken lightly. It takes time and practice to be comfortable and conversant with them. Gender in livelihoods analysis should be central to the development of a research framework and the design and application of an informal livestock research methodology.

Research leadership in understanding gender and livelihoods approaches. It is important to have someone guiding and supporting livestock technology research who is conversant in gender and livelihoods approaches and who respects and understands the need for looking at livestock technology issues in terms of *whole livelihood strategies and systems.* This includes contextualizing research within the gender, age, and other sociocultural structures and relations, as well as understanding technology development and selection criteria in the wider environmental, social, and economic context.

Collection and use of gender and age-disaggregated data. Before going to the field to conduct informal gender-sensitive research into livestock and agricultural livelihoods, it is important to have a clear understanding of the concepts and linkages between gender, local knowledge systems, and broader livelihood. Some of the research team should have extensive experience in the design and collection of gender- and age-disaggregated data. It is important to collect information from men and women on their different gendered livelihood roles, responsibilities, and their criteria for technology development. Moreover, it is important to recognize that gendered livelihood roles and relations are dynamic, adapting or responding to changing situations caused by things such as disease outbreaks, trade and environment policies, and changes in livestock markets.

NOTES

Overview

This Module was written by Catherine L. M. Hill (Consultant) and reviewed by Chitra Deshpande and Catherine Ragasa (Consultants); Deborah Rubin (Cultural Practice); Daniela Battaglia, John Curry, Yianna Lambrou, and Anni McLeod (FAO); Delgermaa Chuluunbaater, Maria Hartl, and Antonio Rota (IFAD); and Jimmy Smith (World Bank).

1. Ian Scoones, "The Growing Demand for Livestock." ID21 Insights 72, February, Brighton, Institute of Development Studies, www.id21.org.

2. For more on typologies of livestock production systems, see FAO (2006c, 2007).

3. This is also leading to a trend in diversity-reducing gene flow, according to FAO (2007).

4. Ida-Eline Engh, Libor Stloukal, and Jacques du Guerny, "HIV/AIDS in Namibia: The Impact on the Livestock Sector," www.fao.org.

5. Women's rights to land and other property are enshrined in international agreements, including the Convention on the Elimination of All Forms of Discrimination against Women (CEDAW), which was adopted by the United Nations General Assembly in 1979. Articles 14, 15, and 16 in particular contain provisions relating to equal access to land, equal inheritance and succession rights, and equal legal capacity.

6. World Bank, personal communication in comments on the outline for this paper.

7. In many areas, particularly in sub-Saharan Africa, numbers of child-headed households engaged in agricultural livelihoods are increasing because of the loss of one or both parents through HIV and AIDS.

8. Suzanne Kindervatter, "Institutionalizing Gender Equality as a Force for Global Development," www.interaction.org.

9. The author's experience is that FAO has conducted capacity building on gender-disaggregated data and supported national agricultural processes. These initiatives showed the value of collecting data disaggregated by sex and age.

10. In many areas affected by the HIV and AIDS epidemic, elder- or child-headed households face different needs and constraints than those typically addressed by those working on livestock technology or extension.

Thematic Note 1

This Thematic Note was written by Catherine L. M. Hill (Consultant) and reviewed by Chitra Deshpande and Catherine Ragasa (Consultants); Deborah Rubin (Cultural Practice);

Daniela Battaglia, John Curry, Yianna Lambrou, and Anni McLeod (FAO); Delgermaa Chuluunbaater, Maria Hartl, and Antonio Rota (IFAD); and Jimmy Smith (World Bank). Biosecurity combines bioexclusion (measures for preventing a pathogen from being introduced to a herd or flock) and biocontainment, which addresses the ability of a pathogen to spread among animal groups within a farm and the possibility of it being released from the farm (Otte and others 2007).

1. Transboundary animal diseases are "those of significant economic, trade and/or food security importance for a considerable number of countries; which can easily spread to other countries and reach epidemic proportions; and where control/management, including exclusion, requires cooperation between several countries" (Otte, Nugent, and McLeod 2004: 6).

2. PowerPoint presentation by Cao Thi Hong Van, "AIERP—Poultry Restocking Impacts for Smallholders," Workshop on the Future of Poultry Farmers in Vietnam after Highly Pathogenic [Avian] Influenza, March 2007.

3. Ellen Geerlings contextualizes this phenomenon in her 2001 thesis "Sheep Husbandry and Ethnoveterinary Knowledge of Raika Sheep Pastoralists in Rajasthan, India," submitted for partial fulfillment of the M.Sc. degree in environmental sciences, Wageningen University.

4. See FAO's Education, Extension, and Communication (www.fao.org).

5. Regulation is an essential tool in preventing the spread of disease and avoiding market shocks. In fact, regulation is the instrument of choice in most Organisation for Economic Cooperation and Development and other high-density livestock countries.

6. Anthony Mugisha, personal communication, October 24, 2007.

7. "Livelihoods at Stake in Rural Egypt," policy brief provided through personal communication with Ellen Geerlings, October 2007.

8. This discussion is based on Linda Mayoux, "Gender Dimensions of Micro-Insurance: Questioning the New Bootstraps," draft paper, www.genfinance.info/Documents/Microinsurance.pdf.

9. This section is adapted from Otte, Nugent, and McLeod (2004) and Otte and others (2007).

10. This section is adapted from ILRI, "African Women Make Their World Go Round," www.ilri.org.

11. For more on developing indicators using participatory approaches, see Dorward and others, "Guide to Indicators and Methods for Assessing the Contribution of Livestock Keeping to Livelihoods of the Poor," Department of Agricultural Sciences Imperial College London, n.d. The framework and approaches can be adapted for use in a Gender in Livelihoods approach and analysis.

Thematic Note 2

This Thematic Note was written by Catherine L. M. Hill (Consultant) and reviewed by Chitra Deshpande and Catherine Ragasa (Consultants); Deborah Rubin (Cultural Practice); Daniela Battaglia, John Curry, Yianna Lambrou, and Anni McLeod (FAO); Delgermaa Chuluunbaater, Maria Hartl, and Antonio Rota (IFAD); and Jimmy Smith (World Bank).

1. Livestock also provides over half of the value of global agricultural output and one-third in developing countries. See also Upton (2004).

2. Katinka de Balogh, personal communication, October 2005.

3. IFAD, Micro-Finance and Technical Support Project (MFTSP) update, 2007.

4. Personal communication with Doborah Rubin, Director, Cultural Practice.

5. IFAD, "Empowerment of Women Producers Association Project," Federation of Bosnia and Herzegovina, signed in May 2005.

6. "Rural Income Diversification Project in Tuyen Quang Province, Vietnam," Supervision Report, September 6–18, 2006.

7. The SL framework outlines a number of these interlinked issues.

Thematic Note 3

This Thematic Note was written by Catherine L. M. Hill (Consultant) and reviewed by Chitra Deshpande and Catherine Ragasa (Consultants); Deborah Rubin (Cultural Practice); Daniela Battaglia, John Curry, Yianna Lambrou, and Anni McLeod (FAO); Delgermaa Chuluunbaater, Maria Hartl, and Antonio Rota (IFAD); and Jimmy Smith (World Bank). See Module 7 for more on this subject.

1. ILRI, "African Women Make Their World Go Round," www.ilri.org.

2. FAO project, Development of Integrated Dairy Schemes in Afghanistan (GCP/AFG/040/GER), 2005-08.

3. This section is adapted from ITDG (1996) and Amuguni (2000).

4. Elite capture refers to situations where those with power and status in a community influence development processes based on their own priorities and potential gains. See World Bank (2008), *CDD and Elite Capture: Reframing the Conversation*, Social Development How to Series, February.

Innovative Activity Profile I

This Innovative Activity Profile was written by Catherine L. M. Hill (Consultant) and reviewed by Chitra Deshpande and

Catherine Ragasa (Consultants); Deborah Rubin (Cultural Practice); Daniela Battaglia, John Curry, Yianna Lambrou, and Anni McLeod (FAO); Delgermaa Chuluunbaater, Maria Hartl, and Antonio Rota (IFAD); and Jimmy Smith (World Bank). This Profile draws heavily on Anderson (2004); Anderson and Centonze (2006); Castro-Gámez and others (n.d.); Gomez, Castro, and Perezgrovas (2001); Perezgrovas, Peralta, and Pedraza (2002).

Innovative Activity Profile 2

This Innovative Activity Profile was written by Catherine L. M. Hill (Consultant) and reviewed by Chitra Deshpande and Catherine Ragasa (Consultants); Deborah Rubin (Cultural Practice); Daniela Battaglia, John Curry, Yianna Lambrou, and Anni McLeod (FAO); Delgermaa Chuluunbaater, Maria Hartl, and Antonio Rota (IFAD); and Jimmy Smith (World Bank). This Profile was prepared based on the extensive inputs provided by Marie-Louise Beerling from her experience as a consultant on the LinKS project, as well as documentation from the LinKS project's and elsewhere. It was edited by the lead module author, who takes responsibility for any mistakes or misrepresentations. The Profile was also based on FAO (2007) and UNDESA (2007).

1. Marie-Louise Beerling, personal communication.

REFERENCES

Overview

Baden, Sally. 1998. "Gender Issues in Agricultural Liberalisation." Topic paper prepared for Directorate General for Development of the European Commission, Report No. 41, Institute of Development Studies, Brighton, U.K.

Bravo-Baumann, Heidi. 2000. "Gender and Livestock: Capitalisation of Experiences on Livestock Projects and Gender." Working document, Swiss Agency for Development and Cooperation, Bern.

de Haan, Nicoline. 2001. "Of Goats and Groups: a Study of Social Capital in Development Projects." *Agriculture and Human Values* 18: 71–84.

Diarra, Marthe, and Marie Monimart. 2006. "Landless Women, Hopeless Women?" Issues Paper 143, International Institute for Environment and Development, London.

Dorward, Andrew, Simon Anderson, Yolanda Nava, James Pattison, Rodrigo Paz, Jonathan Rushton, and Ernesto Sanchez Vera. 2005. "Guide to Indicators & Methods for Assessing the Contribution of Livestock Keeping to Livelihoods of the Poor." Department of Agricultural Sciences, Imperial College, London.

Food and Agriculture Organization (FAO). 1997. "Management of Livestock Resources." Committee on Agriculture (COAG), 14th Session, COAG/97/4, Rome, April 7–11.

———. 2002. "Rural Women: Crucial Partners in the Fight against Hunger and Poverty: Side Event Report." FAO, Rome.

———. 2006a. "Livestock Report 2006." FAO, Rome.

———. 2006b. "Livestock's Long Shadow: Environmental Issues and Options." FAO, Rome.

———. 2006c. "State of Food and Agriculture." FAO, Rome.

———. 2007. "The State of the World's Animal Genetic Resources for Food and Agriculture." FAO, Rome.

Ghotge, Nitya, and Sagari Ramdas. 2002. "Women and Livestock: Creating Space and Opportunities." *LEISA Magazine* 18 (4), (December): 16–17. Also available at www.leisa.info.

GRAIN. n.d. "Participatory Breed Improvement of the Chiapas Sheep." In "Sustaining Agricultural Biodiversity and the Integrity and Freeflow of Genetic Resources for Food and Agriculture." Paper prepared for the Forum for Food Sovereignty. Barcelona: GRAIN; Winnipeg: ETC; Rugby: TDG.

Heffernan, Claire, Louise Nielsen, and Federica Misturelli. 2001. *Restocking Pastoralists: A Manual.* Livestock Production Programme. London: Department for International Development.

Hill, Catherine. 2003. "Livestock and Gender: The Tanzanian Experience in Different Livestock Production Systems. A Glance at LinKS: LinKS Project Case Study No. 3." FAO, Rome.

International Fund for Agricultural Development (IFAD). 2004. "Livestock Services and the Poor: A Global Initiative. Collecting, Coordinating and Sharing Experiences." IFAD, Rome.

Miller, Beth. 2001. "Rights to Livestock." In 2020 Focus No. 06, Brief 04, August, International Food Policy Research Institute, Washington, DC.

Niamir-Fuller, Maryam. 1994. "Women Livestock Managers in the Third World: A Focus on Technical Issues Related to Gender Roles in Livestock Production." IFAD, Rome.

Otte, Joachim, David Roland-Holst, Dirk Pfeiffer, Ricardo Soares-Magalhaes, Jonathan Rushton, Jay Graham, and Ellen Silbergeld. 2007. "Industrial Livestock Production and Global Health Risks." Pro-Poor Livestock Policy Initiative Research Report, June.

Swiss Agency for Development and Cooperation (SDC). 2007. "The Livestock Revolution: An Opportunity for Poor Farmers?" Inforesources Focus No. 1/07, SDC, Bern.

Thomas-Slayter, Barbara, and Nina Bhatt. 1994. "Land, Livestock and Livelihoods: Changing Dynamics of Gender, Caste and Ethnicity in a Nepalese Village." *Human Ecology* 22 (4): 467–94.

Trench, Pippa, John Rowley, Marthe Diarra, Fernand Sano, and Boubacar Keita. 2007. "Beyond Any Drought: Root Causes of Chronic Vulnerability in the Sahel." Sahel Working Group, International Institute for Environment and Development, London.

Upton, Martin. 2004. "The Role of Livestock in Economic Development and Poverty Reduction." Pro-Poor Livestock Policy Initiative Working Paper 10, FAO, Rome.

World Bank. 2005a. "Gender Issues in Monitoring and Evaluation in Rural Development: A Toolkit." Internal report, June, World Bank, Washington, DC.

———. 2005b. "Managing the Livestock Revolution: Policy and Technology to Address the Negative Impacts of a Fast-Growing Sector. Report No. 32725-GLB, World Bank, Washington, DC.

———. 2007. "World Development Indicators." Report, World Bank, Washington, DC.

Thematic Note I

Alders, R., B. Bagnol, M. Harun, H. Msami, L. Sprowles, and M. Young. 2005. "The Impact of Newcastle Disease Control in Village Chickens Using I-2 Thermotolerant Vaccine in Rural Areas of Dodoma and Mtwara Regions, Tanzania." Paper presented at the DFID Livestock Production Programme International Workshop on Improving the Well-Being of Resource-Poor Communities: The Contribution of Small Livestock, Howick, South Africa, September 12–15.

Amuguni, Helen. 2000. "Assessing the Gender Impact of the Community Based Animal Health Programme in Southern Sudan: A Gender Assessment Study in Mading Area, Latjor State, Upper Nile." April, Vétérinaires Sans Frontières–Belgium, Brussels.

AusVet. 2006. "Southern Africa Newcastle Disease Control Project SANDCP July 2002–October 2005 Independent Completion Report." June 26.

Bruschke, Christianne, Alex Thiermann, and Bernard Vallat. 2007. "Implementing Appropriate OIE/FAO Prevention Measures in Different Country Contexts." In *Proceedings of Technical Meeting on Highly Pathogenic Avian Influenza and Human H5N1 Infection*, Food and Agriculture Organization (FAO), June 27–29, 2007, Rome, Italy. Background Paper No. 3.2a.i. Available at www.fao.org/docs/eims/upload//229371/ah656e.pdf.

Curry, John, Rebecca Huss-Ashmore, Brian Perry, and Adrian Mukhebi. 1996. "A Framework for the Analysis of Gender, Intra-Household Dynamics and Livestock Disease Control with Examples from Uasin Gishu District, Kenya." *Human Ecology* 24 (2): 161–89.

de Haan, Nicoline. 2001. "Of Goats and Groups: A Study on Social Capital in Development Projects." *Agriculture and Human Values* 18 (1): 71–84.

Food and Agriculture Organization (FAO). 2005. "The Globalizing Livestock Sector: Impact of Changing Market." Committee on Agriculture, 19th Session, Rome, April 13–16.

Food and Agriculture Organization (FAO)/Ministry of Agriculture and Rural Development (MARD)/Agrifood consulting International (ACI) 2007. "Gender Analysis in Poultry Production in ChúcSontown, Chuong Mỹ District, HàTây Province and ChàLâ Commune, DuongMinhChàu District, TâyNinh Province." PowerPoint presentation at the workshop The Future of Poultry Farmers in Vietnam after Highly Pathogenic Avian Influenza, Hanoi, Vietnam, March 8–9.

FAO/OIE/WHO. 2005. "The Global Strategy for the Progressive Control of Highly Pathogenic Avian Influenza (HPAI)." Draft Report. Rome: FAO (Food and Agriculture Organization); Paris: OIE (World Organisation for Animal Health); Geneva: WHO (World Health Organization.)

Geerlings, Ellen. 2007. "Highly Pathogenic Avian Influenza: A Rapid Assessment of the Socio-Economic Impact on Vulnerable Households in Egypt." Food and Agriculture Organization/World Food Programme Joint Project Report, July, Rome.

Geerlings, Ellen, Evelyn Mathias, and Ilse Köhler-Rollefson. 2002. "Securing Tomorrow's Food: Promoting the Sustainable Use of Farm Animal Genetic Resources: Information for Action." League for Pastoral Peoples, Ober-Ramstadt, Germany. Also available at www.pastoralpeoples.org.

Ghotge, Nitya, and Sagari Ramdas. 2002. "Women and Livestock: Creating Space and Opportunities." *LEISA Magazine* 18, no. 4 (December): 16–17. Also available at www.leisa.info.

Kariuki, G. 2003. "Gender, Environmental and Traditional Knowledge in Managing Malignant Catarrhal Fever in Maasai Herds." Draft, Kenya Agricultural Research Institute, November 5.

Lucas, Caroline. 2007. "Bird Flu's Link with the Crazy Trade in Poultry." *Financial Times,* February 26.

Mugisha, Anthony. 2004. "Socio-Economic and Gender Aspects of Control of Vectorborne Diseases: A Study of Intra-Household Dynamics and Decision-Making in the Pastoralist System of Southwestern Uganda." Ph.D. thesis, University of Reading School of Agriculture, Policy and Development.

Mugisha, Anthony, Anni McLeod, Rachel Percy, and Elizabeth Kyewalabye. 2008. "Socio-economic Factors Influencing Control of Vector-borne Diseases in the Pastoralist System of South Western Uganda." *Tropical Animal Health and Production* 40(4): 287–97.

Otte, Joachim, David Roland-Holst, Dirk Pfeiffer, Ricardo Soares-Magalhaes, Jonathan Rushton, Joay Graham, and Ellen Silbergeld. 2007. "Industrial Livestock Production and Global Health Risks." Pro-Poor Livestock Policy Initiative (PPLPI) Research Report, June.

Otte, Joachim, Rachel Nugent, and Anni McLeod. 2004. "Transboundary Animal Diseases: Assessment of Socio-Economic Impacts and Institutional Responses." FAO Livestock Policy Discussion Paper No. 9, Food and Agriculture Organization, Rome.

Upton, Martin. 2004. "The Role of Livestock in Economic Development and Poverty Reduction." Pro-Poor Livestock Policy Initiative (PPLPI) Working Paper 10, Food and Agriculture Organization, Rome.

World Bank. 2005. "Managing the Livestock Revolution: Policy and Technology to Address the Negative Impacts of a Fast-Growing Sector." June, World Bank, Washington, DC.

Thematic Note 2

Dercon, Stephan, and John Hoddinott. 2005. "Livelihoods, Growth, and Links to Market Towns in 15 Ethiopian Villages." FCND Discussion Paper 194, International Food Policy Research Institute, Washington, DC.

FARM (Food and Agriculture Research Management) Africa. 2002. "Microenterprise Development Best Practices from FARM-Africa's Pastoralist Development Project in Kenya." Booklet, Food and Agriculture Organization, Nairobi. Also available at www.fao.org.

Food and Agriculture Organization (FAO). 2005. "The Globalizing Livestock Sector: Impact of Changing Market." Committee on Agriculture, 19th Session, Rome, April 13–16.

———. 2006. "Livestock Report 2006." FAO, Rome.

Garcia, Zoraida, with contributions from Jennifer Nyberg and Shayma Owaise Saadat. 2006. "Agriculture, Trade Negotiations and Gender." Food and Agriculture Organization, Rome.

Ghotge, Nitya, and Sagari. Ramdas. 2002. "Women and Livestock: Creating Space and Opportunities." *LEISA Magazine* 18 (4) (December): 16–17. Also available at www.leisa.info.

Huss-Ashmore, Rebecca. 1996. "Livestock, Nutrition, and Intra-Household Resource Control in Uasin Gishu District, Kenya." *Human Ecology* 24 (2): 191–213.

International Fund for Agricultural Development (IFAD). 2002. "IFAD in China: The Rural Poor Speak." IFAD, Rome.

———. 2004. "Livestock Services and the Poor: A Global Initiative. Collecting, Coordinating and Sharing Experiences. IFAD, Rome.

Mayoux, Linda. 2005. "'Gender Lens' in Value Chains Analysis for Decent Work, A Practical Guide." Draft for International Labour Organization, Geneva, November.

Oboler, Regina. 1996. "Whose Cows Are They, Anyway?: Ideology and Behaviour in Nandi Cattle 'Ownership' and Control." *Human Ecology* 24 (2): 255–72.

Okali, Christine. 2004. "Gender Issues in Changing Domestic Markets for Livestock Production in Developing Countries." Paper for the expert consultation, Food and Agriculture Organization, Rome, June 22–24.

Upton, Martin. 2004. "The Role of Livestock in Economic Development and Poverty Reduction." Pro-Poor Livestock Policy Initiative Working Paper 10, Food and Agriculture Organization, Rome.

White, Cynthia. 1990. "Changing Animal Ownership and Access to Land among the Wodaabe (Fulani) of Central Niger." In *Property, Poverty and People: Changing Rights in Property and Problems of Pastoral Development,* ed. P. Baxter and R. Hogg, 240–54. Manchester, U.K.: Manchester University.

World Bank. 2005. "Policy and Technology to Address the Negative Impacts of a Fast-Growing Sector." World Bank, Washington, DC, June.

Thematic Note 3

Amuguni, Helen. 2000. "Assessing the Gender Impact of the Community Based Animal Health Programme in Southern Sudan: A Gender Assessment Study in Mading Area, Latjor State, Upper Nile." Vétérinaires sans Frontières–Belgium, Brussels, April.

Food and Agriculture Organization (FAO). 2007. "Maasai Men and Women's Local Knowledge in Breeding Cattle." In *Breeding for a Purpose: Maasai Men and Women's Local Knowledge in Breeding Cattle.* CD-ROM. FAO, Rome.

———. n.d. "Planning Livestock Interventions with a Gender and HIV/AIDS Lens: Why a Gender and HIV/AIDS Focus?" Fact sheet, FAO, Rome.

Geerlings, Ellen, Evelyn Mathias, and Ilse Köhler-Rollefson. 2002. "Securing Tomorrow's Food: Promoting the Sustainable Use of Farm Animal Genetic Resources: Information for Action. League for Pastoral Peoples." Ober-Romstadt, Germany. Also available at www.pastoralpeoples.org.

Gura, Susanne, and League for Pastoralist Peoples. 2003. "Losing Livestock, Losing Livelihoods." *Seedling* (January): 8–12.

International Fund for Agricultural Development (IFAD). 2004. "Livestock Services and the Poor: A Global Initiative. Collecting, Coordinating, and Sharing Experiences." IFAD, Rome. Evaluations are available at www.ifad.org.

———. n.d. (a). "Changing Traditional Practices in Animal Husbandry," IFAD, Rome.

———. n.d. (b). "Lessons from Processing and Marketing." IFAD, Rome.

International Fund for Agricultural Development/Food and Agriculture Organization. 1998. "Agricultural Implements Used by Women Farmers in Africa." September, IFAD, Rome.

ITDG (now Practical Action). 1996. "Discovering Technologists: Women's and Men's Work at Village Level." ITDG, Colombo, Sri Lanka.

Kaaria, Susan, and Jacqueline Ashby. 2001. "An Approach to Technological Innovation That Benefits Rural Women: The Resource-to-Consumption System." Working document No. 13, CGIAR System-Wide Program on Participatory Research and Gender Analysis, Cali.

Tegegne, Azage. 2004. "Urban Livestock Production and Gender in Addis Ababa, Ethiopia." *Urban Agriculture* 12: 29–31.

World Bank. 2008. "CDD and Elite Capture: Reframing the Conversation." Social Development How to Series, February, World Bank, Washington, DC.

Innovative Activity Profile 1

Anderson, Simon. 2004. "Environmental Effects on Animal Genetic Resources: A Review." Commissioned by AGAP, Food and Agriculture Organization, Rome.

Anderson, Simon, and Roberta Centonze. 2006. "Property Rights and the Management of Animal Genetic Resources." CAPRi (CGIAR Systemwide Program on Collective Action and Property Rights), Working Paper No. 48, February, International Food Policy Research Institute, Washington, DC.

Castro-Gámez, Hilda, Gabriel Campos, Reyes López, Raúl Perezgrovas, and Héctor Castillo-Juárez. n.d. "Heritability and Permanent Environmental Effect for Fleece Quality Assessed by an Ancient Tzotzil Indigenous Evaluation System." Unpublished report.

Gomez, Tona, Hilda Castro, and Raul Perezgrovas. 2001. "The Real Sheep of the Tzotzil." *Compass* (December): 29–31.

Perezgrovas, Raul, Marisela Peralta, and Pastor Pedraza. 2002. "Sheep Husbandry among Tzotzil Indians: Who Learns from Whom?" *PLA Notes*. CD-ROM 1988–2001. Also available at www.iied.org/NR/agbioliv/pla_notes/documents/plan_02007.pdf.

Innovative Activity Profile 2

Food and Agriculture Organization (FAO). 2007. "Breeding for a Purpose: Maasai Men and Women's Local Knowledge in Breeding Cattle." Study developed under the LinKS project, FAO, Rome.

United Nations Department of Economic and Social Affairs (UNDESA). 2007. "Indigenous Women and the Food and Agriculture Organization of the United Nations (FAO)." In *Indigenous Women and the United Nations System: Good Practices and Lessons Learned*, 3–8. New York: United Nations. Also available at www.un.org.

FURTHER READING

Overview

Asian Development Bank (ADB). n.d. "Gender Issues in Livestock." In "Gender Checklist: Agriculture." Available at www.adb.org/Documents/Manuals/Gender_Check lists/Agriculture/agri0508.asp?p=genchck.

Food and Agriculture Organization (FAO). 2005. "SEAGA Livestock Guide: Planning with a Gender and HIV/AIDS Lens." June. Available at www.fao.org/sd/dim_pe1/docs/pe1_050901d1_en.pdf.

———. 2006. "Planning Livestock Interventions with a Gender and HIV/AIDS Lens." Fact Sheet. Available at www.fao.org/ag/AGAinfo/subjects/documents/livestock aids0606.pdf.

International Fund for Agricultural Development (IFAD). 1999. "Memory Checks for Programme and Project Design: Household Food Security and Gender: Livestock." Available at www.ifad.org/pub/memory/e/insert2. pdf.

Sere, Carlos, and Henning Steinfeld. 1996. "World Livestock Production Systems: Current Status, Issues and Trends." Animal Production and Health Paper 127, FAO, Rome.

World Bank. 2007. "Gender and the Millennium Development Goals." World Bank, Washington, DC.

Thematic Note 1

Bruschke, Christianne, Alex Thiermann, and Bernard Vallat. 2007. "Implementing Appropriate OIE/FAO Prevention Measures in Different Country Contexts." Background paper, Technical Meeting on Highly Pathogenic Avian Influenza and Human H5N1 Infection, Rome, June 27–29.

McLeod, Anni. n.d. "Socio-Economics of HPAI Control in Viet Nam: the Past and the Future." PowerPoint presentation at the workshop The Future of Poultry Farmers in Vietnam after Highly Pathogenic Influenza, Hanoi, Vietnam, March 8–9.

Thematic Note 2

Bennett, Anthony, Frederic Lhoste, Jay Crook, and Joe Phelan. 2006. "The Future of Small Scale Dairying." In *FAO Livestock Report 2006*. Rome: FAO.

Costales, Achilles, Pierre Gerber, and Henning Steinfeld. 2006. "Underneath the Livestock Revolution." In *FAO Livestock Report 2006*. Rome: FAO.

Joss, Stefan, Hans Schaltenbrand, and Peter Schmidt. 2004. "Clients First: A Rapid Market Appraisal Tool Kit." Theoretical Background and Experiences from Various RMA Events, Helvetas, 2004. Note: Although this is not "gender sensitive," it does propose a participatory methodology for appraising markets. The framework and tools can be "gendered" and adapted to livestock markets.

Van Houten, Helen. 2002. *Microenterprise Development: Best Practices from FARM-Africa's Pastoralist Development Project in Kenya.* Nairobi: FARM (Food and Agriculture Research Management) Africa.

Thematic Note 3

Heffernan, Claire. 2005. "Demand-Led Research, Biotechnology and the Poor: Issues from the Livestock Sector." In *The Role of Biotechnology in Animal Agriculture to Address Poverty in Africa: Opportunities and Challenges,* Proceedings of the 4th All Africa Conference on Animal Agriculture and the 31st Annual Meeting of the Tanzania Society for Animal Production, Arusha, Tanzania, September 20–24.

Nuffic (Netherlands organization for international cooperation in higher eduction). n.d. "Collaborative Application of Empirical Criteria for Selecting High-Quality Fleeces: Tzotzil Shepherdesses and Sheep Scientists Work Together to Develop Tools for Genetic Improvement." Available at www. unesco.org.

Innovative Activity Profile 1

Geerlings, Ellen, Evelyn Mathias, and Ilse Köhler-Rollefson. 2002. "Securing Tomorrow's Food: Promoting the Sustainable Use of Farm Animal Genetic Resources." League for Pastoral Peoples, Ober-Romstadt, Germany. Available at www.pastoralpeoples.org.

Gender and Forestry

Overview

FORESTRY AND LIVELIHOODS: CHANGES AND TRENDS

Forests cover just under 4 billion hectares—30 percent of the earth's land surface (FAO 2005a). They fulfill major economic functions, help maintain the fertility of agricultural land, protect water resources, and reduce the risk of natural disasters such as landslides and flooding. The world's forests are home to at least 80 percent of remaining terrestrial biodiversity and are a major carbon sink that mitigates climate change (World Bank 2002).

More than 1.6 billion people depend to varying degrees on forests for their livelihoods. About 60 million indigenous people are almost wholly dependent on forests. Some 350 million people who live within or adjacent to dense forests depend on them for subsistence and income. In developing countries, about 1.2 billion people rely on agroforestry farming systems that help to sustain agricultural productivity and generate income. Worldwide, forest industries provide employment for 60 million people. Some 1 billion people depend on pharmaceuticals derived from forest plants for their medicinal needs.

Mounting evidence suggests that poverty—and poverty in rural areas in particular—can be reduced only by sustainably managing the natural resources that both generate income and provide environmental services. The forests of the world, which are among the most important of these natural resources, provide support to nearly half of the 2.8 billion people who live on $2 or less a day (World Bank 2002). Thus, forests can and must assume a more prominent role in meeting the United Nations' 2000 Millennium Development Goal of halving extreme poverty by 2015.

"*What happens to forests*" will be largely determined by "*what happens outside forests*" (FAO 2007a: 79) One reason that deforestation and forest degradation will continue in most developing regions is the expansion in agricultural land use for both subsistence and commercial cultivation. Deforestation continues at an alarming rate—about 13 million hectares per year (FAO 2005a). A reversal of the situation would depend on structural shifts in economies to reduce direct and indirect dependence on land. The World Bank's forest strategy *Sustaining Forests* (World Bank 2002) recognizes that forests are always a part of larger economic, environmental, and governance systems that must work together if the goals of poverty reduction, sustainable economic development, and environmental protection are to be met. Total forest area continues to decrease, but the results of the Food and Agriculture Organization's (FAO's) Global Forest Resource Assessment (FAO 2005a) indicate the rate of net loss is slowing. Forest planting, landscape restoration, and natural expansion of forests have significantly reduced the net loss of forest area (FAO 2005a).

Concern about climate change has already focused increased attention on the role of forests in carbon sequestration, reducing carbon emissions and substituting for fossil fuels. Climate change may also affect forests themselves, altering forest ecosystems and increasing the incidence and severity of forest fires as well as pest and disease infestation. At the same time forests will be increasingly valued for the environmental services they provide, which includes their role in conserving biodiversity and in arresting desertification and land degradation. In industrial and rapidly developing countries, recreational use of forests is receiving more attention, requiring changes in forest management.

Geographical shifts in the production and consumption of wood and nonwood forest products are likely to intensify, especially as a result of the rapid growth of the emerging economies in Asia, the Caribbean, Latin America, and the Pacific. This will be countered by slow growth of demand in many industrial countries, due to demographic changes and lower income growth rates. Technological changes, including biotechnology and material technology in wood-consuming industries, will improve productivity and reduce raw material requirements.

For many developing countries, wood will remain the most important source of energy. The rising price of oil and increasing concern for climate change will result in increased use of wood as fuel in both developed and developing countries.

An understanding of how society-forest relationships are likely to evolve is important in preparing the sector to address emerging challenges and opportunities (FAO 2007a). Practitioners and others must not consider natural forests solely in terms of the economic value of timber. Drawing on local knowledge can reveal the full range of social, economic, and ecological functions of these resources and how different groups use and benefit from them. Analyzing the complex interactions between local people and the forests can reveal the impact of forest interventions on livelihoods. By facilitating negotiation between stakeholders, practitioners may support the development of collaborative and adaptive strategies to manage forest resources (FAO 2006a). Successful improvements in forest management quite often resemble and build upon traditional activities already practiced in the area. If innovators do not understand local practices and know which local groups rely on which forest and agroforestry products, they risk introducing innovations that are technically feasible but that result in negative socioeconomic effects.

This Module revisits the gender and forestry analysis and experiences of rural and community forestry themes that were profiled in the 1990s (Rojas 1993)[1] and reexamines gender-related issues in the forest sector in light of recent developments and ongoing trends in the sector (FAO 2007a; World Bank 2002). Drawing on documented evidence, it aims to provide practitioners with a commentary on practical experiences of gender in forestry projects and programs.

The Module is presented under a series of pertinent themes, with lessons learned and best practices.

However thoroughly one recognizes the importance of forests to livelihoods, poverty, sustainability, and conservation, the full potential of forests may never be grasped without an understanding of how women and men use forest resources differently. If decision making in forestry programs and policies follows a "gender-neutral" pathway, the implementation of those programs will not garner the knowledge and skills, nor address the needs, of half of the rural population. Gender- and wealth-disaggregated data on the resource management practices of forest- and agroforestry-dependent communities needs to be consistently and regularly gathered. The Module uses the Sustainable Livelihoods (SL) framework to capture the full scope of gender-related issues as they relate to livelihoods.

The need for gender-disaggregated data on the forestry workforce was recently reinforced by a United Nations Economic Commission for Europe–FAO study on women in forestry in Europe:

> Ideas of specific masculine or feminine qualities are connected to certain roles, positions, tasks and professions in individuals. The perception of what is "appropriate" for men and women forms the basis for the distribution of work, the design and evaluation of different tasks, and the criteria for promotions. Forestry is not an exception to this since it has been generally regarded as an arena mainly for men's work, business and governance. Within organizations, from households to companies and authorities, a gendered organizational logic is at work, which not only reproduces a structure of gender division but also, paradoxically, at the same time, makes gender invisible. Gender invisibility takes many forms. ... In many countries, reliable statistics on the demographics of the forestry workforce are difficult to obtain, and when it concerns women's participation, data are virtually non-existent. (FAO 2006b: 1)

International agencies and nongovernmental organizations (NGOs) such as the International Union for Conservation of Nature are influential in the forest sector and maintain a variety of gender strategies, guidelines, and resources. The World Bank forest strategy, for example, clearly states that "the sustainable use of forests requires the participation of all rural populations, including women" (World Bank 2002: 22). The strategy also states, however, that although women's needs often differ from those of men, many programs continue to overlook women's specific needs regarding forestry. This lack of gender awareness constrains the sustainable use and management of forests and forest ecosystems throughout the world. The World Bank forest strategy also points to a lack of adequate data, information, and methodologies to address this concern. It acknowledges that "gender analysis will be an important tool to provide simple information on resource use, responsibility, perspectives and needs, and serves a critical role in the quality of forest investment design" (World Bank 2002: 22).

A number of concerns regarding forestry and the livelihoods of rural women and men warrant prominent treatment:

- Depletion of forest resources often severely increases women's labor, especially with regard to the time required to gather fuelwood and the cost of purchasing it. Without adequate fuelwood for cooking, household nutrition may be negatively impacted. Conservation measures that bar entrance into forests also increase women's labor.
- Access rights to trees and forests by men and women are often limited by confusion, or lack of clarity between formal and local customary rights. Access to particular nonwood forest products, such as honey and fodder, is often guided by traditional and cultural norms, regardless of whether they are collected for subsistence or for market.
- Both women's and men's knowledge of trees and other forest products should be incorporated in forest management and conservation plans. Including and applying this often heavily gendered traditional and indigenous knowledge can be critical to the success of a project.

Protected areas are specific and unique natural habitats where human encroachment is restricted to preserve biodiversity. In many protected areas around the world, however, people with legitimate or historical land ownership rights live within the established boundaries. Women's and men's relationships with the environment in the protected areas and their buffer zones, in the context of their respective gender roles, are crucial for the very survival of these natural habitats (IUCN 2003). The Innovative Activity Profile on gender, protected areas, and tourism presents an FAO World Heritage national park small enterprise development project that developed and applied an innovative gender strategy.

Although many cases of women successfully managing community groups in participatory forestry and agroforestry field projects can be identified, women continue to be nominal stakeholders in the decision making and planning of decentralized and local forestry programs. The

successful project experiences cited in this Module demonstrate how to overcome this barrier.

Women are the principal practitioners of traditional agroforestry in production systems such as home gardens in Kerala State in India and Sri Lanka (Kumar and Nair 2004). They are also often innovators who develop or adapt new agroforestry technologies, such as dairy fodder and the domestication of indigenous fruits (World Agroforestry Centre 2008). Yet their presence in policy, decision making, and the science of agroforestry remains proportionally minimal.

Women are engaged in many roles in the forest industry in the developing world, often in the most menial jobs in sawmills or plantation nurseries. Women also gain employment in catering and prostitution in forest logging camps. However, an overall lack of data exists with regard to women's employment in large-scale forest enterprises. This lack of visibility of women's employment in forest industry data suggests the likelihood of poorer working conditions and lower remuneration. If women's working conditions and employment opportunities are to improve, gender disaggregated data are required in the forest industries sector. This Module focuses on women's role in small and medium forest enterprises, and more notably the nonwood forest product (NWFP) sector, for which a large body of literature and project experience can be consulted. The entrepreneurship of local people, especially women, in forestry activities and enterprises, may be constrained by centralized ownership, cultural norms, and poor access to extension, training, credit, and markets.

The 2005 Human Development Report identified HIV and AIDS as the factor inflicting the single greatest reversal in the history of human development (UNDP 2005). HIV and AIDS are undermining progress toward the Millennium Development Goals (MDGs), including the third MDG on gender equity. Women in sub-Saharan Africa are infected more often and earlier in their lives than men. By virtue of the gender inequality that is embedded in many cultural traditions, the domestic burden of HIV and AIDS care falls especially heavily on women (UNAIDS 2006). Additional domestic responsibilities to care for the sick translate into a differential use of time in the allocation of other domestic and productive duties, including a differential use of forest products. In high-prevalence areas, women who become caregivers of ill members of the household have less time for agricultural activities on their own plots. As a result, in, for example, *miombo* woodland areas, the household becomes more reliant on forest foods and income from fuelwood that is often gathered by children (FAO 2005b). Pandemics such as HIV and AIDS increase poverty and affect the use of forest resources (Shackleton and others 2006).

Emergencies, such as conflicts and natural disasters, in which populations are massively displaced often lead to additional reliance on forest products for subsistence products. The local forest cover often becomes depleted as people who live in camps, mainly women and children, gather fuelwood in the area. As wood resources are depleted, women and children are obliged to travel longer distances to collect wood, making them vulnerable to gender-based violence (SAFE[2]). Research recommends investing heavily in forested areas during postconflict periods to prevent renewed fighting and help protect the forest itself (Kaimowitz 2005).

Two recently published reports on gender and forestry in Europe (FAO 2006b) and Africa (FAO 2007b) consider the employment and positions of women in forestry services (officers and rangers), forestry education, and the technical and administrative staff of forest ministries. Even the European report recognizes that "quantitative data [are] known to be patchy and insufficient to determine, with confidence, the number of women working in the forest industry, or their roles and employment levels" (FAO 2006b: 11). However, the report also notes that "examples of good practice, have been emerging, which proves that concerted and sustained commitment and planning at senior organizational level can result in quantifiable improvements in the number of professional women foresters employed and the level of seniority they can attain" (FAO 2006b: 11). The Africa report is extremely critical of the status quo, which it characterizes as having a near total absence of data on gender in the forest sector, combined in some cases with a complete lack of motivation by policy and decision makers to address gender issues in the sector.[3] The report emphasizes the need for gender-disaggregated data to better appreciate the gender disparities in forest education, employment, and career opportunities in the formal sector, as well as to appreciate the different roles of rural women and men with livelihoods based on forest-related activities. Such information would also enable the development of more gender-conscious forest sector programs and policies.

Organizational and institutional support to women's groups is required if rural and disadvantaged women are to access resources, credit, technical and entrepreneurial training, and guidance. Having women employed as frontline extension staff, project managers, policy makers, and forest enterprise employees and managers would be advantageous in securing this support. An acknowledged requirement is for more and improved training for women in all cadres of the forest professions, as well as improved facilities to enable women and men to be trained and to accumulate work experience (FAO 2007b).

BENEFITS AND CONSTRAINTS OF GENDER-RESPONSIVE POLICY

Created by the Economic and Social Council of the United Nations in 2000, the United Nations Forum on Forests (UNFF) provides a platform for high-level policy discussions and global cooperation to promote improved management, conservation, and sustainable development of forests. Women are represented at UNFF, as one of the nine Agenda 21 major groups. The other major forest stakeholder groups include indigenous peoples, business and industry, small forest landowners, youth and children, NGOs, local authorities, unions, and representatives of the scientific and technological community (www.un.org/esa/forests).

In some forested countries, the directors of forest departments or ministries of environment and forests are women. This has been shown to enhance the profile of women's role in the forest sector, particularly with regard to smallholder forestry, forest associations, and livelihoods-related issues. In most countries, however, women's role and representation in decision making that pertains to the forest sector are very limited. Considerable efforts can be made through training and job placement in both public and private sectors to enable more women to gain employment in the public sector and be effective forest managers and entrepreneurs, as well as to enhance their advocacy and representational skills (FAO 2006b).

Although an outspoken political commitment exists on nearly all levels to integrate gender considerations into policy development, reality lags behind. Most policy decisions are still taking a gender-neutral approach, ignoring the complementary capacities of women and men in implementing these policies.

Many people working in the forestry sector are familiar with the operationally focused gender materials produced by the Forest Trees and People Program at FAO in the mid-1990s. In recent years, however, mainstream publications pertaining to forests, livelihoods, and poverty became gender neutral, referring, for example, to "rural people," "farmers," and "households." Women per se and recognition of women's specific challenges and acknowledgment of their specific achievements had largely disappeared (FAO 2006a, 2007a). The recent release of PROFOR's *Forests and Poverty Linkages Toolkit* explicitly includes gender in its tools for analysis of livelihoods. Interim results from midterm reports piloting the toolkit in Cameroon, Ghana, Madagascar, and Uganda demonstrate clearly the significance of collecting and analyzing gender- and wealth-disaggregated data.[4] In Madagascar results from one community found that poor women rely significantly more on the forest resource for their livelihoods than do poor men—37 percent of women's income came from the forest compared to 22 percent of men's income. Wealthier men, on the other hand, gained more of their income from the forest than wealthier women.

These kinds of results clearly indicate the contrasting uses and perceptions of forest resources and its products by different members of society. The data also emphasize the vulnerability of poor women and their families, and the likely impacts on the most marginalized segments of a community if they are excluded from decision making about the forest resource base, the products of which often provide one-third of their income (see Technical Note 1 for more details). The data collected in piloting this toolkit could also be indicative of how differential forest product use and access develop between men and women as households move out of poverty.

It is obvious that sustainable development, particularly in forestry, can be achieved only if decision and policy makers continuously connect gender awareness from local to national and global levels. A prerequisite is the continued collection of gender-disaggregated data and the use and application of gender-conscious language and tools in policy texts and field manuals.

INNOVATIVE APPROACHES TO OVERCOME GENDER BARRIERS

The SL conceptual framework for analyzing the agricultural livelihoods of women and men, girls and boys, is an adaptation of the sustainable livelihoods concept and considers assets, risks and vulnerability, information and organization, markets, policies, and institutions. In the forestry context, many of these barriers are probably higher and more intractable than in other rural sectors. Much has to do with traditional management regimes and decision making, but much also relates to the potential wealth of the sector and the dominance of large-scale concessions.

At the local level, groups of women have improved their access to decision making in the management of forest resources through organization and advocacy. Time and again the material presented in this Module will demonstrate that through enhanced organization and representation, they have improved their incomes and the well-being of their households, as well as the educational opportunities of their children.

Women and children are often the most vulnerable in forest conflicts and the most reliant on forest resources

during conflicts and periods of economic hardship. Strong examples of support in advocacy and home visits provide hope that innovative programming will overcome some of the difficulties and alleviate the horrors faced by these families. However, larger initiatives to support the most marginalized families directly have yet to be implemented.

Although training in organizational and representational skills is very important, training in business and negotiation skills for small-scale enterprises is fundamental to the success of identified women's enterprises. For an enterprise to be independently sustainable, training and credit support needs to be provided for at least five years. Projects should not consider engaging for periods less than this.

The gendered nature of resource use, access, control, and responsibility with respect to trees and forests is highly complex (Rocheleau and Edmunds 1997). Women's rights to particular areas of cropping land, trees, and tree products, as well as to "in between spaces" in agricultural landscapes, are often based in negotiable customary law and are often substantial. These rights, however, may be marginalized or not recognized, sometimes regarded as well-meaning efforts to create statutory laws and administrative procedures (Rocheleau and Edmunds 1997). Women's rights are often negotiated and may subsequently not be best served by formal titling of land, which often vests ownership in a single head of household. Agroforestry and forestry projects and programs can better protect women's access rights by allowing for multiple uses of specific spaces and resources by multiple users, and by prioritizing renewable uses, such as the gathering of fruits or harvesting of fallen wood, prunings, coppiced wood, and leaf fodder, which do not preclude most other uses (Rocheleau and Edmunds 1997).

Designers of agroforestry projects and programs are advised to disaggregate gendered knowledge, access, and control further, so as to also include tree products, such as timber, fuelwood, fruits, and fodder. In many cases, although women have substantial labor and management responsibilities for a particular resource, men control the disposal or marketing of the products of that resource, as well as the distribution of its benefits. Reporting gender-disaggregated data on agroforestry practices should also be encouraged. It has long been recognized that women are the principal holders of knowledge and managers of traditional home gardens (FAO 1999), and 60 percent of the practitioners of innovative agroforestry practices such as domestication of indigenous fruit trees and production of dairy fodder are women (see Thematic Note 2). These particular practices are easily adaptable to women's niches on farms. However, the gender aspects of innovative agroforestry practices such as these are perhaps not afforded the profile that they warrant in program reports and scientific publications. Using and applying gender-disaggregated data will raise the profile of women agroforestry practitioners and thereby enable their greater access to technical information, credit, and related extension support.

Gender-related considerations have been integrated in almost all relevant forest policy commitments and related fields, such as climate change. However, a gap still exists in translating these policy commitments into implementation. True change and gender-responsive action can be achieved only if policy and decision makers face their responsibility to ensure an inclusive implementation of their gender-relevant commitments at project and program levels.

The Innovative Activity Profiles demonstrate that gender awareness in implementation needs a strong backup from the policy level to achieve the change of traditional and sometimes obsolete attitudes on the roles of men and women in forest management. Demographic developments and changing family patterns require that women be involved in decision making on all levels to sustain their livelihood and the security of their families. This requires in particular a rethinking of traditional gender-biased land tenure and property rights; greater gender equity in land tenure and rights to forest resources would be building blocks for the sustainable and long-term-oriented development of livelihoods based on forest resources. Policy and decision makers are encouraged to use the potential of gender equity in working toward the Millennium Development Goals on all levels by ensuring universal access to education and training and building entrepreneurial capacity in sustainably managing forest resources.

MEASURING CHANGE: GENDER-SENSITIVE MONITORING AND EVALUATION INDICATORS

Being able to measure the impact that forest policy, training, and management initiatives have on men and women beneficiaries, their families, and communities is important. Table 15.1 gives some ideas for indicators and sources of verification, though clearly modifications are required for each program.

Table 15.1 Monitoring and Evaluation Indicators for Gender and Forestry	
Indicator	**Sources of verification and tools**
Over a set period, an increase of x percent in household incomes from forest-based activities among women-headed households and poor households in program areas	• Household surveys • Project management information system • Socioeconomic data from statistics office
Changes over x-year period of project activities in household nutrition, health, education, vulnerability to violence, and happiness, disaggregated by gender	• Household surveys, before and after • Project management information system • School records
Proportion of annual household income (or consumption) derived from upland farming, agroforestry, or forest activities	• Household surveys
Percentage of women and men actively participating in natural resource management committees (including bank account signatory roles)	• Bank records • Committee meeting minutes • Interviews with stakeholders • Local traditional authorities (such as a chief or local council) • Program and project records
Number of women and men actively involved in management (that is, protection or conservation or production) of protected areas or reserves based on a management framework or plan	• Community monitoring committees • Forest management plans
Capacity-building support provided for community-based resource management, forest enterprises, and others	• Project records • Training records
Change in perceptions of men and women regarding importance of forest protection and management, measured before and after activity	• Focus groups • Stakeholder interviews
Percentage of women and men community extension workers and professional forestry extensionists	• Forest Department records • Project records

(Table continues on the following page)

Indicator	Sources of verification and tools
Level of satisfaction among women and men with access to and quality of extension and training services	• Sample surveys • Stakeholder interviews
Percentage of representations and mentions of women and men in training and awareness-raising materials	• Survey of training and information materials
Number of women and men actively involved in participatory research and innovations in agroforestry or forestry, before and after project activities	• Forestry extension records • Interviews with stakeholders • Observation • Participatory monitoring
Number of women and men involved in seed collection, propagation, and tree nursery techniques in district, before and after project activities	• Forestry department records • Participatory forest management group records • Project records • Stakeholder interviews
Changes to access rights by women- and men-headed households to common property resources (timber and nontimber) in forests	• Case studies • Interviews of local authorities and community leaders • Participatory rapid appraisal
Changes in time taken to collect firewood daily, before and after project activities	• Participatory monitoring • Project records
Number of conflicts over natural resources access or land ownership per year	• Interviews with stakeholders (from all relevant groups in conflicts) • Local traditional authorities (such as a chief or local council) • Program and project records
Number of women and men from district employed in forest enterprises, annually	• Administrative records
Incidence of occupational health and safety problems among workers in plantations and processing plants, disaggregated by gender	• Administrative records • Review of procedures against local and national regulations
Spread of HIV and AIDS, prostitution, alcoholism, and other problems from in-migrant workers, compared with baseline	• Community health surveillance • Health records • Local authority reports
Community satisfaction (disaggregated by gender) with changes in forest access and forest resources dispute treatment	• Group interviews or focus groups • Interviews, before and after

Source: Authors, with inputs from Pamela White, author of Module 16.

Forests as Safety Nets: Gender, Strengthening Rights, and Reducing Vulnerability

Forests have a significant role in reducing vulnerability and providing safety nets and subsistence (food, fuelwood, and incomes) for the rural poor who depend on forests for their livelihoods. Livelihoods vulnerability may arise from natural disasters, human conflict, human and animal disease epidemics, food insecurity, agroecological factors such as water variability, and market and price risks. Poor households are more exposed to these risks and less resilient in coping with them. They tend to have weaker political representation and to experience greater difficulty in securing their rights to land, other resources, and support in times of crisis (see also Module 11). Women are typically the principal agents of food security within a household and tend to suffer the most in terms of increased workload when livelihood shocks occur.

KEY GENDER ISSUES

Several key gender issues face women in regard to forestry issues.

Experiences in community and participatory forest management

One step forward in linking sustainable livelihoods and forests has been approached through community forestry. Too often, however, the community has been viewed as a homogeneous unit in terms of status, influence, wealth, gender, and access to resources (Muckarjee, Jayaswal, and Parihari 2006; Wollenberg and others 2001). Even when these differences have been recognized and participatory processes have been employed, issues of power and the capacity of groups to negotiate solutions have not always been adequately considered. As a result, many women's concerns regarding forest use and access have been neglected in the consultations undertaken in the participatory design

and implementation of projects. Community forestry, however, remains a popular approach to forest management, and the demand for support in carrying out community forestry projects among communities remains high.

Nonwood forest products

Poor households in particular depend on NWFPs, which provide essential food and nutrition, medicine, fodder, fuel, thatch and construction materials, and nonfarm income.[1] NWFPs are particularly important in relieving "hunger periods" in the agricultural cycle; they provide seasonal employment and a buffer against risk and household emergencies. The poor, moreover, tend to have more access to the forest than other natural capital and few land rights elsewhere. Within poor households, gender asymmetry in ownership and access to productive resources such as land causes women to rely disproportionately on NWFPs for income and nutrition (FAO 1995). In many communities women are responsible for the household activities that involve forest-based foods and firewood.

Generally the poor and more marginal households engage in the local trade of nontimber forest products (NTFPs), and this is a particularly important activity for women (Kaimowitz 2003). In a series of studies in Brazil, Cameroon, and South Africa, 40 to 50 percent of those active in this trade were women who headed their own households (Shackelton, Shanley, and Ndoye 2007). In Cameroon the trade in four popular edible NTFPs was dominated by women, who were responsible for most of the harvest and who formed 94 percent of the traders (Ndoye, Ruiz-Perez, and Eyebe 1997). Wholesalers were often men. In eastern Amazonia both poor men and women collect and sell a number of forest fruit species, whereas in the city most fruit wholesalers were men, and most fruit processing was undertaken by poor urban women (Shanley, Luz, and

Swingland 2002). Local trade in many nontimber products is an area in which women are free to earn income with little interference or threat of expropriation by men (Schreckenberg, Marshall, and Te Velde 2006). Where the opportunity cost of women's labor is relatively low, the participation of women can make NTFPs commercially viable.

Global markets for NTFPs often overshadow local trade in traditionally important products. Yet neglect of local trade can lead to further marginalization of low-income groups whose livelihoods depend on that trade (Shackleton, Shanley, and Ndoye 2007). Many households require flexible local income-earning opportunities that allow space for responsibilities such as child care, nursing the ill, maintaining homes, and crop production. The production of NTFPs for local markets can provide part-time, seasonal, occasional, or full-time year-round employment, depending on the product, location, and individual household. This flexibility makes NTFP-related activities particularly appealing to women, enabling them to combine collection and trade of these products with their other domestic duties and responsibilities (Shackleton, Shanley, and Ndoye 2007).

HIV and AIDS and communicable diseases

The most important actions in dealing with the medical and health emergencies created by the HIV and AIDS pandemic are public awareness programs aimed at preventing further spread of the disease. Although this aspect of HIV and AIDS mitigation is generally outside the mandates of agriculture and forestry departments, all sectors of society have a role to play in alleviating the impacts of the disease, both in the immediate and in the long terms. The forest sector can help to mitigate the impacts of AIDS in a number of ways (FAO 2002):

- By enhancing short-term agricultural productivity
- By enhancing long-term agricultural productivity
- By developing education and human resource development strategies in extension and services (forestry training and education)
- By transferring skills from one generation to the next.

One example of the implementation of an HIV and AIDS response within this mandate came as a result of a request of the government of Malawi to support field studies that address the interactions between *miombo* woodlands and the morbidity and mortality caused by communicable diseases, especially HIV and AIDS.[2] The results demonstrated the crucial role of the woodlands in supporting the livelihoods of affected households and documented adjustments in use and access to woodland resources by women and children of households with sick adults, as well as households in which an adult had recently died (box 15.1).

Forests, natural disasters, and conflicts

Natural disasters and civil strife affect large numbers of displaced people who rely on forests for shelter, fuelwood, fodder, and nutrition. Large concentrations of displaced populations in camps place excessive pressure on already degraded natural resources. This can endanger food security and livelihoods in nearby communities and foster resentment within the host population (FAO Forest Department brief prepared for SAFE, 2007). Charcoal and wood are needed for fuel, and branches and timber for shelter constructions and women are typically responsible for collecting them. Many who leave camp to collect forest materials are subject to gender-based violence (Miguel Trossero, personal communication 2007; SAFE 2007).

Alternative fuel, energy saving, and reforestation initiatives undertaken in the vicinity of displaced persons camps may help to reduce women's vulnerability. These can include establishing fast-growing woodlots immediately adjacent to refugee camps, promoting the use of "fireless" cookers, energy-saving mud stoves, and cooking techniques such as soaking beans before cooking them and covering lids while cooking.

Forested areas have been the stage for wars in some two dozen countries that are home to over 40 percent of the world's tropical forests during the last 20 years (box 15.2). Various reasons have been given for this. Forested regions tend to be inaccessible and easy for armies to hide in. Armies have been able to fund their activities by extorting money from petroleum, mining, and logging companies; drug dealers; and farmers in these areas. Some militias carry out mining, logging, and drug trafficking operations themselves. Soldiers often survive by hunting and fishing and preying on isolated farmers in remote forested areas. Many people living in these areas deeply resent the fact that they have been neglected or mistreated by national governments, particularly if they perceive outsiders as benefiting from the local natural resources. The influx of migrants of other ethnic groups often stirs conflicts with local people (box 15.3). Armed groups of various types and inclinations frequently earn a certain degree of local support or acceptance by filling the vacuum left by a national government with weak presence locally (Kaimowitz 2005).

The Malawi country study (Kayambazintu and others 2005) found that because of the gender differentiation in woodland activities within households, the impacts of morbidity and mortality will depend on who in the household is ill or deceased.

Women household members predominantly carry out subsistence woodland activities; they also have the role of primary caregiver when a member of the household is sick. Their labor is therefore typically reallocated for care giving, decreasing subsistence collection of forest products.

In all cases, it was found that less laborious commercial activities remain a viable option for income generation during illness. These include products for which value can be added through home-based work and are less gender differentiated, such as reed mats, baskets, and food processing. The value of such commercial activities

to cope with expenses and productivity losses related to illness is supported by evidence from the case studies.

Commonly, firewood collection duties changed from the adult women to girls and boys when an adult family member was ill. In polygamous households the effect of adult illness on subsistence woodland activities such as firewood collection was less pronounced than in households with only one woman head. Households in which children are old enough to engage in woodland activities also offset the labor reduction caused by adult illness.

In those households for which the importance of woodland activities increased following adult mortality, children were often involved in the collection and sale of forest products. The types of forest products that households reported selling are also products that are typically collected by children and women.

Sources: Kayambazintu and others 2005; UNAIDS 2006.

Angola, Bangladesh, Cambodia, Colombia, Côte d'Ivoire, Democratic Republic of Congo, Guatemala, Guinea, Honduras, India, Indonesia, Liberia, Mexico, Mozambique, Myanmar, Nepal, Nicaragua, Nigeria, Pakistan, Papua New Guinea, Peru, Philippines, Rwanda, Senegal, Sierra Leone, Solomon Islands, Sudan, Surinam, and Uganda.

Source: Kaimowitz 2005.

Immaculate Birhaheka, head of the women's rights group Paif, in Goma, Democratic Republic of Congo, spoke of what happened in villages on the road south from Goma toward Bukavu: "The women who come from there tell us that every woman in every village has been raped over the years. Some were captured and taken into the forest for months, even two years. When they are released some are in such bad condition that they die."

Source: Guardian Weekly, November 16, 2007.

GENDER IN THE IMPLEMENTATION OF POVERTY-FOCUSED FORESTRY PROGRAMS

In 1995 the Forest, Trees and People program at FAO published a series of publications that set out practical methods for gender analysis in the planning and implementation of community-based forest projects and programs. Yet there is little or no indication that gender analysis is systematically

applied in projects and programs at the local level.[3] The design and implementation of gender-equitable interventions that seek to strengthen rights and reduce vulnerability among forest-dependent communitie remain a challenge (box 15.4). (Programs involving wood energy, fuelwood saving, and alternative fuels provide an important exception and do focus on women, although it is evident that women's roles in forestry are far more expansive than these programs' coverage.)

Box 15.4 Gender Analysis in Forestry Programs: Where Is It?

Any rural livelihoods-focused forestry program must analyze the activities and resources available to both men and women as men and women have different experiences, resulting from intergenerational knowledge transfer and years of experimentation in forest product harvesting, processing. and domestication. A few of the questions to be considered are as follows: What forest-related tasks are undertaken by men, women, boys, and girls? Who has access and the power to decide whether and how resources are to be used, and how they are to be allocated? How is knowledge of the forest and its resources gendered? Who has control over the output or product? Market access for harvested and processed forest products is not gender neutral: Who has access to which markets and why? What are the gendered barriers to adding product value and market access? In addition to the gender analysis, an inclusion analysis would shed light on many of the above issues in the initial phases of a forest and livelihoods program: How are men and women included in each aspect of decision making with regard to forest resources, and products for use by the community and by individual households?

Source: Author's adaptation from Feldstein and Poats 1990.

A number of factors contribute to gender blindness, both at the national policy level and in field project design. Field projects and forest offices are predominantly staffed by men forestry officers, who are therefore the majority of those responsible for running participatory rural appraisals and other types of participatory consultation in the villages. In many rural societies, village women are culturally restrained from speaking in public. In many instances it is not considered appropriate for men from outside the community to encourage women to participate in meetings or to suggest separate meetings with women participants. Combined with the common lack of frontline women forestry officers, these cultural proscriptions mitigate against women's perspectives being aired during village discussions and data generation exercises. Although women are ordinarily responsible for the nutrition and food security of their families, the products that women harvest and market to feed their families are generally not included in conventional forest inventories or data collection exercises.

POLICY AND IMPLEMENTATION ISSUES

Three examples illustrate a selection of the key issues facing policy making and the design and management of interventions that effectively capture gender.

Gender and wood energy in Asia

During the Regional Expert Consultation on Gender and Wood Energy in Asia in 1995, discussions raised a number of observations that would be endorsed by the participants. The burden of providing traditional energy supplies for domestic use is commonly the responsibility of women. Rising woodfuel prices, lower woodfuel quality, and reduced access to woodfuels increase this burden. Interventions in the energy sector, such as land use and fuel price reform, often have disproportionately negative implications for women, especially those from lower-income groups. In many Asian countries, the concerns of women are underrepresented in shaping wood energy policies and strategies.

Wood energy plays an important part in women's reproductive tasks. Access to inexpensive, less time-consuming, and sustainable sources of wood energy and to efficient cooking and heating devices will directly benefit women. Women also have increasing energy needs in their productive roles as bread winners. Many self-employed women depend on wood or other biomass energy for commercial activities such as food preparation for sale or are employed in establishments that rely on woodfuel. Others are economically dependent on trading in fuelwood and charcoal, and some have escaped poverty through this trade. The need to understand and to relate to women's needs in regard to these matters is thus of central importance in wood energy planning at all levels.

Forest law, nonwood forest products, and income-earning opportunities for women in Lao PDR

In the Lao People's Democratic Republic, policy makers recognize the importance of NWFPs in alleviating poverty and supporting national economic development. The lack of clear legal guidelines, enforcement mechanisms, support services, and institutional capacity has been recognized as a major constraint to realizing the products' potential in these roles. The government has strengthened a number of institutions and was encouraged in introducing new policies and a legal framework to promote NWFPs. The FAO assisted the government and other involved stakeholders by creating a model for the development of marketing systems for NWFPs using the Market Analysis and Development approach.[4] At the provincial level, stakeholder meetings were held involving local communities, the private sector, and local stakeholders. Between 30 and 50 percent of the membership of the local start-up NWFP enterprises and community groups are women. National-level task forces were established to develop a framework for market information systems. These are the first step in reducing bottlenecks in legislative procedures and access to market information that have thus far restrained the development and application of women's entrepreneurial skills and their access to credit.

HIV and AIDS and national-level policy in the forest sector

The Department of Forestry in Malawi is a pioneer in developing and implemented a Forestry Sector HIV and AIDS Strategy. The government recently launched this strategy covering 2007 to 2011. The major goals of the strategy are as follows:

- To prevent the further spread and transmission of HIV and AIDS among workers, communities, households, and individuals that are dependent on forestry
- To improve sustainably the livelihoods and quality of life of those who are living with and affected by HIV and AIDS.

In line with the National HIV and AIDS Policy and the National Action Framework, the strategy focuses on both

the workplace and core mandate functions of the sector. The document presents the principles that guide the implementation of the strategy, including those that promote gender equality and greater involvement of men, women, and children living with HIV and AIDS, transparency, accountability, and evidence-based programming. The objective is to reduce the further spread of HIV and AIDS and mitigate its impact and to foster the sustainable management and development of forest resources (see also Government of Malawi 2007).

LESSONS LEARNED AND GUIDELINES FOR PRACTITIONERS

The key actions identified in a group of successful projects reviewed as part of the preparation of this thematic note were the empowerment and visibility of women in local-level decision making pertaining to forest resources. Women's self-help groups facilitated better access to and management of resources in all the successful projects. Self-help groups also enabled the women to better represent their views in community decision making and to receive technical and skills training. The North Eastern Region Community Resource Management Project for upland areas in India provides an example of the types of activities undertaken by self-help groups in forest programs (box 15.5). Along with income, the most highly valued components of

---

Box 15.5 India: The North Eastern Region Community Resource Management Project for Upland Areas

Along with natural resource management groups, self-help groups (SHGs) make up the bulk of the activities within the International Fund for Agricultural Development's North Eastern Region Community Resource Management Project for Upland Areas. In Nonglang village in the West Khasi Hills district, poor women have seen the benefit of forming SHGs and working together. Microcredit has been the focus, but women's organization into SHGs has brought other social benefits too.

Women members meet once a week and pool group resources for saving and lending purposes. These savings have been used for income-earning purposes as well as for health and education needs. Over time groups have recognized value in loans for the benefit of the village apart from those for individual members.

SHG members see value in meeting every week to discuss common problems. While meeting to save and lend, women have the opportunity to discuss collectively other needs, such as health and education. Literacy has become one of the goals of the SHG. With the encouragement of the project, the group has organized a school for young children who previously either did not attend classes or did so only in the morning.

According to a survey conducted to assess the impact of SHGs, the most important aspects noted by the group members themselves were "empowerment," "increase in income," and "awareness," in that order. They also appreciated improved consumption patterns and skill development.

Source: Deseng and Yirmeila 2005.

project support through the women's groups were empowerment and awareness.

A review of project experiences led to the following recommended sequencing of support to community-based organizations (CBOs):[5]

1. Identify existing women's groups (CBOs) in the proposed project area, their objectives, activities, successes, and constraints.
2. Provide demand-driven support and training to those groups that already exist following an analysis of problems and opportunities in forest access and resource use.
3. If there are no community-level organizations or associations in which women play an active role, assist local authorities in the creation of self-help groups and village-level development associations in which women can play a more active role.
4. Build capacity and provide management training based on the goals of the groups.

The Jharkhand-Chhattisgarh Tribal Development Program in India applied these steps to empower women and develop their technical skills (box 15.6).

When village-level groups have formed around a common purpose and are active, they are more effective in strengthening their rights and reducing the overall vulnerability of their members. They may come together in associations or more formally in federations (box 15.7).

SHGs do not function in isolation from other forest-related stakeholders, nor are all SHGs women's groups. Depending on the objectives of the group, CBOs and SHGs may have men, women, and youth members. Once a CBO is organized and embarks on an activity such as marketing NTFPs or lobbying for forest resource access, the group is likely to encounter constraints imposed by other forest stakeholders, as well as by forest policy and law beyond the immediate boundaries of the village. Conflicts may occur between the village associations and these stakeholders. Some CBOs have been set up in response to existing conflicts. CBOs often require the additional support of third parties to enhance their negotiation and marketing skills: for instance, when they set out to gain greater access to NTFP value chains. Many documented cases exist of this type of support.[6]

However, other types of conflicts that occur, for example, in the context of illegal logging, mining, or illicit crops, may be violent. CBOs benefit from advocacy by

---

Box 15.6   India: The Jharkhand-Chhattisgarh Tribal Development Program

The program focuses on tribal people in Jharkhand and Chhattisgarh, two of the three Indian states with the highest proportion of tribal people. Tribal peoples are among the poorest in India. The program targets marginal households, women, landless people, hill cultivators, and tribal people. The goal is to empower tribal people to participate in their own development through local self-government. In the Chhattisgarh area, women's productive work consists of agriculture, gathering forest products, and wage labor. Women's workdays are typically 16–18 hours of often physically demanding labor. Women generally go to the forest as a group to collect forest products. Tribal people depend on the forest for their livelihoods, including for nontimber or "minor" forest products. From these they obtain foods such as fruit and oil, as well as needed items for the home, such as bidi, brooms, baskets, mats, rope, home-made toothbrushes, leaf plates, and

medicines. Some forest products are also sold for a small cash income.

The program has two principal subcomponents:

- Grassroots empowerment and technical capacity building
- Livelihood systems enhancement.

The former component provides training to the tribal population, especially women and other marginal groups, on broad-based awareness of tribal rights, gender, and equity issues, as well as legal and managerial strengthening training. The latter component focuses more on technical aspects, such as establishment of nurseries and support for processing and marketing of NTFPs. It works with the village groups in a livelihoods context. A legal defense fund is planned to assist the tribal population in defending its rights.

Sources: IFAD 2006; see also http://cjtdp.nic.in.

Historically, Huoshan County in China's eastern province of Anhui has been one of the country's poorest areas.

The county has abundant natural resources, such as bamboo, tea, mulberry, and medicinal plants. The area is best suited for forestry development because the mountainous topography is generally unsuitable for agriculture. It is not surprising that 75 percent of farmers' income is currently derived from forests.

The Sino-Dutch Forestry Program focuses on household forestry, farmers' self-help organizations, demonstration households, and training in participatory concepts and forestry techniques. It has three basic principles: participatory approaches, gender consciousness, and environmental protection awareness.

Groups created at the village level are subsequently federated into larger networks of groups according to their primary purpose: "farmers' professional associations," "community development fund management organizations," and "forest products processing associations." The primary aim of the farmers' self-help organizations is to improve the

economic and social environment for farmers and their families. By empowering farmers to manage their farms according to their own livelihood preferences, their dependence on the government will hopefully be reduced. Women and men farmers are free to join or drop out of any organization they choose. Each self-help organization has its own rules and regulations, and the farmers themselves elect the management committee.

Xu Jiaqi, a community development specialist for the project, explained that "everyone is involved in project activities. Each person is allowed to share his or her ideas during meetings and discussions. A decision is made by the group by the end of the day. Women are given importance in all activities. In fact, in some groups such as the Bamboo Farmers' Association, most of the members are women (70 percent) are women."

More than 16,000 households have participated in the forestry activities. As a result, the forest cover of the county increased from 59 percent in 1989 to 70 percent in 2002.

Source: Chunguian 2005.

third parties such as NGOs, which may, for instance, publicize their situation and concerns to a wider audience. Successful community-based organizations have been shown to be those that have taken the lead themselves, as they best know the complexities and nuances of the conflict situation and the strengths and weaknesses and history of the various stakeholders involved. The El Balcón, Mexico, case presented in box 15.8 illustrates the significance of different players and the complexities of developing a governable situation around communal forests. Yet it demonstrates how negotiation over confrontation, knowledge and employment over exclusion, and quality leadership, and transparency have reduced conflict and secured livelihoods.

Support for and creation of women's CBOs or subgroups in community-based organizations are not panaceas to mainstreaming gender in livelihood-oriented forestry programs. Women's groups themselves often have many problems in management, corruption, and elite capture such that poor women are marginalized by wealthier, more articulate, and more educated women in the community. Poor women often have less time, further distances to travel, and fewer resources with which to engage in group activities (see also Thematic Note 4, Module 2). However, if women are not organized into entities that represent their needs and rights in forest resource access and use, their voices will not be heard. Local organization is the first step to strengthening rights and reducing vulnerabilities of marginalized women.

Box 15.8   El Balcón, Mexico: Building Peace and Governability around Communal Forests

The Ejido el Balcón is located in the highlands of the sierra, close to the Pacific Ocean in the region called Costa Grande in the Mexican state of Guerrero. The Ejido el Balcón was formed in 1966 when the Mexican government granted collective property rights to 136 family heads of over 2,400 hectares. In 1974 another 19,150 hectares of forestland were given to the ejido (Bray and Merino 2003). This was a time of permanent confrontations over the land. In the initial days of the ejido, nearly 20 percent of El Balcón's community members were widows under 30.

Within the context of Guerrero and rural Mexico, the case of El Balcón is remarkable for several reasons. The ejido has built a forest enterprise that uses modern technology to produce certified timber for export. The enterprise employs all ejido members who want to work for it. Profits have largely been invested in the social welfare of the nearly 600 people living in the ejido (health care, education, and public infrastructure).

From satellite images or by simply traveling through high parts of the sierra, one can readily observe the deterioration of the forests, which constantly suffer from fires and illegal logging. El Balcón is the exception. Its lands are covered with well-preserved forests, and its forest management was certified under the Forest Stewardship Council in 2003.

The most important achievement of El Balcón is the climate of agreement, governability, and peace that it has built amid a region that has fallen victim to illegal logging and drug trafficking. A number of factors may be attributable for the extraordinary institutional development of El Balcón: the quality of its leaders, their preference for negotiation over confrontation in dealing with internal problems as well as with neighboring ejidos, their insistence on the importance of issues such as regulated forest management, transparency of the ejido's business, and association with other forest ejidos of the region.

Source: Merino 2005.

Agroforestry Landscapes: Gendered Space, Knowledge, and Practice

Trees play a crucial role in almost all farming systems and terrestrial ecosystems; they provide a range of essential products and services and play a particularly pivotal role wherever people depend on fragile ecosystems for survival and sustenance. Integrating trees into agricultural landscapes provides a number of environmental services, some of which are essential. Trees maintain soil health and regenerate land that has been cleared of natural vegetation. They provide nutritious foods for human consumption and fodder for livestock, as well as timber, fuelwood, gums, resins, latex, and medicinal substances. Agroforestry is a system of natural resources management that integrates trees on farms and in the agricultural landscape to diversify and sustain production. Farmers throughout the world have practiced agroforestry for millennia. By World Bank estimates, over 1.2 billion people derive their livelihoods from agroforestry systems. Owing to its capacity to enhance multiple functions in agriculture, agroforestry will become increasingly important in land-use practices around the world (World Agroforestry Centre 2008).

Women's knowledge of trees and of tree genetic diversity is extensive, and their roles as both suppliers and users of tree germplasm and genetic resources make them critical agents in scaling up agroforestry practices to improve livelihoods. This is knowledge that is all too often neglected. Women are important to agroforestry, but agroforestry is also very important to them. Farm niches such as dairy fodder and domesticated indigenous fruit trees in home compounds are typically managed by women, and their engagement in these agroforestry activities provides them with access to the products of these activities.

GENDERED TREE TENURE AND ACCESS TO AND DISPOSAL OF AGROFORESTRY TREE PRODUCTS

In 1997 Rocheleau and Edmunds analyzed the gendered nature of resource use, access, control, and responsibility with respect to trees and forests. What emerged from their analysis was a picture of highly complex, often negotiable resource tenure regimes. Women's rights remained substantial, although frequently tenuous and under pressure from a variety of changes in land use, family composition, and household structure (box 15.9). In some cases, evolving customary practices served to maintain women's access to resources and warranted protecting, enhancing, or reconfiguring customary law into more robust, equitable statutory law and administrative procedures. Resource tenure was also clarified when researchers realized that even within seemingly unitary blocks of private household property, complex structures and processes governed how resources were divided and shared by gender. These complex, gendered systems of tree use, access, responsibility, and control require the attention of field workers, planners, and policy makers.

Interventions in community forestry management, farm forestry, and agroforestry frequently invest all access rights in a single "owner," in part for the sake of project implementation simplicity and efficiency, in part on the assumption that such "owners" need exclusive rights to manage their land effectively. This is an erroneous assumption. The nested rights to trees and tree products within tenure domains need to be considered (box 15.10). Agroforestry and forestry projects and programs can better protect women's access rights by allowing for multiple uses of specific spaces and resources by multiple users. These projects and programs can also prioritize renewable uses, such as the gathering of fruits and harvesting of fallen wood, prunings, coppiced wood, and leaf fodder, which do not preclude most other uses (Rocheleau and Edmunds 1997) Women's rights are often negotiated and may, therefore, not be best served by formal titling of land, which often vests ownership in a single head of household.

Designers of agroforestry interventions should be prepared to disaggregate agroforestry products that are controlled by

Ethiopia: Gender Impacts of No-Free-Grazing Trial in Tigray

In the late 1990s a university department undertook an initiative to reduce soil erosion on arable land and to create vegetated soil conservation structures through controlled village-wide trials, which would require the animals that normally grazed on open land near villagers' homesteads to be moved to the low hills surrounding the village. The impact on some of the households was unexpected. One widow had previously used dung from the animals she kept close to her house for cooking and repairing the walls of her compound. Now she had to use the same dung as payment to a wealthier household near the hills where her cattle grazed at night. She was now also obliged to walk six kilometers a day to collect fuelwood from those hills. No complete gender and wealth analysis of space, tenure, agricultural, and forest product access and use had been undertaken before the trial.

Niger: Gender and Customary Tenure in Agroforestry Parklands in Maradi

The village head allocates land to households periodically, and the allocations may change every 5 to 20 years or so. Changes depend on the needs of the village residents and on the number of households requesting to farm on land belonging to the village or village chief. From the allocation, the head of household (usually men) then allocates a portion of that land, usually nearer the homestead, to his wife for the production of domestic food crops and other portions of land to the production of his crops. The wife has a right to plant trees on her portion of land, but then only the right to gather the fruits, leaves, and firewood as by-products, not to harvest the whole tree. She has no right to plant trees on her husband's land. She may, however, have access to certain tree products such as fuelwood or fruits from his land. If, during her married life, she has planted a fruit-bearing tree in the family compound or on her land, she has the right to harvest the fruits from those trees, even after divorce.

Source: Author.

---

men and by women. Attention to customary practices can also inform analysis of how men and women benefit from the products of the resources they use. Men often control and benefit from the products that women are responsible for producing. This is sometimes the case when women are involved in community reforestation projects, caring for nurseries and transplanting seedlings of trees that men ultimately use for poles. Project and policy interventions can make explicit reference to who disposes of tree products and can help women avoid situations in which their labor is exploited largely for the benefit of others.

GENDERED KNOWLEDGE AND HOME GARDENS IN THE SUBHUMID TROPICS OF SOUTH AND SOUTHEAST ASIA

Home gardening is a time-tested example of sustainable, multispecies, agroforestry land use practiced as a subset of farming systems, predominantly in lowland humid tropics. Home gardens contain a vast number of plants, with which the members of the household constantly interact, conserving biodiversity, sequestering carbon, and providing valuable public and private goods. With their ecological similarities to natural forest ecosystems, they provide insurance against pest and diseases outbreaks. They also provide a variety of goods and services that people may otherwise rely on forests for and thus serve as a buffer against pressures on natural forests.

Home gardens are a prominent form of land use in traditionally matrilineal societies such as Kerala, central Java, and west Sumatra. They have remained engines of growth over long periods in these highly populated lowlands. Their productivity is modest compared to intensive monocultures, but they are a far more diversified source of production and income. Planting and maintaining home gardens also reflect the culture and status of the household, and especially women, in local society. In many places women play a vital role in the design and management of these land-use systems.

Growing and harvesting vegetables, fruits, nuts, medicinal plants, and fuel, and rearing animals are often the domain of women, especially in smaller gardens. The possibility of gender equality for participating in garden management and sharing of benefits is perhaps one of the major stimuli for

Box 15.10   Frequency of Trees on Women's Fields in Agroforestry Parklands

Trees located on women's fields generally belong to the men who lend them the piece of land but who may, however, concede women the right of access to them. In central Mali women have the right to trim branches and gather fruit and deadwood without permission from the landowner. Women are also usually responsible for the processing and commercialization of parkland products. Tree protection is as common in women's fields as it is in men's.

In Thiogou in southern Burkino Faso, the density of naturally regenerating trees was found to be significantly higher in women's fields, at 35 trees per hectare, than in the fields of men household heads, at 24 trees per hectare. Women in the area had long-term land loans. Various vegetables and spices as well as some cereals are grown in women's fields, whereas family fields are more exclusively oriented toward staple cereal production. With fields of similar species richness but about one-third the size of fields managed by family heads, the number of tree species per unit was twice as high in women's fields.

Source: FAO 1999.

been reported lost during a 60-year period. Although precise data are not available, the forest diversity of home gardens in most parts of the world appears to have declined. The challenge is now to tie in conversion of the genetic wealth with the formation of economic wealth. The feminization of poverty will continue unabated if the role of women as managers of biological resources is ignored.

Women's knowledge in, and conservation of, genetic material could assist in identifying and promoting species adaptability and domestication to face the challenges posed by the adaptation to and mitigation of climate change. Trees act as reservoirs and potential sources of carbon. The role of tropical forest ecosystems in carbon storage and release is quantified in the global context and recognized in the regulation of atmospheric carbon. According to the Intergovernmental Panel on Climate Change, carbon fixation from forest regeneration, intensified planting and agroforestry, and reduced deforestation could equal 12–15 percent of CO_2 emissions from fossil fuels from 1995 to 2050. Unruh, Houghton, and Lefebvre (1993) estimated the amount of stored carbon in aboveground and underground biomass in 21 different agroforestry systems in sub-Sahelian regions. They concluded that the environmental role of agroforestry in terms of retaining organic matter in the soil and reducing deforestation (and thereby reducing CO_2 emissions) is more important than its straightforward effect of carbon sequestration (FAO 2002).

continued household security enjoyed by home gardeners for generations. Nutritional security and income generation are other factors (Kumar and Nair 2004).

In Sri Lanka women played a key role in diversifying the food and nutritional base by using their knowledge of forest-based resources. Women's home gardens are best described as "genetic gardens." Women have made a significant contribution to the genetic improvement of crop plants and other economically important plants by a continuous selection process. They have also been responsible for domesticating food and medicinal plants that are now found in every home garden (FAO 1999).

However, with the transition of Sri Lankan agriculture from one based on home needs to one catering to markets, women have increasingly been relegated to unskilled work. This is particularly true in the plantation crop sector. Species losses from home gardens are said to be occurring at an unprecedented rate. In Kerala many local varieties of mango and jackfruit and other traditional horticultural crops that were once abundant in home gardens have now become extinct. In West Java 27 varieties of mango have

GENDER, AGROFORESTRY TECHNOLOGY ADAPTATION, AND ADOPTION

Studies are regularly made on the adoption, adaptation, and impact of introduced agroforestry practices. This section gives results of studies that have considered gender aspects to the adoption of agroforestry practices that have been designed and tested to address soil fertility (box 15.11).

Improved fallows and biomass transfer in Kenya and Zambia

In 1999 Franzel and others (2001) surveyed 108 farmers in Kenya and Zambia who had first planted improved fallows in 1994 and 1995 to assess their experiences in managing the technology. Over time, the farmers had managed to increase the land area devoted to fallows from an average of 0.04 to 0.07 hectare between first and third plantings. Neither tree planting nor cutting seemed to be a problem, and the improved fallow system as a whole required 11 percent less labor than a continuous unfertilized maize alternative.

Throughout eastern and southern Africa, farmers cite soil fertility as an important constraint. The World Agroforestry Centre (ICRAF) and its partners responded by undertaking research into agroforestry-related options for soil fertility. Many agroforestry systems were tested, and the more promising systems have been tested in farmer-managed conditions.

Improved fallows are the enrichment of natural fallows with trees. In Kenya most farmers plant improved fallow trees into an existing crop, whereas in Zambia most farmers establish them in an uncultivated field. The dominant crop for which fallows are used is maize in Zambia and maize and beans in Kenya. In western Kenya farmers direct-seed or broadcast at high density one or more of several species; *Crotalaria grahamiana* and *Tephrosia vogelii* are the most

popular. In eastern Zambia, *Sesbania*, the preferred species, is established in a raised bed nursery and then transplanted to the target field. In both countries the tree fallows are cut and the leaves incorporated into the soil during land preparation.

Biomass transfer systems in Kenya involve the growing of trees or shrubs alongside boundaries or contours on farms—or the collection of the same from off-farm niches, such as roadsides—and applying the leaves on the field at planting time and sometimes later in the season. In western Kenya, *Tithonia diversifolia* became the farmers' preferred species. This has been tested on maize, kale, French beans, and tomatoes. Given the small size of farms in Kenya, farmers generally utilize the green manure on smaller plots, often preferring those plots producing higher-value vegetables.

Source: Place and others 2002.

Cutting the fallows generally took less time than planting, could be done by women, and took place during a slack labor period. Analysis of the effects of the gender of household heads on household wealth in four pilot villages found little difference in the use of fallows between men and women; the percentages were 32 and 24 percent, respectively. The use of fallows was higher among wealthier households, who appeared to lead the process of trial and adaptation. Fifty-three percent of the wealthier farmers examined used improved fallows, compared to just 16 percent of the very poor households (Place and others 2002).

Two studies investigated the household characteristics associated with the use of biomass transfer among 747 farmers in the villages of Siaya and Vihiga in western Kenya. In Vihiga, 43 percent of the men-headed households examined continued to use the technology following extension services compared to just 14 percent of households in which the principal decision maker was a woman. Farming households that used biomass transfer were more likely to have a larger number of family members. The frequency of farmers' contact with extension agents was also revealed to be a significant relationship, whereas age, education, and reliance on nonfarm activities were not related (Place and others 2002).

Improved fallows and biomass transfer have been available to farmers for only a few years. Place and his colleagues (2002) found improved fallow and biomass transfer systems

to be feasible and acceptable to farmers, at least at the modest levels at which they are initially used. Economic analysis also found the systems to be profitable to farmers in terms of return to land and labor. Unlike other soil fertility options, improved fallows and biomass transfer appear to be used by large numbers of women farmers. They are also used by poor households more than other agroforestry and soil fertility practices.

Agroforestry practices particularly adapted to farm niches managed by women

Some innovative agroforestry practices are adapted by women and customized to fit the farm niches and products over which they tend to have greater control. In the two examples in box 15.12, an estimated 60 percent of farmers using the technologies are women.

Gender and agroforestry germplasm supply

Improvement of livelihoods for smallholder farmers involves bringing more trees onto farms and into the agricultural landscape. This will require that efficient seed and seedling production and distribution systems reach larger numbers of scattered and relatively isolated small-scale farmers. A well-functioning seed system is one that combines

Gender and tree fodder production for small-scale zero grazing. The low quality and quantity of feed resources are major constraints to dairy farming in central Kenya, parts of Tanzania, and Uganda. In highland areas of Kenya, farm sizes average one or two hectares, and about 80 percent of households own one or two dairy cows. Most farmers grow Napier grass (*Pennisetum purpureum*) as fodder (cut and fed to the cows). Milk yields are low because Napier grass is low in protein. Commercial dairy meal is available, but farmers consider it expensive and most do not use it. In the early 1990s the World Agroforestry Centre (ICRAF) collaborated with the Kenya Forestry Research Institute and the Kenya Agricultural Research Institute to test a number of fodder shrubs near the town of Embu. Most of the trials were farmer designed and managed. *Calliandra calothyrsus* emerged as the best-performing fodder shrub and the one most preferred by farmers. Farmers tested the feasibility of growing *Calliandra* in a range of "neglected niches" on their farms. They found the shrub could be successfully planted in hedges along internal and external boundaries, around the homestead, along contours for controlling soil erosion, or intercropped with Napier grass (Franzel and others 2004). Subsequent to additional project support, it was estimated that 86,450 farmers were planting fodder shrubs in Kenya, Rwanda, Uganda, and Tanzania (Franzel, 2005). About 60 percent of these farmers are women. In Kenya most dairy-related activities are undertaken by women, and studies suggest that they have some control over income derived from these activities. Cash income from a zero grazing enterprise was found to contribute to improved household economies, including payment of school fees and purchase of food and clothing. However, the control of increased income associated with this technology might change hands from women to men. Women will benefit more from commercial dairying under zero grazing if they are better educated and if they have more access to land for planting forages and fodder. Access to credit will enable women to purchase improved dairy breeds and the feed supplements needed for a profitable dairy enterprise (Lauwo and others 2001). Other benefits of fodder trees and shrubs are the provision of bee forage, fuelwood, stakes and poles, fencing, and shade.

Gender and the domestication of indigenous fruits. Many rural households rely on indigenous fruit trees as sources of cash and subsistence in the Southern African Development Community.

Using participatory research to examine domestication, product development, and commercialization, the ICRAF identified a number of priority tree species in each country, including *Uapaca kirkiana, Strychnos cocculoides, Parinari curatellifolia,* and *Sclerocarya birrea.* The goal of domesticating these trees is to increase their quantity, availability, and productivity and to create opportunities for marketing their products. An impact analysis indicated that a robust domestication program will create incentives for farmer-led investment in the cultivation of indigenous fruit trees as an alternative to collecting wild fruit. In Zimbabwe the returns to labor by women and children in collecting wild fruits are two to three times greater than other farming activities. In a survey of roadside market vendors of the indigenous fruit *Uapaca kirkiana* in Dedze, Malawi, the majority of respondents were women or children under 19 years old, and all of them had harvested the fruits from forests and communal lands in areas outside their homesteads and fields (Kadzere and others 2006). Fruits enable women and children to contribute to household income and to assist the household during seasonal periods of food insecurity. In the scaling-up component of this program, 60 percent of the 13,000 farmers reached were women. They were trained in domesticating and propagating trees, establishing nurseries, and managing farms. Indigenous fruit tree seedlings have been tested by farmers in four countries. Akinnifesi and colleagues (2006) found that 86 percent of the planting sites in Malawi and 98 percent in Zambia were located on homesteads. Women were the principal managers of these sites and were likely to benefit the most from production. Women were the principal recipients of training in the local production of fruit concentrates, jam, juice, and other products in Malawi, Tanzania, Zambia, and Zimbabwe (Ham and others 2008).

formal and informal, market and nonmarket channels to stimulate and efficiently meet farmers' evolving demand for quality seeds. The Improved Seed Systems for Agroforestry in African Countries project in Burkina Faso, Malawi, and Uganda was introduced to facilitate access to tree germplasm by men and women farmers.[1] The project entailed considerable analysis of the constraints and opportunities people experience in getting access to germplasm supply for agroforestry. A number of practical lessons from the project experience are discussed by Brandi-Hansen and others (2007):

- Centralized seed supply systems have not provided rural communities with agroforestry tree seed or with messages regarding the importance of seed quality or procedures for collecting quality seed.
- NGOs may be providing agroforestry tree seed, but tree growing is often one among many activities undertaken by an NGO, and their provision of seeds tends to lack the rigor required to ensure quality and adequate returns to the farmers they supply. The majority of large NGOs do not provide accurate and precise information with regard to seed collection and handling. The focus tends to be on volume of seed handled, rather than on quality and site matching. NGOs would appear to have limited connections to most grassroots CBOs. NGOs tend to serve their own clientele, especially "their own" CBOs, and seldom engage with or build on the capacities and networks of existing CBOs.
- A few specialized and highly focused NGOs are providing lessons in quality seed procurement.
- The great majority of persons surveyed who deal in tree seed are women, and members of CBOs that collect tree seed locally, growing trees for their own use.[2] These women and their CBOs are not reached by any of the NGOs.
- Large multipurpose projects or NGOs are therefore not the most appropriate targets of information disseminated about quality seeds. Improved germplasm and information on how to use it should be disseminated directly to women's CBOs, which lie at the heart of the sustainable tree seed supply network. Rural women should be placed at the center of *any* agroforestry tree seed supply system.

Establishing associations and networks of small-scale entrepreneurs is also recommended (Graudal and Lillesø 2007). Yet most such entrepreneurs are men, and focusing on them would likely lead to women being excluded from training opportunities. Youth, who often lack other employment opportunities, also have a role to play in the seed supply system. However, the greatest leverage in terms of quality seed supply and the quality of trees planted on farmland will be in finding mechanisms to train and mobilize the efforts of CBOs, particularly women's groups. These local grassroots institutions already exist.

LESSONS LEARNED AND GUIDELINES FOR PRACTITIONERS

The division of landscapes, farm niches, and products between men and women makes the issue of germplasm access and preference a deeply gendered one. Under the misconception that men are the principal, or only, decision makers with regard to tree planting, management, and use, the basis of women's differentiated decision making is often not recognized in farmers' trials and scaling-up activities. Women require specific targeted information and training as well as access to credit and other services, adjusted to their particular landscape niches and agroforestry product needs. Gender analysis should therefore be considered as nothing less than an essential element of designing and planning agroforestry interventions and should be required periodically throughout the life of an intervention. Women's roles in traditional complex agroforestry systems are acknowledged. Yet their knowledge and experience are not being adequately garnered by policies that will guide the future of traditional agroforestry systems. With the growing influence of the market economy, and the consequent focus on a narrow range of home garden species, a real risk exists that this gendered knowledge, and even certain plant species, will not be passed onto future generations. With regard to the development of innovative agroforestry practices, far greater efforts in considering the gender implications of these developments are required. Recruiting women farmers to participatory agroforestry practice groups, farmer-managed trials, and farmer field schools warrants strong priority. Numbers and categories of individual women and women's CBOs who practice innovative agroforestry should be carefully documented, along with the adaptations they develop.

Agroforestry parklands are widespread throughout much of semiarid Africa. The variety of different types of agroforestry parklands reflects the dynamic nature of these systems and the ability of farmers to adapt them to changes in the natural and socioeconomic environment (FAO 1999). The importance of these parklands as a livelihood buffer and as a pool of forest genetic diversity has brought them to the attention of the policy makers and researchers in recent years. Research into biophysical interactions upon which parkland productivity is based can build on indigenous knowledge to provide management prescriptions more precisely attuned to the needs of different environments. Parkland agroforestry projects could focus on promoting practices and technologies that require minimal labor and capital investments to produce rapid returns, and on increasing opportunities involving parkland tree products (FAO 1999). The promotion of markets and improved processing for parkland products will encourage farmers to invest in the further development of their parkland systems. However, it has been reported that when products such as *Vitellaria* nuts have increased value as a cash crop, men have reduced women's access to the resource. A similar trend resulting from the introduction of domesticated materials or improved processing technologies might develop to the detriment of women. Changes in tree tenure, therefore, need to be monitored and consequences anticipated (FAO 1999).

Finally, although formal credit may be a necessary step for women to adopt efficient forest-related technologies, insecurity of access to land resources currently limits availability to credit collateral. Building the capacity of existing social organizations such as women's groups may be a way of increasing women's access to land resources (including agroforestry tree germplasm and products), making credit more affordable, improving access to markets, and making labor more efficient by task sharing within the groups.

This Note focuses on women practitioners of agroforestry, although the importance of women's representation among professionals who engage in decision and policy making that relates to agroforestry at local, regional, and national levels should not be underestimated. Currently few women agroforestry field workers, scientists, and policy makers are available. Strategies to enhance gender-conscious implementation of agroforestry may be achieved through the following steps:

- Support to existing women's groups active in agroforestry, including tree nursery groups, zero grazing and dairy fodder groups, indigenous fruits marketing groups, and horticulture associations
- Posting of more women frontline staff by the relevant ministries and partner NGOs
- More consciously gender-oriented research, outreach, and scaling-up strategies
- Greater educational opportunities for women in land law and agricultural and forest sciences (box 15.13).

Box 15.13 Examples of Gender Initiatives from Research and Education Institutions

In science and research: Consultative Group on International Agricultural Research (CGIAR) Gender and Diversity Program exists to help the CGIAR Centers leverage their rich staff diversity to increase research and management excellence. The program also has a mentoring and sponsorship program (including a Women's Post Doctoral Fellowship program at the World Agroforestry Centre) and is promoting the education and career of women agricultural scientists.

In education and institutional capacity building: Crucial among the strategies of the Centro Agronomico Tropical de Investigacion y Enseñanza's (CATIE's) gender policy are the following:

- Integrating gender aspects in the design and implementation of research proposals
- Including women farmers in all phases of the outreach strategy
- Steadily increasing the number of women professionals
- Promoting and facilitating the participation of women in graduate education
- Advancing the understanding of gender among students (graduates and courses)
- Developing understanding and implementation of gender focus by CATIE's staff
- Improving CATIE's role in the exchange of knowledge, experience, and expertise.

Sources: Centro Agronomico Tropical de Investigacion y Enseñanza, "Gender Policy," www.catie.ac.cr; World Agroforestry Centre 2008: 45.

Bwindi Impenetrable National Park Enterprise Development Project: Protected Areas and Ecotourism

"Protected areas (PAs) are specific and unique natural habitats, where human encroachment is restricted in order to preserve biodiversity for present and future generations. In many protected areas around the world, however, people with legitimate or historical land ownership rights live within the established boundaries. Women's and men's relationships with the environment in the protected areas and their buffer zones, in the context of their respective gender roles, are crucial for the very survival of these natural habitats.... Women and men have very different approaches to managing the environment: addressing these concrete differences will make people's relationship with the environment more sustainable" (IUCN 2003b: 1).

The Bwindi Impenetrable National Park (BINP) covers 32,092 hectares in southwest Uganda. Its rare afromontane vegetation provides one of the richest habitats for birds, butterflies, trees, and mammals in East Africa. Its mammal populations include chimpanzees and more than half of the world's remaining mountain gorillas—more than 300 individuals. Sections of BNIP have been protected since 1932, and the national park itself was established in 1991. Because of BINP's rare and wide biodiversity, United Nations Educational, Scientific and Cultural Organization accorded it the status of World Heritage Site in 1994.

> **What's innovative?** The project collected gender-disaggregated baseline data, which were incorporated in its design, monitoring, and evaluation. Gender analysis and gender-sensitive framework and criteria were adopted in its microenterprise development component to ensure that priorities of women and other disadvantaged groups were properly taken into account. Women field staff and women entrepreneurs were hired as mentors to encourage more effective women's participation in the project.

Next to the protected area of the BINP are multiple-use zones in 13 of the 21 parishes (some 18 percent of the park area). However, less than 10 percent of the population of these parishes holds licenses to harvest honey, weaving materials, and medical products from the multiple-use zones. Based on the existing harvesting quotas of natural resources, multiple-use zones have limited scope for enterprise development, even among current license holders.

Community-Based Enterprises for the Conservation of Biodiversity at Bwindi World Heritage Site in Uganda was a project carried out by the Mgahinga and Bwindi Impenetrable Forest Conservation Trust Fund from 2001 to 2004. The project was funded by the United Nations Foundation and FAO. It was intended to demonstrate that community-based tree and forest product enterprises can contribute to both poverty alleviation and the conservation of biodiversity.

The project included gender disaggregation of baseline data. During the participatory appraisal, particular attention was devoted to identifying women-headed households and to reviewing educational levels and household livelihood strategies. This included sampling women's and men's daily time profiles. Focus group discussion examined differentials in education, access to training and employment, and access to information and communication. The project also examined management of savings and credit funds by women's groups and identified women entrepreneurs, who were purposefully included in project activities.

FAO'S MARKETING ANALYSIS AND DEVELOPMENT METHODOLOGY

The project employed the Market Analysis and Development approach developed by FAO.[1] This is a step-by-step iterative process that provides forest community members with the capacity to identify and develop viable and successful tree and forest product enterprises and to manage them independently.

The initial idea of the project was to use Market Analysis and Development to improve local livelihoods through the development of income-generating tree and forest enterprises, while protecting those resources. This idea proved to have limitations from the outset of the project because participating communities enjoyed only very restricted access to the park. The project, therefore, had to shift its focus away from "giving value to the forest—and thus protecting it—by using its resources" and toward finding options for reducing pressure on the park (FAO 2006a: 29). These included using products that depend on the biodiversity in the park but that do not come out of the park itself.

During the first two years of the project various products and services were identified, including community-based tourism, support to a local campground, handicrafts, beekeeping, and enterprises dealing with passion fruit, avocados, and mushrooms. Through these enterprises a significant proportion of the local community was able to participate in enterprises that were linked to the conservation of natural resources within the park.

GENDER STRATEGY

During the participatory appraisal undertaken in preparation for the project, particular attention was devoted to identifying women-headed households and the livelihood strategies they employed. Planners reviewed education levels and used focus group discussions to examine differentials in education, and access to training, employment, and information and communication. They also examined the management of savings and credit funds by women's groups. Women entrepreneurs were identified and included in project activities.

A gender strategy was developed to ensure that benefits are equitably shared and that those people with the least access to education, training, and information were provided with opportunities to participate in the project. Hiring women as field staff was deemed crucial to maintaining balanced gender participation. Planners developed a framework and criteria for microenterprise development to ensure that the priorities of women and other disadvantaged groups were properly taken into account, and they applied during the life of the project.

Planners promoted the sustainability of the income from enterprises by building individuals' entrepreneurial capacity through a process that involved the local population in action research and participatory data gathering and analysis. Business literacy and enterprise development stressed negotiating skills. Results of the initial phase of the project indicated that the success of business endeavors undertaken

| Box 15.14 | Other Features of the Project's Gender Strategy |

- Gender disaggregation of project background and baseline data.
- Special attention in the participatory appraisal to identify women-headed households and to review educational levels and household livelihood strategies, including sampling of women's and men's daily time profiles.
- Focus group discussion examining education differentials, access to training and employment, access to information and communication, and the structure of women's groups' management of savings and credit funds.
- Recording of numbers of women's enterprises, women-headed households, women's saving and credit groups, and women's forest user societies, and development of indicators for monitoring and evaluating the participation of women and disadvantaged groups.
- Identification and inclusion of women entrepreneurs in project activities (for example, as mentors to women's enterprises and making presentations to encourage role modeling).

Source: FAO 2006a.

by women entrepreneurs depended on the support of the entire household. The project strived for gender balance rather than focusing exclusively on women or men and took steps to ensure that women and disadvantaged groups were not excluded from extension, marketing, credit, and other activities (box 15.14).

Gender analysis was used as a tool during the initial survey of potential economic opportunities. Both men and women developed criteria; they then decided which enterprise to adopt. When community members were assessing enterprises, the gender strategy ensured that the poorest groups and women participated in the final selection. It was also necessary, however, to involve more educated and experienced community members to promote trade linkages and ensure the proper accounting of finances.

THE BUHOMA VILLAGE WALK: COMMUNITY-BASED ECOTOURISM

The Buhoma village walk was one of the initial community enterprises identified as a result of applying FAO's Market

Analysis and Development approach and the project's gender strategy. In total the enterprise development project worked with 304 entrepreneurs in a range of start-up businesses; 179 of these entrepreneurs were women, and 125 were men.

The Buhoma village walk starts and ends at the Buhoma Community Rest Camp located at the entrance of BNIP. It passes through a typical African village with traditional rural homesteads. The sites along the walk include a local women's handicraft center for a 15-minute craft-making demonstration, a waterfall, tea plantations, a local traditional medicine healer, a school, bird watching in a community woodlot, Batwa (pygmy) music and performance, and brewing facilities for banana beer and a local gin called *waragi. The* walk lasts approximately three hours. The enterprise is made up of eight guides from the local community and a representative for each of the households that manage sites along the route. It is registered under the Buhoma Community Rest Camp Association (BCRCA) of Mukono parish, Kanungu district. The Culture and Tourism Development Committee of the BCRCA supervises its activities. The income earned is shared according to a breakdown that was agreed among all the stakeholders (FAO 2006b).

The aim was to attract an average of five tourist a day (half the people who visit the park), who would pay $7.50 each. The monthly sales target was $750. Promotional strategies included developing a brochure about the walk, listing the walk as one of Bwindi's tourist activities in the Uganda Wildlife Authority (UWA) brochure, and marketing the walk by guides at local tourist lodges. The enterprise received 2,295 visitors between January 2003 and August 2005. In 2004 the village walk generated an extra $27 per month for each guide, $17 per month for each site owner, and $74 per month for the 11 Batwa households (45 households) that managed the sites. This represents significant earnings for people who did not have any access to cash income before, such as the Batwa. Each site owner contributed $1.70 for trail maintenance every month, which was carried out by Batwa community members. All the site owners inspected the trail every fifth day of the month, when there is a general meeting. Site owners have formed a small committee to oversee maintenance of the walk. The village walk guides attend regular training and briefings with UWA rangers. A good working relationship exists among UWA, the community, and the guides.

LESSONS LEARNED AND ISSUES FOR WIDER APPLICABILITY

The project resulted in the establishment of 13 enterprise groups. For each enterprise group, a business plan was developed, technical and entrepreneur capacities were improved, and pilot enterprise activities are up and running. The Mgahinga and Bwindi Impenetrable Forest Conservation Trust Fund is committed to continue giving support to these enterprises, together with a number of local service providers linked with the specific enterprise groups. Some of the enterprises and value-adding technologies that emerged during product selection were of particular interest to women. Yet the support and involvement of the men in their households were found to be critical by the project staff. The design and timing of the training workshops took into account the availability of both men and women. Gender balance was actively sought in market study tours and other enterprise-related activities. All monitoring information was disaggregated by gender so that the impacts of the project for both men and women could be evaluated. The project gave clear indications of the types of strategies necessary to ensure the full participation of women and men (FAO 2006a). There was a common consensus among the stakeholders in the project area that focusing on women yielded better results. The overall attendance and participation of women in workshops was at least 40 percent.

A gender-equitable perspective in the sustained management of protected areas enables practitioners to recognize the following (see also box 15.15):

■ Communities are not homogeneous—consultation with a variety of stakeholders is necessary.

Box 15.15 Maximizing Conservation in Protected Areas: Guidelines for Gender Conservation

Conflicts between community interests and conservation interventions in protected areas are common but not inevitable. Research shows that access to education and training can reduce such conflicts. A gender-equitable perspective additionally asks if both women and men are in a position to participate actively. The poor, who are often women, need education to develop their capacity to manage the environmental resources of protected areas in ways that are sustainable for them and the environment. To invest in the environment is to invest in people.

Source: IUCN 2003b.

- Men and women use and manage different natural resources in protected areas differently.
- The different interests, knowledge, and behavior of women, men, and children have important ramifications for conservation initiatives.
- Strategies to include and facilitate women in extension, entrepreneurial, managerial, and decision-making roles will enhance the sustainability of protected area management initiatives.

NOTES

Overview

This Overview was written by Christine Holding Anyonge and Natalie Hufnagl (Consultants), with inputs from Sophie Grouwels, Simmone Rose, and Dieter Schoene (FAO) and Katuscia Fara (IFAD); and reviewed by Chitra Deshpande and Catherine Ragasa (Consultants); Deborah Rubin (Cultural Practice); Dan Rugabira (FAO); Ilaria Firmian, Maria Hartl, and Sheila Mwanundu (IFAD); and Diji Chandrasekharan Behr and Eija Pehu (World Bank).

1. See also Food and Agriculture Organization, "Gender Analysis and Forestry Training Package," www.fao.org/forestry/foris/pdf/gender/tr-e01/tr-e01.0.pdf.

2. SAFE: The Interagency Standing Committee Task Force on Safe Access to Firewood and Alternative Energy in Humanitarian Settings, Coordinated by the UN Women's Commission for Refugee Women and Children.

3. This contrasts with the European report, which states that "the relatively low level of female representation—both in terms of critical mass and levels of seniority/professional roles—is in stark contrast to the feedback from responding countries that gender/equality is perceived as an important issue in society, [and furthermore] an 'issue' within the forest industries of the respective reporting countries" (FAO 2006b: 11–12).

4. Program on Forests, "Poverty and Forestry Linkages: A Synthesis of Six Case Studies," www.profor.info.

Thematic Note 1

This Thematic Note was written by Christine Holding Anyonge (Consultant), with inputs from Chitra Deshpande and Alessandro Spairani (Consultants), Maria Hartl (IFAD), and Sophie Grouwels and Miguel Trossero (FAO); and reviewed by Catherine Ragasa and Deborah Rubin (Consultants); Simmone Rose and Dan Rugabira (FAO); Katuscia Fara, Ilaria Firmian, and Sheila Mwanundu (IFAD); and Diji Chandrasekharan Behr and Eija Pehu (World Bank).

1. NWFPs consist of goods of biological origin other than wood, as well as services derived from forests and allied land uses (FAO 1995). NTFPs are nontimber forest products (including wood not sold as timber, such as fuel wood/wood energy and wood-carving materials).

2. The *miombo* woodlands, recognized for their floristic richness and widespread occurrence of the genera *Brachystegia, Julbernadia, Isoberlinia,* and their associates (Malaisse 1978), form the dominant natural woodland type in southern Africa. They extend across about 2.7 million square kilometers of the African subhumid tropical zone from Tanzania and Democratic Republic of Congo in the north, through Zambia, Malawi, and eastern Angola, to Mozambique and Zimbabwe. It is estimated that over 75 million people live within the miombo biome and that the woodlands directly support the livelihood of over 40 million people in this African region (Bradley and McNamara 1993; Dewees 1994).

3. FAO, "Regional Wood Energy Development Programme in Asia," Expert consultation in Gender and Wood Energy, http://wgbis.ces.iisc.ernet.in/energy/HC270799/RWEDP/rm22.html.

4. FAO (2006).

5. Thematic Note 4 on Gender, Self-Help Groups, and Farmers' Organisations (Module 2) refers to six types and functions of women's groups in the agricultural sector: producers' associations and cooperatives, self-help groups, rotating savings and credit associations, women's subgroups in village development associations, women's groups in watershed management associations, agricultural extension field schools, or farmer research groups. Terms used in other texts are "farmer's professional associations," "community development fund management organizations," "forest products processing associations," and "agroforestry nursery entrepreneurs." In the context of this Note, the natures of the women's groups to which we are referring are those focused on collective action in relation to their livelihoods and forest resources and may therefore be a range of these alternatives, including self-help groups and village development associations. For the purposes of this Note, we will use the collective term *community-based organizations.*

6. FAO marketing analysis and development methodology, IFAD program support to Phytotrade, and INBAR bamboo and rattan field projects. See Elsie Yang and Yangjing Sucuiwei, "A Gender Assessment Study on Bamboo-Based Rural Development and Utilization Activities—A Case Study in Yunnan, China," Working Paper 53, International Network for Bamboo and Rattan, www.inbar.int/publication/txt/INBAR_Working_Paper_No53.htm.

Thematic Note 2

This Thematic Note was written by Christine Holding Anyonge (Consultant), with inputs from Festus Akinnifesi,

Aichi Kitalyi, and Jens-Peter Barkenow Lilleso (ICRAF); and reviewed by Chitra Deshpande, Catherine Ragasa, and Deborah Rubin (Consultants); Michelle Gauthier, Sophie Grouwels, and Simmone Rose (FAO); Katuscia Fara, Ilaria Firmian, Maria Hartl, and Sheila Mwanundu (IFAD); and Diji Chandrasekharan Behr and Eija Pehu (World Bank).

1. This is a collaboration between DANIDA Forest Seed Centre (now part of Forest and Landscape Denmark) and ICRAF, World Agroforestry Centre, and National Tree Seed Organisations in Burkino Faso, Malawi, and Uganda.

2. In the Uganda study, 602 CBOs were identified, of which most were women's groups, with an average number of 30 members. Some had a small number of men as members. In other words, this survey recorded in two districts of Uganda about 18,000 women as being active in tree seed systems. Most CBOs (82 percent) had no direct affiliation with any organizations, such as NGOs, but nevertheless demonstrated a remarkable level of activity (Brandi-Hansen and others 2007).

Innovative Activity Profile I

This Innovative Activity Profile was written by Christine Holding Anyonge, with inputs from Sophie Grouwels (FAO); and reviewed by Chitra Deshpande, Catherine Ragasa, and Deborah Rubin (Consultants); Simmone Rose and Dan Rugabira (FAO); Katuscia Fara, Ilaria Firmian, Maria Hartl, and Sheila Mwanundu (IFAD); and Eija Pehu (World Bank).

1. FAO's Market Analysis and Development approach: www.fao.org/forestry/site/enterprises/en.

REFERENCES

Overview

Food and Agriculture Organization (FAO). 1999. "Sri Lankan Women and Men as Bioresource Managers." RAP Publication 1999/45, Gender and Bioresources research team of the M. S. Swaminathan Research Foundation, Sri Lanka.

————. 2005a. *Global Forest Resources Assessment (FRA) 2005.* Rome: FAO.

————. 2005b. "Miombo Woodlands and HIV/AIDS Interactions: Malawi Country Report." Forest Policy and Institutions Working Paper No. 6, FAO, Rome.

————. 2006a. *Better Forestry, Less Poverty: A Practitioner's Guide.* FAO Forestry Paper 149. Rome: FAO.

————. 2006b. "Time for Action: Changing the Gender Situation in Forestry." Report of the UNECE/FAO team of specialists on Gender and Forestry, FAO, Rome.

————. 2007a. *State of the World's Forests (SOFO).* Rome: FAO.

————. 2007b. "Mainstreaming Gender in Forestry in Africa." Regional report, FAO, Rome.

International Union for Conservation of Nature (IUCN). 2003. "Maximizing Conservation in Protected Areas Guidelines for Gender Consideration." Policy Brief, IUCN-ORMA, San José, Costa Rica.

Kaimowitz, David. 2005. "Forests and Violent Conflict." In *State of the Worlds Forests,* 117–18. Rome: FAO.

Kumar, B. Mohan, and P. K. Ramachandran Nair. 2004. "The Enigma of Tropical Home Gardens." *Agroforestry Systems* 61: 135–52.

Rocheleau, Dianne, and David Edmunds. 1997. "Women, Men and Trees: Gender, Power and Property in Forest and Agrarian Landscapes." *World Development* 25 (8): 1351–71.

Rojas, Mary. 1993. "Integrating Gender Considerations into Forestry Projects." FAO, Rome.

Shackleton, Sheona, Sarah Kaschula, Wayne Twine, Lori Hunter, Christine Holding Anyonge, and Lisa Petheram. 2006. "Forests as Safety Nets for Mitigating the Impacts of HIV/AIDS in Southern Africa." Forests and Livelihoods Brief No. 4, Center for International Forestry Research, Bogor, Indonesia.

United Nations Programme on HIV/AIDS (UNAIDS). 2006. "Report on the Global AIDS Epidemic." *The Impact of AIDS on People and Societies,* chapter 4. New York: UN.

United Nations Development Programme (UNDP). 2005. *Human Development Report 2005.* New York: UNDP.

World Agroforestry Centre (ICRAF). 2008. *Transforming Lives and Landscapes: The World Agroforestry Centre Strategy, 2008–2015.* Nairobi: ICRAF.

World Bank. 2002. *Sustaining Forests: A Development Strategy.* Washington, DC: World Bank.

Thematic Note I

Bradley, P. N., and K. McNamara, eds. 1993. "Living with Trees: Policies for Forest Management in Zimbabwe." World Bank Technical Paper No. 210, World Bank, Washington, DC.

Chunquian, Jiang. 2005. "Forests of Huoshan County: A Path towards Poverty Alleviation." In *In Search of Excellence. Exemplary Forest Management in Asia and the Pacific,* ed. Patrick B. Durst, Chris Brown, Henrylito D. Tacio, and Miyuki Ishikawa, 175–82. Bangkok: Food and Agriculture Organization.

Deseng, Hembil, and Michael Yirmeila. 2005. "Impact of SHGs on Women's Quality of Life." West Garo Hills NERCAMP, International Fund for Agricultural Development, Rome. Also available at www.enrap.org.

Dewees, P. A. 1994. "Social and Economic Aspects of Miombo Woodland Management in Southern Africa: Options and Opportunities for Research. CIFOR (Center for International Forestry Research) Occasional Paper No. 2, CIFOR, Bogor, Indonesia.

Feldstein, Hilary S. and Susan Poats, eds. 1990. *Working Together: Gender Analysis in Agriculture.* Bloomfield, CT: Kumarian Press.

Food and Agriculture Organization (FAO). 1995. "Non-Wood Forest Products for Rural Income and Sustainable Forestry." Non-Wood Forest Products publication series No. 7, FAO, Rome.

————. 2002. "HIV/AIDS and the Forest Sector." Extension Information Leaflet, FAO, Forest Department, Rome.

————. 2006. "Non-Wood Forest Product Community-Based Enterprise Development: A Way for Livelihood Improvement in Lao People's Democratic Republic." Forestry Policy and Institutions Working Paper Series No. 16, FAO, Rome.

————. 2007. "Mainstreaming Gender in Forestry in Africa." Regional report, FAO, Rome.

Government of Malawi. 2007. "Forestry Sector HIV and AIDS Strategy 2007–2011." Department of Forestry, Lilongwe.

International Fund for Agricultural Development (IFAD). 2006. *North Eastern Region Community Resources Management Project for Upland Areas Interim Evaluation Report no. 1730-IN.* Rome: IFAD.

Kaimowitz, David. 2003. "Not Be Bread Alone ... Forests and Rural Livelihoods in Sub-Saharan Africa." In *Forestry in Poverty Reduction Strategies: Capturing the Potential,* ed. T. Oksanen, B. Pajari, and T. Toumasjukka, 45–64. EFI Proceedings No. 47. Joensuu, Finland: European Forest Institute.

————. 2005. "Forests and Armed Conflict." Editorial in *ETFRN News* 43/44: Forests and Conflicts, 5–6. Wageningen: ETFRN. Also available at www.etfrn.org.

Kayambazintu, Dennis, Marc Barany, Reginald Mumba, and Christine Holding Anyonge. 2005. "Miombo Woodlands and HIV/AIDS Interactions: Malawi Country Report." Forest Policy and Institutions Working Paper No. 6, Food and Agriculture Organization, Rome.

Malaisse, F. 1978. "The Miombo Ecosystem." In "Tropical Forest Ecosystems." United Nations Educational, Scientific and Cultural Organization/United Nations Environment Programme/Food and Agriculture Organization Report, Paris.

Merino, Leticia. 2005. "El Balcón, Mexico. "Building Peace and Governability around Communal Forests." In *ETFRN News* 43/44: Forests and Conflicts, 79–80. Wageningen: ETFRN. Also available at www.etfrn.org.

Mukherjee, Neela, Meera Jayaswal, and Madhumita Parihari. 2006. "Forests as Safety Net: Listening to the Voices of the Poor. A Field Study of 15 Forest Villages in India." Proceedings of REFOFTC 2007, Poverty Reduction and Forests: Tenure, Markets and Policy Reforms, Bangkok, September 3–7, http://recoftc.org/site/index.php?id=445.

Ndoye, Ousseynou, Manuel Ruiz-Perez, and Antoine Eyebe. 1997. "The Markets of Non-Timber Forest Products in the Humid Forest Zone of Cameroon." ODI Rural Development Forestry Network Paper No. 22c, Overseas Development Institute, London.

SAFE. 2007. "UN Task Force on Safe Access to Firewood and Alternative Energy in Humanitarian Settings." Information Template: Agency Roles and Responsibilities Per Issue Area. Geneva: Wood Based Energy.

Schreckenberg, Kate, Elaine Marshall, and Dirk Willem Te Velde. 2006. "NTFP Commercialization and the Rural Poor. More than a Safety Net?" In *Commercialization of Non-Timber Forest Products: Factors Influencing Success. Lessons Learned from Mexico and Bolivia and Policy Implications for Decision-Making,* ed. Elaine Marshall, Kate Schreckenberg, and Adrian C. Newton, 71–76. Cambridge: UNEP World Conservation Monitoring Centre.

Shackleton, Sheona, Patricia Shanley, and Ousseynou Ndoye. 2007. "Invisible but Viable: Recognising Local Markets for Non-Timber Forest Products." *International Forestry Review* 9 (3): 697–712.

Shanley, Patricia, Leda Luz, and Ian R. Swingland. 2002. "The Faint Promise of a Distant Market: A Survey of Belem's Trade in Non-Timber Forest Products." *Biodiversity and Conservation* 11: 615–36.

United Nations Programme on HIV/AIDS (UNAIDS). 2006. "Report on the Global AIDS Epidemic." *The Impact of AIDS on People and Societies,* chapter 4. New York: United Nations.

Wollenberg, Eva, David Edmunds, Louise Buck, Jeff Fox, and Sonja Brodt. 2001. *Social Learning in Community Forests.* Bogor, Indonesia: CIFOR (Center for International Forestry Research).

Thematic Note 2

Akinnifesi, Festus K., Freddie Kwesiga, Jarret Mhango, Thomson Chilanga, Alfred Mkonda, Caroline A. C. Kadu, Irene Kadzere, Dagmar Mithofer, John D. K. Saka, Gudeta Sileshi, Tunu Ramadhani, and Patient Dhliwayo. 2006. "Towards the Development of Miombo Fruit Trees as Commercial Tree Crops in Southern Africa." *Forests, Trees and Livelihoods* 16: 103–21.

Brandi-Hansen, E., Jens-Peter Barnekow Lillesø, S. Moestrup, and J. K. Kisera. 2007. "Do Organisations Provide Quality Seed to Smallholders? A Study on Tree Planting in Uganda, by NGOs and CBOs." Development and Environment No. 8-2007, Forest and Landscape Denmark, Copenhagen.

Food and Agriculture Organization (FAO). 1999. "Agroforestry Parklands in Sub-Saharan Africa." FAO Conservation Guide No. 34, FAO, Rome.

———. 2002. "Trees outside Forests—Towards Better Awareness." FAO Conservation Guide No. 35, FAO, Rome.

Franzel, Steven. 2005. "The Adoption and Impact of Fodder Shrubs in East Africa. 3rd External Programme and Management Review." World Agroforestry Centre, Nairobi, Kenya.

Franzel, Steven, Glenn L. Denning, Jens-Peter Barnekow Lillesø, and Agustin. R Mercado, Jr. 2004. "Scaling Up the Impact of Agroforestry: Lessons from Three Sites in Africa and Asia." *Agroforestry Systems* 61: 329–44.

Franzel, Steven, S. J. Scherr, R. Coe, P. Cooper, and Frank Place. 2001. "Assessing the Adoption Potential of Agroforestry Practices: ICRAF's Experiences in Sub-Saharan Africa." *Agricultural Systems* 69 (1–2): 37–62.

Graudal, Lars, and Jens-Peter Barnekow Lillesø. 2007. "Experiences and Future Prospects for Tree Seed Supply in Agricultural Development Support-Based on Lessons Learnt in DANIDA Supported Programmes 1965–2005." Working Paper, Ministry of Foreign Affairs, Copenhagen.

Ham, Cori, Festus K. Akinnifesi, Steven Franzel, D. du P. S. Jordaan, Chris Hansmann, and Caroline de Kock. 2008. "Opportunities for Commercialization and Enterprise Development of Indigenous Fruits in Southern Africa." In *Indigenous Fruit Trees in the Tropics: Domestication, Utilization and Commercialization,* ed. Festus K. Akinnifesi, Roger R. B. Leakey, Oluyede Ajayi, Gudeta Sileshi, Zac Tchoundjeu, Patrick Matakala, and Freddie R. Kwesiga, 254–72. Nairobi: World Agroforestry Centre; Wallingford, U.K.: CAB International Publishing.

Kadzere, Irene, Christopher B. Watkins, Ian A. Merwin, Festus K. Akinnifesi, John D. K. Daka, and Jarret Mhango. 2006. "Harvesting and Post-Harvesting Handling Practices and Characteristics of *Uapaca kirkiana* (Muell. Agr.) Fruits: A Survey of Roadside Markets in Malawi." *Agroforestry Systems* 68 (2): 133–42.

Kumar, B. Mohan, and P. K. Ramachandran Nair. 2004. "The Enigma of Tropical Home Gardens." *Agroforestry Systems* 61: 135–52.

Lauwo, Apsama, William Mwebembezi, Karwitha Kiugu, and Aichi Kitalyi. 2001. "Is Dairy Zero Grazing as an Enterprise in Smallholder Unit Economical? Experiences in East Africa." RELMA (Regional Land Management Unit) working paper, Nairobi.

Place, Frank, Steven Franzel, Judith DeWolf, Ralph Rommelse, Freddie Kwesiga, Amadou Niang, and Bashir

Jama. 2002. "Agroforestry for Soil Fertility Replenishment: Evidence on Adoption Processes in Kenya and Zambia." In *Natural Resources Management in African Agriculture,* ed. Christopher. B. Barrett, Frank Place, and Abdillahi. A. Aboud, chapter 12. London: CAB International.

Rocheleau, Dianne, and David Edmunds. 1997. "Women, Men and Trees: Gender, Power and Property in Forest and Agrarian Landscapes." *World Development* 25 (8): 1351–71.

Unruh, Jon D., Richard A. Houghton, and Paul A. Lefebvre. 1993. "Carbon Storage in Agroforestry: An Estimate for sub-Saharan Africa." *Climate Research* 3: 39–52.

World Agroforestry Centre (ICRAF). 2008. *Transforming Lives and Landscapes, The World Agroforestry Centre Strategy, 2008–2015* Nairobi: ICRAF.

Innovative Activity Profile 1

Food and Agriculture Organization (FAO). 2006a. "Community Based Enterprise Development for the Conservation of Biodiversity in Bwindi World Heritage Site, Uganda." Forestry Policy and Institutions Working Paper No. 11, FAO, Rome.

———. 2006b. "Community Based Tourism: Income Generation and Conservation in Bwindi World Heritage Site, Uganda the Buhoma Village Walk Case Study." Forestry Policy and Institutions Working Paper No. 12, FAO, Rome.

International Union for Conservation of Nature (IUCN). 2003a. *Gender Matters.* Multimedia video.

———. 2003b. "Maximising Conservation in Protected Areas: Guidelines for Gender Consideration." Policy Brief, IUCN-ORMA, San José, Costa Rica.

FURTHER READING

Overview

Centro Agronomico Tropical de Investigacion y Enseñanza/FAO (CATIE/FAO). 2007a. "Towards an Enabling Environment for Small and Medium Forest Enterprise Development." Policy brief. Turrialba, Costa Rica: CATIE; Rome: FAO.

———. 2007b. *State of the World Forests.* Rome: FAO. Available at www.fao.org/forestry/sofo/en.

Lambrou, Yianna, and Grazia Piana. 2006. "Gender: The Missing Component of the Response to Climate Change." Food and Agriculture Organization, Rome.

Nair, P. K. Ramchandran, M. R. Rao, and Louise E. Buck, eds. 2004. *New Vistas in Agroforestry. A Compendium for the 1st World Congress of Agroforestry, 2004.* Dordrecht: Kluwer.

Swedish University of Agricultural Science. 2006. *Gender and Forestry.* Proceedings of a seminar on Gender and Forestry and IUFRO (Global Network for Forest Science Cooperation) 6.08.01 workshop, Umea, Sweden, June 17–21.

UNFCCC (United Nations Framework Convention on Climate Change). 2006. "Background Paper for the Workshop on Reducing Emission from Deforestation in Developing Countries." Working Paper 1 (a), August 17.

World Bank. 2007. *The World Bank Forest Strategy: Review of Implementation.* Washington, DC: World Bank.

WEB SITES

FAO Forestry: www.fao.org/forestry/en.

FAO Forestry and Climate Change: www.fao.org/forestry/site/35955/en.

FAO Gender and Development Plan of Action 2002–2007: ftp://ftp.fao.org/sd/GADPoA-Factsheet-EN-Final.doc.

FAO Gender and Food Security (Forestry): www.fao.org/GEnder/en/fore-e.htm.

International Fund for Agricultural Development Environment and Natural Resource Management: "Rural Poverty Knowledge Base—A Learning Note": www.ifad.org/rural/learningnotes/pat/4.htm.

PROFOR (World Bank Programme for Forests): www.profor.info/content/livelihood_poverty.html.

World Bank Forestry, key topics: http://web.worldbank.org/WBSITE/EXTERNAL/TOPICS/EXTARD/EXTFORESTS/0,,contentMDK:20628545~menuPK:1605788~pagePK:148956~piPK:216618~theSitePK:985785,00.html.

World Bank Gender and Rural Development Groups Community of Practice: http://web.worldbank.org/WBSITE/EXTERNAL/TOPICS/EXTARD/0,,contentMDK:20445312~menuPK:336688~pagePK:148956~piPK:216618~theSitePK:336682,00.html.

Thematic Note I

GENERAL

Durst, Patrick B., Chris Brown, Henrylito D. Tacio, and Miyuki Ishikawa, eds. 2005. "In Search of Excellence. Exemplary Forest Management in Asia and the Pacific." RAP Publication 2005/02, Asia Pacific Forestry Commission, Bangkok.

Feldstein, Hilary S., and Janice Jiggins, eds. 1994. *Tools for the Field: Methodologies Handbook for Gender Analysis in Agriculture.* West Hartford, CT: Kumarian Press.

Food and Agriculture Organization (FAO). 2007. *State of the Worlds Forests.* Rome: FAO.

FORESTS AND POVERTY ALLEVIATION

Baumann, Pari. 2006. "Forestry-Poverty Linkages in West and Central Asia: The Outlook from a Sustainable Livelihoods Perspective." FAO Livelihood Support Programme Working Paper 34, Food and Agriculture Organization, Rome.

Food and Agriculture Organization (FAO). 2006. "Better Forestry, Less Poverty: A Practitioner's Guide." FAO Forestry Paper 149, FAO, Rome.

———. 2006. "Methodology and Case Studies on Linkages Between Poverty and Forestry: Afghanistan, Iran, Kyrgyzstan and Turkey." FAO Livelihoods Support Programme Working Paper 35, Access to Natural Resources Subprogramme, FAO, Rome.

PROFOR (Program on Forests). n.d. *Forests-Poverty Linkages Toolkit.* PROFOR www.profor.info/content/livelihood_poverty.html.

Regional Community Forestry Training Center for Asia and the Pacific. 2007. "Poverty Reduction and Forests. Tenure, Markets and Policy Reforms." Proceedings of Conference, Bangkok, September 3–7, http://recoftc.org/site/index.php?id=445.

Shepherd, Gill. 2006. "A Quick New Way of Assessing the Forest Dependence of the Poor: The PROFOR Forests—Poverty Toolkit." Developed by ODI, IUCN, CIFOR, and Winrock In Regional Community Forestry Training Center for Asia and the Pacific (RECOFTC). 2007. "Poverty Reduction and Forests. Tenure, Markets and Policy Reforms." Proceedings of Conference, Bangkok, September 3–7, http://recoftc.org/site/index.php?id=445.

FORESTS, GENDER, AND LIVELIHOODS

Food and Agriculture Organization (FAO). 1989. "Household Food Security and Forestry: An Analysis of Socio-Economic Issues." FAO Technical Report, FAO, Rome.

———. 1990. "The Major Significance of 'Minor' Forest Products: The Local Use and Value of Forests in the West African Humid Forest Zone." Community Forestry Note 6, FAO, Rome.

Wilde, Vicki, and Arja Vaino-Mattila. 1995. *Gender Analysis and Forestry.* International Training Package. Rome: Food and Agriculture Organization.

FORESTS AND HIV AND AIDS

Barany, Marc, Christine Holding-Anyonge, Dennis Kayambazinthu, and Almeida Sitoe. 2005. "Firewood, Food and Medicine: Interactions between Forests, Vulnerability and Rural Responses to HIV/AIDs." In Proceedings from the IFPRI Conference: HIV/AIDS and Food and Nutrition Security, Durban, South Africa, April 14–16.

European Tropical Forest Research Network (ETFRN). 2005. "HIV/AIDS and National Forest Programmes." *ETFRN News* 41–42 (autumn 2004): 40–42. Wageningen: ETFRN.

Food and Agriculture Organization (FAO). 2005. "Miombo Woodlands and HIV/AIDS Interactions—Mozambique Country Report." Forest Policy and Institutions Working Paper No. 2, FAO, Rome.

FORESTS AND CONFLICTS

European Tropical Forest Research Network. 2007. "Forests and Conflicts." *ETFRN News* 43/44, www.etfrn.org/ ETFRN/sdfc/background/newsletter_articles.htm.

FORESTS, SOCIAL LEARNING, AND ADAPTIVE
COLLABORATIVE MANAGEMENT

Buck, Louise, Eva Wollenberg, and David Edmunds. 2001. "Social Learning in the Collaborative Management of Community Forests: Lesson from the Field." In *Social Learning in Community Forests,* ed. Eva Wollenberg, David Edmunds, Louise E. Buck, Jeff Fox, and Sonja Brodt. Bogor, Indonesia: Center for International Forestry Research.

Herline Hartanto, Ma, Cristina Lorenzo, Cecil Valmores, Lani Arda-Minas, Erlinda M. Burton, and Ravi Prabu. 2003. *Learning Together: Responding to Change and Complexity to Improve Community Forests in the Philippines.* Bogor, Indonesia: CIFOR.

Wollenberg, Eva, David Edmunds, Louise E. Buck, Jeff Fox, and Sonja Brodt. 2001. *Social Learning in Community Forests.* Bogor, Indonesia: CIFOR.

FORESTS, WOOD ENERGY, AND POVERTY

Food and Agriculture Organization (FAO). 1990. "Guidelines for Planning, Monitoring and Evaluating Cook Stove Programmes." Community Forestry Field Manual 1, FAO, Rome.

———. 2005. "WISDOM—East Africa. Wood fuel Integrated Supply/Demand Overview Mapping (WISDOM) Methodology. Spatial Wood Fuel Production and Consumption Analysis of Selected African Countries." Consultant Report, Forestry Department, Wood Energy, FAO, Rome.

———. 2007. "Wood Energy Supply/Demand Scenarios in the Context of Poverty Mapping. A WISDOM Case Study in Southeast Asia for the Years 2000 and 2015." Environment and Natural Resources Working Paper No. 27, FAO, Rome.

NWFP/NTFPS, LIVELIHOODS, AND POVERTY

Neumann, Roderick P., and Eric Hirsch. 2000. "Commercialisation of Non-Timber Forest Products: Review and Analysis of Research." Bogor, Indonesia: Center for International Forestry Research.

Townson, Ian M. 2005. "Forest Products and Household Incomes. A Review and Annotated Bibliography." Oxford

Forestry Institute. Tropical Forestry Papers 31, CIFOR and OFI, Oxford, U.K.

Wollenberg, Eva, and Andrew Ingles, eds. 1999. "Incomes from the Forest: Methods for the Development and Conservation for Forest Products for Local Communities." Bogor, Indonesia: CIFOR.

Thematic Note 2

Centro Agronomico Tropical de Investigacion y Enseñanza (CATIE). n.d. "Environmental Services in Coffee in Central America, East Africa and India." Available at www.catie.ac.cr.

Dawson, Ian, and James Were. 1997. "Collecting Germplasm from Trees—Some Guidelines." *Agroforestry Today* 9 (2): 6–9.

Food and Agriculture Organization (FAO). 1999. "Sri Lankan Women and Men as Bioresource Managers." RAP Publication 1999/45, FAO, Bangkok.

Franzel, Steven, Peter Cooper, Glenn Denning, and Deborah Eade, eds. 2002. *Development and Agroforestry: Scaling Up the Impacts of Research.* Oxford: Oxfam.

Gladwin, Christina H., Jennifer S. Peterson, Donald Phiri, Robert Uttaro, and Deirdre Williams. 2002. "Agroforestry Adoption Decisions, Structural Adjustment, and Gender in Africa." In *Natural Resource Management in African Agriculture: Understanding and Improving Current Practices,* ed. Christopher B. Barrett, Frank Place, and Abdillahi A. Aboud. London: CAB International.

Kindt Roeland, Jens-Peter Barnekow Lillesø, Anne Mbora, Jonathan Muriuki, Charles Wambugu, Will Frost, Jan Beniest, Anand Aithal, Janet Awimbo, Sheila Rao, and Christine Holding-Anyonge. 2006. *Tree Seeds for Farmers: a Toolkit and Reference Source.* Nairobi: World Agroforestry Centre (ICRAF).

Kitalyi, Aichi, David M. Miano, Sandra Mwebaze, and Charles Wambugu. 2005. "More Forage, More Milk. Forage Production for Small-scale Zero Grazing Systems." RELMA Technical Handbook 33, Nairobi.

Mercer, D. Evan. 2004. "Adoption of Agroforestry Innovations in the Tropics: A Review." *Agroforestry Systems* 61: 311–28.

Nair, P. K. Ramchandran, M. R. Rao, and Louise E. Buck, eds. 2004. *New Vistas in Agroforestry. A Compendium for the 1st World Congress of Agroforestry.* Dordrecht: Kluwer Academic.

Padmanabhan, Marina Aruna. 2005. "Institutional Innovations Towards Gender Equity in Agrobiodiversity Management: Collective Action in Kerala, South India." CGIAR Systemwide Program on Collective Action and Property Rights (CAPRI) Working Paper

No. 39, International Food Policy Research Institute, Washington, DC.

Verchot, Louis V., Meine Van Noordwijk, Serigne Kandji, Tom Tomich, Chin Ong, Alain Albrecht, Jens Mackensen, Cynthia Bantilan, K. V. Anupama, and Cheryl Palm. 2007. "Climate Change: Linking Adaptation and Mitigation through Agroforestry." *Mitigation and Adaptation Strategies for Global Change* 12 (5): 901–18.

WEB SITES

Trees, Agroforestry and Climate Change in Dryland Africa (TACCDA), Hyytiala, Finland, June 30–July 4, 2003: www.etfrn.org/etfrn/workshop/degradedlands/docu ments/TACsynthol5d.pdf.

World Agroforestry Centre and Climate Change: www. worldagroforestry.org/es/climate_change.asp.

Gender Issues in Monitoring and Evaluation

Overview

Common sense tells us that if we do not consciously attempt to measure our progress in life, we will not know whether we have achieved our planned impact—in other words, "what gets measured, gets managed." Given the enormous amounts of money invested in agricultural and rural development by national governments and international donors, monitoring and evaluation (M&E) are accepted as important steps for assessing progress toward specific outcomes and for measuring impact. Although gender and social equity are commonly discussed priorities in agricultural and rural development, little progress has been made in measuring outcomes in these areas. This Module aims to address gender concerns in designing agricultural and rural development projects and to provide ideas for improving the M&E of outcomes and impacts. It addresses the question, "How will my agriculture projects improve if I *track and measure* gender?"

REASONS WE SHOULD MONITOR GENDER

Gender must be addressed in ongoing monitoring and in evaluations for the same reasons we address other issues: in assessing whether an activity is achieving its objectives, we can consider what has been accomplished and what can be learned and fed back into further efforts. Gender is a cross-cutting issue within the development policies of most international donors and national governments. If gender impacts are not evaluated, they are unlikely to be given any attention.

What role do different genders play in agriculture, rural development, and water management? Women are the key agricultural workers in some countries but are not involved at all in others. In many southern African countries, women provide most of the labor for agriculture and small livestock production, yet in many cases they receive little benefit. In Asia different tasks in the agricultural cycle are carried out by men or women. In most countries, large livestock such as cattle are managed by men, although milking may be done by women. Roles (and relative power) in production, processing, and marketing differ by gender—for example, men commonly catch fish and women process or sell them locally. Gender power relations, therefore, lie at the heart of two critical development concerns: who gains access to resources, and who benefits from projects?

When carrying out M&E, the overarching notion of "gender" must be unpacked to reveal the differences within categories of "men" and "women," as neither men nor women form a homogeneous group. Participatory rural appraisal and gender analysis during planning should provide information on different subgroups of men and women and help design appropriate activities and indicators. For instance, in an environmental administration project in Nepal, an assessment of gender and poverty issues related to industry was done to provide a baseline and better understand the impacts of planned activities on different groups (disaggregated by ethnicity, caste, education, employment, rural or urban location, and other characteristics). M&E should provide feedback on how a program's various activities affect different subgroups of men and women. Any disparities in the distribution of benefits must be known for corrective action to be taken.

Women are active in community decision making in some countries, through councils and church groups (for instance, in the Pacific), whereas elsewhere they are almost invisible to outsiders (such as in remote areas of Afghanistan or Nepal). On the other hand, women may have little time for such activities because of their concurrent involvement in household activities and their heavy agricultural work. Such commitments only add to the time constraint when planning for M&E and the inclusion of women in a given program, project, or activity. Box 16.1 lists tools for gender-sensitive monitoring, which is discussed at greater length in all of the Thematic Notes.

Box 16.1   A Selection of Methods and Tools Available for Gender-Sensitive Monitoring

- Monitoring can be based on *quantitative* measures, such as data issued by statistics offices or specifically collected by project staff.
- *Qualitative* monitoring can be done through tools such as interviews, observation, and focus groups.
- *Participation of intended beneficiaries in monitoring* is a means to ensure ownership and to ensure that an activity is truly benefiting the participants.
- *Participatory monitoring*, on the other hand, is a means of involving stakeholders from the start in such activities as identifying activities and indicators that should be monitored, carrying out the monitoring itself, and analyzing the results for improving future processes.
- *External monitoring or evaluation* provides independent, external feedback on progress and outcomes.
- *Impact evaluations* determine whether a program had the desired effects and whether there were any unanticipated effects.
- *Gender audits* are distinct from regular evaluations in that they are based on self-assessments by a project, organization, or ministry of how gender issues are addressed in program portfolios and internal organizational processes. A gender audit is not an external evaluation, but it should be used to facilitate change and develop action plans and monitoring systems.

Source: Author.

"Monitoring" has been defined as the "continuous assessment of project implementation in relation to agreed schedules and use of inputs, infrastructure, and services by project beneficiaries," and "evaluation" has been defined as the "periodic assessment of the relevance, performance, efficiency, and impact (expected and unexpected) of the project in relation to stated objectives" (World Bank n.d.). M&E are broadly viewed as a function of project management that is useful for validating ex ante analysis or for influencing adjustments to project implementation.

Traditionally many donors used the logical framework ("logframe") as the basis for designing M&E. In 2003 the World Bank began using a "results framework" (a simplified logframe) in an effort to focus more on the immediate results of programs and projects. Practitioners now need to link performance with outcomes, with rigorous and credible assessments of progress toward (and achievement of) outcomes. At the "Activity" level in the results framework, "Output Indicators" are used to monitor progress. At the level of "Project Development Objective" and "Components/Results," "Outcome Indicators" are developed. "Outcomes" reflect the quality of outputs produced and behavioral changes in target groups, as well as changes in institutional performance following "adoption" of project outputs. However, to look at the long-term sustainability of a program, the overall development goal should also be considered, and for this purpose the logical framework remains important. Progress toward higher-level goals can be considered in evaluations by developing higher-level "Impact Indicators" (FAO 2001). This topic is discussed in more detail in Thematic Note 1.

INTEGRATING GENDER IN M&E: LESSONS FROM EXPERIENCE

Many donors have observed that project monitoring, evaluation, and reporting commonly focus on processes and inputs rather than outcomes and impacts, with the result that only limited learning is gained about any long-term changes a project may have occasioned in people's lives, including any impacts on gender equity. In fact, M&E *of any kind* are given insufficient attention. For example, a Sustainable Agriculture Systems, Knowledge, and Institutions (SASKI) Thematic Group review of agricultural research and extension projects found that only about 25 percent had adequate M&E plans (cited in World Bank 2006b).

Gender-sensitive monitoring garners even less attention, despite efforts by many donors to promote it and train people to do it (box 16.2). In cases where gender-sensitive indicators

An assessment of project evaluations for the Swedish International Development Cooperation Agency (SIDA) (Peck 1998) probably still applies to most donors. Although 65 percent of the SIDA evaluations conducted during 1997–98 mentioned gender, the quality of analysis was poor. Gender was usually discussed briefly, most often with respect to implementation and not to project objectives or results. Rarely was any link made between an intervention and possible changes that may have occurred in gender relationships and the circumstances of the men and women who were the intended beneficiaries. Most projects lacked gender-disaggregated baseline and monitoring data.

A recent review of development cooperation agencies (OECD 2007) found that only 41 percent used gender-sensitive logframes and noted that agencies that had "come more recently to gender and development" had "yet to develop as full a range of monitoring and accountability mechanisms." On the positive side, however, 70 percent of the agencies surveyed said they used gender criteria for assessing project/program quality.

AusAID (2002) noted that the degree to which gender is monitored in AusAID-funded activities appears to be influenced by the following:

- The extent to which gender is specified in the design documents, logframes, or gender strategies
- The interest of program staff in gender principles and the extent to which they have a sound understanding of the importance of achieving gender and development outcomes
- The degree to which gender issues and strategies have been articulated in the program, regional, or sector strategy.

Several World Bank reports emphasize that weak gender-disaggregated M&E systems in rural projects have been a serious concern. In 2006, for instance, only a third of rural projects had gender-disaggregated M&E indicators (GENRD 2006, 2007)

Sources: Author, based on AusAID 2002; GENRD 2006, 2007; OECD 2007.

do exist, they are more commonly found at the output and outcome level and only rarely at the impact level. Consequently, any assessments tend to be subjective.

Why gender disaggregation is often missing from M&E systems

The Nordic Development Fund's *Gender Equality Study* (NDF 2004) found, "The most commonly cited... major obstacles to women participating and benefiting from development activities include (i) the lack of participation by women in design; (ii) poorly conducted needs analyses; (iii) the lack of baseline data on key gender differences relevant to the specific project; (iv) the failure to address gender issues in project objectives; and, (v) poor monitoring efforts" (NDF 2004: 27).

Even when gender is emphasized at the project design stage, it is sometimes lost in the daily grind of project implementation. The continued collection of gender-specific data (or all monitoring data) can suffer as a result of various difficulties, mainly arising from the lack of time and funds, insufficient follow-up, and poor understanding by local staff of the importance of monitoring. Day-to-day monitoring usually concentrates on project result areas rather than crosscutting issues such as gender, and staff may give gender-specific monitoring insufficient attention.

In summary, gender is insufficiently considered in M&E for several reasons, including the following:

- M&E itself is given insufficient attention, and its usefulness is little understood. Often it is regarded as a task required by the donor, so the step of gender disaggregation is considered an addition to an already burdensome task.
- The leadership of agricultural and water projects and programs may be gender blind. Program managers and staff may not see gender as having any importance in achieving the program's results or its ultimate purpose.
- Field staff may view the work of M&E as gender neutral. Women's opinions may not be recorded, because women are often not present in meetings or are not confident to speak up (particularly if their native language is an indigenous one).

- Gender-disaggregated quantitative data are not easily available from local government sources but must often be collected separately for a program or project, which can be costly and time consuming. By the time a project is under way and attention is turned to M&E, it may be too late to conduct a project-specific baseline study, which ideally is done before the work begins.
- If gender has not been considered at the program design stage, it may be forgotten during implementation. Inclusion of gender-sensitive indicators in the logical framework or results framework is vital.
- Program implementers may consider that national women's unions or other groups that advocate on behalf of women are "taking care of the women's issues," even at the local level, so there is no need to monitor gender.
- External project supervisors and evaluators do not emphasize gender, so it is "forgotten."

Despite this tendency for gender to remain invisible, unacknowledged, or marginalized, much evidence suggests that gender is important to outcomes, and M&E plays a vital role in demonstrating these benefits. For instance, Bamberger (2002) used gender-disaggregated data from borrowers and nonborrowers to demonstrate that the impacts of microcredit in Bangladesh differ substantially based on whether the borrower is a woman or a man and that the marginal impacts of borrowing are often greater for women than men. Such information is vital to building the case for considering gender in rural development programs.

Recent attempts to change gender M&E

A number of recent efforts increase the prospects that gender will be incorporated more explicitly in M&E. The FAO and other United Nations agencies have undertaken to improve the availability of gender-disaggregated data (FAO 2003). Through these data, a much clearer picture should emerge of the relationships between gender inequality and agriculture, rural development, and food security.

At the project and program levels, numerous training materials, toolkits, and guidelines can help in implementing gender-sensitive M&E. Most key donors have prepared guidelines for gender mainstreaming. The OECD's guidelines "support partner efforts to formulate clear, measurable goals and expected results relating to gender equity and women's empowerment (focusing on development impacts,

not just the completion of activities)" (OECD 1999: 24). The guidelines indicate that it is vital to "support partner capacity to monitor and evaluate results achievement in projects, programs, and institutions and to understand the reasons for success or failure." SIDA's evaluation guidelines (SIDA 2004) contain a good section on gender in evaluations, covering preparation, fieldwork, reporting, and dissemination and use. The World Bank's short toolkit, *Gender Issues in Monitoring and Evaluation of Rural Development Projects* (World Bank 2005), presents excellent, simple—and unfortunately underused—guidelines. The most recent report on annual progress toward implementing the World Bank's gender-mainstreaming strategy (World Bank 2006a) urges the Bank to "improve the monitoring and impact evaluation of gender integration into Bank policy and project lending," by investing in gathering statistics disaggregated by gender, developing indicators to measure results and impacts with respect to gender, and ensuring that gender is included "as an independent variable in scientific evaluations of the development impact of Bank operations."

Incentives: ensuring that it happens in practice

Ideally, sufficient training in the purpose and objectives of gender-sensitive monitoring would ensure that the time, funds, and human resources are committed to performing this task and that the results are used. Usually all stakeholders agree in planning meetings and program documents that gender is important and that the gender impacts of a given project should be monitored carefully. Experience has revealed, however, that both a carrot and stick may be needed for gender-sensitive M&E to occur in practice.

External evaluators or donor agency staff can follow up on the issue during monitoring visits: for example, perhaps even requiring compliance with a plan for monitoring gender (box 16.3). The performance evaluations of technical advisers, project staff, or departmental staff might usefully include an assessment of compliance with the gender-monitoring plan. Providing publicity or presenting an award might also offer some incentive to individuals, projects, programs, or government ministries that take very positive action to promote successful gender monitoring. Gender could also be included in the milestones or triggers for annual budget or loan tranche releases (for instance, "Government has recruited new extension staff to reach a minimum of 30 percent women agricultural extension workers in at least 80 percent of districts by March 2008").

One means of ensuring that more attention is given to monitoring and evaluating a project's gender-equity outcomes is to require compliance with a Gender Action Plan. A good example comes from a project implemented by the Asian Development Bank (ADB) in Cambodia: the Northwestern Rural Development Project (Hunt and Kheng 2006). When the loan was designed, a high-quality Gender Action Plan was prepared, stipulating that three requirements had to be met for tranche releases to occur: (1) equal opportunity for employing women in road construction; (2) the involvement of women in prioritizing, planning, implementing, and monitoring village-based infrastructure; and (3) women's participation in training and community-based organizations to reach at least 30 percent.

The plan was based on systematic gender analysis, with targets and strategies for women's participation in each component. An assessment of the results showed that Gender Action Plans "provided a road map for project teams to ensure that women participated and benefited from project activities." Compared with another ADB project in Cambodia, the Northwestern Rural Development Project (with its high-quality Gender Action Plan) was shown to have positive results with respect to gender equity. However, the monitoring of participation and benefits still needed to improve, especially with regard to the collection, reporting, and analysis of gender-disaggregated data. The number of gender-sensitive indicators and strategies was not sufficient, and insufficient information was collected to analyze women's participation, benefits, and progress toward gender equity. Although the loan covenants used in this project were useful for improving compliance with gender-sensitive monitoring requirements, greater leadership, commitment, and ownership of the Gender Action Plan were needed.

Source: Hunt and Kheng 2006.

QUESTIONS TO CONSIDER IN DESIGNING A GENDER-SENSITIVE M&E COMPONENT

Several questions emerge in designing a gender-sensitive M&E component for a project or program. Which levels of participants—spanning the range from donors and recipient governments to management and field implementation—are involved? Which instruments are therefore involved? Should gender be mainstreamed across the institution and all parts of the program, or should there be a specific gender component? How much participatory involvement is appropriate, and what must be remembered when scaling up programs to the national level or moving to newer aid modalities? Is the focus on short-term outcomes or longer-term impacts? How will findings and experiences be shared?

Levels of participants that need to consider gender in project design and M&E

To make it more likely that gender is considered in project design, monitoring, and evaluation, which participants need to consider which issues or actions?

■ *At the management level of the donor agency, implementing ministry, program, or project,* participants should be involved in setting the indicators at the objective level, providing access to statistical data, and dedicating the staff, budget, and tools to ensure that gender-sensitive monitoring can be done.

■ *At various levels within the implementing organization*—specifically, among the staff responsible for the horizontal and vertical coordination of operations and gender-specific and M&E components—participants should be involved in coordinating the work and setting indicators for different components, ensuring that gender is considered. The terms of reference for all staff working on different activities need to assign responsibility for achieving gender objectives, strategies, and outcomes.

■ *At the field level,* participants need to ensure that access to budget, materials, and equipment is considered, as well as timing. For example, the opinions of women and men may not be considered fully during monitoring if meetings to collect their opinions are scheduled when most women are working in the fields, when women are preparing the evening meal for their families, or when most men are out at sea fishing. Extra funds may be required to ensure that monitoring activities can take place at appropriate locations and times.

Mainstreaming versus establishing separate gender components

Gender can be considered as a specific result area or component and monitored as such. This traditional method of treating gender has been used in many projects and is still used in some poverty reduction strategy programs (PRSPs) and other programmatic instruments. Often, however, this approach meant that gender was ignored by many project or program staff and stakeholders, as it was considered "taken care of." As an assessment of development cooperation funded by Finland reports, "Women are sometimes still seen as a separate sector so systematic work to eliminate gender inequalities is not undertaken within other sectors ... In projects 'gender mainstreaming' still usually means small and isolated components dealing with women" (MFA Finland 2003: 11).

Gender mainstreaming across all result areas and activities is now the preferred means of ensuring that gender is considered. "Gender mainstreaming" can be defined as "a commitment to ensure that women's as well as men's concerns and experiences are integral to the design, implementation, monitoring, and evaluation of all legislation, policies, and programs so that women and men benefit equally and inequality is not

perpetuated" (Derbyshire 2002: 9). The drawbacks of this approach are that the impact may be lost, outcomes are much harder to measure, and financial resource allocation by gender becomes increasingly difficult to track (box 16.4). Superficial mainstreaming—in which women are simply mentioned in every project component, or in which gender-differentiated data are collected but not analyzed for program improvements—is also unfortunately too common.

It is important to gain baseline information to ensure that project or program activities do not increase problems in target communities, such as gender-based violence. Gender-mainstreaming activities tend to change gender roles and relations. Unless change proceeds carefully and with adequate awareness raising, domestic violence may arise or worsen as men come to perceive that women's increased empowerment threatens their position as men and heads of the household and community.

How successful has mainstreaming been, and how can we do things differently? Assessments that look at women's participation or benefits derived by women in isolation from the overall project context may be inadequate and misleading. Comparisons between women and men in the target group should be made across every project activity and component,

---

Box 16.4 Mainstreaming Gender and the Implications for Monitoring and Evaluation

The Development Assistance Committee of the Organisation for Economic Co-operation and Development considers that gender should be integral to all development assistance analyses that are undertaken. Steps to carry out gender mainstreaming include the following:

- Ensure that guides and procedural manuals incorporate gender-equity considerations into the methods to be followed by staff, with priority given to promoting gender analysis at the initial stages of the planning process.
- Ensure that the gender-equity objective is reflected in the development of procedures for results-based management, including the specification of results sought, indicators for monitoring achievements, and evaluation criteria.
- Ensure that gender equity and women's empowerment measures and indicators are part of the main-

stream reporting structure and evaluation processes rather than a separate system.
- Develop and maintain statistical systems and project monitoring systems that provide gender-disaggregated data.
- Ensure that gender equity is addressed in all training and staff development initiatives.

Gender mainstreaming should be considered at all levels:

- At the project level, by designing appropriate gender-sensitive indicators for monitoring and by considering gender at all stages of the project cycle, including reporting
- At the program and policy levels, by carrying out gender evaluations and using the results to guide further activities, through checklists and scorecards
- In multilateral and bilateral development organizations, nongovernmental organizations, and government organizations, by carrying out gender audits and self-assessments of their own organizations.

Source: Mason 2007.

and the conclusions about benefits or outcomes should be supported by data and analysis. A risk exists in external evaluations that gender is considered only as a separate chapter, unless the terms of reference explicitly state otherwise.

It is also important that mainstreaming be understood to have the goal of *increasing gender equity,* not simply increasing women's involvement. Increasing women's participation in committees or in monitoring teams is *not* mainstreaming if women are not actively involved in improved gender outcomes and impacts (the extra burden on rural women's limited free time should always be considered). At every step, questions must be asked as to who will benefit from proposed activities. If "policy evaporation" occurs—that is, good policy is not followed through in practice—then gender mainstreaming may not have a real impact on gender equity. Moreover, the real impact may not seen because M&E procedures fail to document what is occurring on the ground.

Box 16.5 presents two ways of treating gender at the national level in PRSPs. One is from Mozambique (where it is compartmentalized) and the other from Vietnam (where it is mainstreamed).

The U.K. Department for International Development (DFID) has chosen to pursue a twin track in which it mainstreams gender by integrating women's and men's concerns in all policies and projects and supports specific activities aimed at empowering women. It may be useful to monitor a targeted output specifically concerned with activities for women, alongside overall mainstreaming (considering outputs for men and women in every activity and result area), in the hope that gender outcomes will improve. It is imperative, however, not to isolate women's activities within one output with a very small claim on resources and no influence on the rest of the policy or project.

Using gender analysis for monitoring

Gender analysis considers women's roles in production, reproduction, and the management of community and other activities. Changes in one aspect of women's lives may produce beneficial or detrimental effects in others. Gender analysis helps to (1) identify gender-based differences in access to resources to predict how different members of households, groups, and societies will participate in and be affected by planned development interventions; (2) permit planners to achieve the goals of effectiveness, efficiency, equity, and empowerment through designing

---

Box 16.5   Compartmentalization versus Mainstreaming of Gender in Poverty Reduction Strategy Programs

Mozambique's second Action Plan for the Reduction of Absolute Poverty—known by its Portuguese acronym, PARPA—treats gender as a separate component. Unfortunately this compartmentalization seems to have led those working on the strategy to believe that they did not need to consider gender outside the gender chapter. Gender is not considered in analyzing the causes of poverty in Mozambique, nor is women's role in economic growth mentioned. The indicators for measuring progress toward development objectives make almost no mention of gender. The causes of gender inequality are not discussed, and few policy interventions are discussed for addressing inequality. National data on school attendance and early childhood growth always include gender, but any differences between boys and girls have vanished in the hands of the government authorities and committees producing the strategy. Gender is considered in the chapter on HIV and AIDS with regard to incidence and causes of infection, but when it comes to the targets and actions to be taken, no further mention is made of women as a key target group.

By contrast, Vietnam's *Comprehensive Poverty Reduction and Growth Strategy 2002* includes many aspects of gender in its analysis of the causes of poverty and mainstreams gender considerations throughout the document. A general instruction is given that monitoring should employ indicators "developed in detail by regions, provinces, rural/urban areas, and genders." Even so, crucial omissions are present. The chapter on targets makes almost no mention of gender—only in the paragraphs specifically on gender equity—and the general economic and social targets are not disaggregated by gender. The indicators provided for monitoring the development objectives do include some gender disaggregation, however, and efforts are being made to improve them.

Source: Author's assessment.

---

policy reform and supportive program strategies; and (3) develop training packages to sensitize development staff on gender issues and training strategies for beneficiaries, such as the World Bank's *Participation Sourcebook* (World Bank 1996).

Comprehensive gender studies are applied mostly in developing policy or planning programs and projects. Aspects of gender analysis may be applied, however, for intermittent monitoring of gender implications of project activities or outcomes. Simple techniques are useful for this purpose, such as direct observation, focus groups, and time-use studies (for example, women's typical daily routine in terms of housework, income generation, and personal time). Performed consistently as part of project M&E, gender analysis helps build a picture of women's growth as individuals and social beings (for instance, it can assess changes in their standing in the household and in the community). Five major categories of information are required for a comprehensive gender analysis: (1) needs assessment; (2) activity profile; (3) resources, access, and control profile; (4) benefits and incentives analysis; and (5) institutional constraints and opportunities (World Bank 1996).

In monitoring and evaluating any benefits arising from a project or program, the gender considerations include developing indicators that define and measure progress in achieving benefits for men and women, ensuring that gender-disaggregated data are collected to monitor impact with respect to gender, and considering ways of involving women in M&E (ADB n.d.).

Gender-disaggregated data and parameters should be included in M&E systems for all projects and presented in all reports. Gender analysis is vital throughout all stages of the program cycle, from identification and design to implementation, monitoring, and evaluation.

Impact assessments

Most monitoring focuses on short-term occurrences, whereas the great challenge is to measure long-term change—the impacts that extend beyond increases in women's participation or incomes during the life of a project or program and that indicate real changes in the lives of poor men and women over the following five or more years. Apart from the design and attribution difficulties, the fact remains that if a project or program has already finished, no one may remain to perform the evaluation, and financing for this activity may not be found. This difficulty is discussed further in Innovative Activity Profile 2 (available in the online version of this *Sourcebook*).

Improved information sharing

Most projects and programs collect much information regularly from staff and beneficiaries, but it is not always shared effectively. Much of it is fed into the management information system, which produces consolidated data and is used to report to government and donors. However, no point exists in collecting such information unless it is used to improve the program to benefit the people from whom it was collected. Different ways may be employed to interpret and use results to make decisions, modify or improve programming, and advocate to different audiences. Examples of changes in gender equity in a practical sense should be collected regularly through monitoring and shared with a wide range of stakeholders. Improved advocacy can have a very positive feedback effect on the project. For example, an agricultural project in South Africa focused on developing producer groups (particularly women-led groups). As part of its qualitative evaluation, the project collected stories and lessons emerging from this process. These were eventually published by a local agricultural magazine that was distributed beyond the original beneficiary groups and reached other departments of agriculture and farmers.

PARTICIPATORY TOOLS AND APPROACHES

The World Bank places considerable emphasis on participatory M&E, which is an important factor in promoting social sustainability. The Bank's *Social Analysis Sourcebook* (World Bank 2003a: 49) cites participatory M&E as a "means to systematically evaluate progress and impact early in the project cycle by bringing the perspectives and insights of all stakeholders, beneficiaries as well as project implementers. All stakeholders identify issues, conduct research, analyze findings, make recommendations, and take responsibility for necessary action." The focus is on the active engagement of primary stakeholders and their shared control of the content, process, and results of M&E. This kind of participation is particularly effective because stakeholders, if they are involved in identifying problems and solutions, develop ownership of the project and tend to be amenable if corrective actions eventually prove necessary. In other words, participation can be both a means and an end. Because they live with the results of a project, participants also have a greater incentive to make changes in project activities and base future interventions on the lessons they have learned. Transparency is enhanced because the intended beneficiaries are involved in making decisions from the start and understand the funding issues. Participatory M&E may also highlight unexpected or unplanned changes, which may not be noticed with traditional indicators and M&E systems. In a project in Vietnam, the gender-disaggregated results of interviews with village women through Most Significant Change monitoring allowed problems with the location of a new road to be raised and dealt with by management (World Bank 2007).

The cost implications (time, money, and other resources; box 16.6) and other considerations of participatory monitoring must be taken into account. For example, it must not be assumed that all women will automatically benefit from efforts to involve some women in project design, implementation, and M&E. Men's and women's groups do not always have the same priorities and understanding of impacts, nor are the opinions of all women the same. In addition, if women are expected to give up their time to participate in monitoring an intervention, a clear means should be present by which their opinions can be fed back into improving future activities. Consultation and true participation in decision making are different and should not be confused.

Participatory M&E can also be a useful tool to improve gender equity, if women are able to take an active role, meet in groups, and build solidarity and confidence (a good example is quoted from Pakistan's Community Infrastructure Project, World Bank 2003b). In many communities, only women can visit other families. Men may not be permitted to speak directly with women who are not family members, so men may not be able to gather essential information for M&E. What may be more difficult is for communities to meet in mixed-sex groups to monitor outcomes and openly discuss how to improve activities. Simple tools may be used to facilitate discussion—for instance, using different-colored voting cards for men and women or for different age or ethnic groups, and then comparing different opinions on topics—or holding separate meetings for different sexes, to prevent men from dominating.

SCALING UP INVESTMENTS

Scaling up of investments usually implies reaching a larger number of beneficiaries via increases in size, scope, and geographic spread of an activity. This has implications for the methods of financing, administering, and monitoring.

Box 16.6   The Cost Implications of Participatory Monitoring and Evaluation: Three Examples

How much participation is enough, and what are the costs of participation? Three projects funded by the World Bank offer insight into these questions. In the Andhra Pradesh Rural Poverty Reduction Project, the participation of more than 600,000 women's self-help groups, as well as a local nongovernmental organization, improved qualitative process monitoring and revealed unexpected outcomes, which made it possible to develop new indicators. Participatory monitoring also significantly reduced project costs: When women's groups identified poor credit recovery rates, they halted disbursement until the rates improved. In the North West Frontier Province of Pakistan Community Infrastructure Project, participatory monitoring of subprojects reduced the number of dropouts among community organizations, produced a cost savings of 40 percent, and increased the quality of work (compared to work done by government-hired contractors). In Mongolia, on the other hand, the full benefits of participatory monitoring in the Sustainable Livelihoods Project were inhibited by the sheer distances involved and the difficulty of holding community meetings. The cost of ensuring full participation—in transport and time—would have been enormous, so the level of participation was modified.

Sources: World Bank 2007 (for Andhra Pradesh), World Bank 2003c for Pakistan, and author for Mongolia (White 2007).

Local to national, project to program

When programs are scaled up in size, either sectorally or geographically, a need exists to scale up the monitoring. The focus on quantitative indicators tends to increase with scaling up, because qualitative measurements such as interviews and focus groups are more difficult to carry out, record, and analyze on a large scale (box 16.7). One example of this problem is the selection of indicators for monitoring global progress in achieving the United Nations Millennium Development Goals. Data on each indicator needed to be available from all countries and may not be too onerous to collect and compare.

Box 16.7   Some Difficulties with Scaling Up Monitoring

In its first phase, the Sustainable Livelihoods Project in Mongolia developed a participatory monitoring and evaluation system. The key issue was to find a balance between information required by the World Bank and the project's national office, and information that would be useful to the community and local project representatives. Planners also had to strike a balance between information that would be good to have and information that was essential. Clearly a risk was present of collecting too much information that would not improve participation. An additional consideration was that communication is very difficult in Mongolia because of the large distances and limited infrastructure and equipment. Although experiences with the initial monitoring and evaluation system were positive, scaling up to much greater national coverage in a later stage of the project has proven less successful and led to more direct monitoring by project staff.

Source: Author.

For large-scale programs, the gender disaggregation of quantitative data should be a basic requirement, even if the softer M&E tools need to be used less often. For instance, interviews and group work could take place in a few sample areas to supplement quantitative data from national monitoring. It is increasingly important for large-scale projects or programs to tie in with national census and living standards surveys rather than duplicate them.

Adapting to reduced international technical assistance inputs

As donors move toward funding larger-scale programs that rely more heavily on national systems and staff and less on specifically recruited international and national staff, local staff will need to build the capacity to incorporate gender considerations into their work. Possibilities for increasing this capacity include the following (OECD 1999):

- Use donor-level gender advisers to regularly support and mentor local gender focal points.
- Give priority to initiatives that focus on partners' capacity to analyze policies, programs, and institutional

cultures and develop change strategies that contribute to gender equity.
- Help partners examine the gender balance within their organizations and identify strategies to increase women's representation at policy- and decision-making levels.
- Increase the availability of gender-disaggregated data by supporting modifications in national and sectoral data collection systems.
- Support research on gender equity by sectoral institutions, research organizations, and advocacy groups to increase the national resources of partners in this area.

Monitoring gender in the new aid modalities

To date, little consideration has been given to gender in monitoring PRSPs, sectorwide approaches (SWAPs), and budget support. This issue is discussed further in Thematic Note 2. Although development cooperation is moving away from projects and toward new aid modalities, the following actions are still vital (OECD 1999):

- Strengthen links between the project and policy levels. Improved communication of lessons from the field can act as a reality check at the national level and ensure greater coherence among gender-equity policy objectives, project-supported activities, and the resulting impacts.
- Support partners' efforts to improve project-level monitoring and impact assessment and gain a greater understanding of how projects can contribute to gender-equity objectives, how obstacles can be overcome, and how project design can be improved.
- Analyze the comparative strengths and weaknesses of different interventions used in specific sectors to increase knowledge about strategies that have positive results and are cost effective.

Sample indicators for a range of agriculture and rural development investments

Although it is not possible to devise sample indicators to match every situation and intervention, sample indicators for output, outcome, and impact, as well as tools and proposed sources of verification, are provided for a range of topics in "Social and Environmental Sustainability of Agriculture and Rural Development Investments: A Monitoring and Evaluation Toolkit" (Punkari and others 2007).

CONCLUSION

Several issues emerge from this overview. Despite the fact that development interventions will be improved if we track and measure their implications with respect to gender, it is clear that M&E of gender issues has been done poorly recently, in projects as well as in the newer aid modalities. The following Thematic Notes focus on how to develop a sound M&E system and discuss other tools for supporting project or program staff, such as gender policies, terms of reference, and training (Thematic Note 1); the experience and tools related to monitoring gender in the newer aid modalities, such as PRSPs, SWAPs, and budget support (Thematic Note 2); and issues related to setting high-quality indicators and the collection and use of data (Thematic Note 3). Two Innovative Activity Profiles are also included, describing methods and practical examples of involving community members in monitoring (Innovative Activity Profile 1) and conducting impact assessments (Innovative Activity Profile 2), the latter in the online version of this *Sourcebook* (www.worldbank.org).

Design of Sound Gendered Monitoring and Evaluation Systems

Gender-sensitive M&E helps project staff, other stakeholders, and beneficiaries themselves to understand how project activities are really changing the lives of men and women. This kind of M&E enables continuous feedback on the status of project implementation, identifying specific problems as they arise. If additional disaggregation is done, monitoring can also follow the impact on young and old, ethnic minorities, people with disabilities, remote residents, and other disadvantaged groups. If the full range of stakeholders has this important information, they can use it to alter the project as needed to ensure maximum benefits and improve performance. The lessons learned by the end of the project can be used to improve project design, change legislation as needed, or change local systems.

Obviously, a well-designed M&E system is needed to carry out gender-sensitive monitoring, along with other supportive tools for staff of the project or program, such as gender policies, term of reference, and training. This Thematic Note discusses specific measures that should be used and offers practical examples of good and bad design.

BASIC STRUCTURES FOR MONITORING GENDER

Women are major players in agriculture and rural development. They are agricultural wage laborers as well as unpaid workers on family farms. Yet women, who form the majority of rural poor, are usually not given equal consideration when agricultural programs are planned, implemented, or monitored. If steps are taken to involve all groups, including women, in such programs, improvement will be seen both in project and program outcomes and in society as a whole. The consideration of gender and involvement of women in M&E can empower women. Every project should meet the following basic requirements:

- Ensure that guidelines and structures are present to support good gendered monitoring at national, local, and project levels.
- Ensure that the goals, purposes, or objectives of the program or project explicitly refer to gender or reflect women's needs and priorities as well as men's. Managers need to formulate clear, measurable objectives and indicators and link them with available annual information sources. M&E must be an integral part of project design, not added as an afterthought.
- Establish M&E mechanisms that will record and track gender differences, and collect baseline data.
- Measure benefits and adverse effects on men and women separately whenever possible, and check whether the needs and interests of women and men are still considered during implementation.
- Insist that project staff make specific and adequately detailed references to gender in supervision forms and project completion reports. Report any gender differences even when no mention was made of gender in project objectives.
- Ensure that staff members obtain the training and tools to understand gender and the reasons for monitoring.

This list applies both to the logical framework and the results framework. The results framework has the following structure: (1) a project development objective and project component statements, (2) indicators for the outcome of the project development objective and for intermediate component outcomes, and (3) an explicit statement on how to use the outcome information. The results framework focuses chiefly on managing the outcomes of project interventions and does not necessarily link into higher-level sectoral goals. However, the project document should describe how the project contributes to these higher-level objectives, including gender objectives, as well as outline project inputs, activities, outputs, and critical assumptions.

The application of a results-based framework may unduly emphasize quantitative indicators for project outcomes and outputs, thus limiting the representation of sustainability concerns in the project M&E framework. This limited representation argues for parallel use of the logical framework in project design to complement the results-based framework, so that the intended links between project outputs and outcomes (the project development objective) and project impacts (the development goal) can be well articulated (Punkari and others 2007).

In the logical framework, the overall objective should link gender outcomes at the project level to provincial or national priorities for a given sector to ensure that the project is not an isolated activity but part of the overall development process for the sector (box 16.8). Indicators at this level will measure change in the broad development goal to which the project contributes.

Qualitative as well as quantitative indicators and data are needed (these are discussed in more detail in Thematic Note 3). The inclusion of gender-sensitive indicators is not enough, however. It is important that there is a means to use the information gathered and to make changes if necessary to ensure that the outcomes will be equitable. Information

from lower-level indicators on inputs and outputs (such as the number of women trained) is useful but insufficient. It must be possible to analyze at the outcome level, for example, whether the training has led women to be empowered and use the training for greater agricultural production. Critical reviews of progress and readjustment should be undertaken, based on information on local constraints—usually the annual work planning stage or midterm review are good moments.

PRINCIPLES AND GUIDELINES FOR INVESTING IN GENDER-SENSITIVE M&E

Different activities are required at national (or international), local government, and project levels to implement gender-sensitive M&E.

National guidelines

Embassies, donor organization representatives, and national representatives should ensure that gender is considered at *all* stages of the planning, implementation, and M&E. National goals regarding the status and participation of women (for example, national gender strategies or specific

---

Box 16.8 Linking Gender Outcomes with the Overall Objective

The specific objective or purpose for a project could be:

To increase the efficiency and impact of existing livelihood, infrastructure, and administrative systems on poverty reduction, economic growth, and equity in project districts.

The corresponding indicators could be the following:

- Percentage of the population below the poverty line for income
- Number of district-commune roads (percentage of communes covered)
- Number of commune-village roads (percentage of villages covered)
- Percentage of households with secure land-use certificates in both husband's and wife's names
- Number of villages having access to reliable market information on relevant agricultural products
- Percentage of women, men, disabled, and minority groups represented in decision-making bodies

- Percentage of women, men, disabled, and minority groups represented in management bodies
- Seventy-five percent of surveyed community members rating their access to livelihood development services as having improved during the life of the project.

But the overall objective could be:

Enhanced, equitable, pro-poor growth in X Province

The corresponding indicators could be the following:

- Implementation of the project resulting in an improvement in living conditions for at least 75 percent of rural households
- The number of acutely poor households in project areas reduced by at least 25 percent by project end
- Percentage of women staff in management roles in provincial agricultural department increased
- Participatory approaches used in socioeconomic development planning by all departments.

Source: Author.

---

goals such as the percentage of women in management committees) must be integrated into project and program planning. Unfortunately, the experience to date is not good. For instance, evaluations of DFID's Country Strategy Papers note that they tend to see the whole community as poor and are less likely to differentiate specific subgroups that should be included in program activities. General statements that gender will be mainstreamed throughout the country program are insufficient unless specific guidance is given. In addition, international conventions and agreements must be observed, such as the United Nations Convention on the Elimination of All Forms of Discrimination against Women. These national representatives should ensure that quantitative and qualitative indicators to promote gender equity are included in project and program documents (logical or results framework), and gender training is included in project or program work plans. Appointing high-level professional women to gender positions in the ministry of agriculture and ensuring that they have the

training and resources to support gender promotion nationally are vital actions. Also, including ministry-level gender focal points in field visits to give them a good understanding of grassroots issues should be done. Examples of program- and policy-related questions that could be asked are given in box 16.9.

Local guidelines

Local authorities may need training; representatives of local government and civil society should be included in capacity-building efforts on gender and M&E. Their inclusion serves several purposes: it ensures that the work of the project or program is well understood, it provides a broader base of understanding about gender issues and monitoring, and it leads to a level of sustainability, by leaving behind a trained cohort to continue the work.

In addition, ways of accessing information, the aims of gender mainstreaming, and the benefits for agricultural

---

Box 16.9 Examples of Program- and Policy-Related Questions

- Do national legislation and policies support gender equity? For instance, in 2003 Vietnam passed a new Land Law, which requires the names of husband and wife to be included on all Land Tenure Certificates. This legislation was a big advance, but strong follow-up is needed to ensure that it is implemented at the local level.
- Are women's voices heard in planning and monitoring? Do representatives from women's unions, nongovernmental organizations, or other groups advocating on behalf of women participate in national committees? What is the gender of the decision makers as well as staff of the finance and agriculture ministries at the national level?
- Are there specific efforts to design and monitor gender-sensitive indicators in national agriculture, transport, and water programs?
- Has gender-disaggregated baseline information been collected prior to commencing program activities, in monitoring national progress toward the Millennium Development Goals, or for undertaking other tasks? Are gender-disaggregated data collected during monitoring. If so, how is this information analyzed, reported, and used to adjust plans?

- Do agricultural extension services reach women and men farmers equally, with information and services given at appropriate times and in culturally appropriate forms? For instance, theoretical training provided in the dominant national language at central locations is more likely to reach men than to reach women who are members of ethnic minorities, who might be the persons responsible for putting the training into practice.
- Are the different roles of women and men farmers considered when new seed, crops, or technologies are researched and developed? In central Vietnam, for example, a seemingly promising larger and stronger rice variety was developed with higher seedling survival and production rates, but it was not successful in farmers' fields. Women are mainly responsible for transplanting rice seedlings, and their larger size meant a heavier load for them. Purely quantitative monitoring would not have discovered why the new variety did not produce the expected higher yields. Qualitative techniques were vital in this case.
- Is agricultural credit equally available to women and men farmers? Usually the answer to this question is tied to the question of collateral: Do both women and men farmers have access to land?

Source: Author.

---

livelihoods all should be promoted in local media. The appointment of women to provincial and district departments should be encouraged.

Project guidelines

Ensure that gender perspectives are incorporated into the following documents and actions:

- *Terms of reference for all staff,* particularly M&E officers
- *Progress reports:* For all components of the project or program, report on progress by gender
- *Staff recruitment:* Encourage the recruitment of a gender-balanced staff, and if one group is particularly disadvantaged, consider recruiting a less-qualified person, but provide intensive training and support
- The subcontracting of local organizations
- Activity monitoring
- Briefings of team members
- Training
- Annual plans
- Project redesign or review
- Project steering and coordinating committee meetings
- Project completion report and ex post evaluation report
- Lessons-learned database, disaggregated by gender
- Project and program steering committees or other coordinating bodies that are monitoring the project, including representatives of women's organizations and gender-equity authorities (ideally as full members).

At the project level, the questions are more relevant to household equality issues:

- Who participates in meetings, planning, and implementation of activities at the community level? A simple gender disaggregation of the data on meeting participants will provide some information but will not give the full picture. Qualitative monitoring is needed to establish how actively different groups are participating.
- What is the division of labor in the household and community?
- Are there differences between men and women in the amounts of time spent on agricultural tasks, and who makes decisions about the time spent?
- Who makes decisions on planting, marketing, and consuming crops and using water for agricultural or domestic purposes?
- What are the patterns of food allocation (sharing, quantity, quality, and so forth) among family members?

Box 16.10 Kyrgyz Republic: Gender Perspectives Reflected in an Agricultural Development Project

At the design stage of an agricultural area development project in the Kyrgyz Republic, rural women were identified as a highly disadvantaged group. Particular attention was given to mainstreaming gender issues, and efforts were made to increase the project's inclusiveness. The monitoring and evaluation of benefits examined the project's effects with respect to gender, including women's ownership of land, their access to and membership in producer organizations, their participation in training and the types of training they were given, changes in women's incomes compared with men's, and the relative social position of women-headed households.

Source: Adapted by author from ADB Web site, www.adb.org, loan/TA case studies on gender.

Box 16.10 gives an example of how some of these perspectives might be incorporated into the design and monitoring of an agricultural development project.

Monitoring formats

When monitoring results, it can be useful to set out the expected results in a *who, what, when, where,* and *how* sense, as in table 16.1 (modified from UNDP 2002). A monitoring planning worksheet can add another level of detail and enable the entire system to be visualized easily (table 16.2).

GOOD PRACTICE: HOW TO INTEGRATE GENDER INTO MONITORING AND EVALUATION

Working through the following checklist is valuable when integrating gendered M&E, both in project planning stages and during implementation.

Stage 1— Identification and preparation:

- Ensure that the benchmark survey or baseline study is gender sensitive.
- Conduct an initial stocktaking: Who are the stakeholders? What are their activities? What is their capacity? What are their roles and needs?
- Undertake an initial gender study or analysis to identify the potential negative impacts of project intervention on women as well as men.

Table 16.1   Monitoring Formats

Type of result	What is measured	Indicators	Who is measuring	How is the information used
Impact	Effectiveness or results in terms of the effect of a combination of outcome activities that improve development. Conditions at a national level, disaggregated by gender.	Use of outcomes and sustained positive development change, such as the change in economic status of women in a district over a five-year period.	Senior donor agency management or government authorities. Usually information comes from an internal impact evaluation, midterm review, final or ex post evaluation, as well as joint reviews of donor and government staff.	Blocks to positive change can be identified—for instance, gender-sensitive legislation may be needed.
Outcome	Effectiveness, or results in terms of access, usage, and stakeholder satisfaction from goods and services generated by projects, programs, partners, and soft assistance, disaggregated by gender.	Use of outputs and sustained production of benefits—for example, the change in attitudes or understanding in a local area regarding women's access to land over a period, or the change in number of women beneficiaries accessing agricultural extension services.	Project and program management and staff and local authorities; information from quarterly and annual reports, discussions at the steering committee level, and visits by donors.	Outcomes are fed back into project or program design. Unexpected negative outcomes—such as an increase in domestic violence arising from changes in gender relationships in the household once the woman has more income—may indicate a need for training, awareness raising, or other adjustments.
Output	Effort or goods and services generated by projects and programs, disaggregated by gender.	Implementation of activities—for example, how many (what percentage) of beneficiaries, participants, or extension staff are women and their satisfaction levels with the project.	Project management and staff, by means of day-to-day monitoring and use of management information system to verify progress, as well as field visits and reports and information received from project management.	If there is an imbalance in the way that the means are being used, then the project or program activities can be redesigned to achieve more gender balance.

Source: Author, adapted from UNDP 2002.

- Identify gender-related goals and priorities based on available information and consultation with stakeholders. Conduct a gender-sensitive social analysis or assessment.
- Assess the institutional capacity for integrating gender into development activities.

Stage 2—Design and appraisal:

- Ensure that gender is integrated into goals and objectives, and set clear targets.

- Plan for developing capacity to address gender issues and to monitor and evaluate progress and outcomes.
- Set up an M&E system. Adopt and "engender" the logical framework or the results framework as included in the project appraisal document, design gender-sensitive indicators, and develop or select the "best" data collection methods. Decide how to organize reporting and feedback processes. Clearly identify who will collect and analyze information, who will receive it, and how it will be used to guide implementation.

Table 16.2 Sample Monitoring Planning Worksheet

		Planning worksheet							
		Data collection					Data analysis and use		
Project objective	**Indicators**	**Information sources**	**Baseline data needed**	**Who is involved**	**Tools and methods**	**How often needed**	**How often used**	**Who is involved**	**How information is to be used**	**Who gets information**
Cost-effective, gravity-fed upland irrigation projects functioning	Women make up at least one-third of membership of irrigation user management committees. Women and ethnic minorities participate actively in decision making on water use and production planning	Minutes; accounts of management committees	None if the committees are new	Project engineers, M&E officer	Observation of user group meetings; minutes of meetings	Four times each year	Four times each year, and especially annual report	M&E officer and project management unit	Fed into annual planning; disseminated in bulletins to beneficiaries	Project management; shared with all user groups

Source: Author.

Stage 3— Implementation:

- Develop capacity to integrate, monitor, and evaluate gender-related issues.
- Collect gender-sensitive data based on the selected indicators.
- Monitor progress against outcome targets set for the period under evaluation, and feed results back into the system to allow for midterm corrections.
- Assess progress and make corrections if needed to obtain expected gender-related outcomes.

Stage 4—Completion:

- Assess the outcomes and impact of gender integration in the overall context of the project.
- Assess outcomes and impact of project interventions on men and women.
- Include gender-differentiated results in reporting lessons learned from implementation.

INSTITUTIONAL STRUCTURES TO SUPPORT MAINSTREAMING GENDER VIA THE MONITORING SYSTEM

Ideally a gender specialist in the donor agency, Ministry, or project team can provide a range of supportive actions, but in lieu of this the following range of steps can be taken to support gender mainstreaming and improved M&E in projects and programs.

Situations when no gender specialist is on the team

Many programs, projects, or government departments have no gender expert. Although this situation might not be ideal, it does not mean that gender mainstreaming and gender-sensitive monitoring cannot happen. Ensuring that guidelines and toolkits are available (those from donors and national departments, and those specially designed for the program or project) and that skills development is a continuing effort is more important. Newly hired and existing staff need training in gender concepts and their application, and gender analysis training must be a regular feature of the staff development program. In addition, the steering committee and management team must take gender issues seriously and ensure both vertical and horizontal integration of a gender approach, including the setting of indicators and regular analysis of monitoring data and the project's

impacts on men and women participants. Ideally short-term inputs from a gender expert could be used to support a team in this situation.

Appointment of a *gender focal point* among staff can ensure that a trained person is available to answer questions, advise other staff, and prevent attention to gender from being lost in everyday work. This person does not need to be a gender expert but should have a good understanding of gender issues and monitoring. A 2007 survey found that 58 percent of projects supported by IFAD had a gender focal point. Of these, 40 percent worked exclusively on gender issues and 60 percent worked on gender in addition to other duties (IFAD 2007).

Job descriptions, responsibilities, and terms of reference

Gender mainstreaming should be an explicit requirement in all job descriptions, job responsibilities, and terms of reference for studies, consulting work, and training. Ideally, projects should aim for a gender balance among technical advisers and field staff, particularly those involved in M&E. A reasonable representation of women among project or program staff gives credibility when the project asks others to take gender into consideration. When employing staff, preference should be given to candidates who not only possess the necessary skills and experience but also have a good working knowledge of gender issues and an appropriate attitude.

Job descriptions of all project staff should include gender-related tasks such as the following:

- Participate in training to gain knowledge and skills, where necessary, to be able to mainstream gender.
- Actively support the inclusion of gender mainstreaming through adherence to the gender-mainstreaming guidelines in all project or program activities.

Specific job descriptions may also need modification to ensure that staff members consider gender in specific topics. For instance, the terms of reference of an agriculture program officer might include such tasks as the following

- Develop and introduce a sustainable extension service in crop husbandry (including plant protection) and forestry that is farmer-centered, market-oriented, and financially feasible; works in close cooperation with other extension agencies; *and meets the needs of both women and men.*

The job description of the M&E officer should also include gender-specific descriptions such as working in close cooperation with *x* staff to:

- Specify quantitative and qualitative indicators at the objective, purpose, result, and subresult levels *that are gender inclusive.*
- Carry out participatory M&E at the activity level and through qualitative evaluations on a regular basis, *ensuring the active participation of women and men, boys and girls, and disadvantaged groups.*
- Assist the project management team in carrying out a participatory rural appraisal, baseline surveys, and other fact-finding activities, *including appropriate gender analyses.*

Management contracts

If the project or program has management contracts with local partners, the requirement of gender mainstreaming should be made explicit. The project or program should support partners to access adequate technical assistance to help mainstream gender in programs and activities, as well as offer training for staff in partner organizations. The contracts should also require that gender considerations are included in monitoring and reporting.

Gender policies, guidelines, and action plans

To put gender-sensitive monitoring into practice in projects, gender policies and guidelines or action plans should be developed, including at least the following instructions to local and international staff:

- Mainstream the promotion of gender equity in all planning and budgeting of project activities and in progress reports. In the project planning exercises, ensure that the anticipated impacts on all groups are considered.
- Provide gender-specific objectives and indicators for the logical framework of the project or program document and annual work plans.
- Develop qualitative and quantitative indicators as measurements of gender-equity promotion at the activity level.
- Disaggregate data by gender in reports and in the information provided to all stakeholders.
- Ensure that project personnel receive gender training.
- Ensure that the project personnel are informed of, and understand, the partner country's national plan for promoting gender equity.

- Ensure that study visits and training opportunities made using project funds include equal numbers of women and men as much as possible.
- Bring up issues connected with promoting the status of women in visits to the field and hold discussions with both women and men workers and intended project beneficiaries.
- Always act in accordance with local laws as well as the gender policies of the donor. In their personal behavior, staff should try to promote the rights of women and men and more equal relations between them.

GENDER CHECKLIST

A gender checklist supports the planning, implementing, and M&E of projects and activities undertaken within a project or program to ensure that gender is mainstreamed and that the outcome is equality of participation and benefits for men and women. Box 16.11 provides key questions that may be asked during the design, implementation, monitoring, or evaluation stage.

Setting times for analysis and encouraging feedback

Clearly a midterm review is a crucial externally imposed time to assess progress and alter program or project activities as necessary. Annual planning should also be used as an opportunity to review what occurred over the last year and consider any differential gender impacts. Many societies have no tradition of giving realistic feedback, either positive or negative. It is likely that many in the community, particularly women and other disadvantaged groups (the very poor or those of low caste), feel constrained and reluctant to complain about problems with project activities. Even if community members report dissatisfaction with an activity, no follow-up discussion of the problem or action may be taken. Both the community and the project or local government authorities need to understand that criticism can be positive, in the sense that it can lead to improvements in the future. Follow-up training and case studies (small-scale gender analyses) of gender impacts may be useful to refresh the minds of staff and potential beneficiaries about the importance of the issue.

Management information system design and use and reporting

The management information system (MIS) devised for the program or project should integrate information flows

General questions:

- Does the project involve most stakeholders in monitoring and evaluating? Are there provisions for women and men (disadvantaged target groups) to participate systematically in the monitoring?
- To what extent may disadvantaged groups be organized and empowered to take corrective action in response to the discovery of weakness or failure during project implementation?
- Are mechanisms in place to ensure that intended project beneficiaries have the ability to change the direction of the project?
- Are mechanisms in place to ensure that any negative impacts of the project can be averted?

Questions related to indicators:

- Will it be possible to assess whether women or men have been disadvantaged socially or economically? For example, will data be collected on changes to the gender division of labor and on access to, and control of, resources (by socioeconomic group)?
- Will it be possible to assess if women's or men's workload increased as a result of program inputs, and if women or men have control over income generated from their labor?
- Will women's (and men's) participation in the project be monitored—for example, the extent to which women (compared to men) receive access to project resources? "Resources" include decision making and training.
- Will it be possible to assess if women's status (or men's) improved because of program inputs?

Source: Author.

on inputs, outputs, impacts, and outcomes using quantitative and qualitative data. The MIS should produce a range of reports according to need—financial reports, time-based reports, monitoring of results or components, reports by socioeconomic groups of beneficiaries, and others. In a rural development setting, the MIS ideally should incorporate a geographic information system that maps data on project activities and outputs. An MIS can provide gender-disaggregated data on stakeholders involved in various aspects of a project and on the indicators selected to monitor change and impact. Both men and women stakeholders should be involved in identifying indicators to monitor change and impact, and both should be involved in providing feedback.

The following information sets should be managed by the MIS:

- *Monitoring of management and administration:* Includes data on staff and personnel (performance, time use, capability), vehicles (mileage, repairs), physical plant (buildings, land, utilities), supplies (stocks, costs, quality), and others.
- *Financial monitoring:* Includes all information about financial resources, such as budget, income, expenditures, and cash flow. In reports, this information may be used to compare income and expenditure over time, changes in sources of revenue, or changes within the organization's expenditures (particularly with regard to gender).
- *Program and process monitoring:* Looks at the management approach, background information, inputs, activities, outputs, and progress toward objectives and impact.

SEAGA (FAO 2001) lists the key components of a monitoring, evaluation, and reporting system:

- A clearly defined purpose and focus
- Indicators for each activity, input, output, outcome, and impact
- Data concerning the indicators
- Analysis of data and presentation of the analysis in useable ways for different people
- Easy access to the information for use in individuals' work.

A deficiency in many MIS designs is that they rely too much on quantitative data and find it difficult to incorporate information derived through qualitative and more participatory approaches (box 16.12). A key decision at the start is to determine what information is needed (compared to what might be interesting). Collecting and recording irrelevant data will complicate the system and waste time. Information should be recorded and entered into the system only if it is going to be used.

Developing and testing computer programs are always more difficult and time consuming than initially expected;

Box 16.12   How Can Participation Be Measured and Reported Meaningfully?

Participation is one of the most important factors to ensure gender equity and thus one of the most important to monitor, yet participation can be difficult and time consuming to measure. Participation can range from attending meetings to initiating empowered activity. Different kinds of participation are desirable in different project activities. For each activity, a decision must be made as to the kind of participation that is desired—for instance, assessing not just the number of women attending meetings but whether they express opinions and ask for more information.

It is particularly difficult to assess program participation and benefits at the community level and to assess any effects on power relationships. Gender-disaggregated data are not the only requirement. Indicators must be identified so that meaningful participation by men and women and real benefits accruing to them can be determined and any resulting power imbalances in the community can be identified clearly. Accurate socioeconomic profiles, including gender analysis, of the target community should inform project activities and assess change. These analyses are not a one-off event but part of the monitoring process.

Each of the following questions can be posed to gain a clearer or richer understanding of true participation in meetings and training sessions:

To what extent did women actively participate in the meeting?

To what extent did women contribute to the meeting outcomes?

To lessen the subjective nature of the answers, development of criteria to form the basis of the answer is

important. For example, criteria to judge "active participation" may include the number of questions asked, the number of comments given, the perseverance of opinion giving in the face of opposition, and attempts to sway others with argument. The answer choice for the questions listed above can be quantified, and change can be noted over time. Initially, for example, 15 percent of women attending meetings may have participated "somewhat" and the remainder "not at all," whereas after a year of involvement in the program, 35 percent of women attending meetings may have participated "a lot," 20 percent "somewhat," and the remainder "not at all."

Note that for the answers to these questions to have any meaning, clarifying how many women the answers refer to is important. Therefore, the questions above need to be followed by another:

To what percentage or fraction of women present at the meeting does this apply?

A range of program impacts are often difficult either to measure or attribute, such as changes in self-confidence, skills, knowledge, and attitudes. Personal attribution is a valid means to gauge program impacts—in other words, a person or group believes that involvement in program activities has occasioned a change in their self-confidence, skills, knowledge, or attitude. Another method is to collect purely qualitative data using a consistent format and record it on an activity fact sheet. This allows effective monitoring and evaluation of project and program activities and their impacts. The use of participatory rural appraisal or gender analysis techniques to monitor indicators is a helpful tool.

Source: Author, adapted from unpublished project documents.

final expenditures of three times the estimated cost are not uncommon. Standard codes can be used in different packages or modules to link related physical activities in the various databases or records to financial budgets. A better approach at the project level may be to rely on a standard, off-the-shelf accounting system, which can be customized with project codes to identify cost centers, components, and activities and to use the same codes in any other packages (such as data-

bases) used to record monitoring data. Keep the quarterly reporting as simple as possible and try to avoid reporting too much numerical data at the activity level. The numerical detail may not add much information that is meaningful to other users of the report and complicates reporting (many numbers need to be reconciled and actual data reported against targets). More detail on results versus expected outputs and outcomes can be included in the annual report.

Operating budgets

Sufficient funds need to be made available for gender-related activities. For instance, funds are needed to purchase gender training materials and to conduct specific studies on the socioeconomic situation of men and women in the project area (gender analysis). Collecting quantitative data disaggregated by gender need not be more costly, but qualitative monitoring of projects, which will pick up on changes in attitudes and changes in gender roles, will require more time and money. The triangulation is important, however, to ensure reliability.

PRACTICALITIES OF M&E

How much M&E is enough? The key is to remember that the purpose of M&E is to guide implementation of a program or project, so a limit exists to the resources that should be used for M&E. The cost of collecting information will usually determine the methods selected and the scope of information collected. A balance must be found between using as few indicators as possible, for reasons of simplicity and cost, and using sufficient indicators to measure the breadth of change and to cross-check results.

Gender in High-Level Programs, Policies, and Newer Aid Modalities: How Should We Monitor It?

The discourse on aid effectiveness has focused on which modality of aid—project or program modalities, in their various forms—has the greatest impact on poverty reduction and economic growth. Arguments in favor of the project approach include the ability to make and monitor change at the local level, to control the work and use of funds closely, and to provide good opportunities for capacity building. The opposing arguments are that delivering aid through projects leads to a proliferation of parallel management systems within or outside the public administration, which hamper coordination, planning, and budgeting and result in heavy transaction costs and insufficient impact. The current paradigm in development thinking, agreed to by many donors in the Paris Declaration on Harmonization of Aid, is to move toward programmatic aid, supporting local governments to run activities directly. The increasing emphasis on harmonization and alignment means that all donors are faced with the dilemma of finding an appropriate balance between their own policy objectives and country-led approaches to development.

Some of the "new" modalities include the following:

- Program support
- Poverty reduction strategy programs/national development plans
- Budget support (general or targeted/sectoral)
- Public financial management
- Sectorwide approaches
- Joint assistance strategies
- Basket funds (usually a precursor to SWAPs).

These newer modalities require the implementation of monitoring measures on a scale that differs to a great extent from those applied in projects, because in most cases an entire country is covered.

KEY ISSUES RELATED TO MONITORING GENDER IN THE NEWER AID MODALITIES

The attention given to gender within these larger initiatives, unfortunately, is not good. Although SWAPs and budget support have many advantages with regard to impact, they can cause gender equity to receive even less priority, unless deliberate steps are taken to monitor gender impacts.

Gender-sensitive M&E in more traditional projects, although perhaps not done well in practice, is usually better understood in theory. The monitoring of gender issues within PRSPs, budget support, and SWAPs, on the other hand, is more problematic, to both plan and implement. It is difficult to link and track the diagnosis of priorities to plans, budgets, expenditures, and outcomes, and they are very often gender blind. Developing countries usually lack the organizations and technical capacity for accurately monitoring how the funds are spent and what gender outcomes are achieved. Although the newer aid modalities have the potential to mainstream gender equity at a national level, experience to date has shown that gender has not been given much consideration. It is rarely considered to be an independent sector, nor is it effectively mainstreamed, and if equity has improved, this happens usually by accident rather than design.

Gender equity is not explicitly addressed in the Paris Declaration. There is a risk that as the influence of donors on resources diminishes under new aid modalities, their ability to encourage partners to pursue gender-sensitive strategies and carry out M&E will diminish. In addition, SWAPs and budget support tend to be implemented from capital cities, in meetings, rather than at the grassroots level. This context may be far away—in distance and perceptions—from what is actually happening on the ground. Competing priorities, discussed by societal leaders (generally men), usually are found, as well as a diminished scope for gender equity. The demands from donors and local government for time and human resources to hold regular working group meetings and joint reviews are enormous. If field visits take place during joint reviews, they often consist of convoys of cars and many visitors sweeping into small villages, with the participation of local leaders and the presence of police for security. Under these circumstances, it is unlikely that the reviewers can collect good qualitative information, and certainly cross-cutting issues or negative results are unlikely to be mentioned.

The Development Assistance Committee review of development cooperation agencies (OECD 2007: 15) found that "a number of respondents believe that the new aid modalities have hampered gender-equity actions. Over half of the mature agencies say the new aid modalities have made gender mainstreaming more difficult—and none say that they have made it less difficult." In addition, problems of attribution often arise when monitoring results at the budget support or SWAP level: did the support of one particular agency make the difference for women in the partner country, or was it a combination of many actions?

REASONS TO MONITOR GENDER SPECIFICALLY IN THE NEW MODALITIES

The Gender Action Partnership (GAP) Web site in Vietnam states, "Experience shows that if Poverty Reduction Strategies do not comprehensively address the gender dimension of poverty throughout the strategy, then it is most likely that the impact of the strategy on poverty reduction and economic growth will be insufficient, inequitable, and less successful (than it could have been had gender been mainstreamed). The responsiveness of income poverty to growth reduction increases significantly as inequality is lowered— that is, '*more equal societies will be more efficient transformers of growth into poverty reduction.*'"[1]

Effective gender mainstreaming and gender-sensitive monitoring in the context of budget support can take place only if the national poverty reduction strategy has captured poverty, vulnerability, and the causes of poverty as gender-specific phenomena and outlined effective measures and interventions to overcome them. Establishing a framework to manage for results that incorporates gender equity requires agreement that gender-equity targets are appropriate and that their monitoring is worth the investment. However, this commitment is not always carried through into action.

The connection between policies, spending commitments, and actual implementation will be strengthened if well-functioning monitoring systems track the introduction of gender-sensitive performance measures and incentives in the public sector and if community organizations lobby for them.

EXPERIENCE AND ACHIEVEMENTS

As noted, the experience of gender-sensitive monitoring of the newer aid modalities has been somewhat weak. The following sections look at monitoring of MDGs, PRSPs, SWAPs, and joint reviews—both experiences to date and possible improvements.

Experience with PRSPs and SWAPs

In these early stages of working with new aid modalities, an emphasis is given to measuring management processes, measuring the consistency of aid flow, and tracking finances and economic performance, rather than measuring progress on achieving development priorities, including gender priorities.

The World Bank's *PRSP Sourcebook* (World Bank 2002) notes that men and women experience poverty differently and that poverty reduction strategies (PRSs) often do not take these differences into account:

A full understanding of the gender dimensions of poverty can significantly change the definition of priority policy and program interventions supported by the PRS. Evidence is growing that gender-sensitive development strategies contribute significantly to economic growth as well as to equity objectives by ensuring that all groups of the poor share in program benefits. Yet differences between men's and women's needs are often not fully recognized in poverty analysis and participatory planning and are frequently not taken into consideration in the selection and design of PRSs.

World Bank (2002: 335)

National statistical data are often insufficient. Normally data on early childhood growth or schooling will record the gender of survey participants, yet this level of detail often disappears by the time the information is summarized in background documents for PRSPs or SWAPs. In addition, household-level income or consumption surveys will not usually indicate gender, unless women-headed households are recorded. Intermediaries processing raw data may make a decision regarding the importance of gender and delete important data for monitoring. Qualitative monitoring and attempts to improve participation have been made using participatory poverty assessments and civil society consultations, and the resulting information used to develop PRSPs, but experience has shown that consultations were usually limited and rushed, at least in the first round of PRSPs. It is also difficult to integrate statistical data with the participatory poverty assessment unless specific examples are presented to support particular topics. Consequently, the recommendations did not appear in the final documents.

Another difficulty faced when working with sectoral basket funding or budget support involving multiple donors is that checklists and monitoring requirements may overlap or even be contradictory, despite the harmonization principle endorsed in the Paris Agreement. As a consequence, some recipient governments have tried to develop their own harmonized guidelines and request that donors use them. The *Harmonized Gender and Development Guidelines* of the Philippines (NEDA 2004) are a good example, but not all recipient governments are strong enough to take a similar action.

Typically PRSPs have had a poor record of including women's organizations in their planning and have lacked a sound gender analysis. Moser and others (2004) identified three types of difficulties in following gender issues in PRSPs: evaporation, "invisibilization," and resistance. "Evaporation" means that although commitments and general statements are made regarding the importance of women in, for example, subsistence agriculture or nutrition, these words do not progress to action. Even if factors exacerbating women's poverty and vulnerability are recognized, plans and objectives may not be developed to counteract them. "Invisibilization" occurs when gender is not monitored or reported, because baseline and monitoring data have not been recorded or passed up to decision makers, because women were not consulted and their perspectives are missing, or because gender information was filtered out as "unimportant." Issues with clear gender dimensions may also become invisible when they are discussed in gender-neutral terms. "Resistance" is the refusal to take problems on board and is perhaps the more traditional obstacle in projects.

One difficulty in a PRSP is the sheer amount of information to be gathered. Too many indicators can overwhelm the abilities of national governments to collect and analyze the information. For instance, although the initial PRSP in Bolivia contained 157 national-level indicators, a subsequent, pared-down draft had 17 (Kusek and Rist 2004). Experience indicates, however, that any data pruning is liable to drop indicators linked to gender.

In the new aid modalities (for instance, in PRSPs or the frameworks for targeted budget support), conscious efforts are needed to mainstream gender and to include gendered indicators. National stakeholders should then collect gender-disaggregated data through national statistics offices and surveys as well as qualitative surveys, to monitor implementation and outcomes. Performance assessment frameworks should consist of a set of indicators that monitor progress against national development strategies and sector programs. However, most assessment tools identified within the Paris Declaration do not monitor gender and social equity. Box 16.13 (below) describes some difficulties encountered in monitoring the PRSP of Mozambique.

Fong, reviewing SWAPs for agriculture implemented between 1989 and 1998, identified SWAPs that successfully integrated a number of gender characteristics, specifically "capacity building on gender in the ministry; using gender objectives to reinforce overall SWAP objectives; a participatory approach with special attention to women stakeholders; mainstreaming gender throughout the program; and strong support of donors." The review also found increasing recognition of the need to address gender issues in agricultural programs: "Fifteen of the 24 SWAPs made efforts to address gender or women in development issues. Analysis of gender issues was undertaken in twice as many SWAPs in the second five-year period as in the first, so there was progress."[2] Although gender needs were recognized in many SWAPs, real action, such as developing activities or earmarking budgets, was limited. The contradiction between the lack of gender considerations in the main document of the Mozambican agricultural SWAP and the practical instructions given for gender-sensitive monitoring is provided in box 16.14.

Experience with monitoring gender progress in the Millennium Development Goals

The Millennium Development Goals (MDGs) developed at the Millennium Summit in 2000 consist of a set of eight goals, 18 targets, and 48 indicators for monitoring socioeconomic and environmental change by 2015 (box 16.15).

Although improvements in gender equity and the status of women are vital for achieving all of the MDGs, gender mainstreaming of the MDGs has not been particularly strong. It has been assumed that if the goals are achieved, progress would occur in social areas at the same time. An analysis of the indicators for monitoring progress shows very little emphasis on gender, other than goal 3. Rather than mainstreaming gender, the goals have seemingly circumscribed it within goals 3 and 5.

The indicators for goal 3 are the ratio of girls' to boys' enrollment in primary, secondary, and tertiary education; the ratio of literate women to men among 15–24-year-olds; the share of women in wage employment in the nonagricultural sector; and the proportion of seats held by women in national parliaments. Clearly, these indicators reflect only a limited subset of activity in education, nonagricultural employment, and political representation. They do not reflect agricultural and rural livelihoods adequately, especially disparities in

Mozambique's second Action Plan for the Reduction of Absolute Poverty (known by its acronym in Portuguese, which is PARPA) shows some improvement in gender monitoring over the first, although many issues remain to be resolved.

Improvements:

- The second version of PARPA has more consideration of gender than the first.
- Specific progress has been made in some areas: a bill on domestic violence is in the pipeline, a Family Law has been passed, and a National Gender Policy is under development.
- A Gender Coordination Group—with representatives from government, donor agencies, United Nations agencies, and civil society—chaired by the United Nations Population Fund, has considered gender issues in the agriculture meetings, although the group has not functioned very well in the joint reviews.

Unresolved issues:

- Key documents focus very little attention on women's economic empowerment. No systematic attention is given to women's rights or to the application of a rights-based approach in general.

- The capacity for stakeholders to conduct gender analyses is low. No strategic approach or results orientation is present. Agriculture has a separate strategy on gender equity, but the substance is weak.
- Progress has been made in institutionalizing gender-mainstreaming mechanisms, such as gender units and the appointment of gender focal points, but their true capacity, resources, and motivation remain unclear.
- Women's advocacy within government is weak in human resources and authority.
- In general, the motivation among government officials to discuss gender issues seems low. Many consider gender-equity strategies to be imposed by donors and feel resistant.
- Much gender training has occurred, yet staff cannot apply the theory in practice.
- Some sectors collect gender-disaggregated data; some do not. Room for improvement exists in all sectors.
- Gender issues are treated in an ad hoc way, not based on analysis. A systematic approach for gender mainstreaming is missing.

Clearly, much work remains to be done, and incentives must be found to mainstream gender in PARPA.

Source: Ministry for Foreign Affairs, Finland, internal memo, May 29, 2007.

---

access to productive resources such as land, credit, and technology. These indicators are also only quantitative in nature and measure equality of access to those areas. They do not measure whether women receive good education or are empowered (World Bank 2007).

Many of the MDGs have a gender dimension. For instance, gender-sensitive activities in agriculture can contribute to goal 3 directly by empowering women farmers and indirectly by reducing women's time burden for domestic tasks. Experience at the project level, however, teaches that if we do not measure the impacts on gender, we cannot assume that benefits will flow equally to women and men. Consequently, various agencies have attempted to strengthen the monitoring. Ideally, at least one gender-sensitive indicator should be used within each MDG. For instance, the United Nations Development Fund for Women (UNIFEM)

has improved the list of indicators, and various groups have reviewed country reports to assess the quality of gender mainstreaming.

In 2006 in a paper for the Development Assistance Committee Network on Gender Equality, Gaynor (2006) noted that gender was not reflected as a cross-cutting issue in any of the 13 MDG country reports reviewed in 2003, and goal 3 (on gender equality) was the only one consistently addressing gender issues across countries. The World Bank reported that "data on all six official indicators of MDG3 are available for only 59 out of 154 developing countries (for 2000–05), and even fewer countries have time-series data that would allow tracking over time for both the official and expanded list of indicators. ... [O]nly 41 countries have current (2000–05) information. This lack of data limits considerably the ability to monitor progress, learn from success, and,

ProAgri, a sectoral program implemented by Mozambique's Ministry of Agriculture and Rural Development (MADER), receives financial support from some 20 donors. Its objective is to protect, conserve, and use agriculture, forestry, and wildlife resources in a sustainable way. The second-phase strategy document for ProAgri emphasized that continued blindness to gender differences in agricultural planning could undermine the program, resulting in poor production, food insecurity, and increased rural poverty. Proposals were made for improved gender-sensitive monitoring and technical support to MADER to develop and apply gender-sensitive socioeconomic participatory methodologies. Interestingly, the targets and milestones listed in this same document make no reference to gender, although the chapter on M&E presents a useful recommendation on including gender concerns in M&E mechanisms, especially the necessity of the following:

- Including explicit and feasible instructions for analyzing equity issues to generate useful data for planning
- Specifying results and relevant indicators, and ensuring that equity goals are reflected in the definition and selection of impact and process indicators and evaluation criteria
- Documenting best practices to build up models.

Source: Strategy Document, ProAgri II, Ministry of Agriculture and Rural Development, Mozambique, www.pwg.gov.mz.

1. Eradicate extreme poverty and hunger.
2. Achieve universal primary education.
3. Promote gender equality and empower women.
4. Reduce child mortality.
5. Improve maternal health.
6. Combat HIV/AIDS, malaria, and other diseases.
7. Ensure environmental sustainability.
8. Develop a global partnership for development.

Source: United Nations, www.un.org/millenniumgoals.

and AIDS and malaria specifically on agriculture and rural development are manifested primarily as the loss of labor and on- and off-farm income. Gender inequality, which is at the core of the epidemic's spread, is one of the main determining factors associated with vulnerability to HIV and AIDS. In the case of goal 7, gender differences in the way natural resources are used are important to outcomes. If women in the boundary zone of a protected area collect nontimber forest products for household use, no point can be seen in monitoring only the forest products sold by men at the local market.

The indicators for many of the MDGs should be expanded, but this task is not simple because data are not available in all countries. Many countries lack basic, gender-disaggregated data on productive assets, including land, livestock, house ownership, ownership of other property, credit, and business ownership. Information on land tenure by gender is included in agricultural censuses or surveys, but it is not usually possible to get national data disaggregated by gender on access to credit (formal and informal) and business ownership; it is necessary to rely on smaller, targeted surveys. Without these data, progress cannot be monitored.

The Ministry of Women's Affairs of Cambodia provides a good example of how the monitoring of goal 3 can be improved. The Ministry improved the collection and handling of statistics and expanded the official indicators for goal 3 to strengthen the focus on gender. It added indicators of gender equity in (1) literacy rates for 25–44-year-olds, to cover women in their prime child-bearing and working years; (2) wage employment in agriculture, industry, and services, to monitor sex segregation within sectors (women are underrepresented in the service sector); and (3) all elected bodies (National Assembly, Senate, and commune councils)

ultimately, to make informed decisions regarding scaling up investments (World Bank 2007: 106). The report strongly recommended that the collection and analysis of gender-disaggregated data be significantly scaled up to permit more accurate and full measurement of progress toward goal 3.

Access to land has considerable influence on progress toward goals 1, 3, and 7 (and others as well, given the links between access to land and access to credit). Gender-sensitive data referring to land rights and security of tenure would provide good information for monitoring progress toward these goals. Links are also present in goals 1, 3, and 6 with respect to the impact of HIV and AIDS on rural households and gender issues in agriculture. The adverse effects of HIV and government positions. In addition, it added a new target focused on reducing all forms of violence against women and children (World Bank 2007).

PRINCIPLES AND GUIDELINES FOR ACTION

With development cooperation increasingly dependent on PRSs, sectorwide strategies, and other country-generated development plans, drawing up gender-equity objectives for these plans and strategies is vital. To minimize policy evaporation, linking policy and strategies with clearly identifiable inputs, outputs, resource allocations, expected outcomes, and their relationship to policy goals is important. A number of indicators, tools, and methods that can support this process are summarized in box 16.16 and discussed in the sections that follow.

MONITORING PRSPS

The *PRSP Sourcebook* (World Bank 2002) recommends three steps for gender-sensitive monitoring of PRSPs:

1. Integrate a gender dimension into the outcome monitoring system.
2. Integrate a gender dimension into the PRS evaluation strategy, and use gender monitoring and impact evaluation results.
3. Build institutional capacity for gender-responsive M&E.

When selecting indicators, tools, and methods to reflect gender outcomes and impacts in PRSPs, PRS managers should consider the following:

- Select *only a few critical goals, outcomes, and indicators* from the PRS for monitoring and evaluating gender outcomes and impacts. In the selection process, consider *how the information is to be used, and by whom,* and assess these needs in light of *budgetary and time constraints.* Ensure that the data are collected.
- Data collection methods are determined by the kinds of information and data needed to monitor change and progress. Optimum results are obtained when traditional and participatory approaches to M&E are used to complement one another.
- Collecting new data on gender is not always necessary. Assess the availability of gender-responsive data before considering the need to collect new data. Gender M&E is frequently done by disaggregating data already being collected and using other available sources of information.

Box 16.16 Summary: Gender Indicators, Tools, and Methods for the New Aid Modalities

In dealing with the new aid modalities, a number of indicators, tools, and methods may be useful for reflecting gender outcomes and impacts.

- Conduct gender analysis, including gender-oriented analyses of PRSPs and other development plans, to track the extent to which partner-country development plans incorporate a gender dimension.
- Conduct participatory assessments, including poverty and social impact analyses and needs assessments.
- Use gender-responsive public financial management tools, such as gender budgeting or gender-disaggregated benefit incidence.
- Include gender indicators as milestones or even triggers for disbursement.
- Ensure that gender is considered when preparing terms of reference for joint reviews or monitoring visits.
- Use gender audits, peer review, and gender-equity markers and indices to study progress.
- Include activities to mainstream gender throughout all levels. Embed gender equity in national monitoring and accountability frameworks and mechanisms.
- Formulate clear, measurable objectives and indicators, and link them with annual information sources.
- Promote capacity building (also for civil society) to contribute to the monitoring process.
- Conduct ex ante assessments of the gender impact of proposed development actions, which in principle identify gender-biased outcomes and permit mitigating actions to be built into a program or project.
- Disseminate good practice and experience locally and internationally.

Source: Author.

Three countries—Mozambique, Uganda, and Vietnam—offer examples of practical steps for monitoring gender in poverty reduction strategy programs, and these are described in box 16.17.

Poverty and social impact analysis reveals the distributional impact of policy reforms on the well-being or welfare of different stakeholder groups, with a particular focus on

Mozambique

Monitoring for Mozambique's Action Plan for the Reduction of Absolute Poverty (PARPA) is being integrated into the regular system of quarterly and annual government reports to parliament. A special annual poverty report will also be prepared, based on quantitative and qualitative data. The PARPA does not specify the form of the poverty report, but ideally it should include monitoring at three levels: sectoral performance, execution of program expenditures and revenues, and changes in welfare as measured by poverty and social indicators. The main quantitative data sources will be administrative data produced by the line ministries and annual household surveys of key welfare indicators (through the Core Welfare Indicators Questionnaires).

The indicator table in PARPA's monitoring section represents an initial attempt to focus on a smaller number of key targets and indicators for each priority area, with a clearer distinction between intermediate and outcome indicators. However, some of these measures are provisional, because in some cases the precise quantities still need to be established and the relevant data sources defined. Targets and indicators are best specified in those sectors that have sectorwide approaches in place. As reporting on the PARPA becomes more institutionalized, further refinement of its indicators may be expected, and the link to poverty outcomes should be strengthened (ideally with more gender consideration).

Uganda

Uganda developed a detailed sectoral information and monitoring system (SIMS) for a water and sanitation program, which includes the monitoring of gender. The system features the following:

- *Sector Management Arrangements*—the institutional framework or system that guides the development, oversight, and coordination of SIMS (Water and Sanitation Sector Working Group, sector performance thematic team).
- *Sector Strategic Monitoring* monitors results for the sector using 10 key "golden indicators," including gender. These indicators are identified by all stakeholders at the start. Various studies also support monitoring, such as national surveys, tracking studies, expenditure analysis, and equity studies.
- *Sector Implementation Monitoring* monitors project/program inputs and outputs through quarterly progress reports, performance assessment framework, monitoring reports, and others.

Some of the lessons learned from this process include the importance of agreeing on definitions, data sources, and data collection methods from the outset and agreeing on annual indicator targets for assessing performance changes over time. Linking SIMS to budgeting and resource allocation within the sector is still a significant challenge, and putting monitoring findings and recommendations into action is still difficult.

Vietnam

Vietnam has included two gender targets in its Comprehensive Poverty Reduction and Growth Strategy. First, 40 percent of newly created jobs should go to women; second, land tenure certificates should be issued in the names of both women and men. To meet the first target, targets are being created for different organizations, gender indicators will be included into the national targeted program on job creation, coordination will take place with concerned agencies, and monitoring and evaluation indicators and processes will be identified. For the second target, the Land Administration will set targets for every year, and the number of certificates to be issued or reissued will be specified. Instructions will be given to district cadastral officers, budget and staff will be allocated, and reporting and evaluation formats established. The concerned ministries and the Women's Union will monitor progress.

Sources: IMF/IDA 2001; Disan Ssozi, "Sector Information and Monitoring System (Uganda Case Study)," www.worldwaterweek.org; Thi Minh Chanh, "Hanoi Action Plan Review," www.unifem-ecogov-apas.org.

the poor and vulnerable (see box 16.18 for an example from Vietnam). Poverty and social impact analysis also addresses sustainability and the risks to policy reform and helps to monitor poverty and social outcomes and impacts of policy changes. It can inform national poverty reduction strategies, specific reform programs, and development bank lending, as well as strengthen evidence-based decision making (World Bank 2004).

Needs assessments can be used to collect information, raise awareness, and understand the priority needs of women based on their different tasks, concerns, and responsibilities. They can divide practical gender needs and strategic needs (which contribute to transforming subordinate relationships between women and men). A needs assessment might be done at the community level but can

also be used right up to the level of national bodies or internationally. The Economic Commission for Latin America and the Caribbean undertook a needs assessment of economic planning units in four Caribbean countries to evaluate their capacity to integrate gender into macroeconomic planning processes (for instance, to carry out gender-sensitive budget analysis of both revenues and expenditures).[3] The study assessed the extent to which the countries sought to integrate gender into macroeconomic planning, as well as the institutional, human resource capacity, and attitudinal factors that facilitated or hindered such integration. It included interviews with Finance and Planning Department staff, NGOs, women's organizations, and training bodies. Current policies and practices were examined as well. The needs assessment formed the basis for designing and implementing subregional training workshops aimed at increasing the capacity of regional economic planners in gender analysis and gender planning. It was a very useful baseline to support gender-sensitive budget analysis in those countries and analyze the constraints to monitoring government commitments to gender equity.

Gender integration in SWAPs should have a number of characteristics to be successful:[4]

- *Capacity building on gender in the ministry:* For example, Kenya's Ministry of Agriculture has given extensive emphasis to building capacity for integrating gender at the ministry, regional, and community levels during SWAp preparation and implementation.
- *Using gender objectives to reinforce overall SWAP objectives:* Enhancing attention to gender will increase the likelihood of reaching overall objectives, such as poverty alleviation and enhanced food security (see box 16.18 for an example from Kenya).
- *A participatory approach, with special attention to gender stakeholders:* To ensure good coverage of ideas and attention to gender issues and increased ownership of the process, groups that do not otherwise participate in the planning or monitoring will need to be tapped at national, regional, and community levels, including a range of government ministries, NGOs, universities, women entrepreneurs, and women farmers, among others. Practical steps may need to be taken to ensure that women have good access to planning meetings (such as ensuring proper timing, providing child care, and identifying a suitable location).
- *Mainstreaming gender throughout the program:* Gender should not be isolated within a separate task force. All

---

Box 16.18 Examples of How Gender Analysis Is Used

Gender Analysis in a Sectorwide Program: Kenya

Between 1996 and 1998, Kenya's Ministry of Agriculture led a study of gender relations in agriculture in three regions, which brought to light constraints and challenges regarding equitable agricultural development, along with institutional inhibitions to change. As a result, a separate objective for gender equity was added to Kenya's Agricultural Sector Investment Program. The objective received a separate budget line, ensuring funding of activities to improve women's economic security. Responsibilities were clearly set for monitoring at each level, and capacities were built.

Gender Analysis of Structural Reforms: Vietnam

An analysis of the gender dimensions of Vietnam's structural reforms focused on links between reform, gender equity, economic growth, and women's welfare in Vietnam during the 1990s. The gender dimensions of key reform policies received special attention. The analysis found that women on the whole are better off as a result of the reforms, but the gains are not evenly distributed across income groups, regions, and ethnic groups. Household and enterprise survey data presented mixed results regarding gendered outcomes and formed the basis for recommendations to enable women to improve their economic and social welfare.

Sources: OECD 2002; Packard 2006.

groups involved in program preparation and monitoring must consider gender as a cross-cutting issue.

■ *Strong donor support.* Strong donor support may be important to the success, for example, of gender focal points in ministries or of including specific, gender-sensitive M&E in the program.

Gender budget analysis tools are used to review general or mainstream budget expenditures (for instance, within the annual budget of a nation or of a specific sectoral program) or to review expenditures specifically targeted to groups of women or men to meet prioritized needs or promote equal opportunities. *Gender budget initiatives* (GBIs) can be defined as "diverse efforts aimed at breaking down the government's budget in order to analyze its impact on women, men, girls, and boys, as well as on other axes of social differentiation (such as race, ethnicity, class, and caste). Their main purpose is to examine whether public expenditures are allocated in an equitable way, and hence promote gender equality" (Balmori 2003: 15). They can also help to reshape government policy goals and resource allocation.

Local organizations have used GBIs to analyze expenditures and link policies to actual spending commitments to women and the poor (for example, in India and Tanzania). This information has been channeled back to governments to promote gender-responsive budgeting. The rationale is to establish a process in partner countries whereby the differential effects on men and women of particular budget decisions are understood and biases are corrected. The most commonly used method takes the government's policy framework and examines it sector by sector, exploring how budget expenditures are used and identifying the longer-term impacts on men and women.

In Morocco a gender-sensitive Economic and Financial Report accompanied the 2006 finance bill and provided a baseline for measuring progress on gender issues in budgets and outcomes in several ministries, including agriculture (for details, see the Web site of the Ministry of Finance and Privatization, www.finances.gov.ma, or the UNIFEM Web site, www.gender-budgets.org). Many examples of gender budget initiatives in other countries are given in World Bank (2007), which identifies the key steps in implementing budget initiatives as upgrading the technical skills of budget officials and gender experts and strengthening government agencies, raising public awareness of gender issues to ensure the sustainability of the initiatives, and supporting well-informed coalitions of NGOs for advocacy. The key challenge for gender-informed budget analysis and policy making is to move beyond gender-targeted interventions to

full and sustained gender mainstreaming in the budget process. A range of tools are available (table 16.3).

One difficulty with GBIs is that results for a given year are usually available only after the following year's budget has been planned, so a lag of one year tends to occur before findings can lead to change.

Linkages with advocacy, research, and training are vital for moving the results of GBIs forward into the development of improved programs. These roles may be carried out by government, but this is unusual. More commonly, governmental "women's machinery" (women's unions, NGOs, and other groups that advocate on behalf of women) may work together with NGOs and university institutions to lobby politicians and raise awareness among the general public. The Tanzania Gender Networking Program, a nongovernmental agency, pioneered the use of gender budgeting (Muro 2007). The gender budgeting process (1997–2000) focused primarily on collecting information, conducting research, disseminating results, lobbying and advocacy, establishing links and recognition, and building capacity of partners and resource persons. Major achievements have been the following:

■ Gender budgeting has been institutionalized. It is now a requirement in the government budget process.
■ There has been a trend of increased budget to social sectors such as health and water.
■ Gender is now a Public Expenditure Review Working Sector Committee.
■ The Tanzania Gender Networking Program is a resource organization for gender budgeting and is called to support other countries that wish to implement it.
■ Public and media engagement in policy debates has increased, along with involvement in GBI campaigns on HIV and AIDS, water, and gender-based violence.

In Kenya, experience has shown that at least three years of capacity building and financial and technical support are needed to ensure that gender-mainstreaming concepts are embedded in national organizations and in strategic and budget frameworks (GTZ 2005).

The *performance assessment framework* (PAF) is a commonly agreed-to matrix or consolidated list of priority policy reforms, measures, and indicators against which progress is monitored and reported on by the government. The PAF is used as the main point of reference for making disbursement decisions. If donors wish to use the PAF as a tool, indicators that measure progress in gender equity and are gender disaggregated could be inserted (although usually a

Table 16.3   Seven Tools for Gender Budget Initiatives and Examples of Their Use

Tool	Application
Gender-aware policy appraisal	Designed to analyze policies and programs from a gender perspective and identify how these policies and the resources allocated to them are likely to reduce or increase gender inequalities.
Gender-disaggregated beneficiary assessment	Implemented to evaluate the extent to which programs or services meet the needs of actual or potential beneficiaries, as identified and expressed by the beneficiaries.
Gender-disaggregated public expenditure benefit incidence analysis	Used to evaluate the distribution of budget resources among women and men, girls and boys, by estimating the unit costs of a certain service and calculating the extent to which this service is being used by each group.
Gender-disaggregated analysis of the impact of the budget on time use	Designed to establish a link between budget allocations, the services provided through them, and the way in which different members within a household spend their time.
Gender-aware medium-term economic policy framework	Designed to incorporate a gender perspective into the medium-term frameworks of policy development, planning, and budgetary allocations, such as by disaggregating variables by gender, combining national income accounts and household income accounts, and highlighting and challenging gender-blind, underlying assumptions about how the economy works.
Gender-aware budget statement	Generated by government agencies for use in reports on the implications of their expenditures on gender-equity objectives.
Disaggregated tax-incidence analysis	Used to assess the differential impacts of taxation on women and men, as well as to evaluate the level of revenue raised in relation to the needs and demands for public expenditure.

Source: Balmori 2003.

reluctance to make the indicators too complicated is encountered). Progress on gender indicators could then be used as a means of conditionality, with disbursement taking place only if agreed-to steps have taken place or if agreed-to results have been achieved. Unfortunately, to date gender has usually not been considered, and much more emphasis has been placed on issues of financial management.

JOINT MONITORING MISSIONS

Programmatic, sectoral, and budget support is usually monitored via regular missions (for instance, six-monthly or annual missions), often consisting of one or many donors and government representatives (joint review missions). To ensure that gender-sensitive monitoring takes place, attention must be given to inserting it in the terms of reference for joint reviews (box 16.19). Guidelines should be established for the review process and missions to ensure that gender-equity issues are included. Meetings with local women's advocacy groups and other relevant persons or agencies should be required as part of data collection. Gender focal points should participate in and support the joint review in their sectors (for example, the focal points in agriculture

ministries). If reliable data can be collected on the outcomes of the support, this information will prove very useful for addressing positive or negative trends in indicators and discussing the reasons at the highest level with all major stakeholders. The development of alliances of donors and local organizations can also be supported and used to promote gender equity by lobbying government decision makers.

EXAMINING GENDER ACTIVITIES OF DONORS

Peer review is a tool developed by the Development Assistance Committee of the OECD (OECD/DAC) in which a panel of peers assesses a multilateral agency's evaluation systems and processes. This tool can be applied equally well to evaluate whether gender is being considered in evaluations.

OECD/DAC has also developed a *gender-equity marker* to allow donors to record whether activities have the explicit goal of achieving gender equity. The marker has been used mainly in social policy areas but not yet in productive areas, which, of course, are highly relevant in agricultural livelihoods. Its use has been limited largely to measuring the policy objectives of a program. The next step is to start using this tool in evaluations, in which it might give some idea of

Box 16.19 Examples of Gender-Specific Topics to Include in Terms of Reference for Joint Review Missions

Poverty and institutional analysis:

- Are gender and other equity, disparity, or human rights issues included in the performance assessment framework reporting instructions and have guidelines been made for the sectors?
- Did government approve any significant new gender legislation or policies during the period in question? Were legal instruments that discriminate against women revised? Has the institutionalization of gender policy and strategy improved in line ministries?
- Have any studies been carried out providing new information on the income, consumption, or other dimensions of poverty from a gender perspective? With what results?
- What progress has been made, and what measures have been taken to improve the production and use of gender analysis and disaggregated data, compared with the previous year?
- Does the analysis consider linkages between sectors, such as links between nutrition and water and sanitation?

Agriculture and nutrition:

- How many women in comparison to men were reached with extension or new technology services, seed, tools, and fertilizer support?
- What is the percentage increase of women having official title to land in comparison with men and the previous year? What actions were taken to increase women's land ownership?
- What is the percentage increase in women having access to credit? What is their average interest rate and loan amount compared to those for men? How do women's and men's loans and repayment rates compare?
- What is the number and position of women in agricultural production and marketing associations?
- What developments have occurred in household food security and nutrition indicators (under-five malnutrition, wasting, and stunting)?
- In related sectors, such as water or transport, in which prices and affordability of services produced by gender have been analyzed, can women afford to pay for transport, energy, and water? What are the utilization rates by gender?

Entrepreneurship and economic development:

- What is women's share of the benefits provided? Examples include the number of women in training courses, as beneficiaries of credit and other funds, as project beneficiaries, and as participants in national and international marketing events.
- What is women's access to capital, credit, and formal banking services?
- How has the number of micro-, small-, or medium enterprises owned by women developed? How many are registered under women's names, compared with the previous year?

Source: Adapted from the Gender Checklist for the Joint Budget Review, Mozambique, unpublished.

how gender equity has been affected. The *gender-equity index* represents another effort to measure progress or regression in gender equity internationally as a result of new aid modalities.[5] The index uses a set of indicators for which data are available in most countries.

Gender audits have been used increasingly as a self-assessment tool for measuring gender equity among institutions, including development agencies and NGOs. Moser (2007: 17) lists the issues that might be considered:

- Analysis of gender issues within organizations in relation to, for example, flexible working hours for both women and men, child care provision, and policies that encourage more flexible gender roles

- Mainstreaming of gender equity in all mainstream policies and creating requirements for gender-sensitive M&E systems
- Human resources, including issues such as gender equity in recruitment
- Technical capacity of staff in gender issues and internal capacity building
- Allocation of financial resources to gender-mainstreaming efforts or women-focused initiatives
- Organizational culture, including a culture of participation and consultation.

The DFID's internal gender audit of its staff in Malawi found that most of them had limited knowledge of gender mainstreaming and very few realized that DFID even had a gender strategy.[6] If staff members are unaware of the importance of gender in projects and programs, they are not likely to ensure gender-sensitive monitoring. It can be extrapolated that local project and government staff will be even less likely to focus on gender in monitoring, if the donor does not actively encourage it. Other NGOs and bilateral and multilateral funding institutions have audited the extent to which gender has been incorporated into their field activities.

CONCLUSION

Evaluation is a much more complex task under the newer aid modalities than in projects because of the greater number of stakeholders, broader geographic coverage, and lack of clear logical frameworks. Tools are gradually being developed for M&E in this new context, however, and their use will be vital for ensuring that gender-equity priorities do not become lost in a myriad of other considerations.

Setting Gender-Sensitive Indicators and Collecting Gender-Disaggregated Data

I f we are to measure progress in gender-related targets, we need gender-sensitive indicators. Indicators are the building blocks of an effective M&E system, but they are highly context specific and uniquely representative of a particular program or project. This Thematic Note examines how to set high-quality indicators and collect the data. Practical examples for projects and programs are provided.

GENDER-SENSITIVE INDICATORS

A gender-sensitive indicator can be defined as "an indicator that captures gender-related changes in society over time" (Beck 2000: 7). The DFID *Gender Manual* (Derbyshire 2002) defines gender-sensitive indicators as follows:

Gender-sensitive indicators allow measurement of benefits to women and men and include the impact/effectiveness of activities targeted to do the following (Derbyshire 2002: 28):

- Address *women's or men's practical needs,* such as new skills, resources, opportunities, or services in the context of their existing gender roles
- Increase gender equality of opportunity, influence, or benefit, such as targeted actions to increase women's role in decision making, opening up new opportunities for women and men in nontraditional skill areas
- Develop gender awareness and skills among policy making, management, and implementation staff
- Promote greater gender equity within the staffing and organizational culture of development organizations, such as, the impact of affirmative action policy.

During the 1970s and 1980s, more emphasis was given to quantitative general (and particularly economic) indicators. Since the 1990s, however, realization has grown of the importance of designing gender-sensitive indicators to monitor the gender impacts of programs and projects. Initially the impact on women was emphasized, but now the emphasis is on gender as it is broadly defined.

REASONS FOR USING GENDER-SENSITIVE INDICATORS

Despite making up half of the population, women are often invisible in society because of their low sociocultural and economic status. Women's invisibility is particularly acute in agriculture, despite the fact that they often do much of the work related to farming. Counting the participation of women and other disadvantaged groups in every activity is a simple way to make them visible to all stakeholders. Even if women are absent, their absence should be mentioned and recorded, and the reasons explained in reports. Because indicators show changes, they can demonstrate that women are participating more or less in project activities over time, and they can prompt discussion among stakeholders as to the reasons.

Gender indicators should show how and if gender equity is being reached, and if the approaches used are effective. They should answer the following questions:

- Is the gap between women and men decreasing in terms of access, income, and power?
- Are project activities the most appropriate and effective activities for achieving an improvement in gender equity?
- Could the project or program do more to benefit different disadvantaged groups?
- How have women and men benefited directly from the activities?
- Are the direct or indirect impacts of the project or program having an adverse effect on the gender situation

(including the socioeconomic position of women and the power relationships between women and men)?

- How do the women and men themselves assess the impact on their lives, and would their situation have been different without the project?

EXPERIENCE AND ACHIEVEMENTS

Most projects tend to collect only basic disaggregated data. Gender-specific monitoring, like monitoring in general, tends to be lost in the day-to-day pressures of implementation.

A survey by the IFAD revealed that the weakest areas for gender-disaggregated data collection are the composition of project-related committees and decision-making bodies, beneficiaries of extension and technical assistance, and beneficiaries of microcredit (IFAD 2007). Given the critical nature of these issues for gender, project monitoring systems are probably missing gender differences.

The FAO is collaborating with other United Nations agencies to collect and provide gender-specific data that will help mainstream gender across the organization. It is hoped that such data will more clearly illustrate gender inequalities in agriculture, rural development, and food security. This effort includes the incorporation of gender-specific demographic data into FAOSTAT (FAO's statistical databases; FAO 2003). Through technical assistance to many national institutions in charge of data collection, FAO has also raised awareness of the importance of gathering gender-disaggregated data through the national agricultural census. The FAO has supported pilot studies to develop a methodology for collecting gender-disaggregated data for countries in transition in Central and Eastern Europe, and it has developed and field-tested sets of gender-sensitive indicators on natural resources management and socioeconomics. Other projects have supported training of FAO field staff in conducting gender-sensitive household surveys and using community appraisal methods. Even so, the FAO progress report noted that "more work is needed in technical units compiling and analyzing statistics, such as from national agricultural censuses and surveys, to assist FAO Members to generate gender-disaggregated data, produce surveys on the gendered nature of work, and provide detailed gender analysis of statistical material and information on data and on data collection methodologies" (FAO 2003: para. 49).

The *Harmonized Gender and Development Guidelines* of the government of the Philippines (NEDA 2004) is an attempt to ensure that gender is mainstreamed across all activities and levels of management. The guidelines include a good set for project management as well as sector-specific monitoring indicators for gender and development.

GUIDELINES IN DESIGNING GENDER-SPECIFIC INDICATORS AND FINDING SOURCES OF VERIFICATION

Many guides for designing appropriate indicators are available. This section provides only a brief overview and some specific examples.

Types of indicators

Indicators can be distinguished in a number of ways.

Input indicators specify the means and resources required for an action. Input indicators are normally part of the project or program document and reporting system, and they describe what is being physically done—for example, how many hours of training are provided to men and women, how much money is spent, or the quantity of fruit trees planted.

Process indicators ensure the effective and efficient use of means and resources for implementing an action. Process indicators are of particular importance for participatory monitoring to ensure that all (primary) stakeholders, disaggregated by gender, have knowledge of and, if appropriate, participate in, progress being made, obstacles encountered, solutions presented, and decisions made, from start to finish.

Output indicators measure the achievement of intended outputs and determine whether project goals are being achieved. *Outcome indicators* measure the immediate impacts produced by the outputs. Typically, output and outcome indicators are used as internal monitoring or evaluation tools. Generally, these are defined prior to the project, but ideally they should be modified in the early stages of implementation to reflect changes that may have taken place and to be certain that data will be available to verify them from baseline and other sources. When output indicators are analyzed, it is essential to consider the influence of gender roles and relations on the distribution of benefits. What measures can verify whether project benefits accrue to women as well as men and identify the different types of women engaged in or affected by the project? Output indicators might include the number of people trained or the number of rural women and men accessing a Web site with agricultural information. An example of an outcome indicator might be the percentage increase in average crop yield among men and women farmers included in the project over the project period.

Impact indicators measure a project's medium- or long-term impacts on poverty and livelihoods among the primary stakeholders. Impact indicators describe the actual change in conditions as a result of a program or project activity, such as changed attitudes of men and women as a result of training, changed practices, or a decrease in the number of households living in poverty over five years. Ideally, indicators for expected local impacts should be established in a participatory manner for any subprojects.

Qualitative versus quantitative indicators

Quantitative indicators are measures of quantity (total numbers, percentages, and others) that show the degree to which a goal or an objective has been attained. Sources of quantitative indicators are data systems and records in which information is presented in a gender-disaggregated manner. They could be project-specific collection systems (specific surveys targeting data related to project outcomes) or existing records, such as the census, agricultural production records, or transport ministry statistics. Traditionally quantitative indicators have been favored because they are more objective and can be verified using data from government records or project-established monitoring systems. In addition, they are easier to incorporate into a management information system and track in reporting. By nature, quantitative indicators may be the simplest means of demonstrating gender differences (and tracking changes) for all audiences. Examples include the number of women participants in technology testing and on-farm trials, gender-disaggregated adoption of new technologies, yields of women's crops, increased incomes for women from cropping, labor time changes by gender, the percentage or number of men and women (or young and old, or ethnic minority women, or members of other groups) receiving training, or the proportion of women farmers adopting new technologies or crops.

Qualitative indicators can be defined as recording people's judgments and perceptions about a given subject. They are useful for understanding processes: Who is participating in decision making? Who benefits? What are the local perceptions of successes and failures? Qualitative indicators are harder to measure because they involve processes and use categories of classification, such as those based on perceptions. Qualitative indicators might relate to levels of participation of women, men, and other groups in meetings, the satisfaction levels of different users of a service, or attitudinal changes. Examples of data sources include interviews, focus groups, user surveys, participant observation, and participatory appraisals.

Quantitative indicators sometimes do not capture the true impacts of a project or program. For this reason, qualitative indicators should be used to complement quantitative ones. In a rural development project in Mongolia, for example, data showed that increased problems were reported in infrastructure construction. Further questioning revealed that the problems had not increased but that community members' involvement in a participatory monitoring process caused more problems to be reported and acted on. If quantitative data alone were considered, they would give an erroneous impression of the project's success. This experience is common, and project and program staff should always question whether increased reporting of a finding really means increased incidence or if it is actually the result of increased awareness or improved consultation. If monitoring by local women in a protected area produces new reports of illegal hunting, it may be that such hunting has always taken place but that only women who collect firewood in the forest see it happening.

Likewise, when recording women's participation in training events or resource management committees, gender-disaggregated quantitative data are insufficient. Finding ways to record whether women participate actively in discussions and are heard (and which group of women), or whether women simply participate to make up the numbers and comply with donor demands.

The power of triangulation

If qualitative data are used to triangulate quantitative results, a powerful and multifaceted case can be built. For instance, direct quotes from participants can be used in reports and explanations provided for quantitative changes. Triangulation is also important to ensure that cultural biases do not affect the results. For instance, in some cultures a woman may not give a truthful answer to a question if it might imply criticism of her husband. In this case, consultation with independent sources is important to confirm the data. Triangulation makes it possible to reduce the sample size and at the same time increase the reliability and validity of the data.

Capacity building is an area that in particular requires qualitative indicators. The interest here lies not only in the number of women trained but also in the extent to which capacity building has increased the social capital of women farmers, extension workers, and the poor, such as access to market information, increased confidence of the poor in their skills, and access to local agricultural extension staff.

Designing indicators

Two acronyms have been used to describe sound performance indicators:

- *TQQ: Time* (time-bound accomplishment), *quantity* (numerically measurable), and *quality* (what level of quality or degree of achievement is desired).
- *SMARTS: Simple* and easily defined, *measurable, attributable, realistic, targeted,* and *specific.* Consideration should be given to whether the indicators selected are relevant (do they provide the necessary information for making decisions?), understandable and meaningful for relevant stakeholders, and feasible (do project staff or stakeholders have the time, skills, and means to monitor it?).

In designing indicators, many issues must be considered.

Comparison to a norm: The use of gender-sensitive indicators should involve comparison to a norm (for example, "the situation of women in a program compared to the situation of men in the program" or "compared to women in the country as a whole"). In this way, the indicator can focus on questions of gender equity rather than only on the status of women. Examples would include "the percentage of women actively participating as members of natural resource management committees" or "numbers of women and men with land certificates in the project province compared with a neighboring province."

Disaggregation: Data should be disaggregated by gender. In an ideal situation (and especially on a larger scale), indicators should also be disaggregated by age, caste, socioeconomic grouping, and by national or regional origin (for instance, "graduates from training course, disaggregated by sex and caste"). This level of detail will allow a broader analysis of which social forces within a society have shaped the particular status of women and men in that society. For instance, in Nepal, high-caste city women are likely to be in a considerably better socioeconomic situation than low-caste rural men.

Ease of access and clarity: Indicators should be phrased in easily understandable language and developed at a level relevant to the institutional capabilities of the country concerned. They must not be ambiguous. An indicator should be understood in the same way by all the project staff carrying out M&E. A potentially ambiguous term can be defined according to an existing definition, or a more precise definition can be formulated until there is no ambiguity whatsoever. For instance, rather than "the *adoption* of a new technique by the target group of men and women farmers," a more precise indicator might be "the *use* of a new technique

over two successive planting seasons by the target group of men and women farmers."

Validity: The information that indicators provide must be close to the reality they are measuring. Ways to ensure this include (1) common sense, (2) whether the indicator reflects similar findings in different situations, and (3) whether different survey instruments yield or uncover the same indicators. In general, the validity of an indicator can be enhanced by triangulation or by using multiple sources of information and data.

Reliability: Reliability means that indicators must be accurate and consistent. For example, an indicator is reliable if multiple uses of the same instrument (such as an interview or a survey) yield the same or similar results. No data are absolutely reliable, but reliability checks should be made: for example, census findings should be compared to findings from microlevel studies for accuracy.

Measurability: Indicators must be about items that are measurable. Concepts such as "women's empowerment" or "gender equity" may be difficult to define and measure. Proxy indicators may have to stand in for less precise concepts: for instance, "the percentage of women enrolling in agricultural training in x province before and after the project intervention" is easier to measure than "the number of women motivated to pursue agricultural training as a result of project empowerment."

What is being measured? Indicators should be relevant to the level: Is a *project's* impact being measured, or the *output* of a particular activity? At the output level, "the number of women and men that participated in x training course" is relevant, but at a higher level, it would be better to measure the result of that training, such as "the number of women and men confidently providing extension advice to farmers" or "the percentage of surveyed women in the target group who rate their access to land titling processes as having improved during the period of the program or project."

Sensitivity and time span: The time covered by the indicator should be specified—for example, "over the implementation period of the program," or "three years after the project has ended." It is also worth considering the sensitivity of indicators; in other words, will the indicator demonstrate a short-, medium-, or long-term change? Although demonstrating a long-term change may be useful for stakeholders, a project time scale of only a few years needs shorter-term indicators if changes are to be recorded and activities fine-tuned as necessary: for example, measurable positive changes are unlikely to be seen in national forest cover during a three-year project (no matter how laudable the goal).

Feasibility of indicators: An indicator makes it possible to focus and structure data collection but serves no purpose as long as the data do not exist. To ensure the feasibility of an indicator, it is necessary to indicate the source of the information to use, for example, land administration office records of land title issuance or questionnaire surveys to be carried out by the project, using specially employed enumerators.

If no source is available or feasible, the indicator should be changed. If no feasible indicator can be found, then the question may need to be excluded.

Simplicity: There should not be too many indicators. Relying upon several indicators allows for cross-checking and strengthens the evidence base for answering a question, but an excessive number of indicators will increase the data collection workload and cost and may not necessarily improve the soundness of the answer. As a rough guide, only six indicators per component/output or project objective should be used.

Be realistic: Make sure that the indicators at the goal and purpose level are realistic and measure achievable benefits. For example, do not anticipate an unrealistic (over 25 percent) increase in household incomes during a short period or do not expect training of women legal advisers to change women's access to land dramatically (use measures of staff capability to measure the benefit of the training instead).

Setting up the system in projects and programs

Baseline and targets: An outcome indicator has two components—a baseline and a target. The baseline is the situation before a program or activity begins. It is the starting point for monitoring results. The target is the expected situation at the end of a program or activity. (Output indicators rarely require a baseline, because outputs are being newly produced and the baseline is that they do not exist [UNDP 2002]).

Project versus program indicators: Indicators at *the project level* are usually limited to the time frame in which a project is implemented (or a set period after completion, for measuring impact). They encompass only the limited geographical and target group focus of a project (for an example, see table 16.4). They usually measure the following:

- Expected or unexpected project outcomes for women and men (compared with project objectives)
- Participation (quantity or quality) of women and men in project activities
- Access to decision making, project resources, and project services by women and men

- Changes in equality of opportunity or decision-making opportunities
- The impact or effectiveness of activities targeted to address women's or men's practical needs, such as new skills, knowledge, resources, opportunities, or services
- Changes in human resources devoted to the project (for example, the number of women or men among project staff or the number of women extension staff)
- The impact and effectiveness of activities targeting improved gender awareness among staff and beneficiaries
- Met or unmet practical and strategic needs of women and men (compared with expressed needs)
- Changes in project budget allocation toward gender at this level
- Emergence of new gender issues in a project or as a result of a project.

The Canadian International Development Agency, in its *Guide to Gender Sensitive Indicators* (CIDA 1997), gives useful examples of how to design gender-sensitive indicators for agriculture.

Indicators at the *program or sectoral level* will usually have a longer time frame and cover a larger geographical area and target group (table 16.5). They might be designed to measure the following:

- Changes in the capacity of staff in government partner organizations, NGOs, and international donor agencies to deal with gender issues
- Development and use of tools and procedures to mainstream gender equity:

  - Changes in recruitment practices relating to equal opportunities
  - Changes in budget allocation toward gender and related outcomes

- Whether subprojects carry out gender-sensitive monitoring
- Whether gender-disaggregated data are collected from the field and used at the national level
- How resources are being transferred to the field level and then spent
- How effective the expenditure on gender-related outputs has been in meeting agricultural program goals.

Gender-sensitive outcomes may include a range of agriculture-related as well as other sectoral indicators, depending on the particular constraints identified in the institutional analysis and the baseline gender analysis.

Expected result	Indicators	Data sources
Result 1: Improved agricultural extension service system	• By project end, all participating communes have at least one trained commune-level extensionist, and a minimum of 20 percent are women • Extension staff carry out their jobs in a confident and competent manner • Provincial and district extension officers in project areas actively support fieldwork at the community level • Willingness to pay is demonstrated: farmers pay 10 percent of the costs of commune extensionists • Women and men farmers are satisfied with their access to quality extension services	• Commune records • Community interviews • Observation • Training records
Result 2: Diversified and strengthened farming systems leading to improved income generation for men and women farmers	• Both women farmers and poor farmers are included as beneficiaries • By the end of the project, income per hectare has increased by 15 percent from productivity gains • More productive and diverse production models are applied and replicated by men and women farmers in project areas • New species or technology does not cause adverse environmental impacts (environmental impact assessed before use) • x number of new models for crop and animal diversification are in use, based on the preferences of men and women farmers	• Extension service records • Project records
Result 3: Cost-effective, gravity-fed upland irrigation schemes completed	• By project end, at least 50 upland irrigation schemes are completed • Irrigation users have an improved understanding of the importance of watershed protection and the potential impact on water quantity and quality • Schemes are self-managed, with revenue collection systems covering the operational and maintenance costs • Women and ethnic minorities participate actively in making decisions regarding water use and in production planning • Women make up at least one-third of the membership of irrigation user management committees	• Commissioning records • Infrastructure bidding and contracting records • Irrigation user agreements • Minutes and accounts of management committees

Source: Adapted from an unpublished program document for the Thua Thien Hue Rural Development Program, Vietnam, 2004.

Designing milestones and triggers for loan disbursement

When development banks are preparing country loans, a set of conditions, triggers, and milestones are developed that are used in clarifying, implementing, and monitoring the overall reform program supported by the development policy operation. Gender has not figured highly in this process thus far, but it would be one means to encourage the consideration of gender in monitoring (box 16.20).

As in designing indicators, specificity—meaning clarity, not excessive detail—is a key attribute of good conditions, triggers, and milestones. Poorly specified conditions or triggers may give rise to disputes about whether the key elements of the reform program are on track.

Table 16.5   Gender-Sensitive Indicators in an Agricultural Sector Program

Development objective	Impact indicators	Targets
Higher and increasingly equal standard of living in program target areas	Level of income generated from agricultural activities for both men- and women-controlled crops	Men: Increase by 15 percent; Women: Increase by 20 percent In Project Year (PY) 15
	Difference in income level between woman- and man-headed households	Decrease by 20 percent in PY 15
	Nutritional status for women and men (targets will be broken down into further detail after preliminary surveys)	n.a.
	Distribution of workload: working hours of rural women	Reduced by 5 percent in PY 15

Immediate objectives	Outcome indicators	Targets
Rights:		
Increased women's control over income and agricultural products	Percentage of women who have control or joint control over family income and farm products	Increased by 15 percent in PY 10
	Number of lawsuits concerning women's access to land under new Land Act	Increased by 20 percent by PY 8
Resources:		
Increased productivity of women-controlled cash and noncash crops	Productivity of agricultural products	Increased by 10 percent by PY 15
	Poultry and vegetable production	Poultry increased by 40 tons, vegetables by 100 tons in PY 8
Marginalized men livestock producers having found new viable sources of income	Percentage of marginalized livestock producers who have created a viable source of income as crop producers, agricultural and industrial workers, and so on	Increased by 30 percent by PY 15

Outputs	Output indicators	Targets
Rights:		
Increased awareness among men and women farmers of gender equity in regard to control over income and products	Percentage of target population who are aware of women's rights to control income and agricultural products	Increased by 30 percent by PY 5
Increased awareness of women's and men's rights to land	Percentage of target population who know basic facts about their rights	Increased by 60 percent by PY 5
Resources:		
Government officials practicing gender-sensitive extension methodologies and promoting gender-sensitive technologies	Percentage of spot checks in which extension is found to be gender sensitive	Increased by 80 percent by PY 8
Increased homestead gardening	Number of households producing vegetables for own consumption	Increased by 20 percent by PY 10
Improved loan access for marginalized livestock producers	Number of loans given to former livestock producers	Increased by 20 percent by PY 10
Cross-cutting issues:		
Improved monitoring of gender issues in the agricultural sector	Gender-sensitive evaluations and annual and semiannual progress reports, including gender-sensitive indicators and monitoring tools, produced	Three reports per year from PY 3
	Lessons learned from monitoring fed back into the planning system	Minimum of two lessons learned from PY 3
	Gender-sensitive databases established	One database by PY 3

(Table continues on the following page)

Table 16.5   Gender-Sensitive Indicators in an Agricultural Sector Program *(continued)*

Outputs	Output indicators	Targets
Improved gender-sensitive planning in the agricultural sector	Number of measurable gender-sensitive targets formulated in annual work plans at all levels by PY 2	At least two targets per plan by PY 2
Strategies concerning woman-headed households implemented	Percentage of all extension officers aware of and practicing the strategy's central elements	80 percent by PY 5

Activities	Process indicators	Targets
Rights:		
Pilot projects to increase women's control over agricultural products identified	Number of pilot projects approved	Four projects approved
Formulation of gender strategy for the agricultural sector at national, regional, and local levels	Strategy has been approved	One approval
Formulation of women's rights in new Land Act	Act has been approved and includes women's inheritance and ownership of land	One approval
Implement information campaigns on women's improved rights concerning access to and control over land	Number of men and women farmers reached by the campaign	Men: 100,000; Women: 100,000

Source: Adapted from DANIDA 2006.

Box 16.20   Designing Conditions, Triggers, and Milestones

Conditions are the actions deemed critical to achieving the outcomes of the program supported by the development policy operation *and* included in the operation documents as legal conditions for disbursements under a World Bank loan, credit, or grant.

Triggers, as used in the context of programmatic development policy operations, are the planned actions in the second or later year of a program that are deemed critical to achieving the outcomes of the program and that will be the basis for establishing the prior actions for later operations. In other words, triggers are the expected prior actions for a subsequent loan, credit, or grant.

Milestones mark the progress in implementing the program. A milestone can be an action or an outcome that is expected to be realized during the implementation period rather than at the end of the operation. Milestones are *not* legal conditions for disbursement or triggers.

Source: World Bank and OPCS 2004.

- *Don't* set too many triggers or conditions, only those of highest priority, as there is a risk for disbursement and progress if they are not met.
- *Don't* use outcomes (that is, monitorable effects of actions) as conditions or triggers unless their realization is largely under the control of the government.
- *Do* indicate what actions are to be done, by which agency of the government, and approximately when.
- *Do* include intermediate outcomes and monitor them carefully.
- *Do* use quantitative indicators, including baselines and targets, whenever possible.

Good examples:

- Condition for first loan: "Parliament has adopted legislation to ensure land certificates are issued to both husband and wife."
- Trigger for second disbursement: "Increase allocation in the 2008 Budget for recruitment of women staff in the agriculture ministry nationwide by at least 10 percent over the allocation in the 2007 budget."

A bad example:

- As a milestone, "improved social indicators" is too vague to be useful.

Practicalities of monitoring and evaluation

How much monitoring is enough? The key issue to consider is that the purpose of M&E is *to guide implementation* of a project or program, so there is a limit to the resources that should be used for M&E. The collection of information has a cost, and that cost will usually determine the methods used and the scope of information collection. Collecting primary data in the field is more expensive than using census data.

Modification of indicators

As a program or project is implemented, it sometimes becomes necessary to modify the logical framework or results framework in light of experience or changed circumstances, then it also becomes important to modify the indicators. Modifying the indicators does not mean lowering the targets to meet the expected outcomes (although this sometimes occurs in national planning systems during the annual cycle). Instead, the types of indicators need to be modified.

For example, if a project was implementing activities to encourage local communities to support the concept of women obtaining legal tenure together with their husbands or as single landowners, the indicators might be "the percentage of certificates including a woman's name, out of the total number of land certificates issued in the district during 2007." However, if the national government changes the law to require that women's names are included, then the awareness-raising activities *may* no longer be required and therefore would probably not be monitored.

GENDER-DISAGGREGATED DATA AVAILABILITY AND COLLECTION

In order to carry out gender-sensitive monitoring, disaggregated data are required. Ideally, for reasons of cost and scale, existing data sources should be used. The following sections look at what is available, how useful it is, selecting data sources, and improving their accuracy.

What data are available now, and how useful are they?

A prerequisite for establishing gender-sensitive indicators is the availability of statistical data disaggregated by gender (and ideally age and ethnicity), as well as qualitative information reflecting differences between women and men. Three main data systems produce useful information for monitoring, some of them gender sensitive: census surveys, the System of National Accounts of the country in question (comprising data from different administrative units), and sample surveys of the population, such as official living standards surveys. Programs and projects usually rely on these systems for baseline and monitoring information, particularly for quantitative data, in addition to developing their own program- or project-specific indicators. In addition, country-level social assessments, such as the Country Social Analysis and Country Gender Assessments, are important references for developing relevant indicators.

Limitations face planners in using statistical information. The accuracy of the data generated from censuses may be subject to various problems, including infrequent collection, gender bias, poor enumeration, and imprecise definition of key terms. For instance, women's economic activity is underrepresented in most censuses and national surveys, because women often work outside of the formal job market, and the contribution of women to economic development is difficult to measure. In many developing countries, statistical data are outdated or inaccurate, and the capacity to collect, analyze, disseminate, and store data is often inadequate.

Gender-sensitive quantitative indicators cannot be used alone. They must be complemented by gender analysis and qualitative monitoring to understand any changes they may demonstrate. As well as designing specific indicators and collecting information, projects and programs may also find it useful to access data from other organizations, such as information gathered by the World Bank in participatory poverty analyses or international crop or forestry data from FAO. For high-level data, the UN Human Development Report may contain useful national information.

As noted earlier, a general lack of gender-specific data exists relevant to agriculture. Most government agencies collect data based on households, products, or regions, which usually means that gender is ignored. Even when disaggregated information is collected, it is often ignored or filtered out of project or program planning. The FAO concluded that a number of fundamental issues were not addressed adequately in agricultural censuses and surveys, such as gender differentiation in land ownership and use, access to credit, training and extension services, technology, and income (FAO 1999). A study of agricultural census data from Africa found that data collection methods were usually inadequate.[1] The authors identified a clear need for capacity building—first, among statisticians to perform gender-explicit analyses of agricultural data, and second, among development planners, so that they can better use census data in general development planning and use gender-disaggregated data in gender-specific planning.

Manasan and Villanueva (2005) tried to analyze how economic contraction in the Philippines affected women's benefits from government programs and noted the difficulty of obtaining gender-disaggregated agricultural data. Even when figures are provided for women and men, they can be quite misleading because they tend to assume that only the "household head"—usually recorded as being a man—is the farmer. Tempelman and Keita observe that, particularly in Africa, the oldest household member who is a man (whether usually present or not) is recorded automatically as the "household head."[2] This tendency potentially contributes to the underestimation of the number of (sub)holdings run by women who manage their own sub-production units within man-headed agricultural holdings. Tempelman and Keita also report that since the 2000 round of the World Census of Agriculture, several African countries have tried to rectify this problem by adopting the concept of "subholder." Defining the concept of "household" carefully is particularly important, as is, with societal norms in mind, to recognize the role played by many women as the main household provider. Economic activity may be defined or understood in varied ways (paid or unpaid work is an obvious difference). But is work on a family farm by a woman considered economic activity? What about household chores? If a nonfamily member is paid to thresh rice, cook, or clean, then this work is counted as economic activity, but if a family member does the work, it usually is not. Women themselves will often discount their own work (both paid and unpaid) as a contribution to the family income. Data from censuses and surveys generally underreport women's paid employment.

Household surveys commonly consider the amount of income spent on food per household per year but do not differentiate between food consumed by men and women household members. If data are to be collected from household surveys, and gender-specific information is required, phrasing the questions so that this information is actually obtained is important.

Women's land ownership rights differ from country to country, but land is often under ownership and control of men (box 16.21). Gender-sensitive indicators may be available from agricultural censuses or land registration records to track land-tenure issues. Because access to credit often depends on access to land, the monitoring of credit activities should take land tenure into consideration.

The FAO's Gender and Population Division is working with its Statistics Division as well as member countries to build capacity through training and technical support in gender and statistics for Ministries of Agriculture and central

---

| Box 16.21 | Culturally Related Questions for Monitoring |

Is land mainly under the control of men or women? What are the consequences for gender relations, decisions about land sales, and cropping patterns?

What are the inheritance practices in the country concerning land? If women can legally inherit land, do they do this in practice?

If women own land, does this also mean that they make key decisions concerning crop selection and marketing?

Has land reform benefited men and women equally?

Do women have equal access to credit facilities? Does such access translate into control over credit in terms of decision making?

Source: Author.

---

statistics offices. The FAO has developed gender-sensitive indicators for the agricultural sector (Curry 2002) and proposed that a gender focus incorporating both age and sex is important for analysis of the agricultural sector, because women and children make important contributions to agricultural production and food security. Gender-sensitive data and indicators on the structure of land ownership, access to and use of productive resources, and cropping and livestock production patterns are required to supplement available data on the age-sex composition of the labor force economically active in agriculture. In anticipation of stakeholders' increased need for information, steps have been taken to improve the indicators and gender sensitivity of data collected through national censuses or to supplement census data with data from other socioeconomic surveys. Examples include the concept of "plot manager," introduced in the national censuses of Guinea, Senegal, and Togo; the collection of gender-disaggregated labor data, including data on unpaid family labor, in Burkina Faso; and the addition of questions on specific topics, such as agroprocessing, in Cape Verde.

In its work with national governments, the DFID supports a stronger focus on generating evidence, statistics, and indicators.[3] For example, the DFID supported Cambodian efforts to integrate gender indicators into the monitoring framework for the national poverty plan, and in Nepal it will support the development of a national poverty monitoring and analysis system using inclusive and disaggregated indicators. These efforts should increase the availability, routine collection, and reporting of gender-disaggregated data from national statistical systems (including more specific data on, for example, income, employment, and access to services) and foster greater use of such data in national monitoring systems. They will also increase the use of gender-disaggregated data in the monitoring sections of national development strategies.

Selecting data sources for gender-sensitive monitoring

Secondary data are not produced specifically for monitoring and evaluation but can have direct and indirect links with a project or program. Secondary data provide baseline information and help monitor a project or program's overall goal and objectives, the form its inputs (investments) have taken, how it is carried out (activities), and its results (outcomes). The main sources of secondary data include official documents such as country development sector plans, sociological and demographic research, reference documents for the project, activity reports, and situation analyses.

FAO maintains databases with information from the censuses of individual countries. These data are derived from periodic agricultural censuses and yearly surveys of agricultural production, including forestry and fisheries. These data collection instruments are designed to monitor the inputs, outputs, and management of agricultural holdings to formulate policy recommendations for sustainable development and reliable food production systems.

The national statistics system in a country can normally provide the following:

- National statistics (census, household, and business surveys), usually gathered by the central statistics agency with support from provincial statistics agencies
- Administrative data (from line ministries and local governments and services)
- Other surveys and datasets (usually from academic and research institutes)
- Qualitative data (these constitute a small but growing data component and include, for example, participatory poverty assessments).

Primary data are collected specifically for monitoring and evaluating a project or program. Data are collected from all project stakeholders (involved directly and indirectly, positively and negatively), using such tools as direct observation, focus group discussions, interviews, and meetings.

In policy and national program monitoring, secondary data sources will be most important, supplemented by field visits to cross-check their validity against local circumstances. In project monitoring, primary data sources are important, because they respond to the specific project indicators. An inventory of available data should be made during planning. What and where are the data, and how can project/program leaders use them for M&E? What additional data need to be collected to cover gaps?

In making decisions about data sources for indicators, consider these questions for each indicator:

- Is the information available from existing sources?
- Is a new data collection effort required?
- How much data do we really need?
- How much data can we really use?
- What data sources are practical?
- Who will pay for data collection?
- Who will do data collection?
- How can staff and other stakeholders be involved in data collection?
- How will the data be analyzed?

For instance, in a rural development program in Vietnam, the plan outlined in the program document was to conduct a thorough baseline survey. However, analysis of existing data available from the government demonstrated that it would be adequate, supplemented by some qualitative and more localized information gathered from participatory rural appraisals and disaggregated by gender, ethnicity, and poverty. This approach saved time and money during the program's busy start-up period. On the other hand, data collection can go too far. A review of the monitoring system of a large, donor-funded rural development project in the Philippines recommended that a reality check should be conducted about the amount of data collected, because the system was overloaded. Projects should make sure that collecting additional data is really worthwhile and should consider the implications of each marginal addition to the data collection. For agricultural projects, recommendations suggest considering the benefits of collecting detailed data on farm household incomes and expenditures from a small sample (such as 10–20 farmers per zone or farming system) to back up broader secondary data. Collected properly, such primary data can provide useful insights into why farm families make the decisions they do, especially when trying to examine the gender impacts. Monitoring data should include a record of how men and women use time and money over the time frame of the program (to determine whether and why they change with the implementation of program interventions).

Steps to improve the accuracy and gender sensitivity of survey data

A numbers of steps can be taken to improve the accuracy and gender sensitivity of data collected through surveys.

- Enumerators should be given gender training. For instance, they could be trained to recognize that many activities done by women are part of general economic activities.
- In the instructions to enumerators, special emphasis should be given to gender issues.
- Local political and cultural sensitivities may mean that enumerators are reluctant to ask questions about "difficult" or "conflictive" issues. The importance of these questions should be explained, and enumerators encouraged to ask them—otherwise the results may not be accurate.
- Instructions to enumerators should emphasize the need to ask probing questions and not simply accept "yes" or "no" answers.

- In recruiting enumerators, efforts should be made to achieve a gender balance. Issues of age, ethnicity, or caste may also be vital to consider in seeking to reduce bias.
- Interviews should be timed to maximize opportunities for meeting with women and men, the young and old—in other words, with a cross-section of the community in question.
- Gathering data on the ages and genders of the head of the agricultural holding and members of the holding's labor force will make it possible to construct extremely useful, gender-sensitive indicators.

Recommendations for improving data collection

Development cooperation organizations should continue to support capacity building in statistics offices, including training in gender sensitization, the development of gender-sensitive indicators, and interview training (for census workers). Support should also be provided to purchase equipment that facilitates data handling.

The information collected by statistics offices and other data collection agencies should be made available as needed, to provide field workers and government staff with data in various formats for monitoring programs and projects.

Training Community Members to Carry Out Project Planning, Monitoring, and Evaluation

Many projects have trained members of participating communities to carry out M&E. The World Bank *Social Analysis Sourcebook* (World Bank 2003: 49) cites participatory M&E as a "means to systematically evaluate progress and impact early in the project cycle by bringing the perspectives and insights of all stakeholders, beneficiaries as well as project implementers. All stakeholders identify issues, conduct research, analyze findings, make recommendations, and take responsibility for necessary action."

Levels of participation and the means of ensuring gender equity vary from project to project. This Innovative Activity Profile discusses lessons from Sri Lanka's Community Development and Livelihood Improvement Project—also known as the Gemi Diriya ("village strength") Project—with some additional insights from Indonesia's Community Empowerment for Rural Development Project.

One difficulty with participatory M&E is that community-driven development programs typically serve a large number of small, widely dispersed communities, and managing such programs requires intense support, especially at start-up and in the early stages of implementation. Using local NGOs, local government staff, and other local resources is not always successful because of high costs, large distances, and insufficient local capacity.

What's innovative? Training women as community professionals or facilitators is a successful step in building confidence and providing a good gender role model. Community facilitators can identify constraints and opportunities in their villages and are effective at instilling confidence and mobilizing their communities. Women facilitators have much better access to women and youth—key decision makers and beneficiaries.

Experience with the Gemi Diriya Project demonstrates that building a network of trained community professionals or facilitators and involving them in all aspects of project implementation is an effective strategy to scale up in a sustainable, cost-effective manner (www.gemidiriya.org; Munshi, Hayward, and Verardo 2006).

PROJECT DESCRIPTION

A Village Self-Help Learning Initiative was piloted in 1999 in three villages in Sri Lanka's poor North Central Province. Its main objective was to introduce and test a model of participatory rural development that focused on empowering local communities to find their own solutions to local development problems. Key actions included mobilizing communities; building inclusive, accountable village organizations; and supporting their self-management.

To scale up the self-help initiative, the World Bank financed the Gemi Diriya Project, starting in October 2004.[1] The Bank has committed $181 million for 12 years to implement the project, which, like the village self-help initiative on which it is modeled, focuses on self-management and learning. To avoid the risk of exclusion of women, the project rules specified at least 30 percent women's representation in decision-making roles and that at least 50 percent of the benefits must be received by women, including capacity building and training. The project contracts external support organizations, such as local NGOs, to carry out an initial information campaign in villages, facilitate participatory planning and appraisals, support formation of village organizations, and offer preliminary training to its office holders. Once established, village organizations have access to a village development fund that finances activities in three main areas: capacity building, community infrastructure services subprojects, and livelihood support. Continued support and guidance are needed to strengthen the village organizations, but continued reliance on project staff would increase dependence and cost, so the idea of training and using community facilitators emerged. The community professionals and facilitators are trained in numerous ways, all supported by the project: through community peer trainers, Community Professionals Learning and Training Centres, and a mobile capacity-building team, which trains, mentors, and monitors community facilitators in the field, building their capacity and confidence in a cost-effective way.

Community professionals and facilitators have a number of advantages. They have a stake in their community's development, are better suited to identifying the constraints and opportunities in their villages, and are much more effective than outsiders in instilling confidence and mobilizing their communities. They also tend to be more accountable to their communities, because they live there and enjoy local legitimacy and trust. They provide a strong local input to Bank supervision missions and are a go-between for the overall implementation team of the project.

The formation of small groups is the foundation of the village organizations; it is the small groups that achieve the objectives of the development programs identified by the community. Training for small group members is thus one of the most important aspects of the project, and this training is provided by community professionals.

LINKING LEARNING, GENDER, AND M&E

The Community Professionals Learning and Training Centres are designed to provide comprehensive training for community professionals in social mobilization skills, M&E, and the Community Operational Manual used by the project, as well as overall social development processes. Based on the knowledge, skills, and field experience gained through this training, facilitators can provide better services to the project (and to other programs assisting with community development) and gain economic benefits for their work. They are paid via the Village Development Funds, but as their skills develop, they also can sell their services on a commercial basis (for instance, to NGOs, donors, or the government). A selection process and a system of grading and promotion are in use. More than 60 percent of community professionals or facilitators are women, who focus on improving gender equity in their communities. Women and poor youth in particular, and poor families more generally, have found the Community Professional Learning and Training Centres to be a very good source of income. The project has conducted a strong information campaign about its objectives and its emphasis on women and youth as project decision makers and intended beneficiaries.

In addition to providing specialized training to community facilitators, the project has had other impacts on improving gender equity, for example, the microfinance program, which provides loans exclusively for livelihood improvement and income-generating projects. Within only two years of its implementation, the program has acquired 71,000 members, who have formed 11,762 small groups. Of these, *80 percent* of the beneficiaries are women.

Six key methods are used to monitor and evaluate the project: a self-monitoring system, a monitoring system based on the project's management information system, internal management reviews, an external process monitoring system, impact evaluations, and social accountability monitoring. The village organization and its various committees continually assess their own performance against the locally developed indicators for capacity building, infrastructure development, livelihood support fund activities, and other activities. This self-monitoring is the main tool for the community to learn from project implementation and build capacity to manage village development.

Process monitoring evaluates how project activities lead to the required outputs, which ultimately produce the desired outcomes and benefits. More specifically, external process monitoring generates the information necessary for project management at all levels and for village organizations to perform their expected roles and responsibilities in the most effective and efficient manner.

One monitoring tool that has proven effective is the Community Report Card, which gathers feedback from the communities about the performance (quality, efficiency, and adequacy) of village organization office holders, community professionals, and project staff, among others. The Report Card is a powerful tool for the community to exert social control on the performance of these teams and alert them as to desired changes.

Another community training scheme with a gender focus was recently implemented in Indonesia and provides good comparisons to the one in Sri Lanka (box 16.22).

LESSONS LEARNED

Community facilitators are a powerful tool for social change and supporting development program activities. In particular, gender, age, and ethnicity should be considered in the selection of community trainers or facilitators (and, indeed,

Box 16.22   Indonesia: Bringing a Gender Focus to Community Empowerment

Between 2000 and 2006, the ADB-funded Community Empowerment for Rural Development Project sought to raise the incomes of about 110,000 poor families in six Indonesian provinces in Kalimantan and Sulawesi. The project supported the development of community-based savings and loan organizations and sought to strengthen rural financial institutions' capacity to extend credit. The project's second major effort was to build capacity for decentralized development planning within villages and within local and provincial levels of government, with an emphasis on infrastructure development.

The economic crisis in Indonesia in the late 1990s highlighted the need for a long-term strategy to reduce poverty significantly by emphasizing social inclusion and skills development among the poor. The Community Empowerment Project supported formal and informal training and decision-making processes to give local communities and government the institutional capacity to direct resources more efficiently to reduce poverty and improve the quality of life in their communities.

The project targeted women as members and decision makers of both savings and loan organizations and village planning committees. The decision to encourage women's full participation in this project was based on the fact that women in the project areas make major economic contributions to their house-

holds. Another reason to include women was to protect and develop women's economic interests in the project.

Despite the fact that women played an important role in the village economy and community affairs, they often felt more constrained than men in participating in village forums. The project was designed to foster women's equitable participation in two ways:

- It offered leadership training for women in the operation of savings and loan organizations, the workings of village planning forums, and the selection of village infrastructure projects.
- It considered women's specific capacities, economic activities, and interests in designing and forming training programs, village organizations, and savings and loan organizations.

Village planning forums were organized and social mobilization and human development training provided to ensure that women's groups participated in the village development planning process. Aside from training community members in planning and monitoring, government officers in the project's executing agency received training on decentralized development planning and gender and development. Gender-based training targets were set to ensure that women government staff received equitable training opportunities.

Source: ADB Gender and Development Web site and specific project documents, Community Empowerment for Rural Development Project, www.adb.org.

---

in all selection processes) to ensure access to the poorest sections of the community. In Gemi Diriya, an ethical framework is applied—the "golden rules" of good governance, equity, transparency, and cost efficiency—when dealing with the use of public finances. Information sharing and awareness raising have also proven to be vital in highlighting the role of all groups in the community, but particularly the key roles played by women and youth.

NOTES

Overview

The Overview was written by Pamela White (Consultant) and reviewed by Chitra Deshpande and Catherine Ragasa (Consultants); John Curry (FAO); Maria Hartl (IFAD);

and Indira Ekanayake, Eija Pehu, and Riikka Rajalahti (World Bank).

Thematic Note I

The Thematic Note was written by Pamela White (Consultant) and reviewed by Chitra Deshpande and Catherine Ragasa (Consultants); John Curry (FAO); Maria Hartl (IFAD); and Indira Ekanayake, Eija Pehu, and Riikka Rajalahti (World Bank).

Thematic Note 2

The Thematic Note was written by Pamela White (Consultant) and reviewed by Chitra Deshpande and Catherine Ragasa (Consultants); John Curry (FAO); Maria Hartl

(IFAD); and Indira Ekanayake, Eija Pehu, and Riikka Rajalahti (World Bank).

1. United Nations (Vietnam), "Gender Action Partnership (GAP)," www.un.org.vn.

2. Monica Fong, "Gender in Sector-Wide Development Policies and Programs," paper presented at the 3rd World Congress of Rural Women, Madrid, October 1-4, www.oecd.org.

3. See "Needs Assessment of Economic Planning Units in Gender Analysis in Selected Caribbean Countries," www.cepa.org.

4. See note 5 above.

5. See "Gender Equity Index 2007," www.socialwatch.org.

6. Caroline Moser, "An Introduction to Gender Audit Methodology: Its Design and Implementation in DFID Malawi," www.enterprise-impact.org.uk.

Thematic Note 3

The Thematic Note was written by Pamela White (Consultant) and reviewed by Chitra Deshpande and Catherine Ragasa (Consultants); John Curry (FAO); Maria Hartl (IFAD); and Indira Ekanayake, Eija Pehu, and Riikka Rajalahti (World Bank).

1. Diana Tempelman and Naman Keita, "Gender Concerns in Agricultural Census in Africa," paper presented at the 3rd International Conference on Agricultural Statistics, Measuring Sustainable Agricultural Indicators, Cancún, November 2–4, www.fao.org.

2. Ibid.

3. "Gender Equality Action Plan 2007–2009," www.dfid.gov.uk.

Innovative Activity Profile 1

The Innovative Activity Profile was written by Pamela White (Consultant) and reviewed by Catherine Ragasa (Consultant); and Natasha Hayward, Meena Munshi, and Eija Pehu (World Bank).

1. See "Community Development and Livelihood Improvement," Gemi Diriya project, www.worldbank.org.

REFERENCES

Overview

Asian Development Bank (ADB). n.d. *Gender Checklist: Agriculture.* Manila: ADB.

Australian Agency for International Development (AusAID). 2002. *Gender and Development: GAD Lessons and Challenges for the Australian Aid Program.* Canberra: AusAID.

Bamberger, Michael. 2002. "Impact Evaluations When Time and Money Are Limited: Lessons from International Development on the Design of Rapid and Economical, but Methodologically Sound, Impact Evaluations." Paper presented at the American Evaluation Association Professional Development Workshop, Impact Evaluation on a Shoestring, November 5.

Derbyshire, Helen. 2002. *Gender Manual: A Practical Guide for Development Policy Makers and Practitioners.* London: Department for International Development.

Food and Agriculture Organization (FAO). 2001. *Project Cycle Management Technical Guide.* Rome: SEAGA Socio-Economic and Gender Analysis Programme, FAO.

———. 2003. *Progress Report on Implementation of the FAO Gender and Development Plan of Action (2002–2007).* Rome: FAO.

Gender and Rural Development (GENRD). 2006. "FY05 Gender Portfolio Review." Internal report, Agriculture and Rural Development, World Bank, Washington, DC.

———. 2007. "FY06 Gender Portfolio Review." Internal report, Agriculture and Rural Development, World Bank, Washington, DC.

Hunt, Juliet, and Samvada Kheng. 2006. *Gender Equality Results in ADB Projects: Cambodia Country Report.* Manila: Asian Development Bank.

Mason, Karen Oppenheim. 2007. *Gender Equality and Aid Delivery: What Has Changed in Development Cooperation Agencies since 1999?* Paris: Organisation for Economic Co-operation and Development.

Ministry for Foreign Affairs (MFA) Finland. 2003. *Strategy and Action Plan for Promoting Gender Equality in Finland's Policy for Developing Countries, 2003–2007.* Helsinki: MFA. Also available at http://formin.finland.fi.

Nordic Development Fund (NDF). 2004. *Gender Equality Study: A Study on Addressing Gender Aspects in Projects Co-Financed by NDF in Developing Countries.* Final Report, March. Helsinki: NDF. Also available at www.ndf.fi.

Organisation for Economic Co-operation and Development (OECD). 1999. *DAC Guidelines for Gender Equality and Women's Empowerment in Development Cooperation.* Paris: OECD. Also available at www.oecd.org.

———. 2007. "Gender Equality and Aid Delivery: What Has Changed in Development Co-Operation Agencies since 1999?" Paris: OECD. Also available at www.oecd.org.

Peck, Lennart. 1998. "Evaluating Gender Equality—Policy and Practise: An Assessment of Sida's Evaluations in 1997–1998." SIDA Studies in Evaluation 98/3, Swedish Agency for Development Cooperation, Stockholm.

Punkari, Mikko, Marlene Fuentes, Pamela White, Riikka Rajalahti, and Eija Pehu. 2007. "Social and Environmental

Sustainability of Agriculture and Rural Development Investments: A Monitoring and Evaluation Toolkit." Agriculture and Rural Development, Discussion Paper 31, World Bank, Washington, DC.

Swedish Agency for Development Cooperation (SIDA). 2004. *Looking Back, Moving Forward*. SIDA Evaluation Manual. Stockholm: SIDA.

White, Pamela. 2007. "Participatory Monitoring and Evaluation Component, Sustainable Livelihoods Project, Mongolia." Final report, unpublished project documents.

World Bank. n.d. *World Bank Operational Manual*. Washington, DC: World Bank.

———. 1996. *The World Bank Participation Sourcebook*. Washington, DC: World Bank.

———. 2003a. *Social Analysis Sourcebook: Incorporating Social Dimensions into Bank-Supported Projects*. Washington, DC: World Bank.

———. 2003b. *Report on Social and Institutional Assessment: Pakistan: NWFP Community Infrastructure Project-II*. Washington, DC: World Bank.

———. 2003c. *Implementation Completion Report: NWFP Community Infrastructure and NHA Strengthening Project*. Washington, DC: World Bank.

———. 2005. *Gender Issues in Monitoring and Evaluation of Rural Development Projects: A Tool Kit*. Washington, DC: World Bank.

———. 2006a. "Implementing the Bank's Gender Mainstreaming Strategy: Annual Monitoring Report for FY04 and FY05." Gender and Development Group, Poverty Reduction and Economic Management, World Bank, Washington, DC, January 11.

———. 2006b. "Monitoring and Evaluation: Measuring and Assessing Agricultural Development Programs." In *Agriculture Investment Sourcebook*, Module 12. Washington, DC: World Bank.

———. 2007. "Process Monitoring in Andhra Pradesh: An Award-Winning Innovation in Project Supervision." Agricultural and Rural Development Notes 22, World Bank, Washington, DC, June.

Thematic Note I

Food and Agriculture Organization (FAO). 2001. *Intermediate Level Handbook*. Rome: Socio-Economic and Gender Analysis Programme, FAO.

International Fund for Agricultural Development (IFAD). 2007. "Exploring Gender Issues in Our Work: Main Findings from a Questionnaire Survey." Paper presented at Looking for New Directions: Gender Mainstreaming and Women's Empowerment Workshop, Rome, May 16–17.

Punkari, Mikko, Marlene Fuentes, Pamela White, Riikkaa Rajalahti, and Eija Pehu. 2007. "Social and Environmental Sustainability of Agriculture and Rural Development Investments: A Monitoring and Evaluation Toolkit." Agriculture and Rural Development, Discussion Paper 31, World Bank, Washington, DC.

United Nations Development Programme (UNDP). 2002. "Handbook on Monitoring and Evaluation for Results." Also available at www.undp.org.

Thematic Note 2

Balmori, Helena Hofbauer. 2003. "Gender and Budgets: Overview Report." BRIDGE (Development-Gender), Institute of Development Studies, University of Sussex, Brighton. Also available at www.bridge.ids.ac.uk.

Deutsche Gesellschaft für Technische Zusammenarbeit (GTZ). 2005. "Kenya." Making Poverty Reduction Strategies Work, Good Practice Sheet, GTZ, Eschborn, Germany, October.

Gaynor, Cathy. 2006. "Paris Declaration Commitments and Implications for Gender Equality and Women's Empowerment." Paper for consideration by the OECD-DAC Network on Gender Equality and the OECD-DAC Working Party on Aid Effectiveness, Organisation for Economic Co-operation and Development, Paris, July 6–7.

International Monetary Fund/International Development Association (IMF/IDA). 2001. "Joint Staff Assessment of the Poverty Reduction Strategy Paper." IMF and IDA, Washington, DC.

Kusek, Jody Zall, and Ray C. Rist. 2004. "Ten Steps to a Results-Based Monitoring and Evaluation System." Washington, DC: World Bank. Also available at www.wi.wur.nl.

Moser, Annalise. 2007. Gender and Indicators: Overview Report." BRIDGE (Development-Gender), Institute of Development Studies, University of Sussex, Brighton. Also available at www.bridge.ids.ac.uk.

Moser, Caroline, Olivia M'Chaju-Liwewe, Annalise Moser, and Naomi Ngwira. 2004. "DFID Malawi Gender Audit: Evaporated, Invisibilized or Resisted?" Department for International Development, London, October.

Muro, Asseny. 2007. Presentation on Tanzania Gender Networking Program to a Seminar on New Aid Modalities of Funding, Ministry for Foreign Affairs of Finland, Helsinki, May 4.

National Economic and Development Authority, Philippines (NEDA). 2004. *Harmonized Gender and Development Guidelines for Project Development, Implementation, Monitoring and Evaluation*. Manila: Asian Development

Bank for NEDA and the National Commission on the Role of Filipino Women.

Organisation for Economic Co-operation and Development (OECD). 2002. *Gender Equality in Sector Wide Approaches—A Reference Guide.* Paris: OECD.

———. 2007. *Gender Equality and Aid Delivery: What Has Changed in Development Co-Operation Agencies since 1999?* Paris: OECD.

Packard, Le Anh Tu. 2006. "Gender Dimensions of Viet Nam's Comprehensive Macroeconomic and Structural Reform Policies," Occasional Paper 14, United Nations Research Institute for Social Development, Geneva.

World Bank. 2002. *PRSP Sourcebook.* Washington, DC: World Bank.

———. 2004. "Using Poverty and Social Impact Analysis to Support Development Policy Operations." Good Practice in Development Policy Note 2, World Bank, Operations Policy and Country Services, World Bank, Washington, DC.

———. 2007. "Promoting Gender Equality and Women's Empowerment." In *Global Monitoring Report 2007: Confronting the Challenges of Gender Equality and Fragile States,* chapter 3. Washington, DC: World Bank.

Thematic Note 3

Beck, Tony. 2000. *Using Gender Sensitive Indicators: A Reference Manual for Governments and Other Stakeholders.* London: Commonwealth Secretariat.

Canadian International Development Agency (CIDA). 1997. *Guide to Gender Sensitive Indicators.* Minister of Public Works and Government Services Canada, Hull. Also available at www.acdi-cida.gc.ca/inet/images.nsf/vLUImages/Policy/$file/WID-GUID-E.pdf.

Curry, John. 2002. "Establishment of a Core Set of Gender-Sensitive Indicators for the Agricultural Sector: A Preliminary Proposal." Paper presented at the United Nations Economic Commission for Europe and Statistical Commission Conference of European Statisticians, Working Session on Gender Statistics, Geneva, September 23–25.

Derbyshire, Helen. 2002. *Gender Manual: A Practical Guide for Development Policy Makers and Practitioners.* London: Department for International Development.

Food and Agriculture Organization (FAO). 1999. *Filling the Data Gap: Gender-Sensitive Statistics for Agricultural Development.* Rome: FAO.

———. 2003. *Progress Report on Implementation of the FAO Gender and Development Plan of Action (2002–2007).* Rome: FAO.

International Fund for Agricultural Development (IFAD). 2007. "Exploring Gender Issues in Our Work: Main Find-

ings from a Questionnaire Survey." Paper presented at Looking for New Directions: Gender Mainstreaming and Women's Empowerment Workshop, Rome, May 16–17.

Manasan, Rosario, and Eden Villanueva. 2005. "The Impact of Fiscal Restraint on Budgetary Allocations for Women's Programs." Discussion Paper Series No. 2005-16. Philippine Institute for Development Studies, Makati City, August.

Ministry of Foreign Affairs of Denmark (DANIDA). 2006. "Gender-Sensitive Monitoring and Indicators." Technical Note, DANIDA, Copenhagen. Also available at www.danidadevforum.um.dk.

National Economic and Development Authority, Philippines (NEDA). 2004. *Harmonized Gender and Development Guidelines for Project Development, Implementation, Monitoring and Evaluation.* Manila: Asian Development Bank for NEDA and the National Commission on the Role of Filipino Women.

United Nations Development Programme (UNDP). 2002. *Handbook on Monitoring and Evaluating for Results.* New York: UNDP.

World Bank and Operations Policy and Country Services (OPCS). 2004. "Designing Development Policy Operations." Good Practice Note for Development Policy Lending 1, World Bank, Operations Policy and Country Services, Washington, DC.

Innovative Activity Profile 1

Munshi, Meena, Natasha Hayward, and Barbara Verardo. 2006. "A Story of Social and Economic Empowerment: The Evolution of 'Community Professionals' in Sri Lanka." Social Funds Innovation Notes 4 (2), World Bank, Washington, DC.

World Bank. 2003. *Social Analysis Sourcebook: Incorporating Social Dimensions into Bank-Supported Projects.* Washington, DC: World Bank.

FURTHER READING

Thematic Note 1

Derbyshire, Helen. 2003. "Progress Report on Implementation of the FAO Gender and Development Plan of Action (2002–2007)." Rome: FAO. Available at www.fao.org.

IFAD. 2002. *Managing for Impact in Rural Development: A Guide for Project M&E.* Rome: International Fund for Agricultural Development.

World Bank. 2002. *PRSP Sourcebook.* Washington, DC: World Bank.

———. World Bank. 2006. "Monitoring and Evaluation: Measuring and Assessing Agricultural Development

Programs." In *Agriculture Investment Sourcebook,* Module 12. Washington, DC: World Bank.

———. 2007. *Social and Environmental Sustainability of Agriculture and Rural Development Investments: A Monitoring and Evaluation Toolkit.* Washington, DC: World Bank.

The Asian Development Bank has an excellent Web site (www.adb.org/Gender/practices.asp) on "Projects Addressing Gender Concerns," with case studies.

Thematic Note 2

Bamberger, Michael, Mark Blackden, Lucia Fort, and Violetta Manoukian. 2002. "Gender." In *A Sourcebook for Poverty Reduction Strategies,* chapter 10. Washington, DC: World Bank.

Budlender, Debbie. 2007. "Financing for Development: Aid Effectiveness and Gender-Responsive Budgets." Commonwealth Secretariat, Eighth Commonwealth Women's Affairs Ministers Meeting Kampala, Uganda, June 11–14.

Department for International Development (DFID). 2006. *Evaluation of DFID'S Policy and Practice in Support of Gender Equality and Women's Empowerment. Thematic Studies,* vol. 3: "Gender and Budget Support," "Gender Equality through Justice and Rights-Based Policies and Programs," "DFID's Efforts to Address Gender Equality Goals in International Partnerships," and "Summary of Research in Gender and DFID'S Support to Pro-Poor Growth." London: DFID, COWI Evaluation Team.

Thematic Note 3

Asian Development Bank (ADB). 2003. *Gender and Development: Our Framework Policies and Strategies.* Manila: ADB. Available at www.adb.org.

Curry, John. 2004. *Establishment of a Core Set of Gender-Sensitive Indicators for the Agricultural Sector: A Preliminary Proposal.* Rome: Food and Agriculture Organization.

Curry, John, and Diana Tempelman. 2006. "Improving the Use of Gender and Population Factors in Agricultural Statistics: A Review of FAO's Support to Member Countries in Gender Statistics." Paper presented at the Inter-Agency and Expert Group Meeting on the Development of Gender Statistics, December 12–14, United Nations, New York. Available at http://unstats.un.org.

Economic Commission for Latin America and the Caribbean. 2002. "Tools and Indicators for Gender Impact Analysis, Monitoring and Evaluation." Interagency Network on Women and Gender Equality, New York, February 26–March 1. Available at www.un.org.

Food and Agriculture Organization (FAO). n.d. Documentation on gender and statistics available at http://unstats.un.org.

———. 2001. *Gender Sensitive Indicators: A Key Tool for Gender Mainstreaming.* Rome: FAO.

———. 2003. "Socio-Economic and Gender-Sensitive Indicators in the Management of Natural Resources." Sustainable Development Department, FAO, Rome. Available at FAO's SD Dimensions Web site: www.fao.org.

———. 2005. *Agricultural Censuses and Gender: Lessons Learned in Africa.* Rome: FAO.

Mayoux, Linda. 2002. "What Do We Want to Know? Selecting Gender Indicators." Available at www.ids.ac.uk.

Whitehead, Ann. 2003. "Failing Women, Sustaining Poverty: Gender in Poverty Reduction Strategy Papers." Report for the UK Gender and Development Network (GADN), GADN and Christian Aid. Available at www.gadnetwork.org.uk.

INDEX

Note: Boxes, figures, notes, and tables are indicated by b, f, n, and t, respectively.

A

AAU. *See* Association of American Universities (AAU)

abandonment, and land rights, 142, 166*n*4

accountability, 24, 25, 56–57, 509

  of CDD projects, 61

  and governance, 33

  mechanisms for, 69

accumulating savings and credit associations (ASCAs), 86, 96, 120*n*1

ACEs. *See* civic extension associations (ACEs)

acquired immune deficiency syndrome (AIDS), 1, 2

  and agricultural markets, 193

  and child-headed households, 603, 635*n*7, 635*n*10

  contract clauses concerning, 380

  coping strategies for, 433, 434*b*10.5

  in fishing communities, 578

  and food security, 14

  and forestry sector, 651, 652*b*15.1, 654, 668*n*2

  impact of, 305, 310*n*1–2

    on MDGs, 645

    on rural households, 613

  and JFFLSs, 305–8, 310*n*107

  and labor rights, 337

  and land and water degradation, 456

  and local knowledge systems, 461*b*10.14

  and rural infrastructure, 368, 374

  as safety risk for women in workforce, 321

  Tanzania, 303

  and training programs, 197

  workplace awareness campaigns, 326

  See also health and health care

ACT. *See* African Conservation Tillage network (ACT)

ActionAid, 544

Action Plan for the Reduction of Absolute Poverty (PARPA), Mozambique, 681*b*16.5, 700*b*16.13, 703*b*16.17

active labor market programs (ALMPs), 324

ADB. *See* Asian Development Bank (ADB)

administration, monitoring of, 694

ADR. *See* alternative dispute resolution (ADR)

advertising, to promote women's economic activity, 101, 120*n*6

advisory services, 265, 268, 269, 270*t*7.3, 271

advocacy, for women's voice in farmer organizations, 70

AET. *See* agricultural extension and training (AET)

affinity groups, and value chains, 210*b*5.17

affirmative action strategies, 323, 324

Afghanistan, poultry farming, 204, 205*b*5.12

Africa

  conservation in Bwindi Impenetrable National Park, 665–68

  dairy farming, 662*b*15.12

  Gender and Rural Transport Initiative, 377, 377*b*9.1

  Improved Seed Systems for Agroforestry in African Countries project, 663

  Indigenous Soil and Water Conservation, 534

  rice farmers, 272

  unproductive soil in, 529, 529*b*12.4

Africa Educational Trust, 393

African Conservation Tillage network (ACT), 303

African Development Bank, 272

African Highland Program, 277

African Women Leaders in Agriculture and Environment (AWLAE), 286

Africa Travel and Transport Project, 379

Agence Nationale d'Appui au Développement Rural (ANADER), 74–76

Agha Khan Rural Support Program, 66

AGRECOL, Bolivia, 393
agribusiness, regional opportunities and constraints in, 174–75
Agribusiness in Sustainable Natural African Plant Products (ASNAPP), 205b5.11
agricultural extension and training (AET)
  good practices and lessons learned from, 283–87
  guidelines and recommendations for, 287–88
  overview, 280
  women's participation in, 280–81
  See also extension services; trainers and training
agricultural extension field schools, 63, 64b2.14
agricultural fairs, 622
agricultural innovation systems (AIS), 258–60, 263, 265
agricultural labor. *See* labor force
agricultural markets
  marketing extension tool, 211–14
  supporting agricultural value-adding strategies, 206–10
  See also markets and marketing
agricultural production. *See* production
agricultural sciences, study in, 280–81, 284, 284b7.12
agricultural services reforms, Côte d'Ivoire project, 74–76
agricultural support, versus food aid and sustenance of social capital, 507–12, 516n3–4
Agricultural Technology Management Agency (ATMA), India, 270–71
Agriculture for Development Policy Brief, 522
agriculture water management (AWM)
  gender mainstreaming in, 229–34
  groundwater development and management, 242–46
  multiple-use water services, 235–41
  See also water services; water supply
agrobiodiversity, 15–16, 433b10.4, 440, 459–62, 468n1
agroenterprises, 278
agroforestry, 211–14, 441, 643, 645
  designers of, 647–48
  domestication programs, 435
  and home gardens, 645, 659–60
  knowledge and practice in, 658–64, 669n2
  See also forests and forestry
Agro-Innovation and Competitiveness Project (INCAGRO), Peru, 261b7.3, 268, 269, 271
agroprocessing, 342, 374, 413n3
aid modalities, 43
  examining gender activities of donors, 706–8
  experience and achievements in, 698–702
  gender indicators, tools, and methods for, 702b16.16
  monitoring gender in, 684, 697–98
  monitoring PRSPs, 702–6
  joint monitoring missions, 706, 707b16.19
AIDS. *See* acquired immune deficiency syndrome (AIDS)
AIS. *See* agricultural innovation systems (AIS)
all-season roads, 378, 413n6
ALMPs. *See* active labor market programs (ALMPs)
ALs. *See* alternative livelihoods (ALs)
alternative dispute resolution (ADR), 149
alternative fuels and energy, 293b7.17, 451
alternative livelihoods (ALs), 580, 582–87, 594n1–2, 594n8

ANADER. *See* Agence Nationale d'Appui au Développement Rural (ANADER)
analytical capacity, 38, 41–42, 44
Andean region, participatory research in, 276–77
Andes community, 298–301
Andhra Pradesh District Poverty Initiatives Project (APDPIP), India, 112–16, 121n1, 210b5.17
Andhra Pradesh Rice Credit Line Project, 17
Andhra Pradesh Rural Poverty Reduction Project (APRPRP), India, 112–16, 121n1, 203, 215–19, 223–24n1–3, 683b16.6
Andhra Pradesh State Cooperative Marketing Federation Limited (APMARKFED), India, 217
animal diseases, 611–16, 636n1, 636n5
animal genetic resources, 435b10.6, 435b10.7, 437, 633–34
animal health, 613–14, 628
animal health workers, 615
animal husbandry, 603, 615, 629
animal production, 603
animal waste, 384, 385
Annan, Kofi, 23
Anthra, 613
APDPIP. *See* Andhra Pradesh District Poverty Initiatives Project (APDPIP), India
APMARKFED. *See* Andhra Pradesh State Cooperative Marketing Federation Limited (APMARKFED), India
APRPRP. *See* Andhra Pradesh Rural Poverty Reduction Project (APRPRP), India
aquaculture, 561–67, 593n1–5
  accessing and managing resources, 568–71, 593n1–3
  alternative livelihoods for fishing communities, 582–87, 594n1–2, 594n8
  aquaculture extension project, 220–22, 224n1
  associations for protecting livelihoods of fishers, processors, and traders, 577–81, 594n1
  CARE Bangladesh, 591–93
  coral reef rehabilitation and management project, 588–90
  family-based systems in Asia, 572–76, 594n1–3
Aqua Finca, Honduras, 581
aquifers, overexploitation of, 243
Aridity Index, 468n4
armed conflicts. *See* conflicts and crises
Armenia, Network and Capacity Building for Rural Women, 396
arsenic poisoning, 243, 243b6.4
artichokes, 179, 180b5.3
artisanal fisheries, 329, 580, 582, 594n1
ASCAs. *See* accumulating savings and credit associations
Asia
  agricultural resource management, 456–57
  family-based aquaculture systems in, 572–76, 594n1–3
  wood energy in, 653
Asian Development Bank (ADB), 568, 620, 621, 679b16.3, 723b16.22
ASNAPP. *See* Agribusiness in Sustainable Natural African Plant Products (ASNAPP)
assessments, gender sensitive, 511–12
assets, 4–6
  access to during crises, 480, 515n7
  in agriculture sector, 16f1.4

asset–sharing strategies, 490
and GAL framework, 427
link to technology development, 629
livestock sector, 605, 606*b*14.1
structural barriers to, 480, 515*n*7
Association of American Universities (AAU), 286
ATMA. *See* Agricultural Technology Management Agency
(ATMA), India
ATMs. *See* automated teller machines (ATMs)
audits and auditing
gender audits, 98–99, 120*n*4, 387, 707
of projects, 509
Australia Agency for International Development (AusAID),
677*b*16.2
automated teller machines (ATMs), 96, 105
avian influenza, 611, 612, 614
AWARD program, 286
AWLAE. *See* African Women Leaders in Agriculture
and Environment (AWLAE)
AWM. *See* agriculture water management (AWM)

B

Badia Livestock Extension Project, Jordan, 628*b*14.3
Bangladesh, 40*b*2.3, 296, 568
CARE Bangladesh, 570–76, 591–93
Centre for Mass Education in Science, 330
crop selection, 535, 535*b*12.8
cyclone in *1991*, 449
Empowerment of Coastal Fishing Communities for Sustainable
Livelihoods Project, 585–86
flooding in, 489–90
food security project, 197
governance issues in, 71–73
Greater Noakhali Aquaculture Extension Project,
220–22, 224*n*1
Greater Options for Local Development through Aquaculture
Project, 591
Livelihood Empowerment and Agroforestry Project, 198,
211–14
Livestock Development Program, 620, 621
marketing extension tool, 211–14
Meghna–Dhanagoda Command Area Development
Project, 568–69
NGOs in, 197
Oxbow Lakes project, 568–69
Rural Roads and Market Project, 379, 379*b*9.3
solar home systems, 388*b*9.5
women in growth center markets, 191*b*5.7
Bangladesh Rural Advancement Committee (BRAC),
296, 568
BBC World Service Trust, 393
BCRCA. *See* Buhoma Community Rest Camp Association
(BCRCA)
Bhairahawa Lumbini Groundwater Irrigation Project (BLGWIP),
Nepal, 244*b*6.5
bicycles, 378
Bill and Melinda Gates Foundation, 286
BINP. *See* Bwindi Impenetrable National Park (BINP)

biodiversity, 428, 432–34, 465*n*3–5
Bwindi Impenetrable National Park, 665–68
Convention on Biological Diversity, 434, 456
in dry lands, 454
good practices and lessons learned from, 434–36
guidelines and recommendations for practitioners, 436–37
impact of intensive agriculture on, 521
and LinKS project, 459–62, 468*n*1
management of, 262, 277
monitoring and evaluation of, 437
overview of, 431–32
policy and implementation issues of, 434, 435*b*10.6, 435*b*10.7,
466*n*8
trends in, 423, 424*b*10.1, 431*b*10.2
bioenergy, 421, 428–29
definition, 467*n*11
gender issues, 443–47, 467*n*1–6
production of, 445
sources of, 443, 467*n*2
trends in, 423, 424*b*10.1
biofortified crops, 521, 554*n*3
biofuels, 443, 444–45, 467*n*6, 467*n*11
Biofuels Association of Zambia, 446
biomass
definition, 467*n*11
transfer of, 660–61
use of, 383–85, 414*n*3, 440, 443, 444, 653
Biorganika, 204
biosecurity, in livestock sector, 611–16, 636*n*1, 636*n*5
biotechnology, 177
BLGWIP. *See* Bhairahawa Lumbini Groundwater Irrigation
Project (BLGWIP), Nepal
Bolivia
adjusting local agriculture to loss of rural labor, 523*b*12.3
AGRECOL, 393
Noel Kempff Climate Action Project, 440
Bosnia and Herzegovina, rural producer organizations in, 201*b*5.9
Botswana, labor-saving technologies for crops, 290*b*7.15
BRAC. *See* Bangladesh Rural Advancement Committee (BRAC)
Brazil, 402, 403*b*9.8, 542*b*12.11
breeding
improvement of local breeds, 627–28
livestock, 461*b*10.13, 607, 633–35
of plants, 262, 436, 437, 541, 543, 543*b*12.13
sheep, 631–32
brewing, 294
bribery, attitudes about, 31*b*2.2
B2B. *See* business to business (B2B)
budgets
budget support, 684
experience with PRSPs and SWAPs, 698–99
gender budget initiatives, 705, 706*b*16.3
gender-responsive, 28*b*2.1, 37, 41, 44, 79*n*3, 405–6
in newer aid modalities, 697–98
operating, 696
reasons to monitor, 698
buffalo milk, 604
Buhoma Community Rest Camp Association (BCRCA), 667

and gender, 322
and working conditions, 341
children, exposure to natural disasters, 449
Chile
informal workers in horticulture, 346, 346t8.11
producer organization for marketing, 266b7.6
China
alternative fuels for domestic cooking, 291b7.17
forestry and farmers' self-help groups, 656b15.7
seed fairs, 543b12.12
women's access to resources, 619b14.2
Wulin mountains minority-areas development project, 457
CIAL-CIAT. *See* Community Agricultural Research Groups (CIAL-CIAT)
CIARA Foundation, 271
CIAT. *See* International Center for Tropical Agriculture (CIAT)
CIFOR. *See* Center for International Forestry Research (CIFOR)
citizens
citizen report cards, 26
as customers, 29
civic extension associations (ACEs), 271
civil service reform, 29–30
civil society
civil society organizations, 579–80
and governance, 25
and reforms, 30
civil status, and land rights, 155
Civil Supplies Corporation, 218
Clean Development Mechanism, 441, 442b10.9
climate change, 421, 428
and disaster mitigation, 486
gender dimensions of, 438–42, 466n1–6, 466n10–11, 466–67n13
impact of desertification on, 454
impact on forests, 643–44
negative impacts of, 438, 439b10.8
and risk management, 489
and rural infrastructure, 368–69
trends in, 423, 424b10.1
coastal storms, 448
codes of conduct, 323
in agricultural labor, 343–44
expansion of, 349
fisheries, 578, 579–80, 581
Guatemala, 339
importance of, 346–47, 353n2
coffee, 203, 203b5.10, 341–42
COHRE. *See* Centre on Housing Rights and Evictions (COHRE)
Collaborative Research Programs, 274
Collaborative Research Support Program (CRSP), 276b7.9
collective association, 185
collective bargaining, 318, 336
collective economic action, in agricultural markets, 200–205
commercial crops, 532
commercialization, 177, 433
Commission for the Verification of Corporate Codes of Conduct, Guatemala, 339

commodities
commodity exchanges, 219
revenues from, 341
and working conditions on plantations, 341–42
common property, 140
communicable diseases, and forestry sector, 651, 652b15.1, 654, 668n2
Communication for Development, 390, 390b9.7
communications
in Hills Leasehold Project, 160
and LinKS project, 461
in sanitation, hygiene, and potable water, 400–402
and seed systems, 543–44
social processes of, 264–65
for women, 59
communities
alternative livelihoods for fishing communities, 582–87, 594n1–2, 594n8
animal health workers in, 614
community-managed procurement centers, 215–19, 223–24n1–3
Community Professionals Learning and Training Centres, 722
community seed fairs, 541, 542b12.11
competition between, 299–300
and ecotourism, 666–67
empowerment of, 487
financial systems in, 112–16, 121n1
forestry programs, 159–61, 167n2, 645, 650
gender issues
building community assets and opportunities, 278
community-based water programs, 291–94
and decision making, 400, 426
to enhance women's participation in community projects, 404, 405t9.7
forest management, 645, 650
IKP project, 112–16, 121n1
and land dispute mechanisms, 148–49
and natural resources management, 426
in watershed development project, 463–65
women representation in community organizations, 265–66
identifying and strengthening community organizations, 587
initiatives to reduce disaster risk-factors, 490
and land rights, 136–37, 151, 166n2
postcrisis assistance in, 507, 508
preventing elite capture of programs, 134
rural poverty reduction projects, 215–19, 223–24n1–3
and seed production, 544–45
self-help groups in, 584
training of to carry out project planning, monitoring, and evaluation, 721–23
Community Agricultural Research Groups (CIAL-CIAT), 262
community-based development (CBD), 53b2.9, 465n4
community-based disaster preparedness (CBDP), India, 487, 487b11.5
Community-Based Enterprises for the Conservation of Biodiversity at Bwindi World Heritage Site, Uganda, 665, 667
community-based natural disaster management, Nepal, 451

community-based natural resource management (CBNRM), 139, 166*n*7, 568, 569
community-based organizations (CBOs), 251, 508
  and agroforestry-related issues, 663, 669*n*2
  and aquaculture extension project, 221
  and forestry-related issues, 655–56
  and gender-sensitive assessments, 511–12
  and marketing extension process, 211–14
  and sanitation, hygiene, and potable water issues, 402, 403*b*9.8
  See also rural producer organizations (RPOs)
Community Based Rural Infrastructure Project (CBRIP), Vietnam, 56, 57*b*2.11
community credit management committees (CCMCs), 248, 253*n*1
Community Development Carbon Fund, 446
community development funds (CDFs), 52, 55
community-driven development (CDD)
  approaches of, 53, 54*b*2.9
  definition, 32, 53*b*2.9
  gender issues, 53–55
    challenges for, 61–62
    gender-responsive actions in, 55–56
    good practices and lessons learned concerning, 56–60
    guidelines and recommendations for practitioners, 60–61
  and governance, 31, 32–33
  overview, 52–53
  in Sri Lanka, 77–79
community e-centers (CeCs), 411–13, 415*n*1
Community Empowerment for Rural Development Project, Indonesia, 723*b*16.22
Community Link Workers, 628
Community Professionals Learning and Training Centres, 722
community seed banks, 541, 542*b*12.11
community seed fairs, 434–35
Comprehensive Poverty Reduction and Growth Strategy 2002, Vietnam, 681*b*16.5, 703*b*16.17
conflict resolution, 489
conflicts and crises
  and access to food, 17
  countries involved in armed conflicts in forested regions, 652*b*15.2
  gender issues
    agriculture during crises, 475–76, 479–81
    conceptual framework for agricultural programming in crises, 481–82
    food aid versus agricultural support and sustenance of social capital, 507–12, 516*n*3–4
    forestry sector, 647, 651, 652*b*15.2, 652*b*15.3, 655–56
    integrating gender perspectives in, 482–83
    and JFFLS approach, 310*n*3
    link between food aid and agriculture in emergencies, 492–98
    managing land and promoting recovery postcrisis, 499–506
    monitoring and evaluation of, 483, 484*t*11.1
    multidimensional issues of agriculture in times of crises, 477–79
    overview, 475
    strategies for, 485–91, 515*n*2
    women entrepreneurs in war zones, 195–96
  impact of natural disasters on, 448

impact on forest products, 646
  See also natural disasters
Congo, Democratic Republic of, rape as weapon in conflict, 652*b*15.3
Conradie v. Hanekom and Another, 339
consensual unions, 156–57
conservation agriculture, 530
Conservation Agriculture and Sustainable Agriculture Development Project, 291
conservation agriculture (CA), 302–4
conservation areas, perceptions about women working in, 573, 573*t*13.3
conservation of natural resources, 298–301
conservation of protected areas, 665–68
conservation tillage, 533
constitutions, and land rights, 503
consultations
  involving communities, 508
  and land policies, 505
Consultative Group on International Agricultural Research (CGIAR), 541
  and IPM, 549*b*12.16
  research initiatives, 262, 274, 277, 664*b*15.13
consumers
  consumer protection, 111
  and livestock technologies, 629
contract labor, 318
Convention on Biological Diversity (CBD), 434, 456
Convention on the Elimination of All Forms of Discrimination against Women (CEDAW), 334, 335*t*8.8, 339, 503*b*11.7, 602, 635*n*5
cool chain distribution, 328–29
cooperative organizations, 67
COPRAUL. *See* Regional Cooperative of United Farmers Ltd. (COPRAUL)
Coral Reef Rehabilitation and Management Program (COREMAP), Indonesia, 569, 588–90
coral resources, 588–90
COREMAP. *See* Coral Reef Rehabilitation and Management Program (COREMAP), Indonesia
corn, 467*n*4
corporate social responsibility (CSR), 323, 342, 343*t*8.9
corporations, and working conditions, 352
corruption, reforms to reduce, 30–31
Costa Rica
  Payment for Environmental Services Programme, 440–41, 466–67*n*13
  solar-powered cookers, 447
costs
  associated with sustainable land reform, 501
  of biosecurity measures, 615–16
  of conservation agriculture implements, 303–4
  of human resource programs, 351
  for multiple-use water services, 238
  of occupational segregation, 192
Côte d'Ivoire, gender in agricultural services reforms, 74–76
cotton growers, 552*b*12.17
Country Economic Memorandum (CEM), 41

of environment, 476, 476*b*11.1
of land, 429, 454–58, 468*n*4, 476*b*11.1
of natural resources, 448
of water, 429, 454–58, 468*n*4
demand-driven mechanisms, 60
demand-oriented approaches, and energy issues, 388
demand-side strategies, 24–26
Democratic Republic of Congo, 493, 652
demographics, in agricultural labor force, 317, 318*t*8.1, 319*t*8.2, 321*t*8.4
Department for International Development (DFID), United Kingdom, 179, 520*b*12.1, 536, 580
conceptual framework for gender equity in sustainable livelihoods, 4–6
gender audits, 707–8
gender mainstreaming, 681
integration of gender-specific indicators into monitoring, 718–19
research in poverty in fishing industry, 180*b*5.2
role of agriculture in poverty reduction, 520*b*12.1
Department of Forests (DOF), Nepal, 159–61, 167*n*2
Department of Livestock Services (DLS), Nepal, 621
desertification, 429, 466*n*6
gender issues of, 454–58, 468*n*4
trends in, 423, 424*b*10.1
design of projects
in agricultural labor, 322–26, 353*n*8
gender-sensitive M&E component, 679–82
ground water development and management, 245–46
LADEP project, 251
multiple-use water services, 240–41
with national extension programs, 269–72
rural roads projects, 409–10
for self-help groups, 68–69
development, 2
development cooperation strategies, 44
East Asia Region CDD operations, 56, 57, 57*b*2.12
interventions for women, 68
strategies and plans for, 36, 79*n*1
development agencies, and energy assistance programs, 383, 413*n*1
Development Assistance Committee (DAC), 43, 680*b*16.4, 698, 700, 706
development cooperation agencies, 677*b*16.2, 678, 698
Development Credit Agreement, 508
DEWA. *See* Division for Early Warning and Assessment (DEWA)
DFID. *See* Department for International Development (DFID), United Kingdom
dietary diversity, 18, 174–75
Digital Broadcast Initiative, 394
Dimitra Project, 395
disaster management, 452–53
disaster risk reduction, 449
discrimination against women, 89
and access to financial services, 87
and disaster recovery, 496
as entrepreneurs, 185
and gender equality strategies, 482
and governance, 25
discrimination in education, 282

diseases
communicable, 651, 652*b*15.1, 654, 668*n*2
livestock, 607, 611–16, 636*n*1, 636*n*5
water borne, 249
See also acquired immune deficiency syndrome (AIDS); health and health care
displacement, 499
displaced persons, 494, 504*b*11.8, 651
internally displaced persons, 477, 482, 499, 501, 502
and rural infrastructure, 368
by transport infrastructure, 375
dispute resolution, and land rights, 133*t*4.1, 147–52, 166*n*1, 166*n*3
dissemination, of labor-savings technologies, 294–96
distance education, 394, 411
distributional gains, mapping of, 180*b*5.3
District Poverty Initiatives Project (DPIP), Andhra Pradesh, India, 112–16, 210*b*5.17
diversification, in agriculture, 433–45, 526
Division for Early Warning and Assessment (DEWA), 488
divisions of labor
in agriculture, 524–25
in fisheries, 562, 582–83, 593*n*2
gender issues in, 230–31
and natural resource management, 425
and risk recovery, 490
and water management, 455
within households, 291
divorce, and land rights, 142, 166*n*4
DLS. *See* Department of Livestock Services (DLS), Nepal
DOF. *See* Department of Forests (DOF), Nepal
domestic animals, and local knowledge, 603
domestic energy, 383–85
domestic markets
for food, 176
growth of, 175
domestic relations, 90
domestic violence, 161
domestic water supplies, 235–37
donor agencies, 53, 79*n*1, 287, 410, 502
for CeCs, 412
donor policy-lending instruments, 42
examining gender activities of donors, 706–8
Downsizing Options Simulation Exercise tool, 41
DPIP. *See* District Poverty Initiatives Project (DPIP), Andhra Pradesh, India
droughts, 618
drug trafficking, 476
drylands, definition, 454, 468*n*4
DTW. *See* deep tubewell (DTW) development
dump pickers' project, 402*b*9.8

E

EALA. *See* East African Legislature Assembly (EALA)
early warning systems, 487–88, 494
earnings
gender gaps in, 329
from informal work, 332
See also income

East African Legislature Assembly (EALA), 38
East Asia, and agribusiness, 174–75
East Asia Region CDD Flagship Report, 56, 57, 58b2.12
eBario project, 412, 415n1
ECLAC. *see* Economic Commission of Latin America and the
    Caribbean (ECLAC)
economic access, 125–26
economic and sector work (ESW), 38, 42, 310n3
Economic Commission of Latin America and the Caribbean
    (ECLAC), 346t8.11
economic development, terms for joint review missions of,
    707b16.19
economic empowerment, 361–62
    gender equity in rural infrastructure, 365–66
    and livestock production, 604
    and market access, 580
    and rural transport, 375
    in sanitation, hygiene, and potable water, 402–3
    and watershed development, 464
economic growth, 375
    and food security, 16
    and women's access to financial services, 87–88
ecosystems, 421, 466n10
    coral reefs, 588–90, 594n8
    destruction of, 477
    impact of intensive agriculture on, 521
    mangrove, 594n8
    role of trees in, 660
    See also biodiversity
ecotourism, 665–68
education, 76
    access to, 262, 367
    addressing imbalances in, 394–95
    agroforestry, 664b15.13
    animal health practices, 614
    curricula, 282–83, 284, 285b7.13, 614, 627
    financial assistance for, 351
    higher, 280–82
    impact of disasters on school attendance, 450
    interventions for women, 283, 283b7.11
    JFFLS approach to, 306
    and labor-saving technologies, 289–97
    and land rights, 505
    management of for disaster mitigation, 488–89, 515n2
    and occupational choices, 325
    in participatory research, 274–79
    in pesticide management, 548
    Radio Teacher, 393
    and rural transport, 375–76
    in sanitation, hygiene, and potable water, 400–402
    women's enrollment in AET, 280
    See also agricultural extension and training (AET); trainers and
        training
efficiency, and women's access to financial services, 87–88
EFTA. *See* European Fair-Trade Association (EFTA)
e-government projects, 395
Egypt, Matruh Resources Management Project, 457
e-Lanka Development Project, 394–95

el Balcon, Mexico, communal forests in, 657b15.8
electric power, 385, 443, 467n6
elite capture, 165n8
    challenges of, 32
    of community programs, 134
    definition, 636n4
    of land, 158
    monitoring of, 630
    risk of, 56
El Niño, 488
El Salvador, 490
e-mails, 393
emergencies
    emergency kits, 489, 515n2
    emergency responses to crises, 480–91
    emergency transport, 367, 374, 375, 380
    and food banks in Niger, 513–15
    link between food aid and agriculture in emergencies,
        492–98
employment, 365
    access to, 337
    for AET graduates, 286–87
    conditions of, 579
    crop production as source of, 522–23
    employee benefits, 351–52
    in fisheries, 562–66
    in forest industry, 645
    generation at local level, 217
    increasing opportunities rural areas, 324
    link to migration, 619–20
    rural opportunities, 323, 324
    seasonal, 324, 328–29, 332, 337, 346
    share by sector, 317, 318t8.1, 318t8.2, 321t8.4
    temporary, 337, 346, 347
    in transport enterprises, 374, 379–80
empowerment of women, 13, 60, 65, 90, 173
    and access to financial services, 88
    in agriculture organizations, 63–65
    in COREMAP project, 588–90
    during crises, 480–81
    in financial sector, 91–92
    and innovations in financial product development, 111
    and insurance, 108–9
    Jharkhand-Chhattisgarh Tribal Development Project
        in India, 655
    organizational models and strategies for, 96–102, 120n1
    practices that increase commitment to, 265
    and remittance transfer services, 103, 104, 110, 111b3.10
    and rural finance, 104, 105b3.6, 121n2
    savings and pensions issues, 107–8
    through group action, 160–61
    through self-managed microfinance associations, 117–20
    versus sustainability, 98, 99b3.3, 120n3
Empowerment of Women in Irrigation and Water Resources
    Management for Improved Food Security, Nutrition and
    Health (WIN project), 13
ENAM. *See* Enhancing Child Nutrition through Animal Source
    Food Management (ENAM)

gender equity, 125, 681
    in accessing markets, 365–66
    in economic empowerment, 365–66
    gender-equity markers, 706–7
    and implementation of staff gender policies, 99–101, 120n6
    and land policy, 126–30
    in management of services, 365
    in newer aid modalities, 697–98
    in planning and decision making, 364
    promotion of through FJJLS, 306–7
    in road maintenance, 408–9, 415n7
gender in agricultural livelihoods (GAL) framework, 426–28
Gender in Agriculture Sourcebook
    considerations in creation of, 6–7
    lessons learned and ways forward, 8–9
    overview, 3–4
    process of, 8–9
    structure of, 7–8, 9n7
    and sustainable livelihoods through a gender lens, 4–5
gender inequalities
    challenges and opportunities for in crises, 496–97
    in fisheries, 565, 593n4
    and food security, 11
    in labor markets, 315
    and women's work, 561, 593n1
Gender Issues in Monitoring and Evaluation of Rural Development Projects toolkit, 678
gender mainstreaming
    at agency level, 405–6
    in agricultural water management, 229–34
    in agriculture sector, 45–51, 76, 80n1–2, 522
    CARE Bangladesh, 591–93
    definition, 45, 80n1
    in financial sector for pro-poor development, 91–92
    Gemidiriya project, 77–79
    implications for M&E, 680–81, 692–93
    irrigation project in Sri Lanka, 510
    livestock sector, 603–5, 635n9–10
    of MDGs, 699
    models and strategies for, 96–102, 120n1, 120n3, 120n8
    and national machineries, 45, 46–47
    perspectives in, 6, 9n6
    and policy making, 38
    in producer organizations, 74–75
    and public administration, 28–31
gender mapping, 575, 594n3
gender pyramid, 579
Gender Responsive Budgeting Initiatives (GRBIs), 79
gender-sensitive indicators, 709
    accuracy of, 720
    in agricultural sector program, 715–16t16.5
    experience and achievements using, 710
    guidelines in designing and verification sources, 710–17
    reasons for using, 709–10
    selecting data sources for, 719–20
gender specialists, 692
gender units, 46, 47–48, 49b2.7
genetically modified (GM) crops, 521, 541, 548, 551

genetic diversity, 431–32, 433
genetic erosion, 433, 465n5
genetic resource management, 277
geographical sourcing of products, 613
geographic information system (GIS), 378b9.2
German Technical Cooperation (GTZ), 446
Germidiriya Community Development and Livelihood Improvement Project, Sri Lanka, 77–79
germplasm supply, 661, 663, 669n2
GGAs. *See* gender and growth assessments (GGAs)
Ghana
    Grains Development Project, 533b12.5
    Land Conservation and Smallholder Rehabilitation Project, 232, 247–49, 253n1
    maize production in, 524
    Volta River Estates, Ltd., 348b8.11
    and women entrepreneurs, 189b5.5
    women's role in fishing industry, 180b5.2
GIS. *See* geographic information system (GIS)
global business environment, 184–85, 187–88
Global Environment Facility (GEF), 435b10.6, 441
Global Forest Resource Assessment, 643
GLOBALGAP standards, 174
globalization, 1–2, 200, 281–82, 372
Global Plans of Action, 434, 435b10.6
Global Positioning System (GPS), 378b9.2
global warming, 438, 466n2, 466n11
GM. *See* genetically modified (GM) crops
GNAEP. *See* Greater Noakhali Aquaculture Extension Project (GNAEP), Bangladesh
GNI. *See* gross national income (GNI)
goats, 607, 611
GOLDA. *See* Greater Options for Local Development through Aquaculture (GOLDA) project, Bangladesh
Gopal Mitras, 464
GoSL. *See* government of Sri Lanka (GoSL)
governance, 48
    and CDD, 52–62
    conceptual framework for reforms, 24–27
    and decentralization, 31–32, 52–62
    definition, 23
    and farmer organizations, 63–70
    Gemidiriya project, 77–79
    global governance, 33–34
    in labor-intensive export agriculture, 342–43
    and land rights, 125–26
    in local government, 71–73
    overview, 23–24
    policy processes for, 27–28
    and public administration and public sector reform, 28–31
    reforms in, 45
    and risk management and preventive action, 486–87
    and rural transport issues, 376–77
    and self-help groups, 63–70
    strengthening of, 409
    See also policies
government of Sri Lanka (GoSL), 507, 508
    See also Sri Lanka

GOWE. *See* Growth Oriented Women Enterprise (GOWE) program, Kenya
Grains Development Project, Ghana, 533*b*12.5
Grameen Bank, 87, 96, 111, 620
grants, to promote AET for women, 286
GRBIs. *See* Gender Responsive Budgeting Initiatives (GRBIs)
Greater Noakhali Aquaculture Extension Project (GNAEP), Bangladesh, 220–22, 224*n*1
Greater Options for Local Development through Aquaculture (GOLDA) project, Bangladesh, 591
greenhouse gas emissions, 441, 442*b*10.9, 466*n*2–3, 466*n*11
    reduction of, 438, 440, 447
    variations of, 467*n*5
Green Revolution technologies, 520–21
gross domestic product (GDP), 16, 341
gross national income (GNI), and food security, 17
groundwater, development and management of, 242–46, 489
group action programs, 262
growth center markets, 191*b*5.7
Growth Oriented Women Enterprise (GOWE) program, Kenya, 198
GRTI. *See* Gender and Rural Transport Initiative (GRTI), Africa
GTZ. *See* German Technical Cooperation (GTZ)
Guatemala
    Commission for the Verification of Corporate Codes of Conduct, 339
    Maria Eugenia Morales de Sierra v. Guatemala, 337
    working conditions in, 326*b*8.3
Guide to Gender-Sensitive Indicators, 713

H
Habitat Agenda, 503*b*11.7
handbooks, for humanitarian action, 490
hand washing, 399
Harmonized Gender and Development Guidelines, 699, 710
healers, 612
health and health care
    and chemical exposures, 338, 345–46, 552, 553
    as factor in food security, 13, 14
    gender issues
        access to, 367
        in agricultural labor, 321–22
        and climate change, 439
        and exposure to pesticides, 553
        in forestry sector, 652*b*15.1
        ICTs to deliver services to poor, 394
        impact for women agricultural workers, 326
        lessons learned and guidelines for practitioners, 403–6
        and natural disasters, 449–50
        and use of traditional bioenergy, 444
        and water quality, 243, 243*b*6.4
    impact of multiple-use water services on, 217
    informal sector, 331, 332
    and insurance products, 109
    link to domestic energy, 384
    link to income, 18
    link to sanitation, hygiene, and potable water, 399
    livestock sector, 612–13

occupational safety and health, 321, 332, 336, 345
    and use of solar cookers, 447
    water-borne diseases, 249
    See also acquired immune deficiency syndrome (AIDS)
Health Unlimited, 394
Heifer Project International, 607
Heifer Zambia, 604
heterogeneity
    of rural infrastructure and services, 363–64
    of women's social class, 68
higher education
    challenges for, 280–81
    opportunities for women in, 281–82
highly pathogenic avian influenza (HPAI), 611, 612, 614
high-value products, 205*b*5.11, 317, 341
    demand for, 176
    informal labor in, 344
    and labor unions, 346
    women's access to, 366
high-yield crops, 433, 465*n*5, 524
Hills Leasehold Forestry and Forage Development Project (HLFFDP), Nepal, 159–61, 167*n*2
HIV. *See* human immunodeficiency virus (HIV)
HLFFDP. *See* Hills Leasehold Forestry and Forage Development Project (HLFFDP), Nepal
hoes, long-handled, 289–90, 295
home-based work, 332, 333*b*8.6
home gardens, 645, 659–60
HomeNet, 332, 333*b*8.6
homestead land purchase program, India, 139–40
Honduras
    ethical fish processing, 581
    improving marketing abilities in, 208, 209*b*5.16
    Land Access Pilot Project (PACTA), 162–65, 167*n*2
    titling systems, 145
horticulture, 322, 326, 346, 347*b*8.9, 535–36
household arrangements
    informal conjugal unions, 156
    and PACTA, 163–64
    See also marriage practices
Household Food Security and Nutrition Project, Ethiopia, 17
household resource management, 283, 285*b*7.13
households
    child-headed households, 603, 635*n*7, 635*n*10
    composition of in rural areas, 1
    division of labor within, 293
    domestic chores, 291, 292, 293*b*7.17
    and domestic energy, 383–85
    food security, 12–13
    househead, 718
    identifying by type, 332
    impact of IKP project on, 115
    and invisible economies of, 373
    link of resources to land rights, 126
    resource poor, 530
    women's responsibility for, 89
household surveys, 718
house ownership, 165–66*n*10

HPAI. *See* highly pathogenic avian influenza (HPAI)
human capital, 103, 602
  access to, 612
  impact of MARENASS project on, 300
  and livestock sector, 608
  and rural infrastructure, 361–62
  and rural transport, 375
human development, 366–67
human immunodeficiency virus (HIV), 1, 2
  and agricultural markets, 193
  and child-headed households, 603, 635n7, 635n10
  contract clauses on, 380
  coping strategies for, 433, 434b10.5
  in fishing communities, 578
  and food security, 14
  and forestry sector, 651, 652b15.1, 654, 668n2
  impact of, 305, 310n1–2
    on MDGs, 645
    on rural households, 613
  and junior farmer field and life schools, 305–8, 310n107
  and labor rights, 337
  and land and water degradation, 456
  and local knowledge systems, 461b10.14
  and rural infrastructure, 368, 374
  as safety risk for women in workforce, 321
  Tanzania, 303
  and training programs, 197
  workplace awareness campaigns, 326
  See also health and health care
humanitarian assistance, 451, 478, 480, 490, 493
  guidelines for, 494
  See also relief efforts
human resource management, 350
hunger, 529, 650
Hurricane Mitch, 500
husbandry, 457–58
hybrid seeds, 538
hygiene, 400–403
  monitoring and evaluation of, 405
  overview, 399
Hyogo Framework, 488

I

IADB. *See* Inter-American Development Bank (IADB)
IAP. *See* indoor air pollution (IAP)
IASC. *See* Inter-Agency Standing Committee (IASC), United Nations
ICARDA. *See* International Center for Research in the Dry Areas (ICARDA)
ICECD. *See* International Centre for Entrepreneurship and Career Development (ICECD), India
ICESCR. *See* International Covenant on Economic, Social and Cultural Rights (ICESCR)
ICICI Bank, India, 96, 97b3.2
ICM. *See* integrated crop management (ICM)
ICP. *See* internally displaced persons (IDP)
ICRAF. *See* World Agroforestry Centre (ICRAF)
ICRC. *See* International Committee of the Red Cross (ICRC)

ICT. *See* information and communications technologies (ICTs)
ICT-enabled procurement centers, 219
IDA. *See* International Development Association (IDA)
IDPs. *See* internally displaced persons (IDPs)
IDRC *See* International Development Research Centre (IDRC)
IFAD. *See* International Fund for Agricultural Development (IFAD)
IFAT. *See* International Federation for Alternative Trade (IFAT)
IFC. *See* International Finance Corporation (IFC)
IFPRI. *See* International Food Policy Research Institute (IFPRI)
IGAs. *See* income-generating activities (IGAs)
IIM. *See* Indian Institute of Management (IIM)
IK. *See* indigenous knowledge (IK)
Ikirezi Natural Products Project, 205b5.11
IKP. *See* Indira Kranthi Patham (IKP), India
illiteracy, 157, 393–94
ILO. *See* International Labour Organization (ILO)
IMF. *See* International Monetary Fund (IMF)
impact indicators, 711
implementation
  gender issues
    and access to land and property, 138–39
    and biodiversity, 434, 435b10.6, 435b10.7, 466n8
    and bioenergy, 445, 447
    and choice of director for gender strategies, 76
    crop protection, 549–53
    and desertification, 456
    family-based aquaculture systems, 574–75
    and farmer organizations, 66–67
    for fishers, processors, and traders, 579–80
    of forestry-related programs, 652–54
    land dispute resolution, 148–50, 166n1, 166n3
    and land rights, 143–45
    livestock sector, 419–20, 604, 608, 613–14, 619–20, 621, 626–27, 636n5
    marketing sector, 619–20, 621
    of multiple-use water services, 238–39
    and natural disasters, 450–51
    and postcrises land issues, 505
    in rural transport, 376–77
    seed production and distribution, 540–41, 545–46
    and self-help groups, 66–67
    and titling of land, 154–55
  partnerships in, 287–88
  of water services, 232–33
Improved Seed Systems for Agroforestry in African Countries project, 663
IMT. *See* irrigation management transfer (IMT)
IMTs. *See* intermediate means of transport (IMTs)
INCAGRO. *See* Agro-Innovation and Competitiveness Project (INCAGRO), Peru
incentives, to ensure monitoring and evaluation, 676–77
income
  in Afghanistan, 205
  in agriculture sector, 17
  fishing sector, 583–84
  households with business income, 388f9.2
  and insurance, 109, 487b11.4

sequencing of interventions in, 364
Vietnam's CBRIP project, 56, 57*b*2.11
See also rural infrastructure
inheritance practices, 128–30, 165–66*n*10–11
and land administration programs, 130–34
and livestock, 617
Rwanda, 504
innovations
in design of loan products, 105, 106*b*3.7
gender issues, 260–63
approaches to overcome gender barriers, 647–48
conservation agriculture for sustainable development, 302–4
emerging trends affecting gender roles in agriculture, 263–67
extension organizations, 268–73
framework for AIS, 258–60
labor-saving technologies, 289–97
overview, 280
in participatory research, 274–79
trends in access to information and technology, 257–58
womens' role in innovation in Africa, 294*b*7.18
in IKP project, 113
in soil fertility management, 533–34
inorganic fertilizers, 531
input indicators, 710
institutions
capacity building, 664*b*15.13
definition, 6
and empowerment versus sustainability, 98, 99*b*3.3, 120*n*3
framework for JFFLS, 308, 310*n*7
and GAL framework, 428
gender issues
for access and ownership of land, 126–31, 134–35, 165*n*7–8, 165–66*n*10
for accessing and managing resources, 568–71, 593*n*1–3
and agriculture sector, 45–51, 80*n*1–2, 325, 525
culture of and empowerment of women, 98–99
and gender equality, 54–55
for groundwater development and management, 242–46
and land dispute mechanisms, 148–49
livestock sector, 608
promoting women's role in, 340
provision of goods and services to women, 58–59
impact of IKP project on, 115
institutional analysis
at community level, 61
for terms for joint review missions, 707*b*16.19
and policies, 5*f*0.1
political processes leading to reform of, 37
rural financial services, 86
rural transport institutional arrangement, 376
strengthening of to support rural livelihoods, 495
Institut Tadbiran Awam Negara (INTAN), Malaysia, 411
INSTRAW. *See* International Research and Training Institute for the Advancement of Women (INSTRAW)
insurance, 103, 104
good practices and innovations in, 108–9
insurance for low-income workers, 487*b*11.4

and livestock sector, 614, 615, 628
social, 331
INTAN. *See* Institut Tadbiran Awam Negara (INTAN), Malaysia
Integrated crop management (ICM), 276*f*7.2
integrated pest management (IPM), 275–76, 549–52
integrated production and pest management (IPPM), 276*f*7.2
Integrated Pest Management Program for Cotton, 552*b*12.17
Integrated Research and Action for Development (IRAD), 384
Integrated Rice and Fish, 591
integrated rural accessibility planning (IRAP), 378
Integrated Rural Resource Management, 275, 275*b*7.8
intellectual property rights (IPR), 436
intelligence-gathering strategies for disease, 615
Interagency Gender and Development Group (INGAD), 40*b*2.3
Inter-Agency Standing Committee (IASC), United Nations, 490, 497
Inter-American Commission, 337
Inter-American Development Bank (IADB), 407
Intercooperation, 211–14
Intergovernmental Panel on Climate Change (IPCC), 438, 466*n*1, 466*n*3–4
intermediate means of transport (IMTs), 378, 388*b*9.2
internally displaced persons (IDPs), 477, 482, 499
location and resettlement of, 502
postcrisis issues, 501
international agreements, 34, 434, 435*b*10.6
International Bioenergy Platform, 445
International Center for Research in the Dry Areas (ICARDA), 178
International Center for Tropical Agriculture (CIAT), 262, 278
International Centre for Entrepreneurship and Career Development (ICECD), India, 198
International Committee of the Red Cross (ICRC), 508
International Covenant on Economic, Social and Cultural Rights (ICESCR), 334, 335*t*8.8
International Development Association (IDA), 478, 507
International Development Research Centre (IDRC), 436
International Federation for Alternative Trade (IFAT), 343, 344*b*8.8
International Finance Corporation (IFC), 189*b*5.5
International Food Policy Research Institute (IFPRI), 3, 38
International Fund for Agricultural Development (IFAD), 654–55, 710
and agroforestry domestication, 435
and extension programs, 257
gender mainstreaming, 3, 55
gender-specific units in, 28–29
HLFFDP project, 159–61, 167*n*2
land policy and administration, 125, 165*n*1
lessons learned from, 41–42
North Eastern Region Community Resource Management Project in India, 65*b*2.15
role of agriculture in poverty reduction, 520*b*12.1
International Institute for Environment and Development, United Kingdom, 536
international labor conventions, 323
International Labour Organization (ILO), 325, 334–36, 353*n*1, 461
gender-sensitive value chain model, 622–23

International Land Coalition, Women's Resource Access
   Programme (WRAP), 160
international law, 334–36, 502
International Livestock Research Institute, 276
International Monetary Fund (IMF), and PRSCs, 42
International Research and Training Institute for the
   Advancement of Women (INSTRAW), 110
International Research Centre for Agroforestry, 436
International Rice Research Institute (IRRI), 290
International Treaty on Plant Genetic Resources, 3, 434
International Union for Conservation of Nature, 644
International Water Management Institute, 236b6.1
Internet, 411
Internet access, 264–65
interventions
   agroforestry-related, 658–59
   in crop agriculture, 526–27, 535
   principles for effective intervention, 481b11.3
   for pro-poor development, 85
   reduction of time spent on domestic chores, 291
   seed systems, 541–45
investments
   in agriculture, 2
   in boats and fishing gear, 562
   in fisheries, 565
   to improve governance, 23, 24t2.1
   in infrastructure, 55
   and multiple-use water services, 235–36
   in research and advisory services, 265
   in roads, 372
   in sanitation, hygiene, and potable water, 399
   scaling up of investments, 683–86
   in soil productivity, 531
invisibility factors, and crop agriculture, 521
invisible economies, 373
IPCC. See Intergovernmental Panel on Climate Change
   (IPCC)
IPM. See integrated pest management (IPM)
IRAD. See Integrated Research and Action for Development
   (IRAD)
IRAP. See integrated rural accessibility planning (IRAP)
IRRI. See International Rice Research Institute (IRRI)
irrigation management transfer (IMT), 230
irrigation systems
   access to, 230
   and agricultural water management, 229–34
   community-focused project to develop, 507–12,
      516n3–4
   The Gambia, 457
   and groundwater issues, 243b6.3, 455
   labor contribution to, 230
   LACOSREP project, 232, 247–49, 253n1
   Sri Lanka, 478–79
irrigation tanks, 507, 516n3
Israeli-Palestinian conflict, 499
ISWC. See Indigenous Soil and Water Conservation (ISWC),
   Africa
IT. See information technology (IT)

J
jatropha oil, 446
JFFLS. See junior farmer field and life schools (JFFLS)
Jharkhand-Chhattisgarh Tribal Development Program,
   India, 655
job markets, for ACT graduates, 285–86
joint ownership, of housing, 452
joint property rights, and PACTA, 162–65
joint staff assessments (JSAs), 41
joint titling of land, 156–57
Jordan
   Badia Livestock Extension Project, 628b14.3
   value chain analysis in, 178
Journal of International Agricultural Research and Extension, 268
JSAs. See joint staff assessments (JSAs)
judicial systems
   and land dispute mechanisms, 148, 149–50, 166n1
   See also legal framework
junior farmer field and life schools (JFFLS), 305–8, 310n1–7

K
Kabarole Research and Resource Centre (KRC), Uganda, 92,
   117–20
Kapitbisig Laban Sa Kahirapan-Comprehensive and Integrated
   Delivery of Social Services Project (KALAE-CIDSS),
   Philippines, 54b2.10, 55
KARI. See Kenya Agricultural Research Institute (KARI)
Karnataka Watershed Development Project (KWDP), India,
   463–65
The Keita Project, Niger, 457–58
Kenya
   agroforestry technologies, 660–61
   Conservation Agriculture and Sustainable Agriculture
      Development Project, 291
   dairy market chains, 617, 618f14.1
   gender analysis in sectorwide program, 704b16.18
   GOWE program, 198
   PARIMA project, 620
   women and community-based water programs, 291, 292b7.16
   and women entrepreneurs, 189b5.5
Kenya Agricultural Research Institute (KARI), 303
Kerala mariculture project, 584–85
knowledge, 4–6, 258b7.1
   agroforestry landscapes, 658–64, 669n2
   differences in agricultural knowledge, 525
   ethnobotanical, 436
   livestock sector, 625–26
   Maasai knowledge of cattle breeding, 633–35
   management of for disaster mitigation, 488–89, 515n2
   pesticide risks, 549
   sharing of, 393–94
   women's access to, 574
   See also indigenous knowledge (IK)
KRC. See Kabarole Research and Resource Centre (KRC), Uganda
KWDP. See Karnataka Watershed Development Project (KWDP),
   India
Kyoto Protocol, 441, 442b10.9
Kyrgyz Republic, 150, 689b16.10

L

labor contracts, 323
labor force, 319–22, 352n5
  agroprocessing industries, 342
  and conservation agriculture, 303–4
  considerations for program and project design, 322–26, 353n8
  definitions of agricultural labor, 316–19
  exploitation of, 579
  in export agriculture, 344–46
  in forestry, 644
  good practices and lessons learned from, 346–47, 353n2
  governance structures, 342–43
  guidelines and recommendations for practitioners, 347–49
  informal sector, 328–33, 353n1
  labor improvement program in Thailand, 250–52
  labor laws, 334–40
  monitoring and evaluation of, 326–27
  overview, 315–16, 341
  participation in by gender, 175
  plantation agriculture, 341–42
  protection of in processing factories, 578
  trends in, 317–19, 352n3
labor force participation (LFP), 315, 316f8.2
labor-intensive export agriculture, 344–46
  agroprocessing industries, 342
  good practices and lessons learned from, 346–47, 353n2
  governance structures in, 342–43
  guidelines and recommendations for practitioners, 347–49
  overview, 341
  plantation agriculture, 341–42
labor-intensive industries, and low wages and skills, 350–52
labor law, 337–38, 352
  and customary law, 336–37
  governing informal sector, 329–30
  international law, 334–36
  lessons learned and guidelines for practitioners, 338–40
  and women agricultural laborers, 334–40
  See also legal framework
labor markets
  flexibility in, 620
  gender equity in access to, 366
  gender inequalities in, 315
labor-saving technologies, 379
  gender issues, 262–63, 289–91
    good practices and lessons learned, 294–97, 309n4
    guidelines and recommendations for, 297
    low-cost water techniques, 291–94
    overview, 289
LACOSREP. See Land Conservation and Smallholder Rehabilitation Project (LACOSREP), Ghana
LADEP. See Lowlands Agricultural Development Programme (LADEP), The Gambia
Lake Chad, 580
Lake Fishing Teams (LFTs), 571
land
  access to land, 136–40, 166n1–4, 166n6–7, 531
  common property, 140
  degradation of, 429, 454–58, 468n4, 476b11.1

and dispute resolution, 133t4.1, 147–52, 166n1, 166n3
land improvement programs, 137–38, 457
landless systems, 619–20
managing land and promoting recovery postcrisis, 499–506
market in, 153–54
ownership issues, 142–43, 166n2, 232, 252, 271, 496
reform programs, 137, 166n3, 501–2
tenure systems, 126–27, 229–31, 531, 537, 602
Land Access Pilot Project (PACTA), Honduras, 162–65
land administration. See land policy and administration
Land Claims Court (LCC), South Africa, 339
Land Conservation and Smallholder Rehabilitation Project (LACOSREP), Ghana, 232, 247–49, 253n1
land husbandry, 534
landless systems, 619–20
land policy and administration
  gender issues, 126–30
  and dispute resolution, 133t4.1, 147–52, 166n1, 166n3
  future of, 134–35
  gendered access to land and property, 136–40, 166nn6–7, 166n1–4
  gender-responsive titling, 153–58
  implementation of land administration programs, 130–34
  importance of gender-sensitive policy, 125–26
  legal reforms and women's property rights, 141–46, 166n2, 166n4–5
  overview, 125, 165n1–3
land reclamation, and LADEP project, 250–52
land rights, 602, 635n5, 718
  Africa, 339
  as economic and social access, 125–26
  enforcement of, 144–45, 146
  and food availability, 15
  impact of disasters on, 449
  importance of, 125
  link to water rights, 242–43
  and natural resources management, 426
  and postcrisis issues, 500
  and sociocultural issues, 130
  tenure systems for, 126–27, 229–31, 531, 537, 602, 688
Land Tenure Certificates, 688
land use systems, 445, 457–58
Lao People's Democratic Republic (PDR), land titling, credit, and gender, 153, 154b4.1, 156, 157, 287, 653–54
LARC. See Legal Assistance to Rural Citizens (LARC), Kyrgyz Republic
Las Hermanas coffee, Nicaragua, 203, 203b5.10
Latin America, 581
  and fertilizer use, 532
  gender and agribusiness, 174
  women entrepreneurs in, 195
Lawler, John, 350
LCC. See Land Claims Court (LCC), South Africa
LDW. See local development window (LDW)
leadership training, 723b16.22
LEAF. See Livelihood Empowerment and Agroforestry (LEAF) Project
Learning for Empowerment Against Poverty (LEAP), Sudan, 109

leasehold forestry, 159–61, 167n2
leasing arrangements, 103, 104, 143
legal aid, 145
Legal Assistance to Rural Citizens (LARC), Kyrgyz Republic,
    150–51
legal framework
    and access to hazardous chemicals, 552–53
    and access to information, 26
    and biodiversity, 434, 435b10.6, 435b10.7, 466n8
    and business environment, 185–87, 188, 191
    crop protection, 549–53
    in fisheries and aquaculture, 579
    forest law, 653–54
    to govern informal sector employment, 329–30
    involved with land, 126–30, 131–35, 153–58, 499–500
    and land dispute resolution, 133t4.1, 147–52, 166n1, 166n3
    multiple-use water services, 238–39
    postcrisis recovery, 502–4
    and risk management, 486–87
    seed systems, 540–51
    for women agricultural workers, 323–24, 334–40
    women's property rights, 141–46, 166n2, 166n4–5
    See also labor law
legal pluralism, and land dispute resolution, 149–50, 166n3
legal services, 146, 339–40
legumes, 534, 535b12.7
leisure, access to, 367
Lesotho, mapping mobility and access in rural areas, 378b9.2
less conservation areas, perceptions about women working in,
    573, 573t13.3
LFP. See labor force participation (LFP)
LFTs. See Lake Fishing Teams (LFTs)
liberalization of trade, 184–85
Liberation Tamil Tigers of Eelam (LTTE), Sri Lanka, 507, 508
LIFE. See Locally Intensified Farming Enterprises (LIFE) project
life skills, teaching of, 305–8
LinKS. See local indigenous knowledge systems (LinKS) project
liquid biofuels, 445, 446
liquid propane gas (LPG), 293b7.17
literacy, 89, 622
    among women, 271
    digital, 394
    financial, 111
    as goal of self-help groups, 65b2.15
    impact of bicycles on literacy program, 378
    and land rights, 151, 502
    and Radio Teacher, 393
    rural indigenous women, 407, 414n4
    and traditional bioenergy, 444
    women farmers, 500
livelihood diversification. See alternative livelihoods
Livelihood Empowerment and Agroforestry (LEAF) Project, 198,
    211–14
livelihood strategies, 4–6
livelihood support activities (LSA), and irrigation project, 508–11
Livestock Development Program, Bangladesh, 620, 621
livestock genetic diversity, 454
Livestock Guru, 628

livestock production, 617, 636n1
livestock sector, 513, 601–3, 635n7
    access to water for, 236b6.1
    and biofuel production, 445
    characteristics of, 601, 602b14.1
    disease control and biosecurity, 611–16, 636n1, 636n5
    knowledge on breeding and selection, 461b10.13, 633–35
    Maasai knowledge of, 633–35
    mainstreaming gender, 603–5, 635n9–10
    management of, 436
    marketing, 617–24, 636n1
    monitoring and evaluation of, 608–10
    SL framework for, 605–8
    technologies to improve agricultural livelihoods, 625–30, 635
    and value chains, 617–24, 636n1
    value of global agricultural output, 636n1
    versus crop production, 455
living infrastructure, 363
loans, 103
    application process, 99b3.3, 120n3
    design of, 105, 106b3.7
    and product design issues, 104, 105b3.6, 121n2
    provided in IKP project, 112
    triggers for loan disbursement, 714, 716, 716b16.20
    women as borrowers, 89, 120n6
    to women who complete training in business development, 101
    See also credit
local authorities, and land rights, 127, 165n7–8
local councils, and land rights, 145
local development window (LDW), 407, 408, 409, 410, 414n3
local government, gender and governance in, 71–73
local indigenous knowledge systems (LinKS) project, 16, 434–35,
    459–62, 468n1, 633–35
local knowledge, 432, 433b10.4, 435b10.7, 465n3
    and biodiversity, 436, 468n1
    cattle breeding, 633–35
    custodians of, 603
    of farmers, 525
    of livestock diseases, 612–13
    and management of drylands, 455
    on value of timber, 644
    See also indigenous knowledge (IK)
Locally Intensified Farming Enterprises (LIFE) project, 139,
    166n7, 591
Local Road Institute, 409
long-term use rights to land, 143
low-external-input technologies, 533
Lowlands Agricultural Development Programme (LADEP), The
    Gambia, 15, 139, 166n6, 250–52
LPG. See liquid propane gas
LSA. See livelihood support activities (LSA)
LTTE. See Liberation Tamil Tigers of Eelam (LTTE), Sri Lanka

M

Maasai livestock keepers, 460, 461b10.13, 633–35
Macallinka Raddiyaha, 393
MACEMP. *See* Marine and Coastal Environment Management
    Project (MACEMP)

machineries, for advancement of women, 26, 28–29, 45, 46–47

MADER. *See* Ministry of Agriculture and Rural Development (MADER), Mozambique

Madhya Pradesh, India, 269

magic boxes, 264*b*7.5

Mainstreaming Hazard Risk Management in Rural Projects, 494, 496

maize production, 533*b*12.5

Malawi
    Department of Forestry, 654
    and forestry studies, 651, 652*b*15.1, 654
    rural travel and transport in, 377*b*9.1
    Smallholder Seed Development Project, 544–45
    WorldFish, 577

Malaysia, community e-centers, 411–13, 415*n*1

Mali, 43*b*2.5, 433*b*10.4, 446

Mali Economic Management Credit, 43*b*2.5

Mali Folke Center, 446

malnutrition, 14, 17

MAMS. *See* Maquette for MDG Simulations (MAMS)

management authority, devolvement to user groups, 30

management boards, 30

management committees, 513–14

management contracts, 693

management information system (MIS), 693–94

management systems, 193–94
    gender equity in, 365
    monitoring of, 694
    for sheep husbandry, 631–32

mandal samakhyas (MS), 112, 114*t*3.3

mapping, 378, 378*b*9.2

Maquette for MDG Simulations (MAMS), 41

MARENASS project, 298–301

marginalization
    of low-income groups, 651
    of women, 480

Maria Elena Cuadro Women's Movement, Nicaragua, 339

Maria Eugenia Morales de Sierra v. Guatemala, 337

mariculture projects, 584–85

marine conservation, 586, 594*n*8

Marine and Coastal Environment Management Project (MACEMP), 584*b*13.2

marital property, 156, 157

market economies
    and inheritance practices, 129, 130
    and property rights, 157–58

marketing cooperatives, 269

marketing extension (ME) process, Bangladesh, 211–14

market-oriented smallholders, 7

markets and marketing
    access to, 4–6, 80*n*3, 103–4, 175–77, 365–66, 480, 515*n*7, 525–26
    agroenterprises, 278
    agroforestry, 663–64
    for allocation of land, 138, 166*n*4
    analysis of value chains in, 178
    in aquaculture, 573–74
    and biodiversity, 433, 465*n*4

capacity development for small-scale women entrepreneurs, 192–99
    collective action and market linkages, 200–205, 218
    entry points of gender integration, 181–82
    for fishers, processors, and traders, 577–78, 594*n*1
    and GAL framework, 427
    impact of changes in, 176–77
    infrastructure, 186–87, 190
    land market programs, 143
    livestock sector, 605–7, 617–24, 636*n*1
    marketing extension tool, 211–14
    market intelligence, 198
    market orientation, 520
    for milk, 201*b*5.9
    monitoring and evaluation indicators, 182–83
    overview, 173–74
    producer organizations for, 266*b*7.6
    regional opportunities and constraints in agribusiness, 174–75
    research in, 111
    and transport issues, 18
    women's role in local markets and seed enterprises, 540
    See also agricultural markets; women entrepreneurs

marriage practices
    and agroforestry, 659*b*15.9
    and land inheritance, 129, 166*n*11
    and land titling, 142, 155, 156–59, 166*n*4

maternity protection, 337

matrilineal communities
    and inheritance practices, 128–30, 165–66*n*10–11
    and land rights, 156, 166*n*5

Mauritius, sustainable land management, 457

MBFOs. *See* membership-based financial organizations (MBFOs)

MDGs. *See* Millennium Development Goals (MDGs)

ME. *See* marketing extension (ME) process

M&E. *See* monitoring and evaluation (M&E)

MEA. *See* Millennium Ecosystem Assessment (MEA)

mechanical energy, 384–85

mediation, 489

Meghna-Dhanagoda Command Area Development Project, Bangladesh, 568–69

membership-based financial organizations (MBFOs), 86, 96–98

mentoring, 272, 286

Mexico, communal forests in, 657*b*15.8

MFAs. *See* microfinance associations (MFAs)

MFIs. *See* microfinance institutions (MFIs)

Mgahinga and Bwindi Impenetrable Forest Conservation Trust Fund, 665, 667

microcredit, 65, 66, 78

microenterprises, 185–86, 190, 666

microfinance associations (MFAs), 117–20

Micro-Finance Associations Program, 117

microfinance institutions (MFIs), 96–98, 108–9, 120*n*3, 120*n*8

microfinance organizations, 111

microfinance programs, 86, 96, 113
    in IKP project, 112–16, 121*n*1
    women's participation in, 87, 88, 89–90

microinsurance, 108–9, 614, 615

Middle East, and women entrepreneurs, 194

MIGEPROFE. *See* Ministry of Gender and Promotion of Women (MIGEPROFE), Rwanda

migrants and migration, 1
    and agricultural labor, 317
    link to employment, 619–20
    as livelihood diversification strategy, 586
    and remittance transfer services, 110, 111*b*3.10

milestones, designing of, 714, 716, 716*b*16.20

milk
    milk collection networks, 201*b*5.9
    procurement of, 217

Millennium Challenge Corporation, 42

Millennium Development Goals (MDGs), 1
    and agriculture sector, 3
    energy services, 367
    and gender equality strategies, 482
    and gender mainstreaming, 45
    hunger, 529
    impact of HIV and AIDS on, 645
    impact of natural disasters on, 448
    list, 701*b*16.15
    and MAMS, 41
    monitoring of, 683, 699–702
    and rural energy, 383
    and water resource management, 237, 239

Millennium Ecosystem Assessment (MEA), 424, 468*n*4, 521

MINECOFIN. *See* Ministry of Economics and Finance (MINECOFIN), Rwanda

Minimum Standards in Disaster Response, 494

Ministries of Agriculture (MOAs), 48, 50, 701*b*16.14

Ministry of Agriculture and Rural Development (MADER), Mozambique, 701*b*16.14

Ministry of Economics and Finance (MINECOFIN), Rwanda, 40*b*2.4

Ministry of Gender and Promotion of Women (MIGEPROFE), Rwanda, 40*b*2.4

miombo woodlands, 645, 651, 652*b*15.1, 668*n*2

MIS. *See* management information system (MIS)

MOAs. *See* Ministries of Agriculture (MOAs)

mobility
    constraints of, 519
    and disaster exposure, 449
    gender restrictions on, 89
    as livelihood diversification strategy, 586
    and rural transport, 372, 374

models, for organizations gender mainstreaming, 96–102, 120*n*1

modern bioenergy, definition, 467*n*11

monetization process, 492

Mongolia, Sustainable Livelihoods Project, 683*b*16.6, 684*b*16.7

monitoring and evaluation (M&E)
    of CDD projects, 61
    codes of conduct, 347, 353*n*2
    dropout records, 283
    gender issues, 409, 410, 686–87, 697–98
        AET graduates, 286–87
        in agriculture sector, 182–83, 326–27, 483, 484*b*11.1, 700, 527–28, 701*b*16.14
        alternative livelihoods, 587

animal disease control, 616
    and biodiversity, 437
    and bioenergy projects, 447
    and climate change, 442
    for crisis, 483, 484*t*11.1
    in crop agriculture, 527–28
    design of gender-sensitive M&E component of projects, 679–82
    ecotourism in BINP, 667
    emergency operations during natural disasters, 453
    examining gender activities of donors, 706–8
    family-based systems, 576
    fisheries and aquaculture, 566–67, 571, 576, 587
    and food security, 19, 20*t*1.1
    in forestry, 648–49
    gender checklist, 693–96
    gender integration in SWAPs, 704
    gender-sensitive assessments, 511–12
    and governance, 34–35
    implementation of gender strategies, 76
    indicators for, 91, 94–95*t*3.1
    integrating gender into M&E, 676–79, 687–89, 689–93
    involvement of women in innovation systems, 266–67
    in irrigation projects, 233, 234*t*6.1
    and land administration programs, 132–34
    land and water degradation, 458
    livestock sector, 604, 608–10, 616, 620–21, 623–24, 629–30, 635*n*9, 636*n*4
    monitoring PRSPs, 702–6
    in natural resources management, 429–30
    PARPA project, 681*b*16.5, 700*b*16.13
    participatory research, 279
    and postcrises land issues, 505
    reasons to monitor gender, 675–76, 698
    and risk management, 487–88
    rural energy, 387–89
    in rural infrastructure, 370–71
    rural transport, 377, 380–82
    in sanitation, hygiene, and potable water issues, 406
    scaling up of investments, 683–86
    soil productivity management, 537
    tools for gender-sensitive monitoring, 676*b*16.1

joint monitoring missions, 706, 707*b*16.19
marketing extension process, 212
of MDGs, 683, 699–702
practicalities of, 696, 717
training communities to carry out project planning, monitoring, and evaluation, 721–23
See also gender-disaggregated data; gender-sensitive indicators

monocultural farming systems and plantations, 445, 465*n*2

monolingual rural indigenous women, 414*n*4

Monterrey Consensus, 45

morbidity, and forestry sector, 651, 652*b*15.1

Morocco, olive oil production, 207*b*5.13

mortality
    and forestry sector, 651, 652*b*15.1
    rates of during crises, 479

Mozambique
    Action Plan for the Reduction of Absolute Poverty, 681*b*16.5, 700*b*16.13, 703*b*16.17
    ProAgri, 701*b*16.14
    Rural Roads and Bridges project, 380
MS. *See mandal smakhyas* (MS)
M. S. Swaminathan Research Foundation, India, 295
multidisciplinary teams, establishing and training of, 197–98
multimedia presentations, 393
multiple use water services, 232–33, 235–41
municipality-level gender committees, 66
Muslim inheritance, 129, 130
mutual financial mechanisms, 86

N

NAADS. *See* National Agricultural Advisory Service (NAADS), Uganda
NABARD. *See* National Bank for Agriculture and Rural Development (NABARD)
name registration, 409, 415*n*8
Namibia, community-based natural resource management in, 139, 166*n*7
NARO. *See* National Agriculture Research Organization (NARO), Uganda
National Agency for Rural Development, 74
National Agricultural Advisory Service (NAADS), Uganda, 268, 269, 271
National Agricultural Research Organization, 275, 275*b*7.8
National Agricultural Services Agency, 74
National Agricultural Services Project, 75
National Agriculture Research Organization (NARO), Uganda, 298
National Bank for Agriculture and Rural Development (NABARD), 113, 116, 121*n*1
national business environment, 185–86, 188–90
National Center for Agricultural Research and Technology Transfer (NCARTT), Jordan, 178
National Commission for Enterprises in the Unorganized Sector (NCEUS), India, 331*b*8.4
National Committee for the Advancement of Women (NCAFW), 40*b*2.3
national coordination units (NCUs), 589
National Development Dairy Cooperative, India, 330
National Fund for Forestry Finance (FONAFIFO), 441
National Gender Service, 75
national legal systems, 336
National Mission on Biofuels, India, 447
National Sample Survey Organisation (NSSO), 330*t*8.7, 332, 719
national project implementation units (NPIUs), 589
natural disasters, 429, 448–53, 467–68*n*1–4
    disaster recovery, 487, 487*b*11.5
    droughts, 618
    economic issues from, 448, 4467*n*1
    food aid versus agricultural support, 492–98, 507–12, 516*n*3–4
    food banks in Niger, 513–15
    forestry sector, 492–98, 646, 651, 652*b*15.2, 652*b*15.3
    impact of, 475, 646
    managing land and promoting recovery postcrisis, 499–506, 499–506

multidimensional issues of agriculture in times of crises, 477–79
    strategies for, 485–91, 515*n*2
    trends in, 423, 424*b*10.1
    See also conflicts and crises
natural resources
    access to, 136–37, 425–26
    and agriculture sector, 15–16, 479–81
    changes in availability of, 13
    conservation of, 298–301
    degradation of, 448
    exploitation of, 586, 594*n*8
    impact of crises on, 475–76
    link to poverty, 643
    rights to, 126, 425–26
    scarcity of, 529
    See also resources
natural resources management (NRM), 130–31, 134, 140, 425–26, 569, 658
    agricultural livelihoods framework, 426–28
    benefits from gender-responsive actions, 428–29
    and bioenergy, 443–47, 467*n*1–6
    and climate change, 438–42, 466*n*1–6, 466*n*10–11, 466–67*n*13
    forest management, 644
    gender and biodiversity, 431–37, 465*n*1–5, 466*n*8, 466*n*12
    Karnataka Watershed Development Project, 463–65
    key issues in natural resources management, 423–25
    land and water degradation and desertification, 454–58, 468*n*4
    and LinKS project, 459–62, 468*n*1
    monitoring and evaluation of, 429–30
    and natural disasters, 448–53, 467–68*n*1–4
    overview, 423
    resource management in India, 654–55
natural resources managers, 395–96
NCAFW. *See* National Committee for the Advancement of Women (NCAFW)
NCARTT. *See* National Center for Agricultural Research and Technology Transfer (NCARTT), Jordan
NCEUS. *See* National Commission for Enterprises in the Unorganized Sector (NCEUS), India
NCUs. *See* national coordination units (NCUs)
needs assessments, 497
Nepal
    asset-sharing strategies in, 490
    biogas program, 446
    community-based disaster management, 451
    Department of Livestock Services, 621
    gender and governance issues in, 71–73
    groundwater irrigation project, 244*b*6.5
    Hills Leasehold Project, 159–61, 167*n*2
    labor-saving technologies for crops, 290*b*7.15
    leasehold of forest land, 139
    Women's Empowerment Program, 65–66
NEPC. *See* North East Provincial Council (NEPC), Sri Lanka
NERICA. *See* New Rice for Africa (NERICA) project
Network and Capacity Building for Rural Women, Armenia, 396
Network of European World Shops (NEWS), 343, 344*b*8.8
Network of Groups of Rural Women, Uruguay, 396

networks and networking, 59, 88
agroforestry, 663
among rural people, 264
Dimitra Project, 395
extended family, 264
financial, 90
and GAL framework, 427
and gender units, 49
in Hills Leasehold Project, 160
informal workers, 332, 333*b*8.6
microfinance, 96
milk collection networks, 201*b*5.9
and natural disasters, 450
NEWS, 343, 344*b*8.8
and PACTA, 163
for RPOs, 202–3
social, 67, 501, 514
Uruguay, 396
Women's World Banking, 87
new aid modalities. *See* aid modalities
Newcastle Disease Programme, South Africa, 514
New Options for Pest Management (NOPEST), 573, 591
New Public Management (NPM), 29
New Rice for Africa (NERICA) project, 272, 551
NEWS. *See* Network of European World Shops (NEWS)
NGOs. *See* nongovernmental organizations (NGOs)
Nicaragua
Las Hermanas coffee, 203, 203*b*5.10
Maria Elena Cuadro Women's Movement, 339
working conditions in, 326*b*8.3
Niger
agroforestry parklands in, 659*b*15.9
credit approaches for women, 190*b*5.6
Food Bank Project, 17
Keita Project, 457–58
preventive action with food banks, 513–15
Noel Kempff Climate Action Project, Bolivia, 440
nonfarm income opportunities, 372
nonfinancial services, 101
checklist for integration in institutional culture, 99, 100*b*3.5
nongovernmental organizations (NGOs), 488
agroforestry-related issues, 663, 669*n*2
Anthra, 613
and aquaculture support, 573–74
Centre for Mass Education in Science, 330
and extension services, 268–69
and financial services, 86, 96–98, 120*n*8
and governance in local government, 72–73
Heifer Zambia, 604
monitoring of working conditions, 339, 347
and multiple-use water services, 239
Pattan, 451–52
promotion of ecological agriculture, 536
and reforms, 30
role in labor rights, 338
role in land dispute resolution, 151
training programs for women, 197
Women for Sustainable Development, 441

nontimber forest products (NTFPs), 650–51, 668*n*1
nonwood forest products (NWFP), 644, 645, 650–51, 653–54, 668*n*1
NOPEST. *See* New Options for Pest Management (NOPEST)
Nordic Development Fund, 677
North Africa
gender and agribusiness, 175
and women entrepreneurs, 194
North East Provincial Council (NEPC), Sri Lanka, 509
Northern Mountains Poverty Reduction Project, Vietnam, 58, 59*b*2.13
Northwestern Rural Development Project, Cambodia, 679*b*16.3
Novartis Foundation, 552
NPIUs. *See* national project implementation units (NPIUs)
NPM. *See* New Public Management (NPM)
NRM. *See* natural resources management (NRM)
NSSO. *See* National Sample Survey Organisation (NSSO)
NTFPs. *See* nontimber forest products (NTFPs)
nutrient management in soils, 530
nutrition and nutritional security, 12, 13*f*1.2, 14, 480
link to income, 18
nutrition education, 307
terms for joint review missions, 707*b*16.19
and utilization of food, 14, 18–19
women's role in, 12–14
NWFP. *See* nonwood forest products (NWFP)

O

obstetric fistula, 374, 413*n*2
occupational safety and health, 321, 332, 336, 345
occupational segregation, 192, 321, 325, 344–45
occupations
choices in, 325
hazardous, 547
Occupied Palestinian Territories, 515*n*7
OECD. *See* Organisation for Economic Co-operation and Development (OECD)
off-farm activities, 293–94, 323
oil imports, 443
Olifants Basin, 237*b*6.2
olive oil production, 207*b*5.13
on-farm activities, 289, 317, 323
organic farming, 536, 551
Organisation for Economic Co-operation and Development (OECD), 324, 579, 636*n*5
Development Assistance Committee, 43, 680*b*16.4, 698, 706
on emergency responses, 493
orphans, empowerment of through junior farmer field and life schools, 305–8, 310*n*1–7
outcome indicators, 710
out-migration, and natural disasters, 450
output indicators, 710
outreach, for AET graduates, 285
outsourcing, 30, 31, 217
Oxbow Lakes Small-Scale Fishermen's Project, Bangladesh, 568–69

and forestry-related programs, 646–67, 652–54
gender and poverty analysis, 404b9.10
and identification of poorest women, 60–61
impact of desertification on, 454–55
impact of PACTA on, 162–63
inclusion of the poorest in CDD, 56–58
and insurance products, 109
link to natural resources, 299, 643
and marketing extension tool, 211–14
role of crop agriculture in, 519–28, 554n1
role of NGOs in, 120n8
rural roads projects, 407–10, 414–15n1–7
and soil fertility management in, 534, 534b12.6
terms for joint review missions, 707b16.19
poverty reduction, 698
and climate change, 438
community-managed rural poverty initiatives projects, 215–19,
223–24n1–3
and compartmentalization versus mainstreaming gender in,
681b16.5
and multiple-use water services, 235–41
Northern Mountains Poverty Reduction Project, 58, 59b2.13
Philippines, 54b2.10
and rural transport, 375
views of agriculture as driver of, 519, 520b12.1
and women's access to financial services, 88
poverty reduction strategies (PRSs), 698, 703b16.17
Poverty Reduction Strategy Papers (PRSPs), 27, 684
development strategies and plans, 36, 79n1
gender dimensions of, 39–41, 681, 681b16.5
gender-sensitive monitoring of, 698–99, 702–6
Poverty Reduction Support Credits (PRSCs), 42, 43b2.5
Poverty Resource Monitoring and Tracking model (PRMT),
119
power and light services, 388b9.5
PPB-PRGA. See Participatory Plant Breeding (PPB-PRGA)
PRADAN. See Professional Assistance for Development Action
(PRADAN)
PRAs. See participatory rapid appraisals (PRAs)
prawn markets, 220–22, 224n1
preventive action
for crises, 494
with food banks in Niger, 513–15
strategies for, 485–91, 515n2
PRGA. See Participatory Research and Gender Analysis (PRGA)
Program
prices
of food, 476
increase in market prices, 217
market prices in India, 264b7.5
private extension services, 268, 269
private sector, 352
financial services in, 86
and food aid, 493
reform in, 30
seed enterprises, 540
Private Sector Development Programme, Noakhali, 221, 224n2
privatization, 30, 31

of biological resources, 465n4
of land and land rights, 137, 138
PRMT. See Poverty Resource Monitoring and Tracking model
(PRMT)
process indicators, 710
processing factories, protecting workers in, 578
processors of fish and fish products, associations for protecting
livelihoods of, 577–81, 594n1
procurement centers, for rural farmers, 215–19
producer associations and cooperatives, 63, 64b2.14
producer organizations (POs), 69, 74–76
product design
and gender issues, 104, 105b3.6, 121n2
in savings programs, 107, 108b3.8
See also design of projects
product development, innovations in, 111
production, 11–12, 289, 375
dependence on natural resources, 15–16
gender in, 153, 154b4.1
impact of food banks on, 514
mechanization in, 564
multiple roles women play in, 258
technologies for, 277, 277b7.10
production groups, facilitating, 571, 593n3
production systems, 522
product markets, gender equity in accessing of, 365–66
Professional Assistance for Development Action (PRADAN), 65, 67
professional women
interventions to promote AET for, 283, 283b7.11
representation in extension services, 272–73
visibility of, 263, 264, 272–73
profitability, and marketing tool, 212
PROFOR, 646–47
PROFOUND, Vietnam, 570, 574–76, 594n3
project management units (PMUs), 509, 589, 590t13.4
Project National d'Appui aux Services Agricoles (PNASA), 74–75
Promoting Farmer Innovations (PFI), 534
propagation techniques, 435
property grabbing, 456
property rights, 89, 499–500
impact of HIV on, 305
promotion of, 629
See also land rights
pro-poor development, gender mainstreaming in financial sector
for, 91–92
protected areas (PAs), 665–68
Provias Descentralizado, 408, 409
PRSCs. See Poverty Reduction Support Credits (PRSCs)
PRSPs. See Poverty Reduction Strategy Papers (PRSPs)
PRSs. See poverty reduction strategies (PRSs)
PTD. See Participatory Technology Development (PTD)
public administration, 26, 28–31
public expenditure management, 28b2.1
public expenditure reviews (PERs), 41
public extension services, 268, 269
public health, 500
public policy, implementation of, 28
public-private partnerships, 30

public sector, seed enterprises, 540
public sector reform, 28–31
public service, 66
public works programs, 324

Q

qualitative data, 717
qualitative indicators, 711
quantitative indicators, 711
Quechua women farmers, 177–78
questionnaires, 389, 389b9.6
quinoa processing, 523b12.3
quotas for women
    on board seats, 232
    to ensure leadership positions, 70
    and legislative reforms, 71
    in local government, 73
    in producer organizations, 69, 80n3
    representation on councils, 145
    in water management organizations, 244, 245

R

radio, 367
    to disseminate information relevant to women, 393–94
    FAO programs, 396
    satellite, 394
Radio Teacher, 393
rape, as weapon in conflicts, 652b15.3
rate of return, 414n2
RCUs. *See* regional coordination units (RCUs)
RDI. *See* Rural Development Institute (RDI)
RDSs. *See* rural development societies (RDSs)
reconstruction, postdisaster, 451, 495–96
recycling, 402
redistributive land reform, 137, 166n3
redistributive water allocation reform, 237b6.2
reforestation, 384
reforms
    civil service reform, 29–30
    conceptual framework for reform governance, 24–27
    to improve agricultural livelihood, 23–24
    and labor rights, 338
    in land rights, 149, 501
    public sector reforms, 29–30
    to reduce corruption, 30–31
    women's property rights, 141–46, 166n2, 166n4–5
    See also agricultural services reforms
refugees, 305–6, 310n3, 482
    location and resettlement of, 502
    and natural disasters, 450
    postcrisis issues, 501
    return of, 477, 499
Regional Cooperative of United Farmers Ltd. (COPRAUL), 163
regional coordination units (RCUs), 589, 590t13.4
registration procedures, 144, 155–56, 501, 504
registry of agricultural workers and employers (RENATRE), 325b8.2

regulatory framework
    conditions for unorganized wage workers, 331b8.4
    standards for livestock disease control, 613, 636n5
relief efforts, 480
    link between food aid and agriculture in emergencies, 492–98
    See also emergencies
remittance transfer services, 103, 104, 110, 111b3.10
RENATRE. *See* registry of agricultural workers and employers (RENATRE)
representative bureaucracies, 29–30
research
    agroforestry, 664b15.13
    in cattle breeding, 633–35
    Consultative Group on International Agricultural Research, 549b12.16
    informal research methods, 634–35
    investment in diverse forms of, 265
    livestock technologies, 626, 627, 628b14.3, 629
    on local and traditional crops, 177
    on multiple-use water services, 239
    participatory research, 261–62, 274–79
    and postcrises land issues, 505
    in sanitation, hygiene, and potable water issues, 403–4
    in sheep improvement research for indigenous women, 631–32
    training women in technology research, 626, 627, 628b14.3
    value chain analysis, 178–81
Réseau des Organisations Paysannes et des Producteurs Agricoles de l'Afrique de l'ouest (ROPPA), 69
resettlement, 138, 499
    of refugees and IDPs, 502
    and rural infrastructure, 368
    and transport infrastructure, 375
resource persons, for agricultural marketing, 217, 223–24n3
resources
    access to, 568–71, 573, 593n1–3, 619b14.2
    control of, 185
    inequity in distribution of, 477, 477b11.2
    and livestock production, 626–27
    management of, 457, 489
    seed sources, 539–40
    See also natural resources
resource tenure, 658, 660b15.10
Revolutionary Armed Forces of Colombia (FARC), 476
revolving savings associations, 107
rice culture, CARE Bangladesh, 591–93
rice farmers, 272
rice-fish culture, 591
rice production, 15, 139, 166n6, 250–52
    and land titling, 154b4.1
    rice seeds, 290
risks and risk management, 4–6
    for disaster management, 452–53
    during crisis or natural disasters, 449–50, 479, 481, 494, 515n2
    exclusion from marketing processes, 214
    and GAL framework, 427–28
    livestock sector, 606–7b14.1, 607–8, 614, 615
    and microinsurance, 614, 615
    pesticides, 548

S

SACEP. *See* South Asia Cooperative Environment Programme (SACEP)

SADC. *See* South African Development Community (SADC)

Safe Access to Firewood and Alternative Energy (SAFE), 646, 668n2

safety
in rural transport, 374
in the workplace, 326

safety nets, 266, 650–57, 668n1–2, 668n5

sanitation, 400–403, 454
lessons learned and guidelines for practitioners, 403–6
monitoring and evaluation of, 405
overview, 399

SARD. *See* Sustainable Agriculture and Rural Development (SARD) initiative

SARI. *See* Selian Agricultural Research Institute (SARI), Tanzania

SASKI. *See* Sustainable Agriculture Systems, Knowledge, and Institutions (SASKI)

savings, 103, 104, 107–8, 121n2

scholarships, to promote AET for women, 286

schools
hygiene promotion in, 402
impact of disasters on attendance, 450
See also education

SDC. *See* Swiss Agency for Development and Cooperation (SDC)

seafood export processing industries, 564

SEAGA. *See* Socio-Economic and Gender Analysis (SEAGA) Programme

seasonal employment, 324, 328–29, 332, 337, 346
Bolivia, 523b12.3
and labor allocations, 525

seaweed farming, 584b13.2

sectoral information and monitoring system (SIMS), 703b16.17

sectorwide approaches (SWAPs), monitoring of, 684, 698–99, 704, 704b16.18

security
in conflict areas, 494
enhanced by rural infrastructure, 368
in postconflict settings, 500
and rural transport, 374

seed banks, 541, 542b12.11

seed dressing, 552, 553b12.18

seeds
community seed fairs, 434–35
Ethiopia, 543
germplasm supply, 661, 663, 669n2
importance of, 538
improvement of seed systems, 663
production and distribution of, 538–46, 555n2
seed aid programs, 495
traditional seed system in Tanzania, 461b10.12
varieties of, 544

Seed Systems Development Project (SSDP), Ethiopia, 543

SEI. *See* Stockholm Environment Institute (SEI)

Self-Employed Women's Association (SEWA), 66, 111, 333b8.6
and insurance for low-income workers in India, 487b11.4
Trade Facilitation Centre, 396

self-employment, in agriculture, 15f1.3

self-help groups (SHGs), 593n1
for community organizations, 584
in financial sector, 113, 114t3.3
forestry-related, 655–56
gender issues
experience, impacts, and benefits from gender-responsive actions, 65–66, 80n1
good practices and lessons learned, 67–69, 80n3
group functions, advantages, and disadvantages, 63–65
guidelines and recommendations for practitioners, 69–70
overview, 63
policy and implementation issues, 66–67
POKMAS, 589
and poverty reduction, 215, 223n2
and procurement centers, 218
resource management in India, 654–55
to sustain watershed management, 463–64
Uruguay, 396
and value chains, 210b5.17

Self-Help Learning Initiative, 60

self-targeting, 58–59

Selian Agricultural Research Institute (SARI), Tanzania, 303

service cooperatives, 30

service delivery, 394

services and service providers, 26–27
capacity building for women in, 197
for marketing extension process, 213
to prevent livestock diseases, 613
women's access to, 263–64

Servicios Integrales a Mujeres Emprendedoras (SIEMBRA), 111

SEWA. *See* Self-Employed Women's Association (SEWA)

SEWA Trade Facilitation Centre (STFC), India, 396

sex discrimination, 336, 337

sex-for-fish exchanges, 564, 565, 577

sexual favors for job security, 321

sexual harassment, 321, 326, 337, 338, 345–46, 578

sexual services, and corruption, 31b2.2

sexual violence, during crises, 479

SFLP. *See* Sustainable Fisheries Livelihoods Programme (SFLSP)

sheep
Chiapas sheep, 604–5
research in sheep improvement for indigenous women, 631–32
shearing of, 277b7.10

shepherds, 631–32

short message system (SMS), 393

shrimp farmers association, 580

shrimp production, 562–63, 564f13.1, 593n2–3

SIDA. *See* Swedish International Development Agency (SIDA)

SIEMBRA. *See* Servicios Integrales a Mujeres Emprendedoras (SIEMBRA)

SIMS. *See* sectoral information and monitoring system (SIMS)

Sino-Dutch Forestry Program, 656b15.7

site management committees (SMCs), 250–51

skills, 70
identifying and addressing gaps in, 193
for informal workers, 330
or women entrepreneurs, 198–99
See also trainers and training

SLA. *See* Sri Lanka Army (SLA); Sustainable Livelihoods Approach (SLA)

SLs. *See* sustainable livelihoods (SLs)

small cooperative groups, 593*n*1

Smallholder Seed Development Project, Malawi, 544–45

small-scale aquaculture, 572–76, 594*n*1–3

small-scale fisheries, 562, 580, 583, 593*n*3

small-scale seed enterprises, 544–45

smart cards, 332*b*8.5, 393

SMCs. *See* site management committees (SMCs)

SMS. *See* short message system (SMS)

social access, role of land in, 125–26

Social Analysis Sourcebook, 682, 721

social assessments, and land titling, 158

social capital, 603
    enhancement of gender equity in, 364
    and food aid, 507–12, 516*n*3–4
    and livestock sector, 608, 611
    strengthening of, 278–79

social class, heterogeneity of , 68

social control, 89

social costs, of biosecurity measures, 615–16

social empowerment, 362
    and livestock production, 604
    and market access, 580
    and rural infrastructure, 364–65

social insurance, 331

social justice, 69

social marketing, 404–5

social mobilization, 73

social networks, 67, 501, 514

social protection, 18
    definition, 353*n*8
    in fisheries, 565, 593*n*5
    improvement of for agricultural workers, 325–26, 353*n*8
    for informal sector, 331, 346–47
    livestock sector, 604

social security, 325*b*8.2, 331

social services, gender equity in accessing, 366

social systems, 264, 500–503

social training, in CARE project, 592

Sociedad de Pequeños Productores Exportadoras y Compradores de Café SA (SOPPEXCCA), 203, 203*b*5.10

society-forest relationships, 644

sociocultural issues, 203
    and access to ICT, 391
    and access to land, 136–37, 166*n*2
    and land rights, 130
    and land titling, 154

Socio-Economic and Gender Analysis (SEAGA) Programme, 310*n*6, 457, 694

socioeconomics, 67, 310*n*2
    and alternative pest control technologies, 548–49
    and delivery of ICT programs, 391
    sources of and access to seeds, 539–40, 555*n*2

socioeconomic status, strengthening of, 570

socioeconomic surveys, 389

soil erosion, 521, 659*b*15.9

soil fertility, 17, 526, 529–30, 660, 661*b*15.11
    gender-responsive approaches to, 530
    management of, 533

soil productivity, 526, 529–37

soil rehabilitation, 455

Sokoine University of Agriculture, Tanzania, 285–86

solar energy systems, 294, 388*b*9.5, 447

solid waste collection, 402, 403*b*9.8

Somalia, Radio Teacher, 393

SOPPEXCCA. *See* Sociedad de Pequeños Productores Exportadoras y Compradores de Café SA (SOPPEXCCA)

South Africa
    Conradie v. Hanekom and Another, 339
    financing value addition, 208*b*5.15
    inequitable water distribution in, 237*b*6.2
    informal workers in horticulture, 346, 346*t*8.11
    Land Claims Court, 339
    Newcastle Disease Programme, 514
    Wine Industry Ethical Trade Association, 349

South African Development Community (SADC), 436

South Asia, 594*n*8
    and gender and agribusiness, 174–75
    home gardens, 659–60
    roles of women in, 2

South Asia Cooperative Environment Programme (SACEP), 594*n*8

Southeast Asia
    home gardens, 659–60
    and women entrepreneurs, 195

South India
    plant variety protection, 545*b*12.15
    seed and crop diversity in, 539*b*12.10

specialty markets, 342

species genetic diversity, 454

Sphere Humanitarian Charter, 494

spillover effects, 179, 323

Sri Lanka
    food aid versus agricultural support and sustenance of social capital, 507–12, 516*n*3–4
    Gemidiriya Community Development and Livelihood Improvement Project, 77–79, 721–23
    and gender integration, 40*b*2.3
    irrigation systems project, 478–79
    women's concerns and the peace, 503, 504*b*11.8
    women's knowledge of forest-based resources, 660

Sri Lanka Army (SLA), 508

SSA. *See* sub-Saharan Africa (SSA)

SSDP. *See* Seed Systems Development Project (SSDP), Ethiopia

standards of living, 159

staple crops, 519, 532

state governments
    and allocation of land, 137
    and land titling, 156

statistics
    concerning natural disasters, 449, 468*n*4
    FAOSTAT, 710, 718
    gender-sensitive, 287

and aquaculture extension project, 220–22, 224*n*1
and extension services, 282
telecenters, 394–95
telecommunications, 411–13, 415*n*1
temporary employment, 337, 346, 347
tenure systems
insecurity of, 6, 455
and land rights, 126–27, 229–31, 531, 537, 602
shared tenure, 142
and water rights, 229–30
Thailand
Cargill's labor improvement program, 338, 350–52
chicken production, 623*b*14.2
time
access to leisure time, 367
addressing of, 369
availability and use of by women, 12–13, 319
and climate change, 439
competing claims on, 373
as economic factor, 362–63
as factor in postcrisis issues, 500
link to labor-saving technology, 379
spent on collecting wood and water, 384, 444, 455
spent on domestic chores, 291
time allocation studies, 524
and use of modern fuels, 385, 414*n*4
titling systems, 130–32, 134–35, 502
gender-responsive, 153–58
Honduras, 145
legal framework for, 143–45
policies to guarantee women's access to, 263*b*7.4
and polygamy, 142
tracer studies, 285, 286
trade
in agricultural commodities, 341
fair trade cooperatives, 201
livestock sector, 605–7, 619
negotiations on global level, 184–85
trade agreements, 184–85, 322*b*8.1
trade associations, 349
Trade Facilitation Centre (STFC), India, 396
Trade-Related Aspects of Intellectual Property Rights (TRIPS), 433, 465*n*4
traders, associations for protecting livelihoods of, 577–81, 594*n*1
trade unions, 325*b*8.2, 346
traditional bioenergy, 444
traditional practices
as obstacle to knowledge sharing, 489
and postcrisis issues, 502
trainers and training
in agricultural development projects, 287
in aquaculture, 572–73
to become service providers, 213–14
for capacity building, 72
to carry out project planning, monitoring, and evaluation, 721–23
in community e-centers, 411, 412
on company values, 351

complementary support for, 198, 199
farmer-to-farmer, 299
in forest-related industries, 647
gender issues, 307, 436, 592–93
access to, 262
addressing imbalances in, 394–95
animal health workers, 615
in COREMAP project, 589, 590*t*13.4
fishing communities, 585*b*13.3
and leadership, 160, 161
livestock technologies, 628
loans to women who complete training, 101
and natural resources management, 426
promotion of safe pesticides, 551–52
rural roads project, 408, 413–14*n*5–6
in sanitation, hygiene, and potable water, 400–402
technology research and development, 626
under PACTA, 163–64
in watershed development project, 464
and women's land rights, 145
informal workers, 332
in land dispute resolution, 151
leadership training, 160, 161, 723*b*16.22
manuals for, 460
marketing skills, 208, 209*b*5.16
in peace building, 489
peer trainers, 722
promotion of training markets, 283
selection of, 196
training-of-trainer programs, 550, 572
on vegetative propagation, 435
for women, 76
See also agricultural extension and training (AET); education
training and visit extension (T&V), 257
transboundary animal diseases, 611, 613, 615, 636*n*1
Transfer of Technology model of extension, 274
transformative programs, 6, 9*n*6
crises recovery, 495–96, 500–503
to end discrimination against women, 483
irrigation project in Sr. Lanka, 510
postdisaster land and recovery issues, 500–503
transparency, 509
and gender budgeting, 28*b*2.1
in transactions, 216
transport, 292–93
access to, 373–74, 413*n*2
of agricultural products, 187, 190
emergency, 367, 374, 375, 380
gender inequality in transport burdens, 373, 413*n*1
link to markets, 18
rural roads projects, 407–10, 414–15*n*1–7
See also rural transport
trees
access to and disposal of agroforestry tree products, 658–59
importance of, 658
located on women's fields, 660*b*15.10
rights and responsibilities concerning, 444
tree domestication program, 435

tree genetic variety, 658

wood and nonwood forest products, 644, 645, 650–61, 668n1

See also agroforestry; forests and forestry

triangulation, power of, 711

triggers for loan disbursement, 714, 716, 716b16.20

TRIPS. See Trade-Related Aspects of Intellectual Property Rights (TRIPS)

tubewells, 244b6.5, 245

Turkey, social security schemes, 325b8.2

T&V. See training and visit extension (T&V)

Tzotzil shepherds, 631–32

U

UER. See Upper East Region (UER)

Uganda, 434b10.5

Bwindi Impenetrable National Park, 665–68

Code of Practice for the Horticulture Sector, 347b8.9

indigenous vegetables, 432b10.3

Kabarole Research and Resource Centre, 92, 117–20

National Agricultural Advisory Service, 268, 269, 271

National Agriculture Research Organization, 298

Rural Outreach Programme, 395

sectoral information and monitoring system, 703b16.17

Uganda Wildlife Authority (UWA), 667

UNCCD. See United Nations Convention to Combat Desertification (UNCCD)

UN Convention on the Elimination of All Forms of Discrimination against Women (CEDAW), 40b2.3

UNDAW. See United Nations Division for the Advancement of Women (UNDAW)

undernourished, estimates of, 11, 12f1.1

UNDHR. See Universal Declaration on Human Rights (UNDHR)

UNDP. See United Nations Development Programme (UNDP)

unemployment, 319, 324, 515n7

UNEP. See United Nations Environment Programme (UNEP)

UNESCAP. See United Nations Economic and Social Commission for Asia and the Pacific (UNESCAP)

UNESCO. See United Nations Educational, Scientific and Cultural Organization (UNESCO)

UNFCCC. See United Nations Framework Convention on Climate Change (UNFCCC)

UNFF. See United Nations Forum on Forests (UNFF)

UNHCR. See United Nations High Commission for Refugees (UNHCR)

UNICEF. See United Nations Children's Fund (UNICEF)

UNIDO. See United Nations Industrial Development Organization (UNIDO)

UNIFEM. See United Nations Development Fund for Women (UNIFEM)

UNIMAS. See Universiti Malaysia Sarawak (UNIMAS)

United Kingdom

Department for International Development, 4–6, 179, 180b5.2, 580, 681, 707–8

integration of gender-specific indicators into monitoring, 718–19

role of agriculture in poverty reduction, 520b12.1

International Institute for Environment and Development, 536

United Nations

Inter-Agency Standing Committee, 490

International Research and Training Institute for the Advancement of Women, 110

and labor rights, 334

Security Council Resolution 1325, 503b11.7

Sub-Commission on the Prevention of Discrimination and Protection of Minorities, 503b11.7

United Nations Children's Fund (UNICEF), 310n5

United Nations Convention to Combat Desertification (UNCCD), 456

United Nations Development Fund for Women (UNIFEM), 28b2.1, 326

United Nations Development Programme (UNDP), 23, 436, 488

United Nations Division for the Advancement of Women (UNDAW), 46

United Nations Economic and Social Commission for Asia and the Pacific (UNESCAP), 411

United Nations Economic Commission for Europe, 644

United Nations Educational, Scientific and Cultural Organization (UNESCO), 280, 281

United Nations Environment Programme (UNEP), 456, 476, 476b11.1

United Nations Forum on Forests (UNFF), 646

United Nations Foundation, 665–68

United Nations Framework Convention on Climate Change (UNFCCC), 441

United Nations High Commission for Refugees (UNHCR), 508

United Nations Industrial Development Organization (UNIDO), 197, 198

olive oil project, 207, 207b5.13

seed dressing project, 552, 553b12.18

United Nations Population Fund (UNPF), 700

Universal Declaration on Human Rights (UNDHR), 19, 334, 335t8.8, 493

Universiti Malaysia Sarawak (UNIMAS), 412

unorganized sectors, 331–32

UNPF. See United Nations Population Fund (UNPF)

Upper East Region (UER), 232, 247–49, 253n1

urban areas

and land rights, 157–58

rural-urban divide, 368

urban agriculture, 554n1

urban finance, 86

Uruguay, Network of Groups of Rural Women, 396

U. S. Agency for International Development (USAID), 139, 145, 166n7, 620

user rights, 66

UWA. See Uganda Wildlife Authority (UWA)

V

VAC. See vuong/ao/chuong (VAC)

vaccination campaigns, 615

value added

calculation of, 179–81

strategies to support in agricultural markets, 206–10

to women's associations, 203

value chains, 177–81